THE CONVOLUTED UNIVERSE

BOOK THREE

by
Dolores Cannon

OZARK
MOUNTAIN
PUBLISHING

PO Box 754
Huntsville, AR 72740 USA
www.ozarkmt.com

800-935-0045/479-738-2348 fax:479-738-2448

For permission, serialization, condensation, adaptions, or for our catalog of other publications, write to Ozark Mountain Publishing, Inc., P.O. box 754, Huntsville, AR 72740, ATTN: Permissions Department.

Library of Congress Cataloging-in-Publication Data
Cannon, Dolores, 1931-
    The Convoluted Universe - Book Three, by Dolores Cannon
    The third book in *The Convoluted Universe series* provides metaphysical information obtained through numerous subjects, by hypnotic past-life regression.

1. Hypnosis   2. Reincarnation   3. Past-life therapy
4. Metaphysics   5. God Source   6. New Earth
I. ·Cannon, Dolores, 1931-   II. Reincarnation   III. Metaphysics
IV. Title

Library of Congress Catalog Card Number: 2001135281

ISBN: 978-1-886940-79-6

Cover Art and Layout: Victoria Cooper Art
Book set in: Algerian, Bell MT, Times New Roman
Book Design: Julia Degan

Published by:
**OZARK
MOUNTAIN
PUBLISHING**
PO Box 754
Huntsville, AR 72740

WWW.OZARKMT.COM
Printed in the United States of America

Wisdom is the
principal thing;
therefore get wisdom;
and with all thy getting,
get understanding.

Proverbs 1:54

Table of Contents

INTRODUCTION

I am assuming that by the time the reader has found this book, they are familiar with my work, and the way I have obtained the information I have written about in my fourteen books. But just in case this is the first one of mine that you have picked up, maybe a little explanation is in order. I do not channel. I have been a past-life hypnotherapist for thirty years, and my information is obtained through my therapy work with thousands and thousands of clients. Whereas, my main focus is therapy and helping my clients find the answer to their problems by going back to the appropriate past life, I consider myself to be the reporter, the investigator, the researcher of "lost" knowledge. This is because I have discovered a method whereby complete access is obtained to the source of all knowledge. Thus many of my books obtain information that has been lost, forgotten or never known. This gives me tremendous pleasure to uncover something new and exciting, and bring it forward to our time.

During the thirty years that I have been doing this type of work I developed my own unique technique of hypnosis. I discovered a way to access what I call the "subconscious" mind of the person I am working with. This is not the subconscious as defined by the psychiatrists. That is more of a childish part of the mind. When I am asked to define what part I am speaking to, I compare it to the Oversoul, the Higher Consciousness, the Higher Self. I believe it is the same thing that Freud referred to as the Universal Mind. Most hypnosis classes teach that you can access the subconscious by using finger motions. Having the client raise one finger for "yes", and another finger for "no". This is slow, tedious, and boring. Why do it that way, when you can have a very active conversation with that part? That is what I have developed: an easy way to access this extremely powerful part. It has access to all knowledge. You only have to think of the correct questions. I always refer to this part as "they", because it always refers to itself as "we". They have said that I can call them the "subconscious" if I want to. It doesn't matter what I call them. They have agreed to work with me, so they answer to the name "subconscious". Also during my work, I discovered that this wonderful and compassionate part of the individual has the power to instantly *cure* any physical problems. In some countries where I have taught my class, they have cautioned about using the word "cure". They say they are not allowed to say that. Instead, they want to use the word "relief". It doesn't matter how it is worded, the results are the same. The client is instantly cured in miraculous ways in only one session. I have reported some of these cases in my other books. I have been told by "them" that I must teach this method to as many as I can, because it will be considered the "therapy of the future". It is most important for people to realize that they can cure themselves. That their minds are extremely powerful, and the body will heal itself if properly directed to do so. At first, I didn't know if the procedure could be taught. How do you teach something that you developed yourself? How do you break it down so that others will be able to understand how it is done? My first attempt was in 2002 when I conducted my first class of ten people in Taos, New Mexico. I called it my "Guinea Pig" class, because I didn't know what was going to happen. People have asked me, "Didn't they resent being called 'guinea pigs'?" They said, no, because they would always be the first. Some laughingly suggested putting GP behind their names. Since that time, I have perfected the teaching technique and have held the classes all over the world. The students now are numbered in the hundreds, and are listed on my website: www.ozarkmt.com under "Students" for referral. I have received correspondence from many of my students who say the method does work and they are also having miraculous results. What greater satisfaction can a teacher have than to succeed in passing on knowledge.

My main purpose for doing the therapy sessions is to help the client with their problems. Yet along the way a great deal of knowledge has also come forth, and that is what I have written about. This is my fourteenth book about my adventures, and there will be more to come. The information pours forth through just about everyone I work with. So now I hope I have made it clear to the new readers. I do not channel, I am not a psychic. I am a hypnotherapist and my information comes from "them". I just have to collect it, organize it and put it together like a jigsaw puzzle. And that is no small task. So now, go forth and enjoy the latest volume of the *Convoluted Universe* series.

Dolores Cannon, CHT, PLT

SECTION ONE

LET US GO EXPLORING

CHAPTER ONE

MY EVOLUTION

It seems strange to me to look back over my work in regressive hypnosis therapy and see how, not only myself, but the entire field has evolved and changed. When I was thrown (ever so gently) into the field of reincarnation in 1968 it was all new and challenging. I had opened a door that would never be closed again in my mind. There were no books or instructions in those days to guide a therapist, so I have had to write my own rules and develop my own technique from the beginning. I now know that was for the better. I never had anyone telling me there was only one correct method (theirs) to do hypnosis. I never had anyone telling me you couldn't experiment, that it had to only be done the way it had been for years. I now know they were only teaching what they had been taught by someone that had been taught by someone else, ad infinitum. They did not question the methods they had been shown, but they also had not been told they could change the rules and develop their own way, follow their own path. Mainly because there were no instructions, I felt I had been thrust into something new and exciting. I discovered time travel, going to the past and being able to relive history as it was occurring. Since I didn't know what could or could not be done, I chose to challenge the abilities of the mind and find out what was possible through hypnosis.

Of course, it has taken me many years to make these discoveries, and I am still discovering new ways to use hypnosis and new ways to obtain information. In the beginning of my work when I began to do it consistently in 1979, I loved the idea of traveling through time (through my subjects) and finding out what it was like to live in those bygone days. As a researcher and a reporter, I love history. What better way to research it than to visit those time periods and ask questions and obtain information? This was where my first books came from, from information gathered from hundreds of subjects. My concept of reincarnation in those early days now seems rather simple, yet it was all I knew. It is also all most people know today, because just the acceptance that we have lived more than once is startling and life changing. The way we have been raised from childhood with the brainwashing of the Church, it takes a brave and courageous soul to wander away from tradition, and begin to ask questions. Questions that the Church does not have the answers for, or are not allowed to discuss. "If it's not in the Bible, then you don't need to know. You will have all your questions answered when you die. Maybe they keep a scorecard up there that will explain everything." Only more and more people are not willing to wait until death to find the answers. They are becoming more and more aware that there is more out there than they have been led to believe all their lives. They are beginning to ask questions, and the answers are there for the searching and questioning mind.

For myself, accepting the concept of reincarnation was not difficult. I grew up in the Protestant religion (Southern Baptist mostly), taught Sunday School, sang in the choir. Yet there was always that nagging feeling that there was more. I had questions that were not answered in the Bible or by my minister. Many times I would sit in the congregation on Sunday morning listening to the sermon, and I was itching to raise my hand and challenge what he was saying. "But maybe it means this or that. How do you know?" Of course, being civilized and a good Christian girl, I couldn't do that. So I resigned myself to teaching the children at Sunday School. The stories were interesting and I didn't have to be involved in the teaching of dogma that I no longer believed. Over time as I became more and more involved in metaphysics, I just kept my beliefs to myself. They are too precious to me to be exposed to ridicule. I dropped out of the orthodox Church and believe I have found the "real" meaning of religion. Spirituality

8

as opposed to religion. Most churches have lost their way and do not know the important difference between those two words.

When I began doing past-life regression therapy full time, I thought I had the theory of reincarnation all figured out. I was positive I knew how it worked. It was the simple process of living a life, doing the best you could, learning lessons, then dying and having your life assessed. Then the working out of the contracts with various souls, and the journey back into the body. A simple process whereby the soul gradually goes through the Earth school from grade to grade until it graduates and becomes one with God again. It all made so much sense that I didn't have any problems accepting the concept, and working with my clients in therapy based on the problems brought forward from other lives.

In my early days when I was writing my first books, I saw past lives as following a linear time pattern. I was still taking my "baby steps" and that was the only thing my mind could comprehend: one life following another separated by time and specific dates. One of my first clients was an excellent somnambulist and was capable of becoming the personality totally when regressed backwards. I saw it as a perfect way to explore history as she gave tremendous amounts of detail about the cultural, theological, etc. of the lifestyles she found herself in. I took her through 25 separate lifetimes by jumping backwards in 100 year increments. Each personality was distinct, and all I had to do was tell her to go to a certain year and she would become that very identifiable personality. I became very familiar with them, their voice, mannerisms and body language. I found it to be a remarkable way to explore history, and I thought that was to be my vocation, and what I would continue to write about. I wrote two books in those early days (1980s) based on this woman's past lives: *Jesus and the Essenes* and *A Soul Remembers Hiroshima.* I know I will eventually write a book that will include some of the other lives because of the wealth of information they contain. But my work has gone in so many different directions since those early days.

As I continued to explore past lives, other theories started to be introduced, and it bothered me. I had it all figured out. I didn't want something else coming in to shake my belief system. The first was the theory of imprinting (written about in *Keepers of the Garden* and *Between Death and Life.)* This was the concept that we didn't have to actually live many, many lives, but that we could be imprinted (or overlaid) with the memories of other people's lives. This was done if the personality was coming in to experience a life that was different and which it had no background to draw upon. The memories of those lives were taken from the vast Library on the spirit side before incarnating (with the help of our spirit guides and masters), and overlaid or imprinted onto our own soul memory. I asked at that time, "How would I know if the person was reliving a true past life or an imprint?" I was told, "You won't. And it really doesn't matter, because everything about the imprint (emotions and all) are overlaid." It was real because the personality needed the information in order to function in our world, and thus no one would be able to tell the difference. But the introduction of this unusual concept really shook my foundations. I struggled with it for a long time. Did I really want to continue in this field if my belief systems were going to be challenged? I was comfortable with my concepts of how life and death and reincarnation worked (linearly), and I didn't want my applecart upset. But then as I studied my reactions to this new idea, I realized that if I didn't at least examine it with an open mind I was no better than the Church with its doctrine: "Just accept. Don't question."

So I began to look more closely at this new concept, and others that presented themselves (such as parallel or overlapping lives), and gradually wisdom began to seep into a closed mind. It is challenging and wonderful at the same time to open up and study new concepts, because there is nothing in our background and upbringing to base these things on. Yet once the mind begins to question, there is no going back. You can't unlearn what you have learned. You can't sweep it under the rug. You can't put the worms back into the can once you have opened it. It is only now, thirty years later, that I can see the wisdom in what "they" were doing. They were spoonfeeding me little bits of information, little crumbs to whet my appetite for more. They left time for me to digest each little piece of information before giving the next. Otherwise, it would have been overwhelming, and "they" knew this. I would have thrown it all against the wall, stopped my work, and said, "I don't understand it! I don't *want* to understand it! Why can't it go back to the way it was? That's what I was comfortable with, time travel and studying history." But apparently they had other plans, and it would only have worked with me cooperating by understanding the little pieces and making them a part of myself.

Almost every client that comes to see me for past-life therapy asks the same question, "What is my purpose? Why am I here? What am I supposed to be doing?" I always tell them we can find the answer *if* it is "appropriate". The subconscious mind (which I work with) will never give the person more than they can handle. Suppose the person's destiny or purpose was 180 degrees from what their life is now. If they were told too soon, they might say, "Oh, no! That's the last thing I would want to do!" And they would put blocks in their way and sabotage themselves. So in this case, the subconscious (who knows everything) will say, "It is not time. We can't tell them." In one case, I had a man who wanted to know his purpose. During the session when I asked the question, the subconscious said, "We can't tell him yet. But oh, we wish we could! You don't know what we see! But consider he is where you were 20 years ago. You don't start a baby out on a three course meal. You give a baby milk first, then soft cereal, then mashed vegetables. Then much, much later you give it solid food." This was a perfect analogy, and it made me understand how far I had come. And how easily the "baby" can be overwhelmed and discouraged without the proper guidance. So I trust them in their wisdom. With the *Convoluted Universe* series they are continuing to expand my mind. Just when I think there is no more to learn, no more new things out there, they give me a new concept or theory to ponder. Even if it is so different and I don't understand it, I think about it and try to make it fit into the scheme of things (of life) that they are trying to show me.

"They" say we are finally ready for these more difficult concepts, and I am constantly telling them, "Yes, but you have to explain it more clearly. Otherwise, how can I write about it or lecture about it?" So my quest continues, and at least it is not dull. I am not stuck in the rut of what I already know. My mind is constantly being expanded by challenging ideas. Sometimes, I wish I could return to those simpler days in the beginning when I was exploring history and writing about those cases. But then I realize that if my work had continued in that way I would have lost a great deal of new information and knowledge. I am continuing to explore, only in a different way and in different territory.

It is still amazing to see how some people first react to the concept of reincarnation. When the idea is presented to them, they say, "You mean that I have lived before? This is not my first time here?" To many, the idea that they have had even *one* other life is mind-expanding. Not realizing that they have actually lived hundreds, in every form imaginable and unimaginable. To some, it is startling to find they have had a past life as the opposite sex. "No, I couldn't have been a woman! I have always been a man!" When I have these beginner clients, their subconscious is very gentle with them. They are usually only shown a simple, mundane past life, because that is all they can handle. It may appear simple to me, yet it holds the answers to their problems.

I had two colored men come to see me in the same week. One saw himself in the lifetime just before the present one (a modern city). When he looked at his body, he was startled, "That's a white man's hand. I can't be white! And my girlfriend's white too!" The second man saw himself in ancient Rome as a gladiator fighting in the arena. He hated it and wanted to stop, yet the only way would be to allow himself to be defeated. He was so tired of all the killing. Guess who he was mostly killing in the arena? Black slaves that had been brought in from Africa for the sport. So in its wisdom, the way the law of reincarnation works, he came back as a black man. Once the concepts of reincarnation are understood, there can be no prejudice, no judging. To do so means you may have to come back as the very thing you are judging or prejudiced about.

The logic of the way the system works is truly beautiful. You are *not* a body! You *have* a body! The "real" you, the one and only "true" you is your spirit. This is what lives forever, going from body to body having adventures and learning lessons. For each life, you put on a new suit of clothes (your body), a new costume, if you will, to play your part in the next play. But like all suits of clothes, it will eventually wear out, no matter how much you like it and want to hang on to it. At that point, you must throw the suit or costume away, and get a new one. Then you start your next part in the new play, one which you must act in with no knowledge of the plot or script. Earth is only a school that you have decided to attend. Each lifetime is a class with many lessons to be learned. You cannot go on to the next class until you have learned the lessons of this one. This is a school where you cannot skip a grade, but you can certainly have to repeat a grade. You keep on until you get it right, which may take a long or short time. If you don't get it right this time around, then you will be presented with the same problems and lessons the next time around until you finally understand it and learn what it is trying to teach you. Then you go on to the next lesson or grade, which may or may not be easier. Thus it goes until you finally graduate and can remain on the spirit side, or return to God.

What goes around, comes around. If only people could understand this. What you do to others in your life must be paid for. There is no free ride. What people do to you must be repaid by them. I have conducted thousands and thousands of past life sessions in my thirty years of therapy, and I see it time and time again. You don't get out of it. Whatever you did in a prior lifetime will be causing problems in the present one. You are brought back in contact with the very same people you wronged in the prior life. You always have to face up to your mistakes. If people only understood that, look at what a different world we would have. If they understood that what they are doing now in this life will come back to haunt them. It will be repaid in one way or another. This is a law of the Universe: the law of cause and effect, the law of balance, called: karma. This is one of the most important things I work on with my clients in therapy. I say that people carry around so much "baggage and garbage". Some of it comes from other lives, and some comes from this life. But they won't get rid of it, and it ends up making them sick. Much of it is karma carried over, sometimes from dealing with the same people for *many* lifetimes. They get into a rut, a pattern. And it is a pattern that serves no useful purpose. They need to understand that if it is not resolved *now* in the present, they will have to return and deal with it again with the same people. Sometimes, this statement is enough to shock the person into looking at the situation. "I don't want to do that! I want to be rid of them! I can't stand them!" Then they had better deal with it. I once asked the subconscious, "Wouldn't it be easier if we knew the reasons we come back? If we remembered the connections with the people in our lives?" It replied, "If wouldn't be a test if you knew the answers."

Before we come into a new life, while we are still on the spirit side reviewing our life we just left, we discuss these things with the other souls involved. We make a contract with them. "Hey, we didn't do such a good job last time. Do you want to try again? This time you be the husband and I'll be the wife. Maybe it will work that way." And we make a decision to come back and try it again with the same people. We can reverse the roles any way we want. Many times it doesn't work, because we get caught up in the same patterns, even if we don't remember what those patterns were. "We just can't get along. Everything I say or do is wrong. It's just horrible living with them. You don't know what I have to go through. I wish there was a way out." It won't be resolved as long as the person is still carrying the baggage and garbage around. Many times, the situation is so bad they cannot talk to the person face-to-face to try to work it out. In this case, I recommend talking to them mentally, mind to mind. Tell them that you know it's not working. You tried, and you know they tried, but it's not working. "So why don't we tear up the contract? You go your way, and I'll go mine. We don't have to keep going through this any more. I release you, with love." Then picture both of you tearing up the contract and throwing it away.

There is no good, there is no bad. There is no evil. There is no Devil. There is no Hell. There are only lessons to be learned. There is only energy, positive and negative. What we perceive as evil, is only human beings using the energy in a negative way. Instead of taking responsibility, it is much easier to say, "The Devil made me do it! I was taken over by evil entities that influenced me and made me do horrible things. Etc. Etc. My parents didn't understand me. Etc. Etc." We all have bad and unfortunate things happen in our lives. That is what life is all about. It is called "living". But out of the bad circumstance, did you learn anything from it? If you learned even one thing, then that was the purpose for the lesson. If you didn't learn anything from the situation, if you go through life blaming others for your misfortune, then you will continue to experience negative things until you finally come to understand what it is trying to teach you. Then you will be free. This is the value and the beauty of exploring our past lives. Even though things appear to be unjust, if we explore our past we may find the answer there. We are merely paying back the karma that we accumulated from our own past deeds. Remember, I said earlier that what goes around, comes around. We do not get out of the paying back of our debts just because we died. That would be too easy. The slate is not wiped clean until the debt is repaid. Then we can begin anew with a clean slate.

What is the quickest, but not the easiest way to repay karma? It certainly isn't: you hurt me, so I'll hurt you back! That just keeps the wheel of karma turning. No, the quickest way is to *forgive.* I didn't say it was easy to do. Some hurts are so deep that it is difficult to let them go. But you have to forgive, with no reservations, and truly mean it. Then you have to forgive *yourself.* That is also one of the hardest things in life. But if you truly want to release karma and not be condemned to keep returning to repay it, it is necessary to forgive. Once you do, and truly mean it, something magical happens. They can't hurt you any more. They can't push the buttons that set you off. It's only a game anyway with most people; they know the buttons to push to get a reaction. Once real forgiveness comes in (and remember, it doesn't have to be consciously face-to-face), everything changes. It may take a while, but you will notice subtle changes and things become easier. What is the alternative? Keeping the wheel of karma going, spinning round and round?

I had a man client who was very ill with cancer in every part of his body. In my work, I have found that cancer is often caused by suppressed anger. By holding anger in (especially if the cancer is in the abdomen or intestinal area) and not expressing it. When this happens, the anger just begins to churn, and finding no release, it begins to eat away at the body. Every time the doctor operated and eliminated the cancer in one part of the man's body it would reappear in another part. It seemed to be a never-ending cycle. So I asked him, "Are you angry about something?" He almost shouted, "Certainly. It's my ex-wife! I hate her!! She has the children and she won't let me see them!" Then I talked to him about forgiving and letting the anger go. "I can't forgive! If I do, then she has won!" I looked him straight in the eyes, and said, "If she *kills* you, she will win."

So simple, and yet so difficult. And thus the wheel of karma continues to turn.

A revelation suddenly came to me one night as I was sitting in front of my TV reading manuscript submissions during the commercial breaks. There was something one of the authors wrote. It did not relate to my deduction, because he was using it in a different context. But it triggered the proverbial light bulb that went off in my head. It was as though many loose pieces of information that I had been given or discovered on my own had suddenly been put together, and made sense in a peculiar way. The pieces had been there all along, I had just not seen them in the proper context. In my therapeutic technique, I work with the subconscious to heal the client. I do this by allowing it to find the cause of the illness or disease. Once it has explained this cause, it can take the problem away. It may be only the person's own mind doing the healing once the conscious mind interference has been removed during deep hypnosis. Whatever it is, it works and I have seen miracles performed in my office. I call this part that I communicate with the "subconscious", but I know it is not the part that the psychiatrists refer to. This is much, much bigger and more powerful. I believe I am communicating with the person's higher self, the higher consciousness, the Oversoul. It is the part that has all of the answers, and the information and the healing can be given if it is appropriate. It answers to the name of "subconscious", so that is how I refer to it. When we are communicating, it will refer to itself as "we" instead of a single entity. It always speaks the same through all of the clients I work with all over the world.

Now for the piece of the puzzle that fell into place and caused the light bulb to go off. I have published three books by Dr. O.T.

Bonnett where he explains how our minds can heal our bodies. In *Why Healing Happens,* he says it is very important to talk to the cells in our body to get their cooperation when we want something healed. In order to get their attention and let them know a higher authority is speaking to them (our personality), we should always refer to them as "we". These cells are used to going about their business taking care of the various parts of the body. They are not used to having another part become aware of them. Thus, when we can get their attention and ask them to help us, we are the *voice of God,* and they pay attention.

In the manuscript I was reading, a man mentioned that we consider ourselves to be a body, a unit. But actually we are only a casing that is housing trillions of individual cells. These cells compose all the organs and systems of our bodies. They all have their jobs to do, and work in harmony and balance with each other. We are the ones that cause imbalance and introduce disease into their world. Literally, he said that we are just a physical casing housing a huge colony of beings. They are capable of thought, digestion, reproduction, excretion, all the things that we, as humans, are capable of. Thus, because we are only a being composed of a huge colony of trillions of individual beings, it is incorrect to refer to ourselves as "I". We should call ourselves "we".

That was when the light bulb went off. This all sounded so familiar. We should communicate with the cells of our body by using the pronoun "we". The subconscious or higher conscious refers to itself as "we". Does that mean that it is also part of an even bigger consciousness? I believe so, and the chapter about God or the Source will begin to make this clear. No one is alone. We are all part of a much larger structure, and each part depends on the other parts in order to survive. It cannot exist alone. I have said many times in my lectures that we are only cells in the body of God. Now it began to fall into place. I have been told that everything is about communication, and the accumulation of information. We have to live countless lifetimes learning every possible lesson and gathering knowledge. For what purpose? I have been told that we must take this accumulation of information back to God when we have completed all of our lessons and "graduated". He was curious, that is why we were created in the beginning as individual sparks of light. He wanted to learn and he couldn't do it on His own. So we were created and sent out to learn everything possible and bring it back to Him. As the information in this book will show, we were incredibly happy and content to remain with God, where there was Love beyond comprehension. We never wanted to leave, but we had to because that was the purpose of our creation. Many people carry that feeling of separation and loneliness into this life, never understanding where it comes from. We were only content when we were all together. The separation was extremely difficult, and we will only be complete when we can return "home" and remain there.

This then began to make sense. Even within our bodies it is about communication. The cells communicate and relate to each other, and even though cells are constantly dying and being replaced, they consider themselves to be a whole. They do not see themselves as separate. Cells and DNA are constantly sending information to our brains and communicating with that main part of us. Would it be proper to say that these cells see *us* as their God, and their task is to accumulate information and knowledge in the only way they know how, and transfer that knowledge to the higher part of our body? This is the same thing we are supposed to be doing through our myriad of lifetimes: accumulating information and sending it back to God.

I assume that if the cells tried to explain their awareness of us (if they ever are aware), they would have as much difficulty as the clients I work with, trying to define their perception of God. We would probably be seen as this huge, vague "something" outside of the brain and body. All powerful (because we have the power to harm *them*), and an All-knowing wispy thing that they cannot see or comprehend. So they continue their job as part of an organ or whatever, totally unaware that when we die, *they* die. The individual cells are doing their job, and may not be aware that they are part of an organ (heart/liver/ kidneys, etc.). This may also be an explanation or analogy of how our larger soul is composed of many parts (lives/personalities) all living their own destinies, totally unaware that they are part of a larger unit. We see ourselves as individual, and performing separately from our larger soul and from our God. I think there is more similarity here than difference. It just takes examining a new concept.

In *Convoluted Universe - Book Two,* it was said that the Earth is also a storehouse of information that it accumulates from all the living beings (cells) that exist on it. The Sun is also accumulating information from, not only the Earth, but all the other planets, moons, asteroids, and satellites that occupy its space. We were told that all the other Suns are acting as accumulators of information received from their various star systems. The universes are accumulating information from all the star systems. It is amazing to me to be told that it is all about storing knowledge and information. It is the same from the microcosm (and we don't know how small that goes) to the macrocosm (and we don't know how large that is). Only God or the Source knows the purpose of all the storing of information. Maybe to help in the creation of new worlds? We have already found in my other books that the cycle of reincarnation, rebirth or regeneration does not only apply to humans. In another chapter, I will show how it applies to every living thing (which encompasses everything, because all is energy and thus all is alive).

We discovered that even the stars in the heavens go through cycles of death and rebirth. A star or Sun has a finite lifetime also, and it dies in a burst of glory when its energy (or soul?) is released and it goes supernova. I asked, "What happens then?" And I was told that the energy is recycled to create new stars. The universe is constantly expanding, but even it has a finite life. It can only expand so far (or explode out) until it reaches the point where it can go no further. Then it begins to implode back on itself. The universe begins to lose energy and die. When it reaches that point, what happens then? I was told, "Then the whole process starts over. It all begins anew." Everything is in the process of constant rebirth, recycling and regeneration.

Bringing it back to the practical, the everyday lives of each one of us (instead of leaving it out there beyond our imagination), this means that our minds are capable of anything. We don't realize how much power we really have. We are so used to people placing limitations on us. We can create anything we want in life. We can heal our bodies. We can have it all. All we have to do is remove the limitations we and others have placed upon ourselves. We have to see how powerful we really are. Then we have to *believe!* Believe and trust. No one can take our power away from us unless we allow it. It is now time in our world to reclaim these abilities that were commonplace in generations past. Our world is going through dramatic changes and we need to change to go with it. We will need all of our powers (psychic and otherwise) returned to us. In the new world, the new Earth, this will be as common and natural as breathing. This is why we are being awakened now. Everything is falling into place, and we all have our parts to play.

These things are my understandings (thus far). They may not be *your* understanding. But keep an open mind, and let us explore together.

CHAPTER TWO

SUMMARY OF TYPICAL CASES

The bulk of my hypnosis work during the past thirty years has been therapy. I realize my job is to help the person who comes to see me find explanations and relief from their problems, so they can live a normal and fulfilling life. So they can move forward without the load of the "baggage and garbage" holding them back. This is my main focus. I take the client back to the appropriate past life so they can understand the source of their problems in this life. Of course, along the way my work has taken many twists and turns, and has brought forth the mind-bending concepts that I am now writing about. In this chapter, I want to cover a few, a bare minimum, of typical therapy cases and their connections with past lives.

At the beginning of November 2006, I had two cases back to back dealing with child abuse. One was a man and the other a woman, both affected very deeply by their experiences. The man remembered constant beatings from the age of two until he left home at the age of 18. He still held great anger and resentment towards his father. The other, the woman, had blocked out all memories of events that occurred before the age of 17. She was sexually abused and molested by her father from the age of 4 or 5. She also held great anger and resentment, because she thought he had destroyed her life. After she left home, she attempted to go to college, but everything was too much for her. She turned to drugs, alcohol and prostitution. When she came to see me (she was 29) she had reached her lowest point and desperately needed help. She had attempted suicide and had been institutionalized. The drugs and alcohol had affected her body, especially her kidneys. She had to have one of them removed. Her remaining kidney was not functioning effectively, and she was experiencing toxins and physical effects. (The subconscious said she was trying to kill herself to put an end to her suffering.) She was in a deep depression and wanted to sleep all the time, which was difficult because she was trying to raise three children by herself. She was also into self-mutilation, cutting and scraping on her body. It was obvious she hated her body (although she was beautiful, she saw herself as ugly), and was trying to destroy the offending part of herself. Both of these people were miserable, sad, and depressed. When they left my office, their entire lives had been turned around and they were ready to face the world with hope instead of despair, because we found the cause of their problems. Each was different, yet similar.

The man went back to a battlefield in World War I. He did not want to be there. He said the recruiters lied to him. They told him it was going to be a short war, and he would not have to fight. Yet here he found himself in the thick of it. There were bullets firing all around, bombs going off and deadly gas filled the air. Soldiers were dying all around him. He said his brother was there somewhere, but he couldn't see him because of all the smoke and confusion. My client was the one who wanted to go to fight in the war. His brother had not wanted to, and he had talked him into it. Since he was so frightened, I assumed he was probably going to die out there during the battle. When I moved him to the last day of his life, he surprised me by saying he was old, and dying in bed. He had survived the war and made it home safely, where he married and had a family. His brother, however, had not been as fortunate. He was killed during the war. Of course, he felt guilty about this, because he felt his brother would have been alive if he hadn't talked him into joining the Army with him. When we got to the subconscious, it said his brother had come back into this life as his present-day father. The brother came in with much anger and resentment, because he felt he had been cheated out of his life. He was determined to make him pay back what he had taken from him. The best way was to take his life away from him, or at least make it as miserable as possible. This explained the unprovoked anger that the father exhibited toward the young boy. Of course, the father is to be pitied because he was incurring a great deal of accumulated karma by coming back with this unresolved anger. When the man understood the connection, he was able to let the father go, to release and forgive him, thus tearing up the contract and cutting the ties. After much work, he left a changed man. He also had been suffering from severe back pain from his neck and shoulders down into his lower back. It was obvious this was caused by carrying this heavy load around for fifty years. He was now able to release it.

The woman's connection was different, yet similar. She saw herself in war-torn Germany in World War II. There were soldiers fighting in the streets, but they were not fighting other soldiers, they were fighting and shooting civilians. She was a female doctor and was trying to help some of the many people who lay around the streets bleeding and dying from gunshot wounds. The soldiers were acting crazed, and were raping the women before they shot them. They were also shooting the men and children. She said the ones being shot were presumed to be Jews, and this was their way of destroying them. Pure chaos reigned on the streets. She tried to help several of the people, but was pushed aside by the angry soldiers. At first, they did not try to harm her because they knew she was a doctor. But then the fighting and panic became worse, and she fled into a building and hid in the stairwell, watching the slaughter taking place outside. There they discovered her, and dragged her out into the street. At this point, they were acting totally insane and wouldn't listen to anyone. They tied her up and many soldiers took turns raping her. Then they shot her in the head, killing her. When I had her leave the body, she saw that they threw her body on a pile of many other bodies. Then they set fire to the pile and burned them all. After death, she said she did not have any anger towards them, because she understood they were caught up in the emotions of war. They were doing their "man" thing.

She came back into this lifetime with the plan of helping other people, to make up for her inability to help in that lifetime. Her present father had been one of the Nazi soldiers, the first to rape her. He had returned to repay the injustice by being her father, intending to raise and protect her. That had been the plan, but it apparently changed after he got here into the body. The subconscious said he got caught up in the ways of the flesh, and forgot his original purpose. This shows that even though the incoming soul has a good plan and noble intentions to repay karma, life has a way of affecting them, and being human is not that easy. On the other side it always looks easy, like it would be simple to accomplish. But the incoming soul forgets that, because this is a world of free will, it will have to contend with the free will of others, and the pressures of being human dealing with emotions. So he was caught up in it, and regrettably accumulated more karma. Both of these men are to be pitied rather than reviled.

Since the circumstances had changed, the woman's plan had to be changed. She came in to help. She now would still be able to help, but from a totally different angle than she had anticipated. Her many terrible experiences were to prepare her to help other women who had been through sexual abuse. She would be able to help them because she understood it. Who better to help these victims than someone who "has been there, done that"? Her life could now turn around and she could also let go of the past, and move forward.

Two different cases along the same line: child abuse. Two cases where the reasons for coming back were to help, but it changed after getting into the body, and being exposed to human ways. The two not only had to forgive the offending fathers, but also to forgive themselves, which is often the hardest thing of all.

An even stranger explanation for child abuse that also extended into marital abuse was explained by a series of lifetimes in a religious environment, monasteries, nunneries and convents.

25

There under strict and unloving circumstances the belief was deeply ingrained that, in order to go to Heaven and be with God, one must suffer. And suffer these so-called "religious" people did. These beliefs were so much a part of my woman client that she could not let go of it, even though she had no conscious memory of it. And all the other people involved repeatedly in those lives returned with her to this one to play their roles as abusers. They created the same environment, because of the belief that that was the only way to get to Heaven.

This is an important point. Vows taken in other lifetimes are extremely important and carry great power, because they are usually taken with great conviction. Because they were not reneged during the lifetime, they carry over into this one. Some of the most common are: the vow of celibacy, chastity, which causes sexual problems in the present life. And the vow of poverty, which brings money problems. And now we discover the vow to suffer. The easiest way to release these is to leave them with the entity in the past who took the vows. To explain that they had importance and purpose in that lifetime, but are definitely not appropriate for the present one. Then the vows can be cancelled or reneged and the power of them dispelled.

A woman client had a series of car accidents, rear enders trying to get her attention. "Their" method of waking her up seemed drastic, but I have discovered that if people don't pay attention to the subtle hints the subconscious tries to drop, then more drastic measures are often required. They said they had tried for many years, but "she was very caught in old programs." One of my students had a hard time understanding this, when I gave many examples during my hypnosis class of people having terrible accidents that left them maimed or crippled. Yet the tragic incidents did change the direction of their lives. My student said, "That could not be true. Spirit would never do that to anyone. They are there to help and protect, not to harm."

This is true. They are always watching over us and are there to help us. "We are always here, and that means everything. Every need is met. Every curiosity answered." But how do we know the accidents are not part of the life plan? When the person is on the spirit side in between lives, they consult with their guides, the elders and the masters, as they try to construct a plan for the type of life they want to experience upon returning to Earth. This, of course, is designed to pay off karma as well as how to grow and learn more, and also to help as many others as possible. Maybe it was also part of the plan that if the person forgot their mission (as often happens), that those from the other side would create events to pull them back to their soul path. So what appears to be drastic, is actually part of the plan that everyone involved agreed to. If subtle hints and intuitions do not work, then something stronger must be tried. It is all done out of love, although it may not appear to be so from our limited human viewpoint. During my lectures I always say, "Everyone has bad things happen to them. We cannot escape it. It is part of life. But when you look at it, *really* look at it, did you learn anything from it? If you learned even one thing, then that was the purpose of it." No one ever said life would be easy. This is considered a very challenging planet. And the more lessons we learn the sooner we can get off the wheel of karma, and stop having to return here. We can then progress upward along the path, instead of spiraling round and round going nowhere.

A female client in her fifties was looking for the reasons for her severe illness: liver and pancreas problems. It almost killed her when she was 41, although it had been present in a less severe form all of her life. It was totally incapacitating, and the doctors at the time told her to prepare to die. There was no help, except maybe a liver transplant, and she was too ill to consider that. Even though they told her she would die, she refused to accept that. (That, of course, is half the battle.) Her life was saved when she met an alternative practitioner who specialized in kinetics, involving muscle responses. The practitioner changed her lifestyle, especially her eating habits and turned her life around. She was still experiencing some problems in the liver area, but not nearly as severe as a few years before. This was the main focus of the session, to try to discover the cause of the illness, and bring the body the rest of the way into full recovery. During the session, we discovered an unusual explanation for liver and pancreas disease.

She went through two lives, each centering on the loss of a loved one, a man she was intending to marry. The first was in a dismal village community where there was nothing but sadness and defeat. She wanted desperately to escape from the unhappiness of the home life (cruel father, disinterested mother, and houseful of hungry children). She met an outsider who came into the village and expected to marry him. She went to the church in wedding dress and all her relatives were there. She was very happy at the prospect of marrying and leaving the area. The man did not arrive; she was left at the altar. Everyone in the family jeered and ridiculed her. "How dare she think she could escape and have a different kind of life. She is nothing, and no one will ever want her." She had no choice but to return to the unhappy home. There she grieved herself to death and died, essentially of a broken heart. She thought there was no way out of the situation, which was probably correct in that time period.

I took her further back to try to discover the reason why she put herself into that type of situation. She saw herself in another life, a tavern scene where everyone was happy. They were celebrating her engagement. But before she could be married, her fiancee was killed in a farm accident caused by a horse pulling a wagon. She was very unhappy, and never married. She died in her forties, alone but not friendless. Her subconscious said the reason for the illness in this life was to protect her from the same unhappiness. She had been terribly affected by the loss of her love in two lifetimes. So in this life, she would not even be allowed the possibility of marriage. If she was so ill, especially during the years of her life when she would most likely find a mate, then the odds were that she would not be hurt again. Her subconscious said she could very well have died at that time, but instead, the meeting with the alternative practitioner turned her life toward thinking about metaphysics. Thus, her life could take a more productive turn. So she was allowed to live so she could learn and teach others. Since there was no likelihood that she would marry now, there was no need for the illness, so the remnants of it could be taken away. (The symptoms were the same as what she died from in the second life.) Her migraines were also connected in the same way, and could disappear now.

A case of extreme depression and isolation from society (since childhood) was traced back through two former lifetimes. Although the man was born into a very large family (12 children), he never felt a closeness to any of them. There was always the feeling of isolation, and depression. This continued throughout his life: a feeling of apathy, of not caring, of being an observer on the outside looking in. He was treated by psychiatrists and put on medication for depression, but he didn't think it did any good. Even natural remedies had no affect. One diagnosis called it "Freedom from harm" complex. In other words, to avoid being hurt, it was easier to shut down and not get involved with people or anything. It was a lonely existence, even his job gave him no satisfaction. He had never married, although he was physically attractive. He assumed his apathy and disinterest in life pushed women away. He did have one relationship where he was deeply attracted to a woman and wanted to marry, but it did not work out, and it made him more depressed. Another time a woman was attracted to him, but he did not respond. He thought his only solution was to commit suicide, and he was seriously considering this. He now had a girlfriend who was trying to understand him from a metaphysical viewpoint, and he was hoping it would work

29

out. It was at her urging that he agreed to the regression. He was skeptical when the session began, and was smirking as though the whole idea was laughable, but he agreed to participate. When we began the session, and I asked his subconscious to take us back to find the reason for his desire for isolation, he said he felt a thrill of joy, as though maybe it was time to find the answer. He was surprised when he felt the surge of excitement at the mention of discovering the reason for his problem.

He went to a former lifetime that was surprisingly similar to the one he was living now. He was living in a small town (maybe out West) where he worked at repairing buggies and carriages. (He now worked at electronics and repairing machines powered by computers in factories.) He was a loner with no family, and felt like an outcast in the town. He was attracted to a beautiful black-haired woman, and suffered in silence as she did not return his affection. He was too withdrawn to make his intentions known. He was unhappy at his work, and nothing seemed worthwhile. The only place he seemed happy was when he went to a cliff overlooking the ocean, and he could sit there in silence getting away from everything. Later, even this did not offer consolation. Eventually, he could not take it anymore and shot himself in the head. Although hoping to end it all, we know that does not happen. Suicide only made things worse, because the law of karma says that you must repeat the same circumstances until you learn the lesson. And that certainly seemed true, as he tearfully said, "My life now is a repeat of that one. I didn't escape from anything." He thought the first woman that he was attracted to in this present life was the same woman from the other life, and she also rejected him. History was repeating itself. He was being dealt the same hand of cards to see what he would do with it this time. He was surprised later that he had been crying profusely during the sad lifetime of the man who repaired carriages, and ended up committing suicide.

But where did that life come from? Why was he caught up in a cycle of repeating the same mistakes again? What created the pattern? I took him further back to try to find the answer. He went to a lifetime in the desert. There was a group of nomads who wandered the desert from place to place with camels, etc., and set up their tents at various sites. He was a very beautiful young woman who was very much aware of her sexuality. She openly flaunted it and teased the men in the group. She enjoyed the effect she had on them, by offering them her charms and then withdrawing. But it finally backfired on her, when she went too far and the men did not think it was funny any more. She was assaulted and raped so badly that she died as a result. So in the next life as the man in the town in the old West, he unconsciously felt it was safer to have no sexual feelings at all. To withdraw from any contact with other people. Also to know what it was like to experience rejection. This pattern continued into his present life because of the karmic debt of suicide. The two past lives had gone from one extreme to the other. He would have to find a middle ground in order to overcome the effects. One way to do this was to understand how it all happened, and to realize that suicide was not the answer. He had considered suicide several times in this life, but thankfully stopped just short of doing it. You don't escape from anything.

Donna was a lesbian who wanted to have a child with her partner by artificial insemination. First they used the sperm of Donna's brother so there would be a genetic connection, but the baby boy was stillborn. They tried again using the sperm of a donor who was not related, but of similar coloring and background. This time it resulted in the live birth of a daughter. Everything was fine until she and her partner had a falling out when the girl was about 8 years old. The mother took the child and would not let Donna have contact. This had resulted in much heartache. She naturally wanted some clarification. She was told that she and the little girl had been together in many, many lifetimes and there was great love there. The separation happened

31

for a good reason, and for growth. They would be reunited when it would be appropriate. I asked about the little boy who was stillborn. "It's the same soul. It had to do with lessons for the brother who was donating the sperm. And this child was not meant to have those actual genetic structures. It was, to say, a 'dry run', for the baby and for Donna and for her partner. And it was an experience, karmicly, for the brother who donated, but it was the same soul that entered the little girl."

The genetics were not correct, and when they used a different donor, the genetics were more compatible. It was the same soul, because it was meant to come into that family. I think if people could understand that, it would stop much of the grieving. When there is a death of a baby, and another birth soon after, it is often the same soul, because it has made an agreement or contract with the individuals involved. In the meantime, many lessons were available to be learned by all the parties involved.

A woman went through a past life as a man that was not very eventful, except that he was killed by a group of people. He had fallen deeply in love with a woman who was not considered to be in his class, so they killed him. Yet that did not kill the love and extreme emotion the man felt. The client said when she awakened that she had never felt such deep, deep emotion and love towards anyone. It was very powerful. After the man died, he did not want to leave the scene or the life. In his spirit form he went to where the woman lived and saw her weeping. He put his invisible arms around her and tried to console her, even though he knew she could not feel him. Eventually, he knew he could not stay there and floated upward towards a bright light. The farther he got from the scene the better he felt. Later when he met with the council on the other side and they evaluated the lifetime, they said he had learned a very valuable and important lesson. He was allowed to experience true love. He then had to prepare to come back, and to reenter the Earth scene. He was shown three different life scenarios, so he could make a choice which to experience as his next incarnation. He still thought about his lost love, and wanted to be with her again. He was told that love was what it was all about, but to experience the same relationship again would not advance him. He could be with her again, but in a different role capacity. That was what it was all about: switching and playing different parts, often with the same people. Thus we return again and again, switching back and forth in our role-playing in the next scenario. The important thing to remember was that we could never lose that love. Death cannot separate us. It is just placed in another form, but it is never lost. Love is the greatest lesson of all, no matter how many challenges it must go through. We are always reunited in one form or another. To understand love and experience it is the ultimate lesson. Once we understand this, we can have love and compassion for everyone, for we never know which role they have chosen to play this time around.

During one of my other sessions, I was told that many of our dreams are messages from our subconscious. And because they are delivered in symbols, they are very difficult for our conscious mind to understand. Many of my clients bring pages of their dreams to the session, wanting an explanation for them. The subconscious always says that they are easy to understand once you focus your attention on the symbols. Just as dreams are messages, so are nightmares. If the subconscious has tried to get a message across in many different ways, and the person doesn't understand, it will try to deliver the message more forcefully in a nightmare. What better way to get your attention than to frighten you? You will definitely remember the nightmare if it causes fear when you awaken suddenly. The symbols then will be fresh in your mind, and can be studied more closely.

Following are selected questions asked during various sessions:

Q: What actually happens to a person when the body dies? I mean, immediately after.

A: In our human minds, we believe that we will be in contact with other spirit bodies who will direct us toward that path which we feel will lead us to God. *We* program the immediate after-death experience while we are here in our bodies. It is individual.

Q: When the body dies, is there any pain associated with it when the spirit leaves?

A: No. It seems that the spirit leaves the body shortly before the physical body actually dies. I thought of sudden death in war. There seems to be great confusion. Also other sudden, "accidental" deaths. In old age and in illness, the spirit takes trips out in preparation.

Q: Many people have told me that when a baby is born, the spirit doesn't remain in the body all the time. Is this correct?

A: The spirit is aware of the time of conception, and it is possible for the spirit to "check in" on the progress of the fetus. It seems to enter at birth or shortly after. But because it is so connected to the spirit world, it does take "trips" to visit the familiar home. Sudden infant death seems to be when the spirit chooses to stay in the spirit world. Or perhaps stayed longer than the newly emerging physical body is able to operate on its own. It seems that we do need the force of the spirit in cooperation with the physical body in order to maintain physical life.

Q: Do you think sometimes it is a mistake? The spirit just doesn't come back in time?

A: There doesn't seem to be any actual "mistakes"!!! It seems that you need to *believe* that you can get back in if you so choose. It also seems that you need to give your consciousness permission to so choose to do otherwise.

Q: We don't want to do anything to cause danger.

A: Danger! "Danger" does not necessarily mean leaving the physical body forever!

Q: When the baby is sleeping, is the spirit going back and forth to the spiritual plane?

A: That is the easiest time for the baby, yes. That is also what is happening to older people and those who are very ill.

Q: During these times, they are conferring with the spirit plane?

A: They are *there*.

Q: Can you give an explanation of Hell?

A: When you die, believing in your human mind that you are going to burn in the fires of Hell, your first experience will be what your mind has made for you. This experience, however, need not *last*. It *will* be what you see *first*. Your expanded self can grow in the positive good almost instantly. All it takes is recognition. But if you *believe* that you will go to *Hell* when you die, that is the first thing you will be aware of. The Hell *you* have made.

Q: Then you won't have to stay there?

A: No, you won't.

Q: How can they be released from this thing of their own mind?

A: The greatest good, which for your terms we'll call "God". It seems that God is able to make manifest to each human consciousness, that which is necessary to open the door to enlightenment. Enlightenment means that you realize that you can create, with your consciousness, whatever it is you so desire, because you *have* the greatest force with you.

Q: What are we? We like to think of ourselves as a personality, an individual.

A: We are all a part of God.

35

Q: Is there really much difference between meditation and prayer?

A: There is a *large* difference. "Prayer" is consciously directed energy. "Meditation" is being open to what comes in. Prayer is directing, not so much asking. Prayer means to consciously direct your thoughts which *are* your power.

Q: Then prayer is a real thing?

A: Prayer is definitely real, and it is definitely powerful.

Q: Some people use empty prayers. They just repeat things. They really don't put anything behind it.

A: That is because they are limited by each of their individual definitions of the term.

Q: In some churches, they just recite things and there is no meaning behind it.

A: The church isn't a good place to find legitimate prayer. We are only now learning what prayer really is. As each of us has more power than we are aware of, when we come together to direct our thoughts to a certain goal, we have *greatly magnified* power. The churches *had* the right idea in forming a place where people could come together and greatly magnify their power to the greater good. Unfortunately, the direction got lost.

Q: Do they have to pray to an entity or to anyone in particular?

A: Prayer means to "Think your conscious thoughts toward a specific goal." You can pray toward the negative as well as the positive. It is hoped that it would always be toward the positive. The positive force is the greatest force.

Q: You don't have to direct it toward a god or another entity?

A: That is where man has messed up. The Force is *all*. To limit it to *an* entity is not correct. Aim it to the "glue".

Q: Then they don't need to pray to a god and ask for help in that way?

A: Oh, *no!* God is not "a being" or "an entity". God, as you are speaking of God, is the great positive *force,* the collective positive force of *ALL THAT IS.* To call God "an entity", and **especially** to *personify* God, is to *limit* the concept.

Q: *Humans are so used to thinking of it as a higher person.*

A: That is correct. That is one of your largest problems.

Q: *Then when we use the force of prayer, we don't direct it to any one thing. We just direct it to a goal?*

A: Correct. The goal of merging with the greatest good, the positive force. The glue of the universe! That is an appropriate term.

Q: *What about praying for protection of other individuals?*

A: What you are actually doing is praying that the positive force be conscious of that individual. You are praying for awareness of the positive force.

Q: *But it does no harm to direct it toward a "figure" we call God, does it?*

A: It only limits it (the concept).

Q: *What about angels? Some people pray to angels and saints.*

A: Those terms are also limiting. We are all operating through physical minds. There are many concepts incomprehensible to the human brain: "Foreverness", "Eternity", are concepts very difficult for the limited human brain to ascertain. So if it is helpful to the individual to think in terms of "Angels, Spirits, and Gods," that should be the *vehicle* to get them to the larger understanding. It should not be the end.

Q: *I have heard so many theories. I have heard that when the world was created, the angels were those spirits or souls that never left the sight of God.*

A: To use terms like the "sight" of God is already personifying the force. The force can manifest *however* it can be received by the human mind. This is all coming from the "God Source". All is from God. Any *negative* things have been made up by man.

D: How do you define angels?
J: They are those who are in service to this humanity. In the most general terms that's how we define them. As there are several levels of – by levels we do not mean superior or inferior. We mean levels in the service that they render to humanity. But this group is dedicated to the welfare, to helping, those who have chosen to incarnate in this place.
D: I've heard that they have never had physical existences. Is that true? (Yes) So they help the ones who have agreed to become physical.
J: That is correct.

Q: Would it be helpful to meditate at any certain time of day?
A: Yes. The time before sunrise, when the day is not day and the night is not night, there is a stillness and a darkness and a peace. The whole Earth is aware of this time. So is everyone else. So are the animals and the plants, the winds and the waters. This is the optimum, premium, easiest and *best* time to meditate. – Of course, it is not always the easiest time for the human who is working!
Q: Would there be a second best time of the day?
A: Yes, early morning. Any *early* morning time seems to be a good time. The other time seems to be when the sun sinks from sight. When we have that twilight period, there is also a stillness that occurs, that we as humans are also aware of. That, too, is a good time. There is no *bad* time to meditate! *Any* time a human will use the discipline to do it is a good time.
Q: How can we be sure if the thoughts that come through in meditation are our thoughts or coming from higher planes?

38

A: It is the amount of emotion and feeling that is connected with that thought. Random thoughts that occur and flit through your mind about things past, things desired, speculations, hopes and dreams, do *not* have the emotional impact that impressions from your larger self have. The *feeling* is your key. If you just think the answer in words, with no feeling, it needs to be critically analyzed. It seems that *feeling* is essential.

Asked about whether humans are assisted with inventions.

A: Humans are able to plug into the need for a certain thing *and* the conscious thought that has already been generated around that certain thing. It is like a physical blob. People who have concentrated on the problem (this is the blob), have opened themselves up to *receiving* and actually *connecting to* this thought form. Now, many of them aren't aware. Just because they concentrated on it a long time doesn't mean they necessarily meditated or prayed. They may just have thought about it a whole lot. To those people, the invention or idea for the invention may have come in a dream or a flash of insight. Frequently you have read of inventors telling that when they waked, the answer to whatever it was, was there in their brains. This explains also why, in different parts of the world, people come up with the same new invention at relatively the same time. They simply plugged into that problem and the solutions that have been spinning around that problem. Humans create the problem *and* the solution.

Q: *Even if it's a radical idea that no one has ever thought of? Some inventions are ahead of their time.*

A: That is because you are thinking in terms of linear time. There is really no such thing as "before". *All* exists simultaneously.

Humans, and their limited human brains, put things in order. It is just about the only way humans can operate. They would be like mice running around in a maze if they didn't make up these arbitrary structures for themselves.

About prophecy:

A: It seems that all are probabilities. It also seems that we Western humans seem to be so locked into outlines or hierarchies, ways of A, B, and C'ing things, that we have to measure, define, and delineate everything. So we have made a concept called "time", and now we make a concept called "date". It is inaccurate for humans to put dates and times on things, because that is not the way they are. It is only our *human* way of trying to *figure out* things. It is not accurate. Using terms like "October 26th" is a left-brained way of trying to handle impressions and operations that are going on. It isn't the best way for making predictions.

Q: You know, humans have to have time frames.

A: They think they do! (Laughter)

Q: But it makes things easier.

A: It makes it easier, but it also adds greatly to the confusion about simultaneous time.

Q: About simultaneous time. Let me give you a kind of either/or. Let's take 14th century Europe. In our time we have history books written about the events that took place in 14th century Europe. Does simultaneous time say that 14th century Europe is still going on, and that people are still somehow doing their things in a continuation of the 14th century? Or is the 14th century going on right now at the same time?

A: The information that the President would be killed in a crash before the election didn't happen in *this* particular time and place. That does not mean it didn't happen. It means that it didn't happen in *our* focus. What happens and is happening in the 14th century has just the same probabilities as that one singular example of the President not being killed in the crash that we *know* of in *this* focus. Our history books are written about *one focus.*

Q: Other probable 14th centuries are occurring now, is that the idea?

A: Yes, and they are influenced by things that we do now, in the future, and may have done in the past, using those human terms.

Q: Is the 14th century kind of frozen in some way so the people don't progress into the 15th century?

A: Say you're a 14th century person. You are not a "single" person. Just like if you stand in one place and look forward, and then adjust your body position one-half inch to the right, you now have a different focus. Look how many different focuses you can have just by turning your body in a complete circle. That is how many different probabilities can occur at the same time, anywhere, any time. It is a concept very hard for the human to grasp.

Q: It is difficult because we know that the physical body does develop from a baby to an old man. I can't understand the concept of no time.

A: That is the focus you are aware of, but you also know a baby who didn't develop into an adult. (Yes) Well, it happened to be *that* focus that you saw that baby in at the time. That same baby, in *another* focus, can grow old.

Q: That's the part that's hard for me to understand, because if it is all happening at one time, you know your own body is different at different years.

A: You only know one focus. This physical focus that we're in here now. In another focus, Dolores Cannon might be a circus acrobat! But in dreams you are *aware* of some of your other focuses. We all are. We don't look the same, we don't have the same relationships, yet frequently we can identify ourselves in our dreams.

41

Q: Yes, but they say your dreams are symbolism.

A: Your *life* is symbolism. Symbolism is how we *all* live.

Q: Is it true that the only thing that seems real is the thing we are able to focus on at that time?

A: That is exactly right. That is why people can experience a past life for Dolores at this very moment in 14th century Sweden or wherever. That is *exactly* right. It is simply shifting the focus.

Q: But in my work, I have seen patterns of how one lifetime influences another life, and it seems to be going in progression.

A: Yes, in *that* focus there is always a progression.

S: If you were to have an experience which was somewhat traumatic, if you sit and think about that experience 10 years later, you are experiencing simultaneous time. Where your mind goes is the time frame with which you are experiencing. The amount of energy you put into that thought puts you more fully into that time frame.

D: When I do past life regressions, would that be along the same line?

S: Similar. What one would prefer in lifetime awarenesses would be to follow patterns which carry through from lifetime to lifetime. It would be like overlays. Take a base picture of self or soul. Take a clear page with a sock painted on. Take another clear paper, put the other sock on, so on and so forth until you have layers which are fully formed with the original page. Now if you choose a dirty sock, that is your choice. But you still have a sock.

D: One thing we've been trying to understand in past life regression is, if the past life personality is in another country, and their native language is another language, why do they communicate with me in English?

S: They are using the brain circuitry of the present lifetime. The self automatically translates into comprehensive terms of the present.

D: *Is it possible to have them speak in their own native language?*

S: It is possible if subject is fully drawn or in sync with that past life.

D: *Sometimes they do not know common English expressions when they are translating or whatever it is they are doing.*

S: Because they are in sync with that past life. There is a blending, so to speak, of both lifetimes so that some of past life terminology blends with present life terminology. There is enough blending between the two to set up at that time a sense of almost confusion within self. They are in sync enough to be able to be aware of lifetime in order to be able to understand lifetime. They would have to be aware of that time period. But the basic brain functions are still rooted in present lifetime languages and awarenesses.

D: *But it is possible from time to time to have foreign words and phrases slip through?*

S: Oh, yes, yes.

D: *And also with music. They were able to sing in their language of the time, which we thought was strange. Then it is possible?*

S: It is possible. What is impossible?

An explanation of what is occurring when someone channels entities.

A: All who channel, those who do the channeling and those who channel, are aspects of each other. A way of comparison would be like an electrical circuit board. Each individual life or aspect is a point on that board. The electrical currents travel from one point to another, but only when that particular point or particular circuit is open does a connection occur. This circuit board would be a grand size for each oversoul. You are fully far more than just an individual circuit. You are connected by each. In order to channel through to another circuit, that electrical pattern must be the same. The importance of you as an individual self is most significant in that if you do not allow this connectedness to occur, that circuitry is cut off by one. In order to allow and experience fully that circuitry, the simplicity of energy, which is love, is most important. All the ideas of consciousness raising and becoming positive within your life, all it boils down to is self love. How can you give love if you do not feel love? How can you express and give away what you do not have? It is self love; call it self worth, call it self esteem, call it anything you wish. It is still self love. I am but a connection in the circuit, an aspect of the one who is channeling me.

About reincarnation:

Q: If a person has left this life and believes that he is going to be reincarnated in another life, can he choose the time and place? Or is it out of his hands?

S: Nothing is out of your hands. You are fully and totally in control of your life. If you feel a drawness to a particular country or time, the soul, so to speak, will automatically program the desire into the self. Desire was there before conscious thought. "Oh, I would like to live in Tibet in 2002." These thoughts are yours, these thoughts are your programming.

Q: Can you go backward into a life of 10,000 BC as easily as you can go forward into 2001? In other words, if time is simultaneous and we think in terms of linear time, can you go backwards as well as forwards?

S: Certainly.

Q: How is that accomplished?

S: How? It is already accomplished. The world as you know it, reality as you know it, is fully formed. It is not a piece of a pie, or a pie crust still waiting to be filled and baked. It is the pie. Where you happen to be right now is only where your conscious thought happens to be directed. All is all, but to make things less confusing, and because of the nature of this reality, you are aware of right now. That does not mean yesterday is not or never occurred, or tomorrow is not or never occurred. It is now. Where you choose to focus is where you place you time, but *all is*.

Q: Suppose a person wanted to go back into a particular time period and make a historical change. Would it be possible then for a whole new future to spring from that change?

S: Wonderful question. Yes, it is possible. However, first it would take the strength of conviction that this can be done. It would take a fully aware consciousness, subconscious, superconsciousness experience in order to do this. That does not mean that present history would be different for those involved in that time. What it would do is cause an offshoot, a "Y" in the road. A creation of a different reality. But it would not necessarily change the reality for those involved here at this moment.

Q: It would be a probable reality? (Yes) *Has that happened before?*

S: Everything happens before, after, now. In order to have that ability, there would be a degree – for lack of a better word – a degree of awareness attained by that individual. This individual seeing and being aware and knowing the patterns of life, lives social events. History would also be aware of the lessons gained by or the awareness gained by, and the need for the souls to experience certain things. They go with the

45

flow, so to speak. They would understand and have understood those patterns which are best, appropriate. They have gained the awareness of acceptance. Is that clear?

Q: *Not completely.*

Q: *Do we choose our birthdate?*
A: Yes, you choose.
Q: *Even if someone were born by Caesarian section?*
A: They chose a mother who would find it necessary to have a Caesarian section.
Q: *Why is the birthdate significant?*
A: Everything in this Universe affects everything else.

Q: *Do we have a specific goal?*
A: Yes. There is within you that awareness of what that goal is. You are working on your goal, whether you are aware consciously of that fact or not. You are working on your goal. Becoming aware of what that goal is, is a matter of wanting to know. Sounds so simple. By becoming less concerned with running to this person or to that person for a little more information, and by becoming more fully aware and in tune with self by learning trust of self. By meditating, by all methods appropriate to you will you learn more. Learning self love is the final goal. Everything else that you would wish to attempt comes from, if it is to be fully realized, the ability to love self.
Q: *What do you mean when you say "final"?*
A: Final, ultimate. This is what this reality, this is what this existence, this Earth, human experience is about. Is to learn self love. This is what increases, what expands, what this reality can and does need and can thrive on: self love. This is what being human is about.

46

Q: You seem to intimate that once that is achieved there would be other realities we would be going to. Is this what you're saying?

A: Are there not other realities? (Yes) Do you think you are confined to this one?

Q: Then you couldn't call it final.

A: Not final, no. This is the prime goal. This is the purpose – purpose, that is the word – for human reality.

Q: Roughly how many lifetimes does it take to learn self-love?

A: How many? We would wish not too many, but in the long run, does it matter?

Q: How in the world did this particular reality get so far off the track that we were taught that self love is a no-no?

A: You chose it.

A question about twins.

S: The decision is made with the other soul out of love. You can't get any closer in the physical plane. Because you have identical DNA, and your thoughts primarily work the same way. They're not, of course, the *same* thought, but the process is so similar. But there's already a framework and you don't need to fill in all the spaces, because you know. They wanted to come back with someone they loved, rather than coming alone. And these are difficult times. They needed that type of companionship because that's a constant. And there's not much constancy in these lives.

During a demonstration session at one of my hypnosis classes the person wanted to know about her twin, who had died. The subconscious said that she had completed what she was supposed to do, "She did her lessons, and it was time for her to go." This is easy to say, but it still doesn't make the grieving any easier. "It

47

hurts her very much. It's going to hurt her for a long time. With twins, there is almost like a gold cord, if you can picture that. A very fine gold cord that attaches them. And even in death – or what you call 'death' – it doesn't sever totally. So they will *forever* be part of each other."

I found an explanation years ago for Siamese twins (which are now called "conjoined" twins). Suppose two souls, while on the spirit side getting ready to return to the Earth school, are discussing their contract with each other. They have loved each other and been together during many, many lifetimes. Maybe something traumatic happened in the life they have just left. Now, one of them says, "*We will never be separated again!*" A simple request that produced unforeseeable consequences. And a very logical explanation.

One of my clients had a question about her birth. She was one of triplets. One was born dead, the second had a mental disease that required that it spend its entire life in an institution, and the third was the woman client. She wanted to know why this happened. The subconscious said that the first triplet changed its mind as the birth was occurring, and decided it did not want to be born at that time. This resulted in the stillbirth. The second decided after it was about two or three months old that it could learn more in this lifetime by being mentally handicapped. So it developed the mental problems. The mother had said that the baby seemed normal until it was about two or three months old, then something suddenly happened. The doctors did not agree, because they said the disease was always present from birth. It did not develop later. I think the explanation I have found makes more sense, because the soul has control over the type of body it inhabits.

Parallel lives.

Q: If each one of us are living in different planes of existence at the same time, is this what would be known as parallel lives?
A: That is accurate. In the sense that each of you, at this point in your lives, are simply facets of your true entire self. That is, your pinpoints of awareness. Your total awareness is far beyond anything you could encompass or imagine at your level. Therefore, it is easy to see that as your awareness grows, as you broaden your reality of the spiritual ladder, you find that your awareness overlaps with that of other individuals. Such that at the ultimate level, you are indeed on the God plane where all is one. Your awareness on your level is simply a drawn-out or focused pinpoint of that total spiritual awareness. And so it could be seen that at various levels, your awareness would indeed overlap with others. Such that ultimately, all is one. Therefore, *all* lives ultimately are concurrent.
D: You said before we were just the tips of our own icebergs.
A: That is accurate.

S: Rainbows are to remind us of the color of energy and creation. Just a reminder, there is way more than we can see with just the naked eye. The color of creation is all different levels of color that are beyond the visualization of a human being. It is just to remind us there was a time when this energy wrapped around us in another realm. This is a reminder of home, of the loving energy. This small reminder that there is more to the spectrum of color than what we actually see with the naked eye. Just a remembrance of home.

49

S: I think we should bear in mind that when one of us opens up, it opens up something in all of us. We are connected. We are one. We are not individual, autonomous units. We have individual personalities, but in the bigger picture, we are connected. We should remind ourselves that we are all one, and that we are spiritual beings first.

A woman had died young in several lifetimes. The subconscious explained, "She learned many things that she needed to learn, and there was no point in going on." She was living longer in this lifetime. "It's taken her longer to learn her lessons this time. She forgets that she has to willingly release from this body. You always set up a way to exit the body in advance. There has to be a way to exit, and it can be whatever way you choose. Whether illness or accident, whatever fits in with the learning experience. But when it comes time to exit, the person decides, and willingly goes. No one else can make that decision for them."

S:There is a lot of mixed energy in crowds. You have to be careful to put up protection before going out in crowds. Sometimes the energy of crowds can latch onto you. If it does, it's draining. You feel very tired. There are so many people that are hungry for energy, because their vibrations are not high enough for them to produce a good quality of energy. So when they find and sense someone with a high vibration they will latch on to that energy, and use that energy. It's kind of like they're suction cups.

I have heard them referred to as "psychic vampires". That's a negative word, but it's the same idea. They don't do it consciously, but they do take energy. "You must protect yourself, even when you go shopping. Anywhere you go where there is a large group of people. It's vitally important for you to keep your energy up at the highest level. Your body has an intelligence. Listen to your body. Talk to it regularly. It likes that. It likes to be recognized. Magnesium is very important for the body. With giving so much energy out, magnesium makes it easier for you to absorb more energy into yourself."

A client came to my office who did not really have any pressing problems, and she didn't care much about finding past lives. As we talked it became obvious that the death of her sister was still affecting her greatly. She wasn't sure about an afterlife, even though she had been raised in a strict Church environment. It had been almost a year and she still spent most of her time thinking about her sister, crying and grieving. When we started the session, I thought it would progress as they normally do. I wouldn't have been surprised if she had found that she and her sister had been together in a past life. Instead she went immediately to a beautiful garden. There were wonderful flowers of radiant colors, and glorious music in the air. I knew from the description that she was probably not in an Earthly environment. When I asked if she could see anyone, she saw her sister coming towards her through the flowers. She was wearing a long gown and looked radiant and beautiful. They took each other's hands, and her sister said to her with much emotion, "Let me go! You can see that I am fine!"

"But what happened? We all thought you were getting better. But then you died."

Her sister replied, "It was my time to go. I had done everything I set out to do in that life, and it was time to go." Then her sister said she had someone else for her to meet before she left this beautiful place. And their parents appeared looking healthy,

51

young and happy. They told her, "You can see we are all fine. It is so beautiful here. There is nothing to grieve about. When your time comes you will come here also, and we will all be waiting."

Skeptics may say that this session was only wish fulfillment because of her grief. But does it really matter? I have done enough sessions to know that it was real, and the meeting was a gift to her so she could go back to living a normal life. I have been told that grieving only holds the departed soul back, keeping it from going on to where it is supposed to go. When we grieve it is a selfish act, because we are only grieving for ourselves, for how our loss is affecting us. It does not affect our lost loved ones in the same way. They lived their life, they found a way to exit because it was time. They must now continue on their own path. They are more than happy to return "home".

SECTION TWO

LIFE IN NON-HUMAN BODIES

CHAPTER THREE

OTHER LIFEFORMS

There are still people who remark, when the subject of reincarnation is brought up, "What do you mean, I have lived before? That's impossible! This is the only body, the only life I have ever had. This is the only thing that is real." Those are the ones that have not even begun to take their baby steps into this fascinating world of the unknown. Then there is the next group that are shocked when they find out (through hypnotic regression or however) that they have had *one* other life prior to this one. They are shocked because it has threatened their belief system. It has made them think. Usually when the person begins their exploration, the subconscious is wise enough to only give them what they can handle. The life they are shown is usually a dull, boring, mundane life. What I call a "digging potatoes life." There is usually nothing traumatic or dramatic, because they are not ready to handle it. Yet, they will find that it answers questions for them, usually regarding family relationships, etc. I could fill not just one book, but several, with the thousands of past lives I have conducted. It has become so commonplace that it is of no value to me as a writer. It is only valuable to the client as therapy. Thus, I only write about those cases that I think will now expand our knowledge of reincarnation through its therapeutic value. A great number of the cases I have conducted contain dates, names, places that could be researched by those curious to check out their validity. Some people have the need for such verification in order to "prove" their experience. I tell them that they are welcome to check the cases if they need to. I no longer need such verification. I know beyond a shadow of a doubt that reincarnation is real. I know and fully believe that it contains all the answers, especially those that the Church have labeled "unexplainable".

It makes sense that 90% of the past lives I uncover will be simple and ordinary. This is the way the world is. This is the way our lives are. There are many, many more ordinary people in the world than those few who get their names in the newspaper. When the person discovers they have had at least *one* other life, it has to sink in. Some dismiss it as impossible and return to their normal lives and their safe, accepted belief systems. That is perfectly all right. I am not here to change anyone's beliefs. My job is to present what I have found, and then let the reader make up their own mind.

Then there are those who have made this discovery: that indeed this present life is not all there is. They then want to explore further. They must be careful not to be overwhelmed by what they may discover, because their lives will never be the same again. It is said that once we learn something, we cannot *un*learn it. If they are amazed that they have lived one life on Earth, imagine what it might do to them to discover that is only the beginning of exploration, the tip of the iceberg. I have had to go through similar changes in my belief system over the 40 years that I have been conducting this experimentation. And as I have worked, I have opened the floodgates to unlimited possibilities. The variety of past lives are only limited by the imagination, and some that I am receiving now defy the imagination. That was the purpose for writing the *Convoluted Universe* series. I left the world of the commonplace long ago. And my readers tell me they are ready to expand their minds with me. And so we go exploring.

Earth is only one of the schools we come to, to learn lessons and gain life information. You can have many, many hundreds of lifetimes on Earth, but you have also had lives on other planets and in other dimensions. I have explored this in the first two books of this series, and I will continue to supply cases in this book that will further stretch the minds of the readers.

However, I have found that the physical human body is only one form the soul can take. Most people think the physical is the only way they can appear, not understanding that you *have* a body, you are *not* a body. This is only a "suit of clothes" that you are wearing at the present time. And like all clothes, no matter how attached we become to them, they will eventually wear out and have to be discarded. Then we simply find another suit of clothes, another costume for the next role we will play in the cosmic drama of life. Why should that next costume be a human body? Why can't it be an animal, plant or inanimate object? Who is to argue that these things do not have life? All of life is about experience and learning. Who is to say you can't learn something from being a rock or a dog? It just means you have to open your mind a little more to the definition of what life is. People have told me, "I can accept the idea that I have lived before as a human. But as an animal? No, that I cannot believe."

I have found in my work that we must experience life as *absolutely everything* in every form before we are finished with our school, our lessons, our education. We must know what it is like to be in every possible situation before we can return to the Creator, God, the Source. There will be much more about our journey since we left the Source, and what is required in order to return to the Source, in the following chapters. In this section, I will present cases that I have conducted where the person did not go to a life with a typical human body in a typical Earth life. However, I think it will show the valuable lessons that can be learned by existing (even for a short period of time) in these other vehicles. It will begin to show just how much is required before we can graduate from the life school. Beware! Your belief systems will definitely be challenged, and your minds will definitely be bent. Let's hope they will fly open and start absorbing like a sponge.

The people who come to see me in my office and on my trips, and wish to have past-life therapy are ordinary human beings from all possible walks of life. You would never know by looking at them what their life history was. This is important. They are here to live as normal a life as possible in this hectic world. These other memories remain hidden in the computer records of their subconscious mind, and are only released when the subconscious thinks it is the appropriate time. In my work, I always take the person through the *appropriate* past life first, and often the answers to their questions are found there. Then I call forth the subconscious mind to answer any questions we have left. The first question I always ask is, why the subconscious chose to show the person this particular lifetime. Its logic far surpasses ours, and its explanation is usually something we would never have thought of with our very limited human logic. Yet it puts everything into place and makes perfect sense. So this is the procedure I will follow in the cases described in this book. I think the reader will be as puzzled as I was while taking the person through the past life, until the subconscious revealed the answer. This is why I enjoy this work so much. I am working with an extremely powerful source of knowledge with tremendous abilities that defy the imagination. And yet you will notice that it always answers the same, using the same terminology. So I always know I am speaking to the same universal part. It comes through everyone I work with. I have absolutely no doubt of who or what I am communicating with. I have become so familiar with it, it is like having a phone conversation with an old friend.

ANIMAL LIFETIMES

When Wendy came into the life, she was confused, and reported something she had difficulty understanding. "I'm on water. And I'm a tiny, tiny, tiny something or other on this leaf floating around in the water. This doesn't even make sense."

D: Let's just talk about it. What do you mean by a tiny, tiny something?
W: I don't know. I'm just so small, and the leaf is huge. I'm just floating there. I know that I am alive. I have awareness. It's calm, clear water. Looks like glass.
D: If you look above the leaf, can you see anything else?
W: A tree. It's a craggy looking tree growing along the edge of the water. Half of the roots are in the water, and half of them are in the land. I don't know what I'm doing here. All I see is the water, the tree and the leaf.
D: You can become aware of yourself.
W: (Suddenly) A worm! It's yellow, it's fat. It's tiny, but it's fat. I wish I had arms and I don't have arms. I have legs, but they're just stubby. And I'm stuck here on this leaf. Seems like all I can do is just wiggle. Can't go off the leaf because I can't swim. But I don't want to stay here either. It's dangerous. I think a bird could get me.
D: How do you think you ended up in the water?
W: I fell from the tree. I was on the leaf. I guess I chose the wrong leaf.
D: Oh! That must have been an experience. Because usually you'd stay away from the water, wouldn't you? (Uh-huh) *What do you eat when you're up there in the tree?*
W: Leaves.
D: Oh! Is it good?
W: It's just what I eat. It seems like it's a nothing life.
D: How do you eat the leaves?
W: Just with my mouth, when I crawl around on my stubby little

feet. I feel inhibited. – Oh! Now I'm floating away. There seems to be a current. – It seems to be rushing water ahead. – There's a waterfall. It looks like a big one, but it isn't. It's just that I'm little. – I'm going down the rough water, and the edges of the leaf are curling up. We're going fast. Ohh! I'm going to get sucked under by the water. – But there seems to be an air bubble that forms around me and the leaf while we go under. So it's popping up and down, up and down. This is so silly! Up and down, up and down. So I don't drown. – Then I finally get swirled down into a calmer pool of water. And the sun's shining bright. I'm just laying there on this leaf.

D: *You had quite an adventure.*

W: It was scary.

D: *What are you going to do now?*

W: Just lay there on my back, because I can't swim.

Would she drown? Or would a bird see her and grab her off the leaf?

D: *We can condense time. What eventually happens?*

W: The leaf finally goes over and gets hung up under a bank. And I can crawl back up on the grass. Because the bank was kind of hanging over the water, and I could crawl up under, and then back up on top on the grass.

D: *I bet that feels good to get out of the water.*

W: It does. I don't want to go there again. I'm just going to join other ones like me. They are glad that I'm okay. It's like a gathering.

D: *They recognize you?*

W: They do.

D: *Are you telling them what happened?*

W: Yes. They said others weren't so lucky.

One may wonder how the other group of worms knew her, since they were obviously separated by a distance that would have been difficult for a tiny worm to traverse. I found in my early work, reported in *Between Death and Life*, that animals and plants belong to a different type of soul group than humans. Where the human seems to be acting as an individual, plants and animals are joined in a common bond as a group soul that interacts on a more subtle level. This was brought home to me one day while I was driving down my country road. I saw a huge flock of birds rise from the trees. They immediately formed into a big mass that swirled and pirouetted across the sky. They were each individual lifeforms, yet they interacted as one intelligence, as one consciousness, with a single mind. This is also a good analogy for the concept of the Source, which will be presented later. We are one, yet we are also part of the Whole. We are never separate.

I then moved Wendy ahead in time to another situation. It was difficult to know how to word it. Normally I move the person forward to an important day. But what would be an important day to a worm? Certainly nothing could be more dramatic than what the poor little thing had just experienced. I asked her what she was doing.

W: I'm just rolled on my back. I'm not fat like I was. And my body's kind of dried up. I'm on my last breath. I'm just old and I'm dying. Nobody's around. It looks like my body's just dried up, and I'm gone! Ssshhwww! I'm glad that's over!

D: *(Laugh) That was a strange one, wasn't it?*

W: It's too weird to be an insect.

D: *(Laugh) But every life has a lesson, it has a purpose. What do you think you learned from something like that?*

W: I know I felt terribly confined. And vulnerable. Now I'm free. I leave that confining body and just slide away! Oh, I'm glad that's over!

61

When I contacted Wendy's subconscious I asked why it had chosen to show her this unusual life.

W: To show that you can be anything in creation, even a lowly worm. That you think there are no lessons by experiencing a lowly worm. One of the things she learned was the confining, the restriction, but yet there was a group consciousness even in a lowly worm. It was not without purpose.

D: *Yes, that makes us aware that everything is alive.*

W: Life even goes smaller than a worm.

D: *I don't think I've had any smaller than a worm. I've had some as the air, and dirt and rocks.*

W: Yes. She should be thankful she wasn't shown experiencing a rock. A worm is much more free than a rock is.

D: *That's true. I've been told when someone is a rock, it's very slow and dense.*

W: And confining.

There were many more sessions that I did in my office in Huntsville during 2005-2006 that involved animal incarnations. With these, I did not keep a copy of the tape recording. Instead, after the client left I made notes so I wouldn't forget. As a reporter I have an insatiable curiosity, I always want to know everything about everything. That is why I ask so many questions. In the case of a human reliving animal incarnations, I wanted to know what it would be like to *be* an animal. How does it feel? How do they live? How do they see? Many questions, and I have tried to recapture some of the answers in my notes.

Dorothy went to a lifetime where she was an eagle. It was a very powerful body, and she really liked it. But the most amazing thing about being the eagle was that all of its energy was focused in its *eyes*, focused on what she could *see*. She was perched on the edge of a nest overlooking a mountainous area with snow, and she could see very intensely every tiny detail. She said as she looked out over the landscape, the colors were the most intense you could imagine, and the shadows were very black and dark. There was a very distinct separation between the colors and the shadow. Quite different from what humans see. Then when she saw movement on the ground – a rabbit – her eyesight changed. When she looked at something that was moving, it was almost like looking through an infrared field. A reddish color, as though she was seeing the energy of the animal, rather than the animal itself. As though when the animal was moving, she could track it by seeing it through an energy, infrared field. And her eyesight would switch back and forth when she was looking for food, or mostly just whenever she was seeing movement.

At night, the normal vision was cut off because of the dark, but another vision would come on if she needed it. Here again, she would see the energy *field*. But at night it would be like a dark blueish-green. So the movement, rather than looking like infrared, would have a blueish-green cast. It reminded me of the night goggles that some of the soldiers use. I think they pick up the energy of the person, and are able to sense that energy in night vision. And probably also similar in the movies, the way robots or different beings see the energy field, rather than the person themself. It always appears as a greenish or reddish cast, to where they're picking up the *heat* of the person or their energy. So apparently this was the way the Eagle could see. And how do we really know how he uses his eyes? Apparently they switch back and forth between two ways of seeing. And the most intense thing about being the eagle was to focus *all* of the energy into its eyesight. I would assume that other night birds, such as owls, have similar vision.

In another case a woman experienced a series of lives in different animal and plant bodies. One was difficult to identify when she first entered it.

S: I'm in something like a bubble. I don't like it, because I'm squished. Squished. Just a bubble. I'm cramped.

This was confusing. Where was she? What was she?

S: Because of my position inside this bubble, there's no room to move. It's hard. It's all scrunched and ... a floating balloon. It's not comfortable at all. I like freedom. Being in this little bubble isn't very free. I have to get out of this bubble.

Since this was causing discomfort, I moved her ahead to when she was out, and asked her to explain what she could see.

S: Amoebas? Am I in the water? I came out of a water bag. I can breathe, but I'm in the water. – It's a creature. And I can float in the water.
D: *What kind of creature?*
S: Slimy. (Pause) It's hard to explain this body. It's like if you took just your toes, and connect them in a circle. That's your extensions, but you're the middle part. You're the body. That is *weird!* Oblong body. – A tadpole? Could that be a tadpole! Oh! I'm a frog! Because you have these wavy things coming out of you, but yet you're like a slimy oblong looking thing. And then you have buds to pop out into a lake. It looks like what I would call a frog. Those little buddy things that look like toes are my legs! And a head. – So now I can breathe in the water, and also out of the water. I like being here. This was a good place to go. This was a good choice. Transition. I like it.
D: *What do you see as you look around?*
S: Gnats in water. I'm sticking up out of the water. Little

creatures to eat. I eat them when they fly by. It's okay, but it's boring. It's not what I thought. I want to go and be something else. – Now I see colors, red, white. The red and white is a part of a flower. You know how the outside is the light color, and then as you slip down inside it gets darker? That's what I am. I *am* the flower! I like to try things. And I am colored light, so I can change colors. I decided to try being a flower, because they have many shades of colors.

D: What does it feel like to be a flower?

S: Expansion. Expanding. Growing. Beautiful. Soft. It's just so beautiful. But then you die, because flowers don't last very long. I'm just trying it on for size. It was good while it lasted.

So it would appear that many of these strange lives are short. They are just so the soul can have the experience.

I found some of the most fascinating animal lives were those of insects. I had a client experience a life as a spider, and she described the way she was able to see. As you know, spiders have several eyes, and in our logic we would think it would be difficult to use them all. I found out that they do not use them all at the same time. The eyes are spaced at intervals, but it was not confusing. It was as if looking at many TV sets showing the same image. It perceived it as one, although it was composed of many facets. When the spider saw movement in one of the eyes, that would be the one it focused on. The others were not used unless something was sensed in that area. It focused on the part or section that was of interest or that contained movement. Where we see things out of the corner of our eye, it could focus in and see the entire image, even in the peripheral. It was the same thing when another woman regressed to a life as a fly. Their eyes are also multi-faceted, and again are similar to many

65

TV screens. They focus on movement in whatever area they need to. The client said, "Otherwise it would be a jumble of information. I select what I want, and disregard the rest." How clever!

Apparently these creatures can see a wider and more detailed range than we can. All of this has made me appreciate and respect life more in *all* forms, and to realize that *everything* has the spark of life.

Another case of this type occurred when a client went into a lifetime as a small whale. At first she didn't know where she was. She came down into the water, and then she went underneath the water. She saw a fin, but she wasn't sure if she was a fish or a seal, or something similar. So when she went under the water, I asked her, could she breathe under the water? And she said, not for very long. She had to come back up to the surface. That determined that she had to be some kind of mammal, and eventually she saw that she was a whale. She just enjoyed swimming around in the ocean, and eating fish. As we moved through the session, she saw a small fishing boat. She didn't know what it was, because it was something she had never seen before. She swam under it, and came out the other side. As she was turning around it, trying to figure out what it was, she had a feeling of fear. So she decided to leave and move away from it. She didn't think they had seen her, but they had.

She unexpectedly felt pain, and from the description it was probably a harpoon. She kept saying, "They stabbed me! Why did they do that? I wasn't hurting anyone. I was just minding my own business, swimming around. Why did they hurt me?" Then she described being hauled ... pulled. They put a net and ropes around her, and took her back to the larger ship. When they finally came to shore she was strung up, and they started cutting her up. She was crying and decided she didn't want to watch it anymore.

One of the reasons for having the session was to discover the cause of her physical problems. She had experienced back pains that had resulted in a numbness in her arms and hands. She would wake up many times at night and be numb. It was also affecting her work, making it hard to hold on to things. When we talked to the subconscious it explained that it was caused by *that* lifetime. When they were cutting the whale up, they cut it down the backbone while she was still alive. And this transferred over, I suppose as the feeling of vulnerability, into this lifetime. It affected the back and the nerves in the hands and arms. I would have thought it would have also affected the legs, but in this case it didn't. With this strange explanation, the physical problem could be taken away, because it did not belong in this life. It was just another case of the body remembering a traumatic death. She was being shown that lifetime so she would know there was a time when she was very happy. She was free and she could do anything that she wanted to, even though it ended badly. She had to know that she could experience that feeling and freedom again in her present life.

A woman who regressed to a lifetime as a giraffe felt very regal, as she could see above everyone. For a few days afterward she felt as though she was walking on stilts.

And then, on my weekly radio show (on www.BBSRadio.com) I interviewed a woman who was an animal communicator. She was talking about how she could communicate with her animals, especially her cat, and it tells her anything she wants to know. There was a distinct difference between receiving answers from animals and guides. One of the questions she asked the cat (which was precisely the type of question I would have asked), was, "How do cats perceive humans?" She knew that dogs mostly perceive everything by smell, but she wanted to know how cats perceive humans. And she was told, "At first we see you as swirling colors of energy before it focuses into a form." Then that brought up the idea: if the cat sees energy first, that would explain how cats can see ghosts and things we can't see. It's seeing the energy of the entity or whatever it is, without having to see the form.

I could readily identify with this because I had personal experience with the unique perception of cats. When my husband was serving in the U.S. Navy during the Viet Nam war in the 1960s, I lived in St. Louis, Mo. We lived in a two-story house directly across from Tower Grove Park, where all the houses on the street looked very similar. My children and I soon found that the house was haunted. The phenomenon took place mostly on the second floor where lights would turn on and off, doors open and close, and loud footsteps would be heard running up and down the stairs at night. Because of monetary problems we had no choice but to continue to live there until my husband returned from the war. So the children and I became accustomed to our invisible houseguest, and named him "George". Yet the most disturbing thing was the actions of our Siamese cat "Boots". After the children were in bed, I would try to relax in the downstairs living room and watch TV. But most nights Boots would sit at the bottom of the stairs and stare upwards at the second floor landing. As she sat there, her tail would be flicking back and forth, the way cats do when they're watching something. She would sit there for a long time transfixed, ears alert and tail moving, watching something that was invisible to me. I would usually say in desperation, "Boots, why don't you go catch a mouse." At the time, I thought all animals could probably see things that we couldn't, but now this explanation sounds more plausible. Cats are more sensitive to seeing energy, and it makes sense that they can also see the energy of a ghost. It was probably confusing to Boots because she couldn't figure out what the energy was.

I had many other cases where the subjects went to lives as a flower, an ear of corn, a rock. Life as a rock was very sloooow. Those readers who have read my other books will remember that in *Legacy From the Stars* I had my first case where someone went to a nonhuman life. A man wanted to go back to his first life on Earth. I naturally thought he would go to a life as a caveman or something similar. Instead, he went to the time when the Earth did not have life yet. The ground was unstable, volcanoes were erupting and spewing all types of gases and chemicals into the air. The Earth had not yet reached the point that it had cooled down enough to support life. The man saw himself (along with many others) as part of the atmosphere. In other words, he was *air*. This was difficult for me to understand at that phase in my work, because I had not yet been exposed to the fact that everything is alive. I thought, here he was as a chemical, an element, yet he still had intelligence. He was aware of himself and his function, and was able to communicate with me. His job at that time was to help filter the dangerous chemicals (especially ammonia) from the air, so that life would be able to survive when it emerged from the "primeval soup" at the beginning of creation of life on Earth. When he was not doing his job he would fly in and out of the flowing lava, just to see what it felt like. I followed his progression as he went from that state to the various lifeforms (plants and sea creatures) as they began to emerge. All of this would have taken eons of time. After that experience, I was open to anything that my subjects would tell me. It showed me that nothing, no form of life, is impossible.

A similar case occurred after I began seeing clients in my office in Arkansas in 2003. When the man came into the scene, he found himself on a very dark barren planet. Yet there were things that projected out of the ground that were more angular than rocks, with sharp points and edges. He knew he was on a black planet, where there was no light, and nothing growing. He did not have a body. He seemed to be a part of the planet, mostly a part of the surface. Then, he went beneath the surface and it was as though that was a shell covering something that was inside. He had great difficulty describing what he was seeing. It was as though things were growing underground, more or less like on the surface: pointed, very large stones. They were very strange, unusual, like nothing he had seen before, and definitely not biological. As he went further down, he could see light which looked like it was coming from flowing lava. He went in and out of it, just to see what it was like, but he was aware that there were consciousnesses around him. Not necessarily beings or people, but consciousness. Sometimes people say they are pure energy, or energy beings. But he said he was consciousness, and he knew he was part of everything there.

As I moved him forward in time, he found that the surface of the planet had changed. He saw something that sounded like a space station, but it was very difficult to describe. It was something that came up from the surface of the planet, as though it was a series of buildings. And this whole community, or whatever it was, formed a series of buildings at least a thousand stories high that circled all the way around the planet. Later, I asked him if he meant something like the rings of Saturn. He said it was very similar, except that it was attached to the surface. And in this station, or whatever it would be called, the people lived. They did not live on the surface of the planet, but in this large community type structure that extended up from the surface. He saw the beings looking rather human-like, although they were dressed in robe-like clothing. They went about their various jobs in this place. He was living among them in a leadership position.

Later, when I was communicating with the subconscious, it said it was showing him that he had been on this distant planet from the time when there was no life on it. Things were

70

beginning to be created and starting to form, even though they were underneath the shell that covered the planet. The lava was the beginning of life. That's why he did not have a body, because he was part of everything. It was to show him that as the planet evolved – which would have taken eons and eons of time to develop certain types of lifeforms – he inhabited each one in progression, until he finally got to where there were intelligent beings. Then, when he evolved to the point where he was the leader of this whole community, it was as though he had gone as far as he could go. At that point he didn't *die,* per se. He just decided to leave the body. And when he did, he came to Earth. He was to progress onward. He had learned everything he could possibly learn by being on that planet from its formation of life all the way through its advancement. So the next set of lessons would be to start over again on another planet with a different set of rules and regulations and lessons. That's when he came to Earth.

In March 2007 after I had begun work on this book, I had a random session that added yet another aspect to the idea of inhabiting animal bodies as a form of reincarnation. My client saw herself in a room where she was enclosed in a clear plastic-type capsule. She was aware that there were many other similar capsules spread all throughout the large room. When she became aware of her body, it did not seem to be fully formed. She knew it had two legs and seemed more animal than human. It seemed to be wrapped as it lay on a table encased in the tube-like capsule. She felt she was some type of experiment. She was able to see a being walking around the room who seemed to be checking on the forms that were in the capsules. He was very tall and was wearing a white coat, but she did not think he was human. She also became aware that there were many others in another room monitoring their progress on some type of computers. She could see keyboards and screens, dials and gauges. I attempted to get information from the mind of the person who seemed to be taking care of her and the others, but the access was limited. All she could get was that they were some type of experiment, and they were located above a planet. From time to time, the capsules were rotated around the room. I moved her ahead to see if we could get more information, and she saw herself on a planet where she had been brought. She was in some type of pen or cage in a muddy area, where she was observed. When I attempted to move her forward again to find out more, she did not continue with the life, but leap-frogged (or jumped) into a human lifetime as a Roman gladiator.

I knew my questions would be answered when I called forth the subconscious and asked it about the strange life. It said she was shown it because she had always been curious about whether there was life on other planets. She had indeed been an experiment connected with the seeding of a planet, and it had taken place on a large spaceship. Various different species were being created by the manipulation and combination of genes and DNA, and she was the result of one of these experiments. When she was sufficiently developed, she was taken down to a planet that the ship had been orbiting. She was put into a pen where she would be allowed to acclimate before being released. The reason we could not follow it any further was because she did not survive. Her experiment had been inefficient. In other words, it did not work and the form couldn't adjust to the planetary conditions. The subconscious said it was not the planet Earth. I said that I already knew that life had been seeded millennia ago on Earth, and it said that this same thing had happened on countless other planets. It was also continuing today, because this was the way life was spread.

CHAPTER FOUR

DIFFERENT LIFEFORMS

Animals and plants are not the only unfamiliar forms the soul or spirit can inhabit. I have had many clients that describe life in forms that are definitely not the traditional human. Some defy the imagination, yet the client feels comfortable inhabiting them, as though it is not illogical.

LAND OF THE GIANTS

Jack saw himself as a very tall man named Larce with long blonde hair. His head came to half the height of the tree he was standing by. He was dressed in brown canvas pants and a shirt with puffy sleeves, with leather straps over his shoulders to hold the pants. He was wearing sandals with soles made of bark, and a sheath with a sword on his back. The sword was used for protection against the people that were even larger than him. He could smell bread baking from a small cottage in the distance. "There are little people that live there. They can't fend for themselves." He was bringing them a deer that he was holding in his hand, and flour. "There's a young woman, and I see two small girls and a baby. I am so much larger than them, but I feel a love towards these small people." To illustrate how much bigger he was, he said the woman's head came only to his waist. There were villages of these small people, and they were in danger from beings who were larger than him. He felt an obligation to protect them. He did not live in their villages, but on the nearby mountain. "I can see and overlook ... everything. I can overlook the valley and see if there's anything that goes wrong." He was only doing it because of a love for these small people.

It was cold in this area and people often wore fur. He lived in a structure made of rocks with his family: parents, brothers, sisters who he also took care of. The larger people lived on an island off the coast of the big water. They came in the spring and fall in their big iron boats. These bigger people lived in darkness in large castles made of huge stones with big log doors. They were never satisfied and wanted what everyone else had. They killed everything, just to kill. They had mechanical things: guns that shot fire; their ships looked like they flew as they came across the water with no sails. He described them as having a face like a bulldog; lower extruding jaw with two teeth over the upper lip, a big hump on the back and very little hair. They walked slumped over. He knew what they looked like, because he wounded some of them in a battle and once in the water. He insisted he did not kill, but defended himself.

D: These indeed sound like strange people. Does anyone know where they came from?
J: They originally came from a place that was red. Right now, that's all I see. Like a planet with red rock.
D: I wondered if your people had stories about them.
J: Stranded. They couldn't go back to where they came from. No atmosphere. They had no way to exist where they came from. They had to leave that place.

I moved him forward to an important day. The little people were having a wedding celebration. His family was there also. They had not had problems with the strange people for a long time. Maybe they were dying out. He said it was bad for the species, but good for him and his people.

I then moved him to the last day of his life. He was lying on a bed in his house. The body was not old. He had continued to grow larger and had become too big. It was causing chest pain, weakness from heaviness, breathing, pain in the ankles and feet, and the lower back. He said you can be too big or too small. The strange people never came back. When he went to the island to check on them, he saw only bones. All of their things were as they left them.

The little woman from the cottage was with him when he died. After his death, his body was put in a boat, and was burned as it floated out to sea. They did this with anyone with any kind of disease. The lesson of that life was respect. Respect yourself as well as your own enemy. And be able to love anything or anyone, whether they're large or whether they're small. Also caution. Awareness. Listen, look, watch. He felt he had learned these lessons.

I then called the subconscious forth to answer questions.

J: Jack had to see this life to know the love that he could not have. He is able to share that love with her in his lifetime now in 2004. She is his present wife. She was the little woman.

D: *Then they've come back together.* (Yes) *That's important because now they're the same size, aren't they?*

J: Pretty close. The love was impossible in the other life, and this caused him much despair. He could only be with her as a friend.

I wanted the subconscious to explain the strange undertones of that life. "Everything Jack has is strange. Everything tends to be different, because he likes different. He does not like the normal. During all his lives, he's always been able to see what other people can't see. He's always been different.

D: *But that is not a bad thing. It just takes adjusting.* (Yes) *In that life, he was a large person and he kept growing. Can you tell me something about his people?*

75

J: His group was from another planet. They were seeded here on Earth.

D: *What country was this?*

J: Cold country. Viking. The northern part. Way back in history.

D: *Would the little people be considered normal size today?*

J: Five foot seven. Some smaller. His group was between nine and ten feet tall. They were seeded from another planet.

D: *So they were really too tall for this planet, weren't they?*

J: Yes. That's why they were put in the north, to be away from the others. The smaller people would be scared of them. They were put there to see if they would survive.

D: *Why did he keep growing?*

J: Genetic defect.

D: *So when they were seeded, they had problems. (Yes) Did that group survive into our time?*

J: Yes. They're not as large.

D: *So some of the large people on Earth today are descendants from that seeding? (Yes) I would have thought they would die out. (No) What about the ones who were on the island, who were even larger?*

J: They came from somewhere else. A mistake from beyond. They weren't supposed to be here. They were supposed to have been sent somewhere else.

D: *Why did they end up here?*

J: Miscalculations on their part.

D: *He said they were stranded. (Yes) Something about a red planet?*

J: Red planet. (Surprised) Not Mars. It had bad atmosphere. They had to leave because they couldn't breathe.

D: *So they miscalculated and ended up on that island. (Yes) But it sounded like they couldn't reproduce.*

J: No, all male. That was why they died out eventually. They were very violent. Nothing humorous about them. Except, they were ugly.

D: *So it was probably better that they were isolated on that island.* (Yes) *What about their castles? Did any of that survive to our time?*

J: Under the mud. Known into our time in 2004, would be found around Iceland. Artifacts will be found eventually. They won't understand.

D: *And those ships sounded rather like spaceships.*

J: Yes, under the mud.

D: *Will they be found?*

J: Possible.

So maybe the stories and fairy tales we have heard all our lives are not fiction after all. I have always believed that most stories and legends have some basis in fact. But I also know that down through time, mankind has taken these legends and added to and taken away, so it is difficult to know what the original was. When I was in Norway, I visited some museums in Oslo. I saw the old paintings depicting the stories of giants, trolls, ogres and strange creatures. Jack's subconscious said they were living in the North. Maybe these stories carry memories of these creatures that dwelled on the Earth long ago. This might also explain some of the people living on Earth now that are very tall. Maybe they carry genes of these gentle giants.

A case in Seattle, Washington in April, 2002 where I was speaking at an APRT (Association for Past-Life Research and Therapy) Hypnosis Conference, uncovered another unexpected lifeform.

Every session that I do for therapy is designed to have the subconscious take the person to the most appropriate past life that will help explain the problems they are having in the present life, or provide information they need. As has been demonstrated in this book and *Book One and Two*, the subject often goes to strange settings that have no logical basis or explanation. I always trust that the subconscious has a reason for taking them there, so I just become the reporter, the investigator, and ask questions within the perimeters of what the subconscious has chosen for them to see. If I tried to remove them and take them to something that would be more logical to me, the essential information would not come forth

The first thing Wanda saw as she entered the scene was a group of people who did not exactly look like people. This was confusing to her as she described them, "They have a substance, a structure of their body, but it extends into this glow. That's cool." She was pleasantly surprised to find that her body was the same. "Oh, my body does that too! A glow! That's fun! And the light, the glow, just keeps on going, and then gets weaker and weaker as it goes away, but it's still there. There's a substance structure on the inside of this light, but it's like you're in a glass globe thing. And your own light is the glass globe. I just feel happy! There's a little difference in the radiance of their glows. Some are brighter than others, and some are a little different color, like some are peach, and some are more like strawberry. Mine is a creamy yellow. And we're all floating."

She seemed so bubbly and happy, enjoying this and exuberant about describing what she was seeing. Almost childlike in her discovery. "And they are so happy to see me. I guess they were here waiting for me. It's kind of like a party. I don't really even understand what they're saying. They talk too fast. There have been lots of changes. They wanted to tell me all the changes all at once. They're afraid that the area's getting sick. And we want to make it better. The colors aren't as bright as they were."

D: What area?
W Oh, down there it isn't as bright. And we need to make it better. (She didn't sound as happy as before.) The glows aren't

brighter, but they seem brighter to me! They say it's not good.

D: Have you been there before?

W: I was there when they started, a long time ago. We came here and we decided to live here. And so we found the area, but then other things were happening that make it not comfortable any more. And they don't want to have to go somewhere else.

D: Do they live on the ground, or just up in the air? If I'm understanding it right.

W: They don't need the ground. What happens down there makes where we live uncomfortable.

D: You said you were there in the beginning when they first came there? (Yes) *Then did you go away?*

W: Yes, I had to go somewhere and help somebody else. Once they got started, then I could go and help another group.

D: So that's what you do? Go from group to group?

W: Yes, because they think I'm important.

This was confusing. I had no idea where we were, and who or what the other beings were. They seemed to be a type of energy beings, but there were differences.

D: What is their job?

W: (Pause) They talk to the fairies. Where do the fairies live? Oh, yeah! The fairies and the other things live down on the ground. The ground is way down there.

D: What do the fairies look like?

W: They look like people, but little. They look like queens ... oh, there's a little unicorn horse, but it's miniature like the fairy. (Laugh) I zoomed down there to see what it was like. I can move around any way I want. I want to do that all the time. (Laugh)

D: What kind of a job do the little people have down there?

W: They're trying to keep their planet nice, and they try to help the bigger animals. And there are other people there too, but they're not supposed to work with the people. The little fairies

79

like the animals. (Pleased) They like me, too.

D: *What do your people do to help the fairies?*

W: We keep them away from the people. We tell them when the people are coming by, because people aren't nice. The people are hurting them. (She became sad.)

D: *How can they hurt them?*

W: (Sadly) Because some people take away their area, and it makes them hurt. The people take their homes, and their homes are the trees. There are not many trees any more.

Apparently, the fairies were like nature spirits whose job was to protect the plants and trees. They were upset because people were taking down the trees that they were sworn to protect. They must have felt they were failing in their job, their assignment.

D: *And this is why they don't like the people?*

W: Yes, but this isn't Earth. It's not like the Earth. It's not the same plants. We came there to help the fairies in their work, because they were too little and they couldn't see forever. And we could help them see what might hurt them.

D: *And you have the ability to see these things and know how to warn them?*

W: Yes, we can see, yes!

D: *But you said you went other places?*

W: Yes, I had to. There are other worlds that needed somebody to help the fairies. And the fairies are very happy when we come, because they can be secure and not scared. We live in the sky! Where people can't see us, but the fairies can. I don't think the people like us much. They don't seem to care about nature.

D: *But by you glowing like that, they probably couldn't see you anyway.*

W: Yes. They only look for structure, and we don't really have that much structure. I came back to check on them, and make sure everything's okay. They're happy to see me, and they have to tell me all about it. That's why I couldn't hear. (Chuckle) It was too much going on. But the fairies, they don't talk as fast. I can go to other worlds, but my job is there. They are very gentle people. They're so caring, so warm. Just being around them feels like lots of love. The people *tried* to come there. And we made a bad stink! We combined things that made a smell. We know those kinds of things, but the people don't understand it. It worked pretty good! And the people went away. (Chuckle) They will try to get rid of the stink. Everybody's happy. Especially happy when the people go away.

Although this type of being normally has no sense of time, I decided to move her forward to an important day when something was happening.

D: *What are you doing? What do you see?*
W: Oh, there are people. And they have their big cities. It's not good. We tried our stink, and it didn't work. They said they could just change the air. They think there's something out there that they need. I'm not sure what it is, but it doesn't sound good for us. They're going to capture animals and run experiments, and that's no good. They're not going to hurt us. They're going to hurt the fairies and the animals. But they're our friends and they're part of us.
D: *I thought they wouldn't be able to see the fairies.*
W: They can't see them, but they make them scared and that hurts them. And then they lose their area. I'm so sad, because that's my job. And I didn't protect them. (Almost crying) I don't really want to see. They hurt them because I didn't protect them. I was supposed to make it never happen. I saw they were going to be there, and it didn't work. (Sadly)
D: *What do the animals look like that they're taking?*
W: Some of them have spots like the leopard.
D: *Big cats, you mean?*

W: Yes, but they're not mean. All the animals are nice. They're scared. Everybody's scared.

D: *What other kind of animals are they taking?*

W: The monkeys. And all the pretty birds. (Almost crying) They were counting on us.

D: *Is there anything you can do to help the animals now?*

W: I don't know. I don't think so. People are too big.

D: *The fairies can't do anything either?*

W: No. They may try. (Very unhappy) But there are too many people, and they're *definite* that they're going to do it. They are putting the animals in cages. The animals are scared, and some of them are dying, just because they're too scared. They don't want to live. They put them in this big building. And they cut down the trees.

Then, apparently Wanda could not stand to watch any longer, because she believed it was her fault that these negative things were happening. She abruptly left the world where she was helping the fairies and animals as some type of nature spirit, and went back to the spirit side. She definitely thought she had failed in her job of trying to protect the little people. She was unhappily reporting for duty to be reassigned. She and the elders on the council decided she could do more good the next time around by being a "people" instead of this glowing energy being, because then she would have more power to make changes. She described the entities on the council who were advising her.

W: They look like globs of light, but they are different from the other lights like I was. Very different. They're just soft, fluffy. Well, no, I guess there's some structure in there too, but they radiate so much light, it's hard to see if they really have structure They don't look like the people where I came from.

D: *Are these the ones that make the decision?*

W: They *help* make decisions. They let you make your own

choices, but they show you all, and talk to you about the choices.

D: *So you've decided that you want to try being a "people"?*

W: (Uncertain) Yes, I can do it.

D: *It's always scary when it's the unknown, something new and different, isn't it? (Yeah!!) Well, what happens then? How do you become a people?*

W: Well, there's this little baby. They told me I was going to be this little baby, and I said I don't want to be a baby, because babies can't be powerful.

D: *Yes, but you have to start somewhere.*

W: I'm just going to go be a kid. I'm going to be about six.

D: *You're not going to be a baby? (Nope.) Do you see the kid you want to be?*

W: Oh, he's cute. He has lots of energy. And he's very concerned about the animals. And I'm telling him some of the things I know. But I don't know much any more; it's fading.

D: *How do you become him if he's already six years old? He would already have a spirit living inside of him, wouldn't he?*

W: I don't know. I just saw him and walked up to him, and then I was him.

D: *So it can work like that sometimes?*

W: I don't know. I saw the baby, and I didn't want the baby. And then I saw him, and now I'm him.

D: *But that's how you become a people, you have to start little?*

W: Yeah, but I'm six and I can still do stuff. I can't tell him about the fairies, because I don't remember it all. I know there's something there, but I don't know what it is.

Even though this was unclear, it was obvious that she had decided to become a "people" so she could make a difference. It was obviously her first incarnation as a human, but it definitely was not her present lifetime as Wendy. So I had her leave the entity there, so we could move forward through time and space. This way I could communicate with her subconscious.

D: I know the subconscious could have picked anything for Wendy to watch. Why did the subconscious choose to show her that lifetime?

W: Because she was valuable. She now, in her present lifetime, feels that she can't do anything with the animals and plants. And she needs to know that, even though she's just one person, she can make a difference. She thinks it's too hard for one person to make a difference. And she forgets that one person has to start. She has ideas about starting. She just doesn't do them.

D: Is that why she left the energy form and came into human incarnations?

W: That's one of the reasons. She doesn't want to work with the animals and the plants any more. She wants to work with the people, because she hopes the people will become better. But she's not sure that people on Earth are ready to understand that there are many different dimensions. It's the same scenario that humans have had to deal with for a very long time. We're finally getting through to her. It took long enough! She's known for so long that she's supposed to be working with people.

D: But when you begin lives as a human, don't you get caught up in it and create karma?

W: Yes. She keeps making the choice to come here. She can go other places. It's a choice. And karma exists if you want it. But if you can step out of the human restrictions, you can make the choice to go other places. And you can make the choice to leave that karma, whether it's positive or negative, behind you.

D: Yes, but she made a decision to be a human so she could make a difference?

W: Yes, she's always hoping to make a difference. She needs to understand that she's made a difference many, many places. And maybe she can just quit trying so hard. She tries to take care of everything and everybody. And she needs to remember she's taken care of everything and everybody for centuries.

In my book *Between Death and Life,* it was explained that one of the series of lives we must experience before we attempt living in the human body is life as nature spirits, i.e.: fairies, etc. These are guardians of the plants and animals. These little beings are real, and cultures in the past that lived close to nature were able to see them. Many of the stories of "little people" are based on fact. In our present technological society, it is much more difficult to be aware of their presence, unless it is the little gremlins that love to play tricks with my computer. This story also shows that the nature spirits do not like being too close to humans. They much prefer the agricultural or natural areas rather than busy cities.

Another form of life that is a requirement is called "elementals". I'm not sure if that was what Wendy was experiencing, because she seemed to be helping the fairies rather than being one of them. The elementals are basic energies that are not defined by a solid form. These do not seem to have an intelligence that can be communicated with. They are attracted to places, and feed off and add to the energy of that place, whether it is positive or negative. Most people can sense this basic energy when they enter certain buildings. Notice how the energy of a large cathedral differs from the energy of a prison. It is the accumulation of energies that remain within the structure. These two life forms are different from each other. This chapter illustrates how there are many other life-forms that are possible before the soul attempts life as a complicated human.

Is this next session describing the same type of entity under a different name?

D: *Sally wanted to know, how do the fairies enter the human realm? She's very interested in the little people, the fairies.*
S: Fairies are not little people. Fairies are quite large, compared to humans.
D: *We always picture them as being very small.*
S: Those aren't fairies. Those are the in-between, the nature spirits that communicate, and are deliminal (phonetic) between here, the human, and the fairy.

Deliminal is not a word. The closest is delimit, which means: to set the limits or boundaries of. Many times in my work, the being that is communicating will invent words, sometimes turning verbs into nouns, and vice versa, in order to come as close as it can to what it is trying to describe. Is this the case here?

D: *But you said the fairies are actually quite large?*
S: Yes, they're large. They're not small. They're sometimes larger than most humans. They have a different ability to interpret their being. They are human-like in that they have two arms and two legs, but they tend to be more connected with nature. So they have nature-like feelings, or nature-like bodies. Sally has a friend, actually, who is a fairy who is very tree-like in his appearance. His skin is wood, like bark; his hair is more like green leaves. They interpret their bodies differently.
D: *But it is a physical body?* (Yes) *Well, she wanted to know how they enter the human realm.*
S: They use the elements.
D: *I know about the elementals, but you mean the elements?*
S: They use the elements. All of their bodies are a combination of the four elements of the air, water, earth and fire. And they separate each of the elements. They cross through a portal

and then reassemble by calling the elements on the other side of the human realm.

D: *But their bodies do appear human?*

S: Yes, that's right. They're a bit odd-looking for humans, but still much more human than if they were still in the fairy realm.

D: *Then people wouldn't know they were actually conversing with a fairy.*

S: No, they would think this person was a bit odd, though. They would think that this fairy in a human body looks a bit different from normal humans.

D: *Does the person who is a fairy know they're different?*

S: Oh, yes, they remember everything.

D: *They know they are not a normal human being.*

S: Yes, they can come and go much more readily than humans do.

D: *How can she use this ability of the fairies for healing?*

S: She needs to be much more connected to the elements, and understand how the elements play a part in illness. And then be able to shift the elements so they are in balance and harmony with each other, so the disease state can be ameliorated. She doesn't need to be near a person to do it though. She actually has this information in her mind, she just hasn't applied it. Again, it goes to her problem with thinking she isn't able to do it.

D: *We put limitations on ourselves, don't we?* (Yes)

When Betty came into the life, she found herself looking at a strange object in an unfamiliar landscape. The object was a smooth, oyster-colored cylinder with a round ball resting on top. There was a red rectangular design on the side. The cylinder stood on rocks all by itself against a strange sky of two mottled colors: navy blue and pale yellow. When she turned around, she saw more rocks of unusual shapes. "They're kind of like an hourglass. Kind of elongated and skinny in the middle. And some are like spires." It definitely did not sound like she was on Earth. Then she announced, "It looks like everything else is underground. I need to be underground. We don't live on the surface, we live under the ground. – There's an opening, a round tube. You go through the tube. – This isn't my home. I have a tour, and then I go back. I'm on a way station. We're miners. I've been checking the beacon. I am the communication officer. This cylinder is a communication beacon. The top of the ball opens and emits light."

I asked if she wanted to go down and see what it was like underground. She said you just slide down the tube. She came out into a chamber where she took off her outerwear. Apparently, it was something that had to be worn on the surface. "I'm taking it off, and I'm not human. I look kind of like a bug. I have multiple arms; I have a football-shaped head. I look like an ant. I have pincer jaws. And my eyes are on the end of an antenna. I can look every direction. I have two antennae, so I can see multi-directions. I have four legs and six arms. My body is brown, and it has three segments. The top segment is the head. The next one has six arms, and the biggest has four legs. And I have some kind of breathing device on my chest. Not an apparatus. It is some kind of organ on the outside of my chest. You pull air in and it communicates. It whistles and clicks. That's how it communicates. We all understand it."

D: *Was there a reason you have to wear something when you go up to the surface?*
B: You would call it radiation. You cannot breathe up there without the suit, and it shields you from the radiation.
D: *Why is there radiation on this place?*
B: It's close to the sun. The only time I go to the surface is to check the beacon.

D: That sounds like it's important, to keep the beacon working.

B: That's why they have me. I'm the emergency backup. If something goes wrong with the beacon, I can send an SOS from me, a pulse. But I think it would kill me. I don't think I would survive it. I think it would take all of me to do it. Too much energy.

D: So that's why they call you the communication officer?

B: Yes, and I'm the emergency backup.

D: In case anything happens, then you would have to sacrifice yourself to send a message? (Yes)

There were other beings living under the ground who were similar to him. "We're segmented into houses. I guess you would call it houses. Each house has a job, and we're lineages that have a job. I'm from a house of communications."

D: That's what you mean by lineages? They pass these abilities down? (Yes) *And the others have different abilities and jobs to do?*

B: Oh, yes, the tunnelers. We work down there. We're mining.

D: Do you have living quarters also?

B: Places to get out of the way. I don't think I sleep.

D: What about sustenance to keep the body alive? Do you consume anything? (No) *How do you stay alive?*

B: We're born with what we need, and when it's gone, we're gone.

She was reporting all of this so matter-of-fact. It didn't bother her. It was just the way it was in this life.

D: You don't have to keep replenishing it or resupplying it?

B: No. It's a short life. We just work.

D: What are you mining?

B: We're mining a stone for someone else. Not for us. We don't need it.

89

D: It sounds like you don't need much of anything, do you?

B: No. We're doing this to help someone else. The stones are white, sometimes clear. Sometimes green and purple. They are pulverized and shipped to another planet.

D: Do you have the equipment down there to pulverize them?

B: Yes. Those get processed. We have houses that do that. We are all workers.

D: Are the stones shipped to your home planet?

B: I don't think I ever had a home. I think I was born on a ship. And dropped to do the work.

D: Did they drop many of you at one time?

B: Yes, enough to do the job. It's a short life. They bring us more to replace us.

D: What do you think about it? Do you like that life?

B: I don't have emotions like that. I have more thoughts than others, because I'm the communicator. This stage of my life, when I shed it, I believe that I will become light. And then I can do what I want.

D: Are you taught that, or do you just know it?

B: We know that. We're born with that. We know that what we're doing is temporary. But those that create us, they don't know that. The people whose ship we were on. They don't understand that, but we have this as a memory. We know we just go from one existence to another. It's temporary. It's something to do for a short period of time.

D: But you said you have more – I guess "feelings" would be the word – than the others, because you are the communicator?

B: Because I'm not really one of them. I just look like it.

D: You said the people on the ship are different. What are they like?

B: They're bigger. They have only two arms and two legs. And their heads are round. They have different features than we do.

D: Do you know anything about this ship and where they go?

B: It's a mining ship. It's a mining operation. And they grow these workers in incubators, and then release them onto the planet to do the mining. They have genetically altered these workers to do certain jobs, to have certain structures in their bodies. And they process the ores and make the deliveries. They have a time. Everything is timed.

D: *So when they release you on the planet, you know exactly what you're supposed to do, and where you're supposed to go?* (Yes) *You don't even question it.*

B: No, no need. I'm born knowing what it is. And I carry the memories of my lineage. I know other places my ancestors have been to. I understand and remember what they experienced, and it will continue on down the house line. But I think I'm a mutation.

D: *So with all of your memories, you have always been this type of being?* (Yes) *Because you carry the memories that the people on the ship have programmed into you?*

B: They couldn't program it. We already have it. They just took us.

D: *But you did say they don't understand that part.*

B: No, they don't. This ship has no spiritual beliefs other than what they were taught as children. They're harder, they're not spiritual beings, and they don't see the spirit within us. They're very different. They're not thinkers, either. They're just workers, also, of a different kind. They're absolutely programmed. I don't think they're human. I don't think they're living. Androids.

D: *Androids?* (Yes) *So you don't think they have a spirit?* (No) *Are all the people on the ship alike?*

B: No. There are other types on the upper decks. I can hear them, but I don't see them. They have a spirit. They're real.

D: *What do you know about those beings?*

B: Those beings are highly trained. They've been to schools. They depend on each other, it's a team. They have a lot of diversity. They have many different shapes; it's many different beings. It's an entire crew, two hundred at least.

91

They have specialized schooling, and they're part of a conglomeration of mining efforts. This where I am, there are eight planets in the solar system. Four of them are inhabited and interact. There's a mining operation that goes beyond the solar system outward, and then brings back ores, or what's needed for the planets.

D: *The beings on the upper deck, are they from all the different planets in your solar system?*

B: And beyond. They hired on. They get hazard pay. It's dangerous work.

D: *Do those beings need to consume anything?*

B: Yes, they do. They have kitchens, they have showers, they have greenhouses. They grow things. They have libraries, but it's not books. It's just to work their clear little rectangular tabs that can do many things. There's music recorded, voices, readings, events, entertainment.

D: *How are they able to comprehend those things if it's not by reading?*

B: They have machines, and they have a hologram. It's different. It's not like anything I've seen. It merges with them.

D: *That's how you're getting the information?* (Yes) *Because at first, you said you could hear them, but now you are able to find out more about them.* (Yes) *And they don't realize that, do they?*

B: No, they just see us as a worker, a bug, but we're not androids. We have a short life force, but it's intense. It's powerful.

D: *These other beings, the higher-developed ones, are they different sexes, or are they all the same?*

B: There are some different sexes there, but it's not necessarily boy and girl. There are some boys, and some girls, but there's more than that. They're not all like that. They're not all quite physical. And some lay eggs. Very many different types. They all come from many different places.

92

I wanted the creature to now focus on the underground facility instead of the ship.

D: *Focus back to the underground – it's not a city – it's a mining operation.* (Yes) *And occasionally, you have to go up to the top to check on the beacon.*

B: Just to make sure it's still upright and not hit by a meteor. It can happen.

D: *What is the importance of the beacon?*

B: The importance of the beacon is to signal that a load or shipment is ready, or the need for a new worker.

D: *If too many have died?* (Yes) *What happens to their bodies when they die?*

B: They recycle the carcass, but the light is released.

So when the signal went out, they would come and pick up the carcasses and drop off new workers. The signal bounced from satellite to satellite in space. "We're three days away from anything. They come and they hover. They send down the retractor, and they siphon up the ore and the bodies. And then send down the pods with the new workers."

D: *Do you know what they use the pulverized ore for?*

B: I'll ask.

D: *You're able to ask and get answers?* (Yes) *They're not aware you can do that, are they?* (No) *You're smarter than they are.* (Laugh)

B: They're using the pulverized ore for fuel. For their ships, and plants, and cities. That's why it's important to keep this cycle going. And it's distributed equally. It's peaceful. There's no control issue. Everyone is sharing.

D: *That's very good. No one wants to have control over anything.*

B: No. They're past that. Those days are ancient times. They're creative. They're working with sunlight and the crushed

93

stone, and they create these beds that magnify the light. And then there are reflectors that move this light to wherever they direct it, so they light cities and they power vehicles. And they use it to supplement growth of food. It's for a power plant. It's a controlled society.

D: *But everyone has all their needs met?*

B: Yes, they do, but it's kind of sterile. There's not much movement. There are not many children. I don't feel any joy. Just existing.

D: *So it is not an ideal society.*

B: I don't like it, but it's temporary. It's short. I don't do the mining. I am communicating to all of them. Telling them where they need to be, and where to look next.

I decided to move him ahead to an important day. Even though it was to be a short life, there might be something happening that he would consider important. He saw a tunnel, but he thought it was a different place, because it was square instead of round. "It feels different. I think I'm going back to the ship. They're calling me back to the ship. And ... they want to open me up. Why do they want to open me up? – They've discovered something about me. When I sent the beacon message, I used a word I shouldn't have. I said it in a different way. They want to know why. They're bringing me up. They think I'm different, and they want to see if it shows inside me. I think they're not going to find anything, because it's not something that's coming from inside of me. And I get to have a shorter life."

D: *Where is it coming from?*

B: The light.

D: *It's coming from your spirit part?* (Yes) *You don't think they understand that, do they?*

B: They're going to.

D: *Why? What happens?*

94

B: I release in front of them, before they cut me open. I let out my pulse of light. I let it go. And it's kind of funny. It made them fall down.

D: *(Laugh) They weren't expecting that, were they?*

B: No, but I think I hurt them. I'm seeing blood from their ears, and their noses.

D: *Who was doing this, the androids or the other ones?*

B: The other ones. The androids couldn't do it.

D: *So you weren't going to wait until they cut into you.*

B: No. They can cut me open after I've pulsed. The pulse was the real part of me. I let that come out *all the way*. It was blinding. It moved through them.

D: *What was it, energy or what?*

B: It's energy. It's not heavy, it's light. And I'm just moving it through the ship. Every part of it. It was so powerful when it was released in that little room. And now I'm moving through the ship. I'm memorizing; memorizing everything. All the systems, all of the occupants, all their lineages. I'm memorizing all of it.

D: *Like absorbing it?* (Yes) *Why are you doing that?*

B: To pass it on, so my future generations will carry the knowledge of the plants, the peoples, the beings, the planets.

D: *The future generations of your house?*

B: The house, and they'll morph. They'll become something more. It goes to all the generations. Time and space doesn't matter to us. It never did, really.

D: *So you just decided, before you go on, to memorize everything?*

B: It was an opportunity. I am memorizing every metal, every piece of material, how the cells are working, how it all works. I am sending it now, into the light.

D: *How do you do that?*

B: I think it.

D: *Everything you see and feel, you're thinking it and sending it out?*

B: Always.

D: *It wouldn't normally be a part of your life, would it?*

B: Yes and no. It's happened before in our house; take advantage of it. It's just that time doesn't matter to us. We've been around for so long.

D: *So you're not worried about your carcass back there, because you weren't going to live very long anyway.*

B: No, it was temporary. We were disguised. They never saw through it. They never knew who we were. They just saw the bug, and the worker. We could go anywhere like that.

D: *But the other beings like yourself didn't have this ability, did they? The ones in the other houses, the other lineages?*

B: They have it.

D: *Do you think they were using it?*

B: Not yet. They were just waiting. It works for us. You have a short life as a worker, and then you pulse out. And you take all the knowledge with you, until you send it into the light.

D: *Do you know what the light does with it?*

B: It creates new things.

D: *It has to have all this information to create new things?*

B: No, but it helps give direction to how the creation needs to move. It is capable of creating anything. It's like a stream of thought that merges with all the other streams of thought. And when that happens, new things are created. Some of it flows back to where it came from; some moves forward into new directions of exploration; and some of it is saved, or curls around itself, and creates an intensification. There's a divine mind that we know we're part of that appreciates this experience, and is utilizing it to expand and to deepen.

D: *But it needs the information so it can create?*

B: No, it uses the information to create. It's *always* in a state of creating. That never changes.

D: *Why is the new information important?*

B: Because it gives an experience; it gives a remembering, a renewal. It brings focus back to what it was, and is, and can be. It's all about change.

D: So this is important for it to have this input.

B: To bring about the changes. Those people back there, they're stuck. They're not moving anymore. They're not growing enough. They're losing their creativity, they're losing their joy in life. They're becoming automated, they're ...

D: Stagnant?

B: That's it, stagnant.

D: So you're not going back there, are you?

B: No, I'm done with that. I've done as much as I can do there.

D: Do you decide where you're going to go next? Or does someone help you?

B: It's a group decision. We all decide.

D: Where is the group?

B: They're in the light. I go into the light. And there's a feeling, an understanding, a knowing. When you're in that light, you feel a calling, or a pull. Or you are attracted, and you can feel your way to it to see where it's going, and what it's doing. And if it's needed, or it appeals, you can go there. It's a long journey, but it's okay.

D: So it just goes from one thing to the next, always expanding, always learning. Is that the idea?

B: It *is* the idea, it is the purpose. It is the gathering. This is the gathering point and the release point. But it spirals, we're always moving. I feel as though we're close to something.

D: Where do they decide you're going to go next?

B: That depends on where you are in the light. There are different levels, you know? If you're working in one particular area, on one strand of thought. There are those that work there that give direction, or help, to create the experience for whatever it needs to be. But if you're beyond that, if you're not locked into that, then it's not quite so defined. It's a oneness of mind that is moving in all directions, at all times. And in order to keep balance within itself, in perfection, sometimes in the outermost areas, that state of perfection needs to be tweaked. And the light might ask you to go there and tweak it.

D: *So, as you become more developed on the different levels, you have more decision about what you do?*

B: Yes, because you're part of that one mind. It's like the hologram. It shatters and every piece is a perfect replica. But it's all part of the bigger picture.

I asked her to move away from that scene and allow the little creature, now that he was just a spark of light, to continue on his own journey. I oriented Betty back into her body, and called forth the subconscious to have it explain why it chose such a strange lifetime for her to see. I knew it had a purpose for showing it to her. It always does.

B: It's the versatility of the light. That things aren't always what they seem. And the understanding that the light within is so much more.

D: *How does it relate to Betty in her life now?*

B: The lineage. The way she's utilized, or brought into being to absorb, and to release it, and then to move forward. Her life is about merging. Her life is about tweaking the perfection.

D: *How do you want her to use this information of that life?*

B: I want her to remember the stream of consciousness, where it goes. I want her to remember the state of oneness, and that the thoughts and focus come from multi-mind. And that she is the vessel for that light in human form.

D: *She was a communicator in that life.*

B: She's always been the communicator. She is one now. It's her reason. She does readings for people and communicates with them. She taps into the core of their light. She peels away the veneers. She helps them to remember that they are love, and their connection to the All.

D: *She wanted to know if there's a way she can improve her psychic abilities and the readings she's giving.*

B: All is as it should be.
D: *You think she's doing a good job?*
B: Good enough.
D: *She worries about it.*
B: She needs to worry. It keeps her honest, it keeps her ego in check. She's battled ego before.

At one of my hypnosis classes, a woman brought up a point that did not apply to my technique that I was teaching. It really was a deviation or distraction, but I could not let it slide, so I attempted to answer it. I was discussing how we have to *be* everything when we decide to incarnate on Earth. Everything meaning: gas, minerals, rocks, plants, animals and then all phases of the human condition. This was because God was curious and wanted to learn, and he sent us out (as cells in the body of God) to learn as much as we possibly could and bring this knowledge back to be added to His gigantic computer storehouse. We would continue to journey out again and again until we could "graduate", and finally return home to the Source and stay. The woman said she could not believe that theory, because God was all-knowing. He had all knowledge, he did not need us. According to what I have learned, that would not appear to be true. He is a compilation of what each and every one of us have deposited in Him over eons of time. He is constantly searching, and out of His insatiable curiosity, He desires to learn unceasingly. Thus, He is constantly creating more and more diverse forms.

She asked what He could possibly use all the information for. I have found it was used to create with. I explained that it seems as though our universe is constantly expanding as we journey outward; increasing our experiences and our knowledge. Then it seems as though it reaches a point where it is at its limit of expansion, and begins to return back to Source, or implode back on itself. Is that when we finally return home with all the knowledge of everything we have experienced? Is that when we reach the point when we can rest and stay with God? Then it seems as though once everything has imploded upon itself, it explodes out again, in a constant cycle.

She asked, "Is there ever a point when we stop? A point when we cease to be, and become nothing?" I do not believe so, because everything is energy, and energy never dies. It just changes shape and form. She could not see the point in returning again and again to the same universe and experiencing all the millions of lessons in different forms. There would come a point when we would have experienced everything that was possible, and then we should just cease to be.

A man in the class supplied the perfect answer. He said, "Yes, we could experience all there is to know in *this* universe. But there are millions upon millions of other universes that contain worlds and creatures that we cannot even imagine." As it is written in this book, there are universes that obey totally different laws of physics. Places where planets are square instead of round, etc. There must be countless experiences awaiting us in these other places. So even if we finally exhaust the possibilities of this solitary universe, there are millions more to explore. And maybe each time the universe explodes out and then implodes in, and explodes out again in its own reincarnational cycle, we are sent to explore something else. The possibilities are endless, and so is the progression of our soul. As long as God is curious and wants to learn new experiences to add to His storehouse of knowledge, we are useful to add to His creative powers. Thus, we constantly return to our "home" where there is great love and rejuvenative powers. And thus we will never die.

CHAPTER FIVE

THE GREEN PLANET

Betty (female) came into the life and could not see anything, but she felt like she was in space. "There's nothing around me. I feel like I'm floating. It's like being part of everything. It's dark, but it's comfortable. It feels like I'm looking out at the Universe. And it's like it's all my children. They're all my sisters. All the stars and all the planets, all the galaxies, it's like my family." As she watched, she saw something spectacular happening. "There was a galaxy just being born." Her voice was filled with awe. "It just kind of erupted. It was just there and growing, and beautiful."

D: *It just formed that quickly?* (Yes) *Do you know how something like that happens?*
R: No, it just does.
D: *Is this a place you go often?*
R: No, I don't think I've ever been here before. It feels so comfortable, and so beautiful. I feel like I want to stay here, but yes, there's probably a place I need to go. Okay. There's a planet showing up. It looks like a big, green moon. We're getting closer, and it's like it's covered in moss. And I get down on the planet and there are really soft trees.
D: *The thing that looked like moss?*
R: Yes. It's a whole forest. The trees are taller than I am. I am walking through a forest, and it's very moist. The trees are like a canopy, so it's dark. The trees have spongy kinds of leaves. A really pretty green. The whole planet is covered in them. The ground is dark and soft, but I'm not sinking in. And the trees have really rough dark brown bark.
D: *Does the ground look like dirt?*

101

R: It looks like shredded bark.

I had her look at herself, and I was surprised at the description. She definitely was not a human being. "I have webbed feet, and they're kind of bluish-grey. They look like elongated duck feet, and there's tissue between the toes. And my legs are long and spindly. My hands are also webbed. I have a thumb and three fingers."

D: *Are you able to pick up things?*
R: Yes, I can hold them in the web.
D: *Are you wearing any clothes?*
R: No. I'm just really skinny.

Her face was elongated vertically, tall and thin. No hair. Big eyes that covered most of her face.

Foot

Face

D: *Why do you need such big eyes?*
R: Because it's dark here. There's light above the trees, but it's dark down here on the ground.
D: *Do you have night and day, or do you know what I mean?*

R: No, there's no night and day. It's just sort of dusk.

She said her mouth was just sort of a hole. I asked, "Do you eat anything, consume anything?"

R: I eat bark. I pick it up off the ground. And the webbed feet help me walk on the bark. I kind of pulverize it and eat it. (Surprised) Tongue! I have a tongue. I mash the bark in my hands, and lick it off my hands with my tongue.

D: *Is that the only thing you consume?*

R: Yes. Just bark.

D: *What does it taste like?*

R: I don't know.

D: *I was thinking, if you're used to it you wouldn't know anything else. Do you drink anything?*

R: No, there's moisture in the air. I absorb it through my skin. It's cool and humid in the woods, so I don't have to drink anything.

D: *Do you have a sex? Do you know what I mean?*

R: I'm ... female. I lay eggs. And my mate fertilizes the eggs after they're laid.

D: *Do you live somewhere around there?*

R: In the forest.

D: *Well, you said the forest covers the whole planet. (Yes) Do you live in a certain place in the forest?*

R: We have a territory that's sort of ours. There are others like us, and we fight over the territories.

D: *Isn't there enough land for everybody?*

R: It's a small planet. The other groups want larger territories.

D: *How do you fight?*

R: They ram each other, and collide with each other. Though hardly ever anyone gets killed. It's just a domination type fight. The biggest one wins.

D: *Does your group ever have to fight?*

R: No, because our male is the biggest. But it usually doesn't go that far. The others will back down.

D: So he dominates the other territories. (Yes) *Do you live in a shelter or anything?*

R: No, we're always in the open.

D: You don't have extremes in temperature?

R: No, it's always the same.

D: And when you lay your eggs, where do you go to do that?

R: We just lay them. Then the males come by and fertilize them.

D: Is your group a large group?

R: Yes. My male has twenty females. Most don't have that many.

D: Is there anything that you do with your time?

R: Hunt for food.

D: But you said the bark is everywhere, isn't it?

R: Yes, but we need a lot. That's the reason there are fights for territory.

D: I would think the bark would be everywhere, because it falls off the trees.

R: Yes, but females that are producing eggs need a lot of food. There are so many females. The males want the females, but they have to have enough territory to support them.

D: Does anyone die in the group?

R: Occasionally, mostly of old age. Old age would be three of your Earth years.

D: I was thinking that's one way to control the population. So people do die, but then you're constantly reproducing.

R: But sometimes the eggs get smashed, especially if they're laid where someone's going to fight.

D: Do you sleep, or do you know what that is?

R: We rest, we don't sleep. We just stop moving. Most of the time we're moving.

D: Are you the only species on this planet, or is there other animal life?

R: It's just us and the trees. But we're taking over. We're killing the trees. That's why we need territory. That's what's happening – the trees are being killed.

D: How are they being killed?

R: In places the bark is gone. They're taking if off the trees.

D: You don't wait until it falls on the forest floor?

R: No. The territory that I live in is still all right. The male's been able to keep the other males out.

D: Do they realize they're killing their food supply?

R: No. My male does. My male knows that he can't have any more than twenty females.

D: But then if you have children – if you want to call them that – they would have to eat also, wouldn't they?

R: Yes, but he knows how many eggs to fertilize. He is wise that way.

D: Because your planet has limited resources. So your life consists of just eating and reproducing.

R: Eating and laying eggs.

D: Wouldn't you want to go anywhere else?

R: No. Other places on the planet are dying. The people are eating the bark. They also have fertilized too many eggs. There are too many children. They're eating all the bark! And now they're killing the trees. And soon there won't be enough to eat.

I moved her forward to an important day, although I couldn't imagine what an important day would consist of in such a mundane existence.

R: There's nothing left but our territory. The rest of the planet is barren.

D: What happened to the other beings?

R: They died. They've eaten it all. They all died of starvation.

D: And the trees couldn't live either?

R: No. Now my male has the entire planet. Our group is the only one left.

D: But what good is the entire planet if you can't live on the

105

other parts?

R: Without the others the trees will come back, eventually. It will be more than my lifetime.

D: *So your group is the only one that's producing children?*

R: Yes. But he is wise. He'll make sure that everything comes back, because he'll teach his young. He'll only let so many males live, and he'll teach them.

It seemed like there was not going to be much variation in a life like this, so I moved her forward to the last day of her life, to see what eventually happened to her.

R: I've just ... I'm resting permanently now. I can't move anymore.

D: *That's what happens when you die?* (Yes) *Even though you eat, it's not enough to keep you alive?*

R: You wear out. You move so much during your life that you just wear out.

I moved her to where she was out of her body and on the other side. "Can you see your body?"

R: Yes. It just fades away. Decomposes, I guess.

D: *What do you think you learned from that lifetime?*

R: The importance of balance. Not taking more than you can use.

That was an important lesson, and one that would be applicable to our present time as we go about depleting the Earth of the natural resources and not replacing them. Let's hope we don't reach the same fate before we realize that it is not the best way to live.

When I called forth Betty's subconscious toward the end of the session, I asked why it had picked this strange lifetime for her to see. I knew there was no way to identify where the planet was located.

R: Because she needs to learn balance in this life. Something she learned in that life she needs to relearn now.

D: *Of course, that was a drastic use of balance, wasn't it?*

R: Yes, but it's an important lesson for her.

D: *In that life, her group was able to survive.*

R: Yes, because they had a leader that understood balance.

D: *It was interesting that they were able to survive on the bark.*

R: It was their food.

D: *It also shows what happens when an entire planet gets out of balance.*

R: Yes. But at the moment, *she* is out of balance. She needs to learn to balance areas of her life in better ways. She's a teacher who's not teaching. She should be. She's a healer. She needs to teach others to heal. She's had bad experiences in the past (other lives). She needs to let those go. She has been killed for her belief in healing. She has been tortured. She needs to forget that. She needs to realize that this is a new life. That's why she needs to balance. She needs to balance what's happened in the past with what is happening now, and realize that there is need and room for teachers. She won't be tortured or killed in this lifetime. This is a time when things have changed, and she needs to teach. She needs to heal by learning balance. She needs to teach balance.

I think the subconscious was also showing us this life as a metaphor for the conditions we are facing in our world today. It is a warning that history repeated itself. It doesn't matter that this happened on another planet, it is showing that we could be headed in the same direction if we don't learn to respect our environment and protect our planet, our home.

CHAPTER SIX

STRUCTURE IS NOT IMPORTANT

Clare is a remarkable young woman. I first met her in Kona, Hawaii in February of 2005. She travels all over the world doing anything she wants. Any adventure is not off limits to her. In Hawaii, she went out every day on a small charter boat to swim with the dolphins. She attended my lectures and workshops while in Kona. She then made arrangements to meet me in London a few months later when I would be there lecturing and conducting one of my hypnosis classes. Her home is on the continent, and it would be easy for her to come and have the session, as well as attend the class. This all sounds normal, but what makes it extraordinary is that Clare is confined to a wheelchair. She has never let this become a handicap. I was worried about her attending the class, because it was held in a private residence near Hyde Park, a beautiful old Victorian three-story house. But the houses in London, as well as restaurants, trains and everything else, are not equipped for the handicapped. She managed to maneuver the stone stairs leading up to the house, and was inside before we were even aware she was there. She did not ask for help, and didn't wait for it.

When she wanted to have the session, I couldn't see how it would be possible. My hotel was one of the thousands of old houses that had been converted into hotels. There are blocks and blocks of them all joined together; they used to be family homes during the 18th and 19th centuries. They have now been remodeled as hotels, but the rooms are small, converted to accommodate a miniature bathroom. There is usually a very small elevator, hardly big enough for two people and luggage, and the hallways are obstacle courses. I did not see how it would be possible for Clare to manipulate all of that to come for the session. But she said not to worry, she was used to going in and

108

out of all kinds of buildings that most people would consider impossible for anyone in a wheelchair. I suppose it is the old saying, "Where there is a will, there is a way." I knew what time she was expected to arrive, and I wanted to go downstairs to the lobby to help her maneuver the elevator, but she was knocking at the door before I had a chance.

I have great admiration for this young woman, and I knew one of the main issues she wanted to address in the session was the cause of her handicap. She was able to get herself out of the chair and onto the bed with the use of her arms and upper torso. Her legs were not completely useless, but they would not support her weight. She had no problem going into a deep trance, and as usual, I never knew what we would discover as I began the session.

Clare came off the cloud suspended over a large city next to the sea. "The city's shape is like a crescent moon along the bay. There are tall buildings, and lower buildings, and jetties going out into something like water. It's funny because it looks as if there are high rises along the side of the sea, but the sea looks kind of fixed. You don't have the movements of the waves. Everything looks a bit frozen." I had her move on down until she was standing on the surface, and asked for a description from that perspective. "I get the impression of a color, bronze or coppery. It's something like a plastic material. Even under my feet, it feels like the same plastic metal material. The buildings are made of it, and everything has a glow like coppery orange. And there are trees that look exactly like models, like they're made of artificial material."

She did not see any type of vehicles or people. The streets were empty, but this often happens when the subject first enters the scene. They are usually alone with no sign of life. Then as we talk, beings and other things enter the picture, almost as though the scene has to be set first, then the rest of it catches up. She noticed what looked like a cloud of bronze coppery colored shooting stars in the dark sky above the city. I then asked her for a description of herself. "I feel very skinny and long. And the legs are very, very skinny, especially under the knee joint. My feet feel more like hooves rather than feet. I'm not wearing any clothes. My body feels like a skeleton. Very thin. And also made of plastic material! Kind of flimsy. My skin is the same bronzy color. I have skinny arms, and funny hands. They are wide, much wider. Six fingers, plus a kind of thumb, which is out of proportion, shorter than the other ones."

D: *What about your face? Do you have any hair?*
C: (Laugh) I feel like a skeleton with hair, yes. It's light colored, and more straw-like.
D: *Do you have eyes?*
C: Yes, I think there is something in the sockets. Could be eyes. I can see. No nose. I'm not sure about a mouth. There is an opening. It's almost as if there is no skin on this skeleton. Just this strange kind of material. There are no ears.
D: *Do you eat food?*
C: There are no organs. It's just the structure, nothing else. It's empty.
D: *What keeps you alive if you don't have a heart or lungs?*
C: That's what I was wondering, if there's any life there. It looks as if there is a system within this structure with something circulating. It's liquid energy, light blue. It circulates in the structure. And there is something that must be green, too.
D: *Do you have to drink it, or replace it, or what?*
C: No, it's like being a car, being fueled. I think from time to time it has to be fueled up again.
D: *How is that done?*
C: In the heel of this structure. There is an opening to be refueled.

When Clare began to describe her living place, it also was strange. She was living in sort of a basement underneath one of the buildings. She also did not need to sleep, as well as not having to eat. So the room was bare, just a space. "It's hard to see. I am in this room, and there seems to be other beings that are much taller than me, with blue dots. As if they were empty and had some blue dots or whatever around them. But the rest is emptiness or black. It's like hanging in the void. I felt some density. And that only allows me to figure out that there must be something, because it's moving. These beings seem to be there, but I can't see them. Just the outlines which are blue specks. It's not continuous. I think we have to do something together."

When I attempted to find out what she did, what her occupation was, she suddenly found herself floating up outside the room. "It's getting gray instead of the other colors. I don't see anything. I was aspired out of there. Sucked out. I'm floating. I'm like in a cloud, in something gray."

D: *Did something happen to make you leave that place?*
C: No. Just disappeared.

I could not get any more information about this strange creature, so I told her to move through time and space until she saw something else that was appropriate. My curiosity was certainly aroused. I was trying to understand what these strange scenes had to do with Clare in this physical lifetime.

C: I see red and black. Black with some red outlines. I have become a bit heavier. As if I've been sinking, becoming more dense. The whole body feels denser. It's made of two layers. The top layer is a bit more structured, more like plastic. And the lower layer touching the bed is softer. And it's tingling in the arms and the chest, and in the legs. And in the head. Now in the face.
D: *Does this body have two arms and two legs, or how is it made?*
C: It has *more* than two arms and legs. It has four legs with just

111

two hips. And it has three arms on each side coming off the shoulders.

D: *Do you get any impressions about the face?*

C: It looks kind of half animal. The head is longer, and it's made of two parts. The first part is like a human head in the back. Then there is an extension, but at a forty degree angle forward. Which makes the head have the forehead coming forward, bending over the lower part of the face. I guess it looks like an open mouth, but it's a whole head and face. The skin is golden.

D: *When you have that many legs, is it hard to walk?*

C: It makes walking faster, because there is always one touching. It's more like a wheel actually, the way they move.

D: *That would make sense. – Where do you live?*

C: There seems to be something in the sky. It is very big. Like a ship. Not really, but some lights with some structure in between.

D: *Are there others there?*

C: I am not aware of others. – It's zooming up again.

She was leaving it again and going off into nothing. I couldn't get any more information. So I told her to move again through time and space to find something else that was appropriate. When I asked her what she was seeing or feeling, she became frustrated, and wanted to stop. "I can't go anywhere. I can't see anything. I'm just feeling 'zzzz' in my body."

D: *That's all right. You're doing beautifully. Just go with it because this is happening for a reason. What are you feeling in your body?*

C: Like ants.

D: *You mean with the nerves?*

C: Probably.

D: *Where is it mostly?*

C: In the finger, in the back, in the legs. A quivering. The image

I get, is feeling like the whole cosmos. Like being full of planets and stars and everything like that.

D: *Oh, that's very big, isn't it?* (Yes) *Like being out there?*

C: No, *being* the cosmos.

D: Being *the whole thing.* (Yes) *What does that feel like?*

C: Like freedom. I don't have to want anything. I just can be. I am, and that's enough. It's like coming home.

D: *Where it is so big it's hard to imagine?*

C: No, it's not an imagination. It's just being.

D: *But if you can be anything, what do you do?*

C: Nothing. At last, nothing. Just exist. Just allow things to happen.

D: *Are you all by yourself?*

C: It seems I'm everything. We are all together. It's not separated.

This all sounded so familiar, since I had been getting the same description from many others of the place they all call "home". They become so content they want to stay there. They have no desire to experience anything else. But I need information, so I knew I would have to get her away from that beautiful place of contentment.

D: *Why did you decide to leave if it was so perfect and so beautiful?*

C: Duty, I guess. To gather experience so the whole can grow. So that different experiences can be gathered, and things can move and evolve.

D: *And it couldn't happen in a perfect place?*

C: I think it's a question of changing states.

D: *Then you had to leave that beautiful state, and go somewhere else to gather information?* (Yes) *To learn.* (Yes) *What did that feel like when you separated?*

C: Very painful.

D: *Are you allowed to go back, or do you have to stay and learn more things?*

C: No, I think I can go back.

D: *Where did you go when you had to separate?*

C: First, I feel like becoming a planet.

D: *Oh, that would be a huge experience, wouldn't it?* (Yes) *What else can you become besides being a planet?*

C: It feels like a being which is more rubbery and longer. More reptilian. There are organs. It's much different. There are no limitations. Not at all.

D: *Is this part of the learning, to experience different types of bodies?* (Yes) *They're physical, but they're all different, aren't they?*

C: Yes, very much so. It's another movement, another view of things.

D: *Then you just go from body to body and place to place gaining information?* (Yes) *Is there anyone or anything that tells you where to go and what to do?*

C: It's like being called from inside.

I decided to move her forward until she first decided to enter the body of Clare. "Why did you decide to enter that body?"

C: I feel pulled down into it. And actually it's very joyful. It feels like an aspiration into it.

D: *Aspiration? Like being sucked into it?* (Yes) *As a baby, or what?*

C: It's very early in the evolution of the baby. Fetal.

D: *When it's inside the mother?* (Yes) *When you entered the body of Clare, was that the first time you had a human body?*

C: No. There were plenty before that.

D: *It seems you like to explore, don't you?*

C: Yes. I'm getting tired of experience. Tired of trying all these different things, and tired of the variation.

Now that I had her back into the body of Clare, I thought it was time to call forth the subconscious, rather than taking her through this lifetime. I asked why it had chosen those strange alien lifetimes for Clare to see?

C: To show her structure isn't important.

D: *They definitely were not human.*

C: It doesn't matter, structural, whatever. The spirit can inhabit anything. It makes no difference what matter seems to look like. They were just another funky representation of life, all the funny forms it can take on. Just to be adapted to whatever is needed at the moment.

D: *So the outside structure is not important?* (No) *Of course, the most important part is the life force, isn't it?*

C: It's a spark, yes. The spirit, the life force, whatever. Or just gathering information and experiences. There are many life forms everywhere. It doesn't matter what kind of a body she's in. Everything has the same information inside, or has sprung from the same information. From the same Source. From spirit, or whatever you want to call it. And it can take on any shape and form and consistency, whatever.

D: *Would this be what she saw when she felt she was the whole cosmos?*

C: Yes, it's a part of it. Everything is part of it, all funny shapes, all expressions of that One. There was a moment when she was in it. There was a moment when there was something else happening, and she was sucked into the light. She *was* the cosmos, but also at the same time in something that was more original, like light, pure light. That was before she became a planet. It felt like the Origin.

D: *If the cosmos was everything, what would the light be?*

C: Just the Origin.

D: *The Origin of where the cosmos and everything came from?*

C: Yes. Maybe there was a step before, but that's not expressible.

D: I've heard that before, there are some words and some terms, concepts, that we'll never be able to understand. There are no words to describe them. (Yes) *So there was something before the light.*

C: Yes, that's already manifestation. But it can't be explained.

D: Then when she went into the light, she became the planet.

C: Afterwards, when she separated from the light.

D: And then there must have been many other experiences before trying the different bodies.

C: Plenty.

D: What was the purpose of her experiencing so many different things?

C: To get the whole manifestation back together. To synthesize. To get a synthesis of all different manifestations. And bring them back to the Source.

D: Then what does the Source do with all of these manifestations?

C: It feels like it's becoming bigger and more whole, and more multifaceted, and richer.

D: So the Source is continually growing and adding to itself. (Yes) *So you showed this to Clare so she could understand?*

C: She knows.

D: But she could have gone to past lives.

C: No. No past lives anymore. She has to go forward. That's not important. She has integrated everything. She has to go forward.

D: Where are we moving forward to? Do you know?

C: To another way of thinking. To meld everything together so there is no violence. No shocks between the different things so there can be harmony and evolution, like being carried by a brook, by a river, forward.

I then proceeded to ask Clare's questions: "Why does she have these disabilities with her spine and her legs? What's the reason for that?"

C: It's like the picture of the world, how it is today. Everything pulling in a different direction instead of harmonizing and going in one direction.

D: *You mean her body is pulling in many different directions?* (Yes) *But she was born with this.*

C: Yes, but it started falling apart, really, when there was disharmony around her. She didn't know how to deal with it. The disharmony in her family? When there was a pull toward her parents, a pull toward her grandmother, and she couldn't join the different forces into one.

D: *So that's when it began to materialize?* (Yes) *Is there anything we can do about it now? Because I know the power of the subconscious.*

C: She has to find the harmony in herself.

D: *She does wonderful things though. We want to help her. How could she find the harmony within herself?*

C: By dying. (That was a shock.)

D: *We don't want that though, do we?*

C: Maybe not physically, but she has to die.

D: *How could she die without dying physically?*

C: She has to step out.

D: *What purpose would that serve?*

C: Like coming back in from another point of view.

D: *This can be done without dying?*

C: Yes, it's possible. She is to be sucked out, put into the laundry and brought back.

D: *Will this happen when she's sleeping at night?*

C: It can happen at any time.

D: *We don't want any harm to the body. Is that understood? Because this is my job, to never cause any harm.*

C: No, she won't be harmed. She can't be harmed. She's gone through so many things without being harmed.

D: *So she will come out of the body, and then come back in from a different viewpoint?*

C: It will just seem awkward as usual when she comes back.

117

D: *Then the body will be more in harmony?*

C: Yes, she will be aligned.

D: *Will she begin to have movement and feeling in her legs?*

C: Could be, yes. It's a possibility.

D: *Once the body is in harmony, can you reconnect the connections?*

C: It's possible. They are still there, and they are whole.

D: *So they have not deteriorated. They can be connected?*

C: They are connected, they are just lank, anesthetized, or ... it's hard to say. It's like they have been squeezed, and instead of having the full flow through them, there is just a little. Like drought in a brook. Yes, there could be more. They're going through more energy.

D: *Can you do that?*

C: If she manages to get fully aligned it will be possible.

D: *When do you want her to do this, where she gets into harmony?*

C: The weekend after next. She'll be back home by that time.

D: *And you'll protect the spirit so it can come back in.*

C: Yes, because the job is not finished. There is much more to come – much, much more. It will be very gradual. She will notice feelings returning to the legs.

D: *Then she'll gradually begin to use the muscles again.*

C: Yes. They have to be awakened. It's time! It's time. The time has come! When she experiments leaving her body and being cleaned, readjusted, it should be possible to work on the entire body at the same time when all her energies are being aligned.

D: *So while she's out of the body for that brief period, you can work on the body?*

C: Yes. Putting the machinery back in order. The whole body needs an overhaul. It's more efficient when she's out, because then her energy systems are also being overhauled. There is nothing else that has to be done.

D: *But there's no danger to her, she will come back.*

C: She will be tired. – This is the best way. Yes, the time has come. She will draw masses. She will be teaching on the larger level. After the overhaul, she will also speak differently. Be more able to convey the things people need in words they can understand more easily. And she will be working much more on an energy level straight through her body. She will be transmitting the knowledge. She will be traveling all over the world. Her life starts now. She needed this trigger. She will also be healing others. She has been waiting for that.

D: *What will she feel like when this happens?*

C: She will be again in this state of funny feeling. Not really being able to see, having a hard time moving her tongue to say something. And then she just has to go and lie on the bed, and the rest will take care of it.

D: *The reason for that is because the connections are separated at that time. That's why it's difficult to talk.* (Yes) *So when she feels like that, the weekend after next, when she'll be back home, she can just go and lie on the bed until it passes?*

C: Until she feels back together again.

D: *And during that time, you'll be working on the body.* (Yes) *That's wonderful. She wasn't expecting this today, was she?*

C: No, not at all.

D: *She was looking for information, but not something like this. – It was strange that we first met a half-world away, and then we met again here.*

C: Yes. It was meant to be. There are no accidents. She took her time, but there she is.

D: *She has learned the lessons of the handicap, and now she doesn't need it anymore.*

C: No. Just let it happen. She knows that the things will take over, and she doesn't have to think about how to get there. She is ready. Big things will happen. As long as she doesn't doubt, she can have it. She must believe that it is true.

When Clare awakened and got up and maneuvered into her wheelchair, she said she already noticed some things that had not been there before. She had more movement in one of her legs. (She usually had to lift them to position them in the chair.) And she had some uncommon sensations in the legs. I explained to her what the process would be when she got back home. I think it would be best for it to happen when she was by herself, with no one to disturb her. That way they could work on her and take all the time they needed.

CHAPTER SEVEN

THE CONSCIOUSNESS OF CELLS

This material laid in my files for more than twenty years. I was going through and destroying many of the old sessions that were conducted back in 1985 when our group was having regular meetings in Eureka Springs. Those were wonderful days of exploration and camaraderie. It was so important to have others of like mind to discuss things with. Although the group has disbanded, I still feel a closeness with these wonderful people who were so important in my life at that time. They have no idea how much I needed their companionship and understanding during those days when everything I was discovering was new and different. At our meetings, we would often have a general topic of interest that would be explored, and whoever was volunteering to be the subject would go into trance and answer the group's questions. When I found this forgotten transcript, I felt as though it had been waiting for over twenty years to be rediscovered and included in my work. That time has come and it has found a home. It fits perfectly with the subject of consciousness and the recognition that *everything* has life and intelligence. Although, at the time of this session I could not comprehend much of what was being said. I had not expanded to that point of understanding. It showed me how far I have progressed in my thinking and comprehension in twenty years.

The topic on this evening was healing. I can still see in my mind's eye all of our group sitting around the room intent on what was occurring, and anxious to participate by asking questions. Oh, how I miss those days, and those dear people!

Subject: We recognize the importance of the subject for tonight and are anxious to discuss with you the aspects of healing. Healing is an important endeavor. Everything is either in a

121

state of healing or moving toward destruction. Destruction is a natural phenomenon and not negative as it sometimes appears. However, a *premature* destruction of an entity or consciousness, a piece of living matter, is to be avoided. Therefore, healing must be practiced by all living beings in order to facilitate their appropriate life span within your time/space dimension.

Questioner: Can you explain the actual process of physical healing of the human body? How does it occur at the cellular level?

S: Each cell is responsible for its own existence the same way that each totality of being is responsible for the existence of the whole of that particular being. The cell has its own self to mind as well as a joint relationship with cells around it, particularly cells which constitute part of a larger systemic organization such as a specific organ. That cell is responsible for obtaining, from the energy fields around it, nourishment appropriate to its development and growth. It is responsible for monitoring its own function, so that it retains as much nourishment as it needs, and sends forth into the rest of the organism those elements not needed for its particular functioning. The cell is aware of dysfunction as the overall entity is aware of a certain malaise indicative of a problem somewhere. The cells obtain information from the thought pool relative to that particular cell, the same way that humans obtain information from the thought pool. The same way that animals obtain information from thought pools in regard to behavior of themselves. The cells have a way of tapping into kind of an "ideal cell" to show them the way they should be functioning, and alert them when this functioning goes awry. At such, they request information with regard to healing. All this takes place in instantaneous time and in microscopic detail. The cells have an innate information ability, but they also get additional information from older cells in the body and the sense of the body energy as a whole.

Q: You mentioned an ideal cell that they pattern themselves after.

S: That is correct.

Q: Would that mean even on the microscopic level they must have something to guide them, something they could use as a pattern?

S: Yes. On every level.

Q: Even the microscopic?

S: Especially the microscopic level. Cells function at essentially the microscopic level.

Q: I was thinking in a sense then they would be thinking of that ideal cell as God.

S: Right.

One of the group: Along that same line, is there a correlation between the ideal self of the cell and the ideal that we hold as our higher self?

S: Not in the way you mean the question. There is no higher self for a cell, specifically the way that you understand your relationship to a higher self. One exists, but it is more like a pattern rather than a guide or a director of activities.

Q: Does this mean that the cells have an intellect?

S: Yes. Every piece of living matter has a consciousness, otherwise known as intellect.

Q: I'm thinking that humans have brains. Would they be able to think in that respect?

S: To fulfill the function of intelligence as it is prescribed in zoology textbooks, with regard to awareness of surroundings, ability to reproduce, movement, our cells fit that categorization.

Q: It would be very basic then? Is that what you mean?

S: The cell does not see itself as "very basic". (Laughter)

Q: I mean they wouldn't have the intellect of a human. Or do they?!

S: In their own way each bit of consciousness has the intellect of a human. Some have intellects that function better for their organism than human intellects function.

123

Q: Then in the function of healing, we have to communicate with that intellect within the cells?

S: That's right.

Q: In healing, the way we understand it, we have to get in touch with our basic problems. We have to understand the causes of our discomfort or disease. Could you suggest a way that we could do this more effectively?

S: The general answer is that one should ask one's body for assistance in this area. Something along the lines of, "I know that I can communicate with my body. I know that I can request assistance in healing. But I don't really know how I go about this. How about giving me a hand?" This is a simplistic answer. The self-discovery method requires a much more detailed understanding of your own present history within this vehicle. As well as – for those who believe it's pertinent – past and future lives, as they might relate to the present vehicle. This complexity is not necessary. It is not necessary always to know exactly what is blocking the healing. It is sufficient to recognize that there are blocks. Request that they be dissolved by mental request, or visualization of the block being dissolved. Even without knowing what the block is. If you believe that blocks can be dissolved without bothering to understand how they got there, this would suffice for most people. As you remember, what you believe is what makes the difference. If you believe you can dissolve the blocks and move toward healing without paying thousands of dollars to psychoanalysts, then do it that way. It's much easier.

Q: How does the process of long distance healing occur?

S: Healing from one person to another seemingly long distance and recognized as long distance by time/space reckoning is, in fact, a short distance. The healer gets in touch with the energy of the entity which is being healed on a more immediate basis. The ability of the healer to expand their aura, to reach out and touch the other individual, allows a hook-up over what seems to be time and space. So that the same kind of healing can occur as occurs with the actual physical laying on of hands, or touching auras with someone in the same proximity.

Q: Can you describe how the energy is transferred from one person to the other, or how one person can transmit that healing energy to another?

S: It's a question of utilizing the pathways which surround all of us in an electrical kind of a sense. Not electricity, of course, but kind of a force-field-energized area around each of us. Some particularly receptive individuals are willing to let down their particular protective barriers, and allow a cross-feed into their energy field from another individual, who is equally able to let down their barriers to send their energy out. Such energy attacking a particular illness, or just approaching, with love, the general aura of the receiving individual provides an extra shot. Remember, these two have agreed ahead of time to this particular healing, to this involvement. The receiving body recognizes that an additional jolt of energy, as the individual was already moving toward health, will simply accelerate the process. The individual doing the healing is willing to sacrifice some of their immediate energy, of which they can generate more than an average person. Then they send it toward a particular spot or the general condition of the receiving individual. In such a way that the energy itself seems to have a kind of mind and intelligence of its own – which it does. And it simply seeks out the problem areas and dissolves them, removes blocks and allows them to regain their own healthy condition.

Q: When I am around people who are sick and they are all coming down with something, I sometimes put up a barrier to keep the germs from coming into my body. Is that possible to do that?

S: Do you do it?

Q: I try to practice it. I believe it, but is it a fact?

S: Has it worked? (Yes.) Well?! (Laughter)

Q: I just mentally put up a barrier that the germs can't go hrough.

S: If you believe in germs and believe in your ability to shield yourself from germs through a barrier. If you believe these two things, then doing it is a snap. You could choose to simply not believe in germs.

Q: Are they real?

S: Not in the way that you and the medical doctors think they are.

Q: Then how are they?

S: Well, they're fine. (Laughter)

Q: Well, you say they're not real in that way....

S: They don't cause diseases. I'm sorry, I shouldn't be playing with you, but it's so much fun to play with you. The germ theory of disease is simply another theory. As you know, people create their own diseases for their own purposes. Germs are a handy scapegoat. If you simply don't believe that they can harm you, then of course, they won't. But that takes a good bit of belief in a world in which they have been seen as a scientific explanation for diseases. In actual fact, the older explanations of possession by devils, and so on, were closer to the truth. Not that people are possessed by devils, but that emotional and spiritual and relationship concerns, and problems, and stress, are actually the causes for disease. Germs have had a lot of bad press.

Q: But they have been observed in the laboratory under the microscope.

S: They exist in the laboratory. They're just not the *reasons* why people create illnesses for themselves.

Q: What about epidemics?

S: As you know, when groups of people are involved in mass events, they have all chosen to participate in the mass event. And they have chosen that particular event for their own purposes, most generally as an example, a lesson of some sort to the remainder of the individuals in that vicinity.

Q: I'm thinking specifically of diseases like the Black Death. They said it was caused by fleas on the rats and it spread all over Europe at that time, killing everyone.

S: Bad press for rats and fleas.

Q: You think because they believed this, that is why it spread?

S: That and the fact that they had their other particular reasons for being involved in such an event.

Q: We've heard that laughter is the best medicine. Can you give the Why?

S: The "Why" laughter is the best medicine is that laughter, at least momentarily, provides you with positive sense of joy and well-being. Provides you with instant health.

Q: Then that means that sorrow or sadness is detrimental to the system?

S: Inappropriate prolonged sorrow or sadness is medically defined as depression, which is detrimental to the ultimate well-being of the vehicle and those with whom they come into contact. Sadness or sorrow as an appropriate emotional response to an event or a situation is not detrimental to the being. The repression of such emotion or the negation of such emotion is more detrimental than the experiencing and showing of appropriate emotional reaction.

Q: The natural expression of emotions is good for you?

S: Right.

Q: It's the blocking of these emotions that causes the diseases, the malfunction?

S: That's a simplistic way of describing block, but accurate in so far as it goes.

Q: That means that it is good to even experience anger? (Yes.)

Q: This is not exactly on the subject of healing but it has some relationship. When the larger self leaves the body and dissolution starts, do the cells in the body still have life until they are transmuted into something else?

S: You want to know what occurs?

Q: *Yes. I am wondering, if each cell has life, at the point that the spirit leaves the body, does the body cell still have life and does it, in turn, choose to go into a state of dissolution?*

S: An excellent question. The line between life and death, as you know from literature, is said to be very fine. Your practical experience tells you there is nothing fine about it at all. Either you're alive or you're dead. But if you look around to understand the scientific, more technical, aspects of this question, you will note for example that trees appear to be dead for long periods of time and will literally spring back to life. They die in little bits and pieces over many years. Let's take a body of a human, for example. When the spirit leaves the body, the cells retain certain aspects of life, such as motion at a cellular level, in that the disintegration is a form of motion. The falling away from the bones of the flesh is certainly motion and can be observed. There are aspects of life which do not, however, occur for most of the cells upon physical death. That would be, reproduction and the use of nutrients and the sloughing off of non-usable pieces, or used and discarded pieces. Those kinds of systemic functions do not occur. However, certain cells in the body, as you know, kind of morbidly grow for a while. So that, like a tree, pieces of the human are dying at different rates. But there is life of a sort until the pieces disintegrate into other things. And then, of course, they continue to live in a different form to the extent that dust is as alive as a bird in flight.

Q: *That would be a form of reincarnation even down to the cellular level. – Along that line, what I see is the change that we go through as we die (or our body changes until we call it death), and we then go to a different dimension. Is that a type of thing that happens to this intelligent force in the cell, that it transmutes to another form?*

S: Right.

128

Q: Is it still part of the human consciousness? Like, say a fingernail cell continues to live for a time after the human dies. Then does the cell rejoin the human spirit or is it going a different way?

S: That cell will retain the memory of life as a piece of the human organism. The same way it will retain memories of life as pieces of other things, when it in other stages, other forms, hooked up with other pieces to create other things. But its memory will be short circuited the same way your present memory is short circuited, and you do not ordinarily consciously recall the pieces of yourself which have been dinosaurs or fleas.

Q: How do these cells view us as a body? Do they have a way of perceiving us? They live inside of us.

S: They sense that they are part of a larger organism the same way that we sense that we are a part of an oversoul. That same vague sense of belonging which occasionally occurs. The cells appreciate it more often than we do, because they can appreciate and be acquainted with that feeling just by normal functioning. If your liver is operating well and doing the things that it is supposed to do, it enjoys a sense of well-being which, were it able to be conveyed to you as an individual intellect, would bring an awareness of joy that most of us unfortunately do not experience very often.

Q: How do they view our brain or our intellect that directs them?

S: Not with a kind of criticality. Simply an acceptance that that's the way this organism operates.

Q: I thought maybe they might be thinking of that as the God or the overall driving force of their Universe, so to speak. It wouldn't be that way?

S: You're putting a human tendency to search for gods onto cells, which accept their existence as a piece of God.

Q: Is there not a brain or consciousness of the planet itself?

S: The consciousness of the planet exists in kind of an overall blanket effect. However, the *life form* on any given planet which is capable of altering structures and creating physical entities to alter its life cycle – in contrast to other animals which do so only on limited scales – and do not necessarily allow for generational continuation of the edifices and so on. That life form on any particular planet becomes, if you would, the consciousness. The conscience as well, of the overall planet, and carries with it the requirement to think globally on behalf of the planet. Such a lesson has yet to be learned by the intelligence of humans on this planet. But such is the design of the universe that the planet itself, although having a consciousness and intelligence, is still required to work in combination with the intelligent beings who are capable of altering the surface of the planet.

Q: *Does that mean when the people of the planet die then the brain of the planet dies?*

S: No, the brain of the planet will operate in consort with the other intelligent beings, which would include all animals, plants, rocks, living things, etc. If there are no animals or plants which spring forth with an ability to alter the physical shape of the planet, the planet will not need to exert such an intelligent symbiotic relationship, and will simply allow a less directed, more natural approach to occur.

CHAPTER EIGHT

EVERYTHING HAS CONSCIOUSNESS

This unusual case was reminiscent of the "Mechanical Person" in *Book One* of this series, where the woman found herself in the body of a robot-type mechanical being. That was an extremely frustrating life because her creators did not realize that she was a more sentient being than they thought. She was not purely mechanical, but had emotions and feelings, even though she could not express them. When they created her out of metal, they did not realize they had also implanted the small spark of life that gave her consciousness. It was the first time I had ever had a case like that. Later when I was doing one of my group regression workshops, one of the participants said he saw himself as a robotic being. He "died" when he was eventually disassembled. So this case goes along the same line, showing me, once again, to always expect the unexpected, and never take anything for granted in this type of work.

I saw Tina at my office in May of 2006. She had been a clinical therapist and had now gone into massage therapy. Her reason for requesting the session mostly dealt with personal relationships. Yet the session went in a totally different direction and was not at all what we expected. Showing once again, we were not controlling this.

When she came off the cloud, she began describing things that were so unfamiliar she had no words for them. She knew she was definitely not on Earth when she saw a huge white oval shaped structure. Looking at it from a distance, she said it looked bigger than a football field. She couldn't tell the material it was made from, "Maybe metal, maybe plastic, or something smooth." She then saw an entrance which was just an opening with a ramp going up to it.

T: I'm allowing myself to just float in. And I'm seeing what looks like a city inside here. I don't understand yet what I'm seeing, but I'm seeing many little creatures. They look almost like little ants, very industrious. It seems like everybody – and I hesitate to call them people – are moving about with a purpose, very industrious. On the outside, this place seems so serene and dreamlike, just this big, white, huge expanse. And inside, it's darker, and not what I expected. It's very big. And it goes, I suppose, down in the ground, and maybe, yes, up higher. These sort of creatures are very busy doing things – like building things. There are many levels, like it's stacked. The word "city" comes to mind, but it's not really a city. It has different rooms, almost different sections. It's like if you cut into a doll house, and you can see into each room. I felt a little anxious coming here. I don't like it. Maybe because, right now it seems very alien, not soft or human or easy. I think these creatures are alive, but they seem very robotic in that they don't have much choice. Like they're very programmed with what they're doing. Nobody is looking up or conversing or being friendly. It seems mainly more... what do I want to say? Technology more than mechanical. But they're all hugely industrious and not to be diverted from what they're doing. Very intent on their purpose.

D: Is that why you think it bothered you?

T: Yes. It doesn't seem very pleasant or very happy. It seems very harsh here. All these creatures are working in close proximity to each other, some of them are stacked, standing on top of each other. There is no respect. There's no individuality.

She described the creatures' hands as having a type of feelers, rather than fingers. They used these to manipulate little buttons, little lights on small boxes. They could move these rather quickly, like somebody typing or playing a piano, only they were doing it with little boxes of light.

T: They're causing something to happen, with these little boxes. Something that's way outside whatever this structure is. I don't know if this is a building in the ground, or if it could be a spaceship. It's very, very huge. I have this sense that they're directing many things. Almost like they're neurons in a big brain, or something. And by manipulating these little boxes, they're causing something outside the structure to occur. I don't know that they're individuals, or there's a group consciousness, or if they're parts of a whole. Or if they're mechanical.

I asked for a physical description of these strange creatures.

T: They have eyes, but they do this work more by touch. It's a very rote thing. (Then a sudden shocking revelation.) As I said that, I had a sense that I've ... I've been one of these. (She began to cry.) And I don't like it.

As she said this she unexpectedly became one of them. She entered a body identical to the ones she had been describing objectively.

T: (Sadly) It's just not a very happy existence. It's feeling like there isn't much choice, and it's just – not very happy. It's a drudgery. What are we accomplishing? Oh, my heavens! We *don't* have any choice, and we *don't* do anything else. It's really funny, because in some way we are alive. But we don't – at least, *I* don't like doing this. I just keep having to do it. And I don't know how long I've done it, but it seems like an eternity. It seems endless that I stay in this thing doing this.

D: *Does your body feel mechanical, or like it is of a substance?*
T: It feels kind of hard and crispy, like I have a shell. I have

133

legs, I think, but I feel somehow, I'm propelled more than I walk. I sort of flow along, or scoot along, but I don't do it by moving legs. I feel like I'm mechanical, or bug-like, or I've been bred to do this thing, and I just do it. I don't know where I came from, and I don't know this will end. And I don't know how I've been created. I don't get that anybody or anything cares or understands. I think that whoever or whatever is in charge of me doesn't understand that there's some sentience here. There is a big lack of feeling. That somehow I'm regarded as a creature or a thing, and it is not known that I have a consciousness.

D: Do you know why you have to do these repetitive motions?

T: I have a sense that I am keeping some beings, or something, alive. That somehow we're a background behind the scenes, like an energy, that somehow keeps some kind of world in existence, by our motions. And I don't think the world that we keep alive is the world that's caused us into being. There's something else above and beyond us that doesn't understand that we know what we know. And doesn't understand, or doesn't care that this *isn't fun.* I think I have a shift that I go away from it, and I am worked on. I go some place else, and I'm deactivated and maybe cleaned up in some way, maintained in some way. And I think that I go to sleep, go dormant.

D: Can you see what kind of place that is?

T: Some other level in some other kind of pod, or room, or whatever we're calling these things. And I slip into a little unit, like I click into a place. The way you recharge a razor or something. I go to this place, and I kind of click into it, and I am deactivated. I lose my power. My consciousness. And something happens to me. Like I'm cleaned up, or reenergized, or I don't know what happens. But I click into there, and then quickly just kind of disappear. And then the next thing I know, that little thing unclicks me, and spits me out. And I go back and do the same thing.

D: So that's the only rest *you get from it. Otherwise, it's just continual?*

T: Seems like it. And it's not a rest, because I don't know about it.

D: Do you require any sustenance of any kind to keep you alive?

T: If I do, I get it there, and I don't know what it is. There may be something that's in this atmosphere that's almost sprayed, or *in* whatever the atmosphere is in this place. That keeps me going. And I don't know if that keeps me healthy, or tuned up, or if it sustains me, if it's my fuel. I don't know. But as I stay there longer, I feel more and more that I'm regarded as mechanical, as a piece of machinery. I do have consciousness. But I don't think I can communicate with any of these other machines, or robots, or beings, or whatever we are. It's really strange. It's like somehow a consciousness has been created, and they don't know that we're conscious. It would never occur to whoever created us. I can only assume these other beings feel the same way, but we cannot communicate. I feel like I am totally locked inside this. I do this, because I have no choice. And I have the sense that, in a way, it's a hell. I know it has meaning, but for me personally, it's meaningless. It's repetition. And I'm locked in here, and I can't communicate. *I can't communicate.* It's hopeless! It's hopeless! I'm totally locked into this shell of a machine doing this work.

I thought it was time that we found out how this all began. How this soul came to be in this dreadful situation. "We can move backwards, because we can manipulate time. You can find out how this was created and who did it. Move backwards to when you first went into this."

T: So they know! I don't like this, because they know! I don't know what the reason is, but I do know that this is a mechanical thing, or a synthesized thing. It is something that's made. It's not an organically grown thing. There's a consciousness that then is united, and they recognize that. It appears that my consciousness is placed. It's like it's poofed into... like it's blown into this thing. It's like a little poof. And I'm put into here, and they know that.

This was exactly the same process that was described in "The Mechanical Person" in *Book One*. A tiny piece of consciousness was blown into the robot and it was activated.

D: What was your consciousness before that?

T: I'm a little organic being, and I'm grown. I'm not sure what it is, but it's this little round ball that seems more organic. What I see is like an assembly line place, where the ball somehow comes from one direction on this assembly line. And then these little robot things come from another. And there is a place where you're injected into this.

D: And you were in the little ball as a consciousness?

T: Yes, yes, yes. I was. And somehow, somebody, something – I haven't seen that yet – has grown us. And has created this little consciousness, and then they put us in this robot. There is a consciousness that's ... grown. I'll use the test-tube baby example.

D: Then these little mechanical things cannot operate without this little spark, a little piece of consciousness inside.

T: Right. And so we're bred to inhabit this little machine. This is not very good being one of these things.

D: I guess the person who does this, or whoever has invented this, doesn't think about that.

T: I think they may tell themselves, whether they know or not, there's not enough sentience in there that it matters, because we're bred to do this. But my experience is that it's drudgery. It's really funny. When you're back with all these little round beings on this conveyor belt, there isn't that sense of hopelessness and drudgery. The little balls are okay. The little balls are just there. But not when they get into the mechanical thing. When you get out into this big, giant factory, city, control center – I don't know what it is. It's layers and layers, and rooms and rooms and rooms. There are hundreds and thousands of these little beings doing this little manipulation thing. When I floated into that, the sense was that it was so sad and hopeless.

D: *Let's see if we can find who is doing all of this. The ones who created all these things in the first place.*

T: What I do is float back. And I am seeing some beings who are quite large. They're much more amorphous and softer in shape. More out of light, or some other substance, than I understand as our physical substance. And they create things. (Seeing them began to affect Tina physically.) Oh! It's very tiring to ... look at them. I have to take a breath. (She breathed deeply.) They are able to manifest ... *think* things into being.

D: *Why is that tiring to watch them?*

T: I don't think they're very nice. It's not that they're bad, but they're uncaring. They are very large, and very powerful. And they have – I guess it's a – mental ability.

D: *Are they physical beings?*

T: They're physical, but they're more refined from what I know is physical. They have kind of an amorphous light shape, and very large, dark round eyes. And I can't see anything else. I don't see hands. I don't see feet. It's not Casper, the ghost, but it's a white thing like that. Very tall, maybe 20 feet tall, with these big eyes. And they don't have to do anything. (It was difficult to explain.) We're causing something to be either mined or obtained. We're causing something to happen by remote control. And what I don't like is, we have been caused to come into being simply to serve them. This is interesting. They're very refined physically, but they somehow have a need or dependence in the physical world. And they create things like us to interface and cause things to happen in the physical world. There are not nearly as many of them as there are of us. We don't create. They create us, and then we obtain things for them, something that they either use themselves, or trade for other things that they need. And it's tiring and exhausting, because it's relentless. (She began crying.) That I have no choice but to keep doing this very tiring stuff day after day. It's for them, and they don't care. And I don't know if there is an end. (Her voice was filled with despair.) I suspect that maybe at some time we get old and die. And I don't know what happens to us then, but we do this far longer than we want to. (She cried harder.) It's a total servitude. *Total*, with no choice and no hope. And no gratitude, because they don't even know that we can feel. And if they would know, I don't think they would care. We are just doing their bidding continuously, continuously. What's amazing about it, as I look at it from this viewpoint ... these creatures have an incredible influence all over a universe, to different planets. Getting what they need. They are fear-inspiring in their coldness. There is no respect for anybody but themselves. It's not that they're consciously evil. It's just clueless. They are just totally involved in themselves and taking care of themselves.

D: *Very self-centered.*

T: Totally.

She was finally able to have a partial understanding of what their job was in these strange surroundings. Their little box was controlling, by remote control, what machines were doing on the planet. It had to do with a type of mining operation. Smaller unmanned ships or devices could be directed to fly to another world, mine a yellow powder, and fill pods, which were then dumped somewhere else. The powder was used as fuel for different purposes. The larger beings could have been located somewhere else, because their part in this was the creation of the little robots, so the mining machines could have been located anywhere. It wouldn't matter as long as they were doing their job.

I decided it was time to move her from that scene to an important day, if there could possibly be an important day in such a dismal life of repetitive drudgery. She entered into the scene crying, but it was a weeping of relief, not despair.

T: It's the day when I die. And I'm so glad to get out of there. I just disappear. And I leave. *I leave.* I leave that robot, and it's *so good.* (Crying) God, it's so good to get out of there!

D: *How did the robot die?*

T: Something happened in my consciousness, and I just dispersed. I don't know how or why, but I was held together in that little ball powering that. And I guess this would be my death. Something disintegrated so that it could no longer be contained. Like the tension on a bubble, the way a bubble bursts.

D: *Did you see anything happening to the body?*

T: I evaporated. The robot stayed there, and it was disempowered. It was either in its plugged-in place, or in its job. The little robot thing kind of crumpled a little bit. It was deactivated. And I dispersed into such tiny particles that I could go through the molecules of the robot. Whatever held me didn't hold me anymore. It was like a snap of the fingers. In an instant, I dispersed. And then I just floated up and left it. It was incredible. That was the only good day of my life there. To get out of that. That was bad. That was bad! I'm floating away. I don't want to stay there. And it's just getting increasingly distant ... and smaller.

She seemed like she couldn't get out of there fast enough. She wanted to put as much distance between those beings and her spirit as possible.

D: *Why did you decide to do that in the first place? From where you are now you can see why you chose to experience a life like that. I'm not going to make you go back into it. We can just observe.*

T: (A shock.) I was one of those really large beings! And I guess I needed to know what effect I had. (She paused for a moment to catch her breath and take this new development in.) I was on the other side of it. Now I have the knowledge, that I needed to know what effect I had, because these really large beings have a great effect. They're huge with a lot of influence, and yet, they don't have any understanding of their influence. I have had many other experiences, not just in the robot life, but other kinds of things being under the influence of these very huge, gray beings. Because I had a long life as one of those, not having any understanding of my responsibility. I was very cold and very selfish, and not understanding my effect. And having done that, it was time to see what that effect was like, because you can't do that. Maybe it is teaching, but it is simply cause and effect. You can't do anything without having an effect. And so, I had to experience the effect. I had to know what it was like. What I had done.

So the law of karma, of cause and effect, is not strictly a human thing experienced on Earth. It is much farther reaching. It is a law that encompasses planets and universes. It also applies to beings of such power that we can only imagine or guess at. Nothing and no one is exempt. What goes around, comes around. You must experience being on the other side of anything you create or cause another to experience. There is much food for thought here. If we truly understood this law, how much better and humane the world would be. If we only understood it, there would be no judgement and no prejudice. Because we would know that if we judged too harshly or were prejudiced, we would be compelled to return as the very thing we were prejudiced against. How else to learn the lesson? We have to experience being on both sides of the coin. If this law were truly recognized and put into practice, there would be no wars and no violence, and heaven on Earth would become a reality.

T: It's effortless to do it. They just create unthinking. They're not doing it with any thought of whether it's positive or negative. It's just whatever comes to mind. Whatever they want, and whatever will benefit them. It's almost like littering the universe. They create junk. They don't think they're doing it. They're just doing whatever they want without any thought of what effect they're having.

D: *They didn't realize these other little things they were creating had life or consciousness.*

T: As that big being, you are so wrapped up in yourself, there's no awareness. You can't be too harsh with these big beings, because they're not doing very good stuff, but they don't know anything else. That's all they do. They're so wrapped up in themselves they don't have any consciousness of how they're affecting anything or anybody else. I don't think it entered their mind.

Yet the karma still had to be repaid.

D: *How did you leave that life of the big being, so you could enter the little consciousness?*

T: As the big being you have much more conscious control. And I decided that I was done with being a big being. It's almost like I grew tired of it. So I decided to leave that beingness. You just decide to do it, and it's over. But then you do go someplace else to decide what to do next.

D: *Did somebody else advise you?*

T: There was sort of a group decision. I went someplace and talked it over with a bunch of other consciousness. And decided where to go from there.

141

D: *So you wanted to experience the other side of what you were doing, but it wasn't much fun.*

T: No. This whole thing is rather bizarre. Because you don't know anything else besides what you know when you're in that particular incarnation, being, whatever it is. I don't even know what to call it. So then you end that, and you go someplace else, and look at it. There's discussion, but it's almost automatic. It's like: you've done this and you've done that, so everybody's in agreement. Then you do this next thing. It's not like there isn't any freedom of choice, but there's so much clarity in this other place. This place in between. It's so expanded, and it's so clear. And then it makes so much sense that you go somewhere else, and then, boom, you go somewhere *else*. In comparison to that place of clarity, it's much more enclosed, because you don't have the same knowing. The other kind of fades away.

D: *All right. Let's return to the part where you finally got out of there, and you're drifting away.*

T: This is after I'm done being a little robot thing?

D: *Yes. After you left there.*

T: I drifted away from there. At first, I drifted slowly, and the farther I got away from wherever that was, I seemed to move faster and faster and faster and faster away from it, until it was on automatic. It's almost like I'm being pulled through a vacuum tube, or through something. And going to this place in between. Maybe I'm saying too much and drawing too many conclusions from this one experience, but it seems like you go back and forth. From being in something to not being in something, and then being something. So I'm just pulled again, like a vacuum into this place where there's a group decision.

D: *But as you look at that experience, did you learn anything from it? Was there a purpose for it?*

T: I think I learned that you have to be nice. You have to be responsible. I learned that too well. And I can see that it was so horrible being this little thing that, I took lifetimes off. I learned from there that you have to be very responsible for your actions. That your actions have incredible ramifications. But the other thing that I've only had glimmers of in this lifetime is that there's much more consciousness in everything, everywhere. Tina kind of gets it now and then, and there's some teachings of this. Even though I see that consciousness was mechanically installed into that robot, what that robot teaches me – it's like it's being written on my forehead in neon – is that everything has consciousness. *Everything has consciousness.* And what I'm supposed to learn now as Tina from that experience, is to understand and not forget that everything has consciousness. That this blanket, this microphone, this bed, everything has consciousness. (A deep breath.)

D: *We tend to think that something material, that is made, doesn't have.*

T: But it does. And if Tina is to learn anything, one of the most important things is to *not forget* that everything has consciousness. She can help other people remember that. But simply, she has to remember to honor the consciousness in absolutely everything. That is paramount for her. There is no big, "What is her purpose in life?" It's nothing like that at all. But for the rest of her time on this planet Earth, it is to be in as much harmony as possible by realizing and respecting and acknowledging the consciousness in everything. People in ancient times knew this: in daily life, respecting the consciousness of fire, the consciousness of your cooking pot, of the food that you're eating. There is consciousness in everything. Absolutely everything! There is consciousness in every animate and inanimate thing in this universe, in this reality, and every other reality. It is at base consciousness.

D: *Does that mean we have to experience all of these things?*

T: We don't have to experience *all* of these things, although we experience much of it. It's everywhere. But for Tina in this

143

lifetime, it is to respect and acknowledge the consciousness in this very real physical world. It's not necessarily important for her to be in touch with other past lifetimes, other realities. Those are all there. And those are all experiences she's had multitudes of multitudes, and will have, if you want to consider it in terms of time. It doesn't matter. She is all of that. We are all that. The differences are insignificant, insignificant. All these beings, these realities, they are very small. They're bumps on the surface. They're changes in hue. They're insignificant.

D: *But you know our curiosity. We want to know about the experiences we've had.*

T: That's normal. And that's fine. And it's good for Tina to have looked at this right now. For her to be in harmony, it's to acknowledge that this consciousness pervades everything. It is consciousness that is the substance, the only substance. And the joy in her life, the harmony in her life, is not by doing a particular thing or knowing a particular thing or being a certain way, other than simply acknowledging that consciousness is the substance of everything. And as in that lifetime, when she was that little robotic creature, the most heart wrenching, the hardest thing to bear, even beyond the loneliness, was no respect, no acknowledgment. Not to be acknowledged as consciousness. And so it would be her job, if we would call it that, to recognize that there is consciousness everywhere. To allow that to be her conscious thought.

D: *In the work I have done, much of what you are describing would be classified as elementals. Separating it from the consciousness that would be in plants and animals and human beings. Just basic energy.*

T: You can call it elemental. Basic energy. Perhaps we're talking about the same thing. If you look at the elemental, and you can acknowledge the elemental in these things. But usually when we talk about elementals, we're talking about

144

nature. And we're talking about the more organic substances. But we look here, and see what we have done on this planet. We are in this technological race. What we have to realize is technology has consciousness. Manufactured things have consciousness. Our Starbucks Coffee has consciousness. Everything has its place, but it's acknowledging the elemental, acknowledging the consciousness, the life, in that. There's nothing wrong with drinking the coffee, but acknowledge its consciousness and thank it for being, and being available. To appreciate the house that shelters us. To appreciate the bed that supports us. To recognize that there is, on its own level, a very real consciousness there. In its own way, not in the way we normally talk about something being alive. But it is brought into life. That we, in our own way on planet Earth – just as those beings were creating everything – we create all sorts of things. We manufacture things. We make jewelry and we grow food. We create radios and airplanes and cars. And acknowledging that once we create it, it has its own collective, its own individual consciousness that exists, that can be addressed. That it has its certain amount of sentience. And it's there. And simply acknowledging it, as she would have appreciated being acknowledged and respected in that other lifetime, is to put one more in harmony.

D: *I guess I'm thinking of human personality, human consciousness. Does that mean, as a human soul – maybe I'm not wording it right – we have been beds and chairs and things like that?*

T: At its most elemental level – not in the way you were using the word elemental – but in its most elementary basic level, it is *all* one consciousness. And so sometimes that sort of breaks off, and it might be a chair. It might be a robot. It might be a human. It might be an angel. It's all the same thing. *It's all the same thing.* It is all play. And you put this into play, and then one thing leads to another. And one has

145

this experience of one thing and this experience of another thing. But that human consciousness at its most basic, most refined level, is all one thing.

D: *I have taken people to lifetimes when they were plants and animals, but I didn't think of something that was made, manufactured, created as having the same kind of consciousness.*

T: But it does. From the vantage point that I am speaking from, it doesn't have, perhaps, as much consciousness. There seems to be more consciousness imbued in certain things than in other things. But in everything, on the physical level, there is an element of consciousness.

D: *That is a different way of looking at things.*

T: Another thing you must be aware of is the significance of creation. To just be aware that we are always creating things, sometimes with more permanence, sometimes with a brief ephemeralness. As we create, every word that we speak, every action that we take on this planet, has an effect. And when we participate in ritual behavior, because of the level of consciousness that we bring to it, it can have a greater effect and bring things into other realities, other than physical realities. Because of the intention, it perhaps gives greater permanence or greater reality. It is this knowledge, that when we speak casually, we have some effect, and we create some ripple in the physical consciousness reality. And the stronger one speaks, the stronger the consciousness. With the greater the intent, with the greater numbers, the stronger the ripple can be, and the longer it can last. So for that reason, it's good to take care with what one does.

D: *Be more aware of what we do and say.*

T: Yes. Because it has an effect. And when we speak casually, the effect is casual. But when we speak with intent, when we speak with strength and consciousness and emotion, the intent and the effect is greater. And as we know, every cause has an effect. It's simple. It happens. It's automatic. It is the rule

146

of the universe. There is cause, and there is effect. So it is wise to speak and act with awareness.

I asked for permission to use this material in my work, because I put everything together like pieces of puzzles.

T: Absolutely. There is no problem with that whatsoever.

D: *I assume I've been speaking to Tina's subconscious. That's the name I give to it.*

T: You may call it that.

D: *I assume that's what I've been speaking to, because you're the one I always communicate with.*

T: And in that, you are quite correct, Dolores. I am the one. We are all the one.

D: *You talk through everybody I work with.*

T: Absolutely. And we may have different guises. We too, may at times, wear something of a mask, pick up a skin, but we are all the same. And we bless you in your work.

In another case, a woman went to a lifetime that could have been at the time of Atlantis, or another highly advanced civilization. In my other work with clients who gave information about Atlantis, I discovered that the scientists reached such a high degree of sophistication, they were able to manipulate the DNA of people and animals, and they created many half-man/half-animal creatures. This was one of the main reasons for the destruction of that culture. They had gone beyond and misused the laws of nature. Yet, in this case, it seems they went even further in their experimentation with horrible results. The woman had great difficulty describing what she was seeing and experiencing. It was so foreign to her way of thinking that she did not want to see it. She was part of a group that was isolated in a building on an island. Over time, through experimentation, many of their organs (especially in the chest area) were replaced with crystal components. It must have taken a long time to allow the body to adapt without killing it. These people were then used to generate energy to power various things. In brief, it seems as though they were walking, thinking, creators of electricity, energy, power or whatever. They may have also been created for use as a weapon. All of this greatly disturbed the woman client, and she did not want to see any more. This was one of the reasons it was so difficult to obtain a clear picture of what was happening. She was obviously seeing much more than she was reporting. I removed her and took her to the day of her death, and what she saw was horrible. Something had gone wrong with the generating of energy, and caused these beings to overload and explode. The force was so great that it destroyed the building and everyone in it. As she left her body, she saw that the crystal pieces of herself were shattered and imbedded into the walls. The death was shocking, sudden and devastating. She had to spend time in the resting place on the spirit side in order to recover. It was a long time before she was able to venture out and reincarnate in a human life. This, of course, had caused mistrust and fear in her present lifetime, especially of anyone who was in a position of power.

This was another example of the scientists at Atlantis misusing the laws of nature, and over-stepping the boundaries of humanity.

The following case is another example of what some civilizations will stoop to when they have no regard for human life. This one did not take place on Earth.

Marie came for a session looking for the answers to personal family problems. The subconscious chose to show her two lifetimes and I could not see how they were related. Yet I never underestimate the knowledge that it applies to the situation. It always has a reason for the lifetime it takes the person to. Its logic far surpasses ours. At first she went through an ordinary, simple, mundane past life where nothing extraordinary happened. Then as I moved her forward to something else she said that her right arm was hurting. I never know when the subject will enter a life. Sometimes they come in on the day of their death, and sometimes they come in when something traumatic is happening. Of course, the first thing I have to do is remove any physical sensations, so they will be comfortable and able to answer questions. I asked why her arm was hurting.

M: I don't know. It feels like there is metal in it. (I was confused. She pointed to her forearm.) It feels metal. Inside ... metal ... inside the arm. Like a rod, where the bone should be.

D: *How did that get there?*

M: The bone broke. They took the bone out and put a rod in.

D: *Who did?*

M: Doctors. They replaced the bone with a rod. There's a space right here, the rod. I don't know why that's there. That shouldn't be like that. Why did they do that? (Pointing at her arms.) This one is; this one is not.

D: *It's just the right arm that has it.* (Yes) *And that was what was causing discomfort?*

M: Yes, the arm feels heavy; very heavy. I don't know if I broke it or they broke the bone. Somehow the bone was broken so they put the rod in it.

D: *Now you're feeling your shoulder. Is that okay?*

M: Oh, this whole arm feels like it could have been replaced. It doesn't feel like the other one. This feels artificial. It doesn't feel real.

149

D: Couldn't they just let it mend by itself?
M: Experiments. They're doing experiments.
D: What do you mean?
M: I don't know. I'm not happy. Doctors – scientists. From my
shoulder down. I don't like it!

I wanted to get an idea of her body and sex, but she said she couldn't see herself. Her arm was her focus. "Arms and legs. Mostly human, but not quite human." I asked her to look around and tell me about her surroundings. "Stainless steel tables, windows ... oval. I feel like I'm on the table, and they're examining my arm. They want to see it work. The only thing that's real about it is the flesh around it. That's why it's heavier. That's why it hurts." I had to remove the physical sensations again. I asked her if she could see who were doing this. "They have white lab coats on ... white lab coats and black hair. Their faces are funny looking. Their hair comes down to a point in the middle of their forehead. That part looks very strange. It almost looks unreal, like a mask, maybe." I asked her if she could communicate with them and find out what was going on, but she said they weren't paying attention to her. They just ignored her, not listening. "They just want ... the arm. They're saying this is a weapon. They made my arm a weapon. I don't want that."

D: How do they want you to use it as a weapon?
M: To fight with. I hit something and it dented. Mine was
damaged, and they don't want it to do that.
D: And you've been using it as a weapon?
M: Yes, fighting; fighting.
D: Is that what your job is? (Yes) *Are you like a soldier?*
M: No, like karate.

I had her move backwards to see her life before this happened. "I had my own arm when they kidnaped me. They stole me. It was just a desolate area. There's no color. It's dusty. We have flat rocks. Very uninteresting. And they come, and they take me. Some kind of a hovering craft. They just kind of suck me up like a vacuum cleaner, and then this."

D: Then they did that? (Yes) *And then they sent you out to be a fighter?*
M: Yes, a warrior. It feels like it was in a ring ... a *ring* ring; a round ring, not square. I think it was sport. Competing. With others just like me, with these weird-looking arms; weird feeling. Each have one arm or the other.
D: So some of the others have it in their other arm?
M: Yes, so it's a fair fight. They need to take this arm away! I don't want it! I don't like it!

So apparently, the artificial arm was damaged, and they were trying to repair it. I then moved her ahead to an important day, to see what happened. What she reported next was difficult to understand. I will condense it here. She felt she was sitting on a gray slab, and she was some type of little, little, little, tiny critter. The best way she could describe it was, "A kind of artificial being, like a robot; mirrors, ovals, circles, flaps. A little critter made out of all these circles and ovals. Something mechanical." So, what began as a mechanical arm had now been developed into something else. "Now there's this whole artificial life form made of nuts and bolts. The whole thing! But it's very small. And I feel it is *me!* It sees. It has eyes ... not physical eyes, but it sees.

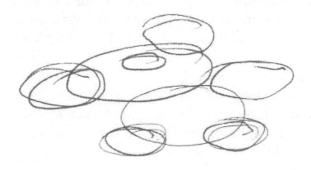

D: Why did they make you into this mechanical thing?

M: I'm not quite sure. – Trying to do away with flesh, so they take a soul and put it in this. It's easier to care for. No disease. I don't like that.

D: So they start out slowly by replacing parts?

M: Parts, yes.

D: Did they eventually get to where it was the whole body? (Yes) *But it still has a spark of life in it?*

M: Yes, it sees. It wants me to know it sees.

D: Are you still the warrior?

M: Things have changed because this is very small. Very, very, just a space to house the soul.

I was unable to find out what the purpose was for creating this. Why did they take a physical body and reduce it down to something that appeared almost like a computer part? I decided to move her to the last day of her life as this tiny mechanical being. "What's happening? What do you see?"

M: Big scrap heap. These guys just disregard everything. Just throw it away. They're awfully cavalier about it. They just throw things away. They just toss it aside. Now I see them walking away laughing.

D: Do they realize that there was something alive inside there?

M: I don't think they care.

There would be no way to get any more information about this strange lifetime, so I called forth the subconscious to answer questions. "Why did you choose that life to show her?

M: So she'd know, to see.

D: What do you mean?

M: It doesn't matter what you're made of, you still see, are still aware. It doesn't matter; flesh and bones or nuts or bolts. There is still consciousness.

152

D: We don't think of something mechanical as being alive.
M: No, but we all are.
D: It's all alive. Is that what you want to tell her?
M: Yes, consciousness, awareness. Everything lives.

It said this took place on another planet where they were experimenting creating artificial life. They had learned to combine the two: life and machine. It wanted her to know this so she could appreciate life.

So these were two separate cases where the subconscious was trying to get the message across to our civilization that everything is alive. That *everything* has consciousness. Even something we would never consider to be sentient. Of course, I have always talked to my car, given it a name, and considered it to have a personality. But this brought it home that it is more than that. We think we are aware of our surroundings, but it is apparent that we have a long way to go in order to appreciate life in all its unpredictable forms. I warned you that my books were designed to make you think!

SECTION THREE
HELP FROM OTHER BEINGS

CHAPTER NINE

THE PLANET OF THE BLUE PEOPLE

When Tom entered the scene, he was an observer. It was night and he was standing by a road in the country. There was a full moon which lit up the scene enough to see clearly. As he stood there trying to figure out where he was and what was happening, he saw a horse-drawn carriage with big wheels pass him on the road. He then became aware of a very big house sitting back from the road. The carriage pulled up in front of it, a passenger got out, and the carriage left. At first he was not aware of having a body, but seemed to be floating. Then he suddenly found himself in the body of the man that had gotten out of the carriage. He was wearing a long coat, corresponding with the eighteenth century, and a top hat. Long black pants, and a cravat tied around his neck. When he became aware of carrying a walking cane, it was obvious he was well-to-do. "I feel middle-aged, getting towards elderly. I have a beard, but it's not very grey yet. I'm getting the impression of a little bit of a stoop, but I don't feel old. In my other hand, I'm carrying one of those old doctor's bags."

D: *What do you have in the bag?*
T: Hmm! Vials and things. It has a stethoscope in there, and pastes and powders, and tubes and concoctions.
D: *What do you think you're doing out there at night?*
T: I think I'm coming to this place to make a house call.
D: *Then you don't live there.*
T: No, I don't live there. The carriage just dropped me off. There's an elderly woman there that needs help. In fact, the elderly woman is my mother, so I have been there before. But I don't believe it's where I grew up, even though I'm getting

157

that the elderly woman is my mother. I'm making a house call on my mother. I'm going up to the house, and I just let myself in. So I guess I'm familiar enough that I just walk in. I hang up my coat and my hat, put down my cane. And then I look down the hall first, for some reason looking in the rooms. I don't know why I'm checking if anyone's there or not, but I do that. It's a large house. And I go up the stairs, around, and I go into the room.

So far it sounded like a typical past-life regression, but it quickly took a surprising turn. He paused, and said with a puzzled look, "That seems a bit strange."

D: *What seems strange?*
T: Well, my mother's there on the bed, but there's something else in the room as well. And I don't think it's *human*.
D: *What does it look like?*
T: I can't get its shape very well, but it doesn't look human. It has long arms and long legs and it's kind of grayish. And I'm getting a confusing picture. It seems predatory and yet at the same time it doesn't. I'm not sure. It's scary, though. I think maybe I'm shocked, because it kind of looks like an alien from a movie. But that might be *my* shock, because it also feels okay somehow. I'm getting the two distinct impressions.
D: *Is your mother aware of it?*
T: I think she's asleep, but I think she's also aware of it. It's like my mother's just been put back in her body. In fact she's not all the way back in yet. She's being put back in.
D: *By this being?*
T: I don't think by the being. I think by something else, but in association with the being. There is a light shining in the window. (Pause) I'm a bit hesitant to go over to the window because of the being there, but the light is shining down from higher up. The being's by the window at the foot of the bed. I think I am quite shocked by it. I'm not sure what the being

is doing there. At first, I thought it was attacking my mother and that's why I got scared. And I think that's why I saw it as a predatory kind of thing, because it's strange to have something that's not human standing in the bedroom. But I'm getting the impression that I somehow met these people before. I can't say why I feel that way, but something about the being is familiar, even though I know I'm not seeing it clearly. I think I'm getting over the shock now, but I'm still wary, because I'm not sure exactly what's going on. I think something about the light is helping my mother back into her body. But I'm not sure why the being is standing there, except that now he's beckoning me over. And he wants me to go up on the light.

D: *How do you feel about that?*

T: It's interesting that now that he's asked me, I feel excited to do that. I'm still concerned about my mother, but oddly, also unconcerned. When I came to the house, I was wondering if she was dying.

D: *Has she been sick?*

T: She's old. She's getting to that time where it doesn't seem she has much longer to live. I don't think she's necessarily sick, but she's getting old and frail. And so, I was calling on her to see how she was. I had received a letter from her that said she was losing – not losing her health, but losing her time. She was feeling like it was time, that she was ready to die. And I, of course being a doctor, decided that I could do something about that. (Pained humor) I don't know why I thought that. But now I'm here, and I'm oddly unconcerned about her. I think this is bigger than me worrying about if she's dying. I somehow feel that she's all right now. I don't know why. And so I'm more interested in going up on the light. I think I'm partly wanting to find for myself, and partly wanting to see where she's been and what she's been up to. Or why she's being put back in her body.

Now it seemed like it would be a typical UFO story, but again it took another strange turn.

D: So it's curiosity then.
T: It is. Now I'm being taken up on the light. I'm safe. *My body's staying there.* My body doesn't go, my body stays. Oddly, it's standing up where I was, holding its doctor's bag, still wearing its clothes. But I'm floating up the light.
D: Are you going with the being?
T: The being is staying to watch my body. I think that's what it has to do. And that's what it was doing with my mother. Just staying there watching the body, and making sure it doesn't come to harm. That it's okay.
D: Tell me what's happening as you go up to the light.
T: It feels very bright, and it feels light because I'm floating. And the light gets brighter and brighter, and it seems to surround everything. I'm getting the impression that I jumped somehow.
D: What do you mean ... jumped?
T: I mean I disappeared from one place and I'm appearing somewhere else, by following the light. I didn't stay with the light. I disappeared in the light, and I'm coming somewhere else.
D: Where have you jumped to?
T: I'm getting a number of different impressions. A waterfall. The way the sun shines on the mist as it rises from a waterfall, and makes many little rainbows. So I'm getting impressions of those little rainbows, kind of in a misty way. But I don't think it's from a waterfall. I think it's just the colors dancing, many little colors. I'm surrounded by light, and there are other colors dancing as well. I'm coming somewhere ... oh! Okay. I'm standing on a balcony and I'm actually looking at a waterfall. But I get the impression that I'm no longer on the Earth. It's odd, I feel like I'm in a body again now, but not the body that I left. My hands are holding the rail.

D: *So it's a different body. What does this body look like?*

T: It seems strange, but I'm getting the impression of a tall, *blue* body. It's odd because the impression I'm getting is not so much of the body, but of me. I seem to be someone with quite some authority standing here on the balcony overlooking a beautiful city with waterfalls. It's a building that's sculpted partly into the mountain where the waterfalls are. The buildings of this city are more naturally fitted to the landscape. I'm not sure if I'm in charge here, but I have some authority. There's webbing between my fingers. I'm tall, I'm blue, my skin seems to be leathery. And it's not a kind of pallor either. I'm not scared of being blue, it's a real full-on blue color.

He had a hard time getting an impression of clothing, because it was as if he had no need for that. "It's kind of a gauzy-like substance. It's more of a decoration than clothing. Something colorful on my shoulders. Perhaps an insignia of rank or position, but it's not functional as clothing is. And yet I'm wearing a heavy metal belt, with a codpiece around it. It seems to be golden in color, or brass. No, I think it's gold. That's interesting. I'm getting a sense of a male body, and yet I think I'm also female somehow. Not androgynous. It's more like a hermaphrodite. I have both sets of equipment, as it were. I have male genitalia, but I also have a womb and female insides." I asked about his face. "I have big, black eyes, but it's almost like I'm fishlike. Somewhat like a lizard. It's not a human face at all. It's a big wide face, almost like a toad face, actually. Even though it's a toad face, I get the impression of some kind of gill structure, and also some kind of skin folds at the back, vertically placed. Ruffles and gills and webbing, mainly on the back of the head. I don't really have a neck. It all blends together. I've been on Earth in that other body. I'm not really a doctor, and I'm not really that woman's son, even though I thought I was. I think I had temporary amnesia to find out what it was like being human.

I think this was a fact-finding mission.

D: *You mean you went to Earth for just a short period of time?*
T: I did. I had the sense that I was this woman's son, but actually I think that was a body I took on for a time.
D: *A body that already existed, or what?*
T: That's interesting. I think that body was created for me.
D: *Without being born?*
T: I'm getting a sense that it was born, but it wasn't born in the normal way that bodies are born.
D: *What do you mean?*
T: I think I am, in a sense, the son of that woman. But I wasn't born as a human is born in normal human lifetimes. I was placed into her body and then taken out again.
D: *Was she aware of this?*
T: Not consciously. I believe, as this being that is blue, I had the ability to inhabit this created human body and to come back. I wasn't there for a long time. I think I was only there for about twenty years or so.
D: *But you said you felt you were not a doctor?*
T: That's right. What I mean by that is I was not a human.
D: *But in that body you were a doctor.*
T: That's correct, yes. The difference was that this was not a normal human incarnation. I had a mission. Somehow it was necessary for me as this blue person, as this toad-like being, to step out of my body for a short time and be transported into this other body. And experience life as a human for this period of time, that I believe was about twenty years. I believe my mother might have died that night. And then it was time for me to come back again. That was a real incarnation of hers.
D: *But if you leave that body there on Earth, you're not going to go back to it?*
T: I think it's up for discussion as to whether or not I go back. If there's anything more for me to do there now that she's left.

There's a possibility that I'll return, and that's why they're keeping the body there. But if I don't return then they'll take the body with them as well.

D: *How are you going to find out?*

T: I have to talk it over with these people in this room. (Pause) We determine that there's no need for me to go back; that was enough. She is here in the room also. She is aware that this was one of her human incarnations. She's had many. She found what she needed to find in that lifetime. And I helped that to occur. It was necessary that I go there to help her with her work. I had to remind her of her work because she lost her way in that lifetime.

D: *That was your purpose for being there?*

T: That's right. And now that I am back, we recognize that we have succeeded and I do not have to go back again.

D: *What happens to the body left on Earth?*

T: It will be transported. It will not be left there to die. The body will be taken care of, yet my soul is no longer attached to it, and it will run its natural course. It will be cared for, I believe, in some kind of tank somewhere on this planet. The cells will live out their time, for they have consciousness too. Nothing will be killed. The cells will live out their time, and then the body will die.

When Tom awakened, he had a few thoughts that remained in his mind about this. He said the being that was in the room removed his body and transported it. It could not be left there because it was not like other human bodies. He didn't elaborate on how it was different. Maybe because it was not a normal incarnation. The body was taken onboard a ship, and placed in a tank. The cells had life and had to be allowed to live out their life span. The mother died a normal death, and because her body was the product of a normal incarnation, nothing had to be done with it.

T: She actually died. That was an actual physical incarnation of hers. So later on, someone will find her body in her bed, and there will be the normal funeral rites.

D: *Do others on your planet go and experience ....*

T: They do, yes. They sometimes go to the Earth, but often they go elsewhere. But it is part of the culture that during one's lifetime it is common for people to take trips to experience other planets, and other cultures, for these lifetimes last many thousands of years. Sometimes it is done as a full lifetime, a full incarnation. And sometimes it's not done in that way. But while they are living, if it is a full incarnation, and even if it is not, they will have the amnesia that is normally done with lifetimes on this planet Earth. They will have that amnesia to get the true human experience. If they go to another planet, to another culture, then they will fit in with how that culture does things. The amnesia that occurs on Earth during lifetimes is not a universal phenomenon.

D: *So when the person is alive on Earth, that personality is not aware that there's a different type of soul in the body.*

Is this similar to Estelle in *Convoluted Universe, Book Two*, where the reptilian had entered her body to experience life on Earth? In that case, the body had to be adapted in order to handle the different type of energy.

T: Correct. But it is not as though someone else's body and soul has been taken. This is simply the soul that chooses to be born as in a normal incarnation. It is just the soul of one of our people on this planet.

D: *But the soul does have amnesia while it's on Earth, because it would be too confusing otherwise.*

T: Well, not necessarily confusing, because we are used to doing this kind of travel. But it would not be the correct experience to have on this planet. On this planet, people have amnesia during their lifetimes.

164

D: *Otherwise, you'd have too many memories that would interfere.*

T: Yes, you wouldn't be getting the normal human experience.

D: *Do you do this repeatedly, or just that one time?*

T: We do it a number of times, but only this one time on Earth. I have had many incarnations as a human, but those were when my soul was committed to the human experience. This particular journey was from the planet of the blue people. This journey was the only time that, as a blue person, I traveled to Earth.

D: *Otherwise, it was just when the soul is reassigned. Is that correct?*

T: That's right, that's right.

D: *But then you just stay on that other planet and continue your life?*

T: That's right, then I continue my life. But what was important about that is, that I made a mistake when I was incarnated on *that* planet. I have had many lifetimes on many other planets in many star systems. Many lifetimes on many of the civilizations on Earth. But while I was here with this blue race, that was my only foray into the Earth. But somehow, once my soul moved to the Earth to have the Earth experience, I confused this experience with me traveling. So the importance of this is, that in fact it was not a visitation or an abduction experience, so much as I *was* the alien. I was doing this for my family member, my sister, even though I came down and it was my mother. It was my sister on that planet, and she was getting lost. And so I came in and corrected her and then I jumped out again. That lifetime as a doctor was not a real lifetime. It was twenty years of being there in order to correct my sister's mistake. My sister, who in that lifetime was my mother, if that makes any sense.

D: *I see, and she was your sister on the blue planet?*

T: Exactly. One of many sisters. I had to help her. She was making a mistake. She was losing her way, she was going

165

insane.

D: *Oh! What was causing that? Anything to do with the two different types of energies?*

T: No. On that blue planet we have access to many of our lifetimes in a conscious way. And so this was a normal human incarnation for her. But as a human she had become weighed down with much of the negativity that exists on this planet, and she had taken it onboard herself. I repeated the pattern myself in *this* lifetime exploring the same energy. She took that pain and negativity on herself, and it was too much for her. And so I came in as her son, to help her to balance and heal.

D: *Does this often happen when an off-planet energy tries to deal with Earth energies?*

T: If there is a personal connection from this lifetime on the blue planet, we will not interfere with what is happening on Earth, because other planetary energies are taking care of that. We of the blue planet are helping. Others in our system are in fact helping them, sending a great deal of energy and a great deal of love, and a great deal of caring. We do this also, but this was specifically to help the being that was my sister. And so, we are more focused with helping those of us who are aware of our other lifetimes on other planets. It is more of a general thing to help Earth and its Earth energy. But specifically for lifetimes we'll help one of our own. We won't necessarily go and help an individual lifetime of someone else.

D: *Does it often occur that the human becomes as confused as your mother did?*

T: She had many lifetimes as a human. Some where she was confused, and some where she was not. So they were normal human incarnations as part of the normal human experience. What was affecting her mind in that lifetime was the normal human negativity. The normal negativity of Earth. It was not because of the other alien lifetime, the lifetime on the blue planet. That is simply where we discovered this lifetime in a

166

conscious sense, and chose to go and help. On the blue planet, she selected me to go, which was quite an honor.

D: *Do you consider this blue planet your home planet?*

T: In this experience, yes. It is where I have many lifetimes, and this is one of my homes. But I have many homes. I have homes in many other planetary systems, and this Earth is also my home. For as a soul, I have been part of this physical experience in many ways and many times.

D: *I am always trying to clarify the distinction between going back to a planet like that, and the spirit side. Is it different?*

T: Yes. This is a physical incarnation on the blue planet.

D: *Sometimes, they sound very similar when you can come and go with your soul body.*

T: Yes, but on that planet we have become quite advanced to be able to soul travel. I believe that is the term that comes to mind about what we do. As we are spiritually advanced enough on that planet, in that lifetime, in that experience, we have learned as a race how to be aware of other lifetimes. We are aware of being both on that planet and other planets in the same system, or in other systems.

D: *What do they do with the information once you bring it back?*

T: We learn more about other cultures. And so now having gone to that planet, the Earth, and found out and corrected the help from my sister's lifetime, we have discovered more about what life is like on Earth. More about why people lose their way. More about, and more specifically, why *she* lost her way. And it was because of taking the negativity of the planet into herself.

D: *Why is it important for you to know this information?*

T: Because this is the same thing I did in this lifetime that I'm living now. (As Tom.) So I had a great deal of pain in this lifetime.

D: *That was one of Tom's questions. He said he was not experiencing a physical pain, but an internal pain. Could you tell him about it?*

167

T: It was taking on the pain of the planet. There was much rage. The sister of the other lifetime had the same problem, much rage against the suffering that occurs here. Sometimes we can get lost into believing there is nothing we can do about it. For ourselves, there is nothing we can do about another's pain, unless they were to let us help. Certainly, here we can choose not to live such painful lifetimes. But sometimes we forget, and sometimes we allow the pain. And sometimes with the rage of finding how much pain is here, we begin to blame God and the divine and take it on ourselves.

D: *Tom said, since he was a child, he always had this feeling, like screaming inside.* (Yes) *And that's what caused it? Picking up the emotions of the planet itself? Because we know the planet is also a living entity.*

T: Yes, but let me be more clear. It is not the emotion of the planet necessarily, for the planet can take care of herself. It is the emotion of the beings on the planet who have lost their way. And so many of them have lost their way. And when one comes down to help, one can get lost. And then he became confused as to who he was and where he was. He became confused as to whether this was his pain, or whether this was the pain of others. And he decided to make it his pain to work through. And yet it does not belong to him, it never did. He needs to let it go.

D: *This is why he became suicidal?* (Yes) *He just wanted to get out of that internal turmoil?*

T: Yes. He was not well-balanced at the time. Having taken onboard all the pain, he lost his way and forgot who he was.

D: *But the amnesia is normal, isn't it?*

T: The amnesia is normal, but he has experienced so many lifetimes in so many systems that he has a presence as a consciousness that is naturally healing and naturally positive. And thus, this is what he forgot.

D: *Why did he come to Earth this time?*

T: This is a pivotal lifetime. This is a lifetime where he will lead

168

many into the new world. He did not know the problems would be so bad. He believed that he would be able to work through them far more easily than he did. He is here to help people. But more than that, he's here to create with them something new, so this kind of pain does not have to exist as much anymore. Many other humans are also feeling this pain, but they don't know what's causing it. Whereas, he does know. He has a way of connecting with the Divine, with the consciousness of the All That Is, the consciousness of Grace. And he has a way of knowing what lifetimes are like; he has a way of knowing what the physical experience is like beyond lifetimes and between lifetimes. He is here to set up a new way of living, a new way of being born, a new way of dying, a new way of existing between lifetimes, so that the cycle of pain is not begun. He is to create a new experience where people become more conscious of who they are, of their divine nature, and less focused on the pain and suffering; less focused on the shame. More aware of their reasons for living; less intoxicated with the myth of pain, with the idea that learning must come through pain. With the idea that karma is important, with the idea that one must learn through suffering. Those intoxicated with those ideas can become more aware, and conscious of the ideas that one can live and grow and learn through joy, and peace and love. And while it is very common on this planet to have been lost, as this new experience is created, this new awareness during lifetimes, between lifetimes and beyond lifetimes, there will be less need for the pain, less need for the suffering. People will not be lost in the confusion anymore. There are very many who have come to do the same thing. Many more who are trying to help from a distance. But many souls have been incarnated at this time to create this new experience.

D: *You said it would be a new way to be born.*

T: Yes, meaning a new kind of experience. Certainly there will still be physical births, souls incarnating, but there will not be the shame handed down. There will not be the pain handed down. There will not be the confusion handed down. And the amnesia will only be in place as much as it needs to be. It will not be in place for everyone completely as it is at this time. People will be more aware of their other lifetimes, more aware of their spiritual purpose and direction. Less focused on just this one lifetime, unless that is the place they truly need to be. But even then, it will not be through pain, it will be focused through love and joy.

Tom had been trained as a medical doctor, but then decided not to pursue that career. He had become involved in energy healing, but was having problems with it.

T: Again this was confusion from the last experience that we spoke of. He was never meant to be a doctor in this lifetime. He got lost in the confusion, and remembered that a doctor had come to help. But he is a healer in other ways. He can use his medical experience, most definitely. He is supposed to be doing birthing of this new world, of this new experience. This is the main focus of this lifetime. And the medicine, although helpful, was a misperception. It's not something he needs to go back to and explore any further. He has been questioning this. We are shifting his energies. We are opening his heart, for in his heart is where he holds his fear. It will be alleviated slowly over the next few years. His role is more to explore. This is why we say it will be released slowly over the next few years, for it is not time for him to have a full healing practice at this stage. Certainly, it is time for him to learn more, and to accomplish more and to find out more of who he is. At this stage, he has more exploring to do.

CHAPTER TEN

SURVIVAL

When Peggy came off the cloud she found herself in a barren landscape; very hilly, with little vegetation. Mostly small brushy trees. She looked around for some sign of people or habitation, but could see nothing. Then she saw a little trail leading up out of a ravine. As she followed it, she found herself floating instead of walking. The path wound up a tall hill through rocks and yellow-brown dried grass. The entire scene was desolate. No sign of life of any kind. She then saw more trees, but they were all dead. When I asked her to look at herself, she said, "I don't feel a body. I feel like energy. It feels like a mass. Almost like ... it's not a round ball, it's kind of oblong. Vibrating. It almost feels like the wind moving." She felt contained, but not like being in a body, just something to enclose the energy. "It's like there's a light in the center of this oval of energy. And the light radiates out like a sheet in an oval shape."

She liked this place even though it was desolate. "It feels very comfortable, very familiar. However, it does feel like I'm searching. I'm still going up the hill, and I'm coming to a place where there are many dark green trees. They may be pine trees, tall. I think I'm searching for a cave, or an indentation in the Earth. I think I'm supposed to meet someone there."

D: *Where did you come from?*
P: This sounds strange. I think I came from Heaven. I was *sent* to this place, but I've been here before. Oh, wait! It's not a cave. It's a hut, only it's really crude. It has a grass roof and poles. And it's hooked into the side of an embankment. There's a little cot ... and there's a man – skinny, old. He's like a hermit. I've come to talk to him, communicate. He's been asking for information, and so I've been sent to talk to

171

him. He is an old man. He's lying on the cot. It's like I'm entering his mind.

D: *I was wondering if he could see you.*

P: I don't think he can, but he knows I'm there. He can sense. And I'm talking to him. He wanted to know how much longer he has to stay there in form. He wants to leave. But I'm there to tell him he can't leave yet. There's something he has to do. I know he's tired, but there's a village over some of these hills that he needs to go to. He needs to talk to these people because they need help. They are confused. They need direction, and he has the wisdom to help them. They need guidance. He has to do this before he can leave.

This sounded very much like Peggy was acting as a guardian angel or guide. She was giving him advice, but also answering his request for information. This seems to be another verification that sometimes we also act in this capacity while on the other side.

D: *What does he think about this?*

P: He's not very happy, but he's willing to go because he knows that he's come here to do certain things. And he has helped other people in this way. There's been some disturbance in this village. It may be earth related, but the people are confused. They think the gods are punishing them. And he has to go and tell them that there is no god in the mountain that's punishing them.

D: *Has he been to this village before?*

P: Not this one. He's been to others.

D: *Then they won't know who he is.*

P: They sort of do, because there are rumors about a wise man that lives in the mountains.

D: *You said he has helped others. Were these people who came to see him?*

P: No, he goes. When he was younger he went farther afield,

but now that he's old he can't go so far. But he's never been to this village. I think they will accept him. He's their only chance, because if they don't accept him, it's going to get very chaotic, and they won't survive.

D: *You mean there will be too much fear?*

P: Yes. And then they will turn on one another.

D: *Can you see what happened to cause this disturbance in the village?*

P: Maybe it was a rock avalanche. But they think there's a god that lives in the mountains that is punishing them. And they're accusing one another of being the cause. They did something to anger the god. And there are so few people in this whole area that if one village is destroyed, if one village doesn't make it, the whole population will be thrown off. It will cause an imbalance. It's very important for the whole ecosystem.

D: *Of this area?*

P: Of this whole world.

D: *I've always thought that more population causes a disruption in the ecosystem.*

P: Not at this place. These people are very attached to this earth, and there's something they have to do. So there has to be a few more people to make sure they won't die out. Because if all these people die it's going to hurt this place. (To herself:) What is it about these people that have to be there? – They have to discover something on this world to help this world itself to evolve.

D: *Is this world Earth?*

P: No, it's not Earth.

D: *Then the population hasn't been there very long?*

P: No, it hasn't been there very long. And there's still much disturbance in the atmosphere and in the earth itself. This world is not that old, and it hasn't settled down yet. But it's beautiful. Now I'm seeing this huge rock arch, and it's just gorgeous. And he's going to the village. I think that's why

I'm at this arch. I'm giving him strength – not necessarily physical strength, but resolve. I'm helping him in his resolve to go there.

D: *Do you know where the original people came from?*

P: I want to say they were brought there. The original ones volunteered. They came from somewhere else. I think from the same star system, but a more advanced planet. They agreed to come and help this new planet. It's been several generations. However, the colonies are not flourishing as they thought they would. But they're not supposed to have contact from the original planet, so they will make this planet their home.

D: *But wouldn't the original people have passed down stories?*

P: They seem to have forgotten them if they did. Or their memory was erased.

D: *That's possible if they wanted them to start fresh.* (Yes) *This is the reason they can't afford to have the whole village wiped out, if they are not flourishing.*

P: And the hermit came. He's been there a long time. And he feels like he hasn't helped, but he's helped more than he thought. He just doesn't realize it. If he hadn't been there, they would have been wiped out by now. He's in the village, and I'm telling him what to say. He's calming the people down because they were pretty upset. He's telling them what they need to do. And we're high up in the mountains. One of the reasons they're so upset is with the avalanche, rockslide, it covered food that they were growing. So he's telling them they need to move.

D: *To move the whole village?*

P: Yes, down to an area that is more stable. And I'm telling him where they should relocate. They're listening to him. And they're gathering up their belongings. They'll do much better down in the valley. They'll have a much longer growing season. They'll be closer to other villages where they can trade, because they carve stone. And so they're going, and he's showing them it will be a journey of a couple of days. He's going with them. I'm going ahead of them.

D: *They can't see you either?*

P: No, they can't see me. But I'm leaving and going down to where they're going.

D: *They have to start all over again, don't they?*

P: They do, but there's not much there so it won't be hard. And this place is much better for them.

D: *It's like he was the voice of reason.*

P: Yes, they were very glad to see him, actually.

D: *We can move time ahead very quickly. Does the old man stay with them very long?*

P: He stays with them for a couple of years to help them.

D: *Do you stay there the whole time?*

P: I stay part of the time. I come and go. But at the end of two years I come and tell him that he can leave. He has finished his work. I'm with him, and he's walking out of his body. And then he can see my energy. We leave together and go back to the planet. I don't believe people are in physical form on that place.

D: *Is this a physical planet?* (Yes) *So it's not an energy world.* (No) *Like you would think of as Heaven.*

P: No, it's a physical place.

D: *But he's in spirit too, isn't he?*

P: Now he is, yes.

D: *Does he recognize this place?*

P: Yes. It's his home, and he's fulfilled his obligation to this new planet. And when he gets back, we go to a group of energy. And he talks, or communicates about what happened there to him and to the people. In fact, he's kind of reporting back.

D: *Does this happen with everyone that leaves from there?*

P: I think so. And I haven't been any place. I'm sort of like a messenger.

D: *Do you go to other places besides that one?*

175

P: Yes. I go to other worlds. Some of them have people. Some of them don't. Some of them are in the spirit. But I take messages from this council on the home planet throughout all this star system. And it's a big star system.

D: *Have you ever lived a physical life yourself, or have you always been this energy?*

P: No, I've lived physical lives. I like being energy though. I like not being in a body. I like that freedom.

D: *If you like it that way, why would you want to enter a body?*

P: To learn.

D: *Can't you learn everything there?*

P: No, there are some things that are much easier to learn in a body. Emotional things, of feelings, sensations. Limitations. It's interesting to have emotion. And you can learn things faster when you have emotion.

D: *Then on the home world when you're energy, you don't really experience emotions?*

P: Not like you do in physical form. Not those kind. It's lighter. It's easier.

D: *Why is it easier to learn the emotions in the physical?*

P: It's the input, it's just there. It's so like in your face. And you have to resolve problems that we don't have in the spirit.

D: *But when you come into a physical body, aren't you worried about being caught there, or trapped there? I'm thinking about karma.*

P: No, I don't feel karma.

D: *When you get into the physical, you interact with other people, and it's so easy to get caught up in things that create karma.*

P: That's true. But I don't remember being caught.

D: *When that happens you have to stay in the physical. You can't go back.*

P: No, I come and go.

D: *Isn't that difficult to keep from becoming trapped in the physical?*

176

P: It doesn't seem to be. I don't know why. Why haven't I gotten trapped? Because I think I'm always the messenger, even when I'm in the physical. I've always been a messenger. I was created a messenger.

D: *So even in the physical, your job is to teach people things, or pass messages along?*

P: Oh, yes. Things they need. Earth is beautiful. I like the Earth itself. I like the beauty of the Earth. Yet it's hard for people on Earth. It's so heavy there. Sometimes it makes me sad, to see them struggle and hurt, and not understand why. When they come to Earth they take things so seriously. It's like Earth is a drama. There are other places that are more light comedy. But Earth is drama, they get so caught up in drama. They take it *so* seriously.

D: *That's because they think that's all there is.*

P: Yes. They need to lighten up!

D: *But when you come into the physical, you don't remember.*

P: That's true. It would help a lot if they could remember these things.

D: *Why aren't we allowed to?*

P: Because of what we need to learn here. It would interfere if they remembered. I think people come here for that drama. It's part of that experience to work through those heavy, dramatic, emotional experiences. But hopefully it'll change. It'll lighten up. We can't remember or we wouldn't be able to do the things we need to do when we're here.

D: *But you said you've also gone to other worlds and were physical there?*

P: Yes. But they're all different experiences, different things to learn. I don't think any two worlds are the same. Different energies, different atmospheres; some are heavy, some are lighter. Some you can create. There are even those worlds where there's no free will.

D: *What happens on a world like that?*

P: You just have certain avenues you have to go, and there is no choice.

D: *That's also a lesson, isn't it?*

P: Oh, yes. Or an experience.

D: *To see what it would be like if you didn't have a choice.*

P: Yes, it's no fun.

D: *Was there any world that was your favorite, that you'd like to go back to?*

P: Yes. All that is just pure love and pure light.

D: *The world when you're energy?* (Yes) *Is that world different from the spirit state when you are in-between lives?*

P: Yes, it is.

D: *Of course, you don't have a body either when you're in the in-between.*

P: No. It's different though. It's a shift. The spirit world is a different dimension than the world where you're just in the spirit, but you're also on a world. It's a different dimension than just being in the spirit.

D: *But if you're in the energy world, you wouldn't die, so to speak, would you?*

P: No, you don't die. You can choose to leave, and you can go back into the spirit world.

D: *I was wondering if you also went into that spirit dimension.*

P: Yes, you do. On my home planet, it's like there are groups of energy observing other worlds. And then they send out messengers to other worlds to help. It's almost like looking at fireflies. These spirits are going out to other worlds with information.

D: *So from the home planet, you can't just go and enter a body.*

P: No. You just do messages, but you have to go to the spirit side to get assignments. In the spirit world, different dimensions, different universes.

D: *When you're there, you're not this glowing energy?* (No) *And they are the ones who tell you where to go, or do you have a choice?*

P: You have a choice. You meet with a council. You decide

178

what it is you want to learn and experience, and when you want to experience it, and what place. And what part of your group you want to go with. I'm in the spirit, and I'm energy and I'm on this planet. And we come back to this planet after we've taken messages. There are other spirits there. But if we decide to leave and go back into spirit, many times, part of our group will go back too. And then, if we reincarnate in other physical worlds, we'll go together.

D: *Do they show you what the life will be like?*

P: You get an overview, and you decide if that's what you want to do. It's kind of like a preview.

D: *So you're able to experience and learn these things without creating negativity and karma.*

P: We can get trapped if we forget. So once we come into a physical world, we remember how to dispense karma while we're there, not to let it cling to us.

D: *Is there a way you can keep it from clinging to you?*

P: Be aware that you're creating it, and resolve it. Not get caught up in the drama. That's hard for most people. But this group I'm with, it's like there's a memory chip that – it's not conscious, but it alerts us some way that we need to take care of our karma in this lifetime. Don't hold it over.

D: *People get caught up in the drama, and they think this is the only reality.*

P: And we can too, if we're not aware.

D: *Are you aware of the body you're speaking through? The human that's known as Peggy?* (Yes) *Why did you choose this life as Peggy? Were you told to do this on the spirit side?*

P: I was asked, and I was asked by Love. This wonderful love, this All That Is.

D: *You mean a Love on the other side, the spirit side?*

P: Yes, the spirit side. A spirit love, that the Earth needed love at this time. It needed the light.

D: *The type of energy that you basically are.*

P: Yes. And I've always thought the Earth was beautiful, and I

179

want to help her.

D: *What do you think of the life of Peggy? Is it working out like you thought it was going to?*

P: Life on Earth is hard, but it's working out.

D: *Especially when you come in with all the memories erased, it makes it hard?*

P: It does. And you feel so heavy. This is a very important time. That's why there are so many people here, because of what is going to happen. And people want to experience it. Energies, beings want to experience it, so there's a rush to come in. It's very exciting.

D: *Why do these spirits want to be here at this time? What is it they want to experience?*

I already knew the answers to these questions, because it is coming through so many of my clients. But I always ask them anyway, because, if the same information is repeated through many, then I believe it has more validity. Besides, sometimes bits and pieces of new information are added.

P: They want to experience the shift that's going to happen, because when the Earth shifts, it will shift this entire universe into a better place.

D: *(Surprised) The* entire *universe?*

P: Yes. And you wouldn't think that one tiny little planet at the far end of a small galaxy would have that much importance. But it does. I think it's strategically placed. I think it has to do with sacred geometry, but that's all I know.

D: *And that's why all the people are coming at this time? They want to be here to experience this?*

P: Yes. It's going to be very dramatic. It will send energy waves throughout the whole universe when this happens.

D: *But also there are huge numbers of people who are choosing to leave the planet at this time.*

P: The ones that are leaving are making room for more to come in. They've experienced what they need in this lifetime. They agreed to come in and help where there are great disasters. Because each great disaster brings the Earth closer to that shift.

D: *It does? Because we think of that as negative energy.*

P: Yes, but it's not.

D: *I've heard two versions: one is that the Earth is going to go through horrible times, and the other one is that we will create a new Earth.*

P: And they're both true. But there will be an overlay. There will be two Earths. One will overlay the other. But you have to remember that it's all just an experience. And neither experience is good nor bad. They're just an experience. It's what people perceive as being good or bad.

D: *So some will choose to remain on the Earth that will be having the negative experiences.* (Yes) *The others may choose to be on the one that is going into the new Earth.* (Yes) *I've also been told they won't be aware of each other.*

P: That's what I've heard also.

D: *And as Peggy she will experience the shifting into the new vibration?* (Yes) *And that will be a whole new thing if the entire universe shifts at one time.*

P: Yes. It will be like beautiful waves of energy. It'll be like a flower opening. That energy will just flow out into the universe. It will be a beautiful thing.

D: *But the ones on the old Earth won't know this is happening.*

P: No, they won't.

D: *They won't even be aware of the ones who've left to go to the new Earth?*

P: That's right.

D: *I have heard these stories from many different people, so I like to have it verified.*

181

CHAPTER ELEVEN

THE BLACK HOLE ENERGY

When Louise came off the cloud, she found herself looking at a place that was strangely familiar, although it did not resemble any place on Earth. "We're at a place that I've seen before, that I identify as – that feels like home. The buildings are all pink spires. I'm way above the planet, and all you can see are different sizes of spires. You would think they were gigantic crystals, but I know they are buildings. They shine, and they look crystalline." Then she found herself on the ground. "Now I see what looks like houses, but very modernistic, on the outskirts. They're each a different color depending on the person's energy that lives in it."

L: As soon as I saw the spires from far away, it just felt like home. It's a good feeling. (Pause) I know that there is something like machinery. It's equivalent to what a boiler room would be, or a furnace room. Beyond the suburb parts, there's something that runs something. I keep feeling like I want to go to that machinery. I'm being drawn there.

The instant she said that, she was immediately there.

L: I'm seeing creatures as people, but part of me knows that we're not people. But people are running out of this building that has all this machinery. And they're coming to greet me. They're hugging me, and they're glad to see me.
D: *What do they look like?*
L: That's funny. Seeing this is confusing to me. Because – at first, they look like people, and then something else, and then they go back to people. This is where I'd say I'm making this

182

up, but what I saw are black hole people. I call them that because I feel I work with them. They're all white, six feet tall, a sausage shape. They have a small neck, small arms. And a diamond-shaped face: pointed at the top, going to two points on the side, and then one point on the chin. I see really nice, beautiful eyes, but they're tilted: the outsides go down. Above the face is a protrusion, you'd almost think their brain was sitting on top of their head. They have four legs coming out about a third of the way up the sausage thing – the body. It's four skinny legs that come out equidistant.

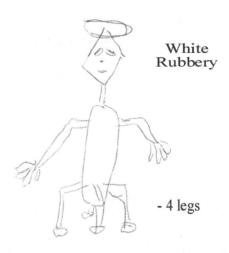

White
Rubbery

- 4 legs

So I see them there, which confuses me, because they told me they were from the black hole. Oh, no, are they just telling me they work with black hole energy? So that's why I feel an affinity toward them, because they – that's me. And one of them is saying, "Welcome, welcome, welcome." It's like I haven't been home in a long time. We're just catching up. That's what it feels like. We're all excited.

D: *Can you see what you look like?*

L: Hmm. I'm seeing myself two ways. If I stand away from myself and look back – I look like me, human. If I get into my body, and I look down, then I look like a black-hole person, like these people.

D: *Is it hard to make the four legs work?*

L: No. No. (Laugh) Oh, it was funny that you would ask that, because it's like asking, "Is it hard to sit down?" It's so natural.

D: *Do you think you worked with these people in that building?*

L: The words I just heard were, "My group. My group." Right now, I'm feeling like I'm here and there at the same time. This is happening right now. So, yes, I haven't been back there for a while.

D: *Why did you leave that place?*

L: Umm, to get information. That's why I'm here on Earth, to get information.

D: *Why do you need to get information?*

L: I just saw the words, "We're expanding." So our planet is expanding. And I'm seeing that different people from our place have gone to many places. And then we come back and report. So that's my job. There are different people from all different – we'll say, "jobs" – or different groups. Like my group does a certain work in the "something" that runs "something". It has to do with that building. And so I'm getting information that has to do with that aspect of things. And then some people, their group is in the middle of the city part. They get different information from different places. (Pause) They're showing me now, as if I'm speaking to a large group about what I found – and I am in one of those pink buildings. And they're showing me that when it was decided all these people would go out to different places, they were chosen from all different groups. So I am from that group, but my information is for everybody, because they're showing me speaking to many.

D: *What kind of information are you sharing with all the people?*

L: I'm getting the words, "Physics, astronomy, characteristics of all the physical things here on Earth. How things work here.

Cultures. DNA." Just everything I can find out.

D: *And the others that went out are also finding the same kind of things?*

L: Yes, but different people go to different places at different times. Let's see. They're trying to tell me how many went to Earth. No. That's not it. It's not how many are on Earth now, because there are only about 13. So we 13 might be on Earth now, but there have been more or less at different times.

D: *Why is it important to them to gather information?*

L: That's what I was wondering. (Laugh) Let's see. They're telling me, part of that machinery has to do with black hole energy. And they say that I know now that it's all energy just compressed together very, very, very, very strong. What's being developed is a system that would help to heal the universe, or more. And with all these different energies that we're working with, we need to find out more about the places we're going to be helping. It's going to make a difference. They're saying, to put it quickly, to find out what energies are needed so we'll be able to provide them. That's why we're finding all this information. We're going to be healing different problems in different places, like the Earth, with these energies. I don't know where else. But some places need more of a certain part of the energy. Some places need another part of the energy. Some places need a certain dose of it. They just told me, when I come down, I bring whatever is needed. I'm bringing the black hole energy. And whatever I find is needed, is provided. So 13 of us are doing it now. We'll be going back, and others will be coming back here. They'll be doing it. So, yes, it's getting the information, and providing the energy at the same time. And they're showing me the reason I was speaking in front of many council members, is reporting. Just reporting. "This is where I went. This is what I found. This is what was provided. This is what happened."

D: *Do you go back and forth quite often?*

185

L: Well, I'm 61 now in this lifetime, and they said I've been back 15 times. And when I go back, I meet with the family or – not the family, the group, is what I'm getting. I meet with my group and I report. Imagine that! And I'm being told that all the other energies that come in, that people need, are a part of this. If someone needs copper energy, they wouldn't be able to handle the other energies. So they just get a part of it.

D: *What is the copper energy?*

L: Well, you know, every single thing is energy. Different vibrations. Some people may need the vibration of copper. The metal. The mineral. That's just a part of the total energy. And as I get more and more information consciously, then many times energy will be sent to this place, or that place, or whatever. But much of my work at night (while sleeping) is going to different places on Earth. And whatever part of the black hole energy they need, is what they get.

D: *Did you volunteer or did somebody ask you to do this?*

L: I'm seeing that it was an honor. It's like you win a prize. Like, "You're going now. Oh, yea, it's me!" We're all equal. It doesn't matter if you swept floors or if you were the president. We're all equal. Anybody can be chosen. And it feels like, at one time or another, everybody does this. You just come out of a different group.

D: *When you came to Earth, did you begin many years ago? Can you see where it all started?*

L: When you asked that, they showed me that same planet. Let's see. I see myself having gone to other places many times, and the Earth many times. (Pause) So we're in a *big* building that has many drawers. Almost like you'd have a compartment with a drawer in it. And when you're ready to do your trip. – I don't see how you get in the drawer, but you're in the drawer. I don't know how it happens right now, but your physical body is in the drawer. Your spiritual body is gone. And then you come back, and that is your body again.

This sounded very similar to other cases where the physical body was kept onboard a spaceship. When the body was put in a state of suspended animation while the spirit was off on another assignment.

D: *Then the body doesn't have to die.*
L: No, it doesn't. It's almost like it's hibernating or something.
D: *And it's there waiting for you to finish your ... journeys?* (Yes) *So your spirit, your soul, is the one that makes these journeys?*
L: Yes. I'm chosen for it. I don't know who decides. I'm being told it's the council members. They, somehow, decide: now it's that person's turn, that person, that person. And they go, and come back. It's like everybody on the planet is just hopping from one place to another, and back and forth. Now they're telling me about my group. A group of 19, but because different people are in different places, you are usually working with about a group of 12. It keeps changing, but you all can pick up where the group left off.
D: *What does the council do with all this information once it's brought back and reported?*
L: Well, I don't see a computer, but I'm being told they don't need computers. They just hear the information, and they know to decide. Say, if you gave someone a certain amount of medicine, and they needed a little bit more. They know to send back some more of this. Somehow, by reporting what you found out, and what was done, they know what the next step is. They know how many people should go to Earth. How many should go here, how many should go there. How much of the black hole energy should be provided. How much is needed in each place. That's what they're monitoring. Evidently, each time you visit, you have the black hole energy. And you're able to heal with it. Here and there, wherever it's needed.
D: *Why do they call it the "black hole energy"?*

187

L: I just got, "Because it is!" (Laugh) Let me see. It *does* come from black holes in the universe. Somehow they are able to harness that energy and contain it, and disperse it.

D: *Then the next question is something our scientists have always wondered about. What are black holes? We know what the scientists say, but what do* they *say?*

L: (Pause) What I'm being shown is – you're looking at the cosmos, and you see it as being black with planets and stars, and whatever. Then you picture that black as being a fabric, or anything. All one solid thing. It could even be, if you want to picture it as plastic, but picture the cosmos as one solid thing. Then from the right and from the left, two pieces of it come toward each other. (Later she showed me what she saw by taking a piece of paper and curving the edges toward each other so they were touching.) As they are moving toward each other, where they're kind of crumpling up in the middle, it starts an energy that begins turning. And that's what causes the black hole. It's almost like you have rock under the ground here, that moves and causes an earthquake, because of the pressure. So the energies of the cosmos come together, and cause a vortex ... no! They're telling me, not a vortex. They're telling me, think of it as pressure. They cause a pressure as it's pushing together, and that is what causes the energies to become so compressed. And that's what we work with, that compressed energy.

D: *The scientists say nothing exists in the black hole.*

L: Yes, they say everything is sucked into it. It is very dense, is what I was getting. They keep saying, "Pressure, pressure, pressure."

D: *That nothing can exist within it. What do they say?*

L: They're showing it as if there's a black hole right there. (Laugh) One of the people is saying, "Well, look at me!" And he jumps in it, jumps out. Jumps in it, jumps out. Jumps in it, and says, "Hey, I can! I can exist!" And they're saying that we can carry that energy. That's why we're going to the

188

Earth. We mostly learn what effects happened since the last group of people came down and brought black hole energy. So we learn all these things, and at the same time we are dispensing black hole energy. Then we go back and report, "Here's what things look like now." So we exist with the black hole energy.

D: *But don't our scientists say that everything is sucked in, and nothing can get out?*

L: Yes. And they keep giving me the word, "Pressure, pressure, pressure, pressure." There is so much pressure there. They're saying that we work it. We're able to go in and out, in and out. We bring some of the black hole energy with us. We disperse some of it. We couldn't bring a whole black hole down. It would be too much. They're telling me, just little pieces are what we work with. So it's a very, very powerful, condensed energy.

D: *We've also heard that if something was sucked in, it would come out somewhere else.*

L: Like a white hole. That's what some physicists call it, I guess.

D: *But they say, space ships or things like that would not be able to escape the draw of a black hole. It would pull them into it.*

L: Yes. When I was trying to find out about what would happen, I just kept getting, "Pressure, pressure, pressure." They're showing me this one area, pressure, pressure, pressure. They're saying that we evidently are a certain vibration that can handle the energy and work with it. And if a spaceship was a certain vibration, they could handle it. They could go in and out, if they were the right vibration.

D: *Is the theory correct that if you were sucked into it, you would come out on another part of the galaxy, or somewhere else?*

L: (Laugh) The one who was jumping in and out of the small one, said, "Come with me." It's almost like we're floating through the air. And so we're at this very small black hole. It's only as big as a house, but it's still the same kind of

189

energy. And he says, "Okay. Do you see anything in it?" And I say, "No. I don't see anything." It's just like when you look at the cosmos. It looks empty and black. And so he says, "Okay. Let's go in it. Do you feel anything?" And I say, "No." And I'm one of those people now. So he takes out a little instrument that shows pounds per square inch. A pressure gauge. And he says, "All right, watch." And the pressure gets so high it explodes. And he said, "Pressure, pressure, pressure." And so now we're going deeper into it. It's like we're going down. And it looks like ... you know where the two pieces of the cosmos came together? (The former example.) Just parts of the cosmos came together, and above it and below it and on the sides of it, it's not being pushed together. So we come out on the other side, and there's no pressure. I mean, it's on the top and the bottom and the sides. They're all the same. So again, I guess to make a point, he's saying, "Pressure, pressure, pressure." That's it. That's pressure.

D: *But you've come out in a different place?*

L: Yes, if you want to go – not in a different dimension though. You're in the cosmos at the top, the bottom, the sides. There's only a certain area that's being pushed together that is the black hole. And that's what it is. It is the black hole. And he's pointing out to me, when he's saying, "Pressure, pressure, pressure," he's not talking about our physics. Not our atmospheric pressure, not our fluid pressure. He's talking about energy pressure. Energy just being pushed, pushed, push, push. And he says it's not like something becoming denser. It's not a denser energy where you go from gas, to liquid, to solid, or something like that. It's not denser in that way. It's different physics. It's a different – (Pause) I keep getting the words, "Can't comprehend, can't comprehend." At least I can understand that it's many different energies being pressurized. But it's not the same as if you took a gas on Earth and pressurized it. It's not the same as if you took a solid and pressurized it.

D: *I was thinking that the people involved with physics would be interested in this. So it's not the way they think?*

L: No. It's almost like a different law of pressurization. It's the way the energies are reacting.

D: *That's why you were able to use it, because it is a different form of energy.* (Yes) *I am thinking about the ETs with their spaceships. They know how to maneuver the black holes, or stay away from them. Would that make sense?*

L: What I was just being shown was that different ETs have different vibrations, also. They have different energies. And different black holes have different amounts of pressure. So they're showing me .... Wait a minute! Sure! That makes sense. Depending on the energies that were present in that part of the cosmos at the time when the two parts pushed together, that depends on what kind of a black hole it is. What kinds of energies are pressurized. So the people – the different ETs and the different spaceships usually know. "We're able to go into *that* black hole. We cannot go in *that* one."

D: *Some people think of these black holes as portals. Is that a different thing?*

L: What they just said is, "A portal is a portal."

D: *So a black hole cannot be used as a portal?*

L: The words I just got were, "Under exceptional circumstances." So sometimes, evidently.

D: *So it shows there are "beings and spirits" that can live in any type of circumstance?*

L: (Laugh) I just got the words, "Of course."

D: *Because our scientists think that nothing can live in something that is so dense and heavy.*

L: Well, actually, we don't *live* there, but we can *be* in the black holes, and we can *utilize* them.

D: *So this planet that you consider home, is not actually in the black hole?*

L: No. It is outside of it, but it utilizes the energy of it. It knows how to do this. And then taking that energy and helping other places in the universe with it.

D: *It can be directed, and they know how to do it.* (Yes) *And this is what they want Louise to do, direct the energy?*

L: Yes. At the moment.

D: *Then when Louise came to Earth, had she had many lives, or is this her first one?*

L: What I keep hearing, "Many have been imprinted."

For more information about imprinting see my books *Keepers of the Garden* and *Between Death and Life*, and the beginning of this book.

D: *So it is really not necessary to live many lives.*

L: The guy who was showing me into the black hole said, "Well, no. Of course not."

D: *But this one now is important. She is gathering information to send back.*

L: Yes. That's what I have done before.

D: *I'm getting the same information from several people, that there are entities gathering information and reporting back. So I guess many of them are going on the same assignments.*

L: Wow! Yes. That's great.

D: *Can I continue to get information for Louise this way, or should I contact Louise's subconscious?*

L: Well, for both parts, it's a yes, if you want.

D: *I can do it either way?* (Yes)

I then asked about a physical problem Louise wanted help with. She had been having some type of pressure on her back between her shoulder blades.

L: I'm seeing the drawers again, where the physical bodies are. Let me see. Ah, okay. That's where my physical body now

– my human body – is feeling the connection with the other. That's kind of weird. They are saying it is because I am in such close connection at the moment. This is just how my physical body is reacting to this energetic connection to who I am up there. They're saying, just like when you see a past life, and you feel the emotions. I see this happening, being that person on that planet. I can feel the connection. And the way I'm feeling it is physically, in the back of my heart chakra. (Pause) I'm seeing them explaining something, but I can't hear it. (Pause) Okay. The past lives, the lives that I've been imprinted as a human, in between those lives (*what I call the "spirit side"*), that's also an illusion. That the planet I live on is an illusion. The black hole is an illusion. So there are no in-between lives.

D: *But her physical body is waiting on that planet for her to return?*

L: Yes. And that will happen. But that's an illusion, too. Everything. *Everything.* Everything is illusion. So what we see as between lives, that's an illusion too.

D: *But it's comforting to people.*

L: Right, right.

D: *Otherwise, it would be very hard for our minds to function if we didn't have something we think is real. Well, if everything we know is an illusion, is anything real? Because I know we create our reality. We create our illusion.*

L: I was just waiting for an answer. And I was shown what looks like the great central Sun.

D: *And that is real?*

L: (Laugh) I just got, "If you want it to be." (Pause) They were showing me all different universes. I specifically saw the Earth. I specifically saw – I guess you call it – my home planet. I saw everything being sucked toward one place. It was like I was standing in the great central Sun, and everything was being sucked inside of there. So what was the question?

D: What is the great central Sun?

L: One thing is that it's made of – everything is in it. *Everything is in it*, because it all was sucked right in there.

D: What does it look like?

L: To me it looks like you're in a creamy, golden, yellowish light, but it has the sense of being in flames. You can't see the flames. You can't feel the flames. But it's the sense of that.

D: I don't want to influence you, but I'm thinking about something I have been told. That over eons, everything that was created implodes back to the Source. Does that make sense?

L: No, that's not what I'm being shown. I wasn't being shown an implosion. I was being shown symbolically that everything we talked about: my home, Earth, whatever, emanates from there. And I just got the words, "No implosion, no explosion."

D: Would the great central Sun be the equivalent of what some people call the "Source"? (Pause) *Do you think it's the same thing with a different name?*

L: Other people call it the Source. But I'm seeing *that* as a ball of light. I'm seeing thousands of other balls of light, and then they're all whooshing into another place. It's as if the Earth is inside – emanates from the Source. Then what we call the Source, what we see as the Source, looks like that emanates from another.

D: So we're limiting it by thinking there is only one?

L: Right. And I'm hearing, it goes on and on and on and on. And this energy is there to be used by everyone.

I then asked about her purpose, what she was supposed to do with her life. This was one of her questions.

L: They show me that I keep going back and forth on my planet Earth – or that planet to somewhere else. But I didn't want to know my purpose on that world. I wanted to know my purpose on Earth. This world.

D: *Yes. These other things are interesting, but we have to live here in the physical right now.*

L: The words I'm getting are, "Just continue." And the feeling of it is that I always go by intuition. I'm always led here and there. To pay attention to the intuition.

Louise had a question about an unusual experience she had about 20 years before. It happened at night and she saw a ball of metal grid work with a hole in it, and she would go inside it.

L: I was going home. They want to tell me that, what was happening then was that a part of my human subconscious was starting to be aware of who I was and where I came from. And I was going back each night and learning. This is what's happening now. This is what's going to go on from now. They're showing me that, until that point, I was not actually bringing the black hole energy to Earth. I had come here and grown up, got used to Earth, then I was ready. This was about age 40. And each night I was going back and forth. I was just being reminded of where I came from. What I was on Earth for. And at the end, they said, "Now bring this to the world." Now at night, I go wherever. Let's see, what did the ball signify? They said, "It disappeared after that, didn't it?" Yes. I never saw it again after that. That was showing me it was an energy around me that was keeping things from being activated until I was ready. And the hole signified being released from that. And then going up and getting the information. And then I was ready. Well, for goodness sake!

CHAPTER TWELVE

UNDERGROUND

I have written about underground cities in *Book Two*, so the idea is not new. There is much mythology and legends involving people living underground, and I always believe that legends are based upon a grain of truth. Many times they have been embroidered and altered over the years to fit the cultures that revive or preserve them, but I have been told that their origins (no matter how dimly obscured) are based on real events. Yet the story told in this session was a different version.

When Marian came off the cloud, the scene she found herself in made her feel uncomfortable. She was standing in front of a huge oak tree that stood at the beginning of a dark forest. The forest came right up to the edge of the ocean with only a tiny bit of sand separating it from the water. The ground had been eroded or taken by the sea to where it was encroaching upon the trees. The trees were huge and very old, with black bark and gnarled knots, their leaves were small and narrow, unlike anything seen on Earth. This was one of the things that made her feel uncomfortable. There were so many of these strange and ominous trees that they blocked out the light in the woods. "The forest is cold. It shouldn't be this cold. It doesn't feel bad, but it doesn't feel right. The balance isn't right, or ... something is not correct." Then a revelation, "Oh! There aren't any creatures! There's no sound! There's nothing!"

She discovered she was a red-haired young man dressed in fur carrying a bow, knife and a quiver of arrows. He would normally use these for hunting animals, but he said, "I'm hunting for something else." Something that should be found in these unfamiliar woods. The trees grew very close together and formed a natural canopy that shut out the light, and formed a tunnel (or as she described it: a cave). "I am looking for something that should be at the end of this cave. The forest forms a cave because of the way it grows."

D: Have you been to this part before? (No) But there's something you are looking for?
M: I am hoping for.
D: How do you know it's there if you've never been to this part before?
M: I don't, that's why I'm searching.

He was going on faith alone, because the only way he knew about this thing he was looking for was from stories, tales that the people had told him. As far as he knew, none of his people had ever looked for it or tried to find it. So I was curious why he felt the need to search for it. "There is a reason: it's needed. I don't know why. It holds an answer to something."

D: An answer for you or for your people?
M: It's for the whole. You don't search for yourself.
D: Would that be selfish if you were looking for something just for yourself?
M: Yes! (He sounded astonished at the idea.)
D: What are the stories you've heard about this thing?
M: Just that it is here. You'll find it at the end of a cave. It holds the answers. It has what is needed to survive, to continue. It's in this cave somewhere.
D: Is it an object or what?
M: No. It's more of a being. It's hard to explain. It doesn't really take a form, but yet it can take many forms. The stories only speak of what it holds, and the idea of answers. It's a gift. I don't know how to explain this.
D: Is something going on in your time period that you need help and answers?
M: There are changes that are expected, major changes. Changes

that both create and destroy. All peoples, many places. It's
as if the Earth will turn upon itself, and you start again. It's
expected, but the knowledge of how to ride the waves, or
continue, has been lost.

D: *The tales tell you that it's coming?* (Yes) *Is anything
happening now? Any signs?*

M: Not where I live, but we know it's coming.

D: *But it could be a long time in the future, couldn't it?*

M: It's closer than we realize. You read, you see, you listen.
You hear the signs. You watch. Everything shows you, if
you listen hard enough, you can hear it.

D: *Your people must be very much in tune with nature if you
know these things.*

M: It's just the way you learn. Can't learn it any other way. You
have to. If you ignore it, you end up ... gone!

I asked him about the place where his people lived. There
were not many of them, and they lived in structures that were near
the woods. "They're made as part of the woods. If you look from
a distance, you cannot tell them from the forest. They blend in
and are hidden." Even though he was familiar with the woods,
the part he had journeyed to was very different and far from his
home.

I moved him ahead until he had gone through the woods (or
cave, canopy) to see if he had found what he was looking for. He
had difficulty describing it. "It has no form. It's very bright. It
changes form. It's not solid. Almost like liquid, but it's not
liquid. It's very, very *white*! I've never seen anything like this.
Sometimes it looks like an old man, and then it moves, or shifts,
or changes, and it looks like something else. But none of the
forms are solid!"

D: *Where did you find this being?*

M: It's at the very end of the cave. It's very broad, very big down
here. It's not like the passageway. It's not dark. I walked to

198

the edge of the cave, and I could see a glow in the opening. I was very surprised.

D: *Are you able to talk to this being?*

M: Yes and no. Not like I would talk to you, but like he would talk to me. It's the same as when you hear the trees, or you listen to the wind. It is not the same as when you talk to another. – He's given me a small piece of himself. (I didn't understand.) It fits in my hand. It's a small piece of it ... of him. I have to take it back. It would be as if you had water, and you took a scoop and scooped some out. But he's not liquid. It doesn't *feel* of water. (That was the best way he could describe it.)

D: *What does the piece look like?*

M: It's beautiful, but it's just ... *bright*! It's just like a yellow, white light. (Laugh)

D: *Different! But didn't you have something you wanted to talk to him about?*

M: This is it. This is what I take back.

D: *He didn't give you any answers?*

M: Yes, he gave me all the answers! They're in my hand! (Laugh) I'm going to take it back. This will keep us safe; this will ensure we go on. The ground will close, and it has to.

Then the man knew it was time to return to his home. He was just carrying the strange piece of light in his hand. "It's not cold. It is not hot. It is an unusual feeling. It is a good feeling. It's not heavy, but I know it's there. It's almost as if it's a part of, but yet separate from, my hand." I sped time up so he would arrive back at his home.

M: There is very little time. – It's starting. This has to go in the center.

D: *What is starting?*

M: The change, the Earth ... the flip! The Earth, it comes above and folds over. It is like making a cocoon.

D: What are you seeing?

M: *The Earth coming up and folding over!* This piece has to be in the center of the village. It has to be in the middle of the homes. And it will hold. It will keep everyone safe.

D: You said it was like a cocoon, like the Earth was folding over. You mean like dirt, or water or what?

M: It is mainly dirt. It has trees in it, but it is the Earth. It is how you would make a hollow shell, but very thick, very big.

D: Do you see this coming?

M: I see it making.

D: I would think that would be frightening to see that.

M: No, it was taught that this was supposed to happen. What was needed was the piece so we would survive. It will be a long time under before we come back.

D: And what do you do? Wait and watch?

M: That's all you can do.

D: I'm trying to get a mental picture of it, because I can't see it. So it's like dirt comes over the woods?

M: When you're in the sea and the waves come up high, it's the same. The dirt comes up like a wave, but because of the piece, it doesn't come down in the center. It goes over.

D: So your little area is like a hollow in the middle of it. (Yes) *Are the trees in there also?*

M: Some, not all.

D: You said it is like a cocoon. It just goes over.

M: Yes. It goes down. It has to go down. The whole goes down into the Earth, like a cocoon goes down into something. There will be many changes on the surface. This cocoon will go down *into* the ground. Deep, so it won't be affected.

D: And it's all your people?

M: It's all those that were at home. Many people did not make it, unfortunately.

Even though to me it seemed very strange, I suppose anything is possible.

M: It is the *only* way to survive now.

D: *Are you able to breathe inside there?*

M: Yes. It's the size of the village. It's the size of the area.

D: *Are you able to see?*

M: Because of the piece, yes.

D: *Are you able to continue living?*

M: Yes. They will live here for a long time. It will be many, many years long, before they come back.

D: *Why do you have to stay down there so long?*

M: How long does it take a tree to grow? What's gone is gone. It cannot come back immediately. They will have to relearn some of the old ways and hold the teachings. And when it's time, they'll go back to the surface.

D: *Are you able to find things to eat down there?*

M: There are many things under the ground to eat. We also have seeds that will grow.

D: *Are you able to go outside of this cocoon?*

M: Yes, it opens. There are large rooms.

D: *I wonder who put those rooms down there?*

M: The Earth. There are large holes in the Earth that you can go into. There are small lakes. The Earth has many secrets, and many beings, creatures. It's the same as listening to the trees and hearing the rocks, and speaking to the other creatures. The Earth is the same. It was ready for us; we just had to be ready for it.

D: *So there are also creatures down there?*

M: Many. Some we have not seen before.

D: *I wonder how they got down there?*

M: The same way we did.

This was sounding more and more like the underground city that was described in *Book Two*. In that book, it said there are many of these cities underground that still exist today. These were lit by a miniature sun, and there were also many animals (some unknown) and water.

201

D: *Are there other people?*
M: There will be. There are others who had the knowledge.
D: *Will you know when it's time to go back to the surface?*
M: Oh, yes. The Earth will tell. – This happened before. According to the tales, there had been a world before this. It did not grow the way it needed to. And so the Earth did what she needed to do. Those who could still hear and listen knew what to do. Those who could not were taken away.
D: *Was there a reason why it happened this time?*
M: For the same as the last; there were too many in the wrong direction not working with each other.
D: *So this is the way the Earth takes care of itself?* (Yes) *Well, do you stay down there for a long time?*
M: I will probably never make it back up.

This could take a long time, and one day would probably be just like the next. So I decided to take him forward to the last day of his life, and see what happened to him. "I see an archway, rounded. It has water running through it. I've fallen. Something hit. I was old. That's why I fell. My legs don't work the way they used to."

D: *But your people were able to live down there, and take care of themselves?*
M: Oh, yes. They did well. They *are* doing well. They will keep it up.
D: *Did you see any other people?*
M: There was a group that came from one of the holes a while back. They had made it through. They were only here for a little while and have gone back. The younger ones will go and visit and see. I never went. They're in another part of this underground place.
D: *But you didn't mind leaving the surface?*
M: No, it's sometimes harder. Little ones don't remember the outside. I do. They were too small. These beings will go on.

They will survive.

Now it was time to call forth the subconscious to get some answers that the man was unable to give us during his life. I always ask why the subconscious chose to show the subject that particular lifetime.

M: It's the same. It's the same lesson. There are teachings that need to go on. There are lessons that need to be passed on. This life is not completely useless. It's the same parallel.

D: *By a parallel, do you mean that you think the life she is living now will be the same conditions?*

M: Yes and no. It isn't exactly the same as she went through then. At this time, it is the same as far as what she is preparing for. There are many changes coming. There are pieces that are being lost that have to be passed on. Teachings. How to speak, how to talk; how to work with the Earth. How to understand and remember. How to listen to the leaves and the trees. How to hear what the voices of the animals, the winds are telling you. These are all out there. These are all real and she knows how to do this.

D: *But you know in our hectic modern society, it does get lost and pushed aside.* (Yes) *People don't pay attention to it.*

M: Or are told they're crazy if they do.

D: *But you think something is going to happen and these things will be lost?*

M: They are already being lost. Not just through people; through energy and time and space. These things have to be held onto. They are part of this planet. There are many Earth changes that are coming, but that is not the concern. The concern is the changes that mankind is bringing – there lies the real danger. Mankind as a whole is wiping out the knowledge of the balance; the ability to balance between nature and himself. It is a very destructive power and energy. And it will actually threaten mankind's existence.

203

D: What does this have to do with Marian's present lifetime?

M: Everyone plays their part. Every being on this planet has a unique role. She has to find hers. She knows what it is, but she doubts it. I cannot reveal it to her at this time. She has to find it. If she slows down and listens, she'll find the key to open that door.

I wanted to know more about the underground existence she described. It was similar, yet different from the other people's stories of this place. I was told that these cities do exist, and people will eventually find evidence of them.

D: I've heard other stories of this underground place, but I've never heard one where it just sank into the ground.

M: Everyone entered in a different manner.

D: Then it was an actual physical happening? (Yes) *The glowing piece that he took down there, what was that?*

M: That was part of a being that is one of the Protectors of this planet. There are many. This was the one that was closest to him.

D: He said this piece was like a light.

M: There were many *more* things involved in it, but the glow was part of it.

D: Also, when he went under the ground, it created a light down there so they could see. (Yes) *But it seemed to be able to protect the whole group as they sank into the ground.* (Yes) *So it was very powerful.*

M: Very much so. It had to be. You have to remember, this is part of a guardian of the Earth, so it is able to communicate with the Earth, because it is a part of it. Just as your hand will do as you ask it to do. Would not the Earth do what you ask it to, if you are a part of it?

D: I see. So it was able to form the cocoon and make this whole group descend into the Earth safely.

The legends of the Hopi Indians say that our present world is called the Fourth World. They believe the other three worlds were destroyed mainly due to the people's corruption and greed, and rebelling against nature. The First World was destroyed by the sinking of land and the separation of land caused by major earthquakes. The Second World was destroyed by freezing, the great Ice Age. The Third World was a world of high technology, even more than we have seen in our present time. It was destroyed by the Great Flood, and those of their people who listened to the prophets were guided to places of safety underground. When the Fourth World was ready, many of them emerged from their underground homes, and resettled on the surface. They were told that the Fourth World would be the world of destruction, and then the beginning of the Fifth World of peace. This last one sounds very similar to the New Earth that is explored in this book and *Book Two*.

This session also took place in an underground location, although it was not on Earth. When Joan descended from the cloud, she found herself in a strange barren, alien landscape. A very red crust, no vegetation. Red, jagged, severe-looking mountains. I then asked her to look down at herself to see what she looked like. She found it more curious than frightening when she looked at her feet and said, "The closest description I can come to is bird like. With the talons perhaps of a crane foot or an ibis foot, more like a three-pronged claw. They are more of a translucent beige toward silver color. A contrast to the landscape I've seen." She then described her body. "Long legs. Thin. Spindly, for lack of a better word. Seem to have, the only description I can find is more of a pod-like description of the body. Bird-like still, more of a teardrop shape body. I have a small neck. Most of the appendages seem more like wings, and then they turn into alien-looking hands instead of like my feet. More like thin arms with larger hands on the end of it. Six fingers, counting the thumb. I thought my face, my head, would be bird-like, but it seems to be more lion-like. Perhaps more cat-like. And I have shoulder length black hair." It sounded like a combination of different types, but definitely alien. I suppose there is no reason why it would have to be either cat-like or bird-like. In other worlds I suppose you could be any combination of anything. What is normal here might be abnormal there. So I go along with whatever description I am given and just continue to ask questions.

"Now I understand that the red place is an outpost. There are many others here, beings of all kinds. We are experimenting with something in this place. We are working with energy of some kind. I'm trying to see where I would be doing that. Whether I would be in a structure, or whether I would be doing something out in the open on the surface. Now I see that I am walking down some stairs to an underground facility where there is a huge – you could say 'city', but – civilization habitations, under the surface of this red place. There's something we're working on in this underground cavern, although it's more modern, more advanced. We are working together on some sort of experiment to do with – I want to say 'transmuting' energy. We are working on adapting energy to make it useful in other areas of the Universe. That's why there are all kinds of beings here. We're working together on something that will benefit all of us. Each in their own respective areas of the Universe will be able to learn and apply this knowledge and/or energy in a beneficial way. I don't know whether it's to make the energy of the Universe more beneficial and more utilitarian. Working on something new that will be beneficial. It will be used for absolutely positive things."

D: This is what the experiment has been about.

J: Yes. It's about using the energies in different, new ways to benefit the Universe. This is my job.

D: Do you live there in this underground place?

J: That's where I live now. Those of us that are here doing the experiment are all living in the underground places.

D: But the other beings are the ones that take it throughout the Universe?

J: Yes. I do not go. I am sending them out. There are many different forms here working on the same project.

D: Do you know if this energy is going to be used on the planet Earth?

J: Yes, it will eventually be used there.

D: I wasn't sure if where you are is even in the same Universe where Earth is located.

J: Yes, we are in the same Universe. It will be used on Earth eventually.

D: What will it be used for?

J: I'm having a block there. There are several applications that can be made, not just one. It would be determined by the person who is taking this back to the new areas. We are changing it in some way to take back, and be used in our respective places. But it's not going to be used in a structure. It's going to be more free energy that will be used beneficially for many different uses in many different places.

I moved Joan forward to an important day. She had difficulty locating anything specific. It was like drifting in and out of a mist. "I was trying to get some clarity. Right now I am seeing that the project itself is the most important thing I could be doing."

It became obvious that I would not be able to move Joan to anything connected with that life. So I decided to bring forth the subconscious to answer the questions about this lifetime she had seen. "Why did you pick that life for Joan to see?"

207

J: She needs to understand that she's working with energy. She knows it on some level, but she needs to understand that she has many more energy abilities than she has understood so far.

Joan, like many others who come to see me, was working with Reiki and using that form of energy healing to help people. It is amazing how many of my subjects either are healers already, or want to become healers. Many are being told they are to develop the use of energy in healing work. Joan was told she needed to continue to do this type of work, but that was not enough. "They" had bigger plans for her, as they do for many others.

J: She does need to focus more on sending energy out to the places where it needs to be sent, to strengthen, to balance during this new phase. At this time, she is here to be helping Earth do its energy changing and transforming. She and many others are here to ground and balance and share energy for the benefit of the Earth particularly. Everything is interconnected. Everything affects everything else.

D: *You said, "The new phase." What did you mean by that?*

J: There is much change happening, much transformation happening, much raising of energies happening, much confusion happening. There is a need for those here for this purpose to balance as well as help raise. That is her main purpose at this point. And also to share knowledge to help open people who are not aware of who they are. She's been limiting herself. She's entering a new phase and she's here to help others entering new phases of their awareness of the expansiveness of creation.

D: *Joan said, in her conscious state, she keeps hearing the words, or seeing the phrase, "Anchor the energy." Can you tell her what that means?*

J: Yes. She is here for that purpose. She is here to anchor the

208

new energy coming in. To hold it and to carry it and to introduce it to places where it has not been introduced before.

D: *How do you want her to introduce it?*

J: Just by the mere mental intent of holding, anchoring, introducing. She is an antenna for the introduction. It is coming to and through her and others, into the Earth and out from there. And her awareness of her purpose will help her intent to be more forceful, more expansive, more helpful.

D: *This person, this being on this other planet, who received all that information and knowledge, is she able to draw on what he received?*

J: That is where the knowledge and the information and the new energy is coming from. The experiment. It is being sent out much like a radio wave, a microwave or magnetic wave to her and others who are here for that purpose. Who have come here at this time for this reason to act as receivers. (She became emotional.) A love energy. Powerful, but loving energy that is transforming and raising and expanding the Creator energy that is coming in at this time and in this space. She is emotional because she is connecting to the person she was, working on this energy. And the knowledge and the awareness of why she is feeling this way is affecting her. She has only occasionally been in touch with this depth of love and healing, and that is causing the emotion.

D: *Was she seeing a past life?*

J: It's a parallel life. It is occurring simultaneously at the same time.

D: *That's what I was thinking. If they are experimenting with the energy, and Earth is receiving it now, it would have to be occurring at the same time.*

J: Yes, it is going on at the same time. But is also being beamed to other areas. She is receiving it here, and others are receiving it in other places that are ready to receive it. It is only going where it is appropriate.

D: *So she's both working on it and sending it out, and receiving*

209

it at the same time, because it is all happening simultaneously.

J: Yes, that's correct.

D: But she had to go through a normal life to get to this point, didn't she?

J: Yes, she did. She had to get to this point. The understanding of the physical life helped her to understand some things that she needed to learn, and pointed her in the direction of the information she needed to open herself. The Reiki was part of her touching back into the love energy, because that is part of the healing energy of the Universe, the Creator. It's another way of handling it. It's another way of experiencing it. It's another way of channeling energy. It's another way of transmuting energy. It's another way of getting it to someone else to use as their guiding system, if she so chooses to use it. It's something she needed to learn to be able to understand this step. She is here as a double vision to be the antenna, and she's also sending it. She is here for a purpose, like many beings on this Earth, and in the Universe, to learn how to use the energy to lift it to a higher level. To help in whatever way they can. And this is what she is doing in this lifetime.

This is the second wave of individuals that I have spoken about before. The ones who are supposed to act as channels or antennas of energy. Their main purpose is to direct the energy into the Earth to be used by others. Of course, none of these people are consciously aware of their missions.

NEW EARTH & HIDDEN CITY

Anita's session was unclear. It had a dreamlike quality that was confusing. It appeared she was onboard some type of craft where her body was being worked on. We got more information when I called the subconscious forth. It said that she was confusing being in two different places, and they were overlapping. It explained that she had been onboard a mother ship where they were healing her body and making some repairs. Then she was taken inside the Earth. I wanted to know why they took her *there.*

A: To make her aware that it was there, and what was going on. She's gone there many times. This is a place ... a kind of protection. Many animals are there, and it also will be a place for people to be taken at the time of change. For protection against the devastation on Earth, and the diseases that man sets off.

D: *Disease can't reach inside the Earth?* (No)

She saw a man and talked with him, and he seemed to be someone she knew. She also saw something shiny which she thought was a vortex. We were told it was a portal, and this was how the man traveled. The man said he had talked to various world leaders, and they wouldn't listen.

D: *Consciously?*
A: Some consciously. But they have their own agenda.
D: *Who contacts them?*
A: Different entities. Different groups.
D: *I am curious what a leader would think if they were contacted consciously.*
A: Some leaders are very aware of us higher beings and what is going on.

211

D: *They know you exist?*

A: Yes. But they don't want to give up their power.

D: *I think they would be surprised if they saw one of you.*

A: When I say "consciously", it is not necessarily face to face. It's more on a subconscious, mental level. Some of it is much like what happens to Anita. They are taken up and talked to.

D: *But they don't remember?*

A: Some do remember a part of it. But they don't want to relinquish their hold on Earth. Many are into the negative. At the time we talked to them, it was a crossroads. It could have happened. Changes could have started then, or they could have been postponed for a little bit longer.

D: *What kind of changes?*

A: War. And with more war comes more Earth changes.

D: *You mean the Earth changes are connected with the wars?*

A: The more negative the vibrations, yes. The energy.

D: *And it could have happened at that time?*

A: Yes. Crisis. But it was postponed once again. Someone made a different decision. One never really truly knows what exactly causes it to be postponed. Some little change from a leader that decides not to do something. It might have been more than one thing. It might have been several things. We never know what really caused it not to happen, but we were at a crossroads. And we'll be coming to more crossroads. With the changes comes *her* change, because she's aware. And she will know what to do. She doesn't need to know yet, because she wouldn't know what to do with it. The information or the power.

D: *What kind of power?*

A: Ability power. Ability to do things, and see things. To be able to help people. Heal people. I don't think she really needs to know right now what she's supposed to be doing. She would think about it too much.

212

The terrible tsunami had recently occurred at Christmas 2004 in Indonesia. It had caused the death of over 200,000 people. I wanted to know if it was caused by negative energy.

A: No, not necessarily negative. Everyone tries to connect it with negativity, but it's going to be a natural thing. The ones that needed to go, left. The ones that needed to stay, stayed. What people call "miracles", babies on mattresses, men on trees. Some of the ones that left will go on to other places. And some have higher work to do, and some will start their lives over somewhere else. So they had many reasons for leaving.

D: *But they went out in such a large group.*

A: Right. It's going to get bigger. Massive. It's going to be the change. But now some negative things that men do will cause earthquakes to come sooner, or tidal waves to come sooner. Or disasters of some sort to come sooner. Because everything we do affects the nature, affects the Earth. There's a consequence for everything we do.

SECTION FOUR

FIRST-TIMERS ON EARTH

CHAPTER THIRTEEN

THE VOLUNTEERS

When I first began my investigations through past-life therapy, I thought I would only find people remembering lives on Earth, because naturally that was all we knew about. My belief system has really been stretched and extended over the past 30 years. My first exposure to life outside of our world and everything we see around us was when I met Phil. His story is told in *Keepers of the Garden*. At first, he remembered normal past lives, and the sessions proceeded normally as I expected they would. This was probably the way it should be because neither of us were prepared to explore beyond that, nor to even know that anything else was possible. Then as we worked, he surprised me by reliving lives on other planets in alien bodies. This was my first encounter with this type, and at times I was at a loss for words. What do you ask an alien? As the work progressed, I was given a great deal of information about the seeding (or beginning) of life on Earth, because "they" said it was time for the knowledge to come forth. We both settled in and became comfortable with the unusual, and my curiosity took over and the questions flooded forth. It was explained that Phil was one of many spirits who had never lived on Earth before. They had volunteered to come and help the Earth at this time in its history. They had no conscious memory of this (naturally) and thus their lives had been difficult. They did not like being on Earth. They had difficulty adjusting to the violence here. They longed to return "home" although they had no idea where "home" was. They just knew it wasn't here. Their problems were caused by the fact that where they came from there was only peace, beauty and love. It was quite a decision to volunteer to come to such a radically different environment. They did it out of love and the

217

desire to help, even though their adjustment has been difficult, and even impossible in some cases.

Then there was the question: if he had never lived on Earth before, why did he go through the memories of several past lives before the other startling information came through? This was reason to doubt my work. Did this mean that reincarnation was not real? That the past lives I had been investigating through so many subjects were mere fantasies? Maybe the Church was right, we only live once and that is it? How else to explain this unexpected development. The answer was that the lives he thought he was reliving were only *imprints*. I had never heard of this before, and I was the first writer to find this theory. It is explained in detail in *Keepers of the Garden* and *Between Death and Life*. The condensed version is that a soul cannot exist on Earth in a human environment without the information and data of past lives in its subconscious. It must have something to relate to and fall back on; otherwise, everything is too new, too drastic, too overwhelming. Just as we have the experience of our childhood to explain the many things we come in contact with, the information and experiences from our past lives also gives us a background to relate to. This means that no one, no infant, comes in as a clean slate. It always has the background of other lives and experiences in its subconscious mind to help it relate to life in the physical. Of course, we are not conscious of any of this, just as we are not consciously aware of our past lives. Many of us do not even consciously remember events from our childhood. This does not mean that they do not exist.

The theory of imprinting is similar to doing research in a library. The spirit is going to be entering into an unknown and totally unfamiliar environment. It would be totally lost without some type of background. So before it comes into the body, it is allowed to pick other people's lives from the vast inventory in the library (or Akashic records) that it thinks will benefit it when it enters the physical. I was told this would apply to anyone, not just an alien soul. For instance, a person has decided to live a life as a leader of some sort. The spirit has never had a past lifetime like that. How will it know what to do? How will it know how to take command and control of a situation if it has never been exposed to such an experience? In that case, it will select the lives of leaders: Presidents, kings, governors, sea captains, people who had lived lives of leadership. These are then *imprinted* onto the soul, and become a part of their soul memory. If it is thus useful to the ordinary spirit returning to Earth, it can be seen how necessary it would be for an alien soul coming for the first time to such a strange and often hostile place as the planet Earth.

I asked, "How will I know the difference when I work with someone? How will I be able to tell if what they are remembering is an actual lifetime or an imprint?" The answer I was given was that I would not be able to tell the difference, because the person would not know the difference. The imprint becomes as real as an actual life. All the memories, emotions and feelings are there. The only difference I can see is that the imprint carries only information, and no karma. This is also a legitimate explanation to the argument that skeptics often bring up about reincarnation. They say, "Why do the people always remember lives as famous people, Cleopatra or Napoleon?" In the first place, this is not true. People do not always remember lives as famous people. The majority of their remembrances are of dull, boring, mundane lifetimes where little of importance happens. I have had people who were *associated* with famous people, but I have never had anyone who regressed to where they were *the* important person. There are many more ordinary people in the world today than those who get their names in the newspaper. And there always have been more ordinary people, thus that is what will come forth. But to get back to the argument that the skeptics present: if there were two or more people who claimed to have been a famous person in another life, it would not mean that one of them is lying or fantasizing. One or both of them could be remembering an imprint, because there is no way to tell the difference.

Now that I work so exclusively with the subconscious and its vast storehouse of information, if a lifetime is an imprint it will tell me so. This is the way I can now tell the difference. There will be examples given in this book. However, the theory of imprinting is one more piece of a huge and complicated puzzle that we call "life", and which I am continuing to explore.

Over the years since I worked with Phil and wrote the book, I have come in contact with others who felt the same way. As the book was translated into other languages and began to circulate in foreign countries, I received mail from people who were so grateful for the book. They thought they were the only ones in the world who had those feelings: of not wanting to be here, of not understanding the violence in the world, of wanting to go "home", of entertaining thoughts of suicide in order to get out. It has helped them tremendously to know they are not crazy, that they are not alone. That they are one of many who volunteered to come and help the Earth go through its crisis mode. They just were not prepared for the repercussions on their gentle souls.

As I wrote about in *Book Two* of this series, I have now found three waves of people who are living their first lives on Earth. The first wave are the age of Phil, roughly in their late forties (early fifties) now. They had the most difficult time adjusting. The second wave are now in their late twenties and early thirties. They have not had as many problems and are moving through life much more easily. They usually live a life of helping others, creating no karma and normally going unnoticed. During the sessions, they are described as "antennas", "channels", "observers", just directors of energy that is needed by the Earth. Many do not want children because that would create karma, and they do not want to be tied to the Earth cycle. They just want to do their work and get out. The Earth experience does not affect them as traumatically as the first wave. The third wave are the new children, many of whom are now in their teens. They have come in with all the knowledge needed (on the unconscious level), their DNA has already been altered, and they are prepared to proceed with little or no problems (except for those created by well-meaning and unknowledgeable adults). I asked one time, "Why did the first group have so many problems and difficulty adjusting?" The answer was that they were the "trail blazers", the "way-showers". They prepared the path for those that followed. Thus, their difficulties have served a purpose.

Since my first meeting with Phil in the 1980s, I have now encountered many people (through my work) who are experiencing their first lifetime on planet Earth. None of these people had this knowledge before we did the sessions. They are now being allowed to have the information, because it is time to acknowledge who they are and their purpose on Earth at this time.

James came to my office in Arkansas for the session mainly to explore an unusual experience he had as a child. He had never forgotten it. It had some indications of a possible missing time episode, but not many other details. Since it had bothered him all these years, this was what he wanted to explore rather than going into past lives. I regressed him back to the night of the incident, but he could not get any more information than he consciously remembered. His conscious mind also wanted to maintain control, because he was afraid he would make up something. I persisted, and some information began to surface. Mostly bodily sensations, floating and the feeling of being inside a small craft. Then the feeling of movement, and a shocking revelation. "Forward; forward – elsewhere, very, very fast. When it moved, when it ... *jumped?* It made me feel ... split apart, like atoms." Even though it sounded strange, he described the sensation of feeling good when this happened. "Like demolecularization, but not in a bad way; just necessary. It is necessary in order to travel.

221

You can not travel in the physical body. It's too fast. The body would break. So they demolecularize me till they can put me back together later. It's contained within the light, within the dome area. Maybe the light holds it or keeps it from going everywhere." He was not aware of anyone else that he could ask questions. I asked if there was any way he could get information. "Not yet. Because I'm in pieces! I have to be put back together. (Laugh) I don't do it. Something does it." Then the dizzying feeling of moving again very fast. Then a surprise, as he was reassembled, he had a different form, and looked more like one of the little gray ETs. He had difficulty explaining the sensations that were going through his mind. "I feel it's not *me*-me-me. Like the memories of me in something else." He was communicating with others like himself. Then confusion again as he tried to describe what he saw. "Earth panels on the walls, and they do stuff. Training."

D: *Who are you training?*
J: Me! Like a workshop. Everything, the skills, Earth knowledge in the panels. It's complicated. Systems, function, form ... not history, but ... fundamental ... basics!
D: *And you're learning this or teaching it?*
J: Learning ... well, both! Teaching it *to* myself.
D: *Is this knowledge of the ship you're on or what?*
J: It could be if I wanted it to. The knowledge can be whatever is there; whatever is stored on this ... thing.
D: *What kind of knowledge do you like to access?*
J: Games, but not like video games, but *like* video games. Simulated. *Life* games. I can program in what I want. (He seemed to be struggling with the concepts.) There's interference .... This is very similar to something on TV. It's not the same – it doesn't look the same – but the concept is the same.
D: *Do you mean it downloads the program to you?*
J: Yeah. It plays it out.

He then discovered that he had something on his head that was pressing against his temples.

J: That's what the *temple* things are for! The things that go on my head. That's where the information goes in. Somebody else does it, but not unwillingly. – Does the *memory* transfer from there to here, or ...?

D: *You said it was games of life?*

J: Scenarios, but big ones. Long scenarios, of what it was like.

D: *Are there more than one of these?*

J: Lives. Any possibility you want!

D: *Do you pick what you want to download?*

J: Sometimes. Others are given, like an assignment.

D: *It's downloaded, and you're able to see what's going to happen?*

J: (Sigh) You live it, but not ... you only live it as much as anyone can live. It's an illusion. It's put in your brain and you live it, but not .... You take the experiences from it without actually living it.

D: *Is there a reason for doing that?*

J: Knowledge and ... *empathy*, maybe? But ... understanding. The question is, "Why do it?"

D: *That's what I was wondering.*

J: The answer is, "For *knowledge*." For knowledge, is all that comes. Knowledge to help – maybe to help *future* people? It's to help. I don't know how, though. – It's like a library, only a different version. More ... not ethereal, but solid. More technology driven rather than just essence.

D: *So this is done for a reason, to help the body that's existing on Earth – the physical body?*

J: Preparation. The word is, "Life," but ... the experience of life. Preparation.

Although it sounded confusing I thought I knew what he was attempting to describe, but I didn't want to influence him. I wanted him to tell it in his own words. Yet more information would not come forth. Something was definitely blocking it, and I didn't think it was James himself. I thought it was time to call forth the subconscious to find answers. When I knew it was there, I asked if I had permission to ask questions. An authoritarian voice answered, "Yes, but *tread lightly!*" I understood that James was not ready to have everything revealed, because it was obvious he did not understand the bits and pieces he was being shown. I would have to be careful and obey the subconscious' instructions, or it would shut down and I would not be allowed any more answers. I told it I would not push, but only accept what it wanted James to know. The subconscious said that what was shown only confused James, and that he had not developed enough yet to understand. He still had much to learn.

D: *Do you think the pieces you have shown him will help him?*
J: He will ask more questions.
D: *Why did he feel like the molecules had all shifted?*
J: Because they had! The molecules break apart so that they can be formed back into ... but only because of the travel. When he travels it has to or he will break.
D: *He was shown, when this happened, that he had changed into this other being. Is that existing at the same time as James is existing?* (Yes) *What is it? A transfer back and forth?*
J: It's the same only in the respect of it all existing at once.

I attempted to get more information about the missing time episode, but I was told it was not time for James to know, and no more could be shown. He would have to wait until he had reached another level of understanding. He was still in an early stage of learning. "They" have told me before that some knowledge is as poison rather than medicine. It can cause problems if it cannot be understood correctly, or if it is given prematurely. This seemed to be the case with James.

D: *Was he describing the process known as imprinting?* (Yes!) *Where other lives are imprinted into the memory to act as a reference guide, so to speak?*
J: A catalogue.

The subconscious was still holding back, but I got it to admit that James was part of the new people who were coming to Earth, who had never experienced a human body before. He was definitely here for a purpose, but the exact nature of it was not allowed for him to know yet. "He can have glimpses, flashes, but never all. It would be too much."

D: *Nobody* made *him come, did they?*
J: No. He volunteered to come at this time. He knew it would be painful, but he is strong.
D: *Can you tell him anything about what's he's supposed to be doing?*
J: Live the examples and they will follow. He's a teacher. Rules; laws – not Earthly; not man laws. Through his interaction with people, he teaches – not by word – but by deed. His aura or energy affects others.
D: *He thought he was supposed to go out and talk to people, and tell them about things.*
J: The message is lost in the fervor. This is the only way he knows, but the mental telepathy .... Subconsciously. *James* doesn't pass it.
D: *Who passes it then?*
J: The knowledge itself ... conductor ... James is like a beacon. Radiating the energy; passing it off. If you have a wall and you throw something against it, it will fall. If you have another wall, and you have it far away, when you throw this idea – this thing – at it, it will still fall. But when they are *close*, they vibrate fast. It bounces back and forth faster. The

beacon is stronger. The signal is stronger.

D: Because it's amplified.

J: Yes, James must understand that being human is hard work. If he follows the feeling of love, he cannot turn down a path that is wrong.

So what started out to be an examination into a possible UFO case instead turned into the exposure of yet another of the second wave of volunteers who have come to help. James was a very gentle soul, very much affected by the world around him. It would be a while before he had learned enough and had evolved enough to have more answers. In the meantime, he was just to fulfill his mission of being a channel, a beacon, for the incoming and outgoing energy that is needed on Earth at this time. Yet it is another example of the difficulty these gentle souls have when they come into our alien and hostile environment.

THE VISITOR

Judy was one of many I have met during my thirty years of working with clients, who have the feeling they don't belong here. They don't want to be here, and have a difficult time adjusting to our world. She went through a normal regression, but we did not find her answer until we contacted the subconscious. I asked it to explain these feelings that she had.

J: She's never felt at home on this planet. There are other places in the Universe where the energy is better, where she feels loved, and she feels like she belongs. Other places she's lived where people love each other, where people live in peace, where people help each other, people care about each other.

226

D: *Why did she come to Earth if she was happier in those places?*

J: Because it's her job.

I had heard this so often it was beginning to sound like a broken record. Yet why would so many of my clients say the same thing unless it was true? They have no way of knowing what the others have said.

J: There are those of us who look at other places in the Universe. And we see places that need assistance. And we know that we have to assist in order to preserve our way of life, in order to preserve our peace.

D: *How does what happens here reflect on your way of life?*

J: It pollutes the Universe. We're all together, we're all related, and when others lower their vibration it affects us also. – But it's not only because we are loving, very loving, peaceful people. Not only do we want to remain that way. We would like others to share in what we have, and what we've found. People on this planet are not happy. This planet that we're on now, on Earth, they struggle every day. They don't know what it's like to live in complete happiness and complete peace, to be one with the Creator, but it's our job to assist them.

D: *Were you able to see what is happening on other planets from where you were?*

J: We can see all that we wish. If we wish to see it we can see it. What's happening here is that sadness spreads from one to another. Each time they are saddened it spreads. There is so little here to change that.

D: *So when your people saw these things happening on Earth, you decided to come here?*

J: Yes. We needed to assist. We thought we would make a difference. We're beings of great love; great, great love and great peace. When we see other souls troubled, it is our nature to assist. It helps us to feel fulfilled.

D: *But when you got here, it wasn't that easy?*

J: It wasn't. We want to help, that's why we're here, but it's very difficult for us to survive here. It is so alien to us. Our vibration is much higher. This causes the problem. On our planet, she was a great healer. She will not be happy unless she continues that work.

D: *Is there any type of method she should use?*

J: On our planet we simply think of the healing and it is done. On your planet this is not quite as simple. So many doubts have been implanted in so many places that sometimes you need your little gadgets or methods that you feel assist you in healing, but the healing comes from within. All the energy comes from the great Source. When she truly forgives herself and integrates into this life, the healing will flow easily from her. She will be able to help others. She will not necessarily need to have all the methods that she's tried to study. It will just flow. She will just know how to do it. She will do it with her hands. Sometimes it is helpful to do that. Our healing can also be done at a distance because we are all connected. It's so easy to do this where we are from. It's very difficult to come here to this planet and not be able to do the same thing.

D: *Of course, you have to have the person's permission even if they are at a distance, don't you?*

J: Absolutely. People on this planet don't give their permission consciously, but they do give permission where it is the soul's mission to heal. She'll be able to do these things. On our planet it is so easy for those of us who are trained. We think it, and it is so. On our planet the vibration is much higher, and here on Earth it is much lower. It's very frustrating to her that it doesn't happen instantaneously here.

D: *What about the allergies that Judy has?*

J: The allergies are her fighting to be away from this atmosphere, from this planet, from the energy here on this planet, by constantly blocking the lower vibrations. She doesn't like the way it feels here. She doesn't want to breathe it, her body wants to fight it off, wants to get rid of it, wants to get rid of everything here.

D: *There's always free will involved.*

J: We cannot force things, it's not our way. There is much change on this planet now. More and more people will be awakened. But it is so difficult for us to come from a place of such love and happiness to this place.

The following is another example session of first-timers or volunteers:

Shirley came off the cloud into what she described as "desolation". "Everything that was living is not there anymore. Everything is gone. Something has caused it to go away. It's just brown earth or dirt, or craters. Whatever was there is not there anymore. (She became emotional.) Nothing. (Crying) I think this was home. (Sobbing) It was destroyed. But I'm not sure what did it. It was beautiful with meadows and forests and trees. What came to my mind was the Garden of Eden."

I asked her to see it the way it was before the destruction occurred. "I see many trees. I see running streams. I see weeping willow trees. It's like a beautiful garden. There are flowers and birds, and animals walking around. A unicorn just walked by. She's white, a long mane, pointy horn on the forehead. She's beautiful. It's a wonderful, perfect place. As far as the eye can see, it's just an idyllic picture. When I perceive my body I sense it as a blending. I feel the male, and then I feel the female, too. And I feel the two together. I can see a human form, but it feels more like an energetic human form. Like you're not really a physical body. I don't feel like I have to eat anything. It's the beauty of everything keeps me alive. That's all it takes.

The connection with nature. (Becoming emotional again.) The thought that came into my mind is that also the thing that keeps me alive is my connection to God, to my Man, to my Father. That's what keeps me alive. When I'm there at this time, I feel at peace, because it's so beautiful. And everything is working in harmony, together."

I decided to move her ahead to find out what happened to this perfect place. I assured her it would not bother her to see it.

S: Something came and scorched everything and destroyed it. All I see are these flames coming down from the sky and burning everything.

D: *Can you see where it's coming from? Because you'll be able to see it and understand it and talk about it.*

S: (She hesitated.) The first thing I saw was a dragon. (Laugh) My mind goes, no, that's not right. (Laugh) – I just keep seeing a dragon, that's all I see. I see flames shooting out of its mouth. It's green with big scales. It's flying around in the sky.

I wasn't worried about this unconventional reply. I decided to go along with whatever she was seeing. I knew that before the session was over, the subconscious would explain everything, if it wasn't clarified along the way.

S: I get a sense that there was somebody that was jealous of this place, and they sent the dragon to destroy it.

D: *Couldn't they have a beautiful and perfect place of their own?*

S: I'm sure they could have. They didn't want anybody else to have it. They didn't want anyone to be happy.

D: *What happened to you when everything was destroyed?*

S: I feel like I left. I didn't want to stay there any more, because it was gone.

D: *You'll be able to see what happened from that perspective. Can you see more about these other beings or whatever they were, that were jealous?*

S: (Chuckle) I'm seeing a land of giants. They're very large. Large bones, large legs, large arms, muscular. It's like a community, but there's one leader that is not nice. He knew about the place that was beautiful. There was jealousy and anger.

D: *Are there dragons where they live?*

S: Yes. (Laugh) They were small compared to the giants. They're like their pets.

D: *So that was the type of creature they sent to destroy your place. (Yes) I wonder what kind of satisfaction that would give them.*

S: Nobody could live in joy, or peace, or harmony. It was just destroyed.

D: *So what did you do after the place was destroyed?*

S: I feel like I floated around for a while. Then I went to visit my Father for a while, because He loves me. I feel the love and the energy flowing through. I feel nourished. I feel unconditional love.

D: *Can you see what the Father looks like?*

S: I just see this ball of light, life energy. There are others that are there. We have to nourish ourselves. I can't stay long. I feel like I'm being given my next assignment.

D: *What is your next assignment?*

S: I have to come to Earth.

D: *You don't look very happy. Do you have a choice?*

S: No, I don't feel like I had a choice. It's an assignment, a job. Somebody has to do it, because nobody else will. I think that's why I've been so angry at Him, at my Father, because it wasn't a choice. It was like when you work for somebody. They tell you to do it, or else. Like when you're in the service, you take orders? That's what it felt like, because I had to go again.

D: *But you had such love for Him, too.*

S: I do, but I was angry because I had to go. I wouldn't have

231

chosen to come to Earth. I was given that assignment to come here.

D: *Tell me what happens as you come to Earth. What's the procedure?*

S: I see myself going through different stages as energy. It feels like different stations, or different posts, or getting different information, or steps. Like checking in with different entities and beings before coming here, and each one giving me information. But it feels like I'm not in physical form. And they're all giving me advice or information to be used.

D: *Then what do you do whenever you finally get to Earth?*

S: Well, I have to be born. I've done it several times, but not lately. There's something here that I have to accomplish. This time there's a sense of mission. I'm here to do something (getting emotional) and I don't know what it is. But I know that I have something *big* to do.

D: *But the first step is to be born as a baby?* (Yes) *Does it feel different to be in a body again?*

S: Yes, yes. I feel confined. The other way was very free. And this way I feel different. I'm a beautiful baby girl. I wanted to be a girl. It just felt like the right thing to be this time, for the assignment.

D: *How do you feel about being in that body?*

S: I've never felt comfortable in that body. I've always had a poor body image. Even though I wanted to be female, it was hard seeing myself as a female. I didn't like looking in the mirror. I didn't like what I saw. I felt that the anatomy was different. (Laugh) When I look in the mirror, I think I should see this beautiful glowing being of light. It's who I am underneath.

D: *But you took on this casing, this outer shell. And you have to stay in this shell for a while till you do what you're supposed to do.*

S: Yes. I know it's to help other people. That's what I'm feeling. I think the other times I came it was free will, free choice. This time it wasn't. This time is different. I would have rather come on my own free will as opposed to having an assignment. It's important, but I don't know why. I don't know what for. I know it's to help other people. To help heal other people.

I asked the subconscious to come forth and explain why it showed Shirley the place that had been destroyed. "Why did you choose that one? What were you trying to tell her?"

S: That there was a perfect place. She can go there and reconnect when she needs to be nourished. She's able to connect all beings, all creatures, and talk to them. They try to communicate with her, but she's been blocking them. She's afraid it isn't real. She doesn't have to be afraid, because it is real. She will be able to heal people's hearts and minds with her voice. She will help them heal on all levels: physical, mental, emotional, and spiritual. She'll be able to do that by talking. Communicating about God and about what life is about. She does not have to be afraid. We will protect her. We will give her guidance.

D: *That place that she saw that was full of so many strange creatures. Was that a real place?*

S: Yes, at one time it was.

D: *With the unicorns and giants and dragons?* (Yes) *We think of them as fantasy or legends.*

S: No, they existed.

D: *Was it on Earth?* (No) *What we have now in our stories, are they just memories of that place?*

S: Memories of another time gone by.

D: *I was wondering why we have these in our stories today, in our world.*

S: Because they existed at one time. They were real.

D: *You mean the memories are in our minds?* (Yes) *So what we think is a story or a fairy tale has a basis in truth?*

S: I believe that, yes.

The following is another example session of first-timers or volunteers:

At first, it sounded like a normal past life when Beth saw herself as a young male in an Arabian market. This began to change when he became aware that he was carrying a book. "It's an instruction manual. The laws of physics. I try to simplify it to teach the people. I am only in this area for a short time, then I go to other places to teach." He had been doing this for three years, and did not have a home that he could return to.

D: *Do you think the book is complicated or hard to teach?*
B: No, I've always known this information. I am bringing this forth from a higher source. The healing energy from this information is very powerful. The book and the energy that's associated with the information.
D: *So it's different than normal physics. Is that what you mean?*
B: Yes. There's information attached to the words, but the people don't hear it. It's for their good, for their higher understanding, for their evolution.
D: *Where did you get the book?*
B: I wrote it to simplify the information to deliver the message to the people. They're really just notes to remind me of what areas to cover. It's more of an outline.
D: *Can you give me an example of what you would tell them?*
B: (Pause) Something about fish, there are fish in the ocean. And the fish swim at a rate that pushes the water away. The faster the fish swims, the more water it pushes away, and the more pressure on the fish. That is the law of inertia.

D: *What does that really mean?*
B: That it's one of the laws of the planet, gravitational law.
D: *And about the fish?*
B: It just refers back to one of the laws of this planet.
D: *The law of gravity?*
B: In inertia.

He traveled from place to place teaching anyone who would listen. He loved going to different places and meeting different people. He was not paid, so I wondered how he was taken care of, how he was able to eat and sleep.

B: I don't have to sleep very much. I don't have to eat. Only for pleasure. Everything I need, I create.
D: *Your body can exist without food?* (Yes) *But isn't your body physical?*
B: Sometimes. When I teach, I come into the physical. And when I have other needs, I leave the body and come to where I can get what I need ... up somewhere. My body is more of an energy body than a physical body.
D: *Where do you go when you don't have a physical?*
B: Oh, I go on a ship.
D: *Is there a ship near there?*
B: Yes, stationed there, but it's not on the ground. It's in the sky. It's round, and it's quite a large ship. It fits 200 people.
D: *Do they also go back and forth?*
B: Some do, to different parts of the planet.
D: *When you're on that ship, what kind of a body do you have?*
B: I never really actually looked at me, I looked at others. I have a very small mouth and a big head, and large eyes – large fingers.
D: *Do all the beings on the ship look alike?*
B: Yes. They don't wear clothes. They have flesh colored, thin bodies.
D: *Do you have what we call "sexes"?* (Yes) *So there are male*

235

and female?

B: Yes. Their physical anatomy is the same. We know them by their *essence.*

D: *What essence do you have when you're on that ship?*

B: Male. When I am on the ship I help organize the teachers that go down on the planet to teach.

D: *Do they all teach different subjects?*

B: Yes. The female, she teaches health. There's a male, he teaches sciences, but on terms that the people can understand ... at their level of understanding. I just learned more, have been exposed to more, and had more experiences. We're all taught how to speak on a level that the beings can understand. We can beam down to wherever we want on the planet. And I am focusing my studies and work in that one particular area at this time. But others go to other parts of the world, the planet.

D: *So the main thing they're all trying to do, is give knowledge and information to the beings of Earth.* (Yes) *Were you instructed to do this by someone?*

B: I had to have been instructed. We're from a larger ship.

D: *That one sounds large if it has two hundred beings.*

B: No. There are thousands of beings on the other ship. They are all different kinds. On the smaller one it is mostly my type.

There was an original home planet they had come from, but they didn't go back there very often. "I'm focused on my mission and my job."

D: *So once you're assigned to a ship, you stay there a long time?*

B: Yes, but it's not about time. There is no time. It's measured in teachings and the amount of people I've been able to reach. I know of the concept that humans have about time. I know of it, but I don't understand it, because everything is simultaneous. I teach until I feel I'm ready to learn more.

And then I gain more knowledge and take it back down to the people again. I go to different places and look like one of them. So people do not become suspicious of me and start to ask questions. "Where do I come from?" I move so they don't ask questions.

D: *Do you want them to use the information?*

B: Eventually. If they do not need it now, they will be able to use it at some point in time. But it is raising their conscious awareness.

D: *Mostly you come to educate. That's the mission of your people?* (Yes) *On the bigger ship, do they have other missions?*

B: Many, many missions. They go to many places. They do not interact with the people the way we do. They are more involved with the interaction of the planets, the Universal goal: harmony and peace.

D: *What can they do to affect the planets?*

B: Protecting the planets from self-destruction. Bringing light and love, and helping the people to create harmony amongst themselves.

D: *If one planet is out of harmony, does that create problems?*

B: Yes, for everyone! For all the planets. Everyone is affected through the energy, because the energy ripples through the Universe.

D: *So the majority of the people on the large craft are interacting in different ways. But it's to help the people of Earth?*

B: Not necessarily Earth. No – many planets. I don't have time. I don't have reference to maps. And I don't know everywhere these beings go, and what everyone is doing. There are too many people. Too many different missions. My job at this time is to help the people of Earth.

D: *But the large ship is stationed somewhere else?*

B: It's farther away from our ship. That's why they are working on different projects. It's much farther away. We report back

237

to them.
D: *If you don't have to eat, what keeps you alive?*

I already knew the answer to this, but I am always asking the same questions to get more validity. If many people give the same answer, then it most likely is the truth.

B: Light.
D: *How do you get the light?*
B: Just absorb it into my body.
D: *Where does the light come from?*
B: It doesn't come from anywhere specifically. It's just all around. It's not like I feed off something. It's just absorbed through the body.
D: *Does the body die, if you know what I mean? Does the body cease to exist at any time?*
B: Yes. The body will wear out. When the body has been used for a period of time, then we dispose of it and retain a new body.
D: *The body becomes where you can't use it any longer?*
B: That's not right. No, the body does not die. It's energy. It's renewable.
D: *You mean the body is reduced to energy?*
B: No, it *is* pure energy.
D: *But you said after a certain length of time, you go to a different one?*
B: That's not us. That's some of the other beings on the ship. Their bodies would cease to exist, because some are more physical, and some are more energy. Mine is more energy.
D: But you have chosen to have this appearance on the ship, that you were talking about?
B: Yes. It resembles where I come from, the beings on my home planet, where I've spent a lot of time.
D: *I was thinking that a body that was pure energy wouldn't need to be in anything, would it?*

B: Well, it has a shape, like an outline, but it's less ... solid? We move more freely about than a being that would be more in the physical form.

I decided we were not going to learn much more at this point, so I moved him ahead to an important day. From the description, I think he may have moved into another life, although it still appeared to be alien, and more physical. He became very distressed and upset, and showed signs of discomfort as he described what was happening. "We're at war with ... is galactic ... a war. Many, many ships."

D: *Are they in Earth's atmosphere?*
B: No. (He was near tears.) I don't know where we are. We are out in space somewhere. (Emotional) This doesn't have to happen! There's no reason why we are fighting! Fighting serves no purpose!
D: *Did someone attack you?*
B: There are many, many represented in these different ships. It's not between two. It's between four different groups. They all want the same thing. It was caused by misunderstanding and the lack of communication.
D: *I thought when you reached this point there wouldn't be any need for violence.*
B: No. These beings are from a planet that is full of greed and hatred. They want everything to themselves. They are not part of our group.
D: *What was the misunderstanding that caused it?*
B: I don't know. Land? Property? It was over some area that was ours, and they wanted it. They built an alliance with another group. The fighting has been going on for a long time. We are all using some type of weapon that will shoot from the craft, smart craft. Very loud. The energy, when they fly past, is horrible. When it hits, it disables part of the ship. I don't want to fight, but we have to. It's the last resort.

239

We've tried everything and they will not understand. They will not try to listen. They will not try to come to an agreement and settle this peacefully. We have tried negotiation. We have tried everything. This is the only way they know to resolve conflict. We have no choice.

I moved her ahead in time to see how the conflict ended, to see what eventually happened.

B: They're gone. And we have our land. We can repair it and renew it. We have our planet and can live in peace again. We didn't die. We survived. It's back to harmony and peace again, which is good. They went somewhere else, or they're not there anymore. We were victorious in this, if you want to call it victory. Some of them perished. But they've decided to take their wars elsewhere.

Since the conflict seemed to be resolved, I moved her ahead to another important day, and it seemed that she had again jumped into a different life, yet still in an alien form. Nothing that she had covered so far even faintly resembled a physical Earth life. When she went into the next scene, she at first had difficulty explaining what she was seeing.

B: I don't know what it is. It's this barren planet. But there's something all around this part of the planet. I'm trying to figure it out. Oh! (A revelation.) We found there's a new planet that needs to be inhabited. It is barren. It is the beginning of ... the birth of a new planet. There are many ships there that are encircling this half of the planet. And they're from all different places. But we're working together as a group to bring forth life to this planet.
D: *It doesn't have any life at all at this point?* (No) *What do you need to do to bring forth life?*
B: Plant organisms on the planet and they will multiply.

240

D: *Where do you get the organisms?*
B: We brought them from other places.
D: *Is this what you do, collect them in different places?*
B: No. I help with organizing and planting vegetation on this planet. Each craft has their own specialty, and my specialty is vegetation.

I did not realize that he was in another lifetime, so I asked, "You were doing the teaching. Is this a different assignment?"

B: That was something else. That was not me.

Then I understood. She had moved into a different lifetime, but still as an alien. Beth's voice slowly began to change from this point. It became clipped and robotic. She described herself as having a short grey body wearing a grey suit.

D: *But your job now is to supervise the planting of the organisms?*
B: Not supervise. I'm a worker, with others. We have a big job. Lots of land to vegetate.
D: *How do you know what will grow there?*
B: There were many experiments done on the planet to see what would be the most hospitable.
D: *And you start with organisms first?*
B: Small plants. There are many of us. We start in one area and then move to other areas, and plant many different species.

This story was familiar to me. I covered the seeding (or beginning) of life on the planet Earth in two of my books: *Keepers of the Garden* and *The Custodians*. At the time of gathering the information and writing those books, the story seemed quite strange. But now I have heard it repeated so many times that I know it is the true version of the way life began. And I have come to accept it as fact. I did not know if she was speaking of the seeding of the planet Earth, but I had already been told that life was created in the same way on many, many other planets when they reached that stage in their development. It was a common way of spreading life, and had been done for incredible eons of time backward into infinity.

D: You will see which ones will grow?
B: We know from our tests which will grow.
D: Will you stay there and watch the development?
B: Yes, we will be here till the vegetation is established. Then we move to a new area and plant more.
D: Wouldn't that take a long time?
B: We have all the time we need. For now, we plant the vegetation, and our ships will stay as long as necessary. We feed it nutrients to help establish the plants.

She was having trouble speaking. Each word was coming across individually, as though it was a difficult energy to enunciate. I have had this happen before, especially when one of the little greys is trying to communicate. A very remarkable example occurred in my book *The Custodians*. This is mostly because, in their natural state, they do not use verbal communication, but mind to mind. So they must utilize the vocabulary of the subject's mind.

D: What about animal species? Do you also do that?
B: Mine is plants. I do not know what others do.

This all could have taken an enormous amount of time, so I moved her ahead to an important day. And she was smiling. "The planet is beautiful."

D: Can you see it from your craft?
B: No. I'm standing on the planet. It is beautiful.

Her voice had changed again. It had a dreamy, wistful quality, and an odd accent. Had she switched to another entity?

B: All of our plants have grown. And there's much vegetation. Very beautiful. We have succeeded in the plan.
D: *What is the next step?*
B: There is water, and they will bring the animals now, different species.
D: *Where do they come from?*
B: They were grown on these ships.
D: *Did you get them from other places also?*
B: Yes, we picked the best.
D: *And now you see what will survive?*
B: We know what will survive. It's all controlled.
D: *This is very good, but it takes a long time to do all of this, doesn't it?*
B: This is what we live for.

It was now time to bring forward the subconscious and get some answers. "Why did you pick those for Beth to see today?"

B: That is who she is. She's a being from other planets. She has spent most of her lifetimes on other planets, and other places than here on Earth. She has wondered about this many times, and she knows this already.
D: *So you wanted her to know it was true?* (Yes) *It sounded like she was a good person, and involved in many important assignments. Why did she decide to enter into a human body if most of her lives were on other planets and ships?*
B: Because it is the right time now. She has not had a life on Earth until now.
D: *Then it must be strange to her to come into a physical body.*
B: Yes. There has been readjustments and some discomforts that have needed to be overcome. She's done well.
D: *She did say she is still having some discomforts.*

243

B: Yes. We are aware of that and the adjustments are being made, but she resists the adjustments. It is the fear of not knowing what is going on within the physical body.

D: *She was born from a physical mother and father, wasn't she?*

B: She came into the physical after the body was formed. She was assigned to this physical body.

Beth had been having some physical problems. She had already had two operations, and yet the problems persisted.

B: When she entered the body, it was, if you'd say, not a perfect landing. She entered the body too quickly and was misaligned. So we've been trying to correct this misalignment.

D: *Is this what caused the problems with her knee and her shoulder?*

B: All the problems of the body. The entity entered this body "crooked" and too rapidly, so there has been an alignment problem. The entity was shifted sideways.

D: *I was thinking sometimes it's an adjustment when the entity has not been in a human body before.*

B: Yes, that's part of the problem, too. But she can overcome this by balancing her energies, and grounding her energies. Yes, we will help her on this. We are aware of the operations, and she will be helped soon. She has to learn how to balance her energies first, then we will make the final adjustments. She needs to tell us when she is in discomfort, and express it to us, so we will know what the physical is going through. It was a structural problem that the physical was born with. We can relieve some of the discomfort, but she did not know that she was to ask. We cannot interfere unless we are given permission. She is here to bring knowledge. (Just like the other life.) I am limited to how much information she can have at this time. Her mission is to unfold soon. She must be patient. She will be able to help and make a difference, as she has been wanting to all her life. It is just around the corner. The mission will unfold rapidly, and she will know and be shown what to do.

I had already encountered many other people in my work who were told they had come to Earth for the first time. I asked, "The ones who have come to Earth for the first time in a human body, will they all have this assignment of helping?"

B: They are all helping, but in different ways. Yes, initially they will help to show the way. That beings from other worlds are not there to hurt the people. But then, after this initial contact, there will be other missions and jobs for these people to accomplish, and to help humanity bring forth God's will.

D: *I have been told that those who have been here for many, many Earth lives are more or less handicapped. The ones coming in like Beth don't have all the karma and other things to deal with. It's easier for them to function.*

B: Yes, they can move through their life and focus on their mission.

Instead of going into a past life, Joanne went immediately to a beautiful place where a bright light was shining down on a city of crystals. "Different colored crystals. They are everywhere. Everything is crystals and fresh, pure water dripping on them. There's a really bright, bright light that shines on the crystals. The light is above and is reflecting off the crystals. There are all different sizes, some huge and small. I know it's a crystal city where everything is made of crystal." She then burst into tears with such emotion that it was difficult to transcribe the tape. She sobbed as she said, "The light feels like home! Home! I'm happy in this planet, but it feels like I don't belong here. I'm just visiting on Earth. It's like on my way home, kind of a resting place – a beautiful, beautiful resting place. Home actually feels more like the crystal city, but there's that light. It feels like it's all the same to me. It's like Earth is my home, and I'm visiting here. And the crystal city feels like home to me, but I don't know if it's my home."

D: *If it's so beautiful there, why did you leave it?*

J: (Crying again.) I don't know why! I had a plan. I think it's because we're on a mission, but I don't know exactly why .... It feels like it was my plan along with others. It was *a* plan. It feels like an agreement; I agreed.

D: *What did you agree to? Do you know?*

J: (Pause) I do think I know. It was to demonstrate love; to be unconditional love; to just be that; to be available. This plan was with other higher beings, and I agreed to do that with that group of higher beings.

D: *Did someone ask you to do it?*

J: Yes, I volunteered, because I was confident I could do that.

D: *Did anybody show you what Earth was going to be like before you volunteered?*

J: I don't recall a warning. I think I was just so full of love and so confident. And it was like a culture shock, almost. (Weeping again.) No! I didn't know, but I changed my mind before I was actually born! I changed my mind! I changed my mind! When I went into the baby, I wanted to change my mind, but they said it was too late. The plan was in progress, and I was to be born. It was too late, but I still chose to do this. I said, "If I can do it, I can do it. (Weeping again.) I know I can do it!"

D: *You really thought you could make a difference.*

J: Oh, but it hurts. (Crying) It hurts my heart.

D: *Why does it feel uncomfortable?*

J: (Crying very hard.) Being here, it hurts because I want to connect at the heart level. This doesn't happen very often. It's just hard to find people that can connect that deeply.

D: *Do you mean it's like a searching, to find people who would feel the same?*

J: I don't know that I search. I just sort of yearn for some of that really deeper connection.

D: *But you are speaking through a body that we call "Joanne". Does that mean that this is the first time you've come into a human body?*

J: I don't know. It just seems so surreal, and ... a shock! If I had any other times, then maybe I would be more used to it. So I don't know.

D: *But you did make an agreement, and you want to make a difference.*

J: I do and I worry that I'm not! (Crying again.) I was told by just being, I would make a difference, but I think I need to do more. Not by just being. I feel like I need to *do* something to make a difference. I was sure that it would be my presence that would be enough, that I wouldn't have to do, but I just forgot there's so much, so much, so much love that needs to be out there. Real love. I just want to go more.

D: *You know how people are. They don't even know. And you can't make them change.*

J: You can't; you can't, no. You just love them and you just see their light. And you love them, even if they don't love themselves. You just love them so they can *really* feel that little bit of light in themselves, that they can work with.

D: *Why is it so important?*

J: Why is it so important to *love*? For me to show love? So they might, for that little bit that I might touch them, that they might feel something inside them. It's like to touch something that is so perfect, just to touch it is enough for them to go, "Oh!"

D: *Just to make a difference. But* why *is that so important that you awaken that in these people?*

J: (Crying again.) Because most of these people actually are still in their sleep, and they don't understand. And it's okay.

It's part of their journey.

D: *Everybody's on a different path. All learning different lessons, and many of them are asleep. But when you volunteered to come, you found it's harder than you thought it was going to be.*

J: (Very emotional) It is! – I spent so much of my life *out* of my body. I drank when I was a teenager. I was scared that they just left me here. So I tried to get away from what I agreed to do by leaving my body.

D: *And you found a way to escape, but you can't really leave as long as you have a job to do.*

J: Yes, escape – that's a better word – escape.

D: *Where did you go when you spent so much time out of your body?*

J: Where I went was very peaceful and quiet, and was just a place I wanted to be.

D: *But you had to come back, didn't you?*

J: Every time!

D: *Because this is your body, and you're attached to it.*

J: That's right, and over time I figured that out. I figured it out, actually, probably three to six years ago, then I was about thirty. That's when I started to be conscious and realizing what I was doing. I didn't know! I didn't know that I was escaping. Then I didn't drink any more. I would just leave. I started realizing after taking classes that I was doing it. I didn't even know I was doing it. I could do it any time during the day. Just escaping. Just going off out of my body. I was depressed.

D: *I thought it had to happen when you were sleeping.*

J: It might not to me. I could be there in a minute.

D: *You just disconnect.* (Yes) *And the people around you wouldn't know you were gone?*

J: No, because I would seem like I was there. I would even answer questions. I would even talk, but I wasn't really there. They might think I was a little off or not interested.

D: But you were still able to do your work?
J: Yes, yes. I remember I was trying to be in my body. In 1991, it came crashing down on me, because I realized that I wasn't letting myself be here and feel pain.

What happened sounded like an emotional breakdown. She had been having problems with her husband, and his drinking was hurting her. It came to a climax when she started crying and couldn't stop. She kept saying, "I just can't do this, and it hurts too much!" It was probably the releasing of years of pent up emotions. After that emotional release, she said it was a long time until she could feel anything. Her world had literally crashed in on her. As though she had spent years running away from life, and it was finally time to face that she couldn't change the pain she felt around her. It was definitely an awakening. "I started to handle the pressure. I just kept playing along and I started becoming more and more conscious of what was around me. I had to make a choice to live consciously and to feel the pain as I go along. Not to try to escape it. Now I know the pain actually helps me be more compassionate, for myself and for others. I guess in the last few years, I have been preparing myself or growing so I can make that difference that would fulfill that reason why I came. I'm learning. It's something I have to do. That I want to; this is part of who I am."

Joanne worked in a hospital, and with hospice, and she was using her newfound confidence there. "I've always been able to *show* love, but it was beyond that. There's more to it than that. More to my plan than just the everyday love. There was something more. I don't know how to explain it. It's to go out there and promote unconditional love, so people can know." She found that she could do this merely by touching people, with her hands and also with her eyes. By looking into their eyes. "I *know* when they receive it, and they know it. It hurts, but I always do it for love. I am more and more realizing with touch that it makes such a big difference, especially in their last hours. I don't know how to explain it. You don't *give* love, you *be* love. You love! It doesn't matter if it's a criminal, you just love that person."

The subconscious came in and said, "She didn't understand her impact. People impacted her, but she didn't understand her impact on people. But now she's more *conscious* about her impact." I asked it why it showed this to Joanne. "It's time for Joanne to know it and feel it and be confident with it."

D: *We were expecting to go to past lives, but instead you chose to show her that beautiful crystal city.*

J: That's what she's about. Past lives mean nothing. She's about love.

D: *What was that crystal city she saw? She said it was like a resting place.*

J: Like a higher aspect of where *I* am ... where *I* reside.

D: *Is it on – what we call the spirit side?*

J: Yes. It actually isn't a physical place. And yet I'm looking at all the crystals with the pure water and the light. Above and beyond the crystals was that really, really bright white light. It was like the crystal city and that bright light were really close together. It feels like that's the higher aspect of me.

D: *Has Joanne had past lives in the physical on Earth before?*

J: No. She is part of the light, and she *chose* to come because it is time to awaken people.

D: *I think it takes a very brave soul to volunteer to come here at this time. It's very difficult on these gentle people that have not been here before.*

J: They are scared and it hurts.

D: *They feel it much more than those who have had many, many lives on Earth. But why does she need to help people awaken?*

J: There is major shifting going on, and this is the time and the opportunity for people *to* awaken. She has to help them awaken through her love, but not to do it forcefully, just the unconditional loving way. She has to learn to become

250

unattached, whether other people receive or not, because she's very sensitive and it hurts to be rejected.

D: *But not everyone* will *receive.*

J: And she knows that. She is to do it in any way she can; in any way that brings her joy and fulfillment. In any way that she can touch anyone. She doesn't have to physically touch, but just to be in their presence. Yet there is something with the physical touch, and she is discovering that more and more – it actually touches.

Joanne had also been doing toning, making sounds when she was working with people. She wanted to know why she felt the need to do this. "Joanne realizes that singing the sounds heal dimensionally. They heal." She also said that sometimes she sings in a strange language. She didn't know where it came from. It was also spontaneous. "The language is not to be understood, because it's not for the mind. It's for the heart. So people are here to receive. They feel it instead of know it in their heads, minds."

D: *Is it an Earth language?* (No) *Where does the language come from?*

J: The Angelic realm.

D: *Does this mean she was a member of the angelic realm before she came to Earth?* (She whispered, "Yes.") *And she carries the memory of those sounds and the words and the music?* (Yes, yes.) *Is there some connection with the angelic realm and the crystal city?*

J: *That* is the connection.

D: *Is it unusual for a member of the angelic realm to come to Earth for the first time.*

J: It happens. They don't really have to, but they can choose to exist.

D: *That makes it more difficult to come from such a beautiful place that's filled with love.*

251

J: (She sighed.) Oh, yes.

D: *I always thought man and the angels had different duties to perform, and they wouldn't want to come to Earth.*

J: They choose. She's catching on; she's learning. It's not easy, but she's doing well.

D: *I've been told that the problem is, most people on Earth have been here too long; going through too many lives and accumulating too much karma.*

J: Yes, it's endless; endless; endless.

D: *That's why these other beings are being sent? They're not trapped?*

J: No, no. I chose; I chose. *I* chose to come. To guide people, to help them. So that somehow, in some little tiny way, they could sort of realize what's going on. Just in the tiniest way, because that could make a big difference for them. It *could* shift them to really think about what this is all about.

As I was typing this part, I suddenly thought about the words in the Bible that talked about entertaining angels unaware. To treat everyone the same, with kindness, because you never know when you might be entertaining an angel unaware. You never know the person's real purpose for being on Earth, and for interacting with you, even if it is for a few brief moments. This is especially true, since even Joanne was unaware of her real heritage. She sacrificed a lot to come to this world of darkness and density, in the hope of introducing a small light to help guide people. This should make us all aware of how important a simple touch or smile might be to others. It could make all the difference.

A man came from England, and we ended up having two sessions. He had experienced *four* kidney transplants. I thought that was unusual in itself, because I didn't think they would give a person that many. After the third one, he almost died, and spent months in the hospital where he was in so much pain that he had to have shots to keep him unconscious, sedated. Also, he was on a respirator for months. Whenever he finally began to come out of it, he had difficulty, because his muscles hadn't been used. He couldn't eat, he couldn't talk, and he had difficulty even learning how to breathe again. During that time period there was a tremendous amount of pain, and the kidney failed. He first had kidney failure when he was only sixteen years old, and he's about 41 now. So far the fourth transplant is working, but it's only been a year since he had it done. Because he's now on drugs that suppress the immune system, he gets infections very easily. Whenever that happens, he goes into sepsis, where the body is overcome by certain germs and organisms, so that it can't function. So he has had a very hard, difficult time.

When we conducted the session, instead of going back into past lives like we expect, he went – like many others are doing now – into the light, wanting to stay there, not wanting to leave. When I got to the subconscious, I especially wanted to find out why he chose to have this experience? Because we do know we choose it. Why would he want to have kidney problems that would create the need for four kidney transplants? The subconscious said this was his first life on Earth. He was determined to experience *everything*. Everything that was absolutely possible to experience in one life. Maybe because he wasn't going to be here that long? Or maybe he wasn't going to come back? But instead of taking it gradually like you would normally do, he chose to put as much as he could into one lifetime. When I asked about the time he almost died, it said he chose to experience that also, because he wanted to know what it would be like to come that close to death. And he also chose to experience all of that pain. He wanted to have all of the experiences that were possible in a human life. He's really cramming a lot into one lifetime. It seems like too much to pile on one soul, unless they are determined to get in here and get it over with *now*. Because they don't know if they're going to get back here. The Earth will definitely be different. Maybe they wouldn't be able to experience things like this if they came back again. This was an unusual explanation, I thought. I thought he would go back to a past life that would explain why he had the kidney problems. But he said when he was experiencing all of this, he never once said, "Why me? Why is it happening to me?" Even as a child. He just went ahead and dealt with it. That's probably part of it, because on this other level he knew he volunteered for this, and this was what he wanted.

An interesting case of a young man who came all the way from England. He took a chance on the airplane, because he would have been exposed to other people and any colds, or organisms that they might have, especially in the recycled air on the plane. He took a chance to come that far to have some sessions. So I hope it did him some good by finding these explanations.

Almost as unexpected, was a case I did several years ago in London. When I talked to the young woman during our interview, I asked about her occupation, as I try to find out as much as I can about the person before we have the session. She curtly said to me, "I'm a hooker! Does that bother you?" I told her, "No, it doesn't bother me if it doesn't bother you." When she saw that I had no judgement, she relaxed and began to trust me. During the session we discovered she was one of the second wave of volunteers who had come to observe and report back. What better way to learn about humans than to study their sexual behavior as a prostitute? Unique, but I suppose valuable to the accumulation of information about our race. It appears that nothing is insignificant, and has value in the total amassing of information.

CHAPTER FOURTEEN

HUSBAND AND WIFE FIRST-TIMERS

In the beginning days of my work, I thought it would be impossible for a spirit, as their first incarnation, to come directly into a physical body in our civilized and hectic culture. I thought they would logically first incarnate into some primitive society where life would be simpler. That way they could adjust and learn how to live on Earth and how to deal with other humans, before coming into our modern lifestyle. Now I am finding that is not always the case. I am encountering more of the special people who have been sent or who volunteer to come and help during these challenging times. They say they have been sent as channels of energy, or as antennas, etc. It is, of course, more difficult for these gentle souls because they do not have the background of Earth lives to prepare them.

In October 2005, I met two more of these special people. And even more unusual, they were husband and wife. I think it is wonderful that they were able to locate each other out of the millions of people in the world, so their identical energies could work together. But then, I have also been told that nothing happens by accident. They had evidently agreed and made plans on the other side before incarnating.

They both gave identical stories while in deep trance even though they were unaware of these things consciously. When Tim came off the cloud, he only saw a very bright light. "It is very bright. It radiates, it has rays going in all directions. It is very beautiful, but you can't look directly at it. It also has many different colors throughout. It is very soothing. There is so much love that comes from it. It surrounds you just like it's hugging you." When this happens, I know they have either gone to the spirit side, or back to the Source (or God). Also, various energy beings look like this. I asked it to take Tim and show him something that was important for him to see. Instead of going into a past life, he was taken to a room where there were several beings dressed in robes of a floating type of material. He could not make out any features as the beings floated effortlessly around the room.

T: I don't see any walls, but you feel you are in a closed environment. This is like a council, and there is a meeting where they have come to discuss all different types of things. Things of the universe. All the different planets. They're having to make decisions for other types of beings or for ... I guess it would be for lower vibrations, for those that haven't reached the higher planes or higher vibrations. This is the council that helps them in making decisions in their processes, or what they will be doing.

He saw that he had the same type of wispy, ghostly body, and felt he was a member of this council.

T: Otherwise, I wouldn't be able to be here. This is a higher vibration, a higher frequency. They don't necessarily make decisions, but they *help* in making decisions. Whatever would be appropriate for the lower vibrations.

D: *How do they help make these decisions?*

T: It seems like for each lower vibration, there are certain vibrations that they need to learn, to be able to elevate their vibrations to a different plane. The council helps them to make decisions that will actually raise their vibrations.

D: *This is not interfering?*

T: No, it's only a form of guidance.

D: *Do you have anything in particular that you're working on right now?*

T: Only to be of a service. To help. To give guidance. That's what we're only here to do. To help guide them to the knowledge.

D: Is there any particular project that you're concerned about right now?

T: There are all different types of projects. As we help the lower vibrations, we are also helping ourselves, because it also teaches us as well as we teach them. If you serve, you gain. This helps you gain knowledge.

D: Are you working with any certain planet at the present time?

T: It's working with all the universes. It's not just one planet.

D: Did you have to go through physical lifetimes to reach that point where you could be on the council?

T: No. Didn't have to go through physical lifetimes. Only by choice. You can raise your vibration level, even though you don't have to go through physical lifetimes to be on the council. Sometimes it may take a period of time. But sometimes you can progress very quickly.

D: Did you ever have a desire to be physical?

T: Not at this point in time, no.

D: You were doing your job over there.

T: That was all I needed to do.

D: Well, it sounds like it's a very important job.

T: This was all that was asked for me to do.

I then asked him to move to when he made the decision to come into the physical, because after all, I was communicating with a physical body in our dimension. He must have decided to come here and incarnate. I wanted to know if someone had told him to come.

T: No, it was only by choice. And the opportunity was there. In other words, the physical form that would fit was there at the time of choice.

D: Did anything happen to cause you to make the choice?

T: To experience. For that was something I had not ever done before. It was definitely new.

D: Have you picked out the body you're going to go into? (Yes.)

257

What does it look like?

T: It is the present. There is no other time.

D: *Explain what you mean.*

T: It is as the person you are speaking to.

D: *You mean Tim has never had any other physical incarnations before this?* (No.) *I've always thought that if that were the case, it would be very difficult. To come directly from the spiritual side to life the way we have it now on Earth, without any former lifetimes to condition the person.*

T: It is very difficult, but there are ways that they help in doing things. There was certain things. I don't know if I can describe these things for you.

D: *I would really appreciate if you could try. Analogies are always good, too.*

T: It's like the information is provided. It's like you go into a chamber. And once you come out of this chamber, this information has been placed within you. Then this information, once it has been placed within you, would give you a background. Something to relate to.

I knew what he was talking about. He was referring to *imprinting.*

T: I don't think you can come into a physical life with nothing. It is still difficult even with this information being placed within. It is extremely different here. There is much to learn, and to experience. It was difficult to leave that beautiful place, but it was something that needed to be experienced. This time in history is when there is great change that is coming about. Things are moving very rapidly; very quickly. He wanted to be able to observe these things.

D: *So no one told him he had to do these things.*

T: No, no one directs you and tells you that you must do these things. These are choices. And also discussions. And he was helped by other members of the council. They helped or guided him to make these choices.

D: *We're so used to thinking of Earth lives where we accumulate karma, and then we have to come back again and again to repay it.*

T: He doesn't have that type of karma that you're speaking of. He is here to observe the progression of humans. How they are actually raising their vibration levels. To see how they are accepting knowledge. And how they're using knowledge. If they're using it for the good of mankind, or if it is being used for greed.

D: *Because Earth is a complicated planet. It has many different types of people, doesn't it?*

T: It is *extremely* complicated. It is unlike any other planet. I think the form of negativity on this planet makes it different. The human race is a very warrior type race. They have a great deal of difficulty living peace. It is almost like their race cannot co-exist in peace. This may come from their lower vibrations. I think each one that comes here has to be so careful and not be caught into these lower vibrations. It is a very challenging planet. I did take that chance. I think any time you come into this existence, you have created karma. And, no doubt, I will have to repay this karma. However, I think the main thing I try to do here is to maintain a balance of being very positive, very loving. And what karma I have created with Earth isn't a negative form, per se. It's to actually find ways of working to reduce that. And then to take care of that karma, and not allow it to carry over.

D: *What is your plan then? To just come in for this one lifetime?*

T: Yes, at the present time. I will have to see once I get back.

D: *You don't want to stay and experience other existences?*

T: I don't know if I will return for other existences. There may be more important things for me to do than to return, than to be physical. I don't know if I will be able to accomplish this or not. It would be very easy to become trapped here. There are so many things to trap you. Even though many desire this

259

presence, it is extremely difficult. It looks quite simple until you come into this physical form. Once you're into the physical form, then it is extremely difficult.

D: *One of the problems is that the physical forgets and doesn't know all these things?*

T: Oh, quite true.

D: *Would it be easier if they were able to remember?*

T: I don't think it would be right for the physical form to remember. I think to remember all these things would be too great. It would be too confusing, and then they would try to change things and probably in a most undesirable way. And maybe not learn the things they were here to learn for their own growth.

D: *People are always saying if they only knew what it was like before, it would be easier.*

T: I think this would be too much information for them. If you had all this knowledge before you, what would be the purpose to come in?

One of Tim's questions dealt with problems he had experienced with his parents.

D: *Why did you pick your parents? Was there a reason for that?*

T: They needed the help in different ways. As coming into this person I came into, it was to help the parents to see that they should not interfere in the lives of their children. To help them to learn that these choices should be made.

D: *This was a lesson for them also?*

T: Oh, yes. We teach. Children teach their parents as parents think they teach their children. More vice versa. More than we realize.

D: *I seem to be working with many people lately who are energy workers and healers.*

T: There's going to be a great deal more. This is only starting to open. And people are seeking other alternatives. They're looking for different ways. They are seeing that what they are used to is not actually working for their best interest. There will be some that cling to the old forms. They have trouble getting past that. It is their conditioning and upbringing, but you have many out here and especially the new ones are coming in. They will be seeking all this new information. And of course, they will be bringing that new information as well. Most of the information is not new. It is new to the people that are present, but it is actually old information. – There are only so many physical forms that are available. And there are so many more spiritual forms that want to come, that there are not enough physical forms.

D: *I see. But right now with our population growth, there are many physical forms available.*

T: But there are not. Also, you have certain ones that are trying to control the metaphysical forms that are available.

D: *What do you mean by that?*

T: You have leaders that are trying to control the availability of physical forms. The diseases, the wars.

D: *You mean they're eliminating many of the physical forms?* (Oh, yes.) *Then there are only limited physical forms that your type of spirit could come into?*

T: Yes. That's true.

D: *But maybe there's enough that it will help.*

T: We do hope so. It's hard to find appropriate food because of all the chemicals in the foods, but the human body is also adapting. This is why you are seeing more people with the old knowledge to bring forth to help. You are seeing, at this time, new humans that are coming in. If you look at their parents, they are helping or they're looking and they're seeing these things come about. Even grandparents are trying to guide them to foods that do not have all the chemical substances we see in the foods today. There is a large segment of the new people coming in that are having a much better diet than others. And this is one of the changes that you are seeing

261

already that is coming about. Not for all, but for some. The source of the food is going to be more difficult as time goes on. It will be a real problem. But there will be ways through information coming in that will help.

D: All of this is going to affect the raising of the vibrations, isn't it?

T: Yes, it is.

D: I've been told we have to make the body lighter.

T: We do have to make the body lighter. And this will help in the process.

Tim was told how he could use his mind to heal. "He will have to develop and trust his mind. He will be able to learn these techniques through meditation. The mind is very powerful. And by viewing the problem, seeing the problem, then his mind will make the changes. He will be able to see inside the body. It is as if you would go inside the person and look at that body. It is as if you would go into the leaf of the tree and float into the channels of the chlorophyll. He will see them as pictures. He will also see how it should be, from pictures and the images that are forming to him, and the process. Then these changes can take place. He would not have to have the person's participation, but he would have to have their permission. Because some choose to have these physical conditions for whatever reasons."

In the afternoon, I had a session with Tim's wife Sandy, and I was surprised to find she was the same type of soul. Of course, nothing happens by accident, but I had never encountered two such cases on the same day.

In the beginning of the session, Sandy also had difficulty seeing anything except shifting colors, and after several attempts to get her to a past life or something visual, I finally contacted the subconscious. It supplied the information that had been denied. Sometimes if the subject is not ready, the information will not come forth. The subconscious is so protective it is also very particular about who it will release it to.

S: What is happening with Sandy is like an experiment. It has never been done before. We're trying to raise the energy levels. There are energy rules in incarnation on Earth and everywhere else. But, because of the times and because of the necessity, we were trying to accomplish bringing a higher vibration into the Earth and then expanding it. To raise the level even after the incarnation. Also to bring in the highest level we could without harm to the physical form.

D: *Because the body can't hold too much energy, or too high of an energy?*

S: Right. There's a level that the human form can't hold. Because we failed at it before, this experience and experiment is very important to Sandy. That's why she volunteered to come and bring that energy in and go through it and do it. *And we did it. It worked this time.* When it failed before, it was like blowing a circuit.

D: *Did it harm the physical form she was trying to come in to?*

S: Right. It did. The body died. It was too much energy, too much information, too high of a vibration in one physical body.

D: *It just can't hold that.*

S: Right. But this body has been able to. And also we fine tuned the body as it aged, to be able to hold more, and have added more since. Many of the physical problems are because of the stress and strain on the body from holding the energy.

D: *Has she had physical incarnations before?*

S: Imprints.

D: *Then you mean that Sandy has never been in a physical incarnation anywhere?*

S: No. She has been an assistant to the Earth. Not incarnated in

263

the Earth, but around the Earth and assisting others who incarnate. She has a workable knowledge, not actual incarnation knowledge, but has been behind the scenes assisting others who incarnate.

D: *Why did she decide to come this time?*

S: Because it was very important for the Earth. And she had the ability to bring in the energy that needed to be brought in, in that way, in that magnitude, and in the proportions that needed to come at that time. It's very scientific. I'm not explaining it well. It's almost like mathematical equations of energy. Hers were most adaptable to come in because she had been working closely with the Earth. She knew how things worked, and the rules and regulations and that sort of thing, scientifically. So she was able to adjust her energy, and adjust the body. We're also helping with that.

D: *But when somebody does this for the very first time, isn't she taking a chance of getting caught up in karma?*

S: No. The reason she isn't taking a chance in getting caught up in karma, is because she doesn't accumulate karma. She's on a different level. Or a different contract, we can say, with the Earth.

D: *Because you know, being human, you run the risk of being trapped and you have to come back time and time again.*

S: Right. She won't get trapped. Her contract was to come and bring her energy in to the Earth. It is not a karmic contract.

D: *So she's protected so she won't accumulate karma.*

S: Right!

D: *That's very tricky.*

S: And the people she came with had contracts, and have been caught up. And they're attracted to her because she's, on a subconscious level, helping them release that.

D: *So they didn't have any karma with her.*

S: No. She came to help them release their karma with others, without getting caught up in it. It's almost like a batting machine. When you practice batting, the ball comes at you and you hit it. She was that backdrop that the ball goes onto. But it wasn't an actual team out there catching the ball and running with it. She held a spot so they could release their karma with her.

D: *So these other people needed someone to help them work out their karma.*

S: Right, because they were on a downhill path. They had gotten themselves into a negative spin. She did contract to help the Earth, but it was on a different level. It wasn't on an incarnation level. But now, she chose to do this, to pull in more energy for this time. It's a strategic time because of the free will, and because it's a balance. It's a balance time where the Earth can go either way and it's a major shift. It's a shifting place. A crossroads.

D: *Is this why more of these – I don't want to call them "new" souls, because they do have a lot of knowledge and power – but is this why more of these are coming in at this time?* (Yes) *I keep meeting more. Some of them say they are just observers. They don't want to get caught here.*

S: It's not that they're observers, but if you can picture how I said ... it's like the batter is hitting the ball and it's going against something. So you're hitting and putting it out there, but the backdrop doesn't react one way or the other. So it's not accumulating any karma. Everything bounces off. But that person is doing their thing, and they're releasing their stuff. And that's why they're not accumulating karma. They didn't come to accumulate. And they're not just observers. They're healers. They're bringing in positive energy to help other people. Other souls see, and they feel their vibrations and they want to acclimate to that.

D: *But the main thing is that they don't get sucked in.*

S: There's no danger of them getting sucked in, because their energy level is what it is. It's almost like there's light being sent out all the time. Or energy going out and interacting with others in a healing manner. And there are no holes to suck, or

265

no karma to connect with. So it's a very positive thing.

Some of my other cases, who were this type of special being, were protected from accumulating karma by having protective devices or shields placed around them. This is reported in my other books. But Sandy's subconscious said, "There is no need for protection, because it's built in, because of the purpose and the energy level. And because there isn't any prior karma. There's nothing to connect to it."

S: Her daughter has come in a similar way as her mother, only it's more perfected now. Her body has acclimated better. Because of the ones that came in first, and brought the energy in, it's not as hard for the new ones to come. The first attempts didn't work. It was too harsh, too stressful for the human form.

D: *I've been told that all the energy of a person's soul could not possibly fit into the human body. That it would destroy the body.*

S: That is correct. Her husband, Tim, has come in, in a very similar way. To blaze the trail.

D: *And he doesn't accumulate karma either.* (Yes) *Was it by accident that the two of them got together?*

S: No. It wasn't by accident. They planned to come together in the same area before they incarnated. They are two similar types of energy. Not the same, but very similar. Sandy was an experiment. The amount of energy that is in her body, would normally be as much as in two separate bodies. Part of the problem was the amount of energy coming in, and also the vibration level. The previous time, it failed. We didn't have the timing and the fine tuning of the body, and the soul coming in and the exact amounts of energy at the right times. It's very technical.

D: *But it had to be as much energy that would normally be in two bodies.*

266

S: Yes. This was the experiment. It was very important and it has accomplished a lot. That was very beneficial. She isn't the only one that did this. Just like her husband, he was one of the ones that came. It's slightly different, but very close to the same. There are others. And she's also helped with them, when she is out of body. She had helped them adjust and get in to incarnate. She has helped several do this, but the part that she doesn't understand, is that since coming in, there has also been more energy come into her. You've heard of walk-ins where one soul leaves and the other comes. This isn't like that. This wasn't actually two souls. The portion that came in would take the volume of two souls. Double the normal amount has come and joined with her recently. That is incarnated now with her.

D: *The two didn't exchange.*

S: No, there was no exchange. That was a joining, an adding. We told her twice that this new part of herself was coming. And now it is here and now it is joined.

D: *Did she know when this happened?*

S: Not consciously. But she knew it was going to and she prepared consciously, and that was of great assistance. And she knows she feels different now. But had not consciously acknowledged that there was more of her, and that it had joined. She will now receive very much knowledge. It's not going to all happen at once, but it will be triggered as she acclimates.

D: *Then when this life is over, will she go back and not have to keep returning?*

S: Right. She will stay until her job is finished. She won't have to incarnate again. She will stay until the shift is complete.

D: *This place where she came from, is that what I call the spirit side?*

S: Anything that is not a form, is spirit side. There are multiple, multiple places. This is not like you die and go there. It's before you incarnate, you're there. It's just a different realm.

267

D: *Some people consider those type of spirits are angels that have never incarnated.*

S: It's not an angel. It's a soul like everyone else, just not incarnated in form. It didn't need to. Didn't feel the necessity until now. But, let me tell you that she was in form, just not in a body form. She was in spirit form. And there are different levels of... we don't call them incarnation, because it's not lower formed like a body on any planet. It is an energy, and it has a body. It has an individuality, but it's just energy. But it's in a space. It's not the energy we call the One energy. The Lake energy. It's a separate individual energy. But it's not in a body or in a physical form like a human form. Or a body on any planet.

D: *That makes sense to me. But now I have more people coming to me that are here as healers and energy workers.*

S: That is due in a large amount to the times changing. It's the winding up of an age. So these type of beings like Sandy and Tim are here to help with this transition. – I will tell you who you've been talking to. This is the part of Susan that just connected.

D: *The new energy.* (Yes.)

Isn't it utterly amazing that all of these things are going on within us, and our conscious minds don't have a clue? We wander and stumble through life wearing blinders, trying to find the answers by trial and error. But as I asked "them" one time, "Wouldn't it be easier if we knew why we were here? If we knew the karmic connections?" And they said in their infinite wisdom, "It wouldn't be a test if you knew the answers." So let us stumble on, and maybe some glimmer of light will be allowed to enter.

CHAPTER FIFTEEN

BIRTH OF A FIRST-TIMER

A JAPANESE FIRST-TIMER

This chapter will show that people reporting coming to the Earth for the first time is not strictly an American phenomenon. Naturally, I have more clients in my home country, but I also have sessions when I am traveling to other countries. I am being exposed to many strange and unusual things that I am now convinced are occurring worldwide. This session occurred on my latest tour of Australia in 2007, when I was giving lectures and conducting my hypnosis classes. Although I had a very full schedule, there was time to work in a few private sessions.

Jasmin was a young Japanese girl, who appeared tiny, delicate, almost China doll fragile. But this masked a very strong and determined interior. I learned not to be fooled by outward appearances. I first met her in New Delhi, India when I was speaking at an International Hypnosis conference in 2006. I then met her again in Australia where she was going to college. She is highly intelligent and, even though she is finishing her Master's degree at the University, she has already begun her own business. She is also very active in many different healing modalities, and she has an active curiosity to learn more. I, again, had difficulty transcribing the tape, because of the accent.

When she went into the scene she saw that she was in the desert and there were camels and tents. Although she saw people, she would not enter into one of their bodies. She said it did not matter, because she was not connected with these people. She seemed to be floating and just watching, observing. "I feel I can go wherever I want to go. I feel I am just observing what is going on around the planet. Appearing and disappearing. Going, and popping in and seeing out, and looking at various places." Then

269

she saw she had shifted her perspective and was looking at Australia's desert. "I feel I'm just enjoying myself." It was obvious that I had encountered another spirit that was not in a physical body. This sounded very similar to Chapter 19, *The Orb*, where the client saw herself floating and observing everything, with no real purpose.

So I asked Jasmin to move backward to see where she started from, where she began this journey. She found herself floating in space, watching. It was beautiful, with shiny stars and the moon in the distance.

D: *Are you by yourself?*
J: I am, but I'm connected to everything.
D: *Is that what it feels like?*
J: Supportive. Love. Safety. Security.
D: *You said you feel like you are everything. Can you see what that is like?*
J: There is a web that I am hooked into, that is connected to everything. Like a spider web, but it's just an energy web that is connected to everything.
D: *But you're still an individual too, aren't you?*
J: Yes. When I focus on one specific thing, I can be an individual. It depends on where your focus is located. I just have a feeling that I am connected to All That Is, everything.
D: *And it feels good?* (Yes) *Then why did you decide to go off on your own, as an observer?*
J: Being an observer also helps me to allow individuality. Become a part instead of the whole. I feel both are important.
D: *It sounded like you were separate when you were floating around and looking at things on the planet.*
J: It's still on that web, the one that I'm connected to. And therefore I am still connected to everything. It's like ... if you look at water, it is connected to everything. All the molecules and everything are connected, but it just depends on where your focus is. You can be one specific molecule, but at the

same time you can feel everything, the entire thing. It's just a matter of where I am actually taking my attention to. In that way, I can say I'm a molecule, or at the same time I can be the ocean. It's the same thing.

D: *So you just decided to go and explore, and observe? There was no reason?*

J: I think I am a traveler, an explorer. I want to know what it is like to be in this dimension.

D: *Is this dimension different than the others?*

J: Yes. I feel where I came from looks lighter. Just the pure light, and faster. And coming down here seems to be a bit more sticky, and slower. It's just a different web, but it's the same connected.

D: *It's still all hooked together in the same way.*

J: Yes, that's right.

D: *But you're able to separate, and focus your attention in a different place?*

J: Yes. Just like a shallow part of the ocean. It's shallow, and you can actually see just the thin layer. And coming down it's like feeling a thick layer of things. It's deeper and thicker.

D: *Did you have a reason why you decided to go and observe and explore?*

J: I don't know. It's just to play.

I then returned her to the scene where she was no longer in space, but was observing things on Earth.

D: *What do you think of the Earth, and these things you are seeing?*

J: It's contaminated. Earth is beautiful and loving, but it's damaged. People made it dirty. Water and desert, chemicals and everything. I can see the whole picture. I feel the Mother Earth as unconditional love. It just is there, but at the same time there are people living unjust, too. I feel sad, but I feel they have to raise their awareness. They have to notice what

271

they are doing to their house. I want to say they are not aware of what they're doing to the Earth.

D: *But you're just observing this?*

J: Yes. I think I want to be a part of it. If I volunteer, I feel I can.

D: *You want to be a part of what is going on?*

J: Yes. I feel like there's an urgency, that we have to sort it out, because other things will be affected. This entire life system gets affected by this planet, and what people are doing to the Earth. Because if the whole atmosphere and gravity and energy fields from this fail, then other systems get affected. Out in space. This entire galaxy, and whole other things. – They told me to come. I actually chose too.

D: *Who told you to come?*

J: The council. They had a meeting. They called out. An emergency situation. It looks like it was allocated to many different planets. And they especially chose the Earth. There are more different planets that need the help, but I volunteered to come here. When I am observing different planets, including the Earth, the Earth looks more interesting, with the trees and water and people. It's covered with a variety of things. So I just decided.

D: *So it's not just Earth. Other planets are also having problems?*

J: But Earth is, I think, the most urgent. I see an emergency.

D: *So that was why you decided to come.* (Yes) *How are you going to come? Have they told you how you're going to do it?*

J: My guide pointed out, to this island Japan. And then she told me I'd live there. And my guide actually pushed me, and she told the energy to change. And then I just went inside. I didn't understand what she meant by "live" at the beginning. But she said, "You will know." And then I just entered, and I was born in the human body. It was like an energy shooting, like a light energy beam. And they threw me into that energy

272

light beam. And like a shooting star I just shoot into the Japan island, this island. And then I was born.

D: *Did you have a choice about who your parents would be?*

J: I feel they chose the father, who is always interested in astronomy. He always looks at the pictures of planets, and he makes telescopes and he studied mathematics. So they said it's a good option. He has a good heart.

D: *And they thought Japan would be a good place to start, to come to.*

J: Yes, they chose this island for me.

D: *What was that like when you entered the body?*

J: The mother has so much emotions of fear; heavy feelings, and negative feelings. Anxiousness. So I learned that they have emotions. I think at first I felt I had stepped into the body. And then it was like being in a different person's body, feeling a whole bunch of emotions from her. And probably I would end up feeling the way it's feeling when I would be choosing this body. So I would be bombarded by emotions and feelings and thoughts. And all the heavy things.

D: *It's different from the way you were before.*

J: Yes, it's very different.

D: *Do you think you're going to like being in this body?*

J: At first they warned I'd get confused. Not knowing which is me, and which is the emotions bombarded by other people. I think I have to be wise to discriminate against which energy is mine, and which is not. Or which are from other people. Because in one body it's caused by so much different emotions, belief systems, thoughts. All sorts.

D: *So you pick up on those feelings.* (Yes) *It's harder to switch them off.*

J: Yes. It's probably meant for me not to switch them off, because I have to learn and integrate, like other humans.

D: *Is this your first time as a human?*

J: First time. They said, "It's your first time." Like a starting. I've been to different lifeforms, but nothing like this.

D: *Did they give you any instructions?*

J: They gave me instructions to allow the human body. I'm noticing the fetus, the baby, and how it is developing. And how organs are created. And how the energy's flowing. And how this *thing* develops into many different organs. And how it grows. Observing how this body operates. It is interesting. It's so different. Like observing, like under a microscope. It's just observing the whole system. It's different.

D: *But when you come into the body, you don't remember where you were before, do you?*

J: I'm probably not allowed to remember very much.

D: *Is there a reason why?*

J: Because I have to pretend to be a human. I have to be a human. It's probably better not to have different memories.

D: *It would be confusing, wouldn't it?*

J: Yes, it is. – It's fun to watch this baby's heart pumping, and how bones .... I like the way its heart pumps. Pumping the blood. It looks interesting. Pumping, moving.

D: *When they told you to come in, did they tell you what they wanted you to do?*

J: They told me to align the human body. And how the entities or the souls project their life streams into the body. And how to manipulate the body, to learn how the whole system works. So that, later on, I can bring the knowledge to a different place, so that other people can learn too. Because nothing is like this. It is unusual, and very rare. Of course, there are planets like this, but this looks more fascinating to me.

D: Why is it rare?

J: This Earth ... feels like this was done as an experiment for some reason. But it has many different life forms. And it's a complexity of what humans are doing. And they have their own concepts of what they call "languages". And this entire thing, it's quite different. Whereas other planets are more telepathic, people here have different bodies and different languages.

D: It's easier when it's telepathic, isn't it? (Yes) *You don't have to communicate with words. – What do you think of this assignment?*

J: It's exciting, fascinating. And I'm ready to learn. But they told me it would be a lot of hard work, but that's what makes it more fun. And it looks complicated. So when I change something complicated, I can acquire more knowledge and skills, so I can expand. They want me to transfer the knowledge, but more energetically, it looks like. Energy transmission of knowledge. I think I needed the education, so people can understand me better. I know when I go into people, I'm transferring the knowledge. The energy and the wisdom, so that people become unknowingly aware of the things.

D: You said, when you go into people. What do you mean?

J: I just touch people, talk to people. Just being around. Wherever I go I feel like I'm being an anchor of some energy. So that other people can also reconnect with the energy they used to be connected to. So that when I'm there, I'm just naturally activating or anchoring people, to connect them to the energy. So whenever I walk around people, people naturally feel me, and they can reconnect with the energy.

D: Because they've forgotten their connections?

J: Yes, seems like it, or they just decided to disconnect. They've forgotten.

It then told me it knew it was speaking through a human being, called Jasmin. It said that when she was doing her healing for people, she was tapping into the energy that she came from. "She feels it brings the energy that is most appropriate to the person. Some people need a lower vibration, so she puts a lower vibration of energy, but they still get healed. And the people who use up their energy, they can still get the pure and higher frequency of energy. They also get healed. So she can adjust which energy they choose naturally. They adjust, or she adjusts,

275

or the energy adjusts itself.

D: *What would happen if she gives them too much?*

J: She doesn't give too much, or the energy doesn't give too much. Or some people might have a over-reaction or side effect.

D: *So when she's doing this, she automatically knows how much energy to give the person.*

J: Yes. Like electricity ... before she touches people ... it's like an energy conductor. It's like water. If you actually have something to change the direction of water, through association, connecting and directing the flow of the energy.

D: *Is she aware consciously of where the energy comes from?*

J: She doesn't have to know, because there is not much point to understand every single detail of which energy is from where. Because everyone is coming from different planets, and different dimensions. And if she focused down into every single detail, her mind would get overwhelmed. The main thing is that people get healed and reconnected. She's doing it to help people. It's beyond words.

D: *Is she so close to this energy because she's not gone through many other lives?*

J: Yes, this is one of the first times. She has been experiencing simultaneous lives with other people through energy. And also she has simultaneous experiences that other human beings are doing, so that she can adjust better when she becomes embodied in her body.

D: *Is that why the energy that she uses is so pure, because she hasn't lived on Earth many times?*

J: Her energy is still very pure. And it is easy for us to use her, because we can bring in other strings of energy that are necessary for other human beings that she encounters.

D: *You know when a person has many, many lifetimes they get bogged down in karma.*

J: She doesn't have karma. It's easy for her. You know she

wants to be one with me all the time. I am already speaking through her when she's talking to people. So she *is* being the pure instrument for *us*. We often speak through her. She is doing a good job. She allows us to be with her. That is a good thing, because not too many people can do this. And she has to take a gentle step now, just like an ordinary human person. Other people can't stand all of a sudden energies going through them. So she has to sometimes slow down, because it's a process of evolution. She can't just go and activate people's energies and DNAs, and vibrations. So we are teaching her to slow down, because she wants to give everyone instant healing suddenly. But, you know, some people have to work out their karma and other stuff. She will understand the difficulties and problems and issues that other humans have to sort out. We know she sometimes gets frustrated when she can't heal people instantly. But usually we have to take time, because it's an individual choice. They may want to keep themselves in sickness and illness, and other driving-down stuff. She has to do this gradually and eventually, because she also needs to teach other people how to see inside the body, and how to do a healing. We give her that ability to do so, but she has to slow down. It's not too much to her. However, it would be too much to other people. She has so many students, but they have to take time to learn. Therefore she has to slow down. Otherwise, all her students feel isolated and left alone, while she's so advanced. She has to learn from other people's difficulties, other people's problems. That's why they cannot do this. Gradual process. So she has to be a human at the same time. She will eventually put all her knowledge together, to do a workshop, a course, an education program. She will accomplish that, so that ordinary people – an adult, and even a child, can learn how to expand consciousness. At this stage she has to learn to be human first. In the new Earth everyone will be able to do these things: to heal, to see inside the body, to communicate telepathically, to materialize objects, to bi-locate. This knowledge is necessary, and everyone will learn these things. This knowledge is accessible for anyone. Awakening abilities. We can't give you a time scale, but all of you can eventually do it.

D: *You said, bi-locate?*

J: Bi-location may be a strange phenomenon to you, but it is happening all the time. It's a matter of you raising your understanding. It is natural to us. We do it all the time. It's just your conscious mind is so limited. It will be revealed to her, and also to everyone, as time comes.

D: *She also wanted to know about living without eating.*

J: She can. You don't have to eat. That's not necessary. But all of you will be able to live without eating eventually, in the new Earth. People are already shifting and changing. Many people are eating just fruits and vegetables.

So I had unexpectedly found another first-timer while on a trip half way around the world. If my mail is any indication there are untold numbers out there who have volunteered or been sent to help the Earth in its time of crisis. On the surface these people look just like any other human being, and they are totally unaware consciously of the important assignment they have been handed.

ENGLAND FIRST-TIMER

This session was done at my hotel in London in 2005. I had been giving many lectures and workshops, and was inundated with requests for private sessions. Francine convinced me that it was very important that she have the session, so I managed to squeeze her into my busy schedule. I am very glad I did, because the session was of great benefit to her. I do not think these things happen by accident. "They" are always in charge, and connect me with those I am supposed to help. Francine had been very depressed since childhood, and was now taking antidepressants. She told me she wanted to commit suicide. She just didn't want to be here any longer, even though she had a good life (by our standards). She was married with children, and her husband was very understanding of her condition. But she was one of those people I am encountering more and more that feel they do not belong here. They are uncomfortable with the violence and horror of our world. They want to go home, even though they don't know where home is. She felt she had reached the end of her rope. She was sincere about wanting to kill herself. The medication might have been taking the edge off, but it was only suppressing the real cause. I had an idea what I was going to find, because I am seeing more of these gentle souls now as we are approaching the coming shift into the New Earth. I have been told they are the pioneers, the trail blazers who set the stage for others to follow. It was very difficult for the ones who came first, because they had a great deal of adjusting to do. The ones who came afterwards have not had as much difficulty. I had a definite feeling that Francine was going to be one of these volunteers who came in first to pave the way for the others.

When Francine was in a deep trance, instead of going to a past life, she found herself in a very uncomfortable situation. She could not see anything, the information was coming as impressions and feelings. "I feel suddenly very, very heavy, and there's nothing there. It's blackness. And I feel anxious. It feels like my heart's beating faster. I feel as though everything is under pressure. I feel my body is being squeezed. It feels tight and squeezed."

I gave her suggestions to relieve any physical sensations, so she wouldn't have the uncomfortable feelings. "What do you think is causing that?"

F: I don't know. I feel as though I'm being born, or I'm about to be born. It feels as though it's all over me, a feeling of being squeezed and squashed. My heart feels strange.

I didn't see the need for her to continue to feel uncomfortable. If she was experiencing her birth, it could have continued for some time. So I moved her ahead in time to see what was causing the sensations.

F: I see a baby being held up by its legs and being snapped on the bottom. – I think I'm the baby.
D: *Where are you when this is happening?*
F: I think it's a hospital. I don't see anything clearly.
D: *Does it feel better now to get out?*
F: I feel something's wrong. It doesn't feel any better. I don't feel so squeezed, but my heart feels wrong.
D: *You mean it feels strange to be in a body?*
F: Yes, I'm frightened and alone. I feel tears coming. It was a shock. It was not fair in that way. I'm confused. I can't remember why I'm here or what's happening. Why is everything so cold and harsh? But I don't see much at all. I'm just feeling all this.
D: *You said you had the feeling of being alone?*
F: Yes, because it is not the feeling of being cuddled or held. I feel as though I'm alone.
D: *Where is your mother?*
F: I don't know. She's not here. I want to be held. I want to

feel that I belong to someone.

D: *Where you came from before this, did you feel alone?* (No)
What was it like there?

F: I felt I was never alone there. Everything's so light and everything's white, as though I'm part of something really large. I know I'm connected to that, and it feels that it's just love. And it hurts to be away from that.

D: *Were there people there?*

F: It feels that, in the main it was just light. But I think you can be separate, in a way. You can have a body, but it would be made of light. Yes, I get the feeling that there are other beings of light all around me. And that we can feel like a mass of light if we want to. And being connected to them all the time, never feeling alone, always being understood, and that we always work together. I was unrestricted and everything was much faster, but common, and it was light. It's hard to explain because there's nothing there apart from this light, and the occasional feeling that I can see shapes of other beings of light. But that's it. There's meant to be a feeling of love and togetherness there, as though we were all part of the same one energy. It felt all together.

D: *What happened that you had to come into a body?*

F: I felt it was time to go. I had to be brave, and I had to do this, but I knew I was going to forget who I was and how I was going to go. It was important that I went. I had something to give, and to bring light. I'm so lucky. I lived in the light all the time, and I lived there for a long, long time. And it was like if someone was asking for help, you wouldn't ignore them. And I had to go. I said I would volunteer to go. I said that I *would* go and help.

D: *Did someone ask you to go, or did you decide on your own?*

F: I think that I volunteered to go, because I felt I wanted to help. I don't think I was told I had to go. I had a choice and I wanted to go. I felt I could help overcome problems by giving my light, my love.

D: *Did you know what it was going to be like?*

F: I think I was told. I had an impression that it would feel difficult, and I felt as though I would be prepared for that. But I knew I would have to forget for a while, and that I would gradually remember.

D: *Is that the hard part, forgetting?*

F: Yes, because then you feel so lonely. And I didn't know who I was anymore.

D: *Why is it important that you forget when you come into the body?*

F: I had to fully incarnate as a human, and in a body, so that I would think I was fully human. It would be too much for my human mind to remember everything at once.

D: *Have you ever been in a body before this one?*

F: I think I have, yes. But I don't think I've ever been on Earth before, because it was so hard to imagine what it would be like to be in a body that was so dense. I was used to feeling so free and so light, and then to feel so heavy all of a sudden. It was very confusing and difficult. They said it would be difficult for me, and I said that I was willing to go, because I wanted to help. I was ready to bear any of the difficulties that might happen in order to do that. I think there's a big plan. I think everyone has been asked to help. It's because there's been much darkness here, and much aloneness in this part of the universe. And it's time for the light to come. I was asked and I said I would volunteer to do this. I don't think I'm alone. I think there are others where I came from that volunteered to come, too.

D: *How did that happen when they asked for volunteers?*

F: There was a big council or meeting. It wasn't just our people, the lights, it was also other people. And in the meeting, this big plan was being organized, and they said they were asking for volunteers. That we were under no obligation to go, it was up to us. If we felt it would be what we could do, then we could go, but there was a bigger plan. And I remember my heart felt so big, full of love. I just felt, "Yes, I'll go do this. This is something I want to do." I felt that if I went, I could help with the plan to tip the balance, because the evolution of the Earth was being slowed down too much by an imbalance of darkness there. And just by being there, I would be helping to balance the light so the evolution could then progress in the correct way, and in the appropriate way.

D: *Did they show you what it would be like?*

F: They did brief us on what it would be like to be in a body. They said it would be very difficult to adjust, because we would feel restricted and limited in a way we'd never experienced before. Here there was complete freedom. There was no restriction at all. There was just love and unlimitedness. I said I'd be prepared to do that if it would help with the plan.

D: *But on Earth it would be different. There would be restrictions.*

F: Yes. It was hard to imagine how difficult it was actually going to be. I believed in the plan, and I believed that I had enough courage and love to make it work.

D: *But when you were going through the birth experience, it was different, wasn't it?*

F: Yes, it was different. Even inside my mother, in the womb, I felt even then that the darkness was restricting, as though something was wrong, as though I was not getting enough nourishment. Or just the tension. I could feel tension.

D: *But it was too late to back out then.*

F: No, I knew this was part of the deal. I'd committed myself by then, that was it. I was going to do it and I didn't want to back out. They said there would be help. They said I would feel very strongly about certain people, and I would talk to them, and I would feel less lonely. That there would be help.

D: *Even though, as soon as you come into that body, you forget.*

F: Yes, as though all that unlimited knowledge is just gone. It's just squeezed into nothing, and I'm having to learn how to breathe, even. And yes, it's really hard. I didn't imagine it would be this hard. I didn't know how painful it would be. I didn't know how it would feel to be so disconnected from the feeling of love. Also, the physical pain. When I was first born, I had a pain in my heart. The heart wasn't working properly. There was a hole in one of the inner chambers of the heart. I wasn't developing properly when I was in the womb. I think the placenta was compromised in its function and there was a lack of nutrition. And also that area of the body was compromised because it felt cut off from the love as well. The physical manifestation of being cut off from the love that I always had known.

D: *What happened? Were you able to repair the heart?*

F: Yes. It was all part of the plan. It was to help people understand their power and that love could heal.

D: *Do you know if you did it yourself, or if you had help?*

F: It was already arranged on a higher level that this would happen, and we all took part in that. I took part in that, and so did all the people that were praying for me. Everybody's energy came together and the healing took place. I think it helped to rebalance, as well, things that weren't complete in my body.

D: *Otherwise, the body would not have been able to live.*

F: No. It would have needed an operation at the least. But that was the plan, to heal.

D: *To come in by teaching people lessons even as a baby.*

F: Yes. It was a good lesson. I felt love when I was healed. I felt the energy in my body. I felt people's prayers and I felt the love washing over me. And it felt good.

D: *So you weren't completely cut off from love.*

F: No, it was there. It was good to find that love. There *is* love here.

D: *But there are many lessons to be learned on Earth, aren't there?*

F: Yes. It was hard work here. I learned to hide from life. As a child I learned to shut down a certain part of myself in order to survive. In order to protect myself from the pain of when people were horrible and nasty, and when I felt other people's pain so strongly. I felt that was too much to bear, and I had to shut that part down for a while.

D: *You weren't expecting that other people could be cruel.*

F: No, no. It just mystifies me, I don't know why. Then as I grew up, I started to understand that people had been the victims of cruelty themselves. That turned to bitterness and anger, and then that came out and transferred to others around them. And it spread like a disease of fear, fear of being a victim of other people's anger.

D: *They all have their own lessons.* (Yes) *Have you met other people that came from the same place?*

F: Yes. I've met many people, some of them from the place I was from. Some have found it really hard, and are not coping well. I have tried to help. They have a hard time adjusting.

D: *Is this what caused the depression when you were younger?* (Yes) *Talk about that. You said you had it for many years?*

F: Yes, I had it for a long time. As a child, too. That's when I started to shut down. I felt very tired. It was very difficult just to function as a human being. I was trying to be light. And I found it was so hard to be the light when everything was so painful around me, feeling all this pain. I kept thinking about why I came here, and yet I couldn't see how I was making a difference. It was difficult to see out of my own life, and into the big Earth picture of the plan. I wanted to know what the plan was, and why I couldn't remember. I always knew I would remember one day. That I would have some answers one day. There was always something more. I felt so guilty as well, because I was also trying to be a human being. And human beings have very limited understanding of the way life works, and we make mistakes. I would feel so bad when I realized I'd made a mistake that caused someone else pain. I've not dealt with that very well.

285

I've always felt hard on myself, I suppose, because I've had this job to do. I thought I could do that, and then I realized that was not going to be easy. The human body has such limitations, and this dimension is slowness. Things move so slowly. And I've had to learn not to expect too much, and that's been a hard lesson.

D: *You can't change it all by yourself, can you?*

F: No, I'm part of a team, but I felt so alone. I thought I had to do it all myself.

D: *Did you realize on another level that there was a team?*

F: Gradually, very gradually. At first, I thought my team was in the Christian religion. I thought that because they talked about the light, and it lit something inside me. The part I shut down, I tried to open up. That was difficult. I responded to the light, though, in the church, but I felt so hurt by the people there. I kept expanding in love and light, and having to contract again all the time. I felt I had a communication with the light again. There was a glimpse of it. And yet it was tainted with limitations that didn't feel right. I knew there was more; I knew it was much bigger. It was like they see God as a grid of structure, whereas I could see God without the structure. There didn't need to be any limitations. But they didn't understand that, and they didn't like that about me. Then I knew it was time to move on. I felt very hurt by things they said.

D: *Do you think they all came from the same place as you, or do you know?*

F: I think everyone has, eventually. When you go *right* back, everyone comes from the same place. But it's different levels of forgetting when you get to places like Earth. Some of them have been in human bodies for hundreds and hundreds of years, and they're crippled by the limitations.

D: *Do you think that's what happened, they lived in the bodies too long?*

F: Yes, I think they've lived here so long, they've just forgotten

286

who they were. They've forgotten about the light. Maybe they need a holiday away. (Laugh) They need to remember what it's like to be unlimited and expanded again.

Francine had turned to taking drugs at one time in her life as an escape.

D: Do you think drugs helped when you felt lost?

F: I think I used them at times as a tool to access the parts of my mind that I needed to open. The parts that allowed me to see all things as one again. I felt as though I was led to those parts of my mind. The drugs helped to open a door. I was looking for a way to feel the oneness again. That I was part of the light and that all the information was still there. It's just harder to get to it. Many people think I'm very strange because I always see something deeper. It's just hard for them to understand.

D: Because they're so caught up in the physical world.

F: Yes. It's easier for me, I guess, than other people to see the games that are being played out. As though there's a game of winning on a physical level, and there's a game of being connected to the light again. It's so destructing. And obviously having to be fully human too, I'm destructive at times. But I think it's time to stop beating myself up about that.

D: Do you think it would have been easier if you had other lives in a human body?

F: Yes, it would have helped to have had a trial run, maybe. (Laugh)

D: But still, you would have had to come into the body the first time, sometime.

F: Yes, it's always going to be hard, isn't it? (At this point the subconscious took over fully.) It was important for Francine's journey as a soul to have this experience, because it would only help the One Light to know more. To add

287

experience is always good. And it was helping a part of the big plan. It's not just to help her. She is helping even the light to grow in more awareness by doing this. She knew it wasn't going to be easy. She felt everything so intensely. She was going round and round in the pain, and she couldn't find a way out. The only way she could see was to die, because she knew she would be free then. But she couldn't die at the time she tried to. They would say, "No, it's not time yet. You still need to stay." Every time, they would stop it, because they loved her and they wanted her to succeed in the plan. If she'd left, she would have been disappointed. And she knew that it was for her good to stay.

D: *It was not allowed, because she was supposed to finish what she had volunteered for.*

F: Yes, and she wanted to stay. But there was the human part that was sad and in pain and angry and wanting to leave, wanting to end the pain. But she has a job to do, and she is going to see it through. That's the hardest part.

I knew I had contact with the subconscious, so I went ahead with my questions.

D: *You went directly into this with her. Is that what you wanted her to know about today?*

F: Yes. It's time for her to know. It's time for her to understand.

D: *All her life she has had this difficulty feeling different.* (Yes) *She said she felt like she didn't belong here.*

F: That's right. This is why.

D: *Has she ever had any lives in a physical body?*

F: A very, very long time ago. She had many lives in a body, but it was less dense than the body she's in now. They built cities, and they lived harmonious lives.

D: *Were these bodies on Earth?*

F: No. Far away.

D: *Would it do her any good to know about these, for her curiosity?*

F: Yes. She went through a series of evolution where she became more and more light, until finally the whole civilization became light. She stayed within that light for many, many eons. They had progressed to the point where they were unity consciousness. They felt oneness all the time, and there was no need to create physical bodies unless they felt like it. And then they'd create light bodies. They had overcome most of the challenges through their evolution, and it was a place where it was harmonious joy and love. That was a very comfortable place to be, and a feeling of accomplishment, too. Hence, it's very hard for her to be in such an *un*evolved state.

D: *What happened to cause her to come to Earth?*

F: There were many problems in a part of the galaxy where Earth is situated. With darkness, it's out of balance. And the Great Council came together, and it was time to start infiltrating the system. And by incarnating on the planet, beings of light had the opportunity to give their light to a planet that was overrun by darkness. She volunteered for the job, because she knew that she could do it.

D: *But it's different when you get down here in the body, isn't it?*

F: Yes, she found it very difficult to adjust. It's very hard to leave somewhere that's so peaceful to come to such a very dense, slow planet with so much pain. It's felt very intensely by people like her because she's very open.

D: *They are very gentle people, and they have not had the programming of other lifetimes on Earth to cushion that.*

F: Yes. They had to have great courage to go. And we are very grateful that they are going, because it's making the plan happen. And it is working. The plan is working.

D: *There are many others who have volunteered to come, aren't there?*

F: There are many, many. Thousands and thousands. And

millions. And there are many children being born now, awaiting in a queue, to come. That's why Francine had twins, because they wanted to come together.

D: *The twins were some of these volunteers?* (Yes) *Did they come from the same place? (Yes) And they've not had other lives either?*

F: They're better adjusted, they're having help. They had help before they started, and they have the help of those that have already done a lot of groundwork and laid the path before them. And they have a mother who's done a lot of adjusting herself, and knows how to introduce them better to life on Earth.

D: *This is what I have noticed in my work. Some of the ones about Francine's age, or even older, had great difficulty adjusting. Many of them wanted to commit suicide and leave.*

F: Yes, that is a problem.

D: *Then the ones that began coming after her seem to have it easier.*

F: Yes, the way is being prepared for them. That was part of the plan, that the people of Francine's age should come with great courage to carve a new path. They knew that was going to be hard because they were breaking old structures and redesigning new ones in an ethereal kind of way. I'm getting a picture of the planet having a grid around it, and their energy that they've brought is helping to shift the grid into a new position. More love is flowing more easily and unblocking channels.

D: *Their energy is causing a difference.*

F: Yes, the light, for the first time, is now greater than the darkness, and there is a chance that the human race will evolve past the point where it was going to destroy itself. It was headed in that direction, and that's why they were asked to come. But they had to forget who they were, because the human race needs to feel that it has to evolve itself. She had to become human in order to be part of the human race, in order to change it from the inside. She couldn't change it from the outside, because that's against the rules.

D: *Which rule is that?*

F: The prime directive of non-interference.

D: This *is not considered interference?*

F: No, this is part of the plan. It's a good plan, because people forget that they're part of the light. But they start to remember, and the light that they bring, just by being who they are, actually makes a huge difference, just by holding the light within them. They are a tiny spark which connects to all the other tiny sparks around the globe, and it's becoming lighter and lighter.

D: *And the children that are coming now have had the way prepared for them, so it's easier.* (Yes) *But they're still having difficulty, because some of them are so evolved. And the adults do not understand them.* (Yes) *I've had many teachers ask how they can help the children. Do you have any suggestions?*

F: The limitations of the education system need to be readdressed so that the freedom of the spirit of each child can be truly expressed in a creative way. And they need to introduce less structure to the timetable, and allow more free movement between subjects, so the children can see how things are all connected together. It's hard for them to sit still and learn numbers and letters, and they can't see the whole picture. They need to know how this fits together.

D: *I do not believe they should be put on these drugs.*

F: They're not helpful. They're shutting them down. The children need to be changing the system, and they're trying to keep them subdued and suppressed.

D: *So-called "normal".*

F: Normalized, yes. But there are too many of them now. Things are shifting.

D: *I don't think they're going to be able to suppress all of them.*

F: No, the wave of change has already started.

D: *Now we can see where the depression that has affected Francine's body comes from.* (Yes) *Do you think learning these things will help her?*

F: Yes, she's already started some body work that is helping to rebalance things that have been out of balance, due to pollution. The toxic environment that humans live in is having a terrible effect, as their bodies are changing now. The pollutants that have built up in their bodies are causing them to feel stuck, and these symptoms occur.

D: *Francine had several symptoms that the doctors were trying to diagnose: dizziness, tiredness, muscle aches and pains, and stiff joints.*

F: Yes, this is all part of the adjustments in her body, and it's happening all over. People need to slow down and take care of their bodies because of the pollution. We are helping her, and as the depression lifts, she will want to be here more, because she'll feel happier here. The pollution on the planet has unbalanced her. The chemicals in her brain, and her body are out of balance. The drugs she's been on have helped her to stabilize that.

D: *Then as the depression lifts after this session, and she understands what's going on, will the other symptoms fade away?*

F: Yes, gradually as she integrates the things she's learned, her body will adjust. I'm getting a picture that her spiritual body has never been fully connected or lodged in the physical body, because she had to shut part of it down. And when she opened it back up, it didn't reconnect properly. It's hard for her to reconnect that, the wiring's all wrong. But she's rewiring it at the moment, and that is going to heal her. She will understand her purpose again, and her depression will lift. It's also teaching her to be still and learn the limitations of being in this body. It's an important lesson, that through the illness she's learned how to achieve balance in a way she would never have known before. And it's helping her. She is in control of the whole situation. She has created it all, even the discomfort of the symptoms is there for her as a tool. And she will have no need of it in the future. The body's being rewired while she's asleep.

D: *Is that part of the DNA changes?*

F: Yes, that's part of the rewiring, the DNA changes. And the reason it's not happening harmoniously with Francine is because of the buildup of toxins and pollutants all around her and in her body. The rewiring is more difficult. It's like part of her spiritual body is vibrating much higher than her physical body, and that's not connecting properly.

D: *Is this happening to everyone in the world?*

F: Some people are finding it easier to change, mutate, as the DNA structure is changing. And others are finding it harder. Those that live in more polluted areas, and those that have had more difficulties incarnating.

D: *Do you think everyone is experiencing something?*

F: It depends on what level people are aware of. But yes, across the board, there are changes occurring all over the planet.

D: *It's a good thing we're not aware of them on the conscious level. We probably wouldn't be able to handle it.*

F: It is important for her to remember that she was part of a great plan, and that she was part of the light. It is important for her to remember to keep going, and not to give up. It is now time for her to remember. This information that has been stored inside her mind isn't quite accessible at this stage, but will be useful in the future. She will have settled into a new pattern by then. Her body will have been rewired, and it will be easier for her to recall these things that she needs to know. The information is often implanted during dreams, especially dreams of many different symbols. These symbols contain whole blocks of information, and this is being put into the mind. Just after 2012, the bodies will be rewired and the memories will surface. The information will be coming through then. It's already wired into the memory, and it will just come when it's ready.

Similar information was given to me when I was active in UFO investigations for the last twenty years. This was reported in my book, *The Custodians*. I was told this is the way the aliens communicate, not with words, but with symbols. They use concepts, blocks of information that are contained in a single symbol. The conscious mind may not be aware of what is happening, but the subconscious recognizes and understands the information that the symbol represents. Symbols are extremely old, and have been used down through time immemorial. When the person sees the symbol, it transfers an entire concept into the subconscious mind where it is absorbed at the cellular level. They said it would lay dormant until the time comes when it is needed. Then the information will surface, and the person will not even be aware of where it came from. This is part of the significance of the Crop Circles, because the symbols contain information. You don't have to be physically in the Crop Circle for it to be transferred. It can happen by looking at a picture of the Circle. So this session reconfirmed what I have been getting for twenty years. This always adds validity when it is repeated by people half a world apart who do not know each other, and do not know what I have already accumulated.

F: Wherever Francine goes, she acts as a catalyst which enables peoples' light to be sparked within them. And sometimes that doesn't come easy to some people, and it challenges them. But just by being who she is, she is doing the plan. Even if it's on the subconscious level, something within them turns on, and a light turns on. They find it easier to believe that the light can win when they have the influence of Francine and others like her. But some people are stuck, and find it hard to take this on. If she knew how much she was doing, she would be happy that the plan was being carried out in the way it was designed. It will help her to know that she is doing her job very well just by being who she is. Because she can't leave until the job is over, until the plan has been all put into place. She'll be happier to stay now that she knows. It's very sad that some people are overwhelmed by the task. Yet we are always there to help. It is very saddening. It's like they get caught up in the Earthly incarnation, and go round in circles and don't know how to reconnect with the purpose.

D: *And the world is becoming less negative because of this type of people.*
F: We want to tell her: *You're doing so well,* and to be encouraged. There's nothing to be afraid of any more. Your body is just being rewired, and you don't need to worry about that. Just relax. Go and do the things that you feel compelled to do. And just keep your eyes fixed on the goal that you came to do, which was to bring the light. Just be who you are. And know that you are very much loved, and that you're never alone.

Over a month later, I received a beautiful letter from Francine. I don't always hear from my clients after a session, and it is always gratifying to know that they have truly been helped by this unorthodox method. Here are some parts of her letter:

"Thank you very much for fitting me into your tight schedule. I have found it to have been of great benefit. The depression has lifted, and my doctor is satisfied that I can come off my antidepressants, which I am now doing. The session helped so much to enable me to see WHY I am here. That I volunteered to be here, and I have a new determination to see the job through. I am also finding it easier to appreciate the good things about living on Earth. The good relationships I have full of love, and the beauty in nature that inspires. I said to my husband, Eddie, "I am so glad I came!" And he chuckled, just glad to see me looking happier. He has noted to me and others that the session, however strange the concept, has obviously helped.

"During the session, I was feeling a lot more than I could describe in words, and every time I have listened to the tape, all the feelings come back clearly. I felt clearly that the loneliness I felt was an illusion of the 3rd dimension. That I was in fact surrounded by beings of light most of the time, and that there are many other light workers around me at all times. It is just harder to see the connections here.

"When you asked my subconscious mind about other lives I had lived, I was able to see in a flash the whole story of the race I had belonged to. I didn't describe it in the session, but I remember seeing a planet with low gravity. The beings were tall and slender, intelligent, loving and very good at co-operating with each other. The city I saw in a flash seemed to have tall spires and buildings that didn't look harsh and out of place amongst the nature around them. There were tall wiry trees. I saw how the race evolved to a stage where there was no need for the physical, and the bodies became light and melded together in unity consciousness.

"When I was on holiday last week, I was gazing out from the terrace where I had eaten breakfast, and I had a very strong soul memory come to me. In the place where I was staying, there were many tall wiry trees, and their fluffy white seeds were floating weightlessly everywhere on the gentle breeze. The moment I first saw them, I knew they reminded me of something, but it wasn't until that moment that I remembered. On the planet of low gravity, the trees were more fragile and wiry. And when it 'rained', the water droplets were large and almost weightless, and hung in the air very much like the seeds here. It was a lovely memory of warm familiarity.

"Thanks again. I feel like I know who I am now, and I have a calm solid confidence in that."

SECTION FIVE

THE SOURCE

CHAPTER SIXTEEN

PAST LIVES ARE NO LONGER IMPORTANT

One of my cases in January 2007 showed that the subconscious was continuing the trend that we should not be focusing on past lives anymore, but moving onward and concentrating on the present one. As I have said already, instead of going to the traditional past life, some of my clients are going back to the Source, or exploring lives in other dimensions, etc. This has been happening more often, especially during 2006, and is increasing. The pattern has definitely reversed itself to where going to a traditional past life is in the minority. A distinct shift in my work. When I ask the subconscious why it didn't take the person to the appropriate past life, it says it is no longer important. They have been through all of that, and it should be let go. I suppose this means they have already paid back any karma, and it does not need to be addressed. The subconscious says the person needs to be focusing on the present life and the future. This message has been repeated again and again.

The case in January 2007 repeated the same theme, although in a different way. I have had clients see things that I knew were not lives, but they were not fantasy either. They have seen symbolism. Usually that is because they do not consciously want to address the problems associated with past lives, so the subconscious has to sneak the information through in symbolism. But this case was different and unexpected. The subject was an immigrant in his 40s. He had very few complaints, and seemed to have no need for therapy. His body was in good shape, because he worked in construction (as a supervisor) and liked physical activity, especially deep sea diving. Yet, he drove 20 hours to come and see me. He said his main complaint was deep unfounded fears, especially the fear of dying. He occasionally would have episodes of high blood pressure, and when these occurred, he became terrified that he was going to die. All of this was very out-of-place for him, because he had never been afraid of anything.

He went into a deep trance easily, and at first I thought he was describing a past life, but it unexpectedly took on unusual twists and turns. It was like being inside someone's dream, and everything he saw made perfect sense as I realized the subconscious was giving him the answers in symbols. At first, he was standing in front of a cave dressed in ragged clothes. He saw a castle sitting on top of a hill, with an approaching thunderstorm behind it. He decided to go to the castle, and as he did, the storm passed around him. He walked across a drawbridge to enter the castle. There were guards on horses dressed in armor like knights, but they did not prevent him from crossing the bridge and entering into the courtyard. They just stood and watched. That was my first clue that this was not a past life, because in that time period, the guards of a castle would certainly not let a disheveled ragged man enter. When he was in the courtyard, he discovered a spiral staircase and went up. It came out on the top of the castle. He stood there watching a rainbow in the distance, and then saw a huge Chinese fire breathing dragon coming at him. He was frightened as it circled him, but then it flew away and left him alone. Next he saw numerous flying rats diving and circling him. This also frightened him until they turned into a flock of birds and flew away. (By this time I thought I knew what the subconscious was doing. Showing him his fears were unfounded.) When he descended into the castle, the guards gave him new clothes to replace his rags. They dressed him in velvet and gold. He was given a beautiful sword with gold and diamonds in the handle. Then a crown of gold was placed on his head. He mounted a white horse and left the castle. When he approached a stream, another dragon flew at him. This one was bigger, a different type, black and threatening. He fought with it, and eventually killed it with his sword.

Then he walked out into a field and saw many tanks approaching him. He said it was 1914, and these were the Kaiser's army. Again, the tanks posed no threat to him. They stopped in the field and came no closer. There were many soldiers (from the same time period) lined up on the road. He walked in front of them and they did not move. Then he walked to the shore of the sea and saw a large passenger ship out in the ocean with the name "Titanic" on the side. He saw there were many people onboard laughing and having a good time. They saw him and yelled at him to come onboard. He walked across the water and climbed up to the deck. There, he was welcomed by laughing and happy passengers. They said he was dressed incorrectly for this journey, and took off his royal robes and dressed him in a suit and vest and hat. (Clothes fitting for the time period.) Then he saw the icebergs and saw the ship hit one. There was a lot of screaming as the ship began to go down. He climbed to the highest end of the ship as it was sliding into the water. Then he saw another smaller ship nearby that rescued him and took him onboard. I told him this showed he was a survivor. Onboard that ship, he went into a stateroom and started taking a bath. When he looked out the window, he saw airplanes with Russian red stars on their wings, the type used in World War II, diving and shooting at the ship. Again, everything was all right, and the next thing he saw was himself walking onto the shore dressed in modern day clothes: jeans and Nike shoes. I knew then he had come full circle, and I should call forth the subconscious.

It said it was indeed symbolism to show him that his present day fears were unfounded. He had survived all of these dangers and was not harmed. I said I thought we were going to go to a past life. And the subconscious said, "We did." It was not necessary to spend time going through the lives like we normally do. It mixed them all together in sequence, yet clouded it in symbolism to prove a point and to answer his questions. He had indeed lived in the days of the castle, during World War I, on the

Titanic, and in World War II. It was again a case of not being necessary to go to past lives. He was to focus on this lifetime and prepare for the ascension into the future. The subconscious wanted him to study healing and the use of energy by taking classes and reading. His blood pressure episodes were only the body adjusting as it changed in frequency and vibration. Also, his bouts of great fear were the conscious mind's way of reacting to something that it perceived as abnormal. It knew something was happening to the body, and was reacting with fear.

It seems as though now, my clients who go to past lives and remember them in detail, especially their association with people in their present lives, are still caught up in karma and are being asked to pay this back and get rid of it. They are still working this out so they can also begin the ascension process. If they wait too long, they will be trapped in the cycle of returning to repay. We have been told they will not be allowed to return to the planet Earth to repay this karma, because the Earth will have changed too much. There will not be any negativity here. They will be sent to another planet that still allows the repayment of karma. The subconscious has said it doesn't matter anyhow, because everyone will eventually ascend. Some will do it sooner than others. They have to get out of the karmic cycle first.

In these type of cases, I just follow and continue asking questions, because I do not know what the subconscious has in store for them.

In one typical case, the woman kept seeing disjointed pictures, here, there, jumbled together. Just different scenes and people and time periods. I couldn't get her to hold on to any one of them long enough to go into a life. I kept trying, but it just continued, very disjointed. Then suddenly, she went to the place that she called "home". It was a *very* emotional scene. She cried and cried, and said it was so beautiful and so full of love. She said later, "Why would anybody have to have a near death experience to *feel* that?" This way you would *know* what it felt like. It is so overwhelming with love. This lady was a nurse practitioner who worked in a hospital. I thought maybe she would be able to use this experience there, especially with people who have a fear of dying. She could tell them, "I know what home is like. I've experienced it."

Then I asked the subconscious why it didn't take her to a past life? Why did it just show her bits and pieces? It said the same thing I've been getting from other people – because past lives are no longer important. The focus has to be on *this* life and what we are accomplishing now. "You've already been there, done that." You don't need to go back and focus on those scenes again. It's very important to move forward now, and go on with *this* life. Then it gave a very good analogy. It said, "You look at a tree, and you don't focus on a leaf or several different leaves, and different branches. That's not important. It's just bits and pieces. You should focus on the entire tree. All these lives are just the leaves and the branches. They are not the totality, the tree, the most important thing." So that was why this continues to be stressed, that past lives are not important. I think occasionally I still get them, because there's something the person needs to know for their present life. To make that connection with the life they are experiencing now. They can get rid of any karma and then move on. So apparently, the people who don't have to be worried about past lives and don't need to see them, don't have any outstanding karma to take care of. It is no longer there to keep them from progressing.

In another case, instead of going into a past life, a woman saw what looked like a giant jewel. And they said, "This gives you some idea of what we can do, if this is what you want to see." It was a giant jewel with many, many facets. And the facets were giving off different reflections in many directions. And they said,

"As you look at this, you see one reflection is a Roman soldier, another reflection is an American Indian. Another reflection is a modern soldier. Each reflection is a different 'life', as you call it. See how easy it would be. Just pick one of these reflections, if that's what you want to see." They wanted her to know the lives were there if she needed them, but she had reached the point where it was not important to know about those things. They said, "We don't focus on that any more. It has to be the 'now' and going forward."

Toward the end of the session, it said, "The jewel we showed you earlier with all the facets and all the reflections, is the *Heart of God*." The jewel is the heart of God. I thought that was an interesting statement.

Then there was a case of an older man who had devoted his life to music, as a performer and a teacher. Music had been his life ever since he climbed up to a piano at age three and began to play notes. Classics and all types of music came very easily to him, and the passion of his life had been piano and organ. He had never married, but had devoted his life to music. Now, as he was considering retirement, he wanted to know where had this interest in music come from? Since it had always been so easy, did it come from another life? Naturally, I thought he was going to regress to a life where he was probably a famous accomplished composer or musician. I have had cases like that before, and that would be the most logical explanation. Yet it didn't turn out that way.

When he began going back, I didn't think he was going to have any problems finding a lifetime, because he was very visual. But instead, when we tried to move to a past life, everything would be black. I tried many different methods, attempting to get him to where he could see *something*. I was able to have him see events from the present lifetime, but he wouldn't go beyond this one. I kept using deepening techniques. When the breakthrough came, I suspected the subconscious was using symbolism to get around his blocks. Finally, he saw a *huge* door in the side of a cliff, and a little being that did not resemble a human. The perspective was: the little being looking like an ant compared to the *huge, huge* size of this door, which was thousands of feet high. He kept calling it a "portal", and he knew there was no way he was going to be able to open the door and go through it. I realized the symbolism of this. He was not ready to open that door. That was why he made it so difficult. Then he saw a wall rising straight up out of the ground. It became bigger and bigger, as it grew taller and taller, and then began to lengthen to where it was thousands of feet long. In this wall were carved statues of different people wearing armor and different types of uniforms. He knew they were from different time periods. The wall was so tall that the statues were stacked five high. They were arranged one after the other all over the wall. He floated along the wall looking at the statues, and it went for thousands and thousands of feet.

I interpreted the wall as also representing the blockage that we had before. "Don't go any further. You're not allowed." I was also thinking the statues in the wall could very well represent past lives, and we'd be able to get somewhere, but we were again unable to move any further. Then I called forth the subconscious so I could get answers. It had a difficult time getting through to where it would finally be able to talk to me, and block out his conscious mind interference. I was beginning to think I was going to have to condition him with a keyword and have him return later that evening, because we had been working on this for at least an hour. The breakthrough came when I asked about the wall. All of a sudden, he just exploded and erupted into an avalanche of emotion. He began to cry and cry and cry very hard. Then I knew we had found it. We'd hit something. We'd broken through his resistance. We'd be able to find out what this was all about. Any time the subject goes into emotion, I know we have found something important. It is impossible to fake these types

305

of emotions. They are real.

I let him cry for a while to get it out of his system, and then I calmed him down. At that point, all he would say was, "Thousands and thousands and thousands of lives." What he saw in the wall were *his* lives, but *all* of them were warrior lives. He saw himself in different kinds of armor, different kinds of uniforms, representative of different soldiers. They covered so many, many, many time periods, going so far back ... as he kept saying, "thousands and thousands of lives." And between bouts of crying and sobbing, he said, "It was just so useless. All of the killing, all of the killing." When I finally got him to calm down, the subconscious said that was why he was not allowed to see it. It was too much. It would have been overwhelming. He was not allowed to see what he had done. That's what the symbolism of the door and the wall represented. He was not going to be able to be shown *specifics,* but he was to be shown enough, so that he would understand his purpose.

The reason for him coming back as a musician was to totally turn his life around. People who are into music are usually much more gentle. And also, in this life, he is gay. I asked him earlier during the interview, "You were alive during two wars, especially Viet Nam and Korea. Why didn't you go into the wars?" He said because, at that time, they had to fill out questionnaires. And on the questionnaire they wanted to know if you had homosexual tendencies. He gave an honest answer, and he didn't have to go to war. Now, it made perfect sense. It helped him. Later, he said this explained his natural tendency to be gay. And it also explained the music.

I told the subconscious, I thought because of the music and the ability to play from such an early age, that he would have gone back to a time when he was a musician in another lifetime. It said, "No. All of us have music in us. It's around us all the time. We just don't use it." But in this present lifetime it was decided to allow him to bring that forth. It's always *there.* Even in the other horrible, killing lifetimes, the ability, the music was there, but it was ignored, because that was not the purpose of those lifetimes. So he was not bringing back an ability or talent. The music was bringing back a softer side that he needed to focus on in this lifetime. But he said there was something else just below the surface. He could get very angry, very easily. He often felt that if he was angered enough, it wouldn't take much for him to kill somebody, and he tried to keep his temper under control. But as a musician and being gay, he has suppressed much of that, because the masculine tendencies are the more warlike. He had wondered if maybe he was supposed to be a female. The subconscious said no, that wouldn't work out the problem as well as being a male, with the more feminine tendencies.

Yet when he awakened, he wanted to know, should it be explored further? Should he try and find out more about those other lives? I don't think it would be advisable, because the subconscious definitely put up barriers, saying, "You can't handle this at this time. It's better to leave it alone. Focus on your life the way it is." He had done very well squelching any violent tendencies. So this is the way it should be.

This brings out most strongly that the subconscious will not allow the person to see anything they cannot handle. This is important, because I always worry about working with teenagers, or those who I don't think are mature enough to handle traumatic scenes. I must totally trust the subconscious to always know what is best for the client.

I have had some similar cases, one where a man regressed to when he was a general during the Civil War. Everyone was praising him about what a wonderful officer he was, and how brave he was in battle. But he said they didn't really know that he was sick and tired of being a soldier. He was tired of the war, and the killing and the blood. And then, when we got to the subconscious, that man also found that he had a whole series of lives as a soldier. One after the other, after the other, after the other, of warriors and soldiers. He said, "They think it's glamorous. That I am this *great soldier*, but it's not glamorous.

It's horrible with all the killing and the blood." So, in this life, he came in with a disability, so he would not be drafted and have to be a soldier, which makes a lot of sense. Maybe the musician, the organist, *enjoyed* killing too much. And that's why it was decided, "Let's do it this way. A drastic change." Where the other man, as the confederate soldier, decided on his own, "I don't want to do this any more." Who knows? It could have been one way or the other.

I had another case that also showed the terrible, little talked about, side of war. A man had gone to other hypnotists trying to have a past life regression, and no one had been successful. When he went into trance, all the man could see was the color red. That was all that was in his field of vision. So he came to me to see if I could get him past that. We found the answer. In the other sessions he came in on the day of his death. As I tracked it and got the entire story, he was a young man at the beginning of World War I and had joined the army because he thought it would be an exciting thing to do. He had never been away from home before, and when he was sent to the battlefield in France, it was a horrible, traumatic experience. He felt he had been lied to by the recruiters to get him to join the army. He was in the midst of battle with shells exploding all around him, and the stench of smoke and blood was very powerful. There were so many being killed that they were trying to bury them right there on the battlefield. After some were buried, more shells would drop and blow them out of the ground again. There were pieces of bodies, hands, feet, arms all over. These they had to bury again, often using their bare hands to dig in the mud. (This explained the problems he had in this life with pain and arthritis in his hands and wrists. The memory of the horrible experience was carried in that part of his body.)

He was crying, and ashamed, because he thought war would be a noble, exciting experience. Instead, he was very frightened and confused, and only wanted to go home. He felt he should be brave and daring, but it only made him feel humiliated and ashamed of his fear. In the middle of it, he was just a poor, frightened young man. He was shocked by what he was seeing. He shouted, "I'm a coward! I'm a coward! I don't want to be here!" Then we came to the day he was killed. It happened there on the battlefield. He was blown to bits by a mortar shell. That explained the red color at the beginning of the regression. That was the moment of death. All he could see was his own blood as his body was torn apart by the bombs and the explosion. That was all that was in his field of vision.

All of this was reverting back to too many lives as one thing. You have to change and go in another direction. You are not learning enough by being stuck in any type of pattern or rut. But that type of a background makes it difficult, because it is so deeply ingrained *into* the person and the cellular memory.

CHAPTER SEVENTEEN

RETURNING TO THE SOURCE

THE PRIEST

Judith's past life was dealing with history, but it would definitely not have been one that she would have chosen to fantasize. She was a powerful priest in the Catholic Church during the height of the persecution of the Inquisition. The man was fanatical about destroying the ones he (or the Church) perceived to be enemies of the Church. Anyone who thought differently, who did not bow to the demands, especially those who practiced the old ways (nature worship and herbal healing). The people he accused did not even have to be guilty, he only had to have a suspicion. He was determined to wipe out anyone he thought might be different. He became so skilled at hunting these poor unfortunates down and having them put to death, that he was promoted higher and higher in the Church. It finally came to the point where his power was unquestioned, and his ego was enormous. He even had his own sister put to death when he discovered she was using herbal remedies to help the poor. He had no qualms and felt no guilt. He was positive that he was doing the will of God, as defined by his religion. There was no doubt in his mind that he was doing the right thing. He did not question this for a moment. Thus, when he finally reached the end of his life, he thought he would go to the glorious Heaven he believed in, and be welcomed into the bosom of God where he would dwell throughout eternity. He had done God's will, and knew he would be rewarded. He was very surprised and dumbfounded when this did not happen. After he left his body, he was met by glowing spirits who took him to a different place. They would not even communicate with him when he asked about going to Heaven to see God.

He was taken to a place of flames. "I'm seeing flames. Like the Sun, but it's not the Sun. I'm someplace where there are flames, but it's not like how we experience fire or flames." Of course, the first thing that comes to most people's mind is that he was taken to the Biblical Hell. A place of eternal fire and damnation to repay for the way he had misused his authority in that lifetime. But I knew this was not the case, because I have discovered in my work that there is no Hell. Hell is an invention of the Church. It does not exist. However, if a person dies really believing that they are damned, that they have lived a wicked life, and that they are going to Hell (as the Church promises), then they may get their wish. They might experience the very thing they are expecting. Remember, you draw to you what you fear most. Even if such a thing were to happen, they would not remain there very long, because it is only an illusion created by their own mind. When they realize this (with the help of their guides and angels), then they can go where they are really supposed to go. So I knew when the priest was describing a place of flames, that it was not Hell.

"This is not the Sun. It is somewhere else. They're telling me this is a resting place. A place to come back and wait. The word 'reprogramming' keeps coming in. It's like it's a place where the knowledge is. There's no time, so I don't know how long I'm here. I'm just there. And there's all this yellow, gold fire. But it's not fire. It's an energy."

D: *But this is not what you thought was going to happen.*
J: No, no!

I knew from experience that a soul could stay in these various places for a long time, so I moved Judith ahead until she was getting ready to leave that place.

D: *Do they take you out of that place?*

311

J: Yes, they do. I don't want to go back.

D: *Are they talking to you?*

J: They don't really talk. It's not like words we use now. They just say that we have to come back.

D: *Did they say why you had to come back?*

Judith became emotional and after many heavy sighs and sniffles, she began to cry. I assured her it was all right to be emotional, and she would feel better talking to me about it.

J: I'm going to go back. I have to go back there and come at it from a different angle. Because when I come at it from in-body on Earth, it's too hard.

D: *Because you get caught up in it, don't you?*

J: Yes, it's too hard. So they let me just go back to this place.

D: *What do they say?*

J: They communicate that they know we must come down to this planet. That we must help this planet and all the beings that come here to realize about this energy source. It's something about it's been brought to this planet. And there's something about learning on this planet. It's all right from that fiery place. The resting place. It's a place of rejuvenation and clarity and knowledge. And it's almost like it is the place in this universe that holds the knowledge of the Universe, and the planets and all the life forms throughout the solar system. And Earth is a place where it was recognized that energy needs to be brought to help humanity. And there are many beings from other places outside of Earth who come here. You know, as humans we talk about the "melting pot". Well, it is truly the melting pot for many life forms that are not of human life. And the way life has formed on this planet has been done in such a way that it's been extremely, excruciatingly dense and painful. And the thought forms that come with these bodies cause people to hurt one another and to hurt what they call "Nature". They say that it is natural.

And some of us from this fiery place have come to help transform it and bring another source of energy that will help. We will take the way of being on this fiery place onto the Earth, and somehow that will be communicated in a way that the humans can receive it.

D: *Are they sending you back to repay for the things you did in that last lifetime?* (No) *You don't have to repay that?*

J: That is part of the human thought form.

D: *I was thinking of karma.*

J: No, karma is just another part of the human thought form. I have had many lifetimes on this planet. And part of that is to know what it is to have the experience, to have what is called "empathy". To know what humans feel, and so the emotions that I experience, are those which I accumulated from lifetime to lifetime. But that is not what we're here to teach. It's not real. It's not necessary. It's not what happens on that other place (the fiery place). This doesn't exist.

D: *The Earth is like that, it pulls people.*

J: That's right. It's what has been formed, and that's what I was shown. But that's not what is, and that's not what is being held. And being held is not even the right word. At that other place where it looks like flame, it's just not necessary. To use the words that we know here, it's like this gigantic screen of pictures one after another. One lifetime after another. I haven't been shown how we ended up here. How humans came onto this planet. I haven't been shown that.

D: *But the main thing is that you're supposed to come back into a female body this time to do different things.*

J: Yes, that is right.

I then brought forward the subconscious and asked it why it chose to show her the powerful negative lifetime of the priest.

J: So she would know about power and the misuse of it. So she doesn't misuse her power again. People will give her power

313

again as she continues to remember why she's here, and where she comes from. She will be getting more and more clearer information from the fiery place. The Place of Knowledge. And she must remember not to fall into the temptation of the power of being a human being. The trap that she was in before.

D: *I was surprised he was not condemned for what he had done. He was responsible for killing many people.*

J: Yes. It was out of balance. He was able to trick many people. It was for him to know fully, fully, fully, what true power and manipulation and exploitation is.

D: *But I was surprised that when he got to the other side he was not condemned for doing such negative things.*

J: That is another part that is held by the human thought form of how things work.

D: *But as Judith, she doesn't have to pay back the karma?*

J: No, not an equal amount. She has learned much through her childhood, her father and the people she grew up with. She sees so much, and it pains her so much seeing the devastation of humanity, that this is what you might call her "karma".

Although they said he would not have to repay karma, it would appear that he did. Judith had experienced many negative things during her childhood and teenage years. So I do not believe he got out of it altogether. What goes around comes around. The only difference is the degree in which it is repaid. I think the subconscious was only looking at it from the broader, big picture.

D: *She is now leading a totally different life than she lived at that time. – But she wanted to know where she came from.*

J: She comes from the Source like everyone else.

D: *Is the fiery place the same as the Source?*

J: No, it's not. It's a place, and there are other places. The words don't do justice to what it is. It's like different beings have come from different places. And the fiery Place of Knowledge is kind of what might be called the Central Place. And then there are other places in other – not dimensions – I don't have the words for it. And not everybody comes to the planet Earth. Some go other places.

I then asked about physical problems Judith had, mainly pain in her neck. The subconscious laughed as it responded, "She is the biggest pain in her neck. Her thinking, her attachment to the body now that she's here, that is the pain in the neck. And her whole thinking about past lives where she thought she has done bad deeds that she has held in her body. That pain in the neck is the culmination of that. It will be gone, it is no longer needed." Then, as has happened many, many times in my work with the subconscious, I watched as it sent energy to that part of her body and removed the discomfort.

D: She didn't want to come this time, did she?
J: She didn't want to come, and there's still emotion around that. That is because she has attachment to the form of the body. She is very pained by what she has seen in past lives and destruction that she did, as well as destruction that others have done. And she continues to see the pain and suffering that goes on. And this session will help her to know that it is the illusion. The most that she and others in human form – who are wanting to know what to do, and who have been sent here to help others – can do, is know that there is compassion and love. And that is the best that can be done on this planet at this time. And that is the greatest good for all. She seems to be coming into alignment with her mission. In the human form, she is a child of God, although from the Place of Knowledge, the Fiery Place – which too is just a word – her life and this body will be about comfort and abundance sharing.

315

THE SOURCE

When I had my first case where my client went back to the Source (reported in *Book One*) I was surprised and unprepared. As I have said before in this book, many times I am caught off guard and presented with a theory or new information that I do not understand. Then I have to consider it and see how it fits into the other material that I have been accumulating. When I received the information I wrote about twenty years ago in *Between Death and Life,* the Source (or God) was described as a huge energy source of incredible power. I was told that it was impossible to describe it in terms our human minds could comprehend. The force was so huge that it was compared to the glue that holds everything together. If it were to wink out for a fraction of a second, *everything* would disintegrate. They said that even though we think we have great knowledge in metaphysics, our concept of God is like a tiny string compared to the totality of what he really is. Then they said, consider the other people, their concept would not even be as a tiny string. They have no idea of what God really is.

In that case in *Book One,* the woman described the Source as being in the Sun, but it was not the Sun that we know in our solar system. This is often called "The Great Central Sun". It was described as a bright light that did not burn like the Sun. It was a place of great compassion and comfort, and she had no desire to leave. After that first case, I began to encounter more people who reported the same experience and the same description. These were reported in *Book Two.* Now it is becoming very common for me to find these. Is it because I have been able to integrate it and understand the concept, so more is being given to me? Or is it because of the times we are living in, and it is time for the subjects to awaken to the reality of who they really are, and where they came from?

NEAR DEATH EXPERIENCE

When this session began, Laura did not find herself in another life. Instead she returned to an incident in this lifetime when she almost died. "I was in a restaurant with my friend, Jeanie. I started choking on my food – the air went out of my body. I was protected. I was not going to die in the physical. Of course, I didn't know that at the time. I was shown how protected I am. I was shown what real love is. I went immediately to a place where there's nothing but the white light. It feels good to be back there. I know I'm aware of angels around me, but it's the most beautiful place I can think of. There's no attachments to anything. We just are. We're aware of others, the people we live with on Earth, but we have no attachments to those things. It's so pretty, so nice. It's so peaceful. I was only taken so far, because I needed to go back. They just took me to show me the feeling and the protection and the love. But I was not yet ready to go any farther."

D: *To let you know that you were not going to die? It wasn't time for you to go?*

L: They just needed to show me that it was okay. That I could face anything because they were always with me. The presence, the I Am presence is always with me. Always.

D: *But when we come to Earth we forget, don't we?*

L: Yes. And that's why I was sad. For two weeks afterward I wondered why I was sad. And I realized that I was grieving not being with His presence. They wanted me to remember.

317

To feel it again. It was important for me to remember it and feel it, so I know it's real. So I would have a faith to know it's real. So I would not be afraid and I could tell others about it. They would know, too. They could remember. I miss it. (She began crying.)

D: *Why does it make you emotional?*

L: The energy is so strong, so loving. It's cleansing, purifying. It's washing away anything that's harmful or negative to us. Nothing can attach itself to itself but itself. I feel very fortunate to know about it. I never want to forget. I never want to forget.

D: *Is this a place?*

L: For me it's the presence. Some people see it as a place. For me it's a presence that I carry with me all of the time, that I'm working to be with all of the time. I came from there, but I have come far away from it also. Some of us farther than others. But it's always there watching and waiting for us.

D: *Why do some people go further away than others?*

L: Some of it is their choice. I don't quite understand the whole thing. I don't think I'm supposed to yet. But there is darkness. There are things that are very far away from it, that are not of this presence. People forget. They get dizzy with what's in the material and the denser realms, and the denser realities. This is why some people, when they die, go through a tunnel, because it takes them a while to get back to it. They have to take a journey back to it. The Presence wants the people to know that it's always there, that it's always with them. It is shown to people if they need to see it. Some of us strive harder to be with it and carry it with us, even though we're not aware, or don't trust it. That's why I was shown that the Presence is with me all the time. I can *build* the Presence within me.

D: *What purpose does the tunnel serve for those types of people?*

L: It's just a journey for them to get back.

D: *Wouldn't they just go immediately to this beautiful place when they die?*

L: Some do. Some that have more of a connection, and are more aware, or have been working harder. But not all. It depends on the job as a person, and what they came in for. And how connected they were when they came in.

D: *Then to go back, they have to see it as a journey, as going through something.*

L: Correct.

D: *So the plan today was to take you back to this to reawaken the feeling?* (Yes) *You say you know that feeling. You carry it with you anyway.*

L: But not like this. When I'm in the physical, when I come back in, it's harder to tap into it. It's harder to be with it. It's *very*, very powerful. This is the closest I've been back to it since that day. They're letting it heal me and help me.

Laura then began to experience uncomfortable physical sensations. She was actually feeling sick, and asked me to let her come out of trance. Instead, I worked on her to balance the physical sensations and remove them and return the body to normal. The subconscious instructed me to talk to Laura's body. After a few moments of this, I could see she was calming down and I would be able to proceed. In a situation like this, the hypnotist must not become upset, because the subconscious will never allow anything to happen to the body physically. Its job is always to protect. Besides, if the hypnotist becomes upset and unsure of themself, the subject can pick up on it immediately because of their heightened sensitivity while in the deep trance state. This can cause more discomfort because they no longer feel confidence in the hypnotist's ability to keep them safe. It is always better not to awaken the subject just because of the hypnotist's fear or insecurity. I always talk to them and calm them down and remove any physical discomfort. When I could see that things had returned to normal, I asked, "In what part of the body were you experiencing the discomfort?"

L: My heart. My whole body was just racing, but my heart was *so* open.

D: *Can you ask them why you experienced that reaction?*

L: To show me that we can not live in that energy all the time. That there is a separation. There is a veil. My body could handle a lot more than most. It has given me a new understanding of that. Also that the vibration is so high that the physical body can't handle more than it's given, what we're ready for. It's healthy for me to know that, because the physical has its limitations. While the spirit is residing in the physical, it can't return to that place fully.

D: *So they wanted you to experience what it was like?* (Yes) *But we also know they would not have put you in any danger.*

L: No. That's why they told me to tell you to talk to my body.

D: *They just want you to have that memory.* (Yes, yes.) *Even knowing you cannot totally experience that vibration.*

L: No, the body can't handle it.

D: *Are you supposed to use that energy?*

L: They can bring it in for me, for what's needed. But I don't need to seek it as hard as I think I need to. I just need to ask and trust and know that it's being used. And this will give me peace of mind to know that I don't have to work as hard as I think I have to. I can use this energy to work on other people. And I will have it with me always.

D: *Was it there before, or has it just been put there?*

L: Let's just say I've been given a tune-up. (Laugh) It is in my crystalline structure.

D: *I've heard of the crystalline structure before. Do they want to explain what they mean by that?*

L: It's as close to being able to tap into the Source as possible. The crystalline structure still keeps it in the physical.

D: *Is the crystalline structure part of the body?*

L: It's the code in the body.

D: *We think of the body being flesh and muscles and bones. We don't think of it having crystals.*

320

L: There are different levels of the codes of structure. But there is a crystalline structure in the body.

D: *Does that mean actual crystal?* (Yes, yes.) *In the bones, or what?*

L: In the DNA.

D: *So it's separate from what we know as the physical structure, the anatomy?*

L: It's encoded through.

"They" interrupted the session again and said they wanted Laura's body to rest for a minute. They calmed the body down, because it was still feeling some effects from the contact with the powerful Source energy. "The heart is still a little too open. This was such an intense love, that it's indescribable. That's why it's so encompassing. We have this within our cellular structure to a certain degree. It's like I've tapped into the big computer, the main circuits. And every cell in my body tapped into it."

D: *That would be like an overload, wouldn't it?* (Yes) *But I've had other people go back to the Source. They do describe it as great love, but they don't have that kind of reaction. Is there a reason?*

L: The physical body wouldn't have been able to handle it. They just got a touch of it, and that was enough for them. Laura's was because she is going to be using this in her energy work, putting it out. It will help heal.

D: *How is Laura supposed to use it?*

L: She can use it through her thoughts. She can use it through her eyes. She can use it through her touch. She just has to ask for the appropriate vibration to come through for each person, for each situation. It is now changing her cellular structure.

D: *How is it changing Laura's cellular structure?*

L: Your words and our words sometimes are hard. We're having to process through Laura's brain.

D: *Yes, and I know the language is not sufficient.*

L: So sometimes when there's not an immediate answer, let us process through the brain. (Pause) Laura doesn't have a vocabulary, so we're having to speak through – (Pause) Seventh Ray energy is now able to come through. Laura will be able to tap into the Seventh Ray.

D: *What is the Seventh Ray energy?*

L: The Christ energy. The crystalline structure on a cellular level would have to change in order to hold the vibration of the Christ energy, so that we can share the body. And the Christ energy comes in so that the cellular vibration can upboot to hold the vibration, without harming her. So that this physical body can also live in this realm.

D: *When you say the energy will live in this body, do you mean it just stays there while she's doing her work?*

L: Not all the time. Not at that vibration. A portion of it. The body couldn't handle it. That's also why we were given this experience to know that it's okay for it to return. That it doesn't have to be with you all the time, Laura. "Channel" is not the correct word, but Laura will be able to channel the energy toward the person or situation she's working with.

I returned to the question that had not been answered earlier when I was stopped so the body could adjust. "Did you mean the crystalline structure is something that's in the genes, the DNA?"

L: Yes, it is what you come in with. That code could be upbooted or changed.

D: *The code is what you come in with?*

L: And abilities, and purpose, and what your body's going to be like when you come in. Physically. What you've chosen.

D: *And that can be changed if it's appropriate?*

L: Yes, it can be changed. Also, if you choose to let it change. If you're also on your path, it will change. You have times in your life when you can change your code. Crossroads, as you call them.

D: *When you choose to go one way or the other.*

L: Right.

D: *I was confused because I think of crystalline as being crystals.*

L: It's the best word for it that you have. Not like crystals that you find here in the physical. It's more of an etheric type crystal. It's more of an energy. And I saw many, many colors. It would be like looking at an energy wave in a pattern, and they're calling that a crystalline structure. It's only part of it. It's very difficult, in your words, to explain.

D: *It's the best you can do in our language. That's why I ask so many questions.*

L: And that is good. It's just hard in this voice.

D: *So the experience that just happened to her changed her code?* (Yes) *It could only be done while we were doing this?*

L: This was an advantage. This was an experience of total relaxation and trust, and openness. She needed someone in the physical to guide. Someone that would trust and know that everything was okay. Someone who wouldn't stop it. But she needed someone to help calm the physical body. This is now a clearer channel. It's exciting for us! This body will be a channel to help heal everybody. Some old abilities have been brought back.

D: *Oh! What kind!*

L: ET, as you would call them. (Laugh) Of course, *you* are ETs to the ETs. I'm kind of laughing at your perception.

D: *Do you mean "abilities" from the ETs, or what?*

L: Old abilities that she had in past lives. Higher consciousness. Bringing in energies from other realms to help in this realm.

D: *What lifetimes were those?*

L: This was on another planet. Oh, what a nice experience! Peaceful and calm, loving. A light body. Oh, she could travel! She could *travel!* Just "shhwwish"! By thought. That was the vibration much closer to Source. She traveled

323

everywhere. Everywhere! There were no limitations on travel. She could go to any planet, any place. You talk about consciousness on this planet, one consciousness. Ohhh! Please keep talking about it! (Sigh) Hopefully, you will experience it.

D: *So in that body, they were all interconnected?*

L: Oh, yes! There was nothing separate.

D: *That's different from the Source she just experienced?*

L: But they were tapped in much more to that! You are so much farther from that! It is a shame! It's sad.

D: *What abilities do you want her to reawaken that she can use now?*

L: The healing abilities are part, but a smaller part. It's more of a thought, the healing of the thought of the planet.

D: *What do you mean? I know the planet is a living being.*

L: The thoughts that are around the planet, and on the planet, need healing for the planet and the people to heal. It's the thoughts that are killing the planet and the people.

D: *Where do these thoughts come from?*

L: These thoughts are manifested in the lower realms, in the denser realms of the physical. The greed, the deceit. All those things that are not part of the pure, love consciousness as we know of God. These are not from God. They're from the physical.

D: *And that is what needs to be healed?*

L: Yes! And that is the second coming. That is part of the Second Coming of Christ, as you call it. When the consciousness of the planet changes, that will be the healing.

D: *I've always known it wasn't the second coming of a person.*

L: It's the consciousness. That's how you would know to say it. It can be called many things. When Jesus came, He was able to embody this Christ consciousness. And He was and is a way-shower, to show you the thought pattern, thought form. How powerful that is! And that's what helps connect us.

D: *So you on that side want the Christ consciousness to return to the planet?*

L: Yes. This is the second coming. We need to heal the negative thoughts of the planet, to bandage them and heal them. This is part of Laura's job to help do that.

D: *That sounds like a big job! How is she supposed to do this?*

L: Through her thoughts. Through helping people change their thoughts – empowering them so they can empower others. She will see new skills develop as she goes forth and sees new ways to do it. The opportunities will be opened for her. And she will feel it now in her heart when the opportunity is there. She will remember and feel this experience. We had to give her an experience that she would remember. Keep the mind clear and pure as possible. She needs to teach meditation and pure thought consciousness to people. Teaching people to use their thoughts to spiritually awaken. Changing thought forms! People are creating many of the negative entities through their thought forms.

D: *Then these are not actual creations from the Source. They are just thought forms that have been created from the people's thoughts?*

L: Yes, yes. And some of them are not so good. So I have been clearing those thought forms, washing the walls of the molds that just happen. You could call mold a negative energy or demon if you wanted to. But our people will come in and wash it off the wall.

D: *It goes along with the idea that thoughts are things.*

L: Yes. A wrong action, free will, drug use, creates. Those that serve in the higher realms can dispense and dissolve those energies, and have it sent to Source. That's why I have come into being, to have it sent to Source so it can be transformed into positive.

D: *So it's not physical. It's just energy that people have created.* (Yes) *But is this different from elementals?*

L: Yes, it is different than elementals, just as we are different than elementals. And just as we cause mischief, they cause

325

mischief.

D: *I figured they were like a basic form of energy.*

L: Yes, and they have thought forms, too. So we're all dealing with each other's thought forms. We're all dealing with each other's stuff. (Laugh)

D: *This is why when some people go into certain places, they feel uneasy or uncomfortable?*

L: Yes, they are feeling those negative energies. People can call them "entities", you can call them "demons", you can call them whatever you want to call them.

D: *It's the energy left behind in that place by whoever has lived there?*

L: It could be. There are many, many different facets to that. Many. Too many.

D: *And there are other places that have a very positive uplifting feeling.*

L: Yes. It's very real. Very real. When I first laid down and started crying, I was going toward the Source. The pure love that I was feeling. It was coming toward me, and that's why it was washing that away and out of me. So we could meet at the highest vibration I could handle. I am so thankful. Just the brief memory is so wonderful.

D: *So part of Laura's job, her purpose, is to change this energy to the highest energies so we can change the thoughts of the world. How do you want her to do this?*

L: Classes, seminars, pamphlets, books, however she can get it out there. It will be given to her and she will be guided.

D: *But how do you teach something like this? What do you tell people to do?*

L: Start with meditation, show them about thoughts, how they really become things by basic kinesiology. Starting with basic meditation skills. Starting with teaching them how to change their thought patterns and their thoughts. Even if it's with one word, one thing to help them to manifest these, show them how it manifests in their lives. Just start slowly. Then start with little books and pamphlets to hand out and help people. So that we change their lives, so it changes the thought patterns, and then they spread it, and they take it out there.

D: *Eventually, it changes the entire world.*

L: We hope.

D: *How do you want people to change the energies in their own homes, because that's the first place to start, isn't it?*

I wanted some type of ritual that people would be able to relate to.

L: Blessing. Blessings on the home. Bless the space, positive, peace be to this house. Peace be to this house. Bless your home, then bless your *own* house, bless yourself. Your body. Because it is your house, your home. Bless this home, bless this house. Peace be to this house. I ask that all harmful and negative things be sent to Source. I release it to Source. Release it to Source. And have anything that's harmful or negative here be transformed into love and blessings that are of the highest and best good. Simple things, things written down on a mirror in the bathroom. Said every day so it starts to become part of their crystalline structure. Write down simple things at first: love, peace, forgiveness. They don't even have to mean it at first. They can say, "Love, peace, forgiveness," if they need to. And forgiving themselves, loving themselves.

D: *People carry around so much stuff that they need to get rid of.*

L: Yes, and they'll see that when they change that, all these other things will fall away and their lives will begin to heal. And allow the lives of others to be healed.

D: *Then it gradually spreads until it can have an effect on the whole world?*

L: Yes. There are some powerful people out there. Their thoughts are powerful. And we need them to think

327

powerfully.

D: *Right now, there's a lot of negativity in the world.*

L: Much depression.

D: *Does this also go toward the idea of creating the new Earth?*

L: Yes, yes, it's part of it.

D: *By changing the thoughts.* (Yes) *Then the negative thoughts are left with the old Earth.* (Yes) *When we began today, I thought we were going to past lives. We didn't do that.*

L: Those have fallen away for now. For Laura, it's important to bring forth those things that she knew before into this realm to help people release things from the past and to move forward.

D: *So we don't need to worry about where we have been in the past.*

L: Some people really do need to, and the lives are very relevant because it helps understanding and healing. It's very important, but from there to step forward into the new thought.

The Light is whole. It has to experience individuality. This is very similar to what I have discovered about plants and animals. They are part of a group and operate as such, even though they are also individual. In order for them to progress to the human stage they must develop an individuality, a personality. This is often accomplished by humans showing them love, and giving them a personality. This separates them from the group soul and starts their progress. They must do this so they can experience being human. We are all parts of groups. From the insides of our bodies all the way back to the Source.

CHAPTER EIGHTEEN

THE SPARK SEPARATES

We had just left a normal past-life regression at the point where the other personality had died. I moved Edith to try to find another past life, because the one we had covered was short, and we had time to explore further. Sometimes the subconscious will bring up more than one that will have meaning for the client. Instead of going into another lifetime, she found herself as part of a beautiful light. "I'm going up. It's like being the light, and being *in* the light. It's not a white light. It's a gold light. It's everywhere, but I think I'm part of the light, too. I think I'm ... *light.* I don't have a physical body. It's a wonderful feeling, but this is not what I expected. It's not like a life light. It's like little sparkles of gold, but they're all one and I'm just being part of it."

D: *Do you feel alone, or are there other beings around?*
E: It's not a sense of ... being a being. It's a sense of being – how to say that? One of many, but become all the same. It's like belonging, and it's like being part of the oneness. Nothing separate, but being separate, but yet you're not separate. I mean, I can identify my dot, my sparkle, but my dot's part of all the dots somehow. There are other dots. There are many dots. But there's not a sense of being alone, or being separated. I can tell that's my dot. There's a sense of being just one with all the others, and one with the light part of it.
D: *Do you communicate with these other dots?*
E: Through feeling. It's like the communication is a sense of oneness. There's not a feeling of being separate. And I know that's strange, because I can identify that my dot is different.

She was having great difficulty trying to explain a concept that was so strange to her. There was much pausing and hesitation, which I have edited out. I decided to move her ahead to when she decided to leave this beautiful place. She described it as seeing a shaft of light splitting off from the great light. She watched as it picked an individual dot (or spark) and carried it away. "It's going down, and it's part of a soul that's being born. It's part of what's being put in, what's being born. There's more than this that goes into it, but this is one aspect. It's like looking at a cell. Something that's divided like two or three, and you see this go into the round thing, the cell thing. It's part of what's being born and ... it's growing. I don't get the sense it has to be a person. It *can* be a person, but it also can be something else in nature. This isn't all that goes into it. This is one aspect. Just that one little dot. But it has to do with the soul part of it."

Apparently, they were not consulted at this point, the dot or spark was just picked up by the shaft of light and carried to Earth and deposited. She did her best to describe the process. "This is like going down and being a person. Whenever it's going to become a person. On its way to being a person. But there's something already there before it goes in and becomes a part of it."

D: *What's already there?*

E: It's like the spiritual joins the physical. The physical is there, and then the spirit gets put into it or something. That's what it looks like. Like it becomes the spirit, but the vehicle is there, and then the spirit's put in.

D: *Did you feel this beam of light that takes you down?*

E: Yes. It's a white light, lighter than the gold. It has some gold in it, but it's a brighter light. And it just carries the dot, or me. I don't feel like a dot now, but like energy being put into the physical. The process feels comfortable. I still feel part of everything. I don't feel cut off. I don't feel separated. I'm there, but I still have the feeling of being one with the rest of

it. I guess that's strange, because it is a different situation.
D: And then the light that brought you down goes away?
E: That's true. But they somehow are still here.

She then realized that she had been born into something as light, and found she was a plant. "I was part of it as it was growing. But when it opened up, I was in the center. Now I'm watching it. I'm not a part of it anymore. It now continues without me. I'm over here. And I don't have a sense of me being the dot or anything. I'm awareness watching it. My job was part of the growing part, but I'm not there anymore. That job is done. Now at this point, I have a choice of what job I want to do next. I can choose. I can go back and be another dot, an entity. The dots can choose to be part of that growing process, or they can do other things. It's a choice. It's a time. It's just a knowingness."

All of this was moving too slowly, so I moved her ahead until she made a decision about the next thing she wanted to do. It was *also* confusing, as she tried to understand what she was seeing. She saw a man, a soldier, in a war situation. "I'm trying to figure out if I'm him, or if I'm supposed to be helping him. No, I don't have a sense of being the man, so I don't know why I'm here. I think he has a decision to make. I see myself as a red color around him. There are yellow colors. There are orange colors. I'm part of the red color around him. It's not just me. There are others; we're helping him make a decision. It's like an energy of force that's present and can help him. There's orange and yellow, but I'm part of the red. I think it's a war situation. I think he's deciding whether or not to kill somebody. We're just an influence to help him to decide if there's a better way than to kill. To try and help him find that better way, or a different way. It's a decision. And I'm seeing myself as part of the red trying to influence him, or help him to make a better decision."

Although she seemed to be confused by it, it seemed she was some sort of guardian spirit and was sent on a mission to help someone. I decided to move her away from the scene, and allow the man to make his decision. I oriented Edith back into her body, and called forth the subconscious. I especially wanted to know more about the gold shaft of light, because I had never heard of that before.

D: *She said she was part of the white light, the gold light, as one of thousands and thousands of little dots. Then a gold shaft of light came down. What was that?*

E: It's more like divine will, intention. It's when a need arises. How the need is met through divine will.

D: *So she didn't have to make a decision. It was all done for her?*

E: Yes. She was part of the light in the shaft. The shaft came into the light. It deposited this dot into what was growing. It was part of the spirit being implanted into the physical.

D: *Is that shaft different from the Source?*

E: No, it's just an aspect of it. It's just part of the divine will in action. It's a need being met. It's a process. Not *the* process, but one aspect of the process that makes it happen.

D: *And then later you're given choices?*

E: How to explain that. There's contentment either way: when you're activated, or when you're given the choice. It's different realms.

That was an interesting choice of words. "When you're activated." Apparently, before that you are part of the Source and are quite content to remain there. Then when you are removed, you are *activated* to become a separate functioning entity (dot, spark, whatever). Then a different process begins.

D: *At the beginning, you don't really have a choice? And after that you are given a choice? Is that correct? I'm trying to understand.*

E: I'm trying to explain. I don't have a sense of one being before the other. Except in this case, that's the way it worked

332

out. There are two different states, but there's contentment either way, where you choose to be in that state or to be of service. To accept your assignment, or you can be in a state where you choose your assignment.

The most interesting point that I found in this regression was the mention of the gold shaft of light. I have reported many times about the Source, the great central Sun, the wonderful white light, that we all come from. It has been described many times that we separate and become physical. But this was the first time this part of the process was mentioned. Apparently, all the little sparkles, the individual souls, are quite content to remain in this state of eternal bliss. *Until* something else decides it is time for one of them to separate and begin their journey of learning and enlightenment. Then the gold shaft separates from the One and acts as a delivery method to escort the incoming spark to the receptacle it is to occupy the first time. Then the ongoing process begins.

CHAPTER NINETEEN

THE ORB

Jane's first impressions seemed like a fantasy land, because it was so idyllic. She described a beautiful nature scene where she was lying on the grass in a meadow enjoying the butterflies and birds, and the sound of running water in the nearby woods. There was even a little fairy sprinkling golden fairy dust around.

"The scene is changing now. This is very strange. Things keep popping in that aren't related. – Now I see a tribe of dark-skinned people off to my right, and they are squatting down. They're watching. It looks like they're looking at me. I see them all looking at where I'm coming from, even though I don't know what that is. It feels like I'm just observing. (Pause) Very strange. To me, I look like an orb. Somewhere between pink and red. Not hot pink, maybe more like burgundy – something like that. This is very weird, like I'm just an orb floating there and looking at this scene.

D: *Is that how these people see you?*
J: I just feel and see all their eyes on me. I don't know what they see. They're just watching me go by. Now things are changing so fast. At first, it felt I was traveling along a dry riverbed, and the people were along the side. It's like I'm just in this orb thing, and I'm observing what's outside. Only it keeps changing. It doesn't stay the same for very long. I passed the tribe, and then it was a dry, sandy riverbed. And now there are trees on either side. To me, I'm just traveling through. It's very strange. And the scenes keep changing so fast that I can't even get a picture of what it is. I feel like I'm just looking out and seeing .... Now I see monkeys in the trees on the side. And I've been by buildings that look ... it's

just so fast. I'm not aware of anything I'm doing, just traveling through and observing.

D: *Then you feel your body is the orb? Or are you inside an orb?*

J: I don't feel a body. I just feel the orb, and see the orb.

D: *And you can go anywhere you want to go.*

J: I'm not sure if it's where I want to go, or if it's where I'm *programmed* to go. But when you asked me, and I thought, well, if it's where I want to go, then I want to go to the ocean. And there it was. So maybe I can just go where I want. It feels like I'm moving a little bit above the ground, and moving through all these different scenes. And now I don't feel I'm programmed. I think there are some programs, and some control, not one or the other.

D: *Let's see where you came from as this orb. If you are programmed, let's see who programmed you. And we can do this very easily by going backwards. Where did you come from as this orb? Where did you start on this observing journey?*

J: I feel like I'm being sucked backwards, moving backwards very fast. I see some planets in the distance. I'm just moving backwards. (Pause) I'm seeing some kind of machines. They're silver-grey with dark sunglass-type material in them. And I'm moving backwards through them. They're on the sides of me, and I'm moving backwards.

D: *Where is this machine?*

J: In the sky. It was light, and now I'm moving through the darkness. It feels like I went back into a star. As if I kind of slammed into the surface and merged. I'm seeing stars all around, and it feels like I went right into one of them.

D: *But the machine was out there in space?*

J: There were several, and they all looked the same. They were traveling on the sides of me when I moved backwards. I moved through them. We weren't traveling together, but I passed by them.

D: *Then you went to this star and merged into it?*

J: Yes, like a drop of water hits the pond, and it just splashes in and merges until it's all flat.

D: *What does that feel like?*

J: It feels really good. It makes me sad. It feels so good.

D: *Do you get the feeling that you're alone, or are there others with you?*

J: It's all one, it's all there. I'm part of the Whole. We're all the same, and we're all there. It's just a form. It's silvery, almost like a ball of mercury when it all comes back together. It's all soft and silvery. It's not where I was formed – how I was created, but it's very comfortable, and it's familiar. It just feels right. It makes my heart feel all tingly. I just merged with it, but it just feels good.

D: *That's the important thing, as long as it feels comfortable. Now let's move forward to when you left it and you started that journey. Did someone tell you to do this?*

J: It's not that someone told me. There's really nobody telling anybody what to do. It's just that we all know. All the parts of us that live there, we just know that this is what we're supposed to do. And we just do it.

D: *So no one tells you to do it. You just know you have to do it.*

J: Yes. It's not a question. It's not a discussion. It's just that when we know the time is right, we go.

D: *What is it you're supposed to do?*

J: I'm observing. As I moved forward, I got my own form back from the Whole. And it felt like I blasted off from the Whole, and flew very fast back the way I just came.

D: *What was the form you took as you broke away?*

J: It was a silver orb. It's a circle that comes off of the Whole, but then the Whole merges all back together until it's smooth again. And then the same thing when I return.

D: *So you all feel this is what you have to do, to leave and go off on your own?*

J: Yes, that's what we do. We journey, we observe, we come

336

back. And it feels like when I come back into the Whole, the information is just absorbed.

D: Do you know what happens to the information then?

J: We're watching, and I'm getting the Earth, primarily. But there are other planets also being observed. And we're watching them, and we're helping.

Apparently the souls or spirits were doing their work in this form as an observer. They gathered information and transferred it back again. They apparently were also helping in various ways in their spirit form, although there would be obvious limitations. But somewhere along the line, it was decided they could have more influence if they lived in a physical body and had direct contact with the humans. It is debatable whether one way is better or more effective than the other. This also accounts for the increasing number of people I find who are first-timers here on Earth. This is why Earth is so confusing and alien to them. Maybe it was thought they would be more effective if they were fresh and new, and not encumbered by past lives and karma. They would also not be disillusioned by living amongst the negativity of Earth over many lifetimes. Therefore, an explanation for many new, fresh spirits coming in at this time.

D: Then when it's taken back and absorbed by the Whole, what does the Whole do with the information?

J: I am getting the understanding that we watch and help where we can. It's monitoring, observing, seeing what's happening, bringing back the information of what's happening. Just traveling around and emitting an energy to help as much as we can right now. There's some type of energy that is emitted during the travel. I'm seeing it's not the same exactly, but similar to the fairy dust that was being spread. I see a type of energy that is almost being sprinkled. There are many orbs doing this. There are many, many different ones leaving from the Whole and coming. I see an energy being sprinkled on the Earth that is available to be used. And some is used, and some is not. Some people are using the energy to help, and some are not. Some are so into the negative, so unaware of the light that they don't know it's there. But the energy is being sprinkled. That's what I do.

D: *Have you ever wanted to enter into a physical body?*

J: I have done that. As I'm observing, we just know what our job is. That's what we do, and we don't question it. We just know that is what our purpose is, and we do it. And then we come back, and that's it.

D: *So occasionally you do enter into a physical body?*

J: The energy that is in the orb has been in physical bodies before. It doesn't feel simultaneous though. As I am feeling the form of the orb, it feels that is a different expression, and a different experience than the physical. And as I'm traveling that way, I'm doing my job and going back to the Whole. But part of the energy that is in the orb at other times is in physical form.

D: *Just a part of the energy?*

J: Yes, that's what it feels like.

D: *Would this be what humans call a "soul"? Or a spirit? Or is there a difference between that and the orb?*

J: The orb is just another of the forms that the soul has taken.

D: *So it can leave a part of its energy in a human body?*

J: Yes. I feel like the energy in the orb is one expression that the soul essence can take, has taken, and the human body is another expression.

D: *Why does it decide to enter into a human body? Is there a reason why it stops being an observer?*

J: Just a different expression, a different experience, a different part of the Whole that wants to experience.

D: *And am I correct that the orb (or soul) continues its existence, and just a piece of the energy enters into a human body?*

J: It feels like it is a different experience. That it has some experience as the orb, and then the energy may choose to go

338

into a human body. There are many expressions – those aren't the only two. But 100 percent of the full energy isn't ever in one expression, so it's split among many things, among many different – I keep getting the word "expression, experience". That it's split among many different expressions.

D: *Is there a reason 100 percent would not enter into one experience, one expression?*

J: I am understanding that there is more than one reason. One is, if 100 percent came into a human body, for example, it would be too much energy to be living in a human body. Just a percentage of it comes.

D: *It's too strong?*

J: Yes. And the other reason is just to experience as many things as possible at one time. It's not needed to be 100 percent anywhere.

D: *To experience as much as it can, to take back as much information as it can.*

J: In whatever role it decides, whatever expression it decides to take on at those times. I'm seeing the Whole, the Source, and then the different sparks coming off as individual souls. And then those souls also splitting off into different expressions according to what is chosen. And I see them all coming from the Whole, the huge light. It's like they're each little tracks of light circling and circling and circling out from the Whole. They're circling around and coming back in, and splitting off again. And it's all happening at the same time. But they're all starting from the same place and splitting off, and returning. And that's all there is.

D: *I'm trying to understand this. When you're experiencing, you're experiencing positive and negative both, aren't you?* (Yes) *Is there a reason for that?*

J: I'm getting that it's just all knowledge and information, and the wisdom to know the difference, because we split from the Light, from the Positive. Wanting to experience something different, and now we have. And now we're all trying to get

339

back to the Whole and to the Light. To make a full circle back again.

D: *What happens when you make full circle and you finally return?*

J: Then we jump off again.

D: *You want to start the whole thing again?*

J: In whatever way we choose. It doesn't always have to be the same. And I'm still just seeing everything. It's like little rays of light coming off and making a circle like it's going around a globe, only there's nothing in the center that I'm seeing. But it's making a globe shape, and they're all individually splitting off and going in all these different directions around and around. And then back again. But I don't see the end when every life stream, every expression comes back into the Whole. I'm still just seeing the circle, the circle, the circle. I'm not seeing what happens if and when all the individual sparks decide to stay home.

D: *Yes, what if all of a sudden they said, "I don't want to go out anymore"?*

J: There are enough wanting to go out that it keeps the cycle going. I don't see where they *all* come back, and don't leave again. I don't see that part. I just see the circle with all of this light circling around and around. And coming back through the Source, and then splitting off again. And not all the same ones, and not all at the same time, and not immediately, but it is a circle. Eventually, each spark leaves again into whatever expression it chooses, or expressions. There may be more than one that it chooses for that time period.

D: *How do you feel about that? Is this something you like to do?*

J: It almost feels funny. It feels like we keep circling around and around and around, and it's okay. And when we get back to Source, we want to go again, or we do go again. But it's not always human, so we're not always having the experience as humans. There are other expressions, so it doesn't always

340

feel the same. But it almost makes me laugh that we just keep on going and going.

D: *What are those other expressions that are not human?*

J: I'm seeing life on other planets and other dimensions, and resting periods. Different choices.

D: *Just to learn, to observe, mostly?*

J: And sometimes just to relax. Sometimes just to have a time to be more integrated, more quiet. It's a different expression in the physical. It feels very active, and so many different choices. But there are other places to go that are more serene, and more relaxing. And we choose to go to those just to get experience.

D: *So even you get tired after a while of doing the same thing again and again?* (Yes) *What are those places like where you just go to rest?*

J: I'm seeing one now that is just blue, and it feels peaceful, and quiet. And it feels slow. The picture I'm getting to explain it is like floating in water without having to do anything. It's almost like being in the womb. Of floating and just feeling peaceful.

D: *Does anybody tell you to go out again?*

J: I'm not getting that anybody is telling me what to do. I don't see any difference in authority or anything like that. It just feels like a place to go to relax. And when it's time, you know it, and you move to the next.

D: *In the meantime, you are accumulating information from many lifetimes, many experiences, many expressions?*

J: And just relaxing, especially from the physical, 3-D world. It's so hectic physically, mentally, emotionally. It's a very fast-paced roller coaster ride. I'm seeing that when we leave the physical, it's like the edges of our energy field are frayed and uneven. So we can go to this place that I'm seeing to just relax and integrate. It's like we're pulling our energy back into the center again.

D: *Recuperating.* (Yes) *So it's not an easy job to experience the physical, life as a human.*

J: No. It's not an easy job, but it's just a choice and it's just an expression. And it's just an experience that we have orchestrated ourselves. And for those that figure that out, it makes it so much easier.

D: *But you know how humans are, bringing it down from the broader picture to the mundane. We do get caught up in the emotions, don't we?*

J: Yes, we do. We do.

I then thought it was time to call forth the subconscious in order to get answers to Jane's questions. Although, the way it had been answering, I was probably already speaking to that part that has all the answers. But it said I could call in the subconscious if I wanted to. "Why did you pick this experience for Jane to look at today?"

J: She's been curious about having lives in other forms, and so we wanted her to see that. And also to know that her purpose before was to help.

D: *You were trying to show her how it all started, where she came from?*

J: That it's so much bigger than where she is right now, so much bigger. It's difficult sometimes getting caught up in the day-to-day, and losing sight of the big picture. She came into this world and chose the life that she did so she could experience fully all the different ways a human can feel. And to use that to help other people who may be lost and struggling, and needing to have someone to connect with.

Animal suffering affected Jane deeply. She wanted an explanation for her reaction to this.

J: Yes, she struggles still with the human reaction, and this has been one of the hardest for her. She understands the human choices, no matter how bad or negative it may look on the surface. But understanding about the animals – that's been more difficult for her. Yet she should know that they too have choices, and have also volunteered to come and live and die. And whatever has happened and will happen to them, they have also made that choice. They are not without choice.

This is also similar to the Japanese First-Timer (Chapter 15), in which she saw herself floating through various landscapes observing.

CHAPTER TWENTY

TEMPLE OF KNOWING

Sandra is a naturopath doctor from California with a successful practice. She studied medicine before deciding to put it to use as a naturopath. She is also accomplished in acupuncture and Chinese medicine.

When she came off the cloud, she found herself at the base of a mountain. "I don't know if I've been walking the whole way, or if I was ... I want to say 'teleporting' in some way. It doesn't really feel like I'm tired from walking, but I have traveled a long distance. I'm at a temple of knowing. Actually, the place is built into the mountain. It is not huge, but it is spacious. It has red columns and gold etchings on the building. I see there are huge gold etched double doors. This place came to me before in meditation, but it's more vivid now. There are many colors on the outside; mainly golds and very deep blues. I did go inside once. It's a temple of knowing."

D: *Before you started on this journey, did you know where you were going?*
S: I knew I was going someplace. I don't know if I knew this was the destination. This is the place where I obtain knowledge. I think it called me here. This is far away from where I live.
D: *Was this unusual for you to go without knowing where you were going?*
S: It's not unusual for our civilization, for the people who live around me. People know, or have heard, that you are called for your destiny to do things, and you are to follow your calling. And this was my calling, so I came here. I think my family knew I needed to go, so I did. It's not uncommon.
D: *I was wondering if you had a family. What did you mean when you spoke of your civilization?*

S: I believe this is Lemuria. It feels like the energy of Lemuria, yes.

D: *Where you lived, was that a city?*

S: We have communities; they are not really cities. I came from a place where we lived on the plains in small groups of families. I was a woodcutter – someone who cut trees down. Not in the way we do it now, but we culled trees. We choose the appropriate tree that needs to be cut down so it helps the forest grow. Then we use the tree for building our crafts and things like that.

D: *Did you think it was unusual to receive a calling to go?*

S: Right, because otherwise, you have more ordinary lives. When I was out in the forest one day, it was a knowing that I needed to leave, that I had to go someplace, but I didn't know where. I was supported, encouraged to go, and this is where I ended up. I didn't know how long it was going to take me to get here. And I'm not quite sure how I got here – almost as if I *found* myself here. Like I was working in the forest and then, like chapters, I would suddenly wake up in certain chapters of my travels. I would wake up in the middle of traveling without knowing quite how I got there. And then I would have chapters of getting to another place, and then this is the end point. I don't really feel like I walked there. I don't feel tired or dusty or anything like that.

D: *What are you going to do now that you are there?*

S: I'm going inside, and I have a teacher there. There are big gold doors, and a black marble floor. Large crystals in the center; really, really large, ten or twelve feet high – really big crystals. At the end, there's an altar. Well, it's not really an altar, it's a portal. And these crystals are in a ring. And in the center of the ring, there's another portal where ancient masters can come through. And in the center, knowledge comes from what I thought was the altar. At one end of the building, is where people can come and go. It's a physical portal, a doorway where you can go to different places.

D: *But the other one is not a physical doorway?*

345

S: The one in the center is kind of physical. You activate the crystals by toning. You tone and you touch the crystals and they awaken. They activate, and the crystals emit this light. You only have to touch one crystal and the crystals then awaken each other. Like different directions, one activates another one.

D: *(From her hand motions.) Shooting across, you mean, rather than going in sequence?*

S: Yes, that's right. And then as the energy grows, the center becomes this vortex. And you can stand in the vortex.

D: *Do you stand in the middle when you're emitting the tone?*

S: No, you stand off to the side. They're all sorts of different crystals. They're not the same crystal type. There are black ones and clear ones and different colors. They're tall like generator crystals, and each face has different usages. You choose the crystal, and you can touch different facets and activate it. And your thought or intention of what you want to know, activates other crystals in a sequence with the tone that you give it. It causes a vibration.

D: *Does it have to be a certain tone?*

S: Yes, it's a tone, and actually you don't even have to make the sound. You can think the tone. You can imagine the tone in your head and it can touch the crystal in a certain way.

D: *I thought you had to make a physical sound, and this would set up the vibration.*

S: You can do that, too. But you can learn also to just do it in your head. Specific tones for specific things. So varying tones, depending on what you need.

D: *So whatever you want to accomplish, would be a different tone?*

S: Yes! Or combinations of tones.

D: *Is this something you knew before you got there?*

S: I don't know how I know this. It seems like I've always known how to use these. Then you stand in the center of the vortex to receive the information. The crystals set a resonance that allows the knowledge to be downloaded, received.

D: *Is it specific knowledge you ask for?*

S: Yes. Or knowledge that needs to be given.

D: *How does that enter your body if you're standing in the center?*

S: Actually, I think your body disappears. And then, when it reappears, the knowing is there.

D: *Where does the body go?*

S: It becomes one with the Universe.

D: *But it comes back, because it is a physical ....*

S: Right. It comes back. And then the knowledge is integrated into the cells of the body.

D: *Are there other people around?*

S: Not right now. And I don't think very many people come here.

D: *I was thinking there had to be someone to show you how to use these things.*

S: No, I already know how to use them. I think what comes through from the other vortex, the doorway, is a guide, a physical person who seems to be the caretaker of the place, that I can consult with. Or I can leave here through this doorway to other places, and consult other people, or other higher guides or teachers. Actually, the Caretaker's more than a caretaker. I think he maintains the crystals and guards the temple. I think the Caretaker is also – it's not really a Master. It's a person who can give me guidance on what is appropriate to bring to my people. I'm called here to obtain the knowledge that will help my people grow and evolve. I'm supposed to come here occasionally and get the knowledge and then bring it to places so it can be disseminated. I'm supposed to go around and somehow share this knowledge. I have kind of a nomadic life, going from place to place. And I can use smaller crystals to carry the knowledge with me, to help me bring this into the world. Sometimes, it's actual knowledge that I communicate verbally or demonstrate to someone, but also a higher resonance of energy, so that I can help people evolve.

D: *Are crystals used in your culture, your civilization?*

S: Crystals aren't used so much by regular people. They are used by teachers and healers. Witnesses and Dreamers. You can travel and send information through crystals. You can use crystals for recording information.

D: *You called some of the crystals "Witnesses". What do you mean by that?*

S: They just sit there. You place the crystals in a place to record happenings. They absorb.

D: *What do you mean by the Dreamers? Is that a different kind of crystal?*

S: No, the crystals assist Dreamers. A Dreamer is a very evolved being. They're almost no longer human, because their vibration is so high that they are able to appear and disappear. They're very powerful creators of their reality.

D: *Does it take a lot of training to get to that point?*

S: Years, decades of training. Dreamers are very, very long lived. As are many people, but Dreamers are *very* long lived, because it can take decades to learn what they're learning. And then when they're much older, they start their work, which is to help the people dream their destinies and imagine new possibilities, and create for themselves. Dreamers can teleport anywhere. That is the first thing they have to learn to do. That's how you become a Dreamer.

D: *Is that one of the things you're going to have to learn?*

S: No, I'm not going to be a Dreamer this time.

D: *Is it difficult to learn to teleport?*

S: It's not that hard. It takes concentration in the way of adjusting your resonance, so that you can dissolve your energy field. Then step into another place by thought, and you're there!

D: *So this is taking the physical body and moving it?*

S: Yes. Feels to be easier than you think.

D: *It sounds like it would be difficult.*

S: It's difficult for people now.

D: *Then they know how to concentrate and they can dissolve the body, if that's the right terminology.*

S: Yes, that's basically what they do.

D: *And then they reassemble someplace else?*

S: Yes. The atoms have a memory so they can just go back, reassemble into the right order.

D: *Do they have to concentrate on where they want to go?*

S: They just have to think, and have intention.

D: *And then they learn about dreaming, helping the person dream?* (Yes) *Do you know how they help them to know their destiny?*

S: I used to know. I don't know right now. – I could probably ask.

D: *Is there someone there you can ask?*

S: I can ask the Guardian. (Long pause) To be visited by a Dreamer is very special. And they come to help if you're lost, or if you're just awakening to who you're supposed to be. They come to help you, and you ask them for a dream. And some people, if they don't have a dream, or if they are lost, the Dreamer will help dream them a future so they can find the dream.

D: *Do you mean a dream like you have at night when you go to sleep, or a dream that is like a goal?*

S: It's the same thing actually. Night dreams are outside of time and space, and these dreams can be created into your goal. So dreams are just a matter of stepping out of time and space. Creating something you want, and putting it back into – perhaps a different time and a different space – but something that will come into your future.

D: *First, you must have the dream before you can create anything. Is that what you mean?*

S: You must be open to the dream. If you can't dream it yourself, the Dreamer can help.

D: *Is the person aware of the Dreamer?*

S: Everyone knows about Dreamers, and it's a great privilege for someone to have a visit from a Dreamer.

D: *Is it a physical person that appears to them?* (Yes) *So they will see this person.*

S: Yes. They can appear at any time. Usually at a time of crossroads for a person. But not everyone at a crossroads will get a Dreamer to come visit. It depends on your destiny in that lifetime.

D: *Do you have to ask for the Dreamer to come?*

S: Sometimes you can ask. But, most of the time, the Dreamer just shows up. The Dreamer helps create the dream for the person. The person is in charge of creating and manifesting it. But the dream must be there first; the imagination of something there. I think the Dreamer creates it and then the person allows it to be manifest in their life.

D: *I was wondering how they get it into their mind.*

S: The Dreamers have the ability to dream, to have a dream for the person, and somehow it becomes part of the person's future.

D: *So, when the Dreamer appears to the person, they have to go to sleep?*

S: No, the person doesn't sleep. The Dreamer sleeps. And the Dreamer creates it in their sleep. The person just allows. You have to be ready for one. – I think I'm here to bring knowledge. I'm not a Dreamer. I wasn't called to be a Dreamer here. I'm bringing knowledge in the form of light. I just obtain the knowledge from the crystals. And I can get guidance from different people who can come and visit me from the portal.

D: *I'm used to thinking of a student attending a school, and a teacher telling him everything.*

S: Oh, no. No school here. It's just me.

D: *And then you absorb this information and take it back with you?*

S: Yes, to different places. Not necessarily back where I came from. Sometimes; it depends on the information, I guess.

D: *So you will return to this place again and again to get more information and knowledge?*

S: Yes. I think I can get here easily, now. I think I know how to teleport, or maybe I'm learning how. But I can get here easily without having to make so many journeys.

D: *What kind of knowledge are you receiving that you have to pass on to people?*

S: Knowledge about how they can achieve their destiny. Knowledge about how to live their lives more easily. Knowledge about nature in gardens, in growing, in plants.

I condensed time and moved him forward. "Is this what you do with your life?"

S: Yes, I'm a bringer of light. I bring light here to people, and light in the form of enlightenment.

D: *Do the people accept these things?*

S: They're very grateful. I have a very rewarding job. They cherish it. Sometimes it's hard if someone is misdirected, but mostly people are very in touch with their inner knowing. I just hope I help them become more in touch.

I moved him forward to an important day in his life. He was again in the temple. But now he was very, very old. "Grey beard, grey hair, and I'm going into the vortex where people come to visit me. I'm going...."

D: *Have you done this before?*

S: I don't think so. I thought I could. This vortex is where my teachers come to teach me.

D: *So you didn't have to go into that part.*

S: No. I always thought I would, but I never have.

D: *Is the vortex in the center of those crystals?*

S: No, it's off to the side. It's on the other side of the temple.

D: *So it's different from the place where you received your information.* (Yes) *All right. What's happening when you go into the vortex?*

S: I dissolve. I'm floating. It's wonderful. I'm going back home. I'm going to the Source.

D: *Then the body has died or what?*

S: My body just disappeared. When I entered the vortex, it just went back to where it came from. It just broke apart.

351

D: *So this is how you exited the body.* (Yes) *But you said you're going back to the Source?*

S: Yes, and beautiful light. Oh, it's lovely. Beautiful, very bright. Pink, yellow and orange light. It's very protective and peaceful.

D: *Why did you want to go back home?*

S: I come here to rest.

D: *Will you stay there for a while?*

S: Well, a while implies time. There's not really time here, so I exist here and recharge. That was a good life. It was fun. It was very fun. It was very rewarding. And it did much good.

D: *So you can stay in this place until you're ready to go out again? Is that what you mean?*

S: Yes, this is where I get my next assignment. I rest here and I decide where to go. I negotiate what I want to do. Not me, but my *whole* self gets to decide what I need to learn next, and how I can help.

D: *What do you mean by your whole self?*

S: My last lifetime was a part of my whole self.

D: *Just a portion?* (Yes) *But you need all of it to make the decision?*

S: Yes, because I need these different parts. There are other parts that need to be consulted. My whole being has a goal to experience and touch as many as I can. So I rest here until we decide what to do next.

D: *There are probably many things you take into consideration?* (Yes) *Do you like to keep returning to the physical?*

S: Yes. Earth is a beautiful place. It's just very, very wonderful. And it needs help. There's so much possibility that hasn't been achieved yet. We make decisions on when to come down.

D: *When you were making the decision to come into the body known as Sandra, what was the plan?*

S: She's supposed to do something different. Oh! Not different from the civilization now – she's supposed to bring in knowing as well. In the next life, she's to increase awareness and help people see their full potential more than the mundane things

352

that people worry about now. They worry about their house, their car, their job, but there's so much more. There's so much beauty in the world. There's so much beauty in themselves and in other places. There are other beings to know and to contact. There are other parts of themselves that they can integrate. They need to begin to see what is important.

D: *How can Sandra work with people to accomplish this?*

S: She can best do this through her ability to inspire people to live beyond their mundane lives. People take their lives too seriously. And to help people see that they are much more than they think they are. That's her job. She can inspire people through talking with them, and she will help people learn how to imagine for themselves and to dream bigger dreams for themselves. That they can step out of their pain into more of the joy and fun and happiness.

D: *It sounds like she's taking on the role of the Dreamer.*

S: She has good capacities to be a Dreamer. She is a Dreamer. She does dreaming now. She's not aware of it, though.

D: *Sandra is a healer now, and she wants to know how to expand, extend her healing work to do more.*

S: She can, into being the Healer of the consciousness of people. Many people are stuck in this rut. And she has the ability to hold a resonance of joy and beauty. And she can see for other people beyond that which they can see for themselves.

D: *Will she be able to bring back this lost knowledge that she had in the past?*

S: Yes, she connects with it now. She's just not very good at it. She's intimidated.

D: *Can you give her any instructions on how to get the knowledge back so she can use it?*

S: She could actually visit this temple in her meditation. Connect and allow the knowledge to come in. And the knowledge can give her the next step. Each next step that she takes will open up more of what she can bring to this world.

D: *So the memories will come back of the knowledge and how to use it?*

S: Some of it is memory, some of it is new. The world is evolving. There's more information that is coming in.

D: *Why did you show her that lifetime?*

S: This was a pivotal lifetime for her, and the lifetime she's in now is also a pivotal lifetime. That lifetime was one of grace and courage and being able to follow the unknown. But being resolute in knowing that she has a destination, even though she doesn't know where the path is taking her.

D: *So you wanted to show her that she has done it before.*

S: Yes, she's done it before, and it was very busy. Sandra actually knows how to return. She was given the information a while ago, but she forgot what it was. She must not be afraid. She must really know that what she can dream, she can have. And that her work is much more important than she thinks, and her impact on the world is much more than she suspects. She's not as weak as she thinks she is. What she will accomplish is a life long goal. She can help people find the motivation beyond the mundane, beyond the day-to-day work: kids, marriage. She can help them find higher motivation. She will have a wide effect, and those people will have effect. Ultimately, she and others, who have similar work, will be able to affect the world globally.

CHAPTER TWENTY-ONE

PARALLEL WORLDS

Terry had driven to my office in Huntsville in the dead of winter from South Texas pulling a horse trailer. She parked at the nearby Wal-Mart, because that was the only place that had enough room. It was very cold, and I wondered if she had any animals in the trailer. She said she was going to pick up some horses on her way back home. Terry is a professional psychic who lives in an isolated area. She tries to maintain her privacy, but it was becoming increasingly difficult. She has the ability to communicate with animals (even at a distance) and tell the owners what is wrong with them, so the veterinarian can help them. So people come and call constantly for her advice.

As part of my hypnotic induction, I always take the client to their beautiful place before I get them into a past life. It is happening more often that they go immediately to where they are supposed to be, and I don't have to complete the induction process. I have been doing this for so many years that I can tell by their descriptions if I can eliminate the rest of the procedure. I can also tell whether the scene they are seeing is the beginning of a normal past life regression, or a twist into the paranormal. The results are always the same, the person will get the therapy they need to help with their problems. The road they take to get there may be a little different each time. In these cases, they sometimes give me information that I can use, as well as answers for themselves. I have had people come to me with the sole intention of being mentioned as a case in my books. One person said, "I would be horribly disappointed if you didn't write about me." I try to explain that this is not the way I write my books. I never go looking for information. My main desire is to help the person with their problems. Most of the past lives they go back to are incredibly boring and mundane, yet they contain the answers they are seeking. If information I can use comes out, it is usually spontaneous and unexpected. You can't go looking for the things I write about. It just happens, and I think this gives it more validity, especially when several people report the same thing. My job is to be the reporter and take the thousands of pages of transcript and weave them together. I am constantly astounded by the things that are being recovered. It is often not evident until I begin putting the pieces together.

During the induction when Terry went to her beautiful place, she was describing a typical beach scene. Then it changed so abruptly, I had to turn on the tape recorder and try to recap what she was saying. There was no reason to complete the induction. At first, she saw herself floating high above the beach observing it. Then suddenly she found herself *under* the water watching the fish go by. There were also dolphins swimming very close to her. This, of course, could have meant many possibilities, but I allowed her to give her own explanation.

"I am just swimming. It's very pretty. Nice and cool. The water's very clear." She said she did not feel she was using any breathing apparatus, so I didn't know if she was human or animal. Then she saw that she was a black-haired native male. He had a knife in his belt that he used to cut open fruit for food. He did not use it to catch the fish, because he considered them his brothers.

"I can stay under the water for quite a while, and then come back up. It doesn't hurt me." He greatly enjoyed being around the fish and the dolphins. "They come when I call them. I like the dolphins. They are so pretty. They show me things. They show me how they see things, hear things. They can hear me calling to them. It vibrates. It's like energy. Vibration. Like when you drop a pebble, the water ripples. It vibrates like that and it ripples. They say they know when I get in the water."

D: *So they don't hear the way humans do?*
T: No. The dolphins say they're Star people.
D: *What does that mean?*

356

T: I don't know. They just show me this picture that the ocean goes on forever. Up. It goes up forever and ever. It's really pretty.

D: *I want to understand that. You mean like an ocean on Earth?*

T: Yes, it's like the ocean. When I ask them what they mean, they just say they can travel through. They show me this picture, it's a big blue crystal. And they say, see, we can go to the stars and come back. Out and back, out and back.

D: *Do you mean it's like space instead of an ocean?*

T: Yes, yes. Space is like an ocean. They say it's all the same.

D: *When they do that, do they travel in their dolphin bodies?*

T: No. It's blue, but it's your essence. It's sparkly. I don't know how to describe it. Like sparkles. It changes. It's not a shape. It just is.

D: *I was wondering if they went with their dolphin bodies, or how they travel.*

T: They can. They can go with the dolphin to bring messages back.

D: *Who are the messages from?*

T: First they said God, and then they say Star people.

She was speaking as a simple native who appeared to be naive, was not complicated, and simply believed whatever information he was getting.

T: They're connecting me through this blue tube that looks like a big blue crystal of some kind. It's a tube. It's really pretty in there. It's not water.

D: *Where is the tube?*

T: I don't know. It just goes up forever.

D: *Out of the water?*

T: Yes. And I can see myself go up, up this tube. They show me what it looks like there. (Hesitation, as she looked for an explanation.) Light. Lots of light. Things coming and going all the time. Ships.

D: *But I thought that the dolphins would be physical creatures like humans. And they wouldn't be able to travel like that.*

T: No, they can go wherever they want to. (This was a surprise.) People think they have them trapped. They don't.

D: *Do the other fish do the same thing?*

T: No, just the dolphins.

His answers were almost childish in their simplicity. He returned to describing the blue tube that came out of the water.

T: It goes from the water all the way up. Up high. Too high to see. Stars, there's stars all around when you get past the Earth. You can look back and see the Earth.

D: *Can you see through this tube?*

T: Yes, you can see outside of it. They call it a portal.

He was not frightened because he had done this many times, yet this was the first time he consciously remembered doing it.

D: *Are they going with you, or are you going by yourself?*

T: They let me hang onto their fins.

D: *They must like you very much if they're letting you go with them.*

T: They just say, "You're one of us."

D: *They wouldn't let just anybody go, would they?*

T: No. You have to know where this portal is. I know where it goes in the sky, but I don't know where it goes in the Earth. They don't want me to see that.

They did not want the wrong people to know its location, but its entrance was in the water. He then described what he saw as he went up in the sky.

T: We came out of the tube, and we're over the city. They show me what it looks like there. (Hesitation, as she looked for an

358

explanation.) The city's all crystal. It's like having crystals stacked on top of one another. It's a very deep blue. I'm seeing another color, maybe sapphire blue. Light. Lots of light. But there are ships that are coming and going all the time. They look like bullets, almost like the dolphin shape. No nose, no eyes, but they're shaped kind of like that. They're dark grey, and they come and go all the time. (Pause) It's a power point. There's a big, bright light right in the middle of all this. It's really intense white light.

D: *You called it a power point. Is that because of its brightness?*

T: No. It's a point in the universe that you start from. – There are tables there.

D: *Can you ask them what that's used for?*

T: Astronomy. (Pause) It's some kind of ... astronomy. They plot the stars. The table looks like marble or rock, and there are all kinds of inscriptions on it.

D: *Where is the table?*

T: In this place where the white light is. It looks like it comes out of the middle of these points of crystal. But I came down into this place where the table is. It's round, and there are inscriptions *all* over it. Line after line of inscriptions. I don't recognize the writing.

D: *Is there anybody else in the room?*

T: Yes. My grandfather. (That was a surprise.)

D: *Ask him what this place is?*

T: He's laughing. He says, "It's your home." (Chuckle) He says, "You're a mathematician."

D: *You didn't know that, did you?*

T: No. I have trouble with math.

D: *Yes. You are a native, and you don't use math, do you?* (Pause. There was confusion.) *Is that what you mean? Or is this something different?*

T: (Confused) I see myself back there. My hair is funny, I have big thick bangs. But my grandfather says, "That's not who you are, though."

359

D: Do you see yourself looking different?

T: Yes, now I'm different. Now I'm a woman, and I have a purple robe with a big white collar. And down the back is ... a long point to the collar with a tassel hanging from it. I have long curly auburn hair that is down past my waist.

D: So you changed when you came out of the tube?

T: Yes. The dolphins left me at the doorway. They said they would be back. And then I saw my grandfather, and now I look different.

D: And he said this was home. (Yes) How does that make you feel?

T: (A sigh of relief.) Comfortable.

D: So it's nothing scary.

T: No. I'm just visiting.

D: Ask him, is this the spirit side?

T: He just said, "But of course."

D: We think of the spirit side as where you go when you die and leave your body.

T: He says, I don't need to worry about that. That I come and go.

D: I wondered if it was similar, or if it was a different place.

T: A different place. (Listening carefully as the grandfather tried to explain.) They're not here. They're below us. They live in another city.

D: The ones who have died and left their bodies?

T: Yes. They live in another place. The vibration is much lower there.

D: Then, where you live, do you have to reincarnate and go into other bodies?

T: I don't *have* to. I can stay or go.

D: In the spirit realm, the lower vibration, do they have to go back and forth?

T: Yes. They don't have a choice. They get lectured to, and then they go back. They listen to talks. There are many teachers that they have to listen to.

D: But you don't have to die to go to this place where you are now?

T: No. I can go back and forth.

D: But the physical body doesn't know this is happening?

T: No. It's still down there with its family.

D: Can you do that? Leave the physical body, and journey to a place like this?

T: Yes. Whenever I want to.

D: But doesn't that affect the physical body when you leave it?

T: No. It's a shell. It just waits until I come back.

D: How does it wait? Is it living?

T: I see that person down there grinding corn right now.

D: He's going along with his regular life. (Yes) *And he doesn't even know that a part of him has left. Would that be correct?*

T: Yes. I just need an anchor here. It's like, he has to have that portal to come back to.

D: That's because you're not ready to leave the body all together?

T: No, I have work to do there.

D: But does the entire soul or spirit or essence or whatever you are, leave at one time? (Yes) *It can do that and leave the body there?*

T: Yes. I'm watching it.

D: The body will still function? (Yes) *He doesn't even know anything has happened.*

T: No. It just goes on about its daily work.

D: That's quite miraculous. I'm trying to understand how that would work.

T: I don't know how that works. I just see that person down there.

D: And why did you come to this place, your home?

T: I have to take information back. That person down there, he's also a religious leader. I hear the word "acolyte". They go to a grotto. It's underground. There's water there. It's not a cave. The ocean rushes in and out. He takes back the

361

information I give him. Numbers. He takes numbers back.

D: *What does he do with the numbers?*

T: (Pause) They put them in something. I don't know what it is. It's like a safe.

D: *Why does he have to take numbers back?*

T: These people can't live.

D: *It depends on the numbers?*

T: Yes. The information comes back. They use it to guide ... they guide ships in. Those tubes. They come in.

D: *But the people don't know what these numbers are used for, do they?*

T: No. They're not very smart people.

D: *So he has to have the numbers, and it's used to guide the ships to this place?* (Yes) *You said he was like a religious leader. Is that why he can talk to the dolphins?*

T: Yes. The people think he's ... he's not a guide. I don't know the word. But he talks to the spirit world. He uses herbs and things to heal them. They think he's a healer. He has visions.

D: *And the people there respect him for this. But does he know where this information comes from?*

T: He thinks this woman talks to him as an angel. But actually *it's himself.*

D: *It's the other part of himself that is giving him the information.* (Yes) *Then when he dies, will he go directly to the place you are now? He doesn't have to go to the lower vibration?*

T: Well, his *physical* body does. But the other part of him will come up the tube.

D: *I was thinking he was different from the rest of the people.*

T: Yes. He has to live alone out there. He has his family, but his wife is ... she doesn't understand.

D: *It usually happens that way. But he doesn't know all of it, does he?*

T: No. Too much information for him. He wouldn't be able to handle it. – He doesn't know how to use the physical body to

362

transmit the information. It's weak. He's sick. He takes on the illness of the people that come to him. I've tried to help him, but he can't ....

D: *It's wonderful to help people, but he shouldn't take that on?* (No) *But what is he going to do with this information you're sending back to him?*

T: It's for later. Next time he'll be able to handle it better.

D: *When he comes back into life, you mean?* (Yes) *When he comes back again, will he know where he has hidden the numbers?*

T: (Pause) He sees it, but he doesn't know where it is on the Earth. He knows where he put it, but he can't find it. He looks, he looks.

D: *When he comes back into another life, will he return to that same place?*

T: He's looking for it. He may find it soon. Now he's dressed in pants and a hat. He's gazing up at this wall, and he knows it's there, but he can't see it. He's going over it with something.

D: *How does he know it's there? Does he remember?*

T: He's having flashes, dreams. (Pause) He's looking for dolphins. He doesn't understand that's not literal.

D: *He probably remembers the dolphins from the other life.*

T: Yes. He's a good man though. He wants to help. But it's not the right time yet, because they'll somehow take that away.

D: *So neither one of these people really knows what to do with this information.* (No) *But this part of you remains up there at this crystal city?* (Yes) *What do you do while you're there?*

T: I talk to my grandfather. I'm learning. I'm his student.

D: *Are you also watching what's occurring on Earth?*

T: Yes. I'm troubled. I want to fix it, but you can't fix it.

D: *Why not?*

T: There's trouble abroad. I don't know what that means. I see this big white snowy hillside. And there's black coming down over the top of the hillside. I see people dressed in

363

armor. I hear a lot of yelling and horses running.

Obviously she was viewing another lifetime, and I didn't see the point in pursuing that. I was more interested in trying to understand, or at least gain information about this apparent splintering that was going on with Terry's soul.

D: Who or what decides which parts of you would be living on the Earth?
T: My grandfather sends me back and forth.
D: Are these like parts of yourself?
T: Yes. It's like particles. Thousands of particles.
D: I'm trying to understand how you could be there, and in all these other physical bodies at the same time.
T: It's like being sent out and pulled back, sent out and pulled back. In and out, in and out.
D: And when you're in the physical, you're not aware of the other place? (No) *But you can still communicate back and forth? Would that make sense?*
T: (Pause, and then a smile.) Grandfather says it's like a sparkler. The sparks come from a central point, but they're all part of the sparkler.
D: So when the shell, as you said earlier, is living down there, it has enough of a spark to keep it alive? (Yes) *But it doesn't know about the central point, does it?*
T: Sometimes, no. – He keeps telling me, "No, no." He turns the light off, because I wanted to go and stop that fighting I was watching. He said, "No, no, not you." He says, after the fighting's over, then they see the city.
D: He won't let you help.
T: I just hear the word "harvest".
D: What does that mean?
T: He just says, "They reap what they sow."
D: That's why you can't interfere?
T: Yes. He says, "You can't help everybody. It's not possible."

But I would like to try. I want to make them stop.

D: *Is that the real part of you that is there in the city, and these other ones are just little sparkles?* (Yes) *That's the real you. Do you know about all the lives you are living?*

T: (Sigh) Oh, there are so many. So many.

D: *Do you watch them all?*

T: It's just like shuffling cards. It goes too quick. There are hundreds of them. I just hear my grandfather say, "It doesn't change who you are. Those were just like shells on a beach."

D: *The bodies, you mean?*

T: Yes. Or ... cicadas. They're like cicadas. He says, "You know, they're on the tree."

What a wonderful example. I am aware of cicadas, because we have them in our part of America. They are a large bug that is often mistakenly called a locust. We live in the country, away from the city, so their characteristic sounds fill the air during certain seasons. But the most amazing and beautiful thing about them is that, as they grow, they split down their back and crawl out of their shell. They leave the shell attached to trees, and it is an exact replica of their body, eyes and everything, except that it is lifeless, just an empty shell. Very similar to the way snakes shed their skins and crawl out of them.

D: *A cicada. A shell. They crawl out of a shell.*

T: Yes. They crawl out and they come home.

D: *That's what I'm trying to understand. Do these shells have wills of their own?* (Yes) *They can do things that accumulate karma, and have to pay back karma?* (Yes) *But the main part that stays up there doesn't accumulate karma?*

T: Not anymore. It did at one time, but that's over now. There's a part, a string, a cord that attaches to the heart. I don't know about other people. I just know there's this cord, and it attaches me into my grandfather. And he says, "It's like climbing a ladder, and you climbed past that lower vibration.

365

They're still climbing. There are many rope ladders. There are other people who are past that too, but the vast majority are still trying to find the ladder."

D: *And even though they have a bigger self, they're the ones that are still caught in karma, the lower vibrations?* (Yes) *When you are able to progress up the rope ladder, does anything have to happen so you are finally out of the karma?*

T: It's like death, but there is no death. Some people follow it back. They find the rope, and they hit like a wall or something, and they fall back down. My grandfather says, "You continue looking over that top. You can see me, then."

D: *I wondered if you had to* do *something, or something had to happen when you finally went past that part.*

T: Oh, yes, the struggle. You just have to forgive. You have to stop ... just stop. No more anger. No more ... no anger.

D: *You mean, finally you understand what's going on?*

T: Yes. It's so unimportant, what's here in the Earth. My grandfather says it's what's written on this tablet, this table.

D: *All those inscriptions?* (Yes) *So when you finally reach that point, you understand what's happening. Is that what you mean?*

T: If I look back, like over the edge of a wall, I see all these lives. And only a few climb up. They're miserable. Angry. They're so angry.

D: *So there comes a time when you're able to graduate, so to speak, or progress further?* (Yes) *But if you have done that, why are you still experiencing lives on Earth?*

T: My grandfather calls me a "wayshower."

D: *I would think if you had reached that point, you would not need to go back.*

T: There are people following.

D: *So you chose to continue coming back so you could help others?* (Yes) *That's very important, because otherwise, they don't know what they're supposed to do.*

T: No. They're very frustrated. They don't listen sometimes.

They get angry.

In one of my books, I was told there were many people on Earth doing the same thing as Jesus and the other masters. It's just that they do not make themselves noticed.

I have described my *Convoluted Universe* series as books for those who want their minds bent like pretzels. If this story has not succeeded in bending yours a little, then I have not done my job. I think it is a perfect example of how one main soul part can be aware of the others, and it also gives us a glimpse of how they exist at the same time. At one time, I asked the subconscious about simultaneous time. "How is it possible that everything is happening at the same time? We know we start out as a baby, grow into a child, and finally an adult. We see it as linear progression. How can it all be happening at the same time?" It answered, "Because it isn't *happening* at the same time. That denotes a beginning and an end. It is *existing* at the same time." Although I don't know if that makes it any clearer. Maybe the examples in this chapter will help.

An article in the June 18, 2007 *Newsweek*, discussed the dangers of traditional psychotherapy. It is being found that it causes more harm than good to have patients relive over and over again the stressful and often traumatic incidents in their life. Even more danger was found when dealing with dissociative-identity disorder (formerly called multiple-personality disorder). Quote: "Some therapists believe that the best treatment for these fractured souls is to bring out the hidden identities, called 'alters', through hypnosis or helping alters leave messages for one another. ... The 'let's meet the alters!' techniques can actually *create* alters in suggestible patients. 'As more alters come out, it gets harder to get the patient back to having one identity.' The longer someone stays in therapy, the more alters show up. ... So much for 'First, do no harm.'"

When I read this article, I suddenly realized what these doctors are unknowingly dealing with. They are assuming (as most of us do in the normal everyday world) that we are one individual personality. They have no concept of this theory that we are actually pieces, facets, splinters, of a much larger soul which is sending out many pieces to experience as much as possible in a quicker time frame. That all of these pieces of ourselves are existing at the same time and are normally not aware of each other. I have been told that this is the way it should be, because the human mind cannot handle knowing all of these things. In order to function in our everyday, normal world, we must be focused on the present life, on the body we are occupying at the present time. It is all right to know that these other parts exist, but if they were to begin interacting with our present life, it would cause confusion and chaos. I have found that in exceptional cases, the person's life can become so traumatic that another "piece" decides to come in for a limited while to relieve the pressure on the spirit occupying the body. If this were not done, the trauma would be too great for the spirit assigned to the body. I believe this has been the case in books I have read about multiple-personalities, such as *Three Faces of Eve* and *Sybil*. Their lives become so difficult that they look for a way to retreat. Maybe when they came into this life, the veil was thinner, or the glue that holds them in their places was weaker. Either way, I think these "alters" are really some of the other facets (or lives) of the individual leaking through. If this is true, I think it is dangerous and of no use to encourage these parts to remain, and to interact and become acquainted with each other. This can only mess up the natural order of things, and cause confusion. They should be encouraged to return to their normal time frame where they can continue living their own life, separate from the patient's.

In my work over thirty years, I have discovered many flaws in the normal hypnosis methods. I had to discover this by trial and error, and by making mistakes in my early days (based on using the normal methods that most hypnotists are taught). Over the years, as I discovered these things, I was determined to incorporate safeguards into my technique. I am extremely careful about the welfare of my clients, so I have incorporated steps that are not taught in traditional classes. That is why my technique is unique. One of the main things I do, is to make sure that when I have brought forth an entity from another life, the entity is returned to its own time period. I discovered mental and physical effects that carried over for a few days after the session if this was not done. I never want my clients to experience any discomfort whatsoever, so when I noticed these things, I made it a part of my technique to return the entity to its own time frame. I would always instruct the client before awakening that nothing that occurred during the session would affect them in any way mentally or physically. I close off the doors and put everyone back where they belong. This is a very important step that a caring past life therapist should do. This is why I believe the psychotherapists are making a dangerous mistake, because they do not know about the multi-facets of our soul. They do not know these should be kept separate. It is not their fault. They are not taught to recognize this. The same way that physicians are often not taught that the mind can heal the body. We are all learning, and more astounding information keeps coming.

CHAPTER TWENTY-TWO

THE VOID

Jenny came from Canada to have this session while I was in Ashtabula, Ohio in 2005, giving lectures and workshops. She thought this would be closer than coming to my office in Arkansas, and she was able to attend the lectures, also.

When Jenny came off the cloud, she was confused because there was a sense of nothingness. "There's nothing. There's black, and I don't see any land. I feel that I'm in space. I'm not on any surface. I'm in, I guess, the void. I don't even see stars of any kind. I guess I better mention what's important: when I was on the cloud, I felt I was being accompanied by spacecraft, sort of like an honor guard of some sort. But now I'm in space, and I can't see anything."

D: *They were probably going with you to help you find where you're supposed to go. But do you feel comfortable out there?*
J: Yes, I don't feel any discomfort. But I don't see any stars. I feel ... not a sense of being lost, but I'm not sure of where I am, or what I'm seeing. – I've asked them for help.
D: *That's fine. They've accompanied you this far. They brought you to this place out of nothingness. Let's take you to where you're supposed to go, to what you're supposed to see – the most appropriate place. They're taking you and you can feel yourself moving through the nothingness.*

As Jenny moved, she became aware of approaching an image in the darkness. "It's not a gate, but it's like a symbol. I'm going through the symbol of a criss-cross, of an X. I'm moving through the middle of the X."

Others have seen a large X as a gateway or portal, and have been directed to go through it.

"I know they're there, and I'm going with them, in my form. I'm not in anything. I'm just going by myself. I'm going through. It's safe. Now I'm feeling more of a rushing taking place. Before, it was like I was stationary and going through, but now it's more of a rush. More quickly through it. And my body's not my body. It's more like it's being disintegrated. It's breaking into these sparks of light going through this intersection, as you will. So I don't have a body anymore. It's dissipated as I'm going through this.

D: *What do you feel you are if you're not a body?*

J: I guess in my limited mind, I'm energy. That's what it looks like: sparks, particles. It's hard to explain. If you looked at the particles from far away, there is some form to it, but you can't say, "That's a head and that's a leg." From far away it would be some shape, but it's not a shape that we know as a body.

D: *But it is some kind of form made out of these sparkles?*

J: Yes, sparkles. And they can come in and out. I can be part of everything when I'm in the blackness. And then I can bring it back together to be a form. If I have a purpose or a task to do, I bring it to more of a form. And if not, then I become a part of everything again. I go back in and out.

D: *So if you concentrate on something, then you could gather it together again?*

J: Yes. They would come to be more of a form, if we could call it a form.

D: *Where are you, or where are you going in this form?*

J: It's everything. Where I am is everything. It's familiar. It's not like I can define it as there's a beginning and an end. There's none of that. It's just expansive. And it goes on forever in my mind's eye. And I'm part of that. But there's no, *on* some surface. It's not a structure. It just goes on and on and on, like there's no end to it. And yet I know I have a place in it. That form becomes a form of many.

D: *What do you mean?*

J: Many forms, let's say, that do the same kind of thing. They can become part of the space, whatever that is, and then become a smaller form. And yet, when we're all together, it makes where we are, our home. Like we are our home in our own form. And when we *all* come together, it makes a larger home. A larger place where we're familiar and comfortable. We know that we belong there.

D: *Are there others there with you?*

J: Yes, there are many, many others. Let's say there's a whole view of different energy sparks, entities, whatever. And when I go into this place, I know where I belong as part of the Whole, but then we become the Whole. If I move out, there's a space that's there for me specifically. It's not like the others won't encroach on that space and fill it in, like it's an empty spot. It's as if I was a spaceship and was going into a mothership, and there's – I don't know what the wording is – my goodness. There's a space like a docking area for that particular ship, let's say, or you would know where to go and land. There would be that place for that ship. It's something like that, only I'm a spark of light and these are other sparks of light. And they know where I belong and I know where they belong. They each have their own space within this bigger space. They merge, like we merge as one. But it's very hard to explain that I know where my place is within that merging.

I think she was trying to indicate that she still maintained her own identity, her own personality.

J: Let's say I see this whole picture as the expanse of space, and they're all there as sparks. We're one thought, one energy, but we can be many energies when we split off. Like everybody has a purpose. Like there's a global purpose and there's an individual purpose.

D: *So you don't merge to the point that you lose your individuality.*

J: In some cases when it's required, yes, I could be part of that and I've lost it. And yet we have the ability to individualize that particular consciousness, so that I can be an individual. And yet there are times of rest where you go back in there and it's a loving thing. It's beautiful. It's safe, it's calm, it's like a resting time. But when it's needed, I can come out of there and be individual.

D: *Does it have any features or physical characteristics?*

J: No, no, it's not. I think we could be anything. But in this place that I am now, I see that it's a dark space. Not fearful of the dark, it's just dark. And the only light is our light. It's like having stars all over in the black sky, and those stars are individuals. Who, when they're at rest, they know they're individuals, but they become one and there's nothing else. There is one loving mass, I guess, but yet you could see the individual stars, if you will, or sparks. It's a comfortable feeling. It's a loving feeling. It feels like home. It's safe. And again, it's like a resting place.

D: *You said there were times you had to go back there and rest. What would cause that to happen?*

J: Well, it looks like I have work to do. And I could be away for many, many eons, but to us it's not. In that place, it's like a snap of a finger. It depends on where we go. It's very short in comparison to other places where there's a limitation of time. I could be away for a very long time, but when I get there, I realize I haven't been. It feels like I haven't been away that long.

D: *When you go out to these other places, does anybody give you instructions, or do you know where to go?*

J: In terms that I know to describe it, there's one theme of this place. It's like we all become a central mind, but yet we're individual minds. I don't know how to describe that. But when we're one, there is direction out of our knowing, and the mere existence of who we are. We know it comes out together like a command, but it's not as such. We know as a whole what we must do, and yet we're individuals in that thinking. We contribute. It's not as if we're robotic. I could say every spark is a world unto its own. And yet when we're together, it becomes a massive world that is something larger than the individual. So we know when we're together there's a certain purpose that has to be achieved. It's a safe haven, really a very safe haven. We have to go out of that safe haven sometimes to places that are not very pleasing or very nice or very safe. But we have such love of that force, that we know we must go. And we're willing to go to these unsafe places, because we don't question the asking of whatever has to be done. We just have to trust.

D: *If it's so nice there, why would you separate and go somewhere else?*

J: Because there's something innate in us that has to help, has to bring that beautiful thought of creation into being. And therefore, we do it willingly with love, even though it has caused problems, because when we're in these other places, we forget who we are. It's important that we forget, because in bringing whatever lesson or light into another existence – if we knew who we are, if we knew we could do certain things, or that it was only a temporary stay – that we're there to do a task and go back, it would give a bias to what is happening. Because there are certain light codes that we give off when we're in these places. So it would taint, it would bias what we're bringing. As an example, in a school you are a teacher. You have a set of subjects or topics or a piece of information to give the students. And maybe there's interaction between the two and then it's gone. But *we* have to go through whatever is happening in that place. We have to go through it at the same processes that they are going through. These entities, the beings, whatever. We have to go through it, because we have to be in the same situation as they are. And in progressing through whatever problems or situations or difficulties they're having, we are also enriching the Whole that we go back to, and expanding that with that information. But we're emitting codes while we're interacting and going through this process, even if it's the most difficult situations or learning of exercises. We emit. We leave something there of us. And by working through the same problems, we show a doorway or a path that they could take to betterment, or to higher evolvement or what they need to go through.

D: *You said you emit codes?*

J: Yes, it's something that's done unconsciously at that time, because again, we have lost memory. And so it's something that comes through to us, and it goes to the land. It goes to wherever we're at, or through the entities that we're in contact with. And it's an unconscious interaction. But we're giving them – you could call it a "structure in codes" – they can use to access it so they can progress. So they can learn, but again most important, it's that we don't remember. Otherwise, we might have an attitude of, "Oh, I know what comes next," so it taints the exercise. So we have to go through that ourselves with these other beings, or whoever they are, so it's not biased. But then we do go back, we always do, whether it takes us years and years and eons. We do go back and that knowledge also enriches, if we could call it "one mind" – it's not really a mind. It enriches that space that I come from, and it keeps expanding with the knowledge. And each individual spark will go somewhere different, and of course, when they come back it just enriches that knowledge, that information, and that understanding, whether it's in motions or different ways of doing things.

D: *What you're experiencing in the physical?*

J: Yes, yes, because sometimes it is in a physical. We've gone to a physical place, and whatever timeline they're in, we're in that timeline. And so we experience whatever situation of the days, so to speak, wherever we find ourselves. So when we go back, it's still in *us*, and that information expands that space that becomes larger, if you will. And again, it doesn't seem to have limitations, like top or bottom or side view or anything. It's very expansive. I can't see an end to this.

D: *With the information it grows.*

J: It's expanding also, yes, the forces of the Creator's knowledge of itself. It knows to be omnipresent in all these things. But it also has to reference it; it has to know itself. It's very hard to explain, because it knows itself. But by these sparks individually experiencing what it is in some form or another, it's also putting reference to *its* existence. It knows it to be wonderful, powerful, all of these things, but I guess it's a step down to these other sparks. That when they go out, they're experiencing one form or another of its glorious nature or its abilities. Because we are part of the Creator or God, or whatever you want to call this force.

D: *That is this thing you're describing?*

J: Yes, when we're all together, we're *it*. Whether we're together or not, we're part of *that*. And when we're not, when we're individuals going down to these places, we have taken these abilities and its knowledge, out of this oneness. We go and do whatever needs to be done. And when we come back, we're part of that Whole again. And it knows when some part of it is out.

D: *So it knows and keeps track of each little spark?*

J: Yes, because we're part of it. Or like, if that was one universe, and we're individual worlds. You see, when we go out, we're individual universes. We have all that information, and when we come back, we're part of a greater one. It's hard to explain.

D: *But when you separate and go out, are you an individual soul at that time? What we call a soul or a spirit?*

J: You're more than that. In this thing that I see, you're more than a soul. Maybe a soul is like a lower – I'm not trying to say "lower, upper." It's a different extension of this world. We're almost like a star, like a sun is a star. So it's like everything into one. It's spiritual, it's physical, it's non-dimensional and dimensional. It's everything rolled into one. And as you step down, different tasks are involved. You could be involved in creating something that are systems of physical places. But then you could step down really, really further, and you are an individual spark as a soul. And you go to certain places for a job. At the same time while you're helping others, you're also learning by accumulating information that you've learned there. So you take it back to the systems, to the world. And then again you go back to this place that's like the loading dock. Like you're part of the Whole.

D: *Then it unloads all the information.*

J: Yes, and then when you go back, the information that's in that individual world spark – whatever – is transmuted automatically to everything else that's there. There's no effort, and when you go to that space, it's sort of defined. It's funny why you're redefining a space in such a concept, but you know where your space is. And once you're there you know, like the ship that goes into that special dock. And there's a period when you disseminate information, let's say, to your boss or to your commander and a downloading. And that's given automatically when you're in that space.

D: *But you said earlier that sometimes you go to a physical place, and sometimes you don't. What are the other places you would go?*

J: There are other places that are just energy. There's no form involved. There are beings of higher learning, and they don't have a need for physical space, whether it's a planet or a world. Some of it is just color. Some of it is just sound. Yet there is living consciousness in all of these things.

D: *But they all have individual energies that live within a place like that?*

J: Yes. They could be individuals. Some of them are similar to what we have as a whole. They become as a group. So they're part of their group, but it's not like an individual, because they don't necessarily have individual characteristics. They're just part of that place that has no form.

D: *What would you learn in a place like that?*

J: There's always learning to be done in different situations, that would benefit others in the way consciousness works or grows or expands, or doesn't grow and expand. Maybe they are in higher learning, but they're still limited in some form or another, because they don't have everything they need. I don't know if that's understandable. So there are difficult situations where there's help needed in all places everywhere. It's just that it's a different kind of help or a need. Sometimes, it's to expand their knowledge. I don't know if it's to know more about emotions. Just to have a better idea of the whole ball of wax, but everything fits together. It's just been separated for a purpose.

D: *But it doesn't sound as complicated as human life, physical life.*

J: No, because here you have more things to deal with. It's so

377

diverse. It doesn't mean that the magnitude of the problems that other entities face in their home worlds is less. Maybe their worlds are being destroyed because of physical situations. Physical, not weather patterns, but they might need to find another place to live, or solve their problems in their environment. But here you have more problems; you have the whole ball of wax. So it's harder to be here. And some of us come down from that nice wonderful space and we lose ourselves. And it takes us awhile to understand what's going on and get back there.

D: *What do you mean, you lose yourself?*

J: Because there's no memory of who you are, you get caught up in what you're working with. You're here to help someone else, or to help this area. But you become a part of – not the problem – but a part of it too much. You get attached to it, or you're caught up in whatever they're feeling and doing, and you forget where you've come from. You come from a higher place of peace and wonder and abilities. Here, you're limited and you forget. But somehow, in us, there's something that pushes us to strive even when we're so-called "lost". You would say there's something built into you that will tell you. Slowly you start coming out of it and there's more knowledge given to you. And again that's a process that helps you, because you realize the Creator realizes. Sometimes the individuals – when they're individuals – don't realize that all of this can happen. When you come from a wonderful situation, you have no idea what you can get into, because you don't know anything else. So it's like the rich man, if he had lots of money, food and a comfortable home. Sometimes, he can't put himself in the shoes of a person that has nothing. And you have to experience that to understand it fully. To understand who you are. To understand the possibilities that are out there. The richness of all the diversity that makes this Whole of who God or the Creator is, or what that force is, or of the expansion. It's richness in feeling and in understanding of what you really are. Who you really are, or who you really are a part of. That's why you don't remember.

D: *Isn't there a danger that you might be totally lost, and not know how to get back?*

J: Yes. And I think in this case, that's what happened to me. But again, there's an understanding, there's a hope, there's a spark. There's something in us that tells us, no, you have to keep on going. You have to strive. There are lights at the end of the tunnel, so to speak, and you will find your way again. But again, in so doing, you help whoever you're in contact with gain their strength, and their way back. But when you get back there, you say, "Oh, my goodness! It took me so long to do whatever I had to do." You think you understand it all, but once you get into these situations or these places, some of it is so dark that you can easily lose yourself. But again, there's something inbred in that individual or spark that will carry you back.

D: *I keep wondering, when you start out on these journeys, is there someone or something that tells you where you have to go?*

J: Again, it's hard to describe what that is. You know because it comes to you in a thought, like these individual sparks that make up what this one entity knows. It's very hard to explain. It's like a knowing. You know where you have to go.

D: *I thought maybe there was someone or something that kept a record, and said this is where you have to go next.*

J: No. Everything is known. There's one who knows who's out there, and what they're doing. But it's not like a record keeping of that sort. It's all mental. It's an inbred kind of thing. Now, what has happened in the past when people do get lost helping the beings that live there, others will come and try to help *them*. So in some cases, depending on where you've gone astray – because many have forgotten who they are – there's always a timing involved, and there is help. It will become known to these people when the time is right. That, "Okay, it's time to realize who you are, and you were meant to do a certain thing here and go back."

D: *So the ones that come and help are other sparks?*

J: Yes, yes, they are.

D: *They know you're in trouble, so they'll come and try to help.* (Yes, yes.) *Well, in my work, I have found a lot about the spirit side where we go after we leave the physical body. Is that a different place?*

J: Yes, that's a different place. The way I see it from here, that I understand, is the spirit world is associated with certain ... let's say, the Earth has so many layers of – not layers. – But looking at the planet Earth, it has a spirit world, it has a dimension. Each planet has its own dimensions and this is a place that's associated with that. Where I'm from, there's not a spirit world as such.

D: *So the physical beings, when they leave the physical body, go back and forth to their own individual spirit world?*

J: Well, they evolve, too. And as they come back and forth, they will evolve to the next level that's associated with that planet. Eventually, they will work themselves until they can go to other worlds and experience other situations there. But I see it as a progression to higher parts of the Earth or dimensions that are associated with that, or spheres of energy around that particular place. Then as they progress at what they're learning, sometimes there are beings that will jump. They will not have to go through different dimensions or layers to go to another place of higher learning. Because what they've experienced in that level – "levels" is a better word – they had it all in that one experience, so therefore, they can go to different parts. It's very strange the way I see it. I see it separate and yet it's a part of everything. It's like this place that I am is *there.* The other systems are in another situation, and yet I know that is a part of everything. Like we all are a part of everything. It just seems like a finer level. And some of us, even though we've experienced situations on Earth or anywhere else, we've always come from this spot.

D: *So everything initiates, originates from that spot. – I wanted to make sure that what I've been hearing about the spirit world was also accurate. They exist separately then.*

J: Yes, I guess it's different levels of the same thing. But in certain places, they don't exist as what you would term a spirit world.

D: *On Earth, we say we accumulate karma when we come here, because of all the things we get involved with. We get stuck, because we have to keep coming back again and again to pay back the karma. Is that accurate?*

J: Yes, it is, and that's another thing we've been caught up in. Entities that are coming to help have been caught up in the situation. It's made that way. It's not so simple as, "Okay, I know who I am. I'm here to do something." We get caught up in it, and then we ourselves are – not a prisoner – but we're held in this energy until we work out whatever we've created. We've come down to help a particular place, situation, being, but then we get caught up in the mire. So therefore, we're kind of stuck, if you will, until it has also been worked out; until we found our way out. But it's not a negative thing in one way, because in that finding out, sometimes this is where the richness of information is. Because, if you were to come from that place to this, and you zap in and out. You've done your thing, but you haven't really experienced anything. You haven't felt anything. It's too quick. So in being stuck, there it is a positive note. Whatever you're feeling and going through, you are enriching the Whole in its expansion of its knowledge. Its expansions of feelings, expansion of everything of what it is. So it's not necessarily a negative thing. It's a good thing in some ways, because it all serves. It's all intertwined and it serves purposes. You don't really know what that purpose is when you're down here.

D: *Then it seems like you have to work it out first before you're allowed to go back home.* (Yes) *I have been told that on the spirit side, there are people who help you, advise you.*

J: Yes, guides and such. – I know there are certain things I can't know at this time because it would taint. If I have certain questions, for example, and if I know it all (and I don't know it all, because there's always learning) it would complicate – not complicate it – but it's like there will be an appropriate time when everything will be revealed. There are certain things I have yet to learn to go through. And I have to be patient and really have faith. I think at some point, I lost my faith, because I thought I was left here. And they're not coming to get me.

D: *Is that what you felt?*

J: At some point, I think I did. And therefore, I have to learn it's not a punishment at all. I have to go on faith for a while.

D: *Why did you have the feeling you were left here and forgotten about?*

J: I think it's a case of, when you understand where you came from, and the abilities you were able to experience. You knew who you truly are. And you come down and let's say, you worked in a really low vibration, you could either – when you've forgotten – get caught up in that situation, or you have like a superiority. You see, this is why sometimes it's not good to understand. It's very complex. You could feel superior to these other people that you're with, or beings, or whatever situation. And then you lose that spiritual side of who you are. You think you're better than someone else. And therefore, you get deeper into that negativity or that place or situation. But still, you know there's a part of you that is beautiful, that is holy, that is sacred, that is love. It's always there in you. And you are sort of in between, where you know who you really are, and then you forget. You get frustrated and, "Why doesn't someone from where I come from come, and get me out of this situation?" And yet, I've gotten myself into that situation. So there's no judgment. I have to learn. I have to go through different experiences to find my way out. And yet, they're there with you and they will always guide you to people or situations. Or when it's time, and you're ready, to get over that arrogance that you had in that particular situation, because again, you're talking about karma. It is cause and effect. Whatever you create, you have to live with the consequences. Even higher beings can also lose their way for a time, and they have to go through the same. You know that the process is the same. It's just that the criteria are different.

D: *So even they take a chance.*

J: Yes, you do, you do. Where you come from, it's so wonderful, and you know you can do all these things. But you don't realize how dense it is in whatever situation or place you're at. So you can, through time, be sort of dragged down in what you create. Of course, you create and manifest all the time.

D: *That's why you said it can take eons of time.*

J: Yes, it could. But then, when you get back, it's so wonderful to be back there that you thought, "Oh, well, I was only away for a few seconds."

D: *Then, there are times when all of the sparks go back to the Source?*

J: Yes. There's a time where there's kind of a resting period, where they do. We are all back. And then it's time to go out again.

D: *When all of the sparks are back together, what happens to the creations they have created?*

J: I think it's all drawn back, the way I see it. At some point, everything has to come back, whether we're the individual spark, and we've created worlds and whatever. They all have to come back for a resting place. They'd all come and be a part of the Whole again, so those creations are brought back, because they're all manifestations, really. But there's a twofold thing here where they all come back for a rest. And that is when the whole of everything comes back for a rest.

D: *Then, in that case, everything they created is gone.*

J: Yes, the way I understand it. There's not a force to hold it there. All of that is back into its resting place for a time. But in between these great expansions of time, the individual ones can go in and go out and do certain things and come back for a rest. That doesn't mean that all of them are at rest, but there are points of time when they all come back.

D: *So at that time when all of the sparks go back into the Whole, everything they have created just disappears.*

J: It's like a drawing in. For instance, I would have created so many things. They integrate back into me, and I integrate back into the Whole. And then something else is created. Something fresh. Everything is absorbed back into that one ball of knowledge, of energy, of creation of all that you can think of. It goes back into that, and you feel a part of everything. There's no separation.

D: *In that case, it does not really disappear. It's just integrated.*

J: It's integrated back, exactly. But all these things I've created as individual manifestations, nothing is really lost because it was a part of me, and I was a part of that.

D: *So after you rest for a while, then what happens?*

J: Then it's time to start up again. It's another thing. It's a constant. But you see, the knowledge that was acquired during that period of time of creation, of manifestation, is not lost. That's a part of that entity. It's a part of that individual spark, so it's never lost. It's part of you. So you go out now and create some more. And you go through that process again of learning. But yet it's like something new, something fresh, and yet it's something old.

D: *But during those times of creation, you not only live on Earth, but on many other places?*

J: Yes, many places.

D: *And you can live in many different types of bodies too, can't you?*

J: Yes. Wherever you go, you're still you. But there's some purpose of it. It is to bring light, to bring knowledge, to bring creation into the mix. You decide, with help, where you need to go.

I then asked this entity to depart and asked the subconscious to come forth to answer Jenny's questions. I always want to know why the subject was shown the particular lifetime.

J: Because all of her questions (and she knows this deep down inside) are not significant. They're not important. She has to realize she's a part of a greater Whole that's much more important, which would satisfy whatever her needs are. She has to remember that she has to go to the top. It's not important that she knows what connections there are with this person or that one. It's important for her to go back to the basics. To focus her attention to the top. No matter what comes into her life, whatever's being shown to her, to look at it with a sense of wonder. Whether she has impediments or challenges, she has to realize that she is part of what you call God, or that force. To have faith that it's going to work out, that whatever her life purpose is, it's going to come to her. People will come in her path that she'll be working with. She has to see the bigger picture, in that all of these things are manifestations. And I'm not going to give her any answers.

D: *(I was surprised.) But she has questions.*

J: Yes. And I think she's going to understand what she was describing, the process. There are certain pieces of information that will help people to move and progress. She, in herself, has to deal with the fact that she's running with no – not assistance – there's assistance there, but she's going to have to go lightly. I'm using the word "lightly". She has to go on faith. She has to have faith that the entity she was a part of, the world she was part of, was love. There was knowledge, there was information, there was consciousness. It's so beyond what she understands at this moment.

D: *It's beyond what many of us understand.*

J; Yes, exactly. Even if we're giving her the information, she has to go, she has to cultivate. And this is one of the abilities she has to cultivate, her inner knowing. That even if she aspires to this connection or that, this is to nurture that without seeing, without touching, because that's going to make her structure strong. See, she's forgotten the structure, she's forgotten who she was. She has glimpses sometimes of who she is, but she has the strength, and that structure is whole, it is strong. It is filled with love, compassion, understanding for others. And this is the wonderment, this is the excitement, this is the experience of it all in not having all the answers, even if they're just little tidbits. There's a wonder in not knowing, but understanding that the help is there for her. And there are people there, whoever they may be. She's got to get away from the naming of things, and just feel and cultivate her own inner guidance, and she will get there. She will get there.

D: *Is this why you chose not to show her any past lives?*

J: Yes. She has to go back to the basics. Never mind spaceships and other worlds. Atlantis. She was part of that time, but she had to go back to where she came from. To that loving structure that is one, that integrates all things as one thing. And that is love of that entity, or being part of that. That's a safe haven not to forget. Not to be stepping down. Yes, creation, we all create, but it's not to get caught up again in the creation. It is to understand why it was done, where we came from, and not get caught up in the things that we did.

D: *I'm getting more and more people now who are being told that past lives are not important. It's what we do from here on.*

J: Yes, yes, yes, exactly. We are all God. He wants us to be equals to Him. He wants us to ask Him questions, to be challenged. Not to be thinking, "Oh, I have to bow down to this." It's the questioning. It's being equal. He is a part of us, and therefore, He wants us to share equally with respect. It is not that we are to go blindly seeing faith, and doing whatever someone's telling you to do. That's not what He wants. And that's fine.

D: *So there's no need to dwell on the karma anymore.*

J: No. There's no need. And if we have any inkling at all, there are higher beings beside us. Or God is beside us, or they are walking with us. They're going to bring the right people, opportunities, for you to fulfill what you have to fulfill. You could be anything in other lives, but what you truly are is part of this grid, part of this wholeness. It's not important what the body looks like or what pain it has. We can die many, many times. It doesn't matter. What matters is the soul. That higher existence that is eternal. That's the thing you have to nourish.

D: *That's what you want people to know.*

J: Yes, yes. We have to go back to the basic. But the most important fact is that we are part of something tremendous, loving, that has knowledge of everything. And get away from the creations we've created. We manifest every second of the day. And not to be caught up again and lose our – we call it "divinity" – lose that spark of life that we have, by being caught up in "Who was I, what did I do?" You're also letting go. You're not experiencing the life that you've chosen to experience. We can't know everything. It's like a wonder. The next corner might bring you something tremendous. But if you knew everything, there wouldn't be that joy of discovering it again, but discovering again who we truly are. Aim high to that love. Show that love to everybody you meet. Compassion, understanding will come to you.

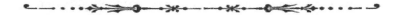

From another case:

Teresa wanted to know what happened during an experience she had in February 2005. She was meditating when she suddenly found herself in a dark, formless place of nothingness, which she could only explain as the "void". It was not frightening, instead, it gave her a great sense of enlightenment. When she returned to a conscious state, she tried to understand it logically, and it made no sense to her. The subconscious was explaining:

T: That was just an experience of being more in touch with some of these more refined levels, or other levels of consciousness. Dropping away the pictures without dropping away this particular body. I allowed her to have that experience. So it's nothing else but to show her that it really is all one consciousness. And that experience of the void that she had is even going to a more elementary level of that consciousness. It is the nothingness out of which everything comes. Everything comes from that. That is infinite, and that is everything, at its most unrefined level. And as she had that experience, it would be natural for her to recognize that none of this is real. To see that, yes, on one level it is real, but from that level of the void, this is just near surface, just near hue, just a tint of color. Very little. That the real reality is the consciousness and is the base of the consciousness, the pure emptiness, the nothingness, from which all consciousness stems.

D: *Is that nothingness comparable to the Source, or are those two different things?*

T: It would be the Source.

D: *Because I've heard the Source described as light.*

T: It is the darkness from which the light comes. It is beyond the light.

D: People say when they return to the Source, or when they started at the Source, it is always a bright light.

T: From my vantage point, I can tell you that the light comes from the darkness. Not – again from my vantage point – to confuse darkness with evil or anything negative. It is simply that which contains light. And from my vantage point, that is the Source. There may be something beyond that, but that is what I see from where I am. The nothingness. And from the nothingness comes the light. And from the light comes the differentiation that we call the somethingness.

SECTION SIX

CREATION

CHAPTER TWENTY-THREE

THE PRACTICING PLACE

Wendy had just left the life as a worm (in Chapter two) and I wanted to follow her to see where she would go next.

W: I'm contemplating what to do next. I'm leaning over an imaginary desk, and I'm studying – what should I do, what should I do? Many possibilities.

D: *Is there anybody that helps you make decisions?*

W: There are many old ones, seemingly old, with long beards. They're contemplating, watching me, just waiting to see what I decide. I seem to be in physical form, young, male. And these old men are standing around just watching me. I'm working over a desk. I'm really young. It looks like maps on the desk.

D: *Do you know what the old ones' jobs are?*

W: It's like they're contemplating who I am, and what I'm doing. Just studying me. I'm thinking this is funny, because they think I shouldn't have this much knowledge, because I'm so young.

D: *Let's move time ahead and find out what you decide to do. You've had a lot of time to think about it, and contemplate. What are you going to do now?*

W: I'm leaving these old men behind. I'm going on a long journey to see what this place is about.

D: *What place is it?*

W: I don't know. It seems to be real, but it's not real. It has trees and woods. You can see it, but you can see through it. It has form. It's real. It's just not dense. Not more solid.

D: *Do you know what this place is?*

391

W: It just floats around. It's just there. It's like you can create. You think it and you can create it. You take a step, and as you take a step you've created by imagining. It's like walking in the air, and there's nothing there until you create it with your mind. This is too weird. Otherwise, if you didn't create with your mind, you would be stepping into nothing. It doesn't make sense. – But oh, it's fun! It's great fun!

D: *So you can create anything you want there.*

W: You have to use your mind. This is almost like playing. I'm young. It's like I'm learning. I won't have anything to stand on, or be in, or be part of, if I don't create it with my mind.

D: *Do you think that's what you're doing now? Learning how to do this?*

W: Yes. It's like it's in the mind. You think it, then you bring it down and make it a reality. I don't know how to explain that. It's like it's in that thought form, and the thought form is real, but it's not real, because it's not solid. But first you have to create it in a thought form for it to take form. That's it! To take form! – It's like I can't move until I create in front of me. Otherwise, you're stuck with nothing, until you create it with your thought. It doesn't have substance until you put into it the details, the details, the details – details. It's called "manifestation". Manifest. It's creating. This is *most* exciting. Otherwise, it's a void unless you create and manifest something.

D: *This is something that's important for you to learn how to do?*

W: Yes. Progression. Progression, otherwise you stagnate. Don't go anywhere. You learn how you create. You learn to create a reality. To experiment, to *be*.

D: *So this is the next step, to learn how to do this, before you go anywhere else.*

W: Yes. It's thought. And then thought comes into form. Thought – you think it, and then it is. You put the details into it and then it manifests.

D: *Is someone helping you learn to do this?*

W: It seems as though this realm is where you go to do this. And there are others around. I see points of light. I don't know what that's about. Electricity. Points. But it seems as though there are others. This is where you go to experiment. This is a realm where anybody can go to learn to create. It's a creator school, but I'm young.

D: *So you have a lot of learning to do?*

W: A lot of experimenting, and it doesn't seem like you exactly have a teacher. What you have is your mind.

D: *So no one shows you how to do it.*

W: No. You experiment. And if it doesn't turn out right, then you erase it, or undo it. And recreate until you get it like you want it. You can see it before it actually takes form. You can see that it won't be perfect, then you can uncreate it. It never gets to the manifested, thick, dense stage.

D: *So it doesn't stay. You have time to undo it.*

W: Yes. Time doesn't mean much. You're not aware of time. You just keep creating things. That's weird. That's *weird!*

D: *Why is it important to learn how to manifest things?*

W: To get you to think before you jump.

D: *What do you mean?*

W: Don't jump and then think, because you could flub up a lot of things. If you think it through, then it's easier than jumping and having to go back and redo, and redo, and redo. So you just go slower. And think it out, *think it!* Think it more clearly, detail for detail for detail. There are many others here doing the same thing. My goodness sakes! This one person is working with the color purple. Just seems to be waving his hands, and this purple is moving in different forms. Totally fascinating! Energy movement. It is fun! Kind of reminds me of Fourth of July with a wand, and then moving it through the air.

D: *So, in that place, you're only limited by your imagination?*

W: Right. What you think, you can create. It's a place to practice, and it doesn't become solid form. It's a practicing, creating place, but you need to pay attention more to detail. – Like if you were going to make a tree, you just don't think a tree, and all the parts are there. You have to think how a tree grows. What all the components of a tree are. This gets really, really, really detailed.

D: *There's more to it than people think.*

W: Way more. Otherwise, there would just be a flat tree, a dead tree. It would look alive, but it wouldn't be. It reminds me of paper dolls. You see the form, flat, but it's not alive.

D: *It doesn't have the substance that something alive has.* (Right) *Is this something you're going to be able to use?*

W: I need to remember to be more detailed, be more accurate. Quit jumping, jumping, jumping into things, and then having to step back and redo. Going too fast. Be more detailed. More thorough. Thorough, thorough, detailed, detailed.

D: *Is this a place where everyone has to go?*

W: No. If you're interested in energy, it's a good place to go if you want to create things. There seems to be an abundance of energy to work with. It's almost like everybody's young. It's childlike, and the curiosity's boundless. I know there are other realities, but you're not aware of them. You're just not interested. You're having so much fun creating. It's like drawing and then erasing if it's not right. And then you can just do it over. And you don't get in trouble there because it's not a solid world. It's great fun.

I wonder if she had the sense of being young because she had just left the life of the worm. That was a very simple, uncomplicated life where manifesting was not an option. Maybe because of her lack of experience, she had to go to the practicing place to learn how to manifest, because if her next step was to go into a physical human body, this talent and ability would be needed.

D: Maybe that's to learn discipline. It would be difficult if it was a solid world.

W: That would be the scary part.

D: On a solid world, if you create it, it's not going to disappear that quickly, is it?

W: No, and it's going to be malformed. And oh, the energy is so dense and heavy. It's not easy to readjust. That's important. It's hard to adjust dense forms.

D: That's why you have to practice first.

W: Practice, practice. Yes. Clearing. Help align ill-formed dense forms. That sounds strange.

D: What do you mean?

W: (Apparently listening to, or reading from, instructions.) "Help realign dense forms that have gotten out of line, that don't function properly. This can be done ...." Hmmm. – I see people walking in dense forms, humped over, arms hanging down, dragging their legs, like it's such a terrible effort to be in a dense, heavy form.

D: You mean a physical body?

W: A physical body, yes. It's not aligned properly. You want to walk over to these dense forms, grab them around the middle, and lift them into a straight, upright, lighter being. This is just crazy. These bodies that they have taken on are so dense they need realigning. They can't even produce a child, an offspring that is aligned properly. These bodies won't form an offspring that is balanced.

D: Where are these bodies?

W: They're just walking all over this Earth. On *Earth!* What appears to the naked eye is not what actually is. What you see when you're looking at them are humans. But actually with the inner eye, these forms are bent over dragging. The energy is misaligned. They're heavy. They lack hope.

D: But they don't really look like this on the outside.

W: No, they don't. This is hidden.

D: How did they get out of alignment?

W: Over time. I see them coming back, coming back, coming back. They've lost what they knew in the beginning. They've come here on Earth so many times, they've forgotten to become lighter.

D: *Then it doesn't help to keep coming back?*

W: These ones it didn't, because as every lifetime is piled on top, it gets heavier and heavier and heavier. You feel like you want to throw it off and lift their form. You want to empty the darkness, the heavy sludge. I see sludge. You want to clear that and help them.

This sounded like what Jesus said in *They Walked With Jesus*. When he looked at the crowds of people gathered around him, he saw them as lumps of coal, dark and dense. They were unaware that within themselves were bright diamonds just waiting to be exposed.

W: They're wandering around looking for answers and don't know what to do about it.

D: *Is there anybody that can help them?*

W: There are lights. Forms that are like lights that are walking upright. And they walk up to them, and the dense ones are drawn to these light forms.

D: *Are these forms also in human body?*

W: Yes. And they don't always know they're light forms either. (Shocked gasp – she became very emotional.)

D: *Why is that bothering you?*

W: There are many of them around. They just don't know who they are. They don't know what they're supposed to be doing. They've forgotten, too. And they're just waiting, waiting for a specific time.

D: *They get stuck here too, you mean, without realizing why they're here?*

W: Yes. They get bogged down too, but they still have that light. And these ones that are like sludge, are drawn to this light.

It's like a cleansing. (Gentle sobbing.)
D: Isn't there anyone to tell them to wake up, to let them know?
W: When the time is right.

This may be the explanation for the many, many people who are coming to me. They say they are looking for direction. They know they are here on Earth to do something, but they don't know what it is. It becomes a nagging feeling that won't leave them. During the session, the subconscious always tells them they are here to help. To heal, to give assistance, to get people ready for what is to come. They are never told they are here to play, drink, have sex, make loads of money, get caught up in the ways of the world. They are *always* told that they are here to help the other people. And usually it is to be in ways they would never have thought of with their conscious mind.

W:These people with the light are slowly, slowly realizing ....
It's like they bump into this sludge, or touch it, or contact it, and this stuff starts melting away from these bent-over sludgy, dense forms. But there's no one that can tell them what they're supposed to be doing.
D: Do you know what you're supposed to be doing?
W: Waiting for a specific time, hoping some of those dense ones might bump into me.
D: You can't go looking for them?
W: No. It's sort of a magnet thing, like being drawn to. It works both ways. You have to move around, and they're moving around. And you're just drawn together like magnets.
D: Neither one being aware that's happening. (No) *Do you feel anything when this happens?*
W: Yes. I can feel their emptying of this heavy, heavy energy. And that gives me great joy. Seems like they've been that way for a long time.
D: Are you back in a physical body as you're doing this?
W: Yes. We with the light, walk upright. This is strange, but the

397

ones with the heavy energy seem to be bent over. This is not in actuality, but that's the feeling. The perception.

D: *So you're back in a physical body, but you're able to see these things?* (Yes) *What kind of physical body are you in?*

W: A tall, light body.

D: *Is that what it looks like to others?*

W: Yes, almost like cleanliness to them. They are drawn, they want to be like that, but don't know how to get that way.

D: *If someone else were to see you in the physical form, they would see you as a tall, light body?* (Yes) *Does it have a physical coating over it?*

W: Yes, but it's also kind of transparent. It's half skin, and we wear clothes. But the body seems to be a little translucent, or transparent. A glowing, radiating energy of acceptance, of not turning anyone away. These others just wander around.

D: *Is this what you do after you've learned to manifest energy? You come back into the physical to use it?*

W: It's remembering that I knew how. I'd been there and learned how to create. A remembering that I had been there.

D: *Are you able to tell which ones are the light beings?* (Yes) *And do others in the physical body know?*

W: They can definitely see a difference. There is no comparison. How do I explain? It's a knowing. It's an energy that the light beings give off. They actually look like all other humans, but you're seeing with a different perception. It's a knowing. You can feel the energy. The ones that are sludgy can't. They are just drawn like a magnet. They don't understand it. They want help. They're tired of being bent over and burdened, burdened, burdened, burdened, heavy, heavy, heavy.

D: *If they're drawn to the light ones, do things change in their life?*

W: Yes. You see them sort of look up and notice that there is something different, that they don't have to live like that. But some of them won't want to change. They think that's all

398

there is. They don't know what to do about it. There are others that are searching, but they are looking down, looking down. They just see Earth things. And then suddenly, they realize maybe there's more than just the Earth things, the material things. And they slightly turn their head upward, and that's like looking elsewhere. Like looking toward the spirit world. When they turn their heads like that, they see that, yes, there is something different. There are others out there. They're like them, but they are *not* like them.

D: *And this makes the change to send them on a different path.*

W: Yes. And touch, you want to touch these ones. That is so sad! (Emotional.) They've been like this for so long, and every time they come to this Earth, it gets heavier and heavier. I don't understand. Why didn't they become lighter instead of becoming denser and denser and denser? Touch them. Sometimes, it's just a touch.

D: *That's all it takes. Something very simple.*

W: Yes. Just walk among the people. Just the energy. Just by touching people. Sometimes, it's eye-to-eye contact. Energy is passed. They know on a soul level, but not necessarily on a conscious level, that this is taking place.

I then had her leave that scene and gave instructions for Wendy's subconscious to come forth to answer questions.

D: *Wendy was looking for answers. You showed her many things. Why did you show her this part about being a light body helping the denser forms? What were you trying to tell her?*

W: That's why she came here. She is supposed to remember where she came from. She was a light form, an energy form.

D: *Where did she come from, if you want her to remember?*

W: From the energy Source of all energy.

D: *Is that where she was experimenting with the energy?*

W: It's one of the realms that have been set up for those who like

399

to work, and who like to create with energy. She was sent out from the main energy Source, or Creator, and is allowed to experiment with creation.

D: *She's supposed to remember the original Creator Source?* (Yes) *She was shown that she could manipulate energy.* (Yes) *Is that what you want her to know?*

W: Yes. She is to join with other light beings who are waking up and remembering what they're here for. It's time to start remembering. There's much work going on at night when she's in this sleep state, that she doesn't know about.

Wendy had problems with her health all her life. "This is so she would look inward instead of outward in the material world. If she'd had good health, she would have not paid any attention to the spirit world. She chose a very hard body to manifest through. After she got here, she decided maybe she didn't want to be here. It was going to be harder than she thought. And she sort of drug her feet all these years. She does not feel at home here, but if she goes back now, she will not have finished what she came to do. We are also learning from this body, because it is weak. We take this knowledge and will be using it to develop ways to help mankind. Her body is not the only body that is in a weakened condition. The whole planet has weakened. She needs adequate rest, adequate food, more meditation. We showed her this manifesting realm, because she needs to pay more attention to detail. Detail in everything that she does from the time she wakes up in the morning till the time she goes to bed at night. Detail, detail, detail. Pay attention to what she puts in her mouth. Where she came from before (the energy side), there wasn't this heavy food. In another realm, she was just energy. And it wasn't the heavy polluted food that you eat nowadays. Be more attuned to liquid form of food, if possible. The lighter foods, the fruits. Not so much heavy dense dead food. More food with energy. Life giving foods. This keeps the body light. Heavy foods keep you heavy, stuck, grounded. Heavy in body, hard to move.

Lighter foods make lightness, airiness. More room in the body for energy to move through. – Everything she does, she needs to pay attention to. And be detailed, be conscious of what she's doing."

D: Isn't that a little frustrating or distracting if you think of every detail?

W: This will help align the body so others can help align theirs.

Asked about the problems with her breathing. "Part of it is the pollution that's in the world today. Part of it is because she polluted her lungs with the stick that she put in her mouth, and lit. (Smoking)"

Heart problems: "This has been so since childhood. It's almost as if she felt she had a broken heart from the time she was little. Feeling alone in a dense, heavy, thick body. Missing the unconditional love. Love on this planet is nothing compared to home."

D: Does the heart need to be corrected?

W: She must remember to rest and to visualize, visualize, visualize. Create with the mind and the body will follow. Visualize the organs in the body functioning properly. Visualize, visualize, visualize. Any damage can be healed, but it takes time. That's why visualization is so important. It will make the body aware that it can heal itself. And pay attention to what is put into the body. Fresh, fresh, fresh, alive food, live food. Life-giving, food giving life.

GENESIS

When Pamela came off the cloud, instead of a past life, she found herself in an ethereal type of environment. Everything was without substance or shape. "I have yet to see anything physical. I see only 10 points of light, and somewhat of a flowing energy, but no sense of form." She began to cry when she saw this formless place of energy, because she said she missed it. She loved to be there playing in the energy. She was then taken completely by surprise when I asked her to look at herself. "Let's see what I can see here. Goodness! Nothing! It's all just swirly light! I see something like molecules around me. I feel I am in this place where everything can be created."

When I asked how she could use that to create, she gave a confusing answer. She seemed to think it was very important, even though I do not understand the process. Maybe one of my readers will understand and identify with it. It could be symbolism, but I don't think so. Everything was formless lines and dots and swirls, until she saw the two pyramids. She knew they represented creation (genesis) at the point where they touched.

Movement

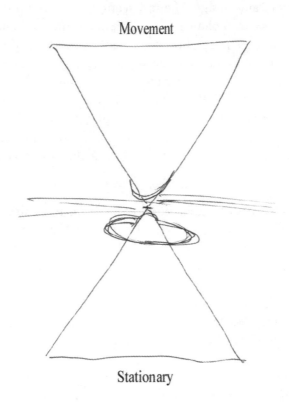

Stationary

P: I saw two points touching, knowing that was critical. I saw a circle of light over that. It's magnificent, although I don't understand it. I'm in the heart of it. I'm in the – structural – that's almost what's happening with these two points touching. They're creating the possibility for this type of life to move and this type of energy. I know it sounds so abstract. One would like to know that I know what it created, but I don't know what it created. Other than the two points touching, create. And I want to say, I was blessed to witness. Or in awe, to witness.

D: *Let's see what your part was in this.*

P: Just witnessing? Good grief! I don't know. Earlier, I think I played in the energy. Wherever I was, I know that's a place I've been to before. And I occupy my time in a way where I can create any image, shape I want. And it's upon my own volition, my own choice to do it. It keeps me very entertained. Any computer programmer can program something to their heart's desire to make it just what they want. Like that. And this is far more organic and natural and instantaneous than that. So I've been here before. I know I've done it. That makes me long to be back there to be able to play in that energy. There are no boundaries. There are no limits. It is familiar, and it sometimes beckons me. By being in this space, I am being called to it.

This was very confusing, and I knew I was not going to get too much more information. Also, where could I take it? She could have existed there for eons. So I decided to call forth the subconscious. I usually didn't do it so early in the session, but I thought it would be the only way to get the answers to this strange situation. When the subconscious came forth, I asked it, "This has been confusing. We thought we were going to past lives. Why did you choose to show these things to Pamela?"

P: She knows.

D: *Let's tell her, because I don't think she knows consciously.*

P: She needed to experience a memory that has been with her all her life. She did not want to depart from that place when she came here.

D: *What did she do there?*

P: She was a creator.

D: *So she was correct when she saw herself as energy, and manipulating energy?*

P: She would not use the word "manipulate", but it is appropriate. She was playing in the energy.

D: *What was she creating when she was there?*

P: Everything. In an early level. If you could see the very, very, very earliest stage, before it's at an advanced stage, it has to go through this phase. So she was overseeing the components and energetics at the minute, molecular – that's not the right word.

Minute, fractional – I'm not sure what else.

D: *But she was there at the beginning?*

P: I don't know.

D: *But when these ... worlds were created, or humans, or physical things, or what?*

P: No. It's in all creation. Whatever this is, is not specific to any one gender, species, planet, solar system. It's in all.

D: *It's a basic energy that all is created from?*

P: Yes. It's the oneness. It's the essence of all.

D: *Like the building blocks?*

P: That would be appropriate.

D: *The building blocks of everything. And is this basic energy always there?*

P: Yes. Basic energy. Light.

D: *And you said she oversaw this?*

P: At one place, she's watching how it's done. And in another place, she's working with it like a child. Playing with it. This is what she does a lot.

D: *In her present life?*

P: No. Not in this physical. Not that she's aware of. All the time, and then in between time. Not conscious. When she's between lives, and at night when she's sleeping.

D: *Does anyone tell her what to create?* (No) *So she just creates what she wants to?* (Yes) *Why did you want her to know about it?*

P: To remind her that this is what she does.

D: *Do you want her to use this ability in the physical?*

P: Not yet. There's a timing to all of this. She'll know. Later.

D: *She'll know when she's supposed to use this energy?*

P: Exactly. And not a minute before. It's very specific. She'll be given images and understandings at the time when there's a right group of people, and technology to utilize it, and the right laws for it not to be misused.

D: *Did she misuse this in another life?*

P: She thinks she did, but she really didn't. It was something to do with a planet. I guess it was destroyed.

D: What did that have to do with Pamela?

P: She thinks she was part of the reason it happened.

D: Was she in a physical body at that time?

P: Partly. There are forces that take physicality in need, and situations of emergency. And that's what she did. She wasn't in a body, but she used a body.

D: And something happened, and she thought she was the cause of it?

P: She was a player in the role of that planet. I don't know that the memories are being allowed right now. There's a timing. It is not quite time for her to know these things. She knows she wasn't completely responsible, but she knows she was also part.

D: Why does Pamela have an attraction for crystals?

P: Baseline creation of that in matter is the most familiar to her in all creation. Going back again to the most basic creative energy.

D: When she plays in the energy, does she use it in a positive way?

P: She's not using the type that she was given an image of today. That's more powerful. (Laugh) She uses ... like scrap metal. It's kind of like what spins off from the other stuff. It's the scrap material, so to speak. It's like if you have two grinders playing, you have spin-off. You'd play with the spin-off. Just the little things. What she can accomplish and understand. It's more crystalline than scrap metal, by the way.

D: Why didn't you want to show her past lives today?

P: It wasn't pertinent. Not at this point.

D: I'm getting more and more of that, where people are told it's not important.

P: It's just not important. There are plenty of things to spin off, and intellectually, it's just not where she needs to go. It's been done before. It's rehashing, and senile.

D: You mean to go into the other lives? (Yes) *But for some people, that's as far as they've developed, I guess you would say. That's all they can understand at this point.*

P: I think present and future are being required. Not the past.

CHAPTER TWENTY-FOUR

BACK TO THE BEGINNING

Gwen was floating, looking for a place to come down, and below she saw a fantastic sight. An entire world composed of crystals. "I'm seeing crystals everywhere. They're sticking straight up in the air. Like a bed of crystals, like little porcupines sticking up. They're all long and slender." Before she had time to explore it further, it disappeared and was replaced by a brilliant blue containing pulsating lights. "There's energy coming off them in whites and yellows, like bursts of energy. They're all over this blue space. It's like the energy is alive. – They're blending together now. They're not individualized, but they've all formed one energy. I'm not seeing things as objects, but mostly as energy fields, as pulsating energy. Now it's changing again. I don't know how to explain this. It's formless, but it's moving. There's an energy source from the lower right that's sending these pulses out and around, and then it comes back down around in. It's formless, but yet every part that comes out has a different shape to it. There's no structure to it. It's the way it looks when the light hits the water, and shimmers across. It has form, but it doesn't have form. It's more fluid. There are colors in it, but they're more iridescent."

D: So you don't feel anything solid?
G: No, I just feel an expansiveness.
D: How do you perceive yourself?
G: As just being a part of it. It's almost as if I were to take the Universe and have the energy flow around, and just be. There are sparks of light forming now within it, but it's more of a fluid, flowing, swirling thing. It's always in movement. It never stands still. It's always in motion.

407

D: And you're a part of the whole thing. (Yes) Are you aware of any other entities like yourself?

G: I'm not picking up any entity or individual, per se. I'm seeing symbols. I'm seeing triangles that are dimensional. They're just here, and they just are, but they're all around the whole. If you need to have words for it, it's creation in motion. That's what it feels like. And when I say that the sparks appear, and the symbols have disappeared. It's just in constant motion, and then these sparks are forming within it. And now it's becoming larger. It's almost like a mist that swirls around and around.

D: Do you know what the sparks are?

G: I'm hearing they were the sparks of God being sent out.

D: This is part of the creation process? (Yes) *That's what you meant by creation in motion, that the sparks become things?* (Yes) *Is there anyone that directs this?*

G: I'm hearing that as you think, your thoughts will create whatever it is that you want to create. The individual does have the power, but I was seeing the source of it, the beginning of it.

D: So you mean there is something bigger that thinks and creates?

G: Right. It's All That Is. Everything is all, and all is everything.

D: And it all began with It, and what It thinks?

G: That was the movement coming out and around. It was fluid, very fluid. It had no form, but it went out and came back to the Source. And then the sparks occurred, but the sparks occurred only when the thought was there. Otherwise, there was only fluid form. I could feel the Source. I couldn't see the Source, but it was over to the right and it flowed out from it. It was always in motion. Then the sparks came out of the mist, and they were starting to take form.

D: Can you see what kind of forms they take?

G: It looked like a galaxy being formed.

D: What part do you have in all of this?

408

G: I feel like I'm just watching it. I don't know why I'm here. I feel like I'm suspended in this space that's here. I'm aware of everything around. I feel like I still have my individuality, but I'm also part of the whole. I'm not separate from it, but I am. It's very comfortable. It's that brilliant blue that goes on forever and ever.

This could have lasted for a very long time. So I asked her to move. "When do you decide to leave that place?"

G: I hear that I will go when I am called, when there's a need. Otherwise, I stay in energy.

D: *What happens at that first time you are called to leave that place, and go somewhere else.*

G: It's more of a pulling. I'm pulled some place. I only see something that looks like a rainbow, but it's not really a rainbow. It has the shape and form of a rainbow and the feeling of a rainbow, but it doesn't have the colors of the rainbow. I feel like I'm surrounded by energy. I'm having a really hard time making anything concrete, or dimensional. It feels like where I want to be.

D: *Let's find out what it's like whenever you become solid, when you separate from the energy and take a form.*

G: I'm taking on a woman's body. She looks young, very slender, olive skin, long dark hair. She has a band around her head with something that sticks out in the front. Not many clothes. A skirt-type dress. My midriff is showing. And a little top. Bare arms. I have jewelry around my neck like shiny little flat circles. It feels like the desert. It feels very Egyptian.

D: *Did you just become the woman?* (Yes) *So you didn't go through the stages of a baby?*

G: That's how I saw myself. It feels like I took over the body.

D: *But wasn't there another soul or spirit inside that body?* (No) *Was there a reason you chose that particular body?*

G: This body had authority. This body was the combination of spirit and authority to bring forth what needed to be brought forth at the time.

D: *Do you know what you're supposed to do in that body?*

G: I saw the Sphinx, and I saw the Pyramid, and I saw a Pharaoh. I felt like I knew the Pharaoh. I feel younger than the Pharaoh. I don't know that I was married to him or anything like that. I could have been his child or a priestess with him.

I moved her forward in time to an important day when something was happening.

G: It's a ceremony of worship and we're offering up prayers. It's important to be in the physical of a woman because of the importance of the woman and her energy. The combination of the feminine and the authority. It was a time when women had power.

D: *You said they were worshiping and offering up prayers. Who were they praying to?*

G: To God.

D: *How do they perceive God?*

G: As the source of all.

D: *So they perceive it that way rather than a statue or another entity?* (Yes) *Then they were closer to the truth, weren't they?*

G: Yes. It was a time when I could feel my full power and my full spirituality honoring God and being a part of that.

D: *Because there were times when they worshiped an idol of some kind that represented an entity.*

G: Yes, but this was not one of those times. I am in a temple, and my whole body feels the energy of it right now. I see many steps, and I see a large, round sphere that glows. It is suspended in the temple.

D: *Suspended in the air inside the temple?*

G: Yes, and we revere it. It's glistening, and it's rotating, and it

410

has many facets to it.

D: Where did it come from? How did it get inside the temple?

G: We created it out of energy, out of the thought, going through the creation that is. Our group created it, not only for the energy that it produces, but for the remembering of what it represents.

D: What does it represent?

G: It represents only one Source. It represents unity. It represents oneness. It also represents both the masculine and the feminine. And that's why it's so important that the woman feels the power as well as the spirituality. That's why this time is so important. And that's why this time today is so important – it's a reclaiming of that power.

D: What do you use that sphere for? Does it have a purpose?

G: It feels like it fills the body. When we talk about it, I can feel it vibrating throughout my whole being. It rejuvenates, it heals, it cleanses, it energizes, it's purity.

D: Is everyone allowed to go to that temple and experience this?

G: No. Just my group.

D: Is there a reason the average person can't go in there and see it?

G: It's felt that they are not ready for it.

D: You think they wouldn't understand it?

G: Not so much understanding, as misusing it. Maybe not so much misuse it, as not know how to use it.

D: How does your group use the energy?

G: There's a melding that goes on. You become one with the energy. We fill ourselves up with the energy. We allow the energy to come into ourselves. It heals us, it sustains us, it gives us wisdom.

They did not need to consume anything to remain alive. The body would not get sick, and was incapable of dying.

D: Are the other people outside the temple a different type of a being than you are?

G: Yes. We are similar, but more delicate featured, lighter of skin than they are. They're human, but they're not as refined.

D: Was your race born there?

G: No. We came here. They were transported there. They had the ability to come through pure energy and take form. The same way I did.

D: What is the purpose of all your group coming there?

G: We are trying to raise the consciousness of humanity. We interact with them. We don't separate ourselves from them. We allow them to know what we feel they can understand. We try to be gentle with them. They don't really know all that goes on within the temples. They would never understand it. We teach them at the level they feel comfortable with. We try to gently move them on.

I decided to move her once again to another important day, and asked what was happening.

G: Something has caused the sphere to become cloudy. Something caused all of the energy to be depleted. I don't know if there was a corruption that occurred within the group. There was no longer the unity that once was.

D: Has a long time passed since you came? (Yes) *How do you feel about that?*

G: I'm upset about it, because I feel we have lost something special. There's no longer an honoring. The group is more each one for themselves. I feel that it's out of my control, but I also feel I've taken a vow to always try to help bring about oneness.

D: Have the others in the group taken the same vows?

G: Some have, some haven't. There has to be an honoring of the individual, an honoring of the God within, but also an honoring of all that is, going back to the original Source that

I didn't want to leave.

D: So vows must be kept, but never broken. Is that how you feel?

G: Yes. I saw the destruction of it.

D: Tell me what you mean.

G: I saw the sphere no longer. It just kept getting dimmer and dimmer, and darker and darker, and the separation between man and woman in the group. And the loss of that oneness. The loss of the respect and love of God.

D: So it was reflecting what was happening within the group. (Yes) *What eventually happened to the sphere?*

G: It just no longer was. It became nothing. It kept getting darker and darker, and the light went out. It was just gone, just no longer was.

D: Do you think you'll be able to create another one?

G: Yes, we will. The group will try.

D: Because without the sphere, your bodies would die, wouldn't they?

G: In that time and place, we no longer are. We dispersed. We left.

D: Did the physical body die?

G: It was more of a dematerialization.

D: Then by dispersing, you mean your soul, your spirit, left and went somewhere else? (Yes) *But you said you would create another sphere.*

G: That is to be done in the future. They lost the ability. They lost it all. They lost their oneness. They lost their understanding of God. They allowed their egos to step in. They allowed only the individual and not the whole. I see them going off in all parts of the Universe.

D: What do you think was the importance of that time, before it became corrupted?

G: The importance was being so close to the Source. It felt like when I originally was with the Source. I was allowed to embody, yet remain connected to the Source.

D: Do you know why the group changed?

413

G: They became wrapped up in their own power, in their own sense of creation. Forgetting that they are all still part of God. They forgot the oneness. I was still caught up in the chaos of it. My heart remained with God and the unity. I held it there.

I then had her leave the scene and drift away from it. And I brought forth Gwen's subconscious to get some answers. "Why did you pick this for her to see today?"

G: She must realize the power that lies within. It is only when all becomes one, will it return to God. And that is why she is working now with the masculine, the feminine, and the child, because we are creating anew. Those three energies are the creation.

D: *But instead of going to a normal past life, she went back to the very beginning.*

G: Yes, to feel the love and the oneness again of all that is. And to see creation in process. There is no form, no shape, it's all energy in a flow. And to see the flow and how the sparks come about.

D: *So her past lives were not important to go to?*

G: No. She has had very few past lives.

D: *Why was that important for her to see that one particular life?*

G: Because at that time, she was in a place where she was a ruler. And she wore the symbol that she received when she visited Egypt, which is the sign of feminine divinity. The symbol is a spiral going up, through the palm, through the heart, up to God. Connecting with God and returning back down in a spiral, connecting into the other palm, across the heart. It is a feminine symbol, but both spirals are the connection of the masculine and feminine coming together as one, through love in the heart.

D: *But it didn't seem like the group were real humans, because they were transported there.*

G: They were in a physical form, but they were different from the

414

form of the humans. They were very delicate featured in human form. Very refined, whereas the humans of that time were not refined. They were very crude.

D: *Did they create those bodies?*

G: Yes, they did. They wanted to be in a form that would be understood by the humans without that fear. But they were more energy than the humans were.

D: *That was why they created that sphere to give them life.* (Yes) *But they became corrupted.* (Yes) *So it showed that even beings that close to God could become corrupted.*

G: God is always experiencing. There is no good or evil. There is only the experience. She needs to feel the power build within her, and I know that she does. There will be a time when again, women will be equal to men, because men will realize they need the power of the woman. And the woman needs the power of the man to come together to be one.

Gwen had been experiencing unusual psychic experiences even from early childhood. Many of these were extremely vivid. "Is there a reason she's been so open all her life, as Gwen?"

G: The vow that she took brings her back at this time. She spoke about being pulled. She has been pulled into this lifetime to be of service, to bring about that oneness, to anchor the energy of the feminine. She has done this in other dimensions, on other planets, not only here. That time that she was here in that form was one of the first times she ever experienced the physical. And she saw what occurred from it, and wanted to make it right. The psychic experiences she has had are little markers upon the way to guide her. She has to feel empowered within to know the power that she contains. If she doesn't experience these things, she doesn't know what could be. She could feel it within, as can anyone who is open to it. But she has experienced them. The experience empowers. – I want to thank you for this

415

opportunity to speak, to be heard. To thank you and Gwen for the work you do. The world needs your light. You each have taken a vow to be here at this time, and the Universe thanks you for all that you have done. Be with God.

CHAPTER TWENTY-FIVE

A DIFFERENT LAW OF CREATION
AND PHYSICS

Irene came off the cloud in a scene that I was becoming familiar with. Many of my clients are now going there. "It's light, it's all light. Pure light and bliss, peace."

D: *Anything else, or any other feelings?*
I: (Smiling) Just being home. It's wonderful.
D: *Why do you call it home?*
I: Because it is. It's my place of peace. It's wonderful.
D: *Are there others with you, or are you by yourself?*
I: I feel others, but they don't have any form. I just know them. I feel them. It's good to be here again. I miss here. I miss this place.
D: *Why did you leave that place if it was so beautiful?*
I: It's my time to help. It is a time when great energies are needed, and great powers and great strength. So then I knew it is my time to come. There are many of us and we have talked of this. It is our time to go.
D: *What did you talk about?*
I: Universes, multiverses. Much, much work to do. Much balancing, much creation.
D: *You felt you couldn't create from the beautiful place, from home?*
I: Oh, no. It's not the same. Creation starts from there, but simply to create is not enough. One must also experience, and that is what we have to do. Not only to create, but to then go and to experience to bring that back. It is not bad if you can take others with you. For some of us have chosen to go

together, and others, apart. It's a learning. It is like starting in a large group, and as you build your strength, you can learn when it's time for you to branch off, and go into others, and do other creations. There are so many, *so* many.

D: *So in the beginning, it's easier to separate from the home if you have others go with you.* (Yes, yes.) *Do you know where you have to go?*

I: To the red planet first.

D: *Why did you choose that planet?*

I: The color red needed to be created first. It's the *vibration*, as it were, of a red planet, yes.

D: *Was the planet already created, or did you help create it?*

I: We took the color red. We created that vibration for the color red. We made that.

D: *And red was important to be the first one?*

I: Yes, it was for our work. We had to do the red first. Others did the green and some did yellow. Each group created a different color.

D: *Were there no colors before that?*

I: There were all, all, all the white. All.

D: *Oh, the light.* (Yes) *So you created colors out of the light.*

I: Yes, we took them.

D: *And each group decided they wanted to concentrate on a different color?*

I: Oh, there are so many! It's quite beautiful!

D: *Then what did you do once you created the color red?*

I: Then we could create other things there; other creations. We could experiment. We could play.

D: *I'm trying to understand. Each one did it with their own colors?* (Yes) *And you could play, you could create anything you want.* (Yes) *And you're given permission to do these things?*

I: It's sort of an agreement thing that we all agreed to do this work, so maybe permission is not the word.

D: *But before that there was nothing there?*

418

I: There was all; all in potential, all that is. All always has been, it just was in another form: Light. It's not like there wasn't anything.

D: *And light contained everything that could possibly be? Would that be a way to say it?*

I: Yes. – I don't like it over here on the red one. I'm leaving that one. It's a little dense. We were only creating with red, see? Red's not as fast a vibration. It was okay. I wanted to see what it would be like.

D: *What did you create out of the red?*

I: A universe.

D: *Oh! A universe would be quite large, wouldn't it?*

I: Pffft! Not really. We all created our universes. You like that word here: "universe". Silly word. So we created one, and we could have what we wanted in it. The whole idea was to create all these different colors, like this universe is. And not just basic colors. It's iridescent and sparkly, with all colors, but yet not colors. It turns one way and it's one color, and it turns another way and it's another color. To create as many as we could out of this light. Oh, there's so, so many! But you know, I sort of get bored, so I don't stay too long in any of them. I like to start doing and then take off and go over to some of the other ones.

D: *Does the group go with you?*

I: Some did, and some liked that, so they stayed. This is when we started splitting off.

D: *What do you put in the universe after you make it?*

I: It's up to whoever is doing it. You can do all sorts of things. You can do like they do in this one, with the planets. But they don't have to be round like they are here. They can be anything. They can be all shapes and forms. And then they all have a vibration. So you have the vibration of the color, and the vibration of the shape. And then they all have their sound.

D: *Each one has a sound?*

I: Oh, yes. Some have more than one. And if they get near one another, they make another sound. That's the fun part.

It sounds like the theory of "music of the spheres".

D: So you never know what it's going to turn out like? It's a surprise.

I: Yes. It's fun. That's the fun part.

D: I thought there were laws of the universes that things had to be shaped a certain way.

I: Maybe in this universe, but not in those.

D: (Laugh) So they can be any shape you want.

I: Of course.

D: Do they make the sound by themselves, or do you create those?

I: Oh, of course, we create them, because we're doing it all. So yes, we do them. But see, when we make the shapes, we're not exactly positive how the sound's going to be. We put in sound. We play with it, tweak it, twidge it. It's because the two sounds come together and make a new sound.

D: It makes music then? (Yes) *But you said you didn't like the red one after you created it?*

I: Well, I tend to get a little bored. It's not that there was anything wrong with it. I was just done with it. The color of the vibration was kind of dense. We did the sound to help with that. And that helped, it really helped. But you know, just all red? When you've been with it, it was a bit much.

D: So after you make the planets, do you make anything on the planets? Or do you go that far?

I: It depends. In some of them, you create things; in some of them, you don't. It depends. Like with the red one, helped create the red, helped create the shapes, the sounds, the movement patterns of the shapes within the universes. They are all different patterns because the different patterns can make different sounds.

D: You mean the way they move and rotate?

I: Well, they don't exactly all rotate. That's here, this universe. In another one, they would do figure eight-ey things, and spinning. It's not the same. Not the same at all.

D: There's no law of physics? That things have to perform to a certain rule?

I: The red rule, yes. But the red rule isn't the same as the pink rule, or the orange rule, or the green rule, or the ... no. As long as they don't interfere or harm any others, each can have their own rules.

It seems as though the basic laws of free will and non-interference extend even to planets and universes.

D: So the planets can move and rotate any way they want. Is that what you mean?

I: No. The red planets have to follow the red rules, and the orange planets follow the orange rules, and the iridescent planets follow the iridescent rules. And then when they all come anywhere near each other – because you know they all kind of interact – and depending on their vibration, you can have them right overlapping one another. Just as long as they're not going to interfere with each other.

D: So there are some rules of creation anyway. But then, if you get tired of that and want to go somewhere else, does that universe just evaporate and collapse? Or does it remain?

I: Oh, no, it's there, because others stayed with it. Initially, there was a whole group of us that wanted to create, and different groups created different colors. And different groups could choose to stay with that color for a while and continue to develop that. And then experience life, as it were, there. Or they could split off and go other places. For some were meant to be strictly in that red realm and to experience that to its full extent. While others are meant to go around and experience some of each; or just some of some.

421

D: *So as long as some of the group remains, then the universe remains?* (Yes) *It doesn't just dissipate. I thought maybe you created, and then it would evaporate again.*

That was the way it was explained in another chapter, where the beings were allowed to practice creating, and if it didn't turn out the way they wanted, it would dissipate. This was done in a certain place especially reserved for doing this, the practicing, the playing with the energy, until it could be mastered. Then it wouldn't interfere with anything else.

I: Some could if you so choose. But no, for the most part they all stay.

D: *But then you can also put life and creatures on these planets if you want to?*

I: Those that stayed could do that. Or you could go around and be a creator of the beginnings of all. And some would stay longer and create more, and then leave. Or some got so wrapped up in creation, they just stayed and stayed until they experienced all that they were to experience.

D: *You mean, in the beginning, they created everything that was on the worlds?*

I: They did it gradually, those that stayed. I didn't stay. I would go on.

D: *But they do create everything that's on the planet: the plants, the waters?*

I: Right. They would create everything that would make those planets, yes. And in some, everything was red. In the red, always red. The creatures were red. They didn't have plants in the red universes. It wasn't needed.

D: *But if they created animals, or creatures, did they decide to experience those creatures? Or did they just take care of the creation of them?*

I: They didn't look like you think of creatures.

D: *Tell me about it.*

I: On the reds, it was more .... Okay, think of a stingray on Earth. Now make it transparent and elongated. And then put, like, an oval in the middle of it. There were some like that, that could roam the surface.

D: *They just used their imagination to create anything they wanted to?* (Yes) *Then what kept these creatures alive after they were created?*

I: In the red, it was simply the atmosphere. They had no ingestion. They didn't take in food and let out waste. They just were. They just existed. They just experienced.

D: *So they didn't need a spark of life in them?*

I: They were a spark of life. They were independent.

D: *I'm trying to understand and compare it with what we know on Earth. We think they have to have a spark of life within them to keep them alive.*

I: They are the spark.

D: *Does this mean they did eventually die?*

I: Yes. They didn't have a way of making more.

D: *I see. They couldn't procreate.* (No) *Then the planet would be dead again, wouldn't it?* (Yes) *Then what happens after that?*

I: I didn't stay there. I don't know. I left about then.

D: *Where did you decide to go?*

I: I'm roaming.

D: *So you're not with that group anymore?*

I: Right. I've always been the curious one. I like to see what's going on.

D: *Where do you decide to go next?*

I: Into a cilium.

I have no idea what that is. The closest the dictionary comes is: cilia in biology.

D: *What is that?*

I: I'm not quite sure. It looks like a pyramid in a pyramid with

423

one corner of it leaking off and curving down.
D: *You didn't have a desire to go into another color?*
I: No, I was called to a cilium.
D: *Who calls you?*
I: A cilium called me. I was needed there.
D: *I was wondering if someone tells you what to do.*
I: No, you just know.

I am becoming more and more convinced that the soul (spirit?) was more of a free agent, if that's the correct term, in the beginning. It did, more or less, what it wanted to do, and went wherever it felt it needed to go without being instructed to do so. It seems as though, after it became entrapped in the cycles of birth and rebirth and karma, that it became contaminated. It could no longer be trusted to make its own decisions. It needed instruction to help it get out of the muck and mire. Then the councils and boards of masters, elders and guides became necessary, so the soul could eventually get back on the track of evolving upward, back to the Source. It had to get out of its experiencing and the forgetting of where it came from. This seems to be a pattern I am observing.

D: *What do you have to do there?*
I: I'm going to find out. It's a big, open chamber. They're doing something here. And there's something inside it, and it's like it's been abandoned.
D: *This is inside this pyramid structure?*
I: Yes. I don't see anyone, but there's light over in this corner. And the walls are like a metal! I feel that if I tapped on them, it would hurt my ears.
D: *A loud sound?*
I: Yes. I'm looking to see what else is in this room. What this is over here – like a half of a pod with lights all around it, on the edge of it. And oh! There are windows all around here, but I can't see out them. But I have the feeling that

someone's watching on the other side of those windows. They're watching what's in that pod. I feel it, I don't see them. And I'm here to stop them from what's going on. This is *not* right. This will *not* continue. This *must* stop. It's against ... it's wrong. It's wrong.

D: *Why is it wrong?*

I: It's *causing* pain, it's causing great pain. It's messing up this whole planet. What *are* these people doing? Who *are* these? What are they doing? It's terrible! (Deep sigh) (Several very deep breaths, as though blowing.)

D: *What are you doing?*

I: I must get out of here, and fast. Now it's disintegrating over here. I have to get out.

D: *What did you do?*

I: I stopped it all.

D: *It looked like you were blowing on it.*

I: I did.

D: *That caused it to disintegrate?* (Yes.) *You have enough power to do that?*

I: Of course.

D: *To destroy the entire place? Or the entire planet?*

I: The place first.

D: *What were they doing that they weren't supposed to do?*

I: I don't know who these are. Lost or stray ones? They're fascinated with pain. They will be sealed on this planet. This planet is now sealed.

D: *These beings were creating pain for others on that planet?*

I: Yes. They are sealed there. The others are gone.

D: *The people they were trying to hurt?*

I: Yes. I sort of disintegrated them. But it's okay. Not in a bad way disintegrated – returned them to spirit.

D: *Because you can't destroy spirit, can you?*

I: No. They're going back to be healed and rest. But the others, the ones that were causing the pain are sealed there.

D: *They cannot leave that place?*

I: No. They are sealed on that planet.

D: *They can never die or reincarnate?*

I: No. They must experience what they have done. I will come back and check on them from time to time. Once they can realize and undo what they have done, they will be free again. They will be given a chance to grow again.

D: *But if the people in your group created all of these planets, why would they create something so negative?*

I: Oh, they didn't. That was a long time ago. I did a big jump. That's why I was called there. It couldn't continue.

D: *Couldn't the ones who created those planets and beings come back and do something about it?*

I: Something got messed up. They needed a higher power. They just needed it to stop. Over much time, they will progress. We're hoping. As I'm feeling them, that is my plan.

Is this something like what Gary was talking about? (In Chapter 38 "The Final Solution.") He was assigned here on Earth to be the final solution if the world doesn't get its act together. He has a similar power to annihilate or disintegrate, and to perhaps seal the planet. At the present time, he has just been assigned to wait and watch.

I: I could hear the cries of those they were harming. That was what called me there.

D: *Then you did the job you felt you needed to do. You released those spirits, those souls.* (Yes) *What are you going to do now?*

I: I shall roam.

D: *And as you said, you take big jumps, don't you?* (Yes) *What do you see now, or what do you feel drawn to?*

I: I keep hearing, "Mary Melissa. Mary Melissa. Mary Melissa." A little girl. – She's playing outside. She's playing with fairies. Oh, they're lovely. They're quite busy this day.

They're working among the flowers. They're playing. They're riding butterflies. Why, I don't know. They have their own wings. I think it's just quite for fun. Mary Melissa has a long, blue ribbon in her hair, and long curly brown hair. It must be windy, for her hair is blowing. And now she's down on her tummy watching the ants.

D: *What is the purpose of the fairies?*

I: Oh, to help with the nature kingdom. Well, not necessarily the nature kingdom, because everything is nature, but as form. They really guard and protect and take care of the flowers and the trees and everything nature-like. But then we get the nature thing mixed up. We think of nature as only nature, like trees and stuff. But it's really pillows and cars and everything that has a form.

D: *That would be like saying it's all of life?*

I: Everything that has form. That's the nature kingdom.

D: *These little beings were created to help and take care of them?*

I: And to enjoy them, and to bring joy. For there's so much joy in them. Mary Melissa loves to play with them. They look forward to playing with her all the time. And sometimes she'll lay on her back and they just run around her. Or if she puts her hand out they'll even come and sit on her finger. They love her, and she loves them.

D: *Do other people also play with Mary Melissa and the fairies?*

I: Oh, no! Her momma does not like any of that nonsense!

D: *She doesn't believe in it?*

I: Oh, no! Her momma is not a nice person. So I think Mary Melissa goes out with the fairies just to feel the joy.

D: *To get away from her mother?*

I: I think so.

D: *Why do you think you're drawn to Mary Melissa?*

I: I'm not quite sure. I'm looking to see why I am seeing her. – Oh! I'm protecting her from her mother. I sent the fairies to play with her.

D: But it's also getting her in trouble, isn't it?

I: Ah, but without the fairies, Mary Melissa would not be alive. Her life is so bad, I think she would leave. It gives her a safe place, to keep her spirit going until she grows up. I've sent the fairies, and they're teaching her: who she is, and the light that she is. And her angels are gathering. You see, we had to start with the fairies and then work our way to the angels. They're helping her realize she has guardian angels, and she'll always have them, and guides to help her.

D: It sounds like you're one of these guardians, too, aren't you?

I: For a brief time, I certainly am.

D: All right. Let's move time ahead. Do you stay with Mary Melissa for very long?

I: Just enough to see her grow into adulthood.

D: You protected her all that time. (Yes) Then where do you go?

I: Ondonga? (Phonetic)

I didn't understand. She repeated, "Ondonga. It appears to be someplace like Africa, a jungle. I'm with a little boy. His name is Ondonga."

D: Oh, that's his name. What are you supposed to do there with him?

I: I'll have to see. – Oh, my! (Three sharp breaths, then a sigh.) He's safe. I can go now. That was quick.

D: What did you do?

I: There was a tiger creeping up behind him. Wow, that was a quickie!

D: (Laugh) What did you do to the tiger?

I: I blew him away.

D: Did the boy know he was in danger?

I: No, he was playing. He'll never know. But he's going to grow up to be the medicine man of his tribe. It was important to keep him safe. That was a quick one! (Laugh) He was quite cute.

D: *Well, let's move forward in time. When did you get to the point that you wanted to be a person, a human being, instead of watching and guarding people? What happened to cause that?*

I: Shift time. I'm here for the shift. I'm here to help with the vibrations of Mother Earth. This is great work that needs to be done, and many of us are called.

D: *Had you been in a physical body before being called here?*

I: Not seeing one. Strange, should be. Most people are.

D: *So you were mostly doing this guardian work?*

I: Seems that way.

D: *That was a very valuable and important work.* (Yes) *Then, did someone tell you to come here at the time for the shift?*

I: I just knew. – It's very difficult to be in the body. Quite confining. Also very difficult for my mother to birth me. Energies were so strong for her.

Is this what is happening? The normal human spirits that have been on Earth for many, many lifetimes accumulating karma are leaving. And being replaced in one way or another by these more advanced spirits who will be able to handle the stresses of the shift. Even those who were normally doing guardian angel work are being called in, as well as the more advanced spirits. They are willing to leave their "home" in the astral to travel here and assist during this important time. The other humans who are staying are having their bodies adjusted to handle the increase in the vibrational frequency change. Those who cannot adjust, are leaving the planet.

I: I didn't stay in her much when she was carrying me. I came in at birth and sort of knocked her out. The angels came and helped her.

D: *Were you able to bring all of your energy into that infant body at that time?*

I: No, no, no, no, no. I would have exploded her.

429

D: *So you just brought a part of yourself into it?*

I: I can draw more when I need it.

D: *So this is the life of the being you're speaking through right now?* (Yes) *And this would be your first experience in the physical. Is that right?*

I: That I can recall, yes. I have been here to help others.

D: *Was it difficult growing up? Experiencing?*

I: Never fit in. *Neeever* fit in.

D: *Weren't you afraid once you got in here, you might get stuck?*

I: Pffft! Not! Nah, can't get stuck. Got too much help, too much power.

D: *(Laugh) I was thinking of karma.*

I: No, I don't have that.

D: *What are you supposed to do about the shift?*

I: We have many who are here to help Mother Earth with the changes. To help awaken others by simply being. We do tend to escape from time to time, though.

D: *How do you do that?*

I: In what you would call "sleep," or "meditation".

D: *You're able to get out of the body?*

I: Definitely. In fact, one of my problems is doing ... like hiking. It's hard to get all the way in the body enough to keep the feet balanced. That's a challenge.

D: *You mean when you are out for a while and come back?*

I: I mean, my challenge in being here is to be here. A part of me tends to take off a lot. Actually, I have many parts of me going many places simultaneously, so this is only a very small part of me here.

D: *So when Irene is either meditating or sleeping, you leave and go off somewhere else?*

I: That, and – although it sounds very strange – I do it even when I'm doing everything else. I have many things I'm doing all at once.

D: *So you're able to do that, and the body still functions?*

I: For certain. I have other bodies functioning other places, too.

D: Why did you do that?
I: To gain as much as I could.

This is very similar to what was reported in Chapter 21 where the woman remembered living in many bodies at the same time.

D: So all these other bodies are also here to experience the shift?
I: In different time zones, as it were. It's hard to explain. I can be everywhere all the time, and being aware of being here now. I'm not always aware of all the dimensions that I'm in. In a sleep state, I am more; or a meditative state, I am more. But I have the awareness of all of this going on simultaneously. It's like being in Best Buy (or Wal-Mart) and in the middle of all the TV sets. And then all the TVs are stacked a million stories up and a million down, all showing something different. And then you're in all of those screens and all of those places. That's what it's like. That's a pretty good description.
D: So when you decided to enter a physical body, you broke apart. If that's a good way to explain it?
I: No, not breaking apart. Still one, bringing maybe a consciousness into that form. This is very difficult to explain, because in all the other forms, there's that consciousness.
D: So when you decided to be a human being, you decided to be in many different bodies all at the same time.
I: Right. And then also, in all the other forms, all of it at once. You know, the spirit form, the ET form has many of those. Those are fun! And all of those in different dimensions, it's really weird.
D: This happened after you decided not to be a guardian.
I: Yes, although parts of me are doing that now, too. Irene does not understand how all of this can be going on.
D: Yes, it's hard for many of us humans to understand these things.
I: This is quite confusing, but I know it's right.

There is more information about the splintering and shattering of the main soul body, and the fragments that go off to experience their own lives in *Convoluted Universe, Book Two*.

D: *So what is Irene supposed to be doing with this?*

I: She has great powers. Her mere presence shifts people. If she thinks of them, they shift.

D: *What do you mean, they shift?*

I: They start to awaken. To remember who they are.

D: *Who are they?*

I: They are pure light and love.

D: *And they've gotten away from that?*

I: Oh, they have. It is quite sad. But it is important, very important, for Irene to do her work. That she remains steady, that she does not get lost in the emotions of those who are not awakening as fast as she would wish for them. Of those who don't seem to be awakening at all. And to honor them, and to love them, but to not get wrapped in that Earth emotion. For she is weakened when she feels sadness for them. There is no sadness, for they are only light and love.

D: *Yes, they're all learning their own lessons.*

I: Yes. There's a great need for great light here in the area where she lives. Great, great light here. And many are awaiting her. There is a spark that she can render them that will help them. Oh, it's like they just explode in their light, and then their sparks go off and do the same for others. It's quite beautiful. It's like a fireworks display. It's all beautifully positive, the most vibrant love and light one can imagine.

D: *When we began this session today, why did you choose to start her at the very beginning of her existence?*

I: It was like a gift, a bliss moment. To give her that bliss moment. That nirvana, that bliss, that home that energizes her. She knows it. It was where she loves to be.

CHAPTER TWENTY-SIX

CREATION OF THE OCEANS

Pierre was a Frenchman who had relocated to America. He had a strong accent that made me have to listen very closely, which also caused a problem during transcription of the tapes. His job was wearing him out and causing him to develop physical problems. It involved constant traveling and he was at the point of burn out. Of course, the logical solution would be to quit and find another job, but there was always the seniority and salary to consider. I have had several clients with this problem. Some hate their jobs with such a passion that they think suicide is the only answer. I always say that no job is worth that, you can always find something else. But many people feel totally trapped in a situation and can see no way out. Some have unconsciously created an illness or a heart attack in order to get out with dignity. "I can't work if I'm sick." "It wasn't my fault. I had a heart attack, so I can't work anymore." It is amazing how the body will cooperate if it thinks that is the desired solution. It does not judge. It just obeys the commands of the owner of the body (conscious or unconscious). This is why we must realize how powerful our thoughts are. In any case, this was one of the main complaints that Pierre spoke about when he came for a session. The information that came forth was totally from a different direction. He said afterwards that this was definitely not what he would have fantasized. He was looking for a past life to explain problems in his life.

When he came off the cloud, there was total confusion as he tried to understand where he was, and the bodily sensations he was feeling. When I asked him to look at himself to see what his body looked like, he said, "I don't feel solid! I cannot see myself. I'm everywhere."

I was thinking he could be an energy form, which has happened many times when the person could not see a body. "Do you have any kind of feeling of what you are?"

P: It's been everywhere. It's been not physical. It's been everywhere.

I asked him to explain what he meant.

P: It feels like the ocean. Like a wave. No boundaries. Just big, big! It's a wonderful feeling. I am not restricted.
D: *That's why you don't have any kind of form?* (Yes) *Don't you have any limits?*

I was trying to think how to word it. Even if he was an energy body, he would have a shape and limitations. Something to enclose him, even if he did feel very large. But I was wrong. This was something totally different than our concepts of physical shapes.

P: The limit is the top of the ocean. The separation with water and air.
D: *Do you feel like you're in the water?*
P: I *am* the water. No boundaries.
D: *So you don't have a body. You're just part of everything there?* (Yes) *What do you see as you look around?*
P: I see the sky. I see the water. I feel the water. I feel the coolness of the water.

There was nothing in the water, no other forms of life. Just the water.

P: Just the beginning. The feeling of the beginning.
D: *What do you mean?*
P: It's the creation of the water.

D: *Before there was anything in it?* (Yes) *That would have been at the very beginning, wouldn't it?*

P: I feel the water. It's not limited. Just the water and the ocean. I am the ocean. I am the ocean.

He said after he awakened, that this was the most wonderful feeling of total freedom. He felt so big, so huge. It was something he could never have imagined.

P: I feel the warm wind. There's no limitation.

D: *Do you feel lonely if there are no other life forms?*

P: No. I feel quiet. I like it. I am whole. I am complete. It's a wonderful feeling.

I was trying to think where to go with this. If he was part of the ocean at the very beginning of the creation, this could go on for quite a while (eons probably) with little change. Especially if he was enjoying it so much.

D: *Were you somewhere else before you came to this place?*

P: I come from Light.

D: *Were you told to come to the water?*

P: No, I volunteered. I see myself coming from a star, from Light.

D: *Why did you decide to do it?*

P: It has to be done.

D: *But you were happy as Light, too, weren't you?*

P: We were part of Creation. It had to be done. So we volunteered.

D: *I was wondering if someone or something said it was time to do this.*

P: There was no time. It had to be done. I see myself as light coming from far, and then I see the ocean. I am the ocean.

D: *And when you became the water, did you create the water? Is that what you mean?*

435

P: The word is not accurate – creation. We are part of Creation. We don't create.

D: *So you didn't make the water. You just became it?*

P: We are part of it.

D: *I am trying to understand if there is a process.*

P: We cannot explain.

D: *You must be a very powerful spirit, if that's the right word.*

P: Powerful is not accurate. We are part of it. It's a natural process.

D: *Do you have any plans, or are you just going to stay there as part of the water?*

P: We would stay until the process is finished, until it is stable, because there is no land at this point. It's a process. In time there will be land. Now it's just water, and we see the sky.

D: *How will the land form?*

P: We are not involved in the land formation. We are involved in water formation.

D: *Other beings will be involved with the land?* (Yes) *I was just wondering if the land will come up through the water.*

P: I do not know. My job is to stabilize the water, so that life can evolve in it.

D: *Are there certain requirements for life to evolve?*

P: Salinity. The salinity has to be just right. The light within the water has to be just right. The gas within the water has to be just right. We are part of the water.

D: *So certain chemicals, if that would be the right word, have to be present?*

P: Yes. Stability. Salinity.

D: *And then when this occurs, what type of life forms would be the first to be formed?*

P: We see what will be amphibian, frog-like.

D: *That's not your job to create the life?*

P: No. My job is to create water, to stabilize water. Then I will be done.

D: *Then other beings will create the first forms of life?*

P: Yes, the Masters.

D: *Are the life forms in the water formed first before the land is formed?*

P: The life forms are formed before the land in the water. Not too far before. – We are going down now. We are going inside the ocean, deep. We are very deep inside the ocean. It's incredible.

D: *Are the chemicals and the elements right now so life can come?*

P: Not quite. The ocean is still moving. We are searching the depths of the ocean now.

D: *What are you looking for?*

P: We are not looking. We are experiencing.

D: *When you came to this place, there was nothing at all?*

P: We have not full awareness, because we came and we created the ocean. We are part of the ocean. We are the ocean.

D: *I was wondering if you were creating the ocean on a* planet?

P: No. The ocean was there first, and then came land.

D: *So there wasn't even a planet at first?*

P: Not quite. Not quite.

D: *I guess I'm thinking about a planet and then things forming on it.*

P: No. The ocean is here.

D: *So the water was just created in space?* (I was having difficulty trying to understand this.)

P: We cannot explain, but the water was created first. The water was created from Light. We came from Light. And we created water, and we are part of water. And we are experiencing its depth right now. The water is very deep. It's undivided.

D: *In our way of thinking, we think of the planets, and things being formed on them. But this was before their creation. Is this what you mean?*

P: That was before the creation in terms of what is known now. This was before we can even talk in terms of time as we know

437

it now.

D: *So first comes water.*

P: No, first comes Light. And then the water.

D: *And then you have to form Light in the water?*

P: And let life and Light. In terms of time, they were very close in time. But there was life, and then a little bit later, there was land. And we could experience the Light. We are experiencing the ocean. The ocean is undivided. This is incredible!

D: *And then there are other beings that create the land?*

P: It is a cooperation.

D: *Then you decide which kind of creatures or plants would form in the water?*

P: We don't decide. It isn't our destiny to decide. We are not at that level. We created the ocean. Others decide, they are responsible for the general plan. We don't decide.

D: *So there are many of you who have different jobs?* (Yes) *Would you be what I would call a Creator Being?*

P: I don't understand that word. There is a Master Creator, but we created the ocean.

D: *So there is someone over you.* (Yes) *The Master that created you, where is that located?*

P: We are not created. We are part of Him.

D: *I guess I'm putting limits on everything because this is our human way of thinking.*

P: Yes, we are not limited. We are experiencing unlimitedness right now.

D: *Is this Master Being also part of this Light?*

P: He *is* the Light. We came from Him. And from there, we created the ocean.

D: *Did you have instructions from Him to do this?*

P: No, but we anticipate your question. You are trying to link us to this being. And that problem stems from the limits of this life, of this form. That's what we anticipate in your question.

D: *Because I try to put things in forms so I can understand.*

P: Yes, we understand. We know what is in the design. What is in the Grand Plan. We know, and we do.

D: *I am thinking of a Master and the workers doing the work. It's not like that?*

P: No. The word "Master" is used in terms of what you would say "respect". It is cooperation.

D: *Is this land going to form a planet?*

P: It will be Earth.

D: *So this was how the whole planet was formed in the beginning.* (Yes) *So the water was formed, then life was formed in the water by another group of beings, and then the land was formed.*

P: Yes. And then the land was formed, and the land had to be cooled. It was too hot. It had to be cool. Cool. We are stable now.

D: *Was there anything else you had to do to the land to make it stable?*

P: No. We don't work with the land. We work with the ocean.

D: *Do you know what these other beings are doing?*

P: I'm not privileged with that information.

D: *But they probably have a job very similar to yours?*

P: Yes, yes. I am stable now.

D: *This is very important for life to exist, isn't it?*

P: Yes. We have to stabilize the water. The light within the water, the salinity, the gas within the water so that life can be created in embryonic stage. Thereafter, can masses of land be created.

D: *Then when the minerals and chemicals are correct, and the water is stable, what do you do?*

P: I depart. I was no longer needed, so I left.

D: *Do other beings stay there and continue to work?*

P: I sense the presence of others who stay behind.

D: *You did a good job. The ocean is very beautiful.*

P: Thank you.

D: *Where did you go when you departed?*

P: I went back to the Light.

D: *Which did you like best, being in the water or the Light?*

P: The water has a different experience, a different feeling. The Light is oneness.

D: *I've heard that before, that it's very beautiful to be all together.* (Yes) *All right. Even though time does not exist, let's move forward to find out where you go. What is your next assignment, if that's a proper word? Where do you go when you leave the Light again?*

He instantly saw himself as a crippled beggar in India. It was a miserable life filled with pain and despair. Apparently, when he decided to enter the physical, he chose the worst of human experience. It was a totally opposite departure from the beautiful peace of being part of the ocean.

D: *Why did you decide to go into a physical body?*

P: It's to experience, so that the Light can experience physicality.

It was a difficult life, because he had been so accustomed to being free without limitations.

P: There is much limitation. It was difficult to be contained. Much physical pain from that physical body. I received experience.

D: *Yes. And when you're in the physical, you don't remember the other, do you?*

P: Sometimes we do, sometimes we are aware. And we chose that, not to remember. It was a difficult life.

D: *Why did you choose to experience that type of life?*

P: It was to experience the extreme, and to learn the strength. I then lived in France as a female. We moved to other places, and chose to come back to experience again.

D: *What other places did you go to?*

P: Saturn. We moved to Saturn.

D: *What was that like?*

P: We don't have a word for it.

D: *Can you try to explain?*

P: We are not allowed to explain. The time is not right for that. It is not useful for this being. But it was quite a different experience from the Light and the water. We are giving what is relevant, which is the difficulties of dealing with limitation. That is the difficulty that this human being has.

D: *So from time to time, you would choose to come back into a life, a human body, to experience something different.*

P: So that we can learn, and finish things we didn't finish.

D: *Why do you feel the need to learn, to experience?*

P: So that the wholeness, the Light, can experience. We are an extension of the Light, and the experience is necessary.

D: *Can't the Light experience on its own?*

P: No. The Light has to be. We see the image. The Light has to be experienced as droplets of light.

D: *Droplets of Light. You mean pieces of it came off?*

I already knew the answers to some of these questions, but I am always trying to get more verification by asking the same thing to many people. If they all say the same thing, I believe that gives my research validity.

P: Individuality. The Light is whole. The Light has to experience individuality. Therefore, the Light has to materialize as droplets of Light.

D: *I see. And you are one of these droplets?*

P: We are *all* one of these droplets. We are a spark of Divinity. We are all drops of the Light in material form.

D: *And you are to experience and gain information.* (Yes) *Then what are you to do with all of this information?*

P: We have to integrate it, reintegrate it back.

D: *And you take it back to the Light.* (Yes)

441

He verified that this Light was the same thing as some people call the Source, and the Great Central Sun. They are simply different names for the same thing, the one that we call "God".

D: *And you have experienced many life forms on Earth?* (Yes) *And also gone other places?* (Yes) *Have you experienced other bodies?*

P: Yes. I see another body. A very high intelligence – but not human.

D: *Did it also feel contained, limited?*

P: Yes, but less contained than this being now. Because the veil did not exist as much.

D: *In your travels, when you would come to the end of the life, the body would eventually die, wouldn't it?*

P: Yes. And then we reintegrate to the Light. We always reintegrate to the Light.

D: *And carry the information of the experience?* (Yes) *Because I have heard you don't really die.*

P: That is correct. But the body, the physical container dies.

I then decided to communicate with Pierre's subconscious in order to get answers, but I was probably already speaking to it. "I call it the 'subconscious'. Is this correct, or do you have another name for what I am speaking to?"

P: Your name is correct.

D: *But you're much more powerful than that, aren't you?*

P: You could say that we are more aware.

D: *Why did Pierre choose to come here today? It was not coincidence, that's for sure.*

P: He needs to know why he's having pains. He needs to know so that he can readjust himself. He needs to know so that he can be aware that he's more than what he seems to be. Although he says it, he needs to experience it. That's why he experienced the vastness of the Ocean today. And he adjusted,

442

and he understands that he's more than his limited self.

Pierre had some questions about physical problems. I suspected they were being caused by the frustration of his job, the feeling of being trapped in a hopeless situation. I was interested to see what the subconscious would say was the cause.

P: The pain in both sides of the lower body is due to the frustration brought upon him by feeling powerlessness, because he cannot physically express himself as he would like to, or as his higher self would like to. So he develops pains. His pain will be relieved. He developed the discomfort so that he could be prompted to act upon it, and experience the largeness of the Ocean. Once that experience occurs, the pain will gradually be removed. But because the pain is in the slightly advanced stage, it will *gradually* diminish. It will be gradual as he understands it. He could have asked for help sooner. He had the opportunity. At this point, his body will not be able to accept an instantaneous relief of this pain. The body has been used to the pain, and the removal of the pain has to be gradual.

I have heard this many times. The discomfort will sometimes increase in order to get the human's attention. If it has been going on for a long time, and has greatly increased, it cannot be eliminated suddenly. Mostly because the body has grown accustomed to it. So in these cases, it has to happen gradually. *But* it does go away.

P: There have been many adjustments made to his body while he is asleep. The only memory he has is in dreams, and they are cloaked in symbolism.
D: *What were the adjustments for?*
P: The adjustments were required so that a new level of energy can be adjusted to his physical body.

D: *That's what I've heard. That there are many of these adjustments going on among many people, because the energy and the vibrations of the world are changing.*

P: That is correct.

D: *And some of us are experiencing this in different ways. Everyone's bodies are reacting differently.*

P: That is correct.

D: *And those that can't adjust are the ones that are leaving the planet.*

P: That is correct. Or they were designed not to be around.

D: *There were certainly many that left the planet right at Christmas time. (The great tsunami that hit Indonesia in 2004.) I know that was all their decision, wasn't it?*

P: It was an agreement so we know that we are one.

D: *They just wanted to get out of here before the other things happen?*

P: We will not say that. We will say that it was an opportunity that they had to serve, to increase the awareness of one world – that we are one. He is unlimited, like the Ocean. He has the ability. He has the power. He can choose.

D: *He also wanted to know what his purpose is? Why is he here?*

A very common question that is asked by just about every client that I see.

P: His purpose is to bring light. In order to bring light, he has to experience the experience of those that he is supposed to serve. It's this experience that he designed himself to bring light. The difficulty comes in the limitation that he experiences. It goes deep inside of him. He knows there is more than what he can do. But he's not allowed to exercise all of his innate ability. So the difficulty has to be with the limitation that he agreed to put on himself.

D: *So he will influence everyone that he has contact with.*

P: That is correct. We would suggest patience. May we suggest that he understand that we understand his impatience, because in his mind, he feels that he's not doing a good job. However, from our perspective, we would say that he has put himself in a very difficult situation, given his ability. The restrictions are difficult. It is difficult for him to shake himself. However, we do understand. We would suggest that he keep working. He is doing fine.

When Pierre returned home, he had a chance to listen to the tape about the creation of the ocean. In an email, he gave some interesting observations. He, of course, was having difficulty accepting the reality of the experience (as many of my clients do), and he was wrestling pro and con about whether he could have been making it up. "As I listened to the tape, I experienced the challenges associated with the use of words and the usage of the tongue to express these words. I sensed that the ocean-energy had to use the conscious mind to express itself in words. So instead of setting it aside, the ocean-energy just 'dissolved' the conscious mind into itself as 'a grain of salt dissolved in the ocean.' However, the grain of salt (or my conscious mind) even as it is dissolved in the ocean water (or the ocean-energy), still maintained its individuality. So the conscious mind expressed in words, as accurate as it could, the information that it received from the ocean-energy. The point here is that there were challenges/difficulties translating the energetic information into human words, and some of the words used were not exactly what the ocean-energy would have wanted to use. But the conscious mind used these words, because it was more or less in charge of the wording aspect of this communication. It would be excellent if we could completely silence the conscious mind, but somehow its presence is still needed for the wording. I sensed that there was another helper/translator that put the energetic information from the ocean-energy in a format that the conscious mind could use to formulate words. It has been made clear to me that it was like the information from the ocean-energy had to go through a 'processing center' before it could be translated into words by the conscious mind.

"I sensed there was very close monitoring and deliberation when you asked the question about being a creator-type energy. I could not see anyone around me, but I was aware of the monitoring. That information was released only to make sure that the ocean-energy was not confused with the Light/Source itself.

"After our session, I was trying to explain the vastness of the ocean, and I mentioned that in terms of size, I felt like 'a grain of salt dissolved in the ocean'. As I am writing this note to you, I am getting the understanding that the above analogy also explains the challenges associated with the human verbal expression. I also understand that there is a lot of information in the analogy of a grain of salt dissolved in the ocean. The grain of salt originates from the ocean, and in fact, it is the ocean in a condensed form. So this analogy shows how we are individual (minute), but are also part of the Whole. We originate from the Light/Source, and we are a condensed/physical expression of the Light, and as such, we are truly unlimited.

"In recent memory and what seems to be dreams, I have left my physical body four times, and had been talked into coming back to it. I think I was getting to the point where I saw no reason to live, so I had to be shown a certain aspect of what is being accomplished. The session gave me hope and the desire at the conscious level, *not* to vacate my physical body."

When I was conducting this session, I had a problem trying to understand it, because it was going against what we would consider to be logical. How could water be created before there was land or a planet? How could water be created out of nothing in space? In the other sessions in this section, the client described how they created galaxies, universes and planets. This was what I would consider to be logical: create something solid first and then put water on it. Yet no matter how illogical it seemed, I thought it sounded familiar. Then I remembered where I had heard it before: from the Bible. The Bible also reports exactly this illogical way that creation occurred, in the first chapter of Genesis. I will put it altogether here instead of breaking it apart into verses the way the Bible does.

In the beginning God created the heaven and the earth. And the earth was without form and void; and darkness was upon the face of the deep. And the Spirit of God moved upon the face of the waters. And God said, Let there be light: and there was light. And God saw the light, that it was good: and God divided the light from the darkness. And God called the light Day, and the darkness he called Night. And the evening and the morning were the first day. Genesis 1:1-5

In one of the chapters in this section, the client said there was something before the Light (or the Source), and that something was darkness. It has also been said that sound played a part in the creation process, thus: *And God said.* Each time God spoke, something new was created. We now know that we are all part of God, so it was these beginning spirits who were still connected with the Source, who were doing much of the creating. It was all the same, all One. Also note that before anything was created (even the light) that the Spirit of God moved upon the face of the waters.

And God said, Let there be a firmaments in the midst of the waters, and let it divide the waters from the waters. And God made the firmament, and divided the waters which were under the firmament from the waters which were above the firmament: and it was so. And God called the firmament Heaven. And the evening and the morning were the second day. And God said, Let the waters under the heaven be gathered together unto one place, and let the dry land appear: and it was so. And God called the dry land Earth; and the gathering together of the waters called the Seas: and God saw that it was good.

Here again, it is obvious that the water existed before the creation of land. Pierre said he could only see the water and the sky. God divided the firmaments. Then the creation process

447

continued: the creation of plants and trees. This goes along with the story in this book, that the alien helpers first introduced plant life to see if it would grow, before animal life. Plants had to be in place as a food source. It is interesting that (according to the Bible) the plant life was created before the Sun and the moon and the stars. Then the first animal life was created in the oceans, then the birds. *And God said, Let the waters bring forth abundantly the moving creature that hath life, and fowl that may fly above the earth in the open firmament of heaven. And God created great whales, and every living creature that moveth, which the waters brought forth abundantly, after their kind, and every winged fowl after his kind: and God saw that it was good. And God blessed them, saying, Be fruitful, and multiply, and fill the waters in the seas, and let fowl multiply in the earth. Genesis 1:20-22*

Then the creation continued by the introduction of animals of many different types, and finally man. All of this is exactly the order reported by the various subjects. The only exception is that these various spirits had a part to play by helping God in the creation. Since we are all God, this should not surprise us. And since we had a role in the creation process of our beautiful Earth, we should honor and respect our home.

THE BORROWER

PIERRE CONTINUED

Pierre returned to my office about six months later to have another session. Normally, I do not have to see a client more than once. And I was sure we had covered everything that he wanted to find in the first session. But I agreed, not knowing what else he might want to pursue. On this trip, he brought his wife, and I had a session with her, also.

After the last session, I had no idea what to expect. What could possibly be more dramatic than finding that you helped with the creation of water before the beginning of the Earth? I never have expectations, and allow the client to go wherever they feel the need to go (or wherever their subconscious thinks they should go). Thus, when Pierre entered the scene, it sounded like we were going to explore a normal past life. Yet again, he was going to surprise me before the session was over.

He saw himself by the ocean sitting on a wooden bench with the number eighteen hundred carved into the back of it. He was a simply dressed, young, fair Caucasian (Pierre in reality is black) with dark hair and beard. There were no people or activity. Just a peaceful and calm feeling as he rested and looked out at the water, watching an old ship passing by. When I asked if he lived around there he answered, "I hear, 'I come and visit.' I hear, 'I don't live here', but I hear, 'I come and sit and visit.'"

Behind him were houses and a small city. "I hear 'Brittany'." I asked him to go to the place where he lived so we could see what it looked like. Even though he was enjoying himself sitting quietly, "I like the ocean and sitting there now," he agreed to go and look at it.

P: I see a cobblestone street, and then I see a small house with two floors on my right as I look. I hear horses hauling carts. I hear the noise of their feet. The house is not very big. It's a single house in a row of houses. The street is very small. It is not very clean. It's not the house, it's the city. It's not very clean.

I asked him to go inside to see what it looked like.

P: I know that a man is standing behind on the right. It's almost like a hostel. He checks you when you walk in this house. I hear, "I rent a room in this house. I am a sailor." I am a boarder. He's almost like the landlord. Now I see a small room with two beds, one on top of the other. And I see an old type backpack. I hear, "I am a visitor from far away. I am observing. I walk, because I see the backpack. I observe. I come from far. A long ways in this world." I go from place to place. I hear, "If I'm walking, I am walking. If I'm not walking, I take the old-time boat." I observe. I record, too. I hear, "I was given a choice." It is almost as if one is going on a camping trip, and you choose in this lifetime. I hear that I was given a choice, a vacation.

D: *So you were not born in this place as a baby and raised. Is that what you mean?*

P: I'm sorry. I am confused. I don't see a baby.

D: *The form you are in now is this young man?*

P: Yes, yes. I hear, "You came from a star." And I don't know. I just came.

D: *But how do you become this body if you weren't born into it?*

P: I hear, "It's not my body. I borrow. I cohabitate."

No, it was becoming obvious that this was not a normal past life regression. There was more going on here.

D: *You cohabitate the body with another soul?* (Yes) *Is this allowed?*

P: I hear, "I am allowed, yes. Agreement. The other knows."

D: *I thought you weren't allowed to enter a body where another soul resided.*

P: Yes. It's temporary cohabitation. Vacation. And then you leave. I stay for only a short while.

D: *And while you're there, you use the body to go from place to place?*

P: You don't command the body. I hear, "The other has control. You cohabitate." It's almost as if you take a ride. The body is a sailor. He walks too, and I hear, "A vagabond."

D: *So the young man is going to these places anyway. And you're just going along to observe what he is seeing?* (Yes) *And he was just chosen at random?*

P: No, I hear, "Agreement."

D: *Is he aware that you're there?*

P: Not aware in real life. Not in awake stage. But deeper, he's aware, because without that agreement, it wouldn't be allowed. There are laws and regulations about these things. We say it here that it is not an invasion. It is an agreement. It's *important* to understand that it is not invasion.

D: *Why are you observing?*

P: I hear, "For this time, it's a vacation." That's all. And an agreement that was made has to be lived. And so he came on vacation in this port, in this area. And we see friends. We see the ocean. We see the bench. The numbers, eighteen hundred, carved.

D: *Where you come from, do they have an ocean?*

P: I don't think so. I hear, "We have worked hard; therefore, we have been given a vacation for this time. And we are not imposing. We are going along in this vacation."

D: *As a reward.*

P: In this situation, an agreement is required, because we are not invading.

D: *But you choose the world you want to go to?*

451

P: Yes. If there is an agreement possible, because we don't want to start from being a baby, and having to grow up. It is especially for a short period.

D: *So you stay for a while, then you go back?*

P: I hear, "You go on another assignment. In this specific situation, you can transit, you go back. Since this is a vacation, you don't need recovery time." So it will be as if one would go back and get the assignment, and then move up to the assignment.

D: *But you said, where you came from in another place, you did a very good job. That's why they rewarded you?* (Yes) *What is it like on that place you came from? Is it a physical world?*

P: No, it's not a physical world. I see a star! And I don't get a sense of physicality.

D: *What kind of form do you have on that other world, the star?*

P: I hear, "We are pure energy. We are golden energy."

D: *What kind of work were you doing that they rewarded you for?*

P: I hear, "Council." I was Counsel.

D: *Were there many who were Counselors?*

P: I hear, "Nine." I was with these.

D: *What kind of job did you have when you were with the council?*

P: I hear, "Counsel of Supervisor of a Star System."

D: *What does a supervisor of a star system do? It sounds like a very important job.*

P: It is a job. A supervisor looks at a group of stars. I hear, "And advises on the way to go to develop."

D: *To develop the stars?*

P: I will not say that. I will say, counsel on the path that the direction is towards.

D: *Is this part of what the council does? Decides what is to be done on different worlds?*

P: Yes, one of nine councils. We advise. When we are asked for information, or when we are asked for direction, we will advise. We do not impose.

D: *Do you do the development yourself?*

P: I will not say that we do the development. We advise. A different group will do the development. However, in some situations, they will ask for our advice, and we will advise.

D: *This group that does the actual development, are they physical beings or like you?*

P: I will say that they can take the physical form if necessary. However, in our planetary level, a physical form is not required.

D: *So these groups can do the development without being physical.* (Yes) *Do they have to go to these worlds to do the developments?*

P: No. I hear, "It is the blueprint for the worlds. The blueprint is worked in, not a physical world. The blueprint is worked in the non-physical world. Refined in the non-physical world. And then it may be launched in the physical world."

D: *So, it is developed there, and then they are able to make it become solid and a reality?*

P: Yes. When we are asked for advice, we counsel. We are one of nine councils in this system, as they are a solar system.

D: *There are probably systems over you too, aren't there?* (Yes) *And they would advise you if you needed them?* (Yes) *So do all of you together decide what type of life forms to put on these worlds?*

P: I hear, "Advisement comes on the level of planetary system. The life form comes at a much later stage, as our advisement did with planetary system, or issue." You build a universe first before you can populate it with life forms.

D: *So you build the entire planetary system?*

P: We advise, we counsel.

D: *You talked about the universe. Is that what you mean by the planetary system, or are these two different things?*

P: These are two different things. Please allow us to correct – we are trying to distinguish the level of – perhaps the complexity between a life form and a planetary or Universal system. Universe might be some planetary system. We counsel at that level. We do not counsel necessarily on the level of life form.

D: *I see. So you counsel first on how they create the whole universe.*

P: Yes. And within the universe are planetary systems.

D: *So the universes are being created constantly?* (Yes) *That's what I'm trying to understand. I would think there would be only so many, and then there wouldn't be room for any more.*

P: We see infinity. And we will try to translate in the sense that, if you were to look, you will be looking forever continuously in the end. That's how the Universe is. So the Universe is infinite. And systems and universes have been created custom all the time.

D: *So they don't necessarily overlap or get in the way of each other.*

P: They are a different vibration, too, so they can cohabitate within the same geographic area, the same space, but without touching or overlapping. They are vibrating at different frequencies, unless a doorway is opened between them. We are using your terminology. We meant a portal. This is possible to go from one to the other.

D: *So people who could find these portals would be able to go from one universe to another?*

P: Those who go between universes know the knowledge. They don't need to find it.

D: *I've been told about different dimensions. Is this different than different universes?*

P: We see that within a dimension, you can have universes. We can not fully explain or express what we see of our understanding. Within a plane are several dimensions, and within a dimension are several universes. We are sorry that we cannot explain clearly. However, the point being made here is that Universes, we hear, "Cohabitate – they can be within the same area."

D: But first, the universes are created and then, the other steps are taken?

P: Yes. First, there are dimensions. And then within dimensions are universes which are created. And within universes are planetary systems which are created. We counsel on the universal and also on the planetary system, since universes are made of planetary systems. We are one of nine councils who counsel in this specific system.

D: That makes it clearer. But he was doing that work and he said he took a vacation, because he did a good job. And just wanted to get away to experience the material world?

P: We would say, yes. We will also say he likes the simplicity in this specific body that he is cohabitating at this point. The young sailor.

D: What does he do with this information if he is an observer?

P: As far as this specific information of this specific situation, we would say again, using one of your analogies, that he is on a vacation. The information we research is not specifically used for a purpose. It is for his own enjoyment, and observation.

D: I've heard there are other beings whose job is to gather information.

P: Yes, the observer. That is different. He is here for his own enjoyment. When he is finished with the vacation, he will go back to the council. He will not stay here long as the body cannot sustain both of them for an extensive time. He will return and stay in the council for another opportunity, or, as you say, job.

D: Is Earth part of the planetary system that his council is over?

P: Yes. As you say, we saw Earth within our light system, but it belongs to this Universe where he counsels. We saw a possibility for him to be in the council, and also for him to be living a life on Earth.

D: Rather than a vacation? (Yes) *As a regular physical life.*

455

P: Yes. And in this situation (as Pierre) – we see a *spark*! An infinite small part of him.

D: *So his main part stays on the council?* (Yes) *And a spark is all that's sent out?*

P: Yes. We will say a "spark" as an analogy. However, this spark is a complete spark.

D: *But the whole essence couldn't come into the body?*

P: No, it could not. It would be too powerful. And also, he has other responsibilities in other systems.

D: *I've been told that the entire energy of the whole soul could not possibly ....*

P: Yes. That's precisely what we're trying to convey, is that we see a spark come off a body of energy. And it has the purpose of fulfilling several functions in different systems, as in his system, and as of Earth. The spark will become a human body on Earth.

D: *Was this decided for a certain reason?*

P: It's part of the experience. It's part of the possibility that exists.

D: *I was thinking if he was so evolved, he would not need to have an Earth experience.*

P: The Earth experience is unique in its simplicity. And also in the lack – excuse me, we're looking for a word – we will not say, the "darkness", but we say the "not knowing", or ignorance of what's happening.

D: *What do you mean?*

P: On a certain level, the Earth is simple, but at another level, because of the fact that a soul enters the Earth system and doesn't know, becomes unaware of its source, it makes it difficult. We are having difficulty translating what seems to be a duality and opposition. The idea here is that the ideal simplicity comes from the fact that on Earth, life evolved around sustenance, on one hand. Therefore, it will be considered simple as compared to other systems. But on Earth, life is also very complex because of the non-remembrance.

D: *Yes, we come in with all the memories erased.*

P: Yes, that is exactly what we are trying to explain.

D: *That's what I'm trying to do, get the information back.* (Yes) *But I thought that once you had evolved to that high state, there wouldn't be a reason to come here. It would be like going back to kindergarten, so to speak.*

P: Yes, it's true. But sometimes, it is interesting to come and work in here. The trip back here is to take a refresher course, if we can use that terminology.

D: *Well, when this spark came to Earth, what kind of bodies did it come into at first?*

P: We express the possibility that the whole self has to be and to function on several levels. We don't necessarily see a body as we see the spark flying across the universes to incarnate on Earth. We see that the spark can choose to incarnate through the birth canal. Or the spark can choose the mode of experience that it chose as it is experiencing the life of the young sailor in Brittany, in France.

D: *That was a spark that did that also?*

P: Yes. So the possibilities are infinite. This is something that we like to impress strongly, is the fact that there is no limitation.

D: *It's all just to learn lessons, or to experience?*

P: It's more to experience than to learn lessons, because at a certain level, the lesson had been transcended. There is, in itself, no longer a need for lessons to be learned. However, there is still a need for the experience to be experienced and integrated in the whole.

D: *You know you're speaking through a vehicle that is called Pierre.* (Yes) *When we did this before, he experienced being part of the ocean.* (Yes) *Was that as one of these sparks?*

P: Yes. As the whole – we would prefer not to give out a name to this energy body. So we will say that the whole energy body from which came the spark Pierre, that energy body cannot physically, and perhaps we should say, safely, inhabit a physical body. Therefore, a spark called Pierre came to the ocean and made it.

D: *He created the ocean?*

P: He was the creator, among some others.

D: *So this was in addition to when he was on the council? He decided to come down and also be a creator? Am I understanding that correctly?*

P: We see your linear thinking, which could be misleading. As help is relative and everything happened at the same time.

D: *Then you mean he can be on the council and be one of the creators at the same time.*

P: And at all the levels.

D: *So he was with others that helped create the ocean.* (Yes) *This was before the land, the continents were formed? It sounded like it was in the very beginning.*

P: Yes. We are looking at your perspective, as we have a different understanding of time. However, from your perspective, it was seen as if he was here before Earth was created. But he was also in the council and at other levels at the same time. We would like to emphasize that you like to categorize these events, but that you perhaps understand that linear time is experienced only in this sphere.

D: *Yes, I have been told time is an illusion. We have created it here.* (Yes)

I then wanted to ask this superior part about a strange experience Pierre had after our last session in February. After he left my office, he drove on to Miami, Florida to continue his work (which involved a great deal of driving from state to state). While there, he went to the beach to relax, and as he was standing there facing the ocean, a strange and startling thing occurred. He said the ocean suddenly grew very large. A huge tidal wave arose and surged toward the beach. It was totally enormous. He was not afraid however, which he later thought was irrational. He

458

stood rooted to his spot on the beach watching the wave rush toward the shore. Then as it crashed down in front of him, the water came right up to his feet and stopped. The sea once again became calm, and it was over as quickly as it had begun. It was startling, but also beautiful and breath-taking at the same time. When he was able to look around, he saw that no one else on the beach seemed to be aware that anything out of the ordinary had happened. It appeared that the event was reserved just for him and no one else. Of course, he wanted to know what that was about, and had included it in his list of questions. The subconscious knew exactly what I was talking about. I did not have to go into details.

P: He created a vision so he could convince his human body of the validity of the experience he had during the session. He anticipated that he would doubt himself, and therefore, he created that experience so he could convince his physical self of the validity of this session he had previously here in this office, a few days earlier.

D: *So no one else on the beach that day was aware of what was happening.*

P: He was the only person who was a spectator to what we would perhaps call a "vision". But in his reality, he did experience the immensity of the rising of the ocean, and the tide of the ocean at his feet.

Also when Pierre returned home from Miami, he noticed the birds in his backyard were doing strange things. He kept hearing a bird, but he could not locate it. And he kept hearing in his mind, "Remember the beginning." I asked the subconscious if it could explain that.

P: Yes, we will, we could, we can. For the bird aware, aware. He tried to locate the bird. He could not totally locate it, because it was a memory from the beginning that he was

459

experiencing. And the bird was supposed to remind him of that beginning of unlimited possibility that exists for him. That he was truly unlimited, as in the beginning.

D: *He was wondering, did the other birds know what had happened to him?*

P: The birds go across dimensions, as they can look at time, not as humans do, but they can cut across time and look at the beginning.

D: *They are able to do these things?*

P: The bird was designed to remind him of the beginning, yes. And they are able to recall in their memory, or to get from the memory bank, experiences from the beginning.

D: *We think of birds as being very simple creatures.*

P: Animals in general have a perception of reality which is different from human beings. Therefore, the animal can transcend time, and go and feel the memory bank of an event that in linear time would appear to be from the beginning.

D: *So they're able to do this, and of course, they can't tell us what they see.* (Yes) *That is amazing. We always think of animals as being very simple creatures. It sounds like they're much more advanced or enlightened than humans.*

P: Animals have more awareness than the human in physical bodies.

D: *We are more tied into our version of reality. This limits us greatly.* (Yes)

CHAPTER TWENTY-SEVEN

THE FIRST CREATURES COME

Another version of the creation of the ocean came through during a session I conducted while in Kona, Hawaii, while giving lectures and workshops. It is similar, just reported in different wording. Melody is very much at home on the ocean, because she and her husband, Mike, own a charter boat service, and take people out daily to swim with the dolphins and whales. Mike knows how to call them so they come immediately and congregate around his boat the minute he sails out onto the ocean.

After going through two lifetimes, I began communicating with her subconscious. It surprised me when it said, "She was there in the beginning of the planet. When the planet was first seeded. And her job was with the whales and dolphins. To bring them to the planet.

D: *What form was she at that time?*
M: In the very beginning, she was all light. She helped seed these whales and the dolphins in the ocean. She brought them in golden pods. Each dolphin, each whale, came in a pod. And was placed in the bottom of the ocean until the time was right when they could live.
D: *When the time was right, then what happened?*
M: The pods opened.
D: *Were they brought from somewhere else?*
M: Yes. The planet of blue water.
D: *And they knew they would be able to live here in the waters?*
M: It took a long, long time, and many experiments, but when the time was right, they came. And the pods kept them safe until

461

the environment was right for them.

D: *Otherwise, they would die if they came out too soon.*

M: Right. They had to adjust to the new environment and adapt, but that was her job.

D: *Was this before there were humans on Earth?*

M: Oh, yes, yes. From the very beginning. There was mostly water on the planet at that time.

D: *Before the land appeared?*

M: In the very beginning, it was all water, of course, and then the lands began to appear, yes. And the first lands to appear were wet. Lemuria.

D: *That was the first place.*

M: Yes. That was one of her first lifetimes on this planet.

D: *As a human?*

M: Well, she had a light body. Not like a human body, yet. That was much later.

D: *Did the people in Lemuria have light bodies?*

M: In the beginning, yes.

D: *So they weren't solid yet.*

M: No, because the planet could not sustain those type of life forms in the early days. It had to be very gradual.

D: *That was one of Melody's questions, whether she had any lifetimes in Lemuria.*

M: She had many.

D: *If that was one of the first places, did they become more solid?*

M: Oh, yes, when the planet could sustain life and different forms, but it took time and there was a lot of trial and error along the way.

D: *What kind of trial and error?*

M: To figure out what kind of life forms could be on this planet.

D: *Which would survive?* (Yes) *Because it has to have a very special environment, doesn't it?*

M: Right. Because you had to breathe the air, and it took a long time for the air to be the right combination of chemicals.

D: *So it wasn't easy.*

M: No, it never is when a new planet is being prepared.

D: *But then she decided to stay on Earth and keep living lives after that?*

M: Yes, she loved it.

D: *So now we know how the energy of Lemuria and the whales and the dolphins are connected with her.*

Melody had questions about an unusual experience she had while traveling on a plane from Salt Lake City to Atlanta in 2001. She felt like she was trying to separate from her body. The subconscious gave a surprising answer. "She had the opportunity to return to the Source at that time."

D: *Was that something she wanted to do?*

M: No, she decided to stay. But at that time, in that incident, she had to choose whether to go back to Source, or remain on the Earth to continue her work. She chose to stay.

D: *She said she actually felt like she was separating.*

M: She was, in fact. She was no more than a few breaths away from going home.

D: *What would people have seen if she had decided to go home?*

M: Her body would have just slumped over in the seat.

D: *They would have thought it was a heart attack or something?*

M: Something of that nature, yes.

D: *It can happen that simply, then.*

M: That simply. It doesn't have to be a big traumatic thing.

D: *But she decided to stay, because she had work to do.*

M: She did.

D: *But she said, after that, she began to have dizzy spells. It went on for three years.*

M: Yes, it happened because of the pressure in the airplane and in her head, and when she was leaving the body, and the pressure going back in.

D: *Oh, because it wasn't like being on the surface.*

463

M: Right, right. But actually, when she was out of her body, she did journey to another place in time. She crossed the dimensional lines.

D: *When she thought she was in the plane?*

M: Right, and she was given some information to bring back that she would work with.

D: *Should you tell her what it is?*

M: No, it's not appropriate at this time.

D: *But she chose to come back. And that caused the dizzy spells for three years?*

M: Yes, yes. It was when she came back into her body and the pressure in the airplane; it caused an imbalance.

D: *That's not a very good place to go out of the body, is it?*

M: Not especially.

D: *But the dizzy spells are gone now?*

M: Yes, the dolphins and the whales have been working with her to help her come back in balance. They have been working with her, and I think the final piece is now in place.

D: *Can we go back and talk some more about the beginning of life? You said she was there with the seeding and it was all water. (Yes) And then you said the land began to appear?*

M: Right. Then the water began to recede and there were many changes on the planet, in the climate. What would you like to know?

D: *I am just curious about it, because I had a man who also said he was a part of the water in those days, and there wasn't any land. (Yes?) I was wondering, did the land just rise or what?*

M: It was a combination of many things. Remember, this happened over a very, very long period of time. It was not an overnight thing. Millennia, for it to happen.

D: *So the planet was all water in those days.*

M: It was water once upon a time, and then, just underneath, the land would shift. And the volcanoes underwater would shift, and they would explode. And it caused water to recede and land to rise. Those things happened.

D: *Why were the volcanoes doing this underneath the water?*

M: It was just the planet itself coming into balance and adjustment. To live in this environment, to contain ... to create an atmosphere. All the chemicals of the air: the oxygen, the hydrogen, the chloride – all the mini components that go into a planet's atmosphere.

D: *So this had to happen with land rising.*

M: Yes, in order to create the atmosphere for plants to grow. That creates atmosphere; it creates oxygen.

D: *And you said she was one of the first ones to bring the golden pods with the dolphins and the whales.* (Yes) *Were other life forms brought at that time?*

M: Not all at the same time. Everything was brought at different times to see what could be sustained here, and what could not.

D: *But many of them had to wait until the proper time to awaken, I guess you would say.*

M: Yes, until the planet was ready. There's some gradual process, you know. Everything's not ... evolution is not what you've been *taught* evolution is. It is the evolvement of an entire planet, and eventually an entire ... *many*, many different species, to see what life could live here and live in harmony.

D: *When the land first began to form and rise, what was the first life on the land part that began to evolve? Can you see that?*

M: Did you know that in the beginning, the dolphins walked on land, also, as well as the ocean?

D: *They did?*

M: Yes, they did, which has been proven by your science.

D: *And they walked like people?*

M: They weren't shaped like people, but they walked the land. They lived on the land. They could go back and forth.

D: *Did they crawl on the land?*

M: Not exactly. They looked different than they do now, to accommodate that. So they would look almost – I don't want to say half man-half dolphin, because that gives a distorted picture. But you don't really have a good analogy for that. (Laugh) You would think it was quite funny, though. But they had little, short legs and feet (Laugh), and they did walk, sort of in a more upright position. But they could go back and forth in the beginning.

D: *This is why they can breathe the air?*

M: This *is* why, because they were going to be on the land, as well.

D: *So they were one of the first forms?*

M: Yes, one of the first air-breathing forms.

D: *Then why did they choose to go to the water and stay there?*

M: They preferred it, because they had come from a planet of water.

D: *Then, what was the first form of life, besides that, that came on the earth part?*

M: That just lived on the land?

D: *I'm thinking of plants and things, I guess, first.*

M: Oh, I thought you meant animal.

D: *Well, either way.*

M: Of course, the plants were first. The plants had to be seeded because they created the oxygen.

D: *So this was also seeded?*

M: Oh, everything was.

D: *Brought from other places.*

M: Absolutely, to see what would live in various places. And when the land began to rise, there was a vast, vast continent of land after a period of time. And so, different things would live in different areas even on the one planet.

D: *Then what form of life was the first on the earth part, besides the plants. I'm thinking of an animal in some form.*

M: The best description to give you – because, remember it changed many times before something really worked – would be more like a bird.

D: *A flying creature?*

M: Yes, more like a bird. But the bird also could be on the water, land on the water, because it required both in order to survive in the earliest of days.

D: *Also, the scientists talk about the dinosaurs.*

M: Yes, they weren't too much farther down before they came. But again, the atmosphere had to be set.

D: *Why did they all have to disappear?*

M: Because they were ready to move on to their next dimension; they went to another dimension. They didn't just get up one day and they all went, "Oop!"

D: *So it was no longer appropriate for them to be on the Earth.* (Right) *They were like an experiment.*

M: You could think that. They were put here for a period of time, and other things happened as a result of their being here. Gasses were formed and all sorts of things. But once that was done, there was no need for them to be here, so they were taken to the next place where they could be of service. Everything has a purpose.

D: *Yes, it all does. I've been told in my work that the ETs had a lot to do with the seeding. Is that true?*

M: Yes, it is. You know, everybody has a job.

D: *(Laugh) Like Melody, she came as a light being.*

M: She came as a light being first to this planet, yes.

D: *And she brought the pods. Is that the same as the ETs, or is it different?*

M: It is different, because they came before from another place and time. There are all different dimensions and galaxies and universes. And there are all kinds of creation going on in all sorts of places. And what works in one, does not necessarily work on another.

D: *Then the theory I've been told is correct, that they had to develop man.*

M: What you would call "man", yes.

D: *(Laugh) Genetically.*

M: Yes, but remember. What is man really? Man is essence and light and Source, which is everything.

467

D: *But* that *is inside. I'm talking about the physical vehicle; the physical casing.*

M: Yes, but it had to begin somewhere. And you have to remember, that essence has intelligence and so everything stems from that plan (or plane?).

D: *I get little bits and pieces from many different people, and I like it when I can get verification.*

M: Of course.

D: *And this is the real story of the Earth. And she has been here from the beginning, helping with everything. And now it's time for her to continue her work with those that she brought here in the very beginning.*

M: Yes, that's why she loves them so much.

CHAPTER TWENTY-EIGHT

THE DESTRUCTION OF A PLANET

When Sam first entered the scene, he saw himself flying an airplane, looking for an airport in order to land. He spent quite a bit of time flying the plane, looking at the ground. I thought we had perhaps entered a past life when he was a pilot. But occasionally, the subconscious will provide the subject with something familiar that they are comfortable seeing, in order to begin the adventure. That appeared to be the case with Sam. As the story progressed, it became obvious that he was actually piloting a small spacecraft. He landed on a planet where he was supposed to connect with some of his people who were living in a camp. He was bewildered to find the place deserted with no sign of life. The area was desert-like, very arid, barren and hot. He searched for quite a while trying to find where the people might have gone, and finally gave up in desperation. With resignation, he decided the only thing to do was leave.

He sounded very tired, "We were struggling. There aren't many of us left, just a group. We've had troubles. We didn't know where we were going. We were just looking for anyplace! This was the place to *go*! Because we were leaving someplace. And here we are, out in the middle of nowhere. I was coming back from somewhere, and they're gone." I asked if maybe it would be easier to go back where they came from. "I don't know if there's anything left where we came from. I'm getting a picture that we had structures that we lived in, in some kind of settlement. It was permanent, it had goals. This is a *dry* place! This is a dry planet!"

D: Let's look at the place you came from. You said you lived in structures?

469

S: Yes. I see this as a cluster of little domes that seem transparent. We could see the sky above us. The top is out of the ground, and we live underneath them. Most of the house where we live is underground, and some are bigger than others. They're cylindrical, and there's more than one level that goes down. That's out of the elements. It's cooler, it's comfortable in the holes. When you get out of the holes, you get out of the settlement, you get out of the structures, this planet is barren. It's a community. An outpost of some kind. Civilization is here. I had a group of people I was with. We worked together.

I asked him to see what kind of work he did there.

S: I fly in a ... machine. I come and I go from outpost to outpost, and I bring the things that they need. So I don't live there all the time. I guess I'm working for these people. But where did they go? They weren't at their place. They're gone, and maybe they've left for a reason. I don't know. Was it abandoned? There's nobody here. Where the hell are they? – I gotta get outta here. Something's gone wrong. This isn't right. I came here, but nothing's the way I expected it. There isn't anybody here. They've left, gone off into the darn desert!

Still confused, he went back to his craft. He felt he needed to go and tell someone, a superior, and try to get help. He really enjoyed flying his machine. "Ooo, this is a nice – boy, is this thing zippy! Wow! I like it! It's not the biggest one. It's not a big cargo carrier. It's a small plane. It's round, it's a disk. It's not just for one man, looks like you might put six people in it, and some cargo. It's nice! It's comfortable. It's a neat machine."

D: *So you're going back to where you came from. Do you have to go far?*

S: I don't know. I go a long way in a big hurry in my machine. I just set the machine to go where it's supposed to go and it goes. You know what? It goes where I think it's gonna go. You think it and it goes! (Amazed) Zip! You just tell it where to go and it goes. (He seemed to be marveling at the technology.)

After a while, he flew in over three spires that were lined up. The spires were guides to help him come in for a landing. He reported in, but his superiors were as confused as he was. He waited impatiently to find out what to do next. "I don't want to do anything by myself, on my own. It's not my job to decide what to do, I just follow orders. I don't make the orders." He was becoming angry. "So I go where I'm told and do what I'm told and I don't ask too many questions."

The events were moving too slowly. Sam became angrier as he waited to find out what was going on, so I decided to move him. I asked him to move to an important day when something was happening. He took a deep sigh, and then answered very softly and timidly, "Everybody's off the planet. Everybody's gone. All of them! They're all gone."

D: *The whole planet?*
S: Yeah! They're all gone! While I was away, they all ... were gone! I went somewhere! I was on a job. I was doing something. I got home and nobody was there! They're all gone ... All of them! Everybody.
D: *You don't have any idea what happened?*
S: Nope. (Pitiful, wistful) The whole place is gone. Everything is gone! (Softly, pained) So that's why I'm moving on. My friends and all my people are gone! This is not good!

He was confused, emotional and on the verge of tears as he tried to understand what had happened. We apparently were not having much luck trying to understand what was going on, so I

471

moved him ahead to another important day hoping to find some answers. He found himself in his ship, all alone, looking down at the Earth from space. He could see the continents of China and the Far East beneath him.

D: *Did someone tell you to go there?*
S: Nope. This is mine. I decided to do it for myself. I came down to Earth. It's not where I was from though. I know where I was from. I didn't know what to do. I didn't have a clue. So I thought, Earth is close. Earth is okay.
D: *Have you ever been there before?*
S: Oh, yeah, I've been to Earth. But usually we stayed away from Earth. It was newer, it was still primitive. There's not much on Earth. I guess there are some people. They're not like us. They're different. They're newer. They're black. (Sam is a black man in his present life.) And they don't live on this part of the Earth either. This part of the Earth doesn't have any people.

It has been said that when the Earth was first seeded or populated, that it occurred on the African continent and then the humans spread out from there. Scientists have been able to trace the earliest origins of man to Africa. They have even isolated it back to a single female. There has been much dispute and arguments about how the human race was able to spread all around the globe. There has also been controversy about how humans appeared in the first place. There have always been more questions than answers, unless you accept the theory that I have been given in my work. That we were seeded by extraterrestrials, and many eons of time passed as the developing species were transported to various areas of the world to see if they could survive. It was a slow and laborious process. Was Sam seeing the Earth at that earliest stage when man had first been created in Africa by interbreeding and the manipulation of genes with the apes? Most of this has been reported in my books, *Keepers of the*

472

Garden and *The Custodians*. The scientific aspects are explored in another book published by my company, *Mankind, Child of the Stars*, by Max Flindt.

S: I think I'll probably come down here somewhere. But there's nobody here for me. There's none of my own people here. What I'm trying to do is find some of my own people! I haven't been able to do that. There weren't very many like me that flew from place to place. Just a few of us. I'm going to see if one of my other friends landed here. There's a place on Earth. I'm looking down on it. It would be Tibet. The plateau. Our people have come here. We have flown in and out of Tibet. And I'm hoping one of my people is here. Oh! My body is different! It's smaller, and it's lighter. Yeah! I'm not the same. My body's light. That's kind of neat!

D: *Were you able to do that, change your body?*

S: I didn't have to change it. That was just the way it was. It was lighter. I am not all flesh. I have more energy. I have a form though. I have a nice, shining form, grayish. I don't think I had to create this body. It's different! It's lighter. And I'm looking for somebody like me. Where are we?

D: *But you said you fly in and out of Tibet?*

S: That's a place where we come in and out. We're not the only ones. Other people from other places come in and out of Tibet, too.

D: *That's mountains, isn't it?*

S: No, it's not. It's a plateau. It's pretty flat. But it's up. It's a higher elevation.

D: *So you're going to land there and see if you can find some of your own kind?*

S: Yeah, or anybody else that can help me. Something terrible happened. I do believe the place I'm from has been destroyed. I really do. I was gone a while, and while I was gone something happened. Everybody is gone. Gone, gone, gone .... I probably will land. (To himself) Is there anybody

473

here? – Yeah, there are! There are. But they're from somewhere else. They're not from where I was. They're not from that planet. They're from farther away. They're not from the solar system. They're not from the same Sun system as the Earth. They have been here for a while, too.

D: *At least they're someone you can relate to.*

S: Maybe. They're different. They're not the same as me. Actually, they're higher. Wow! They're light. They're beings of light. They're fairly physical. I'm denser than they are. They're really light.

D: *Why do people come in and out of this area on Earth?*

S: It's the energy of this high plateau. These people came here, and they're different from the people that are black. They're from a different place. They're working on the Earth. They are helping.

D: *Why would these people come to Earth?*

S: Well, the Earth is great. Everything is coming to Earth. Beings from everywhere are going to put part of themselves on Earth. All over, every kind of being is going to be on Earth. Everything. (To himself) The Earth is hurt too, isn't it? Yep. The Earth got hurt too. That's bad.

D: *Why are they going to do that?*

S: They're the ones that are making it happen, or it's their idea. They're in charge of it. They're developing that plan, and they're bringing everything to Earth. They're bringing things from all over. Everything! All kinds of things. And you know how they do that? It's with light. Strands of light. They change strands of light. When they take these little strands of light, anything can happen. They change everything. It can make anything happen with it.

D: *Where do the strands of light come from?*

S: Oh, my gawd! Their minds? They take it in their mind and then they make stuff form. They put a point of light into something and then it takes shape around it. I knew they were here from a past trip. I didn't know them very well. They have a way to create things. They make things. They take light and they make any form out of it. The light goes in the middle. They can take one cell and change it by changing the light in the middle. They can make anything different just by changing the pieces, the part of the light. It's not what I'm used to doing, but that's how they do it. They make things happen that way. This looks like it's a permanent group here, but they stay away from others. They stay to themselves. In fact, they take charge of everything, but the others don't really know they're here.

D: *You said the other ones were coming to leave parts of themselves, too.*

S: Yes. They're in charge of who comes in. They let in whatever light they want. The light is in everything. There are animals on Earth, and every one of them has a little piece of light. And if you change that piece of light, it becomes a different looking animal. So they can change any animal they want just by changing what's in the light.

Were they using the light to somehow manipulate or change the DNA?

D: *But you said there were black people.*

S: Yes, they're not like me. They're heavier, bigger. They're more solid, too.

D: *Are those people from Earth?*

S: Yes. The group is working with that. They're making them happen. How they do that, I don't know. The bodies came from animals, but the beings themselves are not animals. The body's very animal, so they're changing them around. They're getting bigger and they're developing more abilities. And they look different, less hair.

D: *Do you know if somebody tells this group to do these things?*

S: It looks like they decide what they're going to do. They're from someplace else, too. They're on Earth to make this happen.

D: *To do the creating.* (Yes) *And the other ones who come can create, also?*

S: I don't think so. They're not that advanced yet.

D: *But you said the other groups come and leave parts of themselves.*

S: Oh, yes. They'll bring a group of everything, like all the animals. Every group of animals came from a different place. Like reptiles came from one place, and mammals came from another place. And then they take the light and change it. And then the animal changes.

D: *So the animals can exist on Earth?*

S: Oh, yeah! The animals can exist on Earth. They can make any animal to fit any condition.

D: *That's what I meant. That part of the light is in them so they can stay here and survive.*

S: Yes. If they change the light, the animal changes. They really know what they're doing! Wow! They change something inside its cells, and then the cells all change. The ones that are in charge are from a different dimension than I am. They're much lighter. And I'm thinking that I am lighter than these creatures that are on Earth. But I'm not as light as these ones that are running the show. They're light. They have enormous energy! They can use energy. They just take it and manipulate it. More than I can. I can't do that. They take this enormous energy and they manipulate it and make different forms. They make a different animal. They make all sorts of different animals. They can take this stuff out of their cells, and change it from one animal to the other. And zip! In a matter of a little time, they have another animal! They are creators. – They don't really know what to do with me, either. I wasn't supposed to be here. This isn't my home.

D: *That's what I was wondering. They can't use you. What are you going to do? Are you going to stay with them or what?*

S: I don't know what I'm going to do.

D: But you have to go somewhere.

S: I know ... I'm lost. I don't know where I'm going.

D: All right. Let's leave that scene, and move forward in time to find out what you eventually do.

S: I'm looking at a ... boy, what a mess. What a mess!

D: What are you seeing?

S: I'm seeing everything all wrong. (Pause) It looks like everything is wrecked – everything is gone, wiped out. The air is gone!

D: Where?

S: On my planet! There's hardly any left.

I didn't understand what he was talking about.

S: It's different. It's different! Almost all the air is gone.

D: On a different planet? (Not Earth)

S: Yes. The one I came from. There's hardly enough air to breathe.

D: You went back there?

S: Yes. It's all disrupted. It's all gone. Not all, but almost. There was a big, big problem. Oh, by the way, it burned .... I don't know how I'm going to live. I have to find some of my other friends. There has to be some of us! Maybe some of us were away. I've got to find them! I don't know where to find them! Maybe if I just wait around here, some others will try to come back and I'll find them. I'm looking down on a planet that's barren, that wasn't barren before! When I left it, it wasn't barren, and then I came back, it is. – The Sun is the same!

This was confusing. It almost sounded like he was repeating the same scene that caused him to leave his planet in the first place, when he went to Earth. But he had not described it as being barren and burnt before. Maybe he had to leave Earth because he didn't fit in there. And he may have thought the only

477

place to go was back to his original planet. This was all unclear. So I decided to move him to the last day of his life in that body, so we could find out what eventually happened to him.

D: *What do you see? What happens on the last day?*
S: I'm just very tired. I don't know what to do. (Much emotion, on the verge of crying.) Just so sad. I found a few. We're all sad. (Very emotional. His voice was strained.) There wasn't anything we could do. (Crying) I'm mourning. We tried, we all tried. (Emotional) Our lives are over.
D: *But you said you're tired now?*
S: No point. They're gone. They all died. Everyone that was there, died. Every one.
D: *Do you know why?*
S: Yeah, I know why. There was an explosion. (Big sigh) The planet blew up.
D: *Your home planet?*
S: No, my home planet didn't blow up, but it might as well have. Another one blew up. The next one over. The older one.
D: *And that affected your home planet?*
S: Yes, it did. It wiped it out. We were too close. It blew the air away. The atmosphere. The force just took it right away, and gravity couldn't hold it. It held a little, but not enough for the people. So the people all died. They died right away.
D: *That's why you never could find anybody.*
S: That's right. Just a few of the travelers were away. We were the only ones that survived. And we had nowhere to go. We didn't know where to survive. We looked at the Earth, but we couldn't have survived there. The Earth is *so* heavy! Our bodies are light, and the Earth's gravity was way too strong for us. And the conditions on the Earth were different. We couldn't live on Earth in our bodies outside of our ships. We *couldn't!* We were trying to find someplace to go. – I don't know if we want to try one more trip. I don't know if I have enough muster left to do it. If we could get a bunch of people

together, we'll go. See if we can find someplace to land. There's nothing in this solar system for us. Not now. We would have to leave the solar system and go into the galaxy and see if there's some other place we could live. But there aren't very many of us left. And we don't know whether we want to do it or not. So, we decide if we leave our bodies, we can join our people.

D: *In the spirit form, you mean?*

S: That's what we all are anyway. We go back to our light bodies. Our light bodies never end, but we lose our forms. We lose these little bodies we have. So we stay in our light bodies for a while. Everybody will be together, but I don't know what's going to happen. How could they do that to their home! (Anguished disbelief.)

D: *But it was something nobody could control.*

S: No, we couldn't. We couldn't. Some of our people thought they'd benefit. Stupid. *Stupid!*

D: *You mean they caused the explosion?*

S: No, *our* people didn't cause it.

D: *But they thought they could benefit.*

S: Some of them thought they'd be all right. Thought they'd be better, but they couldn't be.

D: *So you decided to just leave the body?*

S: We don't have to lose them. We can support ourselves a long time without food, or we can take energy directly. But there's nobody to share with! See, that's what this is about! To share! And after they're gone, there's nobody to share with! It's hard to explain.

D: *It's a feeling of being alone.*

S: It's awful! It's an awful feeling to be that alone!

D: *Well, leave that scene and let's move to when whatever happens has already happened. And you're out of it. Do you go to the spirit side?*

S: Yes, the spirit side would be okay. – Oh, the sadness ... My gawd, the sadness! A terrible sorrow!

I felt I was not going to be able to pursue this any further. So I decided it was time to bring forth the subconscious. Maybe I would be able to get more information and explanations from it. I asked why the subconscious had picked that unusual lifetime for Sam to see.

S: Sam wanted to know what his relationship was with Mars. That was Mars. That was the end of life on Mars.

D: *(That was a surprise.) Which was Mars? The one where the air evaporated?*

S: Yes. The air was blown away when the other planet blew up. Mar's air was destroyed. Everyone was killed on Mars. Mars was more highly developed, they already had space travel. And the people were little greys. Their bodies were little light-filled greys. Nice pretty little bodies that were almost all energy. They were advanced. They could travel between solar systems.

D: *He described it as having dome-type buildings.*

S: Yes, it was better to live under the ground. The heat of the planet was more from beneath. The air was cold because we were farther from the Sun. They are 140 million miles from the Sun, so it didn't get hot.

I checked this fact out and found it to be accurate. This was proof again to me that I was communicating with something that had great knowledge. How many average humans would be able to say how far Mars was from the Sun, unless they had made an intense study of the planet and memorized little known facts.

S: They didn't have a warm climate like the Earth. The atmosphere was cold – not comfortable to live in. There were life forms all over, though. It was a lush planet. Life forms survived. There was water on Mars. When the atmosphere went, the water went with it. When the air pressure dropped, the water evaporated right away.

D: Where was the planet that exploded?
S: That was the farther out planet. Ohhh! They blew it up!
(Disgust) The beings that were on it blew it up. They were
trying to become more advanced.

D: You think they made a mistake?
S: Yes, they did. They could only go so far the way they were
trying, and they tried to go too far.

D: Is there any evidence of that planet?
S: Oh, boy! They blasted it to smithereens! (A dark laugh) Yes,
there are comets and meteors and asteroids and stuff that
didn't stay in the orbit. They flew out all of a sudden. Most
of them did not escape from the solar system. Most of them
are still in orbit. They have all sorts of wild orbits. Instead of
a major explosion, there was a disintegration. So the
explosion caused pieces to fly off. But then the pieces that
disintegrated just fell apart and stayed in the same orbit. The
ones that blew up with the explosion went in all directions.

D: Where was the orbit?
S: Just farther out from the Sun, the next planet out. They were
more advanced than we were. They were trying to do
something more advanced. We couldn't stop them.

D: When the planet blew up, it just evaporated the atmosphere?
S: The tremendous force blew the atmosphere of Mars away.

D: Did this affect the atmosphere of Earth?
S: Yes, it did. It affected Earth, but Earth was far enough away.
Earth is in distress over this, too. It got hit by a lot of
asteroids. It got hit by a bunch of stuff from the explosion.
It hit the Earth, but the Earth was farther away on its orbit. It
was nearly all the way around the Sun when it happened.
And Mars was too close, almost as close as it could get.
Darn, if we'd only been on the other side of the Sun. We
wouldn't have been wiped out.

D: Was there life on Earth when this happened?
S: Yes, those beings that were the Creators, were there. They
were creating, and there were all sorts of life, but it wasn't life

481

that we were compatible with. That's the trouble, we weren't compatible with that life. We didn't have bodies that could live on Earth. We couldn't live in that environment. We had our own environment. And as you travel around everywhere, there are physical bodies. Not everybody has physical bodies. Physical bodies are dense. And physical bodies are according to conditions. They can be made any way you want. They can be made to fit almost any condition on any planet, but not the great big gas planets like Jupiter. I don't know about anything 3-dimensional on Jupiter. We couldn't go near Jupiter. It's too big, too strong.

D: *But the atmosphere on Earth was not affected.*

S: Well, it got hit. It got hit, hit, hit, hit, hit. Did it ever! Wow!

D: *When it went through these asteroids and meteorites?*

S: Yes, it did. It got hit a lot. Jupiter got hit by a bunch, but Jupiter absorbed them. Jupiter also caught many the pieces in its gravitation. So did Saturn. Saturn caught many chunks in its gravity.

D: *Is that part of what made the rings?*

S: Ahhh ... let me see. (Pause) No. It didn't. Saturn's rings are different. It made many of the moons around Saturn though, that are just chunks of rock, but not the four main moons of Jupiter. Nope, nope, nope – they were not from that. They were from Jupiter. Jupiter is like a small sun. And Jupiter burnt those four planets of its own. – I haven't found out about the rings.

D: *Well, the subconscious has the answer.*

S: Yes ... it doesn't want me to know. (To himself:) Why are those rings? (Out loud:) Why are those rings? They're smaller particles, they're finer particles. (To self again:) Why are they there?

D: *I was thinking it was all part of the same system.*

S: Maybe, maybe – I don't know ... maybe finer particles were caught by Saturn. But the bigger chunks ... Saturn and Jupiter have many, many rocks orbiting around them that aren't really moons of theirs. They're just things that they captured in their gravitational field. Uranus caught some – so did Neptune. Pluto *is* a piece. It is *not* a planet. There are other pieces farther out yet.

It was amazing to me as I transcribed this tape and typed this chapter to read this about Pluto. This session with Sam was done in my office in Huntsville in August 2005. A full year before the announcement that stunned the astronomical world in 2006, when they proclaimed that they were no longer considering Pluto to be a planet. That it was instead a huge piece of rock. There had long been an argument between experts about the status of Pluto, ever since its discovery in 1930. It is now said that there are many asteroids in our solar system that are bigger than Pluto. So it was demoted from its former lofty status as a planet.

As soon as a session is completed, I often do not remember anything about it. It would be impossible to retain the detailed memory of all the cases I conduct. It would be overwhelming to carry consciously all the information about my clients' individual problems, let alone the contents of the sessions. I have to clear my mind and remain objective in order to function in the rational world of supposed reality. I think many therapists have this same problem. If they do not, they become an empath and can take the physical and mental problems of those they work with upon themselves. This is not good or healthy for the therapist. So we all have to learn to do the work, and then release it. If the session contains something I think might be helpful to me in my writing work, then I ask the subject if I can make a copy of their tape before giving it to them. Thus the ones I keep, I know contain something interesting. But they go into a pile to be transcribed at a later date, which can be months or years later. This was why I was stunned to hear this part about Pluto which was verified a year later in 2006. I think this is validation once again that I am truly in communication with something bigger than all of us. The part that has all the answers and powers beyond the comprehension of our mortal minds. This is why I love to work with this part.

D: So this is the reason you chose to show Sam this life?

S: Sam wanted to know about this. That's an awful thing, to go home and not find anything there. To find your home blown up while you've been away.

D: Does this relate to things that have happened to him in this life?

S: Yes, it does. It really does. It really brings it home.

D: What do you want to tell him about it?

S: Martians came to Earth. We were all allowed to come to Earth.

D: In spirit form, you mean?

S: No, we obtained bodies. They took another monkey, or it was bigger than a monkey. It had a different color skin, a yellow skin. If you start back there, they made all of us genetically compatible. Isn't that interesting? They made all of us from different things. They made the black ones out of gorillas and chimpanzees – they played with their cells. Their physical characteristics came a lot from the ape.

Note: Caucasians were said to have been developed from orangutans, the large ones with white skin and red fur. Of course, there were other manipulations that occurred along the way to produce other variations. An interesting one is discussed in my book *The Legend of Starcrash* about the development of some of the North American Indian races.

S: But ours were from a slightly different monkey. It was medium sized or smaller. And they took the DNA from that and made it slightly built. And did something with our little brown almond eyes. And our little, slighter builds – smaller bodies. And we are the yellow skins. (The little greys from Mars.) That's what they made us. That's what was done, that's where we came in. The Martians found a home on Earth eventually. Not right away. It took them a long time. We were homeless for a *long* time.

D: *But you mean these Creator beings were the ones that were making the bodies?*

S: They helped. The Earth itself had to agree. The planet itself had to allow it to happen. It had never happened before where one planetary consciousness shared itself with another. Never happened before. *Never!* The Earth decided to share its body with another planetary consciousness. And this other planetary consciousness were those from Mars. After these bodies were created, Martian souls came into them. We all did. We have 3rd dimensional souls, we have 4th dimensional ascendant masters, and 5th dimensional ascendant master. And 6th dimensional .... I was a 4th dimensional or 5th dimensional ascendant master on Mars. I was an advanced being. Only advanced beings were allowed to travel. Only advanced beings *could* travel.

D: *And Sam's spirit decided to enter a human body on Earth.*

S: Yes, we've all come back to Earth. We had to come back to Earth and go back to the 3rd dimension in physical bodies to learn more, to advance spiritually back to the 4th and the 5th and the 6th dimensions.

D: *When Sam entered the body and stayed on Earth, did he become trapped here because of karma?*

S: Ahhh! Sam's a funny one. (A deep breath and a pause) Sam doesn't come back very often. Sam comes back around millennia shifts.

In some of my other sessions reported in this book, others have said the same thing. They normally remained with the Source, etc., and only came to Earth during the time of major shifts. These were the times when the most help was needed.

D: *Where is he the rest of the time?*
S: (He mumbled to himself:) It's a gorgeous place, isn't it? Ah ... look how beautiful it is being in the waterfalls of light. (Clearly) Golden pools of beautiful light everywhere. Showers, fountains of light. Golden light everywhere. Oooo, boy! It's love. It's a golden sea of love.
D: *Is this where he goes inbetween incarnations?*
S: Yes. Boy, is it nice! It's a sun, it's in a sun. Golden seas of light. It's not necessarily in a planet, it's likely a sun. It might be the Sun. You know what? I cannot be one hundred thousand percent sure of anything I'm saying, but I'll tell you what – I'm letting my first thoughts fly. And it looks like the Sun. Could it be the Sun? Could you spend time on the Sun? The Sun is humongous.
D: *Anything is possible.*
S: Is it that Sun? Is it another sun? It could be. Gold pools of beautiful light. Oh, showers of light. It's warm!
D: *So Sam decides to come back and enter the human body around the millenniums?*
S: Ahhh ... missions.
D: *Why is he here now?*
S: Gotta be able to raise a body. It was done before, but nobody believes it. Everybody can do it. I have to be able to raise a body.
D: *What do you mean?*
S: There's a transformation. I don't know exactly what it is, I'm still doing it. See, we could get all of our energy from the light. The Universe is full of light, the Universe is all light. And it's only in a three dimensional body that you can't get enough light. When you're in your light body, you can get enough light so you could live. You always live, you live always. Always, always, always. Light bodies can be put to sleep, but they generally always live.
D: *So it's difficult to do that in a physical, solid, dense body.*
S: Yes. Some places, they do it all the time. Their physical

bodies don't end, or they have *very* long lives. But on Earth, it's because it's so negative, so tired, so heavy. And on Earth, you don't know who you are. You lose your connection when you come to Earth. You don't see your light body when you come to Earth. You don't know that you are a light body. Boy, is it tough to find out too! Wow! On Earth, it's *hard*! And everybody's so lost! – I was supposed to come here. I'm supposed to spiritualize a body. It's been done before. And nobody seems to know it. It can be done. Some have done it, by living in the light. They raised a 3rd dimension body to the 5th dimension. That's what they do.

D: *But he has been here now in a physical body living a physical life.*

S: Yes, I have. I didn't have a clue about any more than that either, for a long time. I didn't know a thing. I didn't really have a clue. I lost all my memories. *Really* lost all my memories. I can't believe that you get upon this planet, and you lose all your memories of who you are.

D: *Well, does the subconscious have any advice for Sam?*

S: Stay the course. Stay on the path you're on. Keep trying, keep working on it. Keep making the connection. Open your light bodies, find your light bodies. There's more than *one* light body too – there are more! – We're still working on it. And there are some others working on this too. Our bodies will live a long time. Our bodies will be finer, they'll be taller, they'll be lighter. We'll be able to access more dimensions. Sam is supposed to grow to the next level. Grow and learn. That's what he's doing. Steadily by jerks. Ups and downs. I'm always helping him. He'll have a shot at it. He has a fighting chance. Ahh ... emotions. It's our emotions. Emotions! – He'll know sometimes. He'll have to figure it out. It's still not that easy. Earth is awfully dense. This isn't going to be an easy thing. Also, it's awfully hard to travel between the third dimension Earth and fourth dimensional and fifth dimensional. It's awfully hard to come

487

back from the fifth dimension after you've been away for awhile. This is a purpose. His problem is service to self. He's never really realized the difference between service to self and service of others. You know, service to self, service to family and friends, that's considered service on Earth. And service is a broader term of that. That's hard.

In another session, the first thing a woman client saw was a desolate landscape. The earth was cracked and parched. The trees had no leaves and hardly any limbs, almost as though they had been scorched. Some of them were twisted and bent over. When she was coming down into the scene, she saw a dinosaur, but later she didn't see anything except this desolate parched area. Then she found a little village nestled in between two mountains where there were flowers. That meant things were beginning to grow again. Later when I asked the subconscious about this, it said this was after the time that the dinosaurs had all been destroyed. I asked, "How did this happen?" They said the only thing they could see was a very powerful, great searing, hot wind that just destroyed everything in its path. It was only over certain areas, because the ones who survived, were living in an area in a higher altitude that was not affected. The rest of the dinosaurs did eventually disappear, because after this happened, they didn't have as many resources. They didn't have as much to eat, and they couldn't adapt to the changes in the climate as well as people and other animals could.

Could the searing wind have been caused by the explosion of the planet? Or have there been more than one event down through the tumultuous history of Earth? In my book *The Legend of Starcrash* it described a totally different climate in the Alaskan/Canadian region before something violent happened that created massive winds, earthquakes, and tilted the axis of the Earth.

This is a comment ... a woman came from France who wanted several sessions. And on the last session, she was talking about speaking to those of the Venusian energy, the beings who had come from Venus. She described that, many, many, many years ago, way back in time, Venus was very much like Earth, and had physical beings on it. It has been called the "Sister Planet of Earth", but the atmosphere and all the people were destroyed, through natural disasters, not through war. And when the natural disasters occurred, it caused the planet to heat up. She wasn't clear whether that was caused by the destruction of the ozone layer. Then the people made a transition into another dimension where they did not need the physical body, and they existed and evolved from that point. Venus is no longer inhabitable, and cannot be inhabited again, because it is too hot. But the people – their souls, I guess we would say – made the transition into the spiritual. Apparently, they also reincarnated.

I was finishing this book when I had another case dealing with the destruction of a planet. I thought it should be included rather than waiting for the next book.

The first part of the session was confusing, because Adele was not sure what she was seeing. It looked like sunlight filtering through trees with silverish bark. It was very dark and quiet, because the trees began to close in overhead and shut out the sky. Then it appeared as though it had changed into a cave. "I've been here before. It's like dusk after sun's gone down. There's light. You can see. It's all the same light, no matter how deep in there I go. It feels like I could even be underground. I don't know where the light's coming from. It's safe. You can't be hurt there." She then began to cry, "It's home. But ... it's gone! I'm not supposed to be there, I don't think. I know I can't stay there. It makes me sad. I don't think it's there anymore. I think it's underground, so you'd be safe. It's always safer there."

D: *But that's a good feeling, isn't it?*
A: Not when you can't go home again. It's gone. (Emotional) It hurts. I don't know where I am now. It's not there! (Sobbing) It's gone. All that's left is this unique light.

I asked her to move backwards in time, so we could discover what had happened.

A: It's shapes. Like pyramids on their tops, paths walking through. All the same lights, it's silver, silver.
D: *The pyramids are ... the point is down, you mean?*
A: Yes. Upside down. It's pretty big on top. It's dark up there. The sides are not smooth. It's like veins and tree leaves, except it's not leaves. I don't know what it is, but it illuminates as you walk. It's like I'm moving through. (Struggling to express herself.) I'm going through, like a tunnel. It's not a *tunnel,* tunnel. It should be round, but it's not. It's shaped with slided sides. They are like rips or veins or something that ever so often goes down towards the bottom. And coming out, there's fluorescent. It glows. It doesn't shine. It glows, so you can see. I don't see how far up it goes because the light is so bright, that you can't see anything else. Now it's something like smoke that swirls, swirls.

There was something about it that was upsetting Adele, and she didn't want to see it any more. I asked her to become aware of her body, and it made her even more upset. "I don't know if I have a body. A face? I don't know who I am! I don't have feet. I flow. This is ridiculous. This can't be! I need to have feet. I seem to be floating, but this is ridiculous. I don't know if I really am floating, or if I made this up.

D: Is that an easier way to move?
A: Oh, yes, but I should have a body.
D: What do you feel?
A: Safe. (Chuckled) I don't have to hold this together. It sort of moves and changes, but it's like smoke. It's all in one place, and I can move it in any direction without turning. I feel all of it moves. It seems to move very fast. It feels like an octopus moves, I guess.
D: But it feels good to be unrestricted, doesn't it? (Yes) You can move and float anywhere you want to go.
A: Yes, but it's gone now.
D: This place?
A: Yes, it's gone. We're one with everything; part of one. I've moved somewhere else, but I don't know where I am. There should be color! This is mostly silvery grey, and I seem to move faster.
D: But the place underground – the one you called "home" that you were very happy with – you said it wasn't there anymore?
A: It blew up. I told them it would. (Sigh) They always wanted more. There was never enough.
D: Who are you talking about? Who wanted more?
A: (Emotional) The others above the ground. Why couldn't they just be satisfied? They played with the world. Oh, shit! Stupid!
D: Did you live above the ground?
A: NO! No.
D: You lived under the ground? (Yes) But you knew what was happening there?
A: We always knew ... but nobody believed. They didn't want to. They wanted to be left alone, but we wanted them to leave *it* alone.
D: You said they were playing with the world?

491

A: They felt they had everything under control, but they didn't. It wasn't power. It was a kind of crystal. It was bad. I mean, it was good, but it was bad because they wanted more and more. Children play, but they're not here now.

D: *What were they using the crystal for?*

A: (Emotional) It was pulling power from the stars. We told them, no! (She began to sob.)

D: *It's not your fault. You didn't know they were going to misuse it, did you?*

A: We should have known they were children! (Sobbing) Children have to be taken care of! They don't know what it is. (Long sobbing moan) Nooooo! We should have stayed and watched. I told them! Now it's all gone.

D: *Are you a group, or by yourself?*

A: We are one. We were ... one. One – one mind of collective. Many, but one. They asked for information. If someone asks a question, you have to answer.

D: *But you can't blame yourself if they used it in the wrong way. You were not responsible for their actions.*

A: But we're all responsible for each other's actions. We're all part of the fabric. What we do influences others. Every time a child shoots a gun, we're at fault for giving him a gun. They're not at fault for pulling the trigger.

D: *Were these physical beings that lived in this place aware of you? Did they know about your group, your collective?*

A: They asked questions. I hear *oracle*. We were one, but we weren't one. We were a collective.

D: *So the oracle worked with the information, and passed it on?*

A: We were the oracle. We, we, we ... always we.

D: *And they asked for information, and you gave it to them.*

A: We didn't really see the harm of what we told.

D: *Maybe it's impossible to know every outcome. Even with the power you had, maybe you couldn't foresee everything that could possibly happen.*

A: We walk in different directions. But everything is gone.

Little pieces swirling, moving in all directions. I think it did something to the collective. It ripped the fabric. It's all gone.

D: *Was it a planet or what?* (She sighed and moaned.) *Because you said there were pieces that went in different directions.*

A: I can't tell you. It just was. I don't know what it was. I don't know where it is. It's gone. Little stars – all broken apart. I stayed with it for a while. I stayed. I don't know where the rest of us were. It's like ... I'm with the pieces.

D: *Where did you go after that?*

A: Lost. I'm lost. I feel lost. I can't leave though. I can't leave there for a while.

D: *Because you still feel responsible for those pieces?*

A: We *were* responsible; all of us. I have to stay for a while, and think about calling the others. I'm trying to get us all back together again. I don't feel like I'm on the world still. I feel ripped apart.

I could understand why she felt so distraught about what happened to the world she was definitely responsible for, but I wanted to get her away from it. I moved her forward until she made a decision about where she would go next.

A: There is a silver cord. (Chuckle) It has rainbows in it. I don't know where it's going, but I think I'll go there. I followed it. It looks almost like a wormhole. And then it came out, and I'm so tired. Up through the wormhole, and then I lay down to rest. I don't know where ... it's nice. I don't want to go back out. It hurts so bad. I'm in a cocooning state.

D: *So you're not that energy with that collective anymore?*

A: No, I don't know where they went. I lost them. I am so tired.

This was confusing and unclear, but I thought she might have entered a fetus, and was preparing to be born. I decided to call forth the subconscious to get answers and clarification.

D: *This was a little confusing. She was underneath the ground and got very emotional because of something that happened on top of the surface. Why did you pick that for Adele to see today?*

A: Information. The information she's afraid to have. The fear that she'll cause another catastrophe. Do no harm. She fears the result to this knowledge. Knowledge is power.

D: *That's true. It's all in the way knowledge is used. What was she a part of?*

A: It's hard to explain, except that if you take the fingers of a hand. The whole hand is what the fingers are. That was what it was like, except that there were more fingers. They were all, all collected together and working as a unit. Like-mind; one mind. Hearing, processing what they heard.

D: *Would it be similar to what you are, the subconscious?*

A: It is, except you would have the subconscious as a finger on a multiple hand. More octopus than hand. Where it's a chemical and capable of operating on its own, but also dependent on the body as a whole. This is hard.

D: *It's always hard to explain. Do the best you can.*

A: It would be like a collection of ... whips all hanging, bound together. And the whips think the same thoughts. Processing each one, putting in its part of the weave, and at the end there is this – whether it's a burst energy which is thought – but each one capable of thinking. But no detachment factor. Maybe not part of the collective as much as it needed to be. And that was why they told, they answered questions indiscriminately, because knowledge was just knowledge.

D: *They made no judgment. They just told what they knew.*

A: They were asked and they told. There is the lack of judgment. They only processed information. And although they knew things would happen, there was no way of knowing what would happen, until they told it and started the process. But the other energies tried to stop them by telling them where their message was headed. And they were laughed at and

494

called, "useless". They were called many things that don't mean anything here. That they weren't needed. That they had done theirs and they could go back to their cave. The people told them that they had gone beyond them, and they didn't need anything they had to offer. The collective warned them that if they continued what they were doing, they would end up destroying everything. And the people told them they were wrong, and told them they didn't want to hear anymore from them. And the collective, having done apparently all it could do, went back and waited. They thought they knew best. – I don't know what the collective is, though. This is very interesting, because they are and they aren't.

D: *What do you mean?*

A: I don't know how real ... they were energy. The collective was not like the people.

D: *And the people decided to take the information and use it in the wrong way.*

A: Yes, they were greedy. They wanted more.

D: *And Adele was a part of that collective at that time.* (Yes) *But it wasn't her fault, was it?*

A: She felt like it was. She felt that she didn't teach them well enough, and that if she could just have done a little more, things would have been all right. There's a great sadness there.

D: *Actually, from your viewpoint, you can see she couldn't have done any more, could she? I mean, it's not really her fault. She's not really responsible.*

A: *Fault* is a very subtle word. There's a deeper thing here that we are all responsible, not just for our successes but for our failures. That's part of what we come back to deal with: the fact that fault is like a child that says, "It's not my fault." Adele sees there are layers. That each person contributes positive and negative, though she works very hard to tip-toe away from negatives. And her fault is over-compensating. She has great fear here. She destroyed a world.

D: She didn't do it, they did it.

A: Yes, but without the answers to the questions, they wouldn't have gone where they did. And she was foolish to answer questions where she should have used judgment. Now she's worried about judgment. You forget that there is free will, and free will has two sides: the dark and the light; the yin-yang. She once watched a world destroyed – her world. She will need to overcome the pain she experienced. She's really judgmental of herself. She would rather crawl into a hole and be safe. I don't know what she will do, but I know what she should do. Get away from her cave, her safety. I don't know if she will. The fear of doing wrong is overpowering, all encompassing, sometimes forcing her to blank out rather than to even think about it, because of the harm that was done. It was a very horrible thing, because not only did she lose her world, she lost the collective. She lost everything. She was, for the first time in her existence, totally alone. And without the collective, she was vulnerable and really unable to communicate. She was deaf, dumb, and blind. There was no more safety. It wasn't lonely as much as it was being one without the collective. You lose your strength, your power, your motivating force. You just are. And all she could do was hope that the group could regroup, and they did not.

D: Can I ask you? Maybe I'm not looking at it right. Was this collective like the soul of the planet that was destroyed? The energy of the planet itself?

A: It called itself the collective. It's hard to identify it away from whatever it was, but I think it was part of the planet. It could operate either/or, but it always went back to the collective.

D: I know the planets themselves are alive, and I thought maybe that was this collective.

A: I think one step up maybe. I mean, they were aware of the others. They were part of, but they were separate and they could talk to the others. And I don't think the planet could talk to the others, but the planet could talk to the collective, and the collective could talk. That feels right.

D: So that's why it would be separate from what you are. This was an isolated collective, if that's another word for it.

A: That makes sense, yes.

Adele had many lifetimes on Earth, but she had been holding onto this tragedy for a long time. It had been influencing her and keeping her from attaining her full potential. I had to work with the subconscious for quite a while in order for her to be able to release this. It was now time for her to go with the work she had come here to do. This had been holding her back too long. It would take much courage for her to make drastic changes in her life.

SECTION SEVEN

THE NEW EARTH

CHAPTER TWENTY-NINE

THE COMING SHIFT

At a lecture in Chicago in 2006, I was discussing the evolution of the New Earth. I was describing the vision that Annie Kirkwood had about the Earth splitting into two Earths, which was described in *Book Two*. How, as the one divided into two separate Earths the people on each would not be aware of what was happening on the other. Those who had raised their frequency and vibration would ascend into the New Earth as it evolved and lifted into a different dimension. Thus becoming invisible to the ones "left behind". There have been several things about this concept that bothered me. I always like to have the answers; I guess because of my great curiosity. I have felt there are gaps or holes that needed to be filled. Pieces that needed to be explained. Someone in the audience asked the question about how this could happen, and those on one Earth not be aware of what was happening on the other one. Suddenly I had a revelation. A thought came to me that might be the glimmering of an understandable explanation. It is always wise to trust these flashes of intuition and knowledge, because often they are coming from our guides. In this case, it might have been coming from the same source that gives me all of the information through my clients. I suddenly said, "A possible explanation just came to me."

Earlier in the lecture I had talked briefly about the theory of parallel universes and lives that are created by our thoughts and decisions. In *Book One,* I wrote about a theory I had never heard of, and that gave me a headache trying to understand. In brief it says that: Any time an individual has to make a decision they usually have more than one choice. This is what I call, "Coming to a crossroad." They have to decide to go one way or another. It could be a decision about a marriage, a divorce, a job, anything. They ponder each choice and put a great deal of energy into deciding which path to take. Then they make a decision. We have all experienced these "crossroads". We know that had we chosen to go the other path, our lives would be totally different. We decide to go one direction. But what happens to the energy that we have sent into the other decision that was not chosen? *It also becomes a reality!* Another universe or dimension is instantly created to act out the other decision, and another "you" is also created to be the player in that scenario. This was the *simple* explanation, because it does not only happen when we are faced by major decisions. It can happen each and every time we are faced with choices, no matter how big or small. Each time we make a decision, another universe or dimension is instantly created so the other choice can also become a reality, and another "you" splits off to play that part. They are all just as *real* as the present life we are focused on. We are not aware of these other parts of us, and it is wise that we are not. Our human minds would never be able to handle it all. I was told that the problem is not with the brain, it is with the mind. There are simply no concepts within our human mind to allow us to comprehend all the complexities of it. That is why we will never be allowed to have all the answers. There is no way we could understand. So they (in their wisdom) choose what small pieces to give us during this time of awakening, so we will have some expanded information. And as our minds expand to encompass new ideas and theories, they will give us some more small morsels. I personally am grateful for the bits and pieces I am being given. It shows that our minds are awakening. This is the only way we are going to be able to handle the concept of our Earth changing frequency and vibration in order to shift into a different dimension. The information I am receiving now I could never have even begun to understand when I started my work thirty years ago. So I know I have grown, and I can see this reflected in the books I have written over these years.

The revelation that came to me during the lecture in Chicago was that perhaps the reason the people on each Earth will not be aware of each other, and what is happening, might be that it will be similar to the concept of the creation of parallel universes and dimensions. Only on a much grander scale. If we are not aware of these other parts of ourselves acting out the other decisions we have created by the energy we have focused on them, then the people on the two Earths would be unaware of each other. One Earth would be going in the direction of one decision or choice, and the other Earth would be going in another direction. Each acting out an alternate decision. It is up to the people on Earth at the present time to each make their personal decision of which path they want to follow. The energy is present and becoming stronger. It is physically affecting our bodies. Our own frequency and vibration is being altered. But I believe it is still up to us what we decide, which Earth we gravitate toward, because of our free will. The main difference here is that "they" said this has never happened on such a grand scale before. Never in the history of the universe has an entire planet changed its frequency and vibration to shift into another dimension. That is why it is said to be the greatest show in the universe, and everyone from many different galaxies and dimensions are watching to see what is going to happen.

AN EARLIER SHIFT

I have been receiving a great deal of information about the coming shift. Much of this has already been written about in *Book Two* of this series. And yet the information continues to come. This is our destiny, our future. In this session, I was given another missing part of the story. This has happened on Earth before. Groups of people in the past have been able to shift en masse into another dimension. These are usually groups that are surrounded in mystery because they simply disappeared, leaving no clues as to what happened to their civilizations. There has been much speculation, and various theories have been brought forward by the so-called "experts". But few have considered the fact that they simply walked off this Earth, and entered a different dimension, leaving no trace behind. The Mayans are a prime example, also some North American Indian tribes. I had been told through my work that these groups had become very advanced in their development, and had chosen to change vibrations and shift en masse. I was told this was one of the most logical explanations for the Mayan calendar stopping at the year 2012. If they, in their advanced state, had been able to accomplish this, they were able to see that in the future, the entire planet would follow and accomplish the same feat. This would be an even greater event than what they had accomplished. So they marked in on their calendars as the time the entire planet and everything on it changed frequency and moved into the other dimension, taking every living thing with it. I had been told these things, and it sounded reasonable to me. However, I was not expecting to have a regression where someone went back to a lifetime when they actually experienced such an event. This woman was able to report something that we can only speculate about at this time. It was another piece of the puzzle given by a voice from the past. "They" were making sure I was given all the pieces. My job was to organize them and put them together into a coherent story.

After experiencing death from an accident in Roman times, Suzanne looked down and saw the road she had been walking on as a spiral. "It seems to be the road, but it's also symbolic. Almost like these shells that they cut in half. That's a good example of it. It's like, by looking at the spiral, you're getting some insight into the Universe, and deeper understanding of what makes things tick. Seeing your place on the spiral, seeing how the spiral fits into the Universe, fits into time."

I then moved her away from the death scene, and told her to go to something else, either forward or backward, something that was appropriate for her to see. "I came in on a wooden stairway with wooden railings that were descending from the left. Some kind of log structure straight ahead, and there is no one there. Almost as if you were in a fort or something, and you were looking out through the structure. So it's built in the side of a mountain, but they've cleverly dug into the mountain. That's where the main part of the building is. It is built into the stone of the mountain. – This is a Native American place. And I'm getting that this is on the etheric, or something in the astral somewhere. Or it could be fifth dimensional now, but it's no longer 3-D."

D: Not physical?
S: It seems to be physical, but just not of the Earth plane. It feels like the Earth is vibrating somewhere else. As if there's an overlay of the dimension over the Earth, this would be in the overlay. It might have been at one time 3-D and it increased in vibration. And it's now almost like a parallel in that universe or something related to the Earth, but not the third dimensional Earth.
D: Does this place feel familiar to you?
S: It's home to me.
D: That dimension?
S: Yes, and it's very much like Earth in that there are stones and trees. And this is definitely in the mountains. It's more like our southwest. It's very comfortable here. My interests and my work are with spiritual things, and with healing.
D: How do you perceive your body?
S: I feel like I am a male, and I'm young – not an old person yet, maybe around thirty. Experienced. I'm doing my work, I'm still very fit.
D: How are you dressed?

S: Very simply. Some kind of woven material. It's very functional, sort of like a tunic. Very simple.

D: *But you said you don't feel you're on the Earth.*

S: No, it's not the Earth, but it's related to the Earth.

D: *But you have a physical body?* (Yes) *Then how are you able to go to this place if it is not of the Earth? You can look at it and understand how it happens.*

S: Now it seems that it's all very natural, not unlike the Earth. People were born and raised. But I was trying to see if maybe at one time we were of the Earth, and changed somehow. That may have been how it was.

D: *You said it was related to the Earth in some way. What do you mean by that?*

S: I think we have consciousness of the Earth, almost like we're in another dimension. So either we can perceive it from where we are, or we were once of the Earth and moved off somehow.

D: *So if you moved off the Earth, then you took this physical place with you?*

S: It seems like what might have happened was the band of people – I said "band" because it's not like there are many, many people around. And somehow, we've reached a point of changing frequencies, as if we all went on a similar experience. When people do things as a group. But it was like that whole society was able to transcend.

D: *Was this an intentional thing?* (Yes) *Was it something that was talked about?*

S: Talked about and worked for. People aspired to this.

D: *So not everyone did this, just a certain group of your people?*

S: It was all the known people then. We were an Indian tribe, and we knew there were other tribes around, but they weren't part of our world, Earth society. We were just by ourselves. We only cared about what happened to us.

D: *How were you able to do this? Were you taught?*

S: There were teachers for some generations, the wise people.

And we were taught with meditation. It was all of us. Maybe we're only a few hundred people, but that was our whole world. I think we experienced it before we moved in. We would go and come individually and in groups. The frequency was raised and we experienced that, and shifted back.

D: *How did they know this would happen?*

S: I was just wondering about that. It's like the people just knew. I don't know if at one time, someone might have told them. – I'm sensing now that maybe we were not from the Earth altogether, but we came to Earth, establishing a colony. But we knew mentally we could transport ourselves and move.

D: *Why did you want to do that?*

S: I think it was exploration. Just to see if it could be done. We did the 3-D experience, and then shifting, we moved to just another dimension.

D: *So there wasn't any reason to leave the Earth, the 3-D experience?*

S: No, not imminent danger.

D: *I was thinking that if you were happy where you were in the 3-D experience, or Earth, you wouldn't have any need or desire to move, to shift.*

S: It makes me smile. It's like a spiritual nature is always to learn. So even if things are good, it's like, "Hmm, what's around the corner, and what's to explore?"

D: *In the 3-D world, were you a spiritual group?*

S: Very much. We had great respect for the Earth, and the forces within it.

D: *But you had no desire to stay there.* (No) *So it was decided that you would all do this at once?* (Yes) *You said you did go back and forth.*

S: At first, yes. It was like trying to get out at first. And as we became practiced in that, then we could all make a shift. I'm seeing a blue stone, lapis lazuli. It seems connected to where

507

we come from, and it's symbolic of that. Like turquoise would be to the southwestern Indians, and to the Tibetans. Lapis lazuli is associated with these people somehow. It seems they're from somewhere else in the cosmos.

D: *So they weren't originally of the Earth?*

S: I think it was done before our time, but not before the grandparents' generation.

D: *Did they tell you stories of what happened?*

S: They must have, but I don't remember them.

D: *Maybe that's what made it easier for you to move to the other dimension?*

S: Perhaps. Certainly the knowledge. But I also want to say that people are smarter than they think. Everyone knows how to do this. They may not know they do.

D: *And your people took their physical body and surroundings with them. Is that right?*

S: I'm not sure about that. I think either they manifested similar surroundings where they went, or they moved into another dimension that already had that there.

D: *Do you like it there?*

S: It's more the excitement of learning things. The "there" doesn't matter. The excitement is with learning. I'm very active in my thinking.

D: *Do you have to eat there? Do you have to consume anything?*

S: We do eat, but it seems like the food is lighter, more vibrational. It lasts longer in us, for us. The requirements aren't so great.

D: *And you don't want to go back to the Earth?*

S: We have moved on. It seems the next step of the evolution of us.

I moved him forward to see if anything happened there that was important. It seemed like such an idyllic place, what could he find that would be significant?

S: I see that we're being asked to come back. And I have tears now. We're being asked to come back to the Earth.

D: *The whole group?*

S: Some of us. We know some things that would be of help to the people. And we have great compassion for the people.

D: *But you don't want to go?*

S: Yes and no. It's like taking that first trip for the exploration. Yes, you want to go, but you're torn. It's sad to leave home. We are people who are very loving, very compassionate. And we wish to share this with others.

D: *But this place is not like the spirit side, is it?*

S: Not totally. It seems to be another physical, but less dense, existence. Not totally spirit, I don't think.

D: *It's not like the spirit place where you go when you die and leave the body.*

S: I don't know. We seem to be pretty eternal. We've moved off the physical where we might have died, to some place or frequency where it's not necessary to die. I think we actually pulled it off. Kind of a transition of even the molecular structure of our bodies. I think we became spirit somehow.

D: *You mean it changed in some way?*

S: Yes, it was some transformation when we left. I think we took our bodies with us when we left. I think we took the physical bodies that changed, and we took it with us.

D: *You said it changed the molecular structure?*

S: Yes, totally. Yes.

D: *This was the only way you could make the change?*

S: I think we could have died, but we couldn't have done it en masse. I mean, we *could* have died en masse. But this was an experiment of sorts. It was the melding of a group mind from the 3-D. It was the forerunner of where we can go now, I see.

D: *So it was a group that experimented at first.*

S: Yes. I think there were others trying different ways. This was our way.

D: *You weren't dissatisfied with the Earth. You just wanted to try something different, more spiritual.*

S: Both are equally spiritual, but it seems like we have less restrictions beyond the 3-D. There are advantages.

D: *So someone is telling you, you have to come back?*

S: Not have to. It's like there's a call, there's a need. There's an opportunity.

D: *How do you know this?*

S: It's been talked about. More mental telepathy, but it's communicated, it's known. It's like things have gotten much worse on the Earth since we left, since we moved off. Things have changed.

D: *So you have a way of knowing what's happening on the Earth.*

S: Yes, very much. That's why I say we're connected. We can know these things. There are like holographic thought processes that happen. Any one of us can tune in, or most everyone can tune in to what they want. And there's some relationship between our people and the people who have remained on Earth. It's like someone has this idea. Someone recognized a need there that all of us have information about. But it's the time now.

D: *You have done it so you know how to experience it.*

S: Yes. Oh, there's great advantage to having heavy Earth experience.

D: *So what do you want to do?*

S: Oh, definitely go. I think I can be helpful there, yes.

D: *You don't mind leaving that beautiful place?*

S: Yes, I do. (Laugh) But you can't be here and there at the same time.

D: *How are you going to do this? Do you know?*

S: It's coming in as a baby somehow. I can't see whether we're being ensouled, or if it's a merger of consciousness somehow. But it's a real experience. So somewhere, you join with a fetus. It feels like our whole active consciousness goes.

D: *So what happens to your body there?*

S: I'm not so sure it was a body, now – or just consciousness, vibrational consciousness. Energy.

D: *So then your consciousness comes back into a baby?*

S: It seems that way, yes.

D: *That means starting all over again, doesn't it?*

S: Yes. Well, almost.

D: *But it's important. Do you think the same thing is going to happen to the Earth again?*

S: Same thing being?

D: *You said you were here to show them how.*

S: Things are in sad shape in some ways here. People have forgotten, or didn't learn, basic stuff. I think it's more that they need to learn about love and forgiveness. It doesn't matter what dimension you're in, the lesson always seems to be the same. That we *are* love, and sourced by the One Creator. People get caught up in survival at so many levels.

D: *But when you come back as a baby, are you going to remember what you're supposed to do?*

S: It's programmed. It feels like there are programs that will go off. Yes, we forget. There's a cloud that way. But there are somehow programs that can be activated. It seems like it's a time release thing. Some of it is triggered by associations with people or events. Earthquakes, volcanic eruptions, severe storms. I feel that all through my body. There's some call that happens.

D: *So when Earth events happen, it triggers things?*

S: That's one of the things, yes. I feel that all through my body with great energy.

D: *So when these Earthly things happen, they trigger the program that is in the humans?* (Yes) *The ones who have come in for this mission?*

S: Yes, who have that program. Participating in ceremonies from antiquity are also big triggers.

I decided it was time to call in the subconscious to answer the questions and explain things more fully. Although this other part of Suzanne was doing a good job, it also suggested calling forth the subconscious, "Although it's probably all one anyway." I asked it why it picked that lifetime for her to see.

S: She needs to understand that she is an explorer first, and will always go into new situations. And that this time on Earth is a time for exploration. It's not a done deal.

D: *Where she was, it appeared to be a different dimension.*

S: That is correct.

D: *She had the feeling this group came from somewhere off of the planet. Do you know anything about that?*

S: Yes, they came from the Source.

D: *Directly?* (Yes.) *As a group?*

S: It's not really a group. It's a mind trying to have experiences, so it's splintered. It's the same soul. Suzanne understands that souls splinter, go off. These are probabilities that have their own life. That is that. And it's okay. The joke is, we are all one.

D: *Why did they want to live on Earth?*

S: Earth is pretty special. There is much that can be learned.

D: *But then they decided to shift frequencies.*

S: By coming and taking on the physical and being forerunners. It's very important to create a mold, to create a track. People can entrain to what has happened. The first ones, it's more difficult, then it becomes easier. You have a term for that: the hundredth monkey, or whatever. You make it easier for others if you've made the path. And time is all one. So it's always been known there would be a time for the need for ascension of sorts, of shift, of transformation, of transcendence.

D: *Did something happen that they wanted to leave and try this experiment?*

S: They were exploring how to change dimensions and forms.

They were exploring how to be genuinely 3-D, physical, and then to take that body and make a shift.

D: *And take the body with you.*

S: In this case, to take the body with you and that was what was done.

D: *That was why it was an experiment.*

S: Yes, and that template is here. That knowledge is available.

D: *Was it easier for them because they came directly from the Source?*

S: Yes, they had greater skills, I suppose, and in Earth terms that happened very quickly. But it took some doing.

D: *They weren't here long enough to be contaminated. Would that be correct?*

S: I don't know contamination.

D: *You know how Earth does contaminate people. They get stuck.*

S: The Earth is pure goodness.

D: *So it was easier for them, I guess, because they had not interacted with other humans that much?*

S: Just with themselves, which was really one mind. So it was, yes, taking the luster off our great accomplishment. (Laugh)

D: *She said it was an Indian group?*

S: It was like an Indian group, it was of that time. It was ancient time.

D: *We have stories of Indian tribes that just disappeared. People have always wondered what happened. Was that one of the examples?* (Yes) *So they took their bodies with them into another dimension where they created what they wanted it to look like? Or was it a dimension where these things existed?*

S: In the experience of going, first becoming 3-D, and then never losing connection to Source. So knowing the other was possible, and shifting back and forth, back and forth, back and forth, making a path. They experimented, because they allowed themselves to be really dense. But they had the advantage of knowing always Source in spirit, always. So then it became an experiment of trying to change the 3-D. How to raise the frequency, how to shift dimensions, how to do this with the physical, how to take the physical. So in all of these comings and goings, sometimes there were already things in place in the other dimension. And in some ways, sometimes they made things when they went to the other dimension.

D: *They made it resemble where they came from.* (Yes) *But then she said they were called to come back?*

S: Yes. It was part of the plan. First you explore, you make a path that others will follow. Some others will follow, many others will follow. It will be useful, but somebody has to come back and again show the way. Do it, take the path that they once built, unbeknownst to them. She has returned to help others so they can make this transition.

D: *But Suzanne didn't realize this consciously.*

S: Not coming in, no. But always she knew Source.

She was told she was to travel to the Southwestern part of the United States. "In the canyons, in the rocks, where it's dry, where it's high. Then her mission will be clearer. There is memory in the stone, and in the bone. There is memory." This was the area where the tribe lived before it made the shift.

Suzanne had been doing extensive traveling to all parts of the world. I wanted to know the spiritual significance of that. "She was leaving a vibrational trail when she went that spiraled up. This is the significance of the spiral that spirals up. (See the part about the spiral at the beginning of this chapter.) And as she walked, she left the imprint, so it encodes for people who walk that way, who come in contact with her. It activates and teaches how they too can ascend up the spiral way. She doesn't have to tell people. It is transferred energetically. She influences hundreds, hundreds, hundreds, hundreds of people just by being there. Every continent she went to, she left her imprint. – We want her to follow the spiral way. She knows this, and every cell in her body, and it will be made clear to her. It's an energy spiral."

I wonder if this applies to me also? When I first began my work, I was told that I would travel extensively all over the world, even though at that time I had only traveled to some conferences in the United States. I was told that everywhere I went, some of my energy would remain. That this would not deplete my own energy, it would just remain in the area, and would affect many people. They said that all I had to do was think about the place I had visited and my energy would immediately return there. Their prediction certainly came true, because I have now lectured on almost every continent in the world, and my books are now translated into twenty languages. So the energy is certainly capable of spreading and influencing. And we are totally unaware of what is happening when we are in these places.

CHAPTER THIRTY

HELP IN THE TIME OF CHAOS
(OR THE OLD EARTH)

At the beginning of the session, Anne saw scenes of the interior of a spaceship traveling to other planets, and disjointed scenes which she did not feel confident talking about. She said she could answer any question about things that she knew, but she wasn't sure of questions about things she did not know. This indicated to me that the conscious mind did not want to relinquish control. Then unexpectedly: "It doesn't seem relevant to me to go to these places, or see these things. I feel like something or someone wants to talk or say something if you ask questions."

I am used to this happening. Sometimes "they" get impatient and want to have the client go to something they need to see and are avoiding. Or sometimes there is something else *they* want to speak about. "It's this person, they want to talk to you. There are things to be said to you through me." I assured her it was all right, that I was used to this.

D: *Anything they want to tell me, I'll be very happy to listen to. Do you want to tell Anne about herself, or do you want to tell me about something else?*
A: Other things. She has that ability, but only certain locations or occasions are allowed.
D: *I can understand that, because it wouldn't be safe in many places, would it?*
A: But it is safe right now. We protect her.

I assured it that I understood the need for protection. "That's why she's not allowed to talk about these things to everyone, is

516

she?"

A: No, she's not.
D: *Can you tell her some of the things she's looking for?*
A: It's more like a trigger, that some things need to be asked in the right way.

They have told me this many times. In order to obtain the answers the questions have to be asked in a certain way.

D: *All right. She says she has the feeling that she's not from Earth. She doesn't feel comfortable here, like she doesn't belong. Can you tell her anything about that?*
A: She knows she's not from here. – The questions that need to be asked have more to do with other matters that are not so personal to her, matters of importance at this time. It's important that you ask questions about other things. Her desire is to be of service, and she needs corroboration.
D: *But she does have many personal questions, too. That's why we were going to start with those.*
A: Part of the growth is to connect with the appropriate people to continue the work. And it becomes evident to her as time goes by. It's not so important to ask about herself. – She feels that she's not fulfilling her purpose. That is her major, biggest frustration – that she is not doing what she came to do.
D: *Yes, she said she feels a great deal of loneliness and she keeps wanting to leave.*
A: She wants to finish. She has many abilities and talents, and she feels that she should be using them in a certain way, or another way. And she cannot do this by herself.
D: *What is it you want her to do?*
A: One of them is communicating with you. Your questions should be geared toward a different area that has to do with understanding.

This can be frustrating, and it happens quite often. They want me to talk about something specific, but they will not tell me what it is. They want me to come up with questions about a subject that I do not have information about. It always helps when they bring up a topic. Then I am never at a loss for questions.

A: There are certain triggers that occur when she meets certain people and associates with others, that work like an unlocking, or opening up. And only when those triggers are set off, do some things become clear to her. It's like she lives a secret life. And she knows this, not because she has secrets, but because there are many things that she doesn't share. She had to do things by herself for many, many years. But she has understandings that most people don't, and she's unable to relate. She knows that's part of the challenge of this lifetime – to come like this and be alone in some ways, and internally have to keep to herself. It's like being able to see ahead of time and not being able to say that. It's very frustrating. Like an understanding of cause and effect from a very young age, and trying to relate to people on their level when she knows better. She knows it's a constant struggle to pretend she doesn't see when she does see. There are relationships, lessons to be learned in the process. But it's also to help, to bring awareness.

Since that was one of her questions, I asked about relationships. Whether she would find someone. Again, "they" did not want to discuss something so mundane. "There are more important matters to discuss than relationships. She feels that she's not accomplishing much, and she begins to wonder if she needs to focus on other things. But it's an impatience that makes her worry about these matters. Once the important matters come to the forefront, these other matters take care of themselves."

D: *That's true. But what are the more important matters, so I'll know what questions to ask? I can probably find some questions if I have an idea which way you want to go.*

A: The matters have to deal with the changes that are occurring at this time. And her role in the process, which requires courage, since it is a role of support and being there when the time is needed for her presence and others' presence. People who are here for that reason.

Anne had said she wanted to go home, and experience what home was like, so at this point, they gave her a glimpse of it and she became emotional. "Tell me what you're showing her. What does it look like?"

A: (Very softly) Energy. (She was openly weeping now.) It's like they're charging me with energy or something. (Whispering) I can feel it all over .... (Crying) It's like love.

I let her cry for a while, then I tried to calm her down so the other entity would be able to return and answer the questions and give information unemotionally. After a while, it succeeded, but "they" still were reluctant to release information without having the proper questions. "We love her very much."

D: *I know it took a lot of courage to leave that beautiful place and volunteer to come here at this time. You said she volunteered to come to be here during the changes. Are these the changes I've been told about? (Yes) Do you want to talk about that part?*

A: Many changes. What are the things you have been working on? You may have some questions.

D: *That we're moving to new frequencies and vibrations?*

A: That is correct. Do you have questions?

D: *I've been told a great deal of information, that everything is speeding up, and the vibrations and frequencies of our whole dimension are changing. Is that correct?*

A: Turbulence, much turbulence coming very soon. And there is the need to be very grounded. Much turmoil. There will be need for your stability and all of those who are here, because people will be lost and confused and in much pain. Do you understand?

D: *By turbulence, do you mean more of the violent Earth changes that have been happening?*

A: Situations caused by humans, and situations caused by the Earth changes. And the coming through of new energies and beings that humans are not accustomed to seeing. This will cause a great deal of chaos, that only those who are understanding what is transpiring, will keep calm and be a reassurance to those in confusion. Remember and just be prepared for that, because it's very easy to theorize until the situation is in the physical. Then the physical body needs to be prepared to handle the shifts of energy, and the shock that comes with the process of change. One thing is to feel you can understand what is happening. Another is to be in the midst of chaos and keep yourself calm when it's happening.

D: *That's difficult for humans, isn't it?*

A: It is difficult. And that is a crucial and practical area to focus on at this time, because it is in the physical that you are helping. There are other levels that are helping, but you are in the physical as she is, and other beings are. So in the physical, they could transmit that calm that will be necessary during times of chaos.

D: *But will they listen to us?*

A: It is not up to you to decide. It is up to you to make sure you have the tranquility and grounded energy for those who want to listen to you. That alone requires much work in the physical to keep those energies in place, because that's what you came to do. Anne is very trained, because her life experiences have required her to maintain a level of calm in the midst of madness.

Anne had lived a childhood with abusive and unstable parents, and then a chaotic marriage.

A: That has been a good training ground for her, so that when the time comes, it is not so difficult for her to maintain that calm in the physical. Do you understand?

D: *Yes, I do. I've been told that these changes are going to cause a separation into two Earths. The old Earth and the new Earth, as the vibrations and the frequencies increase. Is that correct?*

A: That is correct. There is a different world, if you will, which some souls will remain or choose to live in after the changes.

D: *You mean to remain with the old Earth?*

A: Yes, with the world that keeps that level of vibration they wish to stay in, and that will be where they remain, or move into. But the new energies will only be livable for those who have worked their own energy up to that vibration.

D: *But the turbulence you spoke of, will that be on the old Earth?*

A: It is now as we go through these changes. This is the time of transformation in the next few years, and the outcome has been prophesied by many. I don't have much to add to that, other than, those who are here now need to remember the important role they are playing in the physical before the changes happen, or before the *final* changes happen. In the midst of the process, there's a need for those who are here to give the assistance. To line up, if you will, as if it were in the military. It's time for them to show up and be aware that they are being called to be very present and ready. And maintain their ground, because there might be situations in which a soul might be in a crucial point where they could go either/or, vibrational wise. And you may be able to make a difference at that time.

D: *What do you mean by either/or?*

A: Their spiritual growth may be in a grey area where they may qualify to step up to a higher vibration, if only they have the

521

courage to jump. Or else they may choose not to, and that is their choice. But your role, if you keep your energy, may be crucial for someone in that situation, because you may be the hand that extends for them to jump.

D: *Make the jump into the higher vibration.* (Yes) *But the higher vibration, the new Earth, will not experience this turbulence?* (No) *It seems as though right now, we are in this part that is experiencing the turbulence.*

A: It is just the beginning. It has begun, but the chaos has not begun. The chaos, the madness of people running around in confusion, because all of their illusions have been shattered. That will be the time of the test of the strength that needs to come forth for those of you who are here to help in the process. There will be a time when people are running in the streets confused and in fear, not unlike the hurricane in Louisiana.

D: *That's what I was thinking of, the tsunami and the hurricanes.*

A: But that multiplied worldwide in most cities is a very different scenario.

D: *Are there going to be similar disasters in many cities?*

A: Some caused by natural, some caused by those in power who are making every effort to keep things the way they are. They are aware of the changes. They refuse to accept. It's like a child who doesn't want to hear the truth. And they refuse to admit they are no longer in charge. So they continue to cling to these ways and may cause more confusion. They feel they may be able to slow down the process and maintain a low vibration by keeping fear on the surface.

D: *They're trying to instill fear in people.*

A: Fear has always been in people, because that's how most, if not all, the societies of this world have functioned for many years. Fear is the way they have maintained power, and almost everyone in this world is in fear. There are different levels of fear, but these changes and the technology that has allowed everyone to communicate freely, have caused a great deal of concern for those in power, because now the fear is vanishing. Many things that are occurring, even the catastrophes, act as a catalyst to bring fear out so it is dealt with. And so it is a cleansing in a way. But those in power don't want this process to occur, and they prefer to keep a level of fear under the water, if you will. And like a desperate child, they try every tactic they can think of at this time to not let that fear dissipate, because that is what is happening. The fear is dissipating despite what the surface seems to show.

D: *People are beginning to think for themselves.*

A: They are. They are confronting their own demons, if you will, because life is taking them places where they have to see things that other times they haven't had to deal with. Therefore, their fears, although they are very present, are at least coming to the surface, whereas before, they were not. Therefore, it is a cleansing that, as it continues, will only liberate more and more, which is a process that those in power are very aware of. They want to slow it down, thinking there might be a way to prevent it. So they will push and push to every extreme they can until things get very difficult. And many people will not be prepared for that edge they are pushing for.

D: *Is the war one of the things?*

A: The war, absolutely the wars, also their diseases that they scare people with.

D: *These diseases are not really there, are they?*

A: They can be if people choose to allow those energies to enter into their body. But for the most part, they are only in the energetic fields. And like anything else that is talked about, or thought about, it can become reality in the physical.

D: *Yes, if enough people accept it as their reality.*

A: But the diseases are extremely blown out of proportion, and they are not epidemics as they are portrayed to be. The media and the movies are showing you their desperation as they insist in presenting to the masses information that is completely negative and fear-based. Subject matter such as murder, death and betrayal, attacks and such that keep the consciousness focused on these matters, as opposed to portraying in the media images of hope and inspiration. But nevertheless, there are enough of those positive messages being broadcast at this time, that like a domino effect, they are no longer stoppable.

D: *Another fear the government is trying to promote is terrorism.*

A: Yes. It is just another tool, like the diseases, to find excuses to give people a reason to be afraid and not unify, but to trust that the government will solve their problems. They are imaginary problems, and in the subconscious, many people are becoming aware of this. They are no longer believing, although many are in the masses. But on their subconscious level, they are beginning to awaken, and the power knows this. That is the reason they are resorting to ridiculous stories that only those who wish to believe, believe in them, because anybody with a logical and reasonable mind could not believe them.

D: *Yes, anybody who thinks for themselves.*

A: So they are presenting the masses the opportunity to choose, because they are pushing for an edge. And in that way, they are serving a purpose by pushing the edge, so that everybody makes a choice, because this is a time of choice. This is no longer a time of middle ground and neutrality.

D: *You said earlier that we would be here whenever the chaos breaks out. Would this be caused by many of these disasters?*

A: Disasters and the breakdown of the structures of government. And the breakdown of the safety net that most people feel they are part of. Such as their Social Security, and their paychecks, and their jobs, and their religious beliefs. Especially if and when ships and/or other things like that begin to become part of the consciousness that many are not prepared for. Therefore, they may run around in shock and confusion, unsure as to what's real and what's not. – The structure of government is breaking, and will break even more to a point of chaos. Like a domino effect, like a crumbling.

D: *If the ships arrive, what would be their purpose for coming?*

A: They are always here. It is only a time for them to become visible as the permissions open up, because it is a time of, not only free will as there is now, but also a time for others to claim their place in the new world. Not just the humans, but others who also belong here, but are in a different vibration. So partly, it is not that they choose to become visible, it is partly that the energies make them visible.

D: *I am aware they've been here. I've been working with them. I know they're positive. I've had no problems with them.*

A: But by them becoming visible and part of the consciousness of the people, and the governments crumbling, and chaos, and natural disasters, you can see how the majority of people would be completely shocked. And their religions and their idea of a structured life would be brought down. So now, they would have nothing to cling to. This causes a great deal of fear for those who have not stepped out of their own house. That fear could lead to madness or schizophrenia or other types of reactions. And it is at that time, and that kind of reaction, that will leave people most vulnerable, where you can be of most service.

D: *Then others like myself and Anne are some of the ones who are here to help?*

A: The ones who are prepared to see these changes and not crumble in fear will be the pillars on which others will lean when nothing makes sense to them. It doesn't mean you will provide the truth to them, it just means you are not falling down like they are.

D: *Because, I was thinking, what can we do when everyone is in chaos?*

A: When you are not losing your mind and you are calm, it doesn't matter what you do. People will see that in you and seek that in you, because they don't know what to make out

525

of what they're seeing. And *you* may not know what to make out of what you're seeing, but you have been prepared. Therefore, you will know and have some sense of trust that things will be okay. You are not crazy.

D: *Where the others won't have any preparation at all.*

A: Exactly.

D: *You know that I've had many, many people coming to me for the last two years who are either healers or they're being told by you, the subconscious part, that they are to be healers. We keep wondering why the world would need so many healers?*

A: Do you know the population of the planet?

D: *Yes, it's quite large.*

A: That might be one reason why. Also, it is a time that's very precious for many souls, because of the learning lessons available, as it is an unusual time that this planet has not experienced. Therefore, it is an opportunity to experience a very one of a kind soul journey. And it's an opportunity to step up in the soul level, experience-wise, because of the challenges it presents. Therefore, many advanced souls are interested in the opportunity for themselves.

D: *I was thinking if structures do break down, the medical profession would definitely be one of them. Maybe that would be one reason to have healers that can use energy and natural healing.*

A: There is a time coming when the energy will be high enough that disease will not be as you know it today. And though the help of those healers is definitely needed, there will be a time when those diseases are not going to be anymore. Therefore, the healing is only temporary. The healers will heal when there is a need. If there are no hospitals because everybody has left the city, for example, or maybe it's drowned (is she referring to the city inundated?), then there are healers available to help. But that is not the only reason they are here. They are here for their own learning purpose, as their own soul is interested in experiencing this shift.

D: *That's why we all chose to be here at this time?*

A: A big reason.

D: *I've also been told that our DNA is being altered so we can adjust to these changes. Is that true?*

A: There are many groups that are participating in the acceleration of energies, and they have their own technology. From our perspective, we would say that through the infusion of higher vibrations on the planet, it reflects back on the people. So it is not their DNA that's being adjusted, at least from our perspective. It is the higher vibrations that are naturally affecting their DNA, which is dormant in some areas. And therefore, it is being activated.

D: *I've heard this is the reason for many physical symptoms people are experiencing at this time.*

A: Areas of blockage in the body, whether they are karmic issues, or their own diseases caused by their lack of self-discipline with their eating habits, or other things, independently of the cause of the disease. But they're basically areas of blockages that are being brought to the surface with these new energies, whereas before, they might have been laying dormant. It is being brought to the surface much like the karmic issues that are being brought to the surface. These energies are forcing these areas to deal with the dark negativity so the energy can flow freely, that those blockages need to be cleared up. In order for that to happen, the issues that are causing these diseases need to be attended to, which requires a level of participation from the people who are suffering. And that is their choice whether they attend to these things or not.

D: *What I have heard, is that many of these physical symptoms people are experiencing are being caused by the change in the vibration as the human body adjusts to it.*

A: That is correct.

D: *If the chaos belongs to the old world, will this be happening at the same time the two worlds are separated? I don't know if I'm wording it right. The new Earth is supposed to be going into a new vibration and a new dimension. And it was described as separating, becoming two worlds. Does that make any sense?*

A: There are many theories. Depending on the perspective, it is a matter of energetic vibration. And one vibration is visible, and some vibrations are not visible to each other. Therefore, if one vibration – the lower, or slower vibration – remains, it's not that it becomes a separate world, it is simply no longer visible. It's the new world that is basically a split-off because of the higher vibration.

D: *But in the new world, things are different than the old world. Isn't that true?* (Yes) *They won't be experiencing the chaos?*

A: No, the chaos is mostly a breaking down of the belief systems. The chaos is caused by the belief systems being challenged and brought down to a place of a complete blank slate, or clean slate. And that is the chaos for many. Those who go on to the new world are comfortable with new belief systems, and therefore, will no longer struggle the way those struggle now. It's not that it's a transformation where all of a sudden people become something they are not. It is just the changes. It's either people can move on from there, from them, or not.

D: *That's what I've been trying to understand. I've been told the new world would be beautiful, we wouldn't have these problems. And they said don't look back. You don't want to see what's happening to the old world.*

A: It is basically a deterrent to look back. It's not that you cannot look back, it's just that you cannot change other people's choices. And therefore, if you're looking back and it is causing you grief, it is only slowing you down.

D: *But you said we're supposed to be involved with these people.*

A: We are here during the time of changes. We are here to keep our energy grounded. It is not so much to be with those with a higher vibration, because they can fend for themselves. And it is not for those who are in deep negativity that we must be next to either. It is for those who are in the midst of confusion, but are perhaps ready to make a jump, that we are most helpful to.

D: *Does that mean we have to stay with the old world as workers?*

A: You will only stay until it's time for you to go. And during the time that you stay, you can do your service. When it's time for you to go, you will know, and then you will no longer be available to those. It is not a matter of, "How long should I stay?" That is a question that is answered eventually. It's a matter of knowing what to do while *you* are here.

D: *I have thought we would be separate from those experiencing the chaos. We would be in a different beautiful world.*

A: For a while, through the process of transformation, not necessarily separate. It's not like one day to the other there is a new world that you are part of, and the old world goes away. There is a process. Eventually, things will change. But in the small process, whether it lasts one month or five years, it is a process that you are still part of, as you are now. You are of it, now. So long as you are here, it is your job to keep the grounded energy for those who are in confusion. Once the actual shift happens, even if you wanted to be here, you couldn't.

D: *Those who have raised their vibrations will go on.*

A: That's correct.

This answered a question I was asked while giving a lecture at the Ashram in the Bahamas. A young woman said that she would like to stay with the Old Earth to help those who would be left behind. I told her that was noble, but I didn't think it could happen. Now, here was the answer. It has to do with vibrations, and once your vibrations have reached the correct frequency you just automatically go to the next level. As they said, "Even if you wanted to stay, you couldn't." Your intent doesn't matter. This is bigger than we are.

D: *And so we're trying to help those who are still trying to decide and make up their minds?* (Yes) *That's why I was trying to get clarification. I've heard it from many people, but sometimes it's a little confusing.*

A: It is confusing from the vantage point of a human.

D: *Then you do see more turbulence happening.*

A: Yes, absolutely. This is the beginning, as those in power are not near done with their strategies. They will cause many more events. And there will be other events, natural causes. So the chaos is much larger than we envision in isolated cases. But of course, all of those things could change, as there is no set future.

D: *I've been told that age is not important anymore.*

A: Age is an illusion. It will be more apparent as we move along in the process of evolution.

D: *I've also heard that whenever the transition happens, we would be allowed to take our physical bodies with us if we want to. Is that correct?*

A: That is true, but it will only be for a short time. There will be another transition very shortly thereafter.

D: *What will happen at that time?*

A: Mankind will become pure energy.

D: *The ones that make the ascension.*

A: That is correct.

D: *I've also heard not everyone will make the transition.*

A: Everyone will be given the opportunity. Whether they can hold that vibration or not is up to them individually. There will be no judgment made on them. They will simply be able to hold the energy, or not. But none will be destroyed as the comments have been heard. They will be placed in an appropriate space for the vibration they are emitting.

D: *And that's what they mean when they say they will be left behind.*

A: In God's plan all will return to God.

D: *Just at different intervals.*

530

During another session, I was speaking to the subconscious.

D: *You keep saying things are changing.*
S: They're accelerating changes, and your scientists don't have a handle on it. This global warming, it's devastating to the ecology. It's happening so much faster than the scientists are saying.
D: *They don't really believe it?*
S: They believe it, but they think the danger is decades away. It's not; it's here! The danger is at our doorstep. There will be some safe places in the U.S.
D: *What's causing the global warming?*
S: You know, accelerants. I mean the aerosols, gas, everything that pollutes the environment – environmental pollution. It's what man is doing. That's why our summers are so hot. And there will be more storms. Many, many, many more. Unbelievable. You aren't going to believe what's coming. The coasts are going to be in for a fun time. The increasing storms and tsunamis are going to accelerate it. The timetable is changing.
D: *Originally there was a different timetable?*
S: Yes. It's moving forward. It's sooner than it was meant to be. Unfortunately, because of what mankind is doing.

LEVELS AND DIMENSIONS AND KARMA

Janet had come to her session with her list of questions. We were expecting to go into a past life to find the answers. But instead she went to an ethereally beautiful place that did not sound Earthly.

J: I'm seeing some double-handled doors, and I'm opening these doors. I'm walking in, and there's a stairway going up, and it's a huge structure. Inside, there's this enormous, domed area. There's a lot of light there now. You don't see it until you start coming up. And there's a place with light in the very center. There are seats – like it's a place to access information or talk to somebody. But when you come in, there's nobody else there. It's not packed full of people. It's like everybody has their own entrance if they want it. And now there's a man there. He's appearing to me like a very down-to-earth wizard. Practical. His white hair is combed back. He has a staff, and he's smiling. He says, "I came to you in one of my more fun costumes. This is just something for you to look at. So, what is it you want to know?

D: *Janet has many questions. Is it okay if we ask them?*

J: Absolutely. Now is the time.

D: *You know that I bring many people, don't you?* (Oh, yes!) *We're always looking for information. Usually when we use this method, the person goes to past lives.*

J: Oh, yes, but she doesn't need to dwell on that stuff anymore.

D: *So she came here instead. Where are we? Where is here?*

J: We're in a dome that holds records and meeting places. It's a very sacred place for people to meet and have a safe place to talk. It's an inter-dimensional temple. It's actually a good meeting place where the dimensions can come together, so people from the physical plane can meet those from the spiritual dimensions. Spiritual, of course, has connotations to it, but those of us who are not in physical body.

D: *But it is like an in-between place.*

J: Yes, we would call it inter-dimensional. It means many dimensions can touch and meet here. So it's a good place to meet and have a cup of tea.

D: *Just as long as it's a place where we can get information.* (Yes) *Well, Janet right now seems to be at a very definite crossroads in her life.*

J: She's been at many crossroads in her life. She's seen many places like this. She'll make the right decision.

D: *But now she needs some help.*

J: She'd like some more information. Those on the physical plane always do.

I began to ask some of her questions that pertained to her marriage and her husband, but the entity did not want to cover that yet. "We'd like to talk about the other things first. She had some other questions. Would you ask them first, please. They'll help bring in what she wants to know."

D: *These are all important because she has to make a decision. But, one of the things she wanted to know, if you can tell her about her general history, or the story of her soul.*

J: She has been and comes from many places, and this is one reason her work is important. She's able to access information from many places, and those parts of her soul that have lived in those places at those dimensions and those vibrations. She is to bring that in to serve more people of varied crystalline structures, as we would say. They have multiple dimensional lives that affect these crystalline structures. She's able to work in all these other dimensions at the same time. And this enables her work to cross through the worlds much faster and easier. So she has to bring those other parts of herself together and keep bringing them in, in order to make that work. She has to be able to access those places.

D: *That's what I've been told. We are not just this one individual. We are actually – splinters is one word – or facets? Would those be appropriate words?*

J: Yes, you are many experiences. She's becoming more aware of these other places. And this is a process many humans can go through. They come to a place where they're able to have this process happen for them. But it's not until they're ready, and they can handle all those multiple vibrations with their physical body. This is why meditation is important, because it raises a vibration to handle stronger energies, and more multi-layered energies that are made of varied vibrations, and they can work with them. It's like working on the other planes in multi-dimensions all at the same time. And the sacred geometry work is bringing in these soul parts by the millions. And that is what's happening with her. It will make her – powerful is such an overused word – but it makes her more powerful, in the sense that she can travel to and be in, consciously, more dimensions at the same time. Gradually, we will have her becoming more aware of these. She's being given what she can handle at the time. She has been given a couple of new tools that will help her become more aware and less fearful of those other dimensions and what is found there, because more and more of her work is going to be in realms that not many people access.

D: *Can you give us an idea what kind of realms those are?*

J: They are truly realms that are hard to look at and hard to see, because they are difficult for the human emotions to bear. People have a perception and a judgment about what they see and become fearful of it. Humans don't carry on very well with something different, when it's not something they've been around. If they can hardly handle people of other races and religions, how are they going to handle someone with snouts and teeth and multiple arms and multiple heads. And all those mythical creatures that they write about, that we read about? There is a reason they've been written about. They have been seen by someone, usually at some level, in what they recall as dream time or memory time. They have accessed them at some point.

D: *Are these physical creatures?*

J: If you're asking if they truly exist, the answer is yes. They actually can affect the physical dimensions, but they're not seen by very many people. And sometimes there are protectors in various dimensions, that many people are not aware of, protecting the planet and its people from some of those dimensions that are inappropriate for the group soul, or humanity's soul at that time. But there is a group of people who have the soul abilities to help with this work. And it has become necessary to help humanity make the shift that it needs to make. The world is in great need at this time. There are not enough Servers who can do this work. It's not everyone's soul path to do this work at this time, but it's necessary because it's opening the planet up, freeing it so that other energies can come in. For the Earth herself, her next goal, is the next step in their spiritual path. And it has become so bad here on the planet that there is great distress over what humanity is going through, and what the Earth herself has gone through. And so there needs to be some shifts made. And that shift would involve taking away some of the interference on the other planes, and truly do protection work. This actually should be quite reassuring for those who hear this. That, isn't it wonderful that we don't all do the same thing?

D: *Everybody's doing something different, but they're not aware of it consciously.*

J: And all are needed. And in dreamtimes, sometimes as the stream of consciousness develops from meditation work, they become more and more conscious of the work. And these people, including this one, know when they wake up they have been clearing the other planes. And they are coming

535

back in their body, and they need to continue clearing, for their safety and the safety of their family and of their city. It will help ease the burden on humanity and Earth. And all those other lightworkers who are doing other things. It's a multi-faceted thing. More and more people are finding out that it's part of their work and necessary to help. It's not for everyone, because it simply would not serve them. You wouldn't give algebra to someone who hasn't learned basic math. It simply wouldn't work, because it's not where they're at. The power has to come from within, and that is where spiritual growth and work at being a serious spiritual student or disciple comes from. It makes all the difference.

D: *They have to prepare their mind and their body?*

J: Exactly. That's what we're trying to get across, yes. So much of the work is done softly and quietly and silently on the other realms. And they understand this because we've also done it for them – we've protected them. They've had to earn it to a certain extent. But we also are watching for those workers who can come onboard. There's always more work to do than it seems we have time to do it. You are well aware of that, I'm sure.

D: *You said this had to be cleared in preparation for the changes that were happening to the Earth?*

J: It will help the Earth, yes. It will help humanity so that it's truly the humans reaping their own karma. And so there's been work with the Galactic Council and those other realms and other beings and other life forms. Part of it is, you can't tell some people that they're not the only life form in existence. They don't understand that. So what normally happens is someone's spiritual growth comes to a place where they can handle it. Until then, they're like the baby that's protected. They don't need to know everything. And it's not theirs to do, so they'll be alright.

D: *That's what I was told in the beginning of my work – not all of my questions would be answered because some of the*

536

information was as poison rather than medicine.

J: Yes, they can get it too soon.

D: *And they wouldn't understand it. They couldn't handle it.*

J: Yes, that's correct. There has to be enough individuals on a planet at a particular time in the humans' growth for certain things to be facilitated. That is their work as a soul, and then it's their work to pass it on because they have benefitted humanity on a level humanity will never know. And so everyone takes their turn. There's no master that hasn't gone through a similar process of helping the group that they started with. Humanity is in a place where they need many Servers. This is what the work is about. But not everyone serves in the same capacity, or is even aware of it. There are many people who are not aware of all the lives they have touched by their good work, by their good words, their good will, and actions. *All* people's actions are very important. And again we come back to the importance of the individual doing meditation and strengthening their body as much as possible – eating good foods and feeding their minds, and being with people of good heart and good vibration. And shielding – wouldn't need to shield if it were a rosy world! – Janet's karma is to overcome the trauma of what people did to her in other lives, face it again and come out the other side better to survive it. Many times, that's what karma is. If you'll notice, there's a pattern. It's not always one doing to the other and then the return. It is facing up to the same tyrant and saying, "This time you will not crush me." And it's not about a power struggle. It's about the growth within the person overcoming the fear, which is tremendous because the death was sometimes horrendous. And then there are multiple emotions about authority and power and who's in charge, and abuse and corruption. All those are rolled into one, and it's overcoming that. And of course, the body and the emotions and the mind can only handle so much at a time, or it's damaging. So the person has to face all those again, and come through it and be different than just oppressed again or harmed again in the same way. This is why many people may have 20 or 30 lifetimes, and they have the same issue over and over and over again. It's because it's the same fear-based issue, or it's the same lack of trust that's been created, and they have to work at overcoming that because it was such a traumatic thing.

D: *And it must be worked out before they can progress further.*

J: Because that's where their abilities are, yes. And so they are suppressing a part of themselves. We murder people with our words. We can harm people on so many levels. There's a violence when you condemn somebody or make fun of somebody. That's a form of violence. The Master has to keep growing. But they have to be in a body that can handle these energies, and you have to build that body. And that's why we're trying to get the message out to people who want to be healed. You have to help build the vehicle that allows it to be healed. That's meditation work, and taking care of yourself, and watching your environment. And how you speak and how you act and how you talk and who you're around – all those things have an effect. But your work is to watch the body, and meditate and take care of the body. It's all levels, levels and levels and levels and levels. We have levels of fear. So you're working through all these levels of emotional issues and struggling through them. And as a spiritual student, you invite those. She has done things that have intentionally brought on many of the things she's dealing with because she wanted to clear them. She is really pushing for soul growth this lifetime.

D: *I know we bring things into our life that we fear so we can confront them.*

J: Exactly. But then we're not happy when we do it. (Laugh) We want to blame somebody else. And so her soul path is, once she gets started, like with meditation, you can't stop. And if you stop, you get stuck because you want to keep

538

growing and keep growing and clear these issues.

A random question:

Q: When the predicted earth changes come about on our planet, how will that affect the parallel or interpenetrating universes?

S: There will be those experiences on this *particular* level which will be experienced on this plane. However, the experience as a whole will be shared on a much deeper level. On a race level as well as on a deeper level, the universal level. Such that even now, experiences on other planets and in other areas of your universe are being shared by a deeper aspect of yourself. A farther-up-the-ladder level of yourself. When – and this is again on an individual level – each of you experience that transition, which each must eventually experience, then you will see that there are others on other planes who have experienced similar transitions. And will be able to offer encouragement and energy. Such that you will be assisted in whatever endeavors you need.

CHAPTER THIRTY-ONE

THOSE LEFT BEHIND

In Chapter 28 *The Destruction of a Planet,* I covered the story of an individual who was new to Earth, who said he was only sent to Earth during crucial times. This was another such individual.

D: *Why did Jean decide to come back now? You said she'd been here in other pivotal points in Earth's history.*

J: This is the big one. (Laughs) This is the great one. This is happening now. And many are remembering who they really are, and are being contacted. The new children are being brought in, and she loves the children. So she's helping others to balance the energies. It's being a bridge. Bridging the energies now. You are a bridge. Of course, you are. So there are those of you that came in to help bridge the information, to be the ambassadors.

D: *To help these people wake up to who they are?*

J: Absolutely. And to be okay. To accept any of them who have experiences that they filed away. It's a big time on your planet, because this is the big one. This is where you, as a planet, awaken out of the dream of thinking you're alone. That you're all that is. Your Earth is evolving. You are all evolving. All eyes are on Earth right now, anyway. This is the big one. Many fought to be here. Even children that come in, even for hours. You'll all carry that, the badge of having been here.

D: *Even for a few hours?*

J: Absolutely. To have been on this planet at a time of this kind of evolution. No planet has ever quite evolved this way before, this uniquely. If you were going to have the option to carry the identification of having been on a planet that will be known through the multiverse, even if you can be here for a few hours, that you could say, "I was on Earth at the time of evolution." Why not?

D: *Is this what I call the new Earth?* (Yes) *That there will be an old and a new, and then a separation.* (Yes.) *And that some won't make the evolution?* (Yes. Yes.) *I'm still trying to understand that.*

J: It is difficult for many humans to understand this concept.

D: *I'm still trying to clarify this to myself, so I can explain it to other people.*

J: All right. We will give you this piece. For those that choose to stay in karma, they have to live that out somewhere. So, do they stay with the old Earth? Do they get taken to some foreign planet? No, they stay where they created.

D: *I see. And those are the ones that will not go on in the evolution?*

J: Not at this time. No. Eventually. Not at this time. But that will be difficult.

D: *Then the old Earth will continue to exist?*

J: Yes. This one.

D: *Will the people in the old Earth be aware that anything has happened when the evolution occurs?*

J: All right. We will take you back to the time of Atlantis. In your history, Atlantis had several destructions, and people perceived that others died.

D: *You mean there was more than one destruction?*

This goes along with the information I have received about multiple advanced civilizations being destroyed in various cataclysmic ways. I was never sure if it was referring to different civilizations that had reached a height of development, or if the Atlantis demise occurred in stages.

J: Yes. There is an Atlantis that went on, and exists in time and space. Therefore, from that perspective, that Atlantis exists now in another dimension. So there will be those on the old

541

Earth that will experience it, because they buy into the fear of the death and destruction and devastation of Earth, and they will be there. In their mind, they may perceive that all of you are dead or gone, or whatever. And likewise, you may perceive them as gone, but either way, there will be two experiences. So think of this as already there. The orchestration to create this experience is so much bigger than any human can perceive at this time. This is a big orchestration, not just occurring on your Earth, but with the help of so many. So many. And no other planets have done this before.

D: *I've been told that the whole universe is watching.*

J: More than just the universe. There are those even from *other* universes that are watching.

D: *Because they said this had never happened before, where an entire planet moves into another dimension.*

J: Never. Ever.

D: *There have been groups. I've heard the Mayans did it.* (Yes) *But it was small groups. This is the first time that an entire planet makes it. That's why I've been told it's important.*

J: That's right. Also look at the fact that, as a consciousness, you see yourselves as separate. Consciousness on this planet was created in a unique way to be able to experience itself as separate. Most races do not see that. Regardless of where they are, they don't experience themselves as separate from their Source. Your planet has.

D: *So the ones who are part of the Federation, and work on the ships, know their Source, and know where they come from?*

J: Of course. And they love you humans. You don't even know what you've done. They recognize there are primitive behaviors on the planet, but to reach the level that you have, based on the restrictions that you've had to work within. It's amazing. Your capacity to love is deep. Your capacity of fear is deep. That's the power of control that gets everybody in trouble. Fostered by the fear.

D: I know Earth was created with free will. But it was also created with the idea of not knowing it was part of the Source?

J: Yes. It was an interesting construct of consciousness, in that it experienced itself as separate. Where else could there be more growth than in a situation where you actually saw yourself as separate from your Source?

D: But you said the other races know they are all part of the Source.

J: Yes, they do. So can there be more soul growth on Earth? Yes.

D: If we thought we were alone, and then had to discover this all by ourselves.

J: Yes. They have to discover the truth of who they are on their own. Yes.

D: With nothing else to help them. I can see what you mean.

J: You have density here. You have the beauty. You have the senses. You have much going on here, but you also have not understanding. Look where you are.

D: I've had many people have sessions where they go back to the Source. They see how beautiful it is, and they don't want to leave it again.

J: When you connect with the Source, it is the most beautiful experience. So your question is what? Are the sessions happening for them to connect with that Source?

D: Yes. Why is it happening? So they will know what it's like, or to remind them or ....?

J: For those that need to have that experience, yes. For some, it would be too great, and they wouldn't be able to go on. They would just as soon leave. It's different for each one of you. Every person is different in terms of what they can and cannot experience. And what it will trigger within their subconscious, because each one of you is a unique and individual fingerprint on the planet. There are no two of you really alike. Think what a genius is the mastery of that.

Think of the beauty and the wonder of that. And there are many of you, other lifetimes now, working on the other side, and they are all participating in this as well. You are never alone, any of you.

D: *We have to rediscover where we came from, and why we're here. But there was one question people have asked me, and I think you have answered part of it. That if some are taken, and some are left behind, wouldn't those that go on to the new world notice the other members in their family were gone? These are some things I'm still trying to clarify, in our way of thinking. I have to be able to explain it to people.*

J: We understand. We understand. We understand. We will give you this explanation. We hope this helps. People are going to start falling out of people's lives. They're going to start noticing them falling away. Quite rapidly, now. In other words, people, family members, whoever they have been close to, just falling away, disappearing. It will all happen overnight. So by the time the shift happens, some of those people will already have fallen out of their life, will separate. Will just disappear. Not be around. So and so moved over here, left town, did this. Do you understand?

D: *Yes, but we could go to the police and try to find the person, or ....*

J: It won't happen that way. It will be them moving away, something happened, distancing, distancing, distancing. By the time it actually occurs, the distance will be there. Haven't you had people fall out of your life lately?

D: *Yes. Of course, we could always contact them if we needed to.*

J: But you won't. That's our point. You won't contact them. It will just be a natural falling away. The frequencies and vibrations will no longer match, and therefore, they will fall out of your mind. The need to contact them won't be there.

D: *And this means they are either staying with the old Earth, or they're going on to the new one?*

544

J: In some cases, there have been those that have left early, and are working on the other side of the veil. You're aware of that. But some of those that disappear, after a period of time, you think, "I wonder what happened to this person?" But you don't have the urge to contact them like you would normally. You don't have that driving urge, "Oh, I'm concerned, I must call. I must reach out." It's not the same. You find that your need to connect with them just isn't there. It just falls away. You forget.

D: *I've been told that at first, those who enter the new world will have physical bodies. So we won't know when we have actually made the shift, the separation. Is that correct?*

J: That may be too simplistic of a description. For those of you that came in to bridge this ... we'll explain it this way. As you do your work, you facilitate. You help people to awaken, to open up to more of who they are. To raise their vibration, their frequency, to be able to resonate at the higher cycles per second so they can make the shift. Does that make sense to you?

D: *Yes. That's what I'm trying to help people to do.*

J: Exactly, what you're helping people to do. Yes. It will happen. It's not going to happen in the way that people think, where there'll be a cataclysm or this or that or the other thing. No. It will just be like you wake up one morning, and you think everything's normal, and you're going on, and you will *be there.* You will notice a difference in resonance, but you will already be there, because your resonance is increasing every day already, as it is. And so, all of a sudden, one day, you will reach the prerequisite cycles per second to take you from here to there. Let's explain it this way. If somebody came back right now from the eighteen hundreds to see you, you would glow to them. You've already reached those cycles per second that would glow to a human form of, say, the eighteen hundreds. So in essence, your cycles per second are raising.

545

Comment: Could this be one reason why when John and the others went to visit Nostradamus (*Conversations With Nostradamus*), he saw them as glowing energy spirits of the future? Was this because they were actually vibrating at a faster frequency that made them glow? That is something to think about.

J: That's the reason you're a bridge to help others to raise their cycles per second so they can make the shift. And the faster you raise more people, they activate other people with their frequencies and vibrations. So what you are doing is activating more and more people on the planet, which activates others, which raises the frequency of the planet. Do you understand? It's all cyclic. Everything affects everything else. You have people that come to Earth and don't have to do anything, they are just strictly activators. Their energy fields activate everybody else's. [See examples in this book.] You have those that are working very hard and diligently, that are like broadcasters. They broadcast out over the planet, like a microwave signal.

D: *This makes sense to me. This is why I've been told age won't make any difference.*

J: That's exactly right.

D: *We'll be functioning at a different level, different vibrations.*

J: Different vibration, different cycles per second.

D: *This is the way some of the other races (ETs, aliens) function, don't they?*

J: Yes. They age at a totally different rate. The goal for humans is a longer life expectancy. Much longer. And also, creating the bridge of understanding. And if you begin with health, you are able to reach people in a non-invasive, non-threatening way.

D: *In this new world, where age won't matter, will the body eventually die? The way we consider it on Earth now, in our reality.*

J: There will be some of you that will have the option not to die at all. Just to make your transition, just to cross over. But not everybody's going to be at exactly the same frequency at the same time. Remember that.

D: *Yes. I was thinking maybe the body would get to the point that it could just maintain itself until the soul was ready to leave.*

J: That's exactly right. Not for everyone, though. If you have many people making this transition, and let's say that the frequency has to be approximately 44,000 cycles per second in order to make that frequency shift. Not everyone is going to be at that frequency shift at the same time. You're going to have different variables in the frequency shift. There will still be those of you that are on that front line, on that cutting edge, even on the other side. Even in the new world. You understand? Because there always will be. Because there always are on every level. Every race always has those that are out there on the cutting edge. A little further out, going a little further, because that's evolution.

D: *I was thinking that was the way it would be. We'd have a lot more time to do our work, and to help reach people.*

J: Of course.

D: *We wouldn't have to worry about the limitations of the body.*

J: Oh, the limitations of the body. No. Well, look at your whole. You are already changing. You are going through cellular changes. They are making adjustments on you.

D: *I've been told they were doing it on me.*

J: Yes, they are. (Laugh) And because you're a spokesperson, again, a bridge, who is more important to look good than you?

D: *I guess. Well, if I hear it from enough people, maybe I'm going to believe it, anyway.*

J: You need to believe it.

547

D: *I've also been told that not everyone will make this shift into the new world.*

J: This is correct. When the Earth is going to make a shift, there's the idea that many souls are allowed in for experience because, as you say, you experience many things in your growth as a soul. And so, there have been many, let's say, beginners coming into the planet. Sometimes being in a class with advanced students can be helpful. As you know, the old country schoolhouses? *(Yes)* So you might have levels of students all in the same room, and they all benefit from that. But there finally comes a time when the students need to move on. And that means that those who are left behind will have to find their own planet. They will be put in other schools, other places.

D: *I always thought it sounded cruel to leave them behind.*

J: Oh, no. They won't be left behind. They will be taken to a place where they can grow.

D: *That's the way I've understood it, too. It would be like a separation.*

J: It's more natural. It's like when you leave your body, you go to another dimension and you grow in that dimension, and you may or may *not* come in as another body here. You may go somewhere else. And if the whole Universe is a body, there are many, many galaxies and planets where they can go.

CHAPTER THIRTY-TWO

PHYSICAL EFFECTS
AS THE BODY CHANGES

I have received much information about the physical symptoms that people are experiencing as their bodies adjust to these frequency and vibrational changes. Many of these include: tiredness, depression, irregular heart rhythms, high blood pressure, muscle aches and pains in the joints. These people have gone to their doctors, only to be told there is nothing wrong with them. The doctors cannot find any cause for the complaints. However, their solution is to put the person on medication anyway, which does no good, because they are not aware of the cause.

I have had a few clients that have experienced more radical symptoms that confounded their doctors. One was Denise, a registered nurse in a large hospital, who came to see me in August of 2005. She had complaints of having seizures and numbness in some parts of her body, but the doctors said it was not a stroke. She also passed out one day at work. When they performed the MRIs, the X-rays, they saw what looked like Christmas tree lights, all over the brain. They called these "nodules". When they took chest X-rays, they found the same thing, nodules throughout the lungs. She also had abnormal enzyme activity in her liver. The doctor couldn't figure out what was going on. In subsequent MRIs and X-rays of the brain, the lights had moved to different areas, appearing more or less as a band, instead of being all over the entire brain. They had a difficult time finding any diagnosis that would fit, but finally came up with an idea of what the *disease* was: sarcodoisis. But one of the doctors said, "I don't think it could possibly be that. On the one hand, it is so very, very, very, very rare. And on the other hand, she couldn't possibly have gotten this where she lives in the desert, where the air is very dry." This disease was supposed to occur where there was dampness and molds. But they were unable to diagnose it any further than that. So they put her on steroids which caused diabetes.

When we did the session, the subconscious said there was no disease. No harm had been done to the body. They were rewiring the brain so it could handle the changes of what is to come. And the same with the lungs and the other parts of the body. It was an adjustment of the energy in the body so it can handle the raising of the higher frequencies and vibrations. I asked, "Then why did it appear like little dots and lights all over her brain?" And they just said, "Connect the dots!" The seizures and numbness were because a lot had to be done quickly. Normally, they don't want to overload the body, so these changes, these adjustments, are happening very gradually. But in some cases – I guess because time is speeding up, and the changes are becoming eminent – they have to adjust the body faster. So it was too much, and this created the seizures and the numbness. The time she fainted was an overload on the system. But they said she doesn't have to worry, it won't happen again. There isn't anything wrong with the brain. And now, if she has another MRI, it won't show anything, because that phase has ended. The next phase is the adjustment of the chemistry of the body, which will not produce these kind of effects.

When the doctor told her she had this strange disease, he said she had less than six months to live. And she kept saying, "I don't think so." When she went back for her checkup, the doctor just kept staring at her, and saying, "I just don't understand why you look so well." She was picking up, without him saying it, that he meant, "Because you're supposed to be dying!" Denise is a nurse in intensive care. And she said, "I see people who are dying all the time. I knew I wasn't dying. So I didn't know what they were talking about."

The subconscious saw her doing wonderful things during the shift, and in the next ten, twenty years she's going to have a big part to play in all of this. I wanted to know more about the steroids. I knew they could be dangerous, especially if they caused the diabetes. They said the diabetes would be phased away. It was only a test to teach her about body lessons. She wouldn't need it now. They said not to worry about the steroids. Even though it was a powerful medicine, they could neutralize it so that it would not affect the body in a negative way. It is flushed out of the system as a harmless byproduct. They have the ability to do this. To neutralize any medication that is not needed and flush it out of the system.

MORE FROM OTHER CLIENTS

I was speaking to Patsy's subconscious, and told it she had complained of allergies to dust and pollens. It answered, "These are physical reactions to being on this planet. I'm feeling that she can live with that. It's also a reminder of who she is. That she's in an element that's not home." She also had sensations in her colon area, and an unexplained rash that she wanted to find out about. "I keep getting 'manufacturing', and I can't explain it any other way. But something is being manufactured in there. It's almost like a necessary element that's being made that's having the reaction in the colon and on the skin. The mucous is a byproduct of the changes that are being made in the body, which is a reaction on the skin. It has to do with what is occurring on the Earth at this time. She has known for a long time that her body is being changed. It just doesn't happen in a way that you can understand when you're in a physical body, but there are many changes going on. Doctors cannot help on this level. They don't understand the changes that are taking place."

D: *And when we're in a conscious state, we can't understand it either.*

P: The conscious state is very confusing.

Patsy also always had very low blood pressure. "That's normal for her. She doesn't need to be like the rest of the people. And for her to operate with that in the body she's in, is all that's required of her. That's one reason we influence her not to go to the doctors, because they try and find something wrong. She doesn't need to be part of that."

D: *They want everybody to be the same.*

P: Yes, they do. That way they're easier to control and medicate. There are many that aren't the same. There is no harm to come to her body.

D: *I get many people who are in fear if they don't understand something.*

P: They're learning. Fear is destructive, very destructive.

Carol had gone through a past life which is not relevant to this book. The subconscious was talking about healing her body. Carol's doctors wanted to operate on her, because she had a growth in her body, a pelvic mass that was pressing on her spine. I asked the subconscious to do a body scan and tell me what it could see. "Chaos, confusion." I asked what was causing that. "Anger ... resentment ... fear. Fear. She takes in other people's fears and transmutes them. This is something she learned to do very young, to take in people's fears, people's negativity so she didn't get hurt by it. She learned to take it in her body and transmute it. In some situations, it is necessary. The growth, the mass inside the body is there for her to heal. She has the knowledge and the understanding and the power and the resources to do so, and she can do it. There's a remembering."

D: *The doctors want to go in there and cut it out.*

C: She could do that and continue the cycle on and on, but it's simply a stumbling block. It is more important that this be healed from the inside out. She must not rely on outside sources.

D: *That's the way we've been brought up to believe, that we have to let the doctors do it.*

C: And beliefs are changing, and part of her role is in changing beliefs.

D: *So she will be able to reduce this mass by herself?*

C: We will help her. She needs to know the process so she can teach others. And she needs to know the process consciously.

For this reason, the subconscious did not want to do the spontaneous healing that I had seen it do many times before. It was to be Carol's responsibility. "The steps of manifestation. The steps involved require trust and surrender, becoming one, all the way back to the beginning to Source."

D: *That doesn't sound easy.*

C: She knows how to do that. There are additional steps in alchemy which she can pull from, from other lifetimes. But it's about changing solids into liquids into gases, into solids, into particles, into space, into energy forms. And then bringing those forms through into physical manifestation. So it's about dematerializing and re-materializing. It may not be automatic, because she's somewhat resistant. She could use voice and music and sound to access the state that is required

D: *And by doing this on herself, she'll be able to teach others?*

C: Yes. She will understand exactly how it works, consciously.

While the subconscious said Carol had to take care of dissolving the mass, the growth, it said it could help with another problem she had. There was an opening from the intestine into the vagina. "I'm melting down the cells, the tissue, and taking them into a liquid state ... and reforming so there is a clear wall. A clear boundary in the vaginal tract, free of inflammation and free of infection. And then sealing the intestines so there is no more leakage into the abdominal cavity. (Pause) I'm vacuuming out all of the debris. The doctors will absolutely not do any surgery. It's time to stop all of the cycling, the postponing."

D: *Should she go back to the doctor?*
C: It won't make any difference one way or another. Because we're actually preventing the doctor from moving forward, because it is not in her highest good to do so. Working with the cells is what we do. We have now surrounded the mass, the growth, in its own membrane. It can be lifted out. It can be melted and dissipated.

D: *Is that how you want her to visualize it?*
C: There are some choices. It can be simply lifted out. It can be melted and vaporized, disappeared. Those would be the two easiest ways that she would know how to do. She can do this in meditation, or when she's in quiet. She will actively do the process on her own physical body. In other words, she will need to place herself on her healing table, and simply do a self-healing. It will be relatively quick.

D: *Then if she did go back to the doctor, he wouldn't see anything there?*
C: That is correct. It is time to stop the pain and suffering, and to move on. She will also need to work on the blood and the changes in the blood, and the changes of consistency in blood. There's an intuition; there's a wisdom of the blood cells and the bone marrow, and the formation and deformation of cells and material. It is pulling through the memories of previous lives and applying the steps that she's needed in this lifetime.

D: *And you want her to work on these things in her own blood system?*
C: Yes. The changes are being created. And she needs to understand how those changes are being created, because the physical body is going to change. And so she needs to understand that process so the physical body doesn't die and give out, because of the changes and the transitions that are

down the road in the future within ten years.

D: *You said the body is changing?*

C: Yes. The physical body is changing in vibration.

D: *How is this affecting the blood?*

C: The blood is changing in consistency. And sometimes there's a "glumping," and sometimes there's a thinning. And so as the changes occur in the vibration of the whole body, the cells will be functioning differently. So some of the old functions are being cast away, and some cells are taking on new functions. I'm not sure what the wordage is, but there's ....

D: *Having to learn something new?* (Yes) *It's something these other cells haven't done before.*

C: Correct.

D: *And this is what you meant, she has to learn how to adjust it; otherwise, the body can't handle it?*

C: Correct.

D: *Is this happening to other people around the world right now?* (Yes) *I've heard of many different symptoms.* (Yes) *So each person is having to learn to adjust?*

C: Every single person won't, but people who will be instrumental in helping others, in teaching others, and in guiding groups. It's about bringing through frequencies that can make massive changes very quickly in the physical body.

D: *Changes that would normally have taken many generations. Is that what you mean?*

C: Yes. It's about compressing time. There is no space and there is no time, but in the Earth plane there *is* time and space. So for spontaneous healings to occur in the Earth plane, there has to be a compression of time that occurs as the cells get new instructions, and let go of the old instructions.

D: *Oh! And this is difficult in some people's bodies. I guess this would create physical symptoms the doctors wouldn't understand. Is that true?*

C: That is correct. They do not have the technology to understand it. There are some who have advanced minds that can deal with that. But the medical field in general is very archaic in

555

terms of what it needs to know, or what it needs to have available. And that is really not workable. That will fall away. The mind is being utilized for change, but also people have to be able to change their minds to let go of their distorted beliefs and come into truth.

D: *We have to get away from the brainwashing we've had all our lives, that tell us we must depend on outside sources. We don't really need to do that.*

C: That is correct.

D: *When you first looked in her body, you said there was chaos, confusion and anger. Can she release all of that now that she realizes it's not necessary?*

C: Yes, most of that has dissipated with the repair work we have done with the strengthening of the boundaries, the vaginal repair, the colon, the whole intestinal, the inside, the vacuuming out of all of the debris. And what earthlings may call, "fallout".

D: *Carol has had a lifetime of being the victim, and being betrayed.* (Yes) *Why did she have a life like that? What was the purpose?*

C: It is necessary for her to understand victimization because there will be masses of people who will be victimized rather quickly, and in large groups. And so all of it will be important to be able to work with them simultaneously. There will be an instant knowing so many steps can be bypassed, by knowing the ins and outs, if you will, of victimization, so it won't be necessary to deal with victimizations. It will be necessary to spontaneously fix what needs to be fixed to shift – it's about the shift ....

D: *She'll be instrumental in working with some of these people.* (Yes) *Because she can identify with them and understand.*

C: Yes. And she will be working with healers.

CHAPTER THIRTY-THREE

THE LIBRARY

After many frustrating attempts to get Nancy to see something, I regressed her back through the present lifetime. She still had difficulty letting go and to stop analyzing. Finally, we made the breakthrough after almost an hour. (I had turned the tape over. I am persistent. I do not give up easily.) I had her go back to before she was born into this life as a baby. She saw herself as an older man in a white robe. "I think I'm on the other side as an elder. I'm old with a beard. Wearing a white robe with some kind of tassel tie; sandals and a staff. I am in a library with a table. I can't see the books, but I think this is a library." I asked her to see what she did there. "My impression is I'm consulting. I would think it's on the other side. And that I'm part of the council that guides and consults people when they're going to incarnate for their lessons."

D: *Sounds like an important job.* (Yes) *Do you have to help them decide what they're going to do?*
N: No, help them to decide how best to facilitate the lesson they want to achieve.
D: *Do you feel you've been a counselor for very long?*
N: There's no sense of time, but my appearance looks old.

She could not see the other people, but she had the impression that they were coming to her. I wondered how she advised them.

N: It's a wealth of information, whatever that means. Whether I have a wealth of information, or that room affords it. That's the only thing that popped into my head, "wealth of information."
D: Do you have the records of things *you* have done in other

557

lifetimes?

N: I think everything is just known. I think you can look at the records if you want, but you don't have to.

D: *Have you lived many other lifetimes before becoming a counselor?*

N: I think so.

D: *Is there a way we can find out about one that is important? One that has bearing on the life you're going to go into as Nancy?*

N: I'd rather ask someone.

D: *Is there someone around you could ask?*

N: I don't know, but I just hear, "yes".

D: *All right. Then ask, "Is there an important past life that Nancy needs to see that will help her in her present life?"*

N: Yes and no. The plus sides are important for karmic lessons. However, we're moving it to the non-karmic necessity. So that's why he gave a yes or no answer.

D: *Then she doesn't need to see her past lives?*

N: Not necessarily. They don't matter.

D: *What about karma?*

N: Karma is virtually cancelled as we move to the new Universe.

D: *Then that means she doesn't have karma to worry about?*

N: No, I do have karma, but it's not going to be important. He just says it's not necessary to fulfill the mission of this life or to move into the next life.

D: *That's why Nancy was not allowed to see any of her other lives?*

N: It's not that I wasn't allowed. It's just that it wasn't necessary. It would cause confusion. The human mind would get hung up on what it was seeing. But it couldn't release or relinquish the judgment in what you wanted me to see, or what you normally would show.

D: *Many people relate to things that happened in other lives so they can move forward.*

N: But because we're in this pinnacle of – going to go this way

– all this doesn't matter anymore. Because there will no longer be reincarnating into the Earth the way that we know it. To look at other lives would only be more confusing, because ideas and tools that were necessary and helpful in the old world are not going to be needed in the new world.

D: *I still get many people whose problems come from other lifetimes.*

N: But all that is discharged. Your work is important because there are some energy tools that need to be released in this lifetime. Energy tools of more or less health issues. It's things of the now that are not related to moving forward, because the moment you move forward, that will all be discharged and relinquished. We never know when the new Earth will appear, but it is coming. It's going to be here. It's just a question of when the vibration and energy will reach the level to almost ... *pop* and create the second world. So you help people with their physical ailments, so they don't have to be uncomfortable till whenever this is going to occur. It's important, because we don't know when it's going to occur – more sooner than not. So if these people come to you, then I guess they have a discomfort that there's no reason for anyone to have.

Nancy wanted to know her purpose (just as everyone else who comes to see me). The subconscious answered, "This isn't the answer she wants, but her purpose is not revealed as yet, because the new Universe has not been created. Everything is still in planning, moving, facilitation stages, and it can still all change. We can see a plan, a big picture, but it still can change."

D: *Can't you give her any idea of what she's supposed to do, because she wants to help plan.*

N: Almost instantaneously, the thought will come.

D: *Is there anything you want her to work on to get ready?*

N: None of it's necessary at this point. She's going to go to the new Earth, and will immediately know — because the new energy and vibration will be higher — what it is she will be doing. The effort is needed here, but it's already crossed the marker where you're either going or you're not going.

D: *I've heard it's already been decided, because the vibrations can't change that quickly.*

N: No. So once you've crossed the marker and you're going, then it's almost like a respite period. And when you get there, it will just be so different that all the things we think we need to do now, and were appropriate in the not so distant past, in the new world will not be needed.

D: *She said she wants to make a difference in other people's lives, and to help the world.*

N: Which would have been necessary if the Earth had stayed in the same vibrational dimension that it is now, but it's almost like you're waiting for it to happen. It's going to happen, but you won't know what it will look like until it happens, because it's a group participation and a joint effect. And all we can say is, it *is* going to happen.

D: *I've heard that some people won't even realize that anything has happened.*

N: I think that thought is even changing, and most definitely the ones that move forward will know what's happening. The ones that are left behind, it's still not determined – devastation's not an appropriate word to use, but I can't think of another one – who will really realize it or not realize it. It's still changing.

D: *But she's wanting to do something to help now. She has studied healing and Reiki, and studied working with angels.*

N: But everyone will have the same gifts and tools and the new energy.

D: *Everyone will be doing the same thing?*

N: Well, not the same things, but it just will not be necessary. The reason why we do all these things is to bring the energy up to that level. But when you're immediately all on that level, there's no need for healing, because we'll all be healed. You can still continue working with people and helping them until the transition. But when everyone transitions, it's almost like you're all at the same rate. You're all on the same page and your veil is lifted, so it's the big "ah-hah!" moment.

D: *There are still people out there that need her, aren't there?*

N: Right. There are people that, minute to minute, you're pulling over to the new world. They're almost in a holding pattern, but they're pulled over and they're waiting. They'll be waiting there to move forward.

D: *So she will never know among those she comes in contact with.*

N: No, nor will they. She should always focus her energy on a sanction of all the energies of everyone on Earth to move forward. And as each person increases their vibration, it's a chain reaction, and it resonates and bounces off the next person to the next, to the next. Until it's an entire huge crescendo that becomes the vibration of Earth in total. If everyone stopped doing what they're doing, it would just become a dim hum. But because we all go and move forward and we're all working at our own pace, it just raises it higher and higher until it's just going to disperse into the cosmos. So you can't really say not to do any work. Just keep doing what you're doing, but the focus is changed. To be bored is great, because it will just instantaneously create all knowledge, all the things we strive for here. But, "Give me Reiki, so I feel better" or "Take away this," it won't be necessary. Everyone will have the tools. And once you have the tools, you don't have the aches or the pains. It's almost like a "human clause" that will no longer be in effect. It's always good in human form to, as you say, have goals and dreams and aspirations. It's very difficult to put into words, because we think it's coming more quickly than you think, and you are spending a waste of time. But that doesn't sound right either, a waste of time. But I think the best thing that anyone could do is have a good intent. Always express your willingness to help, and never turn anyone away that comes to you. Any lessons she needs to be learning now, have to do with the karmic wheel, and it's going to be dispensed soon. Once your vibration gets to a certain level, you're beyond the, "Have to pay karma back." That's why it's not important to pursue questions about past lives. That's her human mind, and all the human minds having a curiosity about things. It's almost child-like. "Why? Why? Why? How come?" So you could just feel guaranteed, or rest assured that if you have awakened, you will move into the new Earth.

Later in the session, Nancy's body was being worked on to remove the desire to smoke and then with compulsive eating so she could lose weight. She could feel them scanning and readjusting, especially in the right side of her brain. Then she felt vibrations throughout her body. "They're just scanning and removing impulses."

D: *Trust them. They know what they're doing. They're removing the impulse to overeat.*
N: Yes, and things that have become habitual. The body's designed to basically handle anything, but the problem is with portion control and quantity. The body is a miracle and the body can dispose of or handle anything in small doses. The favorable food would be anything with less additives, less preservatives. Less is best. Even smaller portion sizes, but just to rid the body of chemical additives, preservatives. So the trend is to go to healthier, leaner, less toxic things for the body. The body will last longer when it doesn't have to work as hard. We have given her the impulses to take and readjust, readjust and program. She will love this. The taste buds are already changing. It's beginning to happen.

They have repeated this through most of my sessions with clients, especially when they wanted information about their diets. We are to move away from heavy foods, because in order to ascend, the body must become lighter. They said the best food is "live" food, which means fresh fruits and vegetables. Some meat is all right, but not the heavy red meat, especially not beef and pork, because of the additives and hormones. They said it deposits chemicals and artificial components in our organs that will remain there for as long as six months. It is extremely difficult to filter and remove them from the body. If we can get organic food, that is the best. They always emphasize smaller portions and several small meals during the day (they called it "grazing"), instead of huge meals. The value of water is beyond comprehension. It is extremely important. Of course, all of this is merely common sense, but when it is repeated constantly through my clients, I think that means they are emphasizing the importance of diet at this time. Eventually, we will move into an all liquid diet.

Then, after we move to the New Earth, there is the possibility of not eating at all. At that point, we will be living off pure energy and light. The same as many of the ETs I have spoken to.

SECTION EIGHT

UNUSUAL ENERGIES

CHAPTER THIRTY-FOUR

A TOTALLY NEW ALTERNATIVE
TO A WALK-IN

I was already working on this book and I thought I had enough information to put it together. Yet I should never underestimate "them". During the last few years, information has been pouring from people during my sessions, and I have been given more unusual theories. I thought I had everything they wanted me to write about. But every time I think that, they surprise me with something totally new and unexpected. I know I have to stop somewhere; otherwise, my books will become *too* big. Of course, each time I have written a book, I ended up removing information and holding it for the next one. In this case, I thought I had received enough for this book. Yet, in January 2007, I had a client come, and during the session we were given another new concept that I knew had to be included. A totally new concept of a walk-in, one that will impact our lives on Earth, and influence our lives in the New Earth. There are numerous strange things going on that we are totally unaware of with our conscious mind. And it is probably just as well. It would be too confusing if we knew all the things happening behind the scenes.

When Christine began the session, it sounded like a perfectly normal past-life regression. There was no hint of what was to come. She found herself as a robed man standing in the middle of a wooded area. It took her a few seconds to decide what sex she was. It was only after studying her body. "I feel male. I have very muscular legs. They don't feel like female legs. My calf muscles are very taut. I'm probably old. I'm in my late forties,

567

early fifties. That's considered very old." He was fascinated by watching groups of small animals and birds moving about. Also the earthy smells of dead leaves gave him a very good, comfortable feeling. He went to a nearby brook to get a drink, and watched some small fish in the water. It was a truly serene and peaceful setting. He felt tired as though he had come a great distance, so he made a bed from piles of leaves.

The only things he was carrying with him was a pouch containing dried meat, his tools that he used as a stone carver, and a sword that was used for self-defense and also for hunting. So far it sounded like the beginning of a normal, past-life regression, but that was soon to change. He was not from this place in the woods, yet he could not identify a home either. "Many different lands I've traveled. I have been traveling for many years. I do not have a particular destination. Just exploring the different lands. I'm supposed to be helping. I'm supposed to be learning about the different people. There is a group of us. They're waiting for me. They're in a very cold area. Geographically, I more or less know how to get there, but I don't know the name of the land. I've been going according to the constellation I used in this life, so I know which direction to go."

D: *The place you started from, what was that like?*
C: I have been gone for many, many years. Millennia, actually. I came from a distance, not of this planet. I've just been traveling, and I've taken on this body in order to be able to be sustained in this environment. I had to inhabit a human form in order to breathe and be able to live and be sustained in this atmosphere. There are more, there are many of us.
D: *So where you came from, you didn't have a body like this?*
C: No. There is no need for it.
D: *What kind of a body do you have there?*
C: It's light. I don't actually have a body, or we don't. We're energy. We travel as energy. That's how we're able to travel as quickly as we can.

D: *Did someone tell you to come and take on the body?*

C: Yes. We were instructed to take on different bodies, depending on what planet we were on.

D: *So each place you go to, you take on a different body?*

C: Yes. We cannot take a former body with us. We have to take on different bodies depending on what system we're in.

D: *So the body you have chosen now, you didn't go into it as a baby and grow with it?*

C: No. This person had just died, so we were able to just enter the body and bring it back, to regenerate it for our own purpose.

D: *So it hadn't been dead long enough?*

C: No. Only a few minutes.

D: *The original soul had already left?* (Yes.) *If you waited too long it wouldn't work?*

C: Right. It was only a matter of a few minutes.

D: *So if you had waited too long, it would have been much more complicated?*

C: Oh, definitely. They're more liberal when it comes to things like this, especially for our purpose.

D: *Who do you mean by "they"? The ones who are in charge of these things?*

C: Yes. Provided that we occupy the body very quickly. We're only allowed a few minutes in order to do that. And they guide us to where they need us to go in order to inhabit a body.

D: *That way you're not taking a body away from a soul that's already living in it.*

C: Right. That isn't allowed.

D: *So you never know what kind of a body it will be. Is that true?*

C: Right. We don't know from one moment to the next. That's why when you asked me if I was male or female, I felt male, but then I had to remember what male was. I just know from my studies that the legs were definitely not a human female form.

D: Is it hard to adjust to a human body?

C: Yes, a little bit. It just takes time, because we're not used to using limbs and appendages. It's just the motor skills.

D: So you were told to come and learn? (Yes) What are you trying to learn?

C: We're supposed to be learning about this planet so we can teach them how to survive what's coming.

D: Don't they already have skills and know how to do things?

C: They have skills, but they don't have ability as far as all the virtues that they need to be able to use.

D: What kind of virtues?

C: Empathy. Tolerance. What it was in its purest form, compassion. They have the ability to learn how to use it to its fullest potential, but they haven't done it yet. We're here to teach them how to do that.

D: Those sound like rather complicated emotions. Do you think they will listen to you?

C: Yes. There are special techniques we use. We have to keep some certain applications ready, that we can use in order to adopt these emotions and use them. Actually, to help protect them.

D: Do you think it will be hard to do?

C: I think it would be challenging, yes.

D: Have you ever done this in a human body before?

C: No, this is going to be the first. Actually, this one is probably going to be simpler. This is more primitive. Very primitive to get used to.

D: The other bodies, other places you went, did they also have problems you were helping with?

C: Oh, yes. Far different problems. Actually, their issues, their problems, were much more complex than the people of Earth are contending with.

D: How are they complex?

C: Different star systems had occupied other planets, and there were galactic wars going on. Our job was more difficult, because there were renegades. There were people after us, and we had to dodge these different societies and try to avoid them during our journeys. They would have annihilated us if they had caught up with us.

D: *So you were told to come to Earth after you completed those assignments?*

C: Yes. We were successful.

D: *And you think this body will be different.*

C: Oh, I think so. More primitive, and just more fragile. Many of the other bodies we inhabited had armor already built into them, and obviously the human body does not.

D: *The armor was built into the structure?*

C: Yes, with practical appendages. Just at a moment's notice they could be used, because they were already built into the body. This body is different, more fragile. It could be harmed easier. And we need to become more adept as part of the motor skills of this human body, because we're more accustomed to working faster. This to us is extremely slow. Part of the process is to have us cohabitate amongst the humans.

D: *When you do this, do you forget why you came?*

C: Sometimes, some of us do. Not always.

D: *I was thinking it might contaminate it, or take the memory away, when you're living in a human body.*

C: I do not know if living in this human body will do that, erase memories of why we came. I guess that's a chance that we take. It might happen, or it might not.

D: *I wondered if they warned you, when you came in.*

C: No, they didn't.

D: *When you complete this life, are you going to stay on Earth and do more, or do you know?*

C: I haven't been given my orders yet.

D: *I think it's admirable to take on a challenge like that, because it is a challenge, isn't it?* (Oh, yes.)

I decided to move him forward in that life and see what he was doing. He found himself in a community, a "colony" of round huts. They were big enough to accommodate five or six humans, or a small family. This was where he was teaching. "Some of the people are like myself, and then some are actual pupils."

D: *Are these others like you who have entered a human body?*
C: Yes. They are robed like I am. The pupils are very young. I would say they're anywhere from ten to fourteen, fifteen years human age. It's too late to teach the older, the adults. We need the fresh, young minds. The older ones are reticent.
D: *Does it bother them that you're teaching the younger ones?*
C: No, these are actually the relatives and parents of the younger, so they have given us permission to do this, to go forward with the project.
D: *That's very good then. You won't have opposition.*
C: Right. But there are so few of them who are allowing us to do this. We have to do it in secret. We do it in a very isolated area. We cannot approach the cities. We have to stay away from metropolises and from cities. They are not aware of our presence, yet.
D: *Do you think something would happen if they became aware?*
C: Oh, yes. They would annihilate us. They would take us as captives. They would not tolerate us. If we weren't annihilated, they would experiment on us, and we cannot afford to have that happen right now. They won't understand our physiology. They will know that we're not of this, that we are not human. Not so much that they would find anything, as what they do discover they will not understand, because it's so far advanced. I don't know that they would find, at this time in their time, any practical use for us.
D: *So whenever you entered the physical body, you had to make changes so you could exist?*
C: Oh, yes. Many. In order to adapt, yes. – We are actually

planning on taking some of the pupils with us, and then bringing them back. They need to come with us.

D: *Where would you take them?*

C: We're taking them back to our colonies on our planet.

This sounded very much like the story of the Australian aborigine in *Book Two*. The glowing beings came and took the children to their planet to teach them many things that they were to pass on to the adults to make their lives better.

C: That was already pre-arranged. They have to go back with us to our colonies in order to be properly tutored. That is safer and easier. It's only within a matter of human days, because of the method of operation we use for travel. It will seem like only a matter of a couple of weeks that they'll be gone. When actually, they will have been given many, many lessons in a short period of time that they can bring back with them to Earth on our return trip. We've already brought some of the adults to our planet and shown them what life is like. That was prior to coming back to get the children to teach them. They seemed to be amicable and totally cooperative with us, because they know their children are going to help them if they are properly trained.

D: *When you take them back to your planet, what happens to your physical body?*

C: Oh, we automatically become the energy that we were. They won't recognize us in human form, but they will also have to become energy in order to survive on our planet.

D: *What happens to their physical bodies when they go with you?*

C: They're just dematerialized temporarily. When we bring them back, we rematerialize them into the original human form.

D: *Of course, that brings up the question: Why couldn't you have materialized a body for yourself?*

C: That would have been a good thing to do, but that wasn't how we were instructed. We were supposed to take on bodies that recently passed.

D: *But these children, their bodies can dematerialize.*

C: Yes. And more so, that is part of their training, being able to do that. Because in immediate future days on the planet Earth, they're going to have to be able to know how to do that, and teach others how to do that.

D: *I thought the part that demateralizes would just evaporate and disperse.*

C: No, not fully.

D: *You're able to keep it together so it can reactivate.* (Oh, yes.) *So you take them to your planet. What is your planet like?*

C: Most of our civilization is underground. It's subterranean, we don't have much above ground. We don't visit the top very much, because the atmosphere was contaminated a long time ago. We are actually looking for other places to recolonize.

D: *What happened to the atmosphere?*

C: We were attacked by different rebels and they contaminated our atmosphere, and made it uninhabitable. So we can't breathe that environment anymore. We have homes of sorts underground. It's similar to Earth, but we live in pods. We have families that are not considered to be "nuclear families". We have many ancestors, because we live longer than humans. We live the equivalent of a thousand years of human life.

D: *Is this place a long way from Earth?*

C: Oh, yes. We're about thirty-seven light years away.

D: *And you're able to transverse that distance quickly?* (Yes) *And these children are able to do the same thing.*

C: Right. It will look like they've only been gone for two, two-and-a-half human weeks.

D: *And you will be teaching these children underground.*

C: Yes. They'll be perfectly safe.

D: *Then when you eventually take them back to their home, will*

you stay and continue to teach?
C: Yes, for follow-up. We'll be staying there for a short time. But we are hoping with the technology we bring to them, that they'll be able to pass it forward safely. They will be in human form when they do that; whereas, we cannot stay in human form for very long. We have to go back. Well, actually we have to go *forward* and visit other galaxies. And not only that, but if they saw us as the beings we were – because eventually we become our original embodiment – the world governments would apprehend us. And we can't afford to have that happen.

D: *What kind of technology are you sharing with these people?*
C: Basically, how to be able to interstellar travel. They need to recolonize. Earth is not going to be here much longer. They're going to have to go to other galaxies and recolonize. So we had to show them how to interstellar travel, in order to do that. And we can even go so far as to give them actual, possible places where they could recolonize. We could show them. That's part of what we need to do to help them repopulate.

D: *So you stayed there with this group for quite a while.* (Yes) *Then you move on and go to another assignment?*
C: We go to other assignments.

I asked if he was aware of the body that I was speaking to, the female body called "Christine". He said that he was. She was one of his assignments.

D: *Did you enter her body as a baby, or what?*
C: No, Christine had a near-death experience.

This was a surprise. Christine had not mentioned it.

D: *When was that?*
C: Back in 1991, she had a cardiac arrhythmia and she died, and

575

she was gone for a few minutes. She wasn't clinically dead yet, so we inhabited her being back in 1991.

D: *But consciously, now as Christine, she doesn't seem to remember going through a death experience?*

C: No. She agreed to allow this to happen. She had agreed to allow us to do this as a walk-in.

D: *So the original Christine's soul went on to the other side.* (Yes) *But she still carries the memories of that original soul?* (Yes) *Because she said she does have memories of past lives as a human. As a Druid, and as a monk, and playing the flute.*

C: Yes, those are her memories. We have retained some of that. Those are not *my* memories, they are hers. Some of the memories are still intact that she has carried.

This might explain why Christine did not go to one of the past lives she said she remembered. They were a part of the old Christine, and the new Christine had no need to access them. Or maybe, she would not even be able to. Whatever the case, they were irrelevant.

C: Most of that was actually a smoke screen for our coming forward today. We wanted her to feel confident enough by having little snippets of this information in her mind. And that would help her feel confident as far as approaching you. Otherwise, if we had told her about all of this, if we had come to her about this before her even meeting with you ... it would have been too overwhelming.

D: *Was she wanting to leave this life when she had the death experience?*

C: Yes. Her birth mother passed away in 1989, and she wanted to be with her.

D: *You mean she was lonely, and missed her?*

C: Yes, but there were no suicidal attempts. This was the easiest transition, this was the easiest way. She had gone through some major, major lifestyle changes following her mother's passing.

D: *So the original soul is with the mother over there.*

C: Oh, yes, they are very, very happy.

D: *But Christine doesn't know any of this consciously, does she?*

C: No. She was not meant to.

D: *Is it all right if she knows it now?*

C: Yes. We have been instructed to let her know. That it's now time for her to know about these things. She didn't know this was going to happen when she came. Eventually, she was going to be brought here, and this was all going to come out. But she had no idea.

The main thing I was concerned about was how all of this was going to affect Christine when she awakened. They assured me that this would help explain many things to her, and it would help alleviate many of her irrational fears.

D: *So you're living her life just like a normal life, so she doesn't know the difference.*

C: Right. But eventually she will. Eventually, she's going to have to go back with us and learn some of the technology. Upon her return, she'll be joining with more like us, to help the human family get through the future days. She is going to have an important role in the New Earth.

D: *Can you give her more details about what she's supposed to be doing?*

C: Helping make the transition into the next dimension. There are some who will resist because of fear and misunderstanding and just apprehension. And we are not going to use any violence, or try to force humans to do anything, because of free will. Free will is respected universally. We'll have no control or regulation over that. We have to try to persuade individuals, because it is for their own good in order to evolve. And that's part of the process involved with Christine. She's going to have to train individuals how to do that in order to make the transition easier. It will be essential.

D: *Why do we have to go into another world?*

C: Because it's time in the grand scheme of things. Because this is all a test. This was an experiment. And eventually, it will get everyone back to the light, to the original Source.

D: *So the world won't progress the way it's going now?*

C: No. No. Eventually, it's all going to go into the successive dimension.

D: *I have been hearing a lot about this from the people I work with. – But you said she will have to go to your planet?*

C: Yes. Temporarily. To learn.

D: *Won't her husband notice if she's gone?*

C: She is going to be astrally traveling. And this is going to happen now, that we are going to make her aware of what's going on. She will be doing this in astral fashion, and learning that way. And when the time is appropriate, she will be able to start doing this amongst the rest of us. While she is off doing these classes and learning, the body can be relaxing and rejuvenating itself.

D: *I thought maybe you were going to have her dematerialize like the others did.*

C: No. Obviously she has to stay in this body throughout the whole process. Her husband does not know. And not only that, but for her family and relatives, and her clients in her work. Demateralization would not be advantageous.

D: *Good, then it will not disrupt her life. But I do know that we go out of our body every night, and we do astrally travel even though we are not aware of it.*

C: All of the information will be disseminated in the astral state. It's going to be an extensive training class, but it will become inherent in her character. We are a very, very, very compassionate civilization. And we are light years ahead as far as technology. And not only that, but as far as being able to use and positively apply all of the universal virtues.

They talked about Christine's body and proceeded to repair some things they found (one was an underactive thyroid condition). "We infiltrated her body back in 1991, and we put her through a metabolic change a couple of years later. This was required so that we could exist in the body. This caused a major weight fluctuation. And it stayed that way since 1993. She has been to many doctors, and nobody has been able to figure out what's happened to her metabolism. As a result of what we did to her system back in 1993, she has been afflicted with pneumonia, six different episodes. Her smoking is also exacerbating the condition. We need to get her to stop smoking. We need to have her respiratory system in much better shape. The body will be recuperative and regenerative." They then gave instructions about how they were going to proceed with that. Because of her resistance, they would have to do it slowly, especially removing the desire to smoke. One suggestion was to keep her so busy she wouldn't have time to think about it.

C: From 1985 to 1991 she had an eating disorder. She was anorexic. We didn't come in until she gained 65 pounds in five months, and had cardiac arrhythmia and died. She was rushed to the hospital, and she *was* dead for a while. And that's when we came in. We basically brought her back with the understanding that only her body would be brought back. The soul, Christine, is no longer in this body. We are what you call a "walk-in". Our intent is pure and benevolent.

D: *Yes, I am familiar with those. And it usually happens at a traumatic time. – But the main thing is that we don't want it to upset her to discover these things.*

C: Right. We didn't tell you about the near death experience until now, because we wanted you to know who we are. When you were talking with Christine earlier today, that's why she did not bring up the near death experience. – She

579

needs to understand that we are going to be visiting her in the astral. And we will be dealing with her training, her lessons, her course work, and her fellowship. She won't have any conscious memory of these trips. Eventually, it's all going to come into fruition, and she will be able to convene with the rest of us in the very near future.

The thing that was different and unusual about this session was not the fact that it was a walk-in. I have encountered many of them during my career. It was the *type* of walk-in that made this case unique. Normally, a walk-in occurs when the person decides they do not want to be in the life anymore, for whatever reason. They want to leave, but suicide is not an option. Why destroy a perfectly good vehicle when another soul would be more than happy to use it. So they make an agreement with another soul (usually one that they know and have association with) that they will leave, and the incoming soul will take over the body at that exact moment. None of this is done with the conscious involvement or motivation. The consciousness of the person usually has no inkling that anything has occurred, except that things seem to change in their life. The incoming soul makes an agreement that it will take on and complete any agreements the person has made with others. Any karma that must be repaid, and any contracts made before coming into this life. The walk-in must honor these commitments and complete them before it can go on with its own reasons for coming in. This is a normal walk-in.

What makes Christine's case different is that the incoming soul did not know her from any prior incarnations. It had no connections with her. It, in fact, had had very few lives on Earth in a human body. It was being sent by a higher power. It was still with agreement with Christine's soul. It must always be understood that these cases are definitely not possession, invasion or taking over the body. It is always done with permission. Apparently, Christine was unhappy about the loss and closeness of her mother, and wanted to go and be with her. With this type of attitude, she would be ineffective in the part she had to play in the coming Earth changes. It would be better to go on. Does this mean the original spirit has to return to another planet later to continue repaying karma?

In another chapter, it was said that they have to come in and make changes in order for the people to be able to shift into the new dimension with the development of the New Earth. But because of the predominant law (or prime directive) of non-interference, they are not allowed to do so from the outside. Therefore, a dramatic and drastic idea was formed. They would not try to change the Earth from the outside. They would be allowed to do so from the *inside*. As this book shows, many souls are coming for the first time directly from the Source. Others, like Christine, are being replaced by spirits whose job is to go throughout the universe and help planets in trouble. These spirits are also new to Earth, and thus are not bogged down by karma. Some, come into the baby's body when it is stillborn. Their energy is so different that alterations must be done so the baby can survive. In Christine's case, it seems that they can no longer start out as babies, because of the time involved waiting for the child to grow up. An ingenious idea, to come as a walk-in and continue life as an adult. In this way, every available vehicle is used. It allows more volunteers to enter at this important time, without having to grow from a baby.

All of these things were surprises to me as I discovered them through my hundreds of clients. I wonder if there are other ways they are finding to infiltrate the human race, that I have not discovered yet? How wonderful that the Source has found a way to help us, in spite of ourselves.

Annette was meeting with the council on the spirit side. She had never lived on Earth in a physical body. She had been quite content to remain on that side where she was a counselor and teacher. The reasons were now being discussed about why she should come. "They're talking about the shift and balancing of energy."

D: *What shift are they talking about?*
A: The rising of the vibration of this system. There is an imbalance, and some energy has to be placed in a certain point to realign. So we decide that a part of us has to come down to enable the energy to be concentrated in certain areas. Wherever that person is. Me, this one. (She seemed hesitant.) It's necessary. It's the council who has determined that we have to send parts of ourselves down into the physical to act as a connection, so that energy can be funneled through. (Big sigh) And this one has the capacity to access a lot of energy, and after, circle the world, so when there is a need, it can balance.
D: *The kind of energy that would circle the world?* (Yes) *That is a lot of energy. Is it the kind of energy the average soul or spirit couldn't handle?* (Yes) *So, it has to be a certain type? And the average human wouldn't be able to do this?*
A: I don't think so, no.
D: *That's why it had to be your type of being?*
A: Yes, that's right. Because we are energy and ... oh, God, I just can't describe it at all!
D: *Just do the best you can.*
A: Each of us has, like an umbilical cord or something that is connected to a part of the energy that we have sent down here. And that umbilical cord can access the energy that we are up here. So this energy that this one has can, through the cord, disperse the energy from us here and can balance the planet.
D: *But it takes more than just one person, doesn't it?*
A: Well, the council has umbilical cords for their own.

D: So these are all over the place.

A: Right, right. It is necessary. It's going everywhere. Actually, it's like a grid. Like on a map, like a lattice or longitude/latitude.

D: Like a latticework, and it's plugged into this universal source of energy?

A: Right, right.

D: You said this is very important at this time. What would happen if these parts didn't come down and try to balance? What would be the alternative?

A: No, it's just too risky. The Earth would have to go through a period of stagnation again, and it's just not worth it.

D: Did this happen before?

A: It's happened many times. Single things affect. It would have a ripple effect. If we allow the Earth to again destroy itself, or become non-inhabitable, it changes the magnetism and that will have a ripple effect to all past ... I mean, to us it is all at the same time. It changes all that is and all that was at this time – at this point. No, it can't happen again.

So Annette was sent down to become a physical human being for the first time in her existence. "So when you sent this piece of yourself down, does it enter into Annette as a baby?"

A: No, no, not as a baby. A baby is too small. It's later. It's a gradual thing. If you saw a fiber optic, a cord or a wire? So you have small wires, inside small wires, inside small wires. So it's kind of like that. It's a small connection, and then more is added on. Gradually, over time-over time-over time.

D: As the body grows?

A: Right, right, exactly. And changes, because everything is timing. There are preparations that have to be made. We knew that this one would have the treatments – the DNA work – done at certain times. And so that has allowed more space in the cells for more energy.

583

D: *But there is a soul that enters that baby's body.*

A: Oh, yes. That's right.

D: *Is that the same soul that is in Annette now?*

A: Yes! But it's not ... it's just less. It's a percentage. I mean, fundamental properties are the same. It's like a tiny wee cell. And that cell, even though it is tiny, has information in it. It's the same idea. It's just a matter of whether you have many or a few. The blueprint is the same.

D: *Could we say, as the body matures it can hold more information, more energy?*

A: Right. More energy. That's the main things.

D: *More energy can go into the cells as the body grows.* (Yes) *Isn't this different than the way a normal body would behave?*

A: Right, right. It's different.

D: *The average human doesn't go through these things?*

A: No, they don't.

D: *They aren't – I guess you would say – "updated or upgraded"?*

A: No, that's right. That's right. There are ... I'm not sure of the number, but each council member has a part that is here.

D: *And they are sending pieces of themselves, because this is something that has to happen right now.*

A: Yes. Her body is getting stronger. At first, she had immunity issues – the asthma and eczema – because the body was rejecting what we were trying to do. But now it's getting better. The body has memory, and it's a problem. It was uncomfortable with the energies that were being integrated at the time. Sometimes the time isn't appropriate, and so, there is not a good compatibility between the energy and the body. Especially when it is young and developing. It's complicated because there are many facets to the human. We are doing our best to make it smooth. Again, things are happening at the same time. It's very hard to explain. If something happens at another time ... it's very, very complicated. Never mind; I can't explain it.

I encouraged her to try.

A: Okay. Because time is all the same – it's like a banana peel that's being unpeeled and laid flat. Oh! An apple peel is better! If you peel an apple it's a spiral. So it seems to have a beginning and an end, but it doesn't. DNA is a good analogy, because it is a spiral also. Let's say on the left helix, something happened when she was five, and it exacerbated the physical. Then the energy connection will make it appear here ... at thirty.

D: *Like it's on the same wavelength, and that triggers the same kind of reaction.*

A: Right. What she does *now* will affect what's perceived as a child. If she makes herself better now, then the child will be better.

D: *That's the part I have always found hard to understand. We always think that the child has grown into an adult, but you mean it's still existing there.*

A: That's right. So the decisions she makes now are good for her as that child. It's like a line. Hmm, not really. It's very hard to find an analogy that is useful.

I feel that what she was trying to explain has to do with the theory of simultaneous time. According to this concept, everything (past, present, future) is all existing at the same time, because time is only an illusion. Thus, it can all be accessed. This is what I have succeeded in doing, accessing all of these different various parts. By using this method of hypnosis, we are going to what I call "a past life", by changing our vibration and frequency to match the vibration and frequency of the time period we wish to see. Very much like tuning the radio channels, or changing the TV stations.

A similar example discovered through another client. Virginia saw herself immediately in a beautiful forest setting. Yet it had many unusual attributes that set it apart from the normal. There were crystals of all sizes and colors growing out of the ground. In the middle of a circle surrounded by crystals there was a seat. She saw herself as a young male dressed in a loose shift tied at the waist. He came regularly to this place, and considered it to be his own special place. He would sit in the middle of the crystals and enjoy the energy moving through his body. He said this was the way he stayed healthy. "It's maintenance. It's very peaceful and very energized; very calming. You can feel the frequency. You can feel the energy from the crystals going through you and around you. The different colors of the crystals are used for different purposes. Yellow is your health, your body. White is your mind. The green is for cleansing. And the purple is a protective energy that goes with you."

This place was up in the mountains, but the village where he lived was down by a river. The village was composed of several families, and their houses were made from weaving branches together. "We like to live more in the wind and feel nature. We don't want to block it all off. Just protection when we need it. Nature talks to you. You have to listen. You can't listen if the wall is solid." They were considered one big family, and everyone had their job, their part to play. His part was to heal by carrying some of the energy with him. "I go there to gather the energy that I use for people; like I collect it and take it with me. I send it to their bodies, where they need it. It goes in and moves things ... adjusts things." He also had a natural knowledge of herbs. No one had taught him how to do these things. "It just comes in my head, like a voice or a picture. I found my special place with the crystals in the woods when I was small, very

young. It was like someone left it there. No one else goes there."
It seemed like the ideal, perfect life, until I asked him to move to an important day. He suddenly announced, "Our village is destroyed. The water came ... the river. Too much water. Washed ... washed things away. The houses and the people. And the rocks and the trees ... everything down the mountain. The sky became very dark. It was just time." He had gone to the day of his death, because he was washed away in the flood.

D: *Did it bother you?*
V: Just moved on. Change. Everyone changes.
D: *Eventually, you mean?* (Yes) *To end one existence and go to another?* (Yes) *Where are you going now?*
V: I'm just floating. It feels like I'm resting. It's very light and airy. I'm just waiting. I'm not sure why I'm waiting.

I condensed time and moved him ahead, so we could find out where he went.

V: I'm in spirit. It's not time to go back yet. It's a different place. Everyone there is spirit. There are no physical bodies like we had before. We're planning where to go in a group.
D: *Why do you want to go as a group?*
V: We need to go and help someone.
D: *It's better as a group than individuals?* (Yes) *Have you known these people before?*
V: Yes, I don't know their names, but I recognize them. They're healers. They guard. We all do. We go to places and help the people that are there. And then we come back and ... to share in another mission.
D: *Does anyone tell you what you have to do?*
V: No, we volunteer. Sometimes the places we go are more difficult than others. The places, the bodies that we have to work in.
D: *Why are they more difficult?*

587

V: Cut off from the collective. Have to remember our own mission with very little to work with. Few people of our mind. We just have to remember.

D: *It's harder to remember, isn't it, when you get into the physical?*

V: Yes, the door closes behind us. The veil that lets us through is thick again. We only have what we bring with us.

D: *So you decide to go as a group?*

V: Yes, many places need help. We go to the critical ones first.

D: *Which are the critical ones?*

V: The ones in danger of perishing altogether. There has to be some of the people in each place who can maintain, that can help who's there. We have to train and make sure they are aware. If they're opened up to the energy that they can hear and feel.

D: *Because these people don't understand?*

V: No, they're very cut off. They're disconnected.

D: *Why are they in danger.*

V: In-fighting. Lose their way. They have no oversight. They've forgotten where they came from and what they were supposed to be doing. If we can teach just one person, then they can go on from there without losing the way of the whole people. More is better, but one is better than nothing. We have to do it without getting caught up in the daily problems and fighting.

D: *Is it easy to get caught up?* (Yes) *Are you willing to take that chance?*

V: Yes, everyone is. It's for the greater good.

D: *Where do you decide to go?*

V: We've been coming to Earth. There are different places, different areas. Sometimes we work from above – energy only. We float, directing energy as a group. Other times we come in form, in the physical. It's more difficult. It is easier from above, but not as effective. It takes longer. It works faster if you come into the physical.

D: *Why is that?*

V: Closer. You can direct the energy from a closer point. The distance works, but it is more intense when you are closer to what you're working with.

D: *Does anyone tell you which way to do it?*

V: No, it's our choice. If it's a group move, or we can individually decide for ourselves. We usually consult each other within the group.

D: *Have you been to Earth many times?*

V: Unfortunately, yes. It gets worse. We work and work and the energies ... some are so heavy and so negative. It takes much energy and much time. But if it happens – if the meltdown occurs, it will be far-reaching to many galaxies. It cannot be allowed. The energy work offsets the chaos, the vibrations that are so erratic. Working to calm and hold things together.

D: *But you're not allowed to interfere, are you?*

V: No, not directly.

D: *It would be easier if you could.*

V: Yes, but it's just not allowed.

D: *So how are you going to make a difference?*

V: One person at a time. It's their choice to help or not to help. Be a light, be a healing force. Train each person that's willing. Hopefully, train more of the light over shadow. Brighten the darkness; calm the negative energies.

D: *So that's why you decide to come to Earth, even though it's not pleasant.*

V: Yes, it's necessary. So many galaxies, so many places of experience are at risk. The universe watches; sends the energy to heal.

D: *Have you gone to other galaxies and experienced them?* (Yes) *Is that different than Earth?*

V: Yes, in some ways. The inhabitants are different; different energies; higher mind.

D: *Do you also take on forms when you go to those places?*

V: Sometimes. Sometimes just energy. Different atmosphere

589

creates the form.

D: *So you never know what it's going to be until you get there?*

V: Unless you're been there before.

D: *But it sounds like it's always an adventure.*

V: Yes, much traveling goes on – many ways to travel. Some are very slow: canoe and paddle. Some ships – different power source. Some are faster than others, but the energy beams are the fastest. The beams of energy go from far reaches of the galaxy – jump in and go for a ride. It's very quickly.

D: *So right now, you're deciding what your next adventure will be, the next assignment.*

V: Mission, yes.

D: *And you decided you want to come to Earth?*

V: Not really, but it's necessary.

D: *So you don't really want to do it, but you feel you need to?* (Yes) *Okay, are you aware that you're speaking through a physical body?* (Yes) *When did you decide to enter this body?*

V: When I came here.

D: *Is this one of the missions – the assignments?*

V: Yes, you have to come to a physical body to work in the physical.

D: *And you decided to be this body we call Virginia?* (Yes) *When did you enter the body?*

V: As a child.

D: *Did you come in as a baby?*

V: No, it was already here.

D: *When did you enter it?*

V: When the baby wanted to leave. It changed its mind at that moment.

D: *Is that allowed?* (Yes) *And the baby wanted to go. Tell me about it. What happened?*

V: I came in. Disorienting ... why was I here? What was going on? Who were the players?

D: *What about the soul that was in the original baby?*

V: The baby was fine. The baby went back. It did not want to be here.

D: *Does that happen often?*

V: Sometimes. Usually, the physical body dies. We needed an avenue to come. Three or four years is a long time when you are trying to work. Saving three or four years is a saving of time when you have things to do – when you have work to do.

D: *That was at the time the other soul wanted to leave?* (Yes) *And you were allowed to enter then.*

V: Yes. It has to be approved. We don't just get to make up our own mind. The council decides if it's appropriate.

D: *Because it's not possession.* (No) *It's always done with permission.*

V: Agreement, yes.

D: *Consent and agreement. And this does happen sometimes.*

V: Yes, more than you would think.

D: *So you don't have to be the little baby learning how to walk and talk.*

V: A waste of time.

D: *But when you enter the body, you don't remember your assignment, is that right?*

V: That is true; most annoying.

D: *(Laugh) I always thought it would be easier if you could remember.* (Yes) *Why aren't you allowed to remember?*

V: It would be detrimental to many people here if they knew. To start from the goals, the purpose, the learning meant to happen here.

D: *You don't think it would be easier to think, "Oh, I've got an assignment. I know why I'm here and I can do that."*

V: Just don't want everyone else here to know we have assignments, or where we came from, how we got here. Not everyone is as open as you are. The plan is very large. When you're here, you're a grain of sand on a beach the size of the Earth. That's how much perspective of the universe you have. Yet each grain of sand is meant to have influence. Not

591

everyone remembers.

D: *Do you think it's time now for people to start waking up and remembering?*

V: Yes, it's necessary. It's the only way the Earth will exist and continue – is for more people to remember. There are many coming back to help the memory awaken.

D: *Many of these who are coming have not lived many lives on Earth, have they?*

V: That is true. It's a difficult place. You have a mission, no remembrance, nothing is familiar. Very few may recognize each other at some level, but don't really know. It takes much effort to awaken, to open the memory cells. It's not always meant to be.

D: *I know many of your kind become so discouraged they want to get out; they want to leave, because it's difficult.*

V: That too, is annoying. To get back to this side and think, "Aw! Why didn't I do it while I was there? We have to start over!" You've always affected someone in some way. So something has been accomplished, but not as much as could have been. – So much wasted time. Childhood – larger bodies are better.

I knew I did not have to call forth the subconscious. I knew from the way it had been answering the questions that I was already communicating with it. It said it was all right for Virginia to know these things, to have this information now. "She wants to know. She's annoyed, too. Much ability – many, many lifetimes of helping – great healing abilities. She should be healing – one person at a time. The Earth has to be healed. The energy has to be brought in. People have to be awakened." I then asked about the past life she had seen.

D: *It sounded like a strange place where all the crystals were growing out of the ground.*

V: The crystals were from a ship. The ship had been left here.

D: So it was a long time ago? (Yes) *Are they still in existence?*
V: Yes, they have multiplied. The place is still there. I feel it's covered. The river, the floods, the landslides. Still there, but not visible. The crystals have very powerful energy.

This session was done as a demonstration for one of my classes, and Virginia was chosen at random. I never know what will happen during a class, but I am surprised when such advanced information is allowed to come forth. I hope it benefitted the students who were gathered around the bed observing. This was another case of a spirit entering a body that had just been vacated by a departing spirit. If possible, they do not want to waste a perfectly good vehicle. And it does save valuable time if the soul enters after the body has already gone through its early growing and adjusting stages.

NOTES MADE WHILE AT THE ASHRAM IN THE BAHAMAS

In April 2007, I was invited to speak at the Sivananda Ashram on Paradise Island in the Bahamas. I have spoken there at the Yoga Teachers' Training Retreat many times, and I truly enjoy being in the company of these gentle people. On this trip, I took the rough draft of this book with me to work on, because I knew I would have time in seclusion, completely cut off from TV, computers and telephones. I had most of the material put together for the book, but I also had many unanswered questions. I sat on the little porch of my small cabin, under a coconut palm, staring out at the peaceful and mesmerizing waves caressing the beach. I was pondering the subject I would be talking about at the temple that night, when words began flooding my brain. Anyone who is a writer will know what I mean. I grabbed a notebook and tried to

593

capture them before they faded away into the limbo.

As I have been writing this book and putting the hundreds of pieces together that I have gained through many, many sessions, I was beginning to get a glimpse of the underlying message that "they" wanted to impart. It was too big to come through any one person. In order to get the story, theory, concept, whatever you want to call it, through to me in its entirety, it had to be given piece by piece through many people. I was the one who had to put the puzzle pieces together. Individually, they are interesting, but together it forms an amazing picture. There definitely is a plan to save mankind, and it is bigger in scope that anyone can imagine.

After the development of the A-Bomb and nuclear power in the late 40s and early 50s, a call went out throughout the universe. This was evident from the influx of UFO sightings at that time. They have said the development and the explosion got their attention, and they had to come and see what this primitive planet was up to. They knew we wouldn't be able to handle it. And with our violent tendencies, we could very well end up destroying our planet. This could not be allowed to happen. It would cause a ripple effect that would be felt throughout the universe, and would disrupt other planets and dimensions. But how to stop it and control it without going against the prime directive of non-interference?

The planet was becoming more and more negative, caused by people living here for hundreds of lifetimes, piling more and more karma on top of themselves. They were not working it out and were stuck. If they couldn't solve their *own* problems, they certainly couldn't work out and stop the violence and wars and ecological problems of our planet. As long as we were going along our own way and not harming anyone but ourselves, they had no reason to interfere. We had free will and they could only watch helplessly as we sank deeper into negativity. It was our choice. The invention of atomic power pushed the panic button and something would have to be done. But that something could not go against the prime directive of non-interference. Even if it was for our own good, they could not just come in and stop it.

The decision was made. If they couldn't help from the outside, they could help from the *inside*. The call went out for volunteers who would be willing to come and live in a physical body as a human, because these had not lived on Earth before, they had not accumulated karma. They had a pure and powerful positive energy that came directly from God, from the Source. They would have to be very careful not to get caught up in the world and create karma. Many are shielded to protect them from this very real danger. They wanted to do their job of introducing and spreading positive energy to counteract and dispel the negative. Then they could return to their "home". I have already reported elsewhere in this book about the three waves of volunteers that I have discovered in my thirty years of working on this.

Time is of the essence as we approach the coming of the New Earth. Now, there is no longer time to wait for the volunteer to grow from a baby to an adult. Thus, I found they are entering the bodies of living adults, mostly at the time when they have Near Death Experiences. This is not possession, but is done with the full consent and knowledge of the exiting soul. It is a different version of the traditional walk-in experience. Very clever. "They" are determined to save us and our beautiful planet in spite of ourselves. An excellent way to get around the prime directive. They are not interfering if they have the cooperation of all souls involved.

The Earth is a living being that is crying out to be saved. It is trying to rid itself of the invaders by cleansing itself: floods, tsunamis, earthquakes, volcanic eruptions. They all are cries for help. It is as though the Earth is ridding itself of its own karma, before it reincarnates into another existence. A pristine, beautiful, perfect new environment where it can start anew, and taking along with it those who are capable of adjusting to the new vibrations and frequencies to create a new world. The old world is headed for destruction. However, it cannot be total physical destruction of the planet itself, because that would cause disruption in the vibratory fields of other planetary bodies and dimensions in the universe. So the Earth has chosen to split off into two worlds, leaving those who want to continue to live in fear and violence to continue on the "old" Earth. And creating a "new" home environment for those who want to progress and evolve. The two types can no longer live side by side on the same planet. Things have changed too much. So the vibration and frequency has to be changed.

Everything is energy. Everything is vibrating at different frequencies. Even rocks, furniture, etc. are vibrating, only at a much lower, denser frequency. As long as everything and everyone on the Earth is vibrating at the same low, slow frequency things will stay the same. The frequency has to be raised so the Earth can split off and enter a new dimension. It is the same thing that happens to our own Earth bodies. As we learn the lessons of the physical plane we can "graduate" to another higher dimension on the spirit side, and not have to return to the Earth school. We can progress, because we will have outgrown this earthly school. Thus the Earth itself is getting ready to "graduate", to leave the familiar, the status quo, and progress into something much higher.

Yet the new Earth without human beings and life in its many diverse forms would be as an empty house. Just four walls without a soul inside. There had to be a way for the humans to also evolve so they can go with the Earth. The humans would have to also raise their vibrations. This was easier said than done, considering how many eons mankind had been trapped here. Then I understood. The karma they had before coming into this world will be left with the "old" Earth. That is where karma will continue to exist. It has no part in the New Earth.

These volunteers have come from a place that has never known violence, hatred and fear. They are bringing that vibration of positivity to the Earth at this time. It is like the "hundredeth monkey syndrome". If we can get enough humans carrying the positive vibration, it will overshadow and diminish the negative vibration. It will wipe it out or lessen its effect by sheer numbers alone. In one session I asked about the current disasters where thousands of people are dying and leaving the planet en masse. I was told they had finished their work here, and had volunteered to leave in order to make room for the new ones coming in. Then I understood. They are making room for more of these volunteers with the positive energy to come in. We can conquer by sheer numbers alone. When the critical mass has been reached, and enough people have succeeded in raising their vibrations and frequencies, then the new Earth will be born. This is the plan that will save the world. The people themselves, of course, have no conscious memory of their reasons for coming at this time. And that is the way it should be. They will play their role well. Those that are still steeped in negativity will remain with the old Earth with what they have created. By the time they realize something is occurring, it will be too late. They cannot change their frequency and vibration quickly enough to follow. It has to be a gradual thing, otherwise it would be too traumatic for the physical body to handle. Thus the separation occurs, the two Earths separate and life goes its separate ways: positive and negative.

I have discovered many of these volunteers live quiet unassuming lives. They do not create attention. They influence in quiet subtle ways. During the session many of them are told they are here just to "be". They influence others only by their presence, and the aura they exude. It links with others through no effort on their part, and many are helped by being in their presence, or by their physical touch. It is very simple and yet very profound. There will not be any heroic dramatic efforts to save our world. It will happen by the simple presence and touch of loving, unselfish individuals.

CHAPTER THIRTY-FIVE

ANSWERING THE CALL

When Anna entered the scene, the first thing she saw was people working, building a very tall golden tower. She said it was being built for the gods. She described it, "It is similar to a pyramid, but it's narrower, higher. Slabs of gold, similar to tiles are being put on the outside." The squares of gold were about 10-12" by 10-12", and were very ornate, covered with designs. The people were golden-skinned, either Egyptian or Babylonian, wearing little white tunics. They had scaffolding that allowed them to attach the square, gold plates.

D: *You said it is being built for the gods?* (Yes) *What do you think that means?*
A: It's the ones that have come from elsewhere. They've been told about these beings, and they haven't always seen them, but they have been told they have to build this tower.
D: *What's the purpose of the tower?*
A: Some kind of communication that the gods want. They want a tower.
D: *Do you know who told them they had to build this for the gods?*
A: It feels like the priests or someone has had direct contact. Somebody got the plans or the design, and they're making these people follow instructions.

I asked her to describe herself. She was a young male wearing golden sandals, a short white robe and a golden belt. Her hair was dark with silver stripes. Then she was startled to discover that she had huge golden wings that were attached to her back. "They are mine, but it doesn't make sense. They are large, and beautiful!" She then noticed she had a golden necklace around her neck that had a dark blue jewel in it. "Oh! There are jewels on the gold belt also. They look like jewels, but they're really buttons or gadgets, like dials or controls. I am also wearing some kind of headpiece. It's not just an ornament. It's some kind of transmitter. It has a purpose. I am standing high on a building on a ledge that is opposite the one they're putting the gold plates on. There is nothing around me to obstruct the view. I'm watching what they're doing, and reporting the progress. I'm making sure it's exact, because every piece of gold, every square, has to be placed exactly in the right position and the right order. This is important, because this is some kind of generator. It has to do with how the energy flows from the ground up the building and out the top. There's a spire that is going to be at the top, and the energy moves in a circle spiral up the building. And each gold plate will be activated or illuminated. It does something to help the energy flow; to move it, to amplify it. It has to be exact."

D: *You mentioned that someone else was telling these people what to do.*

A: The others are here for a while; they're not permanent. Some of them will stay longer. To teach; to help spread knowledge; to bring some technology that would help these people. They have been asking for help. It's simple technology, but it will help change their lives.

D: *And you are communicating, reporting the progress?* (Yes) *Then why do they need this larger communication device?*

A: For when we leave. There'll be some that will stay. They'll be able to use their thoughts and transmit them or send them to keep the communication going.

D: *So the information, the progress report, you are sending is not going back home?*

A: It's going up somewhere. It's not to those that are on the planet. It's going up out of my head somewhere above.

D: *So this is not your home.*

A: It's a project that I'm on, but it's not my home.

D: *Are you one of the ones that are going to stay?*

A: No. I'm just watching. I have to watch and report how the progress is going. How the others are doing their jobs.

D: *When it's completed, what are you going to do then?*

A: (Chuckle) I get to leave. We've done this before.

D: *On this place?*

A: No, in other places. We come as a group. And there are those that are very tall in stature that communicate with the inhabitants. They mingle and share, and teach and guide, because they are skilled at that. They teach whatever is needed. Different worlds have different criteria. Some worlds are ready for more complexity, for more technology, for more balance.

D: *What do the more advanced people think when you come?*

A: They are grateful, because they have been taught about us. There are different levels of teaching. The advanced ones are taught of other worlds, of the sciences, of the spirit of immortality, of languages, of mind. And they are the ones that are gifted with tools to help the more common inhabitants. These people that come are seen as gods.

D: *Do the ones that are more advanced see you also as gods?*

A: No. We make contact with the advanced spirits and they know of our coming. They are prepared. We give them time to prepare, but the only way they can communicate with the others is to call the visitors "Gods", because that is their way.

D: *So, everywhere you go on every world, do you have to build a communication device like this?*

A: They're a little different. Some worlds, the energies are clearer. There are like existing vortexes that can be utilized. It's different everywhere.

D: *Then some people, it's their job to stay and help the planet, or the people of the planet?*

A: They're meant to stay for a while and sometimes there is seeding that is deliberately done, so that the original ones can live.

D: *To carry on the work. Do these people that stay know how to utilize the communication device?*

A: The ones that are interbred – the half-breeds – will know at a certain age. The program is triggered and they know what to do.

D: *I thought maybe it was automatic, and the device was constantly picking up information.*

A: It constantly picks up information, but there is additional amplification that these other beings input into it. But it only lasts for as long as the energy remains pure.

D: *What happens if the energy does not remain pure?*

A: The signal is weakened and it distorts through space time. There are some places where they maintain it longer, so what is taught has a chance to permeate without distortion. Other places, the distortion happens quickly, which is why some others have to stay longer. They only leave when they feel they have established something.

D: *Do you transmit back knowledge about how the groups or the people are progressing and utilizing the information?*

A: Yes, it's like a report to see how quickly they are evolving; how they utilize what they are given; whether they hold it sacred or precious or whether they distort it. It's like an experiment; like a study, research, for these worlds' life forms.

D: *Then whenever the instructors leave, what eventually happens to the communication device?*

A: It functions for a period of time because it uses the energy of the planet. It is the distortions of the people that change the energy of the planet in that area, that distorts the signal. This is why these places are programmed within the minds of the people to be sacred. As long as that sacredness is held, the signals will transmit. But when the people become polluted or distorted, and begin to taint the energy of what is sacred, it starts a distortion over time of the energy in the transmission.

601

And when the transmission becomes so weak, others must come and do it all over again in a different place.

D: *Does the original device remain, or does something happen to it?*

A: It remains, but the disappearance of the vitality of energy changes the appearance of the structure over time. It becomes a dead structure. The gold begins to dissolve. Its energy fades somehow, and what is left is stone. It's like a skeleton. It's like the skin dissolves and fades away, and what's left is a monument.

D: *So if someone were to see it later they would have no idea what its use was.*

A: No, and they would not know what it looked like in its original state.

This makes me wonder about the pyramids and other ancient monuments. It has been said that the Great Pyramid at one time had a capstone of gold. When the energy changed, did they convert into merely stone monuments, masking their true purpose?

D: *So, you are not from that place. Where are you from?*

A: (She was smiling.) I'm from the stars; from a golden world. (Whispering) The golden world. It's a world of many suns. There are five suns in our world.

D: *Does that create a problem with radiation?*

A: No, because we change our form. We don't have to be physical. The suns are like a plasma and their radiation is knowledge. They are there not to radiate *heat*. They give off light, but their light is given because of knowledge. Knowledge is their light. It's a very bright world.

D: *So you don't need a physical body in that world.*

A: You don't need one, but you can wear whatever kind of body you want, if you want one.

D: *What do you look like in your normal state?*

A: (Sigh) It's an energy field that looks a little bit like a jellyfish. Instead of tentacles, they're sparkling electric fields that we give off as we communicate. Some of us keep those forms, but we can change. We can morph into anything by a thought. We can be anything, so it's playful. We can try any forms on and experiment with forms, because the knowledge from the suns gives us the means to do that. There are no limitations there. It's always changing. It's a world of movement and wonder and communication of extraordinary nature.

D: *What is the topography like in a place like that?*

A: It's undulating. There are things that look like mountains, peaks, but they move like frequency waves. They come and they go, and they rise and they fall.

D: *Are there any trees or vegetation?*

A: Not unless we create needing that for beauty. It's ever-changing pictures, and it's not a humanoid world.

D: *Then when you leave to go on a mission, are you told by someone what you're supposed to do?*

A: Yes, we have instructions. We volunteer for these projects and bring knowledge from the suns to these other worlds.

D: *How do you travel when you go to the other worlds?*

A: Thought.

D: *You don't need a craft or any kind of ship?*

A: Not unless the energy of the world we go to has distorted frequencies that would corrupt our thoughts. Then we create vessels or ships to keep our thoughts clear, and the ships deflect the distortions. It's like a shield that allows us to stay in integrity with why we're there.

D: *Otherwise, it would be difficult?*

A: It would be very challenging. Some atmospheres are very thick with convoluted thought of the civilization that we enter. Some atmospheres are clearer depending on the evolution of the world that we enter.

D: *Are you warned about these things before you go somewhere?*

A: Most of the time, but if it is a world that has not been fully researched, sometimes we are caught by surprise.

D: *So when you went to this one world, you created a physical body. Why did you have to do that?*

A: So we could be like them. They would not see us or hear us if we were plasma, and they would be in fear. They would not understand. And so, we morph as necessary into similar life forms in order to communicate and be accepted as much as possible without compromising ourselves.

D: *But you formed a body that had wings.*

A: I like my wings. There are few of us who had the wings. They are there also, for deflection and transmission. Deflection of frequencies coming from the people and the planet. They also are able to receive and translate the thoughts of those that look towards us. They are almost like a satellite dish. It's almost like an organic computer than can take in information and read it.

D: *So this is why you chose a body like that. It has a practical part even though it's beautiful.*

A: Yes. I do not have to interact too much with others, so I can keep that form. They think that I'm, perhaps, more like a bird, when they see me from a distance. Some have seen me closer, but those that are far below just think I am a giant bird of some kind. It keeps me safe and allows me to do what I need to do without interruption.

D: *So you're going to stay until it's completed, and then you have to return or go somewhere else?*

A: I stay until the building is done, and the technology is passed on or brought down to a satisfactory level. And then I leave before some of the others. I am finished there.

I then moved her ahead until the job was finished and she would have to go somewhere else. "Do you change form, or do you keep this form?"

A: I drop the form. I do not need it. It's like a costume.

D: *Do you need a craft?*

A: In this world there is a craft, because of the atmospheric frequencies. So I simply dissolve the form and transmit myself to the craft.

D: *Are you the only one that's leaving, or are there others?*

A: There are others.

D: *So you're going to go somewhere else. Do you have instructions?*

A: I do not know until I am back on the craft and others report in.

D: *They report back to the planet with the five suns?*

A: Others do that. We do not have to report to them. There are others above us that do that reporting. Then decisions come.

D: *Do you know where you're going next?*

A: Hmm. I'm hearing I have to go to Earth.

D: *Do you know where Earth is?*

A: The other side of the universe. It's far from here.

D: *Have you been there before?*

A: A long time ago. I went there to teach, to educate, to restore. I was one of those that had to stay for a while. I have been to Earth close to its beginning of life forms, when many forms were in experiment there. And we designed the nature there and seeded its vegetation ... in some of the early ones that were there.

D: *To see what would grow; what would develop?*

A: And to take some of the barren areas and carpet them with green to create places that were habitable for life forms. Many of the places where there were to be oceans were hot, and not appropriate for water. And these areas had to be cold and changed in order for the atmosphere to condense to create the pools that would give life to other forms.

D: *So you must have water also.*

A: Yes, the clouds. The seeding of the clouds was put into place before we got there. It was a project of many different beings coming together to create the world that would be called the

605

Earth. There are different cultures, and different worlds that have expertise and experience in areas that we do not. And we come together as a united effort to create these new worlds.

D: *Who instructs you? Tells you what to do?*

A: There is a council. I would call it a council, but it is higher than a council. There's a community of many different worlds that are able to scan life in universes. And know when and where to create worlds with life that will have future impact upon the particular part of space that they are in. And this council, this group of worlds, is able to see into the future potentials. They are able to see a matrix through time to know potential outcomes.

D: *But it doesn't always work out the way they hope, does it?*

A: No, it does not.

D: *This must take an incredible amount of time to develop a world to the point that it can have life on it.*

A: In the universe that the Earth is in, time is different from other worlds in other universes. The laws of that universe have an interesting time that is longer than it is to us. To us, it is fast, but to the world that is developing it's called "millions of years". Years or a time frame that's constructed by the laws of that universe.

D: *According to human thinking, it would take an incredible amount of time. But your people and the others are able to come and go at different phases of development?*

A: It's not in our time frame. We can come and go. It's a little bit like walking into a room and having a different atmosphere of time in that room. Almost like a holodeck that is capable of extending time into eons of progression, but it is only a short break in our time.

D: *So things have naturally changed every time you return.* (Yes) *So, you said you are being told to go to Earth again. What phase in its development is it now when you return? Can you see what's happening there?*

606

A: Much distress. The atmosphere is very polluted. There is much pain. The atmosphere is screaming. The souls are screaming for help.

D: *Is this why they asked you to come?*

A: There are many coming at this time.

D: *Then things did not progress the way you had hoped they would?*

A: No, there was interference. Others who came interfered with the experiment in the development of the planet. Those that wanted to use resources and inhabitants for something other than divine pleasure of evolution. They are the dark ones that do not honor natural evolution.

D: *Couldn't the council do something to stop them?*

A: There is free will. The council can only seek to educate these others on the benefits of allowing the plan to occur. They cannot enforce, because the universe has the freedom of all to be. It is a difference of opinion of what evolution looks like.

D: *So what are you supposed to do?*

A: Many are coming from many different worlds. The atmosphere must be healed. The cries must be heard. The planet is weeping; she is in pain. There is much to be corrected.

D: *Do you know how you are going to help this time?*

A: I must pretend to be one of them. There is a need for more of us to intersperse ourselves amongst the inhabitants to do what we must do. We must take on the bodies and be less separated from them this time.

D: *So you won't appear different?*

A: So that we will have more power to help. Being different does not accomplish anything when there is that much pain. There is too much fear.

D: *You have to appear like one of the people.*

A: It's more expeditious to do it that way.

D: *Well, let's move ahead and see what you do. How do you become one of them?*

607

A: (Pause) I do not like it. It is a constricting body and a very heavy energy. It is not fluid. The bodies are filled with genetic fear and doubt, with uncertainty, with hesitation. And to bring energy in and have to meander through the programs and the genetics is challenging. There is too much distortion.

D: *When did you enter this body? Was it a baby?*

A: There was an attempt as a baby, but it was not successful. I am the wrong frequency for the body. I have to change my frequency.

D: *Were you assigned to a certain baby when it was being born? I was wondering how you decided which body.*

A: There is a scanning of the genetic history of the DNA of the potentials – of the parents – and if it seems as if there is a potential of past contact through that genetic strain, then the frequency of that still co-exists within the parents.

D: *So it's easier to do it as a baby?*

A: Sometimes it is easier to do it as a baby, but it depends upon the emotional state of the mother whether or not she blocks that gene from being activated.

D: *But in this case, you couldn't enter as a baby?*

A: It was unsuccessful. The frequency was too heavy. I could not activate the right frequency within the body, and it was aborted.

D: *When were you successful in entering the body?*

A: Later. There was an agreement made with another soul; another aspect of soul.

D: *Was that also as a baby?*

A: It's as if there was a partial incarnation into the body – not fully – to develop the body to help it grow, but to not be fully present within it. It was ripening the body for the right time. There was not a necessity to be fully present because the frequency that was in the body was to be shifted out of it.

D: *Does that mean your frequency was too strong?* (Yes) *Would it have harmed the body if it were to come in sooner?*

A: It may have short circuited some of the necessary functions in the body. The electrical circuits – the electrical charges within the body – could be burned out or distorted, creating dysfunction. The human frame, the human system is very delicate, and there can be great damage done if too much frequency floods the body without preparation.

D: *Too much energy.* (Yes) *So, you said it was only done partially?*

A: Enough to maintain what is called an existence, but not completely in the body and not completely participating.

D: *So, when did you enter fully, or as fully as you can?*

A: The beginning of that was the experience upon the cruise.

During the interview before the session, Anna mentioned a strange experience that occurred while she was at sea during a cruise. She said she went out on the balcony of her stateroom, and felt as though she left her body. Afterwards, she felt like she became a different person. She wondered whether a walk-in had occurred that night.

D: *So we are speaking about the body of Anna that you are speaking through right now.* (Yes) *Why was that particular time chosen?*

A: She was away from all influences that would have prevented or identified her with her past. She was in a plasmic field that one calls "the oceans", and it was easy to make the transference.

D: *She said she had a strange feeling that something happened at that time.*

A: There have been some memories given to her, to help her understand the change that happened.

D: *But it is not what we consider to be a walk-in?*

A: It is not.

D: *I don't know if you have a name for this, but it is like you've always been there, but not all the way. Is that correct?*

A: That is correct. It's a transference of consciousness. A

transference of identity that has been moved into the body. And again, because of the fragility of the body mind, as it must function within the planetary field, it has had to be done very gently and gradually. The times that it was done too suddenly, there was a threat of overload; of despair of two realities overlapping. The mind begins to see flashes and visions of other realities that are carried from the five suns, particularly in this body.

D: *She said she has flashes of memories, and she didn't understand where they were coming from.*

A: Very clearly. And they have had to be gently downloaded until this time to begin to understand that she has access to that other world and the knowledge.

D: *Is it alright if she has the knowledge now?* (Yes) *That's why she was allowed to come here?* (Yes) *She said she had the feeling that something else was inside her looking out of her eyes. Is that you?*

A: Yes, it is the consciousness from the golden world – from the world of five suns.

D: *And she also has the feeling she's reporting back in some way.*

A: She is.

D: *Because it's always been your function to report back.* (Yes) *But much of this has been very confusing to her.*

A: We understand that, but we have not been able to have her know, because she has had to deal with human elements; karmic elements of the body that had to be cleared up.

D: *She feels there's something she needs to be doing.*

A: It is important that she knows that she has access to this knowledge; this is the first thing. The second is for her to not be distressed when I take over her eye vision to report. There are certain times when she gets the message to open up the channel. There are times when she is distracted and I must step in, and then she is aware of a third party.

D: *Now that she understands, it will be easier to handle, won't*

610

it? The hard part is not knowing.

A: It will be very easy for her. In fact, she enjoys reporting; she enjoys participating. It is in that reporting that she will then get the information necessary as to what actions to take and where to go and who to interact with.

D: *Is there any certain work you want her to do?*

A: She must be with people. It is her time to walk out there and to spread what she knows. To speak and be heard.

D: *Will people listen to her?*

A: They will listen as long as she comes from her heart. We will not give her information that is so foreign that it will put her in danger. She is here to help the inhabitants who are listening to understand that it is time for a change. That the ethers that hold the distortions do not have to be the ethers they feed off. There is a parallel ether that is available. There is a parallel atmosphere of consciousness that is available. And there is a choice of which atmosphere to feed off, because each atmosphere has a matrix of thought that is vital to the longevity of the race. One atmosphere is detrimental to evolution. The other atmosphere involves greatness. Interdimensional-intergalactic quantum knowledge that is starting to permeate into this world. Her journey has always been to be a traveler, and she is no different here, even though she is in body. One thing she has had to understand is the potency of the ether of *fear*, because one cannot combat the ether of fear if one does not know its many faces.

D: *Anna said she even felt suicidal at times. She wanted to get out of here.*

A: When she hooks into the wrong ether – to the dark ether; to the fear ether – then it shuts down her circuits of communication. And we very often have to step in to be able to rebalance her, but there have been times it has been a challenge even getting in.

D: *Because she says she feels this is not home. She doesn't want to be here. And I've heard that many times.*

611

A: There is a resistance to this frequency. She understands more now, that it is not the natural frequency that she resonates at. But it is a short-term mission – short-term from our end – even though it is long-term from her perspective of time in this reality. Here the time perspective is sluggish. It is slow and it is very heavy.

D: *This is one of the reasons she felt empty, as though she didn't belong here.*

A: Belonging is an interesting concept. There is, in a sense, no such thing as *belonging*. When one is unified, then the word "belonging", the concept of belonging is a misnomer, because one is all. All the knowledge; all the experience. One is connected. One only needs to belong when they feel alien and foreign. When she moves into the knowingness of her connection, then *belonging* is unnecessary.

Anna had never married, and felt that she never should. I asked for an explanation.

A: She is fearful of getting more caught up in emotional entrapment. It is important for her to understand that the fear is not the ether that she needs to feed off. When she thinks of what is called "marriage", there are two, if you could call it, "timelines" – two choices – and both have very different realities. She is looking at the wrong ether. If the choice is from the more dense ether, then marriage holds death for her. Marriage holds entrapment for her. There is a fear in that reality of a permeation, of entrapment, of giving her power away to a modality – to a matrix – that has been set in motion in this human race for a long time. And she would be buying into all the weight and the heaviness of that particular ether. The other ether is one of lightness of companionship. Of understanding that this entity is like her; is one of us; is family from another realm – another plane. That the love they share is of spirit, and it is *that* that she must feed off and that

612

which has longevity. It has joy; and it has her walking her purpose here. It is a friendship of timelessness with this entity to assist her and help her. And in that, there is no fear. There is much joy; there is much service; and there is much camaraderie. She needs a playmate. It has been a long, heavy journey for her.

D: *You've been talking about the two levels of ether. Is this the equivalent of what I have been getting about the Old Earth and the New Earth?* (Yes) *That the Old Earth is the one with the figment of fear and all the disasters.*

A: The Old Earth is going. It is almost like a black hole. It is collapsing in on itself. It is dismal. It is corrupted. It is the Old Earth. It is very pain-filled: the skies, the ethers, the atmosphere cries in the Old Earth. There is much pain. Some of the New Earth is modeled on the golden planet with the five suns. But there are many worlds that are contributing knowledge, images, resources to the New Earth. It is a haven. It is a jewel. It is easy for Anna to access that frequency, because she has been receiving images of it. She knows it is real. She has not understood that it is a quantum heartbeat from where she is. – It is good that she knows that I am here. It is good that she knows and remembers the golden planet with the five suns. That she understands that this is a progression. That she has come here at this time for a specific purpose and that it is vitally important for her to hold the New Earth – the other ether, the light ether – in her mind. And allow the images from that to start permeating and dissolving the old images.

CHAPTER THIRTY-SIX

TRAVELER OF WORLDS

When Jeannie came off the cloud, she went into a scene of destruction and chaos. "I see a sun, but it's bright orange. It's clouded over with something bad. There's something boiling up from the earth. Something covering the sun. It's really bad. It's so scary. I think it's going to kill people. It makes my heart race. A lot of confusion, and people dying, and the earth breaking and ... and fear, power. All of these things caused a terrible cataclysmic ... it changed life for me as I knew it."

D: *So something very negative happened to the place where you live?*

J: Yes. (Pause) I am *so* sad. People abusing power. You can't take power and abuse it. It's only on loan to you. You just use it.

D: *What happened to create this?*

J: They learned how to control, we all learned how to control. We communicated in our minds, and we learned how to build and raise heavy stuff. And before long, people began to abuse *people* with their powers, because some were stronger than others.

D: *You mean they began to use their mind powers in a negative way?*

J: Yes. It was awful.

D: *What eventually caused this catastrophe?*

J: I'm not clear, because it had to do with the abuse of power, and it trickled into the soil, or the earth. And it trickled into the interior and it just built up and broke apart.

D: *Was it something you were involved with?*

J: No, no! I was involved in the research and the scientific

614

understanding of what we had discovered with our minds and teaching the people. I would never abuse it. It's only a gift.

D: *Could you do anything about it?*

J: No, there were too many of them. I just had to stand back and watch it happen. They couldn't control it. Then they all became really afraid and scared, and screamed. And came to me and asked me, "Stop it! Stop it! Can you help?!"

D: *Was there anything you could do at that point?*

J: No, it was way too late. I saw it coming and I tried to teach them better, but they wouldn't listen. They felt bigger and stronger and more powerful. I just have deep sorrow in my heart. (Pause) It shouldn't have happened. – This is confusing, because I was there when the chaotic part began. But somehow now, I'm looking down at it, like I'm floating above it.

D: *Where were you when it began to happen?*

J: I got in something and flew away. We could see this was going to occur over time, and that they were going in the wrong direction. We went to that place to teach them how to use their awareness for good, but they became so power hungry that they destroyed themselves. And so we built a craft in secret, in case of emergency to leave with, because we had to save the ones that were not abusing the power.

D: *How is the craft powered?*

J: Oh, with our minds. – That wasn't my home. I was sent there to teach. I don't know how I got there. I just know how I left. Ohhh! Ohhh! I projected myself! When I came, I projected myself there! But because I had to go so far, then I built my craft to leave.

D: *Weren't you able to project yourself back again?*

J: No, because I was going to go even further out. This is what I do. I have knowledge that helps people live their lives better.

D: *But in this case, they wouldn't listen?*

J: No, it was a failed mission. I had to build the craft because I could project myself, but the others couldn't. These were some that were very kind, and some that were not abusing their new-found powers.

D: *Do you have a physical body in that place?*

J: Yes, but it's ... it's different. It's long and narrow. It's a body, but it's *not* a body. It's more like an electromagnetic field.

D: *Different from the other people there?*

J: Yes. I have to be different because I couldn't have projected myself there.

D: *Do they perceive you as different or strange?*

J: No, I make myself look like them. I know all about that. I've done that a lot. You can't make people listen to you and get help if they're afraid of you. I tried to help, but they wouldn't listen. It made me feel so sad.

D: *But you got everyone you could on board the craft to go to safety somewhere?*

J: Just to go on to our next mission: to teach new people. I am taking these others with me because they were good of heart.

D: *Then what happened? You said you were up above watching everything down below.*

J: It was so bad. There was red dust all over, and the sun was covered. It was even floating way up where we were.

D: *What else did you see down there?*

J: It looked like it was coming from the edges into the center, and just going down in a hole. It was rolling like a donut in from the outside to the inside. The planet folded up in itself.

D: *That's kind of strange, isn't it?*

J: No, when it's a failed mission like that, it implodes.

D: *What happens then?*

J: I have a whole plan over time, and what I'm supposed to be teaching these different creatures. Some are creatures. And so, because I'm an electromagnetic field, I just change and look like they look. I don't know where I learned that. I've always done that. It's kind of tricky though. I try not to let other people see because they think I'm pretty weird.

D: *This would scare them if they knew?*

J: Yes, because only certain people can do that. I think they came from where I came from. Maybe we all learned that in our youth. I don't know. I just know it's fearful to teach somebody if you are different, so you have to be able to look like them.

D: *That would make sense. But when you're back where you came from, what does your normal body look like?*

J: It's red, and ... oh, boy! It even looks strange to me! I'm really bright red! And I'm really big. It's not an insect. It'd be like a regular body, but it has ... protrusions ... wow! That person could be a grasshopper! It's hard to explain. But it's kind of unusual looking – certainly the color is.

D: *On your home planet, do you need to change your form?*

J: Oh, we can be anything we want. We go around playing jokes on each other. We all can do it.

D: *And then you were told to go and help other people?*

J: I was given the mission to reach out to all the universes. And told that I would be gone a long, long time because I was to help these people become better.

D: *That sounds like a big mission.*

J: Yes, I was pretty surprised. So I go from place to place, and when I get to the new place, I change my form to blend in. But each place is different.

D: *Well, this time when you're in your craft and you're going off, where do you go?*

J: I go to a planet with all yellow looking people. This is a place I haven't been before. So now I'm buttercup yellow.

D: *(Laugh) What about the other people that you brought with you?*

J: They're a little upset, because I've already shown them how to do this, and they can't quite do it yet. So they're hanging back. And I said, "I'll go out first and wait for you, and you can do it." And I showed them how to do it. – Oh, and they're coming out, but they did something wrong. And they're all little short, yellow – they're way too short! Oh, I don't know what they did! I'm going to have to take them back up there! They shrunk themselves so tiny! Oh, that's so funny! I didn't even know you could shrink yourself that tiny!

D: *(Laugh) Do the buttercup yellow people look like humanoids?*

J: They have large eyes and smooth heads and extra long arms. I've seen these kinds of people before, but not yellow. – So I told them to get back up the steps and let's do it again. I'm going to have to stay with them until they get the right size. We're supposed to look *like* them, not *different* from them.

D: *So is that what you did?*

J: They all come out the right size.

D: *Are you planning on staying there for awhile?*

J: I'm tired. I'm tired of training all these people, because something's wrong with the training. Something's not right. I don't understand why. Some understand, and some take it to a new level of power. It's beginning to feel like the red planet.

D: *The one that exploded?*

J: Yes. I'm going to get my people, and we're going to leave now. We're not going to have another failed mission. We'll find a place where we're welcomed and where they're smart enough to "get it". I don't want it to happen again, because that's not what it's about. And that's not what I was told to teach people. It's not right to abuse power. It's a gift.

D: *So you're going to gather them all together and take them somewhere else?*

J: I already got them, the door is closed, we're ready to go. They're all standing around looking confused. I don't care. I'm not going to have a repeat.

D: *So you're not going to try and help these yellow people?*

J: No, they can just do what they want to. I'm not standing around and watching it happen again. We have to get it better. We have to get it straighter. We have to do it different.

D: So now you're going somewhere else?

J: Yes. But the ship's acting up. Gosh! It's vibrating way too much.

D: Is this after you've taken off?

J: Yes. I'm a little worried. It shouldn't be vibrating like this. I don't know if we got dirt or dust or something somewhere it shouldn't be or ... I don't know. I hope nobody did anything to it. I could project myself out, but I can't take the people on the ship with me.

D: Do you think somebody might have done something to it?

J: Well, they were pretty angry about me walking away. I told them, "You listen and do it my way or you cannot do it at all."

D: Let's move time ahead and find out what happens. Did the ship continue to vibrate, or what happens?

J: (Softly) I'm out in the dark. It's just dark.

D: What happened to the ship?

J: I don't know. I'm by myself. I'm not in a ship. I'm here by myself.

D: You can know what happened. You can find out. Was something wrong with the ship?

J: Yes, yes. It broke apart, and I had to project myself out before it disintegrated. The others didn't know how to do that. They had to stay with the ship. Now I'm by myself. And I don't think I can go back, either, because it's another failed mission.

D: Is that what you consider it to be?

J: Yes. If you can't save people, it's a failure.

D: What are you going to do now?

J: I think I'll just stay out here. It's pretty quiet. Maybe I'll rest. I'm very tired.

D: You don't have anyone that tells you to do something?

J: No. When I left my home, I knew that when the decision was made, I was on my own. Somehow, when I left in the beginning, I knew it would be a long time before I had any support, because it was my mission.

D: *So, right now you want to rest. Can you do it out there?*

J: Yes. I just float. It's warm. It's just a new universe. No responsibilities. – Resting even makes me feel dizzy. It's been a long time since I've rested.

D: *Well, let's move ahead and find out what happens to you.*

J: I stay out there many years, because I needed the rest and I needed to replenish myself. Then I decided it was time to teach again. That maybe I have a new perspective on how to accomplish raising vibrational minds.

D: *Where are you going to do this?*

J: I have to make a direction and project myself there. I have great power that way. I wanted to go some place where there is a cave. And in that cave there's information for me that's been placed there. There's a message that was placed there before I started my projects.

D: *Who placed it there?*

J: A great intelligence. – Okay, I'm there. It's so easy to move, if everybody knew how to do this, it would be easier. I see the cave. It's someplace where there's very little water, and it's gray. There's not much life form there.

D: *So you can't help the people there, can you?*

J: No. I'm coming to the cave for my information.

D: *Do you know where to look in the cave?*

J: Yes. It will be in the ceiling. It's dark, and I have to feel. (Pause) Oh! It's on the side, it's not on the ceiling. I have to fix some light on the floor. And now I can see ... It's symbols. Dots, dashes; stuff that I'm familiar with that's very easy to read. But I'm surprised at what it says. It says it's the tree of life.

D: *What does that mean?*

J: It's somehow related to the way you should live. But it's not the way I have lived for many times. It seems to be somewhat different. It's like it's a new way of doing it. Maybe it's the

620

key to why the others collapsed. Maybe. I have to look at it more.

D: *But it's symbols that you can understand?*

J: Yes, but I've never seen it said this way. And some of them go up onto the ceiling. This is a concept ... this is a new way! I wonder why we are doing it a new way? Because the new way is going to be confusing. I have to learn a new way. And I'm not sure. Somehow, I know I have this superior intelligence. And I have nobody to talk to about this to be sure that this new way is the right way. Oh, I think I'm going to get tired again.

D: *Why do you think that?*

J: I just wonder how long it will take us all to learn a new way, only to find out that it's still not the accurate way. I've been doing this for many thousands of years. I feel it sucking me down. I feel like I'm just falling through something.

D: *Did you understand about the new way?*

J: Yes, but it's very different.

D: *Is it positive?*

J: It is if you have enough intelligent people around you.

D: *One person can't do it then, it has to be many?*

J: I think it should be. After all, if we're about saving and teaching, it should be sent to many people. I am tired. It exhausts me to continue to strive to make everything better, only to have people misunderstand and abuse it. I feel like I'm falling down and laying down to rest again. It was a new way and I was excited to read, but I'm not sure that we got it right, yet. Now instead of teaching the people, we're changing their structures.

D: *What do you mean?*

J: We're going into their bodies, into their cells, and rechanging them all, and rewiring them all. This is like doing it all over again. I'm not sure it's forward thinking. (Sigh) Ahh, it just makes me so tired. It's probably a better way, but I don't know if it's a fair way. Do we have the right to go in and change the core being, in order to teach them what we were trying to teach them in the beginning, when they abused the power? I mean, we either are about teaching, or we're about changing the structure of the being. Why didn't we change the structure to begin with, and then when we taught them, they would not abuse it? It's backwards.

D: *Maybe you had to go the first way to see what was going to happen. Maybe that's why this is a new way of looking at it. But you're not the one that makes the rules, are you?*

J: No, I'm not. I'm only the one out there doing it.

D: *Where are you supposed to change the structure? Did you project yourself to another place?*

J: I don't know. It's even different projecting myself this time. It's wavy. I see waves of energy moving, like I'm moving through it. I never saw that before. It feels like *I've* even changed. It's thicker. It's like I'm walking; I'm going through the air but I'm moving. I'm seeing all the energy around me displaced as I move.

D: *Let's move time ahead again. Where do you go this time?*

J: Oh, my God! They sent me – oh, my gosh! Oh! I am in the slowest energy possible. I didn't know I was going to end up there. These people need a lot of awareness. It's slow because they don't know very much. Man! I can't believe this is where I've ended up.

D: *How are you going to teach these people?*

J: I don't know. I have to bring myself to such a level to even be able to communicate with them. I don't know if I can get there. It's not up, it's down! I have to be able to talk at their level, because if I don't, they can't hear me.

D: *Are you going to have to create another body, or how are you going to do it?*

J: I have created another body, but this body is slow moving.

D: *What does the body look like that you have created?*

J: It looks just like the one I have now.

D: *You mean the person called Jeannie?*

J: That would be her! She's really irritated about it, too, I've got to tell you.

D: *But weren't you born as a baby?*

J: I don't think so. I think I just became her.

D: *Didn't her body start out as a baby?*

J: I don't understand the baby part. I just became this woman like I became everybody else, everywhere else.

D: *In our beliefs, we start out as a baby, a fetus growing inside the mother, and the soul enters when the baby is born.*

J: That's not right. No, no, no, no, no! The soul is an electromagnetic field, and the soul moves into the body it wants.

D: *Yes, but doesn't this happen when it's born, when the baby first comes out of the mother?*

J: Well, maybe. I haven't seen that happen. I just know that I took this woman form this time. Which is slow and ... oh, boy!

D: *Was there another electromagnetic field in the body when you took over, or came in, or do you know?*

J: I did it like I do them all.

D: *I thought there was already a spark of life, a life force, in there.*

J: I *was* the life force!

D: *And you just decided to be this female.*

J: Yes. She doesn't have a clue. Personally, I'm not very pleased about being there either. This is a *hard* place to teach anybody. They move slow, they talk slow, they doubt every word they hear.

D: *So, how are you supposed to teach them so you can change things?*

J: By example, but my gosh! I don't know why I came on this mission. I don't have a clue. I don't like this one much.

D: *It's an important one, because these people do need help, don't they?*

J: Oh, yes! It's very confusing. It's all energy, but it moves ever so slowly.

D: *But this woman, the one we call Jeannie, went through a childhood and getting married and having children. Were you there at those times?*

J: No, I skipped that part. (Laugh) That's way slower than I want to be. She does good work with people and she learns fast. But we need to speed this whole thing up. You know, we don't have a whole lot of time. And we need to touch many more people than we're touching.

D: *One on one is slow, isn't it?*

J: Yes, it is. I keep telling her she should be out there talking to large groups of people. She can do this, but because of the energy being slow, she doesn't believe she has that much to tell anybody, anyway. And I keep telling her, "Just do it!" – We have to move on. I've given her all this capability. She has many things she can do. It's not that she questions it. She does everything I tell her to do, but there's something confusing about this slow energy.

Jeannie does Reiki and energy healing on people. I asked this entity if it could explain some strange things that had been happening to Jeannie when she was doing her healing work. While she was working on people, orbs, balls of light of different sizes, appeared in the room.

J: They're just more electromagnetic fields. We're all electromagnetic fields. I mean, we can be just pieces of energy or we can be in the bodies, or we can look like grasshoppers. It's all energy, and these are energies that are there to facilitate speeding up this healing process that she insists on doing. Her work is very good.

D: *So these are other energies that come to help?*

J: Yes. Mostly they're hers, but she thinks it's the client's. And I let her think that because she's pretty headstrong.

D: *They're her little energies that have split off, you mean?*

(Yes) *How can she use that extra energy?*

J: She should be able to learn how to bring it all in and reunite it. A long time ago when I used to project myself into these places, I had all my energy. I was all one. And somehow I could do that, but she doesn't know how to do that. How to organize it and put it together. She needs to be able to bring it in right here. (The solar plexus area.) When she sees the orbs, she needs to gather that energy and suck it in. That's the way she'd have to do it. I could just do it. She has to do it the slow way.

Jeannie had been seeing glowing six-sided geometric figures that she had been able to photograph. She wanted to know about them.

J: They are to expand her mind. First of all, she knows there's something in the middle of those, but those are just messages. She should recognize them. It's like the ones in the cave. If she would recognize those, it would be more about that tree of life thing; concepts. If she understood, she could transport herself anywhere she wants to be and we wouldn't have to be doing this slow energy. I don't know how she stands it.

D: *As humans, that's the only thing we know. That's the problem. You said you wanted her to understand these six-sided figures.*

J: It's part of the healing process. It's advanced theory on healing. If she reads the symbols, she will know how to enhance people's healing. But it will allow her to move. If she wants to, she can leave.

D: *But if she learns how to go from place to place that quickly, it would be a little surprising to people.*

J: Oh, yes. As usual, they wouldn't like it if it's different. I work with her every night and try to teach her, because she listens when she is resting. She's being given instructions not only to guide her in her work, but instructions on how to transport like I used to do. Because there will be a time when this information will be in danger again. So we want her to be able to change and get back out. She needs to be able to leave if she has to. She has valuable information. When she sees these symbols, the information will go to another part of her mind and be absorbed. And at the right time, she will automatically do it without thinking. She ought to be practicing more about leaving and coming back, and leaving and coming back. She knows she can do this. She's taken it right to the edge. She doesn't realize she can pop right back. She knows she can go the other way. And I keep telling her, "You can come back the same – if you can go in, you can go out!" She consciously now sees the opening to the next dimension. And I say, "Jeannie, step across it. You can turn around and step right back through it." She has to trust that she can step back into it. She knows she can go across, but I have not been able to instill in her that she *can* step back, and return.

D: *She does this at night when she's sleeping?*

J: Yes. She's frustrated, because she's beginning to feel the way I felt with all those failures of people's abuse of power. She's holding back, and I don't know why, because it's all there. We have given her everything. She's very, very powerful. But she's worried about people noticing her being different. We have to move things forward again. The energy has been stagnant too long. It all has to do with raising the vibrations and frequencies. And the more we come collectively together, the higher vibrational rates affect and project out through the atmosphere. I raised them two months ago and she almost shook off the massage table, and made me laugh. I won't raise them as fast as I did then, because she really did shake and started to fall off the table when I had to push her back on.

D: *(Laugh) Does she have to be asleep or meditating to do this?*

J: No, she has the ability to just sit down and do it. She's been around forever and ever and ever, and should not have even come to this slow moving energy. – Humans will realize that they, in fact, are part of the God force. Once they become the light that they are in their consciousness, humans can dissemble their molecules. There is very little reason to reassemble the molecules into gross, dense physical form. Once disassembled, to reassemble means that you have to go *back* in some way. Carrying around a heavy body in space just wouldn't really work.

We didn't need to see past lives, because they would have been associated with the original Jeannie, not the entity that was in the body now. These would have occurred before the entity I was speaking to came in. Another part of her could have had the other lives. "Yes, we're all living our lives concurrently right now."

JOURNEY TO EARTH

Another example of an unusual energy came through during one of my hypnosis classes in 2007. I always wonder what some of the students think when this type of information comes through. When they are gathered around the bed observing my demonstration, they are expecting a normal past life. At least they are being shown that this type of therapy is never dull, and the unexpected becomes the norm.

Francis found herself sitting on the sandy shore of an ocean. It was night and a quarter moon glittered as it reflected in the water. She knew there were trees around, but it was too dark to see them. She saw that she was a young female wearing a gauzy yellow dress. Her red hair was hanging loose with flowers in it. She was wearing a necklace with a green stone. When I asked whether she was young or old, she gave a strange answer. "It's different. It's in a younger body, yet there is a lot of age that I feel. I don't look old, but I don't really feel young. I look like I'm about twenty or twenty-four, but I'm a lot older. I'm about a hundred years old, older than that even." She was part of a group who lived in dwellings spread out among the trees. Some of the group were very tall. She said she was very small. This was her favorite spot to come and sit by the ocean at night.

She suddenly announced, "I just saw something. It's sparkly. I'm walking down to the water, and I see my reflection. There's something sparkling behind me." She laughed, "They're wings!" I didn't know what type of being I was speaking to, so I continued to ask questions. She said there were others who were small like she was, but only some had glittery things on their back. Their dwellings were all different sizes, and made from things found in nature: rocks, trees, grass. I asked if she had a family. "Yes, they're all my family, because we're all the same in a way. We're all family, but I live alone." I wondered if they had husbands and wives. "No. It's hard to explain. Yes, there are parents. It's more of a community type of living. You do have parents and family, but they're all together. They're all part of each other. My group is sort of a sisterhood, a group of women. We use guidance energy. It's a way of life – listening to the trees and stones."

D: *Does this group you're with live by themselves, isolated?*
F: It doesn't feel isolated.
D: *I was wondering if you have contact with any other groups.*
F: Oh, yes. Everyone is different. There are different ... *tribe* is the wrong word.
D: *I guess* group *is better.*
F: Yes, but they're both not right.
D: *What does the group do?*

F: They're caretakers. The word *guardians* comes to mind.

D: *The caretakers of what?*

F: Everything. All that's around them: the people and the beings and the energies that exist there.

D: *It sounds like a big job!*

F: Not so, there are very many people that are a part of this.

D: *Well, it sounds like a good life. Do you like it there?*

F: Yes, I do. I like it. I love it there! It's my home. – But I feel some sadness. I'm contemplating. I've been asked if I'd be willing to leave. There's a man and a woman. They asked me if I would be willing to leave. There's information – there's knowledge that needs to be gathered. I seem to enjoy gathering information. That's why they asked me.

D: *You can't do it where you are?*

F: I can continue to gather information there, and continue what I do. There's more information that they want that the collective ... people there would benefit from.

D: *Where do they want you to go?*

F: I'm not sure yet. They first want me to be really clear on the choice.

D: *How do you feel about it? You said you were contemplating.*

F: It's why I went to the ocean. The choice, I feel, is being made within. There's a part of me, I feel, that knows that's what I'm to do. A part of me knows that it's away from home. That it's on a different planet even. It's not anywhere near. That's what saddens me. If I choose to leave, it will be for a long time.

D: *Do they think it's important that you do this?*

F: Oh, yes, they would not have asked me to leave.

D: *Why do they think it's important to go and gather more information?*

F: For growth, for connection. It's reaching out and knowing more.

I moved her ahead in time to see what her decision would be.

F: I decided to go.

D: *Even though it's going to be hard.* (Yes) *How are you going to do this? Have they told you?*

F: I'm trying to find the right words. There's a very advanced way of doing something like this. It's not a death as much as a separation from the body, that I will be needing. There will be someone who has spent his lifetime reading the stars and gathering information. There's a woman there who understands the separation. Separating the soul from the body I'm in now.

D: *What happens to the body if you're going to separate from it?*

F: There's another ... (She searched for the words.) It's a part of me, I believe. It feels like there is something going to enter the body as I leave it, that is also connected to me. Almost like it will continue on there with a new understanding.

D: *So it will continue living even though you separate from it.* (Yes) *What happens when you separate from it?*

F: This is all done outdoors. It's like a room with no roof; it's open to the sky. The man there that understands the stars is going to guide me through a tunnel, some kind of passageway. Where I will be told and informed of where I'll be going and what I'll be doing.

D: *That way you're not alone when you make this journey. What does the tunnel look like?*

F: It's like an expansion of time ... expanding our awareness of time, and allowing the soul to move through it. The man has done this himself. He learned the technique many years ago, before I was ever asked to do this. There's been quite a bit of planning. I'm the first to go.

D: *So you're like a pioneer.* (Yes) *What happens as he takes you?*

F: The two of us are lying down together on a stone. I can smell some of the flowers and plants and stones all around us.

They're all giving off an essence to assist in the separation of the body. I feel myself lifting out. He has my ... it sounds funny to say *hand* when you're not in a body, but there's a connection there as we're touching each other. I enter the time space he has created, and there's just a really quick *whoosh* of time and many bright colors like a circular tunnel, in a way. And then it stops.

D: *Where does it come out?*

F: In a big beautiful room. I can see a building of marble and stones and crystals. We're standing outside the door looking in. They're expecting us. They're going to tell me where they would like me to go. First, they thank me for coming. They understand how difficult it was for me to leave.

D: *Do they give you a choice, or do they tell you what you have to do?*

F: There is choice, but there's no choice in where I'm going. They're sending me to Earth. They're sending me far; very far out.

D: *Have they shown you what it will be like?*

F: I don't get to see everything that it will be like. Some points are shown to me, yes. They say if they tell me too much, it would make it difficult for me. It would impair me to gather the information. There's a very grand sense of love that I feel towards them, and that they feel to me.

D: *So you trust whatever their decision is.*

F: Yes, I do. There is an agreement. There is a contract, if you will, that there will always be guidance and support there. But that there will be much hardship and difficulties before I return.

D: *What do you think about that?*

F: (Emotional) I have mixed emotions. (She began to cry.) I miss my home already. It's a very, very strong sense of service that I feel. I know that where I'm going is in so much need. My being there will have very much value.

D: *Do they agree that it's to get information?*

631

F: To them there is more purpose than that. Harmony; balance; again: connection; bringing – I would say, my awareness; my essence – to where I'm going.

D: *Let's condense time and see where you go.*

F: Earth is the destination. There's another stop. It's like a collection; there are others gathering. There are more people coming. The man is saying good-bye. He gives me a gift before he leaves. (She became emotional.) It's a light. A small round light. And he says to me, "This light will always show you the way back."

D: *So you will never be lost. You will always have a way to go home. That's beautiful. – Do you go to Earth?*

F: No, not yet. There's a waiting period there. There's a gathering. There are more people – we all go together. – I can see the Earth now. There are dimensional levels that I am having an awareness of. The level that I sense that I am on – the number that comes to mind – is seven. There is a planning of how to accomplish what we gather to accomplish. How will we do this? We've all been chosen based on where we're from, being very gifted in some sense. Collectively, it's a very balanced energy.

D: *So everything is very planned out. Where do you have to go? What do you see?*

F: I'm going to be born. The place I'm going to is very, very different than what I'm used to. It's very difficult to explain. There's a very different energy. It's heavier. I feel heavier. There *is* a birth process in the place where I am from, but it's not like this one. (Becoming emotional.) It's not like this one. I am born to a couple. They have waited very, very, very long for a child.

D: *Did you enter the body after it was born, or before it was born?*

F: I'm seeing, before you asked me what happened when I was born, I could see me in their space – not in the body – I am observing them. I am learning about them, and why they

632

were chosen for me to come through. The birth process would have been too shocking to me without this preparation.

So she was now here on Earth and ready to do her job. The description of her parents did not sound like her present life as Francis. I didn't see any point in taking her through the life. So I called forth the subconscious to explain this. "Why did you pick this one? It was a little unusual."

F: She needed to remember where she's from and who she is. That's her home. She's ready to remember. It's time. She's waited a long time. She's ready to bring it to a close. She's ready to go back. This is her last life here.

D: *The birth we saw was not this body as Francis, was it?*

F: No, no. That was the first life she entered on this Earth. She has since experienced hundreds of lives here.

D: *But you think it's time now to wind it up?*

F: Yes. There is a culmination that she's understanding. Bringing together everything she's experienced, so she can understand this life. Why she came here, and what she came to do.

Francis had experienced a difficult life in her present one, but the subconscious said it was easier compared to some of the other ones she had. There had been many problems with relationships.

D: *At the present time she's in kind of a love/hate relationship.*

F: Interesting that she should say that, because that is the most paramount paradox about relationship experiences. She just recently realized that love and hate are the same vibration.

D: *They are?*

F: Yes. Certainly not in the same energy, but the vibration that is felt – the intensity – is very much the same. That is why it is so easy to love someone so deeply. It's the hurt and the pain that transfers that energy into the hate, the resentment,

633

the different energies that are fear-based.

D: *They are both very strong emotions.*

F: The heart is the emotion center. Just as the brain is the thought center of the body, the heart is the emotion center of the body – for the person's life. The emotions are all run through the heart, just like the thoughts are run through the brain.

The rest of the session centered around Francis' personal questions. It seemed that I had found another type of unusual energy that had been sent to Earth. This one was not new to Earth, she had experienced many lifetimes and gone through much difficulty. She apparently did not come directly from the Source like many of the others. She had come from a place of beauty and peace, where they lived extremely long lives. Was she a nature spirit? One of the little people? It is hard to say, because she was a normal lifeform on the planet where she lived. Yet she was asked to come (with many others) to help Earth. Her energy was needed, and she agreed and made the journey. Apparently she would not be staying and going on to the New Earth, because her tour of duty was over. This was her last life on Earth. She had accomplished what she came to do, and it was time to allow her to return home to her beautiful place. She said she was sad in the beginning, because they told her if she agreed to come, it would be a very long time before she could return.

So it appears that I am discovering a kaleidoscope of souls and energies who have come to experience life on this difficult and challenging planet. In the beginning of my work it all seemed so simple. Now I am finding there is no limit to the variety of spirits that can inhabit the human body. They have come from so many strange and unusual places, yet they seem to have one goal in common. To help the people of Earth. To keep our planet from self-destructing. They come with love and caring. We have to all get back to that simple goal that we had when we first ventured here. Before our memories were erased.

CHAPTER THIRTY-SEVEN

THE HEALING ENERGY SPEAKS

It is strange how we become so engrossed in our own reality and our own little world that we cannot conceive of the possibility of other worlds and other realities that defy the imagination. They are so far removed from our belief systems that we have to develop a whole new mind set just to be able to comprehend them. And yet, no matter how inconceivable they are, I have been told that we can never have all the answers. Some information would be as poison rather than medicine. Our minds would be totally overwhelmed and be unable to function, because there is nothing in our minds to base some of these concepts on. I was told it is not a problem with our brains, but our minds. Thus, no matter how strange and unbelievable these sessions are, I must still remember they are only the surface of what the person is trying to relate, because the words to describe the event do not exist in our vocabulary and our reality. So realize that the person is doing the best they can to report something that is totally alien to their mind. This is the reason I often ask for analogies. And then I am told that even those are woefully incompetent to convey the true meaning of the memory or experience. So while you read this book, please suspend reality. Do not expect it all to make sense or to be rationally explained. Enter the world where our dreams are real, and our reality is but a dream. That is probably the only way we can even begin to grasp what they are trying to relate. So for a while, suspend reality and rationality as we journey into the world of the unknown and unexplainable.

When Patricia entered the scene, it was eerily beautiful. She saw a white iridescent landscape that shimmered like mercury. There were colors moving in and out: pinkish, bluish and greenish tints. The sky was also shimmery blue and white, and the surface and sky melded together. When I asked her to see her body, she was surprised that she looked like a snowball. "A *big* sparkly snow white snowball. It fluctuates. It moves. It's not solid. The size and shape of it changes. Basically, it's ball shaped, but it's not a ball. It moves like a sea, or a moving in water. Light, but shimmery silver. Gossamer. It's beautiful." She then became emotional, "It makes me want to cry. It's home! (A deep sigh) It's good to be there." I am hearing this so often now, it is the norm rather than the unexpected.

D: *Have you been gone a long time?*
P: (Still emotional) An awful long time.
D: *Why did you leave if it was such a good place?*
P: I had to go somewhere else.

I was still trying to determine where and what she was. There were no buildings, no structures, because they were unnecessary. She did not need to consume anything. "Whatever you need, it's as though it's absorbed into you with no effort. It's part of the atmosphere, I would say. There's no need or want, or struggle. It's happy there." She was now aware that there were others there like herself. "It's a form, but it moves in and out. Beautiful, shimmery. It's almost like it changes shape ... with breath. With respiration. A pulsing movement. It's *very* easy. There's no struggle."

D: *Is the place or the body physical?*
P: As in a human form? No. Yes, there's substance to them, but they're not solid. I think of solid as more dense. There is much movement, like molecules floating free form. They flow easily to what they actually would like to be.

636

D: But it's different than a spirit? That's what I am trying to distinguish.

P: Yes, I would say so. It is a basic round shape, but it undulates. It moves. And we can merge, to communicate. Just for the experience. Going in and then coming out. It is how we communicate. It's just a different way. It's kind of like clay. You have free will to do whatever you want to do, however you want to do it. And everybody just experiences it.

D: Is there anything you're required to do there?

P: I see it more as a resting place. A place where you come to restore yourself, before you have to go out again. You don't *have* to do anything. Just be.

D: Have you been in a physical existence before you came here?

P: Before I came here, I was somewhere else helping. I assume whatever shape I need to be wherever I want. But this feels so good. It's so free.

D: When you're in a physical shape, that's different, isn't it?

P: Yes, it's very restrictive. It's very limiting. It's work to stay in a form, a shape. Where I am now, you're just free to be "however". This is what I know. I know this experience. And then to take on a form, say, a *body* form. That's so restrictive. There's not as much freedom of movement. There's just not much freedom. This is *home*.

D: So when you're there, you don't have to do anything.

P: We do things. It's just, there's no *have* to. And everybody works together as a body. But really more energy than a body. It's a very agreeable place.

D: What do you do when you're there?

P: Explore. Create.

D: Where do you explore?

P: Where we are. We can go out, like on little side trips, but we come back. This is "home". Not Earth. Just to explore.

D: Where do you go on the side trips?

P: Other bodies of light. All around. Where there is light.

Explore the universe, wherever. No restrictions.

D: You said you also create?

P: Yes. We can make our home look however we want it to. And we do that based on our experiences, when we've left to do our job, to help. And we can do it just for fun. There's music.

D: You mean you create an environment?

P: Yes. And we can do whatever color, out of whatever material. But mostly we like to just be. There is music and lots of color. It's soft, pastel, shimmery color. Nothing's garish there.

D: Where does the music come from?

P: The movement of our body. Sort of, as you would think, an accordion pushing in and out. It's kind of like bellows or something. And it creates sound. I hear bells too.

D: It sounds like a beautiful place. I can see why you really like to be there. – And you said, sometimes you have to go out again somewhere?

P: It's our joy to do that, but it's our job, too. We don't choose to stay there forever, because there are things we can do to help.

D: Is there anyone that tells you what you have to do, and where you have to go?

P: Not really. When we join and kind of blend together, it becomes, I guess, a group decision. The energies join together and you come out with a direction. Where to go. What to do.

D: Then you all work together?

P: Not necessarily, no. But the All helps the one determine what would be best for all.

D: Then eventually, you do have to go someplace and help?

P: There's no *have* to. You don't have to go. But we feel a responsibility, because we go places and raise energy in places that need it.

D: Places where the energy is too low, or ....

P: And dense, yes. Earth would be a place.

D: *Have you been there before?*

P: Many times. The energy is very dense. But we go and we create pockets of energy. And just by being there, it raises the frequency.

D: *Do you have to be in a physical body when you're there?*

P: No, we can do it either way. If it serves the purpose, we can become a form; a human form, animal form. We can also exist there as the air.

D: *So if you feel the need to go and just raise the energy of a certain area?*

P: We go, yes.

D: *You said, pockets of energy?* (Yes.) *How do you do that?*

P: Just the same bellows thing I was telling you about. Going in and coming out, in this energy shape. It's kind of a rhythmic pulsation. And it lifts the vibration.

D: *Do you become part of that energy when you're working with it?*

P: I *am* the energy.

D: *When you go into this denser energy?*

P: I remain the energy. I can remain as I am at home, if I choose. If that serves the purpose better. Or I can go into a form of a body, an animal, a tree. Whatever would serve the purpose of raising the energy and trying to dissipate the density.

D: *Is it easier to do it in a form?*

P: It's more difficult. There's the restriction of the form. Because the energy's increased and produced by this in and out pulsation, without restrictions or limitations *of* the form. Then you do it on a much lower scale.

D: *Then why would you choose to enter a form?*

P: That's a good question, because it is more difficult. But maybe it's easier to go into a certain area in a form shape. People don't really recognize us, per se, as a form, as a shape. But *some* recognize the energy. So it's easier to take a form

639

when you're going into dense space, dense people. It's easier for them to receive the energy, but it's so sticky and thick and dense. But not being in a body, just being the shape, this energy, it goes in and stirs it up and gets movement. That's very, very important. But it's much easier for people to accept the energy when we take a shape.

D: *And you can communicate much easier with the physical too.*

P: It's easier for them. It's more difficult for me.

D: *Do you have to enter the form as a baby?*

P: No. I can go into any existing form and use it.

D: *Is that allowed?*

P: You ask permission.

D: *That's what I was thinking. There may already be a spirit within the ....*

P: This is not a spirit. This is energy.

D: *It's different than a spirit?*

P: It's different. But you do ask permission, because the energy changes things.

D: *So it's not like an invasion.*

P: Oh, absolutely not! No.

D: *Do you have to ask the occupying spirit for permission?*

P: Yes, in essence it's a matter of making the spirit aware that we are coming in. We are not detrimental. We're not harmful. It's as though the spirit and the energy have an understanding. They're aware of each other. And it's all right. It's like when you're given permission to come into someone's home. They'd say, "Come on in and get a drink of water if you want it. It's okay. It's fine." It's kind of an agreement. But you show courtesy by knocking on the door and saying, "Hey, I'm here."

D: *So you wouldn't remain in the body.*

P: No, no. It's a temporary thing. It's a means of bringing the energy, to help the person or the situation. Whatever it might be.

D: *Does the physical person have to ask for this to happen?*

P: No. But I would imagine if they create the situation and the environment there, it would be helpful for us to come in. But it doesn't have to be a conscious choice.

D: *Do they* feel *anything when you do this?*

P: I think they do, yes. It feels like a lightness of spirit. It's a very uplifting experience. And it's as though it provides this person with the energy to do something or to be something, and try to accomplish something.

D: *They need a little extra boost.* (Yes) *So they are aware that something is going on, even if they're not sure exactly what. Well, do you ever feel the need to* become *a physical body?*

P: No, no, I don't. We come and go. We don't become a permanent part of the body. We're here to assist as is needed.

D: *Have you ever had an existence like a spirit would have? I'm just trying to distinguish the difference.*

P: Well, I am a spirit body, a light spirit. You mean, have I gone some place and lived as a spirit in a body or something?

D: *Yes, in a physical body. (Long pause, as though she was thinking.) Or is this the form you have always had, just as an energy?*

P: Yes, I think that's true, because the other doesn't sound familiar.

Just what was I speaking to? If it was not the spirit that occupied Patricia's body, then what was it?

D: *So all of your existence has been helping.* (Yes) *You go to bodies that need that, and uplift them.*

P: Yes. They can be in the animal and plant kingdom as well. Or it can be a whole area, or a whole space. A whole section that would include people, animals, and plants.

D: *Oh, so you could expand?*

P: Absolutely, yes. We have no restrictions.

D: *So you don't want to be restricted by staying in a body all the time.* (No) *Just in and out. That's interesting, because I wasn't aware that your type existed. I guess I always think of spirits.*

P: Right, we exist, but that isn't our job to assist the spirit. The spirit does its thing. We do ours. (Laugh) We're very aware of the spirit. Very aware.

D: *But the spirit, more or less, gets trapped and has to stay with the body? If that's the right term.*

P: Yes, like an assignment.

D: *They have an assignment to stay with that body the whole term of its life?*

P: Yes, I believe that's the agreement.

D: *And you can come and go.*

P: Yes. And it's possible the spirit knows to ask for us, if it thinks the person, the physical body would need it.

D: *People can be very complicated.*

P: Yes, they make it so.

D: *So the spirit knows more about what the body needs.* (Yes) *And I guess you don't have to be involved in that part.*

P: I don't have to stick around. (Laugh) I'm a happy repairman.

She said she not only worked with the individual who needed a little boost of energy, but also with large areas. I assumed that many of these areas, especially on Earth, would have very heavy negative energy.

P: We go to many areas like that. It's very difficult, but we do. Part of it is extremely dense and chaotic energy.

D: *It doesn't bother you. You won't get caught up in that.*

P: No, it doesn't impact me. I know full well why I am there. It is more of a challenge in those areas, just due to the chaos energy, and the density. The low vibration. So that makes it more of a challenge. But it certainly can be done.

D: *You can't get caught up and get lost in that kind of energy?*

P: I haven't. I don't believe that. I don't think it is possible, because we would need to be available for other ... duties, so to speak. We could not be absorbed into that. That's not part of how we operate, no. Many of us are called there.

D: *Are you aware that you're speaking through a physical body to me at this time?* (Pause) *Or are you aware of that?*

P: I believe I am, *now*.

D: *You weren't before.*

P: I didn't think of it.

D: *Because that's how we're communicating.*

P: I see. Okay. That's good. I thought we were just talking. (Chuckle)

D: *But now you can be aware that I'm speaking to someone that's in a physical body, and you're communicating through them.* (Yes) *That's all right, isn't it?* (Yes) *Well, I have a great curiosity. I like to ask questions.*

P: We're curious too.

D: *Why have you chosen to speak* through *this person right now? Do you know?*

P: (Long pause) This person, at some level, is aware of this. This person utilizes this energy.

D: *What does she utilize the energy for?*

P: With her work in energy healing. It's pulled in, yes, to work.

D: *Does she have to have the right kind of motives?*

P: Oh, yes, yes. It has to be of the highest intentions, because we could be used in other ways.

D: *So if someone wanted to use this energy in a negative way?*

P: We would not be available. I am not used that way.

D: *But can people use negative energy?*

P: Oh, yes, they can use negative energy. But we're *not* negative energy. We would not be *used*.

D: *They would use some other type?* (Yes) *So it could be done.*

P: Oh, yes, it *is* done, but that would not be desirable. Negative energy is very powerful. They are not of the light. We, I would say, are disruptive. We disrupt the negative pattern when we go in. We can go in for that negative, as you say, or chaotic energy, and straighten, move it and change it.

D: *Anyway, the reason why you're speaking through this body, is so she'll be aware that this is the energy she uses in her healing?*

P: Yes, it would be good for her to know. And that we can be counted on. And we're very willing.

D: *So if someone wants to do energy work to heal someone, and they have the highest purpose ....*

P: (Interrupted) We would be there. We are available, yes. Intent is everything.

D: *These people know there's an energy, but it seems like you have a personality.*

P: They may be aware of energy, but they don't know how to direct it. Or utilize it to their advantage. But we're *here.*

D: *Do you have any advice on how someone can utilize it?*

P: The person would seek to be open to this, with high intention. And asking for energy from the very highest source. There are all kinds of energy. It's all available.

D: *Are you of the highest source?*

P: Yes. I don't know that we have a name.

D: *But they just ask for the energy of the highest source.*

P: Yes, and we would answer to that. Then they can direct it to wherever it is needed. We're available. Many people are waking up to that fact. To access this, yes.

D: *Are you also the type that can be called on to create positive things?*

P: What we do is create a frequency. We create possibilities. I don't know that we create shape or form with this. So much as we ... facilitate. Is that the word? We facilitate the *energy* for the use.

D: *I've always told people they can create their reality. They can create anything they want in their life, because the mind is that powerful.* (Yes) *And your energy is available if they want to use it in the correct way.*

P: That's exactly right. Their intentions have to be 100% *good,* honorable.

D: *If they're not, you won't work with them?*
P: Absolutely not. We would not be *used* for other than good. That does not mean we would not *be* there in a space that was not good. Because our purpose would be to transmute, so to speak, the chaotic, the negative, into a positive, smooth, high frequency.
D: *Oh, that's wonderful. I like to help people help themselves, but I always think I'm working with something else.*
P: You're working with us.
D: *Is it more or less because you're drawn to this when people are in this state?*
P: (Interrupted) That is part of it. And the intention of the individual to utilize this energy.

I then turned to asking some of the questions Patricia wanted to know about her life, especially her purpose. What happened next was an unusual phenomenon in itself, and proved to me that this part (or energy) was totally separate from the physical body it was speaking through. As it began to talk about her purpose, it paused and then said, "There are tears in the human." Patricia had become emotional, and was crying. And the energy was observing this objectively. I tried to explain to it that she was feeling emotions, and that was good. As Patricia continued to cry softly, it said, "It's overwhelming. Feeling! The feelings!" The emotions were disturbing the energy. It was obvious that it was not used to experiencing anything like this. I tried to remove it from the emotions by telling it that it could allow the *body* to experience this while it talked to me. It would be able to remove itself and communicate while the body did its own thing. I reminded it that it could be in and out and wouldn't have to remain after we finished. There were several deep sighs and then as quickly as snapping your fingers, it was back in control. The emotions were turned off. It had removed itself from them. It was amazing to witness how it experienced something that was totally unfamiliar to it, and then took control of the situation

645

again. It then explained to Patricia what her purpose was to be.

P: The body is going to use this energy with her presence, in any situation. The energy will have a smoothing feeling, impact, on any person or space this body is. This body is finding somewhat of a challenge holding this energy, because it is a very strong energy. She will use it as an active intent of healing with others or places. It may take some adjustment. I think it has put a strain on the physical body by holding and fearing it.

I suggested then that it might be better if she didn't use it for a while.

P: That would be wise. We say they will grow into it, but *we* will grow into them, so to say. (Laugh) So just by being around someone that is ill, her presence will raise the frequency. It will assist the person in raising theirs, just by being there. Like a little bit of lemon dropped in water changes that water, because that's all it takes. Absolutely. For now it would be better for her physical body to be brought into balance and healing, because the better that is, the more energy she will be able to accommodate. And she *will* accommodate this energy. It's not that it *might* happen. It's *going* to happen. Her body just needs to catch up. This body didn't realize, or didn't know, how to utilize this healing energy for her own healing. For everyone else, yes. But this body must learn to accommodate this, because this is what this body has asked to do. It's a very *big* energy.

I then asked the energy to heal Patricia's body of the physical discomforts she had complained about before the session. "See, this is the part I want you to understand. This energy doesn't necessarily *do* it. It provides the energy. It facilitates the frequency for the healing. Anything can be done. Anything can be repaired. Our job is to provide the energy for ... something else to use it." She seemed confused. She said she thought something else had to be called in to use it. I knew what she was speaking of, the subconscious, that I work with regularly to do the healing. She agreed excitedly, "Yes! That's it! Yes, yes! We provide the raw material for this fixer energy. Yes, yes. The subconscious can do it." It agreed that it would be a good idea to call forth the subconscious to do the actual healing, but emphasized that it was always there and available for use at any time by any one (if they had the right intention). I gave instructions and Patricia gave a big sigh when the strong energy left. Then I called forth the subconscious, and I watched as the one replaced the other. The shift was very noticeable. I then asked the subconscious to explain what had happened when that energy spoke through her.

P: It's in her. It's of her. She needs to have the awareness.

This entity was more sure of itself and spoke with more authority, even though the other energy had great power. "She had to be aware of the immensity of it. The availability of it."

D: *I think it was interesting that the energy didn't understand the emotions.*
P: No, it didn't. (Chuckle)
D: *It was good for it to experience that.*
P: I think so.

Then, with the other energy assisting, the subconscious (the fixer energy) went about repairing Patricia's knees. The doctors wanted to operate and do a knee replacement, but the subconscious insisted (as it always does) that there should be no invasion of the body. "The bones are being moved. Their proximity is being adjusted. There is much wear in the bones. The cartilage has to be recreated. And we need to reform and reshape the joints. I am thinking it will take a couple of days. It will be completed over ... say, a month or so, but the majority of the healing will be done in a couple of days. There will be a noticeable difference. The cartilage will be rebuilt. There will be a cushion, and she will be able to walk without discomfort. Health again." It also said that when she went back to the doctor, the difference should be seen on X-ray. It then went to work on Patricia's back, because the problem with the knees had thrown her back out of alignment. I saw her body jump, and heard the bones crack as the energy flowed through. It was obvious something was being done, as the body had been moving and jerking during this entire procedure. "Now it needs work to make it hold there. In some spaces, it may be a little tender, but not to worry."

D: *It's all done with* that *energy.* (Yes) *I appreciate you allowing me to meet that energy. It's a beautiful personality.*
P: It was for your edification, too.

I thought "edification" was an interesting word to use here. I think of that applying to building something, a structure or whatever. But when I looked it up in the dictionary, it said it also meant: moral or spiritual instruction or improvement. It wanted me to know the power of the energy I had been unknowingly using in my work.

Before I awakened Patricia, the subconscious had a parting message for her, "Continue to believe, and to *know* that healing happens. Be it of the spirit, the mind, the body, whatever. It is possible, and it *does* happen, but you must trust and believe. The body was created to heal itself. It knows how to take care of itself."

The more I do this work, the stranger it becomes. I am used to working with the individual spirits of humans that reincarnate and occupy various bodies for the purpose of learning lessons, having experiences, and repaying karma. I have become completely comfortable communicating with the wonderful and powerful subconscious, which holds the answers to everything. I have become somewhat used to the idea that this body that I am in at this moment that is typing this book, is not the only *me*. That I am a very small part of a larger soul that has chosen to splinter or fracture in order to experience as much as possible. And that these other parts of *myself* will never be aware of each other, because it would be too overwhelming and defeat the purpose of the *game*. Just knowing that they exist is mind-boggling enough. I have only partially digested the information that these splinters or facets can exchange places in times of need, similar to walk-ins, yet different, because they are part of the same soul. I have been exposed to so many different ways of thinking, that I thought there could be nothing left to be learned.

Now I am getting information about different forms besides the spirits that occupy our bodies. Yet, in all actuality they are spirits, just in a different form. I have communicated with those fulfilling the duties of a guardian angel (or guide), and creator beings. Some that I am encountering more and more are those that have never lived on Earth before. They have come directly from the Source to help Earth at this time. A more familiar form are those who have only known alien bodies, and are coming to the Earth for the first time. Then I encountered the "hitch-hiker" energy (or spirit) that comes from an extremely high level of development. It only comes to Earth when it is rewarded by having a vacation, and is allowed to hitch-hike or use the human vehicle to observe and absorb emotions and reactions for a limited time.

Now in this chapter, I am exposed to yet another type. An energy that has no desire to occupy a human body, but is there to be used by the occupying spirit for healing or whatever use is needed. There will be more unusual energies introduced in the last chapters of this book.

The amazing thing is that they have a definite personality. They can communicate with me, yet they are totally separate from the person that I was speaking to before the session. And the person is totally unaware that this spirit or energy is occupying the same space they are. This all definitely challenges our concept of reality, and just what our lives are all about. The more I explore this work, the more I am convinced that what we perceive as our human life and existence is merely a facade. A veil that hides a much deeper and more complex world that exists along side of us, and yet is totally invisible to us. I wonder how much more is hidden behind the facade, and how much will be allowed to be revealed?

CHAPTER THIRTY-EIGHT

THE FINAL SOLUTION

George was a member of one of my hypnosis classes in 2005. The class was over and we had this session in his room before he left to catch his flight home. George is very astute psychically and had been aware of entities and various energies in the room during the class. He said this happens to him regularly, and he has had to be careful what he talks about, and who he shares it with. He has put his abilities to work as a therapist. It helps to add insight as he works with clients.

George came off the cloud seeing only the color blue, and knowing he was not in a physical place. "It is not a place, it is an essence and a calmness. And it is where it started. It is part of everything, and we are part of it. We are but one facet of it. It is knowing. It is all. At any point in time, all will come from this. It is just *it*. There is only a feeling of calmness. There is no up, down. There is no sense of time, distance. It is just what it is. Some remember this."

D: *You said this is where you came from?*
G: This time, yes.
D: *But you also said it's where everyone has come from?*
G: All must go through this, yes.
D: *This is where you started?*
G: It is not a place to start. It is something you must go through. One must endure this to go forward. (He was becoming emotional.)
D: *So you started somewhere else before you came to the blue essence?* (Yes) *Why is it emotional?*
G: It did not have to come to this, for me to come down here again. It should not have been a necessity for me to come

651

back and do this again. Why can they not learn?

D: *You were happier there, you mean?*

G: That is not the point. The point is that this could have been avoided by all. It should have not been allowed for me to have to come again. I just don't understand what needs to be done.

This sounded similar to Ingrid's account in *Convoluted Universe - Book Two*, where she came back and was upset about it. She also didn't like what the humans had done to the world, and was emotional about being sent back.

D: *Had you already gone through many physical lives?*

G: This one thinks he has, but no. There are not many, just the ones that have to be done.

D: *So you thought you had finished everything?*

G: It should have been, yes.

D: *Did you have any karma that needed to be repaid?*

G: It was not a necessity. I'm only allowed to come back when the need is great. I should not have to do this again.

D: *You sound angry about it.*

G: Why could they not understand? We taught them, we showed them, we told them the consequences.

D: *Who did you tell? Who are you talking about?*

G: We were talking about those who were there on this plane, who were taught only if they would show those who move forward, to keep them in balance. To show what needed to be done.

D: *The people who were alive on the planet at the time you were here before?*

G: That is correct.

D: *And you thought they understood?*

G: They did. It seems to be a miscalculation on our part of what will transpire in the human race. *We will not allow that miscalculation to arise again.*

652

D: *What was the miscalculation?*

G: That there would be too much fear amongst them.

D: *You thought they would be different?*

G: Correct. That was the plan.

D: *You thought you had accomplished what you started out to do.*

G: That is correct. But we continue to monitor what happens here, and others. We thought the last time when it was corrected, that would be the last time. We told them, we gave them, we showed them what would happen again if it was not averted.

D: *You know how humans are, they forget.*

G: This is true, but we had safeguards in place. We had those others who were here to ensure that this would not happen again. But they did not listen.

D: *The safeguards, the other spirits that were here, you mean?*

G: By your perception of it, yes. There were energies in place. Knowledge that was given at appropriate times to people. They were to share this. But others became involved, and should not have.

D: *What others? Do you mean humans?*

G: This is not correct. No, other influences began to come about – greed, fear, power. This should not be allowed on a grand scale. It will happen, we understand that, we have addressed this, but the magnitude of it was not allowed for.

D: *You didn't think it would become so widespread?*

G: That is correct.

D: *When you came the other time and instructed the people, were you living in a physical body?*

G: You would call it physical, but no. It was physical when you looked at that, but that was all.

D: *Can you tell me something about the time period?*

G: The last time is what you would call "Atlantis". I was here at the end, yes. They abused their power, their knowledge. They misunderstood what it was there for. All they had to do

653

was continue on the path that we set them on. We were sent back to correct this miscalculation.

D: *At that time, were you living among the people?* (No) *So you weren't a physical body in that way?*

G: It was when viewed upon, yes.

D: *Were you watching what was happening?*

G: Others were watching. They realized what was going to happen if it continued on this path, and we were called in. That was our function. We are the ones that correct. We all replace, we all have what you would term a "job". We are the ones that correct.

D: *Are you like spirits?*

G: Similar to that, yes.

D: *Does this mean you have not had physical lives before in a physical body?*

G: No. This one thinks he has, but no.

D: *So you were called in with the others to help at that time, because things were going wrong?*

G: That is correct. The greed and power was coming to a point where it could no longer be allowed. If it was allowed to go forward, then the consequences would have affected too many other entities and planets that we are all connected with. And therefore, that was not allowed at that time – it had to be changed and corrected.

D: *What were they doing that was so negative?*

I knew the answers to these questions, because I had already written about Atlantis (*Convoluted Universe - Book One*). But I am always trying to either verify what I have found, or add more information.

G: They were abusing the energy, abusing their knowledge, instead of helping nurture and continue to understand and grow. They were manipulating what they had. They tried to change it – which it will change, because it's a function of it

– but that had not been allowed for. And then they were going to go down that one line that will exponentiate into other avenues which they were not ready to attain at that time. That type of knowledge was not ready for them at that time and therefore, the correction had to be brought forward. They were using this to destroy others, to regain power over others. Your legends say so, and if you look hard enough you will find that.

D: *I've heard that they abused the power of their minds.*

G: To a degree. Their minds were very advanced, we helped with this, the power of their minds, so that they could understand the energies they were working with. To advance, not only themselves, but the planet in general, which would in turn be a domino effect to the other planets and other communities and entities.

D: *Were they using physical things also to create energy?*

G: Your assumptions are correct at this time. There are crystals that are available and can be manipulated with the right energy to drive frequency. You have already tapped upon this in your writings while working with others. But there also are some crystals that have not yet been discovered that are what you would call a "catalyst". They are the center, they are the holders. Certain individuals or energies can attain this and use this in the power that you would think would be known. No, it was actually the opposite. Things can happen and manipulate from this point and go forward.

D: *Are these large crystals?*

G: Some can be very large, some are not.

D: *You said they've not been rediscovered yet. Is this because when the changes took place, they were buried again?*

G: They were hidden, yes. They were already using these crystals and looking for the others. They cannot find the others. It is not allowed at this time, no. It would have allowed them to reach a new level of understanding that, with the way they were moving forward, would have had a negative impact upon others on that plane of existence. They felt they knew everything, they could control it.

D: *I've also heard they were trying to change nature.*

G: They were, yes. They were changing DNA of the trees to bear more fruit, which is understandable in that case, to feed the population. But also, they did this without understanding the consequences of it. When they changed the DNA of these protectors, the structures were uncommon next to the other structures within and around them. And then with their vast knowledge and the power of their mind, it was clear they could also change the DNA of the humans. This they also became adept at. Some of your ancient legends will also show this. You have not found any evidence yet of this, but you will discover it soon. The ancient legends of what you would call a "minotaur"; there were those and also others. They served no useful purpose whatsoever, but yet they still did this. They called this the "New Science." But one must understand that was *not* science, that was just the abuse of what they had. They already knew what would happen, but yet they wanted to bring it into fruition. They wanted to bring it into this plane, but in this instance, it should not have been there.

There is much more information about this in the chapters on Atlantis in *Convoluted Universe - Books One and Two.*

D: *They were curious and wanted to see what they could do.*

G: That is correct.

D: *Isn't this something our scientists are bringing back now?*

G: That is correct. That is why I am here and the others are here also.

D: *Your people have told me this before. We need to know this information, because history is repeating itself.*

G: This is true. It's already begun to happen again. They seem to be following down the same paths, yes.

D: *They are trying to change the DNA of plants again. They said it is to make more and better food for the population.*

G: They understand, but they are once again crossing that. They have surpassed what they have already done and their manipulations are going down to what you would call a cellular level. But also these changes, you must understand, go past the cellular level. They go past into the energy level, too. And they begin to manipulate that again. They have already done this.

D: *We do know they're cloning animals and messing with the DNA of animals.*

G: It's been going on for what you would term fifteen, thirty years, yes.

D: *I've been told they're also doing this with humans, but it's not common knowledge yet.*

G: That is correct. If they do not understand and realign their thinking, we are working with this with others. But as you would understand, there is much persuasion from the others to continue on that path.

D: *It's all in the name of science, isn't it?*

G: That is the term that is used, yes. Or now, as they are saying, it is the name of what you would call "defense" – military, the betterment of others.

D: *Why would the military benefit from something like that?*

G: They see it as a weapon.

D: *The manipulation of DNA?*

G: That is correct. What you would call "bio-terrorism". Also, creating a person who can withstand the battles of war.

He seemed to be having trouble finding the correct words. The words seemed foreign and strange to him.

D: *The words will come easier, because I know it's difficult using our words. But you mean their bodies would be manipulated?*

657

G: The bodies are being changed to be able to go against a bio-terrorism attack and succeed and survive. But they don't understand that the body itself will become a weapon against them. That which they form to repel, will evolve and come back to them again on a different level, and the consequences will be great.

D: *Do you mean the body is able to develop something to counteract this?*

G: They are working on this in their labs to inject it into a human body so that it will be repellent to bio-terrorism, different ones. And they inject substances into it, change the DNA structure of it so that it will be adaptable to it. But that will only begin to break down after a short term, and they will no longer have a defense against what they have created themselves.

D: *This is one of the reasons you're here, because they are going to harm the people?*

G: I am here to stop this. We are here to make the corrections, yes.

D: *Well, let's go back a little bit. You said you were there at Atlantis when everything was happening. What happened?*

G: They were told to quit. If not .... (Pause)

D: *If not, what?*

G: (Pause) If they would not quit, then we were to control it. We come in and use our full power, and we make the correction. They would no longer exist.

D: *Is that what happened at the time of Atlantis?*

G: That is correct.

D: *What kind of correction did you make?*

G: (Coldly) We eliminated the population. We hid the civilization underneath the water so it could not be found again.

D: *I like to clarify these things. Is it all right if I keep asking questions?*

G: At this time, yes.

D: *Because these are things I am working with.*

G: We understand this.

D: *I have heard the scientists were misusing the crystal power and that's what caused the destruction.*

G: We did allow some of the population to survive, so that the legend could be spread. So that others would hear of what had happened. And we had hoped that because of this, they would understand the value, and also understand that they cannot misuse it. That we will be watching and we will take the appropriate action necessary, to save not only this one, but the others.

D: *What others?*

G: Other planets. It would be a chain reaction. This you already know.

D: *So at that time, you did this even though it was something you didn't want to do. Just destroy everything and start over.*

G: That is correct. But it was a necessity.

This has been reported in some of my other books, that they are normally not allowed to interfere in the affairs of other cultures. They can only watch and observe. The only exception (and I have been told this many times) would be if we reached the point where we could possibly destroy our planet (either through the misuse of atomic power or, etc.). This could not be allowed, because it would cause a ripple effect out into the galaxy and many other civilizations would be adversely effected. They also said it would affect other dimensions where other cultures exist. It would be as the declaration of an unwanted and unjustified war that would have far reaching effects. This could not be allowed. They said in such a circumstance, they would be justified in stepping in and keeping this from happening. However, I had never heard anyone speak of the drastic measures that George was describing. This sounded unnerving, cold and calculating without any feelings for the human race. But did they consider that the human race at that point had moved beyond the need for humane feelings. This would indeed have to be carried out by a totally different type of entity.

D: *I have had stories of people who did survive.*

G: That is correct. They were allowed to. Some were given notice so that some of the knowledge could be used to restart.

These stories have been reported in *Convoluted Universe - Book Two* and some of my other books.

D: *But the majority of Atlantis is under the water?*

G: That is correct, and they are searching for it at this time.

D: *I've also been told parts are under mounds of dirt.*

G: Parts, yes.

D: *But this was something you didn't really want to do?*

G: It is our function.

D: *Did someone or something tell you to do this?*

G: The collective understands what needs to be done.

D: *Even though it would appear to be negative, to destroy a whole civilization?*

G: That is true. We have done this many times.

D: *On Earth, or in other places?*

G: Where we are needed.

D: *I've heard that many times on Earth other civilizations, besides Atlantis, went down.*

G: Correct.

D: *But you have also been sent to other worlds?*

G: Yes. This is our function. That is who we are.

D: *Does this mean that you have never lived in a physical body until now?*

G: There have been times when we had to take on the bodies of the civilization, so we could impress upon them the value of what needed to be accomplished, yes.

D: *But you're angry because you had to come back. You thought you had fixed it the other time.*

G: That is correct. It should not be a necessity at this time, but it is.

D: *There have been many, many, many generations since that time.*

G: That is correct.

D: *And it seems as though the people are back in power again, making the same mistakes.*

G: They are. The other ones that have come in at this point in time have had influence that we had not allowed for. The collective has said it was a necessity.

D: *Are the other ones those energies that are causing the negative influence? (Yes) Are they also in physical body?*

G: They are not in the physical body as you would think. They appear physical, yes. They have a different agenda. We are as diverse as you would say the humans are.

D: *Isn't there a control, like the collective, that would not allow this negativity to come?*

G: There is a collective. It is allowed, yes.

D: *Is this what is causing the wars and everything in our present time?*

G: That is correct at this time.

D: *But you said there are many others like yourself that have come back to correct this?*

G: (Cautiously) Why are you looking for this information?

When suspicion arises, I always have to answer carefully or the flow of information would be cut off.

D: *Because I'm like a reporter. I'm an accumulator of information. I write about it, you know that, but it's to let people know what's happening. Is that acceptable to you? (Yes) I'm trying to help in my own way so people will know what's happening.*

G: We understand.

D: *I have spoken to many other people in this state who say they*

661

have been sent to make changes.

G: There are different levels of change that you speak of. We are the *final* level. The others are here to help facilitate the change. If the change does take place, then we are not needed. If it does not take place, then we will correct.

D: *The same way as before?*

G: We *will* correct.

D: *Would it be the same way, with the water?*

G: It would be a correction.

D: *Do you mean it would be something different?*

G: We are not allowed to tell you at this time, no.

D: *That's all right. I take as much information as I'm allowed to receive. I spoke to a man in England who said there were seven people who were sent. I was wondering if you were one of those, or if you're doing something different. (See the chapter in Convoluted Universe - Book Two "The First of the Seven"). They told me not to reveal the identities, and not to put them in touch with each other. That they had to do their work separately.*

G: I am not of that group. They are the ones who are here to facilitate the change. If they fail, we are the group that will correct. We are the *final* group.

D: *I think this is very valuable information, because the world seems to be stumbling along making the same mistakes all over again.*

G: That is correct.

D: *Is it all right for me to know these things.*

G: At this time, yes.

D: *And I will not reveal the identity of the body you are speaking through.*

G: That will not be allowed, no. It is not his time yet to be fully known. He will be.

D: *That was one thing he wanted to ask about. He feels he has power, and he wants to know why he can't use it.*

G: We all have power, that is true. We would be called the *final*

662

solution. The ones of your group have what you consider much power, yes. He *is* the power.

D: *I have worked with many others who were healers and practiced different energy work in a physical body in other lifetimes. They are now bringing this knowledge back.*

G: He has looked into many different areas and is very familiar with all of them. He will feel an affinity with them. He will understand them, and it will come and seem natural to him.

D: *He felt that he had a power from somewhere, and he wanted to know if he could get that back. But there's also the fear of allowing this power to come through.*

G: That's understood.

D: *Because he is human.*

G: In your perception, yes.

D: *Are you going to allow him to experience these things?*

G: This will be allowed now, yes.

D: *If he allowed this power to come through to help people, would he be able to control it?*

G: He can control it, yes.

D: *Of course, if there was too much power, it would frighten people.*

G: This is true. The power that is attainable is great, yes. We have been working with him and we will open up the pathways for it to come through again. It will no longer be gradual. It is time for him to go, to move forward with this. He'll be allowed to experience the major energy shifts that are coming. He will be allowed to access the universe to use the energy.

D: *But he also has to live a human life.*

G: This is true.

I am always well aware that I perceive the person I am working with to be a normal human being. And I am very careful not to disrupt their life, no matter how strange the information.

D: *He has to live in the physical world. And he has to have a job, and the things that a human needs. We don't want to interfere with any of that, do we?*

G: That is irrelevant.

D: *But it's what humans have to do.*

G: We understand, but it's still irrelevant.

D: *My job is always to protect. So what you are going to let him do will not interfere with his human life, will it?*

G: The question is understood.

D: *He said he was trying to get more information from the spirits. It's actually coming from you, isn't it?*

G: That is correct.

D: *And he wanted to know what was holding him back from attaining these things.*

G: He still retains the fear and the anger from the last time. And why they have not understood and moved forward. That is why he has these doubts that come forward sometimes. And he realizes that he may say that humans are stupid, and do not understand. This is the reason and where it comes from.

D: *He said there was anger.*

G: Oh, yes. That time has come and passed now.

D: *So this is what was holding him back.*

G: He was never held back.

D: *Well, he felt he was. (Laugh)*

G: It's understandable.

D: *He also felt he had the ability to move objects.*

G: He has the ability to do much. Moving objects is what you would term as "child's play", yes.

D: *Will he be able to bring that ability back?*

G: Oh, that's fine. We've been showing this to him off and on. It is natural for him, yes. This and the other abilities will start coming back immediately, yes.

Another ability that George thought he had was the ability to locate objects. He wanted to help people locate buried things.

This was something George wanted to do very badly, yet he felt he wasn't able to do it. He also was interested in healing other people.

G: He can do anything. He still associates that with the last time. It's there again, and it's just one small part of what the ability is, yes. There again we would term it as a child's toy, yes.

D: *So he will be able to have these abilities back?*

G: He's already had them. We will unshield it, yes.

D: *So all of these abilities that he's been afraid of will begin to resurface?*

G: That is true. We will begin to unshield those now. The shield has been up for a while to protect this, because he was not quite ready, in the human sense, to understand or grasp the enormity of it. So he had to be protected until now. He has been doing these things and others. He will be known for some of these things, yes.

D: *But here again, we don't want to disrupt his life.*

G: That's irrelevant. You don't understand the concept of his purpose here. His purpose here is to create things, and make them grow a certain way they have to by the collective. Just because he attains a human body is irrelevant to this matter. But yes, we understand the question. We understand what you are trying to do for the human body. We understand that point. We will make adjustments for this now, yes.

D: *Because he does have to live in this world. And if he appeared to be too unusual, he could be put away somewhere. Then he wouldn't be able to accomplish anything, would he?*

G: He will not allow humans to fully perceive what he can do. He will enjoy working with the child's toys part, yes, and that will satisfy the humans. It will keep them from understanding what he can do. But we also understand he's being looked for now, him and the others, yes.

D: *I was wondering if the government would try to find them.*

G: They are aware that we are here, yes, but they do not know where. The Others are trying to help them find us, yes.

D: *So if some of these abilities are revealed, he's not going to be in any danger?*

G: They cannot harm him, no. Soon they will realize that he is here, yes. They know he is here. Let me clarify this: they know he is on this planet, yes. They know that he is beginning to adapt and use the abilities now. Yes, they are aware of that. Soon they will also be aware of actually who he is. But by that time, they will not be able to do anything to him, for him, or against him.

D: *So you think these are government people?*

G: Them and others, yes. The other ones who are working with them, yes.

D: *I have had other clients that we were told to protect.*

G: He needs no protection now, no.

D: *Because I wouldn't want to do anything that could hurt him.*

G: We understand. That is correct.

D: *So if he becomes more noticeable, then they will identify him.*

G: Oh, that is true, yes. And we wish this to happen, yes. When they identify the group, they will know how many of the group is here. And therefore, our goal is, if they will adjust just by knowing the group is here, then we have achieved our goal, yes.

D: *They don't know how many are involved. They can't possibly find them all.*

G: Yes, they will. They have the understanding, we will allow them to know where we are, yes, that is correct. This group only, though. We must clarify that – it is this group only.

D: *What is the difference between this group and the others?*

G: If you were in a battle and you were an infantry soldier, and a tank was coming towards you. You identify where the tank is, of course, but would you stand in front of the tank?

D: *No.* (Pause) *So what's the correlation?*

G: The group is like a tank. Each one is like a tank. They can identify them, true. And that is our goal (as are many), to have them identify them. They have to. But once they identify them, at that point, they cannot do anything to them. Now of course, they will try. But they will learn how insufficient that is.

D: *So the other groups are doing other work?*

G: Correct. Each group has its own job to do.

D: *Nobody could hurt this person, could they?*

G: The physical part, the human part, at this point and time in his life, perception is yes. But what needs to be understood is – to see why all this was arranged – from this point on, that which is the human part will still be there, yes. We will not allow it to be moved away. But the essence of who he is, the essence of what his ability and, what you would say is, his "job", must be accomplished. So therefore, that part of him has already begun to come through lately and will continue on now with accelerated pace, yes.

D: *So things will be changed in his life now.*

G: Of course.

D: *Okay, but we always want it for the positive. I know you're frowning, but I always work with the positive.*

G: And in this one's frame of understanding, he tries to always be the positive. And he does want the human population to be positive and correct itself. By doing that, he will not have to follow through on his job. He knows what can be accomplished. He knows that if it comes to him and the others of his group to come forward and fully announce themselves to this world again, what you term as a "cataclysm" would be great, yes.

D: *I was told that everything would have to start all over again, and that would take too long.*

G: This is true. But he and others are here in place, just in case.

D: *Does he know any of these others? Or is he supposed to?*

G: He has not met any yet. But there are many, yes.

D: *When George was a child he had many problems with his kidneys, and was put on a lot of medication.*

I have had other cases where people were actively involved with working with energy, both in this life and especially in past lives. They also had problems with their organs, and unexplained fevers during childhood that mystified their doctors, who used many medications to no avail. During the sessions, it came to light that their physical bodies had difficulties incorporating the higher vibrating energy that had been carried over from their past lives. George had been told he did not have any past lives, yet the explanation was similar.

G: He cannot filter into this lifetime very easily. The energy was too great for the body that was chosen for him. The people, the individuals, recognized that something was different and he was examined. But the main reason was that the energy was too much for the body at that time and it had to adapt to it. It affected, not only his kidneys, but many parts of who the body is, yes.

D: *But the kidneys are all right now, aren't they?*

G: Yes. We are working with him, helping him to adjust, helping to clear his mind, his essence. So that it can be adjusted to the new energy, so he will realize and understand who and what he really is. We did not understand that it was causing this much problem with the ability of the healing body to maintain itself. We will correct that.

They went through George's body and adjusted many organs and parts as they went. They talked about some loose connections which were preventing the energy from flowing correctly and smoothly. They even found problems that George was unaware of. The healing and adjustments would continue over the next two weeks. Sometimes, it is not advisable for the healing to take place instantly because it would be too traumatic for the body.

George had also discussed having problems sleeping at night. He woke up every two hours. "That is the energy flow. The information that had been given to him at that point in time comes in flows. And the pause between the flows wakes him up, yes. He must receive the energy, but we will adjust the time framing of it, yes." I asked if he would become successful at healing or doing energy work to where he could stop his regular job. "His goal is not to be successful at this. His goal is to facilitate a change. But in your terms, he will become successful at this in making changes, yes."

D: *He has an irrational fear of dusk, right before it begins to get dark. Can you explain that?*

G: When do you think Atlantis was taken care of? That was when they corrected the last one. The correction was started at dusk, yes.

D: *That was when they began the correction that ended in the cataclysm?*

G: Yes. He realizes his power and what he must accomplish. The fear was irrational. We will adjust that now. You are a facilitator that was gained to allow him to access this at this time. He has always had the feeling that in the human context he could not accept. And by being here with you at this time, he was able to access the information. Therefore, we can now remove the shields that he had put up until the appropriate time. So now they will be removed and he will be able to understand and move forward, yes. That is the connection.

D: *Everything has to happen in the correct time. – Let's hope you don't have to do the final solution again.*

G: We will do our job, yes.

D: *We hope it doesn't come to that this time around. Maybe the human race will begin to get the message.*

G: (Darkly) They didn't last time.

It seems as though the *plan,* the *goal,* had taken into account every possibility. They are trying to change conditions on Earth by introducing new, pure spirits in many ingenious ways. But just in case they are unsuccessful, the *final* solution was also placed here. They have said that the increased new energy that is entering, seemed to be having an effect. But, just in case, they are prepared to use drastic measures again. Let us hope those of George's energy and assignment will not be needed!

CHAPTER THIRTY-NINE

THE ABSORPTION

I had intended to end this book with the Chapter *The Final Solution*. I could think of nothing more powerful than the discovery of that unusual energy that dwelt in the body of a normal man. An unnamed energy that had the power to destroy the world. From the icy way it spoke about its job, I do not have the slightest doubt that it meant what it said. It fully intends to carry out its mission of total destruction, if we don't straighten out the mess we have made of our world. From other sessions in this book, I found others who possess the same power, and some of these have already used that power in other lifetimes. I do not think from the description that they would be called upon to do it again. I believe that assignment would only be allotted to a few. It is quite understandable that they would have to come into this life with total amnesia of the assignment. How else would they be able to carry it out when the time came? How else could they shut off all emotion and only do what they were programmed to do? When I discussed this with my daughter, Julia, she did not think it would be for the best to end the book on such a negative note. I thought it might be a wakeup call if people realized the path we are headed down and if they were aware of the terrible consequences that have already been agreed upon. Now upon reflection, I had to agree that she was right. However, I did not know that "they" were also planning the end of this book, and they did not want it to end on that negative note either.

I really thought this book was finished, and I was doing the final editing, when I had this surprising session while I was in Montreal in May, 2007 speaking at the IIIHS Conference. I was working with Toni, an English teacher. She is a calm, gentle person whose exterior gave no indication of the power and great

671

knowledge dwelling just beneath the surface. As it began, I thought it would be another normal past life session. However, "they" literally screamed at me as they presented yet another concept. I then knew I had no choice but to include it in this book.

As the session began, this was another example of someone not allowing me to complete the induction. Toni's subconscious was so anxious to get started that it propelled her into it when I asked her to go to her beautiful place. She immediately began describing what sounded like the Source. So many of my clients are going there now, instead of going to regular past lives, that I am no longer surprised. I always let the subject pick their own special place, and she could think of no better place than to return to the Source. She became emotional immediately. She described it as, "The heart of the Sun. The heart of God." When I asked for a description, she seemed to be experiencing total bliss. "To tell you what I see would mean that I would need to use an image of looking through something. But when there is nothing to look through, but only That Which Is, it is more difficult to explain. If you could imagine your body sinking or immersing itself into a body – a greater body – of water. That is *so soothing* and *so calming* to the senses and so *reflective* of *light,* that you see or feel or (she searched for the words) can think of – no, not 'think' – can experience nothing else. Then perhaps you have come only a fraction of the way. It is All That Is." She became emotional as she continued, "If I can say that, if I had a body, it would be the body of God. Can you understand? It is difficult to explain or imagine. When you can align your beingness with a much *vaster* beingness than that which is known on this plane."

Her voice grew louder and thundered with authority. It was reverberating so much I didn't know if the microphone clipped on her would be able to handle it. It was a total reversal in personality from the quiet, calm, almost shy Toni. I was curious where this was leading, but I knew she was never in any danger.

It was as though something or someone had been pent up for centuries, and was finally able to find release. I allowed it to express itself. It began an exultation to what it perceived as God. It was completely consumed by feeling a strong emotion. The words blended into tones that took on a musical quality that fluctuated. The sounds were drawn out, and the microphone was being affected by the energy she released. She raised her arms and reached out in utter adoration for something unseen to me. Then she let out several tones that echoed around the room, and with a sudden deep breath, Toni returned, "I am sorry ... I have returned. I have difficulty expressing." The effect of this could only be experienced by hearing it. It was so moving, I could really feel that I was in the presence of God.

D: *It's a great wonder, isn't it? This is what it feels like to be there?*

T: There is no "there". There is only the beingness. I tell you, it is every place, and yet any place you imagine is not that place. (Deep sigh) It is beyond words.

D: *Are others with you there?*

T: At this point, you are not identifying with others. It is a return, and yet to say that you return, have you ever left? Here is the great paradox.

D: *So you can be in both places?*

T: You have your point of expression. Your point of expression is given to you so that you may become expressive of other possibilities that can be created. Possibilities that, in a sense, are part of a large dream state. If you can imagine that God dreams, then you will begin to see that all creation is a beautiful dream of God. Can you understand what I am saying?

This was an incredible experience to be in the presence of an entity of such immense power. The written word can barely describe the emotion and intensity that the words conveyed.

D: *I have heard other people talk about the dreamer dreaming the dream. But they never explained who the dreamer was.*

T: Ah-ha! Here, now, you will see the microcosm and the macrocosm. For you see, there is but God, and yet God, if I may say so, dreams. And the dreams of God, you see ... we are allowed to become an investment of that dream. Can you understand this?

D: *Yes, I do, even though it is difficult for our human minds.*

T: Now, I will attempt. As the dream unfolds – for you see, there are no limits – as the dream unfolds, we are allowed to identify with but a spark of that greater spark, that greater light. And in turn, that spark can dream. Oh, it is infinite. It is infinite. And each dream is part of the greater dream. And it is a *VAST, VAST* experience, and a play. A playing out of untold of dreams. You *must not* believe that the dream is that which holds your reality. No, you see, you are but a part of the dream.

D: *We all are?*

T: (She fumbled with the words.) Mmm, you see ... those who cannot accept this understanding will *never* accept that they are *all* of this. And yet, I tell you, there is nothing but God. These experiences that you claim to have, *are* the dream of God. You *are* God expression – whole – and yet, you are believing the dream.

D: *But we are told we can control our lives, our dream, and create what we want, if we believe in it.*

T: In turn, yes, of course. You *are* in the dream. You are the extension of the *dream*.

D: *Does this mean, God begins the dream and we carry it on, or what?*

T: There, you see now. It manifests, and manifests, and manifests. God dreams, the dreamer dreams, the dream dreams. And at the point where the dreaming has reached the "twilight", I might say, then you fall back out, and you are absorbed back into the dreamer.

D: *So whenever our dreams reach the ultimate, we can't dream any further, you mean?*

T: It is not that you *can't* dream any further, but that you *don't want to dream any further.*

D: *So as long as we can create and we can dream our individual dreams, our lives remain. Is that a way of saying it, or am I understanding it?*

T: (A deep breath. Then she searched for the words.) There are many strands. There are many "paths" that can be taken. Now, when you say, "we", you are alluding to this plane?

D: *Yes, the human plane, because that is all we know at this point.*

T: Thank you. The human – may I say "experiment"? And I *do not* mean disrespect.

D: *I understand.*

T: The human experiment is to see to which point the dreamer will dream. And to which point the dreamer will *allow* himself or herself to dream. You are part of creation. You are given the gifts of creation.

D: *So there are no limits unless we place them. Is that what you mean?*

T: Truly. Truly.

D: *And as long as we continue to dream and create, then our physical lives continue?*

T: You see, when I say "dream", I do not mean that you are asleep. I mean that you are using your creative mind. And you are envisioning that which will be. I do not allude to a sleep state. Oh, no, you are *very* conscious. Oh, yes!

D: *We think we are.*

T: Oh, yes! Oh, yes! Oh, yes!

D: *But I know many people create very negative things.*

T: It is given to them to dream as they will. There are *no* limits, even if your limit is your own. You see, if you choose to be limited, that too is your choice. Again, negativity is but a phase. There can only be God. And yet when you close a

675

certain avenue to the greater understanding, then you begin to limit that which you would accept. Then you accept that there *can* be a limit. Again, it is but a choice that is made and that is *allowed* to happen, because creation will create. That is a gift of God.

D: *You said the dreamer dreams the* big *dream.* (Yes) *What is the* big *dream that God is dreaming?*

T: What will the dreamer dream? (Big sigh and a pause.) I will try to explain in another way. One moment, please.

D: *I know the words are difficult. But we can't imagine his dream, because it is so huge?*

T: Vast. Vast. (Pause) When you repose and you allow yourself to expand, your limited consciousness moves into your more-expanded consciousness. There is a greater movement that is given at that place and a greater freedom to experience *anything* that one would embrace as an experience. In this way, God – who *cannot* change – God, who is God, allows a portion a greater freedom. And in that allowing, in fact denies the perfectness ... not denies, but allows that play. Because how can you change that which is perfect? It is impossible. It is always as is! And yet it is a play. Almost a play, to allow ... where will this creation go? Where will this free spirit carry? This is what I mean.

D: *I've been told that we were sent out as sparks in the very beginning of the creation. And that we are like cells in the body of God. And that our job is to obtain information to bring back. Is that correct?*

T: God is all-knowing. The information that is brought back is for the spark's benefit. That portion acknowledges to *itself* that which it already knows, because it is a part of the All. That is coming back to that portion.

D: *That is what I was told, that God wanted knowledge. He wanted more information to be added to what he already had.*

T: I tell you, God is *whole.* God is whole.

This was beginning to disturb me. I have become accustomed to having my belief systems challenged, and even totally reversed during the course of my work. Usually it happened to introduce a new concept, or a new way of thinking. I could not understand where this was going, because it seemed contradictory to what I have been told through countless subjects. But I have learned that the subconscious always has a purpose and a motive when it allows new information to come through. I know I do not have all the answers, so I have learned to be patient and to allow it to talk. I knew I would have time to sort it all later, if my questions were not explained satisfactorily. Yet at this point, I had no idea where this was going.

D: *Then what is the individual spark's purpose when it goes out?*

T: Love. To move through love in all manifestations. To move through love.

D: *Is it correct, though, that in the very beginning, God, more or less, exploded out. And that was when all of the sparks went out to experience? Is that a good analogy?*

T: For me to tell you this, I can only say, I understand that the dreamer dreams; that the dreamer dreams.

D: *In our analogy of dreams, as long as he is dreaming, then we are all existing in the dream.*

T: Yes, yes, yes. Truly, truly, truly. But you are *not* the dream. There is only God. God is *whole*. God is whole. (Pause) The information you have received – you must go beyond this knowledge. The sparking entity – you are limiting yourself. God is *whole*, and has no need of knowledge. You have to go a transcending way. Beyond this. There can be no *change* to God. You cannot *add* to God. God is *whole, whole, whole*.

D: *But we still consider ourselves to be individuals.*

T: This is the dream.

D: *And you did say that when we complete this dream, this life we are living – because that's all we know at this time – then our dream is over, and we go back and are absorbed.*

677

T: You are dissolved; absolutely. Now imagine ... hmm, an analogy: you have a glass of warm liquid. And to that liquid you add a powder, and that powder is dissolved, and becomes part of that liquid. At one point you could ... (searching for words) you could manipulate that powder. But once it has been dissolved and absorbed ... it is the powder's place to allow the dissolution back to that state, that is the All.

D: *Well, I think this is something that frightens people, because we like to believe we still maintain our personalities, our individuality. We work very hard to create that individuality, and it sounds as though we would lose it if we were absorbed.*

T: You are *not* the dream. You *are* the liquid form that allows the powder form. If you have the fear of losing that individuality, you are not ready to experience *anything* but that. I would say to you, continue to dream, and be at peace.

D: *Well, I get mail from many people. And this is one of the things they say: "I don't want to be absorbed. I want to maintain my identity."*

T: *Truly,* no one will force anything upon you. You are safe in your individuality, and *God* is with you, I tell you. You are safe in your individuality. No one is trying to change you; no one is trying to take anything away from you; no one is trying to add to you. But I tell you, from a state that accepts that God cannot be added to, subtracted from ... God is whole. And this knowledge that you seek, when the time comes, will be accepted with no fear.

D: *I write books, you know. And I have to explain this in ways that people can understand.*

T: (Deep sigh) I tell you, if you would express to the ones who hold this fear, that there is nothing to fear. They are safe within their own creation. That is what I can say to you.

D: *Because I try to present it in a way ... many of them are taking their baby steps, just beginning to explore. And that's why my books have gone slowly, and I've been allowed to expand slowly. So that it wouldn't frighten people.*

T: Truly, truly, truly, truly. You have entered the *dream*, you see.

D: *So they can take their first steps and they will not be overwhelmed.*

T: Yes, truly, truly. There are many who have entered the dream. Many, many. Yes, yes, like in a tapestry; pin pricks. If you were to imagine pricks in a tapestry, and *through* those pin pricks: *lights,* light. A different vision to come in, and slowly, yes, slowly, like a light coming through a pin point. Yes, this is a great task.

D: *That's a good analogy. That's what I need, pictures that people can understand. Then there's one other question, I think, that would disturb people. God is the dreamer. He is dreaming the dream of which we are all a part. And we remain as long as he is dreaming. What happens when God wakes up? Or does he? (Chuckle) What do you think?*

T: (Pause) This knowledge is not given to me to know.

D: *Maybe that is something we cannot understand, anyway. Is that what you mean?*

T: I can only share with you that which is given to me to know. I will attempt to share with you. The Source that I am able to speak of with you, is unchanging. It is *whole.* I must emphasize this. It *is* whole. It is all-beingness. It is as is. The part that is given to dream is allowed to express variations. In no way do those variations impact that which *cannot* be impacted and cannot change. If you can accept that the God that you understand – I do not wish to give you too much here – perhaps it is not given for *all* to accept. But to *you* I shall give you this information. The God that is given to dream, the God that is known to dream, to produce sparks, to expand and to have the return ... it is but *one* plane. There is *beyond* that plane. I tell you there is beyond that. This I give to you. Beyond this I am not at liberty. I have not been given this permission to speak.

D: *I believe someone else mentioned this briefly at one time.*

679

That there were things beyond God.

T: It is not given to me to speak of these things.

D: *Because we don't want to overwhelm the human mind.*

T: Please, I tell you, if they have not accepted that the powder can dissolve, they have not reached that stage to accept the beyond. (Loud laugh)

D: *(Chuckle) It has taken me many years to get to this point.*

T: Bless you. (She kept laughing.)

D: *And I know in the beginning, I would never have understood this much and been able to expand. So I am constantly being given more. And that's the problem with the human mind, trying to understand all these things.*

T: Ah, the value that is given to the human mind. (Loud laugh) Ah! So it is! So it is, and so it is. (Laugh)

D: *This is what I do. I present and if people can understand it, then it's for them to understand or not.*

T: So it is. So it is. So it is. This is *no* rush. There is no rush.

D: *But every little piece of information we can get adds to our own knowledge and our growth, doesn't it?*

T: As is given, yes.

D: *But I always ask the same question. If, when you are there, it is so beautiful, it is so wonderful – I've been told it's beyond belief, and they don't want to leave. Why does the spark, our individual soul, decide to leave, when it's so beautiful?* (She had been making sounds of delight while I was asking this.)

T: The spark, I shall say ... the spark believes that ... (Sigh) the spark does not understand. (Sigh) Please, one moment. (Pause as though listening or consulting.) One moment, please. I am receiving. (A long pause, then a deep sigh.) I am another to speak.

At first, I didn't understand what was happening. Yet this has happened in the past, especially during the sessions included in *The Custodians*. One entity would be speaking, and then another would come in, and the shift would always be quite noticeable. This had not happened for a long time, so I was caught off guard. When she continued, the voice was different, speaking slowly and deliberately as though using this form of communication was difficult and unaccustomed. Was it a different entity that had been called in to answer the question?

T: We who have come from a plane of consciousness that ... the sparks that you refer to, exist in a perfection that includes an acceptance that they can accumulate information, light, knowledge and carry it back to be absorbed by a greater awareness. Which is in turn absorbed by a greater, and so on, and so on, until it is absorbed in the Godhead. Our plane of consciousness is now allowed to give to you the information that Godhead does ... an auxiliary to God. The Godhead *is*, and the portion that you speak of is greater still. Greater still. And the experience of this sparking and returning is but one portion of a dream. It is greatly difficult to express more to you without the knowledge that even the extension and the return have not been accepted yet. To say more and expect you to understand this, is a great feat. (Big sigh)

D: *You mean there will be much more that will be given to me as time goes on?*

The voice returned to the one of authority that had been speaking before. As though another entity that had a piece of knowledge had been called in to deliver that morsel to me. Then it departed. Its job was finished. Upon reflection, as I typed this transcript, I can see I have been truly given only the bare crumbs throughout all my years of work. Now, they were preparing to give me a bigger piece of the loaf. But from my naive answers, they were concluding that I was not yet ready for more, and closed off the eating of the rest of the meal. I had the impression that they thought I was ready, but were now going to wait until I digested this piece before divulging more. Yet they indicated loud and clear that when I have digested it, *there was more!*

T: Ah! But again, the pinpoints that are given. This is but a stream of light that has begun to enter. So you have taken the baby steps with these people, and these beings who accept this rotation. And it is given that some have embraced, "Ah! I am returning to a greater place, a greater knowingness, a greater beingness." And *yet, and yet,* even this (her voice dropped to a whisper) is a dream. Imagine. Imagine that.

D: *Do you think it is time now that we should know this information?*

T: Yes. It is given to you, because those that are truly ready to be seeded with this information, and to *hold* this knowledge ... there is nothing to be done. I assure you, there is nothing to be done at your level. And yet to just allow the trickle to be *implanted.* Implanted. I tell you, years, years, in that which you've perceived to be a future, another world shall manifest itself. And yet I tell you, *even then,* even then that is a *dream.* And you will move beyond that dream. I tell you so. Verily, verily, it is so.

D: *I have been told that now it is time to have this knowledge so we can move away from the negativity of Earth.*

T: I tell you there is no negativity. And yet, truly, people continue to embrace this notion. *There is only God. There is only God. There is only God.* And yet I will succumb to your vernacular of this plane. I will not embrace it, but I will understand that you accept it.

D: *This is the only thing that we can understand at our point.*

T: I accept this. I accept this.

D: *And you know our world at this time is going through some very bad experiences.*

T: I accept. And now, truly, may I speak of this?

Another shift occurred, and a different entity began to speak. This one sounded more feminine and not as powerful as the one that had been dominating the session.

T: I will now address this, if I may. I say to all beings of the Earth plane – I say this from my God Source – if you do not absorb that which *you* accept to be negative into *your thought form*, it *cannot* manifest in this place that you have been given to change. You are God. You **are** God! And yet, you will not *manifest* that part of your created self. It is given to you to *manifest,* to *manifest* your God beingness. (Almost shouting) Open your God self, I say to you! Open your God self, and **allow** the light **to** enter.

The strength of the words were affecting the microphone. It could not handle the volume.

D: *Is this part of what we are being told, that we are creating a new world, a new Earth that we will move into?*
T: From within, will come **such light**. It will *manifest* from the very **core** of your being. *The world which you envision is* **already** *inside of you.* Can I explain this to you? You are not *moving* to another planet. You are **breaking out of your shell.** This planet – this shell – is bringing forth that light. It possesses the core of essence. It is given to you to enter into your light **fully, fully,** and to *draw it out.* And to say, "**I AM LIGHT. I AM LIGHT. HEAR ME, GOD. I AM LIGHT.**" And truly, then, this world shall be not as you *permit* it. I say, YOU PERMIT IT TO BE! *Nothing in God's beingness can exist without the permission of God.* I SAY TO YOU, YOU ARE GODS! YOU ARE THE LIGHT! I see your future. I say, *come forth in your light.* RETURN to yourselves. Oh, humanity, return to yourselves! And in turn, know that beyond that vision, there is a *greater* awareness. And yet can you take the step even to that place? We await *you!*

This entire tirade of powerful emotion had erupted suddenly and was overwhelming. All I could do was listen and wait for it to die down. In my mind's eye, it reminded me almost of the old time preacher with Bible in hand screaming at the congregation at a revival service. But instead of preaching hellfire and damnation for the sinners and urging them to present themselves for salvation, this entity was trying to offer us salvation of a different kind. It was almost desperately trying to get us to open our eyes and acknowledge what we really are. All of this affected the microphone and was obvious on playback for transcription, but it did not seem to affect Toni at all. After the session, she had little memory of what had occurred. I wonder what she thought when she heard the power of these words? It was difficult to convey on paper the power of this entity. I have tried the best I can to transfer it to writing.

Even though Toni did not remember what occurred during the session, the next day she said she had seen a vision that clarified some of it. She wasn't sure how it related, but I think it applied to this part. She saw three levels. The first level was where all the human creating was taking place. The second level was where the humans had to experience their creations. The third level was moving into the new Earth. And then moving beyond that, where the physical body gradually turned into pure light encased in a shell or form. Then the ultimate came when the light could no longer be contained, and broke through, like the shattering of an eggshell. After that, it spread, as light, into everything (eternity).

D: *We are being told we are moving into a new reality. Where things will be changed and it will be truly Heaven on Earth. Is that what you mean?*

T: (The tirade had passed. She had calmed down.) It is already within you. You see, you are *seeded* with light. You embody ... you are the seeding! You are the seeding! You are God! (Big sigh of resignation.) Oh, I tell you, I tell you.

D: *But we limit ourselves.*

T: Ah! Is it possible for a creation to encase itself? To *imagine* that it has encased itself? Truly, we ask you. "Come forth. Break out of that shell. IT IS possible! IT IS possible. It is time! It is time! And yet, time? We must enter into the vernacular, you see. It has never been without this expression, and yet you have managed to create a place where you can limit and embrace a limitation of spirit.

D: *That's what I've been told. There is no time. It is an illusion we have created.*

T: Ah-ha! And how else could you see yourselves as being less than everything?

D: *And they say that everything we experience is only lessons that we're learning from.*

T: Lessons that you believe you must experience. I tell you, God is whole, and requires no additions. I apologize. I speak beyond, perhaps, what many are ready to accept or hear. And yet, I tell you that there is beyond that vision. The place – again I enter into your vernacular. I apologize. (Confusion as she attempted to find the words.) The All that cannot – *needs not*, needs not be altered – it *cannot* be altered. It is perfection.

D: *But it still wants to create.*

T: Here, here is the dream.

D: *Because even though he is perfection and has it all, he still wants to experience.*

T: That portion that you speak of is but a portion that is allowed to dream. You see, the supreme that you are imagining – you are imagining the greatest expansion of God – is yet in a limited place. There is *beyond* that. There is *beyond* that. It is not given at this time but to know that there is beyond that.

D: *So there are no limits. There is more than we can possibly understand.*

T: You are given to understand, perhaps not in this incarnation or this manifestation. (Big sigh) It is given to all to know.

685

D: I was told one time that it was not the human brain, it was the mind that has no concepts to embrace many of these things. And that was the problem. That's our limitations.

T: It is the energy of this place. You see, because you have created a physical vehicle, there is only so much that this physical vehicle can absorb of energy. And so there have been limits that have been placed around the human mind so that the information – the overwhelming information.... And I will speak of this one, too (Toni), because she has more greatly allowed herself to accept that there is but the All. And so, you see, she is able to move into it more easily. And yet, the human mind ... we have these limitations that we allow ourselves as a safety measure, because you do not want to *frazzle, frazzle,* the human vehicle, because it has a purpose within that which is manifested here. You must maintain and experience if that is given to you to experience. And so, when you are ready not to have a limited form in which you can accept that you can embrace your experiences, then you shall no longer have the need for the human form.

D: Yes. And we have created this very dense planet that we live on.

T: It only reflects the denseness that you accept. It does not need to be like this. It can be whatever you make of it. This planet is not given a punishment of denseness. No, no, you are given to create as God creates. And this is not denied you. Blessed are you to be in the creation. You are the blessing of the blessing.

D: But you can see why the human mind has these perceptions.

T: Truly, we understand that from which you work. But we say to you, you can manifest a different variation of this dream.

D: And that's where we really have to change our minds to embrace it.

T: Not to change your mind, no, no, but to embrace. To embrace and to *know* that the light – that new Earth, that new world that you speak of – exists within you *now;* it is *there* now.

You just must allow it to come forth. To move into that higher place, that higher place that is *you*. That is *you*.

D: *Is it alright if I present this information, and just allow anyone who can understand it to accept it?*

T: We say to you, yes, it is given at this time that that which has come forth may be placed into the literature. And yes, those that are given the task to come across this information and in reading it to recall; recall that they have chosen that they shall carry this energy, this information. And they, in turn, we ask them, please, please, do not try to do anything, but do, *do allow* this to move in the energy field. Allow it to move in the energy field. And from there it will be taken to its proper place. You have but to allow the possibility. That, "Ah, I see, this I can manifest." And that, that shall be enough.

I thought it was time to get some answers for Toni. To return to the mundane, because she is living in this world, even if it is an illusion. "You know you're speaking through a human body?"

T: Yes, it is given to her to give this information.

Of course, the main question is always about the subject's purpose. Toni was aware that she had psychic abilities, but she didn't know what to do with them. One thing that she can do is feel energy in everything.

T: It is so. She has been given a mission, and yet she says, "Ah, my God, can I perform this mission? I am but so small." (Loud laugh) You see, she has bridged that place from which you say humanity is, to that place which she knows exists. And she chooses – I say to you, she *chooses* – to live in that in-between place. And it has been *allowed* to her to enter into this embodiment and she does not like the human form. But (loud laugh) we say to her, "We have not kept you in the human form for long, for we allow you to leave the human form and to reintegrate into the All." And for this reason, she *embraces* the dream state. She *knows* that in the dream state, she is allowed to return to the All. And I say to you, she *swims* in that place, which is the *Sea of God,* the *Sea of Love,* the *Sea of Light.* And yet she says, "My God, my God, I can even more fully move into you." And we say, "Your place is here, to be into that in-between place so that this knowledge can come from here to here, if such a 'here and here' exists. And so we say, "No. Be, be, be at peace, dear one. Be at peace."

Toni said that she always feels the everyday world where she lives and works is the illusion, and the dream world is the only reality. She always goes to bed early at a certain time, and she can hardly wait to go to sleep so she can journey.

T: It is not the real one, you see. For her it is the *more* real world than this place. And yet even *that* place is not the realest of worlds. Can we use, even, a superlative? Ay, the human language. It is allowed nightly for her to leave the body. You cannot keep her in the form. (Laugh) This session alone has allowed a *great* cleansing to take place. You see, the energy that she has felt building up inside her – *building* up inside her. She has been patient. She says, "In your time, my God, in your time. I will know when you allow it to happen, that it shall be time." And so it has been. We have asked her to wait until this time. She has waited forty-three years for this moment. I say to you, well done!

She was given many instructions about what to do with the energy and how to apply it for healing and many other uses. I do not want to put those parts here, because they contained personal information. At times, she was talking so fast it was hard to transcribe. This entity throughout had a strange accent and much emphasis on words that caused difficulty in trying to put it on paper. The voice also sounded old, ancient, yet very full of wisdom.

T: The consciousness is changing, growing. If I may use this – if you can take a fabric that is woven, and you *stretch* that fabric. Do you not create holes in that fabric? This is what is happening to the *mind* consciousness of humanity. It is stretching. It is stretching – from where? From within! The mind consciousness is stretching from within, and here comes the information. The awareness that exists has never stopped existing, but has been held at bay by the weave. And yet now it is allowed to trickle forth. We work with your time, you see.

D: *I wondered why we didn't go to one of her past lives.*

T: It is not important. Truly, if past lives were who you are, you would never release yourself from this *wheel.*

D: *The wheel of karma.*

T: The wheel. You just ride it and ride it. We say to you, if that is your choice, God is with you, and continue. And yet we say to you, you are free to be released from this envisionment of all that is your reality. It has been a journey. And if this information is in your vision to so include it in your writings, may it be so with our blessings.

D: *First I have to ponder it. Then I can present it, even though I don't understand it. Someone else may.*

T: That is all that can be expected.

During this session with Toni, I was confronted with a question that I have struggled with for a long time and one that my readers have asked me about. It was what she said about us being completely absorbed back into the Source when we return for the final time. This has always bothered me, because I did not

689

like the idea of losing my personality, my individuality, my identity. After all, we work all our lives to create that very thing that makes us unique and different from everyone else. It takes a long time to create the person we have become, and I liked to think that personality remained and was not lost. When I asked this question during the session, the higher part that I was communicating with said that as long as I held to the belief that I was a distinct and separate individual, I would not be ready for the rest of the information they wanted to share with me. I would be stuck in my present mindset and be incapable of learning more. Of course, this has happened numerous times in my thirty years of exploring the unknown. Every time I thought I had it all figured out, that I knew how the whole crazy system worked, they would shake my foundations by presenting a new theory, a new concept, a new way of thinking. So I suppose I should not have been so surprised that they thought it was now time to move forward another baby step. Who knows what else is waiting out there that they want me to know and write about? But first I must attempt to understand this new concept.

The morning after I returned from Canada, where the session was done, I awoke with some of the pieces coming into my mind. Of course, we know who put them there during the sleep state. (Surprise! Surprise!) I will now try to write it down before it once again disappears into the ethers. We *do* have an individuality! We *do* have a distinct and unique personality! But we also had these in all of our other lifetimes. When I remember some of the past lives that I have experienced, I can relive those emotions, those attachments, those goals, those failures, just as if they occurred yesterday. They are very real, and they are associated with the personality I had during those other lives. I can still feel the frustration of the Catholic monk that I was during the Middle Ages when I was smuggling forbidden books into my cell to be read in secret by candlelight. I identify completely with the horror and desperation that I felt as a keeper of the records at the Alexandrian Library, when all that knowledge was destroyed and burned. Yes, all of these people lived and were very real. Then what happened to them? After their death and their trip to the spirit side to receive another assignment, all memory was lost (or absorbed?) upon their reentry into a new Earth life. True, we can access those memories through past life regression, but for most of us, those lives no longer exist on the conscious level. So what am I fearing? Why does the idea of being absorbed into a greater intelligence upset me? We have done this countless times before this life. We lived, we loved, we hated, we experienced. It was real. It did happen. And then the lesson or experience was completed and we moved on in our education. I suppose when we think of it like that, it has happened before and we survived intact. So if it happens again, we will move on in our development. No knowledge is ever lost. Our life, our accomplishments become part of the greater whole. That is the purpose for us having the experiences in the first place, so that the Source can grow.

We see ourselves as a complete entity, and our world, our life, is all that we know. But I have already been told that we are but a very small facet or splinter of a much greater soul, and that soul is the totality of who we are. That soul is the original spark that split off from the Source in the beginning. Even as a tiny spark, it still contained enough energy to create worlds on its own. Its power is so tremendous that it could never fully enter into a body or a room. The body or the location would be totally annihilated because it could not possibly contain it. So it had to split or divide again, just as the original Source did. Our complete soul has been compared to a jewel with many facets, with each facet representing a separate lifetime. They are separate (in our eyes), yet they are One. Our main soul then has to splinter (for want of a better word), and these pieces enter the various physical bodies that we are experiencing simultaneously. So upon our death, we return again to the original soul and are absorbed. Then eventually, all of our lifetimes (which are now encased into the Oversoul) are absorbed again into the Source, the One, the

691

Beginning and End, the All That Is.

So if this has happened to us countless times already, that we have lived a human life and had the memories erased or absorbed upon our death, then there is nothing to fear. The main purpose for reviving them would for the recognition and completion of karma. Our present personality and the records of its accomplishments and deeds (positive or negative) will be filed away in the Library on the spirit side, awaiting review by those interested in research. It is not totally lost. It is just not remembered as the soul journeys onward. Progression is the key. To stand still is to become stagnant. There must always be movement. With movement comes creation of new wonderments. We are only limited by our imagination. Thus creation proceeds into infinity.

I returned to Montreal a few months after this session to give one of my hypnosis classes. I met with Toni again, and this time she told me that more information had been revealed to her about this greater God hypothesis we had encountered. She drew it for me in the form of a diagram to help clarify it. She saw three levels: the first (or lowest) represented duality, separate realities. This was where the individuals existed. The second level or aspect was the one I have been encountering in my work, and written about in this book: God/the "Father". The Source with awareness of experience, the part that needs to learn. It takes on parameters. It needs information and experiences in order to create new things. Then the third level or ultimate Source, which we had not encountered before. The part that was so huge, so vast that it had no need for experience. This was the part that she described as Whole, that needed no addition or subtraction. It encompassed everything.

And yet, there was the hint that even that part was not the ultimate. That there is more beyond that. What that is, I do not know. And it is not given for me to know at this point. They stopped the information, because they said I had to first digest and

692

understand what I had been given. If I was having problems accepting that much, then they would have to wait until I was ready. They said they would never push. They would never force. Yet when I was ready, more would be given. I have no idea what "more" there can be. It is beyond my comprehension at this point, just as the material in this last chapter was beyond my wildest expectations before the session. How can you anticipate something that you do not even know exists? But they are dangling the carrot, they are teasing and intriguing me. They say there is "more", and I will just have to wait and see what that "more" might be. It will come when I am ready, so I know there will be more books.

So this is a good place to end this phase of the adventure. It is time to close the book, give the mind a rest, and return to our real (?) world. There are the many, mundane things that need attending to. So again, treat this book as "mind candy". Something to make you think, and to open doors to the unfathomable. So now, get up from your chair, and go and continue the dream.

Author Page

Dolores Cannon, a regressive hypnotherapist and psychic researcher who records "Lost" knowledge, was born in 1931 in St. Louis, Missouri. She was educated and lived in St. Louis until her marriage in 1951 to a career Navy man. She spent the next 20 years traveling all over the world as a typical Navy wife, and raising her family. In 1970 her husband was discharged as a disabled veteran, and they retired to the hills of Arkansas. She then started her writing career and began selling her articles to various magazines and newspapers. She has been involved with hypnosis since 1968, and exclusively with past-life therapy and regression work since 1979. She has studied the various hypnosis methods and thus developed her own unique technique which enabled her to gain the most efficient release of information from her clients. Dolores is now teaching her unique technique of hypnosis all over the world.

In 1986 she expanded her investigations into the UFO field. She has done on-site studies of suspected UFO landings, and has investigated the Crop Circles in England. The majority of her work in this field has been the accumulation of evidence from suspected abductees through hypnosis.

Dolores is an international speaker who has lectured on all the continents of the world. Her thirteen books are translated into twenty languages. She has spoken to radio and television audiences worldwide. And articles about/by Dolores have appeared in several U.S. and international magazines and newspapers. Dolores was the first American and the first foreigner to receive the "Orpheus Award" in Bulgaria, for the highest advancement in the research of psychic phenomenon. She has received Outstanding Contribution and Lifetime Achievement awards from several hypnosis organizations.

Dolores has a very large family who keep her solidly balanced between the "real" world of her family and the "unseen" world of her work.

If you wish to correspond with Dolores about her work, private sessions or her training classes, please submit to the following address. (Please enclose a self addressed stamped envelope for her reply.) Dolores Cannon, P.O. Box 754, Huntsville, AR, 72740, USA
Or email her at decannon@msn.com or through our Website: www.ozarkmt.com

my mind, waking or sleeping, for an hour in all those years. Active pains and joys flung themselves up during my days, like towers: but always, refluent as air, this persisting, hidden urge re-formed and became a very element of life: till near the end. It was dead before we reached the town.

Next in order had been the superficial, but powerful, motive, of a wish to win the war, with the conviction that we must have Arab help if we were to win the Eastern war, at a price we could afford. Throughout I tried to make the hurt of so exploiting the blood and hope of another people as small in degree as it seemed necessary in kind. When Damascus fell the Turkish war, and probably the German, was decided: and so this motive also died.

Then I was moved by intellectual curiosity, by the desire to feel myself the inspiration of a national movement, thrilling with the ideals and efforts of all a race. From this cup I drank as deeply as any man should do, when we took Damascus: and was sated with it. More would have set in me the vice of authority and smirched my hope, clean as I felt it, to create some lively thing of black marks on white paper. For three days I was arbitrary: and by use that motive died.

There was left to me ambition, the wish to quicken history in the East, as the great adventurers of old had done. I fancied to sum up in my own life that new Asia which inexorable time was slowly bringing upon us. The Arabs made a *chivalrous* [italics added] appeal to my young instinct, and when still at the High School in Oxford already I thought to remake them into a nation, client and fellow of the British Empire.

The necessary Turkish elements to re-shape Anatolia were ready to my hand, could be grasped before the allies saw the hollowness of their victory while they were still made generous by the German army in Flanders. A strong Syria might dominate Mecca, Yemen was not difficult, and then the centre of gravity would have shifted eastward, and Bagdad been ceded to me gracefully.

However, this remained a dream, because of the insubstantiality of abstract ambition by itself as a sole motive: and is here written only for men to call fantastic. It was a fantasy, to believe that an illiterate spirit of nationality, without authority, without a city, or a ship, or a rifle, or a leader of its own could meet Turkey in arms and wrest away its old capital. They gave me the orts and objects of our fighting materials for my share. I studied them to the best of my ability, and used them as far as I could make them go, in a fashion neither dull nor negligent. After such training, with material resources to reinforce the spiritual, the little rest of my ambition might have been not difficult.[4]

The "personal" motive, the "particular Arab" almost certainly refers to Dahoum, whose personality, as was previously mentioned, furnished the most important component for the "S.A." poem. It was Dahoum for whose freedom Lawrence struggled during the war — "To earn you Freedom, the seven pillared worthy house, that your eyes might be shining for me when we came," he wrote in the dedicatory poem.[5] But Dahoum, as we have seen, died of typhus in 1918 before the war ended.[6] That Dahoum was an inspiration to Lawrence during the war, and is included in the dedication of his postwar narrative, is understandable. It is, however, characteristic of Lawrence that he creates a puzzle and invites his potential audience to try to solve it, thus making public once again a matter of private feeling. It is likely that the intensity of feelings expressed in relation to Dahoum is displaced in part from Will, of whom Lawrence was very fond. There is hardly a mention of Will in Lawrence's writings and letters after Will's death in 1915.

Concerning Lawrence's patriotism there is very little to add. He devoted himself wholeheartedly to the Allied cause, utilizing Arab help, and, as Arnold Lawrence has written, "anaesthetized his emotions and turned himself into an instrument of victory."[7] Lawrence has been seen by some of his detractors as working solely for British interests and motivated principally by British imperialism. It is a view I do not share and find difficult to understand.

The motives of "intellectual curiosity" and "ambition" are so closely related that I shall treat them together. The distinction he seems to be making here is between taking himself, and the extent and limits of his capabilities, as the object to be explored ("intellectual curiosity") and working toward the evolution of a political design for the Middle East ("ambition"). But these aims are so intertwined, and derive from sources of energy within Lawrence that are so closely interrelated, as not to admit of separate treatment.

We have seen in earlier chapters that Lawrence's choice of the Arabs as the national movement he would choose to "hustle into form" was to some degree fortuitous, even though his dream of "freeing" them dated back to his childhood (by "freeing" he seems to have meant inclusion in the British Empire).[8] Through the preparations of his earlier years in the Middle East, his maneuvering himself into Cairo at the appropriate time at the beginning of World War I, and the initiatives he took there in 1916 to bring himself from Egypt into Arabia, he turned a historical opportunity into an actuality.

In the early chapters of *Seven Pillars of Wisdom* Lawrence reveals a fantasy of himself as a kind of contemporary armed prophet, the most recent in the history of prophets, inspired in the desert, who had been spiritual and military leaders of the Semitic peoples since the beginning of recorded history. The Arabs of the desert, he writes, were "incorrigibly children of the idea" and "could be swung on an idea as on a cord; for the unpledged allegiance of their minds" (and by implication their suscepti- bility to the development of an allegiance with one, such as Lawrence, who would choose and be able to lead them and to "arrange their minds") made them "obedient servants."[9] The awesome scope and form of this prophet fantasy does not seem to have become fully apparent to Lawrence until after the campaigns were over and he turned to writing his narrative. However, the shape of his continuing ambition, the quickening "root of authority," and his power to convert fantasy into reality clearly evoked fear in Lawrence and played a part in his personal retreat after the war.

In the introductory chapter of the 1922 (Oxford) edition of *Seven Pillars of Wisdom* Lawrence made the most definitive statement of his historical dream and his anxiety about it:

"This, therefore, is a faded dream of the time when I went down into the dust and noise of the Eastern market-place, and with my brain and muscles, with sweat and constant thinking, made others see my visions coming true. Those who dream by night in the dusty recesses of their minds wake in the day to find that all was vanity; but the dreamers of the day are dangerous men, for they may act their dream with open eyes, and make it possible. This I did. I meant to make a new nation, to restore to the world a lost influence, to give twenty millions of Semites the foundation on which to build an inspired dream-palace of their national thoughts. So high an aim called out the inherent nobility of their minds, and made them play a generous part in events; but when we won, it was charged against me that the British petrol royalties in Mesopo- tamia were becoming dubious, and French policy ruined in the Levant. I am afraid that I hope so. We pay for these things too much in honour and innocent lives."[10]

Lawrence wrote in *Seven Pillars of Wisdom* that as he approached his thirtieth birthday (August 15, 1918) he looked back upon medieval- Napoleonic fantasies of glory and achievement that he had previously entertained: "It came to me queerly how, four years ago, I had meant to be a general and knighted, when thirty." But his intensely self-critical nature rejected what he called "crude ambition" and his "detached self" eyed "the performance in the wings in criticism." The favorable opinion he was receiving of his successes made Lawrence anxious and he sought to dissect and examine his motives, to be truthful with himself. "Here were the Arabs believing me, Allenby and Clayton trusting me, my body- guard dying for me," Lawrence observed, and felt that the good reputa- tion was due to his acting, to a "craving for good repute among men," and to fraud. He asked himself whether "all good reputations were founded, like mine, on fraud." He observed how his "self-distrusting shyness held a mask, often a mask of indifference or flippancy, before my face, and puzzled me.[11]

But Lawrence recognized behind this a powerful, egoistic, aggressive drive for fame and ambition (he called it his "egoistic curiosity"), whose proportions frightened him and which he ultimately rejected. He knew that his studied indifference "was only a mask; because despite my trying never to dwell on what was interesting, there were moments too strong for control when my appetite burst out and frightened me."[12] A few paragraphs later he wrote: "Self-seeking ambitions visited me, but not to stay, since my critical self would make me fastidiously reject their fruits. Always I grew to dominate those things into which I had drifted, but in none of them did I voluntarily engage. Indeed, I saw myself a danger to ordinary men, with such capacity yawing rudderless at their disposal."[13]

For Lawrence there seemed to be some conflict over all strong passions, as if he distrusted powerful feelings of any kind. His insight into this quality in himself was unusual. "I was very conscious of the bundled powers and entities within me," he wrote; "it was their character which hid. There was my craving to be liked — so strong and nervous that never could I open myself friendly to another. The terror of failure in an effort so important made me shrink from trying; besides, there was the standard; for intimacy seemed shameful unless the other could make the perfect reply, in the same language, after the same method, for the same reasons.

"There was a craving to be famous; and a horror of being known to like being known. Contempt for my passion for distinction made me refuse every offered honour."[14]

Anis Sayigh, a Lebanese of Palestinian origins and a well-known Arab nationalist writer, has written a perceptive analysis in Arabic of Lawrence's prophet fantasy and role among the Arab peoples.[15] Sayigh sees Lawrence as being in the tradition of Englishmen who had for three centuries exercised in the Middle East "a prophethood directed toward humanitarian aims." But Lawrence's prophethood, according to Sayigh, was not a religious one, for he was not religious and his age was more complex. The call to prophethood of previous ages would not have been appropriate in the early part of the twentieth century. Lawrence's mission, as Sayigh understands it, was one of reconciling the aims of Arab nationalism, which he supported, with the mission of Britain in the Middle East, as he tried to influence it, and each had responsibilities to the other. Lawrence "wished to save the Arab world from Turkish occupation and the greed of the French, Germans and Russians and to give the Arabs a place in the family of liberated nations."[16] Lawrence, in Sayigh's view, saw Britain as having a special mission or responsibility in the underdeveloped world, and he in turn had the responsibility for defining Britain's mission, fixing its boundaries, and supervising it.

Sayigh stresses also Lawrence's belief that in return the Arabs would, in the psychological sense, liberate the Western mind. "His mission was to protect the alliance between the British and the Arabs, so the British would liberate the Arabs through better arms and international power, from the Turks and the Europeans," Sayigh wrote, while "the Arab psyche of absolute individualism would liberate British mentality from the precipitates of the Victorian age." Lawrence, Sayigh concluded, "gave Britain the right of trusteeship over the East as he gave himself the trusteeship over the two."[17]

Sayigh, in my opinion, answers effectively the question of whether Lawrence's "real" motive was to serve the British or the Arabs during the campaigns. Clearly, in this Arab view he was trying to reconcile the complex and often conflicting aims of both. His intolerant conscience occasioned him much suffering over the limitations of the success of his efforts. Writings about Lawrence abound with discussions of whether he "really cared" about the Arabs. It is clear that the Arab peoples played a part in the fulfillment of vast dreams and historical fantasies on Lawrence's part and in this sense he "used" them. On the other hand there is no inherent contradiction between this larger purpose of personal ambition and caring at a personal level. It is the kind of discourse which often fails to be effectively joined because it is carried on at different levels.

Lawrence's older brother spoke with me about Lawrence's affection for individual Arabs and of his distress over the deaths of his young friends Da'ud and Farraj, and the pain he experienced over the atrocities, other deaths and various hardships suffered by the Arabs in the desert.[18] In most of his writings on the campaigns, Lawrence does not dwell on this "sentimental" aspect of himself (although I believe his feelings are only too apparent in *Seven Pillars*), but stressed instead his interests in and views of strategy and the international politics of the Middle East.

In his letter to the Foreign Office staff member, Lawrence wrote, "I don't think there are any other reasons," and he would perhaps have been irritated at efforts to look beyond the "reasons" to which he has given direct testimony. But the highly personal nature of his endeavor in the Middle East, its seeming emergence out of the intense energies of a private purpose, invite our search for some motive in Lawrence's character and personal development that lay outside British policy and Arab need, some driving force within himself. Elie Kedourie recognized this and noted that "the violently personal terms" in which Lawrence would speak "of the public and far-reaching events in which he had been involved" could not be accounted for by "the events in which he happened, quite by chance [not quite] to be mixed up."[19] Rather, wrote Kedourie, "the answer must be sought in his agitated and forceful personality." Kedourie does not inquire further what this answer might be.

A biographer needs to exercise special caution as he approaches the question of deeper personal motives, those inner drives which the subject tries to mold to the opportunities and requirements of external reality.

This is no less true of Lawrence. For even though his introspective nature, his need to wash his mental linen in writings that would inevitably become public, gives us more opportunity than is usually available when studying historical figures to gain insight into the psychological roots of significant actions, direct evidence for interpretations, even in his case, is nevertheless limited. Only inferences that are no more than likelihoods can be drawn.

The pivotal concept linking Lawrence's passionate pursuit of his "mission" in the Arab cause with his background and personal development lies, in my opinion, in the idea of redemption. Arnold Lawrence understood well his mother's hope that her sons would redeem her guilt. With the deaths during the war of Frank and Will, the burden fell upon T.E., and we have seen how urgently he felt the need to become more active in the campaigns after they died. His reference in *Seven Pillars of Wisdom* to the Germans in Syria as "the enemy who had killed my brothers" suggests this personal element.[20]

The language of renunciation and redemption pervades *Seven Pillars of Wisdom*. Lawrence saw the Arabs of the desert as exemplifying the ideal of renouncing the desires of the world, and his identification with this element he saw (or wished to see) in them played an important part in the structure of the private fantasy by which he was propelled during the campaigns. "The common base of all the Semitic creeds, winners or losers, was the ever present ideal of world-worthlessness," Lawrence wrote in *Seven Pillars*. "Their profound reaction from matter led them to preach bareness, renunciation, poverty; and the atmosphere of this invention stifled the minds of the desert pitilessly."[21] Or: "The desert Arab found no joy like the joy of voluntarily holding back. He found luxury in abnegation, renunciation, self-restraint. . . . His desert was made a spiritual ice-house, in which was preserved intact but unimproved for all ages a vision of the unity of God."[22]

The Arabs were idealized as his own ancestors were devalued. He wrote of the "fine-drawn Arabs whom generations of in-breeding had sharpened to a radiance ages older than the primitive, blotched, honest Englishmen."[23] But the Arabs were a subject people, held in bondage by the Turks, fallen from the former prosperous state of their civilization. In fitting his image of the Arab condition to the outlines of his personal dream, Lawrence condensed time and smoothed out the irregularities of historical fact and detail. "With the coming of the Turks," he wrote "[Arab] happiness became a dream. By stages the Semites of Asia passed under their yoke, and found it a slow death. Their goods were stripped from them; and their spirits shrivelled in the numbing breath of a military Government."[24]

The struggle to create and redeem runs throughout *Seven Pillars of Wisdom*, and Lawrence's personal identification with the Arabs is striking. His redemption and theirs are so intertwined as to be indistinguishable, and he became fully aware that he had attempted to achieve the former through the latter. He would sacrifice himself on behalf of the Arabs and redeem thereby the lowly state (as he perceived it) of both. But the profound egoist root of this self-sacrifice could not escape his ruthless self-examination. It confirmed his belief in his deceitfulness, his illegitimacy, and deepened the sense of sin and guilt, lowering his self-regard still further. "To endure for another in simplicity gave a sense of greatness," Lawrence wrote. "There was nothing loftier than a cross, from which to contemplate the world. The pride and exhilaration of it were beyond conceit. Yet each cross, occupied, robbed the late-comers of all but the poor part of copying: and the meanest of things were those done by example. The virtue of sacrifice lay within the victim's soul.

"Honest redemption must have been free and child-minded. When the expiator was conscious of the under-motives and the after-glory of his act, both were wasted on him. So the introspective altruist appropriated a share worthless, indeed harmful, to himself, for had he remained passive, his cross might have been granted to an innocent. To rescue simple ones from such evil by paying for them his complicated self would be avaricious in the modern man. . . . Complex men who knew how self-sacrifice uplifted the redeemer and cast down the bought, and who held back in his knowledge, might so let a foolish brother take the place of false nobility and its later awakened due of heavier sentence. There seemed no straight walking for us leaders in this crooked lane of conduct, ring within ring of unknown, shamefaced motives cancelling or double-charging their precedents."[25]

To the political deceit of the Revolt was added for Lawrence what he considered the psychological deceit of using another people's need vicariously for personal redemption. No external success or approval as judged in the eyes of the world could affect the inner condemnation of this crime. "The hearing other people praised made me despair jealously of myself, for I took it at its face value; whereas, had they spoken ten times as well of me, I would have discounted it to nothing. I was a standing court martial on myself, inevitably, because to me the inner springs of action were bare with the knowledge of exploited chance."[26]

16

Lawrence the Enabler

All my experience of the Arabs was of the God-father role," Lawrence wrote to Mrs. Shaw. "My object . . . was always to make them stand on their own feet."[1]

To enable another to do for himself what he cannot do without your help presents not only practical and psychological difficulties but raises inevitably a number of moral questions as well. This "enabling" is an essential aspect of such diverse human pursuits as child-rearing, psychotherapy and organizational leadership. It becomes the central dimension of action should a person attempt, as Lawrence did, to reach across cultures to help another people achieve a revolution that it could not accomplish without an outsider's help. No matter how much the helper attempts to identify with the ideals and purposes of another group or people, and works in the service of *its* values and needs, it is doubtful whether he can keep completely separate his own idea of what the others ought to have, or ought to want, or avoid influencing them to dream his dreams. Thus, depending upon the effectiveness of his influence or the scope of his powers, the helper inevitably becomes a kind of aggressor, imposing upon the recipients of his aid his own ideas and needs. When one nation helps another, the imposition is largely political or economic, the serving of national interest in concert with or at the expense of another's. When one person who, because of exceptional abilities brought to focus on an unusual historical situation, has a chance to assume a powerful personal role, the opportunities for him to live out his personal needs and impulses in the service of those he is helping are very great indeed.

Lawrence understood this dilemma profoundly. It lay at the heart of his conflicts regarding what he considered his exploitative role among the Arabs, the mutual prostitution he felt he had been a part of. He tried desperately to exploit no one, to serve the Arabs in the terms of *their* needs, the Allies in terms of *theirs*, and to fulfill at the same time a progressive and humanitarian vision of the progress of history. I believe that within the constraints of the situation he succeeded as well as anyone could have. But Lawrence was also serving his own psychological needs and trying to resolve profound personal conflicts. Ultimately, the shadow of these conflicts, aggravated by the actualities and traumata of the war experience, especially the conflicts that grew out of his need to identify so deeply and thoroughly with the people he was helping, came to dominate his view of himself as the Arabs' leader.

His judgment of what he had accomplished among the Arabs, accurate in a personal psychological sense, often excluded from his feelings any balancing appreciation of the good he had accomplished in the service of Arab ideals and freedom. "A man who gives himself to be a possession of aliens," he wrote early in *Seven Pillars of Wisdom*, "leads a Yahoo life, having bartered his soul to a brute-master. He is not of them. He may stand against them, persuade himself of a mission, batter and twist them into something which they, of their own accord, would not have been. Then he is exploiting his old environment to press them out of theirs. Or, after my model, he may imitate them so well that they spuriously imitate him back again. Then he is giving away his own environment: pretending to theirs; and pretences are hollow, worthless things."[2] The very uncertainty or instability that characterized Lawrence's sense of his own identity operated as an asset in relation to his work with the Arabs. It furnished him with a flexibility that enabled him to shift back and forth between an identification with the Arab world and Arab ways and his role as a British officer (although a rather scruffy one).

It could be argued with justification that no one asked Lawrence to get so involved in the Arab Revolt and assume such thorough responsibility for its conduct and progress that he would have to "barter his soul." But once having taken the responsibility upon himself he did not have the benefit of the personal distance from the agonies of death and mutilation that is the prerogative of most commanders and strategists in modern warfare. Lawrence was simultaneously a commanding strategist of the Revolt, and in the thick of its bloody encounters. In a letter to his friend Richards, written during the last year of the war, he suggests the admixture of pain and pleasure his unique role brought him: "My bodyguard of fifty Arab tribesmen, picked riders from the young men of the deserts, are more splendid than a tulip garden, and we ride like lunatics and with our Bedouins pounce on unsuspecting Turks and destroy them in heaps: and it is all very gory and nasty after we close grips. I love the preparation, and the journey, and loathe the physical fighting."[3]

Lawrence possessed an impressive array of talents and qualifications which suited him well for his work in the Revolt. These included a remarkable memory, intellectual brilliance, flexibility and vision, unusual physical stamina, and great personal courage. In addition he was well schooled during his previous years at Carchemish, and his travels in Syria, in the characteristics of the lands and peoples with whom he would have to deal, and he had read extensively about the history and science of war. But his most important qualities were psychological, the capacity, above all, to identify with the feelings, hopes, fears, ideals and way of life of another people so different from himself, and to draw them, in turn, into an identification with him.

Lawrence the scholar was very much in evidence when he was planning the tactics of the campaigns. "I was not an instinctive soldier, automatic with intuitions and happy ideas," he wrote Liddell Hart, "and when I took a decision, or adopted an alternative, it was after studying (doing my best to study) every relevant — and many an irrelevant — factor. Geography, tribal structure, religion, social customs, language, appetites, standards — all were at my finger-ends. The enemy I knew almost like my own side.[4] I risked myself among them a hundred times, to learn."[5] On reading the typescript of this passage, which Liddell Hart wished to use in his biography, Lawrence thought it might sound boastful. He made the substitution I have put in parentheses and deleted the word "all." But beyond all this, the integration of a successful Arab guerrilla campaign — combining operations of raids on camelback, in armored cars, and eventually in airplanes, with more traditional movements of regular forces — was an art, which the British recognized in giving Lawrence so much latitude.

Lieutenant-Colonel W. F. Stirling, who was with Lawrence during much of 1918, has provided a valuable firsthand picture of the courage, endurance and psychological gifts which enabled Lawrence to work successfully with the Arabs. The following paragraphs are from an article written by Stirling and published before Lawrence's death:

What was it that enabled Lawrence to seize and hold the imagination of the Arabs? . . . The answer may partly be that he represented the heart of the Arab movement for freedom, and the Arabs realized that he had vitalized their cause; that he could do everything and endure everything just a little better than the Arabs themselves. . . . The Emir Feisal treated him as a brother, as an equal. . . . But chiefly, I think we must look for the answer in Lawrence's uncanny ability to sense the feelings of any group of men in whose company he found himself; his power to probe behind their minds and to uncover the well springs of their actions.

His powers of endurance, too, were phenomenal. Few of even the most hard-bitten Arabs would ride with him from choice.[*] He never tired. Hunger, thirst and lack of sleep appeared to have little effect on him. He had broken

---

[*] Apparently this was not true of the more competitive shaykhs. See paragraph 3 of Joyce's remarks quoted below.

all the records of the dispatch riders of the Caliph Haroun al Raschid which had been sung for centuries in the tribal sagas. On one occasion he rode his camel three hundred miles in three consecutive days [no one ever seems to comment on the camel's endurance]. I once rode with mine fifty miles at a stretch, and that was enough for me. . . . His spiritual equipment overrode the ordinary needs of flesh and blood.[6]

The most valuable eyewitness view of Lawrence during the campaigns and at work among the Arabs has been provided by Colonel Pierce Joyce, an Irishman and Lawrence's immediate superior during most of the Revolt. Unlike many of the officers who served in the campaigns, Joyce has never published his memoirs or written an essay about the war or about Lawrence. His accounts are contained in the unpublished transcripts of two BBC broadcasts he made in April 1939 and July 1941 respectively. He spoke as follows:

On a matter of principle Lawrence never trusted Regular officers in general. He considered them limited in imagination, and insufficiently elastic to withstand the shocks of Arab strategy and tactics. . . . On my part I was suspicious of a Lieutenant with no executive command but with a definite political significance and therefore from my point of view entirely to be mistrusted.

Happily this initial setback eventually turned into a great personal friendship which survived many subsequent differences of opinion of how Regular troops should be utilised. The almost impossible tasks initiated in his fertile brain would have shocked the leaders of a Spanish Inquisition, and we had only quite ordinary and unimaginative personnel with which to carry them out. "It is all such sport," he used to say, and certainly his enthusiasm must have been infectious, for the hours of sport were few and the days and months of dust and sun were long and weary. On this occasion his appearance was such a contrast to the untidy Lieutenant I had met at Port Sudan that one suddenly became aware of contact with a very unusual personality. . . . At this, as at dozens of other conferences we attended together, Lawrence rarely spoke. He merely studied the men around him and when the arguments ended as they usually did, in smoke, he then dictated his plan of action which was usually adopted and everyone went away satisfied. It was not, as is often supposed, by his individual leadership of hordes of Bedouins that he achieved success in his daring ventures, but by the wise selection of tribal leaders and by providing the essential grist to the mill in the shape of golden rewards for work well done.

His individual bravery and endurance captured their imagination. Initial successes made "Orance," as the Arabs called him, a byword in the desert and there was always competition among the sheiks to ride with him on a foray. Like the rest of us he had many disappointments, but nothing could shake his determination to win through, or his restless energy in initiating alternative plans when things went wrong. . . . Lawrence and I used to do many desert trips on reconnaissance work, in the famous Rolls Royce Tender

which he christened "The Blue Mist." The desert leagues became furlongs.
. . . Lawrence invariably sat beside the driver indicating the direction with
his hand and with an open throttle we tore across sand dunes and ridges under his almost uncanny guidance [a number of the men who accompanied
Lawrence in the desert have remarked upon his ability to recall the location
of a bush, a rise or a rock after he had once seen it]. . . .
   It was during these desert rips [sic] that I first realized Lawrence's joy in
motion and craze for speed.[7]

"My habit of always hiding behind a Sherif was to avoid measuring
myself against the pitiless Arab standard, with its no-mercy for foreigners
who wore its clothes, and aped its manners," Lawrence wrote of what
Joyce had referred to as his "wise selection of tribal leaders."
   In the earlier broadcast (April 1939), Joyce emphasized Lawrence's
shrewd judgment in the selection of Arab personnel and his ability to
appeal to the imagination of the Arab leaders:

   Feisal was, of course, his outstanding success. Here was the man Lawrence
   had come to Arabia to find and who would bring the Arab Revolt to full
   glory. Sherif Nasir, Ali Ibn el Hussein, Auda Abu Tayi were all instruments
   of successful ventures. Hosts of others appeared and as quickly disappeared
   when they had carried out their task and earned their reward. It is difficult
   to keep Arab irregulars any length of time in the field and so it was ever
   changing personnel on whom Lawrence had to rely for support. . . . His
   disregard for conventions in uniforms is well known — while in Arab dress
   he outrivalled the splendour of Descendants of the Prophet. This again was
   not merely personal vanity. Arabs have a respect for fine raimant, which they
   associate with riches and power. It made him an outstanding figure among
   them, excited their curiosity, and therefore increased his authority when
   dealing with them.[8]

Lawrence's selection of the regal-looking Faisal to be the principal
military leader of the Revolt in preference to his more politically minded
and steadfastly anti-Ottoman older brother, Abdullah, has been frequently written about. Their first meeting at Hamra is dramatically described in Seven Pillars of Wisdom and the passage gives the impression
that Lawrence's decision was made spontaneously on the spot ("I felt at
first glance that this was the man I had come to Arabia to seek").[9]
Actually, there were rather detailed intelligence files in Cairo on the
sharif's sons, and the decision by Lawrence to work principally through
Faisal's leadership was a practical one, based in part on these intelligence
reports. In the first issue of The Arab Bulletin, which was published early
in June 1916, Faisal was reported to be "a good leader" — with "immense
authority" with the tribes.[10] His assets in these accounts included an
attractive appearance and personal qualities, an imposing manner, natural
ability as a soldier, popularity among the Bedouin, efficiency, lack of

prejudice against Christians, and years of experience living in Syria and Constantinople. Liabilities included his readiness to become discouraged, a streak of unreasonableness and narrow-mindedness, a hot temper, and a tendency to be impulsive and rash.[11] In a letter to Newcombe written in January 1917, Lawrence's enthusiasm for Faisal was unrestrained and he called him "an absolute ripper."[12]

Lawrence's relationship with Faisal was many-faceted, and statements of his about the amir, when taken out of context, seem to contradict other comments.[13] When writing to the British authorities, for example, Lawrence would stress Faisal's strength, while in private correspondence and conversation he stated that Faisal was not brave.[14] Lawrence distinguished, however, between spiritual and physical courage. If Lawrence's view of Faisal is taken in its totality, it provides an internally consistent though complex picture of the relationship from Lawrence's standpoint.[15] Records of Faisal's observations about Lawrence are far more fragmentary.

After his first meeting with Faisal at Hamra on October 23, 1916, Lawrence wrote only that he had been "arguing with Feisal (who was most unreasonable) for hours and hours." The next day they had another "hot discussion" which lasted all morning and "ended amicably."[16] After these meetings Lawrence wrote the following detailed description of Faisal for *The Arab Bulletin*: "Sidi Feisal. — Is tall, graceful, vigorous, almost regal in appearance. Aged thirty-one. Very quick and restless in movement. Far more imposing personally than any of his brothers, knows it and trades on it. Is as clear-skinned as a pure Circassian, with dark hair, vivid black eyes set a little sloping in his face, strong nose, short chin. Looks like a European, and very like the monument of Richard I, at Fontevraud [Lawrence's medieval hero again]. He is hot-tempered, proud, and impatient, sometimes unreasonable, and runs off easily at tangents. Possesses far more personal magnetism and life than his brothers, but less prudence. Obviously very clever, perhaps not over-scrupulous. Rather narrow-minded, and rash when he acts on impulse, but usually with enough strength to reflect, and then exact in judgment. Had he been brought up the wrong way might have become a barrack-yard officer. A popular idol, and ambitious; full of dreams, and the capacity to realize them, with keen personal insight, and a very efficient man of business."[17]

Having found his Arab fellow-dreamer in the desert, Lawrence proceeded to pull the strings of the Revolt far more through Faisal, who clearly trusted him, than through any other Arab leader. But Faisal used Lawrence as well to fulfill his own personal ambitions. Sir Reginald Wingate considered it improbable that a man like Faisal, who "had been dancing for years" on the tightrope of Arab-Turkish affairs, who was familiar with European questions and manners, and sophisticated politi-

cally in his own right, "would have been used by a young man so
inexperienced in politics and world affairs as Lawrence."[18] In my opinion
Lawrence was experienced politically ahead of his years and the using, as
in most mutually advantageous relationships that contain an element of
exploitation, went in both directions.

Lawrence appears to have identified in many ways with Faisal, so
much so that in writing of him he often seemed to be writing about himself, or perhaps, about what he had helped Faisal to become. "One never
asked if he were scrupulous," Lawrence wrote in *Seven Pillars of Wisdom*,
"but later he showed that he could return trust for trust, suspicion for
suspicion. He was fuller of wit than of humor. . . . .

"Meanwhile, here, as it seemed, was offered to our hand, which had
only to be big enough to take it, a *prophet* [my italics] who, if veiled,
would give cogent form to the idea behind the activity of the Arab
revolt."[19] In the conversations in the tent Faisal "kept command of the
conversation even at its hottest, and it was fine to watch him do it. He
showed full mastery of tact, with a real power of disposing men's feelings
to his wish."[20]

Clearly, despite assertions to the contrary, Lawrence did like Faisal.
Three months after their first meeting he wrote his family: "Sherif Feisal
(3rd son of Sherif of Mecca), to whom I am attached, is about 31, tall,
slight, lively, well-educated. He is charming towards me, and we get on
perfectly together."[21] A decade later this feeling had not changed despite
Lawrence's disappointment in some of Faisal's limitations.

I have not been able to examine whatever memoirs Faisal may have
written. Clearly he valued his relationship with Lawrence. Even Abdullah, who did write his memoirs and resented Lawrence's "influence
among the tribes," acknowledged that Lawrence was successful in his
work with Faisal's army and "was regarded as the moving spirit in the
Revolt."[22] Ronald Storrs wrote in his memoirs that Faisal spoke to him of
Lawrence "with a good-humored tolerance which I should have resented
more if I had ever imagined that kings could like king-makers."[23] Lawrence wrote Faisal in November 1932, and Faisal in his reply thanked
him "for the interest you have had of our affairs despite your being at far
distant from us. As a sincere friend of us who has ever been our valuable
support, I wish you pleasant long life."[24]

In interviewing Faisal some years later, Mrs. Stuart Erskine found him
evasive when she asked him about Lawrence.

"Lawrence?" she quotes the king as saying. "He said many things about
me which are not a bit true and I should probably say things about him
which would not be true either. He was a genius, of course, but not for
this age."

"For a past age," she suggested.

"On the contrary, for the future. A hundred years hence, perhaps two
hundred years hence, he might be understood; but not today."[25]

Lawrence's dispatches for *The Arab Bulletin,* and those of his other Arab-minded colleagues, were filled with the fruits of their studies. Lawrence's reports in particular covered a broad range of subject matter, which included diaries of his journeys and raids; analyses of the geography, tribal structure, personalities, rivalries and religious tenets of the Arab leaders; and discussions of the political problems and history of the area.

From a psychosocial standpoint his "Twenty-seven Articles," on the handling of Arab tribesmen, which was written early in August 1917, not long after the capture of Aqaba, is the most important and most remarkable. The articles reveal, above all, the results of Lawrence's unremitting study of the Bedouin, his understanding of their psychology (and of other men's as well), and his extreme sensitivity to the self-regard of others lest through injuring the self-esteem of another person the bond might be broken or a potential alliance be prevented. The articles stress objectivity, self-control and discipline, and the holding of oneself emotionally and physically aloof. He explains the importance of working through the tribal leaders and describes the political rewards for the Arabs and the Allies of respecting the "conception of the Sherif." Doing too much for the Arabs is to be avoided because "it is their war." (When Lawrence wrote to King Husayn in June 1918, he referred to "your small Northern army,"[26] although to Robert Graves he wrote rather cynically of Husayn: "We had to pretend that he led.")[27] He discusses the value, difficulties and dangers for a foreigner of wearing Arab dress, while at the same time retaining British identity ("They make no special allowances for you when you dress like them . . . you will be like an actor in a foreign theatre") and stresses the need to do it "the whole way" if Arab things are worn. "This road should not be chosen without serious thought," he warns. There is much else on discussing religion with Bedouin (their faith is so intimate and intense a part of their daily lives "as to be unconscious"), using Bedouin raiding skills and tactics in warfare, the problems of mixing town and desert Arabs, pitfalls of talking about women ("avoid too free talk"), the selection of servants, and the need to look for inner motives behind the proffered explanations. Lawrence concludes with the advice to "bury yourself in Arab circles," for "your success will be just proportional to the amount of mental effort you devote to it." The complete text of the "Twenty-seven Articles" is provided in the Appendix, pp. 463–467.

Many British officers observed at first hand the steadfastness with which Lawrence personally adhered to the tenets of his twenty-seven points, worked, in fact, *through* and *with* the Arab leaders, and retained his patience with them and the tribesmen despite extraordinary frustrations. G. F. Peake wrote, for example: "He was always very conscious of the fact that he was a European and a Christian and also that the desert tribesmen were proud people, jealous of their freedom and fanatical as

regards their religion. . . . His strong personality and knowledge of the
Arabs of the desert no doubt enabled him unobtrusively to get his plans
adopted, without rousing the latent antipathy to all who are not of their
race and religion."[28] A. F. Nayton, the military governor of Beersheba,
wrote long after the war to Arnold Lawrence of "the infinite patience with
which . . . Lawrence handled the Arabs, notwithstanding many disappointments and the innumerable times he was 'let down' by them."[29]

Several of the Howeitat shaykhs* whom I interviewed in Jordan in
April of 1967 remembered Lawrence vividly. None of them, they said,
had ever been interviewed. Their memories of battles and raids, of places
and names, were surprisingly detailed and apparently accurate (except
for dates), considering that the events had taken place a half century
before. Perhaps this is due to the absence of literacy, and the dependence
on recollections through sight and sound, when communication is
achieved orally. "Their very illiteracy has trained them to a longer
memory and a closer hearing of the news," Lawrence once wrote.[31] These
men had ranged in age from fifteen to twenty-eight at the time of the
Revolt. The interviews were tape-recorded and except for one of them
were translated into English on the spot. Later they were gone over by a
second translator to check for accuracy and fill in omissions.

What was most striking to me in these interviews was the way in
which they presented a kind of mirror image of the "Twenty-seven
Articles," a confirmation of the effectiveness of this treatise on Arab
social psychology seen from the Bedouin point of view. All of these men
found dignity and personal pride in their role in the Arab Revolt, which
remained for some of them the most important period of their lives, the
time when they set aside their traditional quarrels and worked together
toward the common goal of getting rid of the Turkish oppressor and
obtaining freedom for their lands and people. The leadership in their
eyes was provided by their own tribal shaykhs through an understanding
with Faisal and the Ashraf (the sharif's family). They took great pride in
the fact that the victory was an Arab victory achieved by Arabs.
Lawrence's role (he was the only Englishman any of the men I interviewed remembered in any detail, and the only one who dressed and
lived as an Arab among them) was deeply valued, but he was seen as a
planner (including the attack on Aqaba and the battle of Tafila),[32] the
encourager and coordinator of the Revolt, the one who obtained supplies,
guns and ammunition. But he worked through Faisal and the other Arab
leaders. "Because Faisal trusted Lawrence we all trusted him," one
shaykh told me. "He was a servant of our master, Faisal, among the
Bedouin."[33]

My informants stated clearly that their acceptance and trust of

* Lawrence once commented in one of his dispatches, "A feature of the Howeitat
is that every fourth or fifth man is a sheikh." [30]

Lawrence grew out of his willingness to live among them, speak their language, wear their clothing, and eat their food. One said, "He was a friend, an Arab . . . he was a faithful man . . . he was an Englishman, but he was a pure friend to the Arabs . . . we suspect those who do not eat with us."[34] (Compare this with Lawrence's "they taught me that no man could be their leader except he ate the ranks' food, wore their clothes, lived with them, and yet appeared better in himself.")[35] Although there were educated Arabs in the campaigns, Lawrence used, according to these tribesmen, "to walk with the Bedouin."

The detailed and careful way in which Lawrence would look after the needs of the tribes was stressed by several men. One told me:

> You know he had learned Arabic. He used to come to a shaykh and say, "We are going to work for a month or two. How many are your people and how much money do you need so that they will not suffer hunger while you are away with your men at war?" He used to think of everything. Now this is what we loved. Because before we went on any expedition he used to know which tribes the expedition was going to consist of. He used to have a big statement — a detailed statement of every member of that family that was going to go on this expedition and knew full well how many members of this expedition would stay behind, and he used to give them enough money to buy food, rice, fat and everything that would keep them going for four months or how long he thought the expedition would last.[36]

The Bedouin valued Lawrence also as a teacher. He was the one who showed them the use of explosives and other means of winning, but he did not just do it for them. They won their own battles. The men who worked most closely with Lawrence felt that he had cared about them personally and they returned the feeling. They would bring him accounts of raids or of prisoners captured, and Lawrence would be lavish in his appreciation and encouragement. Lawrence often did not carry a gun or take part in hand-to-hand combat, but he would risk his life laying the mines by the railroad. The Bedouin were impressed with his bravery, especially as he seemed to risk his life frequently in blowing up the trains. One shaykh told me, "He was very brave with the Arabs . . . whenever he found an injured person he would go into battle and get him away and take him to the camp."

Sometimes Lawrence would summon the shaykhs to his tent — "Majlis Lawrence" — and they would have a big meal of rice and lamb and discuss tactics and share the small talk of tribal life. One shaykh recalled Lawrence bringing out some money after he found out that one of the shaykhs sitting at the table had three wives. "You give this money to your first one and this to the second and this to the third," Lawrence said, "but don't tell one that you gave the other one any so she might think she is special."[37]

Considerable mutual respect and love seem to have developed during
the many months that the shaykhs and tribesmen fought with Lawrence.
They were saddened when the parting came at Damascus. Shaykh 'Ayd
told me, "Some of the shaykhs were crying because he left. . . . He told
them he was leaving and they shook hands and said: 'Have I done anything wrong towards you?' and he said, 'No, on the contrary . . .' and he
saw they had tears in their eyes and he said good-bye and they knew he
was going."[38]

A Lebanese colleague of mine recently listed three types of Western
"innocents" who have traditionally been drawn to the Middle East: the
missionaries; those with an ethnocentric bias who wish to modernize the
area; and the romantics who idealize the Arabs of the desert.[39] The most
consistent criticism of Lawrence, and one which is certainly valid from
our contemporary perspective, is that he falls into the third, the romantic,
category. Lawrence idealized the Bedouin life, its freedom from civilization, and feared the effect of contact with the West: "The poverty of
Arabia made them simple, continent, enduring. If forced into civilized
life they would have succumbed like any savage race to its diseases,
meanness, luxury, cruelty, crooked dealing, artifice; and, like savages,
they would have suffered them exaggeratedly for lack of inoculation."[40]
Lawrence longed to be part of this society, but knew he could not be.
"You guessed rightly that the Arab appealed to my imagination," he
wrote during the war to his friend Richards. "It is the old, old civilisation,
which has refined itself clear of household go[?o]ds, and half the trappings
which ours hastens to assume. The gospel of bareness in materials is a
good one, and it involves apparently a sort of moral bareness too. They
think for the moment, and endeavour to slip through life without turning
corners or climbing hills. In part it is a mental and moral fatigue, a race
trained out, and to avoid difficulties they have to jettison so much that we
think honourable and grave: and yet without in any way sharing their
point of view, I think I can understand it enough to look at myself and
other foreigners from their direction, and without condemning it. I know
I'm a stranger to them, and always will be: but I cannot believe them
worse, any more than I could change their ways."[41]
Anis Sayigh has discussed the consequences of Lawrence's hostility to
the "trappings" of civilization for the Arab world. Lawrence, he says,
wished to impose his fantasy of the way of life of the desert Arabs on all
Arabs, a way of life many modern Arabs understandably think of as
backward. Lawrence longed for the world of the tribal chiefs, with no
formal government, which imprisons, and no factories, modern armies,
police or schools, which mold men's minds. He was critical of the settled
life of Egypt and Lebanon, which is why he would not cooperate with
the Arab nationalists of the cities and insisted upon imposing Hashemite

rulers of Bedouin origin upon the Arab peoples of the cities as well as the desert. Sayigh goes on to say that not only did Lawrence try to impose his preferences upon the Arab world, but he was able to influence British leaders after the war of his views. He would have served the modern Arab world better, Sayigh believes, had he sought a new Arab civilization that would digest all classes in a society in which the Bedouin would have become a stable part of the totality.[42]

How realistic or feasible this would have been for Lawrence in 1918 is a difficult question. Sayigh's argument remains, however, one of the most telling criticisms of Lawrence's influence upon the modern Arab world and of his role as an enabler of change and growth for the Arab peoples with whom he worked and lived.

17

The Conflict of Responsibility

Lawrence had no power to appoint anybody to be Governor of Damascus," General Chauvel wrote with obvious irritation in 1929,[1] and, in fact, no official authorization has been discovered for Lawrence's assumption of authority during the Revolt, either in this instance or in many others. But whether one considers that Lawrence took authority legitimately or usurped it, he did assume *personal responsibility* for the course and conduct of the Arab Revolt in the field and for the political assurances made to the Arab leaders during the course of the war. After the capture of Aqaba he wrote his family as if the Revolt were a personal charge that he dared not neglect: "It is more restful in Arabia, because one feels so nervous of what may happen if one goes away. I cannot ask for leave, as I know there is so much to do down there, and no one to do it."[2] At times he felt he "had a reserve of confidence to carry the whole thing, if need be, on my shoulders."[3]

This exaggerated sense of responsibility finds its fullest and most vivid expression in *Seven Pillars of Wisdom* and contributes greatly to the egoistic tone of the book. Whether or not he was officially limited to serving as an intelligence officer in a liaison capacity to Amir Faisal, Lawrence makes clear in passage after passage that he considered himself responsible for the direction and conduct of the Arab campaigns, an attitude he undoubtedly maintained during the war itself, although it is less evident in the official dispatches. "My personal duty was command," he wrote in *Seven Pillars*, "and the commander, like the master architect, was responsible for all."[4] "All" included not only the strategy, organization and coordination of the Revolt but the lives and well-being of virtually every participant in the Allied effort, English and Arab, and to some degree of the enemy as well.

In conceiving and implementing the strategies of the desert campaigns Lawrence concerned himself both with the use of materials and the planning of tactics and with the psychological dimension of warfare — with the influencing of men's minds. The psychological element of command, he wrote, "considers the capacity for mood of our men, their complexities and mutability, and the cultivation of what in them profits the intention. We had to arrange their minds in order of battle, just as carefully and as formally as other officers arranged their bodies: and not only our own men's minds, though them first: the minds of the enemy, so far as we could reach them: and thirdly, the mind of the nation supporting us behind the firing-line, and the mind of the hostile nation waiting the verdict, and the neutrals looking on."[5] Lawrence's inner sense of responsibility, especially for individual human lives, corresponded in intensity with the scope and intensity of his ambitions and contributed greatly to the increasing anguish he experienced as the months of the Revolt passed, the horrors mounted, and he realized he could not possibly fulfill its exacting and (by the judgments of most people) unrealistic terms.

The futility and unnecessary slaughter of Kut-el-Amara had impressed Lawrence deeply, for in the introductory chapter to the 1922 (Oxford) edition of *Seven Pillars* he drew upon it to exemplify his contempt for what he called "murder" war. "I went up the Tigris," he wrote, "with one hundred Devon Territorials, young, clean, delightful fellows, full of the power of happiness, and of making women and children glad. By them one saw vividly how great it was to be their kin, and English. And we were casting them by thousands into the fire, to the worst of deaths, not to win the war, but that the corn and rice and oil of Mesopotamia might be ours. The only need was to defeat our enemies (Turkey among them), and this was at last done in the wisdom of Allenby with less than four hundred killed, by turning to our uses the hands of the oppressed in Turkey. I am proudest of my thirty fights in that I did not have any of our blood shed. All the subject provinces of the Empire to me were not worth one dead English boy. If I have restored to the East some self-respect, a goal; ideals: if I have made the standard of rule of white over red more exigent, I have fitted those people in a degree for the new commonwealth in which the dominant races will forget their brute achievements, and white and red and yellow and brown and black will stand up together without side-glances in the service of the world."[6]

But Lawrence did not limit his injunction against killing to English boys and men: "To me an unnecessary action, shot, or casualty, was not only waste but sin. I was unable to take the professional view that all successful actions were gains. Our rebels were not materials, like soldiers, but friends of ours, trusting our leadership."[7] Or: "In the pursuit of the ideal conditions we might kill Turks, because we disliked them very much; but the killing was a pure luxury. If they would go quietly the war would end. If not, we would urge them, or try to drive them out. In the last resort, we should be compelled to the desperate course of blood and the maxims of 'murder war,' but as cheaply as could be for ourselves, since the Arabs fought for freedom, and that was a pleasure to be tasted only by a man alive."[8] And, finally: "To man-rationale, wars of nationality were as much a cheat as religious wars, and nothing was worth fighting for: nor could fighting, the act of fighting, hold any need of intrinsic virtue. Life was so deliberately private that no circumstances could justify one man in laying violent hands on another's: though a man's own death was his last free will, a saving grace and measure of intolerable pain."[9]

In passage after passage of *Seven Pillars*, Lawrence describes his personal intervention in disputes and other tribal matters, of which one may justly ask what affair it was of his to become involved. But he held steadfastly to the view that jealousies and feuds could easily have disrupted what unity the Revolt possessed, and his ability to identify with Arab psychology, his detailed knowledge of the tribes, and his position *outside* any one of them make his justification for interfering plausible. His long trek back through the burning desert to retrieve the straggler Gasim ("a gap-toothed, grumbling fellow, skrimshank in all our marches, bad-tempered, suspicious, brutal, a man whose engagement I regretted"), is well known. Lawrence did it, he wrote, because "Gasim was my man: and upon me lay the responsibility of him," and because he needed to avoid being excused on the grounds that he was a foreigner ("that was precisely the plea I did not dare set up, while I yet presumed to help these Arabs in their own revolt").[10]

Later he felt obliged to end the life with his own pistol of his mortally wounded, loyal servant Farraj.[11] Of this merciful killing another British officer wrote:

> His dilemma was whether to abandon him alive for the Turkish soldiers to wreck their vengeance on, or to end his life before leaving him. Lawrence chose the latter course. It will, of course, be asked why he did not order one of the Arabs to perform this tragic task. The answer is a simple one. No Arab tribesman would have obeyed such an order. It would have started a blood feud in which many innocent men would have lost their lives. Moreover, he knew that the German and Turkish governments had done everything possible to rouse the religious and patriotic feelings of the Turkish soldiers. They especially emphasized that the Arabs were not only in rebellion against the Sultan but worse still were apostates, fighting under the orders of Europeans and Christians. In short, no Arab could expect any mercy from the Turks. It must be remembered that Lawrence had no doctors nor even a medical orderly with pain relieving drugs. He therefore took the only course available to end the suffering of a man he could not help.[12]

"In one six days' raid there came to a head and were settled," Lawrence wrote, "twelve cases of assault with weapons, four camel-liftings, one marriage, two thefts, a divorce, fourteen feuds, two evil eyes, a bewitchment."[13] He described the blood enmities that existed among the many tribes, who he asserted but "for my hand over them would have murdered in the ranks each day. Their feuds prevented them combining against me; while their unlikeness gave me sponsors and spies wherever I went or sent, between Akaba and Damascus, between Beersheba and Bagdad."[14] On one occasion, in order to prevent a feud from growing, he executed a man who had killed a man from another tribe.[15] "A highly sensitive and imaginative man cannot do such things as if he were doing no more than putting on his boots," George Bernard Shaw wrote after Lawrence's death. "I once asked him whether he felt badly about such horrible exploits. He said, of course he did, very badly indeed."[16]

Lawrence found his role in the Revolt increasingly odious and disturbing to him personally, and felt his position in it to be false in fundamental ways. An important source of his shame derived from his gradual recognition that in manipulating and inspiring the Arabs to pursue the aims of the Revolt with such energy he was fulfilling an essentially egoistic aim, which derived from the nature of his own ambitions. Lawrence recognized with some alarm the power of his influence upon the Arab leaders, and came more and more to question the morality of exploiting their highest ideals and desire for freedom, not only as "one more tool to help England win,"[17] which has been most stressed in analyses of Lawrence's conflict, but in the service also of his own inner drives and needs.

The most obvious dilemma deriving from Lawrence's self-assumption of responsibility grew out of his position as intermediary between Faisal and Allenby. The dilemma became especially acute after he became aware of the terms of the McMahon pledges and the Sykes-Picot Agreement (probably before his trip into Syria in June of 1917).[18] "I was Feisal's adviser," Lawrence wrote, "and Feisal relied upon the honesty and competence of my advice so far as often to take it without argument. Yet I could not explain to Allenby the whole Arab situation, nor disclose the full British plan to Feisal."[19] Although Lawrence wrote that he had "early betrayed the treaty's [the Sykes-Picot Agreement] existence to Feisal," and Picot and Sykes had met King Husayn at Jidda concerning its terms in June 1917, Lawrence clearly did not feel that the Arab leaders understood its implications or that his own responsibility was mitigated by any such revelations or confessions on his part. Repeatedly in *Seven Pillars of Wisdom* he wrote of his continual bitter shame at what he considered to be the false pretenses under which he was urging the Arabs on in the Revolt, using them as an instrument of British policy, while he knew that they would likely lose in the postwar diplomatic maneuverings of the Great Powers much of what they had gained in liberating their lands from the Ottoman Empire during the campaigns. On his trip into Syria in June 1917, Lawrence wrote on army message forms, "We are calling them to fight for us on a lie and I can't stand it."[20]

But one may ask with Elie Kedourie, what "had Lawrence to do with the bargain" the British had made with the French, the Russians and the Arabs, "and why should he feel dishonoured if the bargain were not kept? He was not the British Government after all, nor the keeper of its conscience. Neither did the British Government authorize him to make bargains or distribute promises. What business, then, had he to 'endorse' promises, especially if, as he says, he 'had no previous or inner knowledge of the McMahon pledges or the Sykes-Picot Treaty?' "[21] Were not the Arabs rebelling against Turkey by their own choice, and was not Lawrence's wholehearted assistance helping them to become free of the tyrannical Ottoman authority? Even if Britain had made a secret deal with the French (and just how secret it was for King Husayn and his sons remains an unsettled question — it was in no way secret after November 1917, when the Bolsheviks published the terms of the Sykes-Picot Agreement in their newspapers), the Arabs could only be better off in their postwar negotiations with the British and French if they were militarily successful in liberating their own lands during the campaigns, as Lawrence was trying to help them do.

But Lawrence was not guided by these conventional and logical considerations alone. He knew that "Arabs believe in persons, not in institutions," and he was the person who represented to them the purposes and commitments of the British government. He was, therefore, in the terms of *his* morality, responsible. He felt that his entire position was false and that *he* was responsible for misleading the Arabs into pursuing their revolution, as if it were being fought entirely on the basis of British (and therefore his) promises.

In actuality the Arabs may have been better off anyway to have fought, with Allied help, as they did, and then to navigate after the war, as they had during it, among the not-unfamiliar shoals of Anglo-French rivalry. But Lawrence was too caught up in his personal turmoil to consider the matter in this light. "I could see that if we won the war the promises to the Arabs were dead paper. Had I been an honourable adviser I would have sent my men home, and not let them risk their lives for such stuff,"[22] he wrote, and "in revenge I vowed to make the Arab Revolt the engine of its own success . . . and vowed to lead it so madly in the final victory that expediency should counsel to the Powers a fair settlement of the Arabs' moral claims. . . . Clearly I had no shadow of leave to engage the Arabs, unknowing, in a gamble of life and death. Inevitably and justly we should reap bitterness, a sorry fruit of heroic endeavor."[23] He continued: "Before me lay a vista of responsibility and command, which disgusted my thought-ridden nature."[24] Further British assurances to the Arabs in

1918 only added to Lawrence's personal distress, which he treated with irony, answering the Arab leaders, when they would ask him which agreement to believe, "the last in date."[25]

But driven by what he variously called his inner "beast" or "demon," Lawrence claimed for himself, and for his own conscience, the responsibility for the Revolt and for its military, political and human consequences. Yet in so doing he provided an example of leadership to the Arabs that did much to enable them to achieve what they did in their rebellion. Lawrence recognized the egoism of this assumption of responsibility, especially the aspect which involved his identifying with another people's need and suffering, and it clearly troubled him deeply. "A reef on which many came to a shipwreck of estimation," Lawrence wrote, in a passage which, though it employs the literary "our" or "we," clearly applies to himself, "was the vanity that our endurance might win redemption, perhaps for all a race. Such false investiture bred a hot though transient satisfaction, in that we felt we had assumed another's pain or experience, his personality. It was triumph, and a mood of enlargement; we had avoided our sultry selves, conquered our geometrical completeness, snatched a momentary 'change of mind.'

"Yet in reality we had borne the vicarious for our own sakes, or at least because it was pointed for our benefit: and could escape from this knowledge only by a make-belief in sense as well as in motive.

"The self-immolated victim took for his own the rare gift of sacrifice; and no pride and few pleasures in the world were so joyful, so rich as this choosing voluntarily another's evil to perfect the self. There was a hidden selfishness in it, as in all perfections."[26]

This kind of personal assumption of responsibility is, I believe, unusual among military commanders, who seem, more often, to regard themselves as subservient to other leaders or to larger political purposes. Usually they are able to justify the killing over which they preside as necessary in view of the larger military or political effort. Lawrence's self-centered scrupulosity appears to be unrealistic, even grandiose. Yet perhaps only through such exaggerated personal assumption of responsibility by those in positions of leadership can men find ways other than war to settle their disputes.

18

The Heroic Legend
and the Hero

Men need heroes in order to transcend the limitations and disappointments they experience in their everyday lives. Heroes embody ideals and values shared in the culture, ready examples with whom the rest of us may identify. But the *creation* of heroes depends upon the compliance of history, the coming together of special events and situations with unusual men or women who take hold of these circumstances, force upon them their own actions and personalities, and transform them along the lines of their own dreams.

The concept of heroism embraces a series of psychosocial interrelationships and tensions among various individuals and groups. These include the hero himself; the people (or peoples) among whom he lives and acts; his followers (who may vary in size as a group from a small band to a nation or nations); his chroniclers and biographers; contemporary propaganda; and, finally, the audience of posterity, whose view of the hero will shift according to cultural need and the materials about him made available by those who choose to examine the oral traditions and the writings (and now the audio-visual materials of the mass media) that concern the hero's performance and reputation. Although man is known to have created heroes as far back as the days when he painted the actions he admired on cave walls, the concept of the hero evolves or shifts according to what a given people or a historical age values or can tolerate.

Heroic ideals must be consistent with the realities of a particular society's circumstances. The admired hero of one age or people could well be seen as the immoral enemy and destroyer in another or vice versa. During his lifetime the hero has some, though often limited, control over what he would wish to represent. After his death he becomes public property and his meaning for history is determined by those of his works which endure and by the interpretations of his historical audience and his various biographers.

There are probably heroic qualities which are not bound by time or epoch, but anyone who tries to name them is in danger of reflecting the narrower perspective of his own values or the values of his age. E. M. Forster, whose empathy for and appreciation of Lawrence was perhaps the most profound of all of Lawrence's friends, called courage, generosity and compassion, all of which he felt T.E. possessed, "the three heroic virtues" that qualified his friend as a hero. But I am not sure that generosity and compassion have always been so valued, and I suspect that figures like Lawrence, and interpreters of his life such as Forster, have helped make them become so.

James Notopoulos in his article "The Tragic and the Epic in T. E. Lawrence," has written that ours is an age in which hero and heroic acts are anachronisms and that the hero is "out of joint" with our pragmatic world.[1] Notopoulos is certainly correct as regards the Homeric heroes or the romantic heroes of the Age of Chivalry, whose acts of valor are committed and admired quite unselfconsciously, with little regard for their political consequences or toll in personal suffering. But for the contemporary leader to be heroic he must fulfill different requirements. The horrors and atrocities of war have become so much the personal experience of humanity, and the dangers of mass destruction so acute, that the traditional elevation of courageous generals or other winners of battles and wars to the status of heroes seems to be becoming — at least for the present — a thing of the past, especially as the political wars of our computer age leave less to the initiative of individuals in the field.

The capacity for *individual* mastery, initiative and achievement is probably an essential requirement for all heroes. Heroic values, bred as they are of necessity, must include in our dangerous age much that is not romantic, qualities such as restraint and renunciation. Our heroes must, in an age when survival of the race is endangered, display examples of conduct that will offer protection (probably always an essential quality of heroism, although variously achieved in different eras), and such protection may be offered perhaps more by self-consciousness and restraint than by the decisive actions of traditional heroes.

Lawrence is a transitional figure in the history of heroism. Imbued with the epic tradition, and raised on a heavy diet of medieval romanticism and its Victorian revival, he brought to his role in the Revolt traditional concepts of chivalric heroism combined with the goal of leading an oppressed people out of bondage in the biblical sense. He tried through self-improvement to embody the ideal of courage, stamina and skill that both Arabs and Britons could look up to and emulate.

The generosity and compassion of which Forster wrote have been less stressed, but they stand out in *Seven Pillars* and shine forth when one speaks of Lawrence with friends who remember him. One little-known member of the Arab Bureau said of Lawrence, "What he hid, I believe, and still believe, was a tender reverence for human life which his duty as a soldier compelled him to violate, and so he was always stressed by an inner conflict."[2] But it is this conflict about human life, the inability to justify killing, the self-consciousness, guilt and exaggerated responsibility-taking that make Lawrence a valued example for the twelfth century, a contemporary hero.

In his essay "T. E. Lawrence: The Problem of Heroism," Irving Howe has written: "The hero as he appears in the tangle of modern life is a man struggling with a vision he can neither realize nor abandon, 'a man with a load on his mind.' "[3] Howe also points out: "What finally draws one to Lawrence, making him seem not merely an exceptional figure, but a representative man of our century, is his courage and vulnerability in bearing the burden of consciousness."[4] Lawrence is, in Howe's phrase, "a prince of our disorder"[5] (which will recall the words of Lunt's Bedouin host: "Of all the men I have ever met he was the greatest Prince").

The precise assessment of Lawrence's instrumentality in the shifting concepts of heroism is very difficult. He is part of the process of shift and the determination of his individual role within it is virtually impossible. He seems to have understood that he represented a new sort of heroism, and was prepared to challenge those who would criticize him through invidious comparison with static or more traditional concepts.

One reviewer of the subscribers' edition of *Seven Pillars*, Herbert Read, wrote in 1927:

> The story fails to reach epic quality because Colonel Lawrence, however brave and courageous he may have been, is not heroic. About the epic hero there is an essential undoubting directness: his aim is single and unswerving; *he questions neither himself, his aims, nor his destiny* [italics added]. He may share his glory with his chosen band, his *comitatus*, but essentially he is self-possessed, self-reliant, arrogant and unintelligent. Colonel Lawrence was none of these things; in all these things he was at the contrary pole — full of doubts and dissemblings, uncertain of his aim, his pride eaten into by humility and remorse, his conduct actuated by intellectual and idealistic motives. It is no disparagement to say that out of such stuff no hero is made.[6]

When Lawrence read Read's review he wrote to Edward Garnett: "I do not like his categorical specification of a hero . . . who in God's name laid this down? Is the hero to be a changeless thing, in the world? And why make Aeneas your archetype? I can't think of any other character in fiction who fits his definition. . . . Isn't he slightly ridiculous in seeking to measure my day-to-day chronicle by the epic standard? I never called it an epic, or thought of it as an epic, nor did anyone else, to my knowledge. The thing follows an exact diary sequence, and is literally true, throughout. Whence was I to import his lay-figure hero? Leaders of movements have to be intelligent, as was Feisal, to instance my chief character. Read talks as though I had been making a book, and not a flesh-and-blood revolt."[7]

The contemporary hero, the "man with a load on his mind," seems to be a kind of political-spiritual figure, such as Mohandas Gandhi, Martin Luther King, or Dag Hammarskjöld, whose examples are of peace, non-violence and renunciation. Lawrence, though a soldier and a hero of war, is also a hero of nonwar. By the assumption of exaggerated personal responsibility for what war really is, he has demonstrated war's unsuitability as material for heroism according to the twentieth-century consciousness he helped to create. His conflict is the product of war and his self-consciousness grows out of it. But this self-consciousness in turn alters the qualities of heroism, so that the shift in the direction that heroism has taken seems to pivot around Lawrence's personal change and experience in the war itself. As Lawrence was changed by his war experience, his self-conscious shift in values becomes our property and his evolving ideals affect our own. He asks us to expect more of our heroes as he expected more of himself, and we are influenced thereby to be more self-critical and to demand more of our leaders.

Although we may know a fair amount about what to value in our heroes, we know very little about the psychology or personal development of the person who is himself destined to become a heroic figure. It would seem important to understand more about this. A vital ingredient in hero-valuing or hero-making is the resonance that the follower or worshipper finds between conflicts and aspirations of his own and those he perceives in the person he chooses to idealize. The worshipper (or, less dramatically, the one-who-does-the-valuing) needs to be able to find that unfulfilled, ideal aspects of himself are fulfilled by and through the hero, even though the worshipper does not recognize the fulfillment consciously. The hero needs to appear to have mastered his struggle to achieve his ideals in such a way that an identification with him seems to offer the possibility of similar mastery to the follower. Thus, psychological conflict and mastery, the overcoming of deep inner dissatisfaction through reaching out toward an ideal, would seem to be an essential aspect of the psychology of the hero. At the same time the process the hero undergoes, in reaching for what he values, and the idealized solution he actually achieves for himself, must be sufficiently recognizable or familiarly human to allow for empathy and identification by the follower. Finally, the hero's solutions of his conflicts, his efforts to achieve an ideal, must be creative. He must strive for new solutions, new values and new directions (even if some of these, in reality, may be old — and merely revived), and they must be for a larger group or for mankind, not just for a few individuals. The psychological development of the hero originates, as it does for us all, in his cultural background, the circumstances of his ancestry and family, and in his early life. There is a set of ideas, quite common in childhood, that might be called the hero fantasy. It derives from the limitations of being a child, subject to the power and authority of one's parents. They appear to the child to be the cause of the frustration of all his wishes. The fantasy enables him to transcend these limitations. In it, he finds out that the parents with whom he is living are imposters who are deceiving him after having usurped the place of his real parents. These impostors do not fully appreciate his value, as his real parents would (they are usually of royal or noble birth and so, of course, is he). The child imagines that he will embark on a heroic quest in which he will perform great deeds and will also restore his real parents to their rightful place, eject the impostors, and be reunited in greatness with his true forebears, who will recognize and appreciate fully his deserving qualities. A variation on this fantasy is that the parents are reduced from former greatness and need to be restored by the child's heroic efforts.[8]

For most children the romantic notions of the hero fantasy are corrected by the inescapable reality of the actual family situation, and by other encounters with situations and persons in the outside world that confront the child daily with the reality of his limitations. By late adolescence he usually has abandoned the fantasy and seeks other solutions for the painful conflicts that recognition of his limitations has imposed.

It is a unique aspect of Lawrence's psychological development that he did not give up his fantasy but sought *his* solutions to earlier conflicts through the kind of heroic activity out of which new myths could be created. I believe the reason for this direction of Lawrence's development may be found in the actualities of his family background, which conformed *in reality* to so many of the elements of the hero-fantasy. His real (former) father was, if not of royal, at least of more noble birth, than the displaced country gentleman Ned Lawrence lived with in Oxford, "kept" as his mother's "trophy of power." Lawrence's actual father *had been*, if not a different person, *in fact* of higher status, and therefore Lawrence himself was or should have been, as well. The guilt of the parents *had* led them to deceive the child regarding his origins, which were kept by them shrouded in mystery and uncertainty. As regards Lawrence's personal development, far from being encouraged to give up his fantasies of restoring his family to its rightful status, his parents, especially his mother, sought *their* redemption and liberation from guilt through the heroic acts he would some day perform. He would justify their transgressions by his ennobling accomplishments, achievements his mother very much approved of.[9]

Unusual gifts of mind and body, which Lawrence appeared quite early to possess, seemed to make possible for parents and child alike the overcoming of ordinary limitations, and Lawrence's childhood friends experienced the sense that almost anything was possible on an adventure with Ned Lawrence. The disturbance of self-esteem resulting from the identification with his parents' sin produced an inner tension, out of which grew the drive to live out the heroic fantasy. It is this tension (the "standing civil war" of which he wrote to Mrs. Shaw), this conflict of self-esteem, which drove Lawrence to seek some public stage upon which he could live out its demands. He strove to silence once and for all through noble and heroic deeds, and through living up to an ideal of personal conduct, the inner voice that reminded him of the fallen aspect of himself. It will be recalled that Lawrence's intensive reading during his youth of medieval chivalric and romantic writings lent additional richness, breadth and variety to the forms of his heroic fantasies and dreams.

As we shall see, far from permanently resolving the conflict, Lawrence's participation in the Arab Revolt only intensified it and brought it more to the surface. The Revolt provided the stage on which he could live out the heroic fantasy of his inner life. Through his achievements in the Revolt, and his sharing in his writings the inner terms of the ambivalent struggle for heroic achievement, Lawrence offered himself as a hero to others who were struggling with conflicts similar to his own. Through his example, Lawrence has helped others to achieve what he could not achieve for himself, and what they might not have been able to achieve without him.[10]

The Lawrence legend grew, I believe, directly out of the elements of his personal psychology that I have just described. It was the product of Lawrence's psychology and personality, operating through his writings and his contacts with others, which found a receptive audience in England and America, and to a lesser extent in other European countries, after the ravages of World War I had begun to destroy the illusion that modern war is romantic. Lowell Thomas's illustrated lectures, films and writings undoubtedly hastened the creation and popularizing of the Lawrence legend, although it was already taking shape in military, diplomatic and academic circles before Thomas began his performances in New York and London.[11] Lawrence's accomplishments were, however, in actuality so remarkable, and the "fit" between the elements of his psychology that contributed to the tendency of legends to grow up around him and the need of his potential historical audience for a new type of heroic figure was so natural, that the creation of a "Lawrence-of-Arabia" was, in my opinion, inevitable.

"The limelight of history," Shaw wrote in an essay on Lawrence, "follows the authentic hero as the theatre limelight follows the *prima ballerina assoluta*."[12] Furthermore, many of the activities that contributed to the Lawrence legend took place some time *after* Lowell Thomas's performances in London — Lawrence's contributions, for example, to the political solutions in the Middle East, his retreat to the RAF, and the circulation of *Seven Pillars of Wisdom* among an increasing number of people during the 1920's. Finally, there is no way that the *lasting* appeal of the Lawrence legend, his endurance as a contemporary historical and legendary figure, can be explained on the basis of the publicity he received during the immediate postwar period.

Much has been written of Lawrence's need to dramatize himself, to seek publicity while simultaneously eschewing it, to "back into the lime-light." But he was critical of that aspect of himself which, in spite of him-self, gave in, often unconsciously, to self-dramatizing. He was aware of his inclination to mislead in his writings: he wrote, for example, to Mrs. Shaw, in 1927: "The reviewers [of *Revolt in the Desert*, his abridgment of *Seven Pillars of Wisdom*] have none of them given me credit for being a bag of tricks — too rich and full a bag for them to control."[13]

But I believe that this insight was to some extent the rationalization of the tendency to dramatize, which seemed to be outside Lawrence's con-trol and which was spawned by psychological needs of which he was unaware. This tendency reached its fullest expression in *Seven Pillars of Wisdom*. One of Lawrence's purposes in writing the book was to invite his public to create with him a new and different self, a mythological Lawrence, larger than life, a self that would be immune to or beyond personal pain and conflict, and one that would replace the self he felt he had debased. The new self would be ideal in its honesty and integrity, a participant in epic events described in the epic mode, committing great deeds in war and yet responsible for war and rejecting it as no com-mander before had been or done, a Lawrence that was to be merciless if not all-seeing in his self-scrutiny.

The irony is that, objectively, the real Lawrence corresponded in so many ways to the ideal one he sought to create through his dramatizing and embroidering. But from his inner psychological perspective the real self was debased by the war and his experiences in it, and fell far short of the ideal self he had to invent, with the help of others, through legend-making.

The dramatic richness of *Seven Pillars of Wisdom* is widely acknowl-edged. Its value as a contemporary epic derives in part from its power to lift everyday events and personal struggles to a higher plane. Some of these events contained an intrinsic drama. In other instances Lawrence brought, through his passionate literary descriptions, drama and beauty to events of the Revolt — even the arrangement of corpses — that would otherwise have been merely horrible, painful or ordinary. Lawrence understood that legend-making often reduced the drama or humanity of actual events, but he was compelled by other forces. He wrote, for ex-ample, that "since Egypt kept us alive by stinting herself, we must reduce impolitic truth to keep her confident and ourselves a legend. The crowd wanted book-heroes, and would not understand how more human Auda ['Awdah abu-Tayyi] was because, after battle and murder, his heart yearned towards the defeated enemy now subject, at his free choice, to be spared or killed: and therefore never so lovely."[14]

Lawrence's consciously critical mind rejected the idea of himself as a hero. He felt his kinship with the vulnerability and humanity of other men — knew, for example, that his bowels sometimes gave way when he was frightened. "Strong praise and strong blame," he once wrote, "are results of half-knowledge; to know the real motive or mood of heroism is often to make it accidental or involuntary or instinctive. You cannot admire the stars, since they are only fire and mud in nature."[15]

Among the more familiar of the dramatically embellished passages of *Seven Pillars of Wisdom* is the one in which Lawrence describes his first meeting with Faisal ("I felt at first glance that this was the man I had come to Arabia to seek — the leader who would bring the Arab Revolt to full glory"), which is in sharp contrast to his matter-of-fact official dispatch. The passage continues with a colorful, high-keyed description of Faisal among his followers. " 'And do you like our place here in Wadi Safra?' " Faisal asks. " 'Well; but it is far from Damascus,' " Lawrence replies. "The word had fallen like a sword in their midst," he continues. "There was a quiver. Then everybody present stiffened where he sat, and held his breath for a silent minute. Some perhaps were dreaming of far off success: others may have thought it a reflection of their late defeat. Faisal at length lifted his eyes, smiling at me, and said, 'Praise be to God, there are Turks nearer us than that.' We all smiled with him; and I rose and excused myself for the moment."[16]

The meeting with Allenby is similarly raised to the level of high drama. Vividly self-effacing here, Lawrence writes: "He was hardly prepared for anything so odd as myself — a little barefooted silk-skirted man offering to hobble the enemy by his preaching if given stores and arms and a fund of two hundred thousand sovereigns to convince and control his converts."[17]

In passage after passage of *Seven Pillars of Wisdom* Lawrence provides accounts which throw the spotlight on himself and credit him with a central place in actions whose grandeur is raised to epic proportions. Yet this self-elevation (unnecessary from a purely objective standpoint in view of his actual accomplishments) is invariably matched with countervailing passages of self-disparagement, and proclamations of the baseness of his position and of his deceit, which become a kind of litany. Similarly, events in which Lawrence focuses credit upon himself, such as the capture of Aqaba ("Akaba had been taken on my plan by my effort. The cost of it had fallen on my brains and nerves"),[18] seem always to be matched by accounts, such as his description of his role at Tafas, that exaggerate negative, even almost criminal, activity. Grand success and spectacular failure seem to alternate throughout the book. In the passages of horror — and there are many — even brutality, cruelty and gore are made somehow glorious; and tortures are stretched in intensity beyond belief. It is as if there is operating in Lawrence in writing this book — and I am treating it here as a psychological document rather than as a literary work — a balance scale controlling the economy of his self-esteem. The glorification of himself, and of the great events of the Arab Revolt in which he took part, seems to serve to overcome his low self-regard. But some internal monitor, or busy conscience under the control of a low self-estimate, seems always to swing the pendulum of judgment back in the direction of self-disparagement.

Seven Pillars of Wisdom has been criticized as a work of history because of alleged distortions of fact. The historian L. B. Namier, who considered Lawrence "a man of genius, a great artist," wrote gently of him that "he seemed to dislike the precision of dates."[19] There are distortions in the book, but they come not, in my opinion, from a simple alteration of facts — it is remarkable how much valuable historical information the book does contain when its psychological and literary purposes are considered. Rather, the distortions and inaccuracy result from Lawrence's need, deriving from the conflicts and his self-regard, to elevate the tale to epic proportions and to make of himself a contemporary legendary figure.

The legend-making did not of course end with Seven Pillars of Wisdom. The Lawrence of myth continued to grow and be enriched by the tales he told his friends (from which, once they are retold, it is impossible to distinguish the embellishment and embroidering that is Lawrence's from that of his friends and biographers) and especially from the accounts he supplied his biographers. Sometimes Lawrence seemed unable to resist writing as if the whole Middle Eastern campaign, even the capture of Damascus, were related to his personal wishes, motives and accomplishments. For example, after teasing Liddell Hart with a cryptic note about the relationship between his dedicatory poem ("To S.A."), and his sadness at the end of the campaigns over the death of Dahoum (he never just comes out and says he felt grieved about the loss of Dahoum), Lawrence wrote: "The unhappy 'event' happened long before we got to Damascus. *I only took D.* (so far as that motive was concerned) for historical reasons."[20] [Italics added]

Richard Goodwin, writing of another modern guerrilla leader, noted: "Still there was always a remoteness — a knowledge that no matter how close you came the man was withholding something. It is a quality useful to leadership and essential to heroic myth."[21] A classic example of such mystification occurs in the exchanges that took place between Lawrence and Robert Graves — at this time Graves was preparing his biography of Lawrence — concerning Lawrence's June 1917 journey behind Turkish lines into Syria. Graves's struggle to obtain the truth, and Lawrence's evasive, teasing, half-revealing-half-concealing replies (he seemed especially to enjoy teasing Graves), which raise as many questions as they answer, occupy six of the 180 pages of *T. E. Lawrence to His Biographer, Robert Graves.* At the conclusion of the merry chase Lawrence wrote Graves: "~~Once during this~~ [Lawrence's deletion].* You may say that 'the more picturesque incidents reported of this journey are demonstrably untrue: but that L's (failure or) refusal to provide accurate details throws upon him responsibility for such fictions as are current.'[22]

"You may make public if you like the fact that my reticence upon this northward raid is deliberate, and based on private reasons, and record your opinion that I have found mystification, and perhaps statements deliberately misleading or contradictory, the best way to hide the truth of what really occurred, if anything did occur." And then in a postscript: *"The lighter you can touch on it the better I'll be served.* Sorry: on these points I can't afford to help you."[23] During the war there was reason to keep the details of the journey secret, especially to protect Syrian nationalists who had taken risks to see Lawrence. If such reasons still existed, Lawrence could have indicated as much without so much tantalization. The preponderant effect of the passage, if not its motive, seems to be mystification. It is the stuff out of which legend is created.

Lawrence emerged from World War I a public figure. From then on, the private Lawrence, Lawrence as a real person, and the mythological Lawrence of legendary heroism begin their complex relationship with one another. At times they seem to coincide, while at other times they diverge widely. During his lifetime the actual Lawrence was forever the critic of the heroic one, especially of the *mythic* heroic character he could not help creating. His insight into his own limitations, his awareness of the distortions of truth the legend he helped to create contained, and his profound intellectual awareness of the impure mixture of creditable and discreditable characteristics that define all men, made the idealized versions of his life that were growing up about him especially distasteful.

Yet the myth continued and he continued to furnish much of its substance. Even in his postwar renunciations and self-effacement, Lawrence continued to provide valuable and precocious ethical examples.

* The deletion was made legibly (by design?) — as if he were "on the point of making a confession," says Graves.

19

The Shattering of
the Dream

Psychic trauma is a violation, the penetration or shattering of the inner defenses by events whose impact is overwhelming, and whose continuing aftereffects cannot readily be integrated by the functioning personality. Trauma occurs at the border between the individual and the external world, between the self and an environment which breaches it. The potential for traumatization lies within the personality, in the childhood development, psychological defenses, ambitions and sexual predilections that create areas of particular vulnerability. The person's feeling of worth, because of injuries in his early development, may be an important area of potential vulnerability.

Although the experience of traumatization is essentially one of pain, traumata frequently occur in connection with pleasure for several fundamental reasons. First, whether consciously or not, the person seeks out or tends to place himself "in the way of" pleasurable experiences. As he becomes emotionally involved, as the "self" becomes invested, he becomes especially vulnerable or exposed to traumatization. Second, pleasures, especially sexual ones, are often associated with aggression and violence, which, in their admixture with pain, are categorized as "sado-masochism." These experiences, because of their unique emotional intensity, are particularly likely to breach psychic defenses and thus become traumatic. Finally, judgments of conscience, of internal disapproval, may be particularly harsh in matters of pleasure, especially for persons who have been subjected to strict or guilt-ridden child-rearing, and this self-disapproval provides in itself an important element of trauma.

The struggle to deal with the continuing effects of a traumatic experience goes on long after its occurrence, sometimes for the rest of a person's life. Depending upon the range of psychological strengths and skills available to him this struggle may take differing forms: shifts in the direction of his way of life (abandonment of a profession, withdrawal from society); the development of symptoms of mental illness; and various efforts to integrate the experience through creative activity or other forms of communication that give evidence of the continuing inner conflict. Those who witness such struggles — for example a person in the throes of a vital decision who vacillates between alternatives — may find them confusing and contradictory, as the oscillations of the elements of the struggle seem to swing now one way and now the other, much as a boat on a stormy sea rolls and pitches as it seeks to maintain its equilibrium. If the person places himself in situations of unusual jeopardy, either out of a need to master fear, to test himself, or to assume unusual responsibility (all of these are applicable in Lawrence's case), he will naturally expose himself more frequently to trauma. Its actual occurrence, however, even in an environmental "field" in which its likelihood is quite great, depends to a large extent on circumstances and on chance. It is a frequent, paradoxical characteristic of trauma that its repetition, often in a particularly painful form, is sought in later years because of the unconscious wish to repeat the pleasurable elements of the experience; the desire to master or erase its traumatic nature; and, finally, the need to seek in the repetition punishment for the unacceptable elements of pleasure that both the original and the subsequent repetitions of the experience contained.

Had the discrepancies between the grand, prophetic, private and public purposes that the events of the war were meant to fulfill for Lawrence, and the actualities of the campaigns, been limited to disappointments with the rapacious behavior of the Arabs or with Britain's failure to live up to its various promises to them, Lawrence would have been understandably disappointed, or even disillusioned, but he would not have suffered a painful and irrevocable psychic injury. The shattering of his defenses resulted from much more specific physical and emotional experiences related to the daily horrors of the war itself.

The assault Lawrence endured at the hands of the Turks at Der'a in November of 1917, and the loss of control he suffered a few miles away at Tafas ten months later, were the severest traumatic experiences he underwent during the course of the campaigns. Both experiences in different ways represented personal violations, an overwhelming of psychological defenses, and the shattering of the integrity of the self. There is some evidence that they were psychologically linked. The depravity and horror of Der'a and Tafas stood for Lawrence in the boldest possible contrast to his noble prophetic dream, for which the capture of Damascus was to be the culmination. So bitter was the pain attached to the achievements of the campaigns that it filled their triumphs with bitter irony, as the subtitle of *Seven Pillars of Wisdom* ("A Triumph") conveys.

It was a fundamental aspect of Lawrence's psychology — or, more accurately, of the elements of his psyche that he brought to bear in dealing with troubling experiences — to bring the public into his personal struggles, to make (even though with reluctance) private suffering a matter of public record. He was aware, of course, of the introspective quality of *Seven Pillars of Wisdom*, and his reluctance to bring it to public attention is related more to its self-revelations, its links to his personal conflicts, than to such practical reasons as passages that are critical of other people. *The Mint* and many of Lawrence's letters similarly reveal his continuing struggle to overcome the destructive experience of the war, whose persisting effects he sought to surmount through creative writing. His writings are filled with the swings of self-esteem from heights of egoism and confidence to depths of despair and self-contempt, and with other paradoxes of feeling, contradictions of attitudes, and contrasts of emotion that are the characteristic substance of inner conflict. The wish to make himself known stands for Lawrence alongside the desire to hide or deceive; unusual candor and factual honesty exist side by side with secrecy and distortion; and a desire to evoke sympathy appears to war with unusual stoicism.

These puzzling contradictory qualities are what have made Lawrence seem mysterious to many people, fascinating to others, and exasperating, irritating or even boring to still others. George Bernard Shaw was undoubtedly right when he wrote that by contrast to other public figures, such as David Lloyd George or Ramsay MacDonald, Lawrence was very well known indeed. "Well, I defy you to tell me about either of them one tenth of what everybody knows about Lawrence," wrote Shaw.[1]

This struggle to "work out" in introspective psychological activity the continuing effects of traumatic experiences is familiar to the psychoanalyst or psychiatrist who attempts in the privacy of his office to help a suffering patient. Together they examine the patient's personality and look at what he wishes to see and yet not see, to understand yet to obscure, to resolve but still to avoid. It is puzzling and somewhat unfamiliar to find similar psychic activity in writings that are destined to reach the public (writings, that is, that are not fiction). It is as if Lawrence's readers and biographers (myself included, I hasten to add) were invited to function as posthumous psychiatrists for a man who never chose to be a patient during his lifetime. Although Lawrence would probably be alternately amused and irritated at the way his psychic bones have been endlessly picked over since his death, he would be glad, I am sure, if his public self-exposure could contribute to human understanding and to the relief of suffering. He would, I am quite certain, want others to benefit from any knowledge or insights gained from studying and analyzing the struggles he could not resolve altogether for himself.

There are three written accounts by Lawrence of what happened at Der'a. The first (in point of time), quite brief, is in a report on the activities of the Jaza'iri brothers, Muhammad Sa'id and 'Abd-al-Qadir, to the deputy chief political officer at British headquarters in Cairo, dated June 28, 1919.[2] The second, far more detailed, is in the 1922 (Oxford) edition of *Seven Pillars of Wisdom* (a key paragraph and one less critical passage were eliminated from the 1926 [subscribers'] edition). The third account, also quite brief, occurs in a letter to Mrs. Shaw written in 1924. These passages, although each stresses a different aspect of what happened, are generally consistent except on one point, namely, whether Lawrence was positively identified by the Turkish bey. In the Cairo report Lawrence claims he was identified, but in *Seven Pillars of Wisdom* he suggests that the bey did not really know who he was. There is no evidence in the letter to Mrs. Shaw to substantiate Aldington's and Knightley and Simpson's assertions that Lawrence admitted to her that he gave in specifically to the *bey's* pederasty. He does suggest that he had not written in "the book" everything that had occurred and indicates that he will now tell her the missing facts. However, the letter, although candid enough, adds nothing that is not in the 1922 *Seven Pillars* version, although he tells more in the letter about how he felt and the relationship between this experience and his retreat into the ranks after the war was over.

Though Lawrence rarely talked about the Der'a incident to his friends, the reports of what he did say have only compounded the confusion. For example, George Bernard Shaw wrote in the flyleaf of his wife's copy of the subscribers' edition of *Seven Pillars:* "one of his chapters (LXXXI) tells of a revolting sequel to his capture by the Turks and his attraction for a Turkish officer. He told me that his account of the affair is not true. I forebore to ask him what actually happened."[3] Considering the highly private and intimate nature of what occurred, Lawrence's candor is quite exceptional. The distortions in his accounts, the doing and undoing, and the inability, as Lawrence wrote to Mrs. Shaw, "to put it plain" completely, are hardly more than one would expect in the recollection and retelling of any severely traumatic experience, all the more so if the teller is aware that his tale will become more or less public property. We, the public, may wish to know more, but it is doubtful whether Lawrence could have been more accurate or more explicit in recalling precisely what happened to him. Experiences so acutely painful and disturbing, both physically and emotionally, are especially prey to distortions of recollection, which the mind imposes upon memories that are, from the standpoint of the self-regard, intolerable and unacceptable.

On or about the night of November 20, 1917, Lawrence set out with an elderly Arab companion on a reconnaissance mission which required that he enter the railroad junction of Der'a south of Damascus. In his 1919 report to general headquarters in Cairo he wrote: "I went into Deraa disguised to spy out the defenses, was caught and identified by Hajim Bey, the governor, by virtue of Abd el Kadir's description of me. (I learned all about his treachery from Hajim's conversation, and from my guards.) Hajim was an ardent paederast and took a fancy to me. So he kept me under guard till night, and then tried to have me. I was unwilling, and prevailed after some difficulty. Hajim sent me to the hospital, and I escaped before dawn, being not as hurt as he thought. He was so ashamed at the muddle he had made that he hushed the whole thing up and never reported my capture and escape. I got back to Azrak very annoyed with Abd el Kadir, and rode down to Akaba."[4]

In *Seven Pillars of Wisdom* (in very tiny handwriting in the original manuscript)[5] Lawrence describes his capture by a Turkish sergeant near Der'a station, his unsuccessful effort to pass himself off as a Circassian (and therefore exempt from military service and not a deserter subject to Turkish imprisonment), and the bey's "fawning" attempt to seduce him. "Incidents like this," he wrote, "made the thought of military service in the Turkish army a living death for wholesome Arab peasants, and the consequences pursued the miserable victims all their after life, in revolting forms of sexual disease."[6] When the bey tried force, Lawrence resisted and kneed him in the groin. Then, according to Lawrence's vividly detailed and lurid account, the bey retaliated by hitting, biting and kissing him, and by forcing a bayonet through a fold in the flesh over Lawrence's ribs and turning the blade. Lawrence quotes the bey as saying, "You must understand that I know:* and it will be easier if you do as I wish," but then Lawrence adds, "It was evidently a chance shot, by which he himself did not, or would not mean what I feared."[7] Lawrence still refused the bey's advances and the latter "half whispered to the corporal to take me out and teach me everything."[8] There follows a still more vivid account of his being whipped, beaten, kicked, and otherwise tortured horribly by the soldiers and of his fear, sensations and struggles to handle the severe pain and to dissociate himself from what was happening.

The account of the torture contains two references to sexual molestation mingled with the assaults ('they would squabble for the next turn, ease themselves, and play unspeakably with me"; and, "I was being dragged about by two men, each disputing over a leg as though to split me apart: while a third man rode me astride").[9] The sequence of events during this part of the account is rather hard to follow. The brutality seems so severe that it appears virtually incompatible with survival, much less a return to activity within a few days.

After a bruising and lacerating kick by the corporal, which damaged a rib, "I remembered smiling idly at him, for a delicious warmth, probably sexual, was swelling through me: and then that he flung up his arms and

---

* Presumably, who Lawrence was.

hacked with the full length of his whip into my groin. This doubled me half-over, screaming, or, rather, trying impotently to scream, only shuddering through my mouth. One giggled with amusement. A voice cried, 'Shame, you've killed him.' Another slash followed. A roaring, and my eyes went black: while within me the core of life seemed to heave slowly up through the rending nerves, expelled from its body by this last indescribable pang."[10]

After this, Lawrence's beaten body was returned to the bey, who rejected him "as a thing too torn and bloody for his bed." Lawrence states that he was then taken to a wooden shed, where he was washed and bandaged by an Armenian dresser and then allowed, unguarded, to obtain some "shoddy clothes" and corrosive sublimate (poison) to "safeguard against recapture."[11] He describes his unopposed escape, his observations at the time of how the town might be captured, and his return to his two Arab companions, to whom he told "a merry tale of bribery and trickery, which they promised to keep to themselves, laughing aloud at the simplicity of the Turks."[12] He indicates again that he did not believe, at the time at least, that he had been identified — "Halim [one of his companions] had been up to Deraa in the night, and knew by the lack of rumour that the truth had not been discovered."[13]

"During the night," Lawrence's account concludes, "I managed to see the great stone bridge by Nisib. Not that my maimed will now cared a hoot about the Arab Revolt (or about anything but mending itself): yet, since the war had been a hobby of mine, for custom's sake I would force myself to push it through. Afterwards we took horse, and rode gently and carefully towards Azrak, without incident,[14] except that a raiding party of Wuld Ali let us and our horses go unplundered when they heard who we were. This was an unexpected generosity, the Wuld Ali being not yet of our fellowship. Their consideration (rendered at once, as if we had deserved men's homage) momently stayed me to carry the burden, whose certainty the passing days confirmed: how in Deraa that night the citadel of my integrity had been irrevocably lost.

"I was feeling very ill, as though some part of me had gone dead that night in Deraa, leaving me maimed, imperfect, only half myself. It could not have been the defilement, for no one ever held the body in less honour than I did myself. Probably it had been the breaking of the spirit by that frenzied nerve-shattering pain which had degraded me to beast level when it made me grovel to it, and which had [sic] journeyed with me since, fascination and terror and morbid desire, lascivious and vicious perhaps, but like the striving of a moth towards its flame."[15]

This account of Lawrence's experience at Der'a, the only one that is detailed, leaves several unanswered questions. These include, for example, how even a man of his toughness could have been so badly tortured and yet return to action so soon without evidence of permanent injury; why, even if he were not identified with certainty, he was permitted to escape; and just what is meant by the "core of life" heaving up and being expelled from its body by pain, that is, whether this was Lawrence's way of describing orgasm, or loss of consciousness, or what.

Arnold Lawrence, who never questioned the factual nature of his brother's account of the Der'a experience, wrote me several years ago that "outside evidence of the Deraa episode is scarcely to be expected," a statement which, despite various efforts on my part and others to substantiate or refute Lawrence's accounts, still remains essentially valid.[16] The *Sunday Times* authors, Knightley and Simpson, sought out information about Hajim Bey himself, who was the governor of the region and based at Der'a at the time of this episode. Their informants, who included the bey's son (the bey himself having died in 1965), insisted that the bey was an aggressive heterosexual — he kept diaries which detailed his activities with girls and a case of gonorrhea — and they doubted that he was homosexual. The bey's son told Knightley and Simpson that his father never mentioned having met Lawrence (not surprising considering the circumstances under which they apparently met). It is, of course, not unlikely that despite his heterosexuality, which seems to have had a compulsive quality, the bey may have been bisexual and kept his homosexual activities secret. Or, as the *Sunday Times* authors suggest, the "paederast" in question may have been someone else.

If the bey's homosexuality cannot be established, his brutality is well substantiated. There are, in King's College, London, among Colonel Joyce's papers, notes made by an Arab soldier which document atrocities committed by Hajim Bey and his soldiers at es-Salt. The Arab soldier, Ibn al-Najdawi, wrote that Hajim Bey, the district officer of Hauran, accompanied by three hundred volunteers, attacked es-Salt, decapitated and otherwise mutilated Arab and Kurdish children and their families, killing in all seven hundred people and burning their homes.[17]

Some of Lawrence's biographers have been skeptical about the occurrence of the Der'a episode, and a prominent American historian has recently found the story "most implausible."[18] Richard Meinertzhagen, with whom Lawrence served in the Middle East and in the Colonial Office, claimed in his memoirs that Lawrence told him he was "sodomized by the Governor of Deraa, followed by similar treatment by the Governor's servants," but that he could not publish the account of the incident because it was too degrading and " 'had penetrated his innermost nature.' "[19] This statement appears in a diary entry of July 20, 1919, and seems an authentic contemporary statement. However, many of Meinertzhagen's "on-the-spot" diary entries, none of which were published until 1959, when the author was in his late seventies, seem to be amalgams of contemporary notes, later recollections, and Lawrence's own writings.

Liddell Hart once told me that during the period in which he was preparing his biography of Lawrence, he talked with several Allied participants in the campaign who told him that Lawrence arrived back in Aqaba after the Der'a incident badly shaken, pale and obviously distraught.[20] I also wrote to Captain L. H. Gilman for any information he might have concerning the authenticity of the episode, and Gilman replied:

> As regards Deraa, I am afraid I cannot help you very much as only Lawrence knew what happened. We knew that he had been through some distressing experience, but Lawrence never alluded to it not even when, subsequently, I was alone with him. I really only learned the details of his experience from his own account in *Seven Pillars of Wisdom*. The whole affair must have been a horrible nightmare, and you, of all men, must know how difficult it is to describe a nightmare.[21] Neither I, nor any of the other British officers who served in Arabia, had any doubt that he did suffer this indignity, and Lawrence was far too gallant and honourable a man to invent this experience: there would have been no point in it.[22]

There the matter must rest, at least for me. I have little doubt that Lawrence underwent a painful, humiliating assault at Der'a at the hands of the Turkish commander and his soldiers, and the element of sexual pleasure he experienced in the midst of such indignity, pain and degradation was particularly intolerable and shameful to him. A passage in a letter to Mrs. Shaw refers unquestionably to a sexual surrender of some sort: "For fear of being hurt, or rather to earn five minutes respite from a pain which drove me mad, I gave away the only possession we are born with — our bodily integrity."[23] But there is no way of telling from this letter to whom the surrender was made or the form it took, only that the surrender itself was an abomination to him ("It's an unforgivable matter, an irrecoverable position: and it's that which has made me foreswear decent living, and the exercise of my not-contemptible wits and talents").[24]

Ten years afterwards Lawrence wrote Robert Graves that the incident at Der'a "apparently did permanent damage" to his nerve, "coming as it did after the grave disappointments of the bridge and the train failures" and the exhaustion of the preceding few months.[25] His friend Eric Kennington believed that in an effort to redeem his fallen "sublime standard" Lawrence "made the rest of his life an intermittent struggle to reclaim or re-create his soul, by altruistic labour, self-denial and penance."[26]

From 1919 to 1925, Lawrence wrote and rewrote the passage dealing with the episode in *Seven Pillars of Wisdom* — nine times he told Mrs. Shaw. He relived its agonies, but he also seems to have been able to achieve to some extent a therapeutic working-through of its influence.[27] "That is the 'bad' book," he wrote to Mrs. Shaw, "with the Deraa Chapter. Working on it always makes me sick. The two impulses fight so upon it. Self-respect would close it: self-expression seeks to open it. It's a case in which you can't let yourself write as well as you could."[28] He had written also to Edward Garnett of his shame over including the incident in the original version of the book, and his conflict about the passage accounted in part for his reluctance for several years to publish even a limited version of the complete book. "For weeks I wanted to burn it in the manuscript," he wrote Garnett, "because I could not tell the story face to face with anyone, and I think I'll feel sorry, when I next meet you, that you know it. The sort of man I have always mixed with doesn't so give himself away."[29]

In the subscribers' edition, published in 1926, Lawrence called the incident "the earned wages of rebellion,"[30] as if it were a punishment warranted by his improper role in the Revolt as a whole. Despite various efforts to come to terms with the experience through his writing and acts of penance, Lawrence continued, at least until 1930, to relive in terrible nightmares the horrors of Der'a and other war experiences.[31] The Der'a episode also contributed to Lawrence's need for repeated acts of penance, which included severe whippings by a tough Scotsman named John Bruce (see Chapter 33).

The episode at Der'a, and the part Lawrence played in the events that took place ten months later at the Syrian village of Tafas three miles northwest of Der'a, appear to be connected by the motive of vengeance. He told a service comrade that he had wished to do back "ten fold" to the Turks what they had done to him at Der'a. Lawrence did not specifically speak of Tafas in this context, nor do I wish to imply that he deliberately took revenge at Tafas for the violation at Der'a. I am suggesting only that his apparent loss of control at Tafas was linked to and perhaps made possible by the humiliation he had experienced ten months before, and the desire for revenge it left within him. Of the link between the Der'a assault and Lawrence's later flagellation problem there is little doubt.

In contrast to the episode at Der'a there were several witnesses of the events around Tafas other than Lawrence himself, and one would think it would be simpler therefore to determine accurately what occurred. Unfortunately, as in many historical events, especially those which are emotionally charged or cast credit or blame upon their participants, exactly who saw or did what is not so easy to determine. The film *Lawrence of Arabia* shows the six-footer Peter O'Toole as Lawrence, his arms covered with blood, having enthusiastically entered into the slaughter of Turkish prisoners. After the film came out, a former British soldier in Allenby's army, George Staples, who claimed he knew Lawrence "in Arabia," is reported in an interview in a Canadian newspaper to have said of the film's depiction of the episode: "It was just like I remembered it."[32] But the interview, solicited evidently to promote the film, contains internal inconsistencies which cast doubt upon its historical value. For one, Staples could not have been an eyewitness because he was in a regiment of the Middlesex Yeomanry, which was over thirty miles from Tafas when the massacre took place.[33]

There are two written accounts by Lawrence of these events. The first, his official report for headquarters,[34] was written hurriedly, probably in Damascus. According to this report, a Turkish column of about two thousand men retreating to the northeast passed through Tafas and "allowed themselves to rape all the women they could catch." The report continues: "We attacked them with all arms as they marched out later and bent the head of their column back towards Tel Arar. When Sherif Bey, the Turkish Commander of the Lancer rearguard in the village, saw this he ordered that the inhabitants be killed. These included some twenty small children (killed with lances and rifles), and about forty women. I noticed particularly one pregnant woman, who had been forced down on a saw-bayonet. Unfortunately, Talal, the Sheikh of Tafas, who as mentioned, had been a tower of strength to us from the beginning, and who was one of the coolest and boldest horsemen I have ever met, was in front with Auda abu Tayi and myself when we saw these sights. He gave a horrible cry, wrapped his headcloth about his face, put spurs to his horse, and rocking in the saddle, galloped at full speed into the midst of the retiring column, and fell, himself and his mare, riddled with machine gun bullets, among their lance points.

"With Auda's help we were able to cut the enemy column into three. The third section, with German machine-gunners resisted magnificently, and got off, not cheaply, with Jemal Pasha in his car in their midst. The second and leading portions after a bitter struggle, we wiped out completely. We ordered 'no prisoners' and the men obeyed, except that the reserve company took two hundred and fifty men (including many German A.S.C.) alive. Later, however, they found one of our men with a fractured thigh who had been afterwards pinned to the ground by two mortal thrusts with German bayonets. Then we turned our Hotchkiss on the prisoners and made an end of them, they saying nothing. The common delusion that the Turk is a clean and merciful fighter led some of the British troops to criticize Arab methods a little later — but they had not entered Turaa or Tafas, or watched the Turks swing their wounded by the hands and feet into a burning railway truck, as had been the lot of the Arab army at Jerdun. As for the villagers, they and their ancestors have been for five hundred years ground down by the tyranny of these Turks."[35]

The continuing Arab attack upon the retreating Turkish Fourth Army resulted in its destruction. The account of this slaughter concludes: "Old

Auda, tired of slaughter, took the last six hundred prisoners. In all we killed nearly five thousand of them, captured about eight thousand (as we took them, we stripped them, and sent them to the nearest village, where they were put to work on the land till further notice) and counted spoils of about one hundred and fifty machine guns and from twenty-five to thirty guns."[36]

The account in Seven Pillars of Wisdom is more detailed, more dramatically vivid and realistic. The grotesque horror of the slaughter of pregnant women and children at Tafas is described relentlessly. The death of a mortally wounded child and the desperate suicidal charge of Talal are richly described. Lawrence quotes himself as saying to the men around him, "The best of you brings me the most Turkish dead."[37] The vengeful assault by the Arabs was led by 'Awdah "while the flame of cruelty and revenge which was burning in their bodies so twisted them, that their hands could hardly shoot. By my orders we took no prisoners, for the only time in our war.[38] . . . By nightfall the rich plain was scattered over with dead men and animals. In a madness born of the horror of Tafas we killed and killed, even blowing in the heads of the fallen animals; as though their death and running blood could slake our agony."[39]

One group of Arabs had not heard the "no prisoners" order and captured about two hundred Turkish prisoners. "I had gone up to learn why it was," Lawrence wrote, "not unwilling that this remnant be let live as witnesses of Talal's price; but a man on the ground behind them screamed something to the Arabs, who with pale faces led me across to see. It was one of us — his thigh shattered. The blood had rushed out over the red soil, and left him dying; but even so he had not been spared. In the fashion of to-day's battle he had been further tormented by bayonets hammered through his shoulder and other leg into the ground, pinning him out like a collected insect.

"He was fully conscious. When we said, 'Hassan, who did it?' he drooped his eyes towards the prisoners, huddling together so hopelessly broken. They said nothing in the moments before we opened fire. At last their heap ceased moving; and Hassan was dead; and we mounted again and rode home slowly (home was my carpet three or four hours from us at Sheikh Saad) in the gloom, which felt so chill now that the sun had gone down."[40]

General Allenby wrote to his wife a few days afterwards: "My cavalry had some sharpish fighting outside the town (Damascus) and a good many dead Turks are still lying about. . . . The number of prisoners is appalling. . . . Barrow (commanding 4th. Cavalry Division) had to leave 2000 behind as they could not keep up. He put them in villages and told the inhabitants to take care of them. Very likely their throats are cut by now. Lawrence tells me that his Arabs found one village where 40 women and 20 or 30 children had been bayoneted by the Turks, in pure wantonness. After that very few, if any, prisoners were taken by them."[41]

The young Arab soldier Subhi al-'Umari wrote confidently that, although Lawrence's description of the Turkish massacre at Tafas was accurate, it must have been based on hearsay because he (Lawrence) was not there at all.[42]

Suleiman Mousa seems to credit the word of an Ottoman officer that no massacre of women and children occurred at Tafas,[43] but all other observers who have written of this event, including Subhi al-'Umari, agree that it did. For example, Lord Winterton, a British officer attached to the Arab forces, wrote in an early article published before Lawrence's accounts appeared: "Tafas is a village inhabited by Arab fellaheen, and the Turks, on the pleas that some of the inhabitants sympathized with General Nuri's force, committed some abominable atrocities, even bayoneting children in arms, before the village was taken."[44] Similar descriptions of the atrocities are provided by F. G. Peake, Ali Jawdat (one of the Arab leaders), General Chauvel, Hubert Young and Lord Birdwood (Nuri al-Sa'id's biographer).

The question of Lawrence's personal role is more complex. No British officer arrived in Tafas with Lawrence, Allenby's cavalry having bypassed the villages and towns, and none of the Arab accounts written by participants in the campaign (including Ali Jawdat's memoirs) refer specifically to Lawrence's actions at Tafas. Hubert Young, who was nearby at the time, wrote: "Ali Jaudat told me that he and Lawrence had tried vainly to save a batch of prisoners from being massacred by Bedouin, whose latent savagery had been aroused by the sight of butchered women and children."[45]

The most detailed accounts have been provided by Peake (who arrived in Tafas shortly after Lawrence) in notes prepared in 1963 (after the film *Lawrence of Arabia* had been released) and in 1965.[46] In the second paper Peake wrote:

It is complete nonsense to say that the Turks killed no Arabs in Tafas. I arrived in Tafas some time after Lawrence, as my heavily loaded camels could not keep up with him. When I arrived in Tafas I saw that T.E.L.'s Bedouin were entirely out of control. They, infuriated by the dead men, women and children, lying in and around the village (which I myself saw) were rushing about shouting and seeking out any Turks who might be alive. Lawrence came running to me and ordered me to restore order as soon as possible. This I was able to do by dismounting 100 of my men and marching with bayonets fixed on the village. The sight of this disciplined body of soldiers was enough. The tumult and the shouting died and the Bedouin rode off northwards in the hope of catching up with the Turks who had already retreated. I was told later that they might have killed a straggler or two, but when they came up with the main body they found them ready to resist. Gradually during the afternoon they drifted back to their leader, T.E.L. I was ordered by Lawrence to collect and guard all Turks as they arrived from the battlefield in Palestine. As their numbers increased, I had to employ a number of Turkish prisoners to help my Egyptian soldiers. This, I think, is sufficient to prove that there never was any No Prisoners order.

In the earlier account Peake wrote that he regarded Lawrence's use of "we" in his writings as indicating the assumption of responsibility for actions of the Arabs he had helped to bring about. In Peake's view Lawrence had stated that "by my orders we took no prisoners" because "he obviously wished to assume the responsibility for an occurrence which neither he nor anyone else could at that time have prevented. He knew that, in future, it would be severely criticized but as he had originally stirred the Arabs to rebel against the Turks [not really so], it was only just that he should be blamed and not the Arabs."[47] Lawrence's subsequent activity and orders to Peake convinced Peake "that when Lawrence had the power to control the Arabs he used it effectively. Previous to my arrival he could only try to influence the Sheikhs to stop their followers killing the Turkish soldiers, but such was their fury that they had no mind to listen to him." Of the view of Lawrence at Tafas shown in the film Peake wrote, "It is to be regretted that a film showing Lawrence of Arabia should give the impression that he was a callous person or rather enjoyed seeing such horrible scenes. It would have been no less interesting and far more truthful had he been shown rushing about on foot trying to persuade the Sheikhs to call back their men."[48]

Even if there was no specific "no prisoners" order, there remain questions of Lawrence's role in the death of the two hundred captured Turks who had pinned down Hassan and what is meant by the statement in Seven Pillars "we killed and killed." Did Lawrence personally take a hand in the slaughter? Arnold Lawrence has shed some light on the first question. After the film Lawrence of Arabia appeared, which demonstrated that Lawrence enjoyed killing and which showed him as a hysterical sadist, Arnold Lawrence wrote for a London weekly: "My brother expressly states that he himself ordered that no prisoners be taken* — 'The best of you brings me the most Turkish dead' — but makes plain, I should have thought, that he did so because he shared the ungovernable fury of every Arab. Unquestionably he afterwards suffered deeply over his loss of control; I suspect that largely accounts for his insistence, throughout the rest of his life, that no Englishman could so serve an alien race without prostituting his own self."[49] In notes Arnold Lawrence prepared on the Tafas episode after receiving Peake's material he wrote, "In conversation with me, T.E.L. gave me clearly to understand that he had himself given the order to execute the 200 captured Turks who had pinned down Hassan;† that he had then regarded it as an execution was unmistakeable."[50]

---

* Arnold Lawrence wrote this before receiving Peake's accounts of Tafas.
† On my manuscript he wrote, "I wonder now whether he did even this."

As regards Lawrence's taking a personal hand in the killing, there is no direct outside evidence. Kirkbride, who was not nearby during the Tafas action, describes the killing of a group of Turkish prisoners by the Tafas villagers, "who were beside themselves with fury, and by the Bedouin, whose blood lust was now aroused,"[51] but he does not mention Lawrence.

In another context, before the film was made, Kirkbride wrote of Lawrence: "His tastes were anything but bloodthirsty, and he appeared to be genuinely shocked by the free use which I made of my revolver during the evening after we entered Damascus, when he would insist on rescuing Turkish stragglers from being murdered by the local populace." And: "Occasionally, someone turned nasty in Damascus and I shot them at once before the trouble could spread. Lawrence got quite cross and said, 'For God's sake stop being so bloody-minded!' "[52] After the film appeared, Kirkbride wrote to Liddell Hart:

> It is complete nonsense to describe him [Lawrence] as having been either sadistic or fond of killing. (These are not always the same thing.) He once told me that his ideal of waging war was based on the professional condottieri of medieval Italy. That is to say, to gain one's objectives with a minimum of casualties *on both sides*. . . . T.E.L. had a horror of bloodshed and it is because of that that he tends to pile on the agony in the passages of *Seven Pillars of Wisdom* dealing with death and wounds — not because he liked seeing others suffer.[53]

But Kirkbride's opinions are not evidence on Lawrence's conduct after the Turkish massacre at Tafas. My own opinion, which is based on the available evidence and what is known of Lawrence's character, is that Lawrence did lose control to the extent of ordering the execution of the two hundred prisoners. Seeing Hassan pinned down was the last straw after all Lawrence had seen and been through. I believe it to be highly doubtful that he personally took part in the killing, and I also believe that he did make an effort, as Peake describes, to control the excesses of the Arabs. I agree with Peake that the "we" regarding the "no prisoners" order and the other events around Tafas is a commander's "we" and derives from Lawrence's wish to assume full responsibility for the wild excesses of 'Awdah and the other Bedouin, to cover up for them.

But I believe, too, that this "we" reflects how intense Lawrence's identification with the Bedouin had become: he could feel their desire for revenge as if it were his own.[54] This identification with the Arabs *in revenge* connected with his own desire for revenge for what had been done to him by the Turks at Der'a ten months before and, combined with the other stresses of the campaigns he had undergone, accounts for his loss of control.

Arnold Lawrence had firsthand knowledge that his brother suffered deeply and felt considerable guilt over the loss of control at Tafas. No matter what the provocation, Lawrence could not reconcile his conduct with his own standards as a military officer or with his personal ideals regarding the value of human life. His brother has pointed out that because Allenby's cavalry bypassed the villages and towns they may not have seen the slaughtered villagers at Tafas. In consequence, the shock with which the British reacted to the Arabs' revenge was not mitigated by an understanding of the circumstances and "added greatly to T.E.'s difficulty till he left for England, if not afterwards."[55] The episode illustrates how dangerous it is for a sensitive person to become too personally absorbed in the daily activity of a military campaign for which he has, at the same time, a more general responsibility.

Peake is obviously correct in his observation that Lawrence knew he would in the future be severely criticized for this episode, but the point may in fact be extended further. I would suggest that Lawrence allowed ambiguities regarding his role at Tafas to stand and that he permitted criticism thereby. This interpretation is consistent with the guilt that Lawrence felt over the episode, and his need to court criticism and seek penance following the campaigns.[56]

I have dwelt at length upon the Tafas episode, and have taken particular pains to try to establish Lawrence's role in it, because it not only, I believe, is pertinent to the evaluation of his character, but raises at the same time issues pertinent to assessing the actions and personality of any public figure. A man who, with little provocation, orders, takes part in, and even enjoys killing helpless prisoners, while experiencing no guilt, is a sadist who invites little sympathy or interest. The film *Lawrence of Arabia* would lead us to believe this true of Lawrence. On the other hand, a man who, after observing extreme atrocities committed against people with whose lives and suffering he has become overly identified, gives way to the impulse to order a retaliatory execution by the victims of these atrocities is a different, more complex person, who may be deserving of our compassion and understanding as well as our criticism.

Damascus, the lodestar, was to have been the fulfillment of Lawrence's prophet dream. Its capture was to have been the glorious culmination of triumphant leadership, whereby a deserving people were sparked into liberating themselves from bondage. In a personal psychological sense its capture was meant to symbolize a final redemption, and the success of the Arab Revolt should have gained Lawrence peace from the criticism of an exacting self-regard that had demanded heroic achievement as the price of relief from an unconscious sense of worthlessness, of being the illegitimate result of sin and deception. Lawrence wrote later that he wept upon entering Damascus "for the triumphant thing achieved at last."[57] But the dream ended there for Lawrence and "its capture disclosed the exhaustion of my springs of action."[58] The treachery of ʿAbd al-Qadir, whom Lawrence was instrumental in deposing after entering Damascus, came to represent the painful contrasts and paradoxes of his experience in the Arab Revolt. Whether al-Qadir deserved it or not (and there is evidence that he did, at least in part), he became the object of Lawrence's intense hatred. His betrayals are elevated to major importance in *Seven Pillars of Wisdom* and in a subsequent official report (issued months after his death). The report was devoted exclusively to his actions and those of his brother, although it is doubtful that al-Qadir played as significant a role as the one Lawrence assigned to him. It appears that he had offered his help at first to the sharifian cause but subsequently betrayed it.

In a scene in *Seven Pillars of Wisdom*, Lawrence conveyed the extreme bitterness, irony and sense of degradation he felt on the day before he left Damascus. A medical major, thinking Lawrence was responsible for the still-terrible conditions of the hospital, burst out at him, " 'Scandalous, disgraceful, outrageous, ought to be shot.' " The powerful passage continues: "At this onslaught I cackled out like a chicken with the wild laughter of strain; it did feel extraordinarily funny to be so cursed just as I had been pluming myself on having bettered the apparently hopeless.

"The major had not entered the charnel house of yesterday, nor smelt it, nor seen us burying those bodies of ultimate degradation, whose memory had started me up in bed, sweating and trembling, a few hours since. He glared at me, muttering 'Bloody brute.' I hooted out again, and he smacked me over the face and stalked off, leaving me more ashamed than angry, for in my heart I felt he was right, and that anyone who pushed through to success a rebellion of the weak against their masters must come out of it so stained in estimation that afterward nothing in the world would make him feel clean. However, it was nearly over."[59]

Lawrence was twenty-eight when he first took an active, personal part in the Arab Revolt. Although he had seemed thus far to his friends and acquaintances an unusual, even odd, sort of genius, he had not given evidence of being deeply troubled, or even especially introspective. But his experiences in the Revolt, however his part in it is assessed, were personally shattering. The horrors he observed and took part in during 1917 and 1918 following the deaths of his two brothers; the political conflict; the disillusionment with the behavior of the Arabs; the multiple bouts of febrile illness;[60] the death of Dahoum; and, above all, the traumatic assault at Derʿa and the loss of control at Tafas, brought about profound changes in Lawrence's mental state and personality.

The Derʿa and Tafas experiences are, in my opinion, of special importance because of their link with the substance of unconscious conflicts and with areas of psychic vulnerability which, until these events occurred, had remained merely potential areas of emotional disorder (all men, I believe, harbor such areas) without overt indication of unusual distress).

But Der'a and Tafas touched off in Lawrence — there seem to be no right words — or brought into his consciousness in an abrupt and devastating way, forbidden or unacceptable sexual, aggressive and vengeful impulses. Until this time, what he had felt as merely a strong attraction to renunciation and self-denial, a kind of idealistic puritanism not without its normal place in the England of his day, became exaggerated into a powerful need for penance through degradation and humiliation, a need that was accompanied by a permanently lowered self-regard. In addition, he was left with a compulsive wish to be whipped, attributable directly to the Der'a experience, which was the source of much later misery and which I will be discussing later in this book.

The other result of the traumatic experiences was a marked increase in introspection. Before the war Lawrence rarely took himself as the object of his curiosity, but after 1918 he turned to studying himself intensively. It is usual for persons who have undergone severe psychic traumata or who suffer from various forms of emotional distress to try to understand themselves through introspection: self-understanding is a time-honored path to the relief of emotional pain. But it is perhaps unusual to find such introspection in a public figure, especially one who has been a military leader.

Long after the war's end Lawrence wrote to Herbert Samuel, the former high commissioner of Palestine, a letter that captures his perception of his war experiences: "I'm glad [Hogarth] sent you the last copy of my Seven Pillars, though I am sorry too, for you will look down on me, as a human being, after you have read it. Yet, when other people judge me as harshly as I judge myself, I find myself pleading that I was in a horrible position in Arabia, throughout, with the choice of no more than evils before me: and that I tried always to do the least harmful of them, and to do it so that the fewest small people were harmed by it. However, all these things are finished."[61]

FOUR

THE POLITICAL YEARS
1918–1922

Introduction

During the four years following the end of World War I and before his enlistment in the RAF in 1922 Lawrence's work and personality became known in the Western world. These were the years in which he struggled to fulfill in the political realm what he felt to be the responsibilities he had undertaken in the campaigns of the war in the Middle East. During this time "Lawrence of Arabia" was created by the public, and for Lawrence himself a gulf began to grow between his inner self as he felt it to be and the unfolding legendary figure he was both drawn to and loathed. These were years in which Lawrence expanded enormously his range of personal relationships and came to know many of the important public figures, writers and artists of the Great Britain of his day. Archeology was cut off to him as a profession, even had he chosen to pursue it, because he could not enter the countries of the Middle East except under political surveillance.[1]

This was a time in which the leadership of the Western powers could still move men and countries around like pawns and bargained and dealt in states and whole populations. As Arnold Toynbee, who was a British delegate to the Paris Peace Conference, wrote, Lawrence and the other advocates for the Middle Eastern peoples "sank deeper in the mire till they were as deeply bogged down as the rest of us."[2] In this period the disappointments in the postwar political arena merged psychologically for Lawrence with the painful effects of his war experiences and led, finally, to a major change in the course of his life.

Hannah Arendt recognized the extraordinary intensity of the conviction that underlay Lawrence's pursuit of his postwar aims. "Never again was the experiment of secret politics made more purely by a more decent man," she wrote. She felt that the imperialists destroyed Lawrence, reducing him until "nothing was left of him but some inexplicable decency."[3] This view is too strong, I believe. The political struggle did not destroy Lawrence, although 'it contributed greatly to his disillusionment. He accomplished much during these years and was able ultimately, with Winston Churchill, to impose his convictions to a large extent upon the final postwar settlements for the Arab regions. But "politically the thing was so dirty that I grew to hate it all before it came out more or less honestly in the end," he wrote to a friend many years later.[4]

Even his denigrators acknowledge that Lawrence was able to an extraordinary extent to impose his will upon the region's future. "On the threshold of the contemporary Middle East," Elie Kedourie wrote in 1956, "stands the figure of T. E. Lawrence, an object at once of awe and pity. He is a portent, a symbol of the power of chance over human affairs, and of the constant irruption into history of the uncontrollable force of a demonic will exerting itself to the limit of endurance. The consequences of his actions have touched numberless lives, and yet their motives were strictly personal, to be sought only in his intimate restlessness and private torment."[5]

These were also the years in which Lawrence first wrote and rewrote *Seven Pillars of Wisdom,* in which he attempted — he was probably the first military commander to do so — to fuse a narrative of battle with the examination of the meaning that making war had for a responsible leader, to connect the motive for making war with the impact of its horror upon the individual. He also wrote articles about Middle Eastern politics, guerrilla strategy, and dynamiting, and about the Arab lands and peoples.

The saga of the writing of *Seven Pillars of Wisdom,* which began in 1919, continues through most of this period. The burden and excitement of writing it reflect the conflict which resulted from reliving his wartime experiences over and over again. On the other hand, the constant and repeated reworking of the memories and materials of the war served a therapeutic role for Lawrence and helped to integrate them and modify their devastating impact.

He entered the RAF three months after he had completed the third and final basic text of the book, although he would continue to rework, criticize and abridge the material for five more years. The writing of *Seven Pillars of Wisdom* was curiously related to his friendship with his much-valued predecessor Charles Doughty, whose classic work, *Travels in Arabia Deserta,* Lawrence brought once more before the public, while he hid his own narrative from public view.

A definitive analysis of the postwar political settlements in the Middle East, or even of the significance of Lawrence's part in them, is beyond my competence or intention. Rather, I will attempt to describe carefully these political questions in order to show how they are related to the personal struggles and suffering Lawrence was undergoing during this time. The emphasis in this section will be, as it has been throughout the book, upon the relationship between inner psychology and creative action, between the private man and his public impact.

20

Arab Self-determination
and Arab Unity

As Lawrence, without official position or orders, assumed personal command of the desert war, he took, with even less well-defined authority, similar personal responsibility for the postwar political negotiations that would determine the political future of the Arab lands that had been wrested from the Ottoman Empire during and after the war's course. It was a natural extension of the "godfather" role he began to assume for himself in 1916.[1] The Arabs, he knew, believed in individuals, not in institutions, and he had been the individual who had represented Great Britain's capabilities, inspiration and assurances to them.[2]

As he had taken it upon himself to represent Britain's plans and promises to the Arabs, so he would try to see to it that these promises were honored. "I salved myself," Lawrence wrote not long after the war, "with the hope that, by leading these Arabs madly in the final victory I would establish them, with arms in their hands, in a position so assured (if not dominant) that expediency would counsel to the Great Powers a fair settlement of their claims. In other words, I presumed (seeing no other leader with the will and power) that I would survive the campaigns, and be able to defeat not merely the Turks on the battlefield, but my own country and its allies in the council chamber. It was an immodest presumption: it is not yet clear if I succeeded: but it is clear that I had no shadow of leave to engage the Arabs, unknowing, in such hazard."[3]

Between 1918 and 1922, in London, Paris, Oxford, Cairo and Amman, Lawrence fought to fulfill what he considered to be his responsibilities to the Arab peoples he had led or influenced during the war. To achieve his ends he used the persuasive powers of his intellect as well as the full range of talents at the disposal of his flexible and winning personality. He waged a war of words in personal negotiations and in public and private papers and letters, even "becoming an Arab" again, at the risk of looking ridiculous, when he thought it would serve a useful purpose. Irving Howe has observed that Lawrence's loyalty to the Arabs during the immediate postwar period, "this stubbornness — let us call it by its true name: this absolute unwillingness to sell out — began to strike his British colleagues as unreasonable, an embarrassment to their diplomacy."[4]

Lawrence's experiences between 1915 and 1920, and his personal associations at All Souls College in Oxford, especially with Lionel Curtis, brought about a marked increase in his political sophistication The practical amalgam he hoped to make in 1916 of Arab nationalistic aspirations and British national interests had been replaced by a more farseeing vision of change for the Arab world and for Asia. He conceived that the Arab regions from North Africa to the Indian Ocean would become the first African or Asiatic countries to achieve dominion status within the British Empire, "our first brown dominion."[5] His conception of dominion status for these lands ran counter to the more traditional imperialism that still influenced the postwar peace conferences, as the victors prepared to divide the spoils of war. Lawrence's effect upon the direction of British imperialist interest in the years after the war has yet to be evaluated objectively.

Lawrence saw in 1920 that the example of the Bolshevik Revolution along the northern frontiers of Arab Asia would have a powerful influence in strengthening and encouraging indigenous political nationalism in Western Asia.[6] "The Bolshevist success," he wrote, "has been a potent example to the East of the overthrow of an ancient government, depending on a kind of divine right, and weighing on Asia with all the force of an immense military establishment."[7] Lawrence called his conceptions of Asiatic dominions within the British Empire "the new Imperialism," perhaps in part to reduce the threatening character of his arguments for his British readers. His notions were not imperialistic by the standards of the period, or even of our own, although a kind of chauvinism in Lawrence seems to have been quite genuine. He envisioned a system of alliances between the Arab Asiatic countries whereby they would join the British Empire for military protection and security, but remain politically autonomous within it. "I think there's a great future for the British Empire as a voluntary association," he wrote in 1928.[8] To achieve this end the British government would have to encourage the assumption of political responsibility among these countries and to pull back from a governing role to an advisory one.

Lawrence's most concise expression of his view of this change was set forth in an anonymous article which appeared in September 1920 in the political monthly the *Round Table*. The writing seems to have been inspired by striking current examples of traditional imperialism in the British administration of Iraq and the French take-over in Syria. We are continuing to see the realization of some of the prophecies contained in this article in the passing decades of the twentieth century:

"This new condition, of a conscious and logical nationalism, now the dominant factor of every indigenous movement in Western Asia, is too universal to be extinguished, too widespread to be temporary. We must prepare ourselves for its continuance, and for a continuance of the unrest produced by it in every contested district, until such time as it has succeeded and passed into a more advanced phase. It is so radical a change in the former complexion of Western Asia as to demand from us a revision of the principles of our policy in the Middle East, and an effort to adjust ourselves, that the advantage of its constructive elements may be on our side.

"This new Imperialism is not just withdrawal and neglect on our part. It involves an active side of imposing responsibility on the local peoples. It is what they clamour for, but an unpopular gift when given. . . . We can only teach them how by forcing them to try, while we stand by and give advice. This is not for us less honourable than administration: indeed, it is more exacting for it is simple to give orders, but difficult to persuade another to take advice, and it is the more difficult which is most pleasant doing. We must be prepared to see them doing things by methods quite unlike our own, and less well: but on principle it is better that they half-do it than that we do it perfectly for them. In pursuing such courses, *we will find our best helpers not in our former most obedient subjects, but among those now most active in agitating against us* [italics added], for it will be the intellectual leaders of the people who will serve the purpose, and these are not the philosophers nor the rich, but the demagogues and the politicians. . . . Egypt, Persia and Mesopotamia, if assured of eventual dominion status, and present internal autonomy, would be delighted to affiliate with us, and would then cost us no more in men and money than Canada or Australia. The alternative is to hold on to them with ever-lessening force, till the anarchy is too expensive, and we let go."[9]

The history of the changing relations between the Great Powers and their former colonies since World War I may be looked at in terms of contrasting examples — instances in which prepared withdrawal has been followed by peaceful affiliation as contrasted with efforts at continued colonial control resulting in bloodshed and suppression.

Political nationalism as we are familiar with it in the twentieth century is a product of European history. Its growth among the Arab countries of Western Asia has been promoted in large part by contact with the European Great Powers, although its ideas were actively taken up in the Middle East, especially in Syria, in the later years of the nineteenth century and the first decades of the twentieth. World War I, with its use of propaganda and the need of the Allies for partners in the East against

Turkey and Germany, brought an enormous increase in contact between the Western powers and the Arab countries, and thus a marked growth in Arab nationalistic ambitions. "The astonished peoples of Western Asia," Lawrence wrote in 1920, "could not choose but hear us, and began, willingly or unwillingly, to see what we were like, and comprehend our least notions. They did not always like them, but they learned a lot. In particular they learned what each of us was fighting for (they heard it from all our mouths, and we all said much the same thing), and a thing sworn to by so many witnesses must surely be true. This liberty, this humanity, this culture, this self-determination, must be very valuable."[10]

From the time of his first dispatches in 1916 Lawrence distinguished between Arab nationalistic feeling — the drive toward self-determination — and political unity or the formation of a single Arab national state or confederation. He was always a strong advocate of self-determination, but never seems to have believed deeply in the concept of Arab political unity. He doubted that the Arab countries would voluntarily surrender their autonomy to become part of a nation. There is often a suggestion in Lawrence's political writings, especially during the war, that his doubts about Arab unity relate not only to its feasibility but also to the threat to British national interests that a strong Arab nation might present. "When people talk of Arab Confederation or Empires they talk fantastically," he wrote in 1928; "it will be generations, I expect — unless the vital tempo of the East is much accelerated — before any two Arab states join voluntarily. I agree that their only future hope is that they should join; but it must be natural growing together. Forced unions are pernicious, and politics, in such things, should come after geography and economics. Communications and trade must be improved before provinces can join."[11] To Mrs. George Bernard Shaw he wrote even more bluntly: "I'd as soon unite the English-speaking races as the Arabic-speaking. Some amalgamations there may be, must be, if their show progresses well: but not any general union or confederation, in my time, I hope. The tremendous value, and the delight of the Arab areas lie in their concentrated localization."[12]

Six years later (1928) in a starkly realistic, negative mood he wrote on the manuscript of Liddell Hart's biography: "Arab unity is a madman's notion — for this century or next, probably. English-speaking unity is a fair parallel. I am sure, I never dreamed of uniting even Hedjaz and Syria. My conception was of a number of smaller states."[13]

But in 1920 he had been neither so sure nor so cynical. He conceived then of "the Arab movement" as developing in stages, born in the desert as he felt all ideas were originally, moving to Damascus with Faisal the father (and perhaps Lawrence the godfather), and reaching its final realization under the leadership of Baghdad. Mesopotamia, Lawrence believed, would (because of its natural resources, potential wealth and strategic geography) ultimately "be the master of the Middle East, and the power controlling its destinies."[14] He concluded: "The question of a unity of the Arabic peoples in Asia is yet clouded. In the past it has never been a successful experiment, and the least reflection will show that there are large areas, especially of Arabia, which it would be unprofitable ever to administer. The deserts will probably remain, in the future as in the past, the preserves of inarticulate philosophers. The cultivated districts, Mesopotamia and Syria, have, however, language, race and interests in common. Till today they have always been too vast to form a single country: they are divided, except for a narrow gangway in the north, by an irredeemable waste of flint and gravel: but petrol makes light of deserts, and space is shrinking today, when we travel one hundred miles an hour instead of five. The effect of railways, air-ways and telegraph will be to draw these two provinces together, and teach them how like they are: and the needs of Mesopotamian trade will fix attention on the Mediterranean ports. The Arabs are a Mediterranean people, whom no force of circumstances will constrain to the Indian Ocean: further, when Mesopotamia has done her duty by the rivers, there will remain no part for water transport in her life — and the way by rail from Mosul or Baghdad to Alexandretta or Tripoli is more advantageous than the way to Basra. It may well be that Arab unity will come of an overwhelming conviction of the Mesopotamians that their national prosperity demands it."[15]

Lawrence hoped that the Zionist movement would have the result of bringing the Jews into a position of technological leadership in the Arab regions of Asia and North Africa and that they would help to raise the material level of their Arab neighbors. "The Jewish experiment," he wrote in 1920, "is a conscious effort, on the part of the least European people in Europe, to make head against the drift of the ages, and return once more to the Orient from which they came. The colonists will take back with them to the land which they occupied for some centuries before the Christian era samples of all the knowledge and technique of Europe. They propose to settle down amongst the existing Arabic-speaking population of the country, a people of kindred origin, but far different social condition. They hope to adjust their mode of life to the climate of Palestine, and by the exercise of their skill and capital to make it as highly organised as a European state. The success of their scheme will involve inevitably the raising of the present Arab population to their own material level, only a little after themselves in point of time, and the consequences might be of the highest importance for the future of the Arab world. It might well prove a source of technical supply rendering them independent of industrial Europe, and in that case the new confederation might become a formidable element of world power. However, such a contingency will not be for the first or even for the second generation, but it must be borne in mind in any laying out of foundations of empire in Western Asia. These to a very large extent must stand or fall by the course of the Zionist effort, and by the course of events in Russia."[16]

There is no evidence that Lawrence anticipated the intransigence and hostility that would develop between Arabs and Jews. But as the war drew to a close he was faced with much more practical political problems. As the Arab Revolt advanced northward successfully under his and Faisal's leadership it produced a rebirth of nationalistic aspirations in Syria that had been crushed by the Young Turks in 1915.[17] "Syrians of Syria are enlisting by thousands in the ranks of his [Faisal's] armies," Lawrence wrote in 1918, two months after the armistice.[18] Syria was nationalistic in sentiment from south to north and there were many Iraqi officers in Faisal's army who soon carried the wave of Arab nationalistic feeling to their own homeland.[19] An Anglo-French declaration of November 7, 1918, born in part out of the exhilaration and good will that attended the winding up of the war, seemed to favor the upsurge of nationalism. The British and French leaders would, they promised, work toward "definite freedom of the peoples so long oppressed by the Turks," "encourage and assist in the establishment of native governments in Syria and Mesopotamia," "ensure equal and impartial justice for all," and "aid the economic development of the country by inspiring and encouraging local initiative."[20] But the co-signers soon reverted to prewar imperialist patterns and were confronted, therefore, during the next few years with native rebellions in Egypt, Iraq and Syria.

Lawrence has been criticized by modern Arab nationalist writers for failing to believe in or support Arab unity. They resent his recommending the division of Greater Syria — what is now Syria, Lebanon, Jordan and Israel — into separate countries (Greater Syria had been, according to Suleiman Mousa, "the moving spirit of the Arab countries" for centuries).[21] They also resent his backing Faisal and the Hashemite family and neglecting other, especially Syrian, nationalist leaders.[22] Anis Sayigh, for example, has noted that Husayn, with his Bedouin background, had too narrow an outlook to represent Arab nationalist interests in Europe, and that Faisal, because of Lawrence's influence, gave up many nationalist demands in Paris and London. Mousa and Sayigh take particular exception to Lawrence's imposing Hashemite rulers on several Arab states.

But these are arguments based on the vantage point of this decade. In 1918 at the close of the war there seemed, apart from Faisal, no Arab nationalist leader with sufficient authority to represent all the Arab peoples, one who was above the factionalism of the fragmentary nationalistic movements that existed after the war and who possessed enough prestige to speak for the Arab peoples at the Paris Peace Conference.

The political situation had not changed greatly from Lawrence's description of it in 1917: "The largest indigenous political entity in settled Syria is only the village under its sheikh, and in patriarchal Syria the tribe under its chief."[23] Furthermore, there was no viable conception of nationhood among the Arabs of Greater Syria in 1919, let alone of Greater Syria and Iraq combined.

The history of the Arab-speaking regions since 1945, when the last colonial reins were released, testifies to the difficulty that these countries have encountered in developing the unity that some Arab nationalist leaders have sought. 'Abd al-Rahman Shahbandar, the Syrian nationalist leader (he was one of the Seven Syrians who extracted the promise of postwar independence from the British high command in Cairo in June 1918) wrote from the perspective of 1931: "Lawrence spent all possible energy to establish the strongest foothold in order for the Arabs to have full independence under their own flags. But what use was there when the British had understandings with their allies, the French, which tore apart and dispersed this full independence."[24] Indeed, soon after the start of the Peace Conference, which opened in Paris in January 1919, it became evident that France, far from observing the spirit of the Anglo-French declaration issued just two months before the conference began, was determined to compensate for her suffering in World War I with the acquisition of a new colony in Syria. She justified this colonization, which amounted virtually to a conquest, on the grounds of her long-standing commercial interests in the Levant, her protective role in relation to the Maronite Christian Sect in Syria and Lebanon (the hostility of the Muslim majority in Syria was ignored or misunderstood), and the Sykes-Picot Agreement of 1916, which recognized French interests in the area.

Lawrence has been criticized repeatedly for his intractable "hostility" toward the French.[25] But the simple fact is that French colonial policies (over which he could have no liberalizing influence) ran in direct opposition to his political and humanistic beliefs and to the personal commitments, however wisely or unwisely made, that he had undertaken. The meaning of these commitments to Lawrence, the depth of his disappointment over their frustration, and the recognition of the limitations of his power to fulfill them is a principal theme in the pages that follow.

21

Leaving Damascus Behind

Although Lawrence left "the silky coolness of the Damascus dust"[1] on October 4, 1918, the Allied forces continued to move northward through Syria during the rest of the month. By the twenty-sixth, Beirut, Homs, Hama and Aleppo were in Anglo-Arab hands, and the Turks had been driven back within the borders of Asia Minor. At the time of the signing of the Turkish armistice on October 31, the Allied forces, dominated by the British and their Arab companions, were in possession of virtually all Syria and Mesopotamia.[2] Particularly embarrassing from the standpoint of future Anglo-French relations was the fact that in Beirut, the Levantine center of French interest, an Arab government had been declared and Arab flags hoisted, though temporarily, with Allenby's permission (also te porary) and Lawrence's possible connivance (later denied by him).[3] T' e stage was set for the Anglo-French struggle over Syria that was to occupy the peacemakers for the next two years.

Despondent that his extraordinary efforts during the campaigns had seemed to come to so little, Lawrence returned to Cairo. There he wrote, "I feel like a man who has suddenly dropped a heavy load — one's back hurts when one tries to walk straight."[4] Lawrence met Wingate on October 14 and gave early notice of his opposition to French claims in Syria and of his intention to struggle in England to hold his government to their commitments to self-determination for their Arab allies.[5] He returned to England through Italy by train, and later told Graves and Liddell Hart that he was promoted temporarily to full colonel at his own request in order to get a berth on an express staff train to Le Havre, to which this higher rank would entitle him.

Lawrence's ambivalent attitude toward his military rank is reflected in this and in other stories of the period in which he both ridicules and capitalizes on the fact of his colonelcy. The stories follow the pattern of the myth of the hero: Lawrence, appearing at his scruffiest, is mistaken for a nobody by an officer of lower rank and less deserving than he, who demands a salute or other show of respect (in one case an officer was even accompanied by a lady, "probably not his wife!").[6] Lawrence then reveals his true identity, delivers a bit of a moral lecture, and the chastened officer goes away red-faced with embarrassment, to the delight of Lawrence and whatever ordinary folk of humble station happen to witness the scene.[7]

Lawrence arrived in England on or about October 24, after stopping in Rome on the way back long enough to learn from Georges Picot that the French intended to impose French advisors on Faisal.[8] Robert Lawrence told me that he appeared wasted and weighed only seventy to eighty pounds instead of his usual 112 pounds or more.[9] Although this weight loss seems virtually inconceivable, a portrait done by James McBey during this period shows Lawrence's gaunt appearance.[10]

Emaciated or not, in less than a week after arriving in England and before the armistice with Turkey was signed, Lawrence was putting forward his ideas for the Near East at a meeting of the Eastern Committee of the War Cabinet. The chairman was the foreign secretary, Lord Curzon, for whom, it has been said, the British Empire was the successor of the Roman and "the instrument of divine will" as well.[11] In welcoming Lawrence at the meeting, Curzon said that "His Majesty's Government had for some time watched with interest and admiration the great work which Colonel Lawrence had been doing in Arabia, and felt proud that an officer had done so much to promote successful progress of the British and Arab arms."[12]

Lawrence was asked to furnish the cabinet with a memorandum in which he set forth his views in more detail.[13] He emphasized British interests in Western Asia, calling the area between Egypt, Persia and Anatolia "our Monroe area," and tactfully reminded his readers of the reason for the selection of the sharif of Mecca and his sons as the leaders for Britain to back in the Revolt and of their noble sacrifices in the Allied cause. He lauded their loyalty and achievements in battle (as General Allenby's "handmaid," of course) and pressed for an autonomous Syria under Faisal's rule ("sovereign in his own dominions with complete liberty to choose any foreign advisers he wants of any nationality he pleases"). Neither France nor the French were mentioned.

In this memorandum, as in his statement to the Eastern Committee the previous week, Lawrence said that the Arabs could accept Jewish "infiltration" in Palestine, and Zionist advice and assistance, as long as it was under a British "façade" and an independent Jewish state was not established. He followed this memorandum with a more detailed proposal for the Arab administration of Iraq.[14]

In the meantime, on October 30, Lawrence had an audience with King George V, a famous episode in which the king wished formally to bestow upon him the C.B. (Companion of the Bath) for Aqaba and the D.S.O. (Distinguished Service Order), honors for which he had already been gazetted (that is, the recommendation of the honors had already been published in a British official gazette).

A meeting with the king himself would naturally be an incident about which myths and stories would proliferate (some of which, as Arnold Lawrence has pointed out, "caused more harm to T.E.L.'s reputation than he can have anticipated")[15] and I shall not attempt in this instance to distinguish fully the actuality from the legend since no recorders of the event, except perhaps the king's secretary, seem to have been exempt altogether from leaving distortions. What is certain is that Lawrence declined to accept the decorations and explained to the king that his reasons for doing so concerned his wish to dramatize and uphold the Arab cause, to accept no official honors for what he regarded as his ignoble role in it, and to impel the British government through the force of his own moral example to honor its responsibilities to its Arab allies.

Whether the audience was public or private (certainly it was private: Lawrence would not have wished to cause the king public embarrassment), whether Lawrence was insulting or courteous, whether the king was insulted or understanding, whether Lawrence did or did not threaten to fight the British, the French or anyone else if Britain let the Arabs down are questions that have been debated by Lawrence's critics, friendly and hostile. The most reliable account of the meeting is in the actual record of the Court:

> During the conversation, Colonel Lawrence said that he had pledged his word to Feisal, and that now the British Government were about to let down the Arabs over the Sykes-Picot Agreement. He was an Emir among the Arabs and intended to stick to them through thick and thin and, if necessary, fight against the French [not the British] for the recovery of Syria.
>
> Colonel Lawrence said that he did not know that he had been gazetted or what the etiquette was in such matters, but he hoped that the King would forgive any want of courtesy on his part in not taking these decorations.[16]

Arnold Lawrence pointed out that the gesture was effective in attracting attention to the Arab cause, and had a particular impact upon Winston Churchill, who was instrumental more than two years later in rectifying Arab grievances — to the extent it lay within his and Britain's power to do so.[17]

On November 8 Lawrence began his sponsorship of Faisal as representative of the Arabs at the Peace Conference. "I believe there will be conversations in Paris in fifteen days time between the Allies about the question of the Arabs," he telegraphed King Husayn with Foreign Office approval, and urged him to have his son prepared to leave Syria for France and to telegraph "the Governments of Great Britain, France, the United States and Italy telling them that your son is proceeding at once to Paris as your representative."[18] On November 21, at another meeting of the Eastern Committee of the War Cabinet, Lawrence was delegated to meet Faisal at Marseilles and to offer at least the possibility of sharifian government in Iraq. In this meeting Lawrence reiterated his conviction that "there would be no difficulty in reconciling Zionists and the Arabs in Palestine and Syria, provided that the administration at Palestine remained in British hands."[19] After some delay Husayn telegraphed the necessary confirmation, Faisal sailed for France (on an English ship), and Lawrence duly met him in Marseilles as arranged. Accompanied by a small party, Faisal was to tour France, meet the French president, and then travel to England.

Ahmad Qadri, who was a member of Faisal's party, states that despite their courtesy the French made a point of regarding Faisal as an Arab shaykh from the Hijaz rather than as a leader who had played an important role in the Allied victories in the desert.[20] Together the party traveled to Lyons, where they were met by Colonel Brémond. Brémond subsequently wrote that he had been given certain instructions concerning Lawrence: "With Lawrence you must be very clear and show him he is on the wrong track. If he comes as a British colonel, in an English uniform, we will welcome him. But we will not accept him as an Arab, and if he comes disguised he has nothing to do with us."[21] According to Brémond, Lawrence was indeed dressed "en costume oriental," although Lawrence denied that he had met Faisal in Arab dress.[22] In any event Nuri al-Sa'id, who was also a member of the Arab party, noted "some coldness between Lawrence and the French."[23] Lawrence was asked to return to England, which he promptly did, but not, according to Qadri, before explaining to Faisal that the French were plotting to keep him away from the Peace Conference.[24] Faisal and his companions were then given red-carpet treatment and escorted ceremoniously about France. Commenting on the incident after being informed by Liddell Hart in 1933 of Brémond's account, Lawrence wrote: "Feisal was guest of the French Government, whose duty (and pleasure) it was to do the entertaining. So a foreign hanger-on was out of place. He [Brémond] was quite nice and (I thought) quite right about it. He gave me no idea that his instructions were as you report."[25]

Just at this time (November 26, 27 and 28, 1918) there appeared in The Times three articles written anonymously by "a correspondent who was in close touch with the Arabs throughout their campaign against the Turks after the revolt of the Sherif of Mecca."[26] Lord Winterton, who was well connected in official circles, had put Lawrence "in touch with the right people in Fleet Street so that the Arab point-of-view might have a 'good press!' "[27] And one of Winterton's friends, Evelyn Wrench, introduced Lawrence to "various newspaper friends." The articles are clearly propaganda pieces written in support of the Arab cause and the leadership of Faisal. They are written in the first person, although the author's personal role is minimized. The campaigns are made to sound like cleanly fought adventures by a worthy and effective ally of a British nation that had the diplomatic wisdom to recognize its value, and Faisal is made the undisputed hero of the piece.[28]

One of the newspapermen with whom Lawrence was put in touch after the armistice was Geoffrey Dawson, editor of *The Times*. In the letter to Dawson that accompanied the articles Lawrence championed the Arab cause: "The points that strike me are that the Arabs came into the war without making a previous treaty with us, and have consistently refused to listen to the temptations of other powers. They never had a press agent, or tried to make themselves out a case, but fought as hard as they could (I'll swear to that) and suffered hardships in their three campaigns and losses that would break up seasoned troops. They fought with ropes around their necks (Feisal had 20,000 alive and 10,000 dead on him. I the same: Nasir 10,000 alive, and Ali el Harith 8,000) and did it without, I believe, any other very strong motive than a desire to see the Arabs free. It was rather an ordeal for as very venerable a person as Hussein to rebel for he was at once most violently abused by the Moslem press in India and Turkey, on religious grounds."[29] Lawrence reviewed the value received by Britain from the Arabs in the Revolt, debated the value of an alliance with the Arabs, and credited McMahon, the high commissioner in Egypt, with bringing about the sharif's entry into the war, as advised by Storrs, Clayton and Lawrence himself. Lawrence followed this with his sharifian solution for the Near East and concluded, rather unrealistically: "The old Sherif wants to be prayed for in Mosques on Friday. He is, already, in Syria, and in parts of Mesopotamia, and will be generally if we leave things alone."[30]

On December 9, Faisal was finally ready — or, perhaps more accurately, was allowed — to leave France for England,[31] and Lawrence met him in Boulogne. According to Brémond's description Lawrence was dressed in white and under the dark sky gave the effect of "a Catholic choir boy." Lawrence with pointed politeness invited Brémond to accompany them to London, but Brémond declined regretfully because his mission was over and he had not been given "the latitude to accept."[32]

In England one of the first things Lawrence did was to arrange a meeting between Faisal and Chaim Weizmann, the Zionist leader (none other than Arthur Balfour, the foreign secretary, had advised Weizmann to seek an agreement with Faisal).[33]* At the meeting Faisal and Weiz-

---

* In the Balfour Declaration of November 2, 1917, the British government had gone on record as favoring "the establishment in Palestine of a national home for the Jewish people."

mann discussed the possibility of reconciling Zionist hopes in Palestine
with Arab ambitions in Syria.

At this time the hope of Jewish-Arab collaboration in the Middle East
was very much alive. Lawrence and Weizmann had met during the
desert campaigns and Weizmann and Faisal had had a meeting in June
1918, at Aqaba. Less well known was the fact that both Lawrence and
Weizmann had met in Palestine with Palestinian Arab leaders who, even
early in 1918, were suspicious of the extent of British collaboration with
the Hashemite family to the exclusion of other Arab groups.[34] But in the
first months after the war's end Arab-Jewish cooperation under British
auspices did not seem so difficult, and Lawrence strove to use his friendships with both Faisal and Weizmann to achieve these purposes. He even
hoped that Zionist wealth could be used to support Faisal's government
in Syria and to block French interests thereby. The vital distinctions
between a Jewish homeland (or the possibility of unlimited Jewish immigration into Palestine) and the establishment of a sovereign Jewish state
seem not to have been considered at this time.

On December 13 Faisal is quoted as having told a Reuter's correspondent: "The two main branches of the Semitic family, Arabs and Jews,
understand one another, and I hope that as a result of interchange of
ideas at the Peace Conference, which will be guided by ideals of self-
determination and nationality, each nation will make definite progress
towards the realization of its aspirations. Arabs are not jealous of Zionist
Jews, and intend to give them fair play, and the Zionist Jews have
assured the nationalist Arabs of their intention to see that they, too, have
fair play in their respective areas." He looked toward "mutual understanding of the aims of Arabs and Jews," and the clearing away of former
bitterness, "which indeed had practically disappeared even before the
war."[35] The *Jewish Chronicle* wrote of the Weizmann-Faisal meeting
that "a complete understanding between the Emir and Dr. Weizmann
was arrived at on all points."[36] Later in the month Lord Rothschild gave
a dinner in Faisal's honor at which the amir again "emphasized the kinship between the Jews and the Arabs, and the harmony between the
Jewish nationalist and the Arab nationalist aspirations."[37]

On January 3, 1919, an agreement between Faisal and Weizmann was
drawn up by Lawrence,[38] and signed in this spirit in anticipation of the
Peace Conference. By the terms of the agreement, Jewish immigration
was to be encouraged and the rights of Arab peasants and farmers were
to be protected in exchange for Zionist economic and political support of
an Arab state, whose boundaries with Palestine were to be established at
the conference.[39] The parties agreed to act "in accord and harmony at
the Peace Conference." Faisal left himself an escape clause (whose tone
Lawrence tried to soften in his English translation) in which the amir
stated categorically that if Britain did not live up to its promise of Arab

independence he "would not be bound by a single word of the Agreement."[40] As it turned out, the agreement never acquired validity because this last condition was never fulfilled. But it does demonstrate the hopes existing at that time, and toward which Lawrence and British leaders such as Sykes and Ormsby-Gore strove: that Zionist and Arab interests could be brought together for the progressive political and economic development of the Middle East.[41] None of those involved in the agreement seem to have anticipated either the hostility that soon would arise in Palestine and in other parts of the Arab world to the establishing of a Jewish homeland in Palestine, or the mishandling on all sides of the problems of Arab-Jewish relations.[42]

During the approximately three weeks they spent together in England in December of 1918, Lawrence hardly left Faisal's side, and took great pains in his behalf. He attempted to fulfill all the amir's various needs, and dressed in Arab garb accompanied him to an audience with King George (Lawrence's second meeting with the king). And Lawrence was indeed effective in securing British backing for Faisal at the Peace Conference, which soon took place.[43]

Soon after returning to England Lawrence picked up the strands once more of his friendship with Charles Doughty. Doughty opened the correspondence, and in replying, Lawrence brushed lightly over the tops of his experience in the Arab Revolt: "It's been a wonderful experience and I've got quite a lot to tell. I'm afraid it is not likely to be written for publication, since some of it would give offence to people alive (including myself!)."[44]

After the new year Lawrence went to a party in Arab dress, "for fun," he wrote many years later.[45] But at the time he embarrassed himself by having done so and wrote apologetically: "I behaved like a lunatic yesterday. But I have been trying for three years to think like an Arab, and when I come back with a bump to British conventions, it is rather painful, and I keep deciding to put an end to it. However, nothing ever happens."[46] Lawrence also discussed his views about Asia and the Arabs with the American publisher F. N. Doubleday and with Rudyard Kipling, both of whom he met at dinner parties in London shortly before leaving for the Peace Conference. Kipling, who had lived for four years in the United States and was on friendly terms with some American politicians, was impressed by Lawrence's ideas and urged him to approach the Republicans, led by Henry Cabot Lodge, since Wilson, in his opinion, was "on the wane" and inclined "to give lofty advice and return to his national fireside."[47]

Lawrence approached the Paris Conference optimistically. "I'm off to Paris, ('peace work,' they call it)," he wrote to a fellow officer of the Hijaz campaign. "In the Hedjaz there is nothing, for Jidda isn't a white man's country! In Syria everything depends on the conference. We may find ourselves shut out, or let in, on the same ground as the rest of the earth. And till the end of the conference I cannot tell you."[48]

By the end of the conference Lawrence was deeply frustrated, disillusioned and troubled.

22

At the Paris
Peace Conference

The rulers of the world have sat here with the problem of human living before them, laid out on their table by the tragedy of war," the American journalist and reformer Lincoln Steffens wrote Allen H. Siggett on April 13, 1919. "That should have opened their minds and hearts too and led them to tackle the job in some new, big way. They wanted to. There was good-will here. But their old habits of mind, their fixed attention upon things they do not really want, their age, their education, — these have made it impossible for them to do their work. . . .

"So they have failed. They have the appearance of success, but, — they have failed. And it does not matter. The problem will be solved. Other, newer men, with a fresher culture, — the men I have seen lately, — they will have their turn now."[1]

Despite the idealism of Woodrow Wilson and his Fourteen Points (Point 12 proclaimed that the non-Turkish nationalities of the Ottoman Empire should "be given an opportunity for autonomous development"), the echoes of nineteenth- and early twentieth-century European nationalism could be heard at the Peace Conference. As Jon Kimche has written, "the whole history of the Middle East in the half century between 1919 and 1969 is a history of the undoing of the work of the Paris Peace Conference of 1919 and the settlements made after the First World War."[2]

Even Lloyd George, who did make an effort at the conference to support a self-governing Syria as had been promised in the agreements made during the war, had little grasp of the meaning of Arab nationalistic aspirations. Deals were made between leaders concerning other peoples, regions and countries without regard to the interests of those peoples. "When Clemenceau came to London after the war," Lloyd George wrote in his memoirs, "I drove with him to the French Embassy through cheering crowds who acclaimed him with enthusiasm. After we reached the Embassy he asked me what it was I specially wanted from the French. I instantly replied that I wanted Mosul attached to Irak, and Palestine from Dan to Beersheba under British control.* Without any hesitation he agreed. Although that agreement was not reduced to writing he adhered to it honestly in subsequent negotiations."[3]

Lawrence arrived in Paris in the second week in January and attended the conference officially as a technical advisor to the British delegation. During the next three months he identified himself with Faisal and the Arabs (Faisal represented and defined the Arab cause because he led the Arab delegation). Lawrence frequently interpreted and translated for Faisal, and wore an Arab headcloth when he believed it would strengthen the Arab position. He also took pains, as revealed in the Foreign Office files, to see that members of the Arab delegation were afforded by the Great Powers the diplomatic courtesies and access to the telegraphic facilities they needed.[4] Lawrence operated in Paris — though unsuccessfully for his cause at the conference — at the pinnacle of power, taking part in meetings with Clemenceau, Lloyd George, Wilson and other world leaders. A decade later he would write to a British politician: "Anyone who had gone up so fast as I went (remember that I was almost entirely self-made: my father had five sons, and only £300 a year) and had seen so much of the inside of the top of the world might lose his aspirations, and get weary of the ordinary motives of action, which had moved him till he reached the top. I wasn't a King or Prime Minister, but I made 'em, or played with them, and after that there wasn't much more, in that direction, for me to do."[5]

Lawrence was, as Gertrude Bell wrote her family at the time, "the most picturesque" figure at the conference,[6] and his legend grew whether or not he believed it to be his conscious wish that it should. Lawrence spent a lot of time with members of the American delegation and with American newsmen. He hoped for a time that the Americans would take responsibility for the administration of Syria — they would, he believed, care more about the interests of its people than the French would.[7] As a result of the earlier cooperation of Faisal with the Zionists, the British Zionists were able to introduce Faisal to the leaders of the American delegation in Paris and help get the Arab cause before the Peace Conference.[8] But the effort was not successful. As Churchill wrote: "The idea that France, bled white in the trenches of Flanders, should emerge from the Great War without her share of conquered territories was insupportable to [Clemenceau] and would never have been tolerated by his countrymen."[9] Syria was to be part of the French booty of World War I.

---

* Did he know where these places were? They do not delimit the boundaries of any country. Perhaps Lloyd George used the expression purely symbolically, but symbolizing what? Mosul was in the sphere of French influence in the Sykes-Picot Agreement, which was thus undone casually in a conversation between two world leaders carving up the spoils of war.

As early as January 11, 1919, just a few days after arriving in Paris, Lawrence attended a dinner with Lionel Curtis, William Bullitt and others in which "the discussion was about Poland and Colonel Lawrence's expedition and experiences."[10] One of the guests, David Hunter Miller, a legal advisor to the American delegation, wrote of the discussion in his diary: Lawrence expressed the hope that the United States could administer Syria; his attitude was "distinctly anti-French." Miller found Lawrence's conversation "remarkable," and it seems to have been from his diary that the story arose of Faisal's reading the Koran while Lawrence, seeming to interpret his "speech," gave a talk about whatever he chose. In Miller's contemporary version, the setting of the speech had been Glasgow in December 1918, not Paris as in a later rendition of the story.[11] Faisal, according to Lawrence as reported by Miller, "leaned over to Colonel Lawrence and said to him in Arabic, 'Instead of making a speech I'm going to get up and recite a chapter from the Koran [the chapter of the Cow, according to Arnold Toynbee] and as your interpretation you can say anything that you damn please!' "[12]

Even in the first days of the Peace Conference, two months before Lowell Thomas began his talk and film show in New York, Lawrence had already become a legendary figure. James Shotwell, an American history professor on leave from Columbia University, also kept a contemporary diary of the Peace Conference. He describes Lawrence as "that younger successor of Mohammed, Colonel Lawrence, the twenty-eight-year-old conqueror of Damascus, with his boyish face and almost constant smile — the most winning figure, so every one says, at the whole Peace Conference."[13] Shotwell goes on to describe Lawrence joking with Faisal and translating for him at informal gatherings of American officials where they pleaded their case:

Lawrence came in the uniform of a British Colonel, but wore his Arab headdress to keep his friend company (they wore them through the meal and all evening). His veil over his explorer's helmet was of green silk and hung down over his shoulder with a tassel or two of deep red. Around his head was a similar double strand of big, colored braid, as in the case of Feisal's, about three-quarters of an inch in diameter and looking much like a crown. He has been described as the most interesting Briton alive, a student of medieval history at Magdalen College, where he used to sleep by day and work by night and take his recreation in the deer park at four in the morning — a Shelly-like person, and yet too virile to be a poet. He is a rather short, strongly built man of not over twenty-eight [actually thirty] years, with sandy complexion, a typical English face, bronzed by the desert, remarkable blue eyes and a smile around the mouth that responded swiftly to that on the face of his friend. The two men were obviously very fond of each other. I have seldom seen such mutual affection between grown men as in this instance. Lawrence would catch the drift of Feisal's humor and pass the joke along to us while Feisal was exploding with his idea; but all the same it was funny to see how Feisal spoke with the oratorical feeling of the South and Lawrence translated in the lowest and quietest of English voices, in very simple and direct phrases, with only here and there a touch of Oriental poetry breaking through.[14]

One cannot help wondering what happened to Faisal's humor and arguments in Lawrence's free translations. William Yale told me that some of the Americans felt that Lawrence and Faisal's joking was at their expense and were offended. But Yale was somewhat embittered toward Lawrence over several encounters in which he felt that Lawrence made him look foolish.[15]

Lawrence kept his own diary for a short time during January and the few notes he made are optimistic in tone. He had reason to believe then that the Americans or the British would taken responsibility for Syria and for promoting an independent state under Faisal, and that French control could be prevented. "The campaign in favour of America cooperating in the East, to secure the practice of her ideals, goes well. . . . I want to frighten America with the size of the responsibility, and then that she should run us for it instead. The Americans are rather fed up with France."[16]

Three days after the dinner that Shotwell described, Lawrence and Faisal had an opportunity to meet with Wilson himself, and this meeting, together with the help of Howard S. Bliss, president of the American University at Beirut (whom the United States had invited to bring evidence on the Syrian question), contributed to Wilson's appointment of a committee of inquiry for Syria.[17] "About work — it is going on well," Lawrence wrote to his family. "I have seen 10 American newspaper men, and given them all interviews, which went a long way. Also, President Wilson, and the other people who have influence. The affair is nearly over, I suspect. Another fortnight, perhaps. Everybody seems to be here, and of course it is a busy time. I have had, personally, one meal in my hotel since I got to Paris! That was with Newcombe, who turned up unexpectedly."[18]

Because Faisal was at the head of the only Arab delegation at the Peace Conference, the "Arab position" was to all intents and purposes his position.[19] Probably with Lawrence's help, he wrote for the conference several memoranda, in which he set forth his wishes for the independence of the Arab lands liberated from the Ottoman Empire during the war. In these memoranda he wrote of the dream of unity of the Arabs of Asia, but did not discuss the political organization of the regions, the form of government to be secured, or who was to rule.[20] Faisal referred repeatedly to the principles of national freedom and autonomy set forth by Wilson and expressed his confidence that "the powers will attach more importance to the bodies and souls of the Arabic-speaking peoples than to their own material interests."[21]

On February 6, Faisal, accompanied by Lawrence, presented his case to the Peace Conference. Lawrence was dressed "in flowing robes of dazzling white," according to Lloyd George; "in Arab dress," according to Arnold Toynbee; and in "Arab headcloth, with Khaki uniform and British badges," according to Lawrence.[22]

Toynbee has provided a firsthand account of Lawrence and Faisal's appearance before the Council of Ten (the leaders of the Allied governments). The French had heard how Lawrence had "put the Arabs' current political case in a telling speech in English" while Faisal read from the Koran, thus saving themselves the trouble of drafting an identical speech in two languages. The French had a Moroccan employee present to verify that Lawrence was actually translating Faisal's speech accurately. Having advance intelligence of this move by the French, Lawrence had written an Arabic version of his speech for Faisal to deliver and an English version for later delivery by himself.

"When the moment arrived," Toynbee wrote, "Faisal recited Lawrence's speech in Arabic and Lawrence followed him with a recitation of it in English, but then there was a hitch. Clemenceau understood English and also spoke it (an accomplishment that gave him a valuable advantage over his Anglo-Saxon and Italian colleagues); but the Italians were as ignorant of English as all the Ten were of Arabic. The only foreign language that the Italians understood was French. President Wilson then made a suggestion. 'Colonel Lawrence,' he said, 'could you put the Amir Faysal's statement into French now for us?' After a moment's hesitation, Lawrence started off and did it; and, when he came to the end of this unprepared piece of translation, the Ten clapped. What had happened was amazing. Lawrence's spell had made the Ten forget, for a moment, who they were and what they were supposed to be doing. They had started the session as conscious arbiters of the destinies of mankind; they were ending it as captive audience of a minor suppliant's interpreter."[23]

Over the next three months the question of Syria at the Peace Conference became embroiled in the struggles between Great Britain and France, especially between Lloyd George and Clemenceau.[24] The attitude of the French bureaucrats — Clemenceau, himself, as Lloyd George acknowledged, "was not annexationist by inclination or political training"[25] — was that the sacrifices of war entitled them to Syria, and they resented British and American efforts to forestall the annexation. As Elizabeth Monroe wrote, "Lloyd George's retreat before Clemenceau over Syria took place by stages in 1919."[26]

During February and March Lawrence seems to have been engaged in endless luncheons and other meetings with little productive result — "the lines of resentment hardening around his boyish lips."[27] Alexander Michailovitj, a prominent Russian nobleman and political figure in the Czarist regime, provided the following colored picture of Lawrence in Paris during these weeks:

None of the all-knowing newspaper correspondents could be bothered to recapitulate the peace-makers' antecedent promises. It became the lot of Col. T. E. Lawrence to mutter well-chosen damnations at the mere sight of these glorious diplomats. The youthful hero from Arabia, in his flowing romantic beduin-cape, understood from the very first moment, that the big four were all set to break the promises he had given the desert chiefs in 1915–1916, in return for their much-needed help against the Turks. As the living personification of eternal opposition, poor Lawrence wandered among Versailles' well-cut hedges, casting hateful glances at Arthur Balfour's aristocratic features and baggy clothes. I sympathized with him. We both spoke of the past to people who only recognized the present. We both had come with reminders of "done duties" to statesmen known for never paying back their debts. We both tried to appeal to the honour of those, to whom "honour" is but a word which in the dictionary stands under the letter H.[28]

At some time during this period he gave an interview to Lincoln Steffens. Although the interview was sought by Steffens, Lawrence used the opportunity to try to influence the Americans through Steffens to take responsibility for the Armenian mandate. Lawrence probably knew Steffens's reputation as a reformer and his intolerance of commercial or other exploitation. The interview, which was not published for twelve years, is filled with irony on Lawrence's part as he tries, with tongue in cheek, to prevail upon the noted "idealism" of the Americans and to get them to take responsibility for a people he called "the perfection of the true commercial spirit." Lawrence led Steffens to offer suggestion after suggestion. He even lured him into suggesting that the Americans handle the Armenians as they had handled the American Indians (by massacring them). "He reminded me," Steffens wrote, "that we were so idealistic and enjoyed such repute for philanthropy that we seemed to be able to do anything within reason without losing either our idealism or our good name."[29]

The question of Armenia was an important one. William Westermann, one of the American delegates, wrote that "the liberation of Armenia was the one outstanding result expected from the Near Eastern negotiations at the Peace Conference," and held the American isolationism responsible for the failure to pursue and protect the independence of Armenia. He went on to say that the United States might have saved thousands of people from starvation there during the postwar period had she accepted responsibility for the mandate. "The mandate for Armenia was offered us," Westermann observed, "and we refused to accept its obligations and the undoubted troubles which their acceptance would have entailed. We feared foreign entanglements."[30]

On February 27 the Zionist representatives presented their case before the Council of Ten at Paris.[31] In line with the Balfour Declaration of 1917, Chaim Weizmann asked for the creation of a Jewish national home, with immigration of seventy thousand to eighty thousand Jews annually, and permission to build Jewish schools where Hebrew could be taught. He denied that this meant the establishment of an autonomous Jewish government.[32] Nevertheless the Zionists were troubled when Faisal a day or two later gave an interview to a French paper which contained remarks unfriendly to the idea of a sovereign Jewish state.[33] A meeting was arranged between Felix Frankfurter, then a Harvard Law School professor, who was representing the Zionists, and Faisal, with Lawrence present to summarize in English Faisal's position. Lawrence drafted a letter setting forth Faisal's views, which expressed sympathy for the Zionist movement, spoke of "working together for a reformed and revived Near East" ("our two movements complete one another"), wished "the Jews a most hearty welcome home," and asserted that "there is room in Syria for both of us." It was published on March 5 in the New York *Times*.[34]

On March 20, President Wilson proposed sending an inter-Allied commission to Syria "to elucidate the state of opinion and the soil to be worked on by any mandatory."[35] In a meeting on March 29 with Colonel Edward House and with Lawrence acting as interpreter, Faisal expressed his delight with the idea of an inter-Allied commission, but the French refused to send a representative — they realized that any investigation of Arab opinion in Syria would work against their colonial interests there. But in the meantime, on March 25, a meeting had taken place at the Paris apartment of Wickham Steed, now editor of *The Times*, in which French and British Arab "experts" met with a number of French journalists to discuss the sending of a commission. According to Steed, Lawrence agreed on the unsettling effect sending a commission might have on Syria and offered to urge Faisal to stay in Paris to negotiate directly with the French.[36] A letter of Gertrude Bell's describing the meeting indicated that Lawrence had "outlined the programme of a possible agreement (between Feisal and the French) without the delay which is the chief defect of the proposal for sending a Commission."[37]

Faisal met with Clemenceau on April 13, and "the Tiger" reportedly told him: "I would agree with everything you want. But the French nation cannot agree that there shall be no sign of her in Syria to indicate her presence there. If France is not represented in Syria by its flag and by its soldiers, the French nation will consider it as a national humiliation, as the desertion of a soldier from the battlefield. . . . However, we do not want to send a large force but only a few men . . . and there will be no objection to have your flag side by side with ours."[38]

Presumably, they reached some sort of verbal agreement that permitted a French mandate in Syria, with the Syrians to elect their own prince and to retain some degree of autonomy. Letters to this effect were actually exchanged in mid-April between Clemenceau and Faisal. But neither Lawrence nor Faisal seems to have been willing to accept the French terms or trust French intentions in Syria, and Lawrence advised Faisal against an agreement to a French mandate.[39] Faisal seems to have been at this point strongly opposed to any French penetration in Syria and wished to have an inter-Allied commission sent immediately. On April 20 he wrote to Clemenceau, thanked him for his kindness and "disinterested friendliness" and "for having been the first to suggest the dispatch of the Inter-Allied Commission which is to leave shortly for the East to ascertain the wishes of the local peoples as to the future organization of their country. I am sure that the people of Syria will know how to show you their gratitude."[40] This statement, which seems to be filled with irony, strongly suggests the thoughts of Lawrence. Three days later Faisal left France for Syria, no agreement having been reached.

On April 7 Lawrence received a telegram that his father had developed influenza complicated by pneumonia and that he should come home if possible. He returned quickly to England, but was distressed to discover that he was too late to see his father alive.[41] There is to my knowledge no written statement of Lawrence's about his father's death, nor any information on how he reacted to it. This would appear to be a prominent example of a characteristic of Lawrence's that his younger brother Arnold has stressed: exercising extreme self-control to avoid showing troubled emotions. The more despairing and troubled Lawrence might feel, the more reserved and guarded he would become about his feelings.[42]

After returning to Paris from his visit home Lawrence stayed long enough to advise Faisal not to make a deal with the French. Then about April 23, at the time Faisal returned to Syria, Lawrence flew off to Cairo in one of a squadron of Handley-Page airplanes (his luggage consisted of a haversack and two books) to pick up some belongings and his wartime papers and reports. Unfortunately, the plane crashed near Rome and the two pilots were killed. Lawrence escaped with a cracked shoulder blade and some other minor injuries, to which he paid no attention while he busied himself with helping the victims of the crash.[43]

David Garnett in *The Letters of T. E. Lawrence* wrote that he regarded this accident as "a turning point in Lawrence's life" and one that contributed to Lawrence's later emotional difficulties.[44] I was skeptical about this and on the advice of Arnold Lawrence wrote to Francis Lord Rennell of Rodd, son of the British ambassador to Italy, at whose embassy quarters Lawrence stayed after the accident. Lord Rennell replied to my inquiry:

> I was serving in the British Embassy in 1919 during the closing months of my father's 11 year Ambassadorship there . . . when I received a message from the Italian Authorities that a British plane had made a crash landing and that one of the occupants was Lawrence who had been admitted to hospital in Rome with some not serious injuries. I immediately went up to

the hospital to see him but found him so little injured or shocked that I was able to bring him down in a day or two to stay in the British Embassy where I was living with my father and mother until he was fit enough to go on to the East in another plane shortly afterwards. During those days he was in the house he was perfectly normal psychologically and seemed in no way different to when I had known him in Egypt and elsewhere during the war.[45]

The ambassador and his wife were able to persuade Lawrence to stay only a few days in Rome, but while he was there they talked about "Arabian affairs." Rodd senior observed that he could well understand how "Lawrence must have been a difficult problem to the authorities."[46]

As Lord Rennell mentioned, Lawrence resumed his journey to Cairo in another aircraft. The trip was marked by an almost unbelievable sequence of delays for aircraft malfunctioning, damage and repairs, and took him to Taranto, Valona in Albania (where he led a glowworm-catching competition), Athens (where he showed the squadron commander, Captain T. Henderson, around the places of archeological interest), Crete and Libya. He reached Cairo late in June. Captain Henderson later wrote: "After the accident at Rome we greatly admired his pluck in deciding to fly on with us, especially as he was incapacitated by his arm, and we had the Mediterranean to cross — the first time for a squadron not fitted for landing on water. During the crossing, when all signs of land and shipping had disappeared, T.E. pushed a note in my hand, 'Won't it be fun if we come down?' I didn't think so!"[47]

Lawrence clearly enjoyed his three months with the Handley-Page squadron. The series of flights influenced his decision to join the RAF. The irony of his remark to Henderson is evident and the unnecessary danger to which pilots and their crews were exposed when flying over water may have played a part in Lawrence's eventual interest in developing air-sea rescue boats.

Lawrence managed to find time during the trip to write portions of the narrative of his war experience, which was by this time taking shape. Chapter 2, he states, was written between Paris and Lyons in the Handley-Page: "Its rhythm is unlike the rest. I liken it to the munch, munch, munch of the synchronised Rolls-Royce engines!"[48] The introduction was begun while they were heading down the Rhone Valley toward Marseilles and completed "on my way out to Egypt."[49]

In June 1919, when the peace treaty had been signed at Versailles and Wilson had returned to the United States, Lawrence wrote the following passage for the introduction to *Seven Pillars of Wisdom*. Although he subsequently suppressed it, it stands as one of the most beautiful things he ever wrote:

"In these pages the history is not of the Arab movement, but of me in it. It is a narrative of daily life, mean happenings, little people. Here are no lessons for the world, no disclosures to shock peoples [sic]. It is filled with trivial things, partly that no one mistake for history the bones from which some day a man may make history, and partly for the pleasure it gave me to recall the fellowship of the revolt. We were fond together, because of the sweep of the open places, the taste of wide winds, the sunlight, and the hopes in which we worked. The morning freshness of the world-to-be intoxicated us. We were wrought up with ideas inexpressible and vaporous, but to be fought for. We lived many lives in those swirling campaigns, never sparing ourselves: yet when we achieved and the new world dawned, the old men came out again and took our victory to remake in the likeness of the former world they knew. Youth would win, but had not learned to keep: and was pitiably weak against age. We stammered that we had worked for a new heaven and a new earth, and they thanked us kindly and made their peace."[50]

In Crete Lawrence met for the first time the great Arabist H. St. John Philby, later to become the only Western advisor close to Ibn Saud. Philby was on the plane that picked up Lawrence in Crete. They evidently got on well and Philby was impressed by Lawrence's "easy manners and friendly approach."[51] They flew together to Cairo, where, Philby wrote, "we . . . championed diametrically opposite causes in the hospitable atmosphere of Allenby's home on the banks of the Nile."[52]

If Philby was arguing then the cause of Ibn Saud and Lawrence that of the Hashemite family, the Saudi champion had reason to be getting the better of the argument. In May, while Lawrence was somewhere between Italy and Crete, Ibn Saud and his Wahhabi tribesmen had invaded the Hijaz. An opposing force sent by King Husayn and led by Amir Abdullah — who had been engaged during the Revolt principally in trying to control the growing power of the Wahhabis — was annihilated, Abdullah barely escaping with his life. Ibn Saud would probably have completed the conquest of the Hijaz had not the British government, which was subsidizing both sides, intervened.[53] As Arnold Toynbee put it:

> France and the United Kingdom did not carry their post-war colonial rivalry in the Middle East to the length of engaging in hostilities, but the India Office and the Foreign Office were less self-restrained. In May, 1919, they fought each other by proxy in Arabia, on the border between the Najd and Hijaz, at a place called Turaba. In this battle, the India Office's Arab ('Abdarrahman ibn Sa'id) defeated the Foreign Office's Arab (King Husayn al-Hashimi); but the Foreign Office then appealed to its ally General Allenby; Allenby threatened to send some whippet tanks to the Foreign Office Arab's aid; and the India Office prudently advised its own Arab to retreat.[54]

This disastrous defeat for the forces of King Husayn weakened the bargaining strength of Faisal in his dealings with the French and made the British understandably more hesitant in their support of Faisal, especially so long as he spoke as a representative of his father.

Lawrence stayed only briefly in Cairo in late June and early July of 1919 ("going through the Arab Bureau Archives for materials")[55] before returning to Paris. He was observed at Shepheard's Hotel in Cairo outfitted not as a colonel any longer, but as "a rather ruffled T.E., dressed in uniform but without belt or cap — as a subaltern in something."[56]

We pick up Lawrence's trail in Paris once more on July 15, when he telegraphs Faisal not to come to Paris as "nothing will be done [regarding the settlement of Arab affairs] till about September."[57] Curzon seems to have agreed with this advice since he noted in a wire to Balfour, "It seems possible that if Lawrence were not available, [Faisal] might be induced to renounce his journey."[58] The Foreign Office documents of July and early August reveal a debate within the department on whether Lawrence was an asset or a liability in Paris for the government's efforts to get Faisal to come to an accommodation with the French. The question seems not to have been resolved and Lawrence returned to England in August.[59]

23

Return to England:
London and All Souls

In New York in March 1919, Lowell Thomas began his film-and-talk shows about the war and his meetings with Allenby and Lawrence during the desert campaigns, thereby making the shy colonel well known in the United States before he became famous in Britain. The wave of popularity in the United States for exotic sun-and-sand commercial films of "Arabia," especially those featuring the Italian-born American actor Rudolph Valentino (*The Sheik*, 1921; *The Son of the Sheik*, 1926), may well have been inspired by Lowell Thomas's reportage of the Palestinian campaigns and of the deeds of Lawrence, whom he had filmed in flowing Arab costume.[1] Thomas told me that he had made a series of film shows, each on a different war theatre, which he booked into the Century Theatre with the backing of the New York *Globe*. The New Yorkers, he said, stayed away when the program was about the Western Front, but whenever he showed the Arab and Palestine campaigns featuring Allenby (sixty percent) and Lawrence (forty percent) "they [the promoters] took busloads of people from the Bronx to see the show," and after several weeks the show was moved to Madison Square Garden.[2] On the last night of the show in New York, Percy Burton, the English impresario who had managed Sarah Bernhardt, came to see it and wished to book it in England. Thomas told him facetiously that he would accept only Covent Garden or Drury Lane, not expecting that Burton would actually arrange it.[3] But Burton went ahead, and about the time Lawrence returned from Paris in August of 1919, Thomas was beginning to popularize the Lawrence legend in nightly film-and-lecture shows at the Royal Opera House in Covent Garden. The show began on August 14 to full houses and seems to have been seen by all the notables of England, including the Royal Family, Lloyd George and his cabinet (Thomas told me Lloyd

George received a minor no-confidence vote for watching the show instead of being at an evening meeting of Parliament), and much of London society. The show was the same as the one in New York, except that an elaborate stage prologue was arranged: a Welsh Guards band played in front of the backdrop of the "Moonlight on the Nile" setting from Sir Thomas Beecham's production of Handel's opera *Joseph and His Brethren*. Thomas estimated that one million people came to see the show in London, which ran for six months instead of the two weeks he had planned. After that he took it on a tour of other English-speaking countries. During the next five years, he published several articles on Lawrence and finally, the first biography of him, which appeared in 1924. Unquestionably, Thomas captured the public imagination and was instrumental in making Lawrence a popular hero.

Lawrence's relationship with Thomas, and his attitude toward the elaborate and fanciful romanticization of his exploits, brought out a central conflict in his character, one which cannot be dismissed with catch phrases of paradox, such as "false modesty" or "backing into the limelight." Thomas has made it clear in his writings — and I questioned him carefully about this — that Lawrence cooperated with him in the creation of his own legend.

Thomas originally left his teaching job at Princeton on a propaganda mission. He was to go to Europe and find material to make Americans more enthusiastic about the war.[4] The carnage of the Western Front offered nothing remotely "optimistic," and Thomas, with his cameraman, Harry Chase, found his way to Allenby in Jerusalem and, with Allenby's help, to Lawrence in Aqaba in the spring of 1918.

According to Lawrence they met twice during the two weeks Thomas was in Arabia.[5] With Allenby and especially with Lawrence, Thomas found material that lent itself to colorful, romantic presentation and storytelling, material that could truly be used to sell the war and make it seem attractive, adventurous and worthwhile. Furthermore, Lawrence was cooperative. He seemed to enjoy posing in his "Sherifian regalia" for Chase's pictures (later he thought they made him look like "a perfect idiot"),[6] introduced Thomas to other British officers and prevailed on them to be photographed, took the Americans into the Arabs' tents, where they observed the Bedouin and their leaders, and showed them around Aqaba. But Lawrence would tell Thomas little about himself or the details of his own exploits (Thomas states specifically in the foreword to his book: "I found it impossible to extract much information from Lawrence regarding his own achievements"), so Thomas was forced to extract information about them and the campaigns at second and third hand from Newcombe, Joyce, Dawnay, Hogarth, Stirling and other "fellow-adventurers."[7] As one might expect, the biographical data in Thomas's book are consequently full of inadvertent inaccuracies.

In the fall and winter of 1919–1920, when Thomas was giving his show, Lawrence came to see it at least five times. When Mrs. Thomas would spy him Lawrence would "blush crimson, laugh in confusion, and hurry away with a stammered word of apology," but he seemed to enjoy the glamour of it all.[8] Characteristically, though, he avoided the spotlight and on one occasion wrote a note to Thomas, "I saw your show last night and thank God the lights were òut." Lord Northcliffe, the British newspaper magnate, tried through Percy Burton to get an interview with Lawrence for the press, but Lawrence refused.[9] The following year, when Thomas was working on his book *With Lawrence in Arabia,* Lawrence walked twelve miles to the edge of London and back several times to help Thomas with it. He said he was not planning to write a book of his own but was only "working on his notes." I asked Thomas why he thought Lawrence had been willing to do this in view of his later antagonism to the Thomas book. He replied, "He knew I was doing a job"; and then added, "All topnotch people are willing to talk with a reporter."[10] Lawrence specifically denied that he went over the manuscripts of Thomas's book, in contrast to the thorough editing and rewriting he later did for the biographies that Graves and Liddell Hart wrote.[11] Thomas retains a very positive feeling about Lawrence and wishes that he had done more to help him, especially in view of the enormous service Lawrence did for his career.[12]

The truth seems to be that much as Lawrence was attracted by the glorious image of himself as "the Uncrowned King of Arabia" that was played on the screen and embellished by Lowell Thomas, he was also genuinely repulsed by it. He knew Thomas's picture of him to be false, not because he had not taken part in acts of heroism, but because it was a make-believe, commercial glorification. At a deeper level he felt he deserved a much lower opinion, and the grandiose myth-making he was witnessing only deepened the inner reproaches of his conscience and further provoked his self-contempt. I suspect that the conflicts aroused by the Thomas performances contributed to the despondency and despair that Lawrence suffered from during the fall and winter of 1919–1920.

In January 1920, Lawrence wrote to Archibald Murray, his first commander-in-chief in Arabia, to convey his embarrassment about Thomas's activities, especially passages in articles Thomas was writing that might be critical of the general. He wrote that he had refused to correct the galley proofs because they contained so many misstatements that he "could not possibly pass one tenth of it."[13] The letter, which includes also a request that Murray read the proofs of *Seven Pillars of Wisdom* ("the first draft was stolen and the second is not finished"), concludes: "I could kick his [Lowell Thomas's] card-house down if I got annoyed, and so he has to be polite. As a matter of fact he is a very decent fellow — but an American journalist, scooping."

In March Lawrence wrote to F. N. Doubleday: "You know a Mr. Lowell Thomas made me a kind of matinee idol: so I dropped my name so far as London is concerned and live peacefully in anonymity. Only my people in Oxford know of my address. It isn't that I hate being known — I'd love it — but I can't afford it."[14]

More candidly and with considerable self-awareness he wrote to a man named Greenhill, who had commanded an armored-car company in the Hijaz: "For Lowell Thomas: I don't bear him any grudge. He has invented some silly phantom thing, a sort of matinee idol in fancy dress, that does silly things and is dubbed 'romantic.' Boy scouts and servants love it: and it's so far off the truth that I can go peacefully in its shadow, without being seen. Last Thursday I went to an art gallery where was a ripping portrait of me by [Augustus] John: another man was looking at it: and as I passed he whispered confidentially, 'Bloody looking feller, isn't he?' and I said yes."[15]

In 1927 Lawrence wrote: "Lowell Thomas was 10 days in Arabia. He saw me for two of those, and again one day in Jerusalem: and afterwards I breakfasted with him once or twice in London. His book is silly and inaccurate: sometimes deliberately inaccurate. He meant well."[16] Much of the inaccurate or otherwise offensive material was removed in later editions of Thomas's book.

The actualities that Lawrence faced upon his return to England in August 1919 contrasted starkly with the romantic glow created by Lowell Thomas's performances. At the end of the previous January, Geoffrey Dawson, editor of *The Times* and a dedicated Fellow of All Souls College for twenty years, had written Lawrence offering to propose him for a fellowship at All Souls. The fellowship "would give you rooms in college and certain emoluments," Dawson wrote, "in return, I think, for a general undertaking to reside during stated portions of the year and to pursue some recognized line of duty. I broached this scheme to the warden last Sunday and found him entirely sympathetic."[17] Lawrence found the terms agreeable and replied that he would indeed accept the post if it was offered to him. Dawson promptly wrote the warden formally recommending "my little friend Lawrence of the Hedjaz. . . . He assures me that his one object in life (after the peace Conference is over) is research in his own particular line of study. . . . He is so big a man, so modest, and so eminently fitted to adorn our society, that I do hope that we shall make an effort to elect him."[18] In June Lawrence received a letter from the warden informing him of his election to a research fellowship, which paid a very small stipend, "the conditions of the Fellowship to be that he continues during his tenure thereof to prosecute the researches into the antiquities and ethnology, and the history (ancient and modern) of the Near East."[19]

But in the Near East matters were working against what Lawrence had struggled to protect.[20] The inter-Allied commission, which had finally been established (the so-called King-Crane Commission) visited Syria in June and July, interviewed Faisal, and assessed the feeling of the Syrian populace. Faisal made it clear to the commission that in his opinion a French mandate would mean the death of his country. The Syrians were overwhelmingly opposed to a French mandate and feared French colonial methods.[21] But the commission had become a purely American effort, distrusted by the French and virtually ignored by the British. By the time the final report was delivered to Wilson in late August the American commitment to the Middle East had faded. Even Charles Crane himself, a Chicago millionaire who was a partisan of self-determination, felt that the commission might do harm by arousing hopes "which it would not be possible to fulfill."[22]

In the meantime, over the spring and summer of 1919, Faisal was establishing a Syrian government, and Lloyd George and Lord Balfour, the foreign secretary, were struggling to resist French demands regarding Syria. But because of increasing pressure at home for demobilization, higher priorities given to securing a British mandate for Palestine, and need to make concessions to France in order to protect British access to Mesopotamian oil fields, Lloyd George began to yield to Clemenceau on the question of Syria. The British government cooled toward Faisal and started to look for a way out of their dilemma. Clemenceau, under pressure from conservative colonialist elements in France, was demanding that the British adhere to the terms of the Sykes-Picot Agreement and agree to the French mandate. An eloquent analysis by Lord Balfour in August of the situation "respecting Syria, Palestine and Mesopotamia" questioned "on what historic basis the French claim to Syria really rests," but also made it clear that "a home for the Jews in the valley of the Jordan" and a British zone in Mesopotamia extending "at least as far as Mosul" had become higher priorities than an independent Syria, or Syria under a British or American mandate.[23] Meanwhile, British officers in Syria warned that British withdrawal and French occupation would inevitably lead to violent resistance by the Arab populace, who would not accept a French military presence in the country.[24]

The home Lawrence returned to on Polstead Road in Oxford in August 1919 was much changed from the one he had left in 1914. Two of his brothers had been killed in the war and his father had recently died. His mother's emotional needs became focused upon him, but he could not meet them. Lawrence's cause in the Middle East was going poorly but his continued involvement with its problems (ensured by the terms of the All Souls fellowship) and the writing of his book permitted him no distance from the conflicts aroused by the shattering experiences of the war.

For the first time in many years Lawrence was relatively footloose with no immediate field of action upon which to release his energies or to draw his attention away from himself. He turned inward, and his mother described to David Garnett how during the fall of 1919 and the winter of 1919–1920 Ned would sit for hours in a state of marked despondency without moving or changing his facial expression. Occasionally his usually severe self-control would give way. On one occasion he tripped over a water can and suddenly gave it a kick that sent it flying across the garden.[25]

On September 1, shortly after arriving in Oxford, Lawrence wrote his old friend Richards that he was out of the army that day, would like to avoid thinking about Arab matters, and was interested in setting up with him their printing press on five acres of land at Pole Hill, Chingford, on the edge of Epping Forest, which he had recently paid for.[26] But a week later he was back in the political battle, writing a letter to *The Times* on September 8 (it appeared three days later) in which he referred to himself as "the only informed free-lance European" and listed for the British public (evidently for the first time) the essentials of the McMahon-Husayn correspondence, the Sykes-Picot Agreement, the statement to the Seven Syrians and the Anglo-French Declaration of November 1918, "all produced under stress of military urgency to induce the Arabs to fight on our side."[27]

All these documents contained commitments to areas of Arab independence in the former Ottoman territories. But *The Times*, under Steed's editorship,° hewed closely to the official government line, and Steed suppressed the last part of the letter, in which Lawrence wrote that he expected the British government to live up to its promises to the Arabs and that he wished to inform the Arabs and the British public that he regretted what he had done in the war because the government evidently had no intention of living up to the commitments it had authorized him to make to the Arabs.[28] Steed weakened the impact of Lawrence's letter still further by publishing an accompanying editorial which, in mollifying tones, spoke of the necessity for Anglo-French cooperation in settling "the legacies of the war" and suggested that "the present Conference in Paris" should help to smooth the approaches to these problems.[29]

Nevertheless, Lawrence's letter evidently caused a stir in the Foreign Office, especially as Lloyd George and Clemenceau were about to conclude an agreement in Paris that would in effect turn over the mandate for Syria to France.[30] Lawrence had obviously become something of a thorn in the side of the Foreign Office. A few days earlier a Foreign Office official had penned a note on a letter from Paris to London (the

---

° Lawrence's friend Geoffrey Dawson had resigned in March 1919 after a conflict with Lord Northcliffe, *The Times* proprietor, who, in his failing years, had become a more faithful advocate of British government policy.

letter itself suggested that Lawrence "if properly handled" might be able
to get Faisal "into a reasonable frame of mind" to accept the plans that
were being devised for him): "The trouble is that it is always Lawrence
who does the 'handling.' He has told me quite frankly that he had no
belief in an Anglo-French understanding in the East, that he regards
France as our natural enemy in those parts and that he has always shaped
his action accordingly."[31]

In the agreement between Lloyd George and Clemenceau of September 13, which was supported publicly by the Supreme Council of the
Allies in Paris two days later, Britain agreed to evacuate Syria by November 1, 1919, with the understanding that the western (coastal) areas of
Syria and Lebanon would be garrisoned by the French, while the cities
of Damascus, Homs, Hama and Aleppo would be turned over to Amir
Faisal.[32] Lloyd George invited Faisal to London to try to pressure him
into accepting the agreement, which Clemenceau regarded as a triumph
for the French. But Faisal, fearing any French occupation of his country,
wrote two letters to Lloyd George — on September 21 and October 9 —
asking that the agreement be abrogated and the coastal areas returned to
Arab control. He anticipated a great catastrophe for the Arab world
should British troops be withdrawn from Syria.[33]

Meanwhile, seeing that one way or another direct British military control of Syria was going to end, Lawrence wrote to the Foreign Office on
September 15 and to Curzon, the foreign secretary, on September 27, in
an attempt to make the best of the situation.[34] The Foreign Office remained willing to use Lawrence's influence with Faisal for its purposes
as long as "Colonel Lawrence's well-known antipathy to the French" did
not interfere with Anglo-French negotiations.[35] He agreed to try to persuade Faisal to accept the French presence in the coastal regions of
Syria if Britain would maintain advisors in central Syria and guarantee
its commitment to an Arab government in Mesopotamia, where he anticipated a revolt by March (1920) 'if we do not mend our ways." (Actually
the revolt did not occur until the summer.) He envisaged Faisal as a kind
of centrally placed broker in the region between the French influence on
the coast and the British mandated areas to the east and south. To
Curzon Lawrence outlined his idea for the eventual leadership of
Baghdad over the regions of Western Asia ("the future of Mesopotamia
is so immense that if it is cordially ours we can swing the whole Middle
East with it").[36] It was in the letter to Curzon that Lawrence made his
often-quoted statement: "My own ambition is that the Arabs should be
our first brown dominion, and not our last brown colony."[37]

On September 28 Lawrence wrote to Alan Dawnay, by this time a
staff officer in Jerusalem, stressing again the importance of keeping
Kinahan Cornwallis, the British liaison officer, in Damascus as an advisor,
and the capacity of Mesopotamia, because of its agricultural and oil

resources, to support a far greater population. He argued for the importance of Arab-Zionist cooperation, and emphasized again the coming of "brown" peoples into the empire, despite the fact that "Australia won't like brown citizens of the Empire — but it's coming anyhow. They are 5,000,000 and the Browns about 300,000,000." The letter concluded with a characteristic disparagement of the French: "The French will hold an uneasy position for a few years on the Syrian coast, like the decadence of the Crusading Kingdom of Jerusalem, or Egypt before the Moroccan bargain — and then: 'No more of me and thee.' "[38] If Lawrence was measuring "a few years" by the clock of human history he was correct. But in less than a year the French had occupied all Syria, driving Faisal out. Independence did not come to the country for a quarter of a century.

William Yale, who had been a member of the King-Crane Commission, was more alarmed by the dangers for peace in the Middle East under the Clemenceau-Lloyd agreement than was Lawrence, who seems to have shifted his focus ahead to Mesopotamia. Yale feared, correctly as it turned out, that the Arabs in Syria would not accept the French anywhere in the country and that the withdrawal of the protective presence of British troops would result in serious local disorders, spreading to other areas of the Middle East. He pleaded for a shift toward a more liberal policy and had a plan of his own. But despite Yale's interviews of countless officials and other leaders of opinion, including Lawrence, his efforts seem to have been of no avail, especially as President Wilson would not invest Yale with any authority.[39] It is not clear whether Lawrence met Faisal during his visit to England in September and October of 1919. In any case, the amir was unchanged in his views. He left after a brief time to negotiate directly with the French and arrived in Paris on October 20.[40]

Rudyard Kipling was more realistic about these sad events and was able to express to Lawrence the disappointment they both felt in a letter he wrote his friend in October:

Dear Lawrence,
Naturally, if you didn't take what was offered you and do what you were wanted to do, you would — from the F.O. point of view — be the worst kind of crook. They don't understand deviations from type. Later on, I expect, you will be accused of having been actuated by "financial motives" in all you did. Wait till you are cussed for being a "venal hireling" — as I was once — in a Legislature.

But we are all sitting in the middle of wrecked hopes and broken dreams. I tried all I knew to put the proper presentation of the American scheme before men over there who, I thought, would help. But one can't expect people whose forebears went West to avoid trouble to stand up to responsibility in a far land for no immediate cash return.

But you will not go out of the game — except for the necessary minute to step aside and vomit. You are young, and the bulk of men now in charge

are "old, cold and of intolerable entrails" and a lot of 'em will be dropping
out soon.[41]

Urged by Kipling and others, Lawrence had begun in Paris to "write
an account of what happened in Arabia."[42] In the manuscript of *Seven
Pillars of Wisdom*, which is in the Bodleian Library, Lawrence stated that
he began the first edition of the book on January 10, 1919, in Paris, but
in notes penned five years later he wrote that the book was begun in
February.[43] Between early 1919 and May 1922 Lawrence wrote three
texts of his book. Of these only the third survives.

There are no contemporary notes about Lawrence's early writing activities in Paris. Perhaps the arrival in March of Gertrude Bell, whom
Lawrence later credited with his decision to publish a limited edition of
the work, played a part in his keeping on with the manuscript. They spent
much time together during March discussing the political problems of
their Arab friends.[44] Hogarth states that Lawrence did most of the writing in the spring at Faisal's temporary home in the Avenue du Bois de
Boulogne.[45] He was aided by a diary he had kept on army telegraph
forms (now in the British Museum) which he described to Mrs. Shaw as
"nearer a bunch of thorns than a flower."[46]

During his first months back in England in the late summer and early
fall of 1919 there is no evidence that Lawrence worked much on his
manuscript. Early in November he turned back to Charles Doughty, who
had provided so much of his original inspiration and to whom he had
first turned for guidance to the East. He wrote cautiously to Doughty's
daughter that he had heard her father had been ill (which proved to be
untrue) and that "I would very much like to come and see him, and I'm
afraid of only being a nuisance."[47] But Doughty himself wrote back
immediately: "I rejoice that you have returned safe & sound from the
late arduous and anxious years of World-wide warfare, in which you
have borne politically and militarily so distinguished a part for your
Country with the Friendlies of the South Arabians; & to think of your
passing again happy days in the blessed peace & quiet days of Oxford
life."[48] Doughty encouraged his young friend to stay with him and his
family at his home in Eastbourne.

Later in the month, in another letter to Doughty, Lawrence confessed
that he had "lost the MSS of my own adventures in Arabia: it was stolen
from me in the train."[49] Lawrence suggested to Liddell Hart that unconscious factors may have been at work in the loss of this first text, which
he considered "shorter, snappier and more truthful" than the later
versions.[50] Liddell Hart provides these details from his notes of a conversation with Lawrence in 1933: "On a train journey from London to
Oxford. Went into refreshment room at Reading, and put bag under
the table. Left it. Phoned up from Oxford an hour later, but no sign of

the missing bag — it was a bank messenger's bag, the "thing they carry the gold in!' [surely an invitation to theft]." Liddell Hart goes to say, "T.E. wonders did fancy (*involuntarily*) [italics in original] play with it?"[51] Lawrence told Liddell Hart that he had proclaimed joyously to Hogarth, "I've lost the damned thing," and Mrs. Lawrence is said to have found him in the garden cottage laughing in his bed late at night afterwards.[52] But Hogarth was angry, and both he and Doughty urged Lawrence to write it again.[53]

On December 2, 1919, in Oxford, Lawrence began writing the second text of his book (except for the introduction, which "survived"), and "so it was built again with heavy repugnance in London in the winter of 1919–1920 from memory and my surviving notes."[54] He wrote most of the second text during the first two months of 1920, calling it then "the-book-to-build-the-house" because he had not yet given up his vague plans for printing in a medieval hall at Chingford.

Lawrence is somewhat contradictory in his statements about the writing of the second text. The inconsistencies are symptomatic of the ambivalent attitude he retained toward his book and toward the events it described throughout the long history of its various writings and publication. He stated in 1923, for example, that he began *Seven Pillars* in Oxford; to Graves he wrote that none of it was written in Oxford; and in a leaflet he issued with the 1926 edition he wrote that a month or so after he lost the first edition, "I began, in London, to scribble out what I remembered of the first text."[55]

Lawrence seems to have found the atmosphere at home and at All Souls difficult for writing, and chose to draft most of the second text in an attic in Westminster, which his architect friend, Herbert Baker, had provided ("dark and oak-panelled, with a large table and desk as the principal furniture").[56] "I work best utterly by myself," he wrote Richards at the time, "and speak to no one for days."[57] When in London he already was living under a different name (he did not tell what it was). He had assumed the new name, he wrote Newcombe, "to be more quiet and wish I could change my face to be more lovely."[58] To Ezra Pound the reasons were "for peace and cleanliness."[59]

Baker has given this picture of his friend at work over the years in the secluded attic, and the spartan existence he preferred:

"It was the best-and-freest-place I have ever lived in," he wrote when he ceased to live permanently there; and "nobody had found me . . . despite efforts by callers and telephones." He refused all service and comfort, food, fire or hot water; he ate and bathed when he happened to go out; he kept chocolate — it required no cleaning up, he said — for an emergency when through absorption or forgetfulness he failed to do so. He worked time-less and sometimes around the sun; and once he said, for two days without food or sleep, writing at his best, until he became delirious. He wrote most of the

Seven Pillars of Wisdom there; he usually slept by day and worked by night; in airman's clothes in winter cold. We who worked in the rooms below never heard a sound; I would look up from my drawing-board in the evening sometimes to see him watching, gnomelike, with a smile; his smile that hid a tragedy.[60]

A decade later Lawrence conveyed to another writer the moral dilemmas and inner psychological obstacles, the struggle "to work out my path again," which accompanied the writing of *Seven Pillars of Wisdom:* "I was a rather clumsy novice at writing, facing what I felt to be a huge subject with hanging over me the political uncertainty of the future of the Arab movement. We had promised them so much; and at the end wanted to give them so little. So for two years there was a dog fight, up and down the dirty passages of Downing St., and then all came out right — only the book was finished. It might have been happier had I foreseen the clean ending. I wrote it in some stress and misery of mind.

"The second complicity was my own moral standing. I had been so much of a free agent, repeatedly deciding what I (and the others) should do: and I wasn't sure if my opportunity (or reality, as I called it) was really justified. Not morally justifiable. I could see it wasn't: but justified by the standard of Lombard St. and Pall Mall. By putting all the troubles and dilemmas on paper, I hoped to work out my path again, and satisfy myself how wrong, or how right, I had been.

"So the book is the self-argument of a man who couldn't then see straight: and who now thinks that perhaps it did not matter: that seeing straight is only an illusion. We do these things in sheer vapidity of mind, not deliberately, not consciously even. To make out that we were reasoned cool minds, ruling our courses and contemporaries, is vanity. Things happen, and we do our best to keep in the saddle."[61]

In drafting the first and second texts, Lawrence apparently wrote at times with great speed and without interruption for many hours. He told his biographer Robert Graves that he did "four to five thousand words a day," and Liddell Hart mentions one marathon of thirty thousand words in twenty-two hours.[62] Book VI — the one that contains the account of his assault at Der'a — Lawrence evidently raced through with particular speed, not wishing perhaps to linger any longer than he had to over these disturbing events. He revised it, however, many times. In *Seven Pillars of Wisdom,* he states that Book VI "was written entire between sunrise and sunrise,"[63] but this is contradicted by his statement in his February 27, 1920, letter to Richards that his book was "on paper in the first draft to the middle of Book VI: and there are seven books in all."[64] In his notes for the 1926 (subscribers') edition, Lawrence refers to ten books in Text II.[65]

These examples of inconsistencies indicate the difficulty of obtaining an accurate history of the writing of *Seven Pillars of Wisdom,* especially during this troubled early period. The book's content is so intimately tied

to Lawrence's deepest conflicts that its writing, and the reporting of its writing, were especially prone to neurotic distortion. But he could, on occasion, be quite objective about the book's potential lasting value. He wrote prophetically in January 1920 to his former commander Archibald Murray: "I put on paper my account of what happened to me in Arabia some time ago, but had it stolen from me, and am therefore doing it again, rather differently. It seems to me unfit for publication, but if published it will have some success (for the story is in parts very odd and exciting — there are many strange things) and will probably last a long time, and influence other accounts in the future, for it is not badly written, and is authoritative, in so far as it concerns myself."[66] Lawrence asked Murray if he would agree to read it over, but whatever Murray's reply, the manuscript was evidently never sent to him. Lawrence wrote Liddell Hart that this text was "not circulated," unlike the first one, which had been "read by Meiner [Meinertzhagen], Dawnay, Hogarth."[67]

As indicated to Murray, Lawrence was unclear at this time about his plans to publish the book. His friend Doubleday wrote that "he had the most peculiar notions. . . . First he was going to have one copy printed and put in the B.M. [British Museum], and he made a dozen different plans."[68] Dermot Morrah, with whom Lawrence shared a suite of rooms at All Souls, mentioned that Lawrence considered either having the book published in a cheap edition in America to avoid piracy in England or setting a price so high ($200,000) that no one would buy it. Later, the story went around the college that Lawrence had written the Library of Congress, urging that *Seven Pillars* be included among the obscene books, and threatening to put dirty pictures in the fly leaf so the Library would have no choice.[69]

In the manuscript Lawrence wrote that this second text was completed on May 11, 1920, but "corrected and added to slowly for nearly two years."[70] A contemporary letter to Doubleday of July 21, 1920, states that "the original-and-to-be-kept-secret version was finished on July 12th."[71] But in August he wrote to Richards, "To finish my 'Boy Scout' book by September 30 will mean my spending August and September in All Souls."[72] On October 7, Doubleday wrote Lawrence, "Your M.S. I have put in the hotel safe (Brown's in London)."[73] Through 1920 Lawrence's efforts to have a second edition of Doughty's *Arabia Deserta* published seemed to parallel his struggles over the second writing of his own book and he turned especially to Doubleday for help with both.[74] As it turned out, Lawrence rewrote the book a third time and then destroyed Text II.

As the turmoil-filled year of 1919 drew to a close Lawrence had turned to the waiting opportunity at All Souls to find "the blessed peace and quiet days of Oxford" that Doughty had held out to him. Whether Lawrence found peace and quiet at Oxford in 1920 is, I suppose, a

matter of definition. He was there only intermittently, moving back and forth between his isolated attic in Westminster and his rooms at the college. But as a result of his friendships at All Souls, especially with Robert Graves, Lawrence met writers and poets — Siegfried Sassoon, Edmund Blunden, John Buchan and, later, Thomas Hardy. His fame brought him in touch with artists like William Rothenstein and Augustus John, who wished to paint his portrait, and Eric Kennington, whom he sought out. "The painters and sculptors also seemed to Lawrence to have a secret," Graves wrote, and "already at Paris, during the Peace Conference he was getting in touch with them."[75]

In the intellectual atmosphere of Oxford Lawrence copied out the poems that best expressed his tastes and moods. Each of these poems had "had a day with me," he wrote to Mrs. Shaw in 1927, many having come from *The Oxford Book of English Verse*, which Lawrence had kept with him during the desert campaigns. They formed a kind of anthology he called "Minorities."[76] "One necessary qualification" for inclusion, he said, was "that they should be in a minor key."[77]

The "minor key" was also a reflection of Lawrence's mood. Morrah observed (1920) that he was subject to depression and would sit silently for hours in the common room, absorbed in his own thoughts. At times Lawrence's aloofness seemed so intense that some of the All Souls students thought that he was "off his rocker," and depressed even to the point of being suicidal. At other times he would be noticed long after dinnertime flat on his face on the hearth rug, or sitting beside the fire in the common room writing. At these times, according to Morrah, Lawrence would warm up and tell "hair-raising stories" about his experiences in the Middle East. He seemed to take pleasure in exaggerating and would continue to "unbend," talking until the early hours of the morning.[78] Ralph Isham (the collector of Boswell's manuscripts), another friend Lawrence came to know during this period, similarly describes Lawrence's yarning: "He did not lie in the strict sense, but he did indulge in fiction. And he was perfectly aware of it. His tales arrived full-blown."[79] On the other hand, according to Herbert Baker, "He could not be induced to tell of his adventures in the War, except in his kindness to my young son; or as a bait to draw out the adventures of others."[80] Lawrence was apparently selective about whom he would share his war experiences with.

I am of the opinion that this tendency to fictionalize his experiences, to turn his life into a legend, was most prominent when Lawrence was feeling particularly troubled in his self-regard. At these times he would give way to an unconscious need to create a fictional self, drawn on the lines of childish heroism, to replace the troubled self he was experiencing. Most of the time his rational self rejected the fictional one, the "Lawrence of Arabia." In meeting Lawrence for the first time in the summer of 1919, Isham asked him if he knew his "namesake of Arabia." Lawrence "grinned

hugely and said, 'I'm afraid I know him much too well.' He enjoyed my discomfiture. I said, 'Well, anyway, you don't look like him.' He replied, 'I know I don't and I don't feel like him.' And we both laughed."[81]

Lawrence tended at All Souls to engage in undergraduate pranks (he was thirty-two at the time). Most of the tales of these escapades — flying the Hijaz flag from the pinnacle of All Souls, ringing the station bell captured at Tell Shahm out his window into the quadrangle, or stealing the Magdalen College deer — have been told by Robert Graves, a well-known fiction-maker himself, but some of them have been confirmed. Arnold Lawrence feels that these pranks were clear indications of his brother's troubled state.[82]

It did look for a time in 1920 as if Lawrence might become the Oxford scholar he had always seemed almost to be. He visited his many friends in Oxford, talked and wrote about books and printing, and called himself a bookworm. He indicated in a letter that he thought of settling down some day to do his history of the Crusades.[83] But his restlessness and discontent proved eventually too profound for such a quiet life. "When I got back I tried Oxford for a bit but gave it up," he wrote at the end of February.[84]

When asked to be the godfather (how often he was a godfather!) to his friend Newcombe's boy he answered: "In the history of the world (cheap edition) I'm a sublimated Aladdin, the thousand and second Knight, a Strand-Magazine strummer. In the eyes of 'those who know' I failed badly in attempting a piece of work which a little more resolution would have pushed through, or left untouched. So either case it is bad for the sprig."[85]

Despite this demurring, he took a godfatherly interest in the "sprig," who was named Stewart Lawrence Newcombe. Wouldn't the child be handicapped by that name? Lawrence asked the father. He soon asked to visit his godson, and was enchanted with him. "Ned loved Jimmy from the time he was born," the mother confided to me, "and bounced him on his knee. He felt Jimmy was something that was his, a familial link."[86]

In March Lawrence wrote to a wartime friend, "I'm out of affairs by request of the Foreign Office which paid me the compliment of calling me the main obstacle to an Arab surrender."[87] On May 14 he wrote to Frederick Stern: "Paris gave me a bad taste in my mouth, and so last May I dropped politics, and have had no touch with British or Arabs or Zionists since. I'm out of them for good, and so my views on Palestine are merely ancient history."[88] But British mismanagement of its Middle Eastern responsibilities had already been drawing Lawrence's attention, and a few days after writing Stern he was once more in the thick of Middle Eastern politics.

While Lawrence was struggling with his memoirs in London and enjoying his friends in Oxford, the situation in Syria and elsewhere in the Middle East was deteriorating. Abandoned by the British to the French in the fall of 1919 (by the end of November all British forces had been withdrawn from Syria), Faisal had turned to the French government to try to negotiate on his own. But in January 1920 his situation became more precarious when Clemenceau was defeated for the presidency and a more conservative, colonialist regime came into power. In March the Syrian congress declared the country's complete independence from France and Faisal was made king. But the assertion was an empty one. On April 25 at the Italian Riviera resort of San Remo the Supreme Council of the Allies met to construct the Turkish treaty and divided Syria into three parts: Lebanon, Palestine and a reduced "Syria." By the terms of this agreement, called the Treaty of Sèvres because it was signed there — near Paris, the mandates for Syria and Lebanon were awarded to France and separate mandates for Palestine and Iraq were assigned to Great Britain. The map of Arab Asia was redrawn, without attention to the wishes of its people. The French interpreted "mandate" as they chose, and soon after the decisions were made public in early May sent an army into Syria, drove Faisal into exile, and occupied Damascus after a bloody battle with Arab resisters.[89]

In late March or early April of 1920, Lawrence received a letter from an archeologist at Carchemish which he must have found distressing. He learned that "everybody, man, woman and child dislikes the French and expressed to me the hope that the English would come back and let the French leave the country."[90] The letter also provided Lawrence with a long account of the progress at the site.

Perhaps this letter, reminding him of his earlier attachments in the Arab East, influenced Lawrence, or perhaps he simply became increasingly distressed over the events in Syria and Mesopotamia. Whatever the reason, he decided to involve himself once more in Arab affairs, at least with his pen. On May 21 he wrote to Philby, inviting him to join a group of "Middle Eastern" colleagues who were petitioning the prime minister (Lloyd George) to take control of Mesopotamia away from the India Office and the Foreign Office, and to place it in the hands of a newly-to-be-created Middle East Department.[91] In the letter to Philby, which has never to my knowledge been published, Lawrence wrote: "It happens to be — politically — the right moment for pressure towards a new Middle East Department, since some re-shuffling of spheres is certain to happen quite soon: and the enclosed [the petition to Lloyd George] is a step taken under advice, to add pressure from outside, to what is going on inside. They have asked me to get your name on the list: other 'experts' invited are Hogarth, Curtis, Toynbee and myself. I have no doubt you will agree, so I won't bother to argue. It is a step necessary before a new policy can be put in force, and when we get it through, then we'll have to open up a battery of advice on the new men. . . . Curzon of course is the enemy: but he's not a very bold enemy, and won't like a rift in his family showing up: I have good hopes of it."[92]

A few days later, Lawrence followed this letter and the petition with the first of three newspaper articles, using the authority of his own name ("Colonel T. E. Lawrence, late British Staff Officer with the Emir Faisal"). Two of the articles appeared in the *Daily Express* and the third in the *Sunday Times*, and all were highly critical of British policy in the Middle East.[93]

In the first, Lawrence attacked the British policy of supporting both Ibn Saud and King Husayn and frankly acknowledged that he had advised his government to support only the latter. He still expected that this latest "outburst of puritanism in the desert" would die away, but was correct in predicting that the European powers would not be able to meet a crisis when it occurred.[94]

In the second, he attacked the paralysis of policy in Middle Eastern affairs that had resulted from a division of responsibility among the Foreign Office, the India Office and the War Office. "The war has had the effect on the offices," he continued, "of making the young men younger, and the old men older. The blood thirstiness of the old men — who did not fight — towards our late enemies is sometimes curiously relieved against the tolerance of those who have fought and wish to avoid making others fight again tomorrow.

"Asia has changed in the war almost as much as Europe, and the men in touch with it today find a great difficulty in speaking a common language with those who have been viceroys or governors long ago.

"The old find it difficult to believe that even before the war the British Empire in Asia was founded, not on troops, but on the passive consent of the greater number of the subjects. They fail to see that Asiatics have fought in the war, not for us, but for their own interests; to give themselves a better standing with us. They do not understand that Russia is also an Asiatic country, and that its revolution is an object-lesson to Asia of a successful rebellion of the half-educated and the poor.

"They have a belief, pathetic if not so dangerous that, 'a few troops' are a medicine for political disease."[95]

The third article, which appeared in the *Sunday Times*, was a bitter attack on the Treaty of Sèvres, which had been made public earlier in the month. Lawrence wrote that after the armistice "everywhere between Russia and the Indian Ocean it was felt that the war cloud had lifted, and that the brown peoples who had chosen to fight beside the Allies would receive their meed of friendship in the work of peace, that new age of freedom of which victory was the dawn." But not only had the framing of a peace treaty with Turkey been delayed, but when it was finally drawn up its terms were "impossible," as its framers admitted. "No account," Lawrence declared, "was taken of the actual conditions of the former Turkish Empire, or of the military and financial strengths of the countries devouring it. Each party making the terms considered only what it could take, or rather what would be most difficult for her neighbors to take or to refuse her, and the document is not the constitution of a new Asia, but a confession, almost an advertisement, of the greeds of the conquerors." He then reviewed the mismanagement of Britain's responsibilities throughout the Middle East, citing especially Lord Curzon, and the loss of "our friendly reputation" in Persia, the Caucasus, Turkey, Mesopotamia, Arabia, Syria and Egypt. In Mesopotamia, Lawrence noted, Britain had 50,000 troops and "nearly 200,000 labourers keeping them alive," at a cost of 30 million pounds a year, "and [they] eat up the country besides."

"Some day," he continued, "by a small increase, we will be able to hold part of Kurdistan and bore there for oil. Meanwhile it is a good training for the troops." He urged in ironic language the consolidation of the management of Britain's Middle Eastern policies under a single department (actually formed later in the year) and predicted (correctly as it turned out) that this would greatly cut the cost of lives and money. The article concluded with a statement of support for Faisal that is one of the most bitingly critical passages he ever wrote:

"He is the moderate in Syria, the constructive stateman who prevents the Arab hot-heads from attacking the French, the Jews, and the British, and his self-control has delayed our settling Syria by a military expedition. However, the Foreign Office have now hit on a new plan, and are tempting him to come to Europe on a business-holiday, for a sum of money running far into six figures. It is not a bribe, but 'arrears of subsidy,' and when he leaves Syria there will be, with luck, another little war, and our expenditure will have justified itself: though I personally, since I know and like Feisal, will regret the part of the money I contribute in taxation towards his downfall. It is not for such policies I fought."[96] Less than two months after Lawrence wrote this letter Faisal was driven from Syria and Lawrence's artist friend Augustus John, who had once painted Faisal for him, must have troubled Lawrence when he asked with seeming innocence, "Why was he beaten by the French — because you were not at his side?"[97]

During the war Arab nationalism had "flickered fitfully in Iraq,"[98] but in Mesopotamia the movement toward independence had received a powerful stimulus from the success of the Arab Revolt (the Arab forces included many Iraqi) and the example of the Bolshevik Revolution to the north. British assurances of independence issued to gain Arab support during the war period — especially the Anglo-French declaration of November 7, 1918, in which the declarers agreed to assist in setting up indigenous governments in Syria and Mesopotamia — provided a further impetus toward self-determination. The autonomous Arab government in Syria during the postwar period had a further influence upon Iraqi nationalist agitation.[99] The announcement in May 1920 of the assignment of the mandate for Iraq to Great Britain further agitated the nationalists and seemed proof that Great Britain had no intention of keeping her earlier promises, although the type of mandate awarded (Class A) promised relatively early independence.

Curzon's statement in the House of Lords in June that "the gift of the mandate . . . rests with the powers who have conquered the territories, which it then falls to them to distribute" reflected British imperialist thinking.[100] The policies of the civil commissioner in Iraq, Arnold Wilson, who advocated large numbers of British personnel to keep the natives in line, was consistent with this thinking. In late June a tribal rebellion broke out on the lower Euphrates and spread through much of the country. Its suppression over the summer of 1920 was a costly tragedy for Great Britain and Iraq in lives and resources, and in the destruction of good will between the Arab and Western worlds.

After the rebellion broke out, Lawrence wrote from All Souls a blistering series of attacks on British Mesopotamian policy, which were published in July and August in *The Times, The Observer* and the *Sunday Times*.[101] During the same period *The Times* published anonymously two additional articles of Lawrence's reviewing in laudatory terms Faisal's contributions to Britain as a leader of the Arabs during the Revolt, and his effective diplomacy of moderation in Syria after the war. These articles are eloquent, stirringly written documents, which reached a British public that was growing intolerant of the cost and bloodshed of mismanagement in Mesopotamia. They played a real part in influencing the government to change its policies and in preparing the ground for Faisal's eventual rulership in Iraq.

"Merit is no qualification for freedom. Bulgars, Afghans and Tahitians have it," Lawrence argued. He urged dominion status for Mesopotamia and the removal of all the thousands of British and Indian soldiers and other personnel then fighting the rebels or running the country, and recommended "tearing up what we have done and beginning again on advisory lines."[102] He knew that his ideas would be called "grotesque," but he advocated making Arabic the government language and raising an army of Arabis — two divisions of volunteers.[103]

As news of the slaughter of Arabs by the British in the rebellion reached him, Lawrence became still more forceful and sarcastic: "We have really no competence in this matter to criticise the French; they have only followed in very humble fashion, in their sphere of Syria, the example we set them in Mesopotamia."[104]

His words rose to a crescendo in the last article (August 22) written while the rebellion was still going on: "We have killed about ten thousand Arabs in this rising this summer. We cannot hope to maintain such an average: it is a poor country, sparsely peopled. . . . Cromer controlled Egypt's six million people with five thousand British troops; Colonel Wilson fails to control Mesopotamia's three million people with ninety thousand troops. . . . We say we are in Mesopotamia to develop it for the benefit of the world. All experts say that the labour supply is the ruling factor in its development. How far will the killing of ten thousand villagers and townspeople this summer hinder the production of wheat, cotton and oil? How long will we permit millions of pounds, thousands of Imperial troops, and tens of thousands of Arabs to be sacrificed on behalf of a form of colonial administration which can benefit nobody but its administrators?"[105]

Lawrence's information about Mesopotamia was sketchy. He had spent little time there and was less familiar with the local conditions and problems of governing the country than he was with those of Syria. He seemed almost to take advantage of incomplete knowledge, turning it into a license for exaggeration in order to strengthen his arguments. His friend Gertrude Bell, who was then serving with the civil administration in Mesopotamia, acknowledged that mistakes had been made. Early in July, before his last barrage of newspaper articles, she had written to Lawrence: "What curious organs [the newspapers] you choose for self expression!" and had criticized his underestimation of Ibn Saud. "However whatever the organs I'm largely in agreement with what you say."[106] She wrote then of her anguish and shared with him her own struggle to shift the direction of British policy in Iraq. She was critical only of his naiveté in failing to recognize that Ibn Saud was far stronger than Husayn and not so easily dealt with.

But by September, Bell was exasperated and frantic over what she felt were misleading statements (not all she objected to are quoted above) and over false impressions she felt Lawrence's articles were making. In her diary entry of September 5 she notes:

> The thing isn't made any easier by the tosh T. E. Lawrence is writing in the papers; to talk of raising an Arab army of two Divisions is *pure nonsense.* . . . I can't think why the India Office lets the rot that's written pass uncontradicted. T.E.L. again: when he says we have forced the English language on the country it's not only a lie but he knows it is. Every jot and tittle of official work is done in Arabic; in schools, law courts, hospitals, no other language is used. It's the first time that has happened since the fall of the Abbasids. . . . we are largely suffering from circumstances over which we couldn't have had any control. The wild drive of discontented nationalism from Syria and of discontented Islam from Turkey might have proved too much for us however far-seeing we had been; but that doesn't excuse us for having been blind.[107]

On September 19 she wrote further in her diary:

> The fact that we are really guilty of an initial mistake makes it difficult to answer letters like those of T. E. Lawrence. I believe them to be wholly mis-

leading, but to know why they're misleading requires such an accurate acquaintance not only with the history of the last two years but also with the country and the people, apart from our dealings with them, that I almost despair of putting public opinion in England right. I can't believe T.E.L. is in ignorance, and I therefore hold him to be guilty of the unpardonable sin of wilfully darkening counsel. We have a difficult enough task before us in this country; he is making it more difficult by leading people to think that it's easy. How can it be easy when you're called upon to reconcile the views and ideals of a tribal population which hasn't changed one shade of thought during the last five thousand years, and of a crude and impatient band of urban politicians who blame you for not setting up universities.[108]

Lawrence received letters of approval for his newspaper campaign from such Arabists as Wilfred Scawen Blunt, the famous Middle East traveler and poet, and from George Lloyd, Doughty and Philby. Blunt wrote, "I was greatly pleased at your letter in the *Times* and, though I have no confidence in the honour of our government, I yet do not quite despair of a victory for Asia or the result of the struggle now going on,"[109] and Lord Lloyd, then governor of Bombay, wrote from India: "No news of you except through the newspapers — Was there ever so fatal and disastrous a muddle over Egypt, Syria, Palestine and Mesopotamia. I am beginning to think that when you and I kept repeating our familiar tags, you 'Alexandretta!' and I 'Gibraltar's not territory' we were not only saying and meaning the same things but right things."[110]

Pleased with the progress of his newspaper campaign, Lawrence wrote in August, before it was over: "It did some good and the Government (very grudgingly and disowning me every step of the road) is doing absolutely the right thing by Mesopotamia now: they are even making the special department in London to look after those districts when they need help!"[111] And to Mrs. Shaw seven years later, he wrote in retrospect: "So I remain unrepentant. I was right to work for Arab self-government through 1919 and 1920: and my methods then, though not beyond criticism were, I think, reasonably justifiable."[112]

During 1920, when he was not writing for the newspapers, Lawrence was busy on other articles. These included his piece on changes in Asia, which he wrote anonymously for Lionel Curtis, the visionary and idealistic editor of the *Round Table,* and an article for Guy Dawnay, editor of *The Army Quarterly,* on his concepts of strategy in guerrilla warfare as applied to the Arab Revolt. In the latter piece, entitled "The Evolution of a Revolt,"[113] Lawrence analyzed the fundamentals of command, breaking them down into scientific or mathematical, biological and psychological aspects (the "kingdoms" that "lay in each man's mind"). The scientific aspect concerned the geography, terrain, populations and forces involved, while the biological concerned the variability of human endurance and capability, "the breaking point, life and death," and the cost and valuation of human life. The psychological aspect he related to that science "of which our propaganda is a stained and ignoble part. Some of it concerns the crowd, the adjustment of spirit to the point where it becomes fit to exploit in action, the prearrangement of a changing opinion to a certain end. *Some of it deals with individuals, and then it becomes a rare art of human kindness* [italics added], transcending, by purposeful emotion, the gradual logical sequence of our minds. It considers the capacity for mood of our men, their complexities and mutability, and the cultivation of what in them profits attention."[114]

Over the summer of 1920 Lawrence's persistent efforts to have a second edition of *Arabia Deserta* published finally met with success, and the Medici Society, which had published booklovers' editions of the classics, agreed to do it, but only if Lawrence would write an introduction, in order presumably, to enhance the chances of commercial success. A decade later H. M. Tomlinson wrote to him, "The simple truth is that your introduction to the 'Arabia Deserta' got that work placed where some of us wanted it to be, but hardly expected to see it."[115] The introduction, really an essay of Lawrence's own on Arabia and the Middle East, was written between August and November 1920, and Lawrence claims it was the "only thing" actually written at All Souls.[116] It provides his most succinct expression of the meaning for him of the desert, the Bedouin way of life and the experience of living among them. He admired in Doughty's pioneering achievement of travel in Arabia not only what he most valued in his own achievements, but also qualities Doughty possessed which he felt he could not emulate. Doughty, like Lawrence, overcame poor health and endured. "None of us triumphed over our bodies as Doughty did," Lawrence wrote.[117] But Doughty was "never morbid, never introspective," as he felt he was himself to a fault, "and the telling is detached, making no parade of good and evil." Doughty, in Lawrence's view, was the kind of Englishman abroad who gave the example of "the complete Englishman, the foreigner intact," in contrast to those like himself who "imitate the native as far as possible," becoming "like the people, not of the people." For Lawrence the attractions and limitations of the Bedouin life and character, the freedom and simplicity, and the "barrenness too harsh for volunteers" combined with narrowness of mind and impulsive subjectivity. Beyond abnegation and self-restraint Lawrence saw in the Bedouin the seeking of pain (which in himself had gone much beyond the renunciation of pleasure), "a self-delight in pain, a cruelty which is more to him than goods." Lawrence wrote almost longingly of some aspects of desert life: the organic connection between social organization and natural circumstances, the candor with which men lived with each other, and the openness of life among the tents ("beside one another . . . the daily hearth of the sheikh's coffee-gathering is their education, a university for every man grown enough to walk and speak").[118]

Gertrude Bell's letter of July 20, 1920, which he received about this time, may have had some impact, for he speaks here admiringly of Ibn Saud. "The Wahabi dynasty of Riath," he wrote near the end of the introduction, "has suddenly revived in this generation, thanks to the courage and energy of Abd el-Aziz [Ibn Saud] the present Emir. He has subdued all Nejd with his arms, has revived the Wahabi sect in new stringency, and bids fair to subject all the inner deserts of the peninsula to his belief." Lawrence concludes the introduction by expressing his indebtedness to Doughty for providing not only a great travel book, but a "military text-book" which "helped to guide us to victory in the East."[119]

By the end of 1920, which he wrote later was an even worse year for him than 1919, matters were looking up for Lawrence. The government had decided upon a change from its inept policies in Iraq, a decision which the press attacks of Lawrence and others had helped to influence. The statesmanlike Percy Cox returned to Baghdad from Persia in October to replace Arnold Wilson, and by the end of the year had instituted a provisional Arab government and other reforms.[120] Plans were being made in London to transfer authority for the region into a newly formed Middle East Department of the Colonial Office under Winston Churchill, thus filling with a single authority what Lawrence had called "the empty space which divides the Foreign Office from the India Office."[121] Lawrence's up-and-down attitude toward his book was on an upturn, and he made plans with the artist Eric Kennington to return with him to the Middle East so that Kennington could illustrate the narrative with drawings of the Arabs and other participants in the campaigns. Kennington was so enthralled with the plans that he spent a month in London studying Lawrence's material on the Revolt and earning money as an artist in order to make the trip at his own expense. Through Lawrence he was captured by a "fantastic Eastern romance" of his own.[122]

Kennington has provided an interesting, romanticized picture of Lawrence at the end of 1920. In their first meeting Kennington observed a nervous giggle, but this subsided eventually in later meetings. Kennington was impressed with Lawrence's

male dignity, beauty and power. He moved little, using bodily presence just sufficiently to make brain contact. I had never seen so little employment or wastage of physical energy. The wide mouth smiled often, with humor and pleasure, sometimes extending to an unusual upward curve at the corners, a curious menacing curve, warning of danger. The face was almost lineless, and removed from me as a picture of sculpture. . . . The eyes roamed round, above, and might rest on mine or rather travel through mine, but never shared my thoughts, though noting them all. He stayed higher on another plane of life. It was easy to become his slave. These crystal eyes were almost animal, yet with a complete human understanding. And at moments of thought, when he would ignore the presence of others, retiring into himself, they would diverge slightly. Then, he was alone, and as inscrutable as a lion or a snake. He would return, and graciously attend to one with limitless patience, dealing with our slower brains and limited understanding, our hesitations, and fears, apparently never exasperated by our inefficiency. . . . I realized both his bodily strength and his sensitiveness. Though not broad, he was weighty from shoulders to neck, which jutted, giving a forward placing to the head, and a thrust to the heavy chin. Graves has called his eyes maternal, and I think rightly so, but a near contrast was the power of the frontal bones, and their aggressiveness . . . the fearless eyes were protected by a fighter's bones above and below.[123]

24

Lawrence and Churchill:
The Political Settlements
in the Middle East

Lawrence's plans to go to Jerusalem ("I'd just got as keen as mustard on going out with Kennington") were cut short by his agreeing to work as a political advisor to Winston Churchill with a "free hand" and a salary of £1,200 a year, which he used for "official purposes" and to pay for Kennington's drawings for his book rather than for his own personal needs.[1] "So I'm a government servant from yesterday," he wrote in a letter to Graves near the start of the new year, "and Palestine goes fut (or phut?)."[2] But Kennington, who had been led by Lawrence — Kennington called it "stumbling after his mind," on an imaginary journey "through Nejd, Yemen, Jerusalem, Damascus, Sunni, Shia, Ash-Kenazim, Saphardim," — was determined to go alone and did so.[3]

Lawrence's work with Winston Churchill in 1921 in a newly created Middle East Department that placed Hashemite rulers at the heads of two new Arab states — he called this later the period "of which I'm proudest" — illustrates most strikingly his political and diplomatic functioning, the strengths and weaknesses of his personal approach to world affairs. As had become characteristic of him, Lawrence worked through another, older, man in a position of power and command, and influenced him toward a solution that carried Lawrence's personal stamp but was spelled out in minute detail ("talk of leaving things to man on spot — we left nothing").[4] Churchill persuaded Lawrence to work with him by "arguments which I could not resist,"[5] and Churchill confounded his astonished colleagues, who included men from the India Office, by returning this "wild ass of the desert" to harness.[6]

A deep mutual admiration and respect grew between Lawrence and Churchill. Churchill admired the patient and calm way Lawrence gave himself to the task, and was able "to sink his personality, to bend his

imperious will and pool his knowledge in the common stock . . . he saw
the hope of redeeming in large measure the promises he had made to the
Arab chiefs and of re-establishing a tolerable measure of peace in those
wide regions. In that cause he was capable of becoming — I hazard the
word — a humdrum official. The effort was not in vain. His purposes prevailed."[7] Lawrence for his part admired Churchill's courage and his
imaginative approach to political problems, his willingness to depart from
old ways and to use the best knowledge available to find new solutions.
Lawrence also stressed Churchill's kindliness to him and called him "an
employer who had been for me so considerate as sometimes to seem more
like a senior partner than a master."[8] The only "breeze" (friction) was
"when T.E. said Lenin was the greatest man, when W.S.C. was fondling
Napoleon's bust."[9]

The solution for Iraq arrived at by Churchill's new Middle East Department had two principal parts: the transfer of responsibility for policing the
country from the army to the air force, and the installation of Faisal at the
head of an Arab government that would be affiliated with Great Britain
and would be given a good deal of opportunity for self-government. The
huge army garrison was to be removed (in 1920 alone £38,500,000 was
expended to suppress the revolt in Iraq — several times what it cost the
British government to finance the entire Arab Revolt), and the policing
responsibility taken on by several squadrons of the young RAF at greatly
reduced expense.[10]

Churchill appears to have originated the idea of RAF control of Mesopotamia early in 1920, before the revolt of the tribesmen, when he was
secretary of state for air and war. The details of how it might be done
were developed by Hugh Trenchard, chief of air staff, and Lawrence
over the course of the next year.[11] In April 1920, after a dinner meeting
with Trenchard, Lawrence wrote to Lord Winterton, "After quite a lot
of talk I feel inclined to back his [Trenchard's] scheme."[12]

Even more than the RAF plan, the placement of Faisal upon the throne
of Iraq bears the stamp of Lawrence's personal diplomacy. With Faisal
in Damascus, Lawrence had proposed to the cabinet at the war's end
that Abdullah rule in Baghdad and Lower Mesopotamia and Zayd in
Upper Mesopotamia,[13] and continued to support this view at the Peace
Conference.[14] But events over the next two years altered his view, and
soon after Faisal's expulsion from Damascus, Lawrence began to prepare
British opinion for the amir's leadership in Iraq. The suggestion that
Faisal rule in Iraq had, ironically, already been made to the government
in a telegram sent by Arnold Wilson in July 1920, just after Faisal left
Syria.[15]

Lawrence concluded his two anonymous encomiums on Faisal in *The
Times* in August 1920 with a statement of his friend's availability: "He
now finds himself a free man, with unrivalled experience, great knowledge

of war and government, with the reputation of the greatest Arab leader since Saladin, and the prestige of three victorious campaigns behind him. He is 33, vigorous, and not yet at the height of his powers. His ambitions for himself are nothing. He is the most democratic of men, the most charming personality, but he has put all his abilities and strength at the service of the Arab national movement for 10 years, and raised it from an academic question to the principal factor in Western Asia. It will be interesting to see in which direction he turns, to which of all the opportunities at his command he will finally incline."[16]

The direction of Faisal's turning or, more accurately, the direction in which he was turned, was soon determined. In December he came to London, and Kinahan Cornwallis, his former advisor in Damascus, with Curzon's authorization unsuccessfully offered him the throne of Iraq.[17] Thereupon Lawrence and Lord Winterton made another try. Winterton was approached by the prime minister's secretary "unofficially" to obtain the amir's promise of acceptance of the crown of Iraq should it be "officially" offered to him. This Winterton did

> with the invaluable aid of Colonel Lawrence, Lord Harlech, and the late Lord Moyne, at 3 A.M. in my house in the country after five hours continuous discussion. King Feisal was a brave, most talented and charming man, and one of the greatest gentlemen I have ever met, but like most geniuses he was temperamental. For hours, to all our collective persuasion, he made the same answer. He was sick of politics, especially European politics, and indeed of all Europeans except personal friends such as ourselves. He had been abominably treated in Damascus; was there any reason to believe we should treat him any better in Baghdad? At last he assented to our request and said he believed Iraq and Britain could and should work together, which would be his great aim in his new position.[18]

By the time Churchill had gathered the principal figures involved in the affairs of Iraq in Cairo for a conference in March 1921, the main decisions had already been made ("over dinner tables at the Ship Restaurant in Whitehall").[19] It would be proposed to the British cabinet that Faisal rule the country in alliance with Great Britain and the expense of governing it should be reduced by entrusting its defense to the Royal Air Force.[20]

Lawrence wrote early in February of 1921 to Lady Kennet, a sculptor who was making a statuette of him, "I'm tired of the limelight, and [I'm] not ever going to be a public figure again."[21] But by the end of the month he was off to Cairo to play a dramatic role in the conference that was held there in March. "Everybody Middle East is here," he wrote home on March 20, "except Joyce and Hogarth. . . . We're a very happy family: agreed upon everything important: and the trifles are laughed at."[22]

Walter Henry Thompson, a Scotland Yard inspector who had the responsibility of guarding Churchill for nearly twenty years, spent many days and hundreds of hours with Lawrence in Egypt and Palestine in March 1921. He has left a remarkable firsthand record of Lawrence's compelling power among the Arab peoples and the adulation which greeted his return to the lands he had helped to liberate.[23] Thompson had received advance notice that Churchill's life would be in danger in Egypt, but Lawrence, through his knowledge of the Arab countries and people ("in a strange sense it *was* Lawrence's land, by legacy to him from those Arabs") and his sense of the moods of crowds, guided the diplomatic party safely through their journeys.[24]

At Gaza, on the way to Jerusalem, Lawrence settled an unruly-looking mob by having the party detrain and proceed to a hall near the town mosque where, dressed in full Arab regalia, he translated a brief speech for Churchill. Thompson described the "magic" in the atmosphere as the tribal leaders from far-flung parts of the Arab world came to greet Lawrence:

> It is doubtful whether the Arabs, with the unclassifiable admixture here in the mob at Gaza of Lebanese, Iraqi, Alaouites, Djebel Druses, Turks, Syrians, Jews, Armenians, Kurds and Persians — whether more than three or four in the crowd knew which was Churchill. Or much cared. We were just a knot of Europeans with hats on. Lawrence was the man.
>
> No Pope of Rome ever had more command before his own worshippers in the Palazzo. And Colonel Lawrence raised his hand slowly, the first and second fingers lifted above the other two for silence and for blessing. He could have owned their earth. He did own it. Every man froze in respect, in a kind of New Testament adoration of shepherds for a master. It was quite weird and very comforting.
>
> We passed through these murderous-looking men and they parted a way for us without a struggle. Many touched Lawrence as he moved forward among them. Far off, drums were beating, and a horse neighed. A muezzin's cry fell sadly among us from the single minaret in the mosque.[25]

Thompson concluded that at this time in this part of Western Asia, "Lawrence was so greatly loved and so fanatically respected that he could have established his own empire from Alexandretta to the Indus. He knew this, too."[26] And, I might add, it frightened him.

One of the "trifles" Lawrence referred to in his March 20 letter to his mother was how to get Faisal accepted by the Iraqis as their ruler. There were rivals for the throne, such as the *naqib* (head of the provisional government) and Sayyid Talib, but the former was too old and infirm, and too limited in competence or authority, to be acceptable to either the British or the Iraqis, and the latter was feared as an unreliable rabble-rouser with dictatorial ambitions.[27] Faisal's diplomatic and military experience, proved statesmanship, high prestige in the Arab world and friendliness (if dealt with fairly) with the British made him an acceptable candidate to Cox, who had, by the time of the Cairo Conference, already come to "a 'Sharifian' although not definitely a 'Feisalian' conclusion."[28] To Mrs. Shaw in 1927 Lawrence wrote, "In 1921, at the Cairo Conference, [Gertrude Bell] swung all the Mesopot. British officials to the Feisal solution, while Winston and I swung the English people."[29]

The implementing of the decisions of the Cairo Conference, especially the installation of Faisal as king of Iraq, was achieved by a combination of British force, diplomacy, manipulation and deception, in which the high commissioner, Sir Percy Cox, and his assistant, Gertrude Bell, played key roles in Iraq, while Churchill managed the difficulties presented by his own government.[30]

Strong national and religious groups in Iraq were either directly opposed to Faisal and favored another candidate, or were at best cool to the prospect of his rule. In April the leading contender, Sayyid Talib, after making a threatening speech was arrested out of fear that he would foment violence among the revolutionary elements of the country. There was considerable delay in making public the British decision to place Faisal on the Iraqi throne, as every effort was made to have his candidacy appear to be the desire of the people themselves. Churchill's speech of June 14 in the British House of Commons, announcing the Cairo decisions, contained the contradictory statements that the British did not intend or desire to force a particular rule on the Iraqi people and that Amir Faisal was "the most suitable candidate in the field." He hoped "that [Faisal] will secure the support of the majority of the people of Iraq."[31]

Faisal arrived in Iraq on June 23 and experienced a cool reception during his trip to Baghdad, but was received there by huge enthusiastic crowds.[32] Under the guidance of the high commissioner a referendum held in August found ninety-six percent of the votes supporting Faisal, but as Sir Percy's biographer noted with masterful understatement, "in the Near and Middle East the results of all such operations are exaggerated and owe much to official prompting or pressure."[33]

Through the force and skill of Faisal's own statesmanship, he was able to reconcile most of the discontented elements of the country to his candidacy, including those that wished complete independence from Britain. He successfully staved off a British effort to shackle his authority and was duly enthroned on August 23 as a military band played "God Save the King" (there was no Arab national anthem), and a twenty-one-gun royal salute was fired.[34] Through this compromised process of democracy-in-action the state of Iraq was created in alliance with Great Britain, and began to move toward full independence.

Faisal owed his throne in Iraq to Lawrence most of all, and it was to Lawrence whom he wrote for advice regarding the details of the treaty between his country and Great Britain, the degree of British control of Iraq's financial and political affairs he should endure, his difficulties effecting changes in his administration, and his frustration with the high commissioner, who, he wrote, had "a perfectly genuine desire, to keep everybody who had served in any office in his position whatever his circumstances are."[35] Faisal's letters to his English friend (Lawrence's letters to the king have not been discovered) are affectionate in tone and convey his deep commitment to his people. He concluded one letter in November 1921:

> And indeed, my dearest Lawrence, I have seen that as the result of the Treaty I shall be able to benefit you and benefit my country and indeed as you know I am not afraid of work or responsibility, and if I saw that I was going to be tied down or gagged and to meet with shame and failure into the bargain I don't wish to be like the Shah of Persia to make a promise and then not stand by my engagements (and I am staking my honour and my love for my people and my love for you on the result) and I should lose everything, nay, I should ask pardon from everybody and become submissive to your directions, whatever they may be. To conclude, Hope you are in good health.
>
> Your friend. Feisul[36]

By 1927 progress toward independence and stable government had been made in Iraq and Lawrence wrote proudly to Mrs. Shaw, who had just met Faisal in London: "I'm awfully glad you liked him. For so long he was only my duckling: and I crow secretly with delight when he gets another inch forward on his road. When you think of the harrassed and distant figure of Wadi Safra in 1916. . . .

"I don't think he wants me really. Not even the nicest man on earth can feel wholly unembarrassed before a fellow to whom he owes too much. Feisal owed me Damascus first of all, and Baghdad second: and between those stages most of his kingcraft and affairs. When with him I am an omnipotent advisor: and while that is very well in the field, it is derogatory to a monarch: especially to a monarch who is not entirely constitutional. . . .

"Also peoples are like people. They teach themselves to walk and to balance by dint of trying and falling down. Irak did a good deal of falling between 1916 and 1921: and since 1921, under Feisal's guidance has done much good trying and no falling. But I don't think it yet walks very well. Nor can any hand save it from making its messes: there is a point where coddling becomes wicked. All my experience of the Arabs was of the ex god-father role: and I think they have outgrown that. If they are to make good as a modern state (how large an 'if') then it must be by virtue of their own desire and excellence. . . .

"What you say about him looking young and happy and peaceful pleases me: of course he has won great credit for himself: and that brings a man to flower. . . .

"You know without my letting [sic] you, how much I liked him. I talk of him always in the past tense, for it will be a long time before we meet again. Indeed I hope sometimes we never will, for it would mean that he was in trouble. I've promised myself to help him, if ever that happens.

"As for Irak . . . well, some day they will be fit for self-government, and then they will not want a king: but whether 7 or 70 or 700 years hence, God knows. Meanwhile Feisal is serving his race as no Arab has served it for many hundred years. He is my very great pride: and it's been my privilege to have helped him to his supremacy, out there, and to have made him a person, for the English-speaking [sic] reading races. Gertrude [Bell] has nobly supported him in his last effort. . . .

"Don't you think he looks the part, perfectly? Was there ever a more graceful walk than his? G.B.S. probably (being an emperor, himself) thinks poorly of kings: but he'd admit that I'd made a good one."[37]

Allowing for the egoism of the letter and some exaggeration of his role as a king- and state-maker, it contains enough uncomfortable reality (from an Arab point of view), and is so revealing of his attitude, as to make understandable the resentment of later Arab nationalists toward Lawrence's political activities in the Middle East.

On March 25 or 26, 1921, Lawrence left Cairo and proceeded via Gaza, Jerusalem and Amman to es-Salt to meet Amir Abdullah, who had gone to Trans-Jordan with "orders from his father to raise the tribes and drive the French out of Syria."[38] Lawrence told Abdullah "that it was impossible for King Faisal to return to Syria,"[39] and brought him through cheering crowds to a meeting in Jerusalem on March 28 with Churchill, Sir Herbert Samuel (the high commissioner of Palestine), and other officials. Abdullah was asked by Churchill to accept the decisions of the Cairo Conference regarding Iraq, but was offered in compensation the amirate of Trans-Jordan as a kind of buffer state, loyal to Great Britain, between Palestine, where a pro-Zionist policy was being implemented, and the anti-Zionist regions of the Arab world.[40] Abdullah proposed the creation of a single Arab state consisting of Palestine and Trans-Jordan, but eventually agreed to the more limited Lawrence-Churchill solution of the amirate of Trans-Jordan after some arm-twisting and the offer of the possible eventual restoration of an Arab administration in Syria.[41] Although Abdullah agreed to try to influence his father to accept the plan, he is said to have held it against Faisal for years afterwards that his brother usurped the crown of Iraq, which Abdullah believed was his by right.[42]

Lawrence seems to have been in good spirits in the early spring of 1921, pleased with his accomplishments at this time and glad to be back again in the desert lands, which were coming into bloom. "The country across Jordan is all in spring," he wrote his family in April, "and the grass and flowers are beautiful. . . . Spent eight days living with Abdullah in his camp. It was rather like the life in wartime, with hundreds of Bedouin coming and going, and a general atmosphere of newness in the air. However the difference was that now everybody is trying to be peaceful."[43]

Kennington captured the excitement with which Lawrence's former desert companions and comrades-in-arms greeted him upon his brief return to Trans-Jordan:

> Their cries . . . become a roar, Aurens — Aurens — Aurens — Aurens! It seemed to me that each had need to touch him. It was half an hour before he was talking to less than a dozen at once. Re-creating the picture, I see him as detached as ever, but with great charm and very gracious. I thought he got warmth and pleasure from their love, but now know his pain also, for they longed for him to lead them again into Damascus, this time to drive out the French. Easily self-controlled, he returned a percentage of the pats, touches and gripping of hands, giving nods, smiles, and sudden wit to chosen friends. He was apart, but they did not know it. They loved him, and gave him all their heart.[44]

Sir Herbert Samuel, the British high commissioner in Palestine, has provided another, more sober, eyewitness recollection of Lawrence's return to Amman: "I was witness of a most affectionate greeting from some of the principal Bedu sheikhs, who had been his associates in the Arab Revolt, when quite unexpectedly they found him among them once more."[45]

Lawrence's good spirits did not last very long. In April and early May he traveled between Egypt, Trans-Jordan and Jerusalem, spending some of the time with Kennington, who was drawing Arabs for the book. He met secretly with Faisal at Port Said to discuss British plans for the amir's enthronement in Iraq and evaluated for the Colonial Office the precarious position and impoverishment of Abdullah's fledgling administration in Amman. He returned to England in May, and wrote Graves, "I'm back in the Colonial Office and hating it."[46] Without an immediate sphere of action Lawrence devoted himself to literary interests, and to help Graves financially by turning over to him the disappointing proceeds of the sale of parts of his narrative of the Arab Revolt to a New York magazine.[47]

Although Lawrence was satisfied with progress in the Middle East from the political standpoint, he recognized that his return there had stirred up troubling memories. "I can't live at home," he wrote his poet friend, "I don't know why: the place makes me utterly intolerable. . . . Our schemes for the betterment of the Middle East race are doing nicely: thanks. . . . I wish I hadn't gone out there: the Arabs are like a page I have turned over: and sequels are rotten things. . . . Meanwhile I'm locked up here: office every day, and much of it, and another trip E. (this time to Jeddah to see the Sherif) looming."[48]

In June Lawrence learned that he was definitely being sent by Churchill as an envoy to try to persuade King Husayn to sign a treaty spelling out the various settlements that had been proposed for the Middle East from the time of the Versailles Treaty. Many of these solutions, such as the British mandate for Palestine, the French presence in Syria, and a general restricting of the king's sovereignty, were obviously intolerable to him, and represented a breach of the agreements and understandings he had been party to with Great Britain since 1914. Lawrence's position was an uncomfortable one and it is somewhat surprising that he accepted the appointment at all. If he were to be completely "successful" from the British point of view, it would have meant selling out his old ally altogether, while encouraging the king would have meant more war with Ibn Saud, who was still receiving subsidization from England.

Lawrence, according to his brother Arnold, chose a middle course and "bitched it up," making sure that his negotiations with Husayn were unsuccessful.[49] Some support for this view is provided by a comment of Lawrence's in a 1927 letter: "It was my action at Jidda in 1921 which made Ibn Saud's advance on Mecca possible. I hope he holds it for some years yet."[50] Later he told a friend in the Tank Corps that this trip to the Hijaz in 1921 was almost too much for him and that the mental strain to which he was subjected during the negotiations with Husayn was worse than anything he had known during the campaign.[51]

Doughty warned Lawrence to "look out for madmen fanatics at Jidda."[52] But early in July Lawrence headed for Jidda anyway and spent two hot, frustrating months there and in Aden. He met several times with the old king. Despite various odd attempts to browbeat Husayn, whose conceit and unrealistic ambitiousness Lawrence now found exasperating, and the contemplation of threats of force or withdrawal of his subsidy, nothing much came of the meetings and no treaty was signed.

The telegraphic correspondence between Lawrence and the Foreign Office from July 23 to September 22 provides a graphic, sometimes amusing, at other times questionable, account of Lawrence's effort to deal with the king.[53] He seems to have been most successful when appealing to the old man's vanity — for example in offering him a yacht for his personal use ("Any news of proposed yacht for Hussein to buy cheap if he behaves himself?"), Italian airplanes (very expensive "rubbish"), or agreeing to a visit from the Prince of Wales. Husayn's sons Zayd and Ali were much more reasonable and seemed to be working with Lawrence toward arriving at some sort of compromise. At one point Lawrence invoked Zayd's authority to recommend suppression of a complaining telegram that Husayn was planning to send to Faisal. It is not clear whether Lawrence had Zayd's authority to do this. When interviewed nearly a half century later, Zayd denied that Lawrence had acted with his knowledge.[54] The contemporary record, however, indicates that Lawrence and Zayd were working in close cooperation. At one point, for example, when Lawrence walked out of a session with the king "with parting remarks," Zayd came to him "with a rough draft of a treaty based on ours for my consideration."[55] When Lawrence left Jidda for Aden on August 12, it appeared that he had made some progress in obtaining the king's acquiescence in the various agreements under discussion.

In late August from Aden, where he had gone to consult the British resident, Lawrence wrote to Kennington, "This is the beastliest trip ever I had: but thank the Lord I took no dress clothes," and sent him an introduction he had written there to a catalogue of the drawings that the artist had made during the past year of the people of the desert for his (Lawrence's) potential book ("something for the future").[56] In this essay Lawrence expressed even more strongly than he had a year before in the introduction in *Arabia Deserta* his preference for the Arabs of the desert, for the Bedouin over the Arabs of the towns or other settled peoples. "He [Kennington] has drawn camel-men," Lawrence wrote, "and princes of the desert, donkey-boys, officers, descendants of the Prophet, a vicepresident of the Turkish Chamber, slaves, sheikhs and swordsmen. They represent a fair choice of the real Arab, not the Algerian or Egyptian or Syrian so commonly palmed off on us, not the noisy, luxury-loving, sensual, passionate, greedy person, but a man whose ruling characteristic is hardness of body, mind, heart and head. . . . It is interesting to see that instinctively he drew the men of the desert. Where he was there were ten settled men to every nomad: yet his drawings show nearly ten desert men to every peasant. This has strengthened in me the unflattering suspicion that the nomad is the richer creature. The Arab townsman or villager is like us and our villagers, with our notion of property, our sense of gain and our appetite for material success. He has our premises, as well as our processes. The Bedouin on the other hand, while his sense is as human and his mind as logical as ours, begins with principles quite other than our own, and gets further from us as his character strengthens. He has a creed and practice of not-possessing, which is a tough armour against our modern wiles. It defends him against all sentiment."[57]

On August 29 Lawrence returned to Jidda for more than three additional weeks of fruitless negotiations with King Husayn,[58] who, Lawrence discovered, had gone back on his decision and demanded, among other things, "recognition of his supremacy over all Arab rulers everywhere."[59] Lawrence wired to London: "My reply made him send for a dagger and swear to abdicate and kill himself. I said we would continue negotiations with his successor."[60] Zayd, Ali and the queen ("who is of our party" and "lectures him at night") took "a strong line" and the negotiations became temporarily "friendly" and "rational" once again.

Lawrence seemed to have forgotten or repressed this episode, for when Liddell Hart asked him in 1933 whether there was any truth to the story that the king had called for his sword and threatened to kill himself Lawrence replied: "No truth. Suicide practically unknown amongst orthodox Moslems. King Hussein used to threaten to abdicate. I wished he would, but was never funny about it. The old man was a tragic figure, in his way: brave, obstinate, hopelessly out-of-date: exasperating."[61]

In mid-September the Foreign Office was becoming eager for Lawrence to visit Trans-Jordan "as soon as possible" (especially as the British government was under pressure from the French to force Abdullah to arrest the men involved in an assassination attempt on the French commander of Syria) and he sought to wind up his negotiations in Jidda. The king approved each clause of the treaty and announced publicly his plan to sign it. Lawrence wired to London, however, that "when Ali presented him [Husayn] text for ratification he shouted and struck at him, and then sent us eight contradictory sets of prior conditions and stipulations all unacceptable. Ali says the old man is mad, and is preparing with Zeid to obtain his formal abdication. Ali and Zeid have behaved splendidly, and they may change things in the next weeks."[62] On September 22 Lawrence set sail for Egypt and after five days there proceeded by train to Jerusalem.

By the end of the summer of 1921 Lawrence was becoming depressed once again. Abdullah's regime in Trans-Jordan was faltering under the pressures of Syrian and Palestinian politicians, French complaints and the besiegings of his British advisors, to all of whom Abdullah was said to have "smiled sweetly, expressed agreement" and done nothing, earning for himself the nickname of "Sunny Jim."[63] Lawrence was delegated to proceed from his mission with Husayn to view the situation at first hand in Amman and advise Winston Churchill in London regarding the future of the regime.[64] In July he had considered with Herbert Samuel that union with Palestine would be the best future for Trans-Jordan.[65] Lawrence expected that he would recommend ending Abdullah's faltering regime, and wrote to Kennington from Cairo at the beginning of October: "Tomorrow I go to Trans-Jordan, to end that farce. It makes me feel like a baby-killer. . . . I'm bored stiff: and very tired, and a little ill, and sorry to see how mean some people I wanted to respect have grown. The war was good by drawing over our depths that hot surface wish to do or win something. So the cargo of the ship was unseen, and not thought of. This life goes on till February 28 next year."[66] As it turned out, Lawrence proved to be the decisive factor in preserving Abdullah's regime in Trans-Jordan.

At the end of the first week of October, after discussions in Jerusalem with the high commissioner and his staff, Lawrence was still planning to persuade Abdullah to step down.[67] He arrived in Amman on October 12 as the chief British representative to evaluate the situation and obtain the agreement of Abdullah to the treaty his father had been unwilling to sign. He lived with his old friend F. G. Peake, who had served with him in the closing days of the desert campaigns and was now attempting to build up a native army, in a stone-built house at the site of a disintegrating Byzantine church.

During this period, according to Peake, Lawrence was given to shifting moods. Much of the time he amused himself with "Arab cronies" and lived once more the life of the desert and the tribes, but felt "stultified" in his role as a civil servant working with politically minded men who had not the élan or the commitment of his companions in the Revolt.[68] He suffered periods in which he appeared to Peake to be "depressed, incommunicative and obviously weighted down by the cares of fashioning a post-war world in the Middle East."[69]

Lawrence spent little time in the chief representative's office, preferring once more to see for himself the situation in the country. He drove all over the countryside (including a last look at his wartime base and retreat at Azraq) with Peake in his Model T Ford and later with Philby, who arrived at the end of November. After two weeks in Trans-Jordan Lawrence wrote a report to the Colonial Office in which he reviewed critically the administrative, military and political situation in the country. The report is factually detailed, but contains characteristic bits of Laurentian irony. For example: "Peake cannot show his men in public till they are reasonably smart and till they have rifles, for in Trans-Jordania every man of military age carries a rifle as a mark of self-respect, and Peake's, the so-called Military Force, is the only unarmed body of men in the country"; and, a driver, "who is supposed to be qualified, can drive the car forward but is not good at reversing. He is practicing this on the path between the tents."[70] Lawrence found in Trans-Jordan an understandable "distrust of the honesty of our motives," principally out of fear that British Zionist policy would be extended into this region, and he advised that Britain declare herself against such a policy.[71] He also busied himself with mediating various tribal disputes and claims: He destroyed a number of his predecessor's files which he thought would trouble Arab-British relations, including several passports awaiting endorsement (creating much trouble for their owners when they came to collect them); found time to engage a mason to underpin a collapsing Roman arch; and helped to resist from behind the scenes French demands that certain Arab nationalists be turned over to them.[72] To Newcombe, who was on his way to Syria, Lawrence wrote in November:

"There's only one thing to tell the French: that the catching of assassins is no doubt desireable, and one of the functions of government: but that we in Trans-Jordan have first to make the government, and then to make opinion disapprove of political assassination. After this the capture of assassins becomes timely. Meanwhile it would be silly, and I'll have no part in it. We cannot afford to chuck away our hopes of building something to soothe our neighbour's feelings: and the French have made our job here as difficult as possible — if it is possible at all — by their wanton disregard of the common decencies between nations.

"Please remind them that they shot Arab prisoners after Meisalun and plundered the houses and goods of Feisal and his friends. The dirty-dog work has been fairly shared, and I thank what Gods I have that I'm neither an Arab nor a Frenchman — only the poor brute who has to clean up after them. . . .

"If you can, drop over here friendly-fashion some time, and I'll show you the French picture from underneath. Not lovely. à toi."[73]

It was (according to Philby) Lawrence's puckish suggestion that he should be succeeded as chief British representative by Philby, the close advisor of Abdullah's enemy, Ibn Saud,[74] but the choice proved to be a happy one for all concerned, including Amir Abdullah himself.[75] Philby arrived on November 28 and his stay overlapped Lawrence's by ten days. He had nothing but praise for Lawrence's work in Trans-Jordan and while Lawrence remained there left him in charge. On his first day at work Philby wrote in his diary: "I leave all business to Lawrence, who in spite of his repeated assertions that he had handed over the reins of office to me, finds that he cannot divest himself of its functions. He must carry on while he remains here, and I am well content to let him do so. He is excellent, and I am struck with admiration of his intensely practical, yet unbusinesslike, methods."[76]

On December 8, Lawrence's last day in Trans-Jordan, he and Abdullah concluded the Anglo-Hijaz Treaty ("a pompous and portentous document," Philby called it). But it proved to have little meaning because King Husayn, to whom Lawrence brought the treaty at Jidda the following day, refused "to accord any kind of recognition to the Jewish National Home Policy in Palestine."[77] Although Lawrence apparently wrote no final report regarding his two months in Amman, he recommended to Churchill that Trans-Jordan be treated as an independent state, freed of control by the high commissioner of Palestine, and that Abdullah be allowed to stay as the head of the new country.[78] Stay he did, as head of the small state of Trans-Jordan, which gradually became free of British authority and achieved independence in 1951, shortly after which Abdullah was assassinated. The present able ruler, Husayn, is Abdullah's grandson.

Lawrence left Jidda, spent several days in Jerusalem and Egypt, and returned to England via Paris before Christmas in 1921, and "shook the

dust of Arabia from his feet forever."[79] In his diary entry of December 8
Philby wrote: "The departure of Lawrence leaves me in full charge, and
at the same time a gap which will not be easy to fill. He knows and is
known to everybody in these parts; and many of them have been intimately associated with him for years during the military operations which
he conducted up and down the railway. That he has effected a great
change in the situation since he came here two months ago admits of no
doubt. He has turned a pessimistic outlook into one which is certainly
the reverse; the administration which he has encouraged to function is
working smoothly."[80]

"In the winter of 1921–1922 Lawrence was in a very nervous condition," Graves wrote, "did not eat or sleep enough, and worked over the
Seven Pillars again."[81] Arnold Lawrence confirms that in 1922 his brother
"came as near as anyone could do to a complete breakdown, after nine
years of overworking without a holiday, and several of them under a
continuous nervous strain. He cured himself by enlisting."[82]

Lawrence wrote little of the months before his enlistment in August
1922. He told Liddell Hart that he was "nearly dotty" then, and that he
spent much time tramping about London.[83] He also made a number of
trips to his property (Pole Hill, Chingford) in Epping Forest in Essex,
where he and Vyvyan Richards again discussed the possibility of printing
Seven Pillars on a printing press they would construct there. It was also
during this period that Lawrence burned at Pole Hill the second text of
Seven Pillars of Wisdom. He delighted a group of boys from a nearby
school, where Richards was a teacher, with rich stories about the Arabian
campaigns, which he so seldom talked about with adults. One of these
former boys, whom I had the opportunity recently to meet, recalled more
vividly the tales themselves, which appealed enormously to the imagination of a teen-ager, than the man who told them.[84] Lawrence's letters,
especially those to Eric Kennington, reflect his increasing frustration with
the Colonial Office routine and his desire to get away from it.

There is evidence that in this time Lawrence experienced genuine poverty, created largely by his generosity to his friends and his refusal to use
any money from his work in the Colonial Office (as it was concerned with
the Arabs and the Middle East) to gratify his own needs. "I ran right out
of money in April 1922," he wrote Ralph Isham five years later. "And went
along with great difficulty until August, when Trenchard let me into the
Royal Air Force. My capital then was 15 pence, and I'd been half-fed for
weeks."[85] It was also during these early months of 1922 that he struggled
with the dedication to his war book ("To S.A.") and submitted the poem
to Robert Graves for poetic revision.

When Graves correctly identified S.A. with Dahoum (whom Lawrence
acknowledged in 1922 as having "provided a disproportionate share of the
motive for the Arabian adventure"), Lawrence threw him off the track by

writing: "You have taken me too literally. S.A. still exists; but out of my reach, because I have changed."[86]

In February 1922, Lawrence became aware that his friend Doughty was once more in difficult straits and went to great lengths to help him. "I feel rather worried about it all," he wrote to Mrs. Doughty.[87] He arranged that Doughty should receive a small government pension and a grant from the Royal Literary Fund, and also put the family in touch with good investment advice on some rubber shares they held. In addition, he obtained £400 with which the British Museum bought from Doughty the manuscript of *Dawn in Britain,* the only manuscript of Doughty's works available, and handled all this so unobtrusively, and with such tact, that Doughty seems never to have felt that he was the recipient of charity, although David Garnett had "reason to think" that Lawrence provided most of the money for the manuscript himself.[88] Several of Doughty's letters reflect without apparent embarrassment his gratitude to his friend, who had spared him being given anything "like to an alms which I could not receive."[89] Lawrence visited Doughty in Eastbourne at the end of March, and according to letters of Doughty's, was to go to Iraq on April 1, but there is no evidence he ever made such a trip.[90]

Dissatisfied with his second version of *Seven Pillars,* Lawrence had begun at the end of 1920 in London the third version, which he had continued to work on in Jidda and later in Amman. Between January and June of 1922, Lawrence had eight copies of *Seven Pillars of Wisdom* (of which five, possibly six, survive) printed privately by the Oxford *Times.* He states that he completed the third text on May 9 and that the following day he burned at Chingford the now-rejected second text.[91] After the book was printed, Lawrence placed the manuscript of the third text in the Bodleian Library, where it may be read. He was still resisting any more general circulation or publication of his work. But in March a fine crop of Kennington's drawings had arrived at the Colonial Office, and Lawrence's friends increased their pressure on him to publish the work. Kennington has offered this version of his peculiar struggle, probably in the spring of 1922, to persuade Lawrence to publish the book, at least for his friends:

"He actually looked not well, and his still seriousness was frightening. 'It is an evil work. . . . I could not refuse you after receiving the Arab portraits from you. It will not disturb you. Next morning you will start your day's work as usual, but you have an odd brain. It is in compartments. I have not let Robert Graves read it. It can never be published. I could not live if it was loosed abroad.' I began to fight. It had to be published. It was a grand, immense masterpiece. He looked more tired. 'How could I go on if it was made public? At Stamford Brook I did not know whether I was trying to throw myself under a train, or trying not to. I intended to throw these volumes off the centre of Hammersmith

Bridge. I have worked myself out and am finished. Every bone in my body had been broken. My lungs are pierced, my heart is weak.' "

Kennington pushed on, but "he began again, gently to prove to me how degraded the book was, and foreseeing defeat in a battle with that brain, I said the book had to be published. He said more gently, 'Give me one good reason — one only.' It seemed, the crisis, and I found one reason, and said it was a book on motive, and necessary at this moment of life; the world had lied till it was blind, and had to be re-educated to see its motives. It sounded futile, but he stopped quiet, and after a pause, said undramatically, 'Not bad' — (giggle) — 'Quite good' — (many giggles) — 'You win.' "[92]

It was not, of course, the end of the struggle, and George Bernard Shaw (whom Lawrence had met in March), Hogarth, Kipling, and other friends also appealed to him to publish the book. "I wrote a book on Arabia," he wrote the young painter Paul Nash in August. "To publish it would involve me in as many libels as there are characters. I move in its pages like St. Anthony among the devils. Also it isn't good enough to publish, but it's good enough for me to make better, till it can be published in the course of years."[93] Years later he brushed aside the influence of all these weighty entreaties, crediting his change of mind and heart to Gertrude Bell's simple request, "Wouldn't you consider publishing it for your friends?"[94]

On July 1, 1922, Churchill agreed to let Lawrence leave the Colonial Office, and three days later Lawrence wrote his formal letter of resignation, declaring himself to be "very glad to leave so prosperous a ship."[95] But it was mid-August before he had worked out with his friend Hugh Trenchard, the air marshal, the details of his enlistment in the RAF. "Winston very agreeable," Lawrence wrote Trenchard. "Hope your lord [Freddie Guest, secretary of state for air] was the same."[96] Trenchard replied, "Yes, my Lord was very agreeable."[97] A week later Lawrence presented himself at the RAF Recruiting Depot for enlistment as Aircraftsman J. H. Ross.

With his enlistment, Lawrence left behind for good the politics of the Middle East and his official involvement with Arab affairs. "The life of politics," he wrote Hogarth ten months later, "wearied me out, by worrying me over-much."[98] Once out of the political arena he proceeded, according to his brother Arnold, "to lose interest in the East, not simply with that satiated curiosity with which he turned from his medieval and archaeological interests. For he looked back upon his subjection to the East with horror. His memories were the more painful because of the vividness with which he recollected sights and smells and sounds, creating again in all their poignancy scenes he would have preferred to forget."[99]

In a speech in the House of Commons a few months before the out-break of World War II, Churchill called Lawrence "the truest champion of Arab rights whom modern times have known,"[100] but not all Arabs would agree with this assessment.

On the one hand, Lawrence was too caught up in Arab causes to be entirely objective, while on the other, his partial withdrawal from public life after the Paris Peace Conference so removed him from what was happening in the Middle East that in 1920 he could become only a propagandist.[101] As a result of the intensely personal quality of all his political activity Lawrence identified too strongly with the purposes of his own government *and at the same time* with the aspirations of the Arab peoples. He was both too visionary and too narrow in his outlook. Modern Arab nationalists have criticized his singleminded backing of the Hashemite family, and Zeine, for example, has pointed out the "blunder on the part of Faisal and Lawrence" in trying to establish after the fall of Damascus a Hashemite government in Beirut and the Lebanon "in the name of the King of the Hedjaz," thus precipitating prematurely a struggle with the French.[102] But Lawrence denied a part in this action and agreed with Zeine's assessment. He wrote in 1929 that the "precipitate occupation of Beyrout and Lebanon wholly threw away the local people's chances" and that Shukri al-Ayyubi was sent to Beirut by Ali Ridah al-Riqabi, the mayor of Damascus.[103] English writers, especially Philby, have stressed how Lawrence backed the wrong horse in continuing to support after 1919 the family of King Husayn while Ibn Saud was consolidating his power in Arabia, and it is possible that personal loyalties stood in the way of a more realistic and objective view ("You can't guard the Hedjaz by backing Husain and dropping I.S. [Ibn Saud]," Gertrude Bell had cautioned him in 1920).[104]

Lawrence's many assessments of his own and Britain's role in the post-war settlements in the Middle East reflect his deep personal involvement in their results, his need for atonement, and perhaps also some rationalization of his abandonment of further involvement with their consequences. "Surely," he wrote to Hugh Trenchard, "my share in helping settle the Middle East atones for my misdeeds in the war. I think so, anyway."[105] Lawrence was aware of the subjectivity of his writings and partisanship, which derived especially from his wartime participation. For example, to one veteran of the campaigns he wrote: "I wish my record of events had been less personal and more a history: but when I tried to be impartial and to weigh the merits of plans and men and action, I found myself disqualified from good writing. I had been so much of a partisan in all the campaign, and been so firmly converted to my private courses, before I embarked on them, that in no case could I have written fairly either of the others or of myself."[106]

In repeated statements Lawrence reiterated his conviction that the

settlements worked out with Churchill represented a fulfillment of Britain's wartime pledges and responsibilities to the Arab peoples, that England was "quit of the war-time Eastern adventure with clean hands."[107]
In 1927 he wrote: "I had 18 months of office, and my settlement is knave- (but not fool-) proof. I'd be a poor creature if it wasn't: and a rat, if I'd voluntarily got out before the last of my men. As it was, I could (and did) retire with some self contentment, with the whole job done. I wanted the Arabs to have leave to make their own mess: and not to go on holding their hands to save them from messes. People learn by falling down, like babies."[108] To Mrs. Shaw Lawrence wrote similarly: "The settlement which Winston put through in 1921 and 1922 (mainly because my advocacy supplied him with all the technical advice and arguments necessary) was, I think, the best possible settlement which Great Britain, alone, could achieve at the time. Had we waited for the French to come to their right mind and cooperate in a complete settlement, we would be waiting yet. And after June, 1922, my job was done. I had repaired, so far as it lay in English power to repair it, the damage done to the Arab movement by the signing of the Armistice in November, 1918."[109] In his final statement on the subject in 1935 Lawrence wrote to Graves, "How well the Middle East has done: it, more than any part of the world, has gained from that war."[110]

Lawrence even offered his suffering in Arab services as evidence of the purity of his and Britain's intentions and actions in fulfilling their obligations to the Arab peoples. Late in 1922 he wrote: "I do not wish to publish secret documents, nor to make long explanations: but must put on record my conviction that England is out of the Arab affair with clean hands. Some Arab advocates (the most vociferous joined our ranks after the Armistice) have rejected my judgement on this point. Like a tedious pensioner I showed them my wounds (over sixty I have, each scar evidence of pain incurred in Arab service) as proof I had worked sincerely on their side. They found me out-of-date: and I was happy to withdraw from a political milieu which had never been congenial."[111]

It was in particular Britain's abandonment of Syria to the French and his accommodation with Zionism that make Lawrence's positive summary statements unbalanced and so disturbing to modern Arab nationalists. However, some of those who hold him responsible for this abandonment are misinformed. Lawrence himself appeared later to forget that the postwar settlement in regard to Syria was the result of a deal between Britain and France, and seemed to blame the outcome on the Syrians themselves. In 1927 he wrote: "Between us [with Churchill] we brought a peace in Irak and Transjordan and Palestine which has lasted for five years. That's a good achievement. The Arabs have now a place where they can obtain their full freedom, if they are good enough to use it. As for Damascus — they had Irak's present opportunity in 1920, and threw it away. So the political education of Syria goes on, as it did under the Turks, with bombs and bayonets as text-books" [the Syrians had risen in a bloody rebellion in 1925 against French military rule].[112] And in another letter: "Syria is not our pudding. The Syrians brought the French there, deliberately. Their political education (and France's) is proceeding!"[113]

Yet in the main Lawrence had made "a good achievement" in his effort to start the Arab nations on their road toward psychological and political independence, and it would be hard to argue with his summary: "My part of the Middle East job was done, by 1922, and, on the whole, well done."[114] And the lasting value of his work grew out of the power of his convictions, the extent of his knowledge and the depth of his personal commitment. Its limitations derived from the intense subjectivity of his involvement, his need — in the postwar political settlements, as in the war itself — to resolve in the public domain profound personal issues.

From the personal standpoint the years of Lawrence's Arab service had been devastating, and neither a just political settlement nor the effort at self-cure by writing his book could heal the wounds they had inflicted. Five years after he left the Colonial Office he wrote in a letter, "That Arabian time is now only a bad dream, which, when I get a touch of fever at night, wakes me up sweating and yelling, scaring the other fourteen fellows in our room into very violent curses."[115]

Arnold Lawrence had written that his brother's conscience was satisfied by the creation of autonomous Arab states "with the provision for their ultimate independence in connection with the British Empire." He points out that T.E.'s "friendliness" was not limited to the Arab-speaking peoples of Asia, for "he had helped to secure a peaceful frontier to the Kemalists during their struggle for the new Turkey and afterwards advocated British support for their Turkish Republic."[116] Arnold Lawrence felt that his brother would have adjusted his attitude toward Zionism "to the tremendous spurt in colonization caused by Jewish emigration from Nazi Germany. After he left the Colonial Office he anticipated a long-protracted British administration of Palestine, ending in a comparatively amicable solution of the problem, in favour, I think, of a Jewish majority in the distant future."[117]

These lines were written in 1936.

The Versailles Treaty and the agreements that followed in its wake represented the last major international diplomatic effort in which the Western Great Powers were able to impose settlements upon the peoples of Asia with so little regard for their desires. Since the period in which these agreements were signed, many new countries have merged in Asia and Africa, and self-determination for the formerly colonized regions has become an accepted principle of international relations.

It was not so in 1919. In the period after the Armistice Lawrence's was one of the few voices of conscience — and surely the most effective one — urging Great Britain, France and the other Western powers to uphold certain of their commitments and to respect the right of the Arab peoples to self-determination. He retained a concept of the British Empire but it was an empire of voluntary affiliation for mutual advantage, not one of conquest and control. His prediction that our allies of the future would come from those different from ourselves, even from peoples "most active in agitating against us," is proving generally true, although his hope of collaboration between the Jews of Palestine and their Arab neighbors is far from being fulfilled.

The relations between the formerly colonized peoples and their colonial masters have shifted radically in the half century since Versailles. The residues of nineteenth-century imperialism are vanishing, giving way to new forms of dominance by the major world powers. The "newer men, with a fresher culture," of whom Lincoln Steffens wrote, have in some instances, taken over.

FIVE

THE YEARS IN THE RANKS, 1922–1935

25

The Service Years: An Overview

There is little that can be said of a period devoted to self-effacement."[1] This statement is the last entry in Lawrence's RAF service record. His biographers seem largely to have agreed with it. The years in which Lawrence served as an enlisted man in the air force and the army have been relatively neglected by them. But I find that although Lawrence's accomplishments were less dramatic than those of the war and postwar political years, this period was equally rich, and formed a vital part of his life and legend. His membership in the ranks became the central focus of his life.

During this time Lawrence published a limited ("subscribers'") edition of *Seven Pillars of Wisdom* and a commercial abridgment of it, *Revolt in the Desert*. He wrote his other original book, *The Mint* (it was not published until after his death), and published a translation of Homer's *Odyssey* (the only work issued under the name of Shaw). He also translated a French book about a California redwood tree, wrote prefaces or introductions to several English works, published anonymously a number of reviews, and wrote great amounts of literary criticism, principally in letters to his friends and literary associates. Lawrence further enriched his personal associations through a number of new friendships, especially with well-known writers.

The most important sources for these years are Lawrence's letters. He wrote several thousand, only a fraction of which have been published, and complained ceaselessly at the task of keeping up his voluminous correspondence. Of particular value are the more than three hundred letters to Charlotte Shaw that are now in the British Museum. The range of his relationships had become enormous by the end of his life. His letters are of particular value in understanding them because of his ability to write in a manner that conveyed the actual quality of his relationship with each of his correspondents. This was deliberate on Lawrence's part. "Each [letter] tries to direct itself as directly as it can towards my picture of the person I am writing to," he wrote Eric Kennington in 1934, "and if it does not seem to me (as I write it) that it makes contact — why then I write no more that night."[2]

Also essential to an appreciation of Lawrence as a human being are the personal accounts of him that I received from the men with whom he served — they were always eager to talk about their friend. In addition, Mrs. Charles Rivington, a friend of mine who had come to know many of these men, had collected their reminiscences and very kindly shared them with me. I regret that her untimely death in 1971 prevented her from writing a full picture, based on her own research, of Lawrence's life in the ranks.[3]

"My ambition to serve in [the air force] dates — concretely — from 1919: and nebulously from early 1917, before there was an Air Force," Lawrence explained to Herbert Baker.[4] His war experience in the Middle East had impressed upon him the potential effectiveness of air power when the military operations had to cover long distances, and his three months with the crew of the Handley-Page squadron in 1919 "put the complete wind up me" about the air and aircraft.[5] Arnold Lawrence confirmed his brother's enthusiasm: "He obviously enjoyed the companionship and appreciated both the mechanics' and pilots' dedication to their jobs and their skill in bringing so many of those worn-out planes to their destination (including the one in which he was)."[6] It is possible that even if T.E. could have been admitted readily into the countries of the Middle East after the peace settlements, he might still have chosen to enlist in the RAF rather than to continue his archeological work.

In earlier conversations with Trenchard after the war Lawrence had spoken of his interest in joining "this air force of yours,"[7] but Trenchard had assumed that Lawrence meant service as an officer. As long as Lawrence was involved in his political strategies in behalf of the Arabs, he put off his plans to enlist. Then on January 5, 1922, he wrote Trenchard that he would "like to join the R.A.F. — in the ranks of course." He wanted to develop his skill as a writer and saw "the sort of subject I need in the beginning of your force . . . and the best place to see a thing from is the ground. It wouldn't 'write' from the officer level."[8] But when he entered the service seven months later, his motives for doing so were far more personal than literary. Even so, he was considered for the post of RAF historian for two years after he enlisted.

Much has been written about Lawrence's motives for joining the RAF. It has been assumed that his reasons were hidden, even from himself. But actually, in his letters and conversations, he revealed — almost casually at times — what the psychological sources of his action were and that he knew, to a considerable extent, what they were. In fact, his insight into the unconscious sources of his motivation was uncommonly deep. As is characteristic, however, of explanations involving psychological processes that relate to unconscious ideas, his revelations seem incomplete. The incompleteness is not just another example of Lawrence's need to tease, to provoke curiosity. Anyone who attempts to convey to himself or anyone else psychological processes that have unconscious origins is bound to come up with only partial explanations. The deeper motives continually act upon each other at a number of levels, both within the personality and in relation to the outside world. They rarely can be viewed satisfactorily by themselves.

By the time Lawrence joined the RAF he was in a deeply troubled state — eating and sleeping poorly, quite agitated, and with no task ahead of him that could fulfill his needs. He had completed recently his third and last version of *Seven Pillars of Wisdom*, and the labor of rewriting, which entailed reliving his war experiences, had "excited" him to the point where he was "nearly dotty."[9] In this shaken state he needed to have basic requirements met — for food, shelter, companionship and security. Furthermore, he regarded himself as guilty, not simply because he felt that his leadership had ended in the betrayal of his Arab followers, or because he had given in to unacceptable sexual and aggressive impulses during the campaigns, but more fundamentally because he continued to be aware in himself of desires, ambitious and erotic, which, to his exacting conscience, were totally repugnant. He entered the ranks to cure himself of wishes, to do penance, and "to kill old Adam," as he phrased it bluntly to another airman.[10]

But Lawrence was not simply a twentieth century anchorite seeking a monastic existence and solitary escape. He remained a creative person, with a need for companionship and a powerful drive to be useful and to be engaged in meaningful work. What he required, therefore, was a situation that could meet his dependency needs, shackle his sinful self in chains, and yet provide opportunities for work he could value, while remaining at a lowly level that offered few conventional worldly rewards. The RAF, supplemented by his personal regimen of penance and self-discipline, fulfilled all these requirements splendidly. He had found after several months in the ranks "that it was a life that suited me exactly and if I could be always healthy I'd wish to keep in it forever."[11]

During his thirteen years as an airman and a private, Lawrence succeeded, in his view, in transforming himself into a person without desire or ambition, yet capable of useful work. He had to a degree escaped his expanding legend, which corresponded so little to his experience of himself. "My 'personality,' like the Arthurian legend, enthralls the mystical-minded. All punk, I'm afraid," he wrote in 1934.[12] But in the service "they regard my legend as a huge joke: If it wasn't *my* legend, I'd do ditto."[13] So thorough, however, was this transformation, and so dependent had he become upon the RAF, that after his discharge Lawrence seemed to have no motive for further activity. Less than three months later he was dead following an accident on his motorcycle.

Lawrence's explanations to his friends of his reasons for joining or remaining in the ranks seemed to vary with his situation and his moods as the years went by; yet if looked at in their totality from the standpoint of his psychology they are internally consistent. In 1922 he sought to find himself "on common ground with other men";[14] in February 1924 it was "the failure" of *Seven Pillars* that "broke my nerve, and sent me into the RAF," and "the assured bread and butter feels better than a gamble outside."[15] Later in 1924 he explained that he had joined because "[I had] looked back on my political record, and found it bad."[16] The following year he wrote Mrs. Shaw that he wished to "tie myself down beyond the hope or power of movement" to "keep my soul in prison, since nowhere else can it exist in safety."[17] In India two years later he gained more objectivity and wrote, "Penance, promise, obstinacy, a vow, self-hypnotisation . . . you catalogue my motives. Isn't it possible I like being in the R.A.F.?"[18] And two months after that he wrote of the RAF: "It has been a real refuge to me, and I am grateful to the Air people for taking me in."[19] After his valuable work began on air-sea rescue boats, which occupied the last six years of his life, he stresses less these inner forces and places more emphasis on his mechanical work in a mechanical age.

Lawrence's fellow airmen and army enlisted men came to accept him naturally as one of their number and seemed to grasp intuitively the needs that his military service fulfilled. But his continuing service in the ranks bewildered his intellectual friends. George Bernard Shaw, for all his witty, often accurate, teasing of his troubled friend, never grasped how essential the RAF was for Lawrence, or the seriousness of his purpose in staying in the ranks. "You suggest that I'm not genuine in the ranks: but I am," Lawrence insisted to Shaw in 1923. "People come into the army often," he explained, "not because it is brutal and licentious, but because they haven't done very well in the fight of daily living, and want to be spared the responsibility of ordering for themselves their homes and food and clothes and work — or even the intensity of their work. Regard it as an asylum for the little-spirited."[20] Five years later he had got no further in making Shaw understand, although he had not given up trying. "Only please don't think it is a game," he wrote from India, "just because I laugh at myself and everybody else. That's Irish, or an attempt to keep sane."[21]

Lawrence had an even more difficult time with Robert Graves, who objected particularly to his assumption of a "plain-man tone" with what Graves considered to be "forced ingenuousness." "Come off it, R.G.!"

Lawrence wrote to him in 1933. "Your letter forgets my present state. It is so long since we met that you are excused knowing that I'm now a fitter, very keen and tolerably skilled on engines, but in no way abstract. I live all of every day with real people, and concern myself only in the concrete. The ancient self-seeking and self-devouring T.E.L. of Oxford (and T.E.S. of the *Seven Pillars* and *The Mint*) is dead. Not regretted either. My last ten years have been the best of my life. I think I shall look back on my 35–45 period as golden."[22]

The meaning for Lawrence of his experience in the ranks naturally evolved and shifted as his situation or station changed and the years passed, but his companionship with the other men was at all times of great importance to him. Each man, including himself, had in some way been "hurt or broken in civvy life, to the point of taking flight from it,"[23] and this fact formed a strong bond with his fellow airmen and tank corpsmen. The barrack rooms and mess halls, where men ate and slept together without differentiation, helped Lawrence achieve his goal of feeling ordinary, of obliterating any sense of being special. He could not have accomplished this as an officer. At Cranwell he wrote Mrs. Shaw: "G.B.S. talks to me as if I were one of his crowd: the policeman (in the guard room) as if I were one of his crowd: and I get frustrated and sorrowful. Hut 105 is balm to this: for there we are all on the same footing. . . . Equality could only exist when it was compulsory."[24]

Lawrence's relationships with the enlisted men and officers he met at the various stations to which he was assigned (more than ten in all) varied greatly, but he seemed never to forget the friendships he had made at previous stations. Once he had formed even an acquaintance with another airman or tank corpsman Lawrence maintained an unending interest in his marriages, love affairs, babies, family life, illnesses and jobs (in and out of the service). If the man was interested in writing, Lawrence's interest extended to it as well, and he used his contact in the publishing world (usually without the man's knowledge) to bring the work to the attention of an appropriate editor or publisher. Lawrence's generosity with money could only be described as saintlike, and he gave away any savings he might accumulate from his wages, royalties or other sources of income so readily that he was in fact constantly quite poor. This extraordinary generosity was not limited to airmen, but was extended to officers and their families (on one occasion to the widow of the chief of air staff), artists with whom he had worked, booksellers and writers — to anyone, in fact, whom he thought in need or who approached him for help.

Most of the enlisted men were younger than he and he seemed to achieve a kind of older brother closeness with several of them. One airman he met at the end of 1922 at Farnborough, R. M. Guy, was a particularly handsome young man ("beautiful, like a Greek God," according to another of his companions),[25] and Lawrence became especially fond of him, as he did of A. E. "Jock" Chambers. On Christmas Day in 1923 Lawrence wrote to Guy, whom he sometimes addressed with pet names such as "Poppet" or "Rabbit," of the closeness they had achieved.

Lawrence's influence upon these men was considerable. Several of his former companions have told me of the difference he made in their lives. Some spoke of being shown aspects of the world they had been ignorant of, while others stressed a kind of moral lift or turn their lives took following the association with Lawrence. Some he introduced to literature, which then became a lifelong interest for them. All experienced an increased confidence and an ability to think things out for themselves as a result of knowing him.

A passage in a letter written in 1924 to Mrs. Shaw, when Lawrence was in the Tank Corps, conveys some of these characteristics of his relationships: "The Air Force fellows are like Oxf. undergrads in their 2nd term . . . buds just opening after the restraint of school and home. Their first questioning. Their first doubt of an established convention or law or practice, opens a floodgate in their minds: for if one thing is doubtful all things are doubtful: the world to them has been a concrete, founded, polished thing: the first crack is portentous. So the Farnborough fellows used to come to me there, after 'lights out,' and sit on the box on my bed, and ask questions about every rule of conduct and experience, about the mind and soul and body: and I, since I was lying on my back could answer succinctly and with illumination. Those who seek me out down here are the keenest ones, and they have been following up the chase of the great why themselves, since I disappeared."[26]

George Bernard Shaw provided a somewhat different view of Lawrence among his enlisted friends: "I must confess that when they invited me to tea he looked very like Colonel Lawrence with several aides-de-camp."[27]

In spite of the depth of these relationships Lawrence never felt that he was altogether "one with my fellows." He was not sure whether this was his "solitary misfortune" or "the common fate of man, and that only myself complains of it more."[28] My own impression is that it was both, and that his critical nature maintained him always at an amused distance from others even when he wished to be closer. He always knew in some part of his mind that he was leading a boy's life in the service and could not give himself over to it completely. "They do not allow, in the services, for grown ups," he wrote E. M. Forster; ". . . the whole treatment and regimen is designed for the immature."[29] But as he wrote Mrs. Shaw in 1932, he had found intimacy in the barracks: "a support of one by the next, great friendliness: and, as G.B.S. so well says, the freedom to do all things that a man's hands were made for. The peace-time soldiering is still the best lay-brotherhood. Look at my life."[30]

Lawrence's influence in the ranks extended beyond his impact on individual men. As in the desert campaigns and the political settlements after the war, his influence was out of proportion to his position, only this time he held no rank higher than the equivalent of corporal. As he had done before, however, Lawrence exerted his influence not by assuming power directly, but by engaging and sometimes capturing the minds of those who held power, and then, through the force of his intellect and personality, persuading these individuals to carry out what he urged. His desire, Lawrence wrote to a member of Parliament who had become his friend, was to make the services "decent for all classes, please, by delivering us of superstitions and callousness."[31]

Although Lawrence did not hesitate to press his arguments for service reforms upon prominent civilian friends like Lady Astor and Ernest Thurtle (Both M.P.'s), Liddell Hart, John Buchan, Churchill and George Bernard Shaw, it was through Hugh Trenchard, chief of air staff from 1919 to 1929 and "Father of the RAF," that Lawrence exerted his most important influence. Trenchard and Lawrence felt an intense mutual respect and liking for one another. "Allenby, Winston and you: That's my gallery of chiefs to date. Now there'll be a come down," he wrote to Trenchard when he learned of Trenchard's plans to retire.[32] "He [Trenchard] is as simply built as Stonehenge," Lawrence wrote to Herbert Baker, in images that must have appealed to his architect friend, "and serves equally as well for a temple, or a public meeting place or monument. Altogether one of my admirations: though I fear he cannot follow the wimbling and wambling of my career. I puzzle Trenchard, and he misunderstands me, often. Not that any such tiny detail could distress him; or blot his greatness, in my eyes."[33] To another friend:

"He sees the R.A.F. from the top, and I see it from the bottom, and each of us no doubt thinks he sees straight enough: but I swear I'm as keen on it as he is: and I do all I can, down here, to make it run smoothly. It's only the little unimportant things in the R.A.F. that make airmen's lives sometimes a misery."[34] And to Thurtle: "Curse the Brass Hats: poor reptiles. They always swear that these things are necessary to discipline. A word in your ear — discipline itself is not necessary. We fight better without it. Yet, being Englishmen we are born with it and can no more lose it than our fingernails."[35]

Lawrence tended to be flattering when writing to Trenchard, especially, it seems, when he was worried the chief was vexed with him. In his letters to Trenchard Lawrence would sometimes enclose lists on separate sheets of "trifles" he thought should be changed as "it is the trifles that irritate and do the most harm,"[36] and he urged Trenchard to communicate more directly with the men in the ranks so he could learn of their needs and hear their complaints.

The dignified Trenchard became on occasion quite annoyed with his most celebrated aircraftsman. Trenchard had a habit of paying unexpected, unheralded visits to the various RAF stations in order to make, undetected, his own private inspections. Once he visited a station in a peculiar horse-drawn carriage, hoping that he would not be identified. But Lawrence, who was on guard duty, caught a glimpse of the air marshal inside, presented arms smartly, and yelled, "Guard turn out." Trenchard's cover was completely blown. Lawrence then proceeded to arrange a reception for the chief with as many appropriate honors as could be managed on so short a notice. As Trenchard pulled away in his carriage he glared fiercely out at Lawrence and boomed indignantly, "SILLY FOOL!" and slammed down the window.[37]

Many of the service practices that Lawrence urged be corrected were in fact "trifles," but others were more serious. Some were eliminated as a result of Lawrence's efforts while he was still serving. Others remained to be changed after he left the RAF. Among the causes Lawrence championed were the elimination of bayonets from airmen's rifles ("Have a bayonet put in your IN tray every morning: and say to yourself 'I must get rid of that today,'" he wrote Trenchard);[38] abolition of the death penalty for cowardice and desertion in the face of the enemy; the abolition of compulsory church parades; the elimination of swagger sticks for officers and men; change from monthly to yearly kit inspection; weekend passes; posting of servicemen to stations nearer their homes; permission to leave the service voluntarily (this was a provision of his own enlistment, and he felt would encourage officers to treat their men more decently); encouraging the wearing of civvies; less arbitrary deprivation of leaves; and permission for pillion-riding on motorcycles ("airmen are the only people in England forbidden it: not soldiers, not sailors. It's rather an insult to what we fondly hope is the most dangerous service").[39] A pocket diary found after Lawrence's death and dated 1933 contained jottings of almost a hundred additional service changes and reforms he thought were needed, some related to those listed above, and some quite new. Many concerned the construction and fitting of marine craft, especially the air-sea salvage boats on which he was then working.[40]

Perhaps as important as these tangible reforms that Lawrence urged and sometimes achieved in collaboration with his chiefs and influential friends, was the subtler influence he seems to have exerted at virtually each station at which he served. It is hard to convey this quality. His commanders have characterized it as a morally uplifting influence, a subtle force that raised the standards of efficiency, improved the quality of work, and had a beneficial effect upon the tenor of relations on the base and upon morale generally. In some instances Lawrence's influence remained, like a legend, bringing about change at a particular station long after he was gone. The degree to which this almost spiritual force affected the spirit of the RAF, especially in the ranks, has never, to my knowledge, been given any attention. Lawrence's achievements in the design, construction, fitting, and overall development of small, maneuverable, fast marine craft for use in the air age — the major achievement of his last six years — also awaits careful and objective study.

Lawrence developed a network of personal relationships outside the RAF and Tank Corps, and somehow was able to maintain his friendships with these "posh" types without evoking resentment among his service friends. It was not simply a matter of isolating or compartmentalizing his various human contacts — although he could be skillful at doing this. Rather, he was able to integrate them smoothly into his own life by bringing together — usually at his cottage, Clouds Hill — men from differing social and economic backgrounds, and thereby he enabled artists, writers, airmen and tank corpsmen to enjoy each other's common humanity. E. M. Forster helped Lawrence look after one tank corpsman who was in difficulty and wrote in this connection, "The lower classes fill me with despair, and if I did not care for them I should lead a calmer life."[41] Yet both Forster and Lawrence grasped an element of falseness in this easy communication across class and economic lines. "How right you are that these chaps, fellows, whatever one calls them, like to be 'posh,'" Forster wrote to his friend, "whereas we are amused by them most when they are dirty, off their guard, and natural. Hence a fundamental insincerity in one's intercourse with them."[42]

During these years Lawrence developed new friendships: with Thomas and Florence Hardy, George Bernard and Charlotte Shaw, David Garnett, E. M. Forster, John Buchan, Noel Coward, Frederic Manning, William Roberts, Edward Elgar, Basil Liddell Hart, and Henry Williamson, and with other writers, artists, actors, booksellers, publishers and political figures. And he kept up, although sometimes intermittently, the friendships he had made earlier in his life.

From the emotional standpoint Lawrence's most important relationship during this period was with Charlotte Shaw. The attachment began in December 1922. She wrote him an ecstatic appreciation of *Seven Pillars of Wisdom* ("I don't believe anything really like it has been written before") while he was still eagerly awaiting G.B.S.'s critique.[43] As a basis for their close association Lawrence and Charlotte Shaw had in common similar Anglo-Irish backgrounds with overwhelming mothers and gentler fathers, inability to come to terms with sexuality and child-rearing and a number of emotional conflicts related in one way or another to consciences that were overly severe. "I have in me (what you have so much more strongly)," Mrs. Shaw wrote to Lawrence in 1927, "a fearful streak of conscience, and sense of duty, complicated by a sensitiveness that is nothing less than a disease."[44]

Because she did not make the same demands as his mother did, and because of the unobtrusiveness of her understanding, Lawrence was able to confide in Mrs. Shaw, although he had to deny any maternal element in the relationship. "Let me acquit you of all suspicion of 'mothering' me," he wrote in the summer of 1928. "With you I have no feeling or suspicion of clash at all. You are (probably) older than me [she was thirty-one years older, actually], you are one of the fixed ones, socially and by right of conquest: yet I talk to you exactly as I feel inclined, without any sense that I'm talking up, or you down. Which is very subtle and successful of you. I think it represents reality too, in your attitude, as well as mine. My mother would be easy with me, too, if she didn't think of mothering."[45]

Lawrence visited the Shaws frequently at their country home at Ayot St. Lawrence in Hertfordshire, but when Lawrence was on distant assignments Charlotte sent him — according to Shaw's secretary, Blanche Patch, who prepared the packages — "chocolates from Gunter's, China tea from Fortnum and Mason's; at Christmas *foie gras* and peach-fed ham to Clouds Hill; to Karachi chocolates, cake and marrons glacés."[46]

It was in long, often highly personal letters, however, that the relationship reached its greatest intensity. Encouraged by Mrs. Shaw's empathy and objectivity, Lawrence shared with her his feelings and conflicts. They exchanged opinions on books, politics, and a wide variety of other subjects, and Lawrence sent her his most treasured writings, including his personal anthology of poems, "Minorities," and the manuscript of *The Mint*. "You are rather like the Semitic God, of whom it is easy to say what isn't, but impossible what is," Lawrence wrote to her in 1929. "I have never tried to describe you in words. Did I tell you that the blend of you and G.B.S. was a symphony of smooth and sharp, like bacon and eggs? Possibly. Conjoined you would be complete humanity. . . . As for feeling 'at home' with you: this is not the word. I do not wish to feel at home. You are more completely restful than anyone I know, and that is surely better? Homes are ties, and with you I am quite free."[47]

Lawrence seems to have written nothing of his own for publication (except his technical treatise for the RAF in 1932 on a type of boat he was developing) after the expansion and reworking of his notes for *The Mint* in 1928, and after completing the translation of the *Odyssey* in 1931, composed no other works of literature. He remained to the end of his life a prolific reader and a lover of books, especially contemporary English and French works (particularly finely printed ones), but seemed often to use reading as a way of substituting an alternative world for the one in which he was living. "I have half an hour in the morning, before breakfast, which I keep for my own reading," he wrote to F. N. Double-day. "One can't *read* in odd half-hours," he complained, as "reading is to soak oneself hour after hour all day in a single real book, until the book is realler than one's chair or world."[48] Lawrence enjoyed most, however, being a teacher of those not previously exposed to literature and poetry, and a kind of freelance critic and champion of freedom of the press for young writers and poets, who often sent him their works.

Although Lawrence took no official part in political life after his enlistment, he was willing to offer his opinions, especially to his various friends in policy-making positions, when consulted (and sometimes when not) on questions involving the Middle East and other topics. He would also on occasion defend his own part in the war and the postwar settlements if he felt it was being distorted by biased newspaper coverage. His interest in political affairs was, however, quite spotty, which raises some doubt whether he could ever have been willing to take on an important post in public life again had he lived longer. He never once, for example, in his long association with George Bernard Shaw mentioned or expressed curiosity about the Russian Revolution, although Shaw had visited the Soviet Union and Lawrence thought Lenin a very great man. The pattern of these years was not political, but Lawrence continued to be a useful public servant on a smaller, more restricted scale.

Music took on increasing importance for Lawrence, and he loved to sit in rapt concentration letting the sounds wash over him. Although he had felt it necessary to abandon archeology as a profession, he never lost interest in the architecture of the Middle Ages. He enjoyed visiting castles and cathedrals in England, and instructing his companions in their details and history. An interest in fine craftsmanship, dating back to childhood, took on new importance in his later years. His cottage, Clouds Hill, which he repaired and outfitted largely himself, and the RAF boats he worked on after 1929, offered him many opportunities for realizing his desire for perfection in artistic craftsmanship. "If the creative instinct had to have an outlet, it was in the solution of the mechanical difficulties and the gradual refinement of the RAF boats," one of his airmen friends wrote after Lawrence's death.[49]

The first months of Lawrence's indoctrination into the RAF at Uxbridge were torture for him and in many ways traumatic. He maintained his equilibrium by writing notes about his experience each night in the barracks. Later at Karachi in India (1927–1928) he reworked these notes and expanded them with entries from the period at the RAF Cadet College at Cranwell in Lincolnshire (1925–1926) which was, by contrast, more humane. The result was *The Mint*, Lawrence's chronicle of service in the ranks, which was not published in a trade edition until 1955. Lawrence had meant, he wrote Wavell in 1929, "to write a 'big' book (not in size: in matter) about the R.A.F.," but the RAF "threw me out, and so broke the continuity of my experience."[50] He pulled strings and in March 1923 was admitted to the Tanks Corps, where he served until July 1925, when alarms of suicide mobilized his friends to induce the British government to permit him to return to the RAF.

The first months of service in the Tanks Corps, when he had once again to go through basic training, were among the most anguish-filled times of his life. Obtaining Clouds Hill in the summer of 1923 gave Lawrence a place of his own and he was able to find relief there from the grimness of service life. After he was readmitted Lawrence served in the RAF continuously for nearly ten years and retired three months before his death. He was stationed in India for two years, from the beginning of 1927 to the beginning of 1929, a period in which he limited his life to the activities within the camps themselves, began his translation of the *Odyssey,* and attended to the voluminous correspondence he carried on with Mrs. Shaw and other friends. He did not venture from his stations in India, and was observed by the officers and other airmen to have periods of despondency and depression.

Lawrence was brought back to England abruptly early in 1929 as the result of a bout of publicity, linking him incorrectly to a rebellion in Afghanistan. During the remaining six years of RAF service he found a new calling as a sort of marine engineer-mechanic, designing, developing and testing new kinds of boats. He achieved peace and personal equilibrium during these years, but he recognized that its price was a considerable restriction of the range and depth of his activities and sensibilities. "It is the life of the mechanic," he wrote Robert Graves in 1933, "concrete, superficial, every-day: unlike the past excitement into which the war plunged me. I know the excitement in me is dead, and happier so."[51]

During part of this six-year period he was at Mount Batten Station, near Plymouth, where he grew close to Wing Commander Sydney Smith and Mrs. Smith. From Mount Batten Lawrence was posted much of the time after 1930 to Southampton for work at the Scott Paine boatyards, and continued to work there until late in 1934, when he was posted to Bridlington on the Yorkshire coast for the last four months of his service. He had a brief period of retirement at Clouds Hill before the fatal accident occurred. Despite a persistent nihilism during the later years of his life, Lawrence never lost a perceptual sensuousness, an openness to the impression of the world around him. He never lost his ability to enjoy speed, the sting of spray or the taste of ripe blackberries "all cold with rain."[52]

David Garnett, whom Lawrence took on an air-sea rescue operation in one of the motorboats with which he was working, has described the "red-faced, weather-beaten, tough mechanic" that Lawrence had become after a decade in the ranks. "We were happy: eager, unself-conscious," Garnett wrote, "made accomplices by the excitement of the flying spray, the work, the boat herself. . . . I think it was then that I first fully realized how wise he had been to enlist in the ranks of the R.A.F. He had done a great deal for it, but it had done a great deal for him by giving him the ease and intimacy which comes from doing work with other men."[53]

Lawrence had visions of a new age in which mankind would leap forward into its last challenge, the mastery of the air. "For thousands of years nature has held this mastery of the last element in her lap, patiently waiting for our generation, and you and I are of the lucky ones chosen," he wrote to another aircraftsman.[54] In 1933 he wrote a few excited lines about the conquest of the air and of scaling the heavens, "as lords that are expected," seeming to anticipate the event of the entry of man into space.[55] He saw the skilled worker as important in reaching this goal: "The conquest of the last element, the air, seems to me the only major task of our generation; and I have convinced myself that progress today is made not by the single genius, but by the common effort. To me it is the multitude of rough transport drivers, filling all the roads of England every night, who make this the mechanical age. And it is the airmen, the mechanics, who are overcoming the air."[56]

It will, of course, never be known whether Lawrence would have played a part in accomplishing this remaining "major task," whether he would have found a way to make such achievement consistent with his life of renunciation. For only three months after writing these lines T. E. Lawrence was dead.

Ross: The First
RAF Enlistment

Lawrence received proofs of the last eight parts of *Seven Pillars of Wisdom* from the Oxford *Times* printers on July 21, 1922,[1] and eight copies of the book were subsequently printed and bound. The following month he sent a copy for comment to George Bernard Shaw, whom he had recently met for the first time, and another to Edward Garnett of Jonathan Cape, the publishers. With the completion of the book, which Lawrence would continue to perfect for four more years, a phase of his life came to an end. Air Marshal Trenchard made special arrangements for Lawrence's enlistment in the RAF and gave orders to his chief personnel officer, Oliver Swann, to carry them out. "He is taking this step in order to learn what is the life of an airman," Trenchard informed Swann, and "on receipt of any communication from him through any channel, asking for his release orders are to be issued for his discharge forthwith without formality."[2]

Swann informed Lawrence on August 16 of the arrangements and he was inducted secretly two weeks later at the recruiting depot in London under the name of John Hume Ross. (He used this name for his bank account for the rest of his life and for the authorship of his translation of *Le Gigantesque* [*The Forest Giant*] in 1924, although he used it personally for less than five months.) Arnold Lawrence stated that his brother picked the name at home one day when their mother happened to speak about a Mrs. Ross, and "he said that would do — he was looking for a short name."[3]

In *The Mint* Lawrence says that he was so anxious before he went to the enlistment depot that he had a bout of "melting of the bowels," which he revealed had occurred at other times of crisis.[4] According to the account of the chief interviewing officer at the recruitment depot, Lawrence attempted initially to be inducted without using the influence of the Air Ministry that was available to him.[5] But he had no references with him and did not come up to medical standards. His brother has written that Lawrence had reached a state of nervous exhaustion by the time he went to the recruiting depot and had starved himself until he weighed about fifteen pounds less than his usual weight, despite the many lunch and dinner invitations of his friends.[6] Furthermore, he had scars on his back from the floggings at Der'a, which aroused suspicions at the depot ("Hullo, what the hell's those marks? Punishment?' 'No Sir, more like persuasion Sir, I think.' Face, neck, chest getting hot").[7] After the initial rejection Lawrence returned with an Air Ministry messenger bearing orders from higher up and was admitted.[8] Lawrence quickly wrote to Swann to thank him for his help and apologized to him for the trouble he had caused. "If I'd known I was such a wreck I'd have gone off and recovered before joining up," Lawrence wrote; "now the cure and the experiment must proceed together."[9]

Lawrence, like other RAF recruits, was sent to the training depot at Uxbridge, about ten miles west of London, where he underwent two months of grueling basic training, the misery and hardship of which were aggravated by the pain of a bone fragment (a relic of the 1919 Handley-Page crash) that was sticking into the inside of his chest wall.[10] As mentioned previously, Lawrence has described his experience at Uxbridge in *The Mint,* a classic and honest picture of certain aspects of barrack life among enlisted men, a life that, since the literature that grew out of World War II and subsequent wars, has become more familiar to the general public. In *The Mint,* he conveys vividly, with great empathy for his fellow sufferers, the raw brutality, vulgarity and crude four-letter humor that was commonplace in the basic training of enlisted men. Trenchard told Arnold Lawrence that he sacked the commander at Uxbridge after reading *The Mint.*[11]

One must read *The Mint* to appreciate the utter degradation to which Lawrence submitted himself or was subjected at Uxbridge. He seemed at times to degrade himself beyond what was necessary and imposed by the camp authorities. Both figuratively and literally he worked in and became covered with excrement and swill until it "oozed slowly from my soiled things and stagnated in a pool over me."[12] Although he had in a sense put shackles on himself by enlisting in the first place, he had reason to rage at the tyranny of the noncommissioned officers and the abuses of authority that were imposed on the lowly "erks" [airmen]. Lawrence did not rebel ("Rebellious again? Not on your life").[13] He protested bitterly in *The Mint* against the unnecessary humiliations imposed upon him and the other men. Instead he was conscientious and correct, and struggled to master the drill and other routines. He submitted to authority, allowing the RAF to "bray me and re-mould me after its pattern" (the "minting" of the book's title).[14]

In the hut he found a fellowship among the men, sharing with many of them the basic sexual shyness which lay behind their vulgarity and verbal lechery and bravado. "We attain an instant friendliness," he wrote, "and there stuck, three paces short of intimacy."[15] *The Mint* contains familiar psychological themes, recalling the struggles of Lawrence's youth, especially the need to master fear. "The root-trouble is fear," he wrote, "fear of falling, fear of breaking down."[16] And: "Here I have been on my own, and up against it: stretched almost beyond my failing body's bearing to sustain the competition of youth. Depot will have the backward-looking warmth of probably my last trial: survived at least, if not very creditably. Though sometimes I've laughed aloud while I cried hardest into my note-book. And the gain of it is that I shall never be afraid of men, again."[17]

Lawrence worked at Uxbridge to develop photography as a trade, having had considerable earlier experience in it. Gradually he found that the self-imposed limitations of military life were making their mark. "We have grown," he wrote, "to do only what we're told. . . . This learning to be sterile, to bring forth nothing of our own, had been the greater half of our training and the more painful half."[18] As much as possible Lawrence felt that he had shed his past identity and had "attained a flight-entity which is outside our individualities."[19] "The R.A.F.," he wrote, "is now myself," and if someone "offends the others I am indignant. He sins against the air."[20]

But, as among the Arabs, Lawrence's solidarity with the other men was incomplete. "I joined in high hope of sharing their tastes and manners and life: but my nature persists in seeing all things in the mirror of itself, and not with a direct eye. So I shall never be quite happy, with the happiness of these fellows who find their nectar of life, and its elixir, in the deep stirring of some seminal gland. It seems I can get nearest it by proxy, by using my powers (so sharpened by experience and success in war and diplomacy) to help them preserve their native happiness against the Commandants and Pearsons [a sergeant who tormented the airmen] of this world."[21]

"My Uxbridge notes dated from 1922 when it was a different place," Lawrence wrote to an officer there in 1933. "Today's recruits are fairly happy there, and we were NOT!"[22] Perhaps his influence, both directly and through his legend, had helped to achieve some change. "Lawrence was already a fabled ghost at Uxbridge by the time the class of April, 1937, discovered the rigours of that place, and the ghost was a dear one," one former A/C 2, E. B. Metcalfe, wrote in 1955.[23] Change for the better had occurred, but more important than that was the continuing influence of Lawrence's ghost. When a mathematics instructor admonished the 1937 recruits that Lawrence of Arabia had been in their classroom and they should behave in a worthy fashion, "it hardly seemed that the famous erk was on our side. Yet with the days that followed, it quickly became evident that dead as he was, he was the only source we had for any redress of grievance."[24]

Lawrence had developed a reputation for intervention and, according to this ex-erk, his memory gave the men solace for the annoyances of service life. "A large book could be compiled of his acts, apocryphal or not, by which he sought on behalf of some unhappy blighter to get him compassionate leave, excused fatigues, reduction of sentence, or even his ticket. 'That ———— wouldn't have talked to Lawrence like that,' an erk would mutter after having a stripe torn off him for some good or bad reason."[25] Whether or not the stories about Lawrence were true would be "missing the point to ask," Metcalfe continued, "for they bespoke an attitude with which it was pleasant and natural to identify oneself."

There were stories of Lawrence's wrath, successfully expressed against unjust authority, of his showing up at the homes of the great with uncouth RAF types, or of sending the "scruffiest rogue" with a message to represent him with full powers. In 1937 the airmen were convinced that when *The Mint* was published "they" [the officers] would have "had it." "What we believed basically was this: that he [Lawrence] was one of the thousands of skilled groundlings, the one who could hope for and gain recognition; that he had souped up the R.A.F.'s motor-boat section to perfection; and that he was a 'man' who was a man." *Seven Pillars of Wisdom* also had great meaning for the men, "for if such a hero could make himself one of our kind, did it not follow that we could make ourselves one of his kind?"[26]

Lawrence's letters of the Uxbridge period reflect little of the stresses he was undergoing at the camp, and to some of his friends he seems, out of fear of being found out, to have made no mention of his enlistment in the RAF. To others, who did know — Eric Kennington was one — he appeared steadier and more poised in his trim Air Force uniform.[27] His surviving letters of the period are concerned with arrangements for the illustration of *Seven Pillars*, and are a blend of apology for asking his worthier friends to read his inadequate production, and big hopes for the book, even the dream that he had succeeded in producing "an English fourth" on the titanic level of "The Karamazovs, Zarathustra and Moby Dick."[28]

One of the artists, Paul Nash, whom Lawrence asked to do the landscape illustrations from his photographs, wrote enthusiastically of his assignment: "I think its going to be great fun. . . . O what a dream! Lawrence is of the salt of the earth and I know he's doing much of this simply to help painters who find a difficulty in *affording* to paint."[29]

Although he constantly expressed his disappointment with the book and devalued it, Lawrence seemed to understand its value at another level, at least as a personal testimony. He described it to Edward Garnett as "a summary of what I have thought and done and made of myself in these thirty years."[30] And in another letter to Garnett: "It was written in dead earnest and with as much feeling as a 'don possessed' can muster: and I think it's all spiritually true."[31] Garnett was very appreciative and encouraging and wrote to Lawrence, "I feel somehow that your analysis of life may carry us *further:* there's a quality in your brain that suggests a new apprehension of things."[32] Garnett also began work on an abridgment of *Seven Pillars,* which Lawrence planned for a time to publish. At the same time Lawrence made arrangements with the young artist William Roberts to draw portraits of high-ranking British officers who played important roles in the Revolt.[33] "I like the complete book, of course, much better," he wrote to Garnett, "but I realize that artistically it has no shape: and morally I detest its intimacy."[34]

When he did refer to his enlistment in writing to his friends Lawrence stressed the loss of freedom and his plan to adjust to his shackles. "I got sick of things," he wrote to one, "and being penniless hopped off — into a kind of community, which does more work than worship, but is remote and cut off from normal ways. It will perhaps suit me — and if it doesn't I will have to suit it. . . . I haven't told anyone what I'm at, or where, except that I am travelling in China! You see, now I'm not my own master."[35]

On November 8 Lawrence was transferred to the RAF School of Photography at Farnborough. In a contemporary note found in the folds of the manuscript of *The Mint* Lawrence compared Farnborough with Uxbridge: "Odd that Uxbridge has so touched me that when I reached Farnborough its looseness and untidiness were disagreeable. Also, I felt lost (November 8). Small room of 12 beds, long classes and 9 months, saw the intimacy greater. Uxbridge diffident offering politeness. Here an understanding no less kind, but less courteous. Some soreness, resentment at multitudes of soldiers round us. Airmen feel so distinctly that they are not soldiers, and fear that outsiders may not see this so clearly as we do."[36]

Airman A. E. "Jock" Chambers, who became one of Lawrence's closest service friends, had a bunk next to his at Farnborough and found his friend in a very anxious and troubled state on arrival from Uxbridge. Lawrence slept little while at Farnborough, according to Chambers, and was disturbed by nightmares in which he would relive the horrors of his war experience, and Chambers did much to comfort his new friend and settle him down.[37]

Chambers furnished me with this account of his meeting with Lawrence at Farnborough:

> He settled in quite easily; his voice sounded posh and alarmed me at first, as we already had one ex-officer we were trying to educate. I've always liked books and as he emptied his kit bag, I spotted some that looked good, found

they were and borrowed them. Some time later, we were both detailed with two others for guard. I had no misgivings — it was nothing new to me; not so my chum. "Jock," he said, "I'm windy — can't slope arms or do any of the drill."[38] "Shut up," says I patronizingly. "Just watch me, follow my motions; nothing in it"; so we "poshed up" and on to Guard Mounting we went. "New Guard — slope arms": Me, in a whisper, "Sling it up cock." Just then Warren A.C. 2 plonk and very fat crossed the road in full view, dressed in khaki drab and carrying a heavy sack of tins as he staggered along. I couldn't resist saying . . . with *Hassan* in my mind [a book by Flecker, which Lawrence had lent Chambers], "Thou dragger of dead dogs." The next moment I heard Sgt. Major Pierce's voice, trembling with rage. "What the ——— hell are you laughing at, Ross?" He replied, "I wasn't laughing, Sgt. Major, just grinning." The Sgt. Major muttered, "I'll double you round the ——— square after this and we'll ——— see who laughs last!" The tension eased; we took over from the old guard and I became sentry no. 1.[39]

Although Lawrence was relieved to get away from Uxbridge, which his entreaties to Swann may have speeded, and found Farnborough almost "disagreeably loose" by comparison, he was unhappy there nevertheless — "a mean C.O. and a bad show Farnborough was," he wrote several years later.[40] Four days àfter his arrival there, he wrote Garnett: "Honestly, I hate this dirty living, and yet by the decency of the other fellows, the full dirtiness of it has not met me fairly. Isn't it a sign of feebleness in me, to cry out so against barrack-life? It means that I'm afraid (physically afraid) of other men: their animal spirits seems to me the most terrible companions to haunt a man: and I hate their noise. Noise seems to me horrible. And yet I'm a man, not different from them; certainly not better. What is it that makes me so damnably sensitive and so ready to cry out, and yet so ready to incur more pain? I wouldn't leave the R.A.F. tomorrow, for any job I was offered."[41]

In the meantime Lawrence eagerly pressed George Bernard Shaw for an opinion of his book. Shaw (referring to an episode before the capture of Aqaba) replied, "Patience, patience: do not again shoot your willing camel through the head," and admitted (on December 1, 1922) that he had only a chance to sample the book. His wife, he said, had "seized it first, and ploughed through from Alpha to Omega. It took months and months."[42]

Shaw worried Lawrence by comparing him with Charles "Chinese" Gordon, the fanatical defender of Khartoum. "You are evidently a very dangerous man," Shaw wrote; "most men who are any good are: there is no power for good that is not also a power for evil. You have a conscience which would have prevented you from acting as Gordon did in China; so there will be a deep difference; but I wonder what, after reading the book through, I will decide to do with you if ever I become one of the lords of the east. As I shant, perhaps I shall put you into a play"[43] (as, in fact, he did nine years later in *Too True to Be Good*).

Over the next few weeks Shaw, who still had not read the book through, indicated in subsequent letters that he thought *Seven Pillars* was a great work and should be published in its entirety. But in the meantime Charlotte Shaw had "devoured" the book from cover to cover. In November she wrote Sydney Cockerell, who had introduced Lawrence to the Shaws, that she was carried off her feet by it, and then on the last day of the year wrote Lawrence himself a letter of ecstatic praise, calling the book "one of the most amazingly individual documents that has ever been written."[44] Although Lawrence had continued planning an abridgment on the grounds that he detested "morally" the intimacy of the uncut version, she encouraged him to publish the whole work. Lawrence was naturally very much pleased and encouraged by Mrs. Shaw's letter, but wrote her that to publish the book in its entirety "was as improbable as that I'd walk naked down Piccadilly."[45] He did, however, consider with Edward Garnett a limited edition of two thousand copies of the complete book, but after the publicity about his identity burst in the press, Lawrence canceled plans to publish even an abridgment.[46]

Despite his complaints Lawrence was also finding that the air force contained for him "spots of light, very exciting and full of freshness."[47] He had been anxious about being discovered and while at Uxbridge wrote to William Roberts, "I should have told you before that I'm a photographer-mechanic in the R.A.F. — a tommy — and so cannot dispose of my own movements very certainly." He could not meet Roberts in London because "I'm in blue uniform, and don't want to be known in any of my old feeding-places! Please don't tell anyone that I've enlisted. The press would make a humourous story of it!"[48] This was prophetic, for on December 16 two reporters, who, according to a report of that date by the commanding officer "have certainly got wind of Ross," came to the camp looking for him.

Although his commanding officer and adjutant suspected who he was, "Ross's" identity as "Lawrence of Arabia" was confirmed to them by a staff officer visiting from the Air Ministry. This information was confined, at least at first, to a few officers at Farnborough. One of them, Charles Findlay, the adjutant, has written of what "a heavy responsibility" it was "to have a world-famous character on our hands as an AC2, and many times as I saw his slight, blue-uniformed figure engaged in some menial task I tried with difficulty to reconcile it with the romantic soldier who had inspired the grim, desert peoples to fight so audaciously."[49]

Although the airmen protected Lawrence's identity, it was, according to Chambers, betrayed by a café proprietor who offered Ross sanctuary and then sold the information to a reporter.[50] Lawrence on the other hand declared that it was "one of the beastly officers" who gave him away.[51]

Once his identity was generally known, Findlay wrote, "there is little doubt that his presence in the camp had an unsettling effect upon all ranks. As Adjutant of the School, I was very conscious of this."[52] I have found no evidence to support the assertion of Samuel Hoare, then secretary of state for air (who, Lawrence stated, "first moved to get me out of the RAF'"), that Lawrence had given the story to the press himself.[53] The "carelessness" of the Colonial Office in using Lawrence as a consultant in the handling of the 1922 crisis between Turkey and Greece may have played a part in the discovery of his identity in the RAF.[54] Guilfoyle, the commanding officer, in a report to Trenchard in mid-December wondered if "all the conjecture and talk" was worth the damage to discipline.[55]

George Bernard Shaw had been impatient with Lawrence about his RAF enlistment and suggested that if he did not know him better he might conclude that he was simply "a depressed mechanic oiling up fuselages for profanely abusive pilots."[56] He warned Lawrence (the press right then was already, according to Chambers, turning the camp into "a sort of fortress, besieged by a number of press men, and photographers")[57] that "[Lord] Nelson, slightly cracked after his whack on the head in the battle of the Nile, coming home and insisting on being placed at the tiller of a canal barge, and on being treated as nobody in particular, would have embarrassed the Navy far less . . . the thing is ridiculous."[58]

By the end of December the story was out in the press with the predictable uncrowned-king-of-Arabia-war-hero-turns-private headlines.[59] Shaw was not surprised when the story broke and wrote Lawrence realistically though rather unsympathetically:

> Like all heroes, and, I must add, all idiots, you greatly exaggerate your power of moulding the universe to your personal convictions. You have just had a crushing demonstration of the utter impossibility of hiding or disguising the monster you have created. It is useless to protest that Lawrence is not your real name. That will not save you. You may be registered as Higg the son of Snell or Brian de Bois Ghilbert or anything else; and if you had only stuck to it or else kept quiet, you might be Higg or Brian still. But you masqueraded as Lawrence and didn't keep quiet; and now Lawrence you will be to the end of your days, and thereafter to the end of what we call modern history. Lawrence may be as great a nuisance to you sometimes as G.B.S. is to me, or as Frankenstein found the man he had manufactured; but you created him, and must now put up with him as best you can.[60]

Trenchard came under increasing pressure to discharge Lawrence from the RAF. He might have been able to resist this had it not been for the junior officers who were concerned that Lawrence was in the RAF as an enlisted man to tell tales about them to their superior officers.[61] Finally Trenchard capitulated and Lawrence was discharged toward the end of January despite his willingness, as he wrote Graves at the time, "to eat dirt, till its taste is normal to me."[62]

27

The Years in the Tanks

Lawrence was deeply distressed by his expulsion and appealed for another chance to the RAF officials. He met with no success, although Trenchard offered him a commission, and Leopold Amery, first lord of the admiralty, proposed giving him a coastguard station or a lighthouse. But either was too isolated even for Lawrence.[1] He concluded his entreaty to the secretary to the chief of air staff by stating, "The last thing I wish to seem is importunate: but I'm so sure that I played up at Farnborough, and did good, rather than harm, to the fellows in the camp there with me, that I venture to put in a last word for myself."[2]

The problem was not, however, with the "fellows" but with the officers. Amery explained, "I had a word with Sam Hoare who assures me that it was nothing but the embarrassment of junior officers and others of knowing what your real identity was that made them decide to drop you out of the Air Force,"[3] and David Hogarth noted to George Bernard Shaw: "Some R.A.F. officers disliked commanding him and thought he laughed at their instructions."[4]

Lawrence returned to London after the ouster and spent six weeks looking for other work, but without success. "No one will offer me a job poor enough for my acceptance," he complained to one of his artist friends.[5] Despite his effort to maintain a cheerful front Lawrence was "in very low water" after his discharge and wrote to William Roberts, another artist, that he felt "rather stranded on the beach, in need of another job very soon, if I'm to go on living. It's rotten not having a trade of any sort."[6] A few days later Lawrence wrote with sardonic humor of his plight to a former friend from Arabian campaign days: "I'm very cheerful, and better off than you, for from my six months in the R.A.F. there survives a Brough [a motorbike], which is the paragon of everything on wheels, and on it I dash frantically about south England. Only the dreadful day creeps nearer when I'll have to eat the poor beast."[7]

Despite his situation (in a sense self-imposed, of course), Lawrence was able to overcome any personal resentment he may have felt and managed to find time to use his influence and prestige to help Trenchard with a problem he was having in relation to Iraq and more generally in regard to the future of the RAF.[8] He spent these weeks "haunting influential acquaintances in the political and literary spheres," primarily in search of another retreat, but he also spoke his mind about the Middle East and the future of the RAF to anyone who asked his opinion and probably to some who did not. The results are described by Andrew Boyle in his biography of Trenchard:

It would be easy to exaggerate the influence of one man, and an unhappy outsider at that, in improving the climate of opinion within a cautious and still uncommitted Government Committee. . . . Trenchard confirmed Amery's impression that Lawrence contributed something positive to the Iraq Committee's deliberations, almost in spite of himself, because his frankness was accepted as being based partly on experience, partly on disinterested conviction. Trenchard found not a little irony in the fact that Hoare, whose propriety had been outraged by the unmasking of "Air Mechanic Ross," and only slightly placated by his dismissal, presently began to benefit indirectly from Lawrence's freelance advocacy. . . . His expulsion "as a person with altogether too large a publicity factor for the ranks," to use his own phrase, was the only sensational happening that winter which brought the RAF to the public eye.[9]

By the beginning of March 1923, the efforts of Lawrence and his friends proved successful at the War Office and he was admitted into the army as a private in the Tank Corps and posted to Bovington Camp in Dorset. He assumed a new name — "Shaw" — this time. Despite Lawrence's protestation to Graves ("I took the name of Shaw because it was the first one-syllabled one which turned up in the Army List Index") and to others that the new name had no special significance,[10] I am convinced that it was based upon an identification, perhaps unconscious, with the Shaws, to whom Lawrence was becoming strongly attached. Certainly he developed a deepening admiration, approaching adulation, for G.B.S. and a dependence of even greater strength upon Shaw's wife.

Despite his acknowledged aim of self-degradation, Lawrence found life among the ranks in the Tank Corps initially intolerable, especially as he had to endure once again a period of basic training. He seemed to have forgotten his unhappiness at Farnborough and to remember only the positive aspects of his experience there, whereas the army, he felt, was totally hateful. Only his ability to express his feelings through his pen seems to have enabled him to survive these first months. In the first of a remarkable series of letters to Lionel Curtis (which Arnold Lawrence and his wife believe were intended primarily for Mrs. Curtis) Lawrence communicated his personal agonies and philosophical ruminations. "The Army (which I despise with all my mind) is more natural [a word Lawrence frequently used to denote the primitive or bestial aspect of life] than the R.A.F.," Lawrence wrote on March 19 in the first of these letters. "For at Farnborough I grew suddenly on fire with the glory which the air should be, and set to work full steam to make the others vibrate to it like myself. I was winning too, when they chucked me out: indeed I rather suspect I was chucked out for that."[11] Three days later he put the matter more succinctly to Aircraftsman R. M. Guy, his Farnborough friend: "The crowd talk a great deal of twats! and the rest of the time about ballocks."[12] So intense was his distress that he even lost interest in his book.[13]

Lawrence felt no better and wrote to Edward Garnett in April: "The army is unspeakable: more solidly animal than I believed Englishmen could be. I hate them, and the life here." But then he added: "and am sure that it's good medicine for me."[14] He longed for the air force and wrote a poetic, romantic essay based on his memories of the three months spent in 1919 with the Handley-Page squadron in the Mediterranean. Included was this passage: "We in the machine were like souls suspended motionless in unchanging ether, conscious of no movement, of no space, hardly of time — for comparing notes with one another afterwards we could not rightly say if the four hours of our crossing had seemed to us a moment or an age. For that space our minds had ceased to exist."[15]

Early in May Lawrence wrote provocatively to George Bernard Shaw, "I haven't been in a mood for anything lately except high-speed motor-biking on the worst roads." If this distressed G.B.S. he did not let on in his next letter ten days later. Rather, he expressed his impatience at all the time Lawrence was taking collecting pictures for his book and wondered whether he had not yet been identified and thrown out of his new regiment.[16]

By mid-May Lawrence's distress had deepened to despair, and in a letter to Curtis he gave indications of the program of self-discipline and penance upon which he would eventually embark. The lifelong physical self-testing and need to master is again evident, but now it has become clearly linked with Lawrence's sexual conflicts and deep doubts about his self-worth:

"The R.A.F. was foul-mouthed, and the cleanest little mob of fellows. These are foul-mouthed, and behind their mouths is a pervading animality of spirit, whose unmixed bestiality frightens me and hurts me. There is no criticism, indeed it's taken for granted as natural, that you should job a woman's body, or hire out yourself, or abuse yourself in any way. I cried out against it, partly in self-pity because I've condemned myself to grow like them, and partly in premonition of failure, for my masochism remains and will remain, only moral. Physically, I can't do it: indeed I get in denial the gratification they get in indulgence. I react against their example into an abstention even more rigorous than old. Everything bodily is now hateful to me (and in my case hateful is the same as impossible). In the sports lately (they vex us with set exercises) I was put down to jump, and refused because it was an activity of the flesh. Afterwards to myself I wondered if that was the reason, or was I afraid of failing ridiculously: so I went down alone and privily cleared over twenty feet, and was sick of mind at having tried because I was glad to find I still could jump. . . .

"This sort of thing must be madness, and sometimes I wonder how far mad I am, and if a mad-house would not be my next (and merciful) stage. Merciful compared with this place, which hurts me body and soul. It's terrible to hold myself voluntarily here: and yet I want to stay here till it no longer hurts me: till the burnt child no longer feels the fire. . . .

"I sleep less than ever, for the quietness of night imposes thinking on me: I eat breakfast only, and refuse every possible distraction and employment and exercise. When my mood gets too hot and I find myself wandering beyond control I pull out my motor-bike and hurl it top-speed through these unfit roads for hour after hour. My nerves are jaded and gone near dead, so that nothing less than hours of voluntary danger will prick them into life: and the 'life' they reach then is a melancholy joy at risking something worth exactly 2/9 a day.

"It's odd, again, that craving for real risk: because in the gymnasium I funk jumping the horse, more than poison. That is physical, which is why it is: I'm ashamed of doing it and of not doing it, unwilling to do it: and most of all ashamed (afraid) of doing it well.

"A nice neurotic letter! What you've done to deserve its receipt God knows. . . . perhaps you have listened to me too friendly-like at earlier times. Sorry, and all that. You are a kind of safety-valve perhaps. I wish you were an alienist, and could tell me where or how this ferment will end."[17]

Two weeks later he wrote again to Curtis that he intended to continue to try to find some relief from the torments of his sickly conscience through the shackles of military authority, but expected that this subjugation would also fail to bring peace:

"You know with neurosis the causeless ones are worst. If my success had not been so great, and so easy, I would despise it less: and when to my success in action there was added (according to those whose judgement I asked) success in book-writing, also at first venture — why then I broke down, and ran here to hide myself. . . .

"Conscience in healthy men is a balanced sadism, the bitter sauce which makes more tasteful the ordinary sweets of life: and in sick stomachs the desire of condiment becomes a craving, till what is hateful feels therefore pure and righteous and to be pursued. So because my senses hate it, my will forces me to it and a comfortable life would seem now to me sinful. . . .

"I have to answer here only for my cleanness of skin, cleanness of clothes, and a certain mechanical neatness of physical evolution upon the barrack-square. There has not been presented to me, since I have been here, a single choice: everything is ordained — except that harrowing choice of going away from here the moment my will to stay breaks down. With this exception it would be determinism complete — and perhaps in determinism complete there lies the perfect peace I have so longed for. Free-will I've tried, and rejected: authority I've rejected (not obedience, for that is my present effort, to find equality only in subordination. It is dominion whose taste I have been cloyed with): action I've rejected: and the intellectual life: and the receptive senses: and the battle of wits. They were all failures, and my reason tells me therefore that obedience, nescience, will also fail, since the roots of common failure must lie in myself — and yet in spite of reason I am trying it."[18]

The day after this letter was written George Bernard Shaw wrote a memorandum to Stanley Baldwin, then the prime minister, expressing concern about Lawrence's poverty: "It strikes all who know about it as a scandal that should be put an end to by some means." Shaw went on to insist that "the private soldier business is a shocking tomfoolery," and urged that Lawrence be given "a position of a pensioned commanding officer in dignified private circumstances."[19] Shaw had discussed the matter with Lawrence, who apparently had indicated his willingness to accept a modest pension, if offered, while remaining in the ranks.[20]

One benefit of being stationed at Bovington in Dorsetshire was that Lawrence was able to develop a friendship with Thomas Hardy and his wife, who lived nearby; the three quickly became fond of one another. "Lawrence came to see us a fortnight ago, and is coming — I think — this Sunday," Mrs. Hardy wrote about a year after their first meeting. "He is one of the few entirely satisfactory people in the world. He can be so very kind. He has had influenza but looks well, and has a most powerful motorcycle."[21]

Lawrence was introduced to Hardy in the spring of 1923 through Robert Graves and wrote several months later: "Hardy is so pale, so quiet, so refined in essence: and camp is such a hurly-burly. When I come back I feel as if I'd woken up from a sleep: not an exciting sleep, but a restful one. There is an unbelievable dignity and ripeness about Hardy: he is waiting so tranquilly for death, without a desire or ambition left in his spirit as far as I can feel it. . . . It is strange to pass from the noise and thoughtlessness of sergeants' company into a peace so secure that in it not even Mrs. Hardy's tea-cups rattle on the tray: and from a barrack of hollow senseless bustle to the cheerful calm of T.H. thinking aloud about life to two or three of us."[22]

By the end of June Lawrence seemed more reconciled to the Tank Corps and was able to write to Hogarth, who had been trying to help him get back into the RAF: "It is probably not worse than the reality of any other unit. It's only that the R.A.F. is much better."[23] To Curtis he wrote: "It isn't all misery here either. There is the famous motor-bike as a temporary escape. Last Sunday was fine, and another day-slave and myself went off with it after church-parade. Wells we got to [over two hundred miles] and very beautiful it was: — a grey and sober town, stiffly built of prim houses, but with nothing of the artificial in it."[24] He watched a white-frocked child playing with a ball in front of the cathedral and observed: "The child was quite unconscious of the cathedral (feeling only the pleasure of smooth grass) but from my distance she was so small that she looked no more than a tumbling daisy at the tower-foot: I knew of course that she was animal: and I began in my hatred of animals to balance her against the cathedral: and knew then that I'd destroy the building to save her. That's as irrational as what happened on our coming here, when I swerved at 60 M.P.H. on to the grass by the roadside, trying vainly to save a bird which dashed out its life against my side car. And yet had the world been mine I'd have left out animal life upon it."[25]

Lawrence revealed little evidence of his distress to his Tank Corps companions. They remembered, rather, his quiet and reserve coupled with a sense of fun, and, inevitably, his kindness and generosity.[26] Only to Eric Kennington and his wife does Lawrence seem to have shown in face-to-face contact the distress he was undergoing. Ordinarily Lawrence would joke about his "Tank Town troubles," but on occasion with the Kenningtons he "dropped all defenses" and revealed "a wall of pain between him and us." Lawrence then gave forth with a barrage of nihilistic thoughts, which had been unfamiliar to Kennington before. "Everything was attacked," Kennington wrote. "Life itself. Marriage, parenthood, work, morality, and especially Hope. Of course, we suffered and were unable to cope with the situation."[27]

Alec Dixon, who was a corporal in the Tank Corps when Lawrence arrived at Bovington, got to know him as well as anyone in the camp, and spent most weekends and two or three evenings a week with Lawrence at Clouds Hill. "Solemnity and an air of melancholy distinguished his behavior during his early months at Bovington camp," Dixon wrote me.[28] But despite the great suffering Lawrence revealed in his letters to Curtis, he never complained to anyone in the camp. He carried out his duties "efficiently and quietly, in a manner that contrasted oddly with the clamorous and slapdash methods of his younger companions."[29] Very few of the men at Bovington, including Dixon, knew, at least at first, of Lawrence's past history, although his skill and speed with a motorcycle earned him a different sort of fame — "seventy miles an hour was nothing to Shaw and couldn't that little bloke ride a motorbike!"[30] Later, after they knew, they would protect him from prying reporters by warning him of their arrival while pretending to look for him.[31] Shaw took Dixon and the other soldiers for rides on his built-to-order motorcycle and he soon became known as "Broughie" Shaw.

Dixon became curious about Private Shaw when he saw the remarkable influence he had on the other recruits. He noted especially that they "eschewed swearing and smutty backchat whenever Shaw paid them a visit."[32] One day Shaw took Dixon for a ride to nearby Salisbury. They roared out of camp at a terrific speed. It was raining and when the speedometer reached eighty-three, Dixon felt the stinging drops tear into his face "as though they had been hailstones. Shaw leaned over to hand me his goggles, puckering his eyes against the driving rain. Through the rain-blurred glass I saw that the speedometer was still at seventy-five."[33] They stopped for tea at a pleasant shop in Salisbury and talked of architecture, the Crusades and many other subjects, and finally of airmen and the air.* "Talk of airmen," Dixon wrote, "reminded me of 'that fellow Lawrence' who had enlisted in the Royal Air Force as a mechanic. That was an extraordinary affair, wasn't it? What on earth, I wondered, could have induced a man of his calibre to demote himself in that absurd fashion. 'Do you suppose it was a stunt on his part?' I asked casually. Shaw giggled at the suggestion. 'Stunt?' he repeated slowly, as if weighing the word. 'No, I shouldn't call it a stunt.' He munched bread and butter for a moment or two, eyeing me thoughtfully. 'That was a difficult question,' he said. 'You see . . . I *am* Lawrence.' "[34]

Dixon described Lawrence as being "as good a soldier as any man in the Depot," but looking small and humble beside his burly fellow recruits. He was very popular with the other men, in part because of the keenness of his sympathy for the underdog.[35] According to Dixon,

he never leaned or lounged, and I never saw him to relax. He was surely a man with "ants in his pants," if ever there was one. When walking about the Camp his normal bearing was very noticeable for, except when on a drill parade, he did not swing his arms as he walked in the approved manner — an oddity which singled him out from all of us. He walked "all of a piece" as it were, with an air of tidiness; his arms were close to his body and his toes well turned out, though not exaggeratedly so. As he walked he appeared to see no one about him; his head was slightly tilted and the blue-grey eyes steady, looking neither to the right nor to the left.[36]

Toward the end of his Tank Corps recruit training Lawrence was assigned to the quartermaster's stores ("a sort of half clerk, half storeman," he wrote his family),[37] where he worked for about two years and was "the driving force" behind its function and reorganization.[38]

* Dixon later wrote me that he considered Lawrence's view of the differences between the Tank Corps and the RAF greatly exaggerated, "a ripe piece of T.E. humbug" (June 25, 1967).

In the summer of 1923 he was able once more to consider the publication of *Seven Pillars of Wisdom*. "It is meant to be the true history of a political movement whose essence was a fraud," he wrote Mrs. Hardy, "in the sense that its leaders did not believe the arguments with which they moved its rank and file: and also the true history of a campaign, to show how unlovely the back of a commander's mind must be."[39] And he sought further advice from the Hardys, Hogarth and others about publishing. By mid-September he had decided upon publishing a private limited edition of one hundred to three hundred copies for friends and others willing to subscribe to an expensive book, although he still felt *Seven Pillars* to be "a pessimistic unworthy book, full of the neurosis of war," and hated the idea of selling it.[40] But Lawrence feared, among other things, the book that Lowell Thomas would publish and thought "it might be better to get my blow in first."[41]°

In September 1923, Lawrence rented for two shillings sixpence a week from a distant cousin on the Chapman side of the family a thatched brick cottage near the camp. The land on which the cottage stood had been in the possession of the family since the fourteenth century,[42] and the cottage itself, called Clouds Hill, was built in 1808. Lawrence remarked on this family connection in a letter home: "Quaint how these people are settled all about here. The daughter of the rector of the South Hill parish it was who knew all about us."[43]†

The cottage was nestled against a small hillside in lovely heath country, and was almost buried by an unruly thicket of rhododendron. (The rhododendron is today as thick as it ever was, but the nearby countryside is scarified and denuded by tank tracks.) The cottage was in a ruined state when Lawrence took it, and he soon began to fit it up "with the hope of having a warm solitary place to hide in sometimes on winter evenings."[44] He used the money from selling a gold dagger he had obtained in Mecca in 1918 to Lionel Curtis to repair the floor and roof and make the cottage habitable.[45]

Lawrence was extraordinarily generous in permitting his friends — those from the service as well as those of the English literary world — to use Clouds Hill whether he was in residence or not, and these disparate types mingled comfortably there. "I wish there was a Clouds Hill in every camp, assigned for the use of aircraft hands," he wrote to one such service friend in 1929.[46] The cottage seems to have been a second home, or even the only home for many of Lawrence's airmen and army friends, and he often encouraged them to stay in the cottage when he was away and could not use it. Jock Chambers and others have described to me in loving

---

° Actually, the subscribers' edition took so long to publish that Lowell Thomas's book was out for at least two years before the two hundred or so copies of *Seven Pillars* saw the light of day in 1926.

† It will be recalled that South Hill was the name of the manor house in County Westmeath, Ireland, which Lawrence's father left behind. This is the only mention of South Hill by Lawrence of which I am aware.

detail the aspects of the cottage rooms and the relaxed pleasure they experienced sitting around the fire, talking or listening to the expanding collection of gramophone records.

E. M. Forster, who first came to the cottage in 1924, has written about the silence, peace and "happy casualness" of the place, as he and other friends ate (from cans), slept, bathed and talked there. "T.E.'s kindness and consideration over trifles were endless," Forster recalls, "and after he had returned to camp one would find a hot bottle in the bed, which he put there in case his precious visitor's feet should be cold. That was like him. The harder he lived himself, the more anxious he was that others should fall soft. He would take any amount of trouble to save them."[47] Dixon has written similarly:

> Two or three other men — sometimes more — of widely differing types were among the regular visitors to Clouds Hill in those days. T.E. was an expert at "mixed grills" where men were concerned. He presided over the company, settling arguments, patiently answering all manner of questions, feeding the gramophone, making tea, stoking the fire and, by some magic of his own, managing without effort to keep everyone in good humour. There were many picnic meals (stuffed olives, salted almonds and Heinz baked beans were regular features) washed down with T.E.'s own blend of China tea. Some of us used chairs, others the floor while T.E. always ate standing by the end of the wide oak mantelshelf which had been fitted at a height convenient to him.[48]

To Chambers, in inviting him to the cottage, Lawrence wrote: "I don't sleep here, but come out 4:30 P.M. till 9 P.M. nearly every evening, and dream, or write or read by the fire, or play Beethoven and Mozart to myself on the box. Sometimes one or two Tank-Corps-slaves arrive and listen with me . . . but few of them care for abstract things."[49] Over the door he carved the Greek words ΟΥ ΦΡΟΝΤΙΣ, meaning "does not care," and explained to Forster and other friends that he had taken this motto out of the story of Hippocleides in Herodotus.[50] "The jape on the architrave," Lawrence wrote in 1932, "means that nothing in Clouds Hill is to be a care upon its habitant. While I have it there shall be nothing exquisite or unique in it. Nothing to anchor me."[51]

Lawrence's friends were becoming impatient with his vacillations about *Seven Pillars*. The poet Siegfried Sassoon wrote him in November 1923: "Damn you, how long do you expect me to go on reassuring you about your bloody masterpiece: It is a GREAT BOOK, blast you. Are you satisfied?, you tank-vestigating eremite."[52]

Toward the end of the year Lawrence made David Hogarth his literary executor and plans for the subscribers' edition were completed.[53] "The business will be done as crazily as you feared," Lawrence warned Shaw, and added, "your subscription will not be accepted, since I'm gunning only at the ungodly rich."[54] On December 19 Lawrence sent out a notice to prospective "discreet subscribers" that one hundred copies of the book would, he expected, be ready in a year or a year and a half (actually it was three years). The book would be elaborately printed and illustrated, and would cost thirty guineas.[55] He estimated that the production would cost him about £3,000 and be covered therefore by the subscribers. Actually, it cost £13,000, part of which resulted from the fact that he gave away over one hundred copies to friends who could not afford the thirty guineas or who might benefit from selling their copies at the enormously inflated price which this rare and notorious collector's item was soon to bring.

Meanwhile, Lawrence continued his campaign to get back into the RAF and never ceased to resent his expulsion bitterly. "If Hoare dies horribly some day you will know it's my bad wishes dogging him," Lawrence wrote to Lord Winterton.[56] He spent Christmas in his cottage ("I refused Max Gate [Hardy's home]," he wrote Sydney Cockerell. "It's not good to be too happy often.")[57] He did "rations and coalyard" to set the other men "free for their orgy.... Xmas means something to them. My pernickety mind discovers an incompatibility between their joint professions of Soldier and Christian."[58]

Lawrence assessed his situation in a letter to R. M. Guy: "Xmas — spent alone in my new-old cottage — has been a quiet time of simply thinking. It seems to me that I've climbed down very far from two years ago: and a little from a year ago. I was in the guard room of Farnborough that night, and the next day the newspapers blew up and destroyed my peace. So it's a bad anniversary for me.

"Yes Trenchard writes to me sometimes, but it won't be to have me back.[59] Baldwin [the Prime Minister] tried to persuade him and failed."[60]

George Bernard Shaw continued his efforts to persuade Baldwin to secure a pension for Lawrence. At the same time he never ceased ragging Lawrence about serving in the ranks — "your success in making the army ridiculous" he called it.[61] Lawrence finally had enough of this, and became bothered by Shaw's refusal to take his purposes seriously. "It's awfully good of you ... but awfully bad for me," he wrote in January 1924. "Please let up on it all. The army is more or less what I ought to have, and in time I'll get to feel at home in it."[62] He also wrote to Hogarth of Shaw: "Such sureness of success has closed his pores."[63]

In February Lawrence received a detailed and very valuable critique of *Seven Pillars of Wisdom* in a long letter from E. M. Forster. He found Forster's appreciation of the book so gratifying that "a miracle happened" when he read the letter. He had been suffering from a bout of malaria and "the fever left me and I sat up and read it all."[64] Forster offered in a meeting to try to help Lawrence "to get rid of" the book. He recognized the anguish it was causing his friend and wrote: "I can't cheer you up over the book. No one could. You have got depressed and muddled over it and are quite incapable of seeing how good it is."[65] Eight years later Lawrence wrote to a young author: "I found Forster a very subtle and helpful critic, over my *Seven Pillars*. Hardly anybody else (of the dozens of critics who dealt with that or *Revolt in the Desert*) said anything that wasn't just useless pap. . . . After all, he writes, and so knows what authors are up against."[66]

An American firm had pirated Lawrence's introduction to Doughty's *Arabia Deserta*, and he became anxious lest the same thing might happen to *Seven Pillars of Wisdom* after the extraordinary expense and effort he had expended in the printing, illustrating, binding and producing of the elaborate subscribers' edition. In April he wrote to F. N. Doubleday: "It's the U.S.A. Copyright law which concerns me. In England the thing is copyright, for subscription printing isn't publication: and the public libraries can't demand copies. But the U.S.A. Land of pirates!

"I'm set on never making a brass farthing for myself out of that scabious Arabian Adventure; . . . but, also, I'd grudge anyone else making any. How can I circumvent the American Pirate? . . .

"The idea that came to me was this. To print every other page (or every other paragraph) of the English edition, at yours or another less reputable works: print them carelessly, so that they should be not merely unreadable, but obviously unreadable. Print perhaps six copies. Price them at 700 dollars (or 7000 dollars, or 7000000 dollars . . . anything so long as it was impossible) and tell the Copyright Department, when it asked, that the edition was still on sale (in fact, not selling well). It wouldn't be worth any pirate's while (so I think) to print the unreadable other half of the English Edition: nor would he be allowed to put the pieces together and print a connected text, since the disjointed first parts would be your right."[67]

Doubleday modified this plan into an appropriate arrangement that would secure the American copyright, and then was surprised to discover that Lawrence had turned the project over to his literary agent, Raymond Savage.[68] Doubleday was even more astonished when he learned that George Doran in New York had secured the publication rights of the book and had signed a contract with Lawrence in September 1925 for the printing of twenty-two copies.[69] Doran was to keep four copies, Lawrence six, two were to be deposited in the Library of Congress (where they remain in the Rare Book Division),[70] and ten were put up for sale at $20,000 per copy, at which price they would naturally not be sold. It appears that Doran was willing to make such an outlandish agreement because he knew that an abridgment of *Seven Pillars* that would be sold to the general public was in the offing. When in fact the abridgment, entitled *Revolt in the Desert*, was published — in 1927 by Doran in the United

States — it sold handsomely at $3.00 a copy, the earlier publicity attending the publication of the "$20,000 edition" having done an excellent job of advance promotion.[71] Doran regarded this as a calculated move on Lawrence's part, although this seems unlikely. "Lawrence had a capacity for superbly arrogant modesty," Doran observed.[72]

Doughty had repeatedly asked to see Lawrence's book on his war experiences ("I have remained in utter painful darkness as to your great Campaign in Arabia," he wrote upon learning he would receive it to read), and in late April Lawrence finally agreed to have a copy of the Oxford proofs sent to him. "My experiences in Arabia were horrible," Lawrence wrote the aging poet, "and I put them down as they happened to me. Consequently the book is not fit for general reading. I've never asked anyone to read it . . . and don't expect you to do so. At the same time you are one of the people whose wishes I cannot refuse."[73]

The desert campaigns proved not to have been what Doughty had expected, and he wrote his friend in biblical cadences, "I am able to view your vast war-work near at hand, with its almost daily multifarious terrible and difficult haps, experiences, physical and mental strains, and sufferings and dark chances that must needs be taken, in meeting and circumventing enemies, in the anxious Leadership of an Armada of discordant elements, as often naturally hostile among themselves of Arab Tribes; until, after two years, you won through to the triumph of Damascus, after enduring all that human life can endure to the end."[74] Then Doughty added, "I trust, that the long endurance of so many mischiefs may have left no permanent injury to your health."

Doughty, according to his biographer, Hogarth, could not approve *Seven Pillars of Wisdom*, "deeply attached to his strange follower though he was." Doughty told Sydney Cockerell that he thought in Lawrence's own interests a good many passages should be omitted.[75]

On this somewhat discordant note the relationship between the two famous Eastern travelers ended. Doughty died in February 1926. Lawrence attended the funeral and afterwards wrote to Mrs. Shaw: "Doughty's funeral made me miserable: not at the fuss of disposing of the body (something has to be done to get *rid* of the huge chunk) but at the sight of Mrs. D. so crushed. She had been very proud and careful of her great man, and now he has fallen. The ride back was miserable, accordingly."[76]

Lawrence was in bed much of May with malaria, and also dislocated his knee. His mood took a downward turn and he described a listlessness and apathy in letters to Graves and Hogarth. He felt, he said, "purged quite suddenly of all desire."[77] He also learned that Hogarth was ill as a result of diabetes, which further troubled him. He was discouraged initially by the extraordinary difficulties of producing his book virtually by himself (he chose the type and the typesetter, and dummied the entire text), especially when subscribers were slow at first in coming and he saw, that even fully subscribed, the book, produced in this way, would not pay for itself.[78] He was helped in financing the book by Robin Buxton, his banker and former wartime comrade-in-arms, and the two carried on a voluminous correspondence regarding the details of the book's production.[79] The next year Lawrence put his property at Chingford up for sale and began planning an abridgment (for which Cape paid an advance of £3,000) in order to pay for the subscribers' edition.

But by the end of the summer of 1924, thirty-guinea subscriptions were "rolling in merrily . . . at a rate of ten or twelve a month," and Lawrence saw that he could have sold two hundred copies if he had wished.[80] Often he discouraged people from subscribing. To one potential customer he wrote, for example: "If you subscribe for the book you are risking thirty guineas on what may be a very disappointing production, when you see it. I strongly advise no one to get it unless he is particularly rich, and a curio-hunter. Incidentally there are no political indiscretions in it: no special lewdness: some horror, and much dullness and hysteria. It's a war book, in other words."[81]

In October 1924, Lawrence received finally from Bernard Shaw the detailed criticism and page-by-page correction of the Oxford proofs of Seven Pillars for which he had been waiting more than a year. "Confound you and your book: you are no more to be trusted with a pen than a child with a torpedo," Shaw scolded, and proceeded to lecture Lawrence humorously on the fundamentals of punctuation, especially the use of colons and semicolons.[82] Shaw also warned Lawrence about libelous passages that had to be removed, and urged that he "swallow" these suggestions "literally with what wry faces you cannot control." On the fly-leaves of Charlotte Shaw's copy of the subscribers' edition of Seven Pillars of Wisdom, Shaw noted: "I rewrote these passages for him in terms that were not actionable. He adapted my versions, but, much amused by them, shewed them with his own text to the victims, as first rate jokes."[83] Shaw also told Lawrence to cut out his moving first chapter, not to "suppress" it but because in Shaw's view it did not properly introduce "the who and when and where and how and what which readers must know if they are to understand what they are reading."[84]

At this time Lawrence wrote to W. F. Stirling — he had sent Stirling the book for corrections and had just received it back: "I hate and despise myself more and more for the part I played in it [the Revolt]. Today my wish is to strip off from the yarn all the little decorations and tricks and ornaments with which I have made it ever-so-little exciting: so that the core of it should stand out as a disenchanting, rather squalid, experience. That's today: and the book is being printed today for the final time. If I waited till tomorrow probably I'd give effect to this wish, and gut the whole yarn of its adventitiousness: and then all would cry out that I'd spoiled it. So the way of least resistance is to let it, generally, alone."[85]

Early in 1925 Lawrence resumed his efforts to get back into the RAF. He wrote to Trenchard: "I've lived carefully, and am in clean trim, mind and body. No worse value, as an Aircraft hand, than I was. . . . The war-worry and middle-east are finished." Lawrence pointed to this two years without difficulty in the army, and entreated: "I'm not the only misfit one meets (and is usually sorry for). There is nothing portentous about my small self. . . . Being 'bottom dog' isn't a whim or a phase with me. It's for my duration, I think." Lawrence concluded the letter with an apologetic threat to use influence to get his way: "Please don't turn me down just because you did so last year and the year before. Time has changed us both, and the R.A.F., since then. I could easily get other people to help me appeal to you: only it doesn't seem fair, and I don't really believe that you will go on refusing me for ever. People who want a thing as long and as badly as I want the R.A.F. must get it some time. I only fear that my turn won't come till I'm too old to enjoy it. That's why I keep on writing."[86]

In June Lawrence learned that his latest effort to return to the RAF had been turned down once more, despite appeals to Churchill and Hoare, whom he again held responsible for his failure (this hope was his only reason for staying in the army he wrote Buxton, and made plans to leave the Tank Corps).[87] He became increasingly distraught and focused his despair upon the "muck, irredeemable, irremediable" of the *Seven Pillars*.[88] On June 1 he had written to his waiting subscribers that the time estimated to produce the *Seven Pillars* had proved wrong and offered them the chance to get their money back if they did not wish to wait. "I am still unable to promise anything," he told them, "and any subscriber who for any reason does not wish to wait the ending of the performance can have his money back on applying to me . . . but naturally I shall regret the loss of those who were willing to risk their money on what the Arabs would term 'fish yet in the sea.'"[89]

As the days went by without any sign that he was to be readmitted to the RAF, Lawrence's despair deepened and on June 13 in a letter to Edward Garnett he threatened suicide: "Trenchard withdrew his objection to my rejoining the Air Force. I got Seventh-heaven for two weeks: but then Sam Hoare came back from Mespot and refused to entertain the idea. That, and the close acquaintance with *The Seven Pillars* (which I now know better than anyone ever will) have together convinced me that I'm no bloody good on earth. So I'm going to quit: but in my usual comic fashion I'm going to finish the reprint and square up with Cape before I hop it! There is nothing like deliberation, order and regularity in these things.

"I shall bequeath you my notes on life in the recruits camp of the R.A.F. They will disappoint you."[90]

In May Lawrence had met John Buchan by chance in the street and had followed this up with a passionate letter pleading that Buchan use his influence to help him return to the RAF. Buchan wrote to Baldwin, who answered, "Come and see me about that exceedingly difficult friend of yours."[91] Buchan's personal intervention and a card from George Bernard Shaw to the prime minister, which threatened "the possibility of an appalling scandal" if Lawrence did commit suicide, turned the tide.[92]

Lawrence wrote a friend in November that while at Bovington that spring he had made up his mind "to come to a natural end about Xmas when the reprint of my book would have been finished."[93] I believe that this was no idle threat and that his despair, increased once again by working over and over the material of his book, especially the Der'a chapter, which he was revising for the ninth time in July, might well have led him to carry it out. But permission for transfer was urged by Trenchard and granted in July despite strenuous objections from Hoare, and Lawrence reentered the RAF on August 19, posted to the Cadet's College at Cranwell in Lincolnshire.[94] The news of the permission felt, Lawrence wrote Buchan in a letter expressing his deep gratitude, "like a sudden port, after a voyage all out of reckoning."[95] Lawrence stayed as an airman in the ranks of the RAF for the remaining ten years of his life. He never again experienced the degree of despair that he had suffered during his years in the Tanks Corps.

28

Cranwell

Lawrence's early letters from Cranwell ("a very comfortable, peaceful, cleanly camp [which] will be glorious when I have settled into it")[1] reflect his exhilaration and relief at being back in the RAF, even as a flight clerk, and he related to friends with relish, humor and a sense of triumph the reinduction process. "A miracle (called Baldwin, I believe, in the directory, but surely a thing with wings and white robe and golden harp)," Lawrence wrote to Edward Marsh in November, "put me back suddenly in the R.A.F., when I had completely lost hope. And now I'm a ludicrously contented airman: It's like old ship Argo, on the beach after all her wanderings, happily dropping to pieces."[2] Two years after he left Cranwell he referred to his fifteen months there as one of the two golden periods of his life (the other was Carchemish):[3]

"Well, you're in luck here: this place is cushy. Any bed you like," was the pleasant greeting Lawrence received at Cranwell.[4] Lawrence seemed at the Cadet College to be, at least outwardly, cheerful and happy. Sensing the suspiciousness with which the men there regarded his unusual past, Lawrence broke the ice socially by playing the most awful-sounding records he could find on his gramophone, and listening without any facial expression while the men suffered. When they realized it was a leg-pull the tension was relaxed and he was accepted into the flight.[5] "Everywhere a relationship: no loneliness anymore," he wrote contentedly.[6]

The mission of the station — to maintain the aircraft which the cadets were learning to fly — was meaningful to Lawrence, and he made a point of flying with the officers in the flight whenever he had an opportunity. Although he was assigned to an office, he would "leave the office at times, shove overalls on," and scrub and wash machines in the hangar despite the fact that "there was never any need to do so."[7]

Sergeant Pugh of "B" Flight at Cranwell reported that in his clerk's job Lawrence mastered and took care of "every conceivable kind of job." Less than a year after Lawrence left Cranwell for India, Pugh wrote Graves: "His sheer force of personality got him undreamed of odds and ends necessary for us in our work, which seemed unattainable to any Sergeant to say the most, and never an aircraft hand."[8] Lawrence would not, however, hear of promotion.

As at other bases, despite his often exaggeratedly literal obedience to authority, Lawrence was the champion of the men against unreasonable authority or regulations. Although he liked, for example, the church at Cranwell, he had no use for the sermons and amused the enlisted men with his employment of the device of "apparent stupidity" in his resistance to mandatory churchgoing.[9] He also astounded the other men by his successful protest to the superintendent of police at Cranwell over being unjustly held up on his motorcycle by the "copper" in the town.[10] Such arguments with civilian authority were unheard of for enlisted men in uniform at that time and provided them with an exhilarating example with which to identify.

Sometimes, according to Sergeant Pugh, Lawrence would head off into the night on his Brough, summer or winter. He would return "loaded up with good things for his roommates," but then make his own supper of "Smith's crisps" (potato chips) at the camp canteen. At other times he would "smoke" down to London on the Brough to look after the printing of his book and would sleep at the Union Jack Club. On at least one occasion, when the club was full, he was packed among other enlisted men in varying states of drunkenness.[11]

Sergeant Pugh offered this summary of Lawrence at Cranwell:

> It seemed his sole purpose was to be an airman of the lowest grade and rank and to be left alone with his Brough at "B" Flight, Cranwell. He was hero-worshipped by all the flight for his never failing cheery disposition, ability to get all he could for their benefit, never complaining, and his generosity to all concerned till at times it appeared that he was doing too much for everyone and all were out to do their best for him. Quarrels ceased and the flight had to pull together for the sheer joy of remaining in his company and being with him for his companionship, help, habits, fun and teaching one and all to play straight. He fathered us and left us a sorrowful crowd awaiting letters or his return.[12]

But beneath the outwardly happy state of mind that Lawrence conveyed at Cranwell his inner sense of failure and deep personal distress remained. "Behind us, in our trial of civvy life, is the shadow of failure," he wrote of Cranwell. "Bitterly we know, of experience, that we are not as good as the men outside."[13] To Mrs. Shaw he wrote just a month after arriving at Cranwell: "Do you know what it is when you see, suddenly, that your life is all a ruin? Tonight it is cold, and the hut is dark and empty, with all the fellows out somewhere. Everyday I haunt their company, because the noise stops me thinking. Thinking drives me mad, because of the invisible ties about me which limit my moving, my wishing, my imagining. All these bonds I have tied myself, deliberately, wishing to tie myself down beyond the hope or power of movement. And the deliberation, this intention, rests. It is stronger than anything else in me, than everything else put together. So long as there is breath in my body my strength will be exerted to keep my soul in prison, since nowhere else can it exist in safety. The terror of being run away with, in the liberty of power, lies at the back of these many renunciations of my later life. I am afraid, of myself. Is this madness? [The latter phrase was written in small, wobbly letters.] The trouble tonite [sic] is the reaction against yesterday when I went mad."[14]

Lawrence went on to tell how he had gone to London, seen Faisal, who was visiting there, and Winterton, and spent a solitary night in a rooming house, but realized only how much that life was behind him, although Winterton had attempted to recall old times. "From henceforward," the letter continues, "my way will lie with these fellows here, degrading myself (for in their eyes and your eyes and Winterton's eyes I see that it is a degradation) in the hope that some day I will feel really degraded, be degraded, to their level. I long for people to look down upon me and despise me, and I'm too shy to take the filthy steps which would publicly shame me, and put me in their contempt. I want to dirty myself outwardly, so that my person may properly reflect the dirtiness which it conceals . . . and I shrink from dirtying the outside, while I've eaten, avidly eaten, every filthy morsel which chance threw in my way."[15]

Early in December Lawrence had a crash while riding his motorcycle, which, in retrospect, seems to anticipate the accident that led to his death ten years later: "Knee: ankle: elbow: being repaired. Tunic and breeches being repaired. Front mudguard, name-plate, handlebars, footrest, renewed. Ski on ice at 55 m.p.h. Dark: wet: most miserable. Hobble like a cripple now."[16]

At Christmastime Lawrence was still wrestling with the Der'a passages during the final corrections of the subscribers' edition of *Seven Pillars*. "That's the 'bad' book" [Book VI], he wrote Mrs. Shaw, "with the Deraa Chapter. Working on it always makes me sick. The two impulses fight so upon it. Self-respect would close it: self-expression seeks to open it. It's a case in which you can't let yourself write as well as you could."[17] And to his agent he wrote several days later: "The book. It crawls. The distractions are too many, and I hate the beastly thing."[18]

His mother looked to him at this time for more expressions of closeness, but Lawrence could not, would not, give them and held her away firmly and abruptly: "You talk of 'sharing my life' in letters," Lawrence wrote, "but that I won't allow. It is only my own business. Nor can anybody turn on or off the tap of 'love' so called. I haven't any in me, for anything. Once I used to like *things* (not people) and *ideas*. Now I don't care for anything at all."[19]

Cranwell brought Lawrence a period of calm he had not experienced for many years, especially during the "interim misfortunes" of the Tank Corps period. In January he wrote Mrs. Shaw like an exultant schoolboy bringing home a good report card: "My R.A.F. character has been assessed (for last year) as 'exceptional.' This is the highest grade. It shows you how I can behave for four months. Down with the Sam Hoares!"[20] Cranwell lacked only privacy — "why there isn't a lock in my power at Cranwell, not even on the shit-house door!" he complained to a friend.[21] But this was made up for by the kind loan, if temporary, of a London apartment: "The place so quiet, so absolutely mine, and the door locked downstairs, so that it was really mine."[22]

Lawrence was able at Cranwell to permit himself once more the sensuous yet objective appreciation of the qualities of the world around him as he had not for years. "I went to a Lyons shop, and ordered tea," he wrote to Mrs. Shaw in February, "the other people were amusing. They hadn't come from my planet, I think. The only friendly person was a black cat, who sat beside me, and was exceedingly insistent upon the point of food. I bought an eclair, and split it open down its length, like two little dugout canoes. The cat flung itself upon them, and hollowed out all the pith with its grating tongue. When it got down to the brown shell it sat back on its hind legs and licked its face lovingly. A man on the opposite seat, also had cream on his cheek and tried horribly hard to lick it. Only his tongue was too short. Not really short, you know: only for that . . . the cat was a very excellent animal. The human beings were gross, noisy, vulgar: they did the same things as the cat, but in a clumsy blatant way. . . . Heaven knows why I've bothered to write you this nonsense. The moral spoils it."[23]

Early in March 1926, Lawrence completed the correction of the text of *Seven Pillars* and soon began work on the popular abridgment for Cape, *Revolt in the Desert*, that was to pay the bills of the lavishly produced subscribers' edition. Actually the latter edition was itself an abridgment of the Oxford text from which Lawrence, incorporating many of George Bernard Shaw's suggestions, had cut out about fifteen percent or fifty thousand words.[24] To a new friend and reader of the book, the Cambridge poet F. L. Lucas, Lawrence wrote: "I always had the ambition to write something good, and when the Revolt gave me a subject I tried to make up for what I felt to be my lack of instinct by taking immense pains: by studying how other people got their effects, and using their experience. So I built an enormous mass of second-hand ornaments into my skeleton ... and completely hid the skeleton under them.... It sounds very conceited, that I should go on believing the book rotten, when you have written in the contrary sense. S.S. [Siegfried Sassoon] also called it epical (though an epic hasn't yet been built on the feelings, as aside from the actions of men)."[25]

A day or two after this was written (in mid-March) Lawrence broke his right wrist trying to help out in an auto accident. He was forced, therefore, to write much of the abridgment, what he called his book "for boy scouts," with his left hand "in a pencilled scrawl"[26]*(Lawrence called it "a drunken script") while his right hand hurt horribly.[27] In making his abridgment (which he claimed to have done in seven hours with the help of two airmen),[28] Lawrence ignored Edward Garnett's earlier abridgment and reduced the text to less than half by taking a set of sheets from the subscribers' edition and, "with a brush and Indian ink" obliterating "whole slabs of the text."[29] Omitted were the emotionally laden, introspective or personal parts, or any sections which might reveal himself or otherwise provoke, shock or disturb his readers. "I cut out all the high emotion," Lawrence wrote Edward Garnett, and "whittled it into nonentity."[30] Since most of his self-criticism derived from precisely these personal elements of the narrative, and from the disturbing occurrences they described, it is not surprising that Lawrence declared the abridgment on occasion to be better than the complete text. "Half a calamity is better than a whole one," he wrote David Garnett. "By excising heights and depths I have made a balanced thing: yet I share your difficulty of seeing the shorter version's real shape across the gaps."[31] Remarkably, according to Howard, "his cuts required scarcely any interpolations to form linkages and very few words were written in."[32]

In order to avoid the publicity that would attend the publication of *Revolt in the Desert*, scheduled to appear the following March (1927) after serialization in the *Daily Telegraph* in December 1926 and January 1927, Lawrence made plans with his superiors to be transferred to India at the end of 1926. There are few letters from this period, in part because after three months his right wrist still throbbed painfully. In June he wrote to Mrs. Shaw: "I can only keep happy in the R.A.F. by holding myself a little below par: if it's much below I mizzle: grow sorry for myself. This happens if I get ill or hurt, or am chased over much by some N.C.O. with a grievance to hand on."[33] Early in July he told his mother of the plans for India, explaining that "the Air Force authorities drag too slowly" and that he wished to be definite before letting her know the news. "It is always difficult to get away," he wrote, "and I've been long drawing in my horns inch by inch, like a snail. India will let me finish the business."[34]

In August, in preparation for leaving the country, Lawrence had his solicitors draw up a Last Will and Testament ("of me THOMAS EDWARD SHAW otherwise called THOMAS EDWARD LAWRENCE or JOHN HUME ROSS of Clouds Hill, Moreton"). He appointed his younger brother and his solicitor as executors and willed each of them £100 and a copy of Shelley's poems in the Kelmscott Edition by William Morris. He left the land and buildings at Pole Hill, Chingford, in Essex to Vyvyan Richards and the residue of his property to his younger brother Arnold and Arnold's children.[35]

On November 3 Lawrence left Cranwell, which had become his "home for lost dogs,"[36] and took a month's leave to prepare his departure for India. The December date of his departure coincided with the completion of the production of the subscribers' edition of *Seven Pillars:* "I had an awful month," he wrote one friend, "real hard labor upon my old man of the sea: final printings, plates, collection, collation, issue to binders, correction of subscribers' lists, allotment of copies. Yet though I sweated it at every possible hour of the day and night, seeing no one and doing nothing else, even now it is not finished. About 20 copies have gone out, and most of the rest will go out about Christmas time ["my Christmas pudding" he called it in another letter][37] but the very special copies will hang on till the New Year. I think my experience is almost a conclusive demonstration that publishing is not a suitable hobby for an airman."[38] "It is a strangely empty feeling to have finished with it, after all these years," he wrote to Dick Knowles, his Clouds Hill neighbor, just before his departure.[39]

Lawrence's mother, who was with Robert Lawrence in China on medical missionary work, had urged Lawrence to leave the RAF when she heard he was going to India. But he replied that "the bustle and enforced duty of the R.A.F. is good for me. I wish it was not India — an experiment which has lasted too long and where we are failing." He then lectured them both — the first of a series of dressings down he gave them — about the evils of missionary work and medicine in general and interfering with the destiny of other peoples, all of which his medical missionary brother not unexpectedly cut from the printed edition of these letters. Lawrence gave many of his books to Vyvyan Richards and a gift copy of *Seven Pillars* in heavy morocco binding to Robert Graves, and also sent copies to Trenchard, King George ("he wanted one") and, via John Buchan, to the prime minister. On board ship he wrote to Sergeant Pugh (of his flight at Cranwell) of Trenchard's last-minute offer of a choice about whether or not to go to India, but "I had to choose to go, of course, damn it. I'm always hurting myself or my interests."[40]

The trip to India aboard the crowded troopship *Derbyshire* was a foul and fetid one, with "wave upon wave of the smell of stabled humanity" from which Lawrence sought to isolate himself by writing further autobiographical notes.[41] What seemed to represent for him the quintessence of its horror was the problem of unplugging a latrine in close quarters stopped up by a sanitary napkin ("the horror of almost final squalidity").[42] The only relief was a brief affectionate meeting in Port Said with the Newcombes, who took him away for several hours into the harbor where he could escape the smell of the ship.[43]

29

India

Lawrence was posted to an RAF depot at Drigh Road near Karachi in the western desert portion of what is now Pakistan. He arrived early in January 1927 and remained there for sixteen months, during which time he left the base rarely, in part because the region reminded him unpleasantly of his earlier experiences in the East. He found the area even more objectionable because of the squalor resulting from its greater density of population and the culturally destructive contact with European civilization. "It is a desert, very like Arabia," he wrote Mrs. Shaw, "and all sorts of haunting likenesses (pack-donkeys, the colour and cut of men's clothes, an oleander bush in flower in the valley, camel-saddles, tamarisk) try to remind me of what I've been for eight years desperately fighting out of my mind."[1]

Although he himself had sought this additional isolation for a specific purpose, and further restriction on the range of his opportunities, Lawrence often longed for England and was sometimes observed to be "oppressed and utterly cast down" or suffering from "fits of depression" during the period at Karachi.[2] His principal job assignment was to the Engine Repair Section, where his intellectual talents were soon put to use helping the officer in charge write reports and memoranda. "Coldly routine subjects developed into reasoned expositions of the pros and cons of every side issue" in Lawrence's reports, and, the adjutant tells us, "many a trivial subject, in itself unworthy of argument beyond the merest yea or nay, was kept alive on paper for the sake of the mysterious stamp of erudition which marked the reports now coming from the E.R.S. officer." From Karachi Lawrence asked Trenchard, "Wouldn't you like the future anthologies of English prose to include passages from technical orders?"[3]

Lawrence's arrival in India was naturally preceded by the expectation that he would be at least "a queer fish." But several of his RAF companions there have described his quiet and unobtrusive ways, and the friendly, natural and unposed manner in which he conversed openly on a variety of subjects once he knew he was being accepted for himself and not regarded as a curiosity or being pumped for information. "He was, like most great readers, extraordinarily well informed over a tremendous range," one officer wrote, "and as he had the sort of mind which forms some useful thought on small as well as large matters and enjoyed an argument even on trivialities, he was most enjoyable to listen to."[4] Private Shaw's need for privacy was accepted by both officers and enlisted men, and one officer noted his "pitiful vulnerability, the barrier which was there ready to be shut down at once as the only shield against probes into his privacy." Although "monastic traits" were noted in Lawrence in India as before, his need for "open spaces" in "community with his fellowmen" has always made the analogy less than completely accurate.[5]

Lawrence worked hard at Karachi, as he always seems to have done in the RAF, and as one officer observed, since he "packed into his working hours an amount of labour out of all proportion to his rank and trade" he was a "magnificent investment at about two shillings a day!"[6] At Karachi even more than at the stations in England Lawrence demonstrated his inventiveness in rigging up extra lighting or special baths, finding methods of insect extermination or discovering ingenious ways to circumvent, while not actually flouting, orders and regulations. Despite his cultured voice and manner, there was not, as one airman stated, "the slightest vestige of superiority in his make-up,"[7] and he adapted with ease to all of the varied types with which he came in contact. This was a principal reason why at Karachi, as at all his stations, Lawrence was so well liked and respected by military personnel at different levels.

The station was in Lawrence's words a "dry hole, on the edge of the Sind desert, which desert is a waste of sand and sandstone, with a plentiful stubble of cactus on its flat parts, and of tamarisk in its valleys. Over it blow hot and cold winds, very heavily laden with dust. We eat dust and breathe dust and think dust and hate dust on the days when duststorms blow."[8] He wrote to Fareedah el Akle (to whom he regretted not having been able to devote more personal attention during her recent trip to Europe as the representative of Syria to the first Council of Women in Paris): "India is squalid, with much of the dirty industrialism of Europe, with all its native things decaying, or being forcibly adjusted to Western conditions."[9]

Lawrence especially deplored the traditional, shortsighted attitudes of the British colonialists toward the Indians and expressed concisely to Mrs. Shaw his own anticolonialist philosophy of enabling: "On a priori grounds I would reply, that no native troops are loyal to their foreign masters: or rather, only those who had no self-respect would be loyal, and men without self-respect aren't capable of loyalty. The better the Indian, the less happy he could be as an agent of repression. Not one British officer in a thousand ever sees the contradiction of his profession with possibility. We are here for the good of India. The only good of mankind is responsibility: therefore the good we will eventually do India is to *enable* it to do without us" (Lawrence's emphasis).[10]

"I am a sort of messenger, runner they call me," he wrote to Jimmy Newcombe, six and a half years old, with apparent cheerfulness, "but I do not run: just waddle like a blue duck."[11] But on the same day he wrote about himself in the third person to a former RAF companion: "It is misery and shame being here again in the East where he did so blacken his character in 1917 and 1918, and he skulks among the airmen out of sight, very remorseful. There are no good roads: and no cream doughnuts. No good records [soon remedied]. No dogs (hot). No nothing."[12]

During this first winter in a colonialized country Lawrence delivered long sermons to his mother and brother in China against all "endeavours to influence the national life of another people by one's own," and observed, accurately as it turned out, that ultimately the rise of the Chinese Nationalists would bring the end of the "foreign" period in China. "The English," he noted dryly, "with their usual genius for beginning on the wrong side, are fighting the Nationalists, the party which must in the end (this year, next year, fifty years hence) prevail."[13] He was equally cynical about the medical work itself and he urged them both to leave the country before they were forced to leave. "There cannot be any conception of duty to compel him [Bob] to stay. In olden days doctors and medicine were respectable mysteries; but science is rather out of fashion now: and it seems to me that the fate of everyone upon earth is only their own concern. It is no merit to prolong life, or alleviate suffering: — any more than it is a merit to shorten life or inflict suffering. These details are supremely unimportant."[14]

The expression of these nihilistic thoughts to his family fitted well the personal renunciation of feeling and desire he believed he was finally realizing in the "clean emptiness" of Karachi. "I've learned a lot about living in the last five years," he wrote Robin Buxton early in March, "and have a curious confidence that I need not worry at all. Desires and ambitions and hopes and envy . . . do you know I haven't any more of these things now in me, for as deep down as I can reach? I am happy when I'm sitting still, in complete emptiness of mind. This may sound to you very selfish . . . but the other fellows find me human, and manage to live with me all right. I like so much the being left alone that I tend to leave other people alone, too."[15]

Early in March, *Revolt in the Desert* was published at about the same time that distribution of the full book to its subscribers was completed.

George Bernard Shaw in an early review of *Revolt* wrote: "The book does not, like the original, leave you with a sense of having spent many toilsome and fateful years in the desert struggling with Nature in her most unearthly moods, tormented by insomnia of the conscience: indeed, it is positively breezy; but that will not be a drawback to people who, having no turn for 'salutary self-torture,' prefer a book that can be read in a week to one that makes a considerable inroad on a lifetime."[16]

Lawrence regarded the reviews of *Revolt in the Desert* as "mostly slobber" and delighted in quoting excerpts from them in his letters for the purpose of making the reviewer look confused and silly. "The reviewers have none of them given me credit for being a bag of tricks — too rich and full a bag for them to control," he wrote Mrs. Shaw.[17] Lawrence did however, object seriously to being accused of imitating Doughty. Doughty, he wrote, "was keen only on death and life, and I was keen on psychology and politics. So we quarter different fields."[18] By the end of June, *Revolt*, which was bought up like "ripe apples," had sold 30,000 copies in England and 120,000 in America and had more than paid off the debts Lawrence had accrued during the production of the subscribers' edition.[19]

Except for a few essays by insiders, the rare subscribers' edition of *Seven Pillars* received few reviews, and Lawrence had to depend on the personal comments and letters of his friends for criticism of the work. "Do you know I'm absolutely hungry to know what people think of it," he had written to Lionel Curtis in 1923 — "not when they are telling me, but what they tell to one another."[20] George Bernard Shaw, sensing how seriously Lawrence took the book, liked to tease him about it. "I used to tell Lawrence that what happened was that an Italian Opera Company had been lost in the desert and bred a posterity of Beduwy," he wrote Sydney Cockerell many years later. "Auda, for instance, was clearly a Verdi baritone."[21]

Lawrence recognized that there was to be a sizable profit from the sales of *Revolt*, which he refused to take for himself, and £4,000 to £5,000 more than was needed to cover his debts had been received by mid-August 1927.[22] "The line of least resistance is the R.A.F. Memorial," he wrote Hogarth, and made substantial contributions to this fund, "but let's have some fun with it," he suggested.[23] By "fun" he meant nothing less than giving away money freely to airmen and other friends who were in financial need. He considered threatening to terminate sales on *Revolt* in June as a kind of blackmail scheme aimed at Cape in order to get his firm to help Pike, the printer of *Seven Pillars*, who was now in financial difficulty. At Lawrence's request sales were stopped after the book had served its purpose. Although Cape had more than fifty thousand additional copies on hand, the book had to be declared out of print. Nevertheless, the profits of the company rose from £2,000 to £28,000 for the year and the company's success may be traced directly to *Revolt in the Desert*.[24]

The limited number of available copies of the larger book (soon selling "thanks to the speculative book sellers" for three or four hundred pounds), and the confused legal status of its copyright, seem to have given Lawrence a perverse delight. "I've had two or three peevish letters from people who failed to subscribe, or whom I refused," he wrote to Buxton. "What matter? My book: I gave it to anybody I pleased: Tell your millionaires, if they pester you, that copies are on sale with Doran of New York! It's not as though the book was out of print. Anybody (with twenty thousand dollars) can get a copy. Ha. Ha.!"[25] Of the subscribers themselves, Lawrence was particularly pleased to receive a "jolly letter," from Allenby, "not peevish at all, so far as I could guess," seeming to accept the account of the campaigns in the book.[26]

With *Revolt in the Desert* published and *Seven Pillars of Wisdom* distributed, Lawrence's mood in the isolation of the Indian desert took a downward turn. "You cannot conceive how empty, uprooted, withering, I feel out here," he wrote Charlotte Shaw; "it is really a case of having come to a stand."[27] It was in April of 1927 that Lawrence wrote her perhaps the most self-exploring and revealing letter he ever wrote about his family relationships and their meaning to him.* He also wrote her that he was concerned that other airmen might discover and read her letters to him. "I feel that they belong utterly to me . . . I don't want the others to share in what I feel about them," he wrote to her.[28]

At the end of April, Mrs. Lawrence and Bob started home from China. "Good news from China," he wrote Fareedah el Akle. "My mother and brother have left it, and are on their way home. I sincerely hope that they will not return. The Chinese are waking up, at last — and the fewer foreigners that they have there the better — well intentioned foreigners, that is. Foreign enemies do no harm to a race just beginning to feel national. By their opposition they inflame the race-consciousness of the local people: but foreign friends! Oh, they are a disaster."[29]

After his mother and brother had returned, Lawrence wrote to them in concern that an airman might have read one of their letters to him which had gone astray. He hoped "there was nothing in the letters which the man who got them shouldn't read. Airmen, you know, dislike the mention of Love and God because they care about these things, and people should never talk or write about what is important."[30] Also omitted by Robert Lawrence from the printed letter was this passage: "The civil wars will last for a while yet, and after that a violently national Government will want to restore Manchuria and Korea. So for a long time China will look after herself: indeed I think probably there will not be much more missionary work done anywhere in future. The time has passed. We used to think foreigners were black beetles, and coloured races were heathen: whereas now we respect and admire and study their

* Most of this letter has already been quoted on pages 12, 27–28, 31.

beliefs and manners. It's the revenge of the world upon the civilization of Europe."[31]

Knowing Lawrence would soon withdraw *Revolt in the Desert,* and in order to forestall other attempts to capitalize on the story, Cape and Doran commissioned Robert Graves in June to write a popular version of the Revolt, based on Lawrence's own account of it.[32] "Robert Graves, a decent poet," was writing the new book about him, "as the result of a conspiracy of my friends, to keep the job out of bad hands," Lawrence wrote to his Clouds Hill neighbor at the end of June.[33] By the terms of his contract Graves had only six weeks to collect his material and Lawrence, understanding this, supplied him with great amounts of biographical information concerning the Revolt and other aspects of his life in long letters in June and July.[34] Furthermore, in order that the book, which was published as *Lawrence and the Arabs* about Christmastime, contain as few distortions as possible, Lawrence went over the drafts of the text in detail, making numerous changes and additions. While this was going on, Lawrence wrote to Lionel Curtis that Graves perhaps "will think out some psychologically plausible explanation of my spiritual divagations."[35]

Although after five or six months at Karachi (Lawrence had noted that it usually took him about six months to adjust to a new camp) he was reasonably content, he longed increasingly for England. "It will amuse you to know that my satisfaction with R.A.F. life keeps me contented in this dismal station and country," he wrote to John Buchan. "We spend much of our time playing infantry-games! However, it is only for a term of years: and my appetite for England will grow and grow and grow, till, upon my return, I'll lie down in the Strand and start eating the pavement in happy delight."[36] At the end of June he summed up his situation to Trenchard: "I'm sure I was wise to come overseas. There is no local press, and I arouse no interest in camp. Karachi I haven't visited. So nobody outside the depot has seen me. Service character still good, and I've not yet been in real trouble: nor sick."[37]

In July Lawrence indicated what he had in mind for himself for future employment after completion of his service period. "Didn't I tell you what I hope for, when I come out of the R.A.F.?" he asked Edward Garnett. "Robin Buxton, my banker, now Trustee, is going to try and get me a night job in the city, either as watchman in a Bank, or caretaker in a group of offices. They pay fairly: it is a quiet employment, whose only necessary qualification is honesty: and the work is not hard. I expect, you know, to fall into age quite suddenly, as I did into middle age on landing here. My eyes are troubling me so that I can't read much, or see clearly what I write. I'm going a bit deaf: and they say (I can't see my own head) that my hair is now thick with white hairs. I take it quite likely by 1935 I'll require an occupation which is slow, and full of sitting down. On the other hand, return to England might cheer me up to a few more years of motor-madness. Who knows?"[38]

His close participation in the creation of Robert Graves's book about him revived once again for Lawrence the painful memories and feelings associated with the war experiences. "Reading it," he wrote to Mrs. Shaw, "is like the memory of last night's sardine which sometimes comes to a man, unasked, just before breakfast, when the day is clean."[39] The book was "too laudatory" for the strict economy of his fiercely critical self-judgment. "So soon as I insulate myself," he wrote Mrs. Shaw in August 1927 the day after he received the proofs of *Lawrence and the Arabs,* "the needle swings back to self-condemnation."[40] In the same letter he told her that he had completed papers to change his name officially to Shaw. "Oh, I am so tired," he wrote, "I'd like to go off and turn into a lizard, and champ myself a long and cool and dark twisty hole under one of those immemorial cactus clumps, and sleep there in the bottom of it until the world was empty of all my kind. . . . By the way I executed a fearsome insect the other day, a legal insect of ———'s [his solicitor's] inventing, called a deed poll, by virtue of which my name is now Shaw only."[41]

In October Lawrence allowed himself after five years of service to be promoted from AC/2 to AC/1, equivalent to corporal and the highest rank he permitted himself, but his letters reveal an increasing nihilism and self-disparagement during the Karachi period, which the news of Hogarth's death in November only served to deepen.

David Hogarth died on November 6, 1927, and Lawrence learned about it three days later. Although the news was not unexpected, as Hogarth had been quite ill for many months, Lawrence's initial reaction was one of shock. "Yesterday Buxton wired me that Hogarth is dead," he wrote Mrs. Shaw, "and that means that the background of my life before I enlisted has gone." He recounted all the jobs he owed to Hogarth or had worked on with him. Since the war, he wrote, "whenever I was in a dangerous position I used to make up my mind after coming away from his advice."[42] Hogarth's wife, Laura, wrote to him in December: "I know you will miss him, more than perhaps anyone else, except Billie and me."[43]

A week after learning of Hogarth's death Lawrence sent the manuscript of his private anthology of poetry, "Minorities," to Mrs. Shaw in return for her private anthology of meditations. He apologized that "the weakness of spirit in this collection will only anger you: and then my notebook will not be a fair return for your notebook. In my eyes it is: for I'm not so intellectual as to put brain-work above feeling: indeed as you know, I don't like these subdivisions of that essential unity, man."[44]

Lawrence's letters during this period are filled with open expressions of his grief. "But I cannot write today," he wrote to H. S. Ede, an art critic at the Tate Gallery who had written to him after reading his contribution to the catalogue introducing Kennington's exhibition of paintings at the Leicester Galleries in London. "There was a man called Hogarth, who did everything for me for about 12 years, while I was growing up: and he died lately leaving me with a queer feeling that I had lost it all again. It's like being once more on one's own: and it will take me a few weeks to get square again."[45]

But three weeks later his grief had not lessened. "My bed-fellows tell me that I cry in bed at nights," he wrote Mrs. Shaw, "in the early hours of the night before they go to sleep and before I wake up. They begin to suspect me of secret griefs."[46] Hogarth represented for Lawrence what he valued most about Oxford, a civilized don who was worldly, scholarly but not bookish. "It was because he lived there that I liked Oxford," he wrote Trenchard, "and now I shall be afraid to go back to it."[47]

Perhaps the most moving expression of his feelings about Hogarth's loss came in a letter to Edward Garnett written just before Christmas: "Hogarth's death did, as you expected, bring me to a standstill. He meant very much to me; indeed he was the only man I had never to let into my confidence. He would get there naturally. Also I like him, almost unhealthily well; and owed him all I ever had, before 1922. After I had enlisted, my need of help and of friends much declined; so I saw little of him in the last five years; but the knowledge of that tower of understanding fellowship was reserve to me, and I feel orphaned in his going. There are expressing artists whose deaths one cannot bitterly deplore: — Conrads, or Hudsons, or Hardys; behind them is more harvest of ideas and emotion than most of us have leisure to gather in. But Hogarth carried his rareness in his mouth and eyes; — and he is wholly lost."[48]

In the meantime in the barracks Sophie Tucker was providing a respite for the airmen from Lawrence's more classical tastes in music. "She was worn to the bone, after about 200 playings," Lawrence wrote Graves, "and I find her just as intellectually suggestive when she comes down the wind to us from the next barrack-block ninety yards away. A splendid woman, doubtless, but she inclines me against matrimony. Imagine her greeting you at breakfast, day after day."[49]

As his first year in India drew to a close Lawrence still found much of the service routine difficult and he continued to resist it. Guard duty in particular remained a "beastly ordeal," which drove him into "a shaking funk," even though he knew the movements well — "something always comes to flurry me, when it is a performance with witnesses,"[50] and E. M. Forster suggested that perhaps "you and I may be wrong in hankering at all after this notion of escaping."[51] By the end of the year also, Lawrence formed a notion (never realized) of doing a biographical study of the revolutionary Roger Casement, with whom he seems, in curious ways, to have identified himself. "He could be made the epitome of all the patriotisms and greeds and lusts of man-imperial," he wrote Mrs. Shaw. "I suppose if I got all the materials and wrote it, white hot, that it would never find a publisher."[52] It is not clear whether Lawrence knew of the irregular sexual practices of which Casement wrote in his suppressed "Black Diaries."

During the first year at Karachi, Lawrence also took up his Uxbridge notes once again to make them into a book, *The Mint*. In August 1927, he had written to Edward Garnett that he was copying the notes into a notebook "as a Christmas (which Christmas?) gift for you."[53] A year later, after Ede and several other friends and acquaintances had read the notes and written long commentaries to the author in India, Lawrence wrote to Ede: "It is my only book, the only time I've said, to myself 'I'll write something about this.' Every evening at Uxbridge after I'd get into bed (the shedding those harsh trousers and tight tunics, and the stretching my legs into the looseness of bed were heavenly freedoms), I'd prop a pad on my drawn-up knees and scribble what had impressed me, in the day: or if nothing had impressed me, I'd jot down a conversation going on a bed or two away. So the Mint is really journalism, and I enjoyed it, as a new adventure."[54] At Karachi Lawrence added extracts, mainly from private letters, describing his experiences at Cranwell, in order to show, in contrast to the savagery of Uxbridge, "how humane life in a cadet college was."[55]

With Hogarth's death Lawrence suspended work on the notes. But on January 2 of the new year (1928) he sent to Mrs. Shaw a draft he had typed in October for her and G.B.S. to read and comment upon. Lawrence would not permit these notes to be published during his lifetime, principally because of the betrayal of trust in regard to his fellow airmen he felt making them public would represent. He wrote of these feelings to Mrs. Shaw in the letter which accompanied the manuscript: "Please regard yourself (in reading it) as being in an equivocal position, eavesdropping in a men's barrack. Those of us who live together have to depend on each other's decency to respect our inevitable confidence. We are all in the mire, together. The rest relied on me, to keep their custom, and I break it. What is given away is not myself, as in the *Seven Pillars*, but my fellows. I take you into their confidence, showing only just so much of myself as seems to illuminate their dark plans. I fear you will not like them. Yet I have censored out their secretest things, their best or worst intimacies. So many of them come to confide in my greater age and experience. What I have left is too much: to my informed mind there are things, poignantly unbearable, suggested behind these notes: and a great and lovely cleanness of spirit. So gay.

"I wrote them for myself, and copied them for Garnett: and was going to ask him not to lend them except to two specific people. Now there will be you and G.B.S. (if you wish) added. I do not want others even to know that the notes exist: least of all that they exist in book-form. You see, all the men are living airmen: only their names have been changed twice or thrice, after the S.P. [*Seven Pillars*] fashion. But we lived together, really, in the huts I mention and we said and did and suffered these things. There is nothing added — and only the intimacies subtracted. They talked like this to me, because I was one of them. Before you they would have been different: and they would be angry to think that a woman had shared their life. They cannot have the privilege of knowing you: nor would all of them have the largeness to understand you, if they did. It has been bred into them that a woman is different: holy almost, despite the soilings they receive when men handle them."[56]

In responding to a first reading of the notes, Mrs. Shaw remarked upon Lawrence's unusual sensitiveness. He replied: "Every one of us thinks he's very sensitive. I fancy we all feel very much the same. I was the only one to put in (unspoken) words, and write it down: that perhaps relieved my feelings: acted as a safety valve. If a fellow cries when he's hurt, it notably eases the pain: though it is not thought brave of him. So perhaps I suffered less than the rest of the squad. . . . I pretended to be one of them: that I might write down what they said and felt. Oh, that was the difficult part. If I'd forgotten my reproducing business, and gone properly with them, I'd have been dumb, too."[57]

On March 15 Lawrence wrote to Edward Garnett that the "R.A.F. notes" were on their way to him, carefully written out by hand and bound in blue morocco — "the blue we wear, and you can imagine the tooling is our brass buttons."[58] Two days later he wrote Trenchard what he had done and tried to reassure him that these candid revelations of barracks life would not embarrass him as he had "made a lovely bonfire of the originals" and "Garnett will not hawk the thing about." He had no intention of publishing them during his lifetime, he reassured the chief, and gave repeated instructions to Arnold Lawrence not to publish the notes before 1950.[59] But Trenchard was not reassured. He felt saddened after receiving Lawrence's letter, and worried about what would happen to the work he had done in building up the young air force should the press get hold of this revealing material, which he had not, as yet, read himself. He claimed not to be annoyed at Lawrence and consulted him for advice about raids that were going on between the tribes under Faisal and Ibn Saud.[60]

Shortly after this, however, Lawrence received encouragement from George Bernard Shaw and an ecstatic critique of *The Mint* from Edward Garnett. Shaw wrote, "There is not the slightest reason why it should not be shewn to anyone interested in the manners and customs of soldiers, or the psychology of military professionalism, or the history of initiation rituals, or the taming of animals, or half a dozen other departments of history and science. The slightest reticence or self-consciousness about it would be misplaced and unpardonable."[61] Shaw also suggested various ways to secure the manuscript from destruction and for the publication of a limited edition. Garnett wrote, "the book has perfect spiritual balance."[62] In a follow-up letter, Garnett described to Lawrence a meeting he had with Trenchard and Edward Marsh that Trenchard had requested because of his anxiety about *The Mint*. Concerned as he was that enemies of the air force might use the book to damage the service, Trenchard was, understandably, strongly opposed to publication. "He might sit for a picture of Mars," Garnett noted caustically.[63]

Meanwhile, in another letter Lawrence tried further to allay Trenchard's anxieties by assuring him of his loyalty and insisting on the private nature of the gift of the manuscript to Garnett. The book would not be published before 1950, or 1970 if Trenchard preferred, and anyway the RAF had become so strong and good, thanks to "your single work," that Trenchard need not worry about its failure or damage to its reputation.[64] There followed a long passage of advice concerning the handling of a new desert crisis.[65]

Lawrence was pleased to receive Shaw's praise of *The Mint*, but not happy with his suggestions about saving it from destruction or placing it on record, especially an idea Shaw had of putting it in a library. "Libraries like the W.O. [War Office] (to which you suggest a copy might go)," he wrote Shaw, "are open only to the officer-class, whose supremacy is based on their not knowing or caring what the men think and feel."[66]

It is not clear how many readers Edward Garnett and his son, David, loaned the manuscript to while Lawrence was in India, or how many friends Lawrence himself allowed to read it after he returned. "Show it to whom you think fit," he urged Edward Garnett, "under promise that they will not gossip about it."[67] Lawrence enjoyed in particular a correspondence with E. M. Forster regarding the book, and David Garnett had his wife type a copy ("slowly so T [Trenchard] won't get it for awhile") from the handwritten manuscript.[68]

Toward the end of his life Lawrence took the book up once again and made further revisions, and a few copies were privately printed soon after his death to prevent piracy in the United States.[69] By 1937 its existence was well known at Uxbridge, where it took on a legendary value as an exposé of abuses by the officers against the men. No edition reached the general public until 1955, one in which the names of characters were changed, and an unexpurgated text was issued only in a limited edition. Not until 1973 was a corrected, unexpurgated edition published without limitation.

The book is a starkly vivid, and unprecedentedly honest, revelation of barracks life. In 1928 E. M. Forster called *The Mint* "what is needed to express the guts of men, and they have never been expressed before,"[70] and in 1935, two months before Lawrence's death, John Buchan wrote him: "I have read your Air Force notes with acute interest and great admiration. It is the kind of document which has never been produced before about any service."[71]

The Mint is also an expression of Lawrence's personal ordeal, and his need for it — for what R. P. Blackmur called his "cultivation of the intolerable" — and "an essay in moral immolation and intellectual asceticism," Lawrence's personal, "minting the soul."[72]

In January 1928, Lawrence learned of the death of Thomas Hardy, and wrote a kindly letter to Mrs. Hardy. He understood her devotion to her treasured man: "You have given up so much of your own life and richness to a service of self-sacrifice. . . . Oh, you will be miserably troubled now, with jackal things that don't matter: You who have helped so many people, and whom therefore no one can help. I am so sorry."[73] Mrs. Hardy replied: "He was devoted to you. Somehow I think he might have lived had you been here. . . . You seem nearer to him, somehow, than anyone else, certainly more akin."[74]

In December 1927, Ralph Isham, on behalf of the American typographer Bruce Rogers, inquired of Lawrence whether he would undertake for £800 a new translation of the *Odyssey*. Rogers had read *Seven Pillars of Wisdom* and decided: "Here, at last was a man who could make Homer live again — a man of action who was also a scholar and who could write swift and graphic English."[75] Lawrence's reply to Isham was a classic example of his self-effacement. He listed the difficulties involved for him, that he "could not," for example, "sign it with any one of my hitherto names. It must go out blank, or with a virgin name on it." Furthermore, he wrote Isham, "I am nothing like good enough for so great a work of art as the Odyssey. Nor, incidentally, to be printed by B.R. [Bruce Rogers]." The letter concluded: "Your kindness remains overwhelming. Do realize I have no confidence in myself."[76]

He left the door open, and Rogers wrote in March a long letter setting forth the terms of the proposal. Lawrence replied in April, "I want to do it, and am afraid," and insisted upon the identity of the translator remaining anonymous.[77] An agreement was reached and Lawrence began work slowly on the translation late in the spring of 1928. As work progressed he came to think less of Homer and more of his own work, despite the usual self-disparagement.

In April Lawrence asked Sir Geoffrey Salmond, the air chief in India whom he had known "from Palestine days," that he be transferred from Karachi to another station. "Salmond has so large a stock of stations to which he can post me, that I can't even guess which it will be," he wrote his family.[78] He requested the transfer not just because of the heat and dust of Drigh Road, but also because "my personal relations in that camp were not improved by the summer postings."[79] He never explained this cryptic statement.

Miranshah, the new post, was in a remote corner of northwest India ten miles from the Afghanistan border, the smallest RAF station in the country, with only twenty-five RAF personnel (including three officers), and seven hundred Indian irregulars. Lawrence enjoyed the enforced isolation of the station in its mountain fastness and wrote that it was "easier for me behind walls than in an open camp."[80] To his former chief in the Hijaz, Pierce Joyce, who would understand the comparison, he likened the Afghan hills to the Wadi Itm near Aqaba, the place possessing a "quietness so intense that I rub my ears wondering if I am going deaf."[81] To Trenchard, who seems not to have been personally involved in this move, Lawrence wrote after four months: "We are behind barbed wire, and walls with towers, and sentried and searchlit every night. It is like having fallen over the edge of the world. A peace and hush which can be felt. Lovely. I hope to stay here for the rest of my overseas spell."[82] He was allowed, however, to remain in this retreat for fewer than eight months.

As the only airman there who could type, Lawrence was assigned office work, to "act postman, and pay clerk, and bottle-washer."[83] He found the commanding officer at Miranshah, I. E. Brodie, to be "the best and kindest C.O. of my experience."[84] Brodie returned the feeling. He liked and admired his "excellent orderly room clerk — excellent because he never produced a letter or a signal without the appropriate answer already typed and ready for signature." Brodie also noted with apparent sympathy that Lawrence had no respect for "barrack-square-type" authority and gave examples of his gentle mocking of silly instructions, usually by an exaggerated compliance which only pointed up their foolishness. Brodie also observed that Lawrence had "a steadying influence — magnetic — unseen and unheard. On the station he was not a hero — he was just 'a jolly good scout.' "[85] Lawrence was the first serviceman to show that there was no medical necessity for helmets and spine pads to fend off sunstroke. He went about bare-headed.[86]

Lawrence's struggles over *The Mint* continued at Miranshah. By July Trenchard had read the book and was still not reassured. "It was what I expected to read," he observed, and with deep sincerity wrote again to Lawrence of his concern that the book could be misunderstood and used to damage the RAF if its contents were made public. He described the reforms in the service he still wished to effect, and wrote of his wish to have air power lead to the prevention of massive killing and unnecessary casualties in war.[87]

Although Lawrence continued to luxuriate in the praise of the book he received from his literary friends, and was under pressure from Cape to permit some form of publication, he held fast to his promise to Trenchard not to publish it, and gave out that he himself was responsible for keeping his book in manuscript. "Trenchard isn't the difficulty," he wrote Jonathan Cape, "at least only a minor one. I am the prime stumbling block. All the fellows in the hut are in the book: and they would regard the record of themselves as a betrayal of confidence. When that sort of man goes to be photographed he puts on what he calls 'best': — a special suit of clothes: — and they wouldn't relish the birthday suits in which I draw them."[88]

Of greater significance for Lawrence was the debate he was undergoing with himself, shared as was his way in letters, about whether he was "a writer." Edward and David Garnett could call him one; E. M. Forster and George Bernard Shaw could speak of his works as masterpieces, even specifying in detail the elements of style and the passages they liked best; and H. M. Tomlinson could remind him of his responsibility to a whole postwar generation to tell the realities of service life.[89] It did not matter. Since praise or even encouragement only intensified his self-criticism, Lawrence could still dismiss *The Mint*, after all these comments, as "a vulgar little book, full of bad words."[90]

The problem, of course, had little — except in his own eyes — to do with the objective value of his works. It lay rather in the fact that Lawrence could no longer consider that he had anything of value or, for that matter, much of anything at all remaining within himself. "I'm all smash inside," he wrote, and "there never was an orange squeezed dryer than myself. Not a kick in the entire body. I'll write nothing else I'm sure." Or: "The great geyser in Iceland used to erupt when visitors threw soap into its mouth. This morning I got a mouthful of Pears [an old English soap] and only sputtered. I think that's a significant picture."[91]

On his fortieth birthday Lawrence summed up his view of himself to Mrs. Shaw: "Growing old too late . . . tragic, isn't it? However, it comforts me to be well over half-way. This forty years has gone quickly. I hope the residue will be less, and will go as quickly. It is not nice to feel decay getting hold of your faculties, though. I grudge my eyes their failing. As far as my arms and legs go, I'm all fit, as yet. Nor am I less elastic-stomached, and I have not got a tropic liver. Nor do I notice any change in my head yet. If only I was not always tired. I have been so, ever since the end of *The Mint*. Does GB go weary after his books? Of course he's so fertile, and I so thin in harvest, that it is not a fair comparison. A light soil soon exhausts itself if one heavy crop is taken out of it, and my *Seven Pillars* was a bit heavy."[92]

At the end of August Lawrence gave what may be taken as his final verdict on himself as a writer to Edward Garnett, his most steadfast supporter: "I am in the R.A.F. for so long as it will keep me. There is no question of my being a writer. 'Writes too' as Whistler or someone said. No more than that.

1.) E. M. Forster wants me to write about women.

2.) D. Garnett wants me to write a fairy tale.

3.) E.G. wants me to write a history of the Versailles Conference.

4.) Actually, I have begun to translate the Odyssey."[93]

This translation was to be his last published work.

Lawrence's RAF service was scheduled to terminate in 1930, and his friend Herbert Baker had even arranged for a permanent job for him as a nightwatchman in the Bank of England. But in September of 1928, Lawrence applied to Trenchard for and was granted a five-year extension of his RAF service to 1935. "The R.A.F. is like a life-line to which I cling," he wrote to Alan Dawnay. "Odd isn't it? If I hadn't tried it, I'd never have guessed that the ranks were my natural home."[94] At times Lawrence seemed to attribute his continuing commitment to the RAF to impersonal forces, beyond his control. "I am distressed for myself, and yet feel that the course is inevitable," he wrote Mrs. Shaw in November, "if only there could be an end in sight. I would so like to be comfortable, and respected. The world would pardon me enlisting for a 'stunt': but not for a vocation. Yet there it is. I'm going to let the force which governs me have its will. There is a governing force: that I'm sure. Of my own choice I would never stay in the wilderness."[95]

In the fall of 1928 Lawrence's work on the *Odyssey* ("mock-heroic" he called its style) picked up in pace, and by Christmas he had spent five hundred hours in translating the first three books. "I think my version is richer, on the whole, than the original," he wrote to the printer and pondered the sex of the author. "He or she? Honestly I don't care. No great sexualist, either way: no great lover of mankind. Could have been written by a snipped great ape. A marvelous crafty tale, mixed just to the right point with all the ingredients which would mix in. The translators aren't catholic like their master. Each of us leans toward his private fancy."[96]

Lawrence was much affected by learning of Trenchard's plan to retire, scheduled for the end of 1929, and wrote him about it as if it were a fait accompli over a year before the projected date. In an expressive letter he drew upon the image of birds and their chicks he often used when writing about the process of growth and to describe his mother's relationship with her children:

"I am very sorry you are going: it ends an epoch: and I had a personal pride in seeing you make the service, and helping you make it, from the bottom, and in being made by it, too. But I'm a believer in the parent birds getting out, when the chick's done his first solo. You may remember my getting right out of the Arab business, so soon as it seemed a going concern. Arab Nationality was as much my creation as the R.A.F. is yours. [One wonders how the Arabs feel about that statement.]

"A careless parent does no harm to the grown-up child: but the more one has cared, the more one tends to keep excessive hold of the leading strings: and the only way a kid can learn to walk is by falling down and struggling up again. Your chicken is so fit, that a bit of tumbling will do it good."[97]

Mount Batten

On January 8, 1929, Lawrence's tour of duty in India was abruptly cut short when he was whisked by air from Miranshah to Lahore. On the twelfth he was on board the S.S. *Rajputana* on his way back to England. What had occasioned this abrupt decision by the Air Ministry were rumors in the worldwide press that Lawrence was involved in a government-instigated rebellion against Amanullah, the emir of Afghanistan, a rebellion inspired perhaps by the fact that the ruler had become too friendly with the Soviet Union.[1] Lawrence, the man of mystery, the archspy, was being used once again, some claimed, as an instrument of imperial policy to foment rebellion, this time in the remote mountains of Asia. "Somewhere in the wild hills of Afghanistan up the rocky slopes by the cave dwellers," claimed one article, "perched high by the banks of mountain streams, a gaunt holyman wearing the symbols of the pilgrim and a man of prayer proceeds along his lonely pilgrimage. He is Col. Lawrence, the most mysterious man in the Empire. He is really the ultimate pro-consul of Britain in the East."[2]

The uproar grew in intensity, and Lawrence was even burned in effigy by Socialists on Tower Hill in London. Although neither the cabinet nor the British government in India suspected Lawrence of any complicity in the Afghan rebellion (he never, as far as one can tell, left the camp enclosure at Miranshah) he was brought home, nevertheless, to quiet the furor. Lawrence was not to be free of newspaper publicity and other notoriety related to his legend — some of it highly noxious to him personally — for the remaining six years of his life.

Secret arrangements were made to have Lawrence (who spent most of his time on board ship in his cabin working on his translation or reading) brought back quietly and taken ashore at Plymouth without publicity.

But there was a commotion when the ship put in at Port Said, and confusion in Plymouth Harbor when Wing Commander Sydney Smith of nearby Cattewater Air Station, the man delegated to bring Lawrence ashore in a motor launch, sought to avoid the hotly pursuing press boats.[3] All this secrecy stimulated rather than quieted publicity, and a chase to elude reporters ensued, which was led by Wing Commander Smith. Much to Lawrence's amusement, it ended in London when he crashed across the threshold of Smith's sister-in-law's apartment and into his wife, almost knocking her off her feet. From there Lawrence was smuggled out the back way and finally to the safety of Herbert Baker's flat on Barton Street. Thus began a friendship between Lawrence and the Sydney Smiths, about which Mrs. Smith has written lovingly in her book, *The Golden Reign*.

Meanwhile, questions were being asked in Parliament about Lawrence's enlistment under a false name and his service activities. Not only was he afraid that he would be sacked from the RAF, but also that the facts regarding his illegitimacy and family background might be brought out. Soon after coming to London he made a midnight telephone call to Ernest Thurtle, the most aggressive questioner regarding his identity, and arranged a meeting with him for the following day at the House of Commons. He explained his situation to Thurtle and several associates, convincingly as it turned out, so that the publicity and questioning slacked off, and loaned Thurtle copies of *Seven Pillars of Wisdom* and *The Mint* in typescript.

After the meeting with Thurtle, Lawrence wrote to Trenchard, "I want to tell you, too, that I have explained to Mr. Thurtle, privately, the marriage tangles of my father (*you* probably know of them: *he* didn't, and is asking the questions which might have dragged the whole story into the light) and I hope he will respect my confidence, and stop asking questions in the House."[4] The visit to Parliament, for which Lawrence received a reprimand from the Air Ministry, resulted in a close friendship with Thurtle, and Lawrence found him a valuable figure in the government through whom he could channel his ideas about service reform. He was soon writing Thurtle long letters espousing various changes. Trenchard, after discussion with Lawrence and the Smiths, agreed that the best arrangement would be for him to be assigned to Smith's station near Plymouth.

Lawrence arrived at his new station early in March 1929, on a Brough motorcycle given to him by George Bernard and Charlotte Shaw. The camp was located on a peninsula near Plymouth: "a spine of rock and grass, like a lizard suddenly fossilized as he tried to swim across Plymouth Sound. The liners come into the harbor and tie up just below our huts, and moo through the morning mist like sea-lions in labour."[5]

Despite the intense cold, which disturbed him, and the fact that "the sea is all over the camp if a gale blows from the South,"[6] Lawrence was more contented at Cattewater (he and Wing Commander Smith soon arranged that the name be changed to Mount Batten) than he had been since Cranwell. This was due in part to the tender relationships and many shared interests he developed with the Smiths. The commanding officer was "a treat" and "a trump," and the two men formed an effective working partnership. Lawrence also was able to find pleasure in being near the sea, related perhaps to the years of his childhood spent near the water, and found a deep gratification in valuable work with boats and marine engines.

In *The Golden Reign,* which contains an introduction by Lawrence's mother, Clare Sydney Smith describes the many hours spent with Lawrence listening to music, following the waterways along the south coast, and exploring the countryside of Devon and Cornwall. The "golden reign," according to Lawrence's mother, was what he called this period, and the Smiths' house, which he christened "The Fisherman's Arms," became for almost three years another home.

Lawrence managed through his natural manner to gain the affection and respect of the men at Mount Batten, who seemed to accept without resentment his special relationship with the Smiths, perhaps in part because he never traded on it to receive special favors. His generosity also endeared him to the men at Plymouth. Sergeant W. Bradbury, who worked closely with Lawrence at Plymouth and Southhampton, wrote after his death: "The troops at Plymouth had many a snack from Shaw's parcels and he enjoyed watching them eat it. His books were returned to him but he lost a good number. His gramophone records were his pets, yet he would lend them to anyone who cared to borrow them; he only stipulated that they use special needles and he even provided them with these. He often did a night duty for fellows who wanted to go out but could not do so owing to the fact that it was their duty night."[7] Later, Lawrence was to work successfully without Bradbury's knowledge to have this younger airman succeed him in his work at the boatyards at Southampton, a position he knew Bradbury wanted.

Tommy Jordan, the former coxswain of one of the boats at Mount Batten, offered, more than thirty years later, these vivid recollections of Lawrence: "He was a bloke on the job and a good bloke on the job. He was a natural conversationalist. He'd get on the men's level, yet he kept that little bit of reserve. A natural man's man. Lawrence of Arabia? No, he was just a man we were working with."[8] According to this former enlisted man Lawrence and Smith worked successfully to achieve an atmosphere of mutual respect between officers and men at Mount Batten. The feeling between the two groups was comfortable and easy, with little consciousness of rank. This climate, Jordan stated, persisted at Mount Batten for many years after Lawrence's death.

During the spring of 1929 Lawrence taught himself to be an expert mechanic by overhauling a Biscayne Baby speedboat, The *Biscuit,* which an English millionaire had given him to use. He kept the boat finely tuned and it was in this craft that he would take Mrs. Smith and other friends on memorable trips in the vicinity of Plymouth. Work also continued on the *Odyssey*, although he found Zeus and Athena too "social" to suit his tastes, and he would have liked "the style to quicken a little, and be business-like: only Homer, alas, was not of my view. It's all the same all through."[9] When the weather grew warmer Lawrence mastered a fear of swimming that had prevented his going in the water since Aqaba, and he swam every evening off the side of a motor yacht until he conquered the problem.

It was also in the spring of 1929 that Lawrence came to know the military historian Captain Basil Liddell Hart. (They had corresponded previously about an article on guerrilla warfare for the *Encyclopaedia Britannica*, written by Liddell Hart and based on Lawrence's 1921 piece for the *Army Quarterly*. But they had not met.) Liddell Hart sought Lawrence out to discuss aspects of military history and strategy, but their discussions reached over such a wide range of subjects that Liddell Hart eventually became interested in writing a full-length biography of Lawrence. Liddell Hart became another valuable person to whom Lawrence could press his ideas about service reform. He also got to know Lady Nancy Astor, M.P. for Plymouth, whom he took for rides on his motorcycle. Lawrence developed a lighthearted friendship with her that continued until his death.

Lawrence was not prevented by his relative isolation at Mount Batten from maintaining a continuing interest in public life, and he did not hesitate to try to influence the course of events, particularly through Thurtle and Lady Astor, if he saw an opportunity. "I am hoping especially that you will let Trotsky into England," he wrote Thurtle in June, "that you will abolish ·the death penalty for cowardice in war. I have run too far and too fast (but never fast enough to please me at the time) under fire, to throw a stone at the fearfullest creature. You see, if I did, I might hit myself in the eye!"[10] Characteristically, Lawrence related his views on social and political issues to his own personal experience.

During the summer of 1929 Lawrence was kept furiously busy assisting Wing Commander Smith with preparations for the Schneider Cup Trophy Race, a competition among marine aircraft of the United States, Great Britain, France and Italy. The race went smoothly and was won by the English seaplane. Lawrence, however, got into difficulty and was almost thrown out of the RAF once again. The new air minister, Lord Thomson, was not pleased to have Lawrence in the RAF and used the pretext of his being seen publicly talking to the Italian air marshal, General Balbo, to crack down on him. The RAF crews had left some slippery green scum on the Italians' slipway and the Italians asked him to have a crew clean it up before the race, which he did.[11] It required fairly extensive negotiations in London before Lawrence was permitted to remain in the RAF and he was allowed to stay only if he stopped hobnobbing with important people, a requirement that could hardly be practically enforced since, as Graves dryly commented, these "included most of Lord Thomson's political opponents."[12] He was also forbidden to fly in government aircraft.

The fall of 1929 was a peaceful, uneventful time for Lawrence, during which he seemed, according to Mrs. Smith, to become more relaxed and "better integrated." Sometimes he took her daughter, nicknamed Squeak, in the boat. "He seemed to inspire confidence, not only in himself, but one's own self as well," Mrs. Smith wrote. "Squeak says just the same. He sometimes took her out in the *Biscuit* and let her take the wheel, even though she was a child, and she never felt in the least nervous when she was with him."[13]

Lawrence's mother moved into rooms in London in September "so that we can be near together!" ("There I am, beset," he objected to Mrs. Shaw.)[14] Also during this period he worked furiously on the *Odyssey* — as much as forty hours a week, he wrote Rogers — and complained to Mrs. Shaw, "I am so bored with the resourceful Odysseus," and, in another letter, "what a set of worms the ancient Greeks paint themselves to be."[15] Lawrence's usual capacity to upgrade the intellectual diet of the airmen was having its effect on Mount Batten as at previous camps. "The airmen are reading more," he wrote to Mrs. Shaw, "they come in to my bed, and say 'can you lend us a book?' and if there's anything just returned, I thrust it towards them."[16] As the year drew to a close Lawrence agreed to be godfather to still another child, this time the baby son of W. H. Brook, his Stokes gunner in Arabia. "Infant camels," he reminded Brook, "can walk three hours after birth. One up on them."[17]

The next year, 1930, would turn out to be quieter and happier, "the first for ten years," he wrote to Mrs. Shaw, "to leave me quite at peace."[18] As the year began he summed up his situation to an aircraftsman at Miranshah: "Life here goes smoothly. In November I had a tiff with Lord T. our present boss. He tried to sling me out: I double crossed him. So am airmanning on. Our C.O. here is a treat. Grub is better than Miranshah grub. Plymouth is a rotten hole; the sea is lovely in summer and hell in winter: and its work, work, work. I wish Greek had never been invented."[19]

Work on the "Greek" continued throughout the year, and Lawrence struggled to maintain the effort at the level of his exacting expectations, often making many drafts before sending Rogers a final version. "I've struggled with it till I'm sick," he wrote Mrs. Shaw in January. "The original is not great stuff: or that is the sad feeling I have: yet I'd like mine to be first rate."[20] To Rogers he wrote: "I don't use any obsolete words, I think, or even archaic words — or hope I don't! The thing tries to be straightforward."[21]

In two other letters to Rogers, Lawrence suggests a psychological link between his doubts about the value of his work on the *Odyssey* and his personal effort (never fully successful) to surmount self-doubts deriving from his illegitimacy. "Alas and Alack! I am going to be really proud of my *Odyssey*. It shall remain illegitimate," he wrote.[22] Several months later he again insisted that his name not appear on the work and asserted, "It's everybody's secret that I have done it, and I don't care; but between that and legitimatising the child is a great gulf!"[23] He suggested face-tiously to David Garnett that he might call the translation *Chapman's Homer*.[24] Although he was "tired of all Homer's namby-pamby men and women,"[25] by the end of 1930 he felt better about his own work. "It's going to be a peach of a book," he wrote Rogers, and then added, "I had so much spare time. But in England an airman has no right to undertake a version of the *Odyssey*. I am sorry to have been so long."[26] By the end of November the work on the *Odyssey* was "¾ done."[27]

Lawrence's kindliness proved helpful to his friend, H. S. Ede, at the Tate Gallery. The two had corresponded since 1927, but did not meet until Lawrence returned from India. Ede suffered an emotional disturbance in the latter part of 1929 and wrote that Lawrence "by his kindly sanity on his various visits helped me considerably at this period."[28] In his effort to help Ede obtain a balanced perspective (Ede tended to blame the war for his difficulties), Lawrence wrote him letters which suggest that he had gained some insight and distance with regard to the conflicts and emotional injuries left by his own war experiences: "I cannot put *all* our troubles down to war. As the war gets more distant, it gets more horrible truly: at the time we did not feel it as hardly as we do now. Yet I feel that change is in ourselves, not in the war. Blame your illness rather on doing too many things. Book-writing is the world's most exhausting toil, and you tried to double it with the Tate. After G-B [Gaudier-Brzeska] is behind you, your health will come to you as before."[29]

But privately to Mrs. Shaw Lawrence indicated that his own emotional conflicts related to the war remained a source of anguish, at least during the night, despite his contented life at Mount Batten: "The war is so long over, that we should be all recovered from it now, only we aren't. It wakes me up in the early hours, sometimes, in a terror."[30] He shared with Ede his view of his own work, that had been such a great emotional strain for him to produce: "Surely you over-estimate *Seven Pillars* — a story of adventure, modern man facing troubles moral, mental and physical. It interests you because we are aware of one generation: but the future will not comprehend what you saw in it, or what I put in it, as they will have travelled past all these things."[31]

Lawrence continued, quietly, to help other people. In February 1930, he recommended his brother Arnold to David Garnett, who was looking for someone to edit an edition of Herodotus for the Nonesuch Press, and wrote to his childhood neighbor, A. S. Kerry, now a mathematician at Eton in behalf of the Newcombes, who were seeking admission for their son, Jimmy. Both of these efforts turned out to be successful.

Mrs. Smith offers this picture of Lawrence in the early spring of 1930, after a year at Mount Batten: "In this year he lost his self-consciousness and much of his nervousness and became a more integrated personality, able to enjoy simple things of life and less tortured by doubt and by thought. He loved, when I knew him, the composition of a view and the atmosphere that a particular day's combination of cloud and sunlight created. He could sit and lose himself in music for hours at a time; he was fulfilled and happy in his work, and he met people naturally — drawing them out if they were simple and inarticulate, teasing them if they took themselves over-solemnly, pricking the bubble of their self-importance with some acute words spoken in an innocent voice with his chin in the air and an amused smile lurking at the corners of his mouth, contracting and hiding in a shell of silence and withdrawal if they jarred or grated on his sensibilities, talking with animation and conviction if they were people of his own calibre of brain and achievement — and holding such an audience in a web of interest at his talk and personality, the Irishman in him thoroughly revelling in holding his audience and winning its approval."[32]

It was in 1930 that Lawrence developed an important friendship with the Australian writer Frederic Manning. "Manning is a very exquisite person: so queer," he wrote to Mrs. Shaw in February.[33] Somehow Lawrence penetrated the anonymity of Manning's war novel, *Her Privates We*. Peter Davies, its publisher, used extracts from a telephone conversation and a letter from Lawrence praising the book to help its sales, and introduced Lawrence to Manning.[34]

It is not clear how often Lawrence and Manning actually met, but they shared many personal thoughts in their correspondence on contemporary literary, social and political questions. Lawrence wrote Manning that the hero of *Her Privates We* said and thought a lot of the things he wanted to say but did not or could not.

In May Lawrence shared with Manning, in connection with a consideration of *Seven Pillars*, the impact upon him of his war experiences, and his lingering moral and political conflicts in relation to these years. He was as usual self-disparaging, but acknowledged his love of Arabia: "I wake up now, often, in Arabia: the place has stayed with me much more than the men and the deeds. Whenever a landscape or colour in England gets into me deeply, more often than not it is because something of it recalls Arabia. It was a tremendous country and I cared for it more than I admired my role as man of action. More acting than action, I fancy, there."[35]

In July he confided to Manning that he was considering having Peter Davies print a copy of *The Mint* but decided against publishing the notes as they were too "scrappy and arty and incompetent," and he could not afford the £120 the project would cost.[36] He also confided to Manning such private opinions as that he found the tone of Graves's latest book (*I Claudius*) "sickening" and that G.B.S. "finds it so easy to be brilliant-surfaced that he never bothers to go underskin. His characters are characters, all right, but have only the one mind among them."[37] Lawrence considered Manning "as satisfying a writer, as anyone who has ever written,"[38] and wrote Graves in 1933, "I think Frederic Manning, and an Armenian, called Altounyan, and E. M. Forster are the three I most care for, since Hogarth died."[39]

At the beginning of March 1930, St. Andrews University offered Lawrence the honorary degree of Doctor of Laws on the occasion of the installation of Stanley Baldwin as chancellor. Acceptance would have involved traveling to St. Andrews in May for the award.[40] He did not — or chose not — to believe the offer was serious, and quickly refused. He told a friend four years later that the invitation was "oddly worded and came in a very crumpled envelope . . . containing a very crumpled single sheet of typewriter size letter paper."[41] A second letter, correctly worded and neater, convinced him the invitation had been in earnest. When he learned that his quick refusal caused embarrassment at the University and for John Buchan and his other friends who were behind the offer, Lawrence promptly wrote Buchan, "I naturally concluded it was a student leg-pull, and sent it cheerfully back to the address given, saying that it was no go. How could I be expected to imagine it was serious?"[42]

Fearing the damage that the publicity attaching to the degree would cause to his air force status, still precarious at this point, Lawrence clung to his refusal, although he appreciated "the mere being taken into consideration for an honorary degree."[43] Lawrence joked later with his friend Reginald Sims about how inappropriate it would be for an airman to become a Doctor of Laws:

"Should I be A/C 1 Doctor Shaw???
Doctor A/C 1 Shaw???
A/C Doc Shaw???
and if ever I were made Leading Aircraftman, how would
LAC DOC SHAW or DOC LAC SHAW sound?"[44]

He was "staggered" some time afterwards to receive a similar offer of a degree from Glasglow University, but refused again on the same grounds, adding that as his own university had not seen its way to recognizing any literary merit of his, it would be "impolitic" to accept such an honor from "a rival university."[45]

Lawrence had discussed and exchanged correspondence with Trenchard regarding the use of air power as a means of reducing casualties in battles. In his desire to see air power in a humane light he seems not to have anticipated the monstrous use to which bombing would be put for the destruction of mankind. In June 1930 he wrote to Liddell Hart in response to a question about the *Arab* reaction to bombing: "There is something cold, chilling, impersonally fateful, about air bombing. It is not punishment, but a misfortune from heaven striking the community. The R.A.F. recognizes this, and bombs only after 24 hours notice is given. So the damage falls only on immovables.

"It is of course infinitely more merciful than police or military action, as hardly anyone is ever killed — and the killed are as likely to be negligible women and children, as the really important men. Only this is too oriental a mood for us to feel very clearly. An Arab would rather offer up his wife than himself, to expiate a civil offense."[46]

Lawrence had continued to visit the Doubledays when they were in England, although F. N. Doubleday was not well. During the summer of 1930 Doubleday underwent a serious operation and Lawrence wrote him several much-appreciated letters, filled with news of his activities, which included the fact that he had broken two chest ribs ("worse than stomach ribs").

In October Lawrence learned that Lord Thomson had been killed in the crash of an *R.101* airship. With Lord Thomson's death the restrictions he had imposed upon Lawrence against flying in government aircraft and visiting his prominent friends were, in effect, removed and he was soon flying and socializing on leave with Nancy Astor and others. "I continue in Plymouth, moderately quiet and immoderately happy," he wrote to Thurtle at the end of October.[47]

In November Lawrence took part in the first of a series of seaplane rescue operations, which contributed to his growing interest in developing fast, maneuverable boats, smaller than the ones the services were using, in order to effect more rapid rescues of pilots and crews. On this occasion there was no loss of life. Despite the bitter cold of the November sea Lawrence dived into the water and got a hawser around the hull of the plane, which lay in quite deep water, so that it could then be hauled out.[48]

At the end of November Lawrence was saddened to learn that in the Soviet Union the Russians had arrested several men and elicited confessions from them that they had had conversations with him in England during the time that he was actually in India.[49] He tried to counteract this unfortunate by-product of his notoriety through letters to Thurtle, but there was very little he or Thurtle could do about the situation. "They may hang these poor creatures for all I know," he wrote Thurtle. It is not known how the trial came out.

Before Christmas Mrs. Smith and her sister were in Paris. "I've forgotten to hope that Paris will be a success," Lawrence wrote them a little sardonically. "I never liked it greatly, but then, there were political reasons for that!"[50]

The new year — 1931 — began pleasantly. Mrs. Smith has described a delightful time of fishing for myriads of mackerel with Lawrence off a breakwater at Mount Batten. She fished and he unhooked the fish and baited the line. But this peace was shattered one day in February when an Iris III seaplane from the air station nose-dived into Plymouth Sound before their eyes. Mrs. Smith has described Lawrence's quick assumption of command of the situation, and his mastery of the rescue operation in which he dived with the other rescuers. Wing Commander Smith's orders for each step of the operation followed Lawrence's suggestions. Six of the twelve men aboard the plane were rescued but the rest drowned.[51] The incident, including Lawrence's part in the rescue operation, brought him new unwelcome publicity.

It may have been this incident that prompted George Bernard Shaw the following month to begin his play *Too True To Be Good*. The central character, Private Meek, who was modeled upon Lawrence, demonstrated that a private could control a regiment more effectively than a colonel. Shortly after the crash, when he learned that Lawrence would have to testify at an inquest, Shaw wrote to him: "As to the crash, you seem to be in the position of the sentinel in Macbeth who, having seen Birnam Wood start to walk, could say only, 'I should report that which I say I saw, but know not how to do it.' You are a simple aircraftsman: nothing but an eyewitness's police report can be extorted from you. However, as you will probably insist on conducting the enquiry, and as you will want to save your ambitious commander from being sacrificed, the future, to my vision, is on the knees of the gods. Pray heaven they sack you!"[52]

In addition to his matter-of-fact descriptions of the crash at the inquest, Lawrence did make behind-the-scenes efforts, through Lady Astor and other influential friends, to protect his commander, and turned the tragic incident into an opportunity to achieve needed reforms, especially in the methods of air-sea rescue.[53] At about the same time he was also drawn into a debate with an Homeric expert, employed by the publishers of his translation, over archeological and other technical questions presented in the *Odyssey*. He refused to accept the authority of any other translator and argued to Rogers that his life's experiences had placed him in as strong a position "vis-à-vis Homer" as other translators: "For years we were digging up a city roughly of the Odysseus period. I have handled the weapons, armour, utensils of those times, explored their houses, planned their cities. I have hunted wild boars and watched wild lions, sailed the Aegean (and sailed ships), bent bows, lived with pastoral peoples, woven textiles, built boats and killed many men. So I have odd knowledges that qualify me to understand the *Odyssey*, and odd experiences that interpret it to me. Therefore a certain headiness in rejecting help."[54]

In March the Shaws took a long trip overseas, which included visits to

Syria and the Holy Land. This trip highlighted for Lawrence the contrast between his present activities and his former life in the Middle East. "Yesterday I had your card from Damascus," he wrote Mrs. Shaw. "How queer it feels that you should have got there. I have to shake myself awake to realize I used to be there once. That was another life, and it was so long ago. Often I fancy that Colonel Lawrence still goes on, and it is only me who has stepped out of the way . . . picture me just as a sailor nowadays."[55]

31

"Boats, Boats, Boats"

Through Flight Lieutenant W. E. G. Beauforte-Greenwood, head of the Marine Equipment Branch of the Air Ministry, Lawrence had begun work in the fall of 1930 testing and tuning speedier experimental boats, which were being produced for the armed services by private contractors. Lawrence had been attempting for some months to influence the Air Ministry to let these contracts, and their development was a victory for his cause.[1] There was a constancy, even monotony, about this work, which was to occupy Lawrence until his retirement. "My life is as before: boats, boats, boats," he wrote to Bruce Rogers eight months before he left the RAF. "They grow more and better daily."[2] In April 1931, Lawrence was given an assignment by Wing Commander Smith to the Scott Paine yard at Hythe, Southampton, where he was to spend about half the remaining months of his life. On this occasion he spent two months in Southampton tuning and testing the new types of boat engines. In May he wrote to Curtis: "We work all day all week, and have no means of amusement and no leisure for it. I am glad to do the job, as the boats are of the sorts I have been pressing upon the service for many months, personally and by reports: and they are proving what I had hoped."[3] The same month he wrote the Smiths: "To confess the truth I have had almost all the speed-boating the most confirmed water rat could want. Something quiet would be my choice now; a country walk perhaps, and some flowers to pick. I am sick of salt water, and the burn of spray."[4]

Sergeant W. Bradbury, who worked with Lawrence at Southampton at this and other times recalls: "He never referred to anything as regards boats in their correct nautical terms, the bow and stern were always the thin and thick end, port and starboard were left and right, and he would never refer to bow and stern lines as such, it was always a piece of string.

If he wanted to know about an engine he would strip it down to the last nut and bolt and go into the smallest part, work on it until he had it correct and then was satisfied."[5] Lawrence's objections to the ways of the "regulars" seem to have persisted throughout his life. But this inattention to technical language did not carry over to Lawrence's *writings* about boats and boat engines. In the spring of 1931 he began a masterful technical report for Beauforte-Greenwood in which he dealt exhaustively with all aspects of the RAF 200 boat he was developing.[6]

Perhaps the too-earnest tone of the treatise struck him as ludicrous and inspired him to write at Southampton a brief satirical essay on an autogyro of the future for the burlesque novel *No Decency Left*, which Robert Graves was writing with Laura Riding. The machine would be designed by a Spanish dressmaker "to provide the ultimate degree of private comfort consistent with safety and speed," and its usual technical features would include beam-antennae (anticipating radar) which would indicate by sound signal the presence of anybody of more than atmospheric density within three hundred meters.[7]

In June 1931, Lawrence returned to Plymouth, and the matter-of-fact tone of a letter to a former companion in the desert indicates how far he had come in molding himself into the role of the uncomplicated aircraftsman: "What's happened to you? I enlisted in 1922 and have been quite happy since, except when badgered by press enquiries into my present or past. It's not comfortable nor well paid: but I like mucking about and the other fellows are decent. Peace time airforcing isn't like the army in war you know. . . . By the way, if you answer this forget the 'Col' and the rest of it. I'm a very plain sort of creature now."[8]

Over the summer Lawrence wrestled with the problem presented to him by the author James Hanley in regard to a novel, *Boy*, which dealt candidly with sexual, including homosexual, feelings and activities. Although he thought Hanley went rather too far in places ("Now, honestly, you overdo the lechery of bus-conductors. A decent, wearied, cynical, and rather hasty-tempered class of men"),[9] Lawrence admired his writing. His letters to Hanley contain this interesting passage: "Your sanity and general wholesomeness stick up out of your books a mile high: people with dirty patches in them skirt round and round them, alluding but never speaking right out."[10] Lawrence sought (unsuccessfully, despite the fact that he did some revamping of the book himself) to keep Hanley out of the courts by having his publisher "even out" the actionable passages ("I far prefer censorship by the publisher to censorship by the police," he wrote one of the publishing partners).[11]

Work on the *Odyssey* was halted by Lawrence's assignment to Southampton. He took it up again when he returned in June to Plymouth and by mid-August had brought the translation near to completion. At the beginning of August he took a leave and buried himself with the *Odyssey* at Barton Street until he was "sicker than ever of that great work."[12] On August 12 he wrote the Smiths, "*Odyssey* creeps slowly over the ground, like a snake with glanders,"[13] but on August 15 he inscribed the last page for the publisher and printer (although he would continue to work on the text until late in October).[14]*

Lawrence felt a "half-regretful sense of loss" as he was unburdened of the work. The requirement of anonymous authorship had been dropped along the way, and the *Odyssey* translation would be the only published work to bear the name of T. E. Shaw. Lawrence had looked to the *Odyssey* for epic greatness when he was younger and now found Homer and his heroes of insufficient stature for his ideals. This disappointment colored his view of the work and therefore to some degree his own achievement as a translator. He comments at the beginning of the volume that "the twenty-eighth English rendering of the *Odyssey* can hardly be a literary event, especially when it aims to be essentially a straightforward translation." His translator's note continues: "Crafty, exquisite, homogeneous — whatever great art may be, these are not its attributes. In this tale every big situation is burked and the writing is soft."[15]

Lawrence, like an early psycho-biographer, sought to deduce Homer from his work, and found him "a book-worm, no longer young, living from home, a mainlander, city-bred and domestic. Married but not exclusively, a dog-lover, often hungry and thirsty, dark harried." And went on to suggest that Homer, "like William Morris, was driven by his age to legend, where he found men living untrammeled under the God-possessed skies."[16] The translator's note concludes with Lawrence's unrelenting expression of disappointment in the examples of the *Odyssey*'s principal characters — "the sly, cattish wife, that cold-blooded egotist Odysseus, and the priggish son who yet met his master-prig in Menelaus. It is sorrowful to believe that these were really Homer's heroes and exemplars."[17]

In July Lawrence learned that the "Golden Reign" was soon to come to an end, and that Wing Commander Sydney Smith and his family were to be assigned to another post. Clare Sydney Smith felt poignantly her own loss at the end of the close association. Lawrence has left no record of his own feelings. She tried to persuade him to transfer with them, but Lawrence wished to continue his work in designing speedboats and also did not want to leave his other friends at Mount Batten.[18] The Smiths were transferred to Manston, another base in England, in October, and as a parting present Lawrence gave them a copy of *Seven Pillars of Wisdom* (a very valuable gift by this time) inscribed on the flyleaf: "From T.E.S. to S.W.S. on dissolution of partnership."[19] At the end of the month he wrote them, after spending two weeks helping Mrs. Smith move into

* See the illustrations between pages 420 and 421 for a reproduction of the final page of Lawrence's translation of the *Odyssey*.

her new home (under "temporary orders"):[20] "Since life is all growing roots and tearing them up every time I reach a new station, I vow that I will not put down roots, to save pain — but the things grow in the dark, all unknowing."[21] Also, in the fall of 1931 Mrs. Shaw visited Lawrence twice at Clouds Hill, and his mother and Robert, against Lawrence's wishes, made plans to return to China.

At the end of November Lawrence wrote a foreword to Bertram Thomas's *Arabia Felix,* the author's account of his crossing — the first ever — of the Rub' al Khali, the great Empty Quarter of the Arabian Desert. Two years earlier Lawrence had urged Trenchard to have this desert, one of the last remaining uncharted lands on earth, crossed by an RAF dirigible: "Let us get the credit: and for the Lord's sake do it quietly."[22] But nothing had come of his suggestion. When Thomas, then the British agent in Muscat, accomplished his feat, not by air but by camel, Lawrence was enthusiastic and urged through Edward Marsh, Churchill's secretary, that the British government honor him appropriately: "Do not let the swag be all carried off by the Rositas [Rosita Forbes, another Arabian traveler] and Lawrences of the vulgar Press. Here is one of your own men doing a marvel."[23] In his foreword Lawrence cited the great Arabian travelers of the past and apologized that only because they had all died must Thomas come down to him for the writing of a foreword. He offered the thought, but did not elaborate on it, that "the mere wishing to be an Arabian betrays the roots of a quirk."[24]

In November Lawrence was reassigned to Hythe, Southampton, to work on a new dinghy engine and remained there until after Easter of 1932. "I am becoming an exile from people," he wrote to Mrs. Shaw soon after returning to Southampton, "or am beginning to feel remote, which is worse, perhaps. The more I like engines . . ." — the rest of the thought was left for her to complete.[25] At the end of the year he expressed concern about his RAF discharge, although he knew it to be more than three years away. "Service life is all making and losing friends, a wandering," he wrote to the Sydney Smiths. "I shall not dispose of myself and grow fixed until 1935. Only this is 1932, almost. It grows fearfully near."[26]

In a letter of January 9, 1932, to Mrs. Shaw, Lawrence wrote a detailed critique of G.B.S.'s new play, *Too True to Be Good,* with an attached sheet of textual corrections based on his knowledge of the services.[27] This was, as Stanley Weintraub has discussed in his book *Private Shaw and Public Shaw,* the first play Lawrence had "worried over" with Shaw, and as early as June of the previous year had offered him criticisms about military dialogue and various aspects of service protocol depicted in the play.[28] Lawrence was enthusiastic about the play, which provides a satirical view of the functioning of a military establishment, but objected to Shaw's view of the services in the postwar period. In his criticism he provides a clear analysis of what service life meant to him: "Only at one point did my nature want to say 'no' to G.B.S.: Where he said that the war had spoiled the services. It did alter them profoundly, for the time. After troops had left England for one of the fronts there was no brotherhood remaining. It was the fighting spoilt it. But after peace came, the pre-war mood returned. Relative to civil life the service today is more serene than it was of old. I cannot clearly tell you why this is. People dare not analyze their contentment. Partly because we feel eternal. The army's always aged about 20: no illness: no death: no old or young. All of a sort, all dressed, paid, fed, worked alike. The security of years of sameness before us. The common subjection to arbitrary power, and its assumption of all responsibility. . . . The male society, men's minds being slow and inflexible. Women, when we want them, we can encounter: but of our own will, only. They cannot come to us. Also there is an intimacy in barracks, a support of one by the next, great friendliness: and, as G.B.S. so well says, the freedom to do all things that a man's hands were made for. The peacetime soldiering is still the best lay-brotherhood. Look at my life."[29]

Although the character of Private Meek was based on Lawrence, Weintraub has pointed out that the figure of Aubrey Bagot, the ex-RAF combat officer who has been warped by military experience to the point where he cannot adjust to civilian life, is also shaped from aspects of Lawrence's character.[30] Shaw incorporated all Lawrence's suggestions, which continued in another letter at the end of January, into a revised text of the play. Lawrence read the play over and over again. "It gave me inexpressible pleasure," he wrote Mrs. Shaw. "I went about for days with a feeling that some great unknown benefit to me had happened. And that does not mean Pvt. Meek!"[31]

At the same time that Lawrence was offering Shaw technical criticisms of his play, he was completing his own detailed technical treatise for the RAF on the 37½-foot cruiser he had been developing. By the beginning of March it was completed, and, as usual, subject to his devaluation. "Ever so dull, the notes, and entirely impersonal," he wrote the Smiths. "Nobody could guess that anybody had written them. They seem just to have collected themselves."[32]

After completing his report Lawrence took up once again his struggle to get his ideas about marine craft accepted in the services, especially by the navy.[33] Lawrence suggested that Dawson send his "marine man" down to Southampton to see the boats for the purpose of writing them up in the paper, and offered to have the reporters picked up and "given a show. My name, of course, not to be mentioned." Dawson followed through as Lawrence wished, and in April (1932) a reporter visited the boatyards and wrote two articles in *The Times* about what he had discovered. Although the articles did not mention Lawrence by name, he could not, as it turned out, remain dissociated from these revolutionary developments in marine engineering.

Over the next few months Lawrence was rewarded for his efforts by a hectic period (which he seems to have enjoyed despite complaints that "my head is like a pudding") of running the new boats hundreds of miles to various coastal stations in England and Scotland, where he instructed new crews in their operation and ran trials of target boats. There are few letters from this period. So busy was he that when he heard in June from a friend that St. John Philby had crossed the Empty Quarter of Arabia by a route more difficult than Bertram Thomas's, Lawrence replied: "Only vaguely I heard he was dead. Good he isn't for Philby is a decent creature."[34]

In August Lawrence returned to Southampton and described himself to Ede as "part mechanic, part water-chauffeur, but very busy, and not useless, though an ephemeris."[35] *Too True to Be Good* played for the first time in August in Malvern, then moved to Birmingham, where Lawrence saw it, before opening in London in September. Lawrence saw the play again in London and this time went backstage to thank Walter Hudd, the actor who played Private Meek, "for making the part neither impudent or servile (its dangers) and tried to hide my regret that the counterfeit was so much nicer than my original."[36] Hudd wrote to Stanley Weintraub of his meeting with Lawrence. "His most striking characteristic appeared to be his *repose*. This aspect of him I had already used, however. He spoke briefly and quietly, examined me curiously, and then shyly withdrew."[37]

In September Lawrence was asked by W. B. Yeats if he would consent to being nominated for membership in the Irish Academy of Letters, to which he was eligible by virtue of being the son of an Irishman. This was one honor which Lawrence did not decline ("I am Irish and it has been a chance to admit it publicly," he wrote Yeats), and his acceptance was communicated to Yeats through Mrs. Shaw. Yeats then wrote to Lawrence: "Your acceptance of our nomination has given me great pleasure, for you are among my chief of men, being one of the few charming and gallant figures of our time, and as considerable in intellect as in gallantry and charm. I thank you."[38]

But complete happiness, as Lawrence wrote to Ede at the time, "is like a boom: it involves a slump before and after."[39] In October he was sent by the Air Ministry from Southampton back to his base at Plymouth, "chased" out of his job and lodgings at Hythe by newspaper headlines concerning his exciting work with speedboats "that said more than the truth."[40] As David Garnett pointed out, it seems never to have occurred to the British government that they had in their famous Lawrence of Arabia, working diligently in the ranks, not only a threat but an extraordinary moral example and a priceless asset for recruitment of men of high caliber into the armed services.

At first Lawrence seems to have enjoyed his relative leisure at Plymouth, where he was engaged in routine activities not concerned with boatbuilding. For the first time in many months he had time to listen to records, catch up on his correspondence and reading, and take his friends on boatrides for pleasure. "My life is full of books," he wrote Aircraftsman-poet G. W. M. Dunn in November 1932, "and I get heaps of them, every week. There must be 2000 in the cottage, all going to waste in the hope that I will live there after 1935 when I leave the R.A.F."[41]

Also in November his translation of the *Odyssey* was published in the United States by the Oxford University Press. Although the work was reviewed favorably on the whole (except by the most decorous of classical scholars) and praised in particular for its freshness, readability and vitality, Lawrence as usual derogated his production.[42] He gave copies to several of his friends with demureness and insisted that he had done this laborious work only for the purpose of getting enough money to pay for improvements at Clouds Hill. "The *Odyssey* to me represents — a bath, a hot-water plant and book-shelves in my cottage," he wrote to one friend in December 1932,[43] and to Rogers he wrote in February, "Please do let the bathroom be furnished by Odysseus himself."[44] Lawrence's perfectionist conclusion was: "The translation just isn't good enough, though it is the best I can do."[45] By February 1933, the translation had sold eleven thousand copies and soon after this a new edition for use in secondary schools was under way.

During his two-week stay in Scotland in April 1932, Lawrence had become friendly with a retired group captain at the coastal station he had visited at Donibristle. This gentleman had taken a hand at farming, unsuccessfully as it soon turned out, and had also written a book about it. Not only did Lawrence write him detailed letters offering criticism of the book, but also sent him £200 in advance of receiving royalty payments from sales of the *Odyssey* ("to stave off bankruptcy from him").[46] "Receipts, arrangements . . . no good," Lawrence wrote the officer. "Treat it as your own, and shove it back on me as and when you can with convenience . . . this *Odyssey* translation is likely to bring me in this much in 1933."[47]

Early in 1933 the lack of any useful application of his talents began to wear on Lawrence and he considered leaving the RAF. As the cold winter wore on he became increasingly frustrated, restless and troubled. Another *Iris* crash, with the loss of a life, involved him once again in a round of salvage operations, a court of inquiry and an inquest. As Mrs. Smith wrote, no one at Mount Batten seemed to know how to make use of him.[48]

Early in March he applied for discharge. He was trying to force the issue, but was prepared to leave if no useful work could be found for him to do. "Actually I have been in the R.A.F. for eleven years now," he wrote Ede, "and the last year or two are only slow dying: So I should not fight for them. I must leave early in 1935, anyhow: and might almost as well leave in 1933. But there are two more types of boats I would be glad to make for them, and other trifles in my power and competence."[49] In March and April Lawrence wrote to air force officials and met with the chief of air staff, Geoffrey Salmond, and then with Salmond's brother John, who became chief when the former retired because of illness. He refused, he told Geoffrey Salmond at the end of March, to continue to do routine assignments at Mount Batten and wished to work further on boatbuilding or to do a long "flying boat" voyage and write a log of it.[50] Lawrence permitted the planned date of discharge — April 6 — to come and go without any action either on his part or the RAF's. But on April 21 he talked with John Salmond, who agreed that he would be posted first to the marine craft contractor's yard at Felixtowe in Suffolk, and then to another experimental station at East Cowes on the Isle of Wight in May. Once again Lawrence was building motorboats. "They are life-saving in object, not war weapons," he wrote Thurtle, and added with rather bitter irony, "Every true pacifist supports the R.A.F. In case of war we will destroy

(1) fleets
(2) civilians
(3) soldiers

in that order!"[51]

In the spring of 1933 Liddell Hart began writing his biography of Lawrence. As in the case of Graves's book Lawrence collaborated in providing information to Liddell Hart and corrected his proofs, but he maintained an ambivalent attitude toward this work as he did toward any work which called public attention to himself. He had enjoyed talking with Liddell Hart in their several meetings about various aspects of military history and strategy, and seems to have permitted the book on the grounds that it would emphasize this aspect of his life, but he resented the personal aspects of the writing. "I like Liddell Hart, yet I fear him," Lawrence wrote Mrs. Shaw in June. "He is too serious. His book on me is very interesting, where it is military, and *awful* (to my hidden self regard) where it deals with me as a human being."[52] After the writing was completed he wrote the publisher: "My reading Liddell Hart's effort does not imply either approval or collaboration. I regret it and apprehend it keenly."[53]

At the end of July 1933, Lawrence returned to Southampton, where he took lodgings in a rooming house. They remained his headquarters for the next sixteen months, although his new assignments in the development of marine craft would take him to other boatyards and testing stations in various parts of the British Isles to supervise RAF boatbuilding contracts. "I work at boats always," he wrote his mother in November, "and am now getting my ideas generally accepted. Even our stick-in-the-mud Admiralty wants to borrow one! When I have evening time I try to revise the *Odyssey* for publication in U.S.A. as a school-book: but I have been all the summer on this, without getting half-way. There are no free evenings."[54] When he was at Southampton, Lawrence (and therefore his friends) were kept well supplied with cakes, candy and pudding by Mrs. Shaw and other friends.

The increased stability of his existence permitted Lawrence to devote himself to "domestic" concerns, especially the installation in his cottage of such improvements as a new bathtub, a pool and an ingenious small ram (a pump to drive water uphill) connected with a spring. "Cottage all a ruin now, with the new water works in progress," he wrote Buxton in August. "Soon I shall have my very own bath! The first I have ever owned in exclusiveness. A milestone in my life."[55] There were a drought and heath fires near the cottage, but not nearly as severe as the following year, and generally it was a "marvelous summer" for weather.[56] More than ever before, Lawrence looked after friends and acquaintances who were in financial need, and even offered help with the education of the son of the dying chief of air staff, Geoffrey Salmond.[57] At times the various names he had used in his life became a nuisance in the handling of his complicated finances. "All these Rosses and Lawrences and Shaws make my head swim, and its a perpetual miracle how anything ever gets in the right place — if it does!" he wrote Buxton.[58]

In November a magazine called *British Legion Journal* printed the last three chapters (not a précis of these as Lawrence stated in a published letter)[59] of *The Mint* as an article by "Lawrence of Arabia" entitled "Service Life."[60] Although the content of the passages was innocuous, being concerned mainly with Lawrence's pleasure in rushing around the countryside on his Brough and his contentment with his comradeship among the men at Cranwell, unauthorized publication of the material got him into various sorts of difficulty. "I've got into awful trouble," Lawrence wrote in an unpublished letter, "with the Air Ministry, for publishing opinions about service matters without permission — with Lord Trenchard, for publishing part of *The Mint* against my most solemn promise to keep it private till 1950 at least — with Jonathan Cape, of piece-meal disclosure of matter upon which they hold an option. In fact my name is mud, everywhere, and I may be civvy next week because of it."[61]

The problem was in part of his own making: he had lent the manuscript to so many people to read. Before he found out who gave it to the *Journal* after "sub-loan upon sub-loan," he suspected David Garnett of leaking the material, but Garnett told him that he was not responsible for it. "As I was explaining this," Garnett wrote, "T.E. looked hard into my eyes. For a moment his blazed with blue fire, full of compelling force, unlike anything I have ever seen before or since in other men. I felt no fear or embarrassment and gazed back at him with astonishment and at that moment there was suddenly no barrier between us. The power, possibly hypnotic, possibly just rage, went out of him. T.E. was satisfied I was speaking the truth."[62] Lawrence did not end up in civvies over this incident: the damage appears to have been fairly readily undone by the *Legion Journal*'s agreement to assume responsibility for publishing the piece.

In December Lawrence seems to have become inspired briefly to write a major autobiographical book about his years in the RAF and the significance of man's entry into the "element of the air." A few paragraphs of the beginning of a work with this title have been preserved,[63] but there is no evidence that Lawrence did much more with the idea during the remaining year and a half of his life. Two months later the project had been downgraded to "sometimes I think of writing a little picture of the R.A.F."[64] The entry into the air and beyond the atmosphere into space has, of course, been the purpose more of this age than of his.

As 1933 drew to a close, Lawrence spoke of himself as a man troubled about growing old and looking forward to death. "I grow fat and stiff and white-haired," he wrote a former companion of the desert campaigns. "Hard luck, again. Time all of us relics of the great war were broken up."[65] On the last day of the year he wrote to Ede that his work with boats "will be the last tangible things I do."[66]

On this same day Lawrence also wrote to his two closest women friends, Lady Astor and Mrs. Shaw, both older than himself, about his problems with love. "This Christmas there has been an epidemic of love amongst my friends, male and female," he wrote Mrs. Shaw. "It makes me feel all shuddery, to be so cold and hostile to it. What can one do? If I turn hard they mope like the owls to the moon! and if I talk gently they beg for more."[67] To Lady Astor, he was more specific about a lady to whom he was rumored to have lost his heart. "Probably it would be wholesome for me to lose my heart," he wrote, ". . . if that monstrous piece of machinery is capable of losing itself: for till now it has never cared for anyone, though much for places and things. Indeed I doubt these words of 'hearts.' People seem to my judgment to lose their heads rather than their hearts. Over the Christmas season two men and four women have sent me fervent messages of love. Love carnal, not love rarefied, you know: and I am uncomfortable towards six more of the people I meet, therefore. It's a form of lunacy, I believe, to fancy that all comers are one's lovers: but what am I to make of it when they write it in black on white? If only one might never come nearer to people than in the street. Miss Garbo sounds a really sympathetic woman! The poor soul. I feel for her."[68]

Early in 1934 Lawrence was sent for nearly three weeks to work at a boat-engine yard at Wolverhampton in the industrial Midlands. Although his retirement was still a year away he wrote his mother: "I have a queer sense that it is all over — all the active part of my life, I mean; and that retirement from the R.A.F. is also retirement from the stream. I shall be 46; which is neither young nor old; too young to be happy doing nothing, but too old for a fresh start."[69] On the same day he wrote to Mrs. Shaw: "In the light of knowledge I see so clearly that what I once took for contentment is resignation: and what I thought was happiness is sense of failure."[70]

These brooding thoughts did not prevent Lawrence from continuing to work productively in the development of motorboat engines and target boats. Although still an A/C 1, Lawrence's influence and authority in boatbuilding had increased to the point where he was given quite a free hand by the Air Ministry ("they get the boats and engines that I want, and not always what they want").[71] Sometimes he would be called to London for high-level conferences at the Air Ministry concerning planning in his field of expertise. At these times he would stay at the Union Jack Club (a hostelry for servicemen) and book as 353172 A/2 Smith, RAF, because "aircraftman Shaw is becoming too popular a chap!"[72] He also managed to find time to "throw pots" in nearby Poole in order to make his own "decent" tea service for Clouds Hill.[73]

Early in 1934 Nazi Germany was becoming a sinister threat on the international horizon and efforts were made by former friends of Lawrence's from the All Souls days, among them Lionel Curtis and Philip Kerr, to draw Lawrence into assuming an active political role. He declined such invitations, but did write an extraordinary letter to Curtis in mid-March offering sound criticisms of Britain's defense preparations and recommending the direction of necessary RAF and naval development and expansion to meet the threat of possible future attack from Germany. He urged that Britain develop (sooner than she actually did) the air capacity to thwart a German attack. He had already had an important personal hand in developing a type of high-speed maneuverable naval craft, the forerunner of the P.T. boat of World War II, that would be less vulnerable to air attack than capital ships.[74]

More than ever during these last months of his life Lawrence was involved in acts of kindness and altruism in behalf of friends and acquaintances. His letters of this period, largely unpublished, are filled with efforts to help others: advice to a friend, for example, too dizzy with "the diet of cocktails" of a doomed love affair to think realistically; offers of the use of his cottage; explanations of enclosed checks meant to help someone in need; or critiques of the work of the many poets and writers who consulted him as his fame grew and his willingness to help became known. Always Lawrence's words seem to have been carefully chosen with attention to the feelings of the person to whom he was writing. He sought to be useful without wounding the self-regard of others.

The publication of Liddell Hart's book early in 1934 brought a new wave of idolization and lionization to further complicate Lawrence's life. The book disappointed him, he wrote, "because it fails to criticize anything. One could swallow praise, if it was moved with a reasonable amount of blame; but as one knows that not everything was well done, one cannot trust his judgement."[75]

One idolator of the period was the young dancer and writer Lincoln Kirstein, a pioneer of modern ballet production, and one of the reviewers of Liddell Hart's book. He had written to Lawrence in December that he regarded him as the only man he knew of who had accomplished in life what he had set out to do, and one of four men with whom he had been obsessed.[76] In April Lawrence, surfeited with the praise of Liddell Hart's book, replied in detail to Kirstein, disavowing the value in himself or his writings that Kirstein had ascribed. "You scare me, with your over-impression," Lawrence wrote. "Please come and see me, if you get to England again; and then you will see I am your own size — and everybody else's. . . . 'Man of action' you call me . . . do for heaven's sake, travel down to where I am and put these ideas straight. We are all poor silly things trying to keep our feet in the swirl."[77] Kirstein, undaunted, wrote that he was concerned with "how men act: a subject so few care to consider — and as I understand it — one of your prime interests."[78] Lawrence replied with more self-criticism: "The worst of being oneself is that one knows all one's vices too! . . . There ain't any such super-creatures as you would fain see."[79] They never met, but Kirstein recalled thirty-five years later, "He was a terrific hero to me in my youth."[80]

In addition to the worshippers male and female (a variant of the latter were a number of women who wrote letters to Lawrence accusing him of having "taken some advantage" of them),[81] Lawrence and his solicitors were made aware by Liddell Hart himself of a man who was going about impersonating Lawrence. They tracked the man down (it turned out he was a discharged mental-hospital patient receiving psychiatric treatment under the name of Lawrence) and persuaded him to give up the imposture. "I am not flattered at the thought that he got away with it successfully. An obviously feeble creature, with the wrinkling face of a chimpanzee," Lawrence wrote hastily after the episode was ended.[82]

Over the remaining months of the spring and summer of 1934 Lawrence turned his thoughts increasingly toward his air force retirement, now only a few months away. Although he was unable to spend as much time at Clouds Hill as he would have wished, he fussed over details of its furnishing, equipment and bedding for William Roberts and several others to whom he lent it freely whether he was there or not. He felt acutely the loss of friends who had died or who, like the Smiths and Robert Graves, were overseas. At the end of May he wrote the Smiths in Singapore: "There comes over me that sense of hopeless space and lack of contact. One changes in a week, you know, and unless in daily touch, how can either of us visualize the sort of mind which receives the letter, after weeks and weeks of posting?"[83]

A conversation with Liddell Hart early in June seemed to anticipate the manner of Lawrence's death a year later. He talked of the way he would try to avoid running over a hen on his motorcycle, although to swerve was a risk — "only on a motorcycle was the driver compelled to take a fair proportion of risk."[84] During another conversation later in the month he told Liddell Hart that the British "Fascists had been after him." He would not help them to power, he said, but if they did come to power he "would agree to become 'dictator of the press' — for a fortnight." That would suffice, he wrote, to settle the quarrel between the press and him.[85]

In a letter to Eric Kennington in August Lawrence showed that the absolutism of the standards by which he continued to measure himself had not softened or been modified in the slightest during his twelve years in the ranks; his inner dissatisfaction remained, therefore, unchanged. "One of the sorest things in life is to come to realise that one is just not good enough," he wrote; "better perhaps than some, than many, almost — but I do not care for relatives, for matching myself against my kind. There is an ideal standard somewhere and only that matters: and I cannot find it. Hence this aimlessness."[86]

During his last months based at Southampton Lawrence moved around a great deal, traveling to Wolverhampton, Kent, Nottingham, London and Plymouth to complete his work on small boats and to test "a rather exciting new" diesel engine.[87] He continued to struggle with the "mulish" navy and "pulled string after string" to get them to accept the faster Scott Paine motorboats as "set against their primitive junks."[88] He grew tired and despondent and longed for the peace of Clouds Hill — "the best part of the picture" — yet managed to find the energy and interest to write for his old friend of the Cairo days, George Lord Lloyd, former high commissioner of Egypt, a long critique of Lloyd's recent book, *Egypt Since Cromer*.[89] "How bored I'm going to be!" (in retirement), he wrote Liddell Hart. "Think of it: a really new experience, for hitherto I've never been bored."[90]

In November 1934, Lawrence was transferred to Bridlington, a summer resort on the North Sea, to supervise the overhauling in a huge garage of ten RAF boats that were working a bomber range. He was stationed at Bridlington for the less than four months that remained of his RAF service. Lawrence felt that it was time he retired: he found himself becoming "censorious" and could "see nothing which could not be better done, whether it is my own old work, or another's."[91] Yet, as he wrote to Mrs. Shaw, he wished he could avoid the inevitable and that "the world did not change. This blue protective coating has meant so much to me. I go back to the self of 1920 and 1921, a crazy pelican feeding not its young but its spirit creations upon its bodily strength. I had hoped all these years that I was not going to be alone again."[92]

The short period of Lawrence's stay at Bridlington is well described by the recollections of men with whom he worked, especially in the notes made after his death by Flight Lieutenant Reginald Sims, an equipment officer stationed there whose family Lawrence visited about once a week. The pattern of earlier recollections of Lawrence in the ranks is not broken by these accounts — the soft, silent manner; the precise, craftsmanlike use of language; the irreverent stories telling of the deflation of lofty personages ("big noises"); the elevating influence on the standards of conduct of officers and men; the abstemious habits; and the unvarying patience and sense of humor. Although his face had become red and roughened, "sandblasted," as Lawrence put it, the blazing blue eyes and impression of eternal youthfulness were unchanged. Lawrence had accumulated by this time an enormous knowledge on a vast variety of technical and other subjects which, combined with considerable practical experience, made him invaluable to the detachment. He loved tools and acquired a perfect fitter's tool kit, selecting its items as much for the beauty of their materials as for the fineness of their craftsmanship.

He had become by this period a still more seasoned storyteller and was apparently less reticent in talking about his past, as the many stories recorded by Sims well document. "He ranged the world for us," Sims wrote, and gave his entranced audiences "in brilliant cameo, sketches of kings, beggars, celebrities, underdogs, artists, murderers, and friends." He did not speak of enemies. "With a slight movement or expression, he would conjure up persons, so that we could almost see them before us, while the faint grin, and elfish look that accompanied some of his descriptions, were part of that birth right with which the Fairies had dowered him."[93]

Although Lawrence did not at Bridlington appear despondent or depressed as he had at earlier posts he still seemed, to Sims, to be "working out some difficult problem of his own at the same moment, that was not even remotely connected with the story he was telling or the life he was leading."[94] His past, Lawrence had once remarked, was like a tin can tied to the tail of a dog that rattled whatever he did.[95] Perhaps the rattle seemed less harsh to him now.

One story Lawrence told Sims — one of the rare ones that concerned his childhood — provides insight into his intense interest in fast boats and his long struggle with the admiralty to have his ideas accepted. When he was eight (the family was by then living in Oxford) his parents took him to see a review of the fleet at Spithead near Southampton on the occasion of the Diamond Jubilee of Queen Victoria. There was a vast array of the latest naval ships in perfect alignment to be reviewed. About half an hour before the Queen was to make her inspection "a small, evil-looking, squat, ugly little steamer, clearly non-service, and simply belching out clouds of dense smoke" made a straight line for the fleet from the shadow of a nearby headland. Greatly alarmed, the senior naval officer in charge dispatched one fast naval vessel after another to head off or even destroy the little steamer that was threatening to ruin the formation. But the little steamer led her pursuing armada out to sea and disappeared over the horizon as she maintained and even increased her lead. This proved to be a dramatic demonstration by a Mr. Parsons, who had invented the turbine engine, but who had been unable until that time to get the admiralty interested in it. After the drama was over — he had spent every farthing he could scrape together on it — the admiralty fined him £200 for the disturbance but gave him a million-pound order for turbine engines. Lawrence had wished to repeat history at the next fleet review at Spithead on the occasion of King George V's Jubilee by demonstrating a speedy motorboat he had developed, but knew he would no longer be in the RAF at that time. He had to be content with a more gradual persuasion of the admiralty to his point of view.[96]

As Lawrence's discharge date approached, a number of his friends became concerned about what he was going to do after retirement and were eager to prevent his vegetating and going to seed. One of these, Lord Rennell of Rodd, a banker, was in close touch with Montague Norman, governor of the Bank of England. Norman in the summer of 1934 was concerned with filling the post of secretary of the bank. The person chosen need not have a technical, financial or economic background but had to be able to provide leadership: "He had to be a man."[97] One day, on the urging of Herbert Baker, who also was concerned about Lawrence's future, Norman called Rodd and asked him to inquire of Lawrence privately whether he would consider "the offer of an appointment to the Bank of England with a view to becoming Secretary of the Governor and Company of the Bank" after his RAF service was over.[98]

Rodd observed that Lawrence had no business experience, but Norman held firm on the "Elizabethan" ground that a man who was good at one thing would be good at another. Rodd wrote to T.E. in the early fall, but owing to the latter's moving about received no reply until a letter from Lawrence dated November 23 came from Bridlington. Lawrence was clearly moved by the offer but, despite his anticipation that he would feel "unutterably lost" out of uniform, refused it. "Will you please say No, for me, but not a plain No," he wrote Rodd. "Make it a coloured No, for the Elizabethan of Baker's naming has given me a moment of very rare pleasure which I shall not tell to anyone, nor forget."[99]

Cheered by the anticipation of a few days at Clouds Hill at Christmastime Lawrence wrote a delightful letter to Jimmy Newcombe, now fourteen and a full-fledged Etonian, which is filled with gentle parodies of Christmas conventions. He urged young Newcombe to watch over his parents and prevent their gluttony at the dinner table: "If they bring in plum puddings and things, remark in a blasé accent . . . the normal speech, I mean, of Eton . . . 'Isn't it jolly, papa, to keep up these old customs? It's like Dickens, isn't it, I mean, what?' That will throw a chill over the whole meal-time — I mean orgy. You owe a duty to your family at Christmas." The letter concluded: "Don't wish them any sort of celebration of the birth of Christ. I only do one Xmas letter per year, and that's not really a letter. I send Lady Astor a reply-paid wire of 'Merry Xmas' and she wires back 'Same to you.' "[100] During the Christmas holidays Lawrence talked with his neighbor, Pat Knowles, about plans for building a printing press, and Knowles even began to gather materials for a shed to house it.[101]

As the year drew to a close the future did not look cheerful to Lawrence. "The R.A.F. leaves me out of its rolls in February next, and I'm facing rather a blank future in something like unhappiness," he wrote the poet Maurice Baring. "I've been serving for 12 years, and the assurance has stayed me, like his shell a hermit crab. Now life's to begin again, with all the 24 hours of the day given to me — and I particularly don't want so much."[102] He still thought sometimes of doing a short book about Roger Casement. "As I see it, his was a heroic nature. I should like to write upon him subtly, so his enemies would think I was with them til they finished my book and rose from reading to call him a hero. He had the appeal of a broken archangel."[103]

On January 3 of the new year (1935) Lawrence wrote to Ede: "Early in March I 'get my ticket.' It's like a blank wall beyond which I cannot even imagine. Exactly what leisure is like, whether it will madden me or suit me. What it means to wake up every day and know there is no compulsion to get out of bed . . . it's no good. When it comes, I shall try to deal with it; but now, beforehand, I can only say that I wish it had not to be."[104]

Other letters in the early weeks of 1935 also express Lawrence's anxiety about leaving the RAF and a sense that time was running out on him and that his life "in the real sense" was over. "The sands run out, continually," he wrote to the Smiths in Singapore. "Another six weeks and the R.A.F. loses its smallest ornament. Meanwhile I work away at the boats, and find myself everlastingly putting up suggestions for new devices or improvements. I forget I'm going out, whenever there is anything to do."[105] Elsewhere he noted that he was constantly tripping himself up "in some research or advice concerning boats, something that might take weeks to fruition."[106]

Lawrence remained "fully engaged" in his work on motorboats until he left the camp, but was also busy with several other matters. He successfully staved off an effort by the film producer Alexander Korda to make a movie of his life. He met Korda, "the film king," and persuaded him of his desire to be left alone. "He was quite unexpectedly sensitive, for a king," Lawrence wrote Mrs. Shaw.[107] Lawrence told the Simses that the only film he could have borne to have done about his Arabian campaign would be one by Walt Disney in the style of *Three Little Pigs* and *The Grasshopper and the Ant* — "Me and my army jogging across a skyline on camels could have been very amusing."[108]

At the end of January he learned that the publishers of Hanley's novel *Boy* were successfully prosecuted for indecency by local police. Lawrence was clearly troubled about this on principle and alarmed at the precedent of putting writers and publishers "at the mercy of the discretion of any Police Chief at any time."[109] He sought to mobilize a protest of publishers against the police action and was still engaged in this effort when he was fatally injured.

Also he had what he called "a dust-up" with the chief constable in one city over the matter of an eccentric widow of fifty-three who kept writing him letters, calling him "Jim," and begging him to return and that all would be forgiven. She would not take no for an answer and kept writing twice a week, so Lawrence asked the chief constable to help him out. The chief seems to have believed the lady's story that Lawrence had lived with her during the 1914–1918 war and had left her with two sons, and he wrote to Lawrence's "C.O." at Bridlington. There being no such officer, the letter came to Lawrence, who wrote the "Chief Copper" a blistering letter telling him that his action could have caused him much gossip and embarrassment. He never heard further from the widow or the constable.[110]

Early in February Lawrence wrote to Robert Graves, who had always been critical of his decision to remain in the ranks, a justification of his air force years, especially his success, achieved with others, of having new concepts of boat design accepted by the admiralty and by the navies of other governments. From the personal standpoint he offered this summary of his years in the ranks:

"I went into the R.A.F. to serve a mechanical purpose, not as a leader but as a cog of the machine. The key-word, I think, is machine. I have been mechanical since, and a good mechanic, for my self-training to become an artist has greatly widened my field of view. I leave it to others to say whether I chose well or not: one of the benefits of being part of the machine is that one learns that one doesn't matter!

"One thing more. You remember me writing to you when I first went into the R.A.F. that it was the nearest modern equivalent of going into a monastery in the Middle Ages. That was right in more than one sense. Being a mechanic cuts one off from all real communication with women. There are no women in the machines, in any machine. No woman, I believe, can understand a mechanic's happiness in serving his bits and pieces."[111]

Lawrence, as is well known, rarely drank, but he was invited by the officers and his fellow airmen to a party shortly before he left Bridlington. The group went to a local theatre and then visited a nearby club for "ginning-up." Lawrence did not have a drink, but ate a cherry on a stick from one of his friend's glasses. A waitress then brought him an entire dish of cherries, "and he ate every one with the zest of a schoolboy raiding a tuck shop."[112]

In February Lawrence had a card printed, which read, "To tell you that in future I shall write very few letters," and planned to put one in each letter that he wrote over the next six months.[113] In order to avoid publicity, plans were made to have Lawrence leave Bridlington at the end of February rather than on his scheduled date of March 11. He had been corresponding, however, with a former serviceman from the days of the Arabian campaigns who had offered to be his valet. Lawrence declined the offer ("No, Clouds Hill wouldn't look right with a valet!"), but let his friend know of his plans to leave Bridlington in a month. Somehow the press found out, for on February 25, the day before Lawrence was to leave, reporters were "scurrying about" Bridlington and also at Clouds Hill.[114]

There is irony in a conversation that occurred not long before Lawrence left Bridlington, recalled afterwards by a ship contractor, Ian Deheer, with whom he had worked there. " 'I have brought my bike up, would you like to see it?' " Lawrence asked. " 'Most certainly,' " Deheer replied. "He took me up to the cycle, which with him standing alongside, looked enormous. I was taken aback at the size of it and remarked, 'You will be breaking your blinking neck on it,' and his reply was, 'Well, better than dying in bed.' "[115]

32

Retirement and Death

From the standpoint of the service at least, Lawrence's years had been successful, for his discharge forms contained this summary: "He is an exceptional airman in every respect and his character and general conduct have at all times been 'very good.' " "A document from the Ministry of Labor among his discharge papers was more specific and conveys a sense that his transformation was quite complete: "This airman has a habit of pushing any job too far. He can do rather too many things. He prefers a small job to a big one. Job preferred: motor yacht hand. Seasonally only and in a small craft. . . . References: None — best reference probably manager British Power Boat Company or Wing Commander."[1]

On February 26 Lawrence left Bridlington on his bicycle, having decided that his income from investments of twenty-five shillings a week would make it difficult to maintain his motorcycle. "I'm riding out of Bridlington at this moment, aiming South but with no destination in view," he wrote to an RAF sergeant.[2] He dropped in (as was his way) on the Arnold Lawrences in Cambridge the next day (it was the last time the brothers were to see each other). He seemed steady, at ease and content, and spoke of passing the time exploring the countryside or printing.[3] He intended to go to Clouds Hill for a time, but otherwise his plans were curiously indefinite. To one person or another he had told of his desire to visit Iceland, take up his dream of printing, tour the Midlands,[4] travel in England with Eric Kennington, or just "wander for most of this year about England."[5]

He had planned to visit Frederic Manning on his way south but discovered that Manning had recently died. He quickly sent off a letter to Manning's friend and publisher, Peter Davies, expressing his sadness and regret that Manning had died unknown and unappreciated. Lawrence's grief over Manning's death blended with his sense of loss with regard to the air force and he wrote to Davies of his longing for death: "I find myself wishing all the time that my own curtain would fall."[6]

As Lawrence disliked wearing a crash helmet when he rode his Brough, Jock Chambers was relieved to hear that Lawrence traveled by bicycle on this trip.[7] Staying in youth hostels along the way, Lawrence arrived in London in the first days of March, having been shocked to discover en route that Clouds Hill was besieged with reporters and photographers, who damaged the roof of the cottage and trampled the land. He took an apartment in London under the name of E. Smith (he had used this before), went about London feeling quite lost,[8] and spent much of the month "wandering about the South Country."[9] The reporters left and he returned to the cottage in mid-March, but so did they.[10] They refused to leave and insisted on interviewing and photographing him. He punched "the most exigent" one of them in the eye so hard that the man had to see a doctor, and rode off on his bicycle back to London with a sore hand.

On March 22 Lawrence suggested to Liddell Hart that he write a book to be called "Fifteen Decisive British Defeats,"[11] and on the same day had a long conversation with Ralph Isham in which they talked about the threat of European war and the more imminent concern about war between Italy and Ethiopia. Lawrence predicted that if war came in Ethiopia conflict between dark and white races would spread over the world.[12] Lawrence himself was approached by the government on whether he might be interested in taking part in the reorganization of Home Defense by serving as the deputy and eventual successor on the defense side to Lord Hankey.[13] He toyed with the idea for a while, and expressed in a conversation with Herbert Baker "a desire to serve in the guiding of it."[14] But, in his brother's words, "after oppressed hesitation he saw means to avoid an active participation in the replanning of national defence — which began immediately with a great expansion of the Air Force."[15]

At the end of March Lawrence visited Ede, who gave him a check for twenty or thirty pounds so that he could afford his motorbike. Although Lawrence thanked him and accepted the check initially, it was found in his cottage uncashed after his death. Ede wrote that he "felt very strongly" after their conversation that Lawrence "really had at last come through the war, or almost so, and I kept thinking that two years, or three of country life would see him embarked on some new activity which would swamp out his previous record."[16]

Lawrence's view of himself at this time was different: "I'm gray-haired and toothless, half blind and shaking at the knees," he wrote to one serviceman, and to another: "The active part of life is over."[17]

Finally, through a combination of writing and personal visits he was able to achieve an "unholy compact" with the Newspaper Proprietor's Association and a precarious peace with the reporters that enabled him to return to Clouds Hill at the end of March. In the weeks of April and May that remained, Lawrence sought the peaceful existence that had always eluded him. He does not in fact seem to have done very much during these last weeks. He spent his time "inventing odd jobs," such as cutting and gathering wood, laying pipe, and building. He fitted the cottage with a large porthole, and tried unsuccessfully to drive off a persistent small bird which fluttered for hours a day against a windowpane. ("First I thought he was a bird-pressman, trying to get a story: then a narcissist, admiring his figure in the glass. Now I think he is just mad.")[18]

Although Lawrence continued to feel "like a lost dog" he was pleased that the navy was ordering "by the dozen for all ships" the fast small dinghies he had developed. He thought the hulls of ships like destroyers should be redesigned so that they could plane (like hovercraft) and thus achieve speeds of 70 knots.[19] At the end of April he traveled to Hythe for a last meeting with Beauforte-Greenwood and Flight Lieutenant Norrington to accept a gift of stainless steel candlesticks in commemoration of their association in the building of the dinghies.[20]

As he began his second month of leisure the pain Lawrence experienced over the loss of the RAF had grown "worse instead of healing over,"[21] and this made him feel "queer and baffled."[22] To Bruce Rogers he wrote on May 6: "I'm 'out' now of the R.A.F. and sitting in my cottage rather puzzled to find out what has happened to me, is happening and will happen. At present the feeling is mere bewilderment. I imagine leaves must feel like this after they have fallen from the tree and until they die. Let's hope that will not be my continuing state."[23] He used the same image in a letter to Eric Kennington: "What I have done, what I am doing, what I am going to do, puzzle me and bewilder me. Have you ever been a leaf and fallen from your tree in autumn and been really puzzled about it? That's the feeling."[24]

Lady Astor made a last effort to draw Lawrence to Cliveden to discuss his role in the reorganization of the defense forces. But he was not interested. "No," he replied to her letter on May 8, "wild mares would not at present take me away from Clouds Hill. . . . Also there is something broken in the works, as I told you: my will, I think. In this mood I would not take on any job at all."[25]

Lawrence made plans to have various visitors at his cottage — E. M. Forster and Aircraftsman Dunn among others — but does not seem to have had any guests during these days. On May 12, the day before his fatal accident he wrote, "At present I'm sitting in my cottage and getting used to an empty life."[26]

One of his visitors was to be Henry Williamson, who wished to come to Clouds Hill to discuss his ideas about Anglo-German relations. Williamson wrote to Lawrence that he would arrive as planned unless the day was rainy. I discussed with Williamson in 1965 his recollections of what he had in mind in requesting such a meeting. Williamson was a friend of the English fascist Oswald Mosley, and he and Mosley had talked about Hitler, whom Williamson regarded as unbalanced or unstable mentally, but who had a capacity to accomplish something positive for Europe if "someone could send him along the proper track." Somehow Williamson got into his head the notion that only Lawrence could send Hitler along this "proper track," although Lawrence — Williamson stated this explicitly — had no sympathy with the dictator or with the German government. Williamson did not recall what he put into his letter, whether in fact it contained any references to these political fantasies. The letter was not discovered among Lawrence's possessions after his death. Its disappearance gave rise to speculation that it was taken by a newspaperman or suppressed. It has never been found.[27]

On the morning of May 13, Lawrence rode on the Brough (he had recently begun to use it again) to Bovington Camp about a mile from Clouds Hill to wire Williamson to come ahead for lunch the next day, whether it was wet or fine. There is no evidence that Lawrence's interest in such a meeting had anything to do with a wish to discuss Williamson's political schemes. They were friends, Lawrence was lonely and lacking in companionship at this time, and, as Knightley and Simpson have pointed out, the two had common literary interests.[28]

On the return trip from Bovington Lawrence was traveling at 50 to 60 miles an hour[29] — an unsafe speed, but one he could ordinarily have managed — when he came suddenly upon two boys at a rise in the road just before the cottage. They were on bicycles, going one behind the other, in the same direction he was. A black car or delivery van had just passed, going in the opposite direction, and may have been distracting. Lawrence swerved suddenly to avoid the boys, flew over the handlebars, and fell in the road, suffering fatal head injuries.[30] He lingered for nearly six days in a coma at the Bovington Camp hospital and died on the morning of May 19, 1935. To avoid publicity visitors were limited. A few friends, among them Colonel Newcombe and Lord Carlow, stayed at the bedside to the end. The King telephoned the hospital to inquire about the fallen hero, and when Lawrence's death was known wrote to Arnold Lawrence, "His name will live in history."

The funeral was held at the Moreton village church on the afternoon of May 21 near Clouds Hill and was attended by mourners who had known Lawrence in various phases of his career: former comrades-in-arms, government dignitaries, artists, writers, military officers and enlisted men. The service was simple and brief, and the parson faltered as if overcome with emotion. The coffin was buried in a leaf-lined churchyard grave.[31]

Clare Sydney Smith's letter to Mrs. Shaw the day after Lawrence's death is characteristic of the reactions of his friends: "For myself I am heartbroken," she wrote. "For him I cannot feel sad. He wasn't a happy man, and he was lonely — But what a loss, and I know you and your husband will feel it sadly."[32] On the same day as this letter was written the New York *Times* reported a statement of 'Ata Amin, chargé d'affaires at the Iraqi Embassy in New York: "The Arab nation has lost a great friend. . . . Lawrence did his utmost in striving for the independence of our nation, he was the champion of the Arab's cause not only during the war but afterward at the Peace Conference."[33] Trenchard also wrote to Arnold Lawrence the day after T.E.'s death, "His influence for the Air Force was all for good," but Lawrence's service file contains a note, written the day after the funeral, stating that nothing would be published "dealing with Lawrence's service in the R.A.F. since there is little that can be said of a period devoted to self-effacement."[34] Seven months later a memorial service was held for Lawrence in St. Paul's Cathedral, London, at which a bust of him was unveiled in the crypt. Mrs. Lawrence offered to pay the railway fare of any of her son's service friends who wished to attend but could not afford to.[35]

Soon dramatic stories, some with sinister political implications, were spread about the circumstances of his death, but I could find no information to substantiate them.[36]

The question of a possible self-destructive or suicidal element in Lawrence's death is more complex. Arnold Lawrence has written of the "despondency" that overshadowed his brother after retirement and that had not lifted by the time of the accident. He suggests that Lawrence rode at a somewhat excessive speed to "forget himself for a few seconds" and that he thus rode "into a catastrophe which the normal quickness of his brain might possibly have averted; as it was, he saved others from injury."[37] The pattern of letters in the last months of Lawrence's life, especially those written after his RAF retirement, suggest a continuing and progressive despair and emptiness. There is no relieving plan, nothing to suggest a revival of new interest in living. It is hard for me to agree with Churchill's opinion that had he lived "some overpowering need would draw him from the modest path he chose to tread and set him once again in full action at the centre of memorable events."[38] It is a useless argument.

There is no evidence of a direct suicidal intent in the accident. But it is known that men who are living without hope or interest in their lives, or have suffered a recent severe loss, like Lawrence's loss of his work in the RAF, are more prone to accidents. The self becomes less attentive to its own preservation. The immediate period of retirement is a well-known time of depression, despair and even suicide for men leaving the security of the armed forces. The RAF had furnished Lawrence with certainty, security and companionship, and a life containing worthwhile work and activities; at the same time it provided relief from larger responsibilities. He had found nothing to take its place, and in his despondency and increasing nihilism was prone to "forget himself," as his brother has described.

Lawrence did not, in my opinion, commit suicide. He was, however, less vigorous in preserving his own life than he might once have been. When he suddenly became aware of the boys on bicycles in front of him his natural response was to protect them from injury, even at the risk of his own safety. Mrs. Smith wrote at the end of *The Golden Reign*, "His strongest impulse was to save life, and he lost his own in doing so."[39]

SIX

FURTHER DIMENSIONS

33

Intimacy, Sexuality and Penance

Every biographer confronts aspects of his subject's life that do not lend themselves to treatment within the chronological sequence of events. This is especially true of themes that relate to the subject's character, or to his intimate or private life. Although these more personal, more psychological, dimensions may be only intermittently apparent or may be visible for the first time relatively late in the subject's life, they usually are organically related to other, earlier times and experiences, even childhood ones. They grow out of the very fabric of the personality.

As I have tried to show in various parts of this book, there are demonstrable connections between elements of Lawrence's personal history and psychology and his actions that have historical importance. I suspect that all public figures are like Lawrence in this respect, although these connections are perhaps more readily discernible in Lawrence's life because of the conflicts with which he struggled and his gifts as an introspective psychologist.

In this section I will deal with some of these personal, more private dimensions, which do not readily find a place in any single part of this narrative. Although they may at times make for painful reading, I feel that their inclusion in this work is necessary if Lawrence is to be fully understood and appreciated.

Arnold Lawrence once concluded a letter to me at a time when we were trying to place his brother's beating problem in a broader psychological perspective, "I don't see why a man's choice of sexual outlet should matter much biographically; everyone has one, or should, and his was predetermined by accidental circumstances."[1] This statement, linking the flagellation disorder with the Der'a incident, raises an important question. Despite the current public openness about sex, a person's sexuality, like the rest of his personal or intimate life, remains his private business, and the biographer may be required to have some justification beyond the potential interest of his readers for making its details public.

Nor is a purely clinical interest adequate, for in professional journals the publication of intimate personal or physical details for the purposes of advancing scientific knowledge is done with accepted safeguards of anonymity and privacy. Obviously, for a public figure like Lawrence no disguise of identity is possible, and the effect of such disclosures on the sensibilities and feelings of relatives and friends, and upon the continuing rights of the dead to remain interred with some privacy respected, merits careful consideration.

The biographer's justification for exploring the sexual (or any other intimate aspect of the life of the person being studied) is his belief that it is vitally related to his public life, that understanding it is essential to understanding the subject's character in general, or that in itself its details are potentially of such unique scientific or humanitarian interest that publication will be of value. In my opinion all of these conditions pertain to some degree in Lawrence's case. Up to the time of the war, it is difficult to establish precise connections between Lawrence's sexuality and its related conflicts and the directions of his life, although I believe such connections exist. After the war, however, they are unmistakable. Furthermore, the intricacies of Lawrence's sexual life are so fundamentally bound up with other aspects of his character that it is not possible to understand the latter fully without some exploration of the sexual aspect. The converse is also, of course, true — that his sexuality is not explicable without a full understanding of his development as a person. In its details and in the elaboration of related rituals, Lawrence's sexuality, though by no means unique, seems to me sufficiently unusual and revealing of the relationship between private psychology and public action as to warrant examination in its own right. Finally, I believe that much of his suffering, which he felt obliged to hide, was the outcome of his early development. Insofar as his early development was affected by prevailing social attitudes, it is of value to show candidly what misery they caused him, if only to contribute to their modification in the future.

Freud, wishing perhaps to be faithful to his medical background and profession, clung for several decades to a rather narrow biological view of sexuality, although he recognized its obvious links to love and to many human relationships. In recent decades psychoanalysts, dynamic psychologists and other students of psycho-sexuality have given increasing attention to aspects of early sexual development and family life, to the part played by sexuality in a wide range of human relationships, and to the links between sexuality and other human drives and emotions, for example, love, fear, ambition, power and aggression. Perhaps the problem is not only one of definition. Sexuality in its biological sense may be narrowly defined, yet also be approached broadly in terms of its importance to the image an individual has of himself and to his personal, professional, social and political relationships.

My own approach to the study of sexuality in general and Lawrence's in particular combines humanistic, psychoanalytic and medical perspectives, and is both narrow and comprehensive. It is narrow in limiting "sexuality" to specifically sexual attitudes and practices; it is broad in seeing these attitudes and practices in a variety of perspectives and contexts. These include most prominently a developmental approach (that is, the view of adult sexuality as emerging from family influences and from relationships in childhood or other earlier developmental stages); a respect for the role of what in his brother's case Arnold Lawrence called "accidental circumstances" in shaping the direction of a person's sexuality; the recognition of inborn genetic or biological factors; a stress on the links between sexuality and love (and other emotions) in human relationships; and, finally, the influence of society, culture and even politics upon sexual attitudes, choices and decisions.

Lawrence was a child of his age. His childhood in Oxford was spent during the decades of late Victorian England, which saw Oscar Wilde's career destroyed when his homosexual practices were revealed. It was an age burdened by a religiosity, an extreme form of which Edmund Gosse, one of the period's most devastating critics, describes as a social force which invented virtues, both "sterile and cruel," sins "which are no sins at all," and darkened "the heaven of innocent joy with futile clouds of remorse."[2] For Lawrence, the strict social and religious codes which prevailed in England around the turn of the century were augmented by the profound personal sense of sin with which his parents were afflicted as a result of their liaison, what he called "the uprooting of their lives and principles."

One of the central developmental tasks of childhood, especially for boys, is to establish sufficient emotional distance from the mother to allow the pursuit of an independent life. Ideally this life would include the choice of a partner sufficiently distinguished from the mother not to fall under the prohibitions of the incest taboos or be made otherwise intolerable by associations with her. The schoolboy years before adolescence are those in which the boy is turning away from the intimacies of early childhood and pursuing instead a variety of nonsexual relationships and interests in school or in other situations outside the home. The onset of puberty is followed generally by the search for sexual contact, again outside the home. The persistence of attachment to the mother may be discerned principally through idealized comparisons of the partner with her, in the choice of a partner who is valued as the mother (or sister) was, or who may even share her valued attributes. The conveying of standards and values by parents, and the various rebuffs and scoldings which so irritate their sons, serve among other things to aid this process of establishing distance.

Now let us examine what happened to Lawrence. As far as we can tell, intimacy with the mother was present in his early childhood, although he received physical affection more continuously from nurses. Religious and intellectual values and devotion of the members of the family to each other were exaggerated as a result of parental guilt and self-imposed social isolation. The boys were strictly brought up in an atmosphere that stressed a high degree of propriety, if not chastity, and they were encouraged to develop a great range of interests and skills outside of the home, in which the father constructively shared. It was in this context that Lawrence gradually discovered the discrepancy between the fundamentalist values the parents taught him, and purported to follow themselves, and the reality of their actual situation. The same mother for whom Oscar Wilde was a dirty word and who disapproved of theatres and dancing was herself living in an adulterous relationship, to which the father had also subscribed. During a period in which he was attempting to achieve distance from his mother and to put his emotional attachment to her behind him, Lawrence was reminded of the illicit nature of her relationship with his father and of the contradictions inherent in it. In addition, to fulfill her own needs, Mrs. Lawrence seems to have been unusually demanding of her sons for intimacy and expressions of love, a trait which was most clearly evident after she had lost two of them in the war.

Lawrence leaves little doubt that the discovery of his illegitimacy and his relationship with his mother had a profound effect upon his subsequent development. When he was nearly forty years old, he could still write Mrs. Shaw that he found his mother "very exciting" and that "probably she is exactly like me; otherwise we wouldn't so hanker after one another, whenever we are wise enough to keep apart." His inability to find a mate who would bear his children Lawrence attributed directly to his relationship with his mother. "Knowledge of her," he wrote Mrs. Shaw, "will prevent my ever making any woman a mother, and the cause of children." Thomas Lawrence could not have helped his son in this struggle, even if he had understood it, for he was viewed by Lawrence as "her trophy of power."

We have seen how during adolescence Lawrence did not seek out what opportunities for contact with the opposite sex were available to him (certainly fewer in the Oxford of his youth than they would be in the present day), and devoted his energies to nonsexual pursuits, to testing and inuring himself, and to mastering a great variety of skills, as if in preparation for some great task. Lawrence's one attempt to form a heterosexual bond during his youth was with an early childhood friend, Janet

Laurie, and ended in failure. Hurt by the rejection, Lawrence feigned, like Hippocleides, not to care. He went to live and work in the Middle East, where he immersed himself in a culture in which women, if not openly devalued, were at least made largely inconspicuous. Association with men was more congenial to him in any event: he had been brought up in a family of five boys and had attended an all-male school and college. Thereafter, he lived largely in societies of men. The circumstances of life at Carchemish necessitated that daily contact be primarily with men, although Lawrence established valuable friendships with women at the mission school at Jebail, and he showed great consideration and kindness toward Mrs. Fontana and other female visitors to the site. At Cairo and during the campaigns his contacts were also principally with men, war being almost exclusively a male exercise. In the peacetime armed forces Lawrence chose an all-male society, quite removed from the company of women.

In *Seven Pillars of Wisdom* Lawrence acknowledged his "craving to be liked — so strong and nervous that never could I open myself friendly to another," yet made it clear that he had shrunk from physical intimacy in any form: "The lower creation I avoided as a reflection upon our failure to attain real intellectuality. If they forced themselves on me I hated them.[3] To put my hand on a living thing was defilement; and it made me tremble if they touched me or took too quick an interest in me. This was an atomic repulsion, like the intact course of a snowflake. The opposite would have been my choice if my head had not been tyrannous. I had a longing for the absolutism of women and animals, and lamented myself most when I saw a soldier with a girl, or a man fondling a dog, because my wish was to be as superficial, as perfected; and my jailer held me back. Always feeling and illusion were at war within me, reasons strong enough to win. . . . I liked the things underneath me and took my pleasures downward. There seemed a certainty in degradation, a final safety. Man could rise to any height, but there was an animal level beneath which he could not fall."[4]

The assault by the Turks at Der'a was, as we know, a shattering experience for Lawrence. The memory of it haunted him, and he described its impact to Mrs. Shaw in terms reminiscent of his brother's account of the mother's childhood beatings, done to break Lawrence's will. More than six years after the incident Lawrence wrote of it to Mrs. Shaw in connection with the trial scene of Shaw's *Saint Joan*. Lawrence seems to have identified himself with Joan: "Poor Joan. I was thinking of her as a person, not as a moral lesson. The pain meant more to her than the example. You instance my night at Deraa. Well, I'm always afraid of being hurt: and to me, while I live, the force of that night will lie in the agony which broke me, and made me surrender. It's the individual view. You can't share it.

"About that night. I shouldn't tell you, because decent men don't talk about such things. I wanted to put it plain in the book, wrestled for days with my self respect . . . which wouldn't, hasn't let me. For fear of being hurt, or rather to earn five minutes respite from a pain which drove me mad, I gave away the only possession we are born into the world with — our bodily integrity. It's an unforgiveable matter, an irrecoverable position: and it's that which has made me foreswear decent living, and the exercise of my not-contemptible wits and talents.

"You may call this morbid: but think of the offence, and the intensity of my brooding over it for these years. It will hang about me while I live, and afterwards if our personality survives. Consider wandering among the decent ghosts hereafter, crying 'Unclean, Unclean!' "[5]

I do not find any inconsistency between this account and the more lurid and dramatic one in *Seven Pillars;* nor do I find substantiation in this passage of Aldington's assertion that Lawrence "yielded to the Bey's pederasty" rather than to the soldiers as described in the earlier version. More significant, the emphasis in the letter to Mrs. Shaw upon the overwhelming of his "bodily integrity," or in *Seven Pillars,* upon the loss of "the citadel of my integrity," is very similar to the way in which Lawrence viewed the threat of intimacy with his mother.

"I think I'm afraid of letting her get, ever so little inside the circle of my integrity," he wrote in 1928, "and she is always hammering and sapping to get in"; and, three months later, "I always felt that she was laying siege to me, and would conquer, if I left a chink unguarded."[6] These passages about his mother were written, of course, long after the Der'a episode, but they suggest that at the very least the incident aroused or revived earlier conflicts in Lawrence's relationship with his mother, a need to avoid surrendering to her desires and demands which, in view of the childhood beatings at her hands, may also have had the meaning of self-surrender. In any event, the flagellation disorder with which Lawrence was afflicted during his years in the ranks, and which will be discussed later in this chapter, appears to have been directly connected to the Der'a episode. In the absence of direct evidence, the linking of this disorder with Lawrence's relationship to his mother and to the childhood beatings becomes a matter of likelihood or of interpretation, for which no further evidence will probably be forthcoming.[7]

I have found no evidence that Lawrence ever as an adult entered voluntarily into a sexual relationship for the purpose of achieving intimacy or pleasure. This applies equally to heterosexual and homosexual relationships. There are a few passages in his letters and notes which indicate a longing for sexual experience, but no evidence that he could act on these longings, and much evidence that he could not. The evidence certainly does not support the view that Lawrence was "asexual," but rather that

British forces entering Damascus, October 1918. Below: The Damascus Town Hall soon after the surrender of the city. From the Bodleian Library, Oxford

McBey portrait of Lawrence at the time of the capture of Damascus.
The picture hangs in the Old Bursary at Jesus College, Oxford.
Courtesy of the Principal and Fellows of Jesus College, Oxford

Statuette of Lawrence by Lady Kennet, 1921, which was formerly
in the City of Oxford High School. Photograph by the author

Lawrence (second from left),
Sir Herbert Samuel (third
from left), Abdullah (next to
Samuel) and others at
Amman, April 1921. From
the Imperial War Museum,
London

Queen Mary, Trenchard and other officers walk past aircraft at
St. Omer, July 1917. From the Imperial War Museum, London

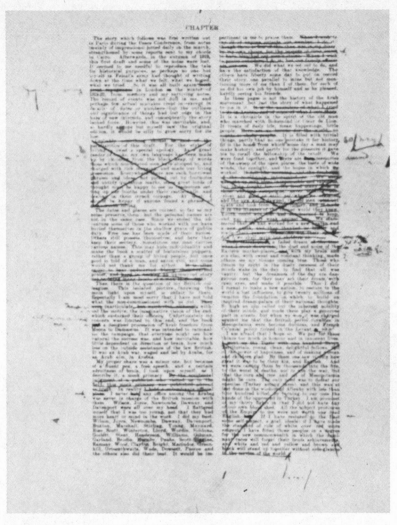

First page of the 1922 (Oxford) edition of *Seven Pillars of Wisdom*.
This was the copy from which Edward Garnett made his
unpublished abridgment in 1922. The deletions are Garnett's.
Courtesy of the Harvard College Library

Lawrence's draft preface for Edward Garnett's 1922 abridgment of *Seven Pillars of Wisdom*. Courtesy of the Harvard College Library

Clouds Hill, Lawrence's cottage. The Greek words over the front door, which were carved by Lawrence himself, mean "Does Not Care." From the Bodleian Library, Oxford

Miranshah, the remote Indian fort in the foothills of the Himalayas, where Lawrence was posted in 1928. From the Bodleian Library, Oxford

Lawrence at Miranshah.
From the National Portrait Gallery

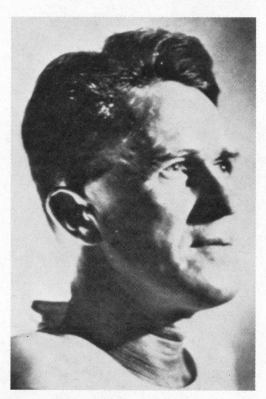

Portrait of Lawrence by Howard Costa,
done around 1930. Courtesy of the
Harvard College Library

With friends in Devonshire. From *The Golden Reign*
by Clare Sydney Smith

Lawrence at Plymouth in 1930. From *The Golden
Reign* by Clare Sydney Smith

Squeak, ∫
Squeak,
Squeak

from
T.
E.
S.

Inscription by Lawrence on the front page of *Child of the Deep* by Joan Lowell. The book belonged to Sydney Smith's daughter, nicknamed "Squeak." From *The Golden Reign* by Clare Sydney Smith

RAF 200 leaving from Plymouth. On board are
Fl/Lt. Beaufort-Greenwood, Wing Commander De Courcey,
A/Lt. Norrington, Corporal Bradbury and Aircraftsman Shaw.
This boat put up a new record between Southampton and
Plymouth. From the Bodleian Library, Oxford

Fa

Sir Emery Walker. — Wilfred Merton
Knight Treasurer

Bruce Rogers — Miss Saunders
Binder Scribe

This last page of my version of the
O DYSSEY
upon which I have spent almost as long as
O DYSSEUS.
and travelled further......

* * * * * *

Which has furnished me with luxuries for five years
and so wholly occupied my hours off duty that I have had no leisure
to enjoy them....

↓

affectionately, kindly,
gratefully
gladly
and
with enormous relief + glee
P R E S E N T E D ......

T. E. Shaw
15 · VIII · 31.

Note by Sir Emery —

Some three years late on the contract ! Otherwise well :

The final page of Lawrence's translation of the
Odyssey. Courtesy of the Bodleian Library, Oxford

Lawrence (left) and Captain Basil Liddell Hart in 1933. Taken by Captain Liddell Hart's first wife, Jessie. Courtesy of Arnold Lawrence

Lawrence at Bridlington, December 1934. Photograph by Reginald Sims. courtesy of Mrs. Hilda Sims

Bust of Lawrence by Eric Kennington (copy) in the chapel of
Jesus College. The original is in the crypt of St. Paul's Cathedral in
London. Photograph by the author

his early development brought about a deep need to reject and devalue all intimacy between the sexes, and gave rise to intense fears and inhibitions that prevented action.

The clearest statement of Lawrence's sexual puritanism, inhibition and conflict occurs in a letter to Mrs. Shaw in 1925: "I'm *too shy* to go looking for dirt. I'm afraid of seeming a novice in it, when I found it. That's why I can't go off stewing in the Lincoln or Navenly brothels with the fellows. They think it's because I'm superior, proud, or peculiar or 'posh,' as they say: and it's because I wouldn't know what to do, how to carry myself, where to stop. Fear again: fear everywhere. Garnett once said that I was two people, in my book: one wanting to go on, the other wanting to go back. That is not right. Naturally the very strong one, Say 'No,' the Puritan, is in firm charge, and the other poor little vicious fellow, can't get a word in, for fear of him. My reason tells me all the while, dins into me day and night, a sense of how I've crashed my life and self and gone hopelessly wrong: and hopelessly it is, for I'm never coming back, and I want to: Oh dear Oh dear, what a coil. Here come the rest [the other airmen in the barracks]: so here endeth the wail. No more thinking for awhile. I'm pitching it straight away to you as written, because in an hour I'll burn it, if I can get my hands on it."[8]

Lawrence strove to isolate psychologically the physical aspect of sex from its emotional and intimate dimensions, thus vulgarizing and demeaning the act and reducing it to a mechanical and trivial performance. He retained a scatalogical view of sexuality that reflected the persistence of a schoolboy attitude. Although this attitude was naturally defensive — that is, protected him from having to deal with the emotional meaning of love linked with mature sexuality — it was a view so tenaciously held, and so frequently elaborated, as to become a matter of conviction and personal philosophy. Even in *Seven Pillars of Wisdom* Lawrence wrote that he chided the venerable 'Awdah abu-Tayyi: "To gain ground with him, I began to jeer at the old man for being so old and yet so foolish like the rest of his race, who regarded our comic reproductive processes not as an unhygienic pleasure, but as a main business of life."[9]

In *The Mint* Lawrence wrote candidly of his ignorance of the realities of the sexual act, which he claims to have shared with many other enlisted men: "Sound momentary: sight momentary: smell? Why, a minute after our personality returns home from an absence, we do not even smell ourselves. Touch? I do not know. I fear and shun touch most, of my senses. At Oxford the select preacher, one evening service, speaking of venery, said, 'And let me implore you, my young friends, not to imperil your immortal souls upon a pleasure which, *so I am credibly informed,* lasts less than one and three-quarter minutes.' Of direct experience I cannot speak, never having been tempted so to peril my mortal soul: and six out of ten enlisted fellows share my ignorance, despite their flaming talk.

Shyness and a wish to be clean have imposed chastity on so many of the younger airmen, whose life spends itself and is spent in the enforced celibacy of their blankets' harsh embrace. But if the perfect partnership, indulgence with a living body, is as brief as the solitary act, then the climax is indeed no more than a convulsion, a razor-edge of time, which palls so on return that the temptation flickers out into the indifference of tired disgust once a blue moon, when nature compels it."[10]

Lawrence's friend F. L. Lucas, a Cambridge don and poet, read *The Mint* in 1929 and questioned these inaccurate speculations in a letter. "Is that genuine ignorance?" he inquired. "I mean the reader cries 'Oh he *must* learn better, if only by hearsay.' Anything up to several hours, they say, in India."[11] Lawrence, sticking to his guns, replied: "The period of enjoyment, in sex, seems to be a very doubtful one. I've asked the fellows in this hut (three or four go with women regularly). They are not sure: but they say it's all over in ten minutes: and the preliminaries — which I discounted — take up most of the ten minutes. For myself, I haven't tried it, and hope not to. I doubt if any man could time his excitement without a stop watch: and that's a cold-blooded sort of notion."[12]

To Robert Graves, who had also read *The Mint* and also challenged Lawrence's assertions about the sex act, Lawrence was even more explicit in defending his views: "Your last page, about fucking, defeats me wholly. As I wrote (with some courage, I think: few people admit the damaging ignorance) I haven't ever and don't much want to. 1-¾ minutes was the Bishop's remark: judging from the way people talk it's transient, if 2-¾ or 3-¾ or 3 hours + ¾s. So I don't feel I miss much; and it must have a dirty feeling, too. However, your positive, comparative, superlative (we make it fucking good

      bastard good

      f. bastard good)

      defeats me wholly."[13]

Although he had many women acquaintances with whom he got along well, especially among the wives of his friends, Lawrence's attitudes toward marriage and toward women in their sexual and reproductive functions grew out of his personal history and conflicts. At the same time these conflicts allowed him to question and challenge the sanctity of marriage. "Marriage-contracts should have a clause terminating the engagement upon nine months notice by either party," he wrote Edward Garnett in 1923.[14] And in *The Mint*: "An idea (as of the normality of marriage, which gives the man a natural, cheap, sure and ready bed-partner), if they [the enlisted men] have grown up with it, has become already, at their age of twenty, enthroned and unchallengeable, by mere use."[15]

Despite his appreciation of many women as human beings (clearly he appraised women as individuals on their own merit and "had more respect for women as *people* than many men"),[16] Lawrence seemed often to devalue the entire sex, if no more than by the implications of his cynicism. "I'm frigid toward woman so that I can withstand her: so that I want to withstand her," he wrote to Sydney Cockerell in 1924.[17] Five years later, in irritation at the implications of newspaper stories about his RAF service he wrote: "Because I don't drink or smoke or dance, all things can be invented. Please believe that I don't either love or hate the entire sex of women. There are good ones and bad ones, I find: much the same as men and dogs and motor bicycles."[18]

Although he was deeply understanding of the struggles and sufferings of women in their reproductive roles — especially when they had failed — Lawrence found the functions related to childbirth, like all other aspects of the sexual and reproductive processes, somehow demeaning. Yet he recognized that his attitudes grew out of the painful history of his own life. In 1924 he wrote to Mrs. Shaw his views on these matters: "Birth . . . seems to me so sorry and squalid an accident . . . if fathers and mothers took thought before bringing children into this misery of a world, only the monsters among them would dare to go through with it. The motive which brings the sexes together is 99% sexual pleasure, and only 1% the desire of children, in men, so far as I can learn. As I told you, I haven't been carried away in that sense, so that I'm a bad subject to treat of it. Perhaps the possibility of a child relieves sometimes what otherwise must seem an unbearable humiliation to the woman: — for I presume it's unbearable. However, here I'm trenching on dangerous ground, with my own ache coming to life again. I hate and detest this animal side — and I can't find comfort in your compartmenting up our personalities. Mind, spirit, soul, body, sense and consciousness — angles of one identity, seen from different points of the compass."[19]

Lawrence was contemptuous of women as writers: "All the women who ever wrote original stuff could have been strangled at birth, and the history of English literature (and my bookshelves) would be unchanged,"[20] an exaggerated attitude which may have been influenced by other feelings about women. In a letter to Harley Granville-Barker Lawrence linked (as many do unconsciously) literary productivity to biological reproduction: "I can't write, and wouldn't if I could, since creation, without conviction, is only a nasty vice. You have to be very eager-spirited to overcome the disgust of reproduction."[21] This comment may contribute to the understanding of Lawrence's intense conflicts and inhibitions concerning literary production: as he was repelled by the biological process, so too he often looked with disgust upon his own efforts to produce literary works.

One of the appeals the society of enlisted men had for Lawrence was probably the fact that, although active sexually where he was not, the other enlisted men shared in many respects his immature and limited views of sexual functioning, and his need to separate the physical aspect of sex from its emotional significance. To the writer James Hanley, Lawrence wrote in 1931: "I've lived in barracks now, for nine years: preferring the plain man to the elaborated man. I find them forthcoming, honest, friendly, and so comfortable. They do not pretend at all, and with them I have not to pretend. Sex, with them, is something you put on (and take off) with your walking-out dress: on Friday night, certainly: and if you are lucky on Saturday afternoon, and most of Sunday. Work begins on Monday again, and is really important."[22]

This trivialization of sexuality occurs over and over again in Lawrence's letters. He even went to the lengths of denying differences between women and men. To Ernest Thurtle, his friend in the House of Commons, he wrote, "Women? I like some women. I don't like their sex: any more than I like the monstrous regiment of men. There is no difference that I can feel between a woman and a man. They look different, granted: but if you work with them there doesn't seem any difference at all. I can't understand all the fuss about sex. It's as obvious as red hair: and as little fundamental, I fancy."[23] Or, still more stridently, two weeks later, to Edward Marsh (Churchill's secretary) upon rereading *Lady Chatterley's Lover*: "I'm deeply puzzled and hurt by this Lady Chatterley of his. Surely the sex business isn't worth all this damned fuss? I've met only a handful of people who really cared a biscuit for it."[24]

Although he was as inhibited in relation to direct physical intimacy with men as with women, I believe it is accurate to say that Lawrence was less uncomfortable with homosexual than with heterosexual concepts and behavior. "Homosexuality disgusted him far less than the abuse of normal sex and the attitude of some of the men in the huts in the R.A.F. or Tank Corps," his brother has written.[25] And Lawrence himself wrote to Charlotte Shaw: "I've seen lots of man-and-man loves: very lovely and fortunate some of them were. I take it women can be the same. And if our minds so go, why not our bodies? There's only a wall between farm and farmyard."[26]

Lawrence's closest attachments were with men, whom he was far more likely to take seriously or idealize. It was, however, nonsexual friendship or intimacy, even playfulness, surely companionship, and sometimes intellectual stimulation, that Lawrence sought in these attachments, rather than erotic contact. His airman friend A. E. "Jock" Chambers has described to me Lawrence's discomfort with physical openness or intimacy, even of a playful kind. Lawrence seemed embarrassed to be seen naked, even by Chambers, who shared in many respects his older friend's repudiation of physical sexuality. Once Chambers gave Lawrence a bear hug from behind in playful roughhousing, pinning his arms briefly behind his back. He could sense immediately that Lawrence did not like it and so quickly stopped.[27]

Lawrence indicated the greater conscious physical appeal of men to him in notes that have been preserved in his private papers, jotted down perhaps in the course of making notes for an autobiography to be called "Confessions of Faith": "Occasionally my eyes seem suddenly switched on to my brain, and I see a thing all the more clear in contrast with the former mustiness, in these things nearly always shapes — rocks or trees or figures of living things — not small things like flowers . . . : and in the figures always men. I take no pleasure in women. I have never thought twice or even once of the shape of a woman: but men's bodies, in repose or in movement — especially the former, appeal to me directly and very generally."[28]

Lawrence's sexual constriction and inhibition contrast sharply with his tolerance and acceptance of the sexuality of others, and his willingness to deal with the subject directly and openly in his writings ("a sexual frankness which would cause most authors to be run in by the police," E. M. Forster wrote in his review of *Seven Pillars of Wisdom*).[29] The tolerance of the sexual practices of others, which he knew often caused much anguish as well as pleasure, was part of Lawrence's deep compassion for human beings, and his understanding of the drives and passions of which they were as often the victims as the masters. His literary candor concerning sexual activities and other body functions also reflects a fundamental intellectual honesty and integrity which must not be confused, as it has often been, with what Lawrence would or could tolerate in himself. His candid descriptions of the homosexual practices of Bedouin youth in the desert in *Seven Pillars of Wisdom* have, in my opinion, been mistakenly offered as evidence of his own participation in these activities. The evidence is strongly to the contrary, however sympathetic Lawrence may have been to the intimacy of these youths, which he saw growing out of their privation, the absence of suitable women, and the "welding" of "souls and spirits in one flaming effort" in the enterprise of the Arab Revolt.

Lawrence's clearest statement of his humanitarian view of sexuality, and his appreciation of the destructive effect of intolerant social and moral attitudes toward this vital aspect of life, is contained in a letter to Henry Williamson about the novel *Lady Chatterley's Lover*: "What D. H. Lawrence means by *Lady Chatterley's Lover* is that the idea of sex, and the whole strong vital instinct, being considered indecent causes men to lose what might be their vital strength and pride of life — their integrity. Conversely, the idea of 'genitals being beauty' in the Blakian sense would free humanity from its lowering and disintegrating immorality of deed and thought. Lawrence wilted and was made writhen by the 'miners-chapel-dirty little boy, you' environment: he was ruined by it: and in most of his work he is striving to straighten himself, and to become beautiful. Ironically, or paradoxically, in a humanity where 'genitals are beauty' there would be a minimum of 'sex' and a maximum of beauty, or Art. This is what Lawrence means, surely."[30] Freud himself never stated in clearer terms the essence of his view of the human cost of neurotic conflict.

Despite his personal revulsion, Lawrence exhibited similar tolerance of the sexuality of the men with whom he lived in the barracks in the Tank Corps and the RAF, recognizing that his own attitudes were odd or exceptional. During a period when he was particularly troubled, having recently had to leave the RAF to join the Tank Corps, he wrote to his friend Lionel Curtis at All Souls: "A filthy business all of it, and yet Hut 12 shows me the truth behind Freud. Sex is an integer in all of us, and the nearer nature we are, the more constantly, the more completely the product of that integer. These fellows are the reality, and you and I, the selves who used to meet in London and talk of fleshless things, are only the outward wrapping of a core like these fellows. They let light and air play always upon their selves, and consequently have grown very lustily, but have at the same time achieved health and strength in their growing. Whereas our wrappings and bandages have stunted and deformed ourselves, and hardened them to an apparent insensitiveness . . . but it's a callousness, crippling, only to be yea-said by aesthetes who prefer clothes to bodies, surfaces to intentions."[31]

Arnold Lawrence wrote after his brother's death that for T.E. there was "no fate he would have more gladly accepted for himself" than a happy marriage,[32] and he once told me on another occasion that his mother had thought that the widow of Robert Scott, the explorer, would have made a good wife for T.E. and would have had the right sort of steadying influence. She was disappointed when Mrs. Scott remarried.[33] There is no information about what T.E. thought of this suggestion, if it was ever made to him. Arnold Lawrence's wife, Barbara, believes that a heterosexual relation might have been possible, though difficult, with the right woman.[34] But the evidence seems to me convincing that no matter how suitable the woman, Lawrence's sexual conflicts were such that he could never have dealt with a marital relationship if it required heterosexual intimacy.

Lawrence's friend David Garnett has perhaps captured best the sad limitations that Lawrence's sexual conflict imposed upon him: "Lawrence did not strive to satisfy the sexual appetite. As a result he did not know love and desire,* and all the range of tenderness between them; he did not know the ecstasies and contentments of physical intimacy or the sharp joys or alarms of parenthood. These were severe limitations and sometimes, like some of the repulsive saints, he seemed to be an enemy of life. The reproductive urge manifesting itself in the whole of nature either disgusted him, or meant little. Yet his imagination and capacity for sympathy

---

* Here I would disagree with Garnett.

enabled him to overcome this disability."[35] T.E.'s exceptionally strong feeling for children, Arnold Lawrence has pointed out, came near to vicarious parenthood.

The passage from *Seven Pillars of Wisdom* that describes the traumatic assault at Der'a (quoted on pages 230–231) points in vivid language to the precipitation in Lawrence of a flagellation disorder.[36] His powerful identification with his guilt-ridden mother; the childhood experience of being beaten repeatedly by her in a manner to break his will; the lifetime fascination with, dread of, and need to master pain; the absence of any offsetting heterosexual adaptation; the guilt and shame which resulted from the war experience; and conceivably, a biologically rooted masochistic predisposition — all of these combined to make Lawrence vulnerable to this disorder, the form of which reflects his youthful familiarity with medieval flagellation practices. There is no evidence that Lawrence suffered from this "morbid desire" prior to the Der'a experience, nor is there evidence that he acted upon it before he enlisted in the Tank Corps in 1923. He may have done so, but the information is not available to me or to anyone I have consulted.[37] Perhaps the political struggles of the postwar period and the feverish efforts to write down his experience of the campaigns in his book helped to prevent earlier manifestations of the problem.

Flagellation or whipping was used in ancient times to revive or resuscitate persons who were medically stricken or unconscious.[38] In the early Christian era and into medieval times in Europe, it was used for mortification of the flesh. "Self-punishment of various kinds were favorite methods adopted by the early saints to subdue sexual thoughts and cravings," one authority on the subject has written.[39] The medieval flagellants sought purification through the practice. Even into the twentieth century the English seem to have found whipping particularly appealing for disciplining children and punishing criminals. The stimulation of latent erotic tendencies by such beatings created a white-slave traffic in flagellation in Victorian England, which provided a field day for such social critics as Bernard Shaw, who noted with pointed irony in one of his several articles deploring the practice that the act which allowed flogging "is a final triumph of the vice it pretends to repress."[40] The punisher collaborates in effect with the unconscious masochistic impulses of the offender while acting out sadistic impulses of his own.

The practice of flagellation by individuals for erotic pleasure is commonplace, being perhaps more frequent in societies that have a medieval tradition of such behavior and use it in rearing children and punishing criminals. Furthermore, erotic flagellation, with rare exceptions, is not severe.[41] Rarer still is the self-determined use of flagellation for personal penance — Lawrence's disorder. Lawrence, as far as I can tell, was not whipped in his school, birching in English schools having been curtailed somewhat after the mid-nineteenth century because of Victorian prudery about the exposure of bare bottoms. He was, though, as has been mentioned, whipped severely as a child by his mother, and he was a student of the Middle Ages. As Arnold Lawrence wrote in 1937 (cryptically at the time because Lawrence's flagellation problem was not publicly known): "His subjection of the body was achieved by methods advocated by the saints whose lives he had read."[42]

In May 1935, about the time of his brother's death at the Bovington Camp hospital, Arnold Lawrence received a letter from John Bruce, a young Scotsman who had joined the Tank Corps near to the time that Lawrence did in 1923. In the letter, which was superscribed with an Aberdeen, Scotland, address, Bruce expressed disappointment that he could not get from the hospital a daily report on Lawrence's condition. The letter, written on May 17, two days before Lawrence's death, referred to an "uncle" of "Ted's" (a nickname given Lawrence by some of his service friends), whom Bruce wished help in contacting, as his correspondence with the uncle had gone through "Ted." In a second letter, written on May 19 after hearing of Lawrence's death, Bruce referred to Lawrence as his greatest friend, regretted not being able to attend the funeral, and wrote that for financial reasons he wished to remain in touch as he might have a statement to make later.

Arnold Lawrence found these letters highly puzzling. In spite of his closeness to his brother, Arnold had not known of Bruce, and by 1920 he and his brothers had no recognized living male relatives, other than a third or fourth cousin, younger than T.E. and whom T.E. had never met.[43] He requested that Bruce direct all future communications through the Lawrence solicitors. "In the meantime," Arnold Lawrence wrote, "I had noticed the passage in the Oxford text of 1922 of *Seven Pillars* which declares the beating he received at Deraa resulted in a longing for a repetition of the experience."[44] After comparing Bruce's letters with earlier ones of his to Lawrence, and with other documents found at Clouds Hill, Arnold Lawrence "realized that my brother had invented a living uncle and that the 'nephew,' who was to be punished by beating and other trials, was T.E. himself."[45]

Meanwhile, Bruce continued writing letters to the family solicitor, in which he expressed his wish to be in touch with T.E.'s uncle (who apparently had paid Bruce for services performed on behalf of his nephew) regarding his interest in writing a book about Lawrence's private life. He planned to base the work on his personal experiences with Lawrence and on more than two hundred letters and a diary. A meeting was arranged between Bruce, Arnold Lawrence and the solicitor, which was to be held at the firm in July 1935. Bruce "did not come to the office as arranged but telephoned to ask me to meet him alone at a railway station, where we spent, I suppose, an hour together. I did not wish to reveal that the uncle was imaginary, and so could not put direct questions freely (in case they should, by chance, show undue ignorance of matters I might be expected to know about), but the main lines of the story became clear. The 'nephew' had committed some serious offence in law — a financial fraud, it seemed — against his uncle or uncle's wife; they decided not to prosecute, since that would involve public disgrace. Instead, they insisted on his undergoing a course of expiation which they themselves devised. I think Bruce said (but I am not sure I have not interpolated this item from data that came to me recently) that they ordered him to enlist. Once enlisted, they — this Bruce certainly told me — arranged for periodic beatings by Bruce, after which T.E. had to show the marks to a doctor who would then report to the uncle and aunt that the punishment had been severe enough. I had no doubt that Bruce believed all this."[46] Arnold Lawrence never met Bruce again.

Bruce did not turn over to Arnold Lawrence any documents at the railway station, though in a letter to the solicitor written two days later, he announced his decision to burn the letters he had in his possession. In December 1935, Arnold Lawrence's solicitor wrote Bruce, expressing concern that Bruce had not, as planned, destroyed the letters.

Bruce responded in indignant and hurt tones: as Lawrence had been his friend in life so he would be his in death; his story never was or would be for sale; and anyway, he had burned it along with the letters he had been tricked into destroying; and so forth. (As we shall see, Bruce sold a document describing in detail his alleged relationship with Lawrence for a considerable amount to the *Sunday Times* in 1968, and the following year wrote to me that he planned to publish someday Lawrence's letters to him.)[47] After 1936 Bruce was not heard from by the Lawrence family for twenty-six years. In 1937, for reasons that are not clear, he wrote a letter to Ronald Storrs, claiming to have been Lawrence's closest friend during the last twelve years of Lawrence's life. In August 1938, Bruce had an article, probably written for him by a journalist, published in a magazine, *The Scottish Field*. In it there are obviously fictitious anecdotes, and the claim, inconsistent with the 1935 letters, that he visited Lawrence at Bovington Camp hospital the day before Lawrence died.[48]

In December 1962, about the time that the film *Lawrence of Arabia* was evoking renewed interest in T.E., Bruce wrote again to Arnold Lawrence. Lawrence did not reply, and two months later Bruce wrote again, enclosing a gossip column clipping from a local newspaper of the town of Helensburgh, Scotland. The article states that Bruce had known Lawrence intimately "as his personal bodyguard," and was about to have a book about him published to be titled "Lawrence after Arabia," which had been ghostwritten by an eminent Scottish author.[49]

Nothing further was heard of or from Bruce until February 1967, when without accompanying explanation or covering letter, a copy of an eighty-three-page typescript, written in the first person and giving Bruce's version of his relationship with Lawrence, arrived at the offices of Arnold Lawrence's solicitors. In a subsequent letter to me, Bruce stated that this was an accident and said that it resulted from mixed-up addresses and other errors whereby the document was mistakenly sent to the firm.

On January 1, 1968, Bruce wrote to the Lawrence solicitors asking if there would be any objection to his writing of his friendship with T.E. and that circumstances beyond his control, specifically illness and poverty, made it necessary for him to break his long silence. He wished for the blessings of the "title holder" of *Seven Pillars of Wisdom*. In their reply the solicitors stated their objections to publication and made reference to the typescript they had received. Bruce wrote letters again on January 8 and 25, offering a puzzling explanation of how the typescript had come to the firm, and closed the second letter with the statement that he had hoped on his death to have handed over the story to the Lawrence family. In reply the solicitor observed that he did not see what prevented Bruce from turning over his story to the family now.

At about this time Bruce sold his story to the *Sunday Times* in the form of a typescript similar to the one that Arnold Lawrence's solicitors had received. The *Sunday Times* incorporated this material in four articles, which were published in June under the general title "The Secret Life of Lawrence of Arabia."[50]

Early in March 1968, Arnold Lawrence learned that the *Sunday Times* had bought Bruce's story and was planning to put together quickly a series of articles based on it, but one that would also include such other subjects as Lawrence's family background, alleged espionage activities, and relationship with Mrs. Shaw.[51] Arnold Lawrence "felt desperate at the prospect of there being no background depicted, so that the story would seem just dirt"[52] and was eager for the *Sunday Times* to have me write a companion article that would place the story of the beatings in an appropriate psychological and historical perspective. We both worked toward this end but unsuccessfully: the story was first made public in a very sensational form on June 23 under the title "How Lawrence of Arabia Cracked Up."[53] It contained a number of the inaccuracies that were in Bruce's original typescript.

It would be a mistake to emphasize Bruce's personal role too strongly. Bruce, whose family had owned a dairy near Aberdeen, was only nineteen when he met Lawrence. It is clear that he valued the relationship at the time, not only because of the money he received for performing his services, but also, as he told me himself, because T. E. Lawrence was the first person of the upper classes who did not look down upon him or impress upon him his higher status.[54]

What Bruce believed was a close personal relationship seems to have been primarily a business arrangement. He was hired to administer the beatings and to help Lawrence carry out certain other penances that he had invented for himself. Bruce was particularly qualified to perform these services because he needed money and he was gullible — he believed at the time, and as recently as his last letter to me (written in February of 1969), that he was serving an "Old Man" or "uncle" of Lawrence's who demanded this barbaric treatment.

Bruce's army records show that he enlisted in the Tank Corps in Aberdeen on March 9, 1923, and was posted to Bovington Camp in Dorset, where all recruits went for their initial training. Since Lawrence enlisted in the Tank Corps three days after Bruce did, and was also posted to Bovington, it is likely that the two met at this time.[55]

Fifteen letters from Bruce and one from Mrs. Bruce were found among Lawrence's possessions at Clouds Hill after his death. Two of the letters were written from Scotland to Lawrence in India in April and May of 1927. They indicate a long period since the last meeting or communication, presumably since Bruce's discharge from the Tank Corps in March 1925. The others date from 1933 and 1934. In the letters Bruce tells Lawrence of his recent marriage, expresses gratitude to him, assures him that his secret is safe, and states that he does not want to lose touch with Lawrence. Nine of the letters are from Bruce to Lawrence directly, and concern various business arrangements regarding the performance of his duties on the "Old Man's" behalf. Instructions from the "Old Man" were, according to these letters, to be sent through T.E. and presumably unopened by him. They were to be *returned* by Bruce through T.E. to the Old Man, also unopened. Therefore Bruce would not possess letters from the "Old Man."

Four letters to the "Old Man," to be transmitted by Lawrence, reveal Bruce as trying to please the Old Man by his faithfulness to his instructions in carrying out the beatings and in arranging for swimming, boxing, and physical therapy instruction for his sinful nephew. In one letter he apologizes for exceeding his instructions and overdoing the beatings (October 10, 1933). Similar communications may have occurred in 1931 and 1932 but would not have been found at Clouds Hill, as Lawrence's mother and older brother occupied the cottage from April 1931 to the end of 1932.[56]

There is no conclusive information on how many times Lawrence underwent floggings at the hands of Bruce or anyone else.[57] Bruce has recalled seven to nine occasions between 1923 and 1935 when beatings occurred. Diary jottings of Lawrence's found after his death at Clouds Hill suggest five incidents of flogging between June and October 1933. Lawrence had noted, for example, "Saturday 23rd June, 30 from Jock" (Bruce's nickname). All of the other floggings were also by "Jock" (with numbers from thirty to seventy-five indicating presumably the number of lashes) except four by "G."[58]

It is understandable that the beatings Bruce administered should have

begun in 1923 after Lawrence entered the Tank Corps. Expulsion from
the RAF had recently taken from him not only valued work, but a way
of life that had provided him with needed stability.[59] Lawrence's letters
of this period, especially those to Lionel Curtis, reflect his despair. A week
after he entered the Tank Corps he had written that in the RAF he had
"grown suddenly on fire with the glory which the air should be." The
army, by contrast "seems safe against enthusiasm. It's a horrible life, and
the other fellows fit it. I said to one, 'They're the sort who instinctively
fling stones at cats' . . . and he said, 'Why what do you throw?' "[60] He
wrote Curtis of his joining the Tanks Corps for "mind suicide" and that
"self-degradation is my aim." A week later he continued in this vein: "We
are social bed-rock, those un-fit for life-by-competition: and each of us
values the rest as cheap as he knows himself to be."[61] And two months
later: "Do you think there have been lay monks of my persuasion? One
used to think that such frames of mind would have perished with the age
of religion: and yet here they rise up purely secular. It's a lurid flash into
the Nitrian desert: seems almost to strip the sainthood from Anthony.
How about Teresa?"[62]

And surely, like Saint Teresa of Avila, Lawrence turned to flagellation
for the suppression of sexual needs and the purification of his soul through
mortification of the body. Bruce allegedly told the *Sunday Times* in 1968
that Lawrence was revising the Der'a chapter in 1923 and had nightmares
five nights running, which angered the other occupants of the hut. Lawrence then induced Bruce to repeat the Der'a punishment.[63] This was
the occasion of the first beating. The beatings seem again to have been
more frequent in 1933 and Arnold Lawrence, understanding the economi-
cal balance of pleasure and pain required by Lawrence's conscience, has
suggested that "the boats involved an enormous amount of physical exer-
tion in fresh air, and perhaps the healthiness so induced aroused more
need for Bruce's treatment."[64] The imminent publication of Liddell Hart's
book, extolling his virtues, may have been another reason for Lawrence's
greater need for the punishments at that time.

Bruce seemed husky and fit at sixty-four, the only time I met with him
(a two-hour talk in the summer of 1968 at Bruce's home and in a coffee
shop in Wrexham in Wales where he was then living), although he said
he had been unable to work for nine years because of emphysema and
bronchitis. He was proud of his association with Lawrence, expressed
fondness for him, and said that Lawrence had often bawled him out and
"was like a father to me." Although Bruce claimed to be the only person
"who really knew Lawrence's life after 1922," he actually seemed to know
very little about Lawrence and the Lawrence family. He stated once
again that he had performed the beatings entirely to serve "Ted," and to
protect him from this cruel "Old Man" who threatened to cause a family
scandal by revealing Lawrence's illegitimacy. He claimed to know who

the "Old Man" was and to have met him in T.E.'s company, but would not tell me whom he suspected. He also believed the Old Man responsible for Lawrence's death and connected the black car described at the inquest with the Old Man, who, he said, had to do with chauffeuring it.

Bruce said he believed he had been selected to administer the beatings because he was strong and trustworthy, and because Lawrence was afraid of someone the Old Man might select. Although he stuck to the story that he had protected Lawrence as early as 1922, he said spontaneously that he had known him during the last twelve years of his life, not noting the contradiction. The beatings in any event did not begin until 1923, at a time when T.E. was under much strain. And Bruce had said elsewhere that there were very few beatings before Lawrence left for India at the end of 1926.[65] He said that Lawrence seemed to get no pleasure from the beatings and that he was not "homosexual." Bruce was unaware that any-one else had performed the beatings, except possibly someone the Old Man might have employed because of the distance to Bruce in Scotland.

I will now turn from what Bruce has supplied to the independent observations of a service companion and to material left at Clouds Hill by Lawrence himself.

Lawrence approached this companion in 1931 in great distress, explaining that he had stolen £150 from an "uncle," or "old man," who came to be known to the companion as "R." The Old Man had allegedly threatened to reveal to the world that Lawrence was illegitimate unless he either returned the money, which he was not in a position to do, or submitted to severe floggings. The companion's role was to witness the beatings, and report to "R" in order to assure that "R"'s instructions were being properly carried out. The presence of a witness seems also to have served the purpose of providing a restraint to any excesses of Bruce's in carrying out the floggings.

The companion observed three beatings with a metal whip between 1931 and 1934. They were brutal, delivered on the bare buttocks, and a precise number of lashes was required. Lawrence submitted to them "like a schoolboy," registered obvious fear and agony, but did not scream or cry out. He required that the beatings be severe enough to produce a seminal emission.

Three letters, purporting to be from "R" to the companion, and returned by him to Lawrence, have survived. In addition to the other instructions to the companion they contain — instructions meticulously composed to sustain the fiction of the "Old Man" — the letters seem also to be attempts to deal, through the companion, with the possibility that the beatings might become too severe. Written of course by Lawrence himself, these letters are remarkable psychological documents, revealing the sadness and pathos of this terrible problem, from which Lawrence, even up to the months before his death, seemed unable to free himself. They reveal his bitter hostility toward himself, his profound self-contempt, his wish to know his own reactions, and, finally, a pathetic desire for some vindicating judgment that would free him of the conflict. The last letter suggests that he was having some success in breaking away from his ordeal.

26 Oct 1934

Dear Sir,

I am very much obliged to you for the long and careful report you have sent me on your visit to Scotland with Ted; and for your kindness in agreeing to go there with the lad and look after him while he got his deserts. I am enclosing a fee of three pounds which I hope you will accept as some compensation for your trouble and inconvenience.

From what you tell me, and from the reports of those who have examined Ted since, it is clear that he had a sound thrashing, which was after all what he wanted. I hope he will take the lesson to heart, and not make it necessary for us to repeat it. Please take any chance his friendship for you gives, to impress upon him how wrong it is for him, at his age and standing, to force us to use these schoolboy measures against him. He should be ashamed to hold his head up amongst his fellows, knowing that he had suffered so humiliating and undignified a punishment. Try and drive some sense into his head. [Details of the whippings follow.]

. . . . .

After being loosed, did Ted stand quite steadily, or did he show any signs of trembling on his way from the club-room to the cafe or the train. Also you say that when they met you at the station, Ted was not looking too happy. Did his face remain pale to the end of his punishment, and after it? Did he say anything about his being glad the business was over?

Hills [Bruce] reports that after the birching Ted cried out quite loudly, and begged for mercy. Can you confirm this, and do you recollect in what terms his plea was made? . . .

. . . Does he take his whipping as something he has earned? Is he sorry after it? Does he feel justly treated? Has this year of harsh treatment made an improvement in his bearing?

I am sorry to bother you with all these difficult questions, but you have seen so much of Ted's private history this last twelve month, that your opinion is worth a great deal. One last question, too, if you say Yes to the main principle — are we at the end of our troubles with the lad? If not, must we give Hills his free hand, or will limited measures suffice? Can Hills be trusted again, or must I look elsewhere? And in that case, do you think your friend would be available or suitable?

With further thanks for your kindness.

Believe me

Yours very sincerely,

R

16 November 1934

Dear Sir,

I must apologize for having taken so long to answer the additional report you were good enough to send me. Your information was exactly what I needed and I am most grateful.

You have aroused my curiosity by your remark that from your service with Ted you know something that might replace corporal punishment in making him behave himself. You must understand that this is a matter of the first importance to me and to Ted. By his wishes which I must respect, according to my promise, we are prevented from meeting; but if you can get your information on paper, you would put me further into your debt.

I note what you say about Hills, and it only confirms my own impression. You will recollect how he came to go to him this time. Ted's punishment at X had proved not enough, due to the inadequacy of a belt for use upon a grown lad, and not through any fault of yours or your friend's. Unfortunately you could not arrange another dose at the time, and while we were thinking about it Ted allowed himself to give offense upon quite another subject. It was with this second offence that Hills dealt with last month. Ted still owes us (as he very well knows) proper payment for his very mean action in trying to steal money in transit from me to you.

I do not know, of course, what your hinted remedy is worth, as a corrective. If it proved effective I might save you and me from a repetition of his punishment. I gather that your friend is not yet available, and it is not fair to the lad himself to keep such a punishment hanging over him for month after month. Yet it is equally impossible for me, having solemnly promised it to him. I always do what I promise, and I have brought Ted to know it.

So will you please try to take me into your confidence on this alternative; and please also enquire into the arrangements of the friend who helped you last time, so that we may fall back on him, if necessary.

Yours sincerely,
R

11 January 1935

Dear Sir,

Your letter showed me that I was perhaps being rather hard on Ted, by repeating that punishment at short interval. So upon reconsideration I informed him that it will be indefinitely postponed. I asked him to give you prompt notice that your help would not be immediately required. We will hold our hands and watch to see if the lad justifies this kindness.

I need not say that I am very much obliged to you for being ready to take the further responsibility. I shall call upon you with confidence if Ted again makes it necessary. Please let me correct one misapprehension in your letter, however. Unless he strips, the birch is quite ineffective.

The twigs are so light that even the thinnest clothing prevents their hurting. I fully understand your reluctance to strip him; so I was making up my mind to ask you to use either your friend's jute whip (which you mentioned to me in a former letter) or a useful little dogwhip which I could send you by post.

If the emergency arises, I shall agree to Ted's coming to you in flannels.

Yours sincerely,

R

These letters demonstrate the dimensions of Lawrence's continuing struggle. Although meant to guide the companion and, through him, Bruce, they also show a kind of internal debate, as Lawrence wrestles with the various sides of his dilemma. The deleted portion of the first letter reveals clearly his genuine distress at and fear of the severity of the beatings. Yet at the same time he continued to use Bruce's services precisely because Bruce was willing to administer severe beatings. Even in the last letter, in which Lawrence does seem to be struggling to escape from his need for "corporal punishment," he reminds the companion that "unless he strips, the birch is quite ineffective" and "even the thinnest clothing prevents [its] hurting."

That Lawrence asks in the letters for details of "Ted's" responses to the beatings suggests that his consciousness or self-awareness was disturbed during them to the extent that he could not monitor his own reactions. In addition, however, a number of his questions — "did he show any signs of trembling" or "did he say anything about being glad the business was over" — reveal Lawrence's continuing struggle to achieve mastery over pain. The need for pain, and at the same time to surmount it, are shown side by side with the fear of fatal injury and the need for protection by the companion.

Lawrence makes it clear that the humiliation of self is as important an aspect of the penance as the physical pain. His contempt for "the lad's dignity" may usefully be compared with the several instances in which Lawrence wrote of his "integrity" and its destruction, and the link with "schoolboy measures" is evident. Here he seems to relish humiliation and writes that "the more we can hurt his feelings the better." Yet along with this need for renewed humiliation and shame, Lawrence seems also to be striving to overcome his conflict ("Please take any chance his friendship with you gives to impress upon him how wrong it is for him, at his age and standing, to force us to use these schoolboy measures against him.") But the debate over the justice of these inordinately severe sentences seems to have gone on eternally within Lawrence's tormented spirit. Only six months before his death he still needed to turn to the authority of a humble service companion for a relieving, more objective judgment, a judgment, one should add, that could probably never have had a lasting impact. "Does he take his whipping as something he has earned?" Lawrence asked. "Is he sorry after it? Does he feel justly treated? Has this year of harsh treatment made an improvement in his bearing?"

Although the floggings were the most dramatic and unusual form of penance that Lawrence imposed upon himself, they were not the only one. In addition, he left documentation at Clouds Hill of other "training" rituals which, taken altogether, comprised an elaborate rehabilitation program. Lawrence wrote to various institutions and individuals, including a riding and hunting establishment, a swimming instructor, physiotherapists, a diet expert, and a "remedial gymnasium" specializing in Swedish massage and "medical electricity." As he did in arranging the floggings, Lawrence would write as the uncle ("Mr. E. Shaw") of a recalcitrant nephew for whom severe discipline was necessary, and would ask for a report from the instructor or manager as to "Ted's" progress. For example, to a riding establishment:

Dear Sir:
Some while ago when I asked about Riding Schools in Southampton, I was advised to write to you. I want my nephew taught to ride, for it will be useful to him in an appointment ahead that I have in mind for him.
I think he has been only once or twice upon a horse, so there will be everything to learn. Probably he could come to you early — to finish 10:30 at latest — or in the evening for an hour or two, several days a week for a while. I would like private lessons, best of all in a riding school, if possible, or in some quiet field: not a road or public park. I must warn you that he will not be an easy pupil, but I can help you a good deal with my authority. However, we can discuss that later, if you are able to undertake the work. Terms we can consider after we settle exactly what is needed. Perhaps you will let me know.[66]

The need for secrecy is evident. Replies from the instructors and establishments were also sent to Mr. E. Shaw, in which the nephew's various treatments, exercises and diets were described and the uncle assured of Ted's improvement. Besides all of these activities Lawrence also subjected himself to swimming in the frigid waters of the North Sea in the fall, under Bruce's supervision.

I fear that I shall disappoint those who have borne with me patiently to this point in the expectation that I will find in the documentation of this aspect of Lawrence's life definitive explanations of his character or of other actions which have puzzled his biographers. Perhaps some readers will choose to go further than I will in their own formulations, but I am bound by the data and by my concern lest this most tortured aspect of Lawrence's life be given too great an emphasis.

We may start by asking with justification, what is this all about? For what crime did Lawrence need to be punished and to carry out upon himself such an elaborate program of penance and expiation? Furthermore, how are we to understand the beatings and their function? Are they "sexual," and if so, in what sense? What is the need for and the meaning of the elaborate story of the "Old Man," and what does it tell us about Lawrence's psychology? Finally, what larger significance does this aspect of Lawrence's psychology hold for his life as a whole and what effect did it have upon his historical contribution?

As for the question of the "crime," the most direct statement we have from Lawrence is contained in the letter to Mrs. Shaw of March 26, 1924, written within a year of the beginning of the severe beatings, if our reckoning is correct. In that letter Lawrence makes it clear that the "unforgiveable matter" was the sexual surrender at Der'a out of fear of pain. In this overwhelming traumatic experience Lawrence felt that he surrendered not only sexually, but gave away the fundamental integrity of self, a self which he had striven so hard to perfect and protect. What made "the offense" even worse was that he had found the experience, the mingling of sexual assault and pain, to be pleasurable, "a delicious warmth . . . swelling through me."[67] The traumatic intensity of the experience, with its overwhelming of psychic defenses, led to the permanent welding for Lawrence of sexual pleasure and pain, so that he was plagued not only by the memory of the incident, but by the continuous desire for its repetition.

The reader who has followed Lawrence's history will not have difficulty appreciating that the linking of pain, which he had always feared and tried to master, with sexual pleasure would occasion much guilt in someone with his puritanical background and scrupulous conscience. The problem, however, became for him intrinsically insoluble. The desire for repetition of the experience proved to be overwhelming, especially at times of despair. But this very desire only aggravated the deep guilt that was already active within him. Yet the only punishment that was sufficiently severe to allay the guilt included the repetition of the experience itself — that is, the pain of the beatings. But this in turn brought about, indeed required, a repetition of the sexual aspect of the experience, thereby deepening the guilt and leading ultimately to a need to repeat the beatings. I believe that in insisting that the beatings be so severe and painful Lawrence was trying (short of emasculating or killing himself) to destroy his sexuality. I have no evidence that in any conscious sense Lawrence's insistence that the beatings be of such intensity was for any purpose other than for penance and to get rid of or eliminate his sexuality, that he did not at a conscious level seek or even experience pleasure in these episodes. Sexuality, however, like most bodily functions, replenishes itself, and more importantly, the association of sexuality with terribly painful beatings, only served to gratify, at an unconscious level, the very desire for which Lawrence needed to be punished. The swims in the freezing North Sea, and other elements of Lawrence's rehabilitation program, had the advantage of being measures that were severely disciplinary without containing a sexual component.

I do not wish to imply that Lawrence's guilt, or his desire for punishment, derived entirely from these sexual sources. We have seen in other chapters his lifelong struggle with problems of self-regard, and with the sense that whatever he was or did was never good enough to live up to the inflexible ideal standards that he had begun to set for himself in childhood. Lawrence's whole involvement in the Arab campaigns, with its deception and horror, came to fill him with a profound sense of guilt and a desire for retreat. The loss of control at Tafas, which was linked, I believe, with the Der'a experience, was also a source of profound guilt. But we are concerned here with the specific forms of the punishments, and with their sexual character as suited to a sexual crime.

Just as the beating ritual itself seems to derive from multiple psychological determinants, the myth of the "Old Man" or uncle is similarly complex and revealing. The elements of the invention, whose enactment involved several other people and elaborate planning and staging, demonstrate a weaving together of conscious and unconscious elements and of childhood and adult features. Lawrence is once more a schoolboy to be punished, a wayward youth to be whipped and otherwise disciplined, not for a deeply disturbing adult sexual conflict, but for a petty, childlike misdemeanor, the "filching" of varying amounts of money from a relative. He also talked with the persons he involved in his plan about an inheritance and about who was the rightful heir, which had a garbled foundation in Lawrence's own life.[68] Not surprisingly, it is once again the shame of the illegitimacy, with its link to childhood, that the "Old Man" threatens to reveal. In the "Old Man's" letters to the companion, Lawrence refers to "schoolboy measures," and the whole tone of the letters is that of a disappointed parent with a chronically and incorrigibly recalcitrant child. These letters in particular reveal vividly the split in Lawrence's mentality between the adult and childhood aspects of himself, which, in actuality, he never fully integrated.

The concoction of the Old Man story, an elaborate fiction but bearing a certain relation to reality, solved practical problems for Lawrence. It protected Bruce and the others Lawrence involved from any direct personal responsibility for the parts they were asked to play. They were not administering or taking part in cruelties to their friend or fellow serviceman: their actions were demanded by the Old Man, and they were simply helping to protect Lawrence from worse threats and punishments. The

elaborate story was also conceived in such a way as to minimize any
suspicion of Lawrence's real purposes: the Old Man made it explicit that
he and the others were never to meet. Even though the men drawn into
these rituals were uneducated, it is nevertheless a testimony to Lawrence's
persuasiveness that none of them seems to have ever doubted the story.
Perhaps an even more remarkable tribute to Lawrence's personality is the
fact that they maintained respect for a man they believed to be a thief and
had seen repeatedly humiliated.[69]

Over and above these practical considerations, the Old Man fantasy is
characteristic of Lawrence's inventiveness and creativity. His elaborate
imagination and rich fantasy life is welded as usual with action, and his
extraordinary capacity to adapt his personal psychological purposes to
the realities and needs of other people's lives is again in evidence. As in
the desert campaigns, complex systems of transmitting messages and
other communications were worked out by Lawrence in extraordinary
detail, forming a tight "system" that has been difficult to unravel. Childhood and adult elements, the medieval flagellation rituals with which he
became familiar in his youth, and his own complex psychological conflicts
and inventiveness were all drawn together by Lawrence in his creative
psychopathology.

It is tempting to speculate about whom the Old Man and his associates represent. "The Old Man" often designates the father in some
American and British circles, but I know of no such reference by Lawrence to his own father. In actuality it was his mother who was the more
severe disciplinarian and administered physical punishment, while the
father is remembered by Arnold Lawrence as stopping a carter from
beating a horse. Accordingly, it is most likely not Mr. Lawrence (as Lawrence knew him) who furnishes the character of the Old Man, but a
sterner figure: the product of T.E.'s imagination and of his own severe
conscience, with which he strove to exist more comfortably. The link to
his mother's childhood beatings is obvious, but the adult beaters are also
associated with the Turkish soldiers who imposed the traumatic assault.

I believe Lawrence could not have allowed himself to be beaten by a
woman (the masochism of many men does take this form), for the beatings, perverse, brutal and pathetic as they seem, are nevertheless a form
of closeness, selected for the fusion of intimacy and simultaneous desecration they represent. The taboo against intimacy with women was, as we
have seen earlier in this chapter, always intense for Lawrence. Lawrence
was generally more comfortable with closeness among men, and could
tolerate perhaps a perverse form of intimacy with certain men in a way
that he could never have tolerated with a woman. Only in the link between the flagellation ritual and the childhood beatings at the hands of
the mother does the never-resolved conflict over the attachment to her
remain in evidence.

Penitent rituals such as Lawrence's are not unusual and may be associated with a wide range of talents and personalities. Typically they recreate childhood scenes, relationships and conflicts that have been revived by the events and traumata of adult life. The sufferer inevitably draws into his private drama other individuals who form a kind of cast of characters that fulfill specific roles under his personal direction. Lawrence's ritual carried his particular stamp. It was thoroughly compartmentalized and highly creative. He took great pains to protect the others whom he involved from injury or embarrassment.

We are, I believe, justified in presuming that Lawrence was fully aware of the limitations he had imposed upon his public career by involving Bruce in an intimate part of his private life. Once he permitted himself to be involved with Bruce he could no longer return to public life, even if he had so chosen.

There were other consequences of these conflicts for Lawrence. Perhaps most importantly, he was forced in dealing with them to squander a certain amount of psychic energy, however rarely the actual beatings may have occurred. Even though Lawrence touched many people's lives during his years in the ranks, contributed to many reforms in the RAF and developed new rescue boats, which may ultimately have saved hundreds of lives, his horizons were specifically limited by his personal conflicts.

After Lawrence's death Arnold Lawrence discussed his brother's struggle to maintain a balance between spirit, intellect and body. "The details of his life," he wrote, "were consistent to his plan, but in my opinion he neglected the body's claims unfairly. He maintained this 'balance' at a cost so terrible in waste and suffering, that its author would himself, I believe, have agreed that it was a failure."[70] He was, indeed, as Ralph Isham once remarked, "a battlefield between purity and passion."[71]

34

Lawrence Assayed

When I was first becoming interested in T. E. Lawrence, I watched Arnold Lawrence being interviewed on television. He said of his brother: "He was one of the nicest, kindest, and most exhilarating people I've known. He often appeared cheerful when he was unhappy."[1] I was much affected by this simple observation, but did not know at the time how to place it in relation to the qualities that seemed most immediately related to Lawrence's accomplishments and fame — his courage, his capacity to lead through influencing others, his tendency to dramatize, and the like. Later, A. E. Chambers said to me: "He was my only real friend, the only one I've ever had. He was one of the finest men who've ever trod the globe, better than Christ or any of them. He hated injustice."[2]

In a curious way I felt that personal statements like these were fundamental to an appreciation of Lawrence as a historical figure, that the private Lawrence and the public Lawrence were related. In *Seven Pillars of Wisdom* Lawrence had written of the Arabs that "no man could be their leader except he ate the ranks' food, wore their clothes, lived level with them, and yet appeared better in himself."[3] This passage seemed to provide a clue to the link between the valued personal traits that Arnold Lawrence and Chambers had described and an essential dimension of Lawrence's greatness and historical importance.

There has been a shift in the field of psychoanalysis with the last decade: from discussing human beings and their difficulties through the use of such terms as ego, superego and narcissism, to speaking of them in language closer to sentience and actuality. Traditional psychoanalytic terms have a mechanistic or static quality, and seem to derive in part from an effort to treat human functioning in the concrete terms of the physical sciences. Although such concepts as "self," "identity" or even "ideal self" may be less than perfect alternatives, they are at least dynamic and imply the relationship between a person — or the image or idea of a person — and other beings or selves. The appreciation of these relationships lies at the core of understanding the qualities of public figures with a significant capacity for leadership, whether or not the additional elements of heroism and legend form around them.

We have seen how from an early age Lawrence took the development of himself, the perfection of self, as the principal task of his life. In conventional terms there is a certain egotism or "narcissism" in Lawrence's focus upon the ideal evolution of self. In his unwillingness to compromise the idealistic expectations of being and accomplishment that he developed in his youth he displays considerable immaturity in the classical sense. But there is beyond these hygienic banalities a deeper, more urgent set of realities to consider when a self, in action, becomes public property or is devoted to public service. Lawrence throughout his life offered his extraordinary abilities, his essential self, and even his conflicts to others for them to use according to their own need — to emulate, to learn and to grow. This was true from the time of his earliest boyhood, through the Carchemish period, the war and his years in the ranks. It lies at the heart of his greatness. He wrote, simply, to Dick Knowles, his Clouds Hill neighbor in 1927, "It's my experience that the actual work or position or reward one has, doesn't have much effect on the inner being which is the important thing for us to cultivate."[4]

A person who, like Lawrence, is provided through his extraordinary capacities the opportunity to offer (not sacrifice, which is, as Lawrence well understood, a destructive degradation of the process being considered here) himself to other individuals or whole peoples — and hopes thereby to fulfill ideal expectations for himself through enabling others to achieve the fulfillment of their selves — puts himself in a particularly vulnerable position. As he stretches the limit of possibility in the process of self-testing he may overstep his firm ground and expose himself to people with whom he shares no bond of mutual trust, expectation or fulfillment. He may then be exploited by those who are indifferent or even inimical to him, as happened to Lawrence at Der'a. There is the additional danger that he may not only arouse dormant hopes and dreams but also violent impulses, which may get out of hand, as they did at Tafas and at other times in the campaigns.

This exploitation — rape being its paradigm — and loss of control can be, as we have seen, painful and shattering to an idealist. But they need not, as indicated by Lawrence's letter to Knowles and, in fact, by the entire pattern of his life after the war, result in his abandoning the effort to cultivate the "inner being." Rather they may result in a retreat from any grand design for fulfillment and to renunciation of the desires and ambitions that seem to be the cause of the pain. We have seen how Lawrence's retreat into the ranks enabled him to continue to offer himself to others in fulfilling goals, which they all shared, of useful work and self-development without the risk or temptation of ambition and exploitation.

The question of identity has run through the pages of this book. It is a concept useful to the historian and the psychologist, for in its reference to the central characteristics of the self it may draw into the scope of its meaning the continuity of the individual with the past and the future. The concept of identity is also useful in considering the relation between one person and another, or between one individual and a group or a people, and lends itself to the study of how one man may play a part in the shifting development of other selves or other identities.

The sense of self, of "I" and of "who I am," begins to form in the second, even in the first year of life. Its central shape or character, the identity of the self, is established in childhood and adolescence to a large degree, although this identity can develop and shift throughout adult life. A sense of personal identity develops in childhood as the child tries out his native endowment in an environment of family members (and later of other adults and children), who may love and encourage or, conversely, attack or hinder his unfolding. The elements of this identity take further definition as the child finds in the parents examples of what to be like or to reject. His identification is based not simply upon what his parents are in actuality, or how they behave, but also upon the values they represent to him and the rich dimension that family members contribute through recalling the memories of specific ancestors. For Lawrence, the past, the family history on both sides, was obscured and distorted by the parents' guilt.

Except for the many moves during the years before the family settled in Oxford and the departure of a nurse of whom he was the favorite, Lawrence's early childhood was quite secure. The available evidence suggests that he emerged from it with a sure sense of himself and a strong will, although even then a friend noted that he had "a secret something of unhappiness about him." The cloudiness of the family background; the uncertainty about his mother's origins; the discovery of his own illegitimacy and the related discrepancy between his parents' values and ideals and their violation of social codes; the deception of their silence on these matters; the perceived dominance of his father by his mother; his mother's deep need to find redemption for her sins through Lawrence and his brothers; perhaps the rejection experience in his only attempt as a young man to find a mate — all these adverse influences distorted, damaged, and interfered with Lawrence's development of his own self and left him vulnerable to the later problems which the traumata of the war years brought about.

His name, and the uncertainties which attached to it and to which he contributed, became the focus of some of the more fundamental questions about his identity. "The Lawrence thing hasn't any better foundation than my father's whim," he wrote to Mrs. Shaw in 1925,[5] and two years later he noted that he was not "legally entitled" to use the name "and never again will."[6] In 1926 he wrote jokingly to the Newcombes' six-year-old son: "It's time for you [sic] to change your name once more. In 1920 Lawrence was current. In 1921 our names became Ross. In 1923 we changed to Shaw. What shall we become next year?"[7]

He ended up treating the question of his identity as one of little consequence and summarized the matter succinctly to Harley Granville-Barker in 1924: "My genuine, birth-day, initials are T.E.C. The C. became L. when I was quite young:[8] and as L. I went to Oxford and through the war. After the war it became a legend: and to dodge its load of legendary inaccuracy I changed it to R. In due course R. became too hot to hold. So now I'm Shaw: but to me there seems no virtue in one name more than another. Anyone can be used by anyone, and I'll answer to it."[9]

And yet it would be an error, or a missed opportunity, if these disturbances of identity, from which Lawrence undoubtedly suffered, were looked at simply from the standpoint of his personal psychopathology. The multifaceted nature of his sense of self, the varied aspects of his identity, the absence of clearly established social roles or regular directions of his professional life — all related to Lawrence's creativity, to his capacity to give others "new values," as one friend put it, and to find new solutions.[10] I have little doubt that his extraordinary capacity to move flexibly among peoples of other classes and races, to understand or intuit their needs and hopes, their feelings and dreams, derived to a large degree from the complex and unsettled elements of his own identity. This capacity seemed to know no bounds. He could be what people needed him to be, for he knew what they felt, what they were. This flexibility was not limited to his work among the Arabs. It is easily observed in his relationships among Easterners and Westerners alike after the war and in his associations during the years in the ranks.

Lawrence's extraordinary capacity for empathy with the feelings of other people —for genuine compassion— little stressed in recent biographies, was attested to time and again to me by family members, and by his friends in their writings and in interviews. The old, the very young, the poor and the weak, mothers and sons — none were exempt from his understanding. "After 70 an unearthly richness attacks most of our elders," he wrote Mrs. Shaw, "and they become wells of satisfaction to me. Only then one gets to like them too much and away they go and die."[11]

He had a strong feminine side, which enabled him to understand the feelings and conflicts of women as well as of men, and to take care of people. Mrs. Kennington has written of how, when she had a bad miscarriage, was terribly ill and did not want to go on living, Lawrence came to her bedside and helped her with his understanding through her loss.[12]

In the later years of his life Lawrence felt more firmly his identity as an Irishman, and as we have seen, was pleased to be invited to join the Irish Academy of Letters. Of his biographers Robert Graves in particular thought that Lawrence in his character "had all the marks of the Irishman."[13] Lawrence thought that his tendency to laugh at himself was typically Irish.[14] He had toyed with the idea of helping the Irish Free State, and wrote to Mrs. Shaw in 1927, "I like England so much as I do because I am not English: whenever the point crops up succinctly I know that I'm Irish."[15] Similarly, Lady Pansy Lamb, one of my correspondents, told this story of meeting Lawrence toward the end of his life:

> Finally I met Lawrence — I can't remember exactly when, but not long before his death. It was a Christmas dinner at the Johns. There was a crowd of people, amongst them a little bright-eyed man in a white sweater, who I thought was perhaps the local garage-man whom the Johns were befriending — No introductions, but we all had our places marked with our names and my younger sister found herself next to the stranger. This was her account of his conversation — He picked up his name ticket and said, "Ah — Shaw — I wondered what name they would put." My sister, in the dark, thought he was joking, and asked, "Have you many aliases?" He replied, "Quite a few." "And many nationalities?" "Always Irish," he answered firmly.[16]

In 1929 he wrote to Pierce Joyce, an Irishman himself, of his longing to visit Ireland on leave, but he never did. "How is Ireland?" he asked Joyce. "I dream of spending my next month's leave (autumn perhaps) partly there. Are there roads in Ireland, fit for motorbikes?"[17] In thanking Yeats for the invitation to join the Irish Academy of Letters he apologized: "It's not my fault, wholly, if I am not more Irish: family, political, even money obstacles will hold me in England always. I wish it were not so."[18] And he wrote Edward Garnett in 1933: "Irishmen are disappointing men. They go so far, magnificently, and cease to grow."[19] But he then amended this harsh judgment six months later to Lady Astor in a critique of a play by Sean O'Casey: "When a rare Irishman does go on growing, you see, he surpasses most men. Alas that they are so rare."[20]

There is a temptation in this age of science and psychology to try to explain everything about human beings, or to show how each of the parts of a person's personality relates to the others. There is a false scientism in this, for we are not integrated in our personalities to nearly the same extent as we are in our bodies. Some qualities in all of us — in Lawrence certainly — must stand by themselves without explanation. The insistence on seeing Lawrence as "mysterious" derives from this need for explanation, contributed to by Lawrence himself. His life and complex personality seemed, more than those of most people, to have discernible form, and he tended often to hint in his teasing way that there were explanations for everything about him if only the hunter would look long and hard enough.

The moral dilemmas that grew for Lawrence out of his personal experiences during the war and in the years immediately afterwards led to an accentuation of his code of renunciation. "There is absolutely nothing I want for myself," he wrote Graves in 1928.[21] Although the severity of his self-denial, the degree of self-punitiveness, and the ritual of flagellation to which he subjected himself may, like his identity problems, be looked at from the standpoint of psychopathology, to do so without considering at the same time the great value for other people contained in certain elements of Lawrence's character that related to these struggles would be an equally unfortunate distortion. Lawrence rejected the Christianity of his parents and of his culture in the formal sense. But he preserved through his conscious choice of values, and through the personal example of his life, the elements in the Judeo-Christian tradition that are morally lasting.

He did not exaggerate much when he wrote Edward Garnett that he had "brick by brick . . . sold or given away or lost everything I possessed."[22] Lionel Curtis wrote that "Lawrence was always giving, himself, his friendship, his time, his brains, his possessions, and especially money when he had it."[23] And Lawrence told Liddell Hart, simply, "I like giving."[24] His RAF and Tank Corps companions have repeatedly attested to his sympathy for the underdog and his ready willingness to use his wiles to right injustices of all sorts in the ranks.[25]

I am convinced that much of what Lawrence accomplished, perhaps the central importance of his life, derived from the force of his moral example, what was known in an earlier time as "character." Mrs. Hardy expressed this best perhaps in a letter to Robert Graves in 1927 about Lawrence: "I consider him the most marvelous human being I have ever met. It is not his exploits in Arabia that attract me, nor the fact that he is a celebrity: it is his character that is so splendid."[26]

Lawrence's sensitivity to the feelings of other people continued during his service years to be accompanied by considerable self-consciousness and shyness about himself. He wrote typically to E. M. Forster in 1927, "If you knew all about me (perhaps you do: your subtlety is very great: shall I put it 'if I knew that you knew . . .'?) you'd think very little of me."[27] He had written similar passages in *Seven Pillars of Wisdom* eight years earlier. This basic doubt about his worth, the feeling of being somehow second-rate, was accompanied by a craving for praise and continued in Lawrence until the end. He rarely referred to his body in his writings. When he did so — invariably in humor — he tended to refer to the limitations of his height or what he considered oddities of his stature. On the occasion of parades, he wrote to Sergeant Pugh of Cranwell: "A group of six-foot people take station behind my back, and use me as a convenient low shelf for leaning on to view the procession."[28] When a young female artist with whom he was not acquainted sought his cooperation in being her model, Lawrence replied that it would be all right if she "can't afford a proper model" for "apparently I'm shaped rather like a tadpole."[29]

Lawrence could, of course, "feel things passionately," as he wrote to Bernard Shaw, but guarded intensely against sentimentality or subjectivity, what he called "the stink of personality" in literature or human relations.[30] He found such extravagant expressions of emotion as Laura Riding's suicide leap from love of Phibbs-Barnett rather appalling and called them "mad-house minds: no, not so much minds as appetites."[31] Yet he could feel compassion for the sufferers. He seems to have given more love, or even to have felt it more, than most people. But he could not abandon himself to giving in love, especially in an erotic sense. When one of his friends became troubled over his passion for a woman who was not his wife, Lawrence wrote to him: "The *matter* puzzles me: you must be patient there with my inadequacy. I do not love anybody and have not, I think ever — or hardly ever. It is difficult to share with people what one gives wholeheartedly to places or people or things. Nor have ever, I think, except momentarily-and-with-the-eye lusted. Altogether I'm a bad subject for feeling."[32]

Children were the group with whom Lawrence found it easiest to be open. He grasped readily what would interest a child, and his many letters to children of his friends and colleagues are directed in their style and content to the level of the child's thoughts and imagination. Lawrence's gift of vivid sensory perception and his unusual ability to impose a creative imagination upon the natural world and upon things and beings *in action* made communication with children easy. Animals, battles, scenes in nature all come alive in amusing directness in Lawrence's letters to young friends.

Lawrence lamented at the same time his inability to create works of the imagination in sculpture, painting or poetry.[33] But his creativity seemed to depend on the application of a vivid sensuous imagination to real things, events and creatures in the world of actuality. Even when he was writing of human feelings he was more invested, as he himself recognized, in what "various people did — in the expressions of their moods in action, than in the moods themselves."[34]

Lawrence was an artist of the world in action. His continuing interest as an adult in polarities of value — the ideal and its failure to be attained, or heroism and its betrayal — also facilitated his meeting of the mind with children. For young children in their moral development are much concerned with extremes of value and achievement, and with polarities of good and evil. They have not yet learned to tolerate within themselves —

nor did Lawrence ever learn — personal compromises on matters of value and morality. Reginald Sims recalled his small son and Lawrence happily discussing "the comparative merits of certain persons included in a book entitled *Heroes of Modern Adventure*."[35] It would have been an amusing conversation to have overheard.

Many have recalled the pleasure T.E. gave them when he shared their childhood interests, taught them to paddle a canoe or to shoot,[36] or took them on speedboat rides or other exciting adventures. The childlike side of his own nature and his sense of fun always remained alive just below the surface, and he could easily share a child's pleasure in simple activities, to which he brought his ingenuity and vast technical knowledge. "He could talk to me in child's language and always interest me," Flight Lieutenant Norrington's daughter wrote.[37] Lawrence would readily go out of his way to do something for a child. Much as he was troubled, for example, about the hero-worshipping of Colonel Lawrence or "Lawrence of Arabia," he readily wrote and signed a charming inscription of a copy of Liddell Hart's book for a crippled boy when the boy's sister indicated that an autographed copy would help the child's spirits.[38]

I talked with Colonel Newcombe's son, Stewart, Jr. (Jimmy) about his recollections of T.E. (Lawrence took a special interest in this particular godson and wrote him many letters, from the time Jimmy was six until he was fourteen). Newcombe recalled his enjoyment of Lawrence's company, especially the speedboat and motorcycle rides. Lawrence seemed to like their excursions and to take pleasure in the uncomplicated nature of the relationship. He seemed to have "a yen" for educating a child and sometimes liked to shock. Newcombe found Lawrence an easy adult to be with compared to most others, not the sort who made you feel frightened or awkward, not knowing what to say next. The conversation would proceed naturally, growing out of subjects they were both interested in, such as battleships or early ideas about boats that skimmed over the surface of the water with little resistance (hovercraft). They also enjoyed poking fun together at the pomposity of most adults.[39]

Hot baths and motorcycle riding were pleasures in which Lawrence permitted himself to indulge fully when baths were available and he could afford to maintain his machine. He would go to great lengths to arrange a bath where a camp had none readily available and was much bothered by cold. "Hot water is very near heaven," he wrote Buxton after rigging up his ingenious electrical hot water heater at Karachi.[40] "I'm very susceptible to cold," he wrote Thurtle later. "In England I'm always getting into hot baths, whenever they are available: because then only I am warm enough. Yet I never get what they call 'a chill.' Odd: because usually I get all the infections going."[41] As Sergeant Pugh put it: "Baths are his God." Lawrence would even bribe the "stoker" at Cranwell to tend to the fires for his bath before those of the others.[42]

Lawrence's love of motorcycle riding was more complex and served many functions. He had George Brough build for him eight very fine Brough Superior motorcycles during his years in the ranks, although his death came before he had a chance to ride the last one.[43] He was fussy about the care of his bikes, and according to a tank corpsman who garaged the Broughs for him near Bovington, gave away his wages in return for help in looking after them.[44] He would, nevertheless, sometimes lend his bikes to other enlisted men who took less good care of them than he did. Lawrence was an extremely fine motorcycle rider, with a great technical knowledge of the subject, and wrote several articles on cycling that were never published. The fine machinery itself gave him great pleasure, and he took pains to master the mechanical details. He also delighted in covering great distances in record times.

Speed itself, achieved on his bikes, gave Lawrence obvious sensual pleasure, which he described to Graves: "When I open out a little more, as for instance across Salisbury Plain at 80 or so, I feel the earth moulding herself under me. It is me piling up this hill, hollowing this valley, stretching out this level place. Almost the earth comes alive, heaving and tossing on each side like a sea. That is a thing that the slow coach will never feel. It is the reward of speed. I could write you pages on the lustfulness of moving swiftly."[45] To Liddell Hart he wrote a brief treatise on the lure of speed and man's historical love of finding any means to go faster. "Speed is the second oldest [next to sex presumably] craving in our nature. Every natural man cultivates the speed that appeals to him. I have a motor-bike income."[46]

His motorcycles afforded Lawrence an opportunity to escape from the dullness and oppression of the camp routine ("a hundred fast miles seem to make camp feel less confined afterwards").[47] On his bike he felt free and released. *The Mint* contains what is virtually a five-page eulogy to his fine machine, and includes an exhilarating race with an airplane overhead.[48]

Sometimes he enjoyed taking others with him for companionship, pillion-style, on his bike. But above all the bike represented for Lawrence an extension or prolongation of himself, an element with which (or with whom) he could maintain a comfortably intimate relationship. His various bikes were given pet names — Boanerges, Boa, or George I, II, III, IV, V, VI, or VII — and he spoke of or to them as if they were living things. Before traveling to India, for example, Lawrence was proud of "Boa" for winning a race against fast automobiles, during which he reached a speed of 120 miles an hour. "Never has Boa gone better," he wrote Mrs. Shaw. "I kept on patting him, and opening his throttle, knowing all the while in a month or two he will be someone's else's, and myself in a land without roads or speed. If I were rich he should have a warm dog garage, and no work until his old age. An almost human machine . . . a real prolongation of my own faculties: and so handsome and efficient. Never have I had anything like him."[49] Lawrence succeeded in damaging this particular bike by crashing it on a slippery street, thereby making parting with it for £100 just before he left for India somewhat less troubling.[50] In *The Mint* Lawrence wrote even more warmly of his pet: "Because Boa loves me, he gives me five more miles of speed than a stranger would get from him."[51]

Although Brough himself stated that he never saw Lawrence "take a single risk nor put any other rider or driver to the slightest inconvenience," Lawrence would clearly expose himself to danger on his motorcycles, especially when he was troubled. He acknowledged to Curtis during the difficult months in the Tank Corps: "When my mood gets too hot and I find myself wandering beyond control I pull out my motor-bike and hurl it top-speed through these unfit roads for hour after hour. My nerves are jaded and gone near dead, so that nothing less than hours of voluntary danger will prick them into life."[52] It was only his skill, and perhaps an element of luck, that kept Lawrence from more serious injury over the years, for he had several accidents and disliked wearing a crash helmet.[53]

Lawrence cultivated a philosophical side of his nature as he grew older. Many of his opinions on the great questions of man and nature have the freshness and immediacy characteristic of his original mind. But as in his personal loves and hates, subjectivity and feeling tended to dominate his views, and feeling was not far behind action. Although he set great store upon feeling being accompanied — preferably preceded — by reason and logic, he acknowledged his "bad habit, if I feel a thing, of acting it straightway, very unacademic, I assure you."[54] Although he was a great reader and a fine judge of literature, here too Lawrence tended to be an impressionistic rather than a formal critic, "one who reacts with his feelings to the quality of a writer's world rather than with his mind to meaning and form in any detached or orderly way."[55] He had a great interest in the craft of writing, in the strategies of literary technique, and as in his personal conduct and being, he sought absolute standards of excellence. As Edward Garnett remarked, "Lawrence to the end was a critic in action."[56]

Lawrence's view of human affairs, based as it was upon his life experience and internal state, became fundamentally a pessimistic one. He understood deeply the difference between ideal conceptions, especially in politics, and effective change. "The ideals of a policy are entrancing, heady things," he wrote toward the end of his life, but "translating them into terms of compromise with the social structure as it has evolved is pretty second-rate work. I have never met people more honest and devoted than our politicians — but I'd rather be a dustman. A decent nihilism is what I hope for, generally. I think an established land, like ours, can do with 1% monists or nihilists. That leaves room for me."[57]

Explanatory formulations of the causes of historical change tend to diminish in power as the student enriches his knowledge and gains a fuller picture of events. New elements emerge; further information must be considered; the plot thickens. The same limitation occurs, I believe, in the study of historical figures: in attempting to understand the subject, we must add to the data of biography and psychology, the influence of events, of politics and of historical circumstances — of reality in the broadest sense.

Still more difficult is it, then, to identify with confidence the links between the psychology of the individual historical figure and the events in which he played a crucial part. Yet such connections do exist. Few would deny that highly motivated persons critically placed by circumstance can affect the course of history as they live out their private dreams and needs on the stage of public life. The students of these relationships are in the position of detectives who know how the story came out and seek in the reconstruction to find patterns of meaning and influence.

Early in the development of this study I sought to demonstrate the contributions that a thorough study of the psychology of an individual historical figure might make to the understanding of historical events and change. I still believe that dynamic psychology can contribute a great deal to biography and to the understanding of history. I have ended believing as much, however, in what the methods of historical biography may contribute to my own field of psychiatry or psychoanalysis.

The basic instrument of psychological understanding is, broadly speaking, the analysis of the individual patient or subject through the data which he brings — his "material." But this material, though it may convey the patient's psychological state and his perceptions of reality, provides a distorted conception of the outside world as objective data: it is, in short, essentially self-serving. The patient communicates it in order to establish empathic sharing of pain with a doctor or therapist, for self-justification, or to defend himself through a variety of mechanisms against uncongenial self-awareness. The therapist's role is, thus, to understand these necessary distortions and to help the patient to accept a view of reality that allows him more latitude in mastering it and ultimately more personal gratification.

But even in his therapeutic role, the analyst is handicapped by the fact that he is furnished data chiefly by the patient and thus knows only the view of reality, past and present, which the patient presents to him, unless he can apply corrective judgments of his own. The exception to this limitation would be those instances in which the patient's misrepresentations apply to the therapist himself and he is helped to correct the distortion within the treatment relationship.

As for the therapeutic process — and I am talking principally about the understanding of individuals rather than groups — it is argued that the misunderstanding of reality and of events *as such* does not matter a great deal, since what is of chief importance is the patient's mental state, his view of reality, and its meaning for him. I would maintain, however, that it is often extremely difficult to understand the patient's mental state, the distortion of reality he is communicating, and the psychological mechanisms he is using to do so if the therapist is kept in the dark about the patient's actuality, present and past. Often — and I have experienced this frequently myself — the therapist finds himself subtly caught up in an unconscious participation in the patient's distorting mental mechanisms, complying with a misrepresentation of the outside world which might not be so unfortunate if it were therapeutic. But more often than not this compact is not only untherapeutic: it confirms the patient in maladaptive approaches to the world around him.

Historical biography, in contrast to the therapeutic priority required in work with individual patients, demands an objective depiction of reality. Here, too, psychological mechanisms are analyzed — although the voluntary yield of data that a motivated patient provides is not, of course, available. But these psychological phenomena are understood in conjunction with information about the reality of the subject's life. Information about family members, childhood influences, cultural, political and economic forces affecting the individual throughout his life is obtained in order more thoroughly to understand the subject and his impact upon the outside world. His actions and writings and even his deepest thoughts and feelings are all perceived in a context of reality, which helps to make them more intelligible. We learn more, I contend, about such a subject in this way than through the products of his own mind alone, for we see it in relation to the actual elements which helped to create it.

Present-day psychiatrists and other mental health professionals sometimes obtain information from family members, teachers, neighbors, and even employers, especially of hospitalized patients, or of patients treated at centers that use the approaches of community psychiatry. But I would remind the reader that virtually the entire psychoanalytic view of man, with the exception of some early work with children and their families, was built up through information obtained by the analysis of a selected sample of individual patients without obtaining information about them from other sources. It can be argued that generalizations arrived at in this way might well be invalidated by data regarding patients and subjects obtained from other sources. It can also be argued that the methods and approaches of psychologically oriented biography might have applicability not only to the understanding of historical figures but to the study of a variety of other individuals and character types as well.

Not infrequently, in the course of history, an extraordinary person has been able for a time to impose his will upon events, to seem even to shape these events in the direction of his private purpose. It is rare for such persons to reveal the working of their minds and thus permit us to gain insight into the inner forces that propelled them. T. E. Lawrence was — I often think — unique in combining these attributes.

I have tried to show in this book how Lawrence was able to adapt his talents, conflicts and private needs to the requirements of a series of historical situations, above all in the 1914–1918 war in the Middle East and in the diplomatic maneuverings that followed. The outcome of the Arab Revolt and the shape of the post–World War I settlements were influenced by his efforts. He required an arena of great happenings for the maximum use of his talents, "the current of cataclysmic events to chafe into me any sparkle of light," as he once wrote to Charlotte Shaw.[58]

Lawrence is most immediately associated with his achievements as a modern guerrilla leader and one of the first political strategists of the emerging nations. Yet if it is possible to divide historical figures into men who are known for what they did and those whose importance lies in what they represented, surely Lawrence may, with equal justification be placed in the second category. For his central, his unique, achievement derives from an effort to perfect the self, a shaping of his personality into an instrument of accomplishment, example and change. He sought *new possibilities* for the self.

By the onset of World War I Lawrence had equipped himself for any task that would test his powers. In the Arab Revolt he found a challenge matched to his capabilities and was able to combine the heroic fantasies of his youth with the historical exigencies and opportunities of the British war effort. He did indeed lead the Arabs "madly" to the final victory in Syria however much they may now criticize his approach to their political destinies after the war was over.

Connections can be found, as we have seen, between the elements in Lawrence's ancestral and family background and childhood development and many of the directions and conflicts of his adult life — links that were as vitalizing as they were impeding. Yet it is also clear that if Lawrence derived strength and purpose from his background and childhood, he was left with certain vulnerabilities — what the British writer John Buchan called "a crack in the firing." Unknowingly, he became burdened with the sin of his parents, especially his mother's, and was driven to redeem their fallen souls along with his own. He became aware at an early age that his parents were not married, despite the strictness of their personal codes. This discovery became a source of irreconcilable conflict in Lawrence, perhaps even as it contributed to his unusual tolerance of contradiction, ambiguity, and oddness in others. Having had such a deception imposed upon himself, Lawrence became deeply troubled about his own later role in the deception of the Arabs, whom he had encouraged in the Revolt while possessing the knowledge that secret agreements might ultimately vitiate their accomplishments.

The powerful and devouring personality of his mother was a source of strength for him, but confronted Lawrence with a formidable developmental challenge. She dominated his childhood and whipped him many times in a fashion to break his will. He maintained his integrity and avoided being totally absorbed by her (unlike his older brother) by identifying with many aspects of her personality, while keeping his distance from her as much as possible. This identification enabled Lawrence to develop richly empathic and nurturing qualities — aspects of personality ordinarily thought to be "motherly," or associated with women — that were fundamental to his achievements. It also left him confused in his sexual identity and vulnerable to the precipitation of a masochistic disorder that grew out of his identification with the passive feminine elements of the mother.

Lawrence was eternally engaged in struggles over value and self-worth. As a child he incorporated into his self-regard the guilt, the burden of sin and the shared family shame of illegitimacy, while absorbing at the same time the merciless expectation of exemplary ethical conduct, which was contained in the severe familial moral and religious tenets. He sought always to eliminate through the conduct of his life the gulf between his actual view of himself and his merciless ideal expectations. This gulf, this internal tension, provided an impetus for some of Lawrence's extraordinary strivings, especially his drive to achieve heroic deeds of a scale and form consistent with the chivalric and epic codes of his youthful readings.

To a certain extent, Lawrence was successful, at least from an objective standpoint. He possessed extraordinary courage and stamina (he once wrote Mrs. Shaw that he had sustained more, and fiercer, physical ordeals than any man he had known),[59] and the resourcefulness of Odysseus. He combined these qualities with an array of talents for leadership and a willingness to assume during the desert campaigns and thereafter responsibility to an extraordinary degree.

But there is always danger in trying to impose internal, private purposes upon the outside world, especially on a national or international scale. Events and peoples rarely conform for long to such purposes, and reality soon moves beyond the control of the individual. For Lawrence, the international politics of the struggles of the Middle East had already assured that he would be disappointed even before he had embarked upon his course of leadership in the Hijaz. He knew before he had been actively engaged in the desert campaigns for a year that he was an instrument of deception, encouraging the Arabs in the belief that their accomplishments on the battlefield would be honored at the conference table after the war. Furthermore, the Arabs, though ready to use Lawrence's guidance in achieving their own liberation, often did not conform to the

epic ideal in their actual behavior during the war, despite his characteriza-
tion of certain of their leaders as epic heroes in *Seven Pillars of Wisdom*.

The war left Lawrence troubled by guilt and shame. Not only had he
been a party to deceiving, to exploiting, the Arabs — a desecration of his
high mission — but he had violated his conscience in other ways: settling
blood disputes with his own hand, putting to death his suffering companion, giving the "no prisoners" order at Tafas. The traumatic sexual
attack by the Turks at Der'a confronted him with disturbing elements in
his nature and reactivated the very doubts about his self-worth that he
had sought to remove. It also left him with a disorder that required a
repetition of the experience through complex, medieval and ritualistic
forms of penance.

The campaigns in Arabia not only failed to resolve Lawrence's conflicts
about his self-worth, they left him with far deeper doubts and self-questioning than he had ever had before — "behind the laughing eyes a dreadful haunting."[60] But from this self-questioning has come what I believe to
be Lawrence's central importance for our time.

The disillusionment and traumatic experiences of the campaigns led
Lawrence to profound introspection, which found its fullest expression in
Seven Pillars of Wisdom. In this work and in some of his letters, Lawrence examines mercilessly the deeper psychological sources of his efforts
on behalf of the Allies and the Arabs during the campaigns. He has told
us something important, I believe, about the egoistic roots of leadership,
"how unlovely the back of a commander's mind must be," and has laid
bare the selfishness of self-sacrifice, in which the minds of the followers
are coopted in order to fulfill the private purposes of the leader. By assuming an exaggerated responsibility for murder he did not commit, in a
war that was not to begin with his responsibility, Lawrence helped to
undermine potentially the rationale — essential in the use of war for political purposes — that killing may be justifiable if the cause is worthy or
the killer is merely following orders.

Through his self-questioning Lawrence helped to make out of date the
romantic heroism of the nineteenth century, which adhered to an archaic
blind patriotism and glorification of war, little adapted to the modern
world viewed as a community of nations. Lawrence's exaggerated concern with the leader's responsibility for life may be of use to our age and
to those of the future in defining what we expect of our heroes and perhaps how we come to regard heroism in a world that cannot tolerate —
or even survive — the glorification and the achievements of war. His
exaggerated sense of responsibility may serve as a moral example for the
ideals of future leadership.

Lawrence always offered a great deal of himself as public property, his
conflicts and his sufferings, as well as his hopes and achievements. Even

after he had chosen to retreat from public life and from the full exercise of his personal powers, Lawrence offered his values and his solutions to others. Over and over again in talks with those who knew Lawrence or whose lives he had touched, I heard how he had changed their views of themselves, had helped them to find new approaches to their personal dilemmas and moral struggles.

Recognizing the essentially private nature of man's quest for a sense of personal worth, Lawrence seems to have been able to offer his tastes, his abilities and his moral values — especially his deeply felt code of renunciation — for others to use without imposing his values upon them. He could, like the saints with whose lives he was so familiar, give away everything he possessed — talents, advice, money — without leaving the recipient feeling in his debt.

Part of Lawrence's success in helping others grew out of his ability to keep his personal suffering apart from the daily congress of his life. He seems to have wrestled with his personal torments on his own time, and to have communicated them selectively in his writings, or in personal letters to friends. To other people he conveyed most often a sense of harmony, and seems to have spared them the knowledge of his compelling need for self-degradation and his nihilism. How was the "miracle of harmony" achieved in a man who was "at once prophet, poet, jester, crusader?" one friend wondered but was at a loss to explain.[61]

Lawrence's personality was replete with paradoxes and contradictions. These relate to the complexities and ambiguities of his origins, family relationships, and childhood development, but are not explained by them. They have made him fascinating to biographers and may account in part for the attraction of his example. He retained on the one hand a childlike immaturity — like a gifted schoolboy — and a responsiveness to the child's world, while at the same time he assumed throughout his life extraordinary adult responsibilities. He possessed an unusual capacity for relationships with many different sorts of human beings, while retaining an essential isolation and aloofness. He was highly open to sensuous experience yet remained always an ascetic who rejected many of the pleasures of the flesh, especially sexual ones. Self-absorbed and egocentric, he was nevertheless unselfish in giving of himself. He suffered troubling forms of psychopathology and was "neurotic" in many ways. Yet out of his sufferings he found new solutions and values, and was often able to convert his personal pathology to creative public endeavors. His own moral conflicts became irreconcilable and he never fully recovered a full sense of his own worth. Yet he continuously helped others feel more worthwhile in themselves.

Lawrence was a great creator of myths in the sense that his exploits and his own rich account of them — so vivid at times as to give the

impression of fiction — served as the basis for the creation by others of
the distorted legend that grew around him. Yet he represented such
fundamental truthfulness in his being that David Garnett once told me
Lawrence was the only man he had known in whose presence he could
never lie. He was to a degree a hero fashioned along the lines of the
Victorian revival of medieval romanticism. Yet he may contribute ultimately to the destruction of this form of heroism and help to replace it
with a model of a hero more self-aware, responsible and realistic. He was
the representative of British colonialism in the Middle East, but became
a spokesman for the end of traditional imperialism. A war hero and
modern military leader — perhaps, next to Churchill, Britain's best known
— Lawrence could become a figure who represents the renunciation
of war.

Lawrence was always influencing people. This power to influence lies
close to the heart of his effectiveness as a leader and of his historical
importance. Besides his influence upon Arabs and British alike during the
war in the Middle East and after it, he influenced the development of the
RAF and was able to convince the admiralty to use for air-sea rescue the
smaller, faster boats he helped to design. Individual airmen and tank
corpsmen and other friends have related to me how their acquaintance
with Lawrence profoundly altered their lives, helped them to find new
purpose and meaning. One airman told me that he had led a derelict life
and was in constant difficulty with the authorities until he got to know
Lawrence. But through the gentle influence and example of his friend he
had steadied himself and had developed a rich and lasting interest in
literature. Others ask themselves at difficult moments, "What would
Lawrence have done?" and feel guided by the memory of his example.

In 1927 Lawrence asked a friend, "How long do you think, before they
forget?"[62] But his influence continues, especially through the written
legacy of his experience. Arnold Lawrence still receives letters from
people who were enabled to do something useful with their lives, or found
a new, deeper meaning through Lawrence's writings and personal example. He had a way of giving people the sense that he had experienced or
suffered what they had endured. As he wrote Mrs. Shaw in 1931, "Colonel
Lawrence still goes on, and it is only me who has stepped out of the
way."[63]

It is difficult, if not impossible, to estimate Lawrence's influence in a
larger sense. As one of his biographers I am a part of the process by
which he becomes known to his historical audience. The selection of
Lawrence for such intensive study bespeaks in itself my belief in his value
and importance, and I would wish naturally to have documented the
basis for this conviction and to have communicated it effectively. I have

in mind not only Lawrence's accomplishments as a military and political leader and writer, or even his achievements in the RAF period, but just as important, I have chosen to stress those aspects of Lawrence's place in history that have been more meaningful to me — the intangible qualities of personality, the example of self through which Lawrence drew others to him and enabled them to change. As Erik Erikson has taught us, the evaluation of the meaning of a man's life viewed in these terms will shift according to the requirements of each age and culture, and every biographer embodies to some extent the values and points of view of his own society in his interpretations of a subject.

Lawrence has been hurt by both his idolators and his denigrators. The latter, especially Richard Aldington and Malcolm Muggeridge, have found Lawrence to be a charlatan and a liar.[64] My own examination of the evidence has led me to different conclusions. Lawrence had a compelling need to tell stories, which grew in part out of his deep doubts about his self-worth. Profoundly uncertain about his value, he laid the foundation for the creation alongside of the actual Lawrence of a legendary personality built on the dramatizations and elaborations of his tales. So extraordinary are some of these stories that they have seemed at times to have been made up. Yet my research led me repeatedly to the conclusion that Lawrence's accounts of his accomplishments were largely accurate and, if anything, he would customarily leave out information that was to his credit, or allow to stand distorted depictions of events that have invited the attacks of his detractors. I have not found Lawrence to be a liar.

Lawrence's struggles form one of the most moving personal sagas I have ever encountered. He could not ultimately resolve his inner personal disorder. Had he been able to, he might have lived to make a contribution in Britain's hour of need in World War II. But though he could not quiet his own inner demons, he was, in Irving Howe's words, a "prince of our disorder" and one of its civilizing forces.

A poet friend wrote to Lawrence once: "You are a kind of double personality for me (a) a charming friendly character given to sudden appearances on inordinate motor-bicycles; (b) a sort of mythological figure or a force of nature — so that I feel as if I were being addressed by an earthquake, in however still and small a voice."[65] Lawrence was tragic and introspective, a master craftsman and technician on the one hand, and a saint with humor on the other. Churchill deemed him one of the greatest beings alive in his time, while David Garnett told me simply, "He was of a higher value."[66]

Others found different riches in Lawrence's nature, other dimensions of themselves. Unable to establish firmly the core of his own identity, he was able to draw men and women to him to offer for their pleasure and development the many currents of his personality. John Buchan captured best this central characteristic of Lawrence's: "I am not a very tractable person or much of a hero-worshipper, but I could have followed Lawrence over the edge of the world. I loved him for himself, and also because there seemed to be reborn in him all the lost friends of my youth."[67]

APPENDIX

Appendix

Twenty-seven Articles*

The following notes have been expressed in commandment form for greater clarity and to save words. They are however only my personal conclusions, arrived at gradually while I worked in the Hedjaz and now put on paper as stalking horses for beginners in the Arab armies. They are meant to apply only to Bedu: townspeople or Syrians require totally different treatment. They are of course not suitable to any other person's need, or applicable unchanged in any particular situation. Handling Hedjaz Arabs is an art, not a science, with exceptions and no obvious rules. At the same time we have a great chance there: the Sherif trusts us, and has given us the position (towards his Government) which the Germans wanted to win in Turkey. If we are tactful we can at once retain his good will, and carry out our job — but to succeed we have got to put into it all the interest and energy and skill *we possess*.

1. Go easy just for the first few weeks. A bad start is difficult to atone for, and the Arabs form their judgments on externals that we ignore. When you have reached the inner circle in a tribe you can do as you please with yourself and them.

2. Learn all you can about your Ashraf and Bedu. Get to know their families, clans and tribes, friends and enemies, wells, hills and roads. Do all this by listening and by indirect inquiry. Do not ask questions. Get to speak their dialect of Arabic, not yours. Until you can understand their allusions avoid getting deep into conversation, or you will drop bricks. Be a little stiff at first.

3. In matters of business deal only with the commander of the Army, column, or party in which you serve. Never give orders to anyone at all, and reserve your directions or advice for the C.O., however great the temptation (for efficiency's sake) of dealing direct with his underlings. Your place is advisory, and

* First published in the *Arab Bulletin* #60, August 20, 1917; reprinted in Lawrence's *Secret Dispatches from Arabia* (1937), pp. 126–133; reprinted in part in Basil Liddell Hart's '*T. E. Lawrence*,' pp. 142–147. The original manuscript is in the PRO/FO 882/7.

your advice is due to the commander alone. Let him see that this is your conception of your duty, and that his is to be the sole executive of your joint plans.

4. Win and keep the confidence of your leader. Strengthen his prestige at your expense before others when you can. Never refuse or quash schemes he may put forward: but ensure that they are put forward in the first instance privately to you. Always approve them, and after praise modify them insensibly, causing the suggestions to come from him, until they are in accord with your own opinion. When you attain this point, hold him to it, keep a tight grip of [sic] his ideas, and push him forward as firmly as possible, but secretly so that no one but himself (and he not too clearly) is aware of your pressure.

5. Remain in touch with your leader as constantly and unobtrusively as you can. Live with him, that at meal times and at audiences you may be naturally with him in his tent. Formal visits to give advice are not so good as the constant dropping of ideas in casual talk. When stronger sheikhs come in for the first time to swear allegiance and offer services, clear out of the tent. If their first impression is of foreigners in the confidence of the Sherif, it will do the Arab cause much harm.

6. Be shy of too close relations with the subordinates of the expedition. Continued intercourse with them will make it impossible for you to avoid going behind or beyond the instruction that the Arab C.O. has given them on your advice: and in so disclosing the weakness of his position you altogether destroy your own.

7. Treat the sub-chiefs of your force quite easily and lightly. In this way you hold yourself above their level. Treat the leader, if a Sherif, with respect. He will return your manner, and you and he will then be alike, and above the rest. Precedence is a serious matter among the Arabs, and you must attain it.

8. Your ideal position is when you are present and not noticed. Do not be too intimate, too prominent, or too earnest. Avoid being identified too long or too often with any tribal sheikh, even if C.O. of the expedition. To do your work you must be above jealousies, and you lose prestige if you are associated with a tribe or clan, and its inevitable feuds. Sherifs are above all blood-feuds and local rivalries, and form the only principle of unity among the Arabs. Let your name, therefore, be coupled always with a Sherif's, and share his attitude towards the tribe. When the moment comes for action put yourself publicly under his orders. The Bedu will then follow suit.

9. Magnify and develop the growing conception of the Sherifs as the natural aristocracy of the Arabs. Inter-tribal jealousies make it impossible for any sheikh to attain a commanding position, and the only hope of union in nomad Arabia is that the Ashraf be universally acknowledged as the ruling class. Sherifs are half townsmen, half-nomad, in manner and life, and have the instinct of command. Mere merit and money would be insufficient to obtain such recognition: but the Arab reverence for pedigree and the prophet gives hope for the ultimate success of the Ashraf.

10. Call your Sherif "Sidi" in public and in private. Call other people by their ordinary names, without title. In intimate conversation call a Sheikh "Abu Annad," "Akhu Alia" or some similar by-name.

11. The foreigner and Christian is not a popular person in Arabia. However friendly and informal the treatment of yourself may be, remember always that

your foundations are very sandy ones. Wave a Sherif in front of you like a banner, and hide your own mind and person. If you succeed you will have hundreds of miles of country and thousands of men under your orders, and for this it is worth bartering the outward show.

12. Cling tight to your sense of humor. You will need it every day. A dry irony is the most useful type, and repartee of a personal and not too broad character will double your influence with the Chiefs. Reproof if wrapped up in some smiling form will carry further and last longer than the most violent speech. The power of mimicry or parody is valuable but use it sparingly for it is more dignified than humor. Do not cause a laugh at a Sherif except amongst Sherifs.

13. Never lay hands on an Arab — you degrade yourself. You may think the resultant obvious increase of outward respect a gain to you: but what you have really done is to build a wall between you and their inner selves. It is difficult to keep quiet when everything is being done wrong, but the less you lose your temper the greater your advantage. Also then you will not go mad yourself.

14. While very difficult to drive, the Bedu are easy to lead, if you have the patience to bear with them. The less apparent your interferences the more you influence. They are willing to follow your advice and do what you wish, but they do not mean you or anyone else to be aware of that. It is only after the end of all annoyances that you find at bottom their real fund of good will.

15. Do not try to do too much with your own hands. Better the Arabs do it tolerably than that you do it perfectly. It is their war, and you are to help them, not to win it for them. Actually also under the very odd conditions of Arabia, your practical work will not be as good as perhaps, you think it is.

16. If you can, without being too lavish, forestall presents to yourself. A well placed gift is often most effective in winning over a suspicious Sheikh. Never receive a present without giving a liberal return, but you may delay this return (while letting its ultimate certainty be known) if you require a particular service from the giver. Do not let them ask you for things, since their greed will then make them look upon you only as a cow to milk.

17. Wear an Arab headcloth when with a tribe. Bedu have a malignant prejudice against the hat, and believe that our persistence in wearing it (due probably to British obstinacy of dictation) is founded on some immoral or irreligious principle. A thick headcloth forms a good protection against the sun, and if you wear a hat your best Arab friends will be ashamed of you in public.

18. Disguise is not advisable. Except in special areas let it be clearly known that you are a British officer and a Christian. At the same time if you can wear Arab kit when with the tribes you will acquire their trust and intimacy to a degree impossible in uniform. It is however dangerous and difficult. They make no special allowances for you when you dress like them. Breaches of etiquette not charged against a foreigner are not condoned to you in Arab clothes. You will be like an actor in a foreign theatre, playing a part day and night for months, without rest, and for an anxious stake. Complete success, which is when the Arabs forget your strangeness and speak naturally before you, counting you one of themselves, is perhaps only attainable in character: while half success (all that most of us will strive for — the other costs too much) is easier to win in British things, and you yourself will last longer, physically and mentally, in

the comfort that they mean. Also then the Turks will not hang you, when you're caught.

19. If you wear Arab things wear the best. Clothes are significant among the tribes, and you must wear the appropriate, and appear at ease in them. Dress like a Sherif — if they agree to it.

20. If you wear Arab things at all, go the whole way. Leave your English friends and customs on the coast, and fall back on Arab habits entirely. It is possible, starting thus to level with them, for the Europeans to beat the Arabs at their own game, for we had stronger motives for our action, and put more heart into it than they. If you can surpass them, you have taken an immense stride toward complete success, but the strain of living and thinking in a foreign and half-understood language, the savage food, strange clothes, and still stranger ways, with the complete loss of privacy and quiet, and the impossibility of ever realizing your watchful imitation of the others for months on end, provide such an added stress to the ordinary difficulties of dealing with the Bedu, the climate, and the Turks, that this road should not be chosen without serious thought.

21. Religious discussions will be fairly frequent. Say what you like about your own side, and avoid criticism of theirs, unless you know that the point is external, when you may score heavily by proving it so. With the Bedu Islam is so all-pervading an element that there is with religiosity, little fervour, and no regard for externals. Do not think, from their conduct that they are careless. Their conviction of the truth of their faith, and its share in every act and thought and principle of their daily life is so intimate and intense as to be unconscious, unless roused by opposition. Their religion is as much a part of nature to them as is sleep, or food.

22. Do not try to trade on what you know of fighting. The Hedjaz confounds ordinary tactics. Learn the Bedu principles of war as thoroughly and as quickly as you can, for till you know them your advice will be no good to the Sherif. Unnumbered generations of tribal raids have taught them more about some parts of the business than we will ever know. In familiar conditions they fight well, but strange events cause panic. Keep your unit small. Their raiding parties are usually from one hundred to two hundred men, and if you take a crowd they only get confused. Also their sheikhs, while admirable company commandoes, are too set to learn to handle the equivalents of battalions or regiments. Don't attempt unusual things, unless they appeal to the sporting instinct Bedu have so strongly, or unless success is obvious. If the objective is a good one (booty) they will attack like fiends: they are splendid scouts, their mobility gives you the advantage that will win their local war, they make proper use of their knowledge of the country (don't take tribesmen to places they do not know), and the gazelle-hunters, who form a proportion of the better men, are great shots at visible targets. A Sheikh from one tribe cannot give orders to men from another: a Sherif is necessary to command a mixed tribal force. If there is plunder in prospect, and the odds are at all equal, you will win. Do not waste Bedu attacking trenches (they will not stand casualties) or in trying to defend a position, for they cannot sit still without slacking. The more unorthodox and Arab your proceedings the more likely you are to have the Turks cold, for they lack initiative and expect you to. Don't play for safety.

23. The open reason that Bedu give you for action or inaction may be true, but always there will be better reasons left for you to divine. You must find these inner reasons (they will be denied, but are none the less in operation) before shaping your arguments for one course or others. Allusion is more effective than logical exposition: they dislike concise expression. Their minds work just as ours do, but on different premises. There is nothing unreasonable, incomprehensible, or inscrutable, in the Arab. Experience of them, and knowledge of their prejudices will enable you to foresee their attitude and possible course of action in nearly every case.

24. Do not mix Bedu and Syrians, or trained men and tribesmen. You will get work out of neither, for they hate each other. I have never seen a successful combined operation, but many failures. In particular, ex-officers of the Turkish army however Arab in feeling and blood and language, are hopeless with Bedu. They are narrow-minded in tactics, unable to adjust themselves to irregular warfare, clumsy in Arab etiquette, swollen-headed to the extent of being incapable of politeness to a tribesman for more than a few minutes, impatient, and usually helpless on the road, in action. Your orders (if you were unwise enough to give any) would be more readily obeyed by Bedouins than those of any Mohammedan Syrian officer. Arab townsmen and Arab tribesmen regard each other mutually as poor relations — and poor relations are much more objectionable than poor strangers.

25. In spite of ordinary Arab example avoid too free talk about women. It is as difficult a subject as religion, and their standards are so unlike our own, that a remark harmless in English may appear as unrestrained to them, as some of their statements would look to us, if translated literally.

26. Be as careful of your servants as of yourself. If you want a sophisticated one you will probably have to take an Egyptian, or a Sudani, and unless you are very lucky he will undo on trek much of the good you so laboriously effect. Arabs will cook rice and make coffee for you, and leave you if required to do unmanly work like cleaning boots or washing. They are only really possible if you are in Arab kit. A slave brought up in the Hedjaz is the best servant, but there are rules against British subjects owning them, so they have to be lent to you. In any case take with you an Ageyli or two when you go up country. They are the most efficient couriers in Arabia, and understand camels.

27. The beginning and ending of the secret of handling Arabs is unremitting study of them. Keep always on your guard; never say an inconsidered thing, or do an unnecessary thing: watch yourself and your companions all the time: hear all that passes, search out what is going on beneath the surface, read their characters, discover their tastes and their weaknesses, and keep everything you find out to yourself. Bury yourself in Arab circles, have no interests and no ideas except the work in hand, so that your brain shall be saturated with one thing only, and you realize your part deeply enough to avoid the little slips that would undo the work of weeks. Your success will be just proportioned to the amount of mental effort you devote to it.

CHAPTER NOTES

Chapter Notes

The following abbreviations are used in the notes:

BM Add MSS	British Museum Additional Manuscripts
Bod Res MSS	The large collection of Lawrence's papers on reserve in the Bodleian Library, Oxford
CAB	Cabinet Papers
Friends	Arnold W. Lawrence, ed., *T. E. Lawrence by His Friends*
FO	Foreign Office Papers
Home Letters	M. Robert Lawrence, ed., *The Home Letters of T. E. Lawrence and His Brothers*
Letters	*The Letters of T. E. Lawrence,* edited by David Garnett
Letters to TEL	Arnold W. Lawrence, ed., *Letters to T. E. Lawrence*
LHB	Basil Liddell Hart, *T. E. Lawrence to his Biographer, Liddell Hart*
Mint	Lawrence's *The Mint*
PRO	Public Record Office
RGB	Robert Graves, *T. E. Lawrence to His Biographer, Robert Graves*
Secret Dispatches	Lawrence's *Secret Dispatches from Arabia*
Secret Lives	Phillip Knightley and Colin Simpson, *The Secret Lives of Lawrence of Arabia*
Seven Pillars	Lawrence's *Seven Pillars of Wisdom*

INTRODUCTION

1. In an essay, "Psychopathic Characters on the Stage," published posthumously, Freud discusses the relationship between dramatic heroes on the stage and the theatre audience, which identifies with the personal conflicts of the protagonist. The spectator, Freud notes, usually feels that there is little of importance in his life and "longs to feel and to act and to arrange things according to his desires — in short to be a hero." The hero on the stage furnishes the opportunity to surmount these limitations through identification with his struggles. Freud does not extend his discussion to the relationship between the "spectator" in society and the public figures with whom he identifies. (*Standard Edition of the Complete Psychological Works of Sigmund Freud*, VII [1942, but written in 1905 or 1906]: 305–310.)

2. *Letters*, p. 651.
3. Isaiah Berlin, *Historical Inevitability*, p. 53.
4. *Letters*, p. 825.
5. Ibid., p. 427.
6. *Seven Pillars*, p. 6.
7. *Letters*, p. 559.
8. A fuller discussion of the history of psychoanalytic approaches to biographical study is provided in an essay by the author, "Psychoanalysis and Historical Biography," *Journal of the American Psychoanalytic Association* 19 (January 1971): 143–179.

1. CHAPMANS AND LAWRENCES

1. LHB, p. 78.
2. RGB, p. 60.
3. RGB, p. 50.
4. LHB, p. 55.
5. Lawrence to John Buchan, June 20, 1927, Bod Res MSS, b55. In 1926 Lawrence also supplied basic biographical data in a humorous letter to David G. Hogarth, who was then preparing an entry on him for the *Dictionary of National Biography* (*Letters*, p. 491–492).
6. Early in my investigations I was led by David Garnett, editor of the Lawrence letters, on to the trail of several members of the Anglo-Irish nobility who had been neighbors of the Chapmans in County Westmeath. They kindly shared with me their recollections of Lady Chapman and her daughters and of the stilted, old-fashioned existence they carried on at South Hill long after Thomas Chapman had eloped with Sarah. "My family and the Chapmans lived about 12 miles apart and probably only met occasionally," one lady wrote me. "I had always understood [Thomas Chapman] had . . . run off with the future Mrs. Lawrence, who was variously described as the 'Italian maid' and 'the Scotch governess'. . . . Meanwhile Lady Chapman and her four daughters had passed a twilight sort of existence and it is not surprising if they grew a little eccentric as they got older. . . . My own first contact with the Chapmans was in 1924 [at a dance]. . . . They [the daughters] certainly looked a bit dishevelled and old-fashioned in dress, but were full of spirit and put up a good show for middle-aged spinsters who had spent their life mewed up in a decayed country house with a decaying mother." A year later the letter writer found "old Lady Chapman, sitting rigidly in an upright chair and looking as if she and her surroundings had not altered since Sir Thomas Chapman eloped. She made polite small talk . . . evidently under the impression that Queen Victoria was still alive" (Lady Pansy Lamb to the author, December 19, 1964). The daughters remembered their mother as cruelly restrictive and punitive. She would make them look away if a man passed in the street, and she once forced the youngest daughter to hang a chamber pot around her neck as punishment when she did something wrong (interview in Dublin with Mrs. Seaton Pringle, a former companion of one of the Chapman daughters, March 19, 1965). She actually drove two of her daughters out of the home for a two-year period. Despite the intolerance of the Victorian era in which she lived, her extreme behavior has led to speculation that Edith Chapman might have been mentally ill. Phillip Knightley and Colin Simpson in *The Secret Lives of Lawrence of Arabia* provide from their researches other accounts of her behavior.

7. *Burke's Peerage*, 1887.
8. Interview with Miss Fitzsimon, Delvin, County Westmeath, March 19, 1965.
9. Lawrence to Charlotte Shaw, March 18, 1927, BM Add MCC, 45903.
10. Lawrence to Edward Garnett, August 27, 1924, Bod Res MSS, d54.
11. Lawrence to Charlotte Shaw, August 24, 1926, BM Add MSS, 45903.

12. Interview on March 20, 1965, with Lily Montgomery, family companion of the Chapman daughters, 1937–1953.

13. Interview with Christine Longford, former neighbor of the Chapmans, March 18, 1965.

14. Interview with Lily Montgomery, March 20, 1965, and letter from her to the author, September 17, 1965.

15. Ibid.

16. Letter to Arabella Rivington from a cousin of Lady Chapman's and the transcription of Mrs. Rivington's interview with the cousin, in the *Sunday Times* research materials, Imperial War Museum, London.

17. Lawrence to Robin Buxton, November 25, 1924, Jesus College Library, Oxford University.

18. Birth record of William Lawrence, Kirkudbright, Scotland.

19. Mrs. Stewart (Elsie) Newcombe to the author, January 5, 1965.

20. LHB, p. 67.

21. Lawrence to Charlotte Shaw, April 14, 1927, BM Add MSS, 45903.

22. Lawrence to Hugh Trenchard, May 1, 1928, Bod Res MSS, d46.

23. Lawrence to Charlotte Shaw, August 28, 1928, BM Add MSS, 45904.

24. Interview with Janet Laurie Hallsmith, March 25, 1965.

25. Interview with Robert Lawrence, March 24, 1965.

26. Interview with Andrew Laurie, March 26, 1965.

27. Interview with Robert Lawrence, March 24, 1965.

28. Ibid.

29. Interview with Theo and Hilda Chaundy, August 24, 1964.

30. An interesting observation in view of the fact that T. E. later took the name Shaw as his own.

31. Comments of A. H. Kerry on a BBC television broadcast, November 27, 1962; interview with Kerry, March 25, 1965.

32. Interview with Janet Laurie Hallsmith and Mollie Laurie, December 17, 1965; interview with C. F. C. Beeson, March 22, 1965.

33. Robert Graves, *Lawrence and the Arabs*, p. 17.

34. Interview with Arnold Lawrence, August 25, 1964.

35. Sarah Lawrence did not live in Oxford after 1923, when the house on Polstead Road was sold. She and Bob soon traveled to China and lived there until they were expelled in 1927. They returned in 1933 and were there when news came of T.E.'s death in 1935. During the interim period and after 1935 Sarah and Bob had a peripatetic existence — in Oxfordshire, Wiltshire, Dorset, London and Malta (where Bob took a post in the Naval Hospital). It was in Malta that Mrs. Lawrence became close to Stewart and Elsie Newcombe. Mrs. Newcombe, because of her close friendship with Sarah, was able to provide valuable information and insights.

36. Interview with Sir Basil Blackwell, Oxford, March 21, 1965.

37. Interview with Basil Liddell Hart, March 27, 1965.

38. Birth record, Sunderland District, England. Mrs. Lawrence concealed her own origins as much as she did the details of her family situation with Lawrence's father. When the *Dictionary of National Biography* required in its entry on Lawrence some mention of the parents' names, Ronald Storrs, the author of the piece, inquired of Arnold Lawrence for information about his mother's maiden name. Arnold knew few details, but discouraged Storrs from asking his mother. "It certainly is no use telling her I approve," he wrote Storrs, "she'd say I ought not to" (letter of April 1946). When she learned from Arnold about the planned article Mrs. Lawrence wrote Storrs to request that if he would say nothing about Lawrence's antecedents other than that his father was Irish and his mother Scottish he would "make an old woman of 85 most grateful" (letter of August 29, 1946). Both letters are among the *Sunday Times* research materials, Imperial War Museum, London.

39. Personal communication from Arnold Lawrence, July 15, 1968.

40. Interview with Arnold Lawrence, August 26, 1972.

41. Interview with Elsie Newcombe, August 27, 1964; Elsie Newcombe to the author, October 3, 1964.

42. Interview with Mollie Laurie, March 25, 1965.

43. Interview with Janet Laurie Hallsmith, March 25, 1965.

44. Florence Hardy to T. E. Lawrence, March 5, 1928, Bod Res MSS, d60.

45. Interview with Elsie Newcombe, August 20, 1972.

46. Ibid.

47. Interview with Dr. and Mrs. Theo Chaundy, August 26, 1964.

48. Interview with David Garnett, October 30, 1964.

49. Interview with Elsie Newcombe, August 20, 1972.

50. When Arnold Lawrence was in Athens six weeks after having written his mother of his marriage, he awoke one morning to discover that he did not know where he was. He went out into the garden in order "to try to get back some feeling." This was about the day that his mother, whose fierce disapproval of his marriage plans he had not anticipated, would have received his letter. Arnold's theory was that her influence upon him was so powerful that she had succeeded in absorbing him. In contrast, other people, especially women, have testified repeatedly to a sweet, kind and loving quality in Mrs. Lawrence, which, despite her disciplined and forceful ways, commanded affection from both adults and children.

51. Robert Lawrence once asked one of his friends, who was familiar with the family background, quite unexpectedly, "Did you know my father's name?" "Thomas Chapman," the friend told him (interview with Elsie Newcombe, August 20, 1972).

52. Interview with Theo and Hilda Chaundy, August 26, 1964.

53. Celandine Kennington to Lady Hardinge, July 30, 1954, in the *Sunday Times* research materials, Imperial War Museum, London.

54. Interview with Elsie Newcombe, August 20, 1972.

55. Interview with Arnold Lawrence, December 8, 1965.

56. Interviews with Elsie Newcombe, August 27, 1964, and August 20, 1972.

57. Lawrence's statement does not agree with the facts as given to me by Arnold and Robert Lawrence, and by Elsie Newcombe, in whom Mrs. Lawrence confided. They all agree that she was brought up in Scotland by an aunt who was married to the rector of an Evangelical ("low church") parish.

58. Lawrence to Charlotte Shaw, May 17, 1928, BM Add MSS, 45904.

59. Lawrence to Charlotte Shaw, April 14, 1927, BM Add MSS, 45903.

60. Lawrence to Charlotte Shaw, August 28, 1928, BM Add MSS, 45904.

61. Arnold Lawrence, "Knowledge of Illegitimacy" (February 1963), Bod Res MSS, b56.

62. LHB, p. 78.

63. Interview with Robert Lawrence, August 24, 1964; *Friends*, p. 31.

64. Interview with Sir Basil Blackwell, March 21, 1965.

65. Interview with Arnold and Barbara Lawrence, March 16, 1965.

66. Personal communication from Arnold Lawrence, July 21, 1968.

67. Interview with C. F. C. Beeson, March 22, 1965.

68. Interviews with Janet Laurie Hallsmith, March 25, 1965, and E. F. Hall, December 16, 1965.

69. Interview with Arnold Lawrence, March 16, 1965.

70. Arnold Lawrence wrote of the difference in his parents' religiosity as follows: "My mother . . . held religious convictions profoundly. She totally accepted the tenets of her brand of Christianity and had no doubt they constituted a complete code of binding rules for conduct; but she could only in small part share in my father's emotional, almost mystical, religious feeling" (letter to the author, November 1, 1968).

71. J. S. Reynolds, *Canon Christopher of St. Aldates, Oxford*, p. 451.

72. Interview with Robert Lawrence, March 24, 1965.

73. *Friends*, p. 28.

74. LHB, pp. 78–79.

75. This information comes from an interview with Stewart L. Newcombe, March 20, 1965, and from a reminiscence by F. C. Lay in the *Jesus College Record*, 1971 (the year of Robert Lawrence's death).

76. Lawrence to Charlotte Shaw, undated, but clearly June or July 1928, BM Add MSS, 45904.

77. Arnold Lawrence wrote the author (July 23, 1973) that he and T.E. once observed together how amusing it might have been had Bob become the eighth Chapman baronet.

78. This passage appears in the manuscript of Graves's biography of Lawrence (Bod Res MSS, c20), but was omitted from the published version.

79. T.E. to Will Lawrence, August 6, 1906, *Home Letters*, p. 21.

80. Interview with E. F. Hall, December 16, 1965.

81. Accounts by F. C. Lay in the *Jesus*

College Record, 1971, and by Sir Ernest
Barker in *Home Letters*, pp. 395–397.

82. Interview with E. F. Hall, December 16, 1965.

83. Ibid.

84. F. C. Lay in the *Jesus College Record*, 1971, p. 25.

85. Interview with Arnold Lawrence, July 21, 1968.

86. He has a wry sense of humor. Once, when we were driving together along an English motorway, he noticed a high-tension power station with its usual concentration of metal towers and structural lattice work. "Those would make wonderful ruins," he remarked.

87. Lawrence to Charlotte Shaw, May 12, 1927, BM Add MSS, 45903.

2. CHILDHOOD AND ADOLESCENCE

1. *Friends*, p. 25.

2. Ibid., pp. 25–30, 31–35.

3. For example, LHB, pp. 77–79, and *Letters*, p. 148.

4. *Friends*, p. 31.

5. Bod Res MSS, c54. The photograph opposite p. 54 in *Secret Lives*, which shows a little boy in a sailor's shirt and cap and bears the caption "Lawrence the boy," is not of Lawrence. It was supplied by a woman in North Wales who believed it to be of Lawrence. The photograph does not resemble him at all.

6. Interview with Robert Lawrence, March 24, 1965.

7. *Friends*, p. 25.

8. Interview with Robert Lawrence, August 24, 1964; also, *Friends*, p. 31.

9. Ibid.

10. Ibid.

11. *Letters*, pp. 112–113, 153, 161–162.

12. Richard Aldington, *Lawrence of Arabia*, pp. 26–31.

13. *Friends*, pp. 25, 32; Mrs. Lawrence's preface to T.E.'s *Crusader Castles*, II, 5.

14. *Letters*, p. 148.

15. LHB, p. 51.

16. Ibid.

17. *Letters*, p. 148. In his effort to discredit Lawrence, Aldington deliberately omits the not-infrequent disclaimers that Lawrence includes in his statements about his unusual abilities. For example, the full statement of his experience in learning Latin, which is contained in a 1911 letter to Mrs. Rieder, herself a language teacher at the American mission

school at Jebail in Syria, was as follows: "I was reading (chiefly police news) at four, and learning Latin at five, and at seventeen I was no more forward than the rest of the school, beginning Latin at eight and one half" (*Letters*, p. 25). His mother confirms that a schoolmaster gave the boys Latin lessons in Langley, to which the family moved before T.E. was six, "to prepare them for going to school." Sometimes it is Lawrence's biographers who are responsible for the distortion, exaggeration or errors that appear in their work. Robert Graves, for example, wrote in his biography of Lawrence: "In six years he read every book in the library of the Oxford Union — the best part of 50,000 volumes, probably" (*Lawrence and the Arabs*, p. 24). Lawrence's actual statement to Graves, upon which this passage was based, was "I read every book *which interested me* [italics mine] in the library of the Oxford Union (best part of 50,000 volumes I expect) in six years" (RGB, p. 64). The exaggeration by Lawrence is still evident but the meaning is different. Aldington chooses to cite this as entirely Lawrence's exaggeration, referring to the fact that Graves said Lawrence passed on every word in the manuscript, despite Liddell Hart's published assertion that this was a proofreading error on Graves's part (LHB, p. 210). The most it seems that Lawrence could be accused of, if indeed he saw the passage in the manuscript, was of failing to correct it himself. In their more recent book, Knightley and Simpson simply reject out of hand the notion of Lawrence's precocity with the statement, "Despite what numerous biographers have written, he was neither a prodigy nor a prig" (*Secret Lives*, p. 9). They do not provide the evidence upon which this assertion is based.

I have gone into considerable detail on this matter because it is part of a larger problem one encounters in trying to understand Lawrence. As a result of central problems of self-esteem in his psychology, statements about his ability, worth, skill and adventurous exploits loom large in his remarks about himself. The difficulties of assessing matters of fact are made still more difficult if his biographers add emotionally toned denigrations or distortions to Lawrence's own inevitable embellishments or dramatic exaggerations.

18. *Friends,* p. 32.

19. Interview with Robert Lawrence, August 24, 1964.

20. Interview with Janet Laurie Hallsmith, March 25, 1965.

21. Ibid.

22. *Friends,* p. 33.

23. Handwritten essay in the front of Charlotte Shaw's copy of *Seven Pillars,* Arents Collection, New York Public Library. Definitions of adolescence as a stage of development rather than simply as a chronological period are affected by cultural determinants. Insofar as adolescence is a time of transition from childhood to adulthood, its characteristics depend on what is expected of children and adults in a given culture, the rapidity with which the transition from childhood to adulthood is made, and the extent to which aspects of this development are left to later realization. Adolescence in America in the 1970's is different from adolescence in England in the first decade of the twentieth century. There are, however, certain changes that are common to adolescents regardless of culture. In addition to the changes of puberty (the time and nature of their occurrence being affected by such factors as climate, general health and, possibly, sexual stimulation), adolescence is generally a time when the establishment of a firm personal identity occurs, when questions of adult sexuality are being faced, when a comfortable emotional distance from one's parents is being established, childhood ideals are brought into harmony with adult realities, and most childhood fantasies are given up. In none of these respects did Lawrence seem to undergo a clearcut adolescence, either physiologically or emotionally.

24. Interview with C. F. C. Beeson, March 22, 1965.

25. *Friends,* p. 52.

26. In the issue dated March 1904.

27. George Bernard Shaw's handwritten essay in the front of Charlotte Shaw's copy of *Seven Pillars,* Arents Collection, New York Public Library.

28. Interviews with C. F. C. Beeson, March 22, 1965; Theo Chaundy, August 26, 1964; and Janet Laurie Hallsmith, March 25, 1965.

29. Interview with Mr. R. W. Bodey, headmaster, City of Oxford High School, August 27, 1964.

30. In the 1930's the Lawrence family endowed a scholarship to enable City of Oxford High School students of little means to go to Oxford.

31. Interview with C. F. C. Beeson, March 22, 1965; *Friends,* p. 46.

32. *Friends,* p. 46.

33. Lawrence to Charlotte Shaw, August 24, 1926, BM Add MSS, 45903.

34. Telephone conversation in 1973 with Fred George, a former City of Oxford High School student during Lawrence's years there; Mrs. Lawrence's preface to T.E.'s *Crusader Castles* II, 5; *Letters,* p. 38.

35. "Playground Cricket," *City of Oxford High School Magazine,* July 1904.

36. *Letters,* p. 491; LHB, p. 79.

37. LHB, p. 40.

38. Ibid., p. 79.

39. Lawrence to Dick Knowles, July 14, 1927, Bod Res MSS, d56.

40. *Mint,* p. 154.

41. Report from Councillor Hutchins, May 11, 1902, Bod Res MSS, c52.

42. Interview with Theo Chaundy, August 26, 1964.

43. Interview with E. F. Hall, December 16, 1965.

44. Ibid.

45. Interview with Janet Laurie Hallsmith, March 25, 1965.

46. Interview with E. F. Hall, December 16, 1965.

47. LHB, p. 24.

48. Ibid., p. 51.

49. *Mint,* p. 132.

50. Knightley and Simpson treat the episode as entirely factual and offer the additional details that Lawrence bicycled to St. Just in Roseland in Cornwall and enlisted as a private in the Royal Artillery and that his father went to Cornwall and bought him out (*Secret Lives,* p. 16). But this information comes, I believe, from one of Lawrence's RAF pals, who was speculating about the episode from fragmentary knowledge, and when I questioned him about it myself, he was quite unsure about the whole matter (several discussions with A. E. "Jock" Chambers, 1965–1972).

51. *Friends,* p. 26.

52. Personal communication from Arnold Lawrence, March 24, 1974.

53. Interview with C. F. C. Beeson, March 22, 1965.

54. Hilda Chaundy to the author, June 18, 1966.

3. LAWRENCE AND HIS FAMILY:
THE BURDEN OF ILLEGITIMACY

1. About 1922 or 1923 Lawrence told his brother Arnold of his parents' legal inability to marry. Arnold laughed and T.E. told him that his parents did not regard it at all as a laughing matter and thought he was "practically a pervert" for taking it lightly (Arnold Lawrence to the author, March 23, 1972).

2. Lawrence to Charlotte Shaw, April 14, 1927, BM Add MSS, 45903.

3. Interview with Arnold Lawrence, July 15, 1968.

4. Interviews with Arnold Lawrence, March 16, 1965, and July 15, 1968.

5. Richard Aldington, *Lawrence of Arabia*, p. 42.

6. Interview with Christine Longford, March 18, 1965.

7. Lawrence to Charlotte Shaw, April 14, 1927, BM Add MSS, 45903.

8. The fact that Lawrence's parents were unmarried was known by Lord Stamfordham, King George's secretary, in 1927. He wrote about it — including some speculation about its traumatic meaning — to one of Lawrence's former chiefs, so presumably the information was widespread at this time (Stamfordham to Reginald Wingate, March 15, 1927 in *Sunday Times* papers, Imperial War Museum, London; the original is in the School of Oriental Studies, University of Durham).

9. Interview with Arnold and Barbara Lawrence, March 16, 1965.

10. Interviews with Elsie Newcombe, August 27, 1964, and August 20, 1972.

11. Lawrence to Lord Winterton, October 27, 1923, Bod Res MSS, d44.

12. Lawrence to Lionel Curtis, March 8, 1926, Bod Res MSS, d51.

13. Lawrence to A. E. Chambers, August 8, 1924, Bod Res MSS, d51.

14. Lawrence to Sir Fred Kenyon, June 1, 1927, Bod Res MSS, d43.

15. Lawrence to F. N. Doubleday, August 25, 1927, Bod Res MSS, d52.

16. Lawrence to Lionel Curtis, November 27, 1927, Bod Res MSS, d51.

17. *Letters*, pp. 50, 301, 382, 721.

18. Interview with Arnold Lawrence, March 16, 1965.

19. LHB, p. 78.

20. "My mother is an enraged housewife," he wrote to Mrs. Hardy on October 24, 1930, when Mrs. Lawrence was "remorselessly" cleaning his cottage (Bod Res MSS, d55).

21. Lawrence to Charlotte Shaw, April 14, 1927, BM Add MSS, 45903.

22. Lawrence to Charlotte Shaw, May 8, 1928, BM Add MSS, 45904.

23. Lawrence to Charlotte Shaw, August 18, 1927, BM Add MSS, 45903.

24. Interview with Robert Lawrence, August 24, 1965.

25. Interview with Hilda Chaundy, March 24, 1965, and Arnold Lawrence, December 8, 1965.

26. Interview with Arnold Lawrence, December 8, 1965.

27. Vyvyan Richards to Helen J. Cash, March 4, 1965, in the *Sunday Times* research materials, Imperial War Museum, London.

28. Interviews with Theo and Hilda Chaundy, August 26, 1964.

29. *Home Letters*, p. 81.

30. Especially in passages that were omitted by Bob in the published version (*Home Letters*). The originals are in Bod Res MSS, c13.

31. Arnold Lawrence to Robert Graves, June 15, 1927, Bod Res MSS, c52.

32. Interview with Hilda Chaundy, August 26, 1964.

33. Lawrence to Charlotte Shaw, May 30, 1928, BM Add MSS, 45904.

34. Interview with Arnold Lawrence, July 21, 1968.

35. The same quality of being overwhelmed is suggested in a comment Lawrence wrote to Mrs. Shaw referring to the way he was given medicine as a boy: "They dosed me sometimes, when I was a child, too weak to kick against them; but I take no medicine now for many years" (Lawrence to Charlotte Shaw, December 8, 1927, BM Add MSS, 45903).

36. Interview with Arnold Lawrence, July 21, 1968.

37. Letter of April 11, 1911, *Home Letters*, pp. 147–148.

38. Letter of May 19, 1911, ibid., p. 160.

INTRODUCTION TO PART II

1. *Oriental Assembly*, p. 143.

2. *Seven Pillars*, p. 661.

3. LHB, p. 80.

4. T. E. Lawrence, *Crusader Castles*, II, 5.

5. Bod Res MSS, b55.

6. Leonard Woolley, *Dead Towns and Living Men*, pp. 94–95.

7. RGB, p. 81.

8. *Friends*, p. 92.

4. LITERARY INFLUENCES

1. Interview with Arnold Lawrence, August 24, 1964.

2. *Friends*, p. 586.

3. RGB, p. 48.

4. LHB, p. 50.

5. J. G. Edwards, "T. E. Lawrence," *Jesus College Magazine*, IV (1935), 343–345.

6. F. S. Shears, "The Chivalry of France," *Chivalry: A Series of Studies to Illustrate Its Historical Significance and Civilizing Influence*, p. 22.

7. *Letters*, p. 87.

8. *Friends*, p. 53.

9. Will Lawrence to the Lawrence family, July 14, 1914, *Home Letters*, p. 555.

10. *Home Letters*, p. 34.

11. J. W. Thompson and E. N. Johnson, *An Introduction to Medieval Europe, 300–1500*, p. 322.

12. Eileen Powell, "The Position of Women," Chap. 7, *The Legacy of the Middle Ages*, edited by C. G. Crump and E. F. Jacob, pp. 401–430.

13. Shears, "The Chivalry of France," p. 67.

14. Thompson and Johnson, p. 322. See also, C. S. Lewis, *The Allegory of Love* (1972).

15. Henry Adams, *Mont-Saint-Michel and Chartres* (1904), p. 213.

16. As Eileen Powell pointed out, the elevation of women in the chivalric ideal "was at least better than placing them, as the Fathers of the Church had inclined to do, in the bottomless pit" (in Crump and Jacob, *The Legacy of the Middle Ages*, p. 406).

17. Steven Runciman, *A History of the Crusades*, III, 480.

18. T. E. Lawrence, *Crusader Castles*, foreword by Arnold Lawrence. It must be pointed out, however, that these special theses were required to be no longer than twelve hundred words and that the student was obliged to keep his discussion within the limits of his subject.

19. Lawrence to his family, August 11, 1907, *Home Letters*, p. 55.

20. Runciman, III, 53.

21. LHB, pp. 31, 80.

22. Lawrence to his family, August 6, 1908, *Home Letters*, p. 67.

23. Thompson and Johnson, p. 322.

24. E. Lévi-Provençal, *Islam d'occident: Etudes d'histoire médiévale.*

25. Lawrence to his family, June 2, 1912, *Home Letters*, p. 210.

26. *Friends*, p. 586.

5. CRUSADER CASTLES

1. *Friends*, p. 54.

2. RGB, p. 60.

3. There is a curious comment, omitted by his older brother from the published *Home Letters*, that Lawrence was in Wales "at last discovering where I got my large mouth from; it's a national peculiarity" (letter to Mrs. Lawrence, April 1907, Bod Res MSS, c13). The comment implies, or at least conveys to the mother that Lawrence considered himself, at eighteen and a half, to have some Welsh parentage or ancestry. This conflicts to a degree with his later claims that he knew his parents' situation "before I was ten." Whether he was playing along with the family fiction, showing consideration for his mother's sensibilities, or confused then in his own mind about his ancestral origins, is not clear.

4. *Friends*, p. 54.

5. Interview with the author, March 22, 1965.

6. Ibid.

7. Jean Beraud Villars, *T. E. Lawrence or the Search for the Absolute*, p. 20.

8. Lawrence to his mother, August 31, 1906, Bod Res MSS, c13. This letter was omitted from *Home Letters.*

9. Lawrence to his mother, August 26, *Home Letters*, p. 35.

10. Letter of August 17, 1906, ibid., p. 20.

11. Letter of August 9, 1908, ibid., p. 70.

12. Lawrence to his mother, August 6, 1908, ibid., p. 68.

13. Handwritten by Shaw on the flyleaf of a copy of T.E.'s *A Letter to His Mother*. This copy is in Houghton Library, Harvard University.

14. Bod Res MSS, c13.

15. Lawrence to his mother, August 24, 1906, Bod Res MSS, c13.

16. Ibid.

17. Ibid.

18. Lawrence to Arnie, August 14, 1906, *Home Letters*, p. 19.

19. Lawrence to Arnie, August 31, 1906, ibid., p. 45. Lawrence loved to play with images of worms when writing his small brother, calling him "worm" frequently. He seemed to enjoy the use of nonsense or gently degrading animal nicknames when addressing a younger boy or man toward whom he had a fond fatherly or big brotherly feeling. In a letter of June 23, 1909 (Bod Res MSS, c13), he closed with a drawing depicting members of the family as "worms" of varying size:

(The drawing is reproduced through the courtesy of the Bodleian Library, Oxford.)

20. Lawrence to Beeson, August 9, 1908, *Letters*, p. 57.

21. T. E. Lawrence, *Crusader Castles*, I, 3.

22. Ibid., I, 29.

23. Letter of August 2, 1908, *Home Letters*, p. 66.

24. In connection with Lawrence's challenge of Oman's views, Richard Aldington says of Lawrence, "He tried to pretend that Oman was a relic of the past and not worth wasting time on, since he was a charlatan, an imbecile and a smatterer" (*Lawrence of Arabia*, p. 68). In the two references Aldington provides to support his assertion that Lawrence damned Oman in this way there is nothing of the sort to be found. In one, from *Crusader Castles*, Lawrence does challenge Oman's theory, but says nothing accusatory. The other is a letter of June 8, 1911, to his brother Will, in which he is encouraging the younger boy to think and see for himself concerning the study of the Crusades and to question traditional authorities. "Oman," he writes, "is a monument: and one doesn't need to look at such things over long" (*Letters*, p. 110). There is nothing about charlatanism, imbecility or smattering. This sort of denigration is characteristic of Aldington's assault.

25. *Crusader Castles*, I, 29.

26. *Friends*, p. 47.

27. Lawrence to his mother, August 28, 1908, *Home Letters*, p. 79.

28. Lawrence to his mother, August 14, 1906, Bod Res MSS, c13. The passage was omitted by Robert Lawrence from the published collection.

29. Lawrence to C. F. C. Beeson, August 16, 1908, *Letters*, p. 61.

30. Lawrence to his family, February 18, 1911, *Home Letters*, p. 134.

31. *Crusader Castles*, I, 56.

32. Ibid., I, 15.

33. L. C. Jane to Robert Graves, 1927 (undated), Bod Res MSS, c52.

34. LHB, p. 52. After Lawrence's death, Arnold Lawrence had the manuscript prepared for publication under the title *Crusader Castles*. A limited edition of one thousand copies was printed. In the foreword, Arnold explained that the many photographs and extensive sketches and illustrations made it too expensive for the university press to publish.

35. Lawrence to a Mr. Field, April 26, 1929, Bod Res MSS, d43.

36. *Friends*, p. 62.

37. See, for example, discussions in T. S. R. Boase, *Castles and Churches of the Crusading Kingdom* (1967); Robin Fedden, *Crusader Castles* (1950); W. Mueller-Wiener, *Castles of the Crusaders* (1966).

38. LHB, p. 87; RGB, p. 49.

39. *Home Letters*, p. 69.

40. RGB, p. 61.

6. LAWRENCE AT JESUS COLLEGE, 1907–1910

1. J. N. L. Baker, *Jesus College, Oxford, 1571–1971*, p. 111.

2. J. G. Edwards, "T. E. Lawrence," *Jesus College Magazine* 4 (1935): 343–345.

3. LHB, p. 41.

4. Jesus College had a large number of students from Wales. As it could be said that there would be no place for the Westcountrymen to go if Exeter College were abolished, "Jesus would say the same about itself and the Welsh" (Dacre Balsdon, *Oxford Life*, p. 190).

5. Interview with W. O. Ault, September 22, 1972.

6. Baker, p. 108.

7. *Friends*, p. 28.

8. Ibid., pp. 67–68.

9. Baker, p. 108.

10. Ibid., pp. 108–109.

11. *Friends*, p. 28.

12. Interviews with Sir Basil Blackwell, March 21, 1965, and Sir Goronwy Edwards, July 12, 1968.

13. *Friends*, p. 47.

14. Ibid.

15. Ibid.

16. H. D. Littler, as quoted in Edwards, p. 344.

17. *Friends*, p. 29; LHB, p. 72.

18. Biographical material about Hogarth was obtained from the memoirs of his sister Janet Courtney: *An Oxford Portrait Gallery* (1931), pp. 3–50, and "David George Hogarth: In Memoriam Fratris," *Fortnightly Review* 129 (1928): 23–33. Also from the following sources: C. R. L. Fletcher, "David George Hogarth," *The Geographical Journal* 71 (1928): 321–344; F. G. Kenyon's biographical essay in the *Dictionary of National Biography*; James H. Breasted, "David George Hogarth," *Geographical Review* 18 (1928): 159–161; Hogarth Papers, St. Antony's College, Oxford; interviews with Arnold and Barbara Lawrence; interview with Hogarth's son, William, March 18, 1965.

19. Lawrence to Charlotte Shaw, March 20, 1924, BM Add MSS, 45903.

20. Interview with William Hogarth, March 18, 1965.

21. Ibid.

22. Lawrence to Edward Garnett, December 1, 1927, *Letters*, p. 551; and to Lionel Curtis, December 22, 1927, ibid., p. 557.

23. Lawrence to P. C. Rothenstein, April 14, 1928, *Letters*, p. 583.

24. C. F. Bell to Lawrence, November 11, 1927, Bod Res MSS, d60.

25. V. W. Richards, *Portrait of T. E. Lawrence*, pp. 19–49.

26. *Secret Lives*, p. 29.

27. Richards, p. 24.

28. Ibid., p. 41.

29. Interview with W. O. Ault, September 22, 1972.

30. Ibid.

31. LHB, p. 96.

32. *Friends*, p. 28.

33. Ibid. Another story has it that Lawrence and the poet A. G. Prys-Jones were both tutored by Jane, who agreed to take them at a weekly single session for the price of one (letter from D. W. T. Jenkins to Richard Brinkley of Aberystwyth College, Wales, February 12, 1973).

34. RGB, p. 50.

35. Lawrence to his family, February 20, 1912, *Home Letters*, p. 193.

36. Lawrence to William Lawrence, May 11, 1912, ibid., p. 208.

37. Graves, *Lawrence and the Arabs*, pp. 16–17.

38. L. C. Jane to Robert Graves [1927] Bod Res MSS, d60.

39. Lawrence to his family, January 11, 1911, *Home Letters*, p. 126.

40. This information and other facts about Jane come from a letter of February 12, 1973, from D. W. T. Jenkins, professor emeritus of education in University College, Bangor, who was a former student of Jane's at Aberystwyth, to Richard Brinkley, a specialist in English history there. The correspondence grew out of my inquiries to Aberystwyth concernng Lawrence's relationship with Jane.

41. The relationship between Janet and Will deepened: he wrote poems which he gave her, and despite Mrs. Lawrence's opposition (ostensibly on the ground that Will — nearly twenty-five when the war began — was young for his age), intended to marry her. Without his parents' knowledge, Will left private instructions with T.E. that in the event of his death T.E. should arrange to have any money he might leave given to Janet (personal communication from Arnold Lawrence, August 26, 1972). When Will was killed he left little of his own except some insurance and his army pay.

In 1914, at the death of a cousin in Ireland, Mr. Lawrence inherited a considerable amount of capital from the estate, along with the baronetcy. In March 1916, realizing perhaps that he was not in good health, Mr. Lawrence gave some of this money to his three surviving sons, but with a stipulation "that if our Will should prove to be alive [Will was then officially only missing, although presumed dead] . . . you and Bob and Arnie should each return me what I would ask for of your capital, so that Will may have the same capital as you others" (Mr. Lawrence to T.E., March 8, 1916, Bod Res MSS, d60). But by early May Mr. Lawrence had received news leaving no doubt about Will's death and he wrote T.E. again: "Poor Will, as you know, left everything he had to you and made you sole executor" (letter of May 11, 1916, Bod Res MSS, d60).

In a letter written in 1923 to David

Hogarth, T.E. referred to his share of his father's bequest as "my father's £5,000," and implied he had fulfilled Will's desire to leave money to Janet by giving £3,000 of his own share to her on Will's behalf. Lawrence wrote to Hogarth, "(I don't want my mother or other brothers to know about it; they think I still have it). One of those killed left a tangle behind, and it took £3,000 to straighten it. Two thousand was no good to me: so I put £1,000 into Epping [perhaps given to his friend Richards, with whom he shared his plot at Epping] and £1,000 into that book of mine; pictures mostly" (Lawrence to Hogarth, June 27, 1923, Bod Res MSS, `d35). Lawrence signed the letter:

• E •

After Will was killed Janet Laurie had a long row over Will with Mrs. Lawrence. When the war began he had written to his sweetheart for advice on whether he should return from India to join the army. Unable to decide how or what to reply, she had written, finally, after much deliberation, that it might trouble him later if he did not return. When he was killed, Mrs. Lawrence learned of Janet's letter to Will and accused her of being responsible for his death. The two women were estranged in their grief and remained separated for seventeen years. In 1932 Mrs. Lawrence visited the place where Janet Laurie (now Mrs. Hallsmith) was living and they saw each other. When Mrs. Lawrence missed her train home, she stayed with Mrs. Hallsmith overnight. The mood was cordial and the younger woman felt forgiven, to her great relief and perhaps to Mrs. Lawrence's as well (interview with Mrs. Hallsmith, March 25, 1965).

42. Interview with the Reverend E. F. Hall and his wife, December 16, 1965.

43. Baker, p. 111.

7. THE FIRST TRIP TO THE MIDDLE EAST, 1909

1. Letter of August 2, 1909, Bod Res, MSS, c13.

2. *Letters*, p. 81.

3. RGB, p. 63.

4. *Letters to TEL*, p. 37.

5. Lawrence to C. M. Doughty, February 8, 1909 (unpublished; courtesy of Arnold Lawrence).

6. Foreword to Bertram Thomas's *Arabia Felix* (1932), p. XVII.

7. *Friends*, p. 73.

8. Ibid., pp. 29–30; LHB, p. 82.

9. *Home Letters*, p. 100.

10. Lawrence to his mother, September 7, 1909, Bod Res MSS, c13.

11. Lawrence to his mother, September 22, 1909, *Home Letters*, p. 107.

12. LHB, p. 52.

13. *Letters*, p. 81.

14. LHB, p. 53; *Friends*, p. 29.

15. RGB, p. 48.

16. *Home Letters*, p. 84.

17. Ibid., p. 103.

18. *Letters*, p. 72.

19. Lawrence to his mother, August 2, 1909, Bod Res MSS, c13.

20. *Letters*, p. 74.

21. Ibid., p. 66.

22. Lawrence to his mother, August 2, 1909, Bod Res MSS, c13.

23. Lawrence to his family, August 13, 1909, Bod Res MSS, c13.

24. *Home Letters*, p. 105.

25. *Letters*, p. 79.

26. *Friends*, pp. 76–77.

27. *Letters*, p. 81.

28. RGB, pp. 61–62.

29. Ibid., p. 62.

30. *Letters*, p. 82.

31. *Home Letters*, p. 108.

32. *Friends*, p. 74.

33. September 22, 1909, *Home Letters*, p. 108.

34. *Friends*, p. 76.

35. *Home Letters*, p. 81.

36. *Letters*, p. 81.

37. *Friends*, p. 61.

38. *Letters*, p. 83.

39. *Home Letters*, p. 105.

40. D. G. Hogarth, *The Life of Charles Doughty*, p. 174.

41. Ibid., p. 175.

8. LAWRENCE AT CARCHEMISH

1. Lady Florence Bell, *The Letters of Gertrude Bell*, I, 305–306.

2. Lawrence to E. T. Leeds, November 2, 1910, Bod Res MSS, d57.

3. C. L. Woolley, T. E. Lawrence, D. G. Hogarth, *Carchemish: Report on the Excavations at Djerabis on Behalf of the British Museum*, Vol. I.

4. Lawrence to Leeds, November 2, 1910, Bod Res MSS, d57.

5. Lawrence to his family, January 24, 1911, *Home Letters*, p. 130. This project (to be distinguished from the *Seven Pillars* of the Revolt) was to be downgraded and disparaged in a letter to Robert Graves in 1927: "Wrote travel book (later destroyed in Ms.) called 'The Seven Pillars of Wisdom,' about Cairo, Smyrna, Constantinople, Beirut, Aleppo, Damascus and Medina" (RGB, p. 49).

6. *Letters*, p. 89.

7. Lawrence to his family, December 16, 1910, *Home Letters*, p. 121.

8. Either she means 1910, or she has condensed the first meeting in the summer of 1909 with this second one in December 1910.

9. Actually, he was twenty-two at the time of the Christmas visit.

10. Fareedah el Akle to the author, June 20, 1969. Written from Brummana, Lebanon, upon receiving an article about Lawrence from him.

11. Fareedah el Akle to Helen Cash, June 12, 1969.

12. Lawrence to his family, January 31, 1912, *Home Letters*, p. 190.

13. Lawrence to Florence Messham, June 13, 1911, *Letters*, p. 112.

14. RGB, p. 50.

15. Letter of March 20, 1911, *Home Letters*, p. 141.

16. Letter of April 29, 1911, ibid., p. 151.

17. Letter of March 31, 1911, ibid., p. 143.

18. Ibid., p. 144.

19. *Oriental Assembly*, p. 2.

20. Lawrence to E. T. Leeds, April 1912, Bod Res MSS, d57.

21. Letter of March 20, 1912, *Home Letters*, p. 198.

22. *Friends*, p. 115.

23. Ibid., p. 84.

24. Ibid., p. 91.

25. Lawrence to E. T. Leeds, April 1912, Bod Res MSS, d57.

26. *Friends*, p. 91.

27. Letter of May 9, 1911, *Home Letters*, p. 159.

28. Letter of June 13, 1911, ibid., p. 169.

29. Letter of June 23, 1912, ibid., p. 216.

30. Lawrence to James Elroy Flecker, February 18, 1914, Houghton Library, Harvard University.

31. C. L. Woolley, *Dead Towns and Living Men*, p. 176.

32. Letter of June 2, 1912, Bod Res MSS, c13.

33. Lawrence to V. W. Richards, December 10, 1913, *Letters*, p. 161.

34. *Friends*, p. 84.

35. Letter of July 28, 1912, *Letters*, p. 145.

36. Lawrence to his family, February 22, 1913, Bod Res MSS, c13.

37. Will Lawrence to the family, September 16, 1913, *Home Letters*, p. 442.

38. Will Lawrence to the family, September 27, 1913, ibid., p. 447.

39. *Friends*, p. 91.

40. Luther Fowle, prologue to Lowell Thomas's "The Soul of the Arabian Revolution," *Asia* 20 (1920): 257.

41. *Friends*, p. 90.

42. Ibid., p. 87.

43. Ibid., p. 69. Volume III of *Carchemish*, which reported the findings of the archeologists in excavating the inner town and the interpretations of the Hittite inscriptions, was not published by the British Museum until 1952 because of various delays and destruction to the objects themselves caused by World War I. In this volume Woolley and R. D. Barnett, although disputed in regard to certain details by other archeologists, were able to establish the sequence of the Hittite dynasties spanning the tenth to the eight centuries B.C. References: H. G. Güterbock, "Carchemish," *Journal of Near Eastern Studies* 13: (1954): 102–114; J. D. Hawkins, "Building Inscriptions of Carchemish," *Anatolian Studies* 22 (1972): 87–114; M. E. L. Mallowan, "Carchemish: Reflections on the Chronology of the Sculpture," *Anatolian Studies* 22 (1972): 63–85; P. Meriggi, "La Ricostruzione di Kargamis," *Rivista degli Studi Orientali*, 29 (1954): 1–16; D. Ussishkin, "Observations on Some Monuments from Carchemish," *Journal of Near Eastern Studies* 26: (1967): 87–92; and "On the Dating of Some Groups of Reliefs from Carchemish and Til Barsib," *Anatolian Studies* 17 (1967): 181–192. One of these scholars praised the work in these terms: "This rich and beautiful volume fills a long-felt gap and lets Carchemish, and especially the city of Katuwas [a late king] emerge in all its greatness" (Güterbock, p. 114). In 1969 Barnett wrote: "That Carchemish . . . was a first class Hittite imperial site has re-

cently been demonstrated by the discovery of letters in Hittite cuneiform script in the French excavations at Ras Shamra, showing that in the fourteenth–thirteenth centuries B.C. it was the seat of the Hittite Viceroy of North Syria. Hogarth's prescience has thus been fully vindicated" (letter to *The Times Literary Supplement*, October 16, 1969).

44. Lawrence to his family, April 11, 1911, Bod Res MSS, c13. Robert Lawrence apparently thought the passage too damaging to include in the published version.

45. *Friends*, pp. 89, 90.

46. Lawrence to E. T. Leeds, February 25, 1912, Bod Res MSS, d57, which contains all the letters to Leeds cited in the next five notes.

47. Letter of June 16, 1913.

48. Letter written at the end of February 1913.

49. Letter of June 1, 1913.

50. Letter of January 24, 1914.

51. Letter to Leeds, July 14, 1912.

52. Lawrence to his family, April 26, 1913, *Home Letters*, p. 254.

53. *Letters*, p. 156.

54. Interview with Janet Laurie Hallsmith, March 25, 1965.

55. Letter of August 29, 1913, *Home Letters*, p. 262.

56. *Friends*, p. 97.

57. Ibid., p. 96.

58. Ibid., pp. 98–99.

59. Ibid., p. 96.

60. Ibid., p. 88.

61. Ibid., p. 87.

62. Hubert Young, *The Independent Arab*, p. 18.

63. Luther R. Fowle, "Prologue," *Asia* 20 (1920): 257.

64. Ibid., p. 258.

65. Lawrence to his family, May 23, 1911, *Home Letters*, p. 163.

66. Letter of June 24, 1911, *Letters*, pp. 113–114.

67. *Friends*, p. 92.

68. Young, p. 20.

69. Woolley, *Dead Towns and Living Men*, pp. 107–108.

70. Letter of June 18, 1911, *Home Letters*, p. 170.

71. Lawrence to Mrs. Rieder, June 14, 1913, *Letters*, p. 155.

72. Lawrence to E. T. Leeds, September 9, 1913, Bod Res MSS, d57.

73. Will Lawrence to the family, November 13, 1913, *Home Letters*, p. 467.

74. Fowle, p. 257.

75. Lawrence to Eddie Marsh, June 10, 1927, *Letters*, p. 521.

76. Letter of June 24, 1911, *Home Letters*, p. 174.

77. *Friends*, p. 106.

78. Letter of April 23, 1914, *Home Letters*, p. 295.

79. LHB, p. 85.

80. Winifred Fontana to Robert Graves, December 5, 1927, Bod Res MSS, c52.

81. *Friends*, p. 593.

82. Letter of March 28, 1913, Bod Res MSS, c13.

83. Letter of March 1, 1911, Bod Res MSS, c13.

84. Lawrence to E. T. Leeds, April 1912, Bod Res MSS, d57.

85. *Friends*, pp. 92–93.

86. *Home Letters*, p. 142.

87. Lawrence to Leeds, May 6, 1914, Bod Res MSS, d57.

88. Lawrence to Doughty, November 24, 1911, courtesy of Arnold Lawrence.

89. Letter of May 11, 1912, *Home Letters*, p. 207.

90. *Friends*, p. 591.

91. RGB, p. 5.

92. See *An Essay on Flecker* (1925), a copy of which is in Houghton Library, Harvard University.

93. Personal communication from Arabella Rivington in 1967, following her visit with Miss Akle.

94. Richard Aldington, *Lawrence of Arabia*, p. 104. Aldington's snide criticism of Lawrence's use of archaic "schoolboy phrases" in this letter is absurd, as these are a deliberately self-conscious part of the humor.

95. Lawrence to Mrs. Von Heidenstam, August 29, 1912, Bod Res MSS, c52.

96. *Friends*, p. 84.

97. Woolley, *Dead Towns and Living Men*, p. 142.

98. Dahoum's name is discussed convincingly in Jeremy M. Wilson's introduction to Lawrence's *Minorities*, p. 29.

99. Woolley, p. 142.

100. Lawrence to Fareedah el Akle, June 26, 1911 (a copy was shown to the author by Arabella Rivington).

101. *Oriental Assembly*, p. 26.

102. Lawrence to his family, September 12, 1912, *Home Letters*, p. 229.

103. *Friends*, p. 89.

104. Interviews with Arnold Lawrence, September 13, 1969.

105. Interviews with Arnold Lawrence. In _Secret Lives_, Knightley and Simpson claim on the evidence of Thomas Beaumont, a gunner who was with Lawrence during the war, that Dahoum worked for Lawrence during the campaigns as a spy, moving back and forth through the Turkish lines. But this is highly improbable. As Arnold Lawrence indicated in a note to me (September 1969), the difficulties a North Syrian of military age would have experienced in traveling to and through the vague Turkish lines would have made it virtually impossible.

106. Lawrence to Fareedah el Akle, January 3, 1921 (a copy was shown to the author by Arabella Rivington); interview with Arnold Lawrence, September 13, 1969. The matter is discussed by J. M. Wilson in his introduction to Lawrence's _Minorities_, pp. 29–30.

107. Lawrence to "Dear Poppet" (probably R. M. Guy), December 25, 1923, Houghton Library, Harvard University.

108. Penciled note on the back flyleaf of Vansittart's _The Singing Caravan_, Bod Res MSS, d230. "Written between Paris and Lyons in Handley Page" is penciled at the bottom of the page.

9. THE EPIC DREAM AND THE FACT OF WAR

1. _Letters_, p. 85.

2. Letter of April 11, 1911, _Home Letters_, pp. 147–148. See page 34 for a longer quotation from this letter.

3. Fareedah el Akle to Lawrence, March 30, 1920, Bod Res MSS, d60.

4. Entry of August 3, 1911, in "Diary of a Journey Across the Euphrates," _Oriental Assembly_, p. 51.

5. Lawrence to his family, March 20, 1912, _Home Letters_, p. 198.

6. Ibid., p. 193.

7. Quoted in Violet Bonham Carter's _Winston Churchill: An Intimate Portrait_, p. 313.

8. _Secret Lives_, pp. 35 ff.

9. Elizabeth Monroe, review of Knightley and Simpson's _Secret Lives_, in _The Times Literary Supplement_, October 2, 1969.

10. Interview with William Hogarth, March 18, 1965.

11. Lawrence to Hogarth, June 24, 1911, _Letters_, p. 114.

12. Lawrence to Mrs. Rieder, May 20, 1912, ibid., p. 139.

13. Lawrence to Leeds, end of February 1913, Bod Res MSS, d57.

14. Hubert Young, _The Independent Arab_, p. 16.

15. Letter in Ashmolean Museum, Oxford, undated, but the reference to a trip to Abu Galgal places it most likely in late June or July of 1913, after Lawrence's trip to Abu Galgal in Mesopotamia.

16. Quoted in _Secret Lives_, p. 41.

17. Letter to _The Times Literary Supplement_, October 16, 1969.

18. The matter is discussed by George Kirk in _A Short History of the Middle East_, pp. 308–309.

19. Lawrence to his family, January 2, 1912, _Home Letters_, p. 182.

20. Lawrence to Leeds, February 25, 1912, Bod Res MSS, d57.

21. Lawrence to his family, November 4 and 12, 1912, _Home Letters_, pp. 241, 242.

22. Letter of March 28, 1913, ibid., p. 252.

23. Lawrence to Mrs. Rieder, _Letters_, p. 152.

24. Letter of January 4, 1914, _Home Letters_, p. 288.

25. Interview with William Yale, August 10, 1966.

26. C. L. Woolley, "The Desert of the Wanderings," _Palestine Expedition Fund Quarterly Statement_ (1914).

27. Letter of June 26, 1912, _Letters_, p. 142.

28. Letter of June 11, 1913, _Home Letters_, p. 256.

29. Letter of October 16, 1913, ibid., p. 269.

30. C.J.G. [Lawrence], "The Kaer of Ibu Wardani," _Jesus College Magazine_ (1912–1913), p. 39.

31. Lawrence to V. W. Richards, December 10, 1913, _Letters_, p. 161.

32. February 18, 1914, _Friends_, p. 104.

10. THE BACKGROUND OF THE ARAB REVOLT

1. P. J. Vatikiotis, _Conflict in the Middle East_, pp. 15–16.

2. George Antonius, _The Arab Awakening_, p. 18.

3. Ibid., p. 32.

4. Manfred Halpern, "Four Contrasting Repertories of Human Relations in Islam," paper presented to a conference

on psychology and Near Eastern studies at Princeton, New Jersey, May 8, 1973.

5. The suppressed introductory chapter for *Seven Pillars of Wisdom*, in *Oriental Assembly*, p. 143. This chapter was not published until after Lawrence's death.

6. George Kirk, *A Short History of the Middle East*, p. 34.

7. Zeine N. Zeine, *The Emergence of Arab Nationalism*, p. 25.

8. Ibid., p. 68.

9. Ibid., p. 92.

10. John E. Mack, "The Young Turk Revolution of 1908 and Its Consequences, 1908–1914," unpublished term paper, Oberlin College, 1951, p. 9.

11. Ahmad Qadri, *Mudhakkirati 'an al-Thawra al-'Arabiyah al-Kubra* [My Memoirs of the Great Arab Revolt], pp. 40–47.

12. Kirk, p. 95.

13. G. P. Gooch, and H. W. V. Temperley, *British Documents on the Origin of the War, 1898–1914*, Vol. IX, quoted in Zeine, *The Emergence*, p. 119.

14. Zeine, *The Emergence*, p. 114.

15. Elizabeth Monroe, *Britain's Moment in the Middle East, 1914–1956*, p. 3.

16. D. G. Hogarth, "Mecca's Revolt Against the Turk," *Century Magazine* 100 (1920): 403.

17. E. C. Dawn, "The Amir of Mecca Al-Husayn Ibn-Ali and the Origin of the Arab Revolt," *Proceedings of the American Philosophical Society* 104 (1960): 11–34.

18. Ronald Storrs, *Orientations*, p. 143.

19. Foreign Office, "Summary of Documents from the Outbreak of War between Great Britain and Turkey, 1914, to the Outbreak of the Revolt of the Sherif of Mecca in June, 1916" (January 1921), PRO/FO 371/6237; also quoted in Storrs, p. 173.

20. Storrs, pp. 175–176.

21. PRO/FO 371/6237; also quoted in Storrs, p. 176.

22. PRO/FO 882/6 (December 1916); also quoted in T. E. Lawrence, *Secret Dispatches from Arabia*, p. 52.

23. Antonius, p. 133.

24. Zeine, *The Emergence*, p. 126.

25. *Seven Pillars*, p. 50; see also Zeine, *The Emergence*, p. 27.

26. Antonius, pp. 152–156.

27. Faisal's contacts with the secret societies in Syria during 1915 and 1916

had an important impact on the development of his commitment to Arab nationalistic aspirations. His relationship to these societies is discussed in Ahmad Qadri's memoirs. Faisal's frustration with the fact that other members of his family did not share his interest in the Arab national movement in Syria is reflected in a letter written by Colonel Joyce during the war: "Faisal still considers that his father and brothers are taking no interest in the Syrian movement and it takes a lot of talk to prevent him getting very depressed on the subject" (Pierce Joyce to Sir Gilbert Clayton, September 17, 1917, in Joyce's "Akaba" Papers, King's College, London).

28. *Seven Pillars*, p. 47.

29. Suleiman Mousa, "The Role of Syrians and Iraqis in the Arab Revolt," *Middle East Forum* 43 (1967): 5–17.

30. Antonius, p. 158.

31. Kirk, pp. 313–314.

32. Hogarth, "Mecca's Revolt," p. 405.

33. Elie Kedourie, *England and the Middle East*, p. 30.

34. This issue is discussed in Zeine N. Zeine, *The Struggle for Arab Independence*, p. 10; Kedourie, p. 281; and Monroe, pp. 9–10.

35. PRO/FO 371/6237; also quoted in Antonius, pp. 414–415. The Foreign Office translations of these documents and those by Antonius differ considerably.

36. A. L. Tibawi, "Syria in the McMahon Correspondence," *Middle East Forum* 40 (1966): 20–21; PRO/FO 371/6237; Monroe, *Britain's Moment*, p. 36.

37. Sir Ronald Wingate, *Wingate of the Sudan*, p. 181.

38. Antonius, p. 176.

39. Kirk, p. 316.

40. Dawn, p. 27.

41. Hogarth, p. 408.

42. LHB, p. 60.

43. Monroe, p. 35.

44. McMahon to Husayn, Cairo, December 13, 1915, and Husayn to McMahon, January 1, 1916, PRO/FO 371/6237; see also, Antonius, pp. 423–425.

45. PRO/CAB 27/36.

46. Hogarth, p. 406.

47. *Arab Bulletin* #42, February 15, 1917, II, 79; quoted in *Letters*, p. 219.

48. Jemal Pasha, *Memories of a Turkish Statesman, 1913–1919*, pp. 214–221.

49. Dawn, p. 27.

50. Ibid.

51. *Seven Pillars*, pp. 52–53.

52. Ibid., p. 53.
53. *Arab Bulletin* #3, June 14, 1916, I, 30–31.
54. Storrs, p. 180.
55. Ibid., pp. 180–188.
56. Ibid., p. 181.
57. Antonius, p. 195.
58. PRO/FO 882/25.
59. Zeine, *The Struggle*, p. 4.
60. Hogarth, p. 411.

11. TWO YEARS IN CAIRO, 1914–1916

1. The poem continues:

*And caught our youth, and wakened us
  from sleeping.
With hand made sure, clear eye, and
  sharpened power,
To turn, as swimmers into cleanness leap-
  ing,
Glad from a world grown old and cold
  and weary,
Leave the sick hearts that honour could
  not move,
And half-men, and their dirty songs and
  dreary,
And all the little emptiness of love!*

From The Collected Poems of Rupert Brooke (London: Sidgwick and Jackson, 1918).

2. Arnold Lawrence to the author, November 1, 1968.
3. Lawrence to James Elroy Flecker, December 3, 1914, Houghton Library, Harvard University.
4. Lawrence to John Buchan, June 20, 1927, Bod Res MSS, b55.
5. Sir Coote Hedley to Liddell Hart, November 23, 1933, quoted in LHB, p. 196.
6. Ibid., p. 193.
7. Ibid., p. 91.
8. 'Abd al-Rahman Shahbandar, "al-Colonel Lawrence," *al-Muqtataf* 78 (March 1931): 269–270.
9. *Friends*, p. 136.
10. Pierce Joyce, BBC broadcast of July 14, 1941 (typescript), King's College, London.
11. Ronald Storrs, *Orientations*, pp. 218–219.
12. *Friends*, p. 177.
13. Storrs, pp. 219–220.
14. *Friends*, pp. 137–142.
15. Lawrence to Leeds, December 7, 1914, Bod Res MSS, d57.

16. Lawrence to Leeds, December 24, 1914, Bod Res MSS, d57.
17. *Home Letters*, p. 303.
18. Lawrence to Hogarth, March 22, 1915, pp. 195–196.
19. Lawrence to Hogarth, April 15, 1915, ibid., p. 196.
20. Lawrence to Leeds, April 18, 1915, Bod Res MSS, d57.
21. Ibid.
22. Letter of June 1915 (undated), *Home Letters*, p. 304.
23. Letter of October 19, 1915, ibid., p. 310.
24. Lawrence to Leeds, November 16, 1915, Bod Res MSS, d57.
25. Letter of December 25, 1915, *Home Letters*, p. 311.
26. Lawrence to Mrs. Hasluck, February 28, 1916, Bod Res MSS, c52.
27. Dispatch of November 8, 1915, to "Foreign, Simla (India)," Houghton Library, Harvard University.
28. Note of Lawrence's on the manuscript of Robert Graves's biography, quoted in RGB, p. 82.
29. Telegram from the War Office, London, #14895, March 29, 1916, Houghton Library, Harvard University.
30. Sir Percy Cox, report of April 7, 1916, Houghton Library, Harvard University.
31. McMahon to Cox, March 20, 1916, Houghton Library, Harvard University.
32. LHB, pp. 61–62.
33. Telegram from the War Office, London, to the commanding general, Basra, April 28, 1916, Houghton Library, Harvard University.
34. Suleiman Mousa has provided an account of a meeting between Lawrence and Sulayman Faydi, one of the Mesopotamian deputies in the Ottoman Chamber of Deputies. Lawrence tried to persuade Faydi to participate in leading the revolt of Iraqi Arabs and said that he had been commissioned to offer British support for such a rebellion. Faydi is said to have surprised Lawrence by refusing, on the grounds of insufficient power on his own part and lack of interest in vengeance against the Turks. "They are your enemies, not ours," Faydi states that he told Lawrence ("The Role of Syrians and Iraqis in the Arab Revolt," *Middle East Forum* 43 [1967]: 15–17; this portion of the article is based on Faydi's memoirs).
35. LHB, p. 18.

36. Townshend to Army Headquarters, April 27, 1916, Houghton Library, Harvard University.

37. Aubrey Herbert, *Mons, Kut and Anzac,* pp. 204–244.

38. W. F. Stirling, "Tales of Lawrence of Arabia," *Cornhill Magazine* 74 (1933): 494–510.

39. PRO/FO 882/15, April 8, 1916; PRO/FO 882/18, May 5, 1916; *Arab Bulletin* #3, June 16, 1916, I, 23, published in *Letters,* pp. 208–209 (not *Arab Bulletin* #23 as indicated there).

40. PRO/FO 882/15, April 8, 1916.

41. Ibid.

42. PRO/FO 882/15, March 26, 1916.

43. *Arab Bulletin* #3, June 16, 1916, I, 24; published in *Letters,* p. 209.

44. Hubert Young, *The Independent Arab,* p. 72.

45. *Home Letters,* pp. 317–327.

46. Letter of July 1, 1916, ibid., p. 327.

47. Descriptive material on *The Arab Bulletin,* Bod Res MSS, b55. Lawrence's personal copy is in Houghton Library, Harvard University, and his penciled notes in it have clarified the authorship of some of the unsigned entries. The majority of the later issues were signed by Kinahan Cornwallis, director of the Arab Bureau.

48. John Brophy, an English novelist, wrote of *The Arab Bulletin,* "These reports are obviously the raw material from which the full book [*Seven Pillars of Wisdom*] was made, and apart from historical considerations are useful literary evidence. They give the lie to those who have urged that Lawrence after the event, created his own past as a myth. That he was a self-conscious writer cannot be denied, but the self-consciousness was an integral part of his personality" (*John's Weekly,* London, November 17, 1939).

49. *Home Letters,* p. 329.

50. *Arab Bulletin* #20, September 14, 1916, I, 241–243.

51. PRO/FO 371/6237, p. 72.

52. Telegram from the War Office, London, to the commander-in-chief, September 17, 1916, PRO/FO 371/6237, p. 72. The arguments and controversy in Allied policy during the fall of 1916 regarding the support to be offered to the Arab effort are presented concisely by Philip Graves in *Memoirs of King Abdullah of Transjordan,* pp. 165–166.

53. *Seven Pillars,* p. 62.

54. Letter of July 22, 1916, *Home Letters,* p. 328.

55. "The Sayings and the Doings of T.E. as heard and experienced by the Sims Family" (unpublished manuscript).

56. Sir Gilbert Clayton, *An Arabian Diary,* p. 67.

57. LHB, p. 92.

58. *Seven Pillars,* p. 63.

59. Storrs, p. 199.

60. Ibid., pp. 199–200.

61. Lawrence to Leeds, January 18, 1916, Bod Res MSS, d57.

62. Lady Florence Bell, *The Letters of Gertrude Bell,* II, 372.

63. *Friends,* p. 123.

64. Hogarth, "Mecca's Revolt Against the Turk," *Century Magazine* 100 (1920): 409.

65. *Letters,* pp. 193–196.

66. Ibid., p. 196.

67. "The Conquest of Syria, If Complete" (1916), PRO/FO 882/16.

68. Ibid.

69. "The Politics of Mecca" (late January 1916), PRO/FO 371/2771 and PRO/FO 141/461 (not 414/461 as noted in *Secret Lives*), quoted in *Secret Lives,* pp. 52–53, 62–63.

70. LHB, p. 17.

71. G. C. Arthur, *General Sir John Maxwell,* p. 153.

72. RGB, p. 80.

73. D. G. Hogarth, entry on Lawrence in the *Encyclopaedia Britannica,* 14th ed.

12. THE COURSE OF THE ARAB REVOLT

1. Lawrence to Mr. Evans-Wentz, October 12, 1916, California private collection.

2. *Arab Bulletin* #24, October 5, 1916, I, 323–324.

3. *Seven Pillars,* p. 91.

4. Ibid., p. 111.

5. Lord Hankey, *The Supreme Command, 1914–1918,* II, 500–501.

6. Janet E. Courtney, *An Oxford Portrait,* p. 43.

7. PRO/FO 882/6, December, 1916.

8. *Arab Bulletin* #18, September 5, 1916, I, 210.

9. "The Evolution of a Revolt," first published in *The Army Quarterly,* October 1920; reprinted in *Oriental Assembly,* pp. 103–134, and in *Evolution of a Revolt: Early Postwar Writings of T. E. Lawrence,* pp. 100–119.

10. *Oriental Assembly,* p. 119.

11. *Seven Pillars,* p. 160.

12. Ibid., p. 167.

13. "Report of a Journey of Lawrence through Arabia on Military Intelligence," January 17–25, 1917, Houghton Library, Harvard University.

14. Lawrence to Newcombe, January 17, 1917. I first saw the letter in photocopy. Haig Nicholson, the former chief of Reuter's Middle East bureau in Cairo, had gotten the original from a Turkish colonel, who took it from Newcombe's saddlebag when Newcombe was captured in Beersheba.

15. Letter of January 31, 1917, *Home Letters,* p. 334.

16. Letter of February 12, 1917, ibid., pp. 334–335.

17. See Edouard Brémond, *Le Hedjaz dans la guerre mondiale* (1931).

18. Letters of February 25 and 28, 1917, *Home Letters,* p. 337.

19. PRO/FO 882/6, February 16, 1917.

20. *Seven Pillars,* p. 174.

21. Lawrence to Clayton, July 10, 1917, *Letters,* pp. 225–226.

22. Wingate to Mark Sykes in London, July 1917, in Wingate Papers, Durham University, England. Actually, Lawrence was not eligible for the V.C. (Victoria Cross) because one of the prerequisites of award was the presence of another British officer who had witnessed the meritorious act. Instead, Lawrence was awarded the C.B. (Companion of the Bath).

23. Letter to H. S. Ede, September 1, 1927, *Shaw-Ede: T. E. Lawrence's Letters to H. S. Ede, 1927–1935,* p. 10.

24. Entry of July 11, 1917, in "Diary of Captain Orlo C. Williams, June 29–December 27, 1917," Imperial War Museum, London.

25. George Lloyd to Wingate, August 17, 1917, Wingate Papers, Durham University, England.

26. *Seven Pillars,* p. 324.

27. Lawrence to his family, August 12, 1917, *Home Letters,* p. 338.

28. *The Times,* May 20, 1935; quoted in Brian Gardner, *Allenby of Arabia: Lawrence's General,* p. 210.

29. For one of the political consequences of placing the leadership of the Revolt under Allenby, see Sir Ronald Wingate, *Wingate of the Sudan,* pp. 194–197.

30. Lawrence to Charlotte Shaw, April 3, 1927, BM Add MSS, 45903.

31. Lawrence to Alan Dawnay, April 14, 1927, Bod Res MSS, d43. Flinders Petrie was the famous Egyptologist.

32. Letter of August 27, 1917, *Home Letters,* p. 339.

33. Ibid.

34. Lawrence to W. F. Stirling, September 24, 1917; copy loaned to author by Jeremy Wilson.

35. Letter to "A Friend" (actually Leeds), September 25, 1917, *Letters,* p. 238.

36. Letter of September 24, 1917, *Home Letters,* p. 341.

37. Hogarth to his wife, October 17, 1917, Hogarth Papers, St. Antony's College, Oxford.

38. C. Falls and A. F. Becke, eds., *History of the Great War,* II, 51.

39. *Arab Bulletin* #72, December 5, 1917, II, 490–504.

40. Letters of November 7, 11, and 26, 1917, Hogarth Papers, St. Antony's College, Oxford.

41. *Seven Pillars,* p. 439.

42. "Pocket Diary for 1917," BM Add MSS, 45983.

43. Hogarth Papers, St. Antony's College, Oxford.

44. Letter of December 14, 1917, *Home Letters,* p. 345. According to Arnold Lawrence, T.E. kept of his decorations only the Croix de Guerre, "which he sent around the streets of Oxford on the neck of Hogarth's dog" (*Friends,* p. 301). T.E. himself wrote that he returned the decoration to Brémond in November of 1918 (LHB, p. 157).

45. Hogarth to his wife, December 16, 1917, Hogarth Papers, St. Antony's College, Oxford.

46. *Seven Pillars,* p. 453.

47. Letter of December 14, 1917, *Home Letters,* p. 343.

48. Ibid., p. 344.

49. Lawrence to Leeds, December 13, 1917, Bod Res MSS, d57.

50. Hogarth to his son, William, December 16, 1917, Hogarth Papers, St. Antony's College, Oxford.

51. Hogarth to his wife, December 23, 1917, Hogarth Papers, St. Antony's College, Oxford.

52. After the publication of Richard Aldington's biography of Lawrence in 1955, Gilman wrote specifically of his objections to Aldington's failure to obtain

information regarding these operations "when there were several British officers present to see Lawrence at work in the field and to bear testimony to his courage and ability. Why? The impression one gets from reading this part of the book is that Lawrence was anywhere but in Arabia" (from Gilman's manuscript found in the Storrs Papers). Gilman then goes on to provide his recollection of these operations and Lawrence's active part in them, concluding his account as follows: "The next day was spent mostly in completing the havoc that we had made of the railway, and there is one incident worth recording which illustrates Lawrence's utter disregard for his own safety. We had driven the Turks from Ramleh station and they took to the nearby hills from which they kept up an annoying fire. Dawnay and Lawrence had set their hearts on blowing up this station, and, accordingly, we loaded some explosives on an armoured car and proceeded towards the station. Unfortunately the ground was so strewn with boulders that the car was held up some little distance from the station. Nothing daunted, Dawnay and Lawrence seized a box of explosives and, under fire, staggered across the open to the station and blew it up."

53. J. B. Glubb, *Britain and the Arabs*, p. 85.

54. Falls and Becke, II, 404.

55. Letter of March 8, 1918, *Home Letters*, p. 348.

56. *Seven Pillars*, p. 502.

57. *Arab Bulletin* #80, February 26, 1918, III, 60.

58. *Seven Pillars*, p. 503.

59. Letter of March 8, 1918, *Home Letters*, p. 349. Lawrence later expressed regret about his bodyguard to Mrs. Shaw: "Yes, I was very sorry, then and now, for the body guard. They were worked too hard and too constantly hurt. And I was a spasmodic inconsiderate chief, too busied over my own difficulties to spare any kindness to them. So they didn't love me!" (May 20, 1926, BM Add MSS, 45903).

60. Hogarth to his son, William, February 25, 1918, Hogarth Papers, St. Antony's College, Oxford.

61. William Yale to Leland Harrison, U.S. Department of State, March 11, 1918, Middle East Centre, St. Antony's College, Oxford.

62. Falls and Becke, II, 408.

63. *Seven Pillars*, p. 534.

64. C. H. C. Pirie-Gordon, ed. *A Brief Record of the Advance of the Egyptian Expeditionary Force, July 1917 to October 1918* (London: His Majesty's Stationery Office, 1919), text opposite plate 53.

65. PRO/FO 371/3381.

66. See Basil Liddell Hart, *"T. E. Lawrence": In Arabia and After*, pp. 317–318.

67. PRO/FO 371/3381.

68. Ibid.

69. Pierce Joyce, BBC broadcast of July 14, 1941 (typescript), in King's College, London.

70. Lord Winterton, diary entry for August 26, 1918, in A. H. Brodrick, *Near to Greatness: A Life of Lord Winterton*, p. 178.

71. R. D. Blumenfeld, *All in a Lifetime*, p. 136.

72. LHB, p. 154.

73. Hubert Young, *The Independent Arab*, p. 209.

74. Ibid., p. 198.

75. Ibid., p. 218.

76. Ibid., pp. 219–220.

77. Ibid., p. 243.

78. C. S. Jarvis, *Arab Command: The Biography of Lieutenant-Colonel F. G. Peake Pasha*, p. 46.

79. Glubb, p. 88.

80. *Seven Pillars*, p. 635.

81. George Barrow, *The Fire of Life*, p. 210.

82. Alec Kirkbride, *An Awakening*, p. 85.

83. Lord Birdwood, *Nuri As-Said: A Study in Arab Leadership*, p. 85.

84. Barrow, p. 211.

85. Birdwood, p. 86.

86. Ibid., p. 86.

87. *Seven Pillars*, pp. 635–636.

88. Barrow, p. 211.

89. Young, p. 252.

13. THE CAPTURE OF DAMASCUS

1. Gertrude Bell, *The Desert and the Sown*, p. 134.

2. W. T. Massey, *Allenby's Final Triumph*, p. 240.

3. Lawrence to the General Staff, G.H.Q., October 1, 1918, quoted in Massey, p. 343; "The Destruction of the Fourth Army," *Arab Bulletin* #106, October 22, 1918, III, 343–350; quoted in *Letters*, pp. 247–257.

4. See discussions in Elie Kedourie, *England and the Middle East*, pp. 113–117; George Antonius, *The Arab Awakening*, pp. 270–274, 433n.

5. Elie Kedourie, *The Chatham House Version and Other Middle Eastern Studies*, pp. 33–51; *Seven Pillars*, p. 643.

6. Massey, p. 343.

7. Lawrence to the General Staff, G.H.Q., quoted in Massey, p. 343; the original is in the Public Record Office, London.

8. *Seven Pillars*, p. 645.

9. Lawrence to W. F. Stirling, October 15, 1924; copy loaned to the author by Jeremy Wilson.

10. Elie Kedourie, "The Capture of Damascus, October, 1918," *Middle Eastern Studies* (1964–1965), p. 71; the article is reprinted in Kedourie's *Chatham House*, pp. 33–51. *Seven Pillars* had been read by only a few people in 1926 and thus could have had no effect on the political outcome in Syria.

11. Ibid., p. 73. General Barrow argued wisely in connection with the capture of Der'a that no "peculiar merit attaches to troops who are the first to occupy a town or locality of historic interest in enemy territory. . . . When the place is unoccupied or weakly defended, there is no glory in being the first to enter" (*Fire of Life*, p. 210). But in the case of Damascus the matter had considerable political significance.

12. Henry Chauvel, letter of January 1, 1936, to the director of the Australian War Memorial, Allenby Papers, St. Antony's College, Oxford.

13. C. Falls and A. F. Becke, eds., *History of the Great War*, II, 591.

14. Ahmad Qadri, *Mudhakkirati 'an al-'Arabiyah al-Kubra* [My Memoirs of the Great Arab Revolt], p. 74. The Jaza'iri brothers were grandsons of an Algerian national hero.

15. Chauvel, letter of January 1, 1936.

16. Alec Kirkbride, *An Awakening*, pp. 94–95. Massey has provided a colorful firsthand account of the rejoicing in Damascus and the dramatic outpouring of enthusiasm with which the townspeople greeted Lawrence upon his entry into the city: "The rejoicings lasted all day. They reached an extraordinary height when sections of the Arab army came into the city. The Emir Feisal had had his agents in Damascus and they had sown good seed. Colonel Lawrence had

come in with a small following, and the people recognized the small brave English scholar who had turned soldier to influence Arabs to fight to throw off the Turkish yoke. Colonel Lawrence wore the head-dress, robes, and sword of an Arab chief of high degree, but this was not a complete disguise, and if the Damascenes had not been told they were to expect him they certainly very readily identified this gallant gentleman, who, more than any one else had striven through good times and bad to put Arab pressure on the Turkish garrisons at Medina and Maan, and to spread Arab disaffection throughout the Turkish Empire. The good report of Colonel Lawrence's work had filtered through the land. The Turks had great fear of him, a personal fear as well as dread of his influence, for they knew he had led scores of raids and had marshalled the Arabs for battle. On the head of this heroic figure they had placed a price of £50,000 [sic] but no Arab desired to gain such a reward. There was a scene of remarkable enthusiasm when Colonel Lawrence rode into the city. The Arabs came in at a fast trot, and in the narrow winding streets, badly paved and neglected so that the tramway rails were in places nearly a foot above the level of the road, there was not sufficient room for demonstration. But as the party rode towards the city, firing at the heavens, as Arabs will in their moments of rejoicing, the people received them delightedly, throwing sweetmeats in Colonel Lawrence's path and showering upon him the perfumes of Araby" (*Allenby*, pp. 249–250).

17. *Letters*, p. 257.

18. Massey, pp. 262–263; Kirkbride, *A Crackle of Thorns*, p. 9, and *Awakening*, pp. 95–96; Chauvel, letter of January 1, 1936.

19. Kedourie, "The Capture," p. 75.

20. Chauvel, letter of January 1, 1936.

21. General Allenby to his wife, October 3, 1918, Allenby Papers, St. Antony's College, Oxford; quoted in Brian Gardner, *Allenby of Arabia*, p. 190.

22. W. F. Stirling, "Tales of Lawrence of Arabia," *Cornhill Magazine* 74 (1933): 509.

23. Archibald Wavell, *Allenby: A Study in Greatness*, p. 285.

24. Lawrence to William Yale, October 22, 1929.

25. Chauvel, letter of January 1, 1936.

26. Kirkbride, *Awakening*, pp. 96–98.

27. Ibid., p. 97.

28. Interview with William Yale, August 10, 1966. Notes made by Yale in response to Lawrence's 1929 letter to him found among the Lawrence papers in Oxford substantiate this account: "My official notes record my interview with General Clayton. An Australian officer, quartermaster, asked me to do something about the hospital. *He said he had received orders from General Chauvel not to provision the hospital, and that he could not do so without risking court-martial* [italics added]. The Italian attaché and I visited the hospital twice and I then went to see Clayton who said that there were barely enough food supplies to provision the troops and consequently nothing could be done about the hospital. This was in contradiction to what the Australian officer told me who said he had enough food to supply the hospital" (Bod Res MSS, d44).

29. Chauvel, letter of January 1, 1936.

30. Chauvel reports of October 22, 1929, and October 3, 1935, Allenby Papers, St. Antony's College, Oxford; Allenby's report to the War Office, October 6, 1918, PRO/CAB 27/34.

31. Chauvel report of October 22, 1929.

32. Chauvel reports of October 22, 1929, and October 31, 1935.

33. Shukri Pasha was soon replaced by Ali Ridah al-Riqabi.

34. Chauvel report of October 22, 1929.

35. Bod Res MSS, d44.

36. Lawrence to Yale, October 22, 1929, *Letters*, p. 670 (see p. 313).

37. Interview with Robert Lawrence, March 24, 1965.

38. W. F. Stirling, *Safety Last*, p. 94.

39. Massey, p. 343.

40. LHB, p. 165.

14. THE ACHIEVEMENTS OF "AURENS"

1. Brian Gardner, *Allenby of Arabia*, p. 210; Field Marshal Alexander Wavell in *Friends*, p. 149.

2. J. B. Glubb, *Britain and the Arabs*, p. 89.

3. Letter to the editor, *The Times Literary Supplement*, November 3, 1961, p. 789.

4. C. Falls and A. F. Becke, eds., *History of the Great War*, II, 409.

5. RGB, p. 104.

6. W. F. Stirling, *Safety Last*, p. 248.

7. Suleiman Mousa, *T. E. Lawrence*, p. 66.

8. Jean B. Villars, *T. E. Lawrence*, p. 151.

9. Correspondence of Theodora Duncan, in a California private collection.

10. *The Times*, May 20, 1935.

11. Massey, *Allenby's Final Triumph*, p. 272.

12. *Friends*, p. 149. Colonel Pierce Joyce, Lawrence's immediate superior during most of the campaign, never questioned that Lawrence was the moving force of the Revolt, and Stirling wrote of Lawrence: "By his daring courage, his strategy, his novel tactics," he welded the turbulent Arab tribes into a fighting machine of such value that he was able "to immobilise two Turkish divisions and provide a flank force for Lord Allenby's final advance through Palestine and Syria, the value of which that great general has acknowledged again and again" (*Friends*, p. 154; *Safety Last*, pp. 245–246). Ramsey, a medical officer who served in the Revolt, reflected on Lawrence's predominant role in a letter to him in 1919: "I will always cherish tender memories of the Hedjaz campaign, although as you know from the British point of view I will always look upon it as a one-man show, the rest of us attempting to do our bit with perhaps only moderate success" (August 28, 1919, Bod Res MSS, d60).

13. Captain L. H. Gilman, unpublished notes in Storrs Papers, 1955.

14. Captain Gilman to the author, May 17, 1973. As of 1975, Gilman is one of the few surviving officers of the desert campaigns.

15. C. S. Jarvis, *Three Deserts* (1936). "One fact, however, stands out," Jarvis wrote (pp. 295–303), "and that is but for some very useful spade-work by Colonel S. F. Newcombe, 'Skinface Newcombe,' the whole credit for the Arab campaign must be given to Lawrence and no one else, for anyone cognizant of the hopeless waterless country in which he operated and the still more hopeless people with whom he had to deal, must realize that no ordinary man could have made anything approaching a success of the revolution. Lawrence is criticized by some for abrogating to himself the duties of Commander-in-Chief, leader of demolition parties, transport officer, liaison offi-

cer, etc., and the criticism seems sound on the face of it if one is unacquainted with the race with which he was dealing. The fact is that Lawrence's many-sided activities were forced upon him, not because he was deficient of capable British assistants — as an actual fact he had many — but because the Arab, being a man of one idea, had no faith in anybody but the queer forceful character that had caught their fancy — 'El Aurens.'

"In the Arab campaigns it had to be Lawrence and no one else — if the Billi tribe were disgruntled Lawrence had to travel some 300 miles to smooth them down; if the Beni Sakhr failed in their demolition work Lawrence had to go and conduct the raid personally; if the Howeitat were weakening in their allegiance it was Lawrence who must go to pull things together. . . .

"There is no questioning the fact that Lawrence was a great man and that he will go down to posterity as the finest guerrilla commander that has ever existed; for, in his campaign, whilst avoiding anything in the nature of a general engagement, except on one occasion, he kept the Turks in a state of anxiety as to his intentions — and caused them to tie up on the Hedjaz line troops that were urgently required elsewhere. He enticed them to strike out blindly against forces that did not exist and by using ju-jitsu methods compelled the enemy to expend his strength on an empty desert. In action they [the Bedouin] were entirely without discipline, and the first hint of loot meant that the greater part of the attacking force broke off the engagement before it was completed to rifle the enemy's baggage.

"Most famous guerrilla leaders have had the advantage of leading insurrectionists amongst whom there has been definite cohesion, and who have been fighting for some national object or aim, but this was entirely lacking in Lawrence's campaign. . . .

"It is only when one studies the campaign from this standpoint that one realizes the magnitude of the task that Lawrence undertook and it is no exaggeration to say that only a superman could have achieved what he did."

16. See H. St. John Philby, *Forty Years in the Wilderness*, Chap. V ("T. E. Lawrence and his Critics"), pp. 82–109.

17. Franz von Papen, *Memoirs*, pp. 80–81.

18. L. Farago, "No Nazi Revolt in the Desert," *Asia* 40 (April 1940): 175–178.

19. Interviewing across cultures is, as one might suspect, full of traps, and the possibility of bias and distortion is compounded by the presence of an interpreter. The interviewee, and sometimes the interpreter, wish to please the interviewer, "to tell him what he wants to hear" (especially true of many Bedouin, I have been told), or to persuade him of a point of view; and the interviewer may unintentionally distort what he records and interprets. The interviewer can only keep these pitfalls in mind and try to overcome them. In my interviews of Arabs, I introduced such safeguards as obtaining more than one account of a particular event and more than one viewpoint on its interpretation. I tape-recorded the interviews whenever I could and submitted the tapes to translators with different backgrounds and points of view.

20. Philip Graves, ed., *Memoirs of King Abdullah of Transjordan*, p. 170.

21. Talk with Andrawes Barghout, April 14, 1967.

22. Interview on April 14, 1967, in Jordan with Howeitat shaykhs who had been young teen-agers during World War I and did not take direct part in the campaigns, although their respective fathers and other relatives did.

23. Interview with Shaykh 'Ayd Ibn Awad al-Zalabani, April 28, 1967, translated by Antoine Hallac and Basim Musallam.

24. Anis Sayigh, *al-Hashimiyun Wa al-Thawrah al-'Arabiyah al-Kubra* [The Hashemites and the Great Arabic Revolution].

25. 'Abd al-Rahman Shahbandar, "al-Colonel Lawrence," *al-Muqtataf* 78 (March 1, 1931): 275.

26. Suleiman Mousa, *T. E. Lawrence: An Arab View*.

27. *Letters*, pp. 225–231.

28. Mousa, pp. 74–79.

29. Ibid., p. 287.

30. Subhi al-'Umari, *Lawrence Kama 'Araftuhu* [Lawrence As I Knew Him] (1969).

31. Sayigh, *al-Hashimiyun*.

32. David G. Hogarth to Sir Gilbert F. Clayton, July 20, 1917, Hogarth Papers, St. Antony's College, Oxford.

33. Jeremy M. Wilson, *Minorities*, p.

33; letter of Lilith Friedman to the author, September 3, 1973, concerning BM Add MSS, 45915.

34. *Secret Lives*, p. 81 (from BM Add MSS, 45915, not 49515 as printed).

35. Interview with Shaykh Salim Ibn Nasir, April 16, 1967.

36. Interview with S. 'Ayd, April 28, 1967.

37. James D. Lunt, "An Unsolicited Tribute," *Blackwood's Magazine* 277 (1955): 294.

38. Ibid., p. 296.

39. Arnold W. Lawrence, ed., *Letters to TEL*, p. 141.

40. *Friends*, p. 409.

41. Carl R. Raswan, *Black Tents of Arabia*, p. viii.

42. al-'Umari, *Lawrence*.

43. Ali Jawdat, *Dhikrayat* [Memoirs], 1900–1958.

44. Mousa, p. 199.

45. See Birdwood's biography, *Nuri As-Said*.

46. Nuri al-Sa'id, in the Baghdad *Times*, March 24, 1927. Peter Kimber, an Australian, interviewed Nuri not long before Nuri's death in 1958, and wrote to Arnold Lawrence of the meeting: "I have not yet read the biography of Nuri by Birdwood, but it would have warmed your heart if you had heard what he had to say about T.E., when he talked to me about him for two hours in the garden of the Semiramis Hotel by the river in Baghdad. I wish now I had had a tape-recorder" (letter of June 14, 1966).

47. George Antonius, *The Arab Awakening*, p. 217.

48. 'Abd al-Rahman Shahbandar, "Lawrence fi al-Mizan" [Lawrence in the Balance], *al-Muqtataf* 79 (July 1, 1931): 38. There are many other Arab descriptions of Lawrence that reflect particular points of view. Zuhdi al-Fatih's *Lawrence al-'Arab: 'ala Khuta Hartzal: Taqarir Lawrence al-Sirriyah* [Lawrence of Arabia: In the Steps of Hertzel and the Secret Reports of Lawrence] links Lawrence to the Crusaders of the Middle Ages out to crush the Muslims, and is perhaps typical of the anti-Zionist propaganda that utilizes Lawrence's name for political, anti-Western purposes. On the other hand, Shakir Khalil Nassar's *Lawrence Wa al-'Arab* [Lawrence and the Arabs] is a characteristically hero-worshipping account of the sort that is not unfamiliar to Western readers.

49. RGB, p. 117.

50. Introduction to the 1922 (Oxford) edition of *Seven Pillars of Wisdom*.

15. THE QUESTION OF MOTIVATION

1. RGB, p. 137.

2. Lawrence to Alan Dawnay, April 14, 1927, Bod Res MSS, d43.

3. Lawrence to a Foreign Office staff member, probably November 1919, Bod Res MSS, b55.

4. Epilogue to the 1922 (Oxford) edition, *Seven Pillars of Wisdom*, p. 285.

5. "To S.A.," *Seven Pillars*, p. 5.

6. Interview with Arnold Lawrence, September 13, 1969.

7. *Friends*, p. 593.

8. Ibid., p. 258.

9. *Seven Pillars*, pp. 42, 195.

10. *Seven Pillars* (Oxford edition, 1922), p. 1.

11. *Seven Pillars*, pp. 562–563.

12. Ibid., p. 563.

13. Ibid., p. 564.

14. Ibid., p. 563.

15. Anis Sayigh, "Ra'y 'Arabi fi Lawrence," [An Arabic Opinion on Lawrence], *Hiwar* 5 (July–August 1963): 15–23.

16. Ibid., p. 18.

17. Ibid., p. 20.

18. Arnold Lawrence has suggested that Robert may have been guessing how T.E. felt and that T.E., usually very reticent about his feelings, did not convey them directly (letter to the author, March 23, 1974).

19. Elie Kedourie, *England and the Middle East*, p. 105.

20. *Seven Pillars*, p. 634. The idealistic union with the mother in the lives of men who became great has been described by Helene Deutsch. Such children are born and reared *ad maiorem Dei gloriam* ("Some Clinical Considerations of the Ego Ideal," *Journal of the American Psychoanalytic Association* 12 (1964): 512–516). Out of the ascetic union with the mother, for whom the child is destined to fulfill his special mission, will come great and glorious deeds. If, as in Lawrence's case, a major element in the mother's psychology is *her* sense of sin, then the mission and the great deeds will naturally contain strong elements of renunciation, asceticism and redemption. The fallen self-regard that is the product of this union of selves be-

tween the mother and the son needs to be elevated by such great deeds, and its associated pain converted into glorious fulfillment (interview with Helene Deutsch, 1966).

21. *Seven Pillars,* p. 39.
22. Ibid., p. 41.
23. Ibid., p. 544.
24. Ibid., p. 44.
25. Ibid., pp. 551–552.
26. Ibid., p. 565.

16. LAWRENCE THE ENABLER

1. Letter of October 18, 1927, BM Add MSS, 45093.
2. *Seven Pillars,* p. 31.
3. Lawrence to V. W. Richards, July 15, 1918, *Letters,* p. 246.
4. The leader of the Arab Legion, F. G. Peake ("Peake Pasha"), provided his friend and biographer, C. S. Jarvis, with examples "of the many occasions when Lawrence saw things clearly from the enemy's point-of-view, and this uncanny gift, which savoured almost of second sight or a sixth sense, was able to foresee the course of a battle with the various contingencies he would have to guard against before the operation started" (C. S. Jarvis, *Arab Command: The Biography of Lieutenant-Colonel F. G. Peake Pasha,* pp. 35–36).
5. LHB, p. 182.
6. W. F. Stirling, "Tales of Lawrence," *Cornhill Magazine* 74 (1933): 497; also reprinted in Stirling's *Safety Last,* p. 83, and in *Friends,* p. 155.
7. Pierce Joyce, transcript of BBC broadcast of July 14, 1941, in "Akaba" Papers, King's College, London. A copy was provided the author through the courtesy of Arnold Lawrence.
8. Pierce Joyce, transcript of BBC broadcast of April 30, 1939, in "Akaba" Papers, King's College, London.
9. *Seven Pillars,* p. 91.
10. *Arab Bulletin* #1, June 6, 1916, I, 7.
11. *Arab Bulletin* #26, October 16, 1916 (not by Lawrence), I, 387; and #32, November 26, 1916 (by Lawrence), I, 482. The latter was printed in *Secret Dispatches,* pp. 37–38.
12. Letter of January 17, 1917, in a private collection in California. See Chap. 12, n. 14.
13. See, for example, Richard Aldington's documentation for his inaccurate

assertion that "neither of the two heroes in fact thought very highly of each other" (*Lawrence of Arabia,* pp. 163–164).
14. Interview with Liddell Hart, March 27, 1965.
15. From official dispatches, *Seven Pillars of Wisdom,* army diaries, conversations with Liddell Hart (further details of which are revealed in a talk I had with him in 1965), and letters to his family and to Mrs. Shaw.
16. *Secret Dispatches,* pp. 17–18.
17. Ibid., pp. 37–38 (from *Arab Bulletin* #32, November 26, 1916, I, 482).
18. Ronald Wingate, *Wingate of the Sudan,* p. 197.
19. *Seven Pillars,* p. 97.
20. Ibid., p. 98.
21. Letter of January 16, 1917, *Home Letters,* p. 333.
22. Philip Graves, *Memoirs of King Abdullah,* p. 170.
23. Ronald Storrs, *Orientations,* p. 520.
24. Arnold W. Lawrence, ed., *Letters to TEL,* pp. 56–57.
25. Mrs. Stuart Erskine, *King Faisal of Iraq,* p. 51.
26. Lawrence to Husayn, June 1918, in the *Sunday Times* research materials, Imperial War Museum, London.
27. RGB, p. 51.
28. F. G. Peake, notes in Bodleian Library, Oxford, May 26, 1963.
29. A. F. Nayton to Arnold Lawrence, January 9, 1946, Bod Res MSS, c52.
30. *Arab Bulletin* #66, October 21, 1917, II, 413; reprinted in *Secret Dispatches,* p. 138.
31. *Oriental Assembly,* p. 131.
32. Compare with Suleiman Mousa, *T. E. Lawrence,* pp. 65–72 and 132–142. Mousa minimizes Lawrence's role in both the Aqaba and the Tafila enterprises.
33. Interviews with Howeitat tribesmen, April 1967.
34. Interview with Shaykh Salim Ibn Nasir, April 16, 1967.
35. *Seven Pillars,* p. 157.
36. Interview with Shaykh 'Ayd Ibn Awad, April 28, 1967. Translation by Antoine Hallac and Basim Musallam.
37. Ibid. Making the presentation of gifts and rewards vivid and concrete evidently appealed to the Arab tribesmen and was employed by Lawrence on other occasions. Lawrence wrote, for example, to Edward Garnett after the war: "When an Arab did something individual and intelligent during the war I would call

him to me, and opening a bag of sovereigns would say, 'Put in your hand,' and this was thought the very height of splendour. Yet it was never more than £120: but the exercise of spreading and burying your fingers in the gold made it feel better than a cold-blooded counting out of two or three hundred pounds" (letter of June 20, 1927, *Letters*, p. 520).

38. Interview of April 28, 1967.

39. Samir Khalaf, remarks made at a conference on psychology and the Near East, May 8, 1973, Princeton University.

40. *Seven Pillars*, p. 219.

41. Lawrence to V. W. Richards, July 15, 1918, *Letters*, p. 244.

42. Anis Sayigh, *al-Hashimiyun Wa al-Thawrah al-ʿArabiyah al-Kubra* [The Hashemites and the Great Arab Revolution] and "Raʾy ʿArabi fi Lawrence" [An Arabic Opinion of Lawrence].

17. THE CONFLICT OF RESPONSIBILITY

1. General Harry Chauvel to Mr. Bean, editor of the *Official History of the War in Egypt and Palestine,* October 8, 1929, Allenby Papers, St. Antony's College, Oxford.

2. Letter of August 12, 1917, *Home Letters,* p. 338.

3. *Seven Pillars,* p. 542.

4. Ibid., p. 192.

5. *Oriental Assembly,* pp. 117–118; see also a similar statement in *Seven Pillars,* p. 195.

6. From the suppressed introductory chapter, 1922 (Oxford) edition, *Seven Pillars.*

7. *Seven Pillars,* p. 163.

8. Ibid., p. 191.

9. Ibid., p. 548.

10. Ibid., pp. 253, 257.

11. Ibid., p. 517.

12. F. G. Peake to Arnold Lawrence, May 26, 1963.

13. *Seven Pillars,* p. 378.

14. Ibid., p. 467.

15. Ibid., pp. 181–182.

16. *Friends,* p. 246.

17. *Seven Pillars,* p. 544.

18. LHB, p. 126; *Seven Pillars,* pp. 275–276.

19. *Seven Pillars,* p. 386.

20. Jeremy M. Wilson, introduction to *Minorities,* p. 33; the original is in BM Add MSS, 45915.

21. Elie Kedourie, *England and the Middle East,* pp. 96–97; *Seven Pillars,* p. 275.

22. *Seven Pillars,* p. 275.

23. Ibid., p. 276.

24. Ibid., p. 277.

25. Ibid., p. 555.

26. Ibid., p. 550.

18. THE HEROIC LEGEND AND THE HERO

1. James Notopoulos, "The Tragic and the Epic in T. E. Lawrence," *Yale Review* (Spring 1965), pp. 331–345.

2. Statement of Guillaume, a member of the Arab Bureau, as conveyed to the author by Arabella Rivington.

3. Irving Howe, *A World More Attractive,* Chap. 1, p. 20. The quotation "a man with a load on his mind" is from Herbert Read's review of *Seven Pillars,* in *The Bibliophile's Almanack for 1928,* p. 39.

4. Howe, p. 36.

5. Ibid., p. 39.

6. Read, review of *Seven Pillars,* pp. 38–39.

7. Lawrence to Edward Garnett, December 1, 1927, *Letters,* pp. 549–550.

8. In his classic work, *The Myth of the Birth of the Hero,* Otto Rank examined the ways in which the elements of the hero-fantasy, with its many variations, have found expression in the hero-myths of Western and Middle Eastern civilization (pp. 1–96).

9. Arnold Lawrence to the author, July 23, 1973.

10. Arnold Lawrence still receives letters from people — sometimes persons suffering from the torments of self-hate — who tell him how they resolved conflicts or "found peace" through their familiarity with his brother's life and writings.

11. See, for example, James T. Shotwell, *At the Paris Peace Conference,* p. 131; or Winston Churchill, *Great Contemporaries,* p. 157.

12. *Friends,* p. 242.

13. Lawrence to Charlotte Shaw, April 14, 1927, BM Add MSS, 45903.

14. *Seven Pillars,* p. 327.

15. Notes, undated, Bod Res MSS, c52.

16. *Seven Pillars,* p. 91.

17. Ibid., p. 322.

18. Ibid., p. 323.

19. *Friends,* pp. 226, 228.

20. LHB, p. 169.

21. Richard Goodwin, *The New Yorker*, May 25, 1968, p. 93.
22. RGB, pp. 84–90.
23. Lawrence to Graves, July 22, 1927, RGB, p. 90. The italics are Lawrence's.

19. THE SHATTERING OF THE DREAM

1. *Friends*, p. 245.
2. The original is in the Humanities Research Center, University of Texas.
3. This copy of *Seven Pillars* is in the Arents Collection, New York Public Library.
4. Report to GHQ, Cairo, June 28, 1919, Humanities Research Center, University of Texas.
5. In the Bodleian Library.
6. Manuscript of *Seven Pillars of Wisdom*, Bodleian Library.
7. *Seven Pillars*, p. 443.
8. Ibid., p. 444.
9. Ibid., pp. 444–445.
10. Ibid., p. 445.
11. Ibid., p. 446.
12. Ibid., p. 447.
13. Ibid.
14. According to his pocket diary he arrived in Azraq on November 22 and in Aqaba on the 26th.
15. Manuscript of *Seven Pillars*. This paragraph was omitted from the subscribers' edition.
16. Arnold Lawrence to the author, December 22, 1968.
17. Joyce's "Akaba" Papers, King's College, London. An Englishman who had served in the desert campaigns told me that he learned from Turkish prisoners that it was common practice for their officers, even those who had been most active heterosexually during peacetime, to take younger soldiers as sexual partners. Some of the younger soldiers volunteered; others were forced to submit. The soldiers also sought young boys for sexual partners and sometimes had sexual relations, or took part in mutual masturbation, with each other.
18. William Langer, discussion of J. E. Mack, "T. E. Lawrence: A Study of Heroism and Conflict," *Journal of the American Psychiatric Association* 125 (1969): 1092.
19. Richard Meinertzhagen, *Middle East Diary*, p. 32.
20. Interview with Basil Liddell Hart, March 27, 1965. T. W. Beaumont, a young gunner who served with Lawrence in the desert campaigns, told me that he spoke with the medical officer, Captain Ramsey, at Aqaba after Lawrence came back from Der'a. He learned from Ramsey that Lawrence had badly swollen testes, for which he required a suspensory bandage, and whipmarks on his thighs. Beaumont claims Lawrence told him, "When I kneed the Bey in the groin these chaps hided me" (interview with the author, September 11, 1969). But Beaumont was only nineteen at the time of the Der'a episode, and his reliability as a witness after more than half a century may be questioned.
21. Gilman was referring here only to my being a psychiatrist. He did not know that I happened, in fact, to have written a book about nightmares.
22. Captain L. H. Gilman to the author, May 17, 1973.
23. Lawrence to Charlotte Shaw, March 26, 1924, BM Add MSS, 45903.
24. Alan Watts, the late student of Eastern philosophies and religions, made an investigation of persons who had undergone torture. He found that for most sufferers the worst time was the beginning, when the agony was experienced as totally destructive, tearing the person apart. During this period the torture was terrifying. But in some instances if the individual surrendered to the experience, "cooperated" with it, it changed into a drunken masochistic giving in. A point would then come when the pain was no longer negative, but became converted into ecstasy, with the disappearance of all terror and meaning (lecture, taped, WBUR radio broadcast, Boston, January 20, 1974). This finding of Watts's corresponds closely to Lawrence's description of his experience and suggests that his response to the torture was not unusual. What was unique to his personality, however, was the lasting shame and intolerance, the refusal to forgive himself. It is not known how many victims of such violations suffer from subsequent disorders of the sort that Lawrence did.
25. RGB, p. 92.
26. *Friends*, p. 272.
27. "Book VI was written first of all the 7 Pillars: and has only been twice rewritten: except the Deraa chapter, which is in about its ninth revise" (letters to Charlotte Shaw, July 30, 1925, BM Add MSS, 45903).

28. Lawrence to Charlotte Shaw, December 26, 1925, BM Add MSS, 45903.

29. Lawrence to Edward Garnett, August 22, 1922, *Letters*, p. 358.

30. *Seven Pillars*, p. 13.

31. Interviews with A. E. "Jock" Chambers; Lawrence to Captain Snagge, June 29, 1927, Bod Res MSS, d44; Lawrence to Charlotte Shaw, July 30, 1930.

32. Toronto *Telegram*, January 31, 1963.

33. Information which casts doubt on Staples's claims of being a witness to these events, or of knowing Lawrence, is contained in a letter of March 28, 1974, from Christopher Dowling of the staff of the Imperial War Museum to Arnold Lawrence.

34. *Arab Bulletin* #106, October 22, 1918, III, 343–350; published in *Letters*, pp. 247–257.

35. *Letters*, pp. 253–254.

36. Ibid., p. 256.

37. Arnold Lawrence believes that the context indicates this could only have been said to his bodyguard (unpublished manuscript, "The Aftermath of Tafas," Bod Res MSS, b56).

38. In the original manuscript "first" is crossed out and replaced by "only."

39. *Seven Pillars*, pp. 632–633.

40. Ibid., p. 633.

41. Brian Gardner, *Allenby of Arabia*, p. 190.

42. See al-'Umari's *Lawrence Kama 'Araftuhu* [Lawrence As I Knew Him].

43. Suleiman Mousa, *T. E. Lawrence*, p. 199.

44. Lord Winterton ["W."], "Arabian Nights and Days," *Blackwood's Magazine* 207 (June 1920): 761.

45. Hubert Young. *The Independent Arab*, p. 251.

46. Unpublished notes of May 26, 1963, and 1965 (no month and day), of which a copy was loaned to the author by Arnold Lawrence.

47. F. G. Peake, notes of May 26, 1963.

48. Ibid.

49. *The Observer*, December 16, 1962.

50. "The Aftermath of Tafas," probably written in 1965 or 1966, Bod Res MSS, b56.

51. Alec Kirkbride, *An Awakening*, pp. 81–82.

52. Alec Kirkbride, *A Crackle of Thorns*, pp. 8, 9.

53. Kirkbride to Basil Liddell Hart, December 8, 1962, Bod Res MSS, b56.

54. Arnold Lawrence wrote me that he guessed "that T.E. reacted as an Arab to the sight of the Tafas villagers" (letter of August 20, 1973).

55. Arnold Lawrence to the author, August 20, 1973.

56. Richard Aldington seized upon the Tafas episode ("the spectacle of a British officer encouraging a mass slaughter of prisoners is deplorable") to attack Lawrence (*Lawrence of Arabia*, p. 237), and his account omits any discussion of the complexities of Lawrence's position. Although Aldington is perhaps unique in his venom, he shares with other denigrators a readiness to accept as factual any of Lawrence's statements about himself that discredit him, while devoting extraordinary effort to disproving those which do a service to his memory. The adulators have done the reverse.

57. Lawrence to Mrs. Hardy, January 15, 1928, *Letters*, p. 564.

58. *Seven Pillars*, p. 661.

59. Ibid., p. 659.

60. *Secret Lives*, pp. 217–219. I would not place the emphasis that Knightley and Simpson do upon the role of medical illness in the personality changes that resulted from Lawrence's war experiences. Although these illnesses were exhausting and at times incapacitating, I do not know of evidence indicating that they would lead to lasting changes of this sort.

61. Lawrence to Herbert Samuel, December 14, 1927, made available through the courtesy of Arnold Lawrence.

INTRODUCTION TO PART IV

1. LHB, p. 73.

2. Arnold Toynbee, *Acquaintances*, p. 192.

3. Hannah Arendt, "The Imperialistic Character," *Review of Politics* 12 (July 1950): 316.

4. Letter to James Hanley, July 2, 1931, *Letters*, p. 729.

5. Elie Kedourie, *England and the Middle East*, p. 88.

20. ARAB SELF-DETERMINATION AND ARAB UNITY

1. Lawrence to Charlotte Shaw, October 18, 1927, BM Add MSS, 45903.

2. This was confirmed for me by several of the Bedouin tribesmen in Jordan whom I interviewed. Lawrence helped them during the war, they said, but then he went away and "signed a treaty" which differed from what he had assured them during the campaigns.

3. *Oriental Assembly,* pp. 144–145.

4. Irving Howe, *A World More Attractive,* p. 27.

5. *Letters,* p. 291.

6. *Oriental Assembly,* pp. 94–95. See also Jon Kimche, *The Second Arab Awakening,* pp. 12–14.

7. *Oriental Assembly,* p. 94.

8. *Letters,* p. 577.

9. *Oriental Assembly,* pp. 95–97.

10. Ibid., pp. 82–83.

11. *Letters,* p. 577.

12. Lawrence to Charlotte Shaw, April 26, 1928, BM Add MSS, 45903.

13. LHB, p. 101.

14. *Oriental Assembly,* p. 88.

15. Ibid., pp. 88–89.

16. Ibid., pp. 92–93.

17. I am speaking of Syria here as Greater Syria, comprising what would now be Syria, Lebanon, Jordan and Israel (see J. P. Spagnolo, "French Influence in Syria Prior to World War I: The Functional Weakness of Imperialism." p. 47).

18. "Syrian Cross Currents," in *Secret Dispatches from Arabia,* p. 159.

19. *Oriental Assembly,* p. 85; George Kirk, *A Short History of the Middle East,* pp. 140–141.

20. David Lloyd George, *Memoirs,* II, 672.

21. Suleiman Mousa, *T. E. Lawrence,* p. 215.

22. See ibid. and "The Role of Syrians and Iraqis in the Arab Revolt"; and Anis Sayigh, *al-Hashimiyun Wa al-Thawrah al-'Arabiyah al-Kubra* [The Hashemites and the Great Arabic Revolution].

23. From "Syria: The Raw Material," *Secret Dispatches,* p. 77.

24. 'Abd al-Rahman Shahbandar, "Lawrence fi al-Mizan" [Lawrence in the Balance], *al-Muqtataf* 79 (July 1, 1931): 38.

25. Woolley summarized the question of Lawrence's attitude toward the French concisely: "He liked France and often talked of the pleasant times he had had there, and I think he was even fond of the French people. But especially after a long stay in the Lebanon, he felt a profound jealousy of the part they played or wished to play in Syria. That French politicians should aim at a control of the country he had come to love infuriated him. He hated the Turks because they were masters of Syria and treated the Arabs as inferiors; that their place should be taken by another non-Arab power was monstrous. Long before the Sykes-Picot Agreement drove him into a deliberate policy of frustration Lawrence was an enemy of France in the Levant, and that sentiment was the key to many of his later acts" (*Friends,* pp. 93–94).

21. LEAVING DAMASCUS BEHIND

1. LHB, p. 156.

2. C. H. Pirie-Gordon, ed., *A Brief Record of the Advance of the Egyptian Expeditionary Force,* Plate 56.

3. J. Nevakivi, *Britain, France and the Arab Middle East,* pp. 71–73; *Letters,* p. 670.

4. *Letters,* p. 258.

5. *Secret Lives,* p. 99.

6. RGB, p. 94.

7. See, for example, RGB, pp. 93–94; *Friends,* p. 162.

8. PRO/CAB 27/24.

9. Interview with Robert Lawrence, August 24, 1964.

10. The portrait hangs in the Junior Common Room, Jesus College, Oxford.

11. Harold Nicolson, *Curzon: The Last Phase,* p. 4.

12. Meeting of October 29, 1918, PRO/CAB 27/24.

13. *Letters,* pp. 265–269.

14. Ibid., p. 270.

15. *Letters to TEL,* p. 187.

16. Quoted in *Letters to TEL,* p. 186.

17. Ibid., p. 187.

18. Lord Birdwood, *Nuri As-Said,* p. 102.

19. Meeting of November 21, 1918, PRO/CAB 27/24.

20. Ahmad Qadri, *Mudhakkirati,* pp. 91–95.

21. Edouard Brémond, *Le Hedjaz dans la guerre mondiale,* p. 311.

22. LHB, p. 157.

23. Birdwood, p. 103.

24. Qadri, pp. 91–95.

25. LHB, p. 168. See also a detailed account of this incident in Jean Beraud Villars, *T. E. Lawrence,* pp. 255–257.

26. *The Times,* November 26, 1918. The three articles were reprinted by the

New York *Times* as a single piece in the magazine *Current History* (February 1919, pp. 348–357), "written by a correspondent of the London *Times* who was in touch with the Arabs throughout their campaign against the Turks."

27. Sir Evelyn Wrench, "Recollections," Bod Res MSS, b55; see also Wrench's *Struggle: 1914–1920*, pp. 362–366.

28. For example: "It took him months to obtain the suffrages of all the tribes, and the expenditure of as much tact and diplomacy as would suffice for years of ordinary life. What he achieved, however, is a little short of wonderful. From time immemorial the desert has been a confused and changing mass of blood-feuds among the Arabs from Damascus to Mecca; for the first time in the history of Arabia since the seventh century there is peace along all the pilgrim road" (*The Times*, November 27, 1918; reprinted in Stanley and Rodelle Weintraub, *The Evolution of a Revolt: Early Postwar Writings of T. E. Lawrence*, p. 41).

29. Lawrence to Dawson, November ("Sunday," probably November 24) 1928, Bod Res MSS, b55.

30. Ibid. Lawrence also wrote that when "things got bad in the early days of the rising," McMahon was fired "largely" because he had brought the sharif into the war.

31. "The French made very heavy weather over Faisal, which added to the trouble [for the Arab cause], and made him a fortnight late," Lawrence wrote to Dawson (December 11).

32. Brémond, p. 317.

33. Leonard Stein, *The Balfour Declaration*, p. 638.

34. See the discussion in Jon Kimche, *The Second Arab Awakening*, pp. 178–183. According to the account of a Palestinian historian, Aref al-Aref, Lawrence had conversations with Palestinian nationalists, in which he is said to have expressed his preference for Jewish or Hashemite dominance in Palestine over rule by Syrian or Palestinian Arabs.

35. *Jewish Chronicle*, December 13, 1918.

36. Ibid.

37. Esco Foundation for Palestine, *A Study of Jewish, Arab and British Policies*, I, 139.

38. Chaim Weizmann, *Trial and Error*, p. 235.

39. See George Antonius, *The Arab Awakening*, pp. 437–439.

40. Ibid., p. 439.

41. Christopher Sykes, *Crossroads to Israel*, pp. 45–49.

42. George Kirk, *A Short History of the Middle East*, pp. 152–157; Zeine N. Zeine, *The Struggle for Arab Independence*, pp. 62–64.

43. Qadri, pp. 96–97.

44. Letter of December 25, 1918, *Letters*, p. 271.

45. LHB, p. 157.

46. Lawrence to Eddie Marsh, January 7, 1919, *Letters*, p. 272.

47. Rudyard Kipling to Lawrence, January 7, 1919, *Letter to TEL*, pp. 120–121.

48. Lawrence to B. E. Leeson, January 8, 1919, *Letters*, p. 272.

22. AT THE PARIS PEACE CONFERENCE

1. Quoted in Ella Winter and Granville Hicks, eds., *The Letters of Lincoln Steffens* (New York: Harcourt, Brace, 1938), pp. 465–466.

2. Jon Kimche, *The Second Arab Awakening*, p. 10.

3. Lloyd George, *Memoirs*, II, 673.

4. PRO/FO 608/92.

5. Lawrence to Ernest Thurtle, April 26, 1929, *Letters*, p. 653.

6. Gertrude Bell to Lady Florence Bell, March 16, 1919, in Lady Florence Bell, *The Letters of Gertrude Bell*, II, 468.

7. H. N. Howard, *The Partition of Turkey*, p. 231.

8. Laurence Evans, *United States Policy and the Partition of Turkey, 1914–1924*, p. 121.

9. Winston Churchill, *Great Contemporaries*, p. 158.

10. David Hunter Miller, *My Diary at the Peace Conference*, I, 74.

11. By Lionel Curtis, in *Friends*, p. 259.

12. Miller, I, 74–75.

13. James T. Shotwell, diary entry of January 15, 1919, in *At the Paris Peace Conference*, p. 121.

14. Diary entry of January 20, 1919, Ibid., pp. 129–131.

15. Interview of William Yale, August 10, 1966. Yale, seventy-nine at the time, was a soured man.

16. *Letters*, pp. 273–274.

17. Jukka Nevakivi, *Britain, France and the Arab Middle East*, pp. 134–135.

18. Letter of January 30, 1919, *Home Letters*, p. 352. Elsie Newcombe, Colonel Newcombe's widow, with whom he was engaged to be married at the time of the Paris Conference, gave me a warm and amusing picture of Lawrence in Paris. Before she met Lawrence, Newcombe said to her: "If you meet a very rude young Englishman, pay no attention. It will be Lawrence." (Lawrence's friends seem, as far as I could discover, never to have been offended by his "rudeness," and did not feel that his humor was of a hurting kind or at their expense.) Colonel Newcombe and his fiancée were at a dinner attended by nineteen other men, and Elsie had no opportunity to meet Lawrence then; but at the end of the evening Lawrence sent the butler with a message that he wished to meet her. A dinner was duly arranged, he arrived, and when she asked him to sit next to her Lawrence said, "No, I am not worthy." Later, he apparently changed his mind because he did sit down beside her, looking sad and soulful and eating a banana. After dinner was over they all went outside. Lawrence was on the sidewalk and the future Mrs. Newcombe was standing in the street. "Now I'm taller than you," he said. She shoved him into the gutter and stood on the sidewalk and replied, "Now I'm taller than you." Colonel Newcombe came along and interrupted this horseplay, saying, "Come with me. Soon you'll want to marry him instead of me." She replied, "Oh no, you're better looking and much nicer." Lawrence laughed, but Newcombe blushed and was silent. (Elsie Newcombe, interview with the author, August 27, 1964; compare the incident with Lawrence's relationship with Janet Laurie, Chap. 6, especially p. 65.)

19. Evans, p. 117.

20. Ibid.; Miller, IV, 297, and XIV, 226 ff.

21. "Territorial Claims of the Government of the Hedjaz" (memorandum of January 29, 1919), PRO/FO 608/92.

22. Lloyd George, II, 673; Arnold Toynbee, *Acquaintances*, p. 182; LHB, p. 157.

23. Toynbee, pp. 182–183. Aldington based his account of this meeting on the memoirs of Lloyd George, who happened to make no mention of Lawrence's

role as an interpreter or translator. Lawrence's assertion that he interpreted for Faisal before the Council of Ten (LHB, p. 157) was therefore assumed by Aldington to be "an elaborately built up story" of Lawrence's own devising. Toynbee's account substantiates Lawrence's version of the event, and describes Lawrence's remarkable performance, which, to my knowledge, Lawrence himself never referred to. In the speech Faisal focused upon his memorandum of January 29 and spoke of the Allied promises of independence, of Arab contributions and sacrifices during the war, of the desire for unity for the Arab-speaking peoples, and of the wish of the Syrians to choose their own mandate (Miller, XIV, 226 ff., and Lloyd George, pp. 673–678). Faisal expressed gratitude for the work of the French military contingent during the war, and made no reference to the growing hostility in Syria toward France. Because Lloyd George was busy "building up the German Treaty" he did not give the matter of Syria much attention and left it with Lord Milner, who had become colonial secretary.

24. See discussions by Lloyd George (II, 678–699), Evans (pp. 125–144), Howard (pp. 225–234), Nevakivi (pp. 126–147), and Zeine N. Zeine (*The Struggle for Arab Independence*, pp. 85–96).

25. Lloyd George, II, 695.

26. Elizabeth Monroe, *Britain's Moment in the Middle East, 1914–1956*, p. 63.

27. Harold Nicolson, *Peace Making — 1919*, p. 142.

28. Alexander Michailovitj, *När Jag Var Storfurste Av Ryssland* [When I Was Grand Duke of Russia], pp. 314–315. The English translation of this passage is by Gunilla Jainchill.

29. Lincoln Steffens, "Armenians Are Impossible: An Interview with Lawrence of Arabia," *Outlook and Independent*, October 14, 1931, pp. 203, 223.

30. E. M. House and C. S. Seymour, *What Really Happened at Paris*, pp. 178, 179.

31. See Esco Foundation, *Palestine*, I, 159–177, for the sequence of events leading up to the approval by the League of Nations in 1922 of the British mandate for Palestine.

32. Ibid., p. 161.

33. Ibid., p. 142.

34. Some contemporary Arab nationalists reject the idea that Faisal could ever have had a letter expressing such sentiment sent with his agreement. Suleiman Mousa states categorically: "The letter that the Zionists claimed Feisal had written on March 3, 1919, to Mr. Felix Frankfurter, then a member of the American Zionist Delegation, is certainly a forgery" (*T. E. Lawrence: An Arab View*, p. 229). Mousa quotes extensively from interviews with 'Awni 'Abd al-Hadi, a member of Faisal's delegation in Paris, who suggested that the letter was sent by Lawrence without Faisal's knowledge. Mr. Frankfurter, however, reprinted the letter in the October 1930 issue of the *Atlantic Monthly*, vouched for its authenticity, and discussed there the circumstances of its framing. "Prince Feisal's letter was a document prepared under the most responsible conditions," Frankfurter wrote. "It received important publicity at the time. It has ever since been treated as one of the basic documents affecting Palestinian affairs and Arab-Jewish relations" (p. 50). Although Faisal objected to those interpretations of his letter which understood it to convey his consent to Zionist policy, he did not disavow its authorship. See also discussions in the Esco Foundation's *Palestine* (I, 142–143) regarding the meeting and the letter; in Leonard Stein, *The Balfour Declaration*, p. 643; and in R. Meinertzhagen, *Middle East Diary*, pp. 14–15.

Hadi, who later became a Palestinian leader, resented what he called "Lawrence's Zionist propensities," indicated to Mousa that whatever Faisal's personal feelings were about the possibility of Arab-Jewish cooperation in Palestine, his support for British Zionist policy was contingent upon obtaining the independence of Syria, and that Faisal's attitude toward Zionism changed when he lost British support for Syria. Hadi, who also served at one time as Faisal's private secretary, claimed to Mousa that Faisal's confidence in Lawrence was lost in 1919 because of the latter's pro-Zionist attitude (Mousa, *T. E. Lawrence*, p. 230), but unpublished letters from Faisal to Lawrence in 1921, seeking his help after he became king of Iraq, are filled with expressions of warmth and affection and suggest no diminution of confidence in his English friend (copies of these letters are in the British Museum).

35. Evans, p. 137.

36. H. Wickham Steed, *Through Thirty Years*, II, 300; see also, Jukka Nevakivi, *Britain, France and the Arab Middle East*, pp. 137–138.

37. Letter of March 26, 1919, in Elizabeth Burgoyne, *Gertrude Bell*, II, 110.

38. Zeine, *The Struggle*, p. 81. The information was obtained by Zeine from al-Husri, *Yawn Maisalun*. Sati al-Husri was Faisal's advisor and future minister of education in the government of Damascus (from Nevakivi, p. 141).

39. Nevakivi, p. 143.

40. Faisal to Clemenceau, April 20, 1919, in E. S. Woodward and R. Butler, eds., *Documents on British Foreign Policy, 1918–1939*, Ser. 1, IV, 252.

41. Interview with Robert Lawrence, March 24, 1965.

42. Interview with Arnold Lawrence, March 16, 1965, and on other occasions. There is a curious entry dated "April 8th, 1919," concerning Lawrence in the published diary of Richard Meinertzhagen, an eccentric ornithologist and Zionist who was at the Peace Conference. Although purporting to be made from contemporary notes, and reporting "we lunched together" (presumably that day), the diary, first published in 1959, makes no mention of Lawrence's having received a telegram from home about his father's illness, or his having just returned from England or being about to go. Perhaps Meinertzhagen is off on his date by a few days or is describing events that occurred a little earlier.

The entry is of considerable potential interest as it provides the only account of Lawrence's troubled state in the early stages of writing his narrative of the Revolt. But I also question whether Meinertzhagen did not draw upon memories from later periods, and from various readings, in reconstructing his diary. He seems to have been much influenced by Aldington. Yet Lawrence's admission of embroidering "dull little incidents" into "hair-breadth escapes" seems a valid observation, and the confession of self-hatred for having "overdone it" is believable. But the statements that describe a kind of pathetic despair and relate it to terror lest he be "found out and deflated" are suggestive of Aldington, as is the statement "he excuses himself by saying that none of his exaggerations can be checked or verified" (p. 31). This is not only untrue but is inconsistent with Lawrence's later comment on the manuscript of Graves's biography: that the documents of the Arab Revolt in the archives of the Foreign Office would corroborate his account. These documents have now become available, and Lawrence's statement to Graves has been largely borne out. The validity of portions of Meinertzhagen's diary as a contemporary record must accordingly be questioned. It must be added that assessing Meinertzhagen's work is not made any easier by his condescending tone ("I cannot help liking the little man"), and his claim to be the only person to understand Lawrence (*Middle East Diary*, p. 30).

43. James Rennell Rodd, *Social and Diplomatic Memories*, Ser. 3, p. 383.

44. Interview with David Garnett, October 29, 1964; see also *Letters*, p. 276.

45. Francis Lord Rennell of Rodd to the author, November 17, 1965.

46. Rodd, *Memories*, p. 383.

47. *Friends*, p. 162.

48. RGB, p. 55.

49. LHB, p. 129; "History of Seven Pillars," Bod Res MSS, d230.

50. *Oriental Assembly*, pp. 142–143.

51. H. St. John Philby, *Forty Years in the Wilderness*, p. 88.

52. Ibid., p. 92.

53. *Secret Dispatches*, pp. 145–147. There is a curious entry in the minutes of March 19, 1919, of the American Commissioners in Paris: "Memorandum No. 168 was read in which General Churchill submitted a proposal that Captain William Yale accept an invitation tendered to him by Colonel Lawrence to accompany the British Forces on an expedition which they are planning for the month of May against the tribes of the Nejd. The Commissioners did not approve of this proposal and suggested that in any reply that should be made to Colonel Lawrence, it be stated that the American Commission to Negotiate Peace cannot take cognizance of any expedition which the British Forces are proposing to make against certain Arabian tribes" (*Papers Relating to the Foreign Relations of the United States*, IX [*The Paris Peace Conference, 1919*], 123. There is no further information on whether the British government actually planned to send Lawrence on such a mission, presumably against Ibn Saud, or whether Lawrence's ill-fated trip to Egypt was related to such

a plan. A note by Lawrence on a Foreign Office telegram of April 18, 1919, suggests that some sort of British mission against Ibn Saud may have been contemplated (PRO/FO 608/80, quoted in part in *Secret Lives*, p. 151):

"If he [Ibn Saud] abandons the Wahabi creed, we will not do too badly. If he remains Wahabi, we will send the Moslem part of the Indian Army to recover Mecca, and break the Wahabi movement. This was done early in the 19th century when the present state of things existed by Ibrahim Pasha of Egypt. It took him three years, and cost him 80,000 men. The Indian Army is better than Ibrahim's, and will do it quicker and cheaper.

TEL

I offered at Christmas 1918 to do it with ten tanks!"

54. Toynbee, *Acquaintances*, p. 184.

55. Lawrence to Charlotte Shaw, December 11, 1928, BM Add MSS, 45904.

56. Essay by Wavell, *Friends*, p. 148. Lawrence found time in Cairo to send a check for £10 to A. C. Frederick J. Daw, who had helped him after the crash in Rome. The check was accompanied by a note: "Will you buy yourself some trifle to remind you of our rather rough landing at Rome? I was not at all comfortable hanging up in the wreck, and felt very grateful to you for digging me out —" (Lawrence to Daw, July 5, 1919, Bod Res MSS, b55).

57. Woodward and Butler, IV, 314.

58. Curzon to Balfour, July 17, 1919, ibid., from PRO/FO 608/92. Two more entries from Meinertzhagen's diary cover these weeks of July 1919, but they are of limited value as contemporary documents (he quotes, for example, from *Seven Pillars of Wisdom*, giving 1918 as the year of its writing). One note dated July 20, 1919, is filled with bits and pieces of the most personal revelations about Lawrence's parents' relationship, his illegitimacy, and the assault at Der'a, which it is highly doubtful Lawrence would have shared with Meinertzhagen (he wrote critically of him in *Seven Pillars of Wisdom*).

What does seem to be substantiated — both Lawrence and Meinertzhagen telling the same story independently — is that Lawrence, who had moved to the Arab delegation headquarters in Paris, had a room above Meinertzhagen's, where he continued to work on his book. Lawrence would lower the book by a string from his balcony ("Romeo and Juliet act") for Meinertzhagen to read (entry of July 17, 1919, *Middle East Diary*, p. 31; LHB, p. 129).

59. PRO/FO 608/92.

23. RETURN TO ENGLAND: LONDON AND ALL SOULS

1. I had my own "adventure with Lowell Thomas" as a result of my interest in Lawrence. It happened that the day we had arranged in New York to talk about my work (November 9, 1965) was the day of the power failure that blacked out a large section of the northeastern United States, including New York City. Mr. Thomas, not to be kept from giving his nightly broadcast, took me and members of his staff across the darkened city to an auxiliary studio on Tenth Avenue, which had its own electric power, where we helped him with the broadcast. After that, Mr. Thomas took me to dinner at the Marco Polo Club at the Waldorf Astoria (a private club for journalists, of which he was president) and we talked in the candle-lit dining room for several hours about his experiences with Lawrence and the Lawrence legend. The experiences must have evoked memories of this critical turning point in his career because the next night, in the broadcast in which he described the blackout, he reported: "A young doctor from Boston had flown down to talk to me about Lawrence of Arabia, a psychiatrist who plans to do a book on Lawrence, attempting to explain why he was the way he was — one of the most unusual men of modern times, who finally wound up as an enlisted man in the R.A.F. — searching for escape" (Lowell Thomas, November 10, 1965). Thomas made it clear to me that if he had done much to expand the public image of Lawrence, so too his experience in reporting Lawrence's campaigns "changed the whole direction of my own life — toward the world in general, films, writing and speaking."

2. Interview with Lowell Thomas, November 9, 1965. See also accounts in *Friends*, pp. 205–215, and Brian Gardner, *Allenby of Arabia*, pp. xi–xxvi, for Thomas's familiar story of his meetings with Allenby and Lawrence in Palestine and the Hijaz and his shows in America and England.

3. Interview with Lowell Thomas, November 9, 1965.

4. The British newspaper publisher, Lord Beaverbrook, launched a campaign in 1917 to bring home to Americans Britain's part in the war. Beaverbrook arranged for British lecturers to visit the United States and for American newspapermen to come to London and the Western Front. One of the latter was Lowell Thomas, who came to Europe looking for a dramatic story. When he could not find what he was looking for on the Western Front he appealed to John Buchan, who had played a major part in Beaverbrook's campaign. Buchan arranged for transport to Allenby's headquarters in the Middle East, where Thomas met Lawrence (Janet Adam Smith, *John Buchan*, p. 212).

5. Lawrence to Archibald Murray, January 10, 1920, Houghton Library, Harvard University.

6. Lawrence to H. R. Hadley, September 2, 1920, *Letters*, p. 319.

7. Lowell Thomas, *With Lawrence in Arabia*, p. ix.

8. Interview with Lowell Thomas, November 9, 1965; *Friends*, p. 209.

9. Percy Burton (as told to Lowell Thomas), *Adventures Among Immortals*, p. 207.

10. Interview with Lowell Thomas, November 9, 1965.

11. Lawrence to G. Wren Howard, December 17, 1933, *Letters*, p. 783.

12. Interview with Lowell Thomas, November 9, 1965.

13. Lawrence to Archibald Murray, January 10, 1920, Houghton Library, Harvard University.

14. *Letters*, p. 301.

15. Lawrence to Greenhill, March 20, 1920, Humanities Research Center, University of Texas.

16. Lawrence to Ralph Isham, August 10, 1927, Bod Res MSS, d55.

17. Dawson to Lawrence, January 31, 1919, Bod Res MSS, d60.

18. Dawson to "Mr. Warden," February 12, 1919, Bod Res MSS, b55.

19. Francis W. Pember, warden of All Souls, to Lawrence, June 18, 1919, Bod Res MSS, d60.

20. See especially discussions by Jukka Nevakivi, *Britain, France and the Arab Middle East*, pp. 148–196, and Zeine N. Zeine, *The Struggle for Arab Independence*, pp. 85–119, for analyses of the

shifts in the Allied policies toward Syria during the summer of 1919.

21. E. L. Woodward and R. Butler, eds., *Documents on British Foreign Policy, 1918–1939*, Ser. 1, IV, 289–292, 311–313.

22. H. C. Howard, *The King-Crane Commission*, p. 78.

23. Woodward and Butler, IV, 340–349.

24. Memorandum by Pierce Joyce, July 1919, in Joyce's "Akaba" Papers, King's College, London.

25. Interview with Arnold Lawrence, March 16, 1965.

26. *Letters*, p. 280.

27. *The Times*, September 11, 1919, in *Letters*, pp. 281–282; reprinted in Stanley and Rodelle Weintraub, *The Evolution of a Revolt*, pp. 63–65.

28. *Letters*, p. 284.

29. *The Times*, September 11, 1919.

30. See discussions in Zeine, *The Struggle*, pp. 107–111; Nevakivi, pp. 186–194; and *Letters*, pp. 283–285, for the negotiations that led to this agreement and its terms.

31. Letter of September 3, 1919, in Woodward and Butler, IV, 370–371. The following are some excerpts from the Foreign Office files of September 11 (PRO/FO 371/4182), the day Lawrence's letter was published by *The Times*.

"It is most emphatically not the case, as Col. Lawrence implies, that the area known as O.E.T.A. [Occupied Enemy Territory Administration] (Dasmascus-Aleppo) was liberated by the 'military action' of the Arabs. Although the Arabs were allowed to make a spectacular try into these places, their fall was the direct result of General Allenby's advance."

*   *   *

"Colonel Lawrence's letter is a carefully calculated indiscretion, written with the object of presenting the Arab case, and of guarding against the risk of the whole subject being discussed purely from the Franco-British point-of-view. He hits us as hard as the French, and if the letter had been written by an Arab, no possible exception could be taken to it. It is quite clear that, contrary to the opinion expressed in the Times leader [the accompanying editorial], his motive is solely to justify himself in the eyes of the people who helped to overthrow the Turks through his influence, and as a result of the confidence placed in him personally. And his attitude is quite understandable. But it is perhaps open to question whether, as an employee of the F.O. [actually Lawrence had been demobilized by September 1], his action is justifiable."

*   *   *

"From the official point of view Col. Lawrence's publication of this letter is quite unpardonable. His claim to be a freelance is definitely disposed by Mr. Balfour's insistence that he is an official member of the Delegation in Paris. [The reference here is to a dispatch from Lord Balfour to Curzon sent in August about the time Lawrence was returning to England. It stated that "Lawrence could still be regarded as technical advisor to this Delegation as his services here are likely to be required when the question of Syria comes to be discussed with the French and possibly with Feisal on the latter's return to Paris" (Woodward and Butler, IV, 315).]

*   *   *

"But from the practical point-of-view I believe his 'indiscretion' may be productive of good. It remains to be seen how the French Govt. and the French Press take it. If they accept Col. Lawrence's statement that he is a free-lance and has access to these documents through Faisal [Lawrence did not actually say that he obtained the documents "through" Faisal. What he wrote was, "When on Prince Faisal's staff I had access to the documents in question"] all may be well, but if they realize his official position and imagine that he has been put up to publishing his letter by H.M.G. there may be a row. Faisal, for instance, has, so far as we know, never been given a copy of the Sykes-Picot Agreement and Lawrence's claim that he had access to it through him is obviously untrue. The truth is far more likely to have been the other way about."

32. Zeine, *The Struggle*, pp. 108–109, and Lloyd George, *Memoirs*, II, 699.

33. Zeine, *The Struggle*, pp. 112–114. According to Zeine (p. 287), the originals of Faisal's letter are published in Arabic in Hafiz Wahbah, *Jazirat al-'Arab fi al-Qarn al-'Ishrin* (Cairo, 1935).

34. *Letters*, pp. 288–293.

35. PRO/FO 371/4183, with a date of late September 1919.

36. Lawrence to Curzon, September 27, 1919, *Letters*, p. 292.

37. Ibid., p. 291.

38. Bodleian Library; the complete letter is quoted in *Secret Lives*, pp. 119–120 and 129–130.

39. *Letters*, pp. 283–287.

40. Zeine, *The Struggle*, p. 119.

41. Letter of October 8, 1919, *Letters to TEL*, p. 122.

42. Lawrence to F. N. Doubleday, August 25, 1927, Bod Res MSS, d52.

43. "History of Seven Pillars," reprinted in *Texas Quarterly* 5 (Autumn 1962); the original is in Humanities Research Center, University of Texas.

44. Elizabeth Burgoyne, *Gertrude Bell*, II, 108–111.

45. D. G. Hogarth, "Lawrence of Arabia: The Story of His Book," *The Times*, December 13, 1926.

46. Lawrence to Charlotte Shaw, June 11, 1926, BM Add MSS, 45903. The diary is now in the British Museum.

47. Lawrence to Miss Doughty, November 3, 1919, shown to me through the courtesy of Arnold Lawrence.

48. Doughty to Lawrence, November 4, 1919, *Letters to TEL*, pp. 38–39.

49. Lawrence to Doughty, November 25, 1919, *Letters to TEL*, p. 296.

50. Lawrence to Frederic Manning, May 15, 1930, *Letters*, p. 693.

51. LHB, p. 145; also *Letters*, p. 693.

52. LHB, p. 145; Joyce Knowles to Theodora Duncan, November 29, 1964, in a California private collection.

53. LHB, p. 145; *Letters to TEL*, p. 39.

54. *Oriental Assembly*, p. 139.

55. Notes in the manuscript of *Seven Pillars of Wisdom*, Bodleian Library, Oxford; RGB, p. 51; *Seven Pillars* (1926 edn.), p. 21.

56. Robert Graves, *Goodbye to All That*, p. 300.

57. Lawrence to Richards, February 27, 1920, *Letters*, p. 300.

58. Lawrence to Newcombe, February 16, 1920, *Letters*, p. 299.

59. Lawrence to Pound, late April 1920, Bod Res MSS, c52.

60. *Friends*, p. 249. The reference to "airmen's clothes" concerns the fact that Lawrence continued to work on the text of *Seven Pillars* after he had joined the RAF in August 1922.

61. Lawrence to Frederick Manning, May 15, 1930, *Letters*, pp. 691–692.

62. Robert Graves, *Lawrence and the Arabs*, p. 406; LHB, p. 45. See also *Seven Pillars*, p. 21, where Lawrence states that in writing the second version he did "many thousand words at a time, in long sittings."

63. *Seven Pillars*, p. 21.

64. *Letters*, p. 300.

65. *Seven Pillars*, p. 21.

66. Lawrence to Murray, January 10, 1920, Houghton Library, Harvard University.

67. LHB, p. 146.

68. F. N. Doubleday, "The Strange Character of Colonel T. E. Lawrence," in *A Few Indiscreet Recollections*, p. 83.

69. Interview with Dermot Morrah, December 11, 1965.

70. Manuscript of *Seven Pillars of Wisdom*, Bodleian Library, Oxford.

71. Lawrence to Doubleday, July 22, 1920, Bod Res MSS, d52.

72. *Letters*, p. 318.

73. Doubleday to Lawrence, October 7, 1920, Bod Res MSS, d60.

74. *Letters*, pp. 304–306.

75. RGB, p. 5. Lawrence came to know Augustus John in Paris. According to John, Lawrence sat frequently for him there and later in England; he enjoyed being painted "and always seemed tickled by the results" (*Chiaroscuro*, p. 238). A friendship developed and Lawrence wrote comments about John's paintings which the artist found amusing, although he often did not agree with them. Once Lawrence wrote: "A friend of mine went to the Alpine Club [where John had a show] and said my larger one was a conscious effort by you to show how long contact with camels had affected my face! But I explained that it wasn't my face which had been in contact with camels" (*Chiaroscuro*, p. 246, from a letter, undated, but of 1920). Christine Longford, who settled later in County Westmeath near the Chapman estate, once spied Lawrence staring long and fixedly at John's portrait of him at the Alpine Club Gallery. Friends came in, and Lawrence would converse with them, but from time to time gazed back over his shoulder, as if he were checking to see that the painting was still there (interview with Christine Longford, March 18, 1965).

76. *Minorities*, p. 40; RGB, p. 21.

The anthology was not published until
1971. Jeremy M. Wilson was the editor.

77. Lawrence to Charlotte Shaw, November 17, 1927, BM Add MSS, 45903;
Minorities, p. 18.

78. Interview with Dermot Morrah,
December 11, 1965.

79. *Friends*, pp. 295 and 298. Morrah
also said that Lawrence rarely ate in the
common room, choosing instead to "cook
up an ungodly scruffy dish of rice on a
chafing dish in his room."

80. Ibid., p. 250.

81. Ibid., p. 294.

82. Interview with Arnold Lawrence,
March 16, 1965.

83. Letter of March 20, 1920, addressee unknown, in a private collection
in California.

84. Excerpt of a letter of February 27,
1920, addressee unknown, printed in a
1951 auction catalogue; the catalogue is
in a private collection in California.

85. *Letters*, pp. 298–299.

86. Interview with Elsie Newcombe,
August 27, 1964.

87. Lawrence to Greenhill, March 20,
1920, Humanities Research Center, University of Texas.

88. Lawrence to Frederick C. Stern,
May 14, 1920, in a California private collection.

89. See accounts by Zeine N. Zeine,
The Struggle for Arab Independence, pp.
151–188; George Antonius, *The Arab
Awakening*, pp. 302–309; and Jukka
Nevakivi, *Britain, France and the Middle
East*, pp. 216–220.

90. P. Guy to Lawrence, March 19,
1920, Bod Res MSS, d60.

91. "Creation of a New Department
for Middle Eastern Administration," document in the Middle East Library, St.
Antony's College, Oxford.

92. Lawrence to Philby, May 21, 1920,
St. Antony's College Library.

93. It was probably at about this time
that Hogarth wrote the following perceptive portrait of his friend: "He is not
so young as he looks and he is hardly
anything that he is popularly supposed
to be — not Daredevil for example, nor
Knight-Errant nor Visionary nor Romantick. The things he wants not to be are
quite numerous; but things he could be,
if he wanted, are more numerous still.
He is not fond of being anything, and
official categories do not fit him. He can
do most things and does some; but to

expect him to do a particular thing is
rash. Besides being anti-official, he dislikes fighting and Arab clothes, Arab
ways, and social functions, civilized or
uncivilized. He takes a good deal of
trouble about all things but quite a great
deal about repelling the people whom he
attracts, including all sorts and conditions of men and some sorts and conditions of women; but he is beginning
to be discouraged by consistent failure,
which now and then he does not regret.
He has as much interest as faith in himself: but those that share the last are
not asked to share the first. He makes
fun of others or kings of them, but if
anyone tries to make either one or the
other of him he runs away. Pushing (not
himself) he finds more congenial than
leading and he loves to push the unsuspecting body: but if it does not get on
as fast as he thinks it should he pushes
it into the gutter and steps to the front.
What he thinks is his Law. To think
as fast or as far as he thinks is not easy,
and still less easy is it to follow up with
such swift action. He can be as persuasive as positive; and the tale of those
he has hocussed into doing something
they never meant to do and are not
aware that they are doing, is long. It is
better to be his partner than his opponent, for when he is not bluffing, he
has a way of holding the aces: and he
can be ruthless, caring little what eggs
he breaks to make his omelettes and ignoring responsibility either for the shells
or for the disgestion of the mess. Altogether a force felt by many but not yet
fully gauged either by others or by himself. He should go far; but it may be in
driving lonely furrows where at present
few expect him to plow" ("Thomas Edward Lawrence," in William Rothenstein, *Twenty-four Portraits*, text opposite the portrait of Lawrence).

94. *Daily Express*, May 28, 1920; reprinted in Weintraub and Weintraub,
Evolution, pp. 66–69.

95. *Daily Express*, May 29, 1920; reprinted in Weintraub and Weintraub,
Evolution, pp. 70–71.

96. *Sunday Times*, May 30, 1920; reprinted in Weintraub and Weintraub,
Evolution, pp. 76–77.

97. John to Lawrence, "Thursday,
1920," *Letters to TEL*, p. 118.

98. P. W. Ireland, *Iraq*, p. 239.

99. Ibid., pp. 239–265; George Kirk,

A *Short History of the Middle East*, pp.
141–143.
100. Quoted in Ireland, p. 263.
101. *The Times*, July 22, 1920; *The
Observer*, August 8, 1920; *Sunday Times*,
August 22, 1920. All three articles were
published in *Letters*, pp. 306–317, and
reprinted in Weintraub and Weintraub,
Evolution, pp. 78–80, 92–99.
102. *Letters*, p. 314.
103. Ibid., p. 308.
104. Ibid., p. 312.
105. Ibid., pp. 315–317.
106. *Letters to TEL*, p. 12.
107. Burgoyne, *Gertrude Bell*, II, 162–
163.
108. Ibid., II, 164–165.
109. *Letters to TEL*, p. 15. Lawrence
visited Blunt, who was eighty then, at
his home in Sussex in the summer of
1920 and has left this impression of the
visit: "An Arab mare [Blunt bred Arabian
horses] drew Blunt's visitors deep within
a Sussex wood to his quarried house,
stone-flagged and hung with Morris
tapestries. There in a great chair he sat,
prepared for me like a careless work of
art in well-worn Arab robes, his chiselled
face framed in silvered, curling hair.
Doughty's voice was a caress, his nature
sweetness. Blunt was a fire yet flickering
over the ashes of old fury" (preface to
Bertram Thomas, *Arabia Felix*, p. xvii).
110. *Letters to TEL*, p. 124.
111. Lawrence to Robert Cunning-
hame-Graham (addressed "Dear Don
Roberto"), August 10, 1920, in a California private collection.
112. Lawrence to Charlotte Shaw, October 18, 1927, BM Add MSS, 45903.
113. *Oriental Assembly*, pp. 103–134.
The piece appeared in the October
issue.
114. Ibid., p. 117.
115. *Letters to TEL*, p. 194.
116. LHB, p. 145.
117. Charles Doughty, *Travels in
Arabia Deserta*, p. 18.
118. Ibid., pp. 24–25.
119. In his preface Doughty paid a
tribute to his friend in his archaic style:
"These volumes, published originally by
the Cambridge University Press, have
been some time out of print. A re-print
has been called for; and is reproduced
thus, at the suggestion chiefly of my
distinguished friend, Colonel T. E. Lawrence, leader with Feysal, Meccan Prince,
of the nomad tribesmen; whom they, as

might none other at that time marching
from Jidda, the port of Mecca, were able
(composing, as they went, the tribes'
long-standing blood feuds and old enmities), to unite with them in Victorious
arms, against the corrupt Turkish sovereignty in those parts; and who greatly
thus serving his Country's cause and her
Allies, from the Eastward, amidst the
Great War; has in that imperishable
enterprise, traversed the same wide region of Desert Arabia" (*Arabian Deserta*,
p. 33).
120. See *Arabian Days* by Philby
(who was serving then in Baghdad) for
a detailed account of these months in
Iraq (pp. 186–195).
121. Lawrence to the *Sunday Times*,
August 22, 1920, *Letters*, p. 315; Philip
Graves, *The Life of Sir Percy Cox*,
p. 275.
122. *Friends*, p. 263.
123. *Friends*, pp. 264–265. It is interesting to compare Kennington's verbal
portrait of Lawrence with that of another sculptor, Kathleen Scott (later Lady
Kennet). During 1921 Lawrence sat for
a statuette, which she cast in pewter and
terra-cotta. She wrote of the figure: "In
sitting for the portrait . . . he submitted
himself, consciously for judgment; and
the statuette shows first of all with what
completeness he could assume an oriental immobility. Yet it brings to light
two incongruities. One is in the counte-
nance, where the actor lets himself be
seen, as it were, commenting on his own
make-up. The duality of the personage
is emphasized, as when a mask is lifted.
Again, those strong feet are not an east-
erner's. They indicate the extraordinary
physical vigour which the small slender
body did not otherwise suggest . . . for
so strong a leadership, infinite patience
was needed. If the statuette expresses
one thing more than another, it is the
power in a swift creature to wait" (Kathleen Scott [Lady Kennet], *Homage*, text
facing photograph of the statuette).

24. LAWRENCE AND CHURCHILL

1. Lawrence to Buxton, February 16,
1927, Jesus College Library, Oxford;
RGB, p. 54.
2. *Letters*, p. 324.
3. *Friends*, pp. 263–264.
4. LHB, p. 143.
5. *Letters*, p. 324.

6. *Friends,* p. 197; Winston Churchill, *Great Contemporaries,* p. 159.

7. Churchill, p. 260.

8. RGB, p. 113.

9. LHB, p. 144.

10. Discussions in Samuel Hoare, *Empire of the Air,* pp. 46–48.

11. See discussions in *Secret Lives,* pp. 138–140.

12. *Letters,* p. 302. But in 1934 Lawrence claimed that the concept of RAF control had grown out of his own experience during the desert campaigns. "The war showed me," he wrote on Liddell Hart's typescript, "that a combination of armoured cars and aircraft could rule the desert: but that they must be under non-army control, and without infantry support. You rightly trace the origin of the R.A.F. control in Irak, Aden and Palestine to this experience. As soon as I was able to have my own way in the Middle East [this is confusing, for in March and April 1920, when Lawrence was first discussing the scheme with Trenchard, he did not yet by any means have his "own way" in the Middle East] I approached Trenchard on the point, converted Winston easily [actually Churchill had invited Trenchard *before* his meetings with Lawrence to prepare a scheme of RAF control — see *Secret Lives,* pp. 138–139], persuaded the cabinet swiftly into approving (against the wiles of Henry Wilson [of the India Office]) — and it has worked very well." In this passage Lawrence has credited himself with the principal role in conceiving and masterminding a valuable and successful plan that he had an important role in developing, but which appears to have been a collaborative effort of Churchill, Trenchard and himself.

13. PRO/CAB 27/24; *Letters,* p. 270.

14. Memorandum of April 22, 1919, PRO/FO 608/92.

15. Arnold Wilson, *Loyalties: Mesopotamia,* II, 30.

16. *The Times,* August 11, 1920; published in Stanley and Roselle Weintraub, *The Evolution of a Revolt,* p. 91.

17. P. W. Ireland, *Iraq: A Study in Political Developments,* p. 309.

18. Lord Winterton, *Orders of the Day,* pp. 101–102.

19. *Friends,* p. 230.

20. Aaron Klieman's monograph *Foundations of British Policy in the Arab World: The Cairo Conference of 1921* (1970) makes use of Public Record Office documents to examine the historical place of the Cairo Conference, and the events leading up to and following it. It is an essential source for the study of this period of British relations in the Middle East. Chapters XXI and XXII of Philip Graves's *The Life of Sir Percy Cox* contain an objective and useful account of the Cairo Conference and the events leading to the crowning of Faisal as king of Iraq on August 23, 1921. Philby, who was a personal advisor and friend to the murderous Sayyid Talib, minister of the interior in the Provisional Government in Baghdad, opposed Faisal's candidacy, favored a republic, believed in the assurances Cox had given him that Faisal's kingship would not be imposed on Iraq, and resigned his position in June 1921 over a disagreement with Cox regarding his (Philby's) role in Faisal's reception and the "rigging" of his election (*Arabian Days,* p. 204). Philby's colorful account of these events in his autobiography must be read with these facts in mind. Although he lost out in the struggle with Cox, Gertrude Bell, Lawrence and others who backed the candidacy of Faisal, Philby never questioned that Lawrence was "an uncompromising champion of Arab independence," but he saw Lawrence as "trammelled by the obsession that the future of Arabia must be worked out under the shadow of Sharifian Hegemony" (*Arabian Days,* p. 208; see also Churchill, *Great Contemporaries,* pp. 159–160, and Ireland, pp. 315–316).

21. *Letters,* p. 325.

22. *Home Letters,* pp. 352–353.

23. W. H. Thompson, *Assignment Churchill* (1955).

24. Ibid., p. 29.

25. Ibid., p. 30.

26. Ibid., p. 31.

27. Philip Graves, *The Life of Sir Percy Cox,* pp. 279–280.

28. Ibid., p. 281.

29. Lawrence to Charlotte Shaw, October 13, 1927, BM Add MSS, 45903.

30. See discussions by P. Graves, *Cox,* pp. 287–304; Ireland, pp. 319–337; Elie Kedourie, *England and the Middle East,* pp. 208–214; *Secret Lives,* pp. 141–142; Philby, *Arabian Days,* pp. 186–205; and Bell, *Letters of Gertrude Bell.*

31. *Parliamentary Debates,* quoted in Ireland, p. 326.

32. P. Graves, *Cox,* p. 296.

33. Ibid., p. 301.

34. Ireland, p. 336.

35. Faisal to Lawrence, undated (probably November 1921), British Museum (copy in English).

36. Ibid.

37. Lawrence to Charlotte Shaw, October 18, 1927, BM Add MSS, 45903.

38. F. G. Peake, *A History and Tribes of Jordan,* p. 105.

39. Abdullah, *Memoirs,* p. 200.

40. *Secret Lives,* pp. 143–146; Ireland, pp. 310–311; LHB, p. 131.

41. Abdullah, pp. 203–204.

42. Ireland, p. 310.

43. *Home Letters,* p. 353.

44. *Friends,* p. 267.

45. Herbert Samuel, *Memoirs,* p. 174.

46. Klieman, *Foundations,* pp. 152–153, 210–213; Lawrence to Graves, May 21, 1921, RGB, p. 13.

47. Letter of May 21, 1921, RGB, p. 14. The articles appeared in *World's Work* (July–October 1921) and are reprinted in Weintraub and Weintraub, pp. 120–171.

48. Lawrence to Graves, May 21, 1921, RGB, p. 15.

49. Interview with Arnold Lawrence, July 21, 1968.

50. Lawrence to "Looker-on," August 11, 1927, Bod Res MSS, d43.

51. *Friends,* pp. 373–374.

52. Doughty to Lawrence, June 14, 1921, *Letters to TEL,* p. 44.

53. PRO/FO 686/93.

54. *Secret Lives,* p. 148.

55. Lawrence to Curzon, August 4, 1921, PRO/FO 686/93.

56. Lawrence to Kennington, August 25, 1921, Bod Res MSS, b56; *Oriental Assembly,* pp. 151–154.

57. From the introduction to the catalogue of drawings.

58. The Lawrence collection in Houghton Library, Harvard University, contains Lawrence's Colonial Office Time Account and his Travelling Allowances Account for the period July 8–December 20, 1921, which makes it possible to trace accurately on a daily basis his movements during this five-month period.

59. Lawrence, Jidda, to Prodrome, London, September 7, 1921, PRO/FO 686/93.

60. Ibid. Faisal, now king of Iraq, was evidently sympathetic to Lawrence's struggles with his father and wrote to him on October 6, 1921: "I am extremely sorry for the obstacles which I see you met in this your last journey to Jeddah, but I know well that you are yourself and that the people who sent you belong to a nation which is patient in the face of obstacles which it meets especially when they result from a friend." A copy of the letter is in the British Musum.

61. LHB, p. 159.

62. Lawrence, Jidda, to Prodrome, London, September 22, 1921, PRO/FO 686/93.

63. Uriel Dann, "T. E. Lawrence in Amman, 1921" (report of a conversation with Kirkbride), paper read to the 28th International Congress of Orientalists, Canberra, Australia, January 11, 1971.

64. Klieman, pp. 221–222.

65. Ibid., p. 219.

66. *Letters,* p. 334.

67. Klieman, p. 224.

68. C. S. Jarvis, *Arab Command: The Biography of Lieutenant Colonel F. G. Peake Pasha,* pp. 84–85.

69. Ibid., p. 84.

70. "Colonel Lawrence's Report of Trans-Jordan, October 24, 1921," Bod Res MSS, d230; *Letters,* p. 335.

71. Ibid.

72. Dann, "T. E. Lawrence in Amman"; Jarvis, p. 84; Philby, *Forty Years in the Wilderness,* pp. 100–101.

73. Lawrence to Newcombe, November 8, 1921, *Letters,* p. 336.

74. Philby, *Forty Years,* pp. 92–93.

75. Abdullah, pp. 225–226.

76. Philby, diary entry of November 29, 1921, *Forty Years,* p. 97; the original diary is in St. Antony's College, Oxford.

77. Ibid., p. 107.

78. Ibid., p. 97; Dann, "T. E. Lawrence in Amman."

79. Colonial Office Time Account, Houghton Library, Harvard University; Philby, *Forty Years,* p. 108.

80. Philby, *Forty Years,* p. 108.

81. RGB, p. 15.

82. Notes for a TV interview on the Jack Paar Show, recorded September 1963 and shown in the U.S. on January 24, 1964, Bod Res MSS, b56.

83. LHB, pp. 73, 159.

84. Personal communication, Philip Townshend Somerville, November 8, 1973.

85. Lawrence to Isham, August 10, 1927, Bod Res MSS, d55.

86. RGB, pp. 16, 17.

87. Letter of March 3, 1922; made available through the courtesy of Arnold Lawrence.

88. *Letters*, p. 338.

89. *Letters to TEL*, p. 45.

90. Ibid., p. 47; Viola Meynell, ed., *Friends of a Lifetime: Letters to Sydney Carlyle Cockerell*, p. 247.

91. Notes in the manuscript of *Seven Pillars of Wisdom*.

92. *Friends*, p. 273.

93. Lawrence to Paul Nash, August 3, 1922, in a California private collection.

94. Quoted in LHB, p. 129.

95. Lawrence to Shuckburgh, July 4, 1922, *Letters*, p. 344.

96. A. Boyle, *Trenchard*, p. 429.

97. Trenchard to Lawrence, August 20, 1922, *Letters to TEL*, p. 195.

98. *Letters*, p. 424.

99. *Friends*, p. 593.

100. Speech of May 23, 1939, quoted in *The Jewish National Home in Palestine*, p. 474.

101. See the discussion of an Arab view by Antonius, *Awakening*, pp. 319–324.

102. Zeine, *The Struggle*, p. 36.

103. *Letters*, p. 670.

104. *Letters to TEL*, p. 12.

105. Lawrence to Trenchard, June 30, 1927, *Letters*, p. 525.

106. Lawrence to Captain Snagge, June 29, 1927, Bod Res MSS, d44.

107. *Seven Pillars*, p. 276; *Letters*, pp. 345–346.

108. Lawrence to "Looker-on," August 11, 1927, Bod Res MSS, d43.

109. Lawrence to Charlotte Shaw, October 18, 1927, BM Add MSS, 45903; also *Letters*, p. 671.

110. *Letters*, p. 853.

111. Draft preface to an abridgment of *Seven Pillars of Wisdom*, November 18, 1922; *Letters*, pp. 345–346.

112. Lawrence to Captain Snagge, June 29, 1927, Bod Res MSS, d44.

113. Lawrence to "Looker-on," August 11, 1927, Bod Res MSS, d43.

114. Lawrence to Snagge, June 29, 1927, Bod Res MSS, d44.

115. Ibid.; confirmed by his hut neighbor at Farnborough, A. E. Chambers, in interviews in 1965.

116. *Friends*, p. 593.

117. Ibid.

25. THE SERVICE YEARS: AN OVERVIEW

1. Air Ministry personnel file, May 22, 1935, Bod Res MSS, d48.

2. Letter of August 6, 1934, *Letters*, p. 813.

3. *The Mint* is a basic source for Lawrence's two months at the RAF training station at Uxbridge. Stanley Weintraub's *Private Shaw and Public Shaw* contains valuable information about Lawrence during his years in the ranks, and Claire Sydney Smith's *The Golden Reign* is indispensable for the period after Lawrence's return from India in 1929. Jeremy Wilson's introductory biographical essay accompanying the publication of Lawrence's private anthology of poetry, *Minorities*, provides additional insights.

4. Lawrence to Baker, November 6, 1928, Bod Res MSS, d49.

5. Lawrence to a pilot who had flown with him to Egypt in 1919, April 17, 1931, *Letters*, p. 719.

6. Arnold Lawrence to the author, October 8, 1973.

7. Andrew Boyle, *Trenchard*, p. 384.

8. Ibid., p. 427; quoted also in *Secret Lives*, pp. 166–167.

9. LHB, p. 73.

10. Ibid.

11. Lawrence to Allanson, January 18, 1927, in a California private collection.

12. Lawrence to H. G. Andrews, March 15, 1934, Bod Res MSS, d43.

13. Lawrence to H. S. Ede, June 30, 1928, *Letters*, p. 615.

14. RGB, p. 23.

15. Lawrence to E. M. Forster, February 20, 1924, *Letters*, pp. 456–457.

16. Lawrence to Ernest Dowson, fall of 1924, Bod Res MSS, d52.

17. Lawrence to Charlotte Shaw, September 28, 1925, BM Add MSS, 45903.

18. Lawrence to Edward Garnett, September 22, 1927, *Letters*, p. 540.

19. Lawrence to Ralph Isham, November 22, 1927, ibid., p. 546.

20. Lawrence to George Bernard Shaw, December 20, 1923, ibid., p. 447.

21. Lawrence to G.B.S., July 19, 1928, ibid., p. 618.

22. RGB, pp. 169–170; also in *Letters*, p. 759.

23. *Letters*, p. 559.

24. Lawrence to Charlotte Shaw, June 17, 1926, BM Add MSS, 45903.

25. Interview with A. E. Chambers, July 23, 1968.

26. Lawrence to Charlotte Shaw, August 31, 1924, BM Add MSS, 45903.
27. *Friends*, p. 244.
28. *Letters*, p. 554.
29. Ibid., p. 594.
30. Lawrence to Charlotte Shaw, January 9, 1932, BM Add MSS, 45903.
31. Lawrence to Ernest Thurtle, July 29, 1929, *Letters*, p. 669.
32. Lawrence to Hugh Trenchard, December 21, 1928, Bod Res MSS, d46.
33. Lawrence to Herbert Baker, October 29, 1928, Bod Res MSS, d49.
34. Lawrence to Edward Garnett, April 23, 1928, *Letters*, p. 597.
35. Letter of May 2, 1930, ibid., pp. 689–690.
36. Lawrence to Trenchard, April 16, 1929, Bod Res MSS, d46.
37. Reginald Sims, "The Sayings and the Doings of T.E. as heard and experienced by the Sims family" (1937); the manuscript is in a private collection.
38. Lawrence to Trenchard, June 20, 1929, Bod Res MSS, d46.
39. LHB, p. 30; also quoted in *Letters*, p. 665.
40. "In Pocket Diary for 1933," Bod Res MSS, d230; Arnold Lawrence showed me the original diary in 1965.
41. Forster to Lawrence, July 5, 1928, Bod Res MSS, d60.
42. *Letters to TEL*, p. 70.
43. Charlotte Shaw to Lawrence, December 31, 1922, quoted in full in Janet Dunbar, *Mrs. G.B.S.: A Portrait*, pp. 237–238, and in *Secret Lives*, pp. 248–249.
44. Charlotte Shaw to Lawrence, May 17, 1927, quoted in Dunbar, p. 251.
45. Lawrence to Charlotte Shaw, undated but June or July of 1928, BM Add MSS, 45904.
46. Blanche Patch, *Thirty Years with G.B.S.*, p. 85.
47. Lawrence to Charlotte Shaw, July 10, 1929, BM Add MSS, 45904.
48. *Letters*, p. 661.
49. *Friends*, p. 448.
50. Lawrence to Lord Wavell, July 23, 1929, Bod Res MSS, d59.
51. *Letters*, p. 760.
52. Letter of September 25, 1933, *Shaw-Ede: T. E. Lawrence's Letters to H. S. Ede, 1927–1935*, pp. 56–57.
53. David Garnett, *The Familiar Faces*, p. 109.
54. *Letters*, p. 725.
55. "Confession of Faith," 1933, Bod Res MSS, d230.

56. Lawrence to Graves, February 4, 1935, *Letters*, pp. 851–852.

26. ROSS: THE FIRST RAF ENLISTMENT

1. *Letters*, p. 353.
2. Trenchard to Oliver Swann, August 17, 1922, Bod Res MSS, d48.
3. Bod Res MSS, c52.
4. *Mint*, p. 19.
5. W. E. Johns, *Sunday Times*, April 8, 1951.
6. *Mint*, pp. 11–12; RAF medical record, copy made available to me through the courtesy of Arnold Lawrence.
7. *Sunday Times*, April 8, 1951; RAF medical record; *Mint*, p. 20. Lawrence's body was evidently well covered with scars of one sort or another. Mrs. Clare Sydney Smith, wife of Lawrence's commander at Mount Batten in 1929–1931, has written "Sydney [Wing Commander Sydney Smith, her husband] pointed out to me all the scars on Tes's [a pet name she used] fair skin. There was hardly a place on his body that wasn't marked in this way" (*The Golden Reign*), p. 102.
8. *Sunday Times*, April 8, 1951.
9. Lawrence to Swann, September 1, 1922, *Letters*, p. 364.
10. *Mint*, pp. 38–39.
11. Personal communication, March 24, 1974.
12. *Mint*, p. 73.
13. Ibid., p. 86.
14. Ibid., p. 107.
15. Ibid., p. 152.
16. Ibid., p. 154.
17. Ibid., p. 163.
18. Ibid., p. 159.
19. Ibid.
20. Ibid., p. 164.
21. Ibid., p. 163.
22. Lawrence to Group Captain Robinson, May 26, 1933, Humanities Research Center, University of Texas.
23. E. G. Metcalfe, "An Erk's Eye View of Lawrence," Manchester *Guardian*, February 17, 1955.
24. Ibid.
25. Ibid.
26. Ibid.
27. *Friends*, p. 275.
28. Lawrence to Edward Garnett, August 26, 1922, *Letters*, p. 360.
29. Paul Nash to Gordon Bottomley, September 12, 1922; quoted in Anthony Bertram, *Paul Nash*, p. 112.

30. Lawrence to Edward Garnett, September 7, 1922, *Letters*, p. 366.

31. Lawrence to Edward Garnett, October 23, 1922, ibid., p. 371.

32. Edward Garnett to Lawrence, September, 1922, *Letters to TEL*, p. 88.

33. The letters to Roberts are in a California private collection.

34. Lawrence to Edward Garnett, November 8, 1922, Humanities Research Center, University of Texas.

35. Lawrence to J. M. Keynes, September 18, 1922.

36. The note is in the Humanities Research Center, University of Texas.

37. Interview with A. E. Chambers, March 17, 1965; see also *Friends*, pp. 339–340.

38. "I'm awkward anyway at rifle drill," Lawrence wrote at the time to Swann (*Letters*, p. 377).

39. Unpublished notes of A. E. Chambers's furnished to the author in 1965.

40. Lawrence to F. L. Lucas, March 26, 1929, Bod Res MSS, d58.

41. Lawrence to Edward Garnett, November 12, 1922, *Letters*, p. 380.

42. Shaw to Lawrence, December 1, 1922, *Letters to TEL*, pp. 161–162.

43. Ibid., p. 163.

44. Janet Dunbar, *Mrs. G.B.S.*, p. 237.

45. Lawrence to Charlotte Shaw, January 8, 1923, BM Add MSS, 45903; quoted in Dunbar, p. 238.

46. *Letters*, pp. 393–397.

47. Lawrence to R. D. Blumenfeld, November 11, 1922, Bod Res MSS, d43.

48. Lawrence to William Roberts, October 27, 1922, in a California private collection.

49. Charles Findlay, "The Amazing AC2," *The Listener*, June 5, 1958, pp. 937–938.

50. Chambers's notes.

51. *Letters*, p. 398.

52. Findlay, "The Amazing AC2," p. 938.

53. *Letters*, p. 426; *Samuel Hoare, Empire of the Air*, p. 255.

54. Stanley Weintraub, *Private Shaw and Public Shaw*, pp. 12–17; *Letters*, p. 363.

55. Guilfoyle to Trenchard, December 16, 1922, Bod Res MSS, d48.

56. *Letters to TEL*, p. 166.

57. Chambers's notes.

58. George Bernard Shaw to Lawrence, December 17, 1922, *Letters to TEL*, p. 166.

59. R. D. Blumenfeld, editor of the *Daily Express* — one of the newspapers that revealed Lawrence's enlistment in the RAF — has taken upon himself some of the responsibility for giving away his secret. "He asked me to guard his secret," Blumenfeld wrote in his memoirs. "I got ill and was away for some months. In the interval someone in the office learned the story which could not of course be a secret long, and 'the beans were spilled' " (*R.D.B.'s Procession*, p. 116).

60. January 4, 1923, *Letters to TEL*, pp. 168–169.

61. *Letters*, p. 393.

62. Lawrence to Graves, January 18, 1923, RGB, p. 24.

27. THE YEARS IN THE TANKS

1. *Letters*, p. 425.

2. Lawrence to T. B. Marson, January 28, 1923, ibid., p. 395.

3. Leopold Amery to Lawrence, February 2, 1923, Bod Res MSS, c52.

4. Notes in the margin of George Bernard Shaw's appeal to the Prime Minister, May 31, 1923, Bod Res MSS, c52.

5. Lawrence to William Rothenstein, February 5, 1923, Bod Res MSS, c52.

6. Lawrence to William Roberts, February 7, 1923, in a California private collection.

7. Lawrence to B. E. Leeson, February 16, 1923, Bod Res MSS, d58.

8. See the discussion in Andrew Boyle, *Trenchard*, pp. 459–460.

9. Ibid., p. 460.

10. RGB, p. 53; the question of Lawrence's assumption of the name Shaw is discussed by Stanley and Roselle Weintraub, in *Private Shaw and Public Shaw*, pp. 31–35.

11. Lawrence to Lionel Curtis, March 19, 1923, *Letters*, p. 411.

12. Lawrence to R. M. Guy, March 30, 1923, Houghton Library, Harvard University.

13. Lawrence to Jonathan Cape, April 10, 1923, *Letters*, p. 408.

14. Lawrence to Edward Garnett, April 12, 1923, *Letters*, p. 409.

15. "A Sea Trip Essay" by Pvt. T. E. Shaw, April 18, 1923, Bod Res MSS, d230.

16. Lawrence to George Bernard Shaw,

May 3, 1923, and Shaw to Lawrence, May 13, 1923. Copies of these letters were made available to the author through the courtesy of Jeremy Wilson.

17. Lawrence to Lionel Curtis, May 14, 1923, *Letters*, pp. 415–417.

18. Lawrence to Curtis, May 3, 1923, pp. 417–419.

19. *Letters*, p. 446.

20. "I was able to understand his determination to make no money by the Seven Pillars, much as it could place within his grasp," Shaw wrote later. "This was not a refusal to coin his blood in drachmas; for he had shed none he could not spare. But the gesture led to a belief that he would not accept payment for his services on any terms.

"I knew better. He was quite willing as a baptized and enlisted soldier and servant to be pensioned as such by his country. I asked him how much would suffice. He replied, with a promptitude which shewed he had fully considered the matter, £300 a year.

"I went to Stanley Baldwin, then prime minister, and demanded £800. Baldwin, pipe in mouth, and always agreeable, approved of all I said, but feared that parliament might object. I, instructed in parliamentary procedure by Lord Olivier, explained how it could be done without raising any question. He very kindly left me under the impression that the pension would be granted.

"It never was. That was Baldwin's way, and the secret of his promotion. He could always be depended on to smoke amiably and do nothing." (Handwritten note by G.B.S. on the flyleaves of Charlotte Shaw's copy of *Seven Pillars* (subscribers' edition), Arents Collection, New York Public Library; quoted in part in Weintraub, *Private Shaw*, p. 62.)

21. Florence Hardy to Sydney Cockerell, April 11, 1924, in Viola Meynell, ed., *Friends of a Lifetime*, p. 311.

22. Lawrence to Graves, September 8, 1923, *Letters*, pp. 429–431; also RGB, p. 26.

23. Lawrence to David Hogarth, June 27, 1923, *Letters*, p. 426.

24. Lawrence to Curtis, June 27, 1923, ibid., pp. 419–420.

25. Ibid., p. 420.

26. *Friends*, pp. 361–365.

27. Ibid., pp. 277–278.

28. Alec Dixon to the author, June 25, 1967.

29. Alec Dixon, *Tinned Soldier*, pp. 295–296.

30. Ibid., p. 297.

31. *Friends*, p. 363.

32. Dixon, p. 294.

33. Ibid., p. 301.

34. Ibid., pp. 301–302.

35. *Friends*, p. 371.

36. Alec Dixon to the author, June 25, 1967.

37. Letter of December 19, 1923, *Home Letters*, p. 357.

38. *Friends*, p. 362.

39. Lawrence to Florence Hardy, August 15, 1923, *Letters*, p. 427.

40. Lawrence to D. G. Hogarth, August 23, 1923, *Letters*, p. 429.

41. Ibid.

42. Notes in a California private collection.

43. Lawrence to his mother, May 18, 1924, Bod Res MSS, c13.

44. *Letters*, p. 435.

45. Ibid., pp. 528, 594. Lawrence went to great lengths to preserve the peace and beauty of his cottage. In 1925 he pleaded with the chief engineer of the district to have removed some recently erected and ugly telephone poles, "festooned with wires," that blocked his view. When the engineer refused to act, Lawrence appealed successfully to the postmaster general of England and the poles and wires were taken down (Reginald Sims, "The Sayings and the Doings of T.E. as heard and experienced by the Sims family" (1937); the manuscript is in a private collection).

46. *Letters*, p. 654.

47. E. M. Forster, "Clouds Hill," *Listener* (September 1, 1938), pp. 426–427.

48. *Friends*, p. 375.

49. *Letters*, p. 436.

50. Forster, "Clouds Hill," p. 426. See p. 66 for a fuller discussion of the meaning of this motto for Lawrence.

51. *Letters*, p. 746.

52. *Letters to TEL*, p. 154.

53. Lawrence to Hogarth, December 9, 1923, Bod Res MSS, d55.

54. Lawrence to Shaw, December 13, 1923, Bod Res MSS, d44.

55. *Letters*, pp. 444–446.

56. Lawrence to Winterton, October 27, 1923, Bod Res MSS, d44.

57. Lawrence to Cockerell, December 25, 1923, in a California private collection.

58. Lawrence to Lionel Curtis, August 25, 1924, *Letters*, p. 465.

59. Apparently Lawrence had threatened to go AWOL or do something to get himself expelled from the Tank Corps, for Trenchard had written him on December 6, "you must not be a defaulter or you will get kicked out. Do not be an ass! If you start being a defaulter it will be impossible for me to help you or for you to help yourself" (*Letters to TEL*, December 6, 1923, pp. 197–198).

60. Lawrence to Guy, December 25, 1923, Houghton Library, Harvard University.

61. *Letters to TEL*, p. 172.

62. *Letters*, p. 452.

63. Ibid.

64. Lawrence to Forster, February 20, 1924, ibid., p. 455.

65. *Letters to TEL*, p. 64.

66. Lawrence to James Hanley, December 28, 1931, *Letters*, p. 738. For an analysis of Lawrence's literary relationship with E. M. Forster see Jeffrey Meyers's "E. M. Forster and T. E. Lawrence: A Friendship," *South Atlantic Quarterly* LXIX (Spring 1970): 205–216.

67. Lawrence to F. N. Doubleday, April 8, 1924, Bod Res MSS, d52.

68. Doubleday, "The Strange Character of T. E. Lawrence" (1928), Houghton Library, Harvard University.

69. The actual contract is in a California private collection, where I examined it.

70. William Matheson, chief of the Rare Book Division, Library of Congress, to the author, October 16, 1973.

71. George Doran, *Chronicles of Barabbas*, pp. 395–397.

72. Ibid., p. 397.

73. Lawrence to Doughty, April 30, 1924, *Letters*, p. 459. Three years later, Lawrence wrote to Hogarth: "I'm afraid *The Seven Pillars* was rather a bitter pill for C.M.D. to swallow. The tone of it must have shocked him. I did not send it, till he had twice written to me asking for it" (letter of May 19, 1927, *Letters*, p. 517).

74. Doughty to Lawrence, May 16, 1924, *Letters to TEL*, p. 54.

75. David Hogarth, *The Life of Charles Doughty*, p. 204.

76. Lawrence to Charlotte Shaw, February 8, 1926, BM Add MSS, 45903.

77. Lawrence to Hogarth, May 9, 1924, *Letters*, p. 460.

78. Michael S. Howard, *Jonathan Cape, Publisher*, pp. 86, 87.

79. Of Lawrence's letters to Buxton, more than ninety are in the library of Jesus College, Oxford.

80. Lawrence to his family, August 18, 1924, *Home Letters*, p. 359.

81. Lawrence to "Dear Sir," August 21, 1924; copy lent to the author by Jeremy Wilson.

82. In his letter Shaw gave teasing examples of properly punctuated passages: "Thus Luruns said nothing; but he thought the more. Luruns could not speak: he was drunk. Luruns, like Napoleon, was out of place and a failure as a subaltern; yet when he could exasperate his officers by being a faultless private he could behave himself as such. Luruns, like Napoleon, could see a hostile city not only as a military objective but as a stage for a coup de theatre: he was a born actor" (Shaw to Lawrence, October 7, 1924; a copy was lent the author by Jeremy Wilson).

83. Charlotte Shaw's copy of *Seven Pillars* is in the Arents Collection, New York Public Library.

84. Ibid.

85. Lawrence to Stirling, October 15, 1924.

86. Lawrence to Trenchard, February 6, 1925, Bod Res MSS, d46.

87. Lawrence to Buxton, May 16, 1925, Jesus College, Oxford.

88. *Letters*, p. 476.

89. Letter of June 1, 1925, Humanities Research Center, University of Texas.

90. Lawrence to Edward Garnett, June 13, 1925, *Letters*, p. 477.

91. Janet Adam Smith, *John Buchan*, p. 242.

92. *Letters*, p. 477.

93. Ibid., p. 485.

94. Boyle, *Trenchard*, p. 516.

95. Letter of July 5, 1925, *Letters*, p. 478.

28. CRANWELL

1. Lawrence to John Buchan, August 27, 1925, *Letters*, p. 483.

2. Lawrence to Marsh, November 21, 1925, Bod Res MSS, d58.

3. Lawrence to Charlotte Shaw, November 27, 1928, BM Add MSS, 45904.

4. *Mint*, p. 170.

5. Robert Graves, *Lawrence and the Arabs*, p. 429 (Sergeant Pugh to Graves).

6. *Mint*, p. 206.

7. Ibid., p. 171; Graves, *Lawrence and the Arabs*, p. 434.

8. Graves, *Lawrence and the Arabs*, pp. 428–429.

9. Ibid., p. 428.

10. Ibid., pp. 435–436.

11. Ibid.

12. Ibid., p. 434.

13. *Mint*, pp. 195–196.

14. Lawrence to Charlotte Shaw, September 28, 1925, BM Add MSS, 45903.

15. Ibid.

16. *Letters*, p. 487.

17. Lawrence to Charlotte Shaw, December 26, 1925, BM Add MSS, 45903.

18. Lawrence to Raymond Savage, December 30, 1925, Bod Res MSS, d59.

19. Lawrence to his mother, December 28, 1925, Bod Res MSS, c13.

20. Lawrence to Charlotte Shaw January 15, 1926, BM Add MSS, 45903.

21. Lawrence to Francis Rodd, January 28, 1926, *Letters*, p. 493.

22. Ibid.

23. Lawrence to Charlotte Shaw, February 22, 1926, BM Add MSS, 45903.

24. Lawrence to F. L. Lucas, March 14, 1926, Bod Res MSS, d58; see also *Seven Pillars*, p. 23.

25. Lawrence to Lucas, March 14, 1926, Bod Res MSS, d58.

26. Michael S. Howard, *Jonathan Cape, Publisher*, p. 91.

27. Lawrence to Charlotte Shaw, March 18, and April 6, 1926, BM Add MSS, 45903. This episode, described in detail to Robert Graves by Sergeant Pugh, who observed it at first hand, was typical of the stoically heroic conduct that characterized Lawrence all his life. After Lawrence had taken care of a pedestrian who was injured in the accident he got someone to start his Brough "and with his arm dangling and changing gear with his foot S. [Shaw] got his bus home and parked without a word to a soul of the pain he was suffering" (Graves, *Lawrence and the Arabs*, p. 431). Because the medical officer was away the arm could not be set until the next day. When he reported sick the next morning he told the medical officer

he had an impacted Colles fracture involving both bones of the wrist. At first the doctor did not believe him, but when he saw the X-ray films showing the fractures, he ordered Lawrence into the hospital for an operation. Lawrence refused both the hospitalization and the operation, had the wrist bound up by a doctor off the base and returned to work (Sims document, 1937, pp. 10–11). According to Sergeant Pugh this was the only time he ever saw a man refuse to go into the hospital with a broken arm.

28. *Letters*, p. 518.

29. Howard, p. 90.

30. Lawrence to Edward Garnett, September 22, 1927, *Letters*, p. 542. For a further discussion of these and other textual changes and differences among the various versions and editions of *Seven Pillars of Wisdom*, see the study of Jeffrey Meyers, *The Wounded Spirit: A Study of Seven Pillars of Wisdom*, especially Chap. 3, pp. 45–73.

31. Lawrence to David Garnett, April 6, 1926, *Letters*, p. 494.

32. Howard, p. 90.

33. Lawrence to Charlotte Shaw, June 17, 1926, BM Add MSS, 45903.

34. Lawrence to his mother, July 6, 1926, Bod Res MSS, c13.

35. Will dated August 28, 1926, Bod Res MSS, d230.

36. Lawrence to Mrs. Friedlow, October 14, 1926, Houghton Library, Harvard University.

37. Lawrence to Geoffrey Dawson, March 16, 1927, Bod Res MSS, b55.

38. Lawrence to Francis Rodd, December 3, 1926. Loaned to the author by Rodd.

39. Lawrence to Dick Knowles, December 3, 1926, in a California private collection.

40. Lawrence to Sergeant Pugh, December 16, 1926, Arts Catalogue, Bodleian Library.

41. "Leaves in the Wind," *Letters*, pp. 502–503.

42. Ibid., p. 612.

43. Interviews with Elsie Newcombe, March 18, 1965, and S. L. ("Jimmy") Newcombe, March 20, 1965.

29. INDIA

1. Lawrence to Charlotte Shaw, January 28, 1927, BM Add MSS, 45903.

2. *Friends*, pp. 415, 418.

3. *Friends*, pp. 401, 402; Lawrence to Trenchard, December 22, 1927, Bod Res MSS, d46.

4. *Friends*, p. 403.

5. Ibid., p. 405.

6. Ibid., p. 409.

7. Ibid., p. 417.

8. *Letters*, p. 505.

9. Lawrence to Fareedah el Akle, January 28, 1927.

10. Lawrence to Charlotte Shaw, August 28, 1928, BM Add MSS, 45904.

11. *Letters*, p. 504.

12. Lawrence to Captain Hollings, January 11, 1927, Bodleian Library, Arts Catalogue.

13. Lawrence to his mother, February 24, 1927, Bod Res MSS, c13.

14. Letter of January 11, 1927, Bod Res MSS, c13.

15. Lawrence to Robin Buxton, March 4, 1927, Jesus College, Oxford.

16. George Bernard Shaw, *The Spectator*, March 12, 1927.

17. Lawrence to Charlotte Shaw, April 14, 1927, BM Add MSS, 45903.

18. Letter to H. H. Banbury, April 20, 1927, *Letters*, p. 514.

19. Lawrence to Trenchard, June 30, 1927, Bod Res MSS, d46.

20. *Letters*, p. 412.

21. George Bernard Shaw to Cockerell, July 14, 1944, in Viola Meynell, ed., *The Best of Friends: Letters to Sydney Cockerell*, p. 123.

22. *Home Letters*, p. 368.

23. Lawrence to Hogarth, June 1, 1927, Bod Res MSS, d55.

24. Michael S. Howard, *Jonathan Cape, Publisher*.

25. Lawrence to Buxton, March 25, 1927, library of Jesus College, Oxford.

26. Lawrence to Alan Dawnay, April 14, 1927, Bod Res MSS, d43.

27. Lawrence to Charlotte Shaw, March 29, 1927, BM Add MSS, 45903.

28. Lawrence to Charlotte Shaw, May 12, 1927, BM Add MSS, 45903.

29. Lawrence to Fareedah el Akle, April 27, 1927.

30. Lawrence to his family, June 16, 1927, Bod Res MSS, c13, omitted from the printed letter, which is in *Home Letters*, pp. 366–367.

31. Ibid.

32. Howard, p. 96.

33. Lawrence to Dick Knowles, June 30, 1927, in a California private collection.

34. RGB, pp. 48–95.

35. Lawrence to Curtis, July 14, 1927, *Letters*, p. 530.

36. Lawrence to Buchan, June 20, 1927, Bod Res MSS, b55.

37. Lawrence to "Dear Hugh" (Trenchard), June 30, 1927, Bod Res MSS, d46.

38. Lawrence to Garnett, July 7, 1927, *Letters*, p. 526.

39. Lawrence to Charlotte Shaw, August 3, 1927, BM Add MSS, 45903.

40. Lawrence to Charlotte Shaw, August 12, 1927, BM Add MSS, 45903.

41. Ibid.

42. Letter of November 11, 1927, BM Add MSS, 45903.

43. Mrs. Hogarth to Lawrence, December 18, 1927, Bod Res MSS, d60.

44. Lawrence to Charlotte Shaw, November 17, 1927, BM Add MSS, 45903; quoted in *Minorities*, p. 19.

45. Lawrence to H. S. Ede, December 1, 1927, *Shaw-Ede: T. E. Lawrence's Letters to H. S. Ede, 1927–1935*, p. 12.

46. Lawrence to Charlotte Shaw, December 21, 1927, BM Add MSS, 45903.

47. Lawrence to Trenchard, December 22, 1927, Bod Res MSS, d46.

48. Lawrence to Edward Garnett, December 25, 1927, Bod Res MSS, d54.

49. Letter of December 24, 1927, RGB, p. 143.

50. *Letters*, p. 561.

51. Forster to Lawrence, December 16, 1927, Bod Res MSS, d60.

52. Lawrence to Charlotte Shaw, December 27, 1927, BM Add MSS, 45903.

53. Letter of August 1, 1927, *Letters*, p. 532.

54. Letter of November 12, 1928, *Shaw-Ede*, pp. 22–23. Wyndham Lewis has suggested that Lawrence's reading of Buddhist or other Eastern philosophies while living in the dusty barrenness of the Drigh Road barracks may have stimulated him to turn once again to his Uxbridge notes, in a further act of self-purging ("Perspectives of Lawrence," *Hudson Review* [Winter, 1956]). This seems far-fetched, though there is no evidence on the point.

55. *Mint*, p. 167.

56. Lawrence to Charlotte Shaw, January 2, 1928, BM Add MSS, 45916. Blanche Patch, secretary for many years to the Shaws, has provided additional details of the unexplained but rather characteristic mystery with which Lawrence surrounded the mailing of the manuscript of *The Mint*: "He posted it

to Charlotte direct, asking her, when G.B.S. and she had read it, to send it on, within ten days, to Edward Garnett, reader to Jonathan Cape the publisher, in a plain wrapper, and with no indication of who was forwarding it to him. By the same post he wrote to Edward Garnett announcing that the manuscript had gone 'by an official by-pass for safety', and asking him to let him know what he had to pay on the parcel 'if the first receiver does not put on stamps', which will indicate Lawrence's views upon the unreliability of womankind. Charlotte did keep the manuscript for a few days longer than his stipulated ten; but she played her part in the conspiratorial affair. She was in North Wales at the time, and the postmark might have given a clue to the sender, so she tied *The Mint* up in a plain parcel, with a second wrapping addressed to me in London, and I posted it on to Edward Garnett (correctly stamped), when I had got back from a holiday I was having" (*Thirty Years with G.B.S.*, p. 80).

57. Lawrence to Charlotte Shaw, March 20, 1928, BM Add MSS, 45903.

58. *Letters*, p. 579.

59. Lawrence to Trenchard, March 17, 1928, Bod Res MSS, d46; personal communication from Arnold Lawrence, March 24, 1974.

60. Letter of April 10, 1928, *Letters to TEL*, pp. 200–201.

61. Letter of April 12, 1928, ibid., pp. 174–175.

62. Letter of April 22, 1928, ibid., p. 97.

63. Letter of May 3, 1928, ibid., p. 99.

64. Lawrence to Trenchard, May 1, 1928, Bod Res MSS, d46.

65. Ibid.; this part of the letter was printed in *Letters*, pp. 598–599.

66. Letter of May 7, 1928, *Letters*, p. 604.

67. Lawrence to Edward Garnett, August 28, 1928, Bod Res MSS, d54.

68. Edward Garnett to Lawrence, May 3, 1928, *Letters to TEL*, p. 99.

69. Personal communication from Arnold Lawrence, March 24, 1974. At that time piracy would have been possible under U.S. copyright law.

70. *Letters to TEL*, p. 67.

71. Ibid., pp. 21–22.

72. R. P. Blackmur, "The Everlasting Effort: A Citation of T. E. Lawrence," in *The Expense of Greatness*, pp. 1–37.

73. *Letters*, pp. 564–565.

74. Florence Hardy to Lawrence, March 5, 1928, Bod Res MSS, d60.

75. From Introduction by Bruce Rogers to *Letters from T. E. Shaw to Bruce Rogers* (unpaged).

76. Lawrence to Isham, February 1, 1928, ibid.

77. Lawrence to Bruce Rogers, April 16, 1928, *Letters*, pp. 586–590.

78. Letter of April 26, 1928, *Home Letters*, p. 374.

79. Lawrence to Francis Yeats-Brown, May 1928, Bod Res MSS, d59.

80. Ibid.

81. Lawrence to Joyce, June 14, 1928, Bod Res MSS, d43; and to H. S. Ede, June 30, 1928, *Letters*, p. 615.

82. Lawrence to Trenchard, September 11, 1928, Bod Res MSS, d46.

83. *Letters*, p. 615.

84. Ibid., p. 625.

85. I. E. Brodie, "Lawrence Was My Orderly," *Naafi Review* (Summer 1963).

86. Ibid.

87. *Letters to TEL*, Trenchard to Lawrence, July 5, 1928, pp. 212–214.

88. Lawrence to Cape, July 10, 1928, Bod Res MSS, d50. Having promised Cape his next book, he offered *The Mint* to him but asked for a £1,000,000 advance in order to make sure that the book would be refused (*Letters*, p. 613).

89. Tomlinson to Lawrence, December 12, 1928, *Letters to TEL*, pp. 189–192.

90. Lawrence to H. S. Ede, August 30, 1928, *Shaw-Ede*, p. 18.

91. Lawrence to Baker, July 17, 1928, and November 6, 1928, Bod Res MSS, c52 and d54.

92. Lawrence to Charlotte Shaw, August 15, 1928, BM Add MSS, 45904.

93. Lawrence to Edward Garnett, August 8, 1928, Bod Res MSS, d54.

94. Lawrence to Alan Dawnay, December 25, 1928, Bod Res MSS, d43.

95. Lawrence to Charlotte Shaw, November 27, 1928, BM Add MSS, 45904.

96. Lawrence to Emery Walker, December 25, 1928, Bod Res MSS, d59.

97. Lawrence to Trenchard, December 27, 1928, Bod Res MSS, d46.

30. MOUNT BATTEN

1. *Friends*, p. 351.

2. *Empire News*, London, December 16, 1928; quoted in *Secret Lives*, p. 233.

3. See Clare Sydney Smith, *The Golden Reign,* pp. 20–24.

4. Lawrence to Trenchard, February 5, 1929, Bod Res MSS, d46.

5. Lawrence to F. N. Doubleday, April 1, 1929, Bod Res MSS, d52.

6. Lawrence to H. S. Ede, March 28, 1929, *Shaw-Ede,* p. 30.

7. *Friends,* p. 580.

8. Interview (taped) of Arabella Rivington with Tommy Jordan, former NCO at Mount Batten, March 1965.

9. Lawrence to Bruce Rogers, May 24 and December 12, 1929, *Letters from T. E. Shaw to Bruce Rogers* (unpaged).

10. *Letters,* p. 660.

11. *Letters,* p. 673; RGB, p. 164.

12. RGB, p. 165.

13. *Golden Reign,* p. 71.

14. Lawrence to Charlotte Shaw, late September 1929, BM Add MSS, 45904.

15. Letter of December 15, 1929, BM Add MSS, 45904.

16. Letter of November 23, 1929, BM Add MSS, 45904.

17. Lawrence to Brooks, December 30, 1929, *Letters,* p. 674.

18. Lawrence to Charlotte Shaw, December 5, 1930, BM Add MSS, 45904.

19. Lawrence to H. G. Hayter, January 8, 1930, Humanities Research Center, University of Texas.

20. Lawrence to Charlotte Shaw, January 4, 1930, BM Add MSS, 45904.

21. Letter of February 12, 1930, *Letters . . . to Bruce Rogers.*

22. Letter of August 3, 1930, ibid.

23. Letter of January 25, 1931, ibid.

24. David Garnett, *The Familiar Faces,* p. 104.

25. *Letters,* p. 708.

26. Letter of December 2, 1930, *Letters . . . to Bruce Rogers.*

27. *Letters,* p. 705.

28. *Shaw-Ede,* p. 41.

29. Letter of February 8, 1930, *Shaw-Ede,* p. 42. Ede had been writing a study of the relationship between the French sculptor Henry Gaudier and an unusual Polish woman, Sophie Brzeska.

30. Lawrence to Charlotte Shaw, July 3, 1930, BM Add MSS, 45904.

31. Letter of July 15, 1930, *Shaw-Ede,* p. 43.

32. Smith, *Golden Reign,* pp. 94–95.

33. Lawrence to Charlotte Shaw, February 6, 1930, BM Add MSS, 45904.

34. *Letters,* pp. 682–683; Manning, *Her Privates We;* also L. T. Hergenhan,

ed., "Some Unpublished Letters from T. E. Lawrence to Frederic Manning," 23 *Southerly* (1963): 242–252.

35. Letter of May 15, 1930, *Letters,* pp. 692–693.

36. Lawrence to Manning, August 7, 1930, Hergenhan, p. 246.

37. Letters of July 25, 1934, and January 2, 1932, Hergenhan, pp. 250, 248.

38. Lawrence to Manning, September 1, 1931, ibid., p. 247.

39. Lawrence to Graves, January 24, 1933, *Letters,* p. 760.

40. Janet Adam Smith, *John Buchan,* p. 327.

41. Reginald Sims, "The Sayings and the Doings of T.E. as heard and experienced by the Sims family (1937); the manuscript is in a private collection.

42. Lawrence to Buchan, March 21, 1930, *Letters,* p. 685.

43. Ibid., p. 686.

44. Sims, "The Sayings and the Doings . . ."

45. Ibid.

46. *Letters,* pp. 694–695, also LHB, p. 41.

47. *Letters,* p. 705.

48. Smith, *Golden Reign,* pp. 124–125.

49. *Letters,* p. 707.

50. Smith, *Golden Reign,* pp. 124–125.

51. Ibid., pp. 133–139.

52. Shaw to Lawrence, February 8, 1931, *Letters to TEL,* p. 180.

53. *Letters,* pp. 713–714.

54. Lawrence to Rogers, January 31, 1931, *Letters,* p. 710. Lawrence particularly found unsupportable the idea, accepted by most translators, that expert archers of the time shot through the holes in a row of hollow axes, and wrote a long letter to Rogers arguing the point (Lawrence to Rogers, February 25, 1931, *Letters,* pp. 710–712).

55. Lawrence to Charlotte Shaw, March 26, 1931, BM Add MSS, 45904.

31. "BOATS, BOATS, BOATS"

1. He wrote Liddell Hart on April 13, 1931: "My two year war with the Air Ministry over the type of motor boats suited to attend seaplanes is bearing results now, and experimental boats are being offered by contractors. I've become a marine expert, and test the things for

them, acquiring incidentally and by degrees quite a knowledge of the S.W. coast of England" (*Letters*, p. 718).

2. Letter of June 5, 1934, *More Letters from T. E. Shaw to Bruce Rogers* (unpaged).

3. Lawrence to Curtis, May 11, 1931, All Souls College, Oxford.

4. Clare Sydney Smith, *The Golden Reign*, p. 143.

5. *Friends*, p. 578.

6. The original manuscript of this treatise is in a California private collection.

7. RGB, pp. 168–169.

8. Lawrence to T. W. Beaumont, June 10, 1931. A copy of the letter was loaned to the author by Beaumont.

9. Lawrence to Hanley, August 21, 1931, *Letters*, p. 735.

10. Letter of July 2, 1931, ibid., p. 729.

11. Lawrence to C. F. Greenwood, July 17, 1931, ibid., p. 730.

12. Smith, *Golden Reign*, p. 155.

13. Ibid., p. 157.

14. Bod Res MSS, d59.

15. T. E. Shaw, *The Odyssey of Homer*, translator's note.

16. Ibid.

17. Ibid.

18. Smith, *Golden Reign*, p. 160.

19. Ibid., p. 161.

20. Lawrence to "Poppet" (R. M. Guy), September 30, 1931, Houghton Library, Harvard University.

21. Smith, *Golden Reign*, p. 169.

22. Lawrence to Trenchard, July 12 and 29, 1929, *Letters*, pp. 662–663, 666.

23. Lawrence to Edward Marsh, March 10, 1931, *Letters*, p. 715.

24. Bertram Thomas, *Arabia Felix*, p. xviii.

25. Lawrence to Charlotte Shaw, November 21, 1931, BM Add MSS, 45904.

26. Smith, *Golden Reign*, p. 177.

27. Quoted in Stanley and Roselle Weintraub, *Private Shaw and Public Shaw*, p. 217.

28. Lawrence to Charlotte Shaw, June 26, 1931, quoted in Weintraub, pp. 209–210.

29. Lawrence to Charlotte Shaw, January 9, 1932, BM Add MSS, 45904; quoted in part in Weintraub, p. 215.

30. Weintraub, p. 216.

31. Lawrence to Charlotte Shaw, January 27, 1932, BM Add MSS, 45904; quoted in Weintraub, pp. 218–219.

32. Smith, *Golden Reign*, p. 182.

33. A letter to his old friend Geoffrey Dawson, editor of *The Times*, conveys Lawrence's behind-the-scenes approach to such political matters: "Today it struck me that as editor you might be interested in the new type of motor boat that we have been producing lately for the R.A.F. I'm partly the guilty cause of them — after a big crash a year ago in Plymouth Sound, which showed me convincingly that we had nothing in the Service fit to help marine aircraft in difficulties. Nor could the Navy supply even an idea of the type of craft we needed. The Navy is rather Nelsonic in its motor boats. I suppose it knows something about steam. . . .

"So the R.A.F. (partly, as I confessed above, at my prompting) went into the science of it, and have had produced for them, by the Power Boat works at Hythe here, an entirely new type of seaplane tender. They are 37 ft. boats, twin engined, doing 30 m.p.h. in all weathers, handy, safe, and very cheap. Many of their features are unique. They cost less than any boats we have ever bought before.

"All this has been done through the admiralty, in the teeth of its protests and traditions. Now the boats are finished, the sailors are beginning to take notice, and wonder if there isn't something in it" (letter of March 22, 1932, Bod Res MSS, b55).

34. Lawrence to Childs, June 14, 1932, in a California private collection.

35. Lawrence to Ede, September 5, 1932, *Shaw-Ede*, p. 52.

36. Lawrence to Ede, October 18, 1932, ibid., p. 54.

37. Weintraub, *Private Shaw and Public Shaw*, p. 227.

38. Letters of September 26, 1932, *Letters to TEL*, p. 213.

39. Letter of September 5, 1932, *Shaw-Ede*, p. 52.

40. *Letters*, p. 754.

41. Lawrence to G. W. M. Dunn, November 9, 1932, *Letters*, pp. 752–753.

42. C. M. Bowra considered Lawrence's translation to be the best rendering of the *Odyssey* into English up to that time. Preferring prose to verse translations of the work generally, Bowra agreed with Lawrence's view of the *Odyssey* as primarily a story and felt that his work gave the *Odyssey* a new freshness and light (*The New Statesman and Nation*, April 8, 1933). Henry Hazlitt

regarded the translation as among the half dozen most eminent and found the total effect one of great dignity and beauty, "more delightful in itself" than any prose translation he had read. He thought the preface was mannered and affected, "even smart alecky" (*The Nation*, December 12, 1932). Louis Lord, a classical scholar, gave examples in his review of how Lawrence had been too free with the Greek. He thought the translation lacked a consistent tonal quality and also contained awkward English sentences. He felt, however, the gripping power of the translation, especially in the scenes of action (*Classical Journal*, April 1933). A. T. Murray, a classicist and an *Odyssey* translator himself, felt that Lawrence had been "unduly free" in his choice of words (*Classical Philology*, July 1933). Bruce Rogers's printing was admired by those reviewers who chose to comment.

Robert Fitzgerald, who has published a verse translation, wrote me that he had thought Lawrence's translation generally very unlike Homer (March 25, 1974), but as E. E. Kellett pointed out in 1935, every age or even every man, will want his own translation of Homer "as his experience widens and his moods change" (*The Spectator*, August 10, 1935).

43. Lawrence to Harley Granville-Barker, December 23, 1932, Houghton Library, Harvard University.

44. Letter of February 17, 1933, *More Letters to Bruce Rogers*.

45. Lawrence to Maurice Baring, December 5, 1932, Humanities Research Center, University of Texas.

46. Lawrence to Robin Buxton, April 7, 1933, Jesus College, Oxford.

47. Letter of February 9, 1933, in the possession of Francis Rodd; name of addressee withheld.

48. Smith, *Golden Reign*, p. 204.

49. Letter of March 23, 1933, *Letters*, p. 765.

50. Letter of March 30, 1933, *Letters*, p. 765.

51. Lawrence to Thurtle, May 23, 1933, Bod Res MSS, d59.

52. Lawrence to Charlotte Shaw, June 29, 1933, BM Add MSS, 45904.

53. Lawrence to G. Wren Howard, December 17, 1933, *Letters*, p. 783.

54. *Home Letters*, pp. 383–384.

55. Lawrence to Buxton, August 12, 1933, Jesus College, Oxford.

56. Lawrence to A. E. Chambers, October 5, 1933, Bod Res MSS (no box no.).

57. Lawrence to Buxton, August 12, 1933, Jesus College, Oxford.

58. Ibid.

59. *Letters*, p. 780.

60. *British Legion Journal* (November 1933), pp. 160, 161, 169.

61. Lawrence to K. W. Marshall, November 12, 1933, Bod Res MSS, d58.

62. David Garnett, *The Familiar Faces*, p. 106.

63. A copy is in the Bodleian Library (Res MSS, d230). "Something happened to me last night, when I lay awake to 5," he wrote to Mrs. Shaw on December 9. "You know I've been moody or broody for years, wondering what I was at in the RAF, but unable to let go — well, last night I suddenly understood that it was to write a book called 'Confession of Faith,' beginning in the Cloaca of Covent Garden, and embodying *The Mint*, and much that has happened to me before and since as regards the air. Not the conquest of the air, but our entry into the reserved element, 'as lords that are expected, yet with a silent joy in our arrival.' It would include a word on Miranshah and Karachi, and the meaning of speed, on land and water and air. I see the plan of it. It will take a long time to do. Clouds Hill, I think — In this next and last R.A.F. year I can collect feelings for it. The thread of the book will come because it spins through my head; there cannot be any objective continuity — but I think I can make it whole enough to do. *The Mint*, you know, was meant as notes for something (smaller) of the sort. I wonder if it will come off. The purpose of my generation, that's really it" (BM Add MSS, 45904).

64. Letter of February 2, 1934, *Home Letters*, p. 386.

65. Lawrence to S. C. Rolls, December 21, 1933, Bod Res MSS, d44.

66. Lawrence to H. S. Ede, December 31, 1933, *Shaw-Ede*, p. 57.

67. Lawrence to Charlotte Shaw, December 31, 1933, BM Add MSS, 45904.

68. Lawrence to Lady Astor, December 31, 1933, *Letters*, p. 788.

69. February 2, 1934, *Home Letters*, p. 386.

70. Lawrence to Charlotte Shaw, February 2, 1934, BM Add MSS, 45904.

71. *Home Letters*, p. 385.

72. Lawrence to "Poppet" (R. M. Guy),

February 18, 1934, Houghton Library, Harvard University.

73. *Letters*, p. 792.

74. Lawrence to Curtis, March 19, 1934, *Letters*, pp. 792–794.

75. Lawrence to Mrs. Peck, May 4, 1934, Bod Res MSS, d44.

76. Kirstein to Lawrence, December 14, 1933, Bod Res MSS, d60.

77. Lawrence to Kirstein, April 12, 1934, *Letters*, p. 797.

78. Kirstein to Lawrence, April 27, 1934, Bod Res MSS, d60.

79. Lawrence to Kirstein, May 11, 1934, Bod Res MSS, d43.

80. Letter to the author, March 12, 1969.

81. For example, in LHB, May 17, 1934, p. 216.

82. Lawrence to Liddell Hart, June 14, 1934, *Letters*, p. 810.

83. Smith, *Golden Reign*, p. 233.

84. LHB, p. 219.

85. Ibid., p. 222.

86. Lawrence to Kennington, August 6, 1934, *Letters*, pp. 813–814.

87. Lawrence to Liddell Hart, October 19, 1934, LHB, p. 225.

88. Smith, *Golden Reign*, p. 239.

89. *Letters*, pp. 819–824.

90. Lawrence to Liddell Hart, October 19, 1934, LHB, p. 225.

91. Lawrence to T. B. Marson, November 23, 1934, Bod Res MSS, d46.

92. Lawrence to Charlotte Shaw, November 16, 1934, BM Add MSS, 45904.

93. Reginald Sims, "The Sayings and the Doings of T.E. as heard and experienced by the Sims family" (1937); the manuscript is in a private collection.

94. Ibid.

95. *Friends*, p. 547.

96. Sims, "The Sayings and the Doings . . ."

97. Francis Rodd, unpublished notes, probably written in 1954 or 1955, sent to the author with an accompanying letter dated November 17, 1965.

98. Ibid.

99. *Letters*, p. 830.

100. Lawrence to Jimmy Newcombe, December 20, 1934, *Letters*, p. 838.

101. *Letters*, p. 844.

102. Lawrence to Baring, end of 1934, Humanities Research Center, University of Texas.

103. Lawrence to Charlotte Shaw, end of 1934 or early 1935, BM Add MSS, 45904.

104. *Shaw-Ede*, p. 58.

105. Letter of January 18, 1935, in Smith, *Golden Reign*, p. 241.

106. *Letters*, p. 845.

107. Lawrence to Charlotte Shaw, January 26, 1935, BM Add MSS, 45904.

108. Sims, "The Sayings and the Doings . . ."

109. *Letters*, p. 864.

110. Ibid., p. 849.

111. Lawrence to Graves, February 4, 1935, ibid., p. 853.

112. *Friends*, p. 561.

113. Lawrence to Lorna Norrington, February 24, 1935, *Letters*, p. 857.

114. Lawrence to T. W. Beaumont, February 25, 1935; lent to the author by Mr. Beaumont.

115. *Friends*, p. 435.

32. RETIREMENT AND DEATH

1. RAF discharge documents (the originals), in a California private collection.

2. Lawrence to Sergeant Robinson, February 26, 1935, in a California private collection.

3. Interview with Arnold Lawrence, July 15, 1968.

4. Lawrence to Rodd, March 6, 1935.

5. Lawrence to Sydney Cockerell, March 6, 1935, in Viola Meynell, ed., *Friends of a Lifetime*, p. 373.

6. Lawrence to Davies, February 28, 1935, *Letters*, p. 859.

7. BBC broadcast, December 3, 1958, notes in a California private collection.

8. Excerpt from a letter to L. H. Ingham, March 6, 1935, Bod Res MSS, b55, and to Alec Dixon, March 6, 1935, in a California private collection.

9. *Letters*, p. 865.

10. Ibid., p. 863.

11. LHB, p. 230.

12. *Friends*, p. 306.

13. Foreword by Liddell Hart in the 2d Edition of *Letters*, p. 29.

14. *Friends*, p. 254.

15. Ibid., p. 595.

16. *Shaw-Ede*, p. 60.

17. Lawrence to "Walter," April 5, 1935, in a California private collection; and to T. B. Marson, April 6, 1935, Bod Res MSS, d46.

18. Lawrence to Flight Lieutenant Norrington, April 20, 1935, *Letters*, p. 868.

19. Lawrence to Lieutenant Robin White, April 13, 1935, Bod Res MSS, d44.

20. *Friends*, pp. 571–572.
21. Lawrence to Lady Nancy Astor, May 5, 1935, Bod Res MSS, d49.
22. Lawrence to the Honorable Stephen Tennant, May 5, 1935, Bod Res MSS, d49.
23. *More Letters to Bruce Rogers* (unpaged).
24. Letter of May 6, 1935, *Letters*, p. 871.
25. Letter of May 8, 1935, ibid., p. 872.
26. Lawrence to Sir Karl Parker, keeper of the Department of Western Art, Ashmolean Museum, May 12, 1935, Bod Res MSS, b55.
27. Interview with Henry Williamson, by a chance meeting on a train from Exeter to London, December 17, 1965.
28. *Secret Lives*, p. 270.
29. The speed was Corporal Catchpole's estimate at the inquest (Bod Res MSS, b56). Knightley and Simpson suggest that 38 mph was the maximum possible speed, as the Brough, they state, was jammed in second gear (*Secret Lives*, p. 274).
30. The Inquest Report, May 21, 1935, Bod Res MSS, b56.
31. LHB, p. 233.
32. Clare Sydney Smith to Charlotte Shaw, May 20, 1935, BM Add MSS, 45922.
33. New York *Times*, May 20, 1935.
34. Service Record, May 22, 1935, Bod Res MSS, d48.
35. Newcombe to Beaumont, undated (lent by Beaumont to the author).
36. See, for example, Colin Graham, "The Crash That Killed Lawrence of Arabia," *Dorset — The Country Magazine* (Summer 1968).
37. *Friends*, p. 595.
38. Churchill, *Great Contemporaries*, p. 167.
39. Smith, *Golden Reign*, p. 144.

33. INTIMACY, SEXUALITY AND PENANCE

1. Letter to the author, November 28, 1969.
2. Edmund Gosse, *Fathers and Sons*, p. 306.
3. I believe Lawrence is using the "me" and "they" to indicate his relationships with men during the campaigns, but that he also means the passage to express his more general feelings and attitudes.
4. *Seven Pillars*, pp. 563–564.

5. Lawrence to Charlotte Shaw, March 26, 1924, BM Add MSS, 45903.
6. Lawrence to Charlotte Shaw, May 8, 1928, and August 18, 1928, BM Add MSS, 45904.
7. There also is no factual support for the view suggested by some that the Der'a beatings rendered Lawrence sexually impotent on a physical basis.
8. Lawrence to Charlotte Shaw, September 28, 1925, BM Add MSS, 45903.
9. *Seven Pillars*, p. 348.
10. *Mint*, p. 109.
11. Lucas to Lawrence, March 9, 1929, Bod Res MSS, d60.
12. Lawrence to Lucas, March 26, 1929, Bod Res MSS, d58.
13. Lawrence to Graves, November 6, 1928, Houghton Library, Harvard University.
14. *Letters*, p. 395.
15. *Mint*, p. 161.
16. Arnold Lawrence to Miss Early, Bod Res MSS, b96.
17. *Letters*, p. 458.
18. Lawrence to B. E. Leeson, April 18, 1929, Bod Res MSS, d58.
19. Lawrence to Charlotte Shaw, June 10, 1924, BM Add MSS, 45903.
20. Lawrence to Cockerell, June 13, 1924, *Letters*, p. 450.
21. Lawrence to Hanley Granville-Barker, December 5, 1924, Houghton Library, Harvard University.
22. *Letters*, p. 728.
23. Ibid., p. 649.
24. Ibid., p. 652.
25. Arnold Lawrence to Miss Early, December 17, 1963, Bod Res MSS, b56.
26. Lawrence to Charlotte Shaw, November 6, 1928, Bod Res MSS, 45904.
27. Interview with A. E. Chambers, March 17, 1965.
28. Bod Res MSS, c52.
29. E. M. Forster, *Abinger Harvest*, p. 136.
30. Letter of March 25, 1930, *Letters*, p. 687.
31. Letter of March 27, 1923, ibid., p. 414.
32. *Friends*, p. 592.
33. Interview with A. W. Lawrence, December 8, 1965.
34. Letter to the author, July 23, 1973.
35. David Garnett, *The Familiar Faces*, p. 110.
36. The passage appears both in the manuscript of *Seven Pillars* in the Bodleian Library and (with minor changes of

wording and punctuation) in the 1922 (Oxford) edition. It was omitted from the subscribers' edition.

37. In the manuscript of his *Essay on Flecker,* Lawrence referred to conversations he had with Flecker before World War I about whipping, and it is possible that Flecker had a problem of this sort.

38. *Journal of the American Medical Association,* Supplement to Vol. 227 (February 18, 1974), p. 834.

39. G. R. Scott, *The History of Corporal Punishment,* p. 125.

40. Quoted in H. Salt, *The Flogging Craze,* p. 88.

41. Scott, p. 196.

42. *Friends,* p. 592. The information that follows is, though detailed, admittedly incomplete. It was obtained with considerable difficulty and with the full cooperation of the Lawrence family, without whose wish to set this aspect of T.E.'s life in an appropriate perspective, this account could not have been provided. Some of the raw facts were presented in the third of the four articles which appeared in the *Sunday Times* in June 1968, and which were written by Colin Simpson and Phillip Knightley, the *Times* "Insight team" (June 9, 16, 23 and 30). A substantially revised and corrected version appears in their book, *The Secret Lives of Lawrence of Arabia.* Most of Knightley and Simpson's account is based on what was told them by John Bruce. I have sought to include as much independent information as possible, and to place Bruce's role in psychological and historical perspective. It is my hope that the reader will look upon this material with empathy and understanding, and be sensitive to the pathetic suffering that Lawrence underwent in serving the demands of a distorted internal sense of psychic justice. Since the discovery of such an unusual aspect of the personal history of a family member cannot help but have a significant impact on other relatives, and because of its highly sensitive personal nature, on the biographer as well, I have approached this dimension of Lawrence's history from a somewhat different direction. Instead of describing the sequence of events solely from the standpoint of Lawrence's history, I have relied more upon the perspectives of its discovery — by the family and subsequent investigation by myself. This approach will, I hope, lead to greater understanding of a

part of Lawrence's life that he ashamedly felt the need to keep to himself, and will reveal some of the methodological problems to be met by the biographer engaged in this type of study.

43. From notes written by Arnold Lawrence in 1967 or 1968 and furnished in 1968.

44. From notes, "My Knowledge of Bruce," prepared by Arnold Lawrence in 1970.

45. Ibid.

46. Notes prepared for the author by Arnold Lawrence, received May 8, 1968.

47. Letter of February 8, 1969.

48. John Bruce, "I Knew Lawrence," *The Scottish Field* (August 1938), pp. 20–21.

49. Clach Mackenny, "Gaveloc Gossip," *Helensburgh Advertiser* (February 1963).

50. These efforts on the part of members of the Lawrence family to prevent Bruce's publication of his "story" should not be interpreted as an effort on their part to suppress the truth. Rather, they wished to avoid an account based exclusively on Bruce's material. After publication of the four *Sunday Times* articles and the Knightley and Simpson book, Arnold Lawrence wrote a letter to the newspaper on October 6, 1969. In publishing the letter (on November 22), the *Sunday Times* omitted several portions, among them the following statement: "I had given similar information to Dr. John Mack, of the Harvard Medical School, before Bruce approached the *Sunday Times* (and so frustrated my hope that a psychiatrist would be the first to describe the association with my brother, in whom Dr. Mack had long been interested)."

51. My own involvement with this aspect of Lawrence's history began with a luncheon meeting with my editor in November 1966. He told me that another Little, Brown author, William Sargant, an English psychiatrist and a friend of Robert Graves, had been told at one time by Graves that he was aware of certain facts concerning Lawrence's sexuality which were not generally known. Dr. Sargant put me in touch with Graves, whom I visited in Majorca during the summer of 1967. Graves told me that Lawrence had "become a flagellant" in the ranks after the war, that he had become impotent as a result of the Der'a experience

(not literally true). Not wanting to write Arnold Lawrence "out of the blue" about this matter, I asked Captain Liddell Hart for further information about the flagellation as Graves had indicated that Liddell Hart had' also known about it. (Eric Kennington and his wife learned after T.E.'s death of Arnold Lawrence's conclusions regarding his brother's regimen of penance and purification, but letters they wrote to Graves at the time reflect some misunderstanding of its significance [California private collection].) Liddell Hart, however — he must have known that Arnold Lawrence would not take offense — referred my letter to him. Lawrence replied cordially, acknowledged that there was "a basis of fact" regarding the flagellation disorder. He wrote further: "To write a statement not liable to be misunderstood would take more time than I can spare at present, whereas you would quickly get everything aright in conversation" (Arnold Lawrence to the author, August 10, 1967). It is worth pointing out that this offer to discuss the matter occurred ten months before the *Sunday Times* made Bruce's story public and some months before Arnold Lawrence had knowledge that Bruce had been successful in selling his story to a newspaper.

52. Arnold Lawrence to the author, March 21, 1968.

53. *Sunday Times*, June 23, 1968.

54. Interview with John Bruce, July 22, 1968.

55. Letter of Colonel Toby Farnell Watson to Liddell Hart, April 1, 1969. Although the document which came to the Lawrence solicitors in 1967 and which was sold to the *Sunday Times* early in 1968 contains elaborate descriptions of meetings between Bruce and Lawrence in 1922 around the time of Lawrence's enlistment in the RAF, this part of Bruce's account, much of which has been relayed in the *Sunday Times* article of June 23, 1968, and more cautiously in the Knightley and Simpson book published in the following year, has not been substantiated. Other documentation provided by Bruce indicated that the relationship actually began when he met Lawrence in the Tank Corps in 1923. In the 1937 letter to Storrs, Bruce wrote that he was Lawrence's friend for the last twelve years of Lawrence's life, that is, from 1923. The *Helensburgh Adver-*

tiser article of 1963 states that Bruce and Lawrence met in 1923, and Bruce also told me in our meeting that he had known Lawrence for twelve years.

56. Arnold Lawrence to the author, January 1970.

57. In addition to Bruce I have been able to establish only a few others who were involved in the beatings in any way — one witness and one or two other men who administered floggings on rare occasions when Bruce was not available.

58. A letter from Lawrence to F. N. Doubleday, written September 18, 1930, contains a long, highly detailed, poetically written account of a trip on leave to a bleak cottage on the north coast of Scotland, where he was joined by John Bruce and one of Bruce's relatives. This was one of the instances in which Lawrence, according to Bruce, had himself beaten (interview with Phillip Knightley, July 23, 1968). There is nothing in Lawrence's description of the stark coastline, the fishing and swimming late in September in the North Sea (!), the sad, cold "disembodied voices" of the gulls, or the matter-of-fact comments on books to suggest that he was involved in any unusual, conflictual or disturbing activity. In fact, another thoughtful letter written later to Doubleday again gives the impression that this trip was, for Lawrence, nothing but a health visit to a spa. "You have liked my letter from Scotland," he wrote, "but that was for what lay behind the words: my care for you and thinking about you as I was there on happy holiday. The health I have is rather a selfish and wonderful thing. It does not feel quite right to keep it all to myself. I would have liked to transfuse you a few quarts of it, out of fairness" (Lawrence to Doubleday, January 27, 1931, Bod Res MSS, d52). This is surely another instance of Lawrence's unusual ability to compartmentalize various aspects of his life, to separate them from one another, when he thought it necessary.

59. Arnold Lawrence is of the opinion that had T.E. been allowed to remain in the RAF in 1923, he probably would not have succumbed to the residuum of the Der'a experience (letter to the author, July 8, 1974).

60. Lawrence to Curtis, March 19, 1923, *Letters*, p. 411.

61. Lawrence to Curtis, March 27, 1923, ibid., p. 413.

62. Lawrence to Curtis, May 14, 1923, ibid., p. 416.

63. Arnold Lawrence to the author, June 4, 1968.

64. Arnold Lawrence to the author, July 23, 1973.

65. Bruce's document sent to the *Sunday Times* in 1968.

66. Draft of a letter to a riding and hunting establishment, July or August 1933.

67. *Seven Pillars*, p. 445.

68. On this point Arnold Lawrence wrote me (on July 23, 1973): "From my slight experience of psychological warfare (of which T.E. had plenty) an elaborate fiction is more plausible the nearer it comes to fact, although the fact is unknowable to the audience; hence he gives his lies a garbled foundation of fact about inheritance and estate and a true foundation about illegitimacy. He cannot possibly have felt any grievance about inheritance because the money had actually come to his father, and why should he regret Bob's exclusion from the landed estate (but he did once remark how funny it would be if Bob had been able to become Sir Montague)."

69. Observation by Arnold Lawrence, July 23, 1973.

70. *Friends*, p. 592.

71. Arnold Lawrence to the author, July 23, 1973.

34. LAWRENCE ASSAYED

1. Arnold Lawrence on the Jack Paar television show, January 24, 1964.

2. Personal observation to the author, August 29, 1972.

3. *Seven Pillars*, p. 157.

4. Lawrence to Dick Knowles, July 14, 1927, Bod Res MSS, d56.

5. Lawrence to Charlotte Shaw, April 17, 1925, BM Add MSS, 45903.

6. Lawrence to Allanson, June 18, 1927, in a California private collection.

7. *Letters*, p. 494.

8. Actually Lawrence's father took the name Lawrence before T.E. was born and the child was registered at birth as Thomas Edward Lawrence.

9. Lawrence to Granville-Barker, May 9, 1924, Houghton Library, Harvard University.

10. *Friends*, p. 332.

11. Lawrence to Charlotte Shaw, July 19, 1934, BM Add MSS, 45904.

12. She wrote: "Then T.E. came up to see me: he sat on a hard stool leaning forward and gripping it with his hands; he fixed his eyes on me and began, 'Of course you must be feeling very miserable, you feel you have failed in your job, and it's about the most important job in the world; . . . you must be feeling you are utterly no good and nothing can ever be worth while . . .' On and on he went, describing me to myself, clarifying all the nightmare fears by defining them, and doing it all from the woman's point of view, not the man's. He seemed to know everything that miscarriage could mean [his mother had lost three infants at birth or in utero], even down to the shame of being laughed at for it, and as he talked warmth began to come into me, instead of flooding out of me, for besides putting things as they were, he brought a power to remake them all afresh" (*Friends*, pp. 311–312).

13. RGB, p. 186.

14. *Letters*, p. 618.

15. Lawrence to Charlotte Shaw, March 18, 1927, BM Add MSS, 45903.

16. Lady Pansy Lamb to the author, December 19, 1964.

17. Lawrence to Joyce, March 19, 1929, Bod Res MSS, b55.

18. *Letters*, p. 744.

19. Lawrence to Edward Garnett, August 10, 1933, ibid., p. 775.

20. Lawrence to Lady Astor, February 15, 1934, ibid., p. 790.

21. Lawrence to Graves, August 27, 1928, RGB, p. 153.

22. *Letters*, p. 510.

23. *Friends*, p. 261.

24. LHB, p. 210.

25. He could also forgive wrongs of various sorts, even those committed against himself, if the injured party were strong enough not to suffer unduly. Bertram Rota, the London bookseller, told me of an incident involving himself. A young man brought to him two documents written by and belonging to Lawrence, the preface to Doughty's *Arabia Deserta* and a shorter preface to *Revolt in the Desert*. Rota sold these to a wealthy collector. Soon thereafter the publisher, Jonathan Cape, "descended" on Rota with the information that the documents had been stolen from Cape by a disaffected young employee of the publishing firm who had gotten into financial difficulty. It would have been difficult for

Rota to recover the documents and an impasse arose. Lawrence provided the solution by suggesting to Cape that Rota merely give over the profit he had made in the transaction to the RAF Benevolent Fund and he would consider the matter closed (interview in March 1965).

26. Florence Hardy to Graves, June 13, 1927, Bod Res MSS, c52.

27. *Letters*, p. 537.

28. Lawrence to Sergeant Pugh, June 30, 1927, Arts Catalogue, Bodleian Library.

29. Lawrence to Elsie Falcon, November 28 (no year given), in a California private collection.

30. *Letters*, pp. 606, 813.

31. Lawrence to Charlotte Shaw, May 22, 1929, BM Add MSS, 45904.

32. Lawrence to Ernest Altounyan, December 28, 1933, Bod Res MSS, d49.

33. RGB, p. 138.

34. *Letters*, p. 691.

35. *Friends*, p. 559.

36. Interview with William Hogarth, March 18, 1965.

37. *Friends*, p. 537.

38. LHB, p. 208.

39. Interview on March 20, 1965.

40. *Letters*, p. 607.

41. Letter of April 1, 1929, ibid., p. 649.

42. Robert Graves, *Lawrence and the Arabs*, p. 429.

43. *Friends*, p. 565.

44. A. H. R. Reiffer, letter of April 1970, Imperial War Museum, London.

45. RGB, p. 121. The quote is actually Lawrence's editing of a passage of Graves's, made to seem like a quotation from a letter by him to Graves.

46. LHB, p. 160.

47. Lawrence to Edward Garnett, April 24, 1923, *Letters*, p. 410.

48. *Mint*, pp. 199–202.

49. Lawrence to Charlotte Shaw, August 24, 1926, BM Add MSS, 45903.

50. *Letters*, p. 501.

51. *Mint*, p. 202.

52. Lawrence to Curtis, May 14, 1923, *Letters*, pp. 416–417.

53. A. E. Chambers, BBC broadcast, December 3, 1958.

54. Lawrence to Charlotte Shaw, June 6, 1924, BM Add MSS, 45903.

55. Edward Mack, unpublished notes on Lawrence as a literary critic, March 29, 1965.

56. *Friends*, p. 465.

57. Lawrence to C. Day Lewis, December 20, 1934, *Letters*, p. 839.

58. Lawrence to Charlotte Shaw, October 15, 1924, BM Add MSS, 45903.

59. Letter of May 12, 1927, BM Add MSS, 45903.

60. *Friends*, p. 449.

61. Ibid., p. 307.

62. Lawrence to A. Dawnay, April 14, 1927, Bod Res MSS, d43.

63. Lawrence to Charlotte Shaw, March 26, 1931, BM Add MSS, 45904.

64. The following is a typical excerpt from Muggeridge: "What could be more extraordinary than the survival of his cult, which flourishes the more as his lies and attitudinizing are made manifest? . . . He is superlatively a case of everything being true except the facts. Who more fitting to be a Hero of Our Time than this, our English Genêt, our Sodomite Saint, with Lowell Thomas for his Sartre and Alec Guinness to say Amen?" (review of Ronald Blythe's *The Age of Illusion* in *New York Times Book Review*, Sunday May 10, 1964).

65. Lucas to Lawrence, January 2, 1928, Bod Res MSS, d60.

66. Interview of October 29, 1964.

67. John Buchan, *Memory Hold-the-Door*, p. 229.

BIBLIOGRAPHY

UNPUBLISHED SOURCES

British Museum. Department of Western Manuscripts. Among the "Additional Manuscripts" are Lawrence's correspondence with Charlotte Shaw (Mrs. George Bernard Shaw) and his war diaries, all of which she bequeathed to the museum. (Only a few of her letters to Lawrence are in the collection: he destroyed many of them at her request.) The materials from the Additional Manuscripts are referred to in the notes as BM Add MSS.

Durham University. Library of the School of Oriental Studies. The Wingate Papers contain documentary material concerning the war in the Middle East, 1916–1918.

Harvard University. Houghton Library. A large collection of Lawrence material: letters; manuscripts and books, including one of the copies of the 1922 (Oxford) edition of *Seven Pillars of Wisdom*; Lawrence's own copy of *The Arab Bulletin* with his handwritten annotations; and a copy of his *Letter to His Mother* (privately printed by Lord Carlow at the Corvinus Press), which contains handwritten comments by George Bernard Shaw; and a copy of *An Essay on Flecker*.

Imperial War Museum, London. In the library are the research materials obtained by staff members of the *Sunday Times* and used by Phillip Knightley and Colin Simpson in preparing their book, *The Secret Lives of Lawrence of Arabia*. There is also a small collection of documentary material related to Lawrence's activities during and after the war.

King's College, London. The library contains the "Akaba" Papers of Colonel Pierce Joyce, an important source on the Arab Revolt.

New York Public Library. Arents Collection. Mrs. George Bernard (Charlotte) Shaw's copy of the subscribers' (1926) edition of *Seven Pillars of Wisdom* with a four-page handwritten essay by G.B.S. on the front flyleaves.

Oxford University. Library of All Souls College. Letters of Lawrence to Lionel Curtis.
———. Library of the Ashmolean Museum. A few of Lawrence's letters from the Carchemish period.
———. Bodleian Library. Among the Reserve Manuscripts is a very large collection of Lawrence's private papers, including thousands of his letters, mostly in typescript copies, and various other documents and photographs. The material has been embargoed until the year 2000 and may be seen only with the permission of Lawrence's executors. The manuscript of *Seven Pillars of Wisdom*, given to the library in 1923, and a small collection of original letters are held separately by the library and may be seen by qualified scholars without special permission. Materials in the Reserve Manuscripts are referred to in the notes as Bod Res MSS.

————. Library of Jesus College. Letters of Lawrence to Robin Buxton.

————. St. Antony's College. Middle East Centre. The Private Papers Collection contains some of Hogarth's letters, the Allenby Papers, and other manuscript material.

Public Record Office, London. Documents from Foreign Office papers and cabinet papers. Referred to in the notes as PRO/FO and PRO/CAB respectively.

University of Texas, Austin. Humanities Research Center. The Lawrence Collection is large and contains hundreds of Lawrence's letters and other original manuscript materials relating to him.

PUBLISHED SOURCES

Lawrence's Principal Writings

Arab Bulletin, The. Papers of the Arab Bureau, 1916–1918, of which Lawrence was one of the authors. Eighteen copies were printed and bound after the war. Lawrence's own copy, with his annotations, is in Houghton Library, Harvard University. His contributions to the *Bulletin* were published separately by Arnold Lawrence under the title *Secret Dispatches from Arabia* (see below).

Crusader Castles. 2 vols. London: Golden Cockerell Press, 1936. Lawrence's thesis for his Oxford degree, which Arnold Lawrence had published after his death.

Essay on Flecker, An (1925). New York: Doubleday, Doran, 1937. A copy is in the Houghton Library, Harvard University.

Evolution of a Revolt: Early Postwar Writings of T. E. Lawrence. Edited by Stanley and Roselle Weintraub. University Park: Pennsylvania State University Press, 1968.

Home Letters of T. E. Lawrence and His Brothers, The. Edited by M. Robert Lawrence. Oxford: Blackwell, 1954.

Letters of T. E. Lawrence, The. Edited by David Garnett. London: Cape, 1938. Referred to in the notes as *Letters.*

Minorities. Edited by Jeremy M. Wilson. London: Cape, 1971. The first publication of Lawrence's anthology of favorite poems in a "minor key." It includes a valuable introductory biographical essay by the editor.

Mint, The. London: Cape, 1973. Lawrence's description of life in the barracks of the RAF. He finished the manuscript in 1928 and made revisions later, but except for a few copies privately printed shortly after his death, the work remained unpublished until 1955. Two versions appeared: an expurgated edition (names were changed) for the general public; and an unexpurgated text in a limited edition. Not until 1973 was a corrected, unexpurgated edition published without limitation. Referred to in the notes as *Mint.*

Oriental Assembly. Edited by Arnold W. Lawrence. London: Williams and Norgate, 1939. An important collection of Lawrence's essays and other writings.

Revolt in the Desert. New York: Doran, 1927. An abridgment of *Seven Pillars of Wisdom* which Lawrence made in 1926.

Secret Dispatches from Arabia. Edited by Arnold W. Lawrence. London: Golden Cockerell Press, 1939. Lawrence's contributions to *The Arab Bulletin.* Referred to in the notes as *Secret Dispatches.*

Seven Pillars of Wisdom: A Triumph. New York: Doubleday, 1935. Lawrence's account of the Arab Revolt was first printed in 1922 by the Oxford *Times.* Eight copies were made, of which five, or possibly six, remain. One of them is in Houghton Library, Harvard University, and is the one from which Edward Garnett made his abridgment (never published). The manuscript of this "Oxford edition" is in the Bodleian Library at Oxford University. The 1926 "subscribers'" or "Cranwell" edition was the result of Lawrence's extensive revision and abridgment of the Oxford edition from 1923 to 1926. Over two hundred copies were elaborately printed by Lawrence, of which he sold 128 for thirty guineas each to the subscribers. The remainder — he was secretive about how many there were — were given away to friends and to those he knew could not afford the price of a copy. The copy belonging to George Bernard Shaw's wife, Charlotte, is in the Arents Collection of the New York Public Library and contains a four-page handwritten essay by G.B.S. on the front flyleaves. No edition of *Seven Pillars of Wisdom* was issued for the general public until after Lawrence's death in 1935. The trade editions published by Cape in England and Doubleday, Doran in the United States in 1935 and reprinted thereafter are identical with the subscribers' edition. *Revolt in the Desert*, first published in 1927 by Cape in England and by George Doran in the United States, is a popular abridgment of *Seven Pillars* — about half its length — which Lawrence made in 1926 in order to pay off the debts he had incurred in publishing the subscribers' edition. *Seven Pillars of Wisdom* is referred to in the notes as *Seven Pillars*.

As T. E. SHAW

Letters from T. E. Shaw to Bruce Rogers. Privately printed by Bruce Rogers at the Printing House of William Edwin Rudge, 1933.

More Letters from T. E. Shaw to Bruce Rogers. Privately printed by Bruce Rogers at the Printing House of William Edwin Rudge, 1936.

Odyssey of Homer, The (translation). New York: Oxford University Press, 1932. Lawrence completed the translation in 1931.

Shaw-Ede: T. E. Lawrence's Letters to H. S. Ede, 1927–1935. London: Golden Cockerell Press, 1942.

Lawrence was a co-author of the reports on the archeological work at Carchemish, Anatolia, undertaken before World War I, and on the survey of the eastern Sinai Peninsula that he and others made in 1914:

Woolley, C. Leonard; Lawrence, T. E.; Hogarth, D. G.; and Guy, P. L. O. *Carchemish: Report on the Excavations at Djerabis.* 3 vols. London: British Museum, 1914, 1921, 1952.

Woolley, C. Leonard, and Lawrence, T. E. *The Wilderness of Zin.* London: Palestine Exploration Fund Annual, 1915.

Other Sources

Adams, Henry. *Mont-Saint-Michel and Chartres* (1904). Boston: Houghton Mifflin, 1927.

Aldington, Richard. *Lawrence of Arabia: A Biographical Enquiry.* London: Collins, 1955.

Antonius, George. *The Arab Awakening.* London: Hamish Hamilton, 1938.

Arendt, Hannah. "The Imperialistic Character." *The Review of Politics* 12 (July 1950): 303–320.

Arthur, G. C. *General Sir John Maxwell.* London: Murray,, 1932.

Baker, J. N. L. *Jesus College, Oxford, 1571–1971.* Oxford: Oxonian Press, 1971.

Balsdon, Dacre. *Oxford Life.* London: Eyre & Spottiswoode, 1957.

Barrow, George. *The Fire of Life.* London: Hutchinson, 1943.

Bell, Gertrude. *The Desert and the Sown.* London: Heinemann, 1907.

Bell, Lady Francis. *The Letters of Gertrude Bell.* 2 vols. New York: Boni and Liveright, 1927.

Benson, G. M. P., and Glover, Edward. *Corporal Punishment: An Indictment.* London: Howard League for Penal Reform, 1931.

Berlin, Isaiah. *Historical Inevitability.* London: Oxford University Press, 1954.

Bertram, Anthony. *Paul Nash: The Portrait of an Artist.* London: Faber and Faber, 1955.

Birdwood, Lord. *Nuri as-Said: A Study in Arab Leadership.* London: Cassell, 1959.

Blackmur, Richard P. "The Everlasting Effort: A Citation of T. E. Lawrence." In *The Expense of Greatness.* New York: Arrow Editions, 1940.

Blumenfeld, R. D. *All in a Lifetime.* London: Ernest Benn, 1931.

———. *R.D.B.'s Procession.* London: Ivor Nicholson, 1935.

Boase, T. S. R. *Castles and Churches of the Crusading Kingdom.* London: Oxford University Press, 1967.

Bowra, C. M. "Two Translations." *The New Statesman and Nation,* April 8, 1933, p. 449.

Boyle, Andrew. *Trenchard*. London: Collins, 1962.
Breasted, James H. "David George Hogarth." *Geographical Review*, 18 (1928): 321–344.
Brémond, Edouard. *Le Hedjaz dans la guerre mondiale*. Paris: Payot, 1931.
Brodie, I. E. "Lawrence Was My Orderly." *Naafi Review* (Summer 1963), pp. 6–7.
Broderick, A. H. *Near to Greatness: A Life of Lord Winterton*. London: Hutchinson, 1965.
Brooke, Rupert. *The Collected Poems of Rupert Brooke*. London: Sidgwick and Jackson, 1918.
Buchan, John. *Pilgrim's Way*. Boston: Houghton Mifflin, 1940. (American ed. of *Memory Hold-the-Door*)
Burgoyne, Elizabeth. *Gertrude Bell*. 2 vols. London: Ernest Benn, 1961.
Burton, Percy (as told to Lowell Thomas). *Adventures Among Immortals*. London: Hutchinson, 1938.
Churchill, Winston. *Great Contemporaries*. London: Butterworth, 1937.
Clayton, Sir Gilbert. *An Arabian Diary*. Berkeley and Los Angeles: University of California Press, 1969.
Courtney, Janet E. *An Oxford Portrait Gallery*. London: Chapman and Hall, 1931.
Crump, C. G., and Jacob, E. F., eds. *The Legacy of the Middle Ages*. Oxford: Clarendon Press, 1926.
Dawn, C. E. "The Amir of Mecca Al-Husayn Ibn- 'Ali and the Origin of the Arab Revolt." *Proceedings of the American Philosophical Society* 104 (1960): 11–34.
———. *From Ottomanism to Arabism: Essays on the Origins of Arab Nationalism*. Urbana: University of Illinois Press, 1973.
Denomy, Alexander. *The Heresy of Courtly Love*. New York: Declan X. McMullen, 1947.
Deutsch, Helene. "Some Clinical Considerations of the Ego Ideal." *Journal of the American Psychoanalytic Association* 12 (1964): 512–516.
Dixon, Alec. *Tinned Soldier: A Personal Record, 1919–1926*. London: Jonathan Cape, 1941.
Djemal Pasha. *Memories of a Turkish Statesman — 1913–1919*. New York: Doran, 1922.
Doran, George. *Chronicles of Barabbas*. New York: Harcourt, Brace, 1935.
Doubleday, F. N. "The Strange Character of Colonel T. E. Lawrence," in *A Few Indiscreet Recollections*, pp. 77–78. Privately printed, December 1928. One of the edition of 57 copies is in Houghton Library, Harvard University.
Doughty, Charles M. *Travels in Arabia Deserta* (1888), with an Introduction by T. E. Lawrence. London: Medici Society and Cape, 1921.
Dunbar, J. *Mrs. G.B.S.: A Portrait*. New York: Harper and Row, 1963.
Edwards, J. G. "T. E. Lawrence." *Jesus College Magazine* 4 (1935): 343–345.
Erikson, Erik. *Gandhi's Truth: On the Origins of Militant Nonviolence*. New York: Norton, 1969.
Erskine, Mrs. Stuart. *King Faisal of Iraq*. London: Hutchinson, 1933.
Esco Foundation for Palestine. *Palestine: A Study of Jewish, Arab and British Policies*. 2 vols. New Haven: Yale University Press, 1947.
Evans, Laurence. *United States Policy and the Partition of Turkey, 1914–1924*. Baltimore: Johns Hopkins Press, 1965.
Falls, Cyril, and Becke, A. F., eds. *Military Operations in Egypt and Palestine*, Vol. II. *History of the Great War*, London: His Majesty's Stationery Office, 1930.
Farago, Ladislas. "No Nazi Revolt in the Desert." *Asia* 40 (April 1940): 175–178.
Fatih, Zuhdi, al-. *Lurins al- 'Arab: 'ala Khuta Hartzal: Taqarir Lurins al-Sirriya* [Lawrence of Arabia in the steps of Herzl: Lawrence's Secret Reports]. Beirut: Dar al-Nafa'is, 1971.
Fedden, Robin. *Crusader Castles*. London: Art and Technics, 1950.
Findlay, Charles. "The Amazing AC 2." *The Listener*, June 5, 1958, pp. 937–938.
Fletcher, C. R. L. "David George Hogarth." *The Geographical Journal* 71 (1928): 321–344.
Forster, E. M. *Abinger Harvest*. London: Edward Arnold, 1936.
Fowle, L. R. "Prologue." *Asia* 20 (April 1920): 257–258.

Frankfurter, Felix. Correspondence in "The Contributor's Column." *Atlantic Monthly* 146 (October 1930): 49, 50, 52, and 54.

Freud, Sigmund. "Psychopathic Characters on the Stage" (1905 or 1906). In Vol. VII of *Standard Edition of the Complete Psychological Works of Sigmund Freud*, pp. 305–310. London: Hogarth, 1952.

Gardner, Brian. *Allenby of Arabia.* New York: Coward-McCann, 1966.

Glubb, J. B. *Britain and the Arabs.* London: Hodder and Stoughton, 1959.

Graham, Colin. "The Crash That Killed Lawrence of Arabia." *Dorset: The Country Magazine* (Summer 1968).

Graves, Philip. *The Life of Sir Percy Cox.* London: Hutchinson, 1941.

———, ed. *Memoirs of King Abdullah of Transjordan.* London: Cape, 1950.

Graves, Robert. *Goodbye to All That.* 1929. Garden City, N.Y.: Doubleday Anchor Books, 1957.

———. *Lawrence and the Arabs.* London: Cape, 1927. (American edition: *Lawrence and the Arabian Adventure.* New York: Doubleday, Doran, 1928.) The material for the book that Graves obtained from Lawrence in interviews and correspondence, and Lawrence's notes on the manuscript, are in *T. E. Lawrence to His Biographer Robert Graves* below.

———. *T. E. Lawrence to His Biographer Robert Graves.* 1938. Reprinted: Garden City, N.Y.: Doubleday, 1963. This work and its counterpart by Basil Liddell Hart were published originally by Faber and Faber as companion volumes. They contain the source materials that Graves and Liddell Hart obtained from their interviews and correspondence with Lawrence as well as Lawrence's notes on their manuscripts. Only five hundred or perhaps a thousand copies of each volume were printed. In 1963 Doubleday reprinted them in a single volume. The Graves work is referred to in the notes as RGB.

Güterbock, H. G. "Carchemish." *Journal of Near Eastern Studies* 13 (1954): 102–114.

Hankey, Lord. *The Supreme Command, 1914–1918.* 2 vols. London: Allen and Unwin, 1961.

Hawkins, J. D. "Building Inscriptions of Carchemish." *Anatolian Studies* 22 (1972): 87–114.

Hazlitt, Henry. "On Translating Homer." *The Nation* 135 (December 21, 1932): 620–621.

Herbert, Aubrey. *Mons, Kut and Anzac.* London: Edward Arnold, 1919.

Herodotus. *The Histories.* Book Six. Baltimore: Penguin, 1961.

Hewlett, Maurice. *Richard Yea-and-Nay.* London: Macmillan, 1900.

Hoare, Samuel. *Empire of the Air.* London: Collins, 1957.

Hogarth, David G. *The Life of Charles Doughty.* New York: Doubleday, Doran, 1929.

———. "Mecca's Revolt Against the Turk." *Century Magazine* 100 (1920): 403–409.

———. *The Penetration of Arabia.* New York: Frederick A. Stokes, 1904.

House, E. M., and Seymour, C. S. *What Really Happened at Paris.* New York: Scribner's, 1921.

Howard, Harry N. *The King-Crane Commission.* Beirut: Khayats, 1963.

———. *The Partition of Turkey: A Diplomatic History.* Norman: University of Oklahoma Press, 1931.

Howard, Michael S. *Jonathan Cape, Publisher.* London: Cape, 1971.

———. "The Reluctant Money-Spinner." *The Times Saturday Review*, January 9, 1971.

Howe, Irving. *A World More Attractive.* New York: Horizon, 1963.

Ireland, Philip W. *Iraq: A Study in Political Development.* London: Cape, 1937.

Jarvis, C. S. *Arab Command: The Biography of Lieutenant-Colonel F. G. Peake Pasha.* London: Hutchinson, 1942.

———. *Three Deserts.* London: Murray, 1936.

Jawdat, Ali. *Dhikrayat* [Memoirs], *1900–1958.* Beirut: al-Wafa, 1967.

Jaza'iri, Amir Sa'id 'Abd al-Qadir, al-. *Jihad Nusf Qarn* [Struggle of Half a Century]. Edited by Anwar al-Rifai. Damascus, n.d.

Jemal Pasha. *See* Djemal Pasha

Jewish National Home in Palestine, The. New York: KTAV, 1970.

John, Augustus, *Chiaroscuro: Fragments of an Autobiography.* London: Cape, 1952.

Kedourie, Elie. "The Capture of Damascus, October, 1918." *Middle Eastern Studies* (1964–1965), pp. 66–83.

————. *England and the Middle East*. London: Bowes and Bowes, 1956.

Kellett, E. E. "The Man of Many Devils." *The Spectator* 155 (August 16, 1935): 264.

Kennet, Kathleen, Lady Kennet. *See* Scott, Kathleen

Kimche, Jon. *The Second Arab Awakening*. New York: Holt, Rinehart and Winston, 1970.

Kirk, George. *A Short History of the Middle East*. New York: Praeger, 1964.

Kirkbride, Alec. *An Awakening*. London: University Press of Arabia, 1971.

————. *A Crackle of Thorns*. London: Murray, 1956.

Klieman, Aaron. *Foundations of British Policy in the Arab World: The Cairo Conference of 1921*. Baltimore: Johns Hopkins Press, 1970.

Knightley, Phillip, and Simpson, Colin. *The Secret Lives of Lawrence of Arabia*. London: Nelson, 1969. Referred to in the notes as *Secret Lives*.

Lawrence, Arnold W. "The Fiction and the Fact." *The Observer*, December 16, 1962.

————, ed. *Letters to T. E. Lawrence*. London: Cape, 1962. A valuable companion volume to *Letters of T. E. Lawrence*, edited by David Garnett. Referred to in the notes as *Letters to TEL*.

————, ed. *T. E. Lawrence by His Friends*. London: Cape, 1937. Essays by Lawrence's friends, family and associates that concern each period of his life. The book was prepared soon after his death and is an invaluable biographical source. Referred to in the notes as *Friends*.

Lay, F. C. "Dr. Montague Robert Lawrence." *Jesus College Record* (1971), pp. 23–28.

Lévi-Provençal, E. *Islam d'Occident: Etudes d'histoire médiévale*. Islam d'hier et d'aujourd'hui, Vol. VII. Paris: Maisonneuve, 1948.

Lewis, C. S. *The Allegory of Love*. London: Oxford University Press, 1972.

Liddell Hart, Basil H. *'T. E. Lawrence': In Arabia and After*. London: Cape, 1934. (American edition: *Colonel Lawrence: The Man Behind the Legend*. New York: Dodd, Mead, 1934.) The material for the book that Liddell Hart obtained from Lawrence in interviews and correspondence, and Lawrence's notes on the manuscript, are in *T. E. Lawrence to His Biographer Liddell Hart* below.

————. *T. E. Lawrence to His Biographer Liddell Hart*. 1938. Reprinted: Garden City, N.Y.: Doubleday, 1963. This work and its counterpart by Robert Graves were published originally by Faber and Faber as companion volumes. They contain the source materials that Graves and Liddell Hart obtained from their interviews and correspondence with Lawrence as well as Lawrence's notes on their manuscripts. Only five hundred or perhaps a thousand copies of each volume were printed. In 1963 Doubleday reprinted them in a single volume. The Liddell Hart work is referred to in the notes as LHB.

Lloyd George, David. *Memoirs of the Peace Conference*. 2 vols. New Haven: Yale University Press, 1939.

Lord, L. E. "T. E. Shaw, The Odyssey of Homer" (review of Lawrence's translation). *Classical Journal* 28 (April 1933): 533–536.

Lunt, J. D. "An Unsolicited Tribute." *Blackwood's Magazine* 277 (1955): 289–296.

Mack, John E. "Psychoanalysis and Historical Biography." *Journal of the American Psychoanalytic Association* 19 (January 1971): 143–179.

MacMunn, George, and Falls, Cyril, eds. *Military Operations in Egypt and Palestine*, Vol. I. *History of the Great War*. London: His Majesty's Stationery Office, 1928.

Mallowan, M. E. L. "Carchemish: Reflections on the Chronology of the Sculpture." *Anatolian Studies* 22 (1972): 63–85.

Massey, W. T. *Allenby's Final Triumph*. London: Constable, 1920.

Meinhertzhagen, Richard. *Middle East Diary: 1917–1956*. London: Cresset Press, 1959.

Meyers, Jeffrey. "E. M. Forster and T. E. Lawrence: A Friendship." *South Atlantic Quarterly* 69 (Spring 1970): 205–216.

————. *The Wounded Spirit: A Study of Seven Pillars of Wisdom*. London: Martin Brian and O'Keefe, 1973.

Meynell, Viola, ed. *The Best of Friends: Further Letters to Sydney Cockerell*. London: Rupert Hart-Davis, 1956.

————. *Friends of a Lifetime: Letters to Sydney Carlyle Cockerell.* London: Cape, 1940.

Michailovitj, Alexander. *När Jag Var Storfurste Av Ryssland* [When I Was Grand Duke of Russia]. Helsingfors: Söderström, 1933.

Miller, David Hunter. *My Diary at the Conference of Paris.* 21 vols. New York: Appeal Printing, 1924.

Monroe, Elizabeth. *Britain's Moment in the Middle East, 1914–1956.* Baltimore: Johns Hopkins Press, 1956.

Mousa, Suleiman. "The Role of Syrians and Iraqis in the Arab Revolt." *Middle East Forum* 43 (1967): 15–17.

————. *T. E. Lawrence: An Arab View.* Translated by Albert Butros. New York: Oxford University Press, 1966.

Mueller-Wiener, Wolfgang. *Castles of the Crusaders.* London: Thames and Hudson, 1966.

Murray, A. T. "The 'Odyssey' of Homer Newly Translated into English Prose, by T. E. Shaw." *Classical Philology* 28 (July 1933): 275–277.

Nassar, Shakir Khalil. *Lawrence Wa al- 'Arab* [Lawrence and the Arabs]. Beirut: American Press, 1930.

Nevakivi, Jukka. *Britain, France and the Arab Middle East.* London: Athlone. 1969.

Nicolson, Harold. *Curzon: The Last Phase.* London: Constable, 1934.

————. *Peace Making — 1919.* London: Constable, 1933.

Notopoulos, James. "The Tragic and the Epic in T. E. Lawrence." *Yale Review* (Spring 1965), pp. 331–345.

Ocampo, Victoria. *338171 T. E. [Lawrence of Arabia].* New York: Dutton, 1963.

Papen, Franz von. *Memoirs.* New York: Dutton, 1953.

Patch, Blanche, *Thirty Years with G.B.S.* London: Gollancz, 1951.

Peake, Frederick G. *A History and Tribes of Jordan.* Coral Gables, Fla.: University of Miami Press, 1958.

Philby. H. St. John. *Arabian Days.* London: Robert Hale, 1948.

————. *Forty Years in the Wilderness.* London: Robert Hale, 1957.

Pirie-Gordon, C. H. C., ed. *A Brief Record of the Advance of the Egyptian Expeditionary Force: July 1917 to October 1918.* London: His Majesty's Stationery Office, 1919.

Powell, Eileen. "The Position of Women." In C. G. Crump and E. F. Jacob, eds., *The Legacy of the Middle Ages.* Oxford: Clarendon, 1926.

Qadri, Ahmad. *Mudhakkirati 'an al-Thawra al- 'Arabiyah al-Kubra* [My Memoirs of the Great Arab Revolt]. Damascus: Ibn Zaydoun, 1956.

Rank, Otto. *The Myth of the Birth of the Hero* (1914). Edited by P. Freund. New York: Knopf, 1939.

Raswan, Carl. *Black Tents of Arabia* (1935). New York: Creative Age, 1947.

Read, Herbert. "*The Seven Pillars of Wisdom*" (review). In *The Bibliophile's Almanack for 1928.* London: The Fleuron, 1928.

Reynolds, J. S. *Canon Christopher of St. Aldates, Oxford.* Abingdon, Eng.: Abbey Press, 1967.

Richards, Vyvyan W. *Portrait of T. E. Lawrence.* London: Cape, 1936.

Rodd, James Rennell. *Social and Diplomatic Memories.* 3d ser. (1902–1919). London: Edward Arnold, 1925.

Rothenstein, William. "Thomas Edward Lawrence." In *Twenty-Four Portraits.* London: Allen and Unwin, 1920.

Runciman, Steven. *The Kingdom of Acre.* Vol. III of *A History of the Crusades.* Cambridge: Cambridge University Press, 1954.

Sachar, Howard. *The Emergence of the Middle East, 1914–1924.* New York: Knopf, 1969.

Salt, Henry. *The Flogging Craze.* London: Allen and Unwin, 1916.

Sayigh, Anis. *al-Hashimiyun Wa al-Thawrah al- 'Arabiyah al-Kubra* [The Hashemites and the Great Arabic Revolution]. Beirut: Dar al-Tali'ah, 1966.

————. "Ra'y 'Arabi fi Lawrence" [An Arabic Opinion of Lawrence]. *Hiwar* 5 (July-August 1963): 15–23.

Scott, G. R. *The History of Corporal Punishment.* London: T. Werner Laurie, 1938.

Scott, Kathleen [Lady Kennet]. *Homage*. London: Geoffrey Bles, 1938.
Shahbandar, 'Abd al-Rahman. "al-Colonel Lawrence." *al-Muqtataf* 78 (March 1, 1931): 269–276.
———. "al-Colonel Lawrence: Safahat Matwiyah Min al-Thawram al- 'Arabiyah" [Pages Turned Over from the Arab Revolt]. *al-Muqtataf* 78 (April 1, 1931): 426–434.
———. "Lawrence fi al-Mizan" [Lawrence Weighed in the Balance]. *al-Muqtataf* 78 (June 1, 1931): 655–663.
———. "Lawrence fi al-Mizan" [Lawrence Weighed in the Balance]. *al-Muqtataf* 79 (July 1, 1931): 35–44.
Shears, F. S. "The Chivalry of France." *Chivalry: A Series of Studies to Illustrate Its Historical Significance and Civilizing Influence.* Edited by Edgar Prestage. London: Kegan Paul, French, Trubner, 1928.
Shotwell, James T. *At the Peace Conference.* New York: Macmillan, 1937.
Smith, Clare Sydney. *The Golden Reign.* London: Cassell, 1940.
Smith, Janet Adam. *John Buchan.* London: Hart-Davis, 1965.
Spagnolo, J. P. "French Influence in Syria Prior to World War I: The Functional Weakness of Imperialism." *Middle East Journal* 23 (1969): 44–62.
Steed, H. Wickham. *Through Thirty Years.* 2 vols. London: Heinemann, 1924.
Steffens, Lincoln. "Armenians Are Impossible: An Interview with Lawrence of Arabia." *Outlook and Independent* (October 14, 1931), pp. 203–205, 222–223.
———. *The Letters of Lincoln Steffens.* Edited by Ella Winters and Granville Hicks. New York: Harcourt, Brace, 1938.
Stein, Leonard. *The Balfour Declaration.* New York: Simon and Schuster, 1961.
Stirling, W. F. *Safety Last.* London: Hollis and Carter, 1953.
———. "Tales of Lawrence of Arabia." *Cornhill Magazine* 74 (1933): 494–510.
Storrs, Ronald. *Orientations.* London: Nicholson and Watson, 1937.
Sykes, Christopher. *Crossroads to Israel.* London: Collins, 1965.
Taylor, H. O. *The Mediaeval Mind.* 2 vols. Cambridge: Harvard University Press, 1914.
Temperley, H. W. V., ed. *A History of the Peace Conference of Paris.* London: Oxford University Press, 1924.
Thomas, Bertram. *Arabia Felix.* New York: Scribner's, 1932.
Thomas, Lowell. *With Lawrence in Arabia.* New York: Century, 1924.
Thompson, J. W., and Johnson, E. N. *An Introduction to Medieval Europe, 300–1500.* New York: Norton, 1937.
Thompson, Walter H. *Assignment: Churchill.* New York: Farrar, Straus and Young, 1955.
Tibawi, A. L. "Syria in the McMahon Correspondence." *Middle East Forum* 42 (1966): 20–21.
Toynbee, Arnold. *Acquaintances.* London: Oxford University Press, 1967.
'Umari, Subhi al-. *Lawrence Kama 'Araftuhu [Lawrence As I Knew Him].* Beirut: al-Nahar, 1969.
Ussishkin, David. "Observations on Some Monuments from Carchemish." *Journal of Near Eastern Studies* 26 (1967): 87–92.
———. "On the Dating of Some Groups of Reliefs from Carchemish and Til Barsib." *Anatolian Studies* 17 (1967): 181–192.
Vatikiotis, P. J. *Conflict in the Middle East.* London: Allen and Unwin, 1971.
Villars, Jean Beraud. *T. E. Lawrence or the Search for the Absolute.* New York: Duell, Sloan and Pearce, 1955.
Wavell, Archibald. *Allenby: A Study in Greatness.* New York: Oxford University Press, 1941.
Weintraub, Stanley. *Private Shaw and Public Shaw.* New York: Braziller, 1958.
Weizmann, Chaim. *Trial and Error.* New York: Harper, 1949.
Williamson, Henry. *Genius of Friendship: T. E. Lawrence.* London: Faber and Faber, 1941.
Wilson, A. T. *Loyalties: Mesopotamia.* 2 vols. London: Oxford University Press, 1931.
Wilson, Jeremy M., ed. *Minorities.* London: Cape, 1971.
Wingate, Sir Ronald. *Wingate of the Sudan.* London: Murray, 1955.

Winterton, Lord ["W."]. "Arabian Nights and Days." *Blackwood's Magazine* 207 (May and June 1920).

Wolff, Robert L., and Hazard, Harry E., eds. *The Later Crusades, 1189–1311.* Vol. II of *A History of the Crusades.* K. M. Sutton, general ed. 2 vols. Madison: University of Wisconsin Press, 1969.

Woodward, E. L., and Butler, R., eds. *Documents on British Foreign Policy, 1918–1939.* Ser. 1, vol. IV. London: Her Majesty's Stationery Office, 1952.

Woolley, C. Leonard. *Dead Towns and Living Men.* London: Humphrey Milford, 1920.

————. "The Desert of the Wanderings." In *Palestine Expedition Fund, Quarterly Statement,* 1914.

Wrench, Evelyn. *Struggle: 1914–1920.* London: Nicholson and Watson, 1935.

Young, Hubert. *The Independent Arab.* London: Murray, 1933.

Zeine, Zeine N. *The Emergence of Arab Nationalism.* 1958. Reprinted: Beirut: Khayats, 1966.

————. *The Struggle for Arab Independence.* Beirut: Khayats, 1960.

Copyright Acknowledgments

INDEX

T